NINTH EDITION

AMERICAN HISTORY

A Survey

VOLUME II: SINCE 1865

ALAN BRINKLEY

Columbia University

McGRAW-HILL, INC.

New York   St. Louis   San Francisco   Auckland   Bogotá   Caracas   Lisbon   London   Madrid
Mexico City   Milan   Montreal   New Delhi   San Juan   Singapore   Sydney   Tokyo   Toronto

"The American Environment"
essays by William Cronon, University of Wisconsin–Madison

About the Author
Alan Brinkley is Professor of History at Columbia University. He is the author of *Voices of Protest: Huey Long, Father Coughlin, and the Great Depression*, for which he won the 1983 American Book Award; *The Unfinished Nation: A Concise History of the American People*; and *The End of Reform: New Deal Liberalism in Recession and War*. He has held Guggenheim, National Endowment for the Humanities, Woodrow Wilson Center, and National Humanities Center fellowships and has written many articles, essays, and reviews for both scholarly and nonscholarly publications.

AMERICAN HISTORY: A Survey
Volume II: Since 1865

Cover photo; Jonathan Fisher, "Morning View of Bluehill Village" (detail). 1824. Oil on canvas, 25 1/2 x 52"; The William A. Farnsworth Library and Art Museum, Rockland, Maine.

This book is printed on acid-free paper.

    4 5 6 7 8 9 0 DOW DOW 9 0 9 8 7

P/N 007957-9
PART OF
ISBN 0-07-912119-5

This book was set in Palatino by York Graphic Services, Inc.
The editors were Peter Labella and Larry Goldberg;
the designer was Wanda Siedlecka;
the production supervisor was Elizabeth J. Strange.
The photo editor was Elyse Rieder.
R. R. Donnelley & Sons Company was printer and binder.

CONTENTS

CHAPTER THIRTY
THE AFFLUENT SOCIETY   793

Where Historians Disagree

Appendices   A-1

PREFACE

HE PAST, OF COURSE, can never change. But our understanding of the past changes constantly. Perhaps at no time has that been more evident than in the last two decades, when historical scholarship has experienced something close to a revolution. Once historians viewed the past largely through the experiences of great men and great events. Today, they attempt to tell a much more complicated story—one that includes private as well as public events, ordinary people as well as celebrated ones, difference as well as unity. The new history is fragmented at times, because it attempts to embrace so many more areas of human experience than the older narrative. It is often disturbing, because it reveals failures and injustices as well as triumphs. But it is also richer, fuller, and better suited to helping us understand our own diverse and contentious world.

This book began its life several decades ago; and like most general histories of its time, it concentrated at first primarily on America's political development and on its expanding role in the world. Nine editions later, it continues to tell those important stories. But it tells many other stories as well. This newest version continues a process of change stretching now over more than a decade. It attempts to present not only the traditional stories of great public events, but also the many areas of the nation's past that historians have more recently revealed.

Despite the many changes, I have tried to retain what I believe has long been the most important strength of this book: a balanced picture of the American past that attempts to connect the newer histories of society, culture, and ordinary people with the more traditional stories of politics, diplomacy, and great public events. The United States is a nation of extraordinary diversity, and we cannot understand its history without understanding the experience of the many different groups that have shaped its society and of the particular worlds that have developed within it based on race, gender, ethnicity, religion, class, or region. But America is not just a collection of different cultures. It is also a nation, whose people share a common political system, a connection to a vast national economy, and a familiarity with a powerful public culture. To understand the American past, it is necessary to examine not just the nation's considerable diversity, but also the powerful forces that have drawn it together and allowed it to survive and flourish despite division.

The process of revision usually means adding things, and this book—like many books that experience periodic revisions—has tended to grow steadily longer. In this edition, I have tried to reverse that process. I have substantially rewritten the entire narrative to make it clearer and more compact, and to make it possible for me to add substantial new material without increasing the length of the book as a whole. I have reorganized several sections to provide a more coherent picture of various elements of the past. Chapter 15 has been restructured to link the extended description of the New South to the account of the Reconstruction process that did so much to shape it. Chapter 16 is now devoted entirely to the history of the trans-Mississippi West in the late nineteenth century and contains a considerably expanded account of that important area of American history. There is a new chapter (27) on the diplomacy of the period between the two world wars, and a new and expanded chapter (28) on World War II itself. There is a new final chapter (34), which contains an account of events since the publication of the previous edition and a significantly expanded discussion of some of the issues that have emerged to shape contemporary society and culture.

There are many other important changes in this edition as well. Throughout the book, there is considerably expanded coverage of the history of the American West and substantially increased attention to the history of Hispanic and Asian people in the United States. There is important new material derived from recent scholarship in women's history. There is a much-expanded discussion of the complicated social and cultural history of the 1950s, a greatly extended account of the origins and impact of the Vietnam War, and a major new section on the rise of the right in the 1970s and 1980s. There are also two new essays in the series entitled "Where Historians Disagree": one on the history of the West (Chapter 16) and the other on women's history (Chapter 32). There are many new illustrations, and there are expanded and updated bibliographies.

The first edition of *American History: A Survey* was the work of three distinguished historians: Richard N. Current, Frank Freidel, and T. Harry Williams. I have had the great privilege of inheriting this book from them and trying to keep alive in a very different time the high standards they established more than thirty years ago. It has now been over fifteen years since I assumed sole responsibility for this book; and as I have attempted to adapt it to the many changes in historical scholarship of the last several decades, it has now evolved into something very different from the book the original authors bequeathed me. Consequently, it now seems to us time for me to accept sole public responsibility for the result. This book will always reflect the extraordinary talents and enduring contributions of its three original authors. But beginning with this edition, it will carry my name alone.

As always, I am grateful to many people for their help in producing this new edition. John Alexander, Sonya Michel, Gary Okihiro, and George Sanchez were among the scholars who read and commented on the previous edition. Their suggestions were of great value. I owe a particular debt to Richard White, both for his thoughtful critique of the coverage of western history in the previous edition of this book and for his excellent history of the American West (*"It's Your Misfortune and None of My Own"*), which introduced me to much of the new work in this rapidly changing field of scholarship. My research assistants Yanek Mieczkowski, Thaddeus Russell, and Charles Forcey made enormous contributions to this edition. So did the many people at McGraw-Hill who steered it through production, among them Peter Labella, Larry Goldberg, Joan Benham, Kathy Bendo, Elyse Rieder, and Sandra Topping. Finally, I am grateful, as always, to the students, teachers, and other readers of this book who have sent me unsolicited comments, criticisms, and corrections. I hope they will continue to offer their reactions by sending them to me in care of the Department of History, Columbia University, New York, N.Y. 10027.

Alan Brinkley

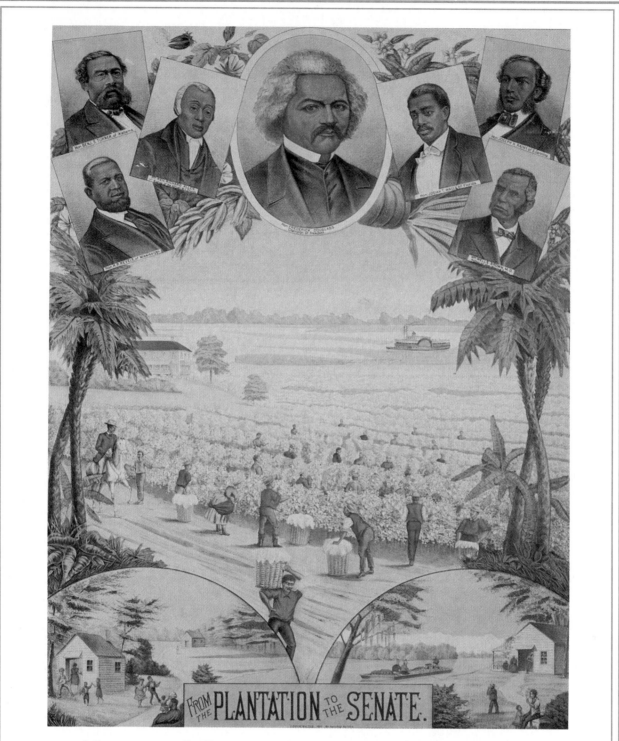

A Reconstruction-Era Tribute to the Election of African Americans to Congress
From left to right: Sen. Hiram R. Revels, Rep. Benjamin S. Turner, the Reverend Richard Allen,
Frederick Douglass, Representative Josiah T. Walls, Representative Joseph H. Rainy, and
writer William Wells Brown. *(Library of Congress)*

CHAPTER FIFTEEN

RECONSTRUCTION AND THE NEW SOUTH

EW PERIODS IN THE history of the United States have produced as much bitterness or created such enduring controversy as the era of Reconstruction—the years following the Civil War when Americans attempted to reunite their shattered nation. Those who lived through Reconstruction viewed it in sharply different ways. To many white Southerners, it was a vicious and destructive experience—a time when vindictive Northerners inflicted humiliation and revenge on the prostrate South and unnecessarily delayed a genuine reunion of the sections. Northern defenders of Reconstruction, in contrast, argued that their policies were the only way to keep unrepentant Confederates from restoring Southern society as it had been before the war; without forceful federal intervention, it would be impossible to stop the reemergence of a backward aristocracy and the continued subjugation of former slaves—no way, in other words, to prevent the same sectional problems that had produced the Civil War in the first place.

To most African Americans at the time, and to many people of all races since, Reconstruction was notable for other reasons. Neither a vicious tyranny, as white Southerners charged, nor a thoroughgoing reform, as many Northerners claimed, it was, rather, a small but important first step in the effort by former slaves to secure civil rights and economic power. Reconstruction did not provide African Americans with either the legal protections or the material resources to assure them anything like real equality. And when it came to an end, finally, in the late 1870s—as a result of an eco-

nomic crisis, a lack of political will in the North, and organized, at times violent, resistance by white Southerners—the freed slaves found themselves abandoned by the federal government to face a system of economic peonage and legal subordination alone. For the remainder of the nineteenth century, those blacks who continued to live in what came to be known as the New South were unable effectively to resist oppression. And yet for all its shortcomings, Reconstruction did help African Americans create institutions and legal precedents that they carried with them into the twentieth century and that became the basis for later efforts to win freedom and equality.

THE PROBLEMS OF PEACEMAKING

In 1865, as it became clear that the war was almost over, no one in Washington knew quite what to do. Abraham Lincoln could not negotiate a treaty with the defeated government; he continued to insist that the Confederate government had no legal right to exist. Yet neither could he simply readmit the Southern states into the Union as if nothing had happened.

The Aftermath of War and Emancipation

The South after the Civil War was a desolate place. Towns had been gutted, plantations burned, fields neglected, bridges and railroads destroyed. Many white

Southerners, stripped of their slaves through emancipation and stripped of the capital they had invested in now worthless Confederate bonds and currency, had almost no personal property. More than 258,000 Confederate soldiers had died in the war; thousands more returned home wounded or sick. Many families had to rebuild their fortunes without the help of adult males. Some white Southerners faced starvation and homelessness.

If conditions were bad for many Southern whites, they were far worse for most Southern blacks—the 4 million men and women emerging from bondage. Some of them had also seen service during the war—as servants to Confederate officers or as teamsters and laborers for the Southern armies. Nearly 200,000 had fought for the Union, and 38,000 had died. Others had worked as spies or scouts for Union forces in the South. Many more had flocked to the Union lines to escape slavery. As soon as the war ended, hundreds of thousands of other former slaves—young and old, healthy and sick—left their plantations in search of a new life in freedom. But most had nowhere to go. Many of them trudged to the nearest town or city, roamed the countryside camping at night on the bare ground, or gathered around Union occupation forces, hoping for assistance. Few had any possessions except the clothes they wore.

In 1865, in short, Southern society was in disarray. Blacks and whites, men and women faced a future of great uncertainty, for which traditional institutions and assumptions were no longer adequate. Yet people of both races faced this future with some very clear aspirations. For both blacks and whites, Reconstruction became a struggle to define the meaning of freedom. But the former slaves and the defeated whites had very different conceptions of what freedom meant.

For African Americans, freedom meant above all an end to slavery and to all its injustices and humiliations. But it also meant the acquisition of rights and protections that would allow them to live as free men and women in the same way white people did. "If I cannot do like a white man," one African-American man told his former master, "I am not free."

Blacks differed with one another on how to achieve that freedom. Some demanded a redistribution of economic resources, especially land, because, as a convention of Alabama freedmen put it in a formal resolution, "The property which they hold was nearly all earned by the sweat of *our* brows." Others asked simply for legal equality, confident that given the same opportunities as white citizens they could advance successfully in American society.

But whatever their particular demands, virtually all former slaves were united in their desire for independence from white control. Freed from slavery, blacks throughout the South began almost immediately to create autonomous African-American communities. They pulled out of white-controlled churches and established their own. They created fraternal, benevolent, and mutual aid societies. When they could, they began their own schools.

For most white Southerners, freedom meant something very different. It meant the ability to control their own destinies without interference from the North or the federal government. And in the immediate aftermath of the war, they attempted to exercise this version of freedom by trying to restore their society to its antebellum form. Slavery had been abolished in the former Confederacy by the Emancipation Proclamation, and everywhere (as of December 1865) by the Thirteenth Amendment. But many white planters wanted to continue slavery in an altered form by keeping black workers legally tied to the plantations. When these white Southerners fought for what they considered freedom, they were fighting above all to preserve local and regional autonomy and white supremacy.

The federal government kept troops in the South after the war to preserve order and protect the freedmen. In March 1865, Congress established the Freedmen's Bureau, an agency of the army directed by General Oliver O. Howard. The Freedmen's Bureau distributed food to millions of former slaves. It established schools staffed by missionaries and teachers who had been sent to the South by Freedmen's Aid Societies and other private and church groups in the North. It made modest efforts to settle blacks on lands of their own. (The Bureau also offered considerable assistance to poor whites, many of whom were similarly destitute and homeless after the war.) But the Freedmen's Bureau was not a permanent solution. It had authority to operate for only one year; and in any case it was far too small to deal effectively with the enormous problems facing Southern society. By the time the war ended, other proposals for reconstructing the defeated South were emerging.

Issues of Reconstruction

The terms by which the Southern states rejoined the Union had important implications for both major political parties. The Republican victories in 1860 and 1864 had been a result in large part of the division of the Democratic Party and, later, the removal of the South from the electorate. Readmitting the South, leaders of both parties believed, would reunite the Democrats and weaken the Republicans. In addition, the Republican Party had taken advantage of the South's absence from Congress to pass a program of nationalistic economic legislation—railroad subsidies, protective tariffs, banking and currency reforms, and other measures to benefit Northern business leaders and industrialists. Should the Democratic Party regain power with heavy Southern support, these programs would be in jeopardy. Complicating these practical questions were emotional concerns. Many Northerners believed the South should be punished in some way for the suffering and sacrifice its rebellion had caused. Many Northerners believed, too, that the South should be transformed, made over in the North's urbanized image—its supposedly backward, feudal, undemocratic society civilized and modernized.

Even among the Republicans in Congress, there was considerable disagreement about the proper approach to Reconstruction—disagreement that reflected the same factional division (between the party's Conservatives and Radicals) that had created disputes over emancipation during the war. Conservatives insisted that the South accept the abolition of slavery, but proposed few other conditions for the readmission of the seceded states. The Radicals, led by Representative Thaddeus Stevens of Pennsylvania and Senator Charles Sumner of Massachusetts, urged that the civil and military leaders of the Confederacy be punished, that large numbers of Southern whites be disenfranchised, that the legal rights of blacks be protected, and that the property of wealthy white Southerners who had aided the Confederacy be confiscated and distributed among the freedmen. Some Radicals favored granting suffrage to the former slaves. Others hesitated, since few Northern states permitted blacks to vote. Between the Radicals and the Conservatives stood a faction of uncommitted Republicans, the Moderates, who rejected the punitive goals of the Radicals but supported extracting at least some concessions from the South on black rights.

Plans for Reconstruction

President Lincoln's sympathies lay with the Moderates and Conservatives of his party. He believed that a lenient Reconstruction policy would encourage Southern Unionists and other former Whigs to join the Republican Party and would thus prevent the readmission of the South from strengthening the Democrats. More immediately, the Southern Unionists could become the nucleus of new, loyal state governments in the South. Lincoln was not uninterested in the fate of the freedmen, but he was willing to defer questions about their future for the sake of rapid reunification.

Lincoln's Reconstruction plan, which he announced in December 1863, offered a general amnesty to white Southerners—other than high officials of the Confederacy—who would pledge loyalty to the government and accept the elimination of slavery. Whenever 10 percent of the number of voters in 1860 took the oath in any state, those loyal voters could set up a state government. Lincoln also hoped to extend suffrage to those blacks who were educated, owned property, and had served in the Union army. Three Southern states—Louisiana, Arkansas, and Tennessee, all under Union occupation—reestablished loyal governments under the Lincoln formula in 1864.

The Radical Republicans were astonished at the mildness of Lincoln's program. They persuaded Congress to deny seats to representatives from the three "reconstructed" states and refused to count the electoral vote of those states in the election of 1864. But for the moment, the Radicals were uncertain about what form their own Reconstruction plan should take.

Their first effort to resolve that question was the Wade-Davis bill, passed by Congress in July 1864. It authorized the president to appoint a provisional governor for each conquered state. When a majority (not Lincoln's 10 percent) of the white males of the state pledged their allegiance to the Union, the governor could summon a state constitutional convention, whose delegates were to be elected by those who would swear (through the so-called Ironclad Oath) that they had never borne arms against the United States—another departure from Lincoln's plan. The new state constitutions would have to abolish slavery, disfranchise Confederate civil and military leaders, and repudiate debts accumulated by the state governments during the war. After a state had met these conditions, Congress would readmit it to the Union. Like the president's proposal, the Wade-Davis bill left up to the states the question of political rights for blacks.

Congress passed the bill a few days before it adjourned in 1864, and Lincoln disposed of it with a pocket veto. His action enraged the Radical leaders, and the pragmatic Lincoln became convinced he would have to accept at least some of the Radical demands. He began to move toward a new approach to Reconstruction.

The Death of Lincoln

What plan he might have produced no one can say. On the night of April 14, 1865, Lincoln and his wife at-

ABRAHAM LINCOLN AND HIS SON TAD
During the last difficult months of the Civil War, Lincoln often found relief from the strains of his office in the company of his young son, Thomas (known as "Tad"), shown here with his father in an 1864 photograph by Mathew Brady. Much has been written about Lincoln's turbulent family life. His wife, Mary Todd Lincoln, was apparently a moody and difficult woman, but the marriage seems generally to have been a happy one. The Lincolns did, however, experience a series of heartbreaking bereavements as three of their four sons died in childhood. Their second child, Edward, died in 1850 at the age of three; their third, "Willie," died of fever in 1862 at the age of eleven; Tad outlived his father by only a few years and died in 1871 at the age of eighteen. Robert Todd Lincoln, the president's eldest son, lived a long, successful, but not very happy life, during which he served as secretary of war, American minister to England, and president of the Pullman Railroad Car Company. *(Library of Congress)*

tended a play at Ford's Theater in Washington. As they sat in the presidential box, John Wilkes Booth, an unsuccessful actor obsessed with aiding the Southern cause, entered the box from the rear and shot Lincoln in the head. The president was carried unconscious to a house across the street, where early the next morning, surrounded by family, friends, and political associates (among them a tearful Charles Sumner), he died.

The circumstances of Lincoln's death earned him immediate martyrdom. It also produced something close to hysteria throughout the North. There were accusations that Booth had acted as part of a great conspiracy—accusations that contained some truth. Booth did indeed have associates, one of whom shot and wounded Secretary of State Seward the night of the assassination, another of whom abandoned at the last moment a scheme to murder Vice President Johnson. Booth himself escaped on horseback into the Virginia countryside, where, on April 26, he was cornered by Union troops and shot to death in a blazing barn. A military tribunal convicted eight other people of participating in the conspiracy (at least two of them on the basis of virtually no evidence). Four were hanged.

To many Northerners, however, the murder of the president seemed evidence of an even greater conspiracy—one masterminded and directed by the unrepentant leaders of the defeated South. Militant Republicans exploited such suspicions relentlessly for months, ensuring that Lincoln's death would help doom his plans for a relatively easy peace.

Johnson and "Restoration"

Leadership of the Moderates and Conservatives fell to Lincoln's successor, Andrew Johnson, who was not well suited, either by circumstance or personality, for the task. A Democrat until he had joined the Union ticket with Lincoln in 1864, he became a Republican president at a moment when partisan passions were growing. Johnson himself was an intemperate and tactless man, filled with resentments and insecurities. He was also openly hostile to the freed slaves and unwilling to support any plans that guaranteed them civil equality or enfranchisement. He once declared, "White men alone must manage the South."

Johnson revealed his plan for Reconstruction—or "Restoration," as he preferred to call it—soon after he took office, and implemented it during the summer of 1865 when Congress was in recess. Like Lincoln, he offered amnesty to those Southerners who would take an oath of allegiance. (High-ranking Confederate officials and any white Southerner with land worth $20,000 or more would have to apply to the president for individual pardons. Johnson, a self-made man, liked the thought of the great planter aristocrats humbling themselves before him.) In most other respects, however, his plan resembled that of the Wade-Davis bill. For each state, the president appointed a provisional governor, who was to invite qualified voters to elect delegates to a constitutional convention. Johnson did not specify how many qualified voters were necessary, but he implied that he would require a majority (as

had the Wade-Davis bill). In order to win readmission to Congress, a state had to revoke its ordinance of secession, abolish slavery and ratify the Thirteenth Amendment, and repudiate the Confederate and state war debts. The final procedure before restoration was for a state to elect a state government and send representatives to Congress.

By the end of 1865, all the seceded states had formed new governments—some under Lincoln's plan, some under Johnson's—and were prepared to rejoin the Union as soon as Congress recognized them. But Radical Republicans vowed not to recognize the Johnson governments, just as they had previously refused to recognize the Lincoln regimes; for by now, Northern opinion had become more hostile toward the South than it had been a year earlier when Congress passed the Wade-Davis bill. Many Northerners were disturbed by the apparent reluctance of some delegates to the Southern conventions to abolish slavery, and by the refusal of all the conventions to grant suffrage to any blacks. They were astounded that states claiming to be "loyal" should elect as state officials and representatives to Congress prominent leaders of the recent Confederacy. Particularly hard to accept was Georgia's choice of Alexander H. Stephens, former Confederate vice president, as a United States senator.

RADICAL RECONSTRUCTION

Reconstruction under Johnson's plan—often known as "presidential Reconstruction"—continued only until Congress reconvened in December 1865. At that point, Congress refused to seat the senators and representatives of the states the president had "restored." Instead, it set up a new Joint Committee on Reconstruction to investigate conditions in the South and to help Congress create a Reconstruction policy of its own. The period of "congressional" or "Radical" Reconstruction had begun.

The Black Codes

Meanwhile, events in the South were driving Northern opinion even more toward the Radicals. Throughout the South in 1865 and early 1866, state legislatures were enacting sets of laws known as the Black Codes, modeled in many ways on the codes that had regulated free blacks in the prewar South. The laws were designed to reestablish planter control over black workers. Although there were variations from state to state, all the codes authorized local officials to appre-

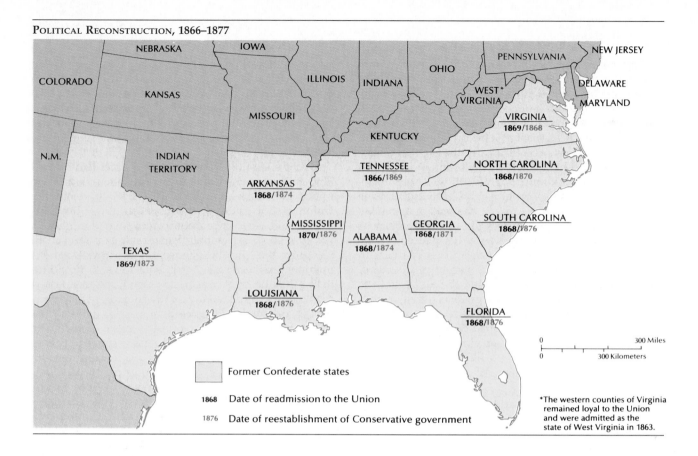

NEBRASKA
IOWA
NEW JERSEY
PENNSYLVANIA
COLORADO
OHIO
KANSAS
ILLINOIS
INDIANA
WEST *
VIRGINIA
DELAWARE
MARYLAND
MISSOURI
VIRGINIA
1869/1868
N.M.
INDIAN
TERRITORY
KENTUCKY
TENNESSEE
1866/1869
NORTH CAROLINA
1868/1870
ARKANSAS
1868/1874
MISSISSIPPI
1870/1876
GEORGIA
1868/1871
SOUTH CAROLINA
1868/1876
TEXAS
1869/1873
ALABAMA
1868/1874
LOUISIANA
1868/1876
FLORIDA
1868/1876

0   300 Miles
0   300 Kilometers

☐ Former Confederate states

1868   Date of readmission to the Union

1876   Date of reestablishment of Conservative government

*The western counties of Virginia
remained loyal to the Union
and were admitted as the
state of West Virginia in 1863.

hend unemployed blacks, fine them for vagrancy, and hire them out to private employers to satisfy the fine. Some of the codes forbade blacks to own or lease farms or to take any jobs other than as plantation workers or domestic servants. To much of the white South, the Black Codes were a realistic approach to a great social problem. To most of the North, and to most African Americans, they represented a return to slavery in all but name.

Congress's first response to the Black Codes was to extend the life of the Freedmen's Bureau and to widen its powers. It could now establish special courts for settling labor disputes, which could nullify work agreements forced on freedmen under the Black Codes. In April, Congress struck again at the Black Codes by passing the First Civil Rights Act, which declared blacks to be citizens of the United States and empowered the federal government to intervene in state affairs when necessary to protect the rights of citizens. Johnson vetoed both the Freedmen's Bureau and Civil Rights bills, but Congress eventually overrode him.

The Fourteenth Amendment

In April 1866, the Radicals acted again. The Joint Committee on Reconstruction submitted a proposed Fourteenth Amendment to the Constitution, which Con-

gress approved in early summer and sent to the states for ratification. Eventually, it became one of the most important of all the provisions in the Constitution.

The amendment offered the first constitutional definition of American citizenship. Everyone born in the United States, and everyone naturalized, was automatically a citizen and entitled to equal protection of the laws by both state and national governments. There could be no other citizenship requirements. The amendment also imposed penalties—reduction of representation in Congress and on the electoral college—on states that denied suffrage to any adult male inhabitants. (This was the first time the Constitution made reference to gender, and the wording clearly reflected the prevailing view in Congress and elsewhere that the franchise was properly restricted to men.) Finally, it prohibited those who had taken an oath to support the Constitution (that is, members of Congress and other federal officials) and later had aided the Confederacy from holding any state or federal office unless two-thirds of Congress voted to pardon them.

Congressional Radicals made it clear that if Southern legislatures ratified the Fourteenth Amendment, their states would be readmitted to the Union. But only Tennessee did so. The refusal of the former Confederate states to ratify, along with the refusal of Kentucky

THE MEMPHIS RACE RIOT, 1866
Angry whites (shown here shooting down blacks) rampaged through the black neighborhoods of Memphis, Tennessee, during the first three days of May 1866, burning homes, schools, and churches and leaving forty-six people dead. Some claimed the riot was a response to strict new regulations protecting blacks that had been imposed on Tennessee by General George Stoneman, the military commander of the district; others argued that it was an attempt by whites to intimidate and control a black population that was trying to exercise its new freedom. Such riots were among the events that persuaded Radical Republicans in Congress to press for a harsher policy of Reconstruction. *(The Granger Collection)*

and Delaware, denied the amendment the necessary approval of three-fourths of the states and temporarily derailed it.

In the meantime, however, the Radicals were growing stronger, in part because of Northern anger at the South's and Johnson's recalcitrance. Bloody race riots broke out in 1866 in New Orleans, Memphis, and other Southern cities in which angry whites rampaged through black neighborhoods, burning homes, schools, and churches. In Memphis, 46 people, almost all blacks, died. Radicals cited the riots as evidence of the inadequacy of Johnson's policy.

In the 1866 congressional elections, Johnson campaigned actively for Conservative candidates, but he did his own cause more harm than good with his intemperate speeches. The voters returned an overwhelming majority of Republicans, most of them Radicals, to Congress. In the Senate, there were now 42 Republicans to 11 Democrats; in the House, 143 Republicans to 49 Democrats. (The South remained largely unrepresented in both chambers.) Nothing now prevented the Republicans in Congress from devising a Reconstruction plan of their own.

The Congressional Plan

The Radicals passed three Reconstruction bills early in 1867. Johnson vetoed them all, and Congress overrode him each time. Finally, nearly two years after the end of the war, the federal government had established a coherent plan for Reconstruction.

That two-year delay significantly affected the South's reaction to the program. In 1865, with the South reeling from its defeat and nearly prostrate, the federal government could probably have imposed almost any plan on the region without much resistance. But by 1867, the South had already begun to reconstruct itself under the reasonably generous terms Lincoln and Johnson had extended. Measures that might once have seemed moderate to most white Southerners now seemed radical and tyrannical, and the congressional Reconstruction plan created deep resentments and continuing resistance.

Under the congressional plan, Tennessee, which had ratified the Fourteenth Amendment, was promptly readmitted. But the Lincoln-Johnson governments of the other ten Confederate states were rejected. Those states were now combined into five military districts, each under a military commander who—in preparation for the readmission of the states—was to register qualified voters, defined as all adult black males and those white males who had not participated in the rebellion. After the completion of registration, voters would elect a convention to prepare a new state constitution, which had to include provisions for black suffrage. Once voters ratified the new constitution, states could hold elections for a government. Finally, if Congress approved the state's new constitution, if the state legislature ratified the Fourteenth Amendment, and if enough other states ratified it to make the amendment part of the Constitution, then the state was to be restored to the Union.

By 1868, seven more of the former Confederate states (Arkansas, North Carolina, South Carolina, Louisiana, Alabama, Georgia, and Florida) had fulfilled these conditions (including ratification of the Fourteenth Amendment, which now became part of the Constitution) and were readmitted to the Union. Conservative whites held up the return of Virginia and Texas until 1869 and of Mississippi until 1870. By then, Congress had added an additional requirement for readmission: ratification of another constitutional amendment.

The Fifteenth Amendment

This was the Fifteenth Amendment, which forbade the states and the federal government to deny suffrage to any citizen on account of "race, color, or previous condition of servitude." Several Northern and border states refused to approve it, and it was adopted only with the support of the four Southern states that had to ratify it in order to be readmitted to the Union.

The Fifteenth Amendment was important in theory, but in practice it had little effect on black suffrage for many years. It was, the historian Henry Adams once wrote, "more remarkable for what it does not than for what it does contain." The amendment guaranteed African Americans the right to vote, but not the right to hold public office. It did nothing to prohibit the literacy, property, and educational tests and the poll taxes that would be used by generations of white Southern leaders to prevent most blacks (and many poor whites) from voting.

Nor did the amendment make any reference to women. That was a particularly bitter blow to some feminists, because they had worked since the Civil War to ensure that any efforts to extend suffrage would link the black vote with the female vote. In 1866, Elizabeth Cady Stanton, Susan B. Anthony, Lucy Stone, and others had joined together in the Equal Rights Association, which worked to incorporate woman suffrage in state constitutions. In 1868, they created the Working Women's Association, which embraced a broad agenda of feminist and labor causes, including woman suffrage. And in 1869, Stanton and Anthony (now leading the National Woman Suffrage Association) opposed the Fifteenth Amendment because of its failure to include women in its provisions and because, some said, it elevated black men over white women. Without woman suffrage, Stanton argued, political power would flow to "the lower orders of Chinese, Africans, Germans, and Irish, with their low ideals of womanhood." By opposing the Fifteenth Amendment, Stanton and Anthony alienated many more moderate feminists (among them Lucy Stone) and caused a final breakdown of the alliance between feminists and abolitionists, who had worked together so closely since the 1840s.

The limits of the Fifteenth Amendment reflected the politics of its principal sponsors. Southern Republicans and Northern Radicals did not want to guarantee universal suffrage, because they feared that in doing so they would assure former Confederates the right to vote. Many Northern politicians, moreover, wanted to preserve voting restrictions in their own states. Some western states, for example, prohibited Chinese from voting, and several New England states retained property and literacy requirements. Republicans, in other words, wanted to expand their own electoral strength in the South (by enfranchising former slaves while disenfranchising former Confederates) without upsetting existing voting restrictions in the North, some of which also helped the Republicans.

Impeaching the President, Assaulting the Courts

To stop the president from interfering with their designs, Radicals in Congress passed two remarkable laws in 1867. One, the Tenure of Office Act, forbade the president to remove civil officials, including members of his cabinet, without the consent of the Senate. The principal purpose of the law was to protect the job of Secretary of War Edwin M. Stanton, the only Lincoln appointee still in the Cabinet, who was cooperating with the Radicals. The other law, the Command of the Army Act, prohibited the president from issuing military orders except through the commanding general of the army (General Grant), whose headquarters were to be in Washington and who could not be relieved or assigned elsewhere without the consent of the Senate.

President Johnson had long since ceased to be a serious obstacle to the passage of Radical legislation. But he was still the official charged with administering the Reconstruction programs, and as such, the Radicals believed, he was a serious impediment to their plans. Early in 1867 they began looking for a way to remove him. The only constitutional grounds for impeachment were "high crimes or misdemeanors." Republicans could find nothing on which to base such charges until Johnson gave them what they considered a plausible reason for action. He deliberately violated the Tenure of Office Act—in hopes of bringing a test case of the law before the courts. He dismissed Secretary of War Stanton even after Congress had refused to agree.

In the House of Representatives, elated Radicals impeached the president on eleven charges and sent them

THADDEUS STEVENS
Stern, uncompromising, and severe, Thaddeus Stevens of Pennsylvania was the incarnation of the North's vindictive designs, according to many Southerners during (and long after) Reconstruction. Others admired him as one of the few white leaders who remained firmly committed to racial equality. He served in the House of Representatives from 1849 to 1853 and again, more prominently, from 1859 until his death in 1868. He spent much of the last year of his life organizing and managing the impeachment trial of Andrew Johnson. *(Library of Congress)*

lated. On the first three charges to come to a vote, seven Republicans joined the twelve Democrats to support acquittal. The vote was 35 to 19, one short of the constitutionally required two-thirds majority. After that, the Radicals dropped the impeachment campaign.

The congressional Radicals also took action to stop the Supreme Court from interfering with their plans. In 1866, the Court had declared in *Ex parte Milligan* that military tribunals were unconstitutional in places where civil courts were functioning, a decision that seemed to threaten the system of military government the Congress was establishing in the South. Radicals immediately proposed legislation to require a two-thirds majority of the justices to overrule a law of Congress, to deny the Court jurisdiction in Reconstruction cases, to reduce its membership to three, and even to abolish it. The justices apparently took note. Over the next two years, the Court refused to accept jurisdiction in any cases involving Reconstruction. The bills affecting the Court never passed.

THE SOUTH IN RECONSTRUCTION

When white Southerners spoke bitterly in later years of the effects of Reconstruction, they referred most frequently to the governments Congress helped impose on them—governments they claimed were both incompetent and corrupt, that saddled the region with enormous debts, and that trampled on the rights of citizens. When black Southerners and their defenders condemned Reconstruction, in contrast, they spoke of the failure of the national and state governments to go far enough to guarantee freedmen even the most elemental rights of citizenship—a failure that resulted in a harsh new system of economic subordination. (See "Where Historians Disagree," pp. 432–433.)

The Reconstruction Governments

In the ten states of the South that were reorganized under the congressional plan, approximately one-fourth of the white males were at first excluded from voting or holding office. That produced black majorities among voters in South Carolina, Mississippi, and Louisiana (states where blacks were also a majority of the population), and in Alabama and Florida (where they were not). But the government soon lifted most suffrage restrictions so that nearly all white males could soon vote. After that, Republicans maintained control only with the support of many Southern whites.

to the Senate for trial. The first nine counts dealt with the violation of the Tenure of Office Act. The tenth and eleventh charged Johnson with slandering Congress and with not enforcing the Reconstruction Acts.

The trial before the Senate lasted through April and May 1868. The president's accusers argued that Johnson had defied Congress and was indeed guilty of high crimes and misdemeanors. His defenders claimed that he had acted properly in challenging what he considered an unconstitutional law. Radicals put heavy pressure on all the Republican senators, but the Moderates (who were losing faith in the Radical program) vacil-

THE BURDENED SOUTH
This Reconstruction-era cartoon expresses the South's sense of its oppression at the hands of Northern Republicans. President Grant (whose hat bears Abraham Lincoln's initials) rides in comfort in a giant carpetbag, guarded by bayonet-wielding soldiers, as the South staggers under the burden in chains. More evidence of destruction and military occupation is visible in the background. *(Culver)*

Critics called these Southern white Republicans "scalawags." Many were former Whigs who had never felt comfortable in the Democratic Party—some of them wealthy (or once wealthy) planters or businessmen interested in the economic development of the region. Others were farmers who lived in remote areas where there had been little or no slavery and who hoped the Republican program of internal improvements would help end their economic isolation. Despite their diverse social positions, scalawags shared a belief that the Republican Party would serve their economic interests better than the Democrats.

White men from the North also served as Republican leaders in the South. Critics of Reconstruction referred to them pejoratively as "carpetbaggers," which conveyed an image of penniless adventurers who arrived with all their possessions in a carpetbag (a common kind of cheap suitcase covered with carpeting material). In fact, most of the so-called carpetbaggers were well-educated people of middle-class origin, many of them doctors, lawyers, and teachers. Most were veterans of the Union army who looked on the South as a new frontier, more promising than the West. They had settled there at war's end as hopeful planters, or as business and professional people.

But the most numerous Republicans in the South were the black freedmen, most of whom had no previous experience in politics and who tried, therefore, to build institutions through which they could learn to exercise their power. In several states, African-American voters held their own conventions to chart their future course. One such "colored convention," as Southern whites called them, assembled in Alabama in 1867 and announced: "We claim exactly the same rights, privileges and immunities as are enjoyed by white men—we ask nothing more and will be content with nothing less." The black churches freedmen created after emancipation, when they withdrew from the white-dominated churches they had been compelled to attend under slavery, also helped give unity and political self-confidence to the former slaves.

African Americans played a significant role in the politics of the Reconstruction South. They served as delegates to the constitutional conventions. They held public offices of practically every kind. Between 1869 and 1901, twenty blacks served in the U.S. House of Representatives, two in the Senate (Hiram Revels of Mississippi and Blanche K. Bruce of Virginia). African Americans served, too, in state legislatures and in various other state offices. Southern whites complained loudly (both at the time and for generations to come) about "Negro rule" during Reconstruction, but no such thing ever actually existed in any of the states. No black man was ever elected governor of a Southern state (although Lieutenant Governor P. B. S. Pinchback briefly performed gubernatorial duties in Louisiana). Blacks never controlled any of the state legislatures, although they held a majority in the lower house in South Carolina for a time. In the South as a whole, the percentage of black officeholders was always far lower than the percentage of blacks in the population.

The record of the Reconstruction governments is mixed. Critics at the time and since denounced them for corruption and financial extravagance, and there is some truth to both charges. Officeholders in many states enriched themselves through graft and other illicit activities. State budgets expanded to hitherto unknown totals, and state debts soared to previously un-

SENATOR HIRAM REVELS
White Southerners complained bitterly of "Negro rule" during Reconstruction. In fact, African Americans never occupied more than a small minority of elected positions in the Reconstruction South. One of the most prominent was Hiram R. Revels, who served as a United States Senator from Mississippi in the 1870s. *(United States Senate)*

dreamed-of heights. In South Carolina, for example, the public debt increased from $7 million to $29 million in eight years.

But the corruption in the South, real as it was, was hardly unique to the Reconstruction governments. Corruption was at least as rampant in the Northern states. And in both North and South, it was a result of the same thing: a rapid economic expansion of government services (and revenues) that put new strains on (and new temptations before) elected officials everywhere. The end of Reconstruction did not end corruption in Southern state governments. In many states, in fact, corruption increased.

And the state expenditures of the Reconstruction years were huge only in comparison with the meager budgets of the antebellum era. They represented an effort to provide the South with desperately needed services that antebellum governments had never offered: public education, public works programs, poor relief, and other costly new commitments. There were, to be sure, graft and extravagance in Reconstruction governments; there were also positive and permanent accomplishments.

Education

Perhaps the most important of those accomplishments was a dramatic improvement in Southern education—an improvement that benefited both whites and blacks. In the first years of Reconstruction, much of the impetus for educational reform in the South came from outside groups—from the Freedmen's Bureau, from Northern private philanthropic organizations, from many Northern women, black and white, who traveled to the South to teach in freedmen's schools—and from Southern blacks themselves. Over the opposition of many Southern whites, who feared that education would give blacks "false notions of equality," these reformers established a large network of schools for former slaves—4,000 schools by 1870, staffed by 9,000 teachers (half of them black), teaching 200,000 students (about 12 percent of the total school-age population of the freedmen). In the 1870s, Reconstruction governments began to build a comprehensive public school system in the South. By 1876, more than half of all white children and about 40 percent of all black children were attending schools in the South. Several black "academies," offering more advanced education, also began operating. Gradually, these academies grew into an important network of black colleges and universities, which included such distinguished schools as Fisk and Atlanta Universities and Morehouse College.

Already, however, Southern education was becoming divided into two separate systems, one black and one white. Early efforts to integrate the schools of the region were a dismal failure. The Freedmen's Bureau schools, for example, were open to students of all races, but almost no whites attended them. New Orleans set up an integrated school system under the Reconstruction government; again, whites almost universally stayed away. The one federal effort to mandate school integration—the Civil Rights Act of 1875—had its provisions for educational desegregation removed before it was passed. As soon as the Republican governments of Reconstruction were replaced, the new Southern Democratic regimes quickly abandoned all efforts to promote integration.

Landownership and Tenancy

The most ambitious goal of the Freedmen's Bureau, and of some Republican Radicals in Congress, was to

THE SOUTHERN PLANTATION BEFORE AND AFTER EMANCIPATION: BARROW PLANTATION, OGLETHORPE COUNTY, GEORGIA

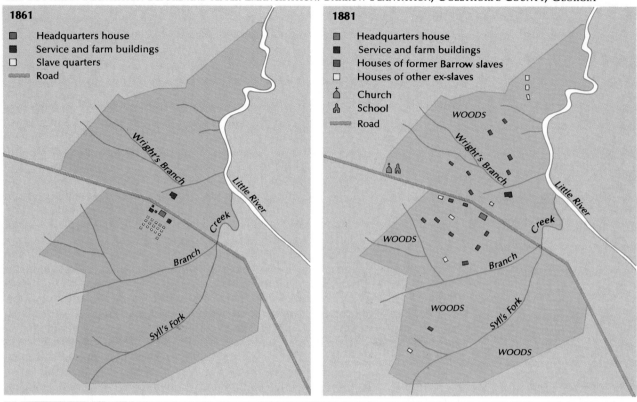

make Reconstruction the vehicle for a fundamental reform of landownership in the South. The effort failed. In the last years of the war and the first years of Reconstruction, the Freedmen's Bureau did oversee the redistribution of substantial amounts of land to freedmen in a few areas—notably the Sea Islands of South Carolina and Georgia, and areas of Mississippi that had once belonged to the family of Jefferson Davis. By June 1865, the Bureau had settled nearly 10,000 black families on their own land—most of it drawn from abandoned plantations—arousing dreams among former slaves throughout the South of "forty acres and a mule."

By the end of that year, however, the experiment was already collapsing. Southern plantation owners were returning and demanding the restoration of their property, and President Johnson was supporting their demands. Despite the resistance of the Freedmen's Bureau, the government eventually returned most of the confiscated land to the original white owners. Congress, moreover, never had much stomach for the idea of land redistribution. Very few Northern Republicans believed that the federal government had the right to confiscate property.

Even so, distribution of landownership in the South changed considerably in the postwar years. Among whites, there was a striking decline in landownership, from 80 percent before the war to 67 percent by the end of Reconstruction. Some whites lost their land because of unpaid debt or increased taxes; some left the marginal lands they had owned to move to more fertile areas, where they rented. Among blacks, during the same period, the proportion who owned land rose from virtually none to more than 20 percent. Many black landowners acquired their property through hard work or luck or both. But some relied on assistance from white-dominated financial or philanthropic institutions. One of them was the Freedman's Bank, established in 1865 by antislavery whites in an effort to promote landownership among blacks. They persuaded thousands of freedmen to deposit their modest savings in the bank, but then invested heavily in unsuccessful enterprises. It was ill prepared, therefore, for the national depression of the 1870s and it failed in 1874.

Still, most blacks, and a growing minority of whites, did not own their own land during Reconstruction; and some who acquired land in the 1860s had lost it by the 1890s. These people worked for others in one form or another. Many black agricultural laborers—perhaps 25 percent of the total—simply worked for wages. Most, however, became tenants of white landowners—working their own plots of land and paying their landlords either a fixed rent or a share of their crop. (See pp. 437–440.)

The new system represented a repudiation by blacks of the gang-labor system of the antebellum plantation, in which slaves had lived and worked together under the direction of a master. As tenants and share-croppers, blacks enjoyed at least a physical independence from their landlords and had the sense of working their own land, even if in most cases they could never hope to buy it. But tenantry also benefited land-lords in some ways, relieving them of any responsibility for the physical well-being of their workers.

Incomes and Credit

In some respects, the postwar years were a period of remarkable economic progress for blacks. If the material benefits they had received under slavery are calculated as income, then prewar blacks had earned about a 22 percent share of the profits of the plantation system. By the end of Reconstruction, they were earning 56 percent. Measured another way, the per capita income of blacks rose 46 percent between 1857 and 1879, while the per capita income of whites declined 35 percent. This represented one of the most significant redistributions of income in American history.

But these figures are somewhat misleading. For one thing, while the black share of profits was increasing, the total profits of Southern agriculture were declining—a result of the dislocations of the war and a reduction in the world market for cotton. For another thing, while blacks were earning a greater return on each hour of labor than they had under slavery, they were working fewer hours. Women and children were less likely to labor in the fields than in the past. Adult men tended to work shorter days. In all, the black labor force worked about one-third fewer hours during Reconstruction than it had been compelled to do under slavery—a reduction that brought the working schedule of blacks roughly into line with that of white farm laborers. Nor did the income redistribution of the post- war years lift many blacks out of poverty. Black per capita income rose from about one quarter of white per capita income to about one-half in the first few years after the war. And after this initial increase, it rose hardly at all.

For blacks and poor whites alike, whatever gains there might have been as a result of land and income redistribution were often overshadowed by the ravages of the crop lien system. Few of the traditional institutions of credit in the South—the "factors" and banks—returned after the war. In their stead emerged a new system of credit, centered in large part on local country stores, some of them owned by planters, others by independent merchants. Blacks and whites, landowners and tenants—all depended on these stores for such necessities as food, clothing, seed, and farm implements. And since farmers did not have the same steady cash flow as other workers, customers usually had to rely on credit from these merchants in order to purchase what they needed. Most local stores had no competition (and went to great lengths to ensure that things stayed that way). As a result, they were able to set interest rates as high as 50 or 60 percent. Farmers had to give the merchants a lien (or claim) on their crops as collateral for the loans (thus the term "crop lien system," generally used to describe Southern farming in this period). Farmers who suffered a few bad years in a row, as often happened, could become trapped in a cycle of debt from which they could never escape.

This burdensome credit system had a number of effects on the region, almost all of them unhealthy. One was that some blacks who had acquired land during the early years of Reconstruction gradually lost it as they fell into debt. So, to a lesser extent, did white small landowners. Another was that Southern farmers became almost wholly dependent on cash crops—and most of all on cotton—because only such marketable commodities seemed to offer any possibility of escape from debt. Thus Southern agriculture, never sufficiently diversified even in the best of times, became more one-dimensional than ever. The relentless planting of cotton, moreover, was contributing to an exhaustion of the soil. The crop lien system, in other words, was not only helping to impoverish small farmers; it was also contributing to a general decline in the Southern agricultural economy.

The African-American Family in Freedom

One of the most striking features of the black response to Reconstruction was the effort to build or rebuild family structures and to protect them from the interference they had experienced under slavery. A major reason for the rapid departure of so many blacks from plantations was the desire to find lost relatives and reunite families. Thousands of African Americans wandered through the South looking for husbands, wives, children, or other relatives from whom they had been

AFRICAN-AMERICAN WORK AFTER SLAVERY
Black men and women engaged in a wide range of economic activities in the aftermath of slavery. But discrimination by white Southerners and the former slaves' own lack of education limited most of them to relatively menial jobs. Many black women (including this former slave) earned money for their families by working as "washer women," doing laundry for white people. *(Historic New Orleans Collection)*

separated. Former slaves rushed to have marriages, previously without legal standing, sanctified by church and law. Black families resisted living in the former slave quarters and moved instead to small cabins scattered widely across the countryside, where they could enjoy at least some privacy.

Within the black family, the definition of male and female roles quickly came to resemble that within white families. Many women and children ceased working in the fields. Such work, they believed, was a badge of slavery. Instead, many women restricted themselves largely to domestic tasks—cooking, cleaning, gardening, raising children, attending to the needs of their husbands. Some black husbands refused to allow their wives to work as servants in white homes. "When I married my wife I married her to wait on me," one freedman told a former master who was attempting to hire his wife as a servant. "She got all she can do right here for me and the children."

Still, middle-class notions of domesticity were often difficult to sustain in the impoverished circumstances of most former slaves. Economic necessity required many black women to engage in income-producing activities, including activities that they and their husbands resisted because it reminded them of slavery: working as domestic servants, taking in laundry, or helping in the field. By the end of Reconstruction, half of all black women over the age of sixteen were working for wages. And unlike white working women, most black female income-earners were married.

THE GRANT ADMINISTRATION

Exhausted by the political turmoil of the Johnson administration, American voters in 1868 yearned for a strong, stable figure to guide them through the troubled years of Reconstruction. They did not find one. Instead, they turned trustingly to General Ulysses S. Grant, the hero of the war and, by 1868, a revered national idol. Grant was a failure as president. During his two terms in office, he faced problems that would have taxed the abilities of a master of statecraft. Grant, however, was a dull and unimaginative man with few political skills and little vision.

The Soldier President

Grant could have had the nomination of either party in 1868. But believing that Republican Reconstruction policies were more attuned to public opinion than the Democratic alternatives, he accepted the Republican nomination. The Democrats nominated former governor Horatio Seymour of New York. The campaign was an exceptionally bitter one, in large part because the Democrats, desperate to revive their party's declining fortunes, chose to make opposition to Reconstruction and an open defense of white supremacy the basis of their appeal. The Ku Klux Klan (see p. 430), in the meantime, terrorized Southern Republicans, both black and white, in an effort to discourage them from voting. One member of Congress from Arkansas and three members of the South Carolina legislature were assassinated in the violence and terror that accompanied the campaign in the South.

The 1868 election was also the first in which Northern capitalists united behind the Republicans, making the party the principal defender of industrial growth in American politics, as it would remain for several generations. It was also in 1868 that the so-called Stalwarts established their dominance within the party. Fervently committed to the economic interests of Northern capitalists, they worked from within to shift the party's concerns away from issues related to the South and the freedmen and toward industrialization.

Grant's triumph in the end was surprisingly narrow, an indication, perhaps of how unpopular Reconstruction was already becoming. He carried twenty-six states to Seymour's eight. But Grant's popular majority was a scant 310,000 votes, a result of 500,000 black votes in the reconstructed states of the South.

Grant entered the White House with no political experience of any kind, and his performance in office was clumsy and ineffectual from the start. Except for Hamilton Fish, whom Grant appointed secretary of state and who served for eight years with great distinction, most members of the cabinet were as dull and inept as the president. Grant relied chiefly, and increasingly, on the machine leaders in the party—the group most ardently devoted to the spoils system.

Grant used the spoils system even more blatantly than most of his predecessors. And in doing so, he provoked the opposition of Senator Charles Sumner and other Republican leaders, who joined with reformers to agitate for a new civil service system to limit the president's appointive powers. Nothing came of their efforts. Grant soon attracted the hostility of other Republicans as well. Many Northerners were growing disillusioned with Reconstruction, disgusted by stories of corruption, extravagance, and incompetence in the South. They opposed Grant's continuing support of radical programs there. Some Republicans suspected (correctly) that there was corruption in the Grant administration itself. Still others criticized Grant because he did not support a tariff reduction.

The Liberal Republicans

By the end of Grant's first term, therefore, a substantial faction of the party—those who called themselves Liberal Republicans—had come to oppose what they called "Grantism." They had many disagreements with the president, but among the most important was their distaste for the way he used the patronage system to reward political cronies. They agitated, therefore, for a civil service system, which would limit the president's powers of appointment and, presumably, raise the quality of those working in government. Such scholarly journalists as E. L. Godkin of *The Nation* and

George William Curtis of *Harper's Weekly* argued that the government should base its appointments not on services to the party but on fitness for office as determined by competitive examinations, as the British government already was doing. Grant reluctantly agreed to establish a civil service commission, which Congress authorized in 1871, to devise a system of hiring based on merit. It proposed a set of rules that Grant seemed to approve; but the president was not really much interested in reform, and even if he had been he could not have persuaded his followers to accept a new system that would undermine the very basis of party loyalty—patronage. Nothing came of the commission's work.

Debate over civil service reform remained one of the leading political issues of the next three decades. The debate involved more than simply an argument over patronage and corruption. It also reflected basic differences of opinion over who was fit to serve in public life. Middle-class reformers were saying, implicitly, that only educated, middle-class people (the "best men") should be permitted access to government office. Their concerns grew in large part out of their alarm over the character of those who served in the Reconstruction governments and their fear that the growing immigrant population of the North would produce similarly unfit leaders there. As Charles Francis Adams, Jr., one of the leaders of the Liberal Republicans, once said: "Universal suffrage can only mean in plain English the government of ignorance and vice:—it means a European, and especially Celtic proletariat on the Atlantic coast, an African proletariat on the shores of the Gulf, and a Chinese proletariat on the Pacific." Civil service reform would, in short, help limit the power of democracy to debase public life.

Those opposing civil service reform included not just party leaders but immigrants, workers, some farmers, and others. They argued that the establishment of an elite corps of civil servants would be undemocratic. It would exclude them from participation in government and restrict power to the upper classes. That was precisely what the reformers hoped to do.

In 1872, hoping to prevent Grant's reelection, the Liberal Republicans deserted the party and nominated their own presidential candidate: Horace Greeley, veteran editor and publisher of the *New York Tribune*. The Democrats, somewhat reluctantly, named Greeley their candidate as well, hoping that the alliance with the Liberals would enable them to defeat Grant. But the effort was in vain. Grant won a substantial victory, polling 286 electoral votes and 3,597,000 popular votes to Greeley's 66 and 2,834,000. Greeley had carried only two Southern and four border states. Three weeks later, apparently crushed by his defeat, Greeley died.

Le voleur de « troisième mandat. » — Dessin de Houssot, d'après une gravure originale.

THE GRANT SCANDALS
This hostile cartoon suggests the growing popular discontent at the many scandals plaguing the Grant administration in its last years. Although the president himself was never proved to have been involved in any illegality, the scandals damaged his reputation nevertheless and helped thwart his hope of winning a third term as president. *(Bettmann)*

The Grant Scandals

During the 1872 campaign, the first of a series of political scandals came to light that would plague Grant and the Republicans for the next eight years. It involved the Crédit Mobilier, a French-owned construction company that had helped build the Union Pacific Railroad. The heads of Crédit Mobilier had used their positions as Union Pacific stockholders to steer large and fraudulent contracts to their construction company, in the process bilking the Union Pacific (and the federal government, which provided large subsidies to the railroad) of millions. To prevent investigations, the directors had transferred some Crédit Mobilier stock to key members of Congress. But in 1872, Congress did

investigate and revealed that some highly placed Republicans—including Schuyler Colfax, now Grant's vice president—had accepted stock.

One dreary episode followed another in Grant's second term. Benjamin H. Bristow, Grant's third Treasury secretary, discovered that some of his officials and a group of distillers operating as a "Whiskey ring" were cheating the government out of taxes by filing false reports. Among those involved was the president's private secretary, Orville E. Babcock. Then a House investigation revealed that William W. Belknap, secretary of war, had accepted bribes to retain an Indian-post trader in office; it became known as the "Indian ring." Other, lesser scandals added to the growing impression that "Grantism" had brought rampant corruption to government.

The Greenback Question

Compounding Grant's, and the nation's, problems was the financial crisis known as the Panic of 1873. It began with the failure of a leading investment banking firm, Jay Cooke and Company, which had invested too heavily in postwar railroad building. There had been panics before—in 1819, 1837, and 1857—but this was the worst one yet. The depression it produced lasted four years.

Debtors now pressured the government to inflate the currency, which would have made it easier for them to pay their debts. More specifically, they urged the government to redeem its war bonds with "greenbacks"—paper currency of the sort issued during the Civil War—which would increase the amount of money in circulation, lower the value of the dollar, and hence reduce the value of their debts. But Grant and most Republicans favored a "sound" currency—based solidly on gold reserves—which would favor the interests of banks and other creditors by keeping the dollar, and hence the value of the debts owed to them, high.

The greenback question would not go away. For one thing, there was the approximately $356 million in paper currency issued during the Civil War that was still in circulation. And in 1873, when the Supreme Court ruled in *Knox* v. *Lee* that greenbacks were legal, the Treasury issued more in response to the panic. The following year, Congress voted to raise the total further. But Grant, under pressure from eastern financial interests, vetoed the measure—over the loud objections of many Republicans.

In 1875, Republican leaders in Congress, in an effort to crush the greenback movement for good, passed the Specie Resumption Act. This law provided that after January 1, 1879, the greenback dollars, whose value constantly fluctuated, would be redeemed by the government and replaced with new certificates, firmly pegged to the price of gold. The law satisfied creditors, who had worried that debts would be repaid in debased paper currency. But "resumption" did nothing for debtors, because the gold-based money supply was not able to expand enough to help them.

In 1875, the greenbackers, as the inflationists were called, formed their own political organization: the National Greenback Party. It was active in the next three presidential elections, but it failed to gain widespread support. It did, however, keep the money issue alive. And in the 1880s, the greenback forces began to merge with another, more powerful group of currency reformers—those who favored silver as the basis of currency—to help produce a political movement that would ultimately attain enormous strength. The question of the proper composition of the currency was to remain one of the most controversial and enduring issues in late-nineteenth-century American politics.

Republican Diplomacy

The Johnson and Grant administrations achieved their greatest successes in foreign affairs. The accomplishments were the work not of the presidents themselves, who displayed little aptitude for diplomacy, but of two talented secretaries of state: William H. Seward, who had served Lincoln and who served throughout the two terms of the Grant administration.

An ardent expansionist and advocate of a vigorous foreign policy, Seward acted with as much daring as the demands of Reconstruction politics and the Republican Party's hatred of President Johnson would permit. Seward agreed to a Russian offer to sell Alaska to the United States for $7.2 million. Only with great difficulty was he able to persuade Congress to authorize the purchase, and he faced criticism from many who considered Alaska a useless frozen wasteland and called it "Seward's Folly." But Seward knew that Alaska was an important fishing center and a potential source of valuable resources such as gold. In 1867, Seward also engineered the American annexation of the tiny Midway Islands west of Hawaii.

In contrast with its sometimes shambling course in domestic politics, the diplomatic performance of the Grant administration under Hamilton Fish was generally decisive and firm. Fish was in many ways the personification of northeastern conservatism and, while officially a Republican, had opposed virtually all the party's Reconstruction policies. But he was a skilled and effective diplomat. His first major challenge was resolving a burning controversy with England. Many Americans believed that the British government had violated the neutrality laws during the Civil War by permitting English shipyards to build ships (among them the *Alabama*) for the Confederacy. American demands that England pay for the damage these vessels had caused became known as the "Alabama claims."

Seward had tried to settle the Alabama claims through the Johnson-Clarendon Convention of 1869, which would have submitted the matter to arbitration. But the Senate rejected it because it contained no British apology. In 1871, Fish succeeded in forging a new agreement: the Treaty of Washington, which provided for international arbitration of the claims and in which Britain expressed regret for the escape of the *Alabama* from England.

THE ABANDONMENT OF RECONSTRUCTION

As the North grew increasingly preoccupied with its own political and economic problems, interest in Reconstruction began to wane. The Grant administration continued to protect Republican governments in the South, but less because of any interest in ensuring the position of freedmen than because of a desire to prevent the reemergence of a strong Democratic Party in the region. But even the presence of federal troops was not enough to prevent white Southerners from overturning the Reconstruction regimes. By the time Grant left office, Democrats had taken back (or, as white Southerners liked to put it, "redeemed") the governments of seven of the eleven former Confederate states.

For three other states—South Carolina, Louisiana, and Florida—the end of Reconstruction had to wait for the withdrawal of the last federal troops in 1876, a withdrawal that was the result of a long process of political bargaining and compromise at the national level. (One former Confederate state, Tennessee, had never been part of the Reconstruction process.)

The Southern States "Redeemed"

In the states where whites constituted a majority—the states of the upper South—overthrowing Republican control was relatively simple. By 1872, all but a handful of Southern whites had regained suffrage. Now a clear majority of the electorate, they needed only to organize and vote for their candidates.

In other states, where blacks were a majority or the populations of the two races were almost equal, whites used intimidation and violence to undermine the Reconstruction regimes. Secret societies—the Ku Klux Klan, the Knights of the White Camellia, and others—used terrorism to frighten or physically bar blacks from voting or otherwise exercising citizenship. Paramilitary organizations—the Red Shirts and White Leagues—armed themselves to "police" elections and worked to force all white males to join the Democratic Party and to exclude all blacks from meaningful political activity.

The Ku Klux Klan was the largest and most effective of these organizations. Organized in 1866 and led by former Confederate General Nathan Bedford Forrest, it gradually absorbed many of the smaller terrorist organizations. Its leaders devised rituals, costumes, secret languages, and other airs of mystery to create a bond among its members and make it seem even more terrifying to those it was attempting to intimidate. The Klan's "midnight rides"—bands of men clad in white sheets and masks, their horses covered with white robes and with hooves muffled—created terror in black communities throughout the South.

Many white Southerners considered the Klan and the other secret societies and paramilitary groups proud, patriotic societies. Together such groups served, in effect, as a military force (even if a decentralized and poorly organized one) continuing the battle against Northern rule. They worked in particular to advance the interests of those with the most to gain from a restoration of white supremacy—above all the planter class and the Southern Democratic Party.

Even stronger than the Klan in discouraging black political power, however, was the simple weapon of economic pressure. Some planters refused to rent land to Republican blacks; storekeepers refused to extend them credit; employers refused to give them work.

In the meantime, Southern blacks were losing the support of many of their former supporters in the North. After the adoption of the Fifteenth Amendment in 1870, some reformers convinced themselves that their long campaign in behalf of black people was now over; that with the vote, blacks ought to be able to take care of themselves. Former Radical leaders such as Charles Sumner and Horace Greeley now began calling themselves Liberals, cooperating with Democrats, and at times outdoing even the Democrats in denouncing what they viewed as black and carpetbag misgovernment. Within the South itself, many white Republicans joined the Liberals and eventually moved into the Democratic Party.

The Panic of 1873 further undermined support for Reconstruction. In the congressional elections of 1874, the Democrats won control of the House of Representatives for the first time since 1861. Grant took note of the changing temper of the North and made use of military force to prop up the Republican regimes that were still standing in the South.

By the end of 1876, only three states were left in the hands of the Republicans—South Carolina, Louisiana, and Florida. In state elections that year, Democrats (after using terrorist tactics) claimed victory in all three. But the Republicans challenged the results and claimed victory as well, and they were able to remain in office because of the presence of federal troops. Without federal troops, it was now clear, the last of the Republican regimes would quickly fall.

The Compromise of 1877

Grant had hoped to run for another term in 1876, but most Republican leaders—shaken by recent Democrat successes, afraid of the scandals with which Grant was associated, and concerned about the president's failing health—resisted. Instead, they sought a candidate not associated with the problems of the Grant years, one who might entice Liberals back and unite the party again. They settled on Rutherford B. Hayes, a former Union army officer, governor, and congressman, champion of civil service reform. The Democrats united behind Samuel J. Tilden, the reform governor of New York who had been instrumental in overthrowing the corrupt Tweed Ring of New York City's Tammany Hall.

Although the campaign was a bitter one, there were few differences of principle between the candidates, both of whom were conservatives committed to moderate reform. The November election produced an apparent Democratic victory. Tilden carried the South and several large Northern states, and his popular margin over Hayes was nearly 300,000 votes. But disputed returns from Louisiana, South Carolina, Florida, and Oregon, whose total electoral vote was 20, threw the election in doubt. Tilden had undisputed claim to 184 electoral votes, only one short of a majority. But Hayes could still win if he managed to receive all 20 disputed votes.

The Constitution had established no method to determine the validity of disputed returns. It was clear that the decision lay with Congress, but it was not clear with which house or through what method. (The Senate was Republican, the House Democratic.) Members of each party naturally supported a solution that would yield them the victory.

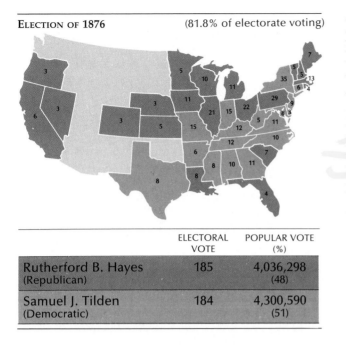

ELECTION OF **1876**   (81.8% of electorate voting)

	ELECTORAL VOTE	POPULAR VOTE (%)
Rutherford B. Hayes (Republican)	185	4,036,298 (48)
Samuel J. Tilden (Democratic)	184	4,300,590 (51)

Finally, late in January 1877, Congress tried to break the deadlock by creating a special electoral commission to judge the disputed votes. The commission was to be composed of five senators, five representatives, and five justices of the Supreme Court. The congressional delegation would consist of five Republicans and five Democrats. The Court delegation would include two Republicans, two Democrats, and an independent. But the independent seat ultimately went to a justice whose real sympathies were with the Republicans. The commission voted along straight party lines, 8 to 7, awarding every disputed vote to Hayes. Congress accepted their verdict on March 2. Two days later, Hayes was inaugurated.

Behind the resolution of the deadlock however, lay a series of elaborate compromises among leaders of both parties. When a Democratic filibuster threatened to derail the commission's report, Republican Senate leaders met secretly with Southern Democratic leaders to work out terms by which the Democrats would allow the election of Hayes. According to traditional accounts, Republicans and Southern Democrats met at Washington's Wormley Hotel. In return for a Republican pledge that Hayes would withdraw the last federal troops from the South, thus permitting the overthrow of the last Republican governments there, the Southerners agreed to abandon the filibuster.

Actually, the story behind the "Compromise of 1877" is somewhat more complex. Hayes was already

on record favoring withdrawal of the troops, so Republicans needed to offer more than that if they hoped for Democratic support. The real agreement, the one that won over the Southern Democrats, was reached well before the Wormley meeting. As the price of their cooperation, the Southern Democrats (among them some former Whigs) exacted several pledges from the Republicans in addition to withdrawal of the troops: the appointment of at least one Southerner to the Hayes cabinet, control of federal patronage in their areas, generous internal improvements, and federal aid for the Texas and Pacific Railroad. Many powerful Southern Democrats supported industrializing their region. They believed Republican programs of federal support for business would aid the South more than the states' rights policies of the Democrats.

In his inaugural address, Hayes announced that the South's most pressing need was the restoration of "wise, honest, and peaceful local self-government"— a signal that he planned to withdraw federal troops and let white Democrats take over the state governments. That statement, and Hayes's subsequent actions, supported the widespread charges that he was paying off the South for acquiescing in his election and strengthened those who referred to him as "his Fraudulency." Hayes tried to counter such charges by projecting an image of stern public (and private) rectitude. But the election had already created such bitterness that even Hayes's promise to serve only one term could not mollify his critics.

The president and his party had hoped to build up a "new Republican" organization in the South drawn from Whiggish conservative white groups and committed to some modest acceptance of African-American rights. But all such efforts failed. Although many white Southern leaders sympathized with Republican economic policies, popular resentment of Reconstruction was so deep that supporting the party was politically impossible. At the same time, the withdrawal of federal troops was a signal that the national government was giving up its attempt to control Southern politics and to improve the lot of blacks in Southern society.

The Legacy of Reconstruction

Reconstruction made some important contributions to the efforts of former slaves to achieve dignity and equality in American life. There was a significant redistribution of income, from which blacks benefited. There was a more limited but not unimportant redistribution of landownership, which enabled some former slaves to acquire property. There was both a relative and an absolute improvement in the economic

RECONSTRUCTION

DEBATE OVER THE NATURE of Reconstruction—not only among historians, but among the public at large—has created so much controversy over the decades that one scholar, writing in 1959, described the issue as a "dark and bloody ground." Among historians, the passions of the debate have to some extent subsided since then; but in the popular mind, Reconstruction continues to raise "dark and bloody" images.

For many years, a relatively uniform and highly critical view of Reconstruction prevailed among historians, a reflection of broad currents in popular thought. By the late nineteenth century, most white Americans in both the North and the South had come to believe that few real differences any longer divided the sections, that the nation should strive for a genuine reconciliation. And most white Americans believed as well in the superiority of their race, in the inherent unfitness of blacks for political or social equality. Out of this mentality was born the first major historical interpretation of Reconstruction, through the work of William A. Dunning. In *Reconstruction, Political and Economic* (1907), Dunning portrayed Reconstruction as a corrupt outrage perpetrated on the prostrate South by a vicious and vindictive cabal of Northern Republican Radicals. Reconstruction governments were based on "bayonet rule." Unscrupulous and self-aggrandizing carpetbaggers flooded the South to profit from the misery of the defeated region. Ignorant, illiterate blacks were thrust into positions of power for which they were entirely unfit. The Reconstruction experiment, a moral abomination from its first moments, survived only because of the determination of the Republican Party to keep itself in power. (Some later writers, notably Howard K. Beale, added an economic motive—to protect Northern business interests.) Dunning and his many students (who together formed what became known as the "Dunning school") compiled state-by-state evidence to show that the legacy of Reconstruction was corruption, ruinous taxation, and astronomical increases in the public debt.

The Dunning school not only shaped the views of several generations of historians. It also reflected and helped to shape the views of much of the public. Popular depictions of Reconstruction for years to come (as the book and movie *Gone with the Wind* suggested) portrayed the era as one of tragic exploitation of the South by the North. Even today, many white southerners and many others continue to accept the basic premises of the Dunning interpretation. Among historians, however, the old view of Reconstruction has gradually lost all credibility.

The great black scholar W. E. B. Du Bois was among the first to challenge the Dunning view in a 1910 article and, later, in a 1935 book, *Black Reconstruction*. To him, Reconstruction politics in the Southern states had been an effort on the part of the masses, black and white, to create a more democratic society. The misdeeds of the Reconstruction governments, he claimed, had been greatly exaggerated, and their achievements overlooked. The governments had been expensive, he insisted, because they had tried to provide public education and other public services on a scale never before attempted in the South. But Du Bois's use of Marxist theory in his work caused many historians who did not share his philosophy to dismiss his argument; and it remained for a group of less radical, white historians to shatter the Dunning image of Reconstruction.

In the 1940s, historians such as C. Vann Woodward, David Herbert Donald, Thomas B. Alexander, and others began to reexamine the record of the Reconstruction governments in the South and to suggest that their record was not nearly as bad as most historians had previously assumed. They also looked at the Radical Republicans in Congress and suggested that they had not been motivated by vindictiveness and

WHERE HISTORIANS DISAGREE

partisanship alone. By the early 1960s, a new view of Reconstruction as emerging from these efforts, a view whose appeal to historians grew stronger with the emergence of the "Second Reconstruction," the civil rights movement. The revisionist approach was summarized by John Hope Franklin in *Reconstruction After the Civil War* (1961) and Kenneth Stampp in *The Era of Reconstruction* (1965), which claimed that the postwar Republicans had been engaged in a genuine, if flawed, effort to solve the problem of race in the South by providing much-needed protection to the freedmen. The Reconstruction governments, for all their faults, had been bold experiments in interracial politics. The congressional Radicals were not saints, but they had displayed a genuine concern for the rights of slaves. And Andrew Johnson was not a martyred defender of the Constitution, but an inept, racist politician who resisted reasonable compromise and brought the government to a crisis. There had been no such thing as "bayonet rule" or "Negro rule" in the South. Blacks had played only a small part in Reconstruction governments and had generally acquitted themselves well. The Reconstruction regimes had, in fact, brought important progress to the South, establishing the region's first public school system and other important social changes. Corruption in the South had been no worse than corruption in the North at that time. What was tragic about Reconstruction, the revisionist view claimed, was not what it did to Southern whites but what it did not do for Southern blacks. By stopping short of the reforms necessary to ensure blacks genuine equality, Reconstruction had consigned them to more than a century of injustice and discrimination.

By the 1970s, then, the Dunning view of Reconstruction had all but disappeared from serious scholarly discussion. Instead, historians seemed to agree that Reconstruction had in fact changed the South relatively little; and they began to debate why Reconstruction fell as far short as it did of guaranteeing racial justice. Some

scholars have claimed that conservative obstacles to change were so great that the Radicals, despite their good intentions, simply could not overcome them. Others have argued that the Radicals themselves were not sufficiently committed to the principle of racial justice, that they abandoned the cause quickly when it became clear to them that the battle would not easily be won.

In recent years scholars have begun to question the revisionist view—not in an effort to revive the old Dunning interpretation, but in an attempt to draw attention to those things Reconstruction in fact achieved. Leon Litwack's *Been in the Storm So Long* (1979) reveals that former slaves used the relative latitude they enjoyed under Reconstruction to build a certain independence for themselves within Southern society. They strengthened their churches; they reunited their families; they refused to work in the "gang labor" system of the plantations and forced the creation of a new labor system in which they had more control over their own lives. Eric Foner, in *Nothing but Freedom* (1983) and *Reconstruction: America's Unfinished Revolution* (1988), compared the aftermath of slavery in the United States with similar experiences in the Caribbean and concluded that what is striking about the American experience in this context is not how little was accomplished, but how far the former slaves moved toward freedom and independence in a short time, and how large a role African Americans themselves played in shaping Reconstruction. During Reconstruction, blacks won a certain amount of legal and political power in the South; and even though they held that power only temporarily, they used it for a time to strengthen their economic and social positions and to win a position of limited but genuine independence. Through Reconstruction they won, if not equality, a measure of individual and community autonomy, building blocks of the freedom that emancipation alone had not guaranteed.

circumstances of most blacks. Perhaps most of all, there was a large, and largely successful, effort by blacks themselves to carve out a society and culture of their own within the American South, to create or strengthen their own institutions, and to convince themselves that they were, indeed, no longer slaves.

Reconstruction was not as disastrous an experience for Southern whites as most believed at the time. The region had emerged from a prolonged and bloody war defeated and devastated, and yet within little more than a decade, the white South had regained control of its own institutions and, to a great extent, restored its traditional ruling class to power. Former Confederate leaders received no severe punishments. The federal government imposed no drastic economic reforms on the region, and indeed few lasting political changes of any kind other than the abolition of slavery. Not many conquered peoples have fared as well.

But Reconstruction was as notable for its limitations as it was for its achievements. For in those years the United States failed in its first serious effort to resolve its oldest and deepest social problem—the problem of race. What was more, the experience so disappointed, disillusioned, and embittered white Americans that it would be nearly a century before they would try again in any serious way.

Why did this great assault on racial injustice not achieve more? In part, it was because of the weaknesses and errors of the people who directed it. But in greater part, it was because attempts to produce solutions ran up against conservative obstacles so deeply embedded in the nation's life that they could not be dislodged. Veneration of the Constitution sharply limited the willingness of national leaders to infringe on the rights of states and individuals. A profound respect for private property and free enterprise prevented any real assault on economic privilege in the South. Above all, perhaps, a pervasive belief among many of even the most liberal whites that African Americans were inherently inferior served as an obstacle to equality. Given the context within which Americans of the 1860s and 1870s were working, what is surprising, perhaps, is not that Reconstruction did so little, but that it did even as much as it did.

Considering the odds confronting them, therefore, African Americans had reason for pride in the gains they were able to make during Reconstruction. And future generations had reason for gratitude for two great charters of freedom—the Fourteenth and Fifteenth Amendments to the Constitution—which, although largely ignored at the time, would one day serve as the basis for a "Second Reconstruction" that would renew the drive to bring freedom and equality to all Americans.

THE NEW SOUTH

The agreement between southern Democrats and northern Republicans that helped settle the disputed election of 1876 was supposed to be the first step toward developing a stable, permanent Republican Party in the South. In that respect, at least, it failed. In the years following the end of Reconstruction, white southerners established the Democratic Party as the only viable political organization for the region's whites. Even so, the South did change in the years after Reconstruction in some of the ways the framers of the Compromise of 1877 had hoped.

The "Redeemers"

By the end of 1877—after the last withdrawal of federal troops—every southern state government had been "redeemed." That is, political power had been restored to white Democrats. Many white southerners rejoiced at the restoration of what they liked to call "home rule." But in reality, political power in the region was soon more restricted than at any time since the Civil War. Once again, the South fell under the control of a powerful, conservative oligarchy, whose members were known variously as the "Redeemers" (to themselves and their supporters) or the "Bourbons" (a term for aristocrats used by some of their critics).

In a few places, this post-Reconstruction ruling class was much the same as the ruling class of the antebellum period. In Alabama, for example, the old planter elite—despite challenges from new merchant and industrial forces—retained much of its former power and continued largely to dominate the state for decades. In most areas, however, the Redeemers constituted a genuinely new ruling class. They were merchants, industrialists, railroad developers, and financiers. Some of them were former planters, some of them northern immigrants who had become absorbed into the region's life, some of them ambitious, upwardly mobile white southerners from the region's lower social tiers. They combined a commitment to "home rule" and social conservatism with a commitment to economic development.

The various Bourbon governments of the New South behaved in many respects quite similarly. Conservatives had complained that the Reconstruction governments fostered widespread corruption, but the Redeemer regimes were, if anything, even more awash in waste and fraud. (In this, they were little different from governments in every region of the country.) At the same time, virtually all the new Democratic regimes lowered taxes, reduced spending, and drastically diminished state services—including many of the most important accomplishments of Reconstruction. In one state after another, for example, state support for public school systems was reduced or eliminated. "Schools are not a necessity," an economy-conscious governor of Virginia commented.

By the late 1870s, significant dissenting groups were challenging the Bourbons: protesting the cuts in services and denouncing the commitment of the Redeemer governments to paying off the prewar and Reconstruction debts in full, at the original (usually high) rates of interest. In Virginia, for example, a vigorous "Readjuster" movement emerged, demanding that the state revise its debt payment procedures so as to make more money available for state services. In 1879, the Readjusters won control of the legislature, and in the next few years they captured the governorship and a U.S. Senate seat. Other states produced similar movements, some of them adding demands as well for greenbacks, debt relief, and other economic reforms. (A few such independent movements included significant numbers of blacks in their ranks, but all consisted primarily of lower-income whites.) By the mid-1880s, however, conservative southerners—largely by exploiting racial prejudice—had effectively destroyed most of the dissenting movements.

Industrialization and the "New South"

Many white southern leaders in the post-Reconstruction era hoped to see their region become the home of a vigorous industrial economy. The South had lost the war, many argued, because its economy had been unable to compete with the modernized manufacturing capacity of the North. Now the region must "out-Yankee the Yankees" and build a "New South." Henry Grady, editor of the *Atlanta Constitution,* and other prominent spokesmen for a New South seldom challenged white supremacy, but they did advocate other important changes in southern values. Above all, they promoted the virtues of thrift, industry, and progress—qualities that prewar southerners had often denounced in northern society. "We have sown towns and cities in the place of theories," Grady boasted to a New England audience in the 1880s, "and put business above politics. . . . We have fallen in love with work."

But even the most fervent advocates of the New South creed were generally unwilling to break entirely with the Southern past. That was evident in, among other things, the popular literature of the region. At the same time that white southern writers were extolling the virtues of industrialization in newspaper editorials and speeches, they were painting nostalgic portraits of the Old South in their literature. Few southerners advocated a literal return to the old ways, but most whites eagerly embraced romantic talk of the "Lost Cause." And they responded warmly to the local-color fiction of such writers as Joel Chandler Harris, whose folk tales—the most famous being *Uncle Remus* (1880)—portrayed the slave society of the antebellum years as a harmonious world marked by engaging dialect and close emotional bonds between the races. Thomas Nelson Page similarly extolled the old Virginia aristocracy. The white leaders of the New South, in short, faced their future with one foot still in the past.

Even so, New South enthusiasts did help southern industry expand dramatically in the years after Reconstruction and become a more important part of the region's economy than ever before. Most visible was the growth in textile manufacturing, which increased ninefold in the last twenty years of the century. In the past, southern planters had usually shipped their cotton out of the region to manufacturers in the North or in Europe. Now textile factories appeared in the South itself—many of them drawn to the region from New England by the abundance of water power, the ready supply of cheap labor, the low taxes, and the accommodating conservative governments. The tobacco-processing industry, similarly, established an important foothold in the region, largely through the work of James B. Duke of North Carolina, whose American Tobacco Company established for a time a virtual monopoly over the processing of raw tobacco into marketable materials. In the lower South, and particularly in Birmingham, Alabama, the iron (and, later, steel) industry grew rapidly. By 1890, the southern iron and steel industry represented nearly a fifth of the nation's total capacity.

Railroad development increased substantially in the post-Reconstruction years—at a rate far greater than that of the nation at large. Between 1880 and 1890, trackage in the South more than doubled. And the South took a major step toward integrating its transportation system with that of the rest of the country when, in 1886, it changed the gauge (width) of its trackage to correspond with the standards of the North. No longer would it be necessary for cargoes heading into the South to be transferred from one train to another at the borders of the region.

Yet southern industry developed within strict limits, and its effects on the region were never even remotely comparable to the effects of industrialization on the North. The southern share of national manufacturing doubled in the last twenty years of the cen-

THE CROP-LIEN SYSTEM: THE SOUTH IN 1880

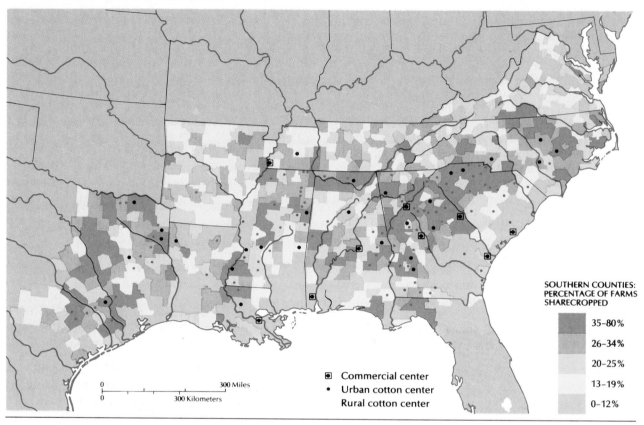

SOUTHERN COUNTIES:
PERCENTAGE OF FARMS
SHARECROPPED

	35–80%
	26–34%
	20–25%
	13–19%
	0–12%

◪ Commercial center
• Urban cotton center
   Rural cotton center

tury, to 10 percent of the total. But that percentage was the same the South had claimed in 1860; the region, in other words, had done no more than regain what it had lost during the war and its aftermath. The region's per capita income increased 21 percent in the same period. But at the end of the century, average income in the South was only 40 percent of that in the North; in 1860 it had been more than 60 percent. And even in those areas where development had been most rapid—textiles, iron, railroads—much of the capital had come from the North. In effect, the South was developing a colonial economy.

The growth of industry in the South required the region to recruit a substantial industrial work force for the first time. From the beginning, a high percentage of the factory workers (and an especially high percentage of textile workers) were women. Heavy male casualties in the Civil War had helped create a large population of unmarried women who desperately needed employment. Factories also hired entire families, many of whom were moving into towns from failed farms. Hours were long (often as much as twelve

hours a day) and wages were far below the northern equivalent; indeed one of the greatest attractions of the South to industrialists was that employers were able to pay workers there as little as one-half what northern workers received. Life in most mill towns was rigidly controlled by the owners and managers of the factories. They rigorously suppressed attempts at protest or union organization. Company stores sold goods to workers at inflated prices and issued credit at exorbitant rates (much like country stores in agrarian areas), and mill owners ensured that no competitors were able to establish themselves in the community. At the same time, however, the conditions of the mill town helped create a strong sense of community and solidarity among workers (even if they seldom translated such feelings into militancy).

Some industries, textiles for example, offered virtually no opportunities to African American workers. Others—tobacco, iron, and lumber, among others—did provide some employment for blacks, usually the most menial and lowest-paid positions. Some mill towns, therefore, were places where black and white

TUSKEGEE INSTITUTE, 1881
From these modest beginnings, Booker T. Washington's Tuskegee Institute in Alabama became the preeminent academy offering technical and industrial training to black men. It deliberately deemphasized the traditional liberal arts curricula of most colleges. Washington considered such training an unnecessary frill and encouraged his students to work on developing practical skills. *(Bettmann)*

culture came into close contact. That proximity contributed less to the growth of racial harmony than to the determination of white leaders to take additional measures to protect white supremacy.

At times, industrialization proceeded on the basis of no wage-paying employment at all. Through the "convict-lease" system, southern states leased gangs of convicted criminals to private interests as a cheap labor supply. The system exposed the convicts to brutal and at times fatal mistreatment. It paid them nothing (the leasing fees went to the states, not the workers).

And it denied employment in railroad construction and other projects to the free labor force.

Tenants and Sharecroppers

Despite significant growth in southern industry, the region remained primarily agrarian. The most important economic reality in the post-Reconstruction South, therefore, was the impoverished state of agriculture. The 1870s and 1880s saw an acceleration of the process that had begun in the immediate postwar years: the

THE ORIGINS OF SEGREGATION

Not until after World War II, when the emergence of the civil rights movement forced white Americans to confront the issue of racial segregation, did historians pay much attention to the origins of the institution. Most had assumed that the separation of the races had emerged naturally and even inevitably out of the abolition of slavery. It had been a response to the failure of Reconstruction, the weakness and poverty of the black community, and the pervasiveness of white racism. It was, in effect, the way things had always been.

The first major challenge to these assumptions, indeed the first serious scholarly effort to explain the origins of segregation, was C. Vann Woodward's *The Strange Career of Jim Crow* published in 1956. Not only was it important in reshaping scholarship. It had a significant political impact as well. As a southern liberal, Woodward was eager to refute assumptions that segregation was part of an unchanging and unchangeable southern tradition. He wanted to convince scholars that the history of the South had been one of sharp discontinuities; and he wanted to convince a larger public that the racial institutions they considered part of a long, unbroken tradition were in fact the product of a particular set of historical circumstances.

In the aftermath of emancipation, and indeed for two decades after Reconstruction, Woodward argued, race relations in the South had remained relatively fluid. Blacks and whites did not often interact as equals, certainly, but black Southerners enjoyed a degree of latitude in social and even political affairs that they would subsequently lose. Blacks and whites often rode together in the same railroad cars, ate in the same restaurants, used the same public facilities. Blacks voted in significant numbers. Blacks and whites considered a number of different visions of how the races should live together, and as late as 1890 it was not at all clear which of those visions would prevail. By the end of the nineteenth century, however, a great wave of racist legislation—the Jim Crow laws, which established the basis of segregation—had hardened race relations and destroyed the gentler alternatives that many whites and blacks had considered viable only a few years before. The principal reason, Woodward argued, was the populist political insurgency of the 1890s, which mobilized blacks and whites alike and which frightened many white southerners into thinking that blacks might soon be a major political power in the region. Southern conservatives, in particular, used the issue of white supremacy to attack the populists and to prevent blacks from forming an alliance with them. The result was disenfranchisement and segregation.

Woodward's argument suggested that laws were important in shaping social behavior—that laws had made segregation and, by implication, other laws could unmake it. Not all historians agreed. A more pessimistic picture of segregation emerged in 1965 from Joel Williamson's study of South Carolina, *After Slavery*. Williamson argued that the laws of the 1890s did not mean very much, that they simply ratified a set of conditions that had been firmly established by the end of Reconstruction. As early as the mid-1870s,

imposition of systems of tenantry and debt peonage on much of the region; the reliance on a few cash crops rather than on a diversified agricultural system; and increasing absentee ownership of valuable farmlands (many of them purchased by merchants and industrialists who paid little attention to whether the land was being properly used). During Reconstruction, perhaps a third or more of the farmers in the South were tenants; by 1900 the figure had increased to 70 percent. That was in large part the result of the crop-lien system that had emerged in the aftermath of the Civil War. Farmers who owned their own land often lost it

WHERE HISTORIANS DISAGREE

Williamson claimed, the races had already begun to live in two separate societies. Blacks had constructed their own churches, schools, businesses, and neighborhoods; whites had begun to exclude blacks from white institutions. The separation was partly a result of pressure and coercion from whites, partly a result of the desire of blacks to develop their own, independent culture. Whatever the reasons, however, segregation was largely in place by the end of the 1870s, continuing in a different form a pattern of racial separation established under slavery. The laws of the 1890s did little more than codify an already established system.

More recently, scholars have revised or challenged both these interpretations by attempting to link the rise of legal segregation to changing social and economic circumstances in the South. Howard Rabinowitz's *Race Relations in the Urban South* (1978) links the rise of segregation to the new challenge of devising a form of race relations suitable to life in the growing southern cities, into which rural blacks were moving in substantial numbers. The creation of separate public facilities—schools, parks, waiting rooms, etc.—was not so much an effort to drive blacks out of white facilities; they had never had access to those facilities, and few whites had ever been willing to consider granting them access. It was, rather, an attempt to create for a black community that virtually all whites agreed must remain essentially separate a set of facilities where none had previously existed. Without segregation, in other words, urban blacks would have had no schools or parks at all. The alternative to segregation, Rabinowitz suggests, was not integration, but exclusion.

In the early 1980s, a number of scholars began examining segregation anew in light of the rising American interest in South Africa, whose system of *apartheid* seemed to them to be similar in many ways to the by-then largely dismantled Jim Crow system in the South. John Cell's *The Highest Stage of White Supremacy* (1982) used the comparison to construct a revised explanation of how segregation emerged in the American South. Like Rabinowitz, he considered the increasing urbanization of the region the principal factor. But he ascribed different motives to those whites who promoted the rise of Jim Crow. The segregation laws, Cell argues, were a continuation of an unchanging determination by southern whites to retain control over the black population. What had shifted was not their commitment to white supremacy but the things necessary to preserve it. The emergence of large black communities in urban areas and of a significant black labor force in factories presented a new challenge to white southerners. They could not control these new communities in the same informal ways they had been able to control rural blacks, who were more directly dependent on white landowners and merchants than their urban counterparts. In the city, blacks and whites were in more direct competition than they had been in the countryside. There was more danger of social mixing. The city therefore required different, and more rigidly institutionalized, systems of control. The Jim Crow laws were a response not just to an enduring commitment to white supremacy, but to a new reality that required white supremacy to move to its "highest stage," where it would have a rigid legal and institutional basis.

---

as merchants seized it for payment of liens. Farmers who rented could never accumulate enough capital to buy land.

Tenantry took several forms. Farmers who owned tools, equipment, and farm animals—or who had the money to buy them—usually paid an annual cash rent for their land. But many farmers (including most black ones) had no money or equipment at all. Landlords would supply them with land, a crude house, a few tools, seed, and sometimes a mule. In return, farmers would promise the landlord a large share of the annual crop—hence the term "sharecropping." After paying their landlords and their local furnishing merchants (who were often the same people), sharecroppers seldom had anything left to sell on their own.

The crop-lien system was one of several factors contributing to a particularly harsh social and economic transformation of the southern backcountry, the piney woods and mountain regions where cotton and slavery had always been rare and where farmers lived ruggedly independent lives. Subsistence agriculture had long been the norm in these areas; but as indebtedness grew, many farmers now had to grow cash crops such as cotton instead of the food crops they had traditionally cultivated in order to make enough money to pay off their loans.

But the transformation of the backcountry was a result of other factors as well. Many backcountry residents had traditionally subsisted by raising livestock, which had roamed freely across the landscape. In the 1870s, as commercial agriculture began to intrude into these regions, many communities began to pass "fence laws," which required farmers to fence in their animals (as opposed to fencing off their crops, as had once been the custom). There were widespread protests against the new laws, and at times violent efforts to resist them. But the existence of the open range (which had once been as much a part of life in the backcountry South as it was in the American West) could not survive the spread of commercial agriculture. Increasingly, therefore, opportunities for families to live largely self-sufficiently were declining. At the same time, opportunities for profiting within the market remained slim. The people of the backcountry, perhaps even more than other groups for whom agriculture had always been a business, felt the pain of losing their economic independence. They would be among the most important constituents for the populist protests of the 1880s and 1890s.

The crop-lien system was particularly devastating to southern blacks, few of whom owned their own land to begin with. These economic difficulties were compounded by social and legal discrimination, which in the post-Reconstruction era began to take new forms and to inspire new responses.

African Americans and the New South

The "New South creed" was not the property of whites alone. Many African Americans were attracted to the vision of progress and self-improvement as well. Some blacks succeeded in elevating themselves into a distinct middle class—economically inferior to the white middle class, but nevertheless significant. These were former slaves (and, as the decades passed, their off-

spring) who managed to acquire property, establish small businesses, or enter professions. A few blacks accumulated substantial fortunes by establishing banks and insurance companies for their race. One of those was Maggie Lena, a black woman who became the first female bank president in the United States when she founded the St. Luke Penny Savings Bank in Richmond in 1903. Most middle-class blacks experienced more modest gains by becoming doctors, lawyers, nurses, or teachers serving members of their own race.

A cardinal tenet of this rising group of blacks was that education was vital to the future of their race. With the support of northern missionary societies and, to a far lesser extent, a few southern state governments, they expanded the network of black colleges and institutes that had taken root during Reconstruction into an important educational system.

The chief spokesman for this commitment to education, and for a time the major spokesman for his race as a whole, was Booker T. Washington, founder and president of the Tuskegee Institute in Alabama. Born into slavery, Washington had worked his way out of poverty after acquiring an education (at Virginia's famous Hampton Institute). He urged other blacks to follow the same road to self-improvement.

Washington's message was both cautious and hopeful. African Americans should attend school, learn skills, and establish a solid footing in agriculture and the trades. Industrial, not classical, education should be their goal. Blacks should, moreover, refine their speech, improve their dress, and adopt habits of thrift and personal cleanliness; they should, in short, adopt the standards of the white middle class. Only thus, he claimed, could they win the respect of the white population, the prerequisite for any larger social gains. Blacks should forgo agitating for political rights, he said, and concentrate on self-improvement and preparation for equality.

In a famous speech in Georgia in 1895, Washington outlined a philosophy of race relations that became widely known as the Atlanta Compromise. "The wisest among my race understand," he said, "that the agitation of questions of social equality is the extremest folly." Rather, blacks should engage in "severe and constant struggle" for economic gains; for, as he explained, "no race that has anything to contribute to the markets of the world is long in any degree ostracized." If blacks were ever to win the rights and privileges of citizenship, they must first show that they were "prepared for the exercise of these privileges."

Washington offered a powerful challenge to those whites who wanted to discourage African Americans from acquiring an education or winning any economic gains. He helped awaken the interest of a new gener-

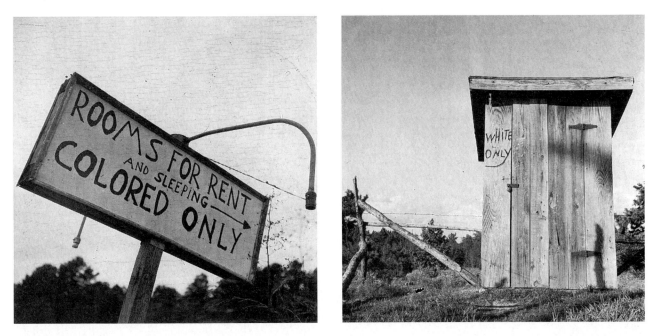

JIM CROW AT WORK
The formal separation (or "segregation") of the races spread through the South in the 1890s and early twentieth century, producing signs such as these—many of which survived into the 1960s. *(Library of Congress)*

ation to the possibilities for self-advancement through self-improvement. But his message was also an implicit promise that blacks would not challenge the system of segregation that whites were then in the process of erecting.

The Birth of Jim Crow

Few white Southerners had ever accepted the idea of racial equality. That the former slaves acquired any legal and political rights at all after emancipation was in large part the result of federal support. That support all but vanished after 1877. Federal troops withdrew. Congress lost interest. And the Supreme Court effectively stripped the Fourteenth and Fifteenth Amendments of much of their significance. In the so-called civil rights cases of 1883, the Court ruled that the Fourteenth Amendment prohibited state governments from discriminating against people because of race but did not restrict private organizations or individuals from doing so. Thus railroads, hotels, theaters, and the like could legally practice segregation.

Eventually, the Court also validated state legislation that institutionalized the separation of the races. In *Plessy* v. *Ferguson* (1896), a case involving a Louisiana law that required separate seating arrangements for the races on railroads, the Court held that separate accommodations did not deprive blacks of equal rights if the accommodations were equal, a decision that survived for years as part of the legal basis of segregated schools. In *Cumming* v. *County Board of Education* (1899), the Court ruled that laws establishing separate schools for whites were valid even if there were no schools for blacks comparable to the white schools from which they were excluded.

Even before these decisions, white southerners were working to strengthen white supremacy and to separate the races to the greatest extent possible. One illustration of this movement from subordination to segregation was black voting rights. In some states, disfranchisement had begun almost as soon as Reconstruction ended. But in other areas, black voting continued for some time after Reconstruction—largely because conservative whites believed they could control the black electorate and use it to beat back the attempts of poor white farmers to take control of the Democratic Party.

In the 1890s, however, franchise restrictions became much more rigid. During those years, some small white farmers began to demand complete black disfranchisement—both because of racial prejudice and because they objected to the black vote being used against them by the Bourbons. At the same time, many

A LYNCH MOB, 1893
A large, almost festive crowd gathers to watch the lynching of a black man accused of the murder of a three-year-old white girl. Lynchings remained frequent in the South until as late as the 1930s, but they reached their peak in the 1890s and the first years of the twentieth century. Lynchings such as this one—publicized well in advance and attracting whole families who traveled great distances to see them—were relatively infrequent. Most lynchings were the work of smaller groups, operating with less visibility. *(Library of Congress)*

members of the conservative elite began to fear that poor whites might unite politically with poor blacks to challenge them. They too began to support further franchise restrictions.

In devising laws to disfranchise black males (black females, like white women, had never voted), the southern states had to find ways to evade the Fifteenth Amendment, which prohibited states from denying anyone the right to vote because of race. Two devices emerged before 1900 to accomplish this goal. One was the poll tax or some form of property qualification; few blacks were prosperous enough to meet such requirements. Another was the "literacy" or "understanding" test, which required voters to demonstrate an ability to read and to interpret the Constitution. Even those

African Americans who could read had difficulty passing the difficult test white officials gave them.

Such restrictions were often applied unequally. Literacy tests for whites, for example, were sometimes much easier than those for blacks. Even so, the laws affected poor white voters as well as blacks. By the late 1890s, the black vote had decreased by 62 percent, the white vote by 26 percent. One result was that some states passed so-called grandfather laws, permitting men who could not meet the literacy and property qualification to be enfranchised if their ancestors had voted before Reconstruction began, thus barring the descendants of slaves from the polls while allowing poor whites access to them. In many areas, however, ruling elites were quite content to see poor whites, a potential source of opposition to their power, barred from voting.

The Supreme Court proved as compliant in ruling on the disfranchising laws as it was in dealing with the civil rights cases. The Court eventually voided the grandfather laws, but it validated the literacy test (in the 1898 case of *Williams* v. *Mississippi*) and displayed a general willingness to let the southern states define their own suffrage standards as long as evasions of the Fifteenth Amendment were not too glaring.

Laws restricting the franchise and segregating schools were only part of a network of state statutes—known as the Jim Crow laws—that by the first years of the twentieth century had institutionalized an elaborate system of segregation reaching into almost every area of southern life. Blacks and whites could not ride together in the same railroad cars, sit in the same waiting rooms, use the same washrooms, eat in the same restaurants, or sit in the same theaters. Blacks had no access to many public parks, beaches, picnic areas; they could not be patients in many hospitals. Much of the new legal structure did no more than confirm what had already been widespread social practice in the South since well before the end of Reconstruction. But the Jim Crow laws also stripped blacks of many of the modest social, economic, and political gains they had made in the more fluid atmosphere of the late nineteenth century. They served, too, as a means for whites to retain control of social relations between the races in the newly growing cities and towns of the South, where traditional patterns of deference and subjugation were more difficult to preserve than in the countryside. What had been maintained by custom in the rural South was to be maintained by law in the urban South.

More than legal efforts were involved in this process. The 1890s witnessed a dramatic increase in white violence against blacks, which, along with the Jim Crow laws, served to inhibit black agitation for equal rights. The worst such violence—lynching of blacks by white mobs, either because the victims were accused of crimes or because they had seemed somehow to violate their proper station—reached appalling levels. In the nation as a whole in the 1890s, there was an average of 187 lynchings each year, more than 80 percent of them in the South. The vast majority of victims were black.

The most celebrated lynchings occurred in cities and towns, where large, well-organized mobs—occasionally with the tacit cooperation of local authorities—seized black prisoners from the jails and hanged them in great public rituals. Such public lynchings were often planned well in advance and elaborately organized. They attracted large audiences from surrounding regions. Entire families traveled many miles to witness the spectacles. But such great public lynchings were relatively rare. Much more frequent, and more dangerous to blacks because less visible or predictable, were lynchings performed by small vigilante mobs, often composed of friends or relatives of the victim (or supposed victim) of a crime. Those involved in lynchings often saw their actions as a legitimate form of law enforcement; and indeed, some victims of lynchings had in fact committed crimes. But lynchings were also a means by which whites controlled the black population through terror and intimidation. Thus, some lynch mobs killed blacks whose only "crime" had been presumptuousness. Others chose as victims outsiders in the community, whose presence threatened to disturb the normal pattern of race relations. Black men who had made any sexual advances toward white women (or who white men thought had done so) were particularly vulnerable to lynchings; the fear of black sexuality, and the unspoken fear among many men that white women might be attracted to that sexuality, was always an important part of the belief system that supported segregation. Whatever the reasons or circumstances, the victims of lynch mobs were denied the protection of the laws and the opportunity to prove their innocence.

The rise of lynchings shocked the conscience of many white Americans in a way that other forms of racial injustice did not. Almost from the start there was a substantial anti-lynching movement. In 1892 Ida B. Wells, a committed black journalist, launched what became an international anti-lynching movement with a series of impassioned articles after the lynching of three of her friends in Memphis, Tennessee, her home. The movement gradually gathered strength in the first years of the twentieth century, attracting substantial support from whites in both the North and South (particularly from white women). Its goal was a federal anti-lynching law, which would allow the national government to do what state and local governments in the South were generally unwilling to do: punish those responsible for lynchings.

But the substantial white opposition to lynchings in the South stood as an exception to the general white support for suppression of African Americans. Indeed, just as in the antebellum period, the shared commitment to white supremacy helped dilute class animosities between poorer whites and the Bourbon oligarchies. Economic issues tended to play a secondary role to race in southern politics, distracting people from the glaring social inequalities that afflicted blacks and whites alike. The commitment to white supremacy, in short, was a burden for poor whites as well as for blacks.

SIGNIFICANT EVENTS

1863 Lincoln announces preliminary Reconstruction plan

1864 Louisiana, Arkansas, and Tennessee readmitted to Union under Lincoln plan

Wade-Davis bill passed

1865 Lincoln assassinated; Andrew Johnson becomes president (April 14)

Johnson readmits rest of Confederate states to Union under Lincoln plan

Black Codes enacted in South

Freedmen's Bureau established

Congress reconvenes (December) and refuses to admit Southern representatives; creates Joint Committee on Reconstruction

1866 Freedmen's Bureau Act renewed

Congress approves Fourteenth Amendment; most Southern states reject it

Republicans gain in congressional elections

Ex parte Milligan challenges Radicals' Reconstruction plans

Ku Klux Klan formed in South

1867 Military Reconstruction Act (and two supplementary acts) outlines congressional plan of Reconstruction

Tenure of Office Act and Command of the Army Act restrict presidential power

Southern states establish Reconstruction governments under congressional plan

U.S. purchases Alaska

1868 Most Southern states readmitted to Congress under congressional plan

Andrew Johnson impeached but not convicted

Fourteenth Amendment ratified

Ulysses S. Grant elected president

SUGGESTED READINGS

Reconstruction: General Studies. E. Merton Coulter, *The South During Reconstruction* (1947). W. E. B. Du Bois, *Black Reconstruction* (1935). William A. Dunning, *Reconstruction, Political and Economic, 1865–1877* (1907). Eric Foner, *Reconstruction: America's Unfinished Revolution, 1863–1877* (1988). John Hope Franklin, *Reconstruction After the Civil War* (1961). Rembert Patrick, *The Reconstruction of the Nation* (1967). Kenneth M. Stampp, *The Era of Reconstruction, 1865–1877* (1965).

Early Reconstruction. Richard H. Abbott, *The First Southern Strategy: The Republican Party and the South, 1855–1877* (1986). Herman Belz, *Reconstructing the Union* (1969). Louis S. Gerteis, *From Contraband to Freedman* (1973). William B. Hesseltine, *Lincoln's Plan of Reconstruction* (1960). Willie Lee Rose, *Rehearsal for Reconstruction: The Port Royal Experiment* (1964). Brooks D. Simpson, *Let Us Have Peace: Ulysses S. Grant and the Politics of War and Reconstruction, 1861–1868* (1991).

Congressional Reconstruction. Howard K. Beale, *The Critical Year: A Study of Andrew Johnson and Reconstruction* (1930). Herman Belz, *A New Birth of Freedom* (1976); *Emancipation and*

Equal Rights (1978). Michael Les Benedict, *A Compromise of Principle: Congressional Republicans and Reconstruction, 1863–1869* (1974); *The Impeachment and Trial of Andrew Johnson* (1973). Richard Franklin Bensel, *Yankee Leviathan: The Origins of Central State Authority in America, 1859–1877* (1990). William R. Brock, *An American Crisis* (1963). Fawn Brodie, *Thaddeus Stevens* (1959). La Wanda Cox and John H. Cox, *Politics, Principles, and Prejudice, 1865–1867* (1963). Richard N. Current, *Old Thad Stevens* (1942). David Donald, *Charles Sumner and the Rights of Man* (1970); *The Politics of Reconstruction* (1965). Charles Fairman, *Reconstruction and Reunion* (1971). William Gillette, *The Right to Vote* (1965). Harold Hyman, *A More Perfect Union* (1973). Stanley Kutler, *The Judicial Power and Reconstruction Politics* (1968). Eric McKitrick, *Andrew Johnson and Reconstruction* (1960). Mark W. Summers, *Railroads, Reconstruction, and the Gospel of Prosperity* (1984). Hans L. Trefousse, *The Radical Republicans* (1963); *The Impeachment of a President* (1975); *Andrew Johnson: A Biography* (1989).

The South in Reconstruction. Roberta Alexander, *North Carolina Faces the Freedmen: Race Relations During Presidential*

SIGNIFICANT EVENTS

1869 Congress passes Fifteenth Amendment

First "redeemer" governments elected in South

1870 Last Southern states readmitted to Congress

"Force acts" passed

1871 Alabama claims settled

1872 Liberal Republicans defect

Grant reelected president

1873 Commercial and financial panic disrupts economy

1875 Specie Resumption Act passed

"Whiskey ring" scandal discredits Grant administration

1877 Rutherford B. Hayes elected president after disputed election

Last federal troops withdrawn from South after Compromise of 1877

Last Southern states "redeemed"

1879 Readjusters win control of Virginia legislature

1880 Joel Chandler Harris publishes *Uncle Remus*

1883 Supreme Court upholds segregation in private institutions

1890s "Jim Crow" laws passed throughout South

Lynchings increase in South

1895 Booker T. Washington outlines Atlanta Compromise

1896 *Plessy* v. *Ferguson* upholds "separate but equal" racial facilities

1898 *Williams* v. *Mississippi* validates literacy tests for voting

Reconstruction, 1865–1867 (1985). James D. Anderson, *The Education of Blacks in the South* (1989). George Bentley, *A History of the Freedmen's Bureau* (1955). Dan Carter, *When the War Was Over: The Failure of Self-Reconstruction in the South, 1865–1867* (1985). Richard N. Current, *Those Terrible Carpetbaggers* (1988). Barbara Fields, *Slavery and Freedom on the Middle Ground* (1985). Eric Foner, *Nothing but Freedom: Emancipation and Its Legacy* (1983). William Gillette, *Retreat from Reconstruction, 1869–1879* (1980); *The Right to Vote: Politics and Passage of the Fifteenth Amendment* (1969). William C. Harris, *The Day of the Carpetbagger: Republican Reconstruction in Mississippi, 1867–1875* (1979). Robert Higgs, *Competition and Coercion: Blacks in the American Economy, 1865–1914* (1977). Thomas Holt, *Black over White: Negro Political Leadership in South Carolina During Reconstruction* (1977). Elizabeth Jacoway, *Yankee Missionaries in the South* (1979). Jacqueline Jones, *Soldiers of Light and Love: Northern Teachers and Georgia Blacks, 1865–1873* (1980); *Labor of Love, Labor of Sorrow: Black Women, Work, and the Family from Slavery to the Present* (1985). Peter Kolchin, *First Freedom: The Responses of Alabama's Blacks to Emancipation* (1972). Leon Litwack, *Been in the Storm So Long: The Aftermath of Slavery* (1979). Richard Lowe, *Republicans and Reconstruction in Virginia, 1865–1870* (1991). Peyton McCrary, *Abraham Lincoln and Reconstruction* (1978). William S. McFeely, *Yankee Stepfather: General O. O. Howard and the Freedmen* (1968). Otto Olsen, *Carpetbagger's Crusade: Albion Winegar Tourgé* (1965). Michael Perman, *Reunion Without Compromise* (1973); *The Road to Redemption: Southern Politics, 1869–1979* (1984). L. N. Powell, *New Masters: Northern Planters During the Civil War and Reconstruction* (1980). Roger L. Ransom and Richard Sutch, *One Kind of Freedom: The Economic Consequences of Emancipation* (1977). C. Peter Ripley, *Slaves and Freedmen in Civil War Louisiana* (1976). James Sefton, *The United States Army and Reconstruction* (1967). Crandall A. Shifflett, *Patronage and Poverty in the Tobacco South: Louisa County, Virginia, 1860–1900* (1982). Joel G. Taylor, *Louisiana Reconstructed* (1974). Allen Trelease, *White Terror: The Ku Klux Klan Conspiracy and Southern Reconstruction* (1967). Michael Wayne, *The Reshaping of Plantation Society: The Natchez District* (1983). Vernon Wharton, *The Negro in Mississippi, 1865–1890* (1965). Sarah Wiggins, *The Scalawag in Alabama Politics, 1865–1881* (1977). Joel Williamson, *After Slavery: The Negro in South Carolina During Reconstruction* (1965).

The Grant Administration. William B. Hesseltine, *U. S. Grant, Politician* (1935). Ari Hoogenboom, *Outlawing the Spoils* (1961). David Loth, *Public Plunder* (1938). William McFeely, *Grant* (1981). Allan Nevins, *Hamilton Fish* (1936). K. I. Polakoff, *The Politics of Inertia* (1973). John G. Sproat, *"The Best Men"* (1968). Margaret S. Thompson, *The "Spider Web": Con-*

gress and Lobbying in the Age of Grant (1985). Irwin Unger, *The Greenback Era* (1964). C Vann Woodward, *Reunion and Reaction* (1951).

The New South. Edward L. Ayers, *The Promise of the New South: Life After Reconstruction* (1992). Paul Buck, *The Road to Reunion* (1937). Orville Vernon Burton, *In My Father's House* (1985). Orville Vernon Burton and Robert C. McMath, Jr., eds., *Toward a New South?* (1982). W. J. Cash, *The Mind of the South* (1941). Paul Gaston, *The New South Creed* (1970). J. Morgan Kousser and James M. McPherson, eds., *Region, Race, and Reconstruction (1982).* Jonathan Wiener, *Social Origins of the New South: Alabama, 1860–1885* (1978). C. Vann Woodward, *Origins of the New South* (1951); *The Burden of Southern History* (rev., 1968); *American Counterpoint* (1971); *Thinking Back* (1986); *The Future of the Past* (1989).

Politics in the New South. Kenneth E. Davison, *The Presidency of Rutherford B. Hayes* (1972). Carl Degler, *The Other South: Southern Dissenters in the Nineteenth Century* (1974). Vincent P. DeSantis, *Republicans Face the Southern Question: The New Departure Years, 1877–1897* (1959). Sheldon Hackney, *Populism to Progressivism in Alabama* (1959). Stanley P. Hirshson, *Farewell to the Bloody Shirt: Northern Republicans and the Southern Negro* (1962). V. O. Key, Jr., *Southern Politics and the Nation* (1949). J. Morgan Kousser, *The Shaping of Southern Politics: Suffrage Restriction and the Establishment of the One-Party South, 1880–1910* (1974). Paul Lewinson, *Race, Class, and Party* (1932). David Potter, *The South and the Concurrent Majority* (1972). Francis B. Simkins, *Pitchfork Ben Tillman* (1944). Joseph F. Wall, *Henry Watterson: Reconstructed Rebel* (1956). C. Vann Woodward, *Reunion and Reaction* (1951); *Tom Watson: Agrarian Rebel* (1938).

Race, Economics, and Social Structure. Francis Broderick, *W. E. B. DuBois* (1959). David Carlton, *Mill and Town in South Carolina, 1880–1920* (1982). Melvin Greenhut and W. Tate Whitman, eds., *Essays in Southern Economic Development* (1964). Steven Hahn, *The Roots of Southern Populism: Yeoman Farmers and the Transformation of the Georgia Upcountry* (1983). Steven Hahn and Jonathan Prude, eds., *The Countryside in the Age of Capitalist Transformation* (1985). Jacquelyn Dowd Hall et al., *Like a Family: The Making of a Southern Cotton Mill World* (1987). Louis R. Harlan, *Booker T. Washington: The Making of a Black Leader, 1856–1901* (1972); *Booker T. Washington: The Wizard of Tuskegee: 1901–1915* (1983). Robert Higgs, *Competition and Coercion: Blacks in the American Economy, 1865–1914* (1977). Melton A. McLaurin, *Paternalism and Protest: Southern Cotton Mill Workers and Organized Labor* (1971). James M. McPherson, *The Abolitionist Legacy: From Reconstruction to the NAACP* (1975). August Meier, *Negro Thought in America* (1963). Cynthia Neverdon-Morton, *Afro-American Women of the South and the Advancement of the Race, 1895–1925* (1989). Howard Rabinowitz, *Race Relations in the Urban South, 1865–1890* (1978). Roger Ransom and Richard Sutch, *One Kind of Freedom* (1977). Elliott M. Rudwick, *W. E. B. DuBois: Propagandist of Negro Protest* (rev., 1969). Altina L. Waller, *Feud: Hatfields, McCoys, and Social Changes: Appalachia, 1860–1900* (1988). Joel Williamson, *After Slavery* (1965); *The Crucible of Race: Black-White Relations in the American South Since Emancipation* (1985); *A Rage for Order* (1986), an abridgment of *The Crucible of Race*. C. Vann Woodward, *The Strange Career of Jim Crow* (rev., 1974). Gavin Wright, *Old South, New South: Revolutions in the Southern Economy Since the Civil War* (1986).

***American Progress*, 1872**
John Gast, an artist in Brooklyn, New York, painted this tribute to westward expansion—a
picture of hardy pioneers marching toward the frontier, protected by the goddess of
progress—at the request of a publisher of travel guides. Engravings adapted from the painting appeared in one guide book, and color reproductions were offered to customers as a
bonus for subscribing to others. It is an example of the wide-ranging promotional effort—by
railroads, landowners, farm-equipment manufacturers, even guidebook publishers—designed
to persuade Americans to move into the western territories in the late nineteenth century.
(Gene Autry Western Heritage Museum)

CHAPTER SIXTEEN

THE CONQUEST OF THE FAR WEST

THROUGH MUCH OF THE first half of the nineteenth century, relatively few English-speaking Americans considered moving into the vast lands west of the Mississippi River. For some the obstacle was distance; for others it was lack of money; for many more it was the image of much of the Far West, popularized by some early travelers, as the "Great American Desert," unfit for civilization.

By the mid-1840s, however, enough migrants from the eastern regions of the nation had settled in the West to begin to challenge that image. Some were farmers, who had found fertile land in areas once considered too arid for agriculture. Others were ranchers, who had discovered great open grasslands on which they could raise large herds of cattle or sheep for the market. Many were miners, including some of the hundreds of thousands of people who had flocked to California during the 1848–1849 gold rush. By the end of the Civil War, the West had already become legendary in the eastern states. No longer the Great American Desert, it was now the "frontier": an empty land awaiting settlement and civilization; a place of wealth, adventure, opportunity, and untrammeled individualism; a place of fresh beginnings and bold undertakings.

In fact, the real West of the mid-nineteenth century bore little resemblance to either of these images. It was a diverse land, with many different regions, many different climates, many different stores of natural resources. And it was extensively populated, with a number of well-developed societies and cultures. The English-speaking migrants of the late nineteenth century did not find an empty, desolate land. They found Indians, Mexicans, French and British Canadians, Asians, and others, some of whose families had been living in the West for generations.

The Anglo-American settlers helped create new civilizations in this vast and complicated land, but they did not do so by themselves. Although they tried, with considerable success, to conquer and disperse many of the peoples already living in the region, they were never able to make the West theirs alone. They interacted in countless ways with the existing population. Almost everything the Anglo-Americans did and built reflected the influence of these other cultures.

Most of all, however, English-speaking Americans transformed the West by connecting it with, and making it part of, the growing capitalist economy of the East. And despite their self-image as rugged individualists, they relied heavily on assistance from the federal government—land grants, subsidies, and military protection—as they developed the region.

THE SOCIETIES OF THE FAR WEST

The Far West (or what many called the "Great West")—the region beyond the Mississippi River into which millions of Anglo-Americans moved in the years after the Civil War—was in fact many lands. It contained some of the most arid territory in the United States, and some of the wettest and lushest. It contained the flattest plains and the highest mountains. It contained vast treeless prairies and deserts and great forests. And it contained many peoples.

The Western Tribes

The largest and most important western population group before the great American migration was the Indian tribes. Some were members of eastern tribes—Cherokee, Creek, and others—who had been forcibly resettled west of the Mississippi to "Indian Territory" (later Oklahoma) and elsewhere before the Civil War. But most were members of tribes indigenous to the West.

The western tribes had developed a number of patterns of civilization. More than 300,000 Indians (among them the Serrano, Chumash, Pomo, Maidu, Yurok, and Chinook) had lived on the Pacific Coast before the arrival of Spanish settlers. Disease and dislocation decimated the tribes, but in the mid-nineteenth century 150,000 remained—some living within the Hispanic society the Spanish and Mexican settlers had created, many still living within their own tribal communities.

The Pueblos of the Southwest had long lived largely as farmers and had established permanent settlements there even before the Spanish arrived in the seventeenth century. The Pueblos grew corn; they built towns and cities of adobe houses; they practiced elaborate forms of irrigation; and they participated in trade and commerce. In the eighteenth and nineteenth centuries, their intimate relationship with the Spanish (later Mexicans) produced, in effect, an alliance against the Apaches, Navajos, and Commanches of the region.

The complex interaction between the Pueblos and the Spanish, and between both of them and other tribes, produced an elaborate caste system in the Southwest. At the top were the Spanish or Mexicans, who owned the largest estates and controlled the trading centers at Santa Fe and elsewhere. The Pueblos, subordinate but still largely free, were below them. Apaches, Navajos, and others—some captured in war and enslaved for a fixed time, others men and women and they had left their own tribes—were at the bottom. They were known as *genizaros*, Indians without tribes, and they had become in many ways part of Spanish society. This caste system reflected the preoccupation of the society of the Spanish Empire in America with racial ancestry; almost everyone in the Southwest—not just Spanish and Indians, but several categories of mulattoes and mestizos (people of mixed race) had a clear place in an elaborate social hierarchy.

The most widespread Indian groups in the West were the Plains Indians. They were, in fact, many tribal

BUFFALO CHASE
The painter George Catlin captured this scene of Plains Indians in the 1830s hunting among the great herds of buffalo, which provided the food and materials on which many tribes relied. *(National Museum of American Art/Art Resource)*

and language groups. Some formed alliances with one another; others were in constant conflict. Some lived more or less sedentary lives as farmers; others were highly nomadic hunters. Despite their differences, however, the tribes shared some traits. Their cultures were based on close and extended family networks and on an intimate relationship with nature. Tribes (which sometimes numbered several thousand) were generally subdivided into "bands" of up to 500 men and women, usually made up of highly interrelated people. Each band had its own governing council, but the community had a decision-making process in which most members participated. Within each band, tasks were divided by gender. Women's roles were largely domestic and artistic: raising children, cooking, gathering roots and berries, preparing hides, and creating many of the impressive artworks of tribal culture. They also tended fields and gardens in those places where bands remained settled long enough to raise crops. Men worked as hunters and traders and supervised the religious and military life of the band. Most of the Plains Indians practiced a religion centered on a belief in the spiritual power of the natural world—of plants and animals and the rhythms of the days and the seasons.

Many of the Plains tribes—including some of the most powerful tribes in the Sioux nation—subsisted largely through hunting buffalo. Riding small but powerful horses, descendants of Spanish stock, the tribes moved through the grasslands following the herds. Permanent settlements were rare. When a band halted, it constructed tepees as temporary dwellings; when it departed, it left the landscape almost completely undisturbed, a reflection of the deep reverence for nature that was central to Indian culture and religion.

The magnet that drew the hunters and guided their routes was the buffalo, or bison. This huge grazing animal provided the economic basis for the Plains Indians' way of life. Its flesh was their principal source of food, and its skin supplied materials for clothing, shoes, tepees, blankets, robes, and utensils. "Buffalo chips"—dried manure—provided fuel; buffalo bones became knives and arrow tips; buffalo tendons formed the strings of bows.

THE TRANSCONTINENTAL RAILROAD
This complicated trestle under construction by the Union Pacific was one of many large spans necessary for the completion of the transcontinental railroad. It gives some indication of the enormous engineering challenges the railroad builders had to overcome. *(Union Pacific Museum)*

The Plains Indians were proud and aggressive warriors, schooled in warfare from their frequent (and usually brief) skirmishes with rival tribes. The male members of each tribe were, in effect, a warrior class. They competed with one another to develop reputations for fierceness and bravery both as hunters and as soldiers. By the early nineteenth century, the Sioux had become the most powerful tribe in the Missouri River Valley and had begun expanding west and south until they dominated much of the Plains and were the most important military force in the region.

The Plains warriors proved to be the most formidable foes white settlers encountered. But they also suffered from several serious weaknesses that in the end made it impossible for them to prevail. One weakness was the inability of the various tribes (and often even of the bands within tribes) to unite against white aggression. This was a problem that had plagued Native Americans in the East for centuries and had contributed to their ultimate undoing. The western tribes, like the eastern ones, were culturally ill-disposed toward political or military centralization. Not only were they seldom able to draw together a coalition large enough to counter white power, they were also frequently distracted from their battles with whites by conflicts among the tribes themselves. And at times, tribal warriors faced white forces who were being assisted by guides and even fighters from other, usually rival, tribes.

Even so, some tribes were able to overcome their divisions and unite effectively. By the mid-nineteenth century, for example, the Sioux, Arapaho, and Cheyenne had forged a powerful alliance that dominated the northern Plains. The more important weaknesses of the western tribes in their contest with white society were, in fact, ecological and economic. Indians were tragically vulnerable to eastern infectious diseases. Smallpox epidemics, for example, decimated the Pawnees in Nebraska in the 1840s and many of the California tribes in the early 1850s. And the tribes were, of course, at a considerable disadvantage in any long-term battle with an economically and industrially advanced people. They were, in the end, outmanned and outgunned.

Hispanic New Mexico

For centuries, much of the Far West had been part of, first, the Spanish Empire and, later, the Mexican Republic. Although the lands the United States acquired in the 1840s did not include any of Mexico's most populous regions, considerable numbers of Mexicans did live in them and suddenly became residents of American territory. Most of them stayed.

Spanish-speaking communities were scattered throughout the Southwest, from Texas through New Mexico and Arizona, and into California. All of them were transformed in varying degrees by the arrival of Anglo-American migrants and, equally important, by the expansion of the American capitalist economy into the region. For some, the changes created opportunities for greater wealth. But for most it meant an end to the more communal societies and economies they had built over many generations.

In New Mexico, the centers of Spanish-speaking society were the farming and trading communities the Spanish had established in the seventeenth century. (See p. 12.) Descendants of the original Spanish settlers (and more recent migrants from Mexico) lived alongside the Pueblo Indians and some American traders and engaged primarily in cattle and sheep ranching. There was a small aristocracy of great landowners, whose estates radiated out from the major trading center at Santa Fe. And there was a large population of Spanish (later Mexican) peasants, who worked on the great estates, farmed small plots of their own, or otherwise scraped out a subsistence. There were also large groups of Indian laborers, some enslaved or indentured.

When the United States acquired title to New Mexico in the aftermath of the Mexican War, General Stephen Kearney—who had commanded the American troops in the region during the conflict—tried to establish a territorial government that excluded the established Mexican ruling class (the landed aristocrats from around Santa Fe and the most influential priests). He drew most of the officials from among the approximately 1,000 Anglo-Americans in the region, ignoring the over 50,000 Hispanics. There were widespread fears among Hispanics and Indians alike that the new American rulers of the region would confiscate their lands and otherwise threaten their societies. In 1847, Taos Indians rebelled; they killed the new governor and other Anglo-American officials before being subdued by United States army forces. New Mexico remained under military rule for three years, until the United States finally organized a territorial government there in 1850.

By the 1870s, the government of New Mexico was dominated by one of the most notorious of the many "territorial rings" that sprang up in the West in the years before statehood. These were circles of local businesspeople and ambitious politicians with access to federal money who worked together to make the territorial government mutually profitable. In Santa Fe, the ring used its influence to gain control of over 2 million acres of land, much of which had long been in the possession of the original Mexican residents of the territory. The old Hispanic elite in New Mexico had lost much of its political and economic authority.

Even without its former power, Hispanic society in New Mexico survived and even grew in the face of the expansion of Anglo-American settlement in the Southwest. The U.S. Army finally did what the Hispanic residents had been unable to accomplish for 200 years: it broke the power of the Navajo, Apache, and other tribes that had so often harassed the residents of New Mexico and prevented them from expanding their society and commerce. The defeat of the tribes led to substantial Hispanic migration into other areas of the Southwest and as far north as Colorado. Most of the expansion involved peasants and small tradespeople who were looking for land or new opportunities for commerce. The pattern of large estates and a self-conscious aristocracy did not repeat itself in the newer Hispanic settlements.

Hispanic societies survived in the Southwest in part because they were so far from the centers of English-speaking society that Anglo-American migrants (and the railroads that carried them) were slow to get there. But Mexican Americans in the region also fought at times to preserve control of their societies. In the late 1880s, for example, Mexican peasants in an area of what is now Nevada harassed English-speaking cattle ranchers who were attempting to move into the region and successfully fended off their encroachments.

But by then, such successes were already the exception. The Anglo-American presence in the Southwest grew rapidly once the railroads established lines into the region in the 1880s and early 1890s. With the railroads came extensive new ranching, farming, and mining. The expansion of economic activity in the region attracted a new wave of Mexican immigrants— perhaps as many as 100,000 by 1900—who moved across the border (which was unregulated until World War I) in search of work. But the new immigrants, unlike the earlier Hispanic residents of the Southwest, were coming to a society in which they were from the beginning subordinate to Anglo-Americans. The English-speaking proprietors of the new enterprises restricted most Mexicans to the lowest-paying and least stable jobs.

Hispanic California and Texas

In California, Spanish settlement began in the eighteenth century with a string of Christian missions along the Pacific coast. The missionaries and the soldiers who accompanied them gathered most of the coastal Indians into their communities, some forcibly

THE CALIFORNIOS
Before the arrival of large waves of immigrants from the United States, California was the home of a flourishing Mexican ranching and mission culture, with a wealthy aristocracy—as this 1850 painting of the Don Manuel family suggests. *(Courtesy W. Graham Arader, III, San Francisco)*

and some by persuasion. The Indians were targets of the evangelizing efforts of the missionaries, who baptized over 50,000 of them. But they were also a labor force for the flourishing and largely self-sufficient economies the missionaries created; the Spanish forced most of these laborers into a state of servitude little different from slavery. The missions had enormous herds of cattle, horses, sheep, and goats, most of them tended by Indian workers; they had brickmakers, blacksmiths, weavers, and farmers, most of them Indians as well. Few of the profits of the mission economy flowed to the workers.

In the 1830s, after the new Mexican government began reducing the power of the church, the mission society largely collapsed, despite strenuous resistance from the missionaries themselves. In its place emerged a secular Mexican aristocracy, which controlled a chain of large estates (some of them former missions) in the fertile lands west of the Sierra mountains. For them, the arrival of Anglo-Americans before and after the Civil War was disastrous. So vast were the numbers of English-speaking immigrants that the *californios* (as the Hispanic residents of the state were known) had little power to resist the onslaught. In the central and northern parts of the state, where the Anglo population growth was greatest, the *californios* experienced a series of defeats. English-speaking prospectors organized to exclude them, sometimes violently, from the mines during the gold rush. Many *californios* also lost their lands—either through corrupt business deals or through outright seizure (sometimes with the help of the courts and often through simple occupation by squatters). Years of litigation by the displaced Hispanics had very little effect on the changing distribution of landownership.

In the southern areas of California, where there were at first fewer migrants, some Mexican landowners managed to hang on for a time. The booming Anglo communities in the north of the state created a large market for the cattle that southern *rancheros* were raising. But a combination of reckless expansion, growing indebtedness, and a severe drought in the 1860s devastated the Mexican ranching culture. By the 1880s, the Hispanic aristocracy in California had largely ceased to exist.

Increasingly, Mexicans and Mexican Americans became part of the lower end of the state's working class, clustered in *barrios* in Los Angeles or elsewhere, or becoming migrant farmworkers. Even small landowners who managed to hang on to their farms found themselves unable to raise livestock, as the once communal grazing lands fell under the control of powerful Anglo ranchers. The absence of herding destroyed many

family economies and, by forcing farmers into migrant work, displaced much of the peasantry.

A similar pattern of dispossession and exploitation occurred in Texas, where many Mexican landowners lost their land after the territory joined the United States. (See pp. 352–354.) This occurred as a result of fraud, coercion, and the inability of even the most substantial Mexican ranchers to compete with the enormous Anglo-American ranching kingdoms that were emerging. In 1859, Mexican resentments erupted in an armed challenge to American power: a raid on a jail in Brownsville, led by the rancher Juan Cortina, who freed all the Mexican prisoners inside. But such resistance had little long-term effect. Cortina continued to harass Anglo communities in Texas until 1875, but the Mexican government finally captured and imprisoned him. As in California, Mexicans in southern Texas (who constituted nearly three quarters of the population there) became an increasingly impoverished working class relegated largely to unskilled farm or industrial labor.

On the whole, the great Anglo-American migration was less catastrophic for the Hispanic population of the West than it was for the Indian tribes. Indeed, for some Hispanics, it created new opportunities for wealth and station. For the most part, however, the late nineteenth century saw the destruction of Mexican Americans' authority in a region they had long considered their home; and it saw the movement of large numbers of Hispanics—both longtime residents of the West and more recent immigrants—into an impoverished working class serving the expanding capitalist economy of the United States.

The Chinese Migration

At the same time that ambitious or impoverished Europeans were crossing the Atlantic in search of opportunities in the new world, many Chinese crossed the Pacific in hopes of better lives than they could expect in their own poverty-stricken land. Not all came to the United States. Many Chinese moved to Hawaii, Australia, Latin America, South Africa, and even the Caribbean—some as "coolies" (indentured servants whose condition was close to slavery).

A few Chinese had come to California even before the gold rush (see pp. 364–366), but after 1848 the flow increased dramatically. By 1880, more than 200,000 Chinese had settled in the United States, mostly in California, where they constituted nearly a tenth of the population. Almost all came as free laborers. For a time, white Americans welcomed the Chinese as a conscientious, hardworking people. In 1852, the governor of California called them "one of the most worthy classes of our newly adopted citizens" and called for more Chinese immigration to swell the territory's inadequate labor force. Very quickly, however, white opinion turned hostile—in part because the Chinese were so industrious and successful that some white Americans began considering them rivals, even threats. The experience of Chinese immigrants in the West became, therefore, a struggle to advance economically in the face of racism and discrimination.

In the early 1850s, large numbers of Chinese immigrants worked in the gold mines. Many of them were well-organized, hardworking prospectors, and for a time some of them enjoyed considerable success. But opportunities for Chinese to prosper in the mines were fleeting. In 1852, the California legislature began trying to exclude the Chinese from gold mining by enacting a "foreign miners" tax (which also helped exclude Mexicans). A series of other laws in the 1850s were designed to discourage Chinese immigration into the territory. Gradually, the effect of the discriminatory laws, the hostility of white miners, and the declining profitability of the surface mines drove most Chinese out of prospecting. Those who remained in the mountains became primarily hired workers in the mines built by corporations with financing from the East. These newer mines—which extended much deeper into the mountains than individual prospectors or small, self-financed groups had been able to go—replaced the early, smaller operations.

As mining declined as a source of wealth and jobs for the Chinese, railroad employment grew. Beginning in 1865, over 12,000 Chinese found work building the transcontinental railroad. In fact, Chinese workers formed 90 percent of the labor force of the Central Pacific and were mainly responsible for construction of the western part of the new road. The company preferred them to white workers because they worked hard, made few demands, and accepted relatively low wages. Many of the workers were recruited for the railroad in China by agents for the Central Pacific. Once employed, they were organized into work gangs under Chinese supervisors.

Work on the Central Pacific was arduous and often dangerous. As the railroad moved through the mountains, the company made few concessions to the difficult conditions and provided their workers with little protection from the elements. Work continued through the winter, and many Chinese tunneled into snow banks at night to create warm sleeping areas for themselves. The tunnels frequently collapsed, suffocating those inside; but the company allowed nothing to disrupt construction.

But the Chinese laborers were not always as docile as their employers imagined them to be. In the spring of 1866, 5,000 Chinese railroad workers went on strike demanding higher wages and a shorter workday. The company isolated them, surrounded them with strikebreakers, and starved them into submission. The strike failed, and most of the workers returned to their jobs.

In 1869 the transcontinental railroad was completed. Thousands of Chinese were now out of work. Some

AN ANTI-CHINESE RIOT
White citizens of Denver attacked the Chinese community of the city in 1880, beating many of its residents and vandalizing their homes and businesses. It was one of a number of anti-Chinese riots in the cities of the West. They were a result of a combination of racism and resentment by white workers at what they considered unfair competition from Chinese laborers who were willing to work for very low wages. *(Bettmann)*

hired themselves out on vast drainage and irrigation projects in the agricultural valleys of central California. Some became common agricultural laborers, picking fruit for low wages. Some became tenant farmers, often on marginal lands that white owners saw no profit in working themselves. Some managed to acquire land of their own and established themselves as modestly successful truck farmers.

Increasingly, however, Chinese immigrants flocked to cities. By 1900, nearly half the Chinese population of California lived in urban areas. By far the largest single Chinese community was in San Francisco. Much of community life there, and in other "Chinatowns" throughout the West, revolved around organizations—usually formed by people from the same clan or community in China—that functioned as something like benevolent societies and filled many of the roles that political machines often served in immigrant communities in eastern cities. They were often led by prominent merchants. (In San Francisco, the leading merchants—known as the "Six Companies"—often worked together to advance their interests in the larger community of the city and state.) These organizations became, in effect, employment brokers, unions, arbitrators of disputes, defenders of the community against outside persecution, and dispensers of social services. They also organized the elaborate festivals and celebrations that were such a conspicuous and important part of life in Chinatowns.

Other Chinese organizations were secret societies, known as "tongs." And some of the tongs were violent criminal organizations, involved in the opium trade and prostitution. Few people outside the Chinese communities were aware of their existence, except when rival tongs engaged in violent conflict (or "tong wars"), as occurred frequently in San Francisco in the 1880s.

Life was hard for most urban Chinese, in San Francisco and elsewhere. The Chinese usually occupied the lower rungs of the employment ladder in the western cities in which most lived. Many worked as common laborers, servants, and unskilled factory hands. Some established their own small businesses, especially laundries. They moved into this business not because of experience—there were few commercial laundries in China—but because they were excluded from so many other areas of employment. Laundries could be started with very little capital, and required only limited command of English. By the 1890s, Chinese constituted over two-thirds of all the laundry workers in California, many of them in shops they themselves owned and ran.

The relatively small number of Chinese women fared even worse. During the earliest Chinese migra-tions to California, virtually all the women who made the journey did so because they had been sold into prostitution in China. As late as 1880, nearly half the Chinese women in California were prostitutes. Both Anglo and Chinese reformers tried to stamp out the prostitution in Chinatowns in the 1890s, but more effective than their efforts was the growing number of Chinese women in America. Once the sex ratio became more balanced, Chinese men were more likely to seek companionship in families.

Anti-Chinese Sentiments

As Chinese communities grew larger and more conspicuous in western cities, anti-Chinese sentiment among white residents became increasingly virulent. In fact, next to the Indians, the Chinese probably suffered the most intense persecution from white Americans in the West. Anti-coolie clubs emerged in the 1860s and 1870s seeking a ban on employing Chinese and organizing boycotts of products made with Chinese labor. Some of these clubs attacked Chinese workers in the streets and were suspected of setting fire to factories in which Chinese worked. These activities reflected the resentment of many white workers toward Chinese laborers for accepting low wages and thus undercutting union members. As the political value of attacking the Chinese grew in California, the Democratic Party took up the call. So did the Workingmen's Party of California—created in 1878 by Denis Kearney, an Irish immigrant—which gained significant political power in the state in large part on the basis of its hostility to the Chinese. By the mid 1880s, anti-Chinese agitation and violence had spread up and down the Pacific Coast and into other areas of the West.

But the denunciations of the Chinese did not rest on economic grounds alone. They rested on cultural and racial arguments as well. For example, the reformer Henry George, a critic of capitalism and a champion of the rights of labor (see p. 490), described the Chinese as products of a civilization that had failed to progress, that remained mired in barbarism and savagery. They were, therefore, "unassimilable" and should be excluded.

In 1882, Congress responded to the political pressure and the growing violence by passing the Chinese Exclusion Act, which banned Chinese immigration into the United States for ten years and barred Chinese already in the country from becoming naturalized citizens. Support for the act came from representatives from all regions of the country. It reflected the growing fear of unemployment and labor unrest throughout the nation and the belief that excluding "an industrial army of Asiatic laborers" would protect

"American" workers and help reduce class conflict. Congress renewed the law for another ten years in 1892 and made it permanent in 1902. It had a dramatic effect on the Chinese population, which declined by more than 40 percent in the forty years after its passage.

The Chinese in America did not accept the new laws quietly. They were shocked by the anti-Chinese rhetoric that lumped them together with African Americans and Indians. They were, they insisted, descendants of a great and enlightened civilization. How could they be compared to people who knew "nothing about the relations of society"? White Americans, they said, did not protest the great waves of immigration by Italians ("the most dangerous of men," one Chinese American said) or Irish or Jews. "They are all let in, while Chinese, who are sober, are duly law abiding, clean, educated and industrious, are shut out." The Six Companies in San Francisco organized strenuous letter-writing campaigns, petitioned the president, and even filed suit in federal court. Their efforts had no significant effect.

Migration from the East

The great wave of new settlers in the West from the eastern United States came on the heels of important earlier migrations. California and Oregon had substantial Anglo-American settlements and were both already states of the Union by 1860. There were large and growing Anglo- and African-American communities in Texas, which had entered the Union in 1845 and had been part of the Confederacy during the war. And from Texas and elsewhere, traders, farmers, and ranchers had begun to establish Anglo-American outposts in parts of New Mexico, Arizona, and other areas of the Southwest.

But the scale of the postwar migration dwarfed everything that had preceded it. In previous decades, the settlers had come in thousands. Now they came in millions, spreading throughout the vast western territories—into empty and inhabited lands alike. Most of the new settlers were from the established Anglo-American societies of the eastern United States, but substantial numbers—over 2 million between 1870 and 1900—were foreign-born immigrants from Europe: Scandinavians, Germans, Irish, Russians, Czechs, and others.

They came for many reasons. Settlers were attracted by gold and silver deposits, by the shortgrass pasture for cattle and sheep, and ultimately by the sod of the Plains and the meadowlands of the mountains, which they discovered were suitable for farming or ranching. The completion of the great transcontinental railroad line in 1869, and the construction of the many subsidiary lines that spread out from it, also encouraged settlement.

The land policies of the federal government also worked to encourage settlement. The Homestead Act of 1862 permitted settlers to buy plots of 160 acres for a small fee if they occupied the land they purchased for five years and improved it. The Homestead Act was intended as a progressive measure. It would give a free farm to any American who needed one. It would be a form of government relief to people who otherwise might have no prospects. And it would help create new markets and new outposts of commercial agriculture for the nation's growing economy.

But the Homestead Act rested on a number of misperceptions. The framers of the law had assumed that mere possession of land would be enough to sustain a farm family. They had not recognized the effects of the increasing mechanization of agriculture and the rising costs of running a farm. Moreover, they had made many of their calculations on the basis of eastern agricultural experiences that were inappropriate for the region west of the Mississippi. A unit of 160 acres was too small for the grazing and grain farming of much of the Great Plains. Although over 400,000 homesteaders stayed on Homestead Act claims long enough to gain title to their land, a much larger number abandoned the region before the end of the necessary five years, unable to cope with the bleak life on the windswept plains and the economic realities that were making it difficult for families without considerable resources to thrive.

Not for the last time, beleaguered westerners looked to the federal government for solutions to their problems. In response to their demands, Congress increased the homestead allotments. The Timber Culture Act (1873) permitted homesteaders to receive grants of 160 additional acres if they planted 40 acres of trees on them. The Desert Land Act (1877) provided that claimants could buy 640 acres at $1.25 an acre provided they irrigated part of their holdings within three years. The Timber and Stone Act (1878), which presumably applied to nonarable land, authorized sales at $2.50 an acre. These laws ultimately made it possible for individuals to acquire as much as 1,280 acres of land at little cost. Some enterprising settlers got much more. Fraud ran rampant in the administration of the acts. Lumber, mining, and cattle companies, by employing "dummy" registrants and using other illegal devices, seized millions of acres of the public domain.

Political organization followed on the heels of settlement. After the admission of Kansas as a state in 1861, the remaining territories of Washington, New Mexico, Utah, and Nebraska were divided into smaller

SODBUSTERS

As farmers moved onto the Great Plains in Nebraska and other states on the agrarian frontier, their first task was to cut through the sod that covered the land to get to soil in which they could plant crops. The sod itself was so thick and solid that some settlers (including the Summers family of West Custer County, Nebraska, pictured here in 1888) used it to build their houses. The removal of the sod made cultivation of the plains possible; it also removed the soil's protective covering and contributed to the great dust storms that plagued the region in times of drought. *(Nebraska State Historical Society)*

units that would presumably be easier to organize. By the close of the 1860s, territorial governments were in operation in the new provinces of Nevada, Colorado, Dakota, Arizona, Idaho, Montana, and Wyoming. Statehood rapidly followed. Nevada became a state in 1864, Nebraska in 1867, and Colorado in 1876. In 1889, North and South Dakota, Montana, and Washington won admission; Wyoming and Idaho entered the next year. Congress denied Utah statehood until its Mormon leaders convinced the government in 1896 that polygamy (the practice of men taking several wives) had been abandoned. At the turn of the century, only three territories remained outside the union. Arizona and New Mexico were excluded because their scanty white populations remained minorities in the territories, because their politics was predominantly Democratic in a Republican era, and because they were un-

willing to accept admission as a single state. Oklahoma (formerly Indian Territory) was opened to white settlement and granted territorial status in 1889–1890.

THE CHANGING WESTERN ECONOMY

Among the many effects on the Far West of the new wave of Anglo-American settlement was a transformation of the region's economy. The new American settlers tied the West firmly to the growing industrial economy of the East (and of much of the rest of the world). Mining, timbering, ranching, commercial farming, and many other economic activities relied on the

East for markets and for capital. Some of the most powerful economic institutions in the West were great eastern corporations that controlled mines, ranches, and farms.

Labor in the West

As commercial activity increased, many farmers, ranchers, and miners found it necessary to recruit a paid labor force—not an easy task for those far away from major population centers and unable or unwilling to hire Indian workers. The labor shortage of the region led to higher wages for workers than were typical in most areas of the East. But working conditions were often arduous, and job security was almost nonexistent. Once a railroad was built, a crop harvested, a herd sent to market, a mine played out, hundreds and even thousands of workers could find themselves suddenly unemployed. Competition from Chinese immigrants, whom employers could usually hire for considerably lower wages than they had to pay whites, also forced some Anglo-Americans out of work. Communities of the jobless gathered in the region's few cities, in mining camps, and elsewhere; other unemployed people moved restlessly from place to place in search of work.

Those who owned no land were highly mobile, mostly male, and seldom married. Indeed, the West had the highest percentage of single people (10 percent) of any region in the country—one reason why single women found working in dance halls and as prostitutes among the most readily available forms of employment.

Despite the enormous geographical mobility in western society, actual social mobility was limited. Many Americans thought of the West as a land of limitless opportunity, but as in the rest of the country, advancement was easiest and most rapid for those who were economically advantaged to begin with. Studies of western communities suggest that social mobility in most of them was no greater than it was in the East. And the distribution of wealth in the region was little different from that in the older states as well.

Even more than in many parts of the East, the western working class was highly multiracial. English-speaking whites worked alongside African Americans and immigrants from southern and eastern Europe, as they did in the East. Even more, they worked with Chinese, Filipinos, Mexicans, and Indians. But the work force was highly stratified along racial lines. In almost every area of the western economy, white workers (whatever their ethnicity) occupied the upper tiers of employment: management and skilled labor. The lower tiers—unskilled and often arduous work in the mines, on the railroads, or in agriculture—consisted overwhelmingly of nonwhites.

Reinforcing this dual labor system was a set of racial assumptions developed and sustained largely by white employers. Chinese, Mexicans, and Filipinos, they argued, were genetically or culturally suited to manual labor. Because they were small, those who promoted these racist stereotypes argued, they could

MINING TOWNS, 1848–1883

COLORADO BOOM TOWN
After a prospector discovered silver nearby in 1890, miners flocked to the town of Creede, Colorado. For a time in the early 1890s, 150 to 300 people arrived there daily. Although the town was located in a canyon so narrow that there was room for only one street, buildings sprouted rapidly to serve the growing community. Like other such boom towns, however, Creede's prosperity was short-lived. In 1893 the price of silver collapsed, and by the end of the century, Creede was almost deserted. *(Henry Ford Museum)*

work better in deep mines than whites. Because they were accustomed to heat, they could withstand arduous work in the fields better than whites. Because they were unambitious and unconcerned about material comfort, they would accept low wages and live in conditions that white people would not tolerate.

These racial myths served the interests of employers above all, but white workers tended to embrace them too. That was in part because the myths supported a system that reserved whatever mobility there was largely for whites. An Irish common laborer might hope in the course of a lifetime to move several rungs up the occupational ladder. A Chinese or Mexican worker in the same job had no realistic prospects of doing the same. Poor whites in the American South often believed they had more in common with wealthy planters than they did with black workers. Similarly in the West, white laborers—when forced to choose sides—often supported white bosses over nonwhite fellow workers. That was one reason why workers in

the West, like those in the South, often had difficulty organizing effectively to challenge their employers.

The western economy was, however, no more a single entity than the economy of the East. In the late nineteenth century, the region produced three major industries, each with a distinctive history and distinctive characteristics: mining, ranching, and commercial farming.

The Arrival of the Miners

The first economic boom in the Far West came in mining, and the first part of the area to be extensively settled by migrants was the mineral-rich region of mountains and plateaus, where settlers hoped to make quick fortunes by finding precious metals. The life span of the mining boom was relatively brief. It began in earnest around 1860 (although there had, of course, been some earlier booms, most notably in California), and flourished until the 1890s. And then it abruptly declined.

News of a gold or silver strike in an area would start a stampede reminiscent of the California gold rush of 1849, followed by several stages of settlement. Individual prospectors would exploit the first shallow deposits of ore largely by hand, with pan and placer mining. After these surface deposits dwindled, corporations moved in to engage in lode or quartz mining, which dug deeper beneath the surface. Then, as those deposits dwindled, commercial mining either disappeared or continued on a restricted basis, and ranchers and farmers moved in and established a more permanent economy.

The first great mineral strikes (other than the California gold rush) occurred just before the Civil War. In 1858, gold was discovered in the Pike's Peak district of what would soon be the territory of Colorado; the following year, 50,000 prospectors stormed in from California, the Mississippi Valley, and the East. Denver and other mining camps blossomed into "cities" overnight. Almost as rapidly as it had developed, the boom ended. Eventually, corporations, notably the Guggenheim interests, revived some of the profits of the gold boom, and the discovery of silver near Leadville supplied a new source of mineral wealth.

While the Colorado rush of 1859 was still in progress, news of another strike drew miners to Nevada. Gold had been found in the Washoe district, but the most valuable ore in the great Comstock Lode (first discovered in 1858 by Henry Comstock) and other veins was silver. The first prospectors to reach the Washoe fields came from California; and from the beginning, Californians dominated the settlement and development of Nevada. In a remote desert without railroad transportation, the territory produced no supplies of its own, and everything—from food and machinery to whiskey and prostitutes—had to be shipped from California to Virginia City, Carson City, and other roaring camp towns. When the first placer (or surface) deposits ran out, California and eastern capitalists bought the claims of the pioneer prospectors and began to use the more difficult process of quartz mining, which enabled them to retrieve silver from deeper veins. For a few years these outside owners reaped tremendous profits; from 1860 to 1880 the Nevada lodes yielded bullion worth $306 million. After that, the mines quickly played out.

The next important mineral discoveries came in 1874, when gold was found in the Black Hills of southwestern Dakota Territory. Prospectors swarmed into the area, then (and for years to come) accessible only by stagecoach. Like the others, the boom flared for a time, until surface resources faded and corporations took over from the miners. One enormous company, the Homestake, came to dominate the fields. Popula-

tion declined, and the Dakotas, like other boom areas of the mineral empire, ultimately developed a largely agricultural economy.

Although the gold and silver discoveries generated the most popular excitement, in the long run other, less glamorous natural resources proved more important to the development of the West. The great Anaconda copper mine launched by William Clark in 1881 marked the beginning of an industry that would remain important to Montana for many decades. In other areas, mining operations had significant success with lead, tin, quartz, and zinc. Such efforts generally proved more profitable in the long run than the usually short-lived gold and silver extraction.

Life in the boomtowns had a hectic tempo and a gaudy flavor unknown in any other part of the Far West. A speculative spirit, a mood of heady optimism, gripped almost everyone and dominated every phase of community activity. And while relatively few of the prospectors and miners who flocked to the bonanzas ever "struck it rich," there was at least some truth to the popular belief that mining provided opportunities for sudden wealth. The "bonanza kings"—the miners who did become enormously wealthy off a strike—were much more likely to have come from modest or impoverished backgrounds than the industrial tycoons of the East.

The conditions of mine life in the boom period—the presence of precious minerals, the vagueness of claim boundaries, the cargoes of gold being shipped out—attracted to the camps outlaws and "bad men," operating as individuals or gangs. When the situation became intolerable in a community, those members interested in order began enforcing their own laws through vigilance committees, an unofficial system of social control used earlier in California. Vigilantes were unconstrained by the legal system, and they often imposed their notion of justice arbitrarily and without regard for any form of due process. Sometimes criminals themselves secured control of the committees. Some vigilantes continued to operate as private "law" enforcers after the creation of regular governments.

Men greatly outnumbered women in the mining towns, and younger men in particular had difficulty finding female companions of comparable age. Those women who did gravitate to the new communities often came with their husbands, and their activities were generally (although not always) confined to the same kinds of domestic tasks that eastern women performed. Single women, or women whose husbands were earning no money, did choose (or find it necessary) to work for wages at times, as cooks, laundresses, and tavern keepers. And in the sexually imbalanced mining communities, there was always a ready market for prostitutes.

The thousands of people who flocked to the mining towns in search of quick wealth and who failed to find it often remained as wage laborers in corporate mines after the boom period. Working conditions were almost uniformly terrible. The corporate mines were deep and extremely hot, with temperatures often exceeding 100 degrees Fahrenheit. Some workers died of heatstroke (or of pneumonia, a result of experiencing sudden changes of temperature when emerging from the mines.) Poor ventilation meant large accumulations of poisonous carbon dioxide, which caused dizziness, nausea, and headaches. Lethal dusts stayed in the stagnant air to be inhaled over and over by the miners, many of whom developed silicosis (a disabling disease of the lungs) as a result. There were frequent explosions, cave-ins, and fires, and there were many accidents with the heavy machinery they used to bore into the earth. In the 1870s, before technological advances eliminated some of the dangers, one worker in every thirty was disabled in the mines, and one in every eighty was killed. That rate fell later in the nineteenth century, but mining remained one of the most dangerous and arduous working environments in the United States.

The Cattle Kingdom

A second important element of the changing economy of the Far West was cattle ranching. The open range—the vast grasslands of the public domain—provided a huge area on the Great Plains where cattle raisers could graze their herds free of charge and unrestricted by the boundaries of private farms. The railroads gave birth to the range-cattle industry by giving it access to markets. Eventually, the same railroads ended it by bringing farmers to the plains and thus destroying the open range.

The western cattle industry was Mexican and Texan by ancestry. Long before citizens of the United States invaded the Southwest, Mexican ranchers had developed the techniques and equipment that the cattlemen and cowboys of the Great Plains later employed: branding (a device known in all frontier areas where stock was common), roundups, roping, and the gear of the herders—their lariats, saddles, leather chaps, and spurs. Americans in Texas adopted these methods and carried them to the northernmost ranges of the cattle kingdom. Texas also had the largest herds of cattle in the country; the animals were descended from imported Spanish stock—wiry, hardy longhorns—and allowed to run wild or semiwild. From Texas, too, came the horses that enabled the caretakers of the herds, the

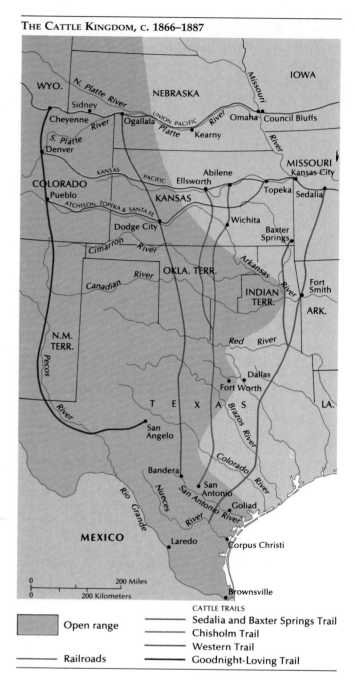

THE CATTLE KINGDOM, C. 1866–1887

CATTLE TRAILS
——— Sedalia and Baxter Springs Trail
——— Chisholm Trail
——— Western Trail
——— Goodnight-Loving Trail

Open range

——— Railroads

cowboys, to control them—small, muscular broncos or mustangs well suited to the requirements of cattle country.

At the end of the Civil War, an estimated 5 million cattle roamed the Texas ranges. Eastern markets were offering fat prices for steers in any condition, and the

THE CATTLE DRIVE
Cowboys round up a herd near Cheyenne, Wyoming, during one of the great cattle drives that briefly characterized the ranching economy of the West. *(American Heritage Center, University of Wyoming)*

challenge facing the cattle industry was getting the animals from the range to the railroad centers. Early in 1866, some Texas cattle ranchers began driving their combined herds, some 260,000 head, north to Sedalia, Missouri, on the Missouri Pacific Railroad. Traveling over rough country and beset by outlaws, Indians, and property-conscious farmers, the caravan suffered heavy losses, and only a fraction of the animals arrived in Sedalia. But the drive was an important experiment. It proved that cattle could be driven to distant markets and pastured along the trail, and that they would even gain weight during the journey. This earliest of the "long drives," in other words, established the first, tentative link between the isolated cattle breeders of west Texas and the booming urban markets of the East. The drive laid the groundwork for the explosion of the industry—for the creation of the "cattle kingdom."

With the precedent of the long drive established, the next step was to find an easier route through more accessible country. Market facilities grew up at Abilene, Kansas, on the Kansas Pacific Railroad, and for years the town reigned as the railhead of the cattle kingdom. Between 1867 and 1871, cattlemen drove nearly 1.5 million head up the Chisholm Trail to Abi-

lene—a town that, when filled with rampaging cowboys at the end of a drive, rivaled the mining towns in rowdiness. But by the mid-1870s, agricultural development in western Kansas was eating away at the open range land at the same time that the supply of animals was increasing. Cattlemen therefore had to develop other trails and other market outlets. As the railroads began to reach farther west, Dodge City and Wichita in Kansas, Ogallala and Sidney in Nebraska, Cheyenne and Laramie in Wyoming, and Miles City and Glendive in Montana all began to rival Abilene as major centers of stock herding.

A long drive was a spectacular sight, and it is perhaps unsurprising that it became the most romanticized and mythologized aspect of life in the West. It began with the spring, or calf, roundup. The cattlemen of a district met with their cowboys at a specified place to round up stock from the open range; these herds contained the stock of many different owners, with only their brands to distinguish them from one another. As the cattle were driven in, the calves were branded with the marks of their mothers. Stray calves with no identifying symbols, "mavericks," were divided on a pro-rata basis. Then the cows and calves were turned loose to pasture, while the yearling steers (year-old males) were readied for the drive to the north. The combined herds, usually numbering from 2,000 to 5,000 head, moved out. Cowboys representing each of the major ranchers accompanied them. Most of the cowboys in the early years were veterans of the Confederate army. The next largest group consisted of African Americans—over half a million of them. They were more numerous than white northerners or Mexicans and other foreigners. They were usually assigned such jobs as wrangler (herdsman) or cook.

Every cattleman had to have a permanent base from which to operate, and so the ranch emerged. A ranch consisted of the employer's dwelling, quarters for employees, and a tract of grazing land. In the early years of the cattle kingdom, most ranches were relatively small, since so much of the grazing occurred in the vast, open areas that cattlemen shared. But as farmers and sheep breeders began to compete for the open plains, ranches became larger and more clearly defined; cattlemen gradually had to learn to raise their stock on their own fenced land.

There had always been an element of risk and speculation in the open-range cattle business. At any time, "Texas fever"—a disease transmitted to cattle by parasite-carrying ticks—might decimate a herd. Rustlers and Indians frequently seized large numbers of animals. But as settlement of the plains increased, new forms of competition joined these traditional risks. Sheep breeders from California and Oregon brought their flocks onto the range to compete for grass. Farmers ("nesters") from the East threw fences around their claims, blocking trails and breaking up the open range. A series of "range wars"—between sheepmen and cattlemen, between ranchers and farmers—erupted out of the tensions between these competing groups. Some of the wars resulted in significant loss of life and extensive property damage.

Accounts of the lofty profits to be made in the cattle business—it was said that an investment of $5,000 would return $45,000 in four years—tempted eastern, English, and Scottish capital to the plains. Increasingly, the structure of the cattle economy became corporate; in one year, twenty corporations with a combined capital of $12 million were chartered in Wyoming. The inevitable result of this frenzied, speculative expansion was that the ranges, already severed and shrunk by the railroads and the farmers, became overstocked. There was not enough grass to support the crowding herds or sustain the long drives. Finally nature intervened with a destructive finishing blow. Two severe winters, in 1885–1886 and 1886–1887, with a searing summer between them, stung and scorched the plains.

Hundreds of thousands of cattle died, streams and grass dried up, princely ranches and costly investments disappeared in a season.

The open-range industry never recovered; the long drive disappeared for good. Railroads displaced the trail as the route to market for livestock. But the established cattle ranches—with fenced-in grazing land and stocks of hay for winter feed—survived, grew, and prospered, eventually producing more beef than ever.

Although the cattle industry was overwhelmingly male in its early years, there were always a few women involved in ranching and driving. As ranching became more sedentary, the presence of women greatly increased. By 1890, more than 250,000 women owned ranches or farms in the western states (many of them as proxies for their husbands or fathers, but some in their own right). Indeed, the region provided women with many opportunities that were closed to them in the East—including the opportunity to participate in politics. Wyoming was the first state in the Union to guarantee woman suffrage; and throughout the West, women established themselves as an important political presence (and occasionally as significant officeholders).

The Romance of the West

The supposedly unsettled West had always occupied a special place in the Anglo-American imagination, beginning in the seventeenth century when the first white settlers along the Atlantic coast began to look to the interior for new opportunities and for refuge from the civilized world. But the vast regions of this "last frontier" had a particularly strong romantic appeal to many whites. Some of the reasons were obvious. The Great Plains, the Rocky Mountains, the basin and plateau region beyond the Rockies, and the Sierra Nevada–Cascade ranges beyond that—all constituted a landscape of brilliant diversity and spectacular grandeur, different from anything white Americans had encountered before. It was little wonder that newcomers looked on it with reverence and wonder. Painters of the new "Rocky Mountain School"—of whom the best known was Albert Bierstadt—celebrated the new West in grandiose canvases, some of which were taken on tours around the eastern and midwestern states and attracted enormous crowds, eager for a vision of the Great West. Such paintings emphasized the ruggedness and dramatic variety of the region, and reflected the same awe toward the land that earlier regional painters had displayed toward the Hudson River Valley and other areas.

Even more appealing than the landscape, perhaps, was the rugged, free-spirited lifestyle that many Americans associated with the West—a lifestyle that supposedly stood in sharp contrast to the increasingly stable and ordered world of the East. Many nineteenth-century Americans came to romanticize, especially, the figure of the cowboy and transformed him remarkably quickly from the low-paid worker he actually was into a powerful and enduring figure of myth. Admiring Americans seldom thought about the many dismal aspects of the cowboy's life: the tedium, the loneliness, the physical discomforts, the relatively few opportunities for advancement. Instead, in western novels such as Owen Wister's *The Virginian* (1902), they romanticized his freedom from traditional social constraints, his affinity with nature, even his supposed propensity for violence. The cowboy became a powerful and enduring symbol of what had long been an important ideal in the American mind: the ideal of the natural man (the same idea that had shaped such earlier novels as James Fenimore Cooper's *The Deerslayer* and *The Last of the Mohicans*). That symbol has survived into the late twentieth century—in popular literature, in song, in film, and on television.

Yet it was not simply the particular character of the new West that made it so important to the nation's imagination. It was also the fact that many Americans considered it the last frontier. Since the earliest moments of European settlement in America, the image of uncharted territory to the west had always comforted and inspired those who dreamed of starting life anew. Now, with the last of that unsettled land being slowly absorbed into the nation's civilization, that image exercised a stronger pull than ever. Mark Twain, one of the great American writers of the nineteenth century, gave voice to this romantic vision of the frontier in a series of brilliant novels and memoirs. In some of his writings—notably *Roughing It* (1872)—he wrote of the Far West, and of his own experience as a newspaper reporter in Nevada during the mining boom. His greatest works, however, dealt with life on an earlier frontier: the Mississippi Valley of his boyhood. In *The Adventures of Tom Sawyer* (1876) and *The Adventures of Huckleberry Finn* (1885), he produced characters who repudiated the constraints of organized society and attempted to escape into a more natural world. For Huck Finn, the vehicle of escape might be a small raft on the Mississippi, but the yearning for freedom reflected a larger vision of the West as the last refuge from the constraints of civilization.

One of the clearest and most influential statements of this romantic vision of the frontier came not from an artist but from the historian Frederick Jackson Turner, of the University of Wisconsin. In 1893, the thirty-three-year-old Turner delivered a memorable paper to a meeting of the American Historical Association in Chicago entitled "The Significance of the Frontier in American History." In it, he cited the findings of the 1890 census that the unsettled area of the West had been "so broken into by isolated bodies of settlement" that a continuous frontier line could no longer be drawn. The passing of that line, he argued, ended an era in the nation's history. For, as Turner stated, "the existence of an area of free land, its continuous recession, and the advance of settlement westward, explain American development." This experience of expansion into the frontier had stimulated individualism, nationalism, and democracy. It had kept opportunities for advancement alive. It had made Americans the distinctive people that they were. "Now," Turner concluded portentously, "four centuries from the discovery of America, at the end of a hundred years of life under the Constitution, the frontier has gone and with its going has closed the first period of American history."

In fact, Turner's assessments were both inaccurate and premature. The West had never been a "frontier" in the sense he meant the term: an empty, uncivilized land awaiting settlement. White migrants into the region had joined (or displaced) already established societies and cultures. At the same time, considerable unoccupied land remained in the West for many years to come. A vast public domain still existed in the 1890s, and during the forty years thereafter the government was to give away many more acres than it had granted as homesteads in the past. But Turner did express a growing and generally accurate sense that much of the best farming and grazing land was now taken, that in the future it would be more difficult for individuals to acquire valuable land for little or nothing.

In accepting the idea of the "passing of the frontier," many Americans were acknowledging the end of one of their most cherished myths. As long as it had been possible for them to consider the West an empty, open land, it was possible to believe that there were constantly revitalizing opportunities in American life. Now there was a vague and ominous sense of opportunities foreclosed, of individuals losing their ability to control their own destinies. The psychological loss was all the greater because of what historian Henry Nash Smith would later call, in *Virgin Land* (1950), the "myth of the garden": the once widely shared belief that the West had the potential to be a virtual Garden of Eden, where a person could begin life anew and where the ideals of democracy could be restored. That, too, was a theme in late-nineteenth-century fiction. For

THE FRONTIER AND THE WEST

THE AMERICAN WEST, AND the process by which people of European descent settled there, has been central to the national imagination for at least two centuries. It has also, at times, been central to American historical scholarship.

Through most of the nineteenth century, the history of the West reflected the romantic and optimistic view of the region beloved by many Americans. The lands west of the Mississippi River were places of adventure and opportunity. The West was a region where life could start anew, where brave and enterprising people endured great hardships to begin building a new civilization. Francis Parkman's *The Oregon Trail* (1849), a classic of American literature, expressed many of these assumptions and in the process shaped the way in which later generations of Americans would view the West and its past. But the emergence of western history as an important field of scholarship can best be traced to the famous paper Frederick Jackson Turner delivered at a meeting of the American Historical Association in 1893. It was entitled "The Significance of the Frontier in American History." The "Turner thesis" or "frontier thesis," as his argument quickly became known, shaped both popular and scholarly views of the West (and of much else) for two generations.

Turner stated his thesis simply. The settlement of the West by white people—"the existence of an area of free land, its continuous recession, and the advance of American settlement westward"—was the central story of American history. The process of westward expansion had transformed a desolate and savage land into modern civilization. It had also continually renewed American ideas of democracy and individualism and had, therefore, shaped not just the West but the nation as a whole. "What the Mediterranean Sea was to the Greeks, breaking the bonds of custom, offering new experiences, calling out new institutions and activities, that, and more, the ever retreating frontier has been to the United States."

The Turner thesis shaped the writing of American history for a generation, and it shaped the writing of western American history for even longer. In the first half of the twentieth century, virtually all the major figures in the field echoed and elaborated at least part of Turner's argument. Ray Allen Billington's *Westward Expansion* (1949) was for decades the standard textbook in the field; his skillful revision of the Turner thesis kept the idea of what he called the "westward course of empire" (the movement of Europeans into an unsettled land) at the center of scholarship. In *The Great Plains* (1931) and *The Great Frontier* (1952), Walter Prescott Webb similarly emphasized the bravery and ingenuity of white settlers in Texas and the Southwest in overcoming obstacles (most notably, in Webb's part of the West, aridity) to create a great new civilization.

The Turner thesis was never without its critics. But serious efforts to displace it as the explanation of western American history did not begin in earnest until after World War II. In *Virgin Land* (1950), Henry Nash Smith examined many of the same heroic images of the West that Turner and his disciples had presented; but he treated those images less as descriptions of reality than as myths, which many Americans had used to sustain an image of themselves that the actual character of the modern world contradicted. Earl Pomeroy, in an influential 1955 essay and in many other works, challenged Turner's notion of the West as a place of individualism, innovation, and democratic renewal. "Conservatism, inheritance, and continuity bulked at least as large," he claimed. "The westerner has been fundamentally imitator rather than innovator. . . . He was often the most ardent

WHERE HISTORIANS DISAGREE

of conformists." Howard Lamar, in *Dakota Territory, 1861–1889* (1956) and *The Far Southwest* (1966), emphasized the highly diverse experiences of different areas of the West and thus challenged the emphasis of the Turnerians on a distinctive western environment as the crucial determinant of western experience.

The generation of western historians who began to emerge in the late 1970s launched an even more emphatic attack on the Turner thesis and the idea of the "frontier." Echoing the interest of historians in other fields in issues of race, gender, ethnicity, and culture, "new" western historians such as Richard White, Patricia Nelson Limerick, William Cronon, Donald Worster, Peggy Pascoe, and many others challenged the Turnerians on a number of points.

Turner saw the nineteenth-century West as "free land" awaiting the expansion of Anglo-American settlement and American democracy. Pioneers settled the region by conquering the "obstacles" in the way of civilization—the "vast forests," the "mountainous ramparts," the "desolate, grass-clad prairies, barren oceans of rolling plains, arid deserts, and a fierce race of savages." The "new western historians" have rejected the concept of a "frontier" and emphasize, instead, the elaborate and highly developed civilizations (Native American, Hispanic, mixed-blood, and others) that already existed in the region. White, English-speaking Americans, they have argued, did not so much settle the West as conquer it. And that conquest was never complete. Anglo-Americans in the West continue to share the region not only with the Indians and Hispanics who preceded them there, but also with African Americans, Asians, Latin Americans, and others who flowed into the West at the same time they did. Western history, these recent scholars have claimed, is a process of cultural "convergence," a constant competition and interaction—economic, political, cultural, and linguistic—among diverse peoples.

The Turnerian West was a place of heroism, triumph, and above all progress, dominated by the feats of brave white men. The West the new historians describe is a less triumphant (and less masculine) place in which bravery and success coexist with oppression, greed, and failure; in which decaying ghost towns, bleak Indian reservations, impoverished barrios, and ecologically devastated landscapes are as characteristic of western development as great ranches, rich farms, and prosperous cities; and in which women are as important as men in shaping the societies that emerged. This aspect of the "new western history" has attracted particular criticism from those attached to more traditional accounts. The novelist Larry McMurtry, for example, has denounced the new scholarship as "Failure Studies." He has insisted that in rejecting the romantic image westerners had of themselves, the revisionists omit an important part of the western experience.

To Turner and his disciples, the nineteenth-century West was a place where rugged individualism flourished and replenished American democracy. To the new scholars, western individualism is a self-serving myth. The region was inextricably tied to a national and international capitalist economy; indeed, the only thing that sustained Anglo-American settlement of the West was the demand in other places for its natural resources. Western "pioneers" were never self-sufficient. They depended on government-subsidized railroads for access to markets, federal troops for protection from Indians, and (later) government-funded dams and canals for irrigating their fields and sustaining their towns.

And while Turner defined the West as a process—a process of settlement that came to an end with the "closing of the frontier" in the late nineteenth century—the new historians see the West as a region. Its history does not end in 1890. It continues into our own time.

example, In *Ramona* (1884), the novelist Helen Hunt Jackson wrote of California before American settlement as an agrarian paradise of rugged Hispanic pioneers and saintly missionaries. The setting for utopia, once the New World as a whole, had shrunk to the West of the United States. And now even that West seemed to be vanishing.

THE DISPERSAL OF THE TRIBES

Having imagined the West as a "virgin land" awaiting civilization by white people, many Americans tried to force the region to match their image of it. That meant, above all, ensuring that the Indian tribes would not remain obstacles to the spread of white society.

White Tribal Policies

The traditional policy of the federal government was to regard the tribes simultaneously as independent nations and as wards of the president, and to negotiate treaties with them that were solemnly ratified by the Senate. This limited concept of Indian sovereignty had been responsible for the government's attempt before 1860 to erect a permanent frontier between whites and Indians, to reserve the region west of the bend of the Missouri River as permanent Indian country. However, treaties or agreements with the tribes seldom survived the pressure of white settlers eager for access to Indian lands. The history of relations between the United States and the Native Americans was, therefore, one of nearly endless broken promises.

By the early 1850s, the idea of establishing one great enclave in which many tribes could live gave way, in the face of white demands for access to lands in Indian Territory, to a new reservations policy, known as "concentration." In 1851, each tribe was assigned its own defined reservation, confirmed by separate treaties—treaties often illegitimately negotiated with unauthorized "representatives" chosen by whites, people known sarcastically as "treaty chiefs". The new arrangement had many benefits for whites and few for the Indians. It divided the tribes from one another and made them easier to control. It allowed the government to force tribes into scattered locations and to take over the most desirable lands for white settlement. But it did not survive as the basis of Indian policy for long.

In 1867, in the aftermath of a series of bloody conflicts, Congress established an Indian Peace Commission, composed of soldiers and civilians, to recommend a new and presumably permanent Indian policy.

The commission recommended replacing the "concentration" policy with a new one. The government would move all the Plains tribes into two large reservations—one in Indian Territory (Oklahoma), the other in the Dakotas. At a series of meetings with the tribes, government agents cajoled, bribed, and tricked representatives of the Arapaho, Cheyenne, Sioux, and other tribes into agreeing to treaties establishing the new reservations.

But this "solution" worked little better than previous ones. Part of the problem was the way in which the government administered the reservations it had established. White management of Indian matters was entrusted to the Bureau of Indian Affairs, located in the Department of the Interior. The bureau was responsible for distributing land, making payments, and supervising the shipment of supplies. Its record was appalling. The bureau's agents in the West, products of political patronage, were often men of extraordinary incompetence and dishonesty. But even the most honest and diligent agents were generally ill-prepared for their jobs, had no understanding of tribal ways, and had little chance of success. The poor and usually corrupt administration of the reservations was one reason for the constant conflicts between the tribes and the whites who were surrounding them.

But the problem was also a result of what was, in effect, economic warfare by whites: the relentless slaughtering of the buffalo herds that supported the tribes' way of life. Even in the 1850s, whites had been killing buffalo at a rapid rate to provide food and supplies for the large bands of migrants traveling to the gold rush in California. After the Civil War the white demand for buffalo hides became a national phenomenon—partly for economic reasons and partly as a fad. (Everyone east of the Missouri seemed to want a buffalo robe from the romantic West, and there was a strong demand for buffalo leather, which was used to make machine belts in eastern factories.) Gangs of professional hunters swarmed over the Plains to shoot the huge animals. Some hunters killed merely for the sport of the chase, although the lumbering victims did not present much of a challenge. Railroad companies hired riflemen (such as Buffalo Bill Cody) and arranged large shooting expeditions to kill large numbers of buffalo, hoping to thin the herds, which were obstructions to railroad traffic. Some Indian tribes (notably the Blackfeet) also began killing large numbers of buffalo to sell in the booming new market.

But it was not just the hunting that threatened the buffalo. It was the ecological changes that white settlement brought to the region—the reduction and in some areas virtual disappearance of the open plains on which the buffalo depended. The southern herd was virtually exterminated by 1875, and within a few years the smaller northern herd had met the same fate. In 1865, there had been at least 15 million buffalo; a decade later, fewer than a thousand of the great beasts survived. The army and the agents of the Bureau of Indian Affairs condoned and even encouraged the killing. By destroying the buffalo herds, whites were destroying the Indians' source of food and supplies and their ability to resist the white advance. They were also contributing to a climate in which Indian warriors felt the need to fight to preserve their way of life.

The Indian Wars

There was almost incessant fighting between whites and Indians from the 1850s to the 1880s, as Indians struggled against the growing threats to their civilizations. Indian warriors, usually traveling in raiding parties of thirty to forty men, attacked wagon trains, stagecoaches, and isolated ranches, often in retaliation for earlier attacks on them by whites. As the United States Army became more deeply involved in the fighting, the tribes began to focus more of their attacks on white soldiers.

At times, this small-scale fighting escalated into something close to a war. During the Civil War, the eastern Sioux in Minnesota, cramped on an inadequate reservation and exploited by corrupt white agents, suddenly rebelled against the restrictions imposed on them by the government's policies. Led by Little Crow, they killed more than 700 whites before being subdued by a force of regulars and militiamen. Thirty-eight of the Indians were hanged, and the tribe was exiled to the Dakotas.

At the same time, fighting flared up in eastern Colorado, where the Arapaho and Cheyenne were coming into conflict with white miners settling in the region. Bands of Indians attacked stagecoach lines and settlements in an effort to regain territory they had lost. In response to these incidents, whites called up a large territorial militia, and the army issued dire threats of retribution. The governor urged all friendly Indians to congregate at army posts for protection before the army began its campaign. One Arapaho and Cheyenne band under Black Kettle, apparently in response to the invitation, camped near Fort Lyon on Sand Creek in November 1864. Some members of the party were warriors, but Black Kettle believed he was under official protection and exhibited no hostile intention. Nevertheless, Colonel J. M. Chivington, apparently encouraged by the army commander of the district, led a volunteer militia force—largely consisting of unemployed miners, many of whom were apparently drunk—to the

unsuspecting camp and massacred 133 people, 105 of them women and children. Black Kettle himself escaped the Sand Creek massacre. Four years later, in 1868, he and his Cheyennes, some of whom were now at war with the whites, were caught on the Washita River, near the Texas border, by Colonel George A. Custer. White troops killed the chief and slaughtered his people.

At the end of the Civil War, white troops stepped up their wars against the western Indians on several fronts. The most serious and sustained conflict was in Montana, where the army was attempting to build a road, the Bozeman Trail, to connect Fort Laramie, Wyoming, to the new mining centers. The western Sioux resented this intrusion into the heart of their buffalo range. Led by one of their great chiefs, Red Cloud, they so harried the soldiers and the construction party—among other things, burning the forts that were supposed to guard the route—that the road could not be used.

But it was not only the United States military that harried the tribes. It was also unofficial violence by white vigilantes who engaged in what became known as "Indian hunting." In California, in particular, tracking down and killing Indians became for some whites a kind of sport. Some who did not engage in killing offered rewards (or bounties) to those who did; these bounty hunters brought back scalps and skulls as proof of their deeds. Sometimes the killing was in response to Indian raids on white communities. But often it was in service to a more basic and terrible purpose. Considerable numbers of whites were committed to the goal of literal "elimination" of the tribes, a goal that rested on the belief in the essential inhumanity of Indians and the impossibility of white society's coexisting with them. In Oregon in 1853, for example, whites who had hanged a seven-year-old Indian boy explained themselves by saying simply "nits breed lice." In California, civilians killed close to 5,000 Indians between 1850 and 1880—one of many factors (disease and poverty being the more important) that reduced the Indian population of the state from 150,000 before the Civil War to 30,000 in 1870.

The treaties negotiated in 1867 brought a temporary lull to many of the conflicts. But new forces soon shattered the peace again. In the early 1870s, more waves of white settlers, mostly miners, began to penetrate some of the lands in Dakota territory supposedly guaranteed to the tribes in 1867. At the same time, the federal government, responding to the recommendations of a commission, decided that it would no longer recognize the tribes as independent entities and would no longer negotiate with tribal chiefs. This step was intended to undermine the collective nature of Indian

THE BATTLE OF THE LITTLE BIG HORN: AN INDIAN VIEW
This 1898 watercolor by one of the Indian participants portrays the aftermath of the Battle of the Little Big Horn, June 25–26, 1876, in which an army unit under the command of General George Armstrong Custer was surrounded and wiped out by Sioux and Cheyenne warriors. This grisly painting shows Indians on horseback riding over the corpses of Custer and his men. Custer can be seen lying at left center, dressed in yellow buckskin with his hat beside him. The four standing men at center are Sitting Bull, Rain-in-the-Face, Crazy Horse, and Kicking Bear (the artist). At lower right, Indian women begin preparations for a ceremony to honor the returning warriors. *(Southwest Museum, Pasadena, California)*

life and to force the Indians to assimilate into white culture—a goal cherished by many white reformers, who believed that only through assimilation could the Indians achieve genuine "civilization."

Indian resistance flared anew, this time with even greater strength. In the northern plains, the Sioux, in response to the entrance of miners into the Black Hills and in anger at the corrupt behavior of white agents, rose up in 1875 and left their reservation. When white officials ordered them to return, bands of warriors gathered in Montana and united under two great leaders: Crazy Horse and Sitting Bull.

Three army columns set out to round them up and force them back onto the reservation. With the expedition, as colonel of the famous Seventh Cavalry, was the colorful and controversial George A. Custer, golden-haired romantic and glory seeker. At the Battle of the Little Bighorn in southern Montana in 1876—perhaps the most famous of all conflicts between whites and Indians—the tribal warriors surprised Custer and part

of his regiment, surrounded them, and killed every man. Custer has been accused of rashness, but he seems to have encountered something that no white man would likely have predicted. The chiefs had gathered together between 2,500 and 4,000 warriors, one of the largest Indian armies ever assembled at one time in the United States.

But the Indians did not have the political organization or the supplies to keep their troops united. Soon the warriors drifted off in bands to elude pursuit or search for food, and the army ran them down singly and returned them to Dakota. The power of the Sioux was soon broken. The proud leaders, Crazy Horse and Sitting Bull, accepted defeat and the monotony of life on reservations. Both were later killed by reservation police after being tricked or taunted into a last pathetic show of resistance.

One of the most dramatic episodes in Indian history occurred in Idaho in 1877. The Nez Percé were a small and relatively peaceful tribe, some of whose members had managed to live unmolested in Oregon into the 1870s without ever signing a treaty with the United States. But under pressure from white settlers, the government forced them to move into a reservation that another branch of the tribe had accepted by treaty in the 1850s. With no realistic prospect of resisting, the Indians began the journey to the reservation; but on the way, several younger Indians, drunk and angry, killed four white settlers.

The leader of the band, Chief Joseph, persuaded his followers to flee from the expected retribution. American troops pursued and attacked them, only to be driven off in a battle at White Bird Canyon. After that, the Nez Percé scattered in several directions and became part of a remarkable chase. Joseph moved with 200 men and 350 women, children, and old people in an effort to reach Canada and take refuge with the Sioux there. Pursued by four columns of American soldiers smarting from their defeat at White Bird Canyon, the Indians covered 1,321 miles in seventy-five days, repelling or evading the army time and again. They were finally caught just short of the Canadian boundary. Some escaped and slipped across the border; but Joseph and most of his followers, weary and discouraged, finally gave up. "Hear me, my chiefs," Joseph said after meeting with the American general Nelson Miles. "I am tired. My heart is sick and sad. From where the sun now stands, I will fight no more forever." He surrendered to Miles in exchange for a promise that his band could return to the Nez Percé reservation in Idaho. But the government refused to honor Miles's promise, and the Nez Percé were shipped from one place to another for several years; in the process, many of them died of disease and malnutrition (although Joseph himself lived until 1908).

The last Indians to maintain organized resistance against the whites were the Chiricahua Apaches, who fought intermittently from the 1860s to the late 1880s. The two ablest chiefs of this fierce tribe were Mangas Colorados and Cochise. Mangas was murdered during the Civil War by white soldiers who tricked him into surrendering, and in 1872 Cochise agreed to peace in exchange for a reservation that included some of the tribe's traditional land. But Cochise died in 1874, and his successor, Geronimo—unwilling to bow to white pressures to assimilate—fought on for more than a decade longer, establishing bases in the mountains of Arizona and Mexico and leading warriors in intermittent raids against white outposts. With each raid, however, the number of warring Apaches dwindled, as some warriors died and others drifted away to the reservation. By 1886, Geronimo's plight was hopeless. His band consisted of only about thirty people, including women and children, while his white pursuers

numbered perhaps ten thousand. Geronimo recognized the odds and surrendered, an event that marked the end of formal warfare between Indians and whites.

The Apache wars were the most violent of all the Indian conflicts, perhaps because the tribes were now the most desperate. But it was the whites who committed the most flagrant and vicious atrocities. In 1871, for example, a mob of white miners invaded an Apache camp, slaughtered over a hundred Indians, and captured children, whom they sold as slaves to rival tribes. On other occasions, white troops murdered Indians who responded to invitations to peace conferences, once killing them with poisoned food.

Nor did the atrocities end with the conclusion of the Apache wars. Another tragic encounter occurred in 1890 as a result of a religious revival among the Sioux—a revival that itself symbolized the catastrophic effects of the white assaults on Indian civilization. The Sioux were by now aware that their culture and their glories were irrevocably fading; some were also near starvation because corrupt government agents had reduced their food rations. As other tribes had done in trying times in the past, many of these Indians turned to a prophet who led them into a religious revival.

This time the prophet was Wovoka, a Paiute who inspired an ecstatic spiritual awakening that began in Nevada and spread quickly to the plains. The new revival emphasized the coming of a messiah, but its most conspicuous feature was a mass, emotional "Ghost Dance," which inspired ecstatic visions that many participants believed were genuinely mystical. Among these visions were images of a retreat of white people from the plains and a restoration of the great buffalo herds. White agents on the Sioux reservation watched the dances in bewilderment and fear; some believed they might be the preliminary to hostilities.

On December 29, 1890, the Seventh Cavalry (which had once been Custer's regiment) tried to round up a group of about 350 cold and starving Sioux at Wounded Knee, South Dakota. Fighting broke out in which about 40 white soldiers and more than 300 of the Indians, including women and children, died. What precipitated the conflict is a matter of dispute. An Indian may well have fired the first shot, but the battle soon turned into a one-sided massacre, as the white soldiers turned their new machine guns on the Indians and mowed them down in the snow.

The Dawes Act

Even before the Ghost Dance and the Wounded Knee tragedy, the federal government had moved to destroy forever the tribal structure that had always been the cornerstone of Indian culture. Reversing its policy of

BURIAL AT WOUNDED KNEE
Soldiers bury some of the Sioux Indians killed at Wounded Knee. This mass grave held over 100 bodies, many of them women and children. The Wounded Knee massacre was the last major episode in a year-long effort by whites to suppress the Sioux religious revival known as the Ghost Dance. *(Amon Carter Museum)*

nearly fifty years of creating reservations in which the tribes would be isolated from white society, Congress abolished the practice by which tribes owned reservation lands communally. Some supporters of the new policy believed they were acting for the good of the Indians, whom they considered a "vanishing race" in need of rescue by white society. But the action was frankly designed to force Indians to become landowners and farmers, to abandon their collective society and culture and become part of white civilization.

The Dawes Severalty Act of 1887 (usually known simply as the Dawes Act) provided for the gradual elimination of tribal ownership of land and the allotment of tracts to individual owners: 160 acres to the head of a family, 80 acres to a single adult or orphan, 40 acres to each dependent child. Adult owners were given United States citizenship, but unlike other citizens, they could not gain full title to their property for twenty-five years (supposedly to prevent them from selling the land to speculators). The act applied to most of the western tribes. The Pueblo, who continued to occupy lands long ago guaranteed them, were excluded from its provisions.

In applying the Dawes Act, the Bureau of Indian Affairs relentlessly promoted the idea of assimilation that lay behind it. Not only did they try to move Indian families onto their own plots of land; they also took Indian children away from their families and sent them to boarding schools run by whites, where they believed the young people could be educated to abandon tribal ways. They also moved to stop Indian religious rituals and encouraged the spread of Christian-

ity and the creation of Christian churches on the reservations.

Few Indians were prepared for this wrenching change from their traditional collective society to capitalist individualism. In any case, white administration of the program was so corrupt and inept that ultimately the government simply abandoned it. Much of the reservation land, therefore, was never distributed to individual owners. Congress attempted to speed the transition with the Burke Act of 1906, but Indians continued to resist forced assimilation.

Neither then nor later could legislation provide a satisfactory solution to the problem of the Indians, largely because there was no entirely happy solution to be had. The interests of the Indians were not compatible with those of the expanding white civilization. Whites successfully settled the American West only at the expense of the region's indigenous people.

THE RISE AND DECLINE OF THE WESTERN FARMER

The arrival of the miners, the empire building of the cattle ranchers, the dispersal of the Indian tribes—all served as a prelude to the decisive phase of white settlement of the Far West. Even before the Civil War, farmers had begun moving into the plains region, challenging the dominance of the ranchers and the Indians and occasionally coming into conflict with both.

By the 1870s, what was once a trickle had become a deluge. Farmers poured into the plains and beyond, enclosed land that had once been hunting territory for Indians and grazing territory for cattle, and established a new agricultural region.

For a time in the late 1870s and early 1880s, the new western farmers flourished, enjoying the fruits of an agricultural economic boom comparable in many ways to the booms that eastern industry periodically enjoyed. Beginning in the mid-1880s, however, the boom turned to bust. American agriculture—not only in the new West but in the older Middle West and the South as well—was producing more than it ever had, too much for the market to absorb. For that and other reasons, prices for agricultural goods declined. Both economically and psychologically, the agricultural economy began a long, steady decline.

Farming on the Plains

Many factors combined to produce this surge of western settlement, but the most important was the railroads. Before the Civil War, the Great Plains had been accessible only through a difficult journey by wagon. But beginning in the 1860s, a great new network of railroad lines developed, spearheaded by the transcontinental routes Congress had authorized and subsidized in 1862. They made huge new areas of settlement accessible.

The building of the transcontinental line was a dramatic and monumental achievement. Thousands of immigrant workers—mostly Irish on the eastern route, Chinese on the western—labored in what were at times unimaginably difficult conditions to penetrate mountain ranges, cross deserts, protect themselves against Indians, and—finally—connect the two lines at Promontory Point in northern Utah in the spring of 1869.

But while this first transcontinental line captured the public imagination, the construction of subsidiary lines in the following years proved of greater importance to the West. State governments, imitating Washington, encouraged railroad development by offering direct financial aid, favorable loans, and more than 50 million acres of land (on top of the 130 million acres the federal government had already provided). Although operated by private corporations, the railroads were essentially public projects.

It was not only by making access to the Great Plains easier that the railroads helped spur agricultural settlement there. The railroad companies themselves actively promoted settlement, both to provide themselves with customers for their services and to increase the value of their vast landholdings. In addition, the companies set rates so low for settlers that almost anyone could afford the trip west. And they sold much of their land at very low prices and provided liberal credit to prospective settlers.

Contributing further to the great surge of white agricultural expansion was a temporary change in the climate of the Great Plains. For several years in succession, beginning in the 1870s, rainfall in the plains states was well above average. White Americans now rejected the old idea that the region was the Great American Desert. Some even claimed that cultivation of the plains actually encouraged rainfall.

Even under the most favorable conditions, farming on the plains presented special problems. First was the problem of fencing. Farmers had to enclose their land,

HELD UP BY BUFFALO
Once among the most numerous creatures in North America, the buffalo became almost extinct as a result of their indiscriminate slaughter by white settlers and travelers, who often fired at herds from moving trains simply for the sport of it. This scene was painted around 1880 by N. H. Trotter. *(Smithsonian Institution)*

SIGNIFICANT EVENTS

1847 Taos Indians rebel in New Mexico, killing American governor and precipitating military rule

1848–1849 California gold rush begins

1851 "Concentration" policy devised for western tribes

1852 California legislature passes "foreign miners' tax" to exclude Chinese from gold mining

1858 Comstock Lode silver deposits discovered in Nevada

1859 Colorado gold rush launches western mining bonanza

Mexicans in Texas raid Brownsville jail

1861 Kansas admitted to Union

1862 Homestead Act passed

1864 Nevada admitted to Union

1865 U.S. troops massacre Arapaho and Cheyenne at Sand Creek

1865–1867 Sioux War

1866 "Long drives" launch western cattle bonanza

Chinese workers strike against Union Pacific

1867 Nebraska admitted to Union

Indian Peace Commission establishes "Indian Territory" (later Oklahoma)

1868 Black Kettle and his Cheyenne warriors captured and killed by U.S. forces

1869 Union Pacific, first transcontinental railroad, completed

1872 Cochise, chief of Chiricahua Apaches, agrees to treaty with U.S.

1873 Barbed wire invented

Timber Culture Act passed

1874 Gold rush begins in Black Hills, Dakota Territory

1875 Sioux uprising begins

Southern buffalo herd virtually extinguished

1876 Battle of Little Bighorn

Colorado admitted to Union

---

if for no other reason than to protect it from the herds of the open-range cattlemen. But traditional wood or stone fences were too expensive and were ineffective as barriers to cattle. In the mid-1870s, however, two Illinois farmers, Joseph H. Glidden and I. L. Ellwood, solved this problem by developing and marketing barbed wire, which became standard equipment on the plains and revolutionized fencing practices all over the country.

The second problem was water. Water was scarce even when rainfall was above average. After 1887, a series of dry seasons began, and lands that had been fertile now returned to semi-desert. Some farmers dealt with the problem by using deep wells pumped by steel windmills, or by turning to what was called dryland farming (a system of tillage designed to conserve moisture in the soil by covering it with a dust blanket), or by planting drought-resistant crops. In many areas of the plains, however, only large-scale irrigation could save the endangered farms. But irrigation projects of the necessary magnitude required government assistance, and neither the state nor federal governments were prepared to fund the projects.

Most of the people who moved into the region had previously been farmers in the Middle West, the East, or Europe. In the booming years of the early 1880s, with land values rising, the new farmers had no problem obtaining extensive and easy credit and had every reason to believe they would soon be able to retire their debts. But the arid years of the late 1880s—during which crop prices were falling while production was becoming more expensive—changed that prospect. Tens of thousands of farmers could not pay their debts and were forced to abandon their farms. There was, in effect, a reverse migration: white settlers moving back east, sometimes turning once-flourishing communities

SIGNIFICANT EVENTS

1877   Desert Land Act passed

Nez Percé Indians resist relocation

1878   California Workingmen's Party founded and attacks Chinese immigration

Timber and Stone Act passed

1881   Anaconda copper mine begins operations in Montana

1882   Congress passes Chinese Exclusion Act

1884   Helen Hunt Jackson publishes *Ramona*

1885–1887   Harsh winters help destroy open-range cattle raising

1885   Mark Twain publishes *Huckleberry Finn*

1886   Geronimo surrenders, ending Apache resistance

1887   Dawes Act passed

Prolonged drought in Great Plains begins

1889   North Dakota, South Dakota, Montana, and Washington admitted to Union

Oklahoma (formerly "Indian Territory") opened to white settlement

1890   Indian "Ghost Dance" revival

Battle of Wounded Knee

Wyoming and Idaho admitted to Union

1891   Hamlin Garland publishes *Main-Traveled Roads*

1892   Congress renews Chinese Exclusion Act

1893   Frederick Jackson Turner proposes "Turner thesis"

1896   Utah admitted to Union

1902   Congress makes Chinese Exclusion Act permanent

Owen Wister publishes *The Virginian*

1906   Congress passes Burke Act to speed assimilation of tribes

into desolate ghost towns. Those who remained continued to suffer from falling prices (for example, wheat, which had sold for $1.60 a bushel at the end of the Civil War, dropped to 49 cents in the 1890s) and persistent indebtedness.

Commercial Agriculture

American farming by the late nineteenth century no longer bore very much relation to the comforting image many Americans continued to cherish. The sturdy, independent farmer of popular myth was being replaced by the commercial farmer—attempting to do in the agricultural economy what industrialists were doing in the manufacturing economy.

Commercial farmers were not self-sufficient and made no effort to become so. They specialized in cash crops which they sold in national or world markets.

They did not make their own household supplies or grow their own food but bought them instead at town or village stores. This kind of farming, when it was successful, raised the farmers' living standards. But it also made them dependent on bankers and interest rates, railroads and freight rates, national and European markets, world supply and demand. And unlike the capitalists of the industrial order, they could not regulate their production or influence the prices of what they sold.

Between 1865 and 1900, agriculture became an international business. Farm output increased dramatically, not only in the United States but in Brazil, Argentina, Canada, Australia, New Zealand, Russia, and elsewhere. At the same time, modern forms of communication and transportation—the telephone, telegraph, steam navigation, railroads—were creating new markets around the world for agricultural goods. American commercial farmers, constantly opening new lands, produced much more than the domestic market could absorb; they relied on the world market to absorb their surplus, but in that market they faced major competition. Cotton farmers depended on export sales for 70 percent of their annual income, wheat farmers for 30 to 40 percent; but the volatility of the international market put them at great risk.

Beginning in the 1880s, worldwide overproduction led to a drop in prices for most agricultural goods and hence to great economic distress for many of the more than 6 million American farm families. By the 1890s, 27 percent of the farms in the country were mortgaged; by 1910, 33 percent. In 1880, 25 percent of all farms had been operated by tenants; by 1910, the proportion had grown to 37 percent. Commercial farming made some people fabulously wealthy. But the farm economy as a whole was suffering a significant decline relative to the rest of the nation.

The Farmers' Grievances

American farmers were painfully aware that something was wrong. But few yet understood the implications of national and world overproduction. Instead, they concentrated their attention and anger on more immediate, more comprehensible—and no less real—problems: inequitable freight rates, high interest charges, and an inadequate currency.

The farmers' first and most burning grievance was against the railroads. In many cases, the railroads charged higher rates for farm goods than for other goods, and higher rates in the South and West than in the Northeast. Railroads also controlled elevator and warehouse facilities in buying centers and charged arbitrary storage rates.

Farmers also resented the institutions controlling credit—banks, loan companies, insurance corporations. Since sources of credit in the West and South were few, farmers had to take loans on whatever terms they could get, often at interest rates of from 10 to 25 percent. Many farmers had to pay these loans back in years when prices were dropping and currency was becoming scarce. Increasing the volume of currency eventually became an important agrarian demand.

A third grievance concerned prices—both the prices farmers received for their products and the prices they paid for goods they bought. Farmers sold their products in a competitive world market over which they had no control and of which they had no advance knowledge. A farmer could plant a large crop at a moment when prices were high and find that by the time of the harvest the price had declined. Farmers' fortunes rose and fell in response to unpredictable forces. But many farmers became convinced (often with some rea-

son) that "middlemen"—speculators, bankers, regional and local agents—were combining to fix prices so as to benefit themselves at the growers' expense. Many farmers also came to believe (again, not entirely without reason) that manufacturers in the East were conspiring to keep the prices of farm goods low and the prices of industrial goods high. Although farmers sold their crops in a competitive world market, they bought manufactured goods in a domestic market protected by tariffs and dominated by trusts and corporations.

The Agrarian Malaise

These economic difficulties produced a series of social and cultural resentments. In part, this was a result of the isolation of farm life. Farm families in some parts of the country—particularly in the prairie and plains regions, where large farms were scattered over vast areas—were virtually cut off from the outside world and human companionship. During the winter months and spells of bad weather, the loneliness and boredom could become nearly unbearable. Many farmers lacked access to adequate education for their children, to proper medical facilities, to recreational or cultural activities, to virtually anything that might give them a sense of being members of a community. Older farmers felt the sting of watching their children leave the farm for the city. They felt the humiliation of being ridiculed as "hayseeds" by the new urban culture that was coming to dominate American life.

The result of this sense of isolation and obsolescence was a growing malaise among many farmers, a discontent that would help create a great national political movement in the 1890s. It found reflection, too, in the literature that emerged from rural America. Writers in the late nineteenth century might romanticize the rugged life of the cowboy and the western miner. For the farmer, however, the image was often different. Hamlin Garland, for example, reflected the growing disillusionment in a series of novels and short stories. In the past, Garland wrote in the introduction to his novel *Jason Edwards* (1891), the agrarian frontier had seemed to be "the Golden West, the land of wealth and freedom and happiness. All of the associations called up by the spoken word, the West, were fabulous, mythic, hopeful." Now, however, the bright promise had faded. The trials of rural life were crushing the human spirit. "So this is the reality of the dream!" a character in *Jason Edwards* exclaims. "A shanty on a barren plain, hot and lone as a desert. My God!" Once, sturdy yeoman farmers had viewed themselves as the backbone of American life. Now they were becoming painfully aware that their position was declining in relation to the rising urban-industrial society to the east.

SUGGESTED READINGS

General Works. Ray A. Billington and Martin Ridge, *Westward Expansion*, 5th ed. (1982). Thomas D. Clark, *Frontier America* (rev. 1969). William Cronon et al., eds., *Under An Open Sky: Rethinking America's Western Past* (1992). Robert V. Hine, *The American West*, 2nd ed. (1984). Patricia Nelson Limerick, *The Legacy of Conquest: The Unbroken Past of the American West* (1987). Patricia Nelson Limerick et al., eds., *Trails: Toward a New Western History* (1992). Frederick Merk, *History of the Westward Movement* (1978). Rodman W. Paul, *The Far West and the Great Plains in Transition, 1859–1900* (1988). Rodman W. Paul and Richard W. Etulain, *The Frontier and the American West* (1977). Richard White, *"It's Your Misfortune and None of My Own": A History of the American West* (1991).

Migrations and Communities. Gunther Barth, *Bitter Strength: A History of the Chinese in the United States, 1850–1870* (1964). Albert Camarillo, *Chicanos in a Changing Society: From Mexican Pueblos to American Barrios in Santa Barbara and Southern California* (1979). Sucheng Chan, *This Bittersweet Soil: The Chinese in California Agriculture, 1860–1910* (1986). Richard Griswold del Castillo, *La Familia: Chicano Families in the Urban Southwest, 1848 to the Present* (1984); *The Los Angeles Barrio, 1850–1890* (1979). Arnold De Leon, *They Called Them Greasers: Anglo Attitudes Toward Mexicans in Texas, 1821–1900* (1983). Sarah Deutsch, *No Separate Refuge: Culture, Class, and Gender on the Anglo-Hispanic Frontier in the Early Southwest, 1880–1940* (1987). Mario T. Garcia, *Desert Immigrants: The Mexicans of El Paso, 1880–1920* (1981). Robert V. Hine, *Community on the American Frontier* (1980). Richard Hogan, *Class and Community in Frontier Colorado* (1979). Howard R. Lamar, *Dakota Territory, 1861–1889* (1956); *The Far Southwest, 1846–1912* (1966); *Texas Crossings: The Lone Star State and the American Far West, 1836–1986* (1991). Timothy R. Mahoney, *River Towns in the Great West* (1990). Leonard Pitt, *The Decline of the Californios: A Social History of the Spanish-Speaking Californians, 1846–1890* (1960). Earl Pomeroy, *The Pacific Slope: A History of California, Oregon, Washington, Idaho, Utah, and Nevada* (1965). Andrew F. Rolle, *California: A History* (2nd ed., 1969). Robert J. Rosebaum, *Mexicano Resistance in the Southwest* (1981). Alexander Saxton, *The Indispensable Enemy: Labor and the Anti-Chinese Movement in California* (1971). Lillian Schlissel, *Women's Diaries of the Westward Journey* (1982). Thomas Sheridan, *Los Tucsonenses: The Mexican Community in Tucson, 1854–1941* (1986). Ronald Takaki, *Strangers from a Different Shore: A History of Asian Americans* (1989). Shih-shan Henry Tsai, *The Chinese Experience in America* (1986). Oscar O. Winther, *The Transportation Frontier: The Trans-Mississippi West, 1865–1890* (1964).

Miners and Cattlemen. Andy Adams, *The Log of a Cowboy* (1927). Lewis Atherton, *The Cattle Kings* (1961). Gunther Barth, *Instant Cities* (1975). Edward E. Dale, *The Range Cattle Industry*, rev. ed. (1969). Philip Durham and Everett L. Jones, *The Negro Cowboys* (1965). Robert K. Dykstra, *The Cattle Towns* (1968). Odie B. Faulk, *Tombstone: Myth and Reality* (1972). Joe B. Frantz and Julian Choate, *The American Cowboy: The Myth and the Reality* (1955). Marion S. Goldman, *Gold Diggers & Silver Miners: Prostitution and Social Life on the Comstock* (1981). William S. Greever, *Bonanza West: Western Mining Rushes* (1963). Ralph Mann, *After the Gold Rush: Society in Grass Valley and Nevada City, California, 1849–1870* (1982). Ernest E. Osgood, *The Day of the Cattleman* (1929). Rodman W. Paul, *Mining Frontiers of the Far West, 1848–1880* (1963); *The Far West and the Great Plains in Transition, 1859–1900* (1988). Wilson P. Rodman, *Mining Frontiers of the Far West* (1963). J. M. Skaggs, *The Cattle Trailing Industry* (1973). Richard W. Slatta, *Cowboys of the Americas* (1990). Duane A. Smith, *Rocky Mountain Mining Camps* (1967); *Mining America: The Industry and the Environment, 1800–1980* (1987). L. Steckmesser, *The Western Hero in History and Legend* (1965). Donald E. Worcester, *The Chisholm Trail* (1980).

Indians. Ralph K. Andrist, *The Long Death: The Last Days of the Plains Indians* (1964). Robert F. Berkhofer, Jr., *The White Man's Indian* (1978). Donald J. Berthrong, *The Southern Cheyennes* (1963). Dee Brown, *Bury My Heart at Wounded Knee: An Indian History of the American West* (1970). Margret Coel, *Chief Left Hand: Southern Arapaho* (1981). Angie Debo, *Geronimo* (1976). Richard Drinnon, *Facing West: The Metaphysics of Indian-Hating and Empire-Building* (1980). Thomas W. Dunlay, *Wolves for the Blue Soldiers* (1982). Loretta Fowler, *Arapahoe Politics, 1851–1978: Symbols in Crisis of Authority* (1982). William T. Hagan, *The Indian Rights Association: The Herbert Welsh Years, 1882–1904* (1985); *American Indians* (1961). Howard L. Harrod, *Renewing the World: Plains Indians Religion and Morality* (1987). Dwight L. Hoover, *The Red and the Black* (1976). Frederick E. Hoxie, *A Final Promise: The Campaign to Assimilate the Indians, 1880–1920* (1984); *The Crow* (1989). Peter Inverson, *The Navajos* (1990). Robert Mardock, *Reformers and the American Indian* (1971). Janet A. McDonnell, *The Dispossession of the American Indian, 1887–1934* (1991). John G. Neihardt, *Black Elk Speaks* (1932). James C. Olson, *Red Cloud and the Sioux Problem* (1965). Theda Perdue, *The Cherokee* (1989). John Powell, *People of the Sacred Mountain: A History of the Northern Cheyenne Chiefs and Warrior Societies, 1830–1879*, 2 vols. (1981). Francis P. Prucha, *American Indian Policy in Crisis* (1976); *The Great White Father: The United States Government and the American Indians* (1984). Willard H. Rollings, *The Comanche* (1989). Mari Sandoz, *Crazy Horse* (1961). Edwin R. Sweeney, *Cochise: Chiricahua Apache Chief* (1991). Robert M. Utley, *Last Days of the Sioux Nation* (1963); *Frontiersmen in Blue: The United States Army and the Indian, 1848–1865* (1967); *Frontier Regulars: The United States Army and the Indian* (1973); *The Indian Frontier of the American West, 1846–1890* (1984). Wilcomb E. Washburn, *The Indian in America* (1975); *Red Man's Land/White Man's Law* (1971). Richard White, *The Roots of Dependency: Subsistence, Environment, and Social Change Among the Choctaws, Pawnees, and Navajos* (1983). Charles F. Wilkinson, *American Indians, Time, and the Law: Native Societies in a Modern Constitutional Democracy* (1987).

Western Women. Susan Armitage and Elizabeth Jameson, eds., *The Women's West* (1987). John Mack Faragher, *Women and Men on the Overland Trail* (1979). Elizabeth Hampsten,

Read This Only to Yourself: The Private Writings of Midwestern Women, 1880–1910 (1982). Dolores Janiewski, *Sisterhood Denied* (1985). Julie Jeffrey, *Frontier Women: The Trans-Mississippi West, 1840–1880* (1979). Polly Welts Kaufman, *Women Teachers on the Frontier* (1984). Ruth Moynihan, *Rebel for Rights: Abigail Scott Dunaway* (1983). Sandra L. Myres, *Westering Women and the Frontier Experience, 1880–1915* (1982); *Westering Women and the Frontier Experience, 1800–1915* (1982). Peggy Pascoe, *Relations of Rescue: The Search for Female Moral Authority in the American West, 1874–1939* (1990). Glenda Riley, *Women and Indians on the Frontier, 1825–1915* (1984); *A Place to Grow* (1992). Joanna L. Stratton, *Pioneer Women: Voices from the Kansas Frontier* (1981).

Western Agriculture.   Allan Bogue, *From Prairie to Corn Belt* (1963). Everett Dick, *The Sod-House Frontier* (1937). John Mack Faragher, *Sugar Creek: Life on the Illinois Prairie* (1986). Gilbert Fite, *The Farmer's Frontier, 1865–1900* (1966). Paul W. Gates, *History of Public Land Development* (1968). Norris Hundley, Jr., *The Great Thirst: Californians and Water, 1770s–1990s* (1992).

D. Aidan McQuillen, *Prevailing over Time: Ethnic Adjustment on the Kansas Prairies, 1875–1925* (1990). Nell Irvin Painter, *Exodusters: Black Migration to Kansas After Reconstruction* (1976). Fred A. Shannon, *The Farmer's Last Frontier, 1860–1897* (1945). Walter Prescott Webb, *The Great Plains* (1931). Thomas A. Woods, *Knights of the Plow: Oliver H. Kelley and the Origins of the Grange in Republican Ideology* (1991). (See also bibliography for Chapter 19.)

The Idea of the West and the Western Environment.   Ray A. Billington, *Frederick Jackson Turner* (1973). William Cronon, *Nature's Metropolis: Chicago and the Great West* (1991). John Mack Faragher, *Daniel Boone: The Life and Legend of an American Pioneer* (1992). Richard Slotkin, *The Fatal Environment: The Myth of the Frontier in the Age of Industrialization* (1985); *Gunfighter Nation* (1992). Henry Nash Smith, *Virgin Land* (1950). Frederick Jackson Turner, *The Frontier in American History* (1920). Donald Worster, *Under Western Skies: Nature and History in the American West* (1992); *Rivers of Empire* (1985).

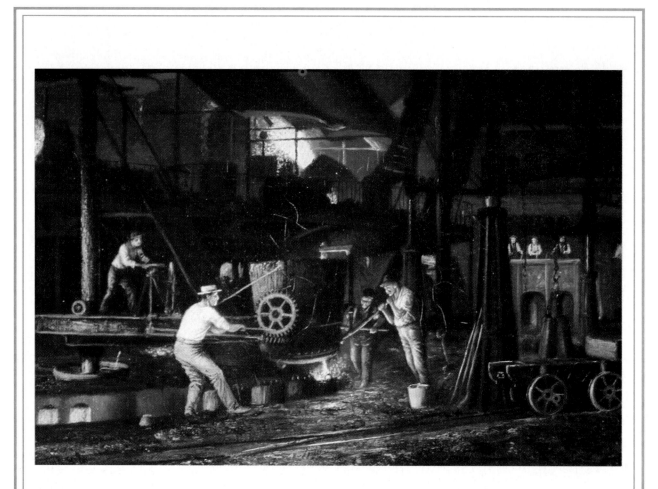

THE STEEL MILL
This 1895 painting of a Bethlehem Steel Company mill shows workers preparing to pour (or "teem") a ladle of molten steel, the product of a Bessemer converter, into cast iron molds to form steel ingots. The ingots will later be rolled into various shapes. Bessemer was one of the two leading processes for converting iron into steel; the other was the open-hearth method. Together, these processes propelled the American steel industry—and through it the industrial economy as a whole—into a period of dramatic growth. *(Bethlehem Steel)*

INDUSTRIAL SUPREMACY

ITH A STRIDE THAT astonished statisticians, the conquering hosts of business enterprise swept over the continent; twenty-five years after the death of Lincoln, America had become, in the quantity and value of her products, the first manufacturing nation of the world. What England had accomplished in a hundred years, the United States had achieved in half the time." So wrote the historians Charles and Mary Beard in the 1920s, expressing the amazement many Americans felt when they considered the remarkable expansion of their industrial economy in the late nineteenth and early twentieth centuries.

In fact, America's rise to industrial supremacy was not as sudden as such observers suggested. The nation had been building a manufacturing economy since early in the nineteenth century, and industry was well established before the Civil War. But Americans were clearly correct in observing that the accomplishments of the last three decades of the nineteenth century overshadowed all that had come earlier. Those years witnessed nothing less than the transformation of the national economy.

The remarkable growth did much to increase the wealth and improve the lives of many Americans. But the benefits were not universal. While industrial titans and a growing middle class were enjoying a prosperity without precedent in the nation's history, workers, farmers, and others were experiencing a disorienting and often painful transition that slowly edged the United States toward a great economic and political crisis.

SOURCES OF INDUSTRIAL GROWTH

Many factors contributed to the growth of American industry: abundant raw materials; a large and growing labor supply; a surge in technological innovation; the emergence of a talented, ambitious, and often ruthless group of entrepreneurs; a federal government eager to assist the growth of business; and a great and expanding domestic market for the products of manufacturing.

New Technologies and New Industries

The rapid emergence of new technologies and the discovery of new materials and productive processes were prerequisites to late-nineteenth-century industrial growth. In the entire history of the United States up to 1860, the government had granted only 36,000 patents. For the period from 1860 to 1890, the figure was 440,000. Americans also benefited from comparable technological advances in Europe.

Some of the most important innovations were in communications. In 1866, Cyrus W. Field laid a transatlantic telegraph cable to Europe. During the next decade, Alexander Graham Bell developed the first commercially useful telephone; and by the 1890s, the American Telephone and Telegraph Company, which handled his interests, had installed nearly half a million telephones in American cities. Other inventions that speeded the pace of business organization were the typewriter (by Christopher L. Sholes in 1868), the cash register (by James Ritty in 1879), and the calculating or adding machine (by William S. Burroughs in 1891).

Among the most revolutionary innovations was the introduction in the 1870s of electricity as a source of light and power. Two pioneers of electrical lighting were Charles F. Brush, who devised the arc lamp for street illumination, and Thomas A. Edison, who invented the incandescent lamp (or light bulb), which could be used for both street and home lighting. Edison and others designed improved generators and built large power plants to furnish electricity to whole cities. By the turn of the century, electric power was becoming commonplace in street railway systems, in the elevators of urban skyscrapers, in factories, and increasingly in offices and homes.

A process by which iron could be transformed into steel—a much more durable and versatile material—had been discovered in the 1850s almost simultaneously by an Englishman, Henry Bessemer, and by an American, William Kelly. The process consisted of blowing air through molten iron to burn out the impurities and became known as the Bessemer process, and after the Civil War it transformed the metal industry. In 1868, the New Jersey ironmaster Abram C. Hewitt introduced from Europe another method of making steel—the open-hearth process. These techniques made possible the production of steel in great quantities and in large dimensions, for use in the manufacture of locomotives, steel train tracks, and girders for the construction of tall buildings.

The steel industry emerged first in western Pennsylvania and eastern Ohio, a region where iron ore and coal were abundant and where there was already a flourishing iron industry. Pittsburgh quickly became the center of the steel world. But the industry was growing so fast that new sources of ore were soon necessary. The upper peninsula of Michigan, the Mesabi range in Minnesota, and the area around Birmingham, Alabama, became important ore-producing centers by the end of the century, and new centers of production emerged in cities that were at once near the mines and close to waterways: Cleveland, Detroit, Chicago, and Birmingham, among others.

The oil industry emerged in the late nineteenth century largely in response to the steel industry's need for lubrication for its machines. (Not until later did oil become important primarily for its potential as a fuel.) The existence of petroleum reserves in western Pennsylvania, where oil often seeped to the surface of streams and springs, had been common knowledge for some time. At first, however, no one was sure what it was or what

to do with it. Then, in the 1850s, experiments commissioned by the Pennsylvania businessman George Bissell showed that the substance could be burned in lamps and that it could also yield such products as paraffin, naphtha, and lubricating oil. Bissell then raised money to begin drilling; and in 1859, Edwin L. Drake, one of his employees, established the first oil well near Titusville, Pennsylvania. It was soon producing 500 barrels of oil a month. Demand for petroleum grew quickly, and promoters soon developed other fields in Pennsylvania, Ohio, and West Virginia. By the 1870s, oil had advanced to fourth place among the nation's exports.

Thirty years later, the demand for oil had expanded dramatically, as its value as a fuel became apparent. But the available reserves in the East had begun to run out. A search began in other parts of the country for new oil deposits, much of it spearheaded by ambitious independent explorers (known as "wildcatters") whose search for the "black gold" resembled the search for actual gold in California and elsewhere decades before. In 1901, explorers discovered the Spindletop oil field in Texas, one of the greatest oil deposits in the world, and Standard Oil (the dominant firm in the industry) quickly established facilities there. A few years later, more discoveries followed in other parts of Texas and in Oklahoma. Those states became the leading oil producers in the nation and remained so for decades. Other important oil fields were discovered in California at about the same time. The emergence of these great new oil fields soon broke Standard Oil's monopoly of the industry. It was unable to dominate the vast new producing regions in the way it had dominated the fields in Pennsylvania and Ohio.

By the beginning of the twentieth century, other great innovations were emerging. In the 1890s, the Italian inventor Guglielmo Marconi was taking the first steps toward the development of radio. The Wright brothers launched the first airplane flight at Kitty Hawk, North Carolina, in 1903. Perhaps most important, the automobile was in development. In the 1870s, designers in France, Germany, and Austria—inspired by the success of railroad engines—were already beginning to develop motors that might drive independently controlled vehicles. They achieved early successes with an "internal combustion engine," which used the expanding power of burning gas to drive pistons; and with this new engine they created the first automobiles.

Charles and Frank Duryea built the first gasoline-driven motor vehicle in America in 1893. Three years later, Henry Ford produced the first of the famous cars that would bear his name. By 1910, the industry had become a major force in the economy, and the automobile had begun to reshape the American landscape.

THE ASSEMBLY LINE
Workers in the Ford Motor Company's plant in Highland Park, Michigan, guide auto bodies down a ramp onto chassis that have moved into position from below. This was the final stage of the assembly line, which Henry Ford pioneered and which by 1914 (when this photograph was taken) had become common in other industries as well. *(Henry Ford Museum & Greenfield Village)*

In 1895, there had been only four automobiles on the American highways. By 1917, there were nearly 5 million.

The Science of Production

Central to the growth of the automobile and other industries were changes in the techniques of production. By the turn of the century, many industrialists were turning to the new principles of "scientific management." Those principles were often known as "Taylorism," after their leading theoretician, Frederick Winslow Taylor. Taylor's ideas were controversial during his lifetime and have remained controversial since. Taylor himself, and his many admirers, argued that scientific management was a way to manage human labor to make it compatible with the demands of the machine age. But scientific management was also a way to increase the employer's control of the workplace, to make working people less independent.

Taylor urged employers to reorganize the production process by subdividing tasks. This would speed up production; it would also make workers more interchangeable and thus diminish a manager's dependence on any particular employee. And it would reduce the need for highly trained skilled workers. If properly managed by trained experts, Taylor claimed,

workers using modern machines could perform simple tasks at much greater speed, significantly increasing productive efficiency.

Manufacturers also began placing greater emphasis on industrial research. In part because of the phenomenal success of Thomas Edison's famous industrial laboratory in Menlo Park, New Jersey, dozens of corporations were, by the early years of the twentieth century, establishing laboratories of their own. By 1913, Bell Telephone, Du Pont, General Electric, Eastman Kodak, and about fifty other companies were budgeting hundreds of thousands of dollars each year for research by their own engineers and scientists.

The most important change in production technology in the industrial era was the emergence of mass production and, above all, the moving assembly line, which Henry Ford introduced in his automobile plants in 1914. This revolutionary technique cut the time for assembling a chassis from twelve and a half to one and a half hours. It enabled Ford to raise the wages and reduce the hours of his workers while cutting the base price of his Model T from $950 in 1914 to $290 in 1929. Ford's assembly line became a standard for many other industries.

Railroad Expansion

The principal agent of industrial development in the late nineteenth century was the expansion of the railroads. Railroads promoted economic growth in many ways. They were the nation's main method of transportation and gave industrialists access to distant markets and distant sources of raw materials. They were the nation's largest businesses and created new forms of corporate organization that served as models for other industries. And they were America's biggest investors, stimulating economic growth through their own enormous expenditures on construction and equipment.

Every decade in the late nineteenth century, total railroad trackage increased dramatically: from 30,000 miles in 1860 to 52,000 miles in 1870, to 93,000 in 1880, to 163,000 in 1890, and to 193,000 by 1900. Subsidies from federal, state, and local governments—as well as investments from abroad—were vital to these vast undertakings, which required far more capital than private entrepreneurs in America could raise by themselves. Equally important was the emergence of great railroad combinations that brought most of the nation's rails under the control of a very few men. Many railroad combinations continued to be dominated by individuals. The achievements (and excesses) of these tycoons—Cornelius Vanderbilt, James J. Hill, Collis P. Huntington, and others—became symbols to much of the nation of great economic power concentrated in in-

RAILROADS, 1870–1890

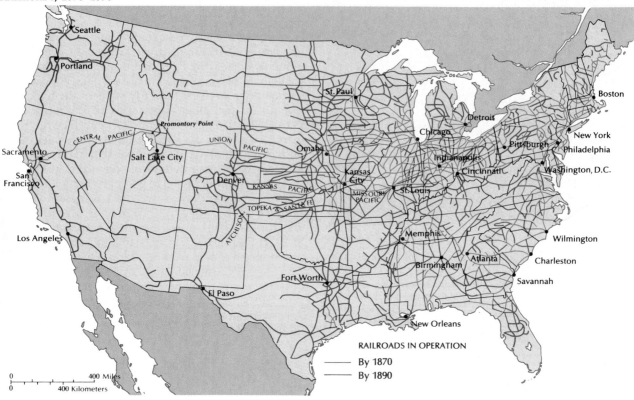

dividual hands. But railroad development was less significant for the individual barons it created than for its contribution to the growth of a new institution: the modern corporation.

The Corporation

There had been various forms of corporations in America since colonial times, but the modern corporation emerged as a major force only after the Civil War, when railroad magnates and other industrialists realized that no single person or group of limited partners, no matter how wealthy, could finance their great ventures.

Under the laws of incorporation passed in many states in the 1830s and 1840s, business organizations could raise money by selling stock to members of the public; after the Civil War, one industry after another began doing so. At the same time, affluent Americans began to consider the purchase of stock a good investment even if they were not themselves involved in the business whose stock they were purchasing. What made the practice appealing was that investors had only "limited liability"—that is, they risked only the amount of their investments; they were not liable for any debts the corporation might accumulate beyond that. The ability to sell stock to a broad public made it possible for entrepreneurs to gather vast sums of capital and undertake great projects.

The Pennsylvania Railroad and others were among the first to adopt the new corporate form of organization. But it quickly spread beyond the railroad industry. In steel, the central figure was Andrew Carnegie, a Scottish immigrant who had worked his way up from modest beginnings and in 1873 opened his own steelworks in Pittsburgh. Soon he dominated the industry. His methods were much like those of other industrial titans. He cut costs and prices by striking deals with the railroads and then bought out rivals who could not compete with him. With his associate Henry Clay Frick, he bought up coal mines and leased part of the Mesabi iron range in Minnesota, operated a fleet of ore ships on the Great Lakes, and acquired railroads. Ultimately, he controlled the processing of his steel from mine to market. He financed his undertakings not only out of his own profits but out of the sale of stock. Then, in 1901, he sold out for $450 million to the banker J. Pierpont Morgan, who merged the Carnegie interests with others to create the giant United States Steel Corporation—a $1.4 billion enterprise that controlled almost two-thirds of the nation's steel production.

There were similar developments in other industries. Gustavus Swift developed a relatively small Chicago meatpacking company into a great national corporation, in part because of profits he earned selling to the military in the Civil War. Isaac Singer patented a sewing machine in 1851 and created I. M. Singer and Company, one of the first modern manufacturing corporations.

Many of the corporate organizations developed a new approach to management. Large, national business enterprises needed more systematic administrative structures than the limited, local ventures of the past. As a result, corporate leaders introduced a set of managerial techniques—the genesis of modern business administration—that relied on the division of responsibilities, a carefully designed hierarchy of control, modern cost-accounting procedures, and perhaps above all a new breed of business executive: the "middle manager," who formed a layer of command between workers and owners. Beginning in the railroad corporations, these new management techniques moved quickly into virtually every area of large-scale industry. Efficient administrative capabilities helped make possible another major feature of the modern corporation: consolidation.

ANDREW CARNEGIE
Carnegie was one of a relatively small number of great industrialists of the late nineteenth century who genuinely rose "from rags to riches." Born in Scotland, he came to the United States in 1848, at the age of thirteen, and soon found work as a messenger in a Pittsburgh telegraph office. His skill in learning to transcribe telegraphic messages (he became one of the first telegraphers in the country able to take messages by sound) brought him to the attention of a Pennsylvania Railroad official, and before he was twenty, he had begun his ascent to the highest ranks of industry. After the Civil War, he shifted his attention to the growing iron industry; in 1873 he invested all his assets in the development of the first American steel mills. Two decades later he was one of the wealthiest men in the world. In 1901 he abruptly resigned from his businesses and spent the remaining years of his life as a philanthropist. By the time of his death in 1919, he had given away some $350 million. *(Culver)*

Consolidating Corporate America

Businessmen created large, consolidated organizations primarily through two methods. One was "horizontal integration"—the combining of a number of firms engaged in the same enterprise into a single corporation. The consolidation of many different railroad lines into one company was an example. Another method, which became popular in the 1890s, was "vertical integration"—the taking over of all the different businesses on which a company relied for its primary function. Carnegie Steel, which came to control not only steel mills, but mines, railroads, and other enterprises, was an example of vertical integration.

The most celebrated corporate empire of the late nineteenth century was John D. Rockefeller's Standard Oil, a great combination created through both horizontal and vertical integration. Shortly after the Civil

War, Rockefeller launched a refining company in Cleveland and immediately began trying to eliminate his competition. Allying himself with other wealthy capitalists, he proceeded methodically to buy out competing refineries. In 1870, he formed the Standard Oil Company of Ohio; within a few years it had acquired twenty of the twenty-five refineries in Cleveland, as well as plants in Pittsburgh, Philadelphia, New York, and Baltimore.

So far, Rockefeller had expanded only horizontally. But soon he began expanding vertically as well. He built his own barrel factories, terminal warehouses, and pipelines. Standard Oil owned its own freight cars and developed its own marketing organization. By the 1880s, Rockefeller had established such dominance within the petroleum industry that to much of the nation he served as the leading symbol of monopoly. He controlled access to 90 percent of the refined oil in the United States.

Rockefeller and other industrialists saw consolidation as a way to cope with what they believed was the greatest curse of the modern economy: "cutthroat competition." Most businessmen claimed to believe in free enterprise and a competitive marketplace, but in fact they feared the existence of too many competing firms, convinced that substantial competition could spell instability and ruin for all. A successful enterprise, many capitalists believed (but did not say publicly), was one that could eliminate or absorb its competitors.

As the movement toward combination accelerated, new vehicles emerged to facilitate it. The railroads began with so-called pool arrangements—informal agreements among various companies to stabilize rates and divide markets (arrangements that would in later years be known as cartels). But the pools did not work very well. If even a few firms in an industry were unwilling to cooperate (as was almost always the case), the pool arrangements collapsed.

The failure of the pools led to new techniques of consolidation resting less on cooperation than on centralized control. At first, the most successful such technique was the creation of the "trust"—pioneered by Standard Oil in the early 1880s and perfected by the banker J. P. Morgan. Over time, the word "trust" became a term for any great economic combination. But the trust was in fact a particular kind of organization. Under a trust agreement, stockholders in individual corporations transferred their stocks to a small group of trustees in exchange for shares in the trust itself. Owners of trust certificates often had no direct control over the decisions of the trustees; they simply received a share of the profits of the combination. The trustees themselves, on the other hand, might literally own

only a few companies but could exercise effective control over many.

In 1889, the state of New Jersey helped produce a third form of consolidation by changing its laws of incorporation to permit companies actually to buy up other companies. Other states soon followed. That made the trust unnecessary and permitted actual corporate mergers. Rockefeller, for example, quickly relocated Standard Oil in New Jersey and created there what became known as a "holding company"—a central corporate body that would buy up the stock of various members of the Standard Oil trust and establish direct, formal ownership of the corporations in the trust.

By the end of the nineteenth century, as a result of corporate consolidation, 1 percent of the corporations in America were able to control more than 33 percent of the manufacturing. A system of economic organization was emerging that lodged enormous power in the hands of a very few men: the great bankers of New York such as J. P. Morgan, industrial titans such as Rockefeller (who himself gained control of a major bank), and others.

Whether or not this relentless concentration of economic power was the only way or the best way to promote industrial expansion became a major source of debate in America in the late nineteenth century and beyond. But it is clear that, whatever else they may have done, the industrial giants of the era were responsible for substantial economic growth. They were integrating operations, cutting costs, creating a great industrial infrastructure, stimulating new markets, creating jobs for a vast new pool of unskilled workers, and opening the way to large-scale mass production. They were also creating the basis for some of the greatest public controversies of their era.

CAPITALISM AND ITS CRITICS

The rise of big business was not without its critics. Farmers and workers saw in the growth of the new corporate power centers a threat to notions of a republican society in which wealth and authority were widely distributed. Middle-class critics pointed to the corruption that the new industrial titans seemed to produce in their own enterprises and in local, state, and national politics. The growing criticisms challenged the captains of industry to create a defense of the new corporate economy, to convince the public (and themselves) that it was compatible with the ideology of individualism and equal opportunity that had long been central to the American self-image.

"MODERN COLOSSUS OF (RAIL) ROADS"
Cornelius Vanderbilt, known as the "Commodore," accumulated one of America's great fortunes by consolidating several large railroad companies under his control in the 1860s. His name became a synonym not only for enormous wealth, but also (in the eyes of many Americans) for excessive corporate power—as suggested in this cartoon, showing him standing astride his empire and manipulating its parts. *(Culver)*

The "Self-Made Man"

The rationale for modern capitalism rested squarely on the older ideology of individualism. The new industrial economy, its defenders argued, was not reducing opportunities for individual advancement, it was expanding them. It was providing every individual with a chance to succeed and attain great wealth.

There was an element of truth in such claims, but only a small one. Before the Civil War there had been few millionaires in America; by 1892 there were more than 4,000. Some were in fact what almost all millionaires claimed to be: "self-made men." Carnegie had worked as a bobbin boy in a Pittsburgh cotton mill; John D. Rockefeller had begun as a clerk in a Cleveland commission house; E. H. Harriman, a great railroad tycoon, had begun as a broker's office boy. But most of the new business tycoons had begun their careers from positions of wealth and privilege.

Nor was their rise to power and prominence always a result simply of hard work and ingenuity, as they liked to claim. It was also a result of ruthlessness, arrogance, and, at times, rampant corruption. The railroad magnate Cornelius Vanderbilt expressed the attitude of many corporate tycoons with his belligerent question: "Can't I do what I want with my own?" So did his son William, with his oft-quoted statement: "The public be damned." Once, when the elder Vanderbilt's lawyers warned him that a move he contemplated was illegal, he bellowed: "What do I care about the law? H'aint I got the power?"

Industrialists made large financial contributions to politicians, political parties, and government officials in exchange for assistance and support. And more often than not, politicians responded as they hoped. Cynics said that Standard Oil did everything to the Ohio legislature except refine it. A member of the Pennsylvania legislature once reportedly said: "Mr. Speaker, I move we adjourn unless the Pennsylvania Railroad has more business for us to transact." During the notorious "Erie War" of 1868, in which Cornelius Vanderbilt did battle against Jay Gould and Jim Fisk for control of the Erie Railroad, both sides in the dispute offered lavish bribes to members of the New York State legislature to support measures favorable to their cause. The market price of legislators during the fight was $15,000 a head. One enterprising politician collected $75,000 from Vanderbilt and $100,000 from Gould. Politicians were not innocent victims of this corruption. Many of them openly demanded bribes and in effect blackmailed businessmen.

The average industrialist of the late nineteenth century was not, however, a Rockefeller or a Vanderbilt, but a more modest entrepreneur engaged in highly risky ventures in an unstable economy. For every successful millionaire, there were dozens of aspiring businessmen whose efforts failed. Some industries fell under the monopolistic control of a single firm or a small group of large firms. But many more industries remained fragmented, with many small companies struggling to carve out a stable position for themselves in an uncertain, highly competitive environment. The annals of business did indeed include real stories of individuals rising from rags to riches. They also included stories of people moving from riches back to rags.

Survival of the Fittest

Most tycoons liked to claim that they had attained their wealth and power through hard work, acquisitiveness, and thrift—the traditional virtues of Protestant America. Those who succeeded, they argued, deserved their success. "God gave me my money," explained John D. Rockefeller, expressing the assumption that riches were a reward for worthiness. Those who failed had earned their failure—through their own laziness, stupidity, or carelessness. "Let us remember," said a prominent Protestant minister, "that there is not a poor person in the United States who was not made poor by his own shortcomings."

Such assumptions became the basis of a popular social theory of the late nineteenth century: Social Darwinism, the application to human society of Charles Darwin's laws of evolution and natural selection among species. Just as only the fittest survived in the process of evolution, so in human society only the fittest individuals survived and flourished in the marketplace.

The English philosopher Herbert Spencer was the first and most important proponent of this theory. Society, he argued, benefited from the elimination of the unfit and the survival of the strong and talented. Spencer's books were popular in America in the 1870s and 1880s. And his teachings found prominent supporters among American intellectuals, most notably William Graham Sumner of Yale, who promoted similar ideas in lectures, articles, and a famous 1906 book, *Folkways.* Sumner did not agree with everything Spencer wrote, but he did share Spencer's belief that individuals must have absolute freedom to struggle, to compete, to succeed, or to fail.

Many industrialists seized on the theories of Spencer and Sumner to justify their own power. "The growth of a large business is merely the survival of the fittest," Rockefeller proclaimed. "This is not an evil tendency in business. It is merely the working out of the law of nature and a law of God." Carnegie, who became the leading exponent of Social Darwinism among American industrialists, later described his reaction on first reading Spencer: "I remember that light came as in a flood and all was clear."

Social Darwinism appealed to businessmen because it seemed to legitimize their success and confirm their virtues. It appealed to them because it placed their activities within the context of traditional American ideas of freedom and individualism. Above all, it appealed to them because it justified their tactics. Social Darwinists insisted that all attempts by labor to raise wages by forming unions and all endeavors by government to regulate economic activities would fail, because economic life was controlled by a natural law, the law of competition. And Social Darwinism coincided with another "law" that seemed to justify business practices and business dominance: the law of supply and demand as defined by Adam Smith and the classical economists. The economic system, they argued, was like a great and delicate machine functioning by natural and automatic rules, by the "invisible hand" of market forces. The greatest among these rules, the law of supply and demand, determined all economic values—prices, wages, rents, interest rates—at a level that was just to all concerned. Supply and demand worked because human beings were essentially economic creatures who understood and pursued their own interests, and because they operated in a free market regulated only by competition.

But Social Darwinism and the ideas of classical economics did not have very much to do with the realities of the corporate economy. At the same time that businessmen were celebrating the virtues of competition and the free market, they were actively seeking to protect themselves from competition and to replace the natural workings of the marketplace with control by great combinations. Rockefeller's great Standard Oil monopoly was the clearest example of the effort to free an enterprise from competition. But many businessmen made similar attempts on a smaller scale. Vicious competitive battle—something Spencer and Sumner celebrated and called a source of healthy progress—was in fact the very thing that American businessmen most feared and tried to eliminate.

The Gospel of Wealth

Some businessmen attempted to temper the harsh philosophy of Social Darwinism with a more gentle, if in some ways equally self-serving idea: the "gospel of wealth." People of great wealth, advocates of this idea argued, had not only great power but great responsibilities. It was their duty to use their riches to advance social progress. Andrew Carnegie elaborated on the creed in his 1901 book *The Gospel of Wealth,* in which he wrote that the wealthy should consider all revenues in excess of their own needs as "trust funds" to be used for the good of the community; the person of wealth, he said, was "the mere trustee and agent for his poorer brethren." Carnegie was only one of many great industrialists who devoted large parts of their fortunes to philanthropic works—much of it to libraries and

HORATIO ALGER
Horatio Alger (1834–1899) wrote over 100 novels describing plucky young boys who worked their way up "from rags to riches." Indeed, the phrase "Horatio Alger story" became a widely recognized synonym for upward mobility and individual success. In fact, very few of the great industrial tycoons of the late nineteenth century really ascended from poverty. Alger's novels were less reflections of reality than promoters of a powerful myth. This portrait was painted long after Alger's death by Stephen Dohanos, a popular magazine artist of the 1950s. *(UPI/Bettmann)*

schools, institutions he believed would help the poor to help themselves.

The notion of private wealth as a public blessing existed alongside another popular concept: the notion of great wealth as something available to all. Russell H. Conwell, a Baptist minister, became the most prominent spokesman for the idea by delivering one lecture, "Acres of Diamonds," more than 6,000 times between 1880 and 1900. Conwell told a series of stories, which he claimed were true, of individuals who had found opportunities for extraordinary wealth in their own backyards. (One such story involved a modest farmer who discovered a vast diamond mine in his own fields in the course of working his land.) "I say to you," he told his rapt audiences, "that you have 'acres of diamonds' beneath you right here . . . that the men and women sitting here have within their reach opportunities to get largely wealthy. . . . I say that you ought to get rich, and that it is your duty to get rich." Most of the millionaires in the country, Conwell claimed (inaccurately), had begun on the lowest rung of the economic ladder and had worked their way to success. Every industrious individual had the chance to do likewise.

Horatio Alger was the most famous promoter of the success story. Alger was originally a minister in a small town in Massachusetts but was driven from his pulpit as a result of a sexual scandal. He moved to New York, where he wrote his celebrated novels—more than 100

in all, which together sold more than 20 million copies. The titles varied: *Andy Grant's Pluck*, *Ragged Dick*, *Tom the Bootblack*, *Sink or Swim*. But the story and message were invariably the same: A poor boy from a small town went to the big city to seek his fortune. By work, perseverance, and luck, he became rich.

Alternative Visions

Alongside the celebrations of competition, the justifications for great wealth, and the legitimization of the existing order stood a group of alternative philosophies, challenging the corporate ethos and at times capitalism itself.

One such philosophy emerged in the work of the sociologist Lester Frank Ward. Ward was a Darwinist, but he rejected the application of Darwinian laws to human society. In *Dynamic Sociology* (1883) and other books, he argued that civilization was not governed by natural selection but by human intelligence, which was capable of shaping society as it wished. Unlike Sumner, who believed that state intervention to remodel the environment was futile, Ward thought that an active government engaged in positive planning was society's best hope. The people, through their government, could intervene in the economy and adjust it to serve their needs.

Other Americans skeptical of the laissez-faire ideas of the Social Darwinists adopted more drastic approaches to reform. Some dissenters found a home in the Socialist Labor Party, founded in the 1870s and led for many years by Daniel De Leon, an immigrant from the West Indies. De Leon attracted a modest following in the industrial cities, but the party failed to become a major political force. It never polled more than 82,000 votes. De Leon's theoretical and dogmatic approach appealed to intellectuals more than to workers. A dissident faction of his party, eager to forge ties with organized labor, broke away and in 1901 formed the more enduring American Socialist Party.

Other radicals gained a wider following. One of the most influential was Henry George of California. His angrily eloquent *Progress and Poverty*, published in 1879, became one of the best-selling nonfiction works in American publishing history. George tried to explain why poverty existed amidst the wealth created by modern industry. "This association of poverty with progress is the great enigma of our times," he wrote. "So long as all the increased wealth which modern progress brings goes but to build up great fortunes, to increase luxury and make sharper the contrast between the House of Have and the House of Want, progress is not real and cannot be permanent."

George blamed social problems on the ability of a few monopolists to grow wealthy as a result of rising land values. An increase in the value of land, he claimed, was a result not of any effort by the owner, but of the growth of society around the land. It was an "unearned increment," and it was rightfully the property of the community. And so George proposed a "single tax," to replace all other taxes, which would return the increment to the people. The tax, he argued, would destroy monopolies, distribute wealth more equally, and eliminate poverty. Single-tax societies sprang up in many cities. George himself moved east to New York; and in 1886, with the support of labor and the socialists, he narrowly missed being elected mayor.

Rivaling George in popularity was Edward Bellamy, whose Utopian novel *Looking Backward,* published in 1888, sold more than 1 million copies. It described the experiences of a young Bostonian who went into a hypnotic sleep in 1887 and awoke in the year 2000 to find a new social order where want, politics, and vice were unknown. The new society had emerged from a peaceful, evolutionary process. The large trusts of the late nineteenth century had continued to grow in size and to combine with one another until ultimately they formed a single great trust, controlled by the government, which absorbed all the businesses of all the citizens and distributed the abundance of the industrial economy equally among all the people. Society had become a great machine, "so logical in its principles and direct and simple in its workings" that it almost ran itself. "Fraternal cooperation" had replaced competition. Class divisions had disappeared. Bellamy labeled the philosophy behind this vision "nationalism," and his work inspired the formation of more than 160 Nationalist Clubs to propagate his ideas.

The Problems of Monopoly

Relatively few Americans shared the views of those who questioned capitalism itself. But by the end of the century a growing number of people were becoming deeply concerned about a particular, glaring aspect of capitalism: the growth of monopoly (control of the market by large corporate combinations).

By the end of the century, a wide range of groups had begun to assail monopoly and economic concentration. Laborers, farmers, consumers, small manufacturers, conservative bankers and financiers, advocates of radical change—all joined the attack. They blamed monopoly for creating artificially high prices and for producing a highly unstable economy. Beginning in 1873, the economy fluctuated erratically, with severe recessions creating havoc every five or six years, each recession worse than the previous one, until finally, in 1893, the system seemed on the verge of total collapse.

Adding to the resentment of monopoly was the emergence of a new class of enormously and conspicuously wealthy people, whose lifestyles became an affront to those struggling to stay afloat in the erratic economy. According to one estimate early in the century, 1 percent of the families in America controlled nearly 88 percent of the nation's assets. Some of the wealthy—Andrew Carnegie, for example—lived relatively modestly and donated large sums to charities. Others, however, lived in almost grotesque luxury. Like a clan of feudal barons, the Vanderbilts maintained, in addition to many country estates, seven opulent mansions on seven blocks of New York City's Fifth Avenue. Other wealthy New Yorkers lavished vast sums on parties. The most notorious, a ball on which Mrs. Bradley Martin spent $368,000, created such a furor that she and her husband fled to England to escape public abuse.

Observing their flagrant displays of wealth were the four-fifths of the American people who lived modestly, and at least 10 million people who lived below the commonly accepted poverty line. The standard of living was rising for everyone, but the gap between rich and poor was increasing. To those in difficult economic circumstances, the sense of relative deprivation could be almost as frustrating and embittering as poverty itself.

INDUSTRIAL WORKERS IN THE NEW ECONOMY

The American working class was both a beneficiary and a victim of the growth of industrial capitalism. Many workers in the late nineteenth century experienced a real rise in their standard of living. But they did so at the cost of arduous and often dangerous working conditions, diminishing control over their own work, and a growing sense of powerlessness.

The Immigrant Work Force

The industrial work force expanded dramatically in the late nineteenth century as demand for factory labor grew. The source of that expansion was a massive migration into industrial cities—migration of two sorts. The first was the continuing flow of rural Americans into factory towns and cities—people disillusioned with or bankrupted by life on the farm and eager for new economic and social opportunities. The second was the great wave of immigration from Mexico, Asia, Canada, and above all Europe in the decades following the Civil War—an influx greater than that of any previous era. The 25 million immigrants who arrived in the United States between 1865 and 1915 were more than four times the number who had arrived in the fifty years before.

In the 1870s and 1880s, most of the immigrants to eastern industrial cities came from the nation's traditional sources: England, Ireland, and northern Europe. By the end of the century, however, the major sources of immigration had shifted, with large numbers of southern and eastern Europeans (Italians, Poles, Russians, Greeks, Slavs, and others) moving to America and into the industrial work force. In the West, the major sources of immigration were Mexico and, until the Chinese Exclusion Act of 1882, Asia. No reliable figures are available for either group, but an estimated 1 million Mexicans entered the United States in the first three decades of the twentieth century, many of them swelling the industrial work force of western cities.

The new immigrants were coming to America in part to escape poverty and oppression in their homelands. But they were also lured to the United States by expectations of new opportunities. Sometimes such expectations were realistic, but often they were the result of false promises. Railroads tried to lure immigrants into their western landholdings by distributing misleading advertisements overseas. Industrial employers actively recruited immigrant workers under the Labor Contract Law, which—until its repeal in 1885—permitted them to pay for the passage of workers in advance and deduct the amount later from their wages. Even after the repeal of the law, employers continued to encourage the immigration of unskilled laborers, often with the assistance of foreign-born labor brokers, such as the Greek and Italian *padrones* who recruited work gangs of their fellow nationals.

The arrival of these new groups introduced heightened ethnic tensions into the dynamic of the working class. Low-paid Poles, Greeks, and French Canadians began to displace higher-paid British and Irish workers in the textile factories of New England. Italians, Slavs, and Poles emerged as a major source of labor for the mining industry in the East, traditionally dominated by

OCCUPATIONAL DISTRIBUTION, 1880 AND 1920

ELLIS ISLAND
The great photographer Lewis Hine took this picture of an Italian mother with her three children arriving on Ellis Island, the processing center for the millions of immigrants who entered the United States through New York City. *(Bettmann)*

native workers or northern European immigrants. Chinese and Mexicans competed with Anglo-Americans and African Americans in mining, farmwork, and factory labor in California, Colorado, and Texas. Even within industries, moreover, workers tended to cluster in particular occupations (and thus, often, at particular income levels) by ethnic group.

Wages and Working Conditions

The average standard of living for workers rose in the years after the Civil War, but for many laborers, the return for their labor remained very small. At the turn of the century, the average income of the American worker was $400 to $500 a year—below the $600 figure widely considered the minimum for a reasonable level of comfort. Nor did workers have much job security. All workers were vulnerable to the boom-and-

bust cycle of the industrial economy, and some lost their jobs because of technological advances or because of the cyclical or seasonal nature of their work. Even those who kept their jobs could find their wages suddenly and substantially cut in hard times. Few workers, in other words, were ever very far from poverty.

American laborers faced other hardships as well. For first-generation workers accustomed to the patterns of agrarian life, there was a difficult adjustment to the nature of modern industrial labor: the performance of routine, repetitive tasks, often requiring little skill, on a strict and monotonous schedule. To skilled artisans whose once-valued tasks were now performed by machines, the new system was impersonal and demeaning. Factory laborers worked ten-hour days, six days a week; in the steel industry they worked twelve hours a day. Many worked in appallingly unsafe or unhealthy factories. Industrial accidents were frequent and severe. Compensation to the victims, either from their employers or from the government, was often limited, until many states began passing workmen's compensation laws in the early twentieth century.

For many workers, the most disturbing aspect of factory labor in the new industrial system was their loss of control over the conditions of their work. Skilled workers had been accustomed to running their own shops. Even semiskilled workers and common laborers had managed to maintain some control over their labor in the relatively informal working conditions of the early and mid-nineteenth century. As the corporate form of organization spread, employers set out to make the factory more efficient (often in response to the principles of scientific management). That meant, they believed, centralizing control of the workplace in the hands of managers, ensuring that workers had no authority or control that might disrupt the flow of production. This loss of control, as much as the low wages and long hours, lay behind the substantial working-class militancy in the late nineteenth century.

Women and Children at Work

The decreasing need for skilled work in factories induced many employers to increase the use of women and children, whom they could hire for lower wages than adult males. By 1900, women made up 17 percent of the industrial work force, a fourfold increase since 1870; and 20 percent of all women (well over 5 million) were wage earners. Some of these working women were single and took jobs to support themselves or their parents or siblings. Many others were married and had to work to supplement the inadequate earnings of their husbands; for many working-

CHILDREN OF WEALTH
The children of the wealthy railroad executive George Jay Gould (son of the notorious financier Jay Gould) ride through a Paris park in "voiturettes," miniature automobiles manufactured in France. *(Culver)*

class families, two incomes were required to support even a minimal standard of living. Even so, in some communities the aversion to seeing married women work was so strong—among both men and women—that families struggled on inadequate wages rather than see a wife and mother take a job.

Women industrial workers were overwhelmingly white and mostly young, 75 percent of them under twenty-five. The vast majority were immigrants or the daughters of immigrants. There were some women in all areas of industry, even in some of the most arduous jobs. Most women, however, worked in a few industries where unskilled and semiskilled machine labor (as opposed to heavy manual labor) prevailed. The textile industry remained the largest single industrial employer of women. (Domestic service remained the most common female occupation overall.) Women worked for wages as low as $6 to $8 a week, well below the minimum necessary for survival (and well below the wages paid to men working the same jobs). At the turn of the century, the average annual wage for a male industrial worker was $597; for a woman, it was $314. Even highly skilled women workers made about half what men doing the same job earned. Advocates of a minimum wage law for women created a sensation when they brought several women to a hearing in Chicago to testify that low wages and desperate poverty had driven them to prostitution. (The testimony was not, however, sensational enough for the Illinois legislature, which promptly defeated the bill.)

At least 1.7 million children under sixteen years of age were employed in factories and fields, more than twice the number of thirty years before. Ten percent of all girls aged ten to fifteen, and 20 percent of all boys, held jobs. Under the pressure of outraged public opinion, thirty-eight state legislatures passed child labor laws in the late nineteenth century; but these laws were of limited impact. Sixty percent of child workers were employed in agriculture, which was typically exempt from the laws; such children often worked twelve-hour days picking or hoeing in the fields. And even for children employed in factories, the laws merely set a minimum age of twelve years and a maximum workday of ten hours, standards that employers often ignored in any case. In the cotton mills of the South, children working at the looms all night were kept awake by having cold water thrown in their faces. In canneries, little girls cut fruits and vegetables sixteen hours a day. Exhausted children were particularly susceptible to injury while working at dangerous machines, and they were maimed and even killed in industrial accidents at an alarming rate.

As much as the appalling conditions of woman and child workers troubled the national conscience, conditions for many men were at least equally dangerous. In mills and mines, and on the railroads, the American accident rate was higher than that of any industrial nation in the world. As late as 1907, an average of twelve railroad men a week died on the job. In factories, thousands of workers faced such occupational diseases as lead or phosphorus poisoning, against which few employers took precautions.

The Struggle to Unionize

Labor attempted to fight back against such conditions by adopting some of the same tactics their employers had used so effectively: creating large combinations, or unions. But by the end of the century their efforts had met with little success.

There had been craft unions in America, representing small groups of skilled workers, since well before the Civil War. Alone, however, individual unions could not hope to exert significant power in the new corporate economy, and in the 1860s some labor leaders began to search for ways to combine the energies of the various labor organizations. The first attempt to federate separate unions into a single national organization came in 1866, when William H. Sylvis founded the National Labor Union—a polyglot association, claiming 640,000 members, that included a variety of reform groups having little direct relationship with labor. After the Panic of 1873 the National Labor Union disintegrated and disappeared.

The National Labor Union, like most of the individual unions that joined it, excluded women workers. Male workers argued (not entirely incorrectly) that women were used to drive down their wages; and they justified their hostility by invoking the ideal of domesticity. "Woman was created to be man's companion," a National Labor Union official said, "to be the presiding deity of the home circle." Most women workers agreed that "man should be the breadwinner," as one female union organizer said. But many argued that as long as conditions made it impossible for men to support their families, women should have full and equal opportunities in the workplace.

Unions faced special difficulties during the recession years of the 1870s. Not only was there widespread unemployment, which depression conditions created; there was also widespread middle-class hostility toward the unions. When labor disputes with employers turned bitter and violent, as they occasionally did, much of the public instinctively blamed the workers (or the "radicals" and "anarchists" they believed were influencing the workers) for the trouble, rarely the employers. Particularly alarming to middle-class Americans was the emergence of the "Molly Maguires," a militant labor organization in the anthracite coal region of Pennsylvania. The Mollies operated within the Ancient Order of Hibernians, an Irish fraternal society, and sometimes used terrorist tactics. They attempted to intimidate the coal operators through violence and occasionally murder, and they added to the growing perception that labor activism was motivated by dangerous radicals. Much of the violence attributed to the Molly Maguires, however, was instigated or performed by informers and agents employed by the mine owners, who wanted a pretext for ruthless measures to suppress unionization.

Excitement over the Molly Maguires paled beside the near hysteria that gripped the country during the railroad strike of 1877, which began when the eastern railroads announced a 10 percent wage cut and which soon expanded into something approaching a class war. Strikers disrupted rail service from Baltimore to St. Louis, destroyed equipment, and rioted in the streets of Pittsburgh and other cities. State militias were called out, and in July President Hayes ordered federal troops to suppress the disorders in West Virginia. In Baltimore, eleven demonstrators died and forty were wounded in a conflict between workers and militiamen. In Philadelphia, state militia opened fire on thousands of workers and their families who were attempting to block the railroad crossings and killed twenty people. In all, over 100 people died before the strike finally collapsed several weeks after it had begun.

The great railroad strike was America's first major, national labor conflict, and it illustrated how disputes between workers and employers could no longer be localized in the increasingly national economy. It illustrated as well the depth of resentment among many American workers toward their employers (and toward the governments allied with them) and the lengths to which they were prepared to go to express that resentment. And finally, it was an indication of the frailty of the labor movement. The failure of the strike seriously weakened the railroad unions and damaged the reputation of labor organizations in other industries as well.

The Knights of Labor

The first major effort to create a genuinely national labor organization was the founding in 1869 of the Noble Order of the Knights of Labor, under the leadership of Uriah S. Stephens. Membership was open to all who "toiled," a definition that included all workers and most business and professional people. The only excluded groups were lawyers, bankers, liquor dealers, and professional gamblers. Unlike most labor organizations of the time, the Knights welcomed women members—not just female factory workers, but domestic servants and women who worked in their own homes. Leonora Barry, an Irish immigrant who had worked in a New York hosiery factory, ran the Woman's Bureau of the Knights. Under her effective leadership, the Knights enlisted 50,000 women members (both black and white) and created over a hundred all-female locals.

The Knights were loosely organized, without much central direction. Members met in local "assemblies," which took many different forms. They were loosely affiliated with a national "general assembly." Their program was similarly vague. Although they championed an eight-hour day and the abolition of child labor, the leaders were more interested in long-range reform of the economy. Leaders of the Knights hoped to replace the "wage system" with a new "cooperative system," in which workers would themselves control a large part of the economy.

For several years, the Knights remained a secret fraternal organization. But in the late 1870s, under the leadership of Terence V. Powderly, the order moved into the open and entered a spectacular period of expansion. By 1886, it claimed a total membership of over 700,000, including some militant elements that the moderate leadership could not always control. Local unions or assemblies associated with the Knights launched a series of strikes in the 1880s in defiance of Powderly's wishes. In 1885, striking railway workers forced the Missouri Pacific, a link in the Gould system, to restore wage cuts and recognize their union. But the victory was temporary. In the following year, a strike on another Gould road, the Texas and Pacific, was crushed, and the power of the unions in the Gould system was broken. Their failure helped discredit the organization. By 1890, the membership of the Knights had shrunk to 100,000. A few years later, the organization disappeared altogether.

The AFL

Even before the Knights began to decline, a rival organization based on a very different organizational concept appeared. In 1881, representatives of a number of existing craft unions formed the Federation of Organized Trade and Labor Unions of the United States and Canada. Five years later, it changed its name to the American Federation of Labor (AFL), and it soon became the most important and enduring labor group in the country. Rejecting the Knights' idea of one big union for everybody, the Federation was an association of essentially autonomous craft unions and represented mainly skilled workers. It was generally hostile to organizing unskilled workers, who did not fit comfortably within the craft–based structure of existing organizations.

Toward women, the AFL adopted an apparently contradictory policy. On the one hand, the male leaders of the AFL were essentially hostile to the idea of women entering the paid work force. Because women were weak, they believed, employers could easily take advantage of them by paying them less than men. As a result, women workers drove down wages for everyone. "It is the so-called competition of the unorganized, defenceless woman worker, the girl and the wife, that often tends to reduce the wages of the father and husband," Samuel Gompers, the powerful leader of the AFL, once said. He talked often about the importance of women remaining in the home, and argued, incorrectly, that "There is no necessity of the wife contributing to the support of the family by working." More than that, female labor was, the AFL newspaper wrote, "the knife of the assassin, aimed at the family circle."

Though hostile to the idea of women workers, the AFL nevertheless sought equal pay for those women who did work and even hired some female organizers to encourage unionization in industries dominated by women. These positions were, in fact, less contradictory than they seem. By raising the pay of women, the AFL could make them less attractive to employers and, in effect, drive them out of the work force.

Gompers accepted the basic premises of capitalism; his goal was simply to secure for the workers he represented a greater share of capitalism's material rewards. Gompers rejected the idea of fundamental economic reform; he opposed the creation of a worker's party; he was generally hostile to any government efforts to protect labor or improve working conditions, convinced that what government could give it could also take away. The AFL concentrated instead on the relationship between labor and management. It supported the immediate objectives of most workers: better wages, hours, and working conditions. And while it hoped to attain its goals by collective bargaining, it was ready to use strikes if necessary.

As one of its first objectives, the AFL demanded a national eight-hour day and called for a general strike if workers did not achieve the goal by May 1, 1886. On that day, strikes and demonstrations for a shorter workday took place all over the country, most of them staged by AFL unions but a few by more radical groups.

In Chicago, a center of labor and radical strength, a strike was already in progress at the McCormick Harvester Company when the general strike began. City

SAMUEL GOMPERS
Gompers migrated to the United States from England as a boy and began work at the age of thirteen as a cigar maker, rising to become head of his local union. When the American Federation of Labor was organized in 1886, Gompers became its first president, a position he held (with only a single, one-year interruption) until 1924. Gompers helped the AFL to become the premier labor organization in the United States; he also helped commit the organization to a narrow, craft-oriented view of unionism that excluded an increasing proportion of workers as mass-production industries rose to prominence. He is shown here during a union-organizing drive in West Virginia. *(George Meany Memorial Archives)*

police had been harassing the strikers, and labor and radical leaders called a protest meeting at Haymarket Square. When the police ordered the crowd to disperse, someone threw a bomb that killed seven officers and injured sixty-seven other people. The police, who had killed four strikers the day before, fired into the crowd and killed four more people. Conservative, property-conscious Americans, frightened and outraged, demanded retribution, even though no one knew who had thrown the bomb. Chicago officials finally rounded up eight anarchists and charged them with murder, on the grounds that their statements had incited whoever had hurled the bomb. All eight scapegoats were found guilty after a remarkably injudicious trial. Seven were sentenced to death. One of the condemned committed suicide, four were executed, and two had their sentences commuted to life imprisonment.

To most middle-class Americans, the Haymarket bombing was an alarming symbol of social chaos and radicalism. "Anarchism" now became a code word in the public mind for terrorism and violence, even though most anarchists were relatively peaceful visionaries dreaming of a new social order. For the next thirty years, the specter of anarchism remained one of the most frightening concepts in the American middle-class imagination. It also became a constant obstacle to the goals of the AFL and other labor organizations, and it was particularly devastating to the Knights of Labor, which, as the most radical of the major labor organizations, never recovered from the post-Haymarket hysteria. However much they tried to distance themselves from radicals, unions were always vulnerable to accusations of anarchism, as the violent strikes of the 1890s occasionally illustrated.

The Homestead Strike

The Amalgamated Association of Iron and Steel Workers, which was affiliated with the American Federation of Labor, was the most powerful trade union in the country. Its members were skilled workers, in great demand by employers and thus able to exercise significant power in the workplace. Employers sometimes called such workers "little shopfloor autocrats," and they resented the substantial control over working conditions these skilled laborers often had. The union had a rulebook with fifty-six pages of what workers called "legislation" limiting the power of employers. In the emerging corporate world of the late nineteenth century, such challenges to management control were beginning to seem intolerable to many employers.

By the mid-1880s, the steel industry had introduced new production methods and new patterns of organization that were streamlining the steelmaking process and, in the process, reducing the companies' dependence on skilled labor. In the Carnegie system, which was coming to dominate the steel industry, the union had a foothold in only one of the corporation's three major factories—the Homestead plant near Pittsburgh.

By 1890, Carnegie and his chief lieutenant, Henry Clay Frick, had decided that the Amalgamated "had to go," even at Homestead. Over the next two years, they repeatedly cut wages at Homestead. At first, the union acquiesced, aware that it was not strong enough to wage a successful strike.

In 1892, the company stopped even discussing its decisions with the Amalgamated, in effect denying the union's right to negotiate at all. Finally, when Frick announced another wage cut at Homestead and gave the union two days to accept it, the Amalgamated called for a strike. Frick abruptly shut down the plant and called in 300 guards from the Pinkerton Detective Agency to enable the company to hire non-union workers. The hated Pinkertons were well-known strikebreakers, and their mere presence was often enough to incite workers to violence.

The Pinkertons approached the plant by river on barges on July 6, 1892. The strikers prepared for them by pouring oil on the water and setting it on fire, and they met the guards at the docks with guns and dynamite. After several hours of pitched battle, which brought death to three guards and ten strikers and injuries to many others, the Pinkertons surrendered and were escorted roughly out of town.

But the workers' victory was temporary. The governor of Pennsylvania, at the company's request, sent the state's entire National Guard contingent, some 8,000 troops, to Homestead. Production resumed, with strikebreakers now protected by troops. And public opinion turned against the strikers when a radical made an attempt to assassinate Frick. Slowly workers drifted back to their jobs; and finally—four months after the strike began—the Amalgamated surrendered. By 1900, every major steel plant in the Northeast had broken with the Amalgamated, which now had virtually no power to resist. Its membership shrank from a high of 24,000 in 1891 (two-thirds of all eligible steelworkers) to fewer than 7,000 a decade later. Its decline was symbolic of the general erosion of union strength in the late nineteenth century, as factory labor became increasingly unskilled and workers thus became easier to replace. The AFL unions were often powerless in the face of these changes.

The Pullman Strike

A dispute of greater magnitude and equal bitterness, if less violence, was the Pullman strike in 1894. The Pullman Palace Car Company manufactured sleeping and parlor cars for railroads, which it built and repaired at a plant near Chicago. There the company built the 600-acre town of Pullman and rented its trim, orderly houses to the employees. George M. Pullman, owner of the company, considered the town a model solution to the industrial problem; he referred to the workers as his "children." But many residents chafed at the regimentation and the high rents.

In the winter of 1893–1894, the Pullman Company slashed wages by about 25 percent, citing the declining revenues the depression was causing. At the same time, Pullman refused to reduce rents in its model town, which were 20 to 25 percent higher than for comparable accommodations in surrounding areas. Workers went on strike and persuaded the militant American Railway Union, led by Eugene V. Debs, to support them by refusing to handle Pullman cars and equipment. Opposing the strikers was the General Managers' Association, a consortium of twenty-four Chicago railroads. It persuaded its member companies to discharge switchmen who refused to handle Pullman cars. Every time this happened, Debs's union instructed its members who worked for the offending companies to walk off their jobs. Within a few days thousands of railroad workers in twenty-seven states and territories were on strike, and transportation from Chicago to the Pacific Coast was paralyzed.

Most state governors responded readily to appeals from strike-threatened businesses; but the governor of Illinois, John Peter Altgeld, was a man with demonstrated sympathies for workers and their grievances. Altgeld had criticized the trials of the Haymarket anarchists and had pardoned the convicted men who were still in prison when he took office. He refused to call out the militia to protect employers now. Bypassing Altgeld, railroad operators asked the federal government to send regular army troops to Illinois, on the pretext that the strike was preventing the movement of mail on the trains. President Grover Cleveland and Attorney General Richard Olney, a former railroad lawyer and a bitter foe of unions, complied. In July 1894, over Altgeld's objections, the president ordered 2,000 troops to the Chicago area. A federal court issued an injunction forbidding the union to continue the strike. When Debs and his associates defied it, they were arrested and imprisoned. With federal troops protecting the hiring of new workers and with the union leaders in a federal jail, the strike quickly collapsed.

Sources of Labor Weakness

The last decades of the nineteenth century were years in which labor, despite its organizing efforts, made few real gains and suffered many important losses. In a rapidly expanding industrial economy, wages for

THE PULLMAN STRIKE
Railroad workers, striking in sympathy with the employees of the Pullman Palace Car Company, burned 600 freight cars in the Chicago railroad yards in July 1894. *(Bettmann)*

workers rose hardly at all, and not nearly enough to keep up with the rising cost of living. Labor leaders won a few legislative victories: the abolition by Congress in 1885 of the Contract Labor Law; the establishment by Congress in 1868 of an eight-hour day on public works projects and in 1892 of an eight–hour day for government employees; state laws governing hours of labor and safety standards; and gradually some guaranteed compensation for workers injured on the job. But many of these laws were not enforced, and neither strikes nor protests seemed to have much effect. The end of the century found most workers with less political power and considerably less control of the workplace than they had had forty years before.

Workers failed to make greater gains for many reasons. The principal labor organizations represented only a small percentage of the industrial work force. Four percent of all workers (fewer than 1 million people) belonged to unions in 1900. The AFL, the most important, excluded unskilled workers, who were emerging as the core of the industrial work force, and along with them most women, blacks, and recent immigrants. Women responded to this exclusion in 1903 by forming their own organization, the Women's Trade Union League. But the WTUL was mostly interested in securing protective legislation for women workers, not in a general organization and mobilization of labor; and the WTUL would have found little support within the AFL or other male-dominated organizations even if its goals had been more expansive. Other divisions within the work force contributed fur-

SIGNIFICANT EVENTS

1851 I. M. Singer and Company, one of first modern corporations, founded

1859 First oil well drilled in Pennsylvania

1866 William H. Sylvis founds National Labor Union

First transatlantic cable laid

1868 Open-hearth steelmaking begins in America

1869 Knights of Labor founded

1870 John D. Rockefeller founds Standard Oil

1873 Carnegie Steel founded

Commercial and financial panic disrupts economy

1876 Alexander Graham Bell invents telephone

1877 Railroad workers strike nationwide

1879 Thomas A. Edison invents electric light bulb

Henry George publishes *Progress and Poverty*

1881 American Federation of Labor founded

1882 Rockefeller creates first trust

1886 Haymarket bombing blamed on anarchists

1888 Edward Bellamy publishes *Looking Backward*

1892 Workers strike Homestead plant

1893 Depression begins

1894 Workers strike Pullman Company

1901 J. P. Morgan creates United States Steel Corporation

American Socialist Party founded

Spindletop oil field discovered in Texas

1903 Women's Trade Union League founded

Wright brothers make first successful flight at Kitty Hawk, North Carolina

1906 Henry Ford produces his first automobiles

William Graham Sumner publishes *Folkways*

1914 Ford introduces assembly line in his factories

---

ther to union weakness. Tensions between different ethnic and racial groups kept laborers divided.

Another source of labor weakness was the shifting nature of the work force. Many immigrant workers came to America intending to remain only briefly, to earn some money and return home. The assumption that they had no long-range future in the country (even though it was often a mistaken one) eroded their willingness to organize. Other workers—natives and immigrants alike—were in constant motion, moving from one job to another, one town to another, seldom in one place long enough to establish any sort of institutional ties or exert any real power. A study of Newburyport, Massachusetts over a thirty-year period shows that 90 percent of the workers there vanished from the town records in those years, many of them because they moved elsewhere.

Even workers who stayed put often did not remain in the same job for long. The rags-to-riches stories of

the Horatio Alger novels had few counterparts in reality. But some real social mobility did exist. Workers might move from unskilled to semiskilled or skilled jobs during their lifetimes; their children might become foremen or managers. The gains were small, but they were enough to inspire considerable (and often unrealistic) hopes and to persuade some workers that they were not part of a permanent working class.

Above all, workers made few gains in the late nineteenth century because of the strength of the forces arrayed against them. They faced corporate organizations of vast wealth and power, which were generally determined to crush any efforts by workers to challenge their prerogatives—not just through brute force, but also through infiltration of unions, espionage within working-class communities, and sabotage of organizational efforts. And as the Homestead and Pullman strikes suggest, the corporations had the support of local, state, and federal authorities, who were willing to send in troops to "preserve order" and crush labor uprisings on demand.

Despite the creation of new labor unions, despite a wave of strikes and protests that in the 1880s and 1890s reached startling proportions, workers in the late nine-

teenth century failed on the whole to create successful organizations or to protect their interests in the way the large corporations managed to do. In the battle for power within the emerging industrial economy, almost all the advantages seemed to lie with capital.

SUGGESTED READINGS

General Histories. Daniel Boorstin, *The Americans: The Democratic Experience* (1973). Thomas C. Cochran and William Miller, *The Age of Enterprise* (1942). Carl Degler, *The Age of the Economic Revolution* (1977). John A. Garraty, *The New Commonwealth* (1968). Ray Ginger, *The Age of Excess* (1963). Samuel P. Hays, *The Response to Industrialism, 1885–1914* (1957). Robert L. Heilbroner, *The Economic Transformation of America* (1977). Robert Higgs, *The Transformation of the American Economy, 1865–1914* (1971). Edward C. Kirkland, *Industry Comes of Age: Business, Labor, and Public Policy, 1860–1897* (1961). Alan Trachtenberg, *The Incorporation of America: Culture and Society in the Gilded Age* (1982). Robert Wiebe, *The Search for Order, 1877–1920* (1968).

Technology. Robert W. Bruce, *Bell* (1973). Roger Burlingame, *Engines of Democracy: Inventions and Society in Mature America* (1940); *Henry Ford* (1957). Robert Conot, *A Streak of Luck* (1979). Richard N. Current, *The Typewriter and the Men Who Made It* (1954). George Daniels, *Science and Society in America* (1971). Frank E. Hill, *Ford* (1954). Thomas P. Hughes, *Networks of Power: Electrification in Western Society, 1880–1930* (1983). Judith McGaw, *Most Wonderful Machine: Mechanization and Social Change in Berkshire Paper Making, 1801–1885* (1988). Martin V. Melosi, *Coping with Abundance: Energy and Environment in Industrial America* (1985). Elting E. Morison, *Men, Machines, and Modern Times* (1966). Lewis Mumford, *Technics and Civilization* (1934). Allan Nevins, *Ford*, 3 vols. (1954–1962). David F. Noble, *America by Design: Science, Technology, and the Rise of Corporate Capitalism* (1977). Leonard S. Reich, *The Making of American Industrial Research: Science and Business at GE and Bell, 1876–1926* (1985). Nathan Rosenberg, *Technology and American Economic Growth* (1972). Peter Temin, *Steel in Nineteenth Century America* (1964). Wyn Wachhorst, *Thomas Alva Edison: An American Myth* (1981). Frederick A. White, *American Industrial Research Laboratories* (1961).

Railroads. Lee Benson, *Merchants, Farmers, and Railroads* (1955). Edward G. Campbell, *The Reorganization of the American Railroad System* (1938). Thomas C. Cochran, *Railroad Leaders* (1953). Robert Fogel, *Railroads and American Economic Growth* (1964). Edward C. Kirkland, *Men, Cities, and Transportation*, 2 vols. (1948). Gabriel Kolko, *Railroads and Regulation, 1877–1916* (1965). George H. Miller, *Railroads and the Granger Laws* (1971). Richard C. Overton, *Burlington West* (1941); *Gulf to Rockies* (1953). John F. Stover, *The Life and Decline of the American Railroad* (1970); *The Railroads of the South, 1865–1900* (1955). George R. Taylor and I. D. Neu, *The Amer-*

ican Railroad Network, 1861–1890 (1956). Anthony F. C. Wallace, *St. Clair: A Nineteenth-Century Coal Town's Experience with a Disaster-Prone Industry* (1987).

The Corporation. Alfred D. Chandler, Jr., *Strategy and Structure: Chapters in the History of the American Industrial Enterprise* (1962); *Pierre S. DuPont and the Making of the Modern Corporation* (1971); *The Visible Hand: The Managerial Revolution in American Business* (1977); *Scale and Scope: The Dynamics of Industrial Capitalism* (1990). David F. Hawkes, *John D.: The Founding Father of the Rockefellers* (1980). Matthew Josephson, *The Robber Barons* (1934). Maury Klein, *The Life and Legend of Jay Gould* (1986). Norma R. Lamoreaux, *The Great Merger Movement in American Business, 1895–1904* (1985). Harold C. Livesay, *Andrew Carnegie and the Rise of Big Business* (1975). Allan Nevins, *Study in Power: John D. Rockefeller*, 2 vols. (1953). Glenn Porter and Harold C. Livesay, *Merchants and Manufacturers* (1971). Joseph Wall, *Andrew Carnegie* (1970). Bernard Weisberger, *The Dream Maker* (1979). Olivier Zunz, *Making America Corporate, 1870–1920* (1990).

Ideologies. Charles A. Baker, *Henry George* (1955). Robert C. Bannister, *Social Darwinism: Science and Myth in Anglo-American Social Thought* (1967). Samuel Chugerman, *Lester F. Ward: The American Aristotle* (1939). Sidney Fine, *Laissez Faire and the General Welfare State: A Study of Conflict in American Thought, 1865–1901* (1956). Louis Galambos, *The Public Image of Big Business in America, 1880–1940* (1975). Richard Hofstadter, *Social Darwinism in American Thought* (rev. ed., 1955). Edward C. Kirkland, *Dream and Thought in the Business Community, 1860–1900* (1956). T. J. Jackson Lears, *No Place of Grace: Antimodernism and the Transformation of American Culture, 1880–1920* (1981). Robert G. McCloskey, *American Conservatism in the Age of Enterprise* (1951). Arthur E. Morgan, *Edward Bellamy* (1944). Daniel T. Rodgers, *The Work Ethic in Industrial America, 1850–1920* (1978). David Thelen, *Paths of Resistance: Tradition and Dignity in Industrializing Missouri* (1986). John L. Thomas, *Alternative America: Henry George, Edward Bellamy, Henry Demarest Lloyd, and the Adversary Tradition* (1983). Irvin G. Wylie, *The Self-Made Man in America* (1954).

Labor. Paul Avrich, *The Haymarket Tragedy* (1984). John Bodnar, *Immigration and Industrialization: Ethnicity in an American Mill Town* (1977). Stanley Buder, *Pullman* (1967). John T. Cumbler, *Working-Class Community in Industrial America* (1979). Henry David, *The Haymarket Affair* (1936). Ileen A. De-

Vault, *Sons and Daughters of Labor: Class and Clerical Work in Turn-of-the-Century Pittsburgh* (1990). Melvyn Dubofsky, *Industrialism and the American Worker, 1865–1920* (1975). Melvyn Dubofsky and Warren Van Tine, eds., *Labor Leaders in America* (1987). P. K. Edwards, *Strikes in the United States, 1881–1974* (1981). Leon Fink, *Workingmen's Democracy: The Knights of Labor and American Politics* (1983). Samuel Gompers, *Seventy Years of Life and Labor*, 2 vols. (1975). David M. Gordon, Richard Edwards, and Michael Reich, *Segmented Work, Divided Workers: The Historical Transformation of Labor in the United States* (1982). Brian Greenberg, *Worker and Community: Response to Industrialization in a Nineteenth-Century American City, Albany, New York, 1850–1884* (1985). Herbert G. Gutman, *Work, Culture, and Society in Industrializing America* (1976). Willam F. Hartford, *Working People of Holyoke: Class and Ethnicity in a Massachusetts Mill Town, 1850–1960* (1990). Stuart Kaufman, *Samuel Gompers and the Origins of the American Federation of Labor* (1978). Alexander Keyssar, *Out of Work: The First Century of Unemployment in Massachusetts* (1986). S. J. Kleinberg, *The Shadow of the Mills: Working-Class Families in Pittsburgh, 1870–1907* (1989). David Montgomery, *Beyond Equality* (1975); *Workers' Control in America: Studies in the History of Work, Technology, and Labor Struggles* (1979); *The Fall of the House of Labor: The Workplace, the State, and American Labor Activism, 1865–1925* (1987). Daniel Nelson, *Managers and Workers: Origins of the New Factory System in the United States, 1880–1920* (1975). Richard J. Oestreicher, *Solidarity and Fragmentation: Working People and Class Consciousness: Detroit, 1875–1900* (1986). Henry Pelling, *American Labor* (1960). Peter Rachleff, *Black Labor In Richmond, 1865–1890* (1984). Roy Rosenzweig, *"Eight Hours for What We Will": Workers and Leisure in an Industrial City, 1870–1920* (1983). Steven J. Ross, *Workers on the Edge: Work, Leisure, and Politics in Industrializing Cincinnati, 1788–1890* (1985). Peter R. Shergold, *Working Class Life* (1982). Sheldon Stromquist, *A Generation of Boomers: The Pattern of Railroad Labor Conflict in Nineteenth-Century America* (1987). Philip Taft, *The A. F. of L. in the Time of Gompers*, 2 vols. (1957–1959). Daniel J. Walkowitz, *Worker City, Company Town: Iron and Cotton Workers Protest in Troy and Cohoes, New York, 1855–1884* (1978). Leon Wolff, *Lockout: The Story of the Homestead Strike of 1892* (1965).

Women. Mary Blewett, *Men, Women, and Work Culture: Class, Gender, and Protest in the New England Shoe Industry* (1988). Patricia Cooper, *Once a Cigar Maker: Men, Women, and Work Culture in American Cigar Factories, 1900–1919* (1987). Tamara Hareven, *Family Time and Industrial Time: The Relationship Between the Family and Work in a New England Industrial Community* (1982). Paula Hyman, Charlotte Baum, Sonya Michel, *The Jewish Woman in America* (1975). Susan E. Kennedy, *If All We Did Was to Weep at Home: A History of White Working-Class Women in America* (1979). Alice Kessler-Harris, *Out to Work: A History of Wage-Earning Women in the United States* (1982). Susan Levine, *Labor's True Women: Carpet Weavers, Industrialization, and Labor Reform in the Gilded Age* (1984). Elizabeth Anne Payne, *Reform, Labor, and Feminism* (1988). Barbara Wertheimer, *We Were There: The Story of Working Women in America* (1977).

The Left. Mari Jo Buhle, *Women and American Socialism, 1870–1920* (1981). Melvyn Dubofsky, *We Shall Be All: A History of the Industrial Workers of the World* (1969). Gerald N. Grob, *Workers and Utopia* (1961). J. H. M. Laslett, *Labor and the Left* (1970). Margaret M. Marsh, *Anarchist Women: 1870–1920* (1981). Nick Salvatore, *Eugene V. Debs: Citizen and Socialist* (1982).

THE AMERICAN ENVIRONMENT

THE LOCOMOTIVE'S MAGIC WAND

THE RAILROAD WORKED A revolution in the nineteenth-century American land-scape. The story of the railroad's construction is among the most familiar narratives of American history. For contemporary observers, the locomotive was the great icon of the age, a "magic wand" that transformed city and country alike. Most saw in it the central symbol of American progress. The writer Caroline Kirkland was typical in describing the railroad as "the resistless chariot of civilization with scythed axles mowing down ignorance and prejudice as it whirls along," driving "the shadows of the past . . . into the dim woods." Among the "shadows" that fled before it were some of the most familiar features of American ecosystems.

The basic achievement of the railroad, in the most abstract economic terms, was to reduce the cost of space by accelerating the speed at which one could move across it. In the 1830s, traveling from New York to Chicago by lake and canal took roughly three weeks. By railroad in the 1850s, it took less than two days. The difference was even more impressive for roads. Whereas a team of horses was doing well to haul a wagonload of grain a dozen miles in a day, a railroad could transport the same grain *hundreds* of miles in the same time. No less important, the railroad liberated America's rural economy from the forced hibernation of winter. While roads and canals sat idle under winter ice, locomotives kept hauling goods to market no matter how cold the weather. As a result, the entire economy became more productive.

This was why the railroad seemed such a symbol of progress. Wherever it went, farms and towns sprang up in response to the new opportunities it brought. The pace of western development increased dramatically as settlers followed the railroads out onto the midwestern prairies in increasing numbers. As they plowed up the sod to raise grain, they dismantled the tallgrass prairie, so much so that it had almost disappeared by the end of the century. The same fate befell the white pine forests of northern Michigan, Wisconsin, and Minnesota. Sawed into lumber and shipped south on Lake Michigan or the Mississippi River, pine trees were delivered by rail to prairie farmers who used them for fences and houses. By 1900, the pines had nearly vanished from their former homes, and midwestern lumber companies were moving their operations elsewhere.

Farther west, an equally dramatic fate befell the great bison herds which had been the mainstay of Great Plains Indian life for generations. With the coming of the Union Pacific in the north and the Kansas Pacific in the south, bison were slaughtered at an almost unimaginable rate. A single hunting party could gun down hundreds in a day for their skins, while tourists could shoot from the windows of their trains without even stopping to inspect their kills. Within half a decade of the arrival of the railroads, over 4 million bison died on the southern plains alone. By 1883, the last major herd had vanished from the plains. An animal that had numbered in the tens of millions less than a quarter-century before now teetered on the brink of extinction. It was no accident that the last major battles between Plains Indians and the U.S. Army took place at exactly the same time. In addition to facili-

THE AMERICAN ENVIRONMENT

tating the movement of soldiers in such conflicts, the railroad had helped destroy the ecological foundation of the Indian economy.

The railroad also introduced the herds of livestock that soon replaced the bison. The drives that brought longhorn steers from Texas to the Kansas cattle towns did so for only one reason: to reach the railroad. As livestock expanded into the grasslands where bison had once grazed, it was the railroad that permitted them to be shipped to market. The result was a newly integrated regional economy that fundamentally altered the environments that sustained it. By the late nineteenth century, the old shortgrass prairies of the high plains were raising range-fed cattle, their native bison having almost entirely disappeared. The tallgrass prairies of Iowa and Illinois had been converted to corn production. Their native bluestem grasses had been plowed under, and much of the grain they now raised was used in feedlots where western cattle were fattened for final sale. Whether raised in Texas, Mon-

EARLY RAILROAD CONSTRUCTION CREW
For many nineteenth-century Americans, the appearance of railroad surveyors and construction crews seemed to herald a new era. The locomotive symbolized progress, bringing in its wake a sudden growth of farms, factories, and towns. *(Bettmann)*

THE AMERICAN ENVIRONMENT

tana, or Illinois, cattle eventually made their way to Chicago's great Union Stockyard. There they were slaughtered and shipped to the eastern markets, where they were finally eaten.

Without the railroad, none of this would have occurred when and how it did. By the end of the century, the new technology had linked together the different regional environments of the continent with great urban markets. No matter where they lived, no matter what the time of year, Americans relied on the railroad to satisfy their basic needs with products from distant places: Minnesota flour, Texas beef, and Washington lumber all reached their customers via the iron horse. The widespread availability of such products liberated Americans from the constraints of local resources and created a truly national market. These benefits had been earned at the cost of immense ecological changes, but those changes were rarely evident to customers living hundreds of miles from landscapes they never saw. Had they seen the ties between their own lives and the slaughtered bison herds, vanished prairies, and disappearing forests, they would almost certainly have joined Caroline Kirkland in regarding them as reasonable costs of civilized progress.

Just how thoroughly the railroads altered the landscape of the United States can be suggested by one further change. Until the 1880s, every community in America had its own "local" time. People set their clocks according to the rules of astronomy: noon was the moment when the sun stood highest in the midday sky. When it was noon in Chicago, it was 11:50 A.M. in St. Louis, 11:27 A.M. in Omaha, and 12:18 P.M. in Detroit, with every possible variation in between. For the railroad companies, trying to keep track of hundreds of different times was a nightmare, since a train leaving a station at one local time arrived at its destination at an entirely different local time. Such scheduling problems could even cause train wrecks. And so, on November 18, 1883, the major railroad companies carved up the continent into four uniform time zones and declared that they intended to ignore all local times. Henceforth, for railroad purposes, every community in a time zone would have the same time. The U.S. government did not finally ratify this change until 1918, but most communities adopted railroad "standard" time very quickly. The magic wand of the locomotive had managed to change not just the many natural environments of North America, but time itself.

***The Bowery at Night*, 1895**
This painting by Louis Sontag of lower Manhattan portrays many of the new technologies
that were transforming American cities in the late nineteenth century. The elevated railroad
and electric streetcars move alongside older, horse-drawn vehicles. Shops are illuminated
by new electric lights.   *(Muesum of the City of New York)*

CHAPTER EIGHTEEN

THE AGE OF THE CITY

THE INDUSTRIALIZATION AND COMMERCIALIZATION of America changed the face of society in countless ways. Nowhere were those changes more profound than in the growth of cities and the creation of an urban society and culture. Having begun its life as a primarily agrarian republic, the United States in the late nineteenth century was becoming an urban nation.

The change did not come easily. Cities grew so rapidly that their facilities and institutions could not keep pace. Housing, transportation, sewers, social services, governments—all lagged far behind the enormous demands the new urban population was placing on them. American sensibilities lagged behind as well. Many people rebelled at the new and intimidating pace of urban life and at the dazzling and at times uncomfortable diversity of the urban population. "Our cities," wrote the sociologist Charles Horton Cooley, "are full of the disintegrated materials of the old order looking for a place in the new."

THE URBANIZATION OF AMERICA

The great migration from the countryside to the city was not unique to the United States. It was occurring simultaneously throughout much of the Western world in response to industrialization and the factory system. But America, a society with little experience of great cities, found urbanization particularly jarring—but also particularly alluring.

The Lure of the City

"We cannot all live in cities," Horace Greeley wrote shortly after the Civil War, "yet nearly all seem determined to do so." The urban population of America increased sevenfold in the half-century after the Civil War. And in 1920, the census revealed that for the first time, a majority of the American people lived in "urban" areas—defined as communities of 2,500 people or more. New York and its environs grew from 1 million in 1860 to over 3 million in 1900. Chicago had 100,000 residents in 1860 and more than a million in 1900. Cities were experiencing similar growth in all areas of the country.

Natural increase accounted for only a small part of the urban growth. In fact, urban families experienced a high rate of infant mortality, a declining fertility rate, and a high death rate from disease. Without immigration, cities would have grown relatively slowly, if at all. The city attracted people from the countryside because it offered conveniences, entertainments, and cultural experiences unavailable in rural communities. But it attracted people most of all because it offered more and better-paying jobs than were available in rural America or in the foreign economies many immigrants were fleeing.

AMERICA IN 1900

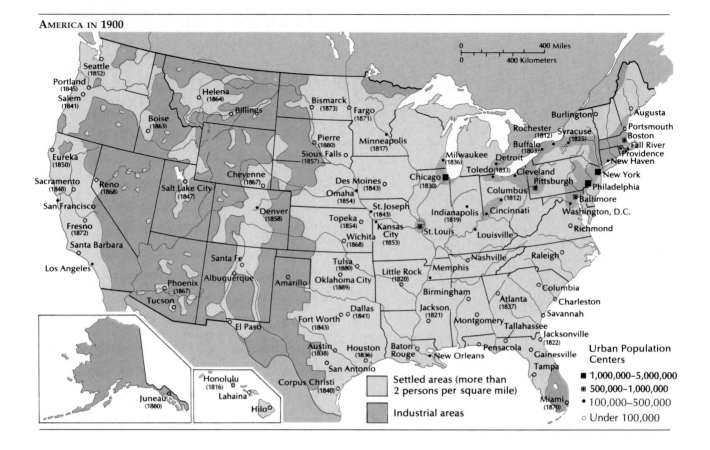

Urban Population Centers

■ 1,000,000–5,000,000
⊞ 500,000–1,000,000
• 100,000–500,000
○ Under 100,000

Settled areas (more than 2 persons per square mile)

Industrial areas

People moved to cities, too, because new forms of transportation made it easier for them to get there. Railroads made simple, quick, and relatively inexpensive what once might have seemed a daunting journey from parts of the American countryside to nearby cities. The development of large, steam-powered ocean liners created a highly competitive shipping industry in which Europeans and Asians could cross the oceans to America much more cheaply and quickly than they had in the past.

Migrations

As a result, the late nineteenth century was an age of unprecedented geographical mobility, as Americans left the declining agricultural regions of the East at a dramatic rate. Some who left were moving to the newly developing farmlands of the West. But almost as many were moving to the cities of the East and the Midwest.

Among those leaving rural America for industrial cities in the late nineteenth century were young rural women, for whom opportunities in the farm economy were limited. As farms grew larger, more commercial, and more mechanized, they became increasingly male preserves; and since much of the work force on many farms consisted of unskilled and often transient workers, there were fewer family units than before. Farm women had once been essential for making clothes and other household goods, but those goods were now available in stores or through catalogs. Hundreds of thousands of women moved to the cities, therefore, in search of work and community.

Southern blacks were also beginning what would be a nearly century-long exodus from the countryside into the city. That was a testament to the poverty, debt, violence, and oppression African Americans encountered in the late-nineteenth-century rural South, because the opportunities they found in cities were limited. Factory jobs for blacks were rare and professional opportunities almost nonexistent. Urban blacks tended to work as cooks, janitors, domestic servants, and in other low-paying service occupations. Since many such jobs were considered women's work, black women often out-

EVOLVING ETHNIC AND CLASS SEGREGATION
IN MILWAUKEE, 1850–1890

Italians, Greeks, Slavs, Slovaks, Russians, Jews, Armenians, and others. By the 1890s, more than half of all immigrants came from these new regions, as opposed to fewer than 2 percent in the 1860s.

In earlier stages of immigration, most new immigrants from Europe (with the exception of the Irish) were at least modestly prosperous and educated. Germans and Scandinavians in particular had headed west on their arrival, either to farm or to work as businessmen, merchants, professionals, or skilled laborers in midwestern cities such as St. Louis, Cincinnati, and Milwaukee. Most of the new immigrants of the late nineteenth century lacked the capital to buy farmland and lacked the education to establish themselves in professions. So, like the poor Irish immigrants before the Civil War, they settled overwhelmingly in industrial cities, where most of them took unskilled jobs.

The Ethnic City

By 1890, most of the population of some major urban areas consisted of foreign-born immigrants and their children: 87 percent of the population of Chicago, 80 percent in New York, 84 percent in Milwaukee and Detroit. (London, the largest industrial city in Europe, by contrast had a population that was 94 percent native.) New York had more Irish than Dublin and more Germans than Hamburg. Chicago eventually had more Poles than Warsaw.

Equally striking was the diversity of the new immigrant populations. In other countries experiencing

numbered black men in the cities. By the end of the nineteenth century, there were substantial African-American communities (10,000 people or more) in over thirty cities—many of them in the South, but some (New York, Chicago, Washington, Baltimore) in the North or in border states. Much more substantial African-American migration was to come during World War I and after; but the black communities established in the late nineteenth century paved the way for the great population movements of the future.

The most important source of urban population growth in the late nineteenth century, however, was the arrival of great numbers of new immigrants from abroad: 10 million between 1860 and 1890, 18 million more in the three decades after that. Some came from Canada, Mexico, Latin America, and—particularly on the West Coast—China and Japan. But by far the greatest number came from Europe. After 1880, the flow of new arrivals began for the first time to include large numbers of people from southern and eastern Europe:

POPULATION GROWTH, 1860–1900

IMMIGRATION'S CONTRIBUTION TO
POPULATION GROWTH, 1860–1920

heavy immigration in this period, most of the new arrivals were coming from one or two sources: Argentina, for example, was experiencing great migrations too, but almost everyone was coming from Italy and Spain. In the United States, however, no single national group dominated. In the last four decades of the nineteenth century, substantial groups arrived from Italy, Germany, Scandinavia, Austria, Hungary, Russia, Great Britain, Ireland, Poland, Greece, Canada, Japan, China, Holland, Mexico, and many other nations. In some towns, a dozen different ethnic groups might find themselves living in close proximity.

Most of the new immigrants were rural people, and their adjustment to city life was often a painful one. To help ease the transition, many national groups formed close-knit ethnic communities within the cities: Italian, Polish, Jewish, Slavic, Chinese, French-Canadian, Mexican and other neighborhoods (often called "immigrant ghettoes") that attempted to re-create in the New World many of the features of the Old.

Some ethnic neighborhoods consisted of people who had migrated to America from the same province, town, or village. Even when the population was more diverse, however, the community offered newcomers much that was familiar. They could find newspapers and theaters in their native languages, stores selling their native foods, churches or synagogues, and fraternal organizations that provided links with their national pasts. Many immigrants also maintained close ties with their native countries. They stayed in touch with relatives who had remained behind. Some (per-

haps as many as a third in the early years) returned to Europe or Asia or Mexico after a relatively short time; others helped bring the rest of their families to America.

The cultural cohesiveness of the ethnic communities clearly eased the pain of separation from the immigrants' native lands. What role it played in helping immigrants become absorbed into the economic life of America is a more difficult question to answer. It is clear that some ethnic groups (Jews and Germans in particular) advanced economically more rapidly than others (for example, the Irish). One explanation is that, by huddling together in ethnic neighborhoods, immigrant groups tended to reinforce the cultural values of their previous societies. When those values were particularly well suited to economic advancement in an industrial society—as was, for example, the high value Jews placed on education—ethnic identification may have helped members of a group to improve their lots. When other values predominated—maintaining community solidarity, sustaining family ties, preserving order—progress could be less rapid.

But other factors were at least as important in determining how well immigrants fared in the New World. Immigrants who aroused strong racial prejudice among native-born whites—most notably African Americans, Asians, and Mexicans—found it very difficult to advance whatever their talents. Among others, however, those who arrived with a valuable skill did better than those who did not. Those who arrived with at least some capital had an enormous advantage over those who were penniless. And over time, those

TOTAL IMMIGRATION, 1860–1900

SOURCES OF IMMIGRATION, 1860–1900

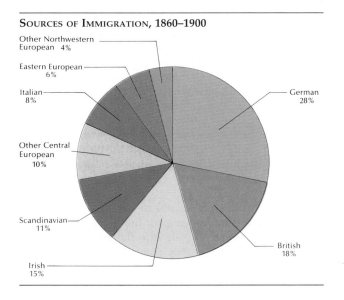

Other Northwestern European 4%

Eastern European 6%

Italian 8%

Other Central European 10%

Scandinavian 11%

Irish 15%

German 28%

British 18%

who lived in cities where people of their own nationality came to predominate—for example, the Irish in New York and Boston, or the Germans in Milwaukee—gained a tremendous advantage as they learned to exert their political power.

Assimilation

Despite the substantial differences among the various immigrant communities, virtually all groups of the foreign-born had certain things in common. Most immigrants, of course, shared the experience of living in cities (and of adapting from a rural past to an urban present). Most were young; the majority of newcomers were between fifteen and forty-five years old. And in virtually all communities of foreign-born immigrants, the strength of ethnic ties had to compete against another powerful force: the desire for assimilation.

Many of the new arrivals from abroad had come to America with romantic visions of the New World. And however disillusioning they might find their first contact with the United States, they usually retained the dream of becoming true "Americans." Even some first-generation immigrants worked hard to rid themselves of all vestiges of their old cultures, to become thoroughly Americanized. Second-generation immigrants were even more likely to attempt to break with the old ways, to try to assimilate completely into what they considered the real American culture. Some even looked with contempt on parents and grandparents who continued to preserve traditional ethnic habits and values.

The urge to assimilate put a particular strain on relations between men and women in immigrant communities. Many of the foreign-born came from cultures in which women were even more subordinate to men, and even more fully lodged within the family, than women in the United States. In some immigrant cultures, parents expected to arrange their children's marriages and to control almost every moment of their daughters' lives until marriage. But either out of choice or out of economic necessity, many immigrant women (and even more of the American-born daughters of immigrants) began working outside the home and developing friendships, interests, and attachments outside the family. The result was not the collapse of the family-centered cultures of immigrant communities; those cultures proved remarkably durable. But there were important adjustments to the new and more fluid life of the American city, and often considerable tension in the process.

Assimilation was not, of course, entirely a matter of choice. Native-born Americans encouraged it, both deliberately and inadvertently, in countless ways. Public schools taught children in English, and employers often insisted that workers speak English on the job. Although there were merchants in immigrant communities who sold ethnically distinctive foods and clothing, most stores by necessity sold mainly American products, forcing immigrants to adapt their diets, wardrobe, and lifestyles to American norms. Church leaders were often native-born Americans or more assimilated immigrants who encouraged their parishioners to adopt American ways. Some even reformed their theology and liturgy to make it more compatible with the norms of the new country. Reform Judaism, imported from Germany to the United States in the mid-nineteenth century, was an effort by American Jewish leaders (as it had been among German ones) to make their faith less "foreign" to the dominant culture of a largely Christian nation.

Exclusion

The arrival of so many new immigrants, and the way many of them clung to old ways and created culturally distinctive communities, provoked fear and resentment among some native-born Americans, just as earlier arrivals had done. Some people reacted against the immigrants out of generalized fears and prejudices, seeing in their "foreignness" the source of all the disorder and corruption of the urban world. "These people," a Chicago newspaper wrote shortly after the Haymarket bombing, referring to striking immigrant workers, "are not American, but the very scum and offal of Europe . . . Europe's human and inhuman rubbish." Native-born Americans on the West Coast had a similar cultural aversion to Mexican, Chinese, and Japanese immigrants. Others had economic concerns. Native laborers were often incensed by the willingness of the immigrants to accept lower wages and to take over the jobs of strikers.

The rising nativism provoked political responses. In 1887, Henry Bowers, a self-educated lawyer obsessed with a hatred of Catholics and foreigners, founded the American Protective Association, a group committed to stopping the immigrant tide. By 1894, membership in the organization had reportedly reached 500,000, with chapters throughout the Northeast and Midwest. That same year a more genteel organization, the Immigration Restriction League, was founded in Boston by five Harvard alumni. It was dedicated to the belief that immigrants should be screened, through literacy tests and other standards designed to separate the desirable from the undesirable. The league avoided the crude conspiracy theories and the rabid xenophobia of the American Protective Association, and its more sophisticated nativism made it possible for many educated, middle-class people to support the restrictionist cause.

Even before the rise of these new organizations, politicians were struggling to find answers to the "immigration question." In 1882 Congress had responded to strong anti-Asian sentiment in California and elsewhere and excluded the Chinese, even though they made up only 1.2 percent of the population of the West Coast. (See pp. 456–457.) In the same year, Congress denied entry to "undesirables"—convicts, paupers, the mentally incompetent—and placed a tax of 50 cents on each person admitted. Later legislation of the 1890s enlarged the list of those barred from immigrating and increased the tax.

But these laws kept out only a small number of aliens, and more ambitious restriction proposals made little progress. Congress passed a literacy requirement for immigrants in 1897, but President Grover Cleveland vetoed it. The restrictions had limited success because many native-born Americans, far from fearing immigration, welcomed it and exerted strong political pressure against the restrictionists. Immigration was providing a rapidly growing economy with a cheap and plentiful labor supply; many argued that America's industrial (and indeed agricultural) development would be impossible without it.

The Urban Landscape

The city was a place of remarkable contrasts. It had homes of almost unimaginable size and grandeur, and hovels of indescribable squalor. It had conveniences unknown to earlier generations, and problems that seemed beyond society's capacity to solve. Both the attractions and the problems were a result of the stunning pace at which cities were growing. The expansion of the urban population helped spur important new technological and industrial developments. But the rapid growth also produced misgovernment, poverty, congestion, filth, epidemics, and great fires. Planning and building simply could not match the pace of growth. "The problem in America," a municipal reformer wrote, "has been to make a great city in a few years out of nothing."

One of the greatest problems of this precipitous growth was finding housing for the thousands of new residents who were pouring into the cities every day. For the prosperous, housing was seldom a worry. The availability of cheap labor and the increasing accessibility of tools and materials reduced the cost of building in the late nineteenth century and let anyone with even a moderate income afford a house. Many of the richest urban residents lived in palatial mansions in the heart of the city and created lavish "fashionable districts." These wealthy residents were the principal force behind the creation of the great art museums, concert halls, opera houses, and parks that cities began to build in the late nineteenth century.

The moderately well-to-do (and as time went on, increasing numbers of wealthy people as well) took advantage of the less expensive land on the edges of the city and settled in new suburbs, linked to the downtowns by trains or streetcars or improved roads. Chicago in the 1870s, for example, boasted nearly one hundred residential suburbs connected with the city by railroad and offering the joys of "pure air, peacefulness, quietude, and natural scenery." Boston, too, saw the development of some of the earliest "streetcar suburbs"—Dorchester, Brookline, and others—which catered to both the wealthy and the middle class. New Yorkers of moderate means settled in new suburbs on the northern fringes of Manhattan and commuted downtown by trolley or riverboat. Real estate developers worked to create and promote suburban communities that would appeal to the nostalgia for the countryside that many city dwellers felt. Affluent suburbs, in particular, were notable for lawns, trees, and houses designed to look manorial. Even more modest communities strove to emphasize the opportunities suburbs provided for owning land.

Most urban residents, however, could not afford either to own a house in the city or to move to the suburbs. Instead, they stayed in the city centers and rented. And because demand was so high and space so scarce, they had little bargaining power in the process. Land-

STREETCAR SUBURBS IN NINETEENTH-CENTURY NEW ORLEANS

lords tried to squeeze as many rent-paying residents as possible into the smallest available space. In Manhattan, for example, the average population density in 1894 was 143 people per acre—a higher rate than that of the most crowded cities of Europe (Paris had 127 per acre, Berlin 101) and far higher than in any other American city then or since. In some neighborhoods—the lower East Side, for example—density was more than 700 people per acre, among the highest levels in the world.

Landlords were reluctant to invest much in immigrant housing, confident they could rent dwellings for a profit regardless of their conditions. In the cities of the South—Charleston, New Orleans, Richmond—poor blacks lived in crumbling former slave quarters. In Boston, they moved into cheap three-story wooden houses ("triple deckers"), many of them decaying fire hazards. In Baltimore and Philadelphia, they crowded into narrow brick row houses. And in New York and many other cities, more than a million people lived in tenements.

The word "tenement" had originally referred simply to a multiple-family rental building, but by the late nineteenth century it was being used to describe slum dwellings only. The first tenements, built in 1850, had been hailed as a great improvement in housing for the poor. "It is built with the design of supplying the laboring people with cheap lodgings," a local newspaper commented, "and will have many advantages over the cellars and other miserable abodes which too many are forced to inhabit." But tenements themselves soon became "miserable abodes," with many windowless rooms, little or no plumbing or central heating, and perhaps a row of privies in the basement. A New York state law of 1870 required a window in every bedroom of tenements built after that date; developers complied by adding small, sunless air shafts to their buildings. Most of all, tenements were impossibly crowded, with three, four, and sometimes many more people crammed into each small room.

Jacob Riis, a Danish immigrant and New York newspaper reporter and photographer, shocked many

A NEW YORK TENEMENT, 1910
This photograph of a woman and her children in a rear tenement bedroom was meant to illustrate the crowding and squalor of urban immigrant life. The photographer was Lewis Hine, who from 1907 to 1914 worked for a government committee investigating child labor and whose efforts to expose social conditions helped spur legislative action. He was also a pioneer in industrial photography and created some of the classic early images of factory production. *(George Eastman House)*

century, more and more streets were paved, usually with wooden blocks, bricks, or asphalt; but paving could not keep up with the number of new thoroughfares the expanding cities were creating. By 1890, Chicago had paved only about 600 of its more than 2,000 miles of streets.

But it was not simply the conditions of the streets that impeded urban transportation. It was the numbers of people who needed to move every day from one part of the city to another, numbers that mandated the development of mass transportation. Streetcars drawn on tracks by horses had been introduced into some cities even before the Civil War. But the horsecars were not fast enough, so many communities developed new forms of mass transit. In 1870, New York opened its first elevated railway, whose noisy, filthy steam-powered trains moved rapidly above the city streets on massive iron structures. New York, Chicago, San Francisco, and other cities also experimented with cable cars, towed by continuously moving underground cables. Richmond, Virginia, introduced the first electric trolley line in 1888, and by 1895 such systems were operating in 850 towns and cities. Boston in 1897 opened the first American subway when it put some of its trolley lines underground. At the same time, cities were developing new techniques of road and bridge building. One of the great technological marvels of the 1880s was the completion of the Brooklyn Bridge in New York, a dramatic steel-cable suspension span designed by John A. Roebling.

Cities were growing upward as well as outward. The first modern "skyscraper"—by later standards a relatively modest building, ten stories high, constructed in Chicago in 1884—launched a new era in urban architecture. Once builders perfected the technique of constructing tall buildings with cast iron and then steel beams, and once other inventors produced the electric elevator, no obstacle remained to even higher buildings. The greatest figure in the early development of the skyscraper was the Chicago architect Louis Sullivan, who introduced many of the modern, functional elements to the genre—large windows, sheer lines, limited ornamentation—in an attempt to emphasize the soaring height of the building as its most distinctive feature. Sullivan's students, among them Frank Lloyd Wright, expanded the influence of these innovations still further and applied them to low buildings as well as tall ones.

Strains of Urban Life

The increasing congestion of the cities and the absence of adequate public services produced serious hazards. One was fires. In one major city after another, fires destroyed large downtown areas, where many buildings

middle-class Americans with his sensational (and some would say sensationalized) descriptions and pictures of tenement life in his 1890 book *How the Other Half Lives.* Slum dwellings, he said, were almost universally sunless, practically airless, and "poisoned" by "summer stenches." "The hall is dark and you might stumble over the children pitching pennies back there." But the solution many reformers (including Riis) favored, and that governments sometimes adopted, was to raze slum dwellings without building any new housing to replace them.

Urban growth posed monumental transportation challenges. Old downtown streets were often too narrow for the heavy traffic that was beginning to move over them. Most were without a hard, paved surface and resembled either a sea of mud or a cloud of dust, depending on the weather. In the last decades of the

CHICAGO IN FLAMES
The great Chicago fire of 1871 (which legend attributes to a kerosene lantern kicked over by "Mrs. O'Leary's cow") devastated much of the central part of the city, just as great fires destroyed parts of other large cities (among them San Francisco and Boston) in the late nineteenth century. The fires were tragedies for those who lost their property or their lives; but they were opportunities for speculators and developers, who used the destruction as an opportunity to build new, "modern" city centers. *(Chicago Historical Society)*

were still constructed of wood. Chicago and Boston suffered "great fires" in 1871. Other cities—among them Baltimore and San Francisco, where a tremendous earthquake produced a catastrophic fire in 1906—experienced similar disasters. The great fires were terrible and deadly experiences, but they were also important events in the development of the cities involved. They encouraged the construction of fireproof buildings and the development of professional fire departments. They also forced cities to rebuild at a time when new technological and architectural innovations were available. Some of the modern, high-rise downtowns of American cities arose out of the rubble of great fires.

An even greater hazard than fire was disease, especially in poor neighborhoods with inadequate sanitation facilities. But an epidemic that began in a poor neighborhood could (and often did) spread easily into other neighborhoods as well. Few municipal officials recognized the relationship of improper sewage disposal and water contamination to such epidemic diseases as typhoid fever and cholera; and many cities lacked adequate systems for disposing of human waste until well into the twentieth century. Flush toilets and sewer systems began to appear in the 1870s, but they could not solve the problem as long as sewage continued to flow into open ditches or streams, polluting cities' water supplies.

Above all, perhaps, the expansion of the cities spawned widespread and often desperate poverty. Despite the rapid growth of urban economies, the sheer number of new residents ensured that many people would be unable to earn enough for a decent subsistence. Public agencies and private philanthropic or-

CITY STREETS
The unpaved streets of many major cities became almost impassable seas of mud after rain storms. The garbage and horse manure that accumulated with the mud also made them major health hazards. Some of the terrible epidemics of the late nineteenth century were a direct result of the unsanitary conditions in city streets. *(Library of Congress)*

ganizations offered very limited relief, and even they were generally dominated by middle-class people, who tended to believe that too much assistance would breed dependency and that poverty was the fault of the poor themselves—a result of laziness or alcoholism or other kinds of irresponsibility. Most tried to restrict aid to the "deserving poor"—those who truly could not help themselves (at least according to the standards of the organizations themselves, which conducted elaborate "investigations" to separate the "deserving" from the "undeserving"). Other charitable societies—for example, the Salvation Army, which began operating in America in 1879, one year after it was founded in London—concentrated more on religious revivalism than on the relief of the homeless and hungry. Tensions often arose between native Protestant philanthropists and Catholic immigrants over religious doctrine and standards of morality. Middle-class faith in the idea of self-improvement led to a widespread inattention to the structural roots of urban poverty. Middle-class people grew particularly alarmed over the rising number of poor children in the cities, some of them orphans or runaways, living alone or in small groups scrounging for food. These "street arabs," as they were often called, attracted more attention from reformers than

any other group—although that attention produced no lasting solutions to their problems.

Poverty and crowding naturally bred crime and violence. Much of it was relatively minor, the work of pickpockets, con artists, swindlers, and petty thieves. But some was more dangerous. The American murder rate rose rapidly in the late nineteenth century (even as such rates were declining in Europe), from 25 murders for every million people in 1880 to over 100 by the end of the century. That reflected in part a very high level of violence in some nonurban areas: the American South, where lynching and homicide were particularly high; and the West, where the rootlessness and instability of new communities (cow towns, mining camps, and the like) created much violence. But the cities contributed their share to the increase in crime as well. Native-born Americans liked to believe that crime was a result of the violent proclivities of immigrant groups, and they cited the rise of gangs and criminal organizations in various ethnic communities. But even in the cities, native-born Americans were as likely to commit crimes as immigrants. The rising crime rates encouraged many cities to develop larger and more professional police forces. But police forces themselves could spawn corruption and brutality, particularly since jobs on them were often filled through political patronage. Some members of the middle class, fearful of urban insurrections, felt the need for even more substantial forms of protection. Urban national guard groups (many of them created and manned by middle-class elites) built imposing armories on the outskirts of affluent neighborhoods and stored large supplies of weapons and ammunition in preparation for uprisings that, in fact, virtually never occurred.

Americans and Europeans alike reacted to life in the city with marked ambivalence. It was a place of strong allure and great excitement. Yet it was also a place of alienating impersonality, of a new feeling of anonymity, of a different kind of work with which the individual could feel only limited identification. To some, it was also a place of degradation and exploitation. Theodore Dreiser's novel *Sister Carrie* (1900) exposed one troubling aspect of urban life: the plight of single women (like Dreiser's heroine, Carrie) who moved from the countryside into the city and found themselves without any means of support. Carrie first took an exhausting and ill-paying job in a Chicago shoe factory, then drifted into a life of "sin," exploited by predatory men. Many women were experiencing in reality the dilemmas Carrie experienced in fiction. Living in conditions of extreme poverty and hardship, some moved into prostitution—which, degrading and dangerous as it was, also produced a livelihood and a sense of community for desperate people.

The Machine and the Boss

Newly arrived immigrants, many of whom could not speak English, needed help in adjusting to American urban life: its laws, its customs, usually its language. Some ethnic communities created their own self-help organizations. But for many residents of the inner cities, the principal source of assistance was the political machine.

The urban machine was one of America's most distinctive political institutions. It owed its existence to the power vacuum that the chaotic growth of cities (and the very limited growth of governments) had created. It was also a product of the potential voting power of large immigrant communities. Any politician who could mobilize that power stood to gain enormous influence, if not public office. And so there emerged a group of urban "bosses," themselves often of foreign birth or parentage. Many were Irish, because they spoke English and because some had acquired previous political experience from the long Irish struggle against the English at home. All were men (unsurprisingly, since in most states women could not yet vote).

The principal function of the political boss was simple: to win votes for his organization. That meant winning the loyalty of his constituents. To do so, a boss might provide them with occasional relief—baskets of groceries, bags of coal. He might step in to save those arrested for petty crimes from jail. When he could, he found jobs for the unemployed. Above all, he rewarded many of his followers with patronage: with jobs in city government or in such city agencies as the police (which the machine's elected officials often controlled); with jobs building or operating the new transit systems; and with opportunities to rise in the political organization itself.

Machines were also vehicles for making money. Politicians enriched themselves and their allies through various forms of graft and corruption. Some of it might be fairly open—what George Washington Plunkitt of New York's Tammany Hall called "honest graft." For example, a politician might discover in advance where a new road or streetcar line was to be built, buy an interest in the land near it, and profit when the city had to buy the land from him or when property values rose as a result of the construction. But there was also covert graft: kickbacks from contractors in exchange for contracts to build streets, sewers, public buildings, and other projects; the sale of franchises for the operation of such public utilities as street railways, waterworks, and electric light and power systems. The most famously corrupt city boss was William M. Tweed, boss of New York City's Tammany Hall in the 1860s and 1870s, whose excesses finally landed him in jail in 1872.

"KEEPING TAMMANY'S BOOTS SHINED," C. 1887
This lithograph by cartoonist Joseph Keppler shows the heavy foot of New York City's Tammany Hall sitting atop City Hall, while Hugh Grant, a Tammany sheriff later elected mayor, applies the patronage polish that was the organization's lifeblood. The strap dangling from the boot bears the name of Richard Croker, who emerged as one of Tammany's principal leaders after the fall of Boss Tweed and who served as the undisputed chief of the organization from 1886 until 1901. *(Bettmann)*

Middle-class critics saw the corrupt machines as blights on the cities and obstacles to progress. In fact, political organizations were responsible not just for corruption, but also for modernizing city infrastructures, for expanding the role of government, and for creating stability in a political and social climate that otherwise would have lacked a center. The motives of the bosses may have been largely venal, but their achievements were often greater than those of the more scrupulous reformers who challenged them.

Several factors made boss rule possible. One was the power of immigrant voters, who were less concerned with middle-class ideas of political morality than with obtaining the services that machines provided and reformers did not. Another was the link between the political organizations and wealthy, prominent citizens who profited from their dealings with bosses and resisted efforts to overthrow them. Still another was the structural weakness of city governments. Within the municipal government, no single official usually had decisive power or responsibility. Instead, authority was generally divided among many officeholders and was limited by the state legislature. The boss, by virtue of his control over his machine, formed an "invisible government" that provided an alternative to the inadequacy of the regular government. Through his organization, he might control a majority of those who were in office even if (as was usually the case) he did not hold public office himself.

The urban machine was not without competition. Reform groups frequently mobilized public outrage at the corruption of the bosses and often succeeded in driving machine politicians from office. Tammany, for example, saw its candidates for mayor and other high city offices lose almost as often as they won in the last decades of the nineteenth century. But the reform organizations typically lacked the permanence of the machine, and more often than not, their power faded after a few years. Thus, many critics of machines began to argue for more basic reforms: for structural changes in the nature of city government.

SOCIETY AND CULTURE IN URBANIZING AMERICA

For urban middle-class Americans, the last decades of the nineteenth century were a time of dramatic advances. Indeed, it was in those years that a distinctive middle-class culture began to exert a powerful influence over the whole of American life. Much of the rest of American society—the majority of the population, which was neither urban nor middle class—advanced less rapidly or not at all; but almost no one was unaffected by the rise of the new urban, consumer culture.

The Rise of Mass Consumption

The growth of American industry could not have occurred without the expansion of markets for the goods being produced. Much of the emerging mass market for industrial goods consisted of the increasingly wealthy middle class. But much of it consisted of less affluent people, who consumed more because their incomes were increasing too, even if modestly, and because mass production and mass distribution were making consumer goods less expensive.

Incomes in the industrial era were rising for almost everyone, although at highly uneven rates. While the most conspicuous result of the new economy was the creation of vast fortunes, more important for society as a whole was the growth and increasing prosperity of the middle class. The salaries of clerks, accountants, middle managers, and other "white collar" workers rose on average by a third between 1890 and 1910—and in some parts of the middle class salaries rose by much more. Doctors, lawyers, and other professionals, for example, experienced a particularly dramatic increase in both the prestige and the profitability of their professions. Working-class incomes rose too in those years, although from a much lower base and considerably more slowly. Iron and steel workers, despite the setbacks their unions suffered, saw their hourly wages increase by a third between 1890 and 1910; but industries with large female, African-American, or Mexican work forces—shoes, textiles, paper, laundries, many areas of commercial agriculture—saw very small increases, as did almost all industries in the South. Still, even some workers in these industries experienced a rise in family income because women and children often worked to supplement the husband's and father's earnings, or because families took in boarders or laundry or otherwise supplemented their incomes.

Also important to the new mass market was the development of affordable products and the creation of new merchandising techniques, which made many consumer goods available to a broad market for the first time. A good example of such changes was the emergence of ready-made clothing. In the early nineteenth century, most Americans had made their own clothing—usually from cloth they bought from merchants, at times from fabrics they spun and wove themselves. More affluent people contracted with private tailors to make their clothes. But the invention of the sewing machine and the spur that the Civil War (and its demand for uniforms) gave to the manufacture of clothing created an enormous industry devoted to producing ready-made garments. By the end of the century, virtually all Americans bought their clothing from stores. Partly as a result, much larger numbers of people became concerned with personal style. Interest in women's fashion, for example, had once been a luxury reserved for the relatively affluent. Now middle-class and even working-class women could strive to develop a distinctive style of dress.

Another example of the rise of the mass market was the way Americans bought and prepared food. The development and mass production of tin cans in the 1880s created a large new industry devoted to packaging and selling canned food and (as a result of the techniques Gail Borden discovered in the 1850s) condensed milk. Refrigerated railroad cars made it possible for perishables—meats, vegetables, dairy products, and other foodstuffs—to travel over long distances without spoiling. The development of artificially frozen ice made it possible for many more households to afford iceboxes. Among other things, the changes

THE DEPARTMENT STORE, C. 1892
This detail from an advertisement shows an interior cross section of the Abraham and Straus department store in Brooklyn, New York. Early department stores boasted not just of the amount and variety of their merchandise but also of the magical qualities of the consumer world they created. *(New-York Historical Society)*

meant improved diets and better health; life expectancy rose six years in the first two decades of the twentieth century.

Changes in marketing also altered the way Americans bought goods. Small local stores faced competition from new "chain stores." The Great Atlantic & Pacific Tea Company (the A & P) began creating a national network of grocery stores in the 1870s. F. W. Woolworth built a chain of dry goods stores. Sears Roebuck established a large market for its mail-order merchandise by distributing an enormous catalog each year. Even people in remote rural areas could order its products.

In larger cities, the emergence of great department stores (which had appeared earlier in Europe) helped transform buying habits and turn shopping into a more alluring and glamorous activity. Marshall Field in Chicago created one of the first American department stores—a place deliberately designed to create a sense of wonder and excitement. Similar stores emerged elsewhere: Macy's in New York, Abraham and Straus in Brooklyn, Jordan Marsh and Filene's in Boston, Wanamaker's in Philadelphia.

The rise of mass consumption had particularly dramatic effects on American women, who were generally the primary consumers within families. Women's clothing styles changed much more rapidly and dra-

matically than men's, which encouraged more frequent purchases. Women generally bought and prepared food for their families, so the availability of new food products changed not only the way everyone ate, but also the way women shopped and cooked. Canning and refrigeration meant greater variety in the diet. It also meant that food did not always have to be purchased on the day it was eaten. The consumer economy produced new employment opportunities for women as sales clerks in department stores and as waitresses in the rapidly proliferating restaurants. And it spawned the creation of a new movement in which women were to play a vital role: the consumer protection movement. The National Consumers League, formed in the 1890s under the leadership of Florence Kelley, attempted to mobilize the power of women as consumers to force retailers and manufacturers to improve wages and working conditions.

Leisure and Sport

Closely related to the growth of consumption was an increasing interest in leisure time, which for many people was expanding rapidly. Members of the urban middle and professional classes had large blocks of time in which they were not at work—evenings, weekends, even vacations (previously almost unknown

THE AMERICAN NATIONAL GAME
Long before the modern major
leagues began, local baseball clubs
were active throughout much of the
United States establishing the game
as the "national pastime." This
print of a "grand match for the
championship" depicts an 1866
game at Elysian Fields, a popular
park just across the river from New
York City in Hoboken, New Jersey.
*(National Baseball Library, Cooperstown,
N.Y.)*

among salaried workers). Working hours in many factories declined, from an average of nearly seventy hours a week in 1860 to under sixty in 1900. Even farmers found that the mechanization of agriculture gave them more free time. The lives of many Americans were becoming compartmentalized, with clear distinctions between work and leisure that had not existed in the past. The change produced a search for new forms of recreation and entertainment.

Among the responses to this search was the rise of organized spectator sports, and especially baseball, which by the end of the century was well on its way to becoming the "national pastime." A game much like baseball, known as "rounders" and derived from cricket, had enjoyed limited popularity in Great Britain in the early nineteenth century. Versions of the game began to appear in America in the early 1830s, well before Abner Doubleday supposedly "invented" baseball. (Doubleday, in fact, had almost nothing to do with the creation of baseball and actually cared little for sports. Alexander Cartwright, a member of a New York City baseball club, defined many of the rules and features of the game as we know it today in the 1840s.)

By the end of the Civil War, interest in baseball had grown rapidly. More than 200 amateur or semiprofessional teams or clubs existed, many of which joined a national association and agreed on standard rules. As the game grew in popularity, it became a source of profit. The first salaried team, the Cincinnati Red Stockings, was formed in 1869. Other cities soon fielded professional teams, and in 1876, at the urging of Albert Spalding, they banded together in the National League. A rival league, the American Association, soon appeared. It eventually collapsed, but in 1901 the American League emerged to replace it. In 1903, the first modern World Series was played, in which the American League Boston Red Sox beat the National League Pittsburgh Pirates. By then, baseball had become an important business and a great national preoccupation (at least among men), attracting paying crowds at times as large as 50,000.

Baseball had great appeal to working-class males. Baseball players tended to be men from modest backgrounds, and in the beginning at least, baseball crowds were made up largely of male urban laborers. The second most popular game, football, appealed at first to a more elite segment of the male population, in part because it originated in colleges and universities. The first intercollegiate football game in America occurred between Princeton and Rutgers in 1869, and soon the game began to become entrenched as part of collegiate life. Early intercollegiate football bore only an indirect relation to the modern game; it was more similar to what is now known as rugby. By the late 1870s, however, the game was becoming standardized and was taking on the outlines of its modern form.

As college football grew in popularity, it spread to other sections of the country, notably to the midwestern state universities, which were destined soon to replace the eastern schools as the great powers of the game. It also began to exhibit the taints of professionalism that have marked it ever since. Some schools used "ringers," tramp athletes who were not even registered as students. In an effort to eliminate such abuses, Amos Alonzo Stagg, athletic director and coach at the University of Chicago, led in forming the Western Conference, or Big Ten, in 1896, which established rules governing eligibility. Football also became known for a high level of violence on the field; eighteen college students died of football-related injuries and over a hundred were seriously hurt in 1905. The carnage prompted a White House conference on organized sports convened by President Theodore Roosevelt. As a result of its deliberations, a new intercollegiate association (which in 1910 became known as the National College Athletic Association, the NCAA) revised the rules of the game in an effort to make it safer and more honest.

Other popular spectator sports were emerging at about the same time. Basketball was invented in 1891 at Springfield, Massachusetts, by Dr. James A. Naismith, a Canadian working as athletic director for a local college. Boxing, which had long been a disreputable activity concentrated primarily among the urban lower classes, became by the 1880s a more popular and in some places more reputable sport, particularly after the adoption of the Marquis of Queensberry rules (by which fighters wore padded gloves and fought in three-minute rounds). The first modern boxing hero, John L. Sullivan, became heavyweight champion of the world in 1882. Even so, boxing remained illegal in some states until after World War I.

The major spectator sports of the era were activities open almost exclusively to men. But a number of other sports were emerging in which women became important participants. Golf and tennis seldom attracted crowds in the late nineteenth century, but both experienced a rapid increase in participation among relatively wealthy men and women. Bicycling and croquet also enjoyed widespread popularity in the 1890s among women as well as men. Women's colleges were beginning to introduce their students to more strenuous sports as well—track, crew, swimming, and (beginning in the late 1890s) basketball—challenging the once prevalent notion that vigorous exercise was dangerous to women.

Leisure and Popular Culture

Other forms of popular entertainment developed in the cities in response to the large potential markets there.

Many ethnic communities maintained their own theaters, in which immigrants listened to the music of their homelands and heard comedians making light of their experiences in the New World. Urban theaters also introduced one of the most distinctively American entertainment forms: the musical comedy, which evolved gradually from the comic operettas of European theater. George M. Cohan, an Irish vaudeville entertainer, became the first great creator of musical comedies in the early twentieth century; in the process of creating his many shows, he wrote a series of patriotic songs—"Yankee Doodle Dandy," "Over There," and "You're a Grand Old Flag"—that remained popular many decades later.

Vaudeville, a form of theater adapted from French models, was the most popular urban entertainment in the first decades of the twentieth century. Even saloons and small community theaters could afford to offer their customers vaudeville, which consisted of a variety of acts (musicians, comedians, magicians, jugglers, and others) and was, at least in the beginning, inexpensive to produce. As the economic potential of vaudeville grew, some promoters—most prominently Florenz Ziegfeld of New York—staged much more elaborate spectacles.

Vaudeville was also one of the few entertainment media open to black performers. They brought to it elements of the minstrel shows they had earlier developed for black audiences in the late nineteenth century. Some minstrel singers (including the most famous, Al Jolson) were whites wearing heavy makeup (or "blackface"). But most were black. Performers of both races performed music based on the gospel and folk tunes of the plantation and on the jazz and ragtime of black urban communities. Performers of both races also tailored their acts to prevailing white prejudices, ridiculing blacks by acting out demeaning stereotypes.

The most important form of mass entertainment (until the invention of radio and television), and the one that reached most widely across the nation, was the movies. Thomas Edison and others had created the technology of the motion picture in the 1880s. Not long after, short films became available to individual viewers through "peep shows" in pool halls, penny arcades, and amusement parks. Soon larger projectors made it possible to project the images onto big screens, which permitted substantial audiences to see films in theaters. By 1900, Americans were becoming attracted in large numbers to these early movies—usually plotless films of trains or waterfalls or other spectacles designed mainly to show off the technology. D. W. Griffith carried the motion picture into a new era with his silent epics—*The Birth of a Nation* (1915), *Intolerance* (1916), and others—which introduced serious plots and elaborate productions to filmmaking. Some of them also contained notoriously racist messages, an indication, among other things, that the audiences for these early films were overwhelmingly white. Motion pictures were the first truly mass entertainment medium, reaching all areas of the country and almost all groups in the population.

Particularly striking about popular entertainment in the late nineteenth and early twentieth centuries was its public quality. Americans of diverse classes and backgrounds spent their leisure time in places where they would find not only entertainment, but also other people. Thousands of working-class New Yorkers flocked to the amusement park at Coney Island, for example, not just for the rides and shows, but for the excitement of the crowds, as did the thousands who spent evenings in dance halls, vaudeville houses, and concert halls. More affluent New Yorkers enjoyed afternoons in Central Park, where a principal attraction was seeing other people (and being seen by them). Moviegoers were attracted not just by the movies themselves, but by the energy of the audiences at the lavish "movie palaces" that began to appear in cities in the early twentieth century, just as sports fans were drawn by the crowds as well as by the games.

Mass entertainment did not always bridge differences of class or race; there were relatively few places where people of widely diverse backgrounds gathered together. When the classes did meet in public spaces—as they did, for example, in city parks—there was often considerable conflict over what constituted appropriate public behavior. Elites in New York City, for example, tried to prohibit anything but quiet, "genteel" activities in Central Park, while working-class people wanted to use the public spaces for sports and entertainments. But even divided by class, leisure and popular entertainment did help sustain a vigorous public culture.

Not all popular entertainment, however, involved public events. Many Americans amused themselves privately by reading novels and poetry. The so-called dime novels, cheaply bound and widely circulated, became popular after the Civil War, with tales of the Wild West, detective stories, sagas of scientific adventure (such as the Tom Swift stories), and novels of "moral uplift" (among them those of Horatio Alger). Publishers also distributed sentimental novels of romance, which developed a large audience among women, as did books about animals and about young children growing up. Louisa May Alcott's *Little Women,* most of whose readers were women, sold more than 2 million copies.

Mass Communications

Urban industrial society created a vast market for new vehicles for transmitting news and information. And so American publishing and journalism experienced an important change in the decades following the Civil War. Between 1870 and 1910, the circulation of daily newspapers increased nearly ninefold (from under 3 million to more than 24 million), a rate three times as great as the rate of population increase. And while standards varied widely from one paper to another, American journalism began to develop the beginnings of a professional identity. Salaries of reporters increased; many newspapers began separating the reporting of news from the expression of opinion; and newspapers themselves became important businesses.

One striking change was the emergence of national press services, which made use of the telegraph to supply news and features to papers throughout the country and which contributed as a result to the standardization of the product. By the turn of the century important newspaper chains had emerged as well. The most powerful was William Randolph Hearst's, which by 1914 controlled nine newspapers and two magazines. Hearst and rival publisher Joseph Pulitzer helped popularize what became known as "yellow journalism"—a deliberately sensational, often lurid style of reporting presented in bold graphics, designed to reach a mass audience. Another major change occurred in the nature of American magazines. Beginning in the 1880s, a new kind of magazine appeared, also designed for a mass audience. One of the pioneers was Edward W. Bok, who took over the *Ladies' Home Journal* in 1899 and, by targeting a mass female audience, built its circulation to over 700,000.

HIGH CULTURE IN THE AGE OF THE CITY

In addition to the important changes in popular culture that accompanied the rise of cities and industry, there were profound changes in the realm of "high culture"—in the ideas and activities of intellectuals and elites. Even the notion of a distinction between "highbrow" and "lowbrow" culture was relatively new to the industrial era. In the early nineteenth century, most cultural activities attracted people of widely varying backgrounds and targeted people of all classes. By the late nineteenth century, however, elites were developing a cultural and intellectual life quite separate from the popular amusements of the urban masses.

The Literature of Urban America

Many foreign observers and even some Americans in the late nineteenth century viewed the culture of the United States with contempt. Critics claimed that American life, despite its glittering surface, was essentially acquisitive and corrupt, with little cultural depth. But whatever the quality of culture and society in late-nineteenth-century America, the growth of industry and the rise of the city were having profound effects on them. Some writers and artists—the local-color writers of the South, for example, and Mark Twain, in such novels as *Huckleberry Finn* and *Tom Sawyer*—responded to the new civilization by evoking an older, more natural world. But others grappled directly with the modern order.

One of the strongest impulses in late-nineteenth- and early-twentieth-century American literature was the effort to re-create urban social reality. This trend toward realism found an early voice in Stephen Crane, who—although best known for his novel of the Civil War, *The Red Badge of Courage* (1895)—was the author of an earlier, powerful indictment of the plight of the working class. Crane created a sensation in 1893 when he published *Maggie: A Girl of the Streets*, a grim picture of urban poverty and slum life. Theodore Dreiser was even more influential in encouraging writers to abandon the genteel traditions of earlier times and turn to the social dislocations and injustices of the present. He did so both in *Sister Carrie* and in other, later novels (including *An American Tragedy*, perhaps his greatest work, published in 1925).

Many of Dreiser's contemporaries followed him in chronicling the oppression of America's poor. In 1901 Frank Norris published *The Octopus*, an account of a struggle between oppressed wheat ranchers and powerful railroad interests in California. Upton Sinclair's *The Jungle* (1906) exposed abuses in the American meat-packing industry and helped inspire legislative action to deal with the problem. Kate Chopin, a southern writer who explored the oppressive features of traditional marriage, encountered widespread public abuse after publication of her shocking novel *The Awakening* in 1899. It described a young wife and mother who abandoned her family in search of personal fulfillment. It was formally banned in some communities. William Dean Howells, in *The Rise of Silas Lapham* (1884) and other works, described what he considered the shallowness and corruption in ordinary American lifestyles.

Other critics of American society responded to the new civilization not by attacking it but by withdrawing from it. The historian Henry Adams published an autobiography in 1906, *The Education of Henry Adams*, in which he portrayed himself as a man disillusioned with and unable to relate to his society, even though he continued to live in it. The novelist Henry James lived the major part of his adult life in England and Europe and produced a series of coldly realistic novels—*The American* (1877), *Portrait of a Lady* (1881), *The Ambassadors* (1903), and others—that showed his ambivalence about the merits of both American and European civilization.

Art in the Age of the City

American art through most of the nineteenth century had been overshadowed by the art of Europe. By 1900, however, a number of American artists, although some continued to study and even live in Europe, broke from the Old World traditions and experimented with new styles. Winslow Homer was vigorously American in his paintings of New England maritime life and other native subjects. James McNeil Whistler was one of the first Western artists to appreciate the beauty of Japanese color prints and to introduce Oriental concepts into American and European art.

By the first years of the new century, some American artists were turning decisively away from the traditional academic style, a style perhaps best exemplified in America by the brilliant portraitist John Singer Sargent. Instead, many younger painters were exploring the same grim aspects of modern life that were becoming the subject of American literature. Members of the so-called Ashcan School produced work startling in its naturalism and stark in its portrayal of the social realities of the era. John Sloan portrayed the dreariness of American urban slums; George Bellows caught the vigor and violence of his time in paintings and drawings of prize fights; Edward Hopper explored the starkness and loneliness of the modern city. The Ashcan artists were also among the first Americans to appreciate expressionism and abstraction; and they showed their interest in new forms in 1913 when they helped stage the famous and controversial "Armory Show" in New York City, which displayed works of the French post-impressionists and of some American moderns.

The work of these and other artists marked the beginning in America of an artistic movement known as modernism, a movement that had counterparts in many other areas of cultural and intellectual life as well. Rejecting the heavy reliance on established forms that characterized the "genteel tradition" of the nineteenth-century art world, modernists rejected the past and embraced new subjects and new forms. Where the genteel tradition emphasized the "dignified"and

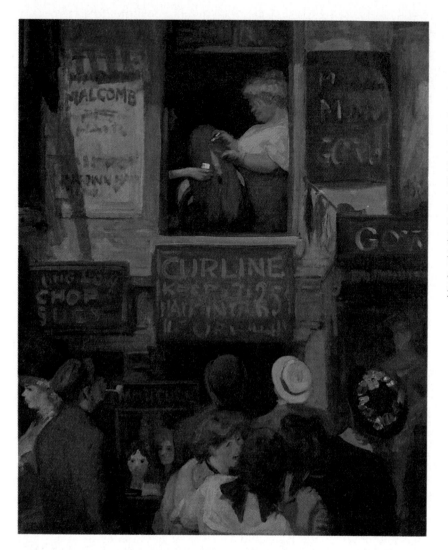

HAIRDRESSER'S WINDOW
This 1907 painting is by John Sloan, an American artist who belonged to the so-called Ashcan School. Sloan and others were in revolt against what they considered the sterile formalism of academic painting and chose instead to portray realistic scenes of ordinary life. In 1913 they stirred the art world with a startling exhibition in New York, known as the Armory Show. In it they displayed not only their own work (which was relatively conventional in technique, even if sometimes daring in its choice of subjects) but also the work of innovative European artists, who were already beginning to explore wholly new artistic forms. *(Wadsworth Atheneum, Hartford)*

"elevated" aspects of civilization (and glorified the achievements of gifted elites), modernism gloried in the ordinary, even the coarse. Where the genteel tradition placed great importance on respect for the past and the maintenance of "standards," modernism looked to the future and gloried in the new. Eventually, modernism developed strict orthodoxies of its own. But in its early stages, it seemed to promise an escape from rigid, formal traditions and an unleashing of individual creativity.

The Impact of Darwinism

The single most profound intellectual development in the late nineteenth century was the widespread acceptance of the theory of evolution, associated most prominently with the English naturalist Charles Darwin. Darwinism argued that the human species had evolved from earlier forms of life (and most recently from simian creatures similar to apes) through a process of "natural selection." It challenged the biblical story of the Creation and almost every other tenet of traditional American religious faith. History, Darwinism suggested, was not the working out of a divine plan, as most Americans had always believed. It was a random process dominated by the fiercest or luckiest competitors.

The theory of evolution met widespread resistance at first from educators, theologians, and even many scientists. By the end of the century, however, the evolutionists had converted most members of the urban professional and educated classes. Even many middle-

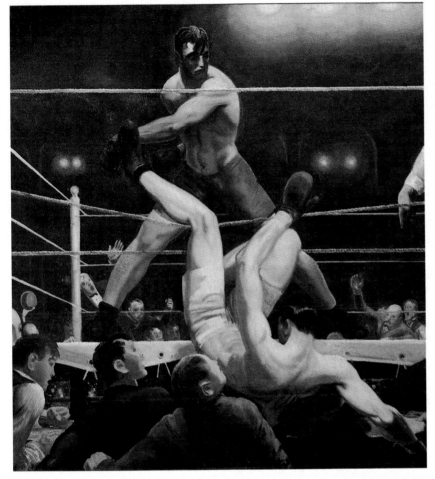

DEMPSEY AND FIRPO
The artist George Bellows began painting fight scenes in the first years of
the twentieth century, when boxing
appealed primarily to working-class
urban communities. By 1924, when
he painted this view of the Dempsey-
Firpo fight, prizefighting had become
one of the most popular sports in
America. *(Whitney Museum of American
Art, New York; gift of Gertrude Vanderbilt
Whitney)*

class Protestant religious leaders had accepted the doctrine, making significant alterations in theology to accommodate it. Evolution had become enshrined in
schools and universities; virtually no serious scientist
any longer questioned its basic validity.

Unseen by most urban Americans at the time, however, the rise of Darwinism was contributing to a deep
schism between the new, cosmopolitan culture of the
city—which was receptive to new ideas such as evolution—and a more traditional, provincial culture
located mainly (although not wholly) in rural areas—
which remained wedded to more fundamentalist religious beliefs and older values. Thus the late nineteenth
century saw not only the rise of a liberal Protestantism
in tune with new scientific discoveries. It also saw the
beginning of an organized Protestant fundamentalism,
which would make its presence felt politically in the
1920s and again in the 1980s.

Darwinism helped spawn other new intellectual
currents. There was the Social Darwinism of William
Graham Sumner and others, which industrialists used
so enthusiastically to justify their favored position in
American life. But there were also more sophisticated
philosophies, among them a doctrine that became
known as "pragmatism," which seemed peculiarly a
product of America's changing material civilization.
William James, a Harvard psychologist and brother of
the novelist Henry James, was the most prominent
publicist of the new theory, although earlier intellectuals such as Charles S. Peirce and later ones such as
John Dewey were also important to its development
and dissemination. According to the pragmatists, modern society should rely for guidance not on inherited
ideals and moral principles but on the test of scientific
inquiry. No idea or institution (not even religious faith)
was valid, they claimed, unless it worked and unless

CHARLES DARWIN
Darwin's theories of natural selection, or evolution, revolutionized biological science. They also had a stunning impact on religious and even social thought. By challenging large parts of traditional religion and by suspecting that species were changeable, Darwinism opened the way for decades of theological controversy and for a series of spurious applications of his ideas to contemporary social problems. *(Bettmann)*

it stood the test of experience. "The ultimate test for us of what a truth means," James wrote, "is the conduct it dictates or inspires."

A similar concern for scientific inquiry was intruding into the social sciences and challenging traditional orthodoxies. Economists such as Richard T. Ely and Simon Patten argued for a more active and pragmatic use of scientific discipline. Sociologists such as Edward A. Ross and Lester Frank Ward urged applying the scientific method to the solution of social and political problems. Historians such as Frederick Jackson Turner and Charles Beard argued that economic factors more than spiritual ideals had been the governing force in historical development. John Dewey proposed a new approach to education that placed less emphasis on the rote learning of traditional knowledge and more on a flexible, democratic approach to schooling, one that enabled students to acquire knowledge that would help them deal with the realities of their society.

The relativistic implications of Darwinism also promoted the growth of anthropology and encouraged some scholars to begin examining other cultures—most significantly, perhaps, the culture of American Indians—in new ways. A few white Americans began to look at Indian society as a coherent culture with its own norms and values that were worthy of respect and preservation, even though different from those of white society. But such ideas about native Americans found very little support outside a few corners of the intellectual world until much later in the twentieth century.

Toward Universal Schooling

A society that was coming to depend increasingly on specialized skills and scientific knowledge was, of course, a society with a high demand for education. The late nineteenth century, therefore, was a time of rapid expansion and reform of American schools and universities.

One example was the spread of free public primary and secondary education. In 1860, there were only 100 public high schools in the entire United States. By 1900, the number had reached 6,000 and by 1914 over 12,000. By 1900, compulsory school attendance laws were in effect in thirty-one states and territories. But education was still far from universal. Rural areas lagged far behind urban-industrial ones in funding public education. And in the South, many blacks had access to no schools at all.

Educational reformers, few of whom shared the more relativistic views of anthropologists, sought to provide educational opportunities for the Indian tribes as well, in an effort to "civilize" them and help them adapt to white society. In the 1870s, reformers recruited small groups of Indians to attend Hampton Institute, a primarily black college. In 1879, Richard Henry Pratt, a former army officer, organized the Carlisle Indian Industrial School in Pennsylvania. Like many black colleges, Carlisle emphasized the kind of practical "industrial" education that Booker T. Washington had urged on blacks. Equally important, it isolated Indians from their tribes and tried to force them to assimilate to white norms. The purpose, Pratt said, was to "kill the Indian and save the man." Carlisle spawned other, similar schools in the West. The tribes themselves resisted this new approach to Indian education, both because of the hostility of the white educators to tribal culture and because the schools were often dreary and dangerous places. Ultimately, the reform efforts failed, although less because of Indian resistance than because of inadequate funding, incompetent administration, and poor teaching.

Colleges and universities were also proliferating rapidly in the late nineteenth century. They benefited particularly from the Morrill Land Grant Act of the

SIGNIFICANT EVENTS

1836   Mount Holyoke College founded as seminary for women

1839   Abner Doubleday establishes rules for baseball

1865   Vassar College founded

1869   Princeton and Rutgers play first intercollegiate football game

1870   New York City opens elevated railroads

Wellesley College founded

1871   Great fires destroy much of Chicago and Boston

Smith College founded

1872   Tammy's Boss Tweed convicted of corruption

1876   Baseball's National League founded

Johns Hopkins University creates first modern graduate school

1879   Carlisle Indian Industrial School founded in Pennsylvania

1882   Congress restricts Chinese Immigration

1884   First "skyscraper" built in Chicago

William Dean Howells publishes *The Rise of Silas Lapham*

1887   American Protective Association founded

1890   Jacob Riis publishes *How the Other Half Lives*

1891   James Naismith invents basketball

1894   Immigration Restriction League founded

1895   Stephen Crane publishes *The Red Badge of Courage*

1897   Boston opens first subway in America

1899   Kate Chopin publishes *The Awakening*

1900   Theodore Dreiser publishes *Sister Carrie*

1901   Baseball's American League founded

1903   Boston Red Sox win first World Series

Henry James publishes *The Ambassadors*

1906   Earthquake and fire destroy much of San Francisco

Upton Sinclair publishes *The Jungle*

1910   National College Athletic Association founded to regulate collegiate football

1913   Ashcan School artists stage Armory Show in New York City

Civil War era, by which the federal government had donated land to states for the establishment of colleges. After 1865, states in the South and West took particular advantage of the law. In all, sixty-nine "land-grant" institutions were established in the last decades of the century—among them the state university systems of California, Illinois, Minnesota, and Wisconsin. Other universities benefited from millions of dollars contributed by business and financial tycoons. Rockefeller, Carnegie, and others gave generously to such schools as Columbia, Chicago, Harvard, Northwestern, Princeton, Syracuse, and Yale. Other philanthropists founded new universities or reorganized and renamed older ones to perpetuate their family names—Vanderbilt, Johns Hopkins, Cornell, Duke, Tulane, and Stanford.

Education for Women

The post-Civil War era saw, too, an important expansion of educational opportunities for women, although such opportunities continued to lag far behind those available to men and were almost always denied to black women.

Most public high schools accepted women readily, but opportunities for higher education were few. At the end of the Civil War, only three American colleges were coeducational. In the years after the war, many of the land-grant colleges and universities in the Middle West and such private universities as Cornell and Wesleyan began to admit women along with men. But coeducation played a less crucial role in the education of women in this period than the creation of a network of women's colleges. Mount Holyoke, which had begun its life in 1836 as a "seminary" for women, became a full-fledged college in the 1880s. At about the same time, entirely new female institutions were emerging: Vassar, Wellesley, Smith, Bryn Mawr, Wells, and Goucher. A few of the larger private universities created separate colleges for women on their campuses (Barnard at Columbia and Radcliffe at Harvard, for example). Proponents of women's colleges saw the institutions as places where female students would not be treated as "second-class citizens" by predominantly male student bodies and faculties.

The female college was part of an important phenomenon in the history of modern American women: the emergence of a distinctive women's community. Most faculty members and many administrators were women (usually unmarried). And the life of the college produced a spirit of sorority and commitment among educated women that had important effects in later years, as women became the leaders of many reform activities. Most female college graduates ultimately married, but they married at a later age than their non-college-educated counterparts and in some cases continued to pursue careers after marriage and motherhood. A significant minority, perhaps over 25 percent, did not marry at all, but devoted themselves exclusively to careers. A leader at Bryn Mawr remarked, "Our failures marry." That was surely hyperbole. But the growth of female higher education clearly became for some women a liberating experience, persuading them that they had roles to perform in society in addition to those of wives and mothers.

SUGGESTED READINGS

General Histories. Howard Chudacoff, *The Evolution of American Urban Society*, rev. ed. (1981). Charles N. Glaab and Andrew T. Brown, *A History of Urban America* (1967). Constance M. Green, *The Rise of Urban America* (1965). Blake McKelvey, *The Urbanization of America* (1963). Lewis Mumford, *The Culture of the Cities* (1938); *The City in History* (1961). Arthur M. Schlesinger, *The Rise of the City, 1878–1898* (1933). Jon C. Teaford, *City and Suburb: The Political Fragmentation of Urban America* (1979); *The Twentieth-Century American City: Problem, Promise, and Reality* (1986). Sam Bass Warner, Jr., *The Urban Wilderness* (1972); *Streetcar Suburbs* (1962).

Mobility and Race. Howard Chudacoff, *Mobile Americans: Residential and Social Mobility in Omaha, 1880–1920* (1972). Michael Frisch, *Town into City* (1972). Clyde Griffen and Sally Griffen, *Natives and Newcomers* (1977). Gerald D. Jaynes, *Branches Without Roots: Genesis of the Black Working Class in the American South, 1862–1882* (1986). David M. Katzman, *Before the Ghetto* (1966). Kenneth L. Kusmer, *A Ghetto Takes Shape* (1976). Roger Lane, *The Roots of Black Violence in Philadelphia, 1860–1900* (1986). Gilbert Osofsky, *Harlem: The Making of a Ghetto* (1966). Richard Sennett, *Families Against the City* (1970). Allan H. Spear, *Black Chicago* (1967). Stephan Thernstrom, *Poverty and Progress* (1964); *The Other Bostonians* (1973). Stephan Thernstrom and Richard Sennett, eds., *Nineteenth Century Cities* (1969). Olivier Zunz, *The Changing Face of Inequality: Urbanization, Industrial Development, and Immigrants in Detroit, 1880–1920* (1982).

Immigration. Thomas J. Archdeacon, *Becoming American: An Ethnic History* (1983). Josef Barton, *Peasants and Strangers: Italians, Rumanians, and Slovaks in an American City* (1975). John Bodnar, *The Transplanted: A History of Immigrants in America* (1985); *Immigration and Industrialization* (1977). John W. Briggs, *An Italian Passage* (1978). Jack Chen, *The Chinese of America* (1980). Robert D. Cross, *The Church and the City* (1967). Leonard Dinnerstein and David Reimers, *Ethnic Americans: A History of Immigration and Assimilation* (1975). John B. Duff, *The Irish in the United States* (1971). Elizabeth Ewen, *Immigrant Women in the Land of Dollars: Life and Culture on the Lower East Side, 1890–1925* (1985). Lawrence H. Fuchs, *The American Kaleidoscope: Race, Ethnicity, and the Civic Culture* (1990). Mario T. Garcia, *Desert Immigrants: The Mexicans of El Paso, 1880–1920* (1981). Nathan Glazer and Daniel P. Moynihan, *Beyond the Melting Pot* (1963). Susan A. Glenn, *Daughters of the Shtetl: Life and Labor in the Immigrant Generation* (1990). Milton M. Gordon, *Assimilation in American Life* (1964). Victor Greene, *For God and Country: The Rise of Polish and Lithuanian Ethic Consciousness in America* (1975). Oscar Handlin, *The Uprooted*, rev. ed. (1973). Marcus Hansen, *The Immigrant in American History* (1940). John Higham, *Strangers in the Land* (1955); *Send These To Me: Jews and Other Immigrants in Urban America* (1975). John Higham, ed., *Ethnic Leadership in America* (1978). Francis L. K. Hsu, *The Challenge of the American Dream: The Chinese in the United States* (1971). Maldwyn A. Jones, *American Immigration* (1960). Edward R. Kantowicz, *Polish-American Politics in Chicago* (1975). Thomas Kessner, *The Golden Door: Italian and Jewish Immigrant Mobility* (1977). Harry Kitano, *Japanese-Americans: The Evolution of a Subculture* (1969). Alan M. Kraut, *The Huddled Masses: The Immigrant in American Society, 1880–1921* (1982). Matt S. Maier and Feliciano Rivera, *The Chicanos: A History of Mexican-Americans* (1972). Gwendolyn Mink, *Old Labor and New Immigrants in American Political Development: Union, Party, and State, 1875–1920* (1986). Ewa Morawska, *For Bread and Butter: The Life-Worlds of East Central Europeans in Johnstown, Pennsylvania, 1890–1940* (1985). Stanley Nadel, *Ethnicity, Religion, and Class in New York City, 1845–1880* (1990). Humbert S. Nelli, *The Italians of Chicago* (1970). Moses Rischin, *The Promised City: New York's Jews* (1962). Barbara Solomon, *Ancestors and Im-*

migrants (1965). Thomas Sowell, *Ethnic America* (1981). Philip Taylor, *The Distant Magnet: European Emigration to the U.S.A.* (1971). David Ward, *Cities and Immigrants* (1965). Virginia Yans-McLaughlin, *Family and Community: Italian Immigrants in Buffalo, 1880–1930* (1977).

Urban Poverty and Reform.   Robert H. Bremner, *From the Depths* (1956). Stephan F. Brumberg, *Going to America, Going to School* (1986). James H. Cassedy, *Charles V. Chapin and the Public Health Movement* (1962). Allen F. Davis, *Spearheads for Reform* (1967). Barbara Gutmann Rosencrantz, *Public Health and the State* (1972). Marvin Lazerson, *Origins of the Urban School* (1971). James T. Patterson, *America's Struggle Against Poverty* (1981). Thomas L. Philpott, *The Slum and the Ghetto* (1978). James F. Richardson, *The New York Police* (1970). Jacob Riis, *How the Other Half Lives* (1890); *Children of the Poor* (1892); *The Battle with the Slum* (1902). Selwyn K. Troen, *The Public and the Schools* (1975). David B. Tyack, *The One Best System: A History of American Urban Education* (1974).

Urban Politics.   John M. Allswang, *Bosses, Machines and Urban Voters* (1977). Alexander B. Callow, *The Tweed Ring* (1966). Brian J. Cudahy, *Cash, Tokens, and Transfers: A History of Urban Mass Transit in North America* (1990). Lyle Dorsett, *The Pendergast Machine* (1968). Lori Ginzberg, *Women and the Work of Benevolence: Morality, Politics, and Class in the Nineteenth-Century United States* (1990). Roger Lane, *Policing the City: Boston, 1822–1885* (1967). Seymour Mandelbaum, *Boss Tweed's New York* (1965). Christine M. Rosen, *The Limits of Power: Great Fires and the Process of City Growth in America* (1986). John Sproat, *The Best Men* (1968). Zane L. Miller, *Boss Cox's Cincinnati: Urban Politics in the Progressive Era* (1968).

Social Thought and Urban Culture.   Martha Banta, *Imaging American Women: Idea and Ideals in Cultural History* (1987). Stuart Blumin, *The Emergence of the Middle Class: Social Experience in the American City, 1760–1900* (1989). Gunther Barth, *City People: The Rise of Modern City Culture in Nineteenth-Century America* (1980); *Instant Cities: Urbanization and the Rise of San Francisco and Denver* (1975). Susan Porter Benson, *Counter Cultures: Saleswomen, Managers, and Customers in American Department Stores, 1890–1940* (1986). Henry C. Binford, *The First Suburbs: Residential Communities on the Boston Periphery, 1815–1860* (1985). Paul Boyer, *Urban Masses and Moral Order in America, 1820–1920* (1978). Marc Carnes, *Secret Ritual and Manhood in Victorian America* (1989). Clifford E. Clark, *The American Family Home, 1800–1960* (1986). Lawrence Cremin, *The Transformation of the School* (1961). Perry Duis, *The Saloon: Public Drinking in Chicago and Boston, 1880–1920* (1983). Lewis A. Erenberg, *Steppin' Out: New York Nightlife and the*

Transformation of American Culture, 1890–1930 (1981). Charles V. Forcey, *The Crossroads of Liberalism* (1961). Timothy J. Gilfoyle, *City of Eros: New York City, Prostitution, and the Commercialization of Sex, 1790–1920* (1992). Eliot Gorn, *The Manly Art: Bare-Knuckle Prize Fighting in America* (1986). Harvey Green, *Fit for America: Fitness, Sport, and American Society* (1986). Allen Guttmann, *A Whole New Ball Game: An Interpretation of American Sports* (1988). Karen Halttunen, *Confidence Men and Painted Women: A Study of Middle-Class Culture in America, 1830–1870* (1982). Neil Harris, *Cultural Excursions: Marketing Appetites and Cultural Tastes in Modern America* (1990). Daniel Horowitz, *The Morality of Spending: Attitudes Toward the Consumer Society in America, 1875–1940* (1985). Kenneth T. Jackson, *The Crabgrass Frontier: The Suburbanization of the United States* (1985). John F. Kasson, *Amusing the Million: Coney Island at the Turn of the Century* (1978); *Rudeness and Civility: Manners in Nineteenth-Century Urban America* (1990). William Leach, *True Love and Perfect Union: The Feminist Reform of Sex and Society* (1980); *Land of Desire: Merchants, Power, and the Rise of a New American Culture* (1993). T. J. Jackson Lears, *No Place of Grace: Antimodernism and the Transformation of American Culture, 1880–1920* (1981). T. J. Jackson Lears and Richard Wightman Fox, eds., *The Culture of Consumption* (1983). Godfrey M. Lebhar, *Chain Stores in America* (1962). Lawrence Levine, *Highbrow/Lowbrow: The Emergence of a Cultural Hierarchy in America* (1988). John A. Lucas and Ronald Smith, *Saga of American Sport* (1978). D. W. Marcell, *Progress and Pragmatism* (1974). Jay Martin, *Harvests of Change* (1967). Martin V. Melosi, ed., *Pollution and Reform in American Cities* (1980). Steven Mintz and Susan Kellogg, *Domestic Revolutions: A Social History of American Family Life* (1988). Frank Luther Mott, *American Journalism*, rev. ed. (1962). Donald R. Mrozek, *Sport and American Mentality, 1880–1910* (1983). Lewis Mumford, *The Brown Decades* (1931). David Nasaw, *Going Out: The Rise and Fall of Public Amusements* (1993); *Schooled to Order: A Social History of Public Schooling in the United States* (1979). James D. Norris, *Advertising and the Transformation of American Society, 1865–1920* (1990). Kathy Peiss, *Cheap Amusements: Working Women and Leisure in Turn-of-the-Century New York* (1986). Alexander Saxton, *The Rise and Fall of the White Republic: Class Politics and Mass Culture in Nineteenth-Century America* (1990). Robert W. Snyder, *The Voice of the City: Vaudeville and Popular Culture in New York* (1989). Dale Somers, *The Rise of Sports in New Orleans* (1972). Susan Strasser, *Satisfaction Guaranteed: The Making of the American Mass Market* (1989). Christopher Tunnard and H. H. Reed, *American Skyline* (1955). Morton White, *Social Thought in America* (1949). Larzer Ziff, *The American 1890s: Life and Times of a Lost Generation* (1966).

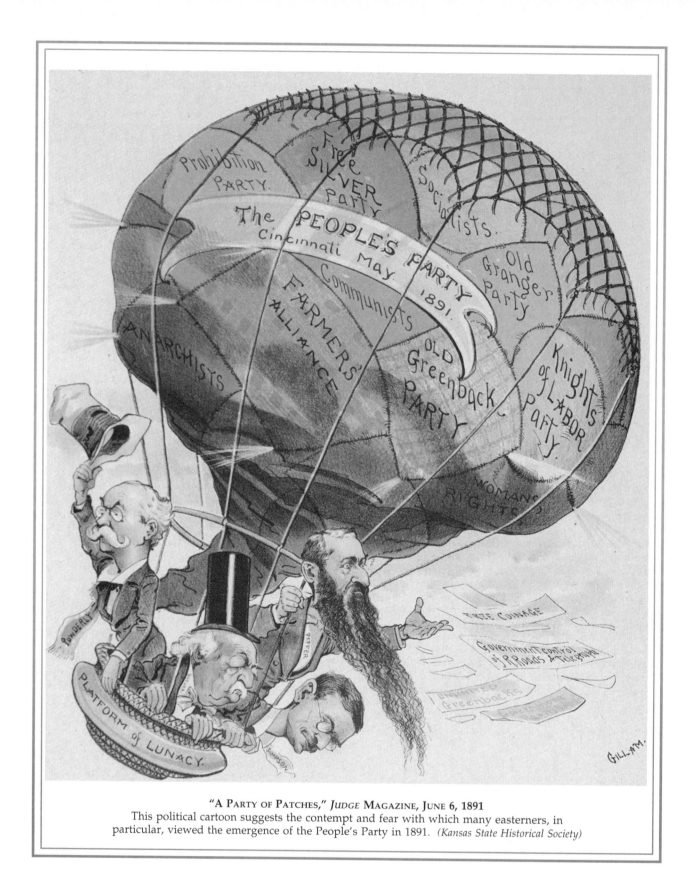

"A PARTY OF PATCHES," JUDGE MAGAZINE, JUNE 6, 1891
This political cartoon suggests the contempt and fear with which many easterners, in
particular, viewed the emergence of the People's Party in 1891. *(Kansas State Historical Society)*

CHAPTER NINETEEN

FROM STALEMATE TO CRISIS

HE ENORMOUS CHANGES AMERICA was experiencing in the late nineteenth century strained not only the nation's traditional social arrangements but its political institutions as well. Economic growth brought both progress and disorder. And it was to government, gradually, that Americans began to look for leadership in their search for stability.

Yet American government during much of this period was ill equipped to deal with the new challenges confronting it. In the face of unprecedented dilemmas, it responded with apparent passivity and confusion. Its leaders, for the most part, seemed political mediocrities. The issues with which it was concerned were often irrelevant to the nation's most serious problems. Rather than taking active leadership of the nation's dramatic transformation, the American political system for nearly two decades after the end of Reconstruction was locked in a rigid stalemate—watching the remarkable changes that were occurring in the nation and doing little to affect them. The result was a set of problems and grievances that festered and grew without any natural outlet. And it was not surprising, under the circumstances, that in the 1890s the United States entered a period of national crisis.

THE POLITICS OF EQUILIBRIUM

To modern eyes, the nature of the American political system in the late nineteenth century appears in many ways paradoxical. The two political parties enjoyed a strength and stability during those years that neither was ever to know again. And yet the federal government, which the two parties were struggling to control, was doing relatively little of importance. In fact, most Americans in those years engaged in political activity less because of their interest in national issues than because of broad regional, ethnic, or religious sentiments. Party loyalty had less to do with positions on public policy than with the way Americans defined themselves culturally.

The Party System

The most striking feature of the late-nineteenth-century party system was its remarkable stability. From the end of Reconstruction until the late 1890s, the electorate was divided almost precisely evenly between the Republicans and the Democrats. Loyalties fluctuated almost not at all. Sixteen states were solidly and consistently Republican, and fourteen states (most of them in the South) were solidly and consistently Democratic. Only five states were usually in doubt, and it was there that national elections were commonly decided, often on the basis of voter turnout. The Republican Party captured the presidency in all but two of the elections of the era, but the party was not really as dominant as that suggests. In the five presidential elections beginning in 1876, the average popular-vote margin separating the Democratic and Republican candidates was 1.5 percent. The congressional balance was similarly stable. Between 1875 and 1895, the Republicans generally controlled the Senate and the Democrats generally controlled the House; in any given election, the number of seats that shifted from one party to the other was very small.

As striking as the balance between the parties was the intensity of public loyalty to them. In most of the country, Americans adhered to their party affiliations with a passion and enthusiasm that are difficult for later generations to understand. Voter turnout in presidential elections between 1860 and 1900 averaged over 78 percent of all eligible voters. Even in nonpresidential years, from 60 to 80 percent of the voters turned out to cast ballots for congressional and local candidates. Large groups of potential voters were disfranchised in these years: women in most states; almost all blacks and many poor whites in the South. But for adult white males outside the South, there were few franchise restrictions. The remarkable turnout represented a genuinely mass-based politics.

Party politics in the late nineteenth century occupied a central position in American culture, comparable in some ways to the role that spectator sports and mass popular entertainment play today. Political campaigns were often the most important public events in the lives of communities. Political organizations served important social and cultural functions. Political identification was almost as important to most individuals as identification with a church or an ethnic group. Partisanship was an intense, emotional force, widely admired and often identified with patriotism.

What explains this remarkable loyalty to the two political parties? It was not, certainly, that the parties took distinct positions on important public issues. Both parties were solidly committed to the growth of the corporate industrial economy. Both were hostile to all forms of economic and social radicalism. Both were committed (at least until the 1890s) to a "sound currency" and to the existing structure of the financial system.

What determined party loyalties was less concrete issues than other factors. Region was perhaps the most important. To white southerners, loyalty to the Democratic Party was a matter of unquestioned faith. It was the vehicle by which they had triumphed over Reconstruction, the vehicle for the preservation of white supremacy. To many old-stock northerners, white and black, Republican loyalties were equally intense for the opposite reason. The party of Lincoln had freed the slaves and preserved the Union; it was a bulwark against slavery and treason.

Religious and ethnic differences also shaped party loyalties. The Democratic Party attracted most Catholic voters, most recent immigrants, and most of the poorer workers; those three groups, of course, often overlapped. The Republican Party appealed to northern Protestants and citizens of old stock. Among the few substantive issues on which the parties took clearly different stands were matters concerning immigrants. The Republicans tended to be more nativist and to support measures restricting immigration. They also tended to favor temperance legislation. Catholics and immigrants viewed such proposals as an assault on their culture and lifestyle and opposed them, and the Democratic Party followed their lead.

For many Americans, in other words, party identification was usually more a reflection of vague cultural inclinations than a calculation of economic interest. Individuals might affiliate with a party because their parents had done so, or because it was the party of their region, their church, or their ethnic group. Most clung to their party loyalties with great persistence and passion.

The National Government

One reason the two parties managed to avoid substantive issues was that the federal government (and for the most part state and local governments as well) did relatively little. The government in Washington was responsible for delivering the mails, for maintaining a national military, for conducting foreign policy, and for collecting tariffs and taxes. It had few other responsibilities. And it had few institutions with which to engage in additional responsibilities even if it chose to do so.

There was one significant exception. From the end of the Civil War to the early twentieth century, the federal government administered a system of annual pensions for Civil War veterans who had retired from work, and for their widows. At its peak, this pension system was making payments to a majority of the male citizens (black and white) of the North, and to many women as well. Some activists hoped to see it made permanent and universal; they pressured the government to create a system of old-age pensions for all Americans. But their efforts failed. That was in part because the Civil War pension system was awash in party patronage and was widely viewed as corrupt. Other reformers—believers in "good government"—saw elimination of the pension system as a way to fight graft, corruption, and party rule. When the Civil War generation died out, the pension system died with it.

In most other respects, the United States in the late nineteenth century was a society without a modern, national state. The most powerful national political institutions were the two political parties and the federal courts (a fact that has led one scholar to refer to the American government of that era as a "state of courts and parties"). The national leaders of both parties were primarily concerned not with policy but with office—with winning elections and controlling patronage.

Both parties were dominated by powerful bosses and machines chiefly concerned with controlling and dispensing jobs. The Democrats relied on the big city organizations (such as New York's Tammany Hall), which enabled them to mobilize the voting power of immigrants. The Republicans tended to depend on strong statewide organizations such as those of Roscoe Conkling in New York and Matt Quay of Pennsylvania.

Presidents and Patronage

The power of party bosses had a significant effect on the power of the presidency. The office had great symbolic importance, but its occupants were unable to do very much except distribute government appointments. A new president had to make almost 100,000 appointments (most of them in the post office, the only really large government agency); and to do that, he had to rely on a tiny staff working in a few rooms in the White House. James Garfield, who became president in 1881, once complained, "I have heretofore been treating of the fundamental principles of government, and here I am considering all day whether A or B should be appointed to this or that office." Even in making appointments, presidents had limited latitude, since they had to avoid offending the various factions within their own parties.

Sometimes that proved impossible, as the presidency of Rutherford B. Hayes demonstrated. The victor of the disputed election of 1876, Hayes was harried by angry Democrats (who called him "His Fraudulency") from the moment he entered office to the moment he left. But he was crippled as well by his own party. By the end of his term, two groups—the Stalwarts, led by Roscoe Conkling of New York, and the Half-Breeds, captained by James G. Blaine of Maine—were competing for control of the Republican Party and threatening to split it. The dispute between the Stalwarts and the Half-Breeds was characteristic of the political battles of the era. It had virtually no substantive foundation. Rhetorically, the Stalwarts favored traditional, professional machine politics while the Half-Breeds favored reform. In fact, neither group was much interested in political change; each simply wanted a larger share of the patronage pie. Hayes tried to satisfy both and ended up satisfying neither.

The battle over patronage overshadowed all else during Hayes's unhappy presidency. His one impor-

PRESIDENT AND MRS. RUTHERFORD B. HAYES
Hayes was one of a series of generally undistinguished late-nineteenth-century presidents whose subordination to the fiercely competitive party system left them with little room for independent leadership. This photograph captures the dignity and sobriety that Hayes and his wife sought to convey to the public. His wife was a temperance advocate and refused to serve alcoholic beverages in the White House, thereby earning the nickname "Lemonade Lucy." Hayes attracted less whimsical labels. Because of the disputed 1876 election that had elevated him to the presidency, critics referred to him throughout his term as "His Fraudulency." *(Library of Congress)*

tant substantive initiative—an effort to create a civil service system—attracted no support from either party. And his early announcement that he would not seek re-election only weakened him further. He had virtually no power in Congress. The Democrats controlled the House throughout his presidency, and the Senate during the last two years of his term. And Senate Republicans, led by Roscoe Conkling, opposed his efforts to defy the machines in making appointments. Hayes's presidency was a study in frustration.

The Republicans managed to retain the presidency in 1880, in part because they managed to agree on a ticket that made it possible for the Stalwarts and the Half-Breeds briefly to paper over their differences. After a long convention deadlock, they nominated a "dark horse," James A. Garfield, a veteran congressman from Ohio and a Half-Breed; to conciliate the Stalwarts, the convention gave the vice presidential nomination to Chester A. Arthur, a Conkling henchman. To oppose Garfield, the Democrats nominated General Winfield Scott Hancock, a minor Civil War commander with no national following. Garfield won a decisive electoral victory, but his popular vote margin was very thin. The Republicans also captured both houses of Congress.

Garfield began his presidency by trying to defy Conkling and the Stalwarts in his appointments and by showing support for civil service reform. He soon found himself embroiled in an ugly public quarrel with both Conkling and Thomas Platt, the other senator from New York and another important Stalwart leader. But before it could be resolved, Garfield was victimized by the spoils system in a more terrible sense. On July 2, 1881, only four months after his inauguration, Garfield was shot twice while standing in the Washington railroad station by an apparently deranged gunman (and unsuccessful office seeker) who shouted, "I am a Stalwart and Arthur is president now!" Garfield lingered for nearly three months and finally died, a victim as much of bungled medical treatment as of the wounds themselves.

Chester A. Arthur, who succeeded Garfield, had spent a political lifetime as a devoted, skilled, and open spoilsman and a close ally of Roscoe Conkling. But on becoming president, he tried—like Hayes and Garfield before him—to follow an independent course and even to promote reform. The terrible circumstances that had brought him to the presidency undoubtedly shaped his behavior. He realized that the Garfield assassination had to some degree discredited the traditional spoils system.

The "new" Arthur dismayed the party bosses. He kept most of Garfield's appointees in office. He also supported civil service reform, aware that the legislation was likely to pass whether he supported it or not. In 1883, finally, Congress passed the first national civil service measure, the Pendleton Act, which identified a limited number of federal jobs to be filled by competitive written examinations rather than by patronage. Relatively few offices fell under civil service at first, but its reach extended steadily so that by the mid-

twentieth century most federal employees were civil servants.

The Return of the Democrats

The unsavory election of 1884 was typical of national political contests in the late nineteenth century in its emphasis on personalities rather than policies. The Republicans repudiated Arthur (who was in any case already suffering from an illness that would kill him two years later) and chose instead their most popular and controversial figure, Senator James G. Blaine of Maine—known to his adoring admirers as "the plumed knight" but to thousands of other Americans as a symbol of seamy party politics. An independent reform faction, known derisively by their critics as the "mugwumps," announced they would bolt the party and support an honest Democrat. Rising to the bait, the Democrats nominated Grover Cleveland, the "reform" governor of New York. He differed from Blaine on no substantive issues but had acquired a reputation as an enemy of corruption.

In a campaign filled with personal invective, what may have decided the election was the last-minute introduction of a religious controversy. Shortly before the election, a delegation of Protestant ministers called on Blaine in New York City; their spokesman, Dr. Samuel Burchard, referred to the Democrats as the party of "rum, Romanism, and rebellion." Blaine was slow to repudiate Blanchard's indiscretion, and Democrats quickly spread the news that Blaine had tolerated a slander on the Catholic church. Cleveland's narrow victory may well have been a result of a heavy Catholic vote for the Democrats in New York. Cleveland won 219 electoral votes to Blaine's 182; his popular margin was only 23,000.

Grover Cleveland was respected, if not often liked, for his stern and righteous opposition to politicians, grafters, pressure groups, and Tammany Hall. He had become famous as the "veto governor," as an official who was not afraid to say no. He was the embodiment of an era in which few Americans believed the federal government could, or should, do very much. His administration was characterized from beginning to end by an unwavering commitment to economy in government. No one should forget, he explained, that "though the people support the Government, the Government should not support the people."

Cleveland did grapple with one major economic issue. He had always doubted the wisdom of protective tariffs. And he concluded finally that the existing high rates were responsible for the annual surplus in federal revenues, which was tempting Congress to pass

THE STATE, WAR, AND NAVY BUILDING
This sprawling Victorian office building was one of the largest in Washington when it was constructed shortly after the Civil War. It housed the State, War, and Navy Departments until not long before World War II. It suggests both the degree to which the federal government was growing in the late nineteenth century and, more importantly, the degree to which it remained a tiny entity compared to what it would later become. This building, which stands directly next door to the White House, today houses a part (but only a part) of the president's staff. *(Library of Congress)*

the "reckless" and "extravagant" legislation he so frequently vetoed. In December 1887, therefore, he asked Congress to reduce the tariff rates. Democrats in the House approved a tariff reduction, but Senate Republicans defiantly passed a bill of their own actually raising rates. The resulting deadlock made the tariff an issue in the election of 1888.

The Democrats renominated Cleveland and supported tariff reductions. The Republicans settled on former Senator Benjamin Harrison of Indiana, who was obscure but respectable (and the grandson of President William Henry Harrison); and they endorsed protection. The campaign was the first since the Civil War to involve a clear question of economic difference between the parties. It was also one of the most corrupt (and one of the closest) elections in American history. Harrison won an electoral majority of 233 to 168, but Cleveland's popular vote exceeded Harrison's by 100,000—making this one of only two presidential elections in American history (the other was 1876) in which the loser in the popular vote was the victor in the electoral college.

Tariffs, Trusts, and Railroads

Benjamin Harrison's record as president was little more substantial than that of his grandfather, who had died a month after taking office. One reason for Harrison's failure was the intellectual drabness of the members of his administration—beginning with the president himself and extending through his cabinet. Another was Harrison's unwillingness to make any effort to influence Congress. And yet during Harrison's dreary administration, public opinion was beginning to force the government to confront some of the pressing social and economic issues of the day. Most notably, perhaps, sentiment was rising in favor of legislation to curb the power of trusts.

By the mid-1880s, fifteen western and southern states had adopted laws prohibiting combinations that restrained competition. But corporations found it easy to escape limitations by incorporating in states such as New Jersey and Delaware that offered them special privileges. If antitrust legislation was to be effective, it would have to come from the national government.

THE TOURNAMENT OF TO-DAY.—A SET-TO BETWEEN LABOR AND MONOPOLY.

LABOR AND MONOPOLY

This 1883 cartoon appeared in *Puck,* a magazine popular for its satirical treatment of American politics. It expresses a common sentiment of the Populists and many others: that ordinary men and women (portrayed here by the pathetic figure of "labor" and by the grim members of the audience) were almost hopelessly overmatched by the power of corporate monopolies. The knight's shield, labeled "corruption of the legislature," and his spear, labeled "subsidized press," make clear that—in the view of the cartoonist at least—corporations had many allies in their effort to oppress workers. *(Culver)*

Responding to growing popular demands, both houses of Congress passed the Sherman Antitrust Act in July 1890, almost without dissent. Most members of Congress saw it as a largely symbolic measure to help deflect public criticism, not likely to have any real effect on corporate power.

For over a decade after its passage, the Sherman Act had virtually no impact. As of 1901, the Justice Department had instituted only fourteen suits under the law against business combinations and had obtained few convictions. It had used the law much more frequently against labor unions. The courts, meanwhile, weakened the bill considerably. In *United States* v. *E. C. Knight Co.* (1895), in which the government charged that a single trust controlled 98 percent of refined sugar manufacturing in the country, the Supreme Court rejected the government's case. The sugar trust was engaged in manufacturing, not in interstate commerce, the Court declared; and since Congress's authority to control interstate commerce was its only authority for regulating corporations, the trust, despite its obviously monopolistic characteristics, was not illegal.

A SENATE FOR REVENUE ONLY.

SHACKLED BY THE TARIFF
This 1894 cartoon by the political satirist Louis Dalrymple portrays an unhappy Uncle Sam bound hands and feet by the McKinley Tariff and by what tariff opponents considered a closely related evil—monopoly. Members of the Senate are portrayed as tools of the various industries and special interests protected by the tariff. The caption, "A Senate for Revenue Only," is a parody of the anti-tariff rallying cry, "A tariff for revenue only," meaning that duties should be designed only to raise money for the government, not to stop imports of particular goods to protect domestic industries. *(The Granger Collection)*

The Republicans were more interested, however, in the issue they believed had won them the 1888 election: the tariff. Representative William McKinley of Ohio and Senator Nelson W. Aldrich of Rhode Island drafted the highest protective measure ever proposed to Congress. Known as the McKinley Act, it became law in October 1890. But Republican leaders apparently misinterpreted public sentiment, for the party suffered a stunning reversal in the 1890 congressional election. Their substantial Senate majority in the Senate was slashed to 8; in the House, they retained only 88 of the 323 seats. McKinley himself was among those who went down to defeat. Nor were the Republicans able to recover in the course of the next two years. In the presidential election of 1892, Benjamin Harrison once again supported protection and Grover Cleveland, renominated by the Democrats, once again opposed it. Only a new third party, the People's Party, with James B. Weaver as its candidate, advocated any serious economic reform. (See p. 540.) Cleveland won 277 electoral votes to Harrison's 145 and had a popular margin of 380,000. Weaver ran far behind. For the first time since 1878, the Democrats won a majority of both houses of Congress.

The policies of Cleveland's second term were much like those of his first—devoted to minimal government and hostile to active state measures to deal with social or economic problems. But this time, a major economic crisis (see p. 545) created popular demands for a more active government. For the most part, Cleveland resisted those pressures.

Again, he supported a tariff reduction, which the House approved but the Senate gutted. Cleveland denounced the result but allowed it to become law as the Wilson-Gorman Tariff. The bill threw one small crumb to agrarian interests: a small federal income tax (2 percent of incomes over $4,000). But the Supreme Court declared it unconstitutional. Only after approval of the Sixteenth Amendment in 1913 was the federal government able to tax incomes. Public pressure was also growing in the 1880s for regulation of the railroads. Farm organizations in the Midwest (most notably the Grangers—see pp. 538–539) had persuaded several state legislatures to pass regulatory legislation in the early 1870s. But in 1886, the Supreme Court—in *Wabash, St. Louis, and Pacific Railway Co.* v. *Illinois,* known as the *Wabash* case)—ruled one of the Granger laws in Illinois unconstitutional, calling it an attempt to control interstate commerce that infringed on the exclusive power of Congress. Later, the Courts limited the powers of the states to regulate commerce even within their own boundaries.

Railroad regulation, it was now clear, could only come from the federal government. Congress grudgingly responded to public pressure in 1887 with the Interstate Commerce Act, which banned discrimination in rates between long and short hauls, required railroads to publish their rate schedules and file them with the government, and declared that all interstate rail rates must be "reasonable and just"—although the bill did not define what that meant. A five-person agency, the Interstate Commerce Commission (ICC), was to administer the act. But it had to rely on the courts to enforce its rulings. For almost twenty years after its passage, the Interstate Commerce Act—haphazardly enforced and narrowly interpreted by the courts—was without practical effect.

The controversies over the tariff, the trusts, and the railroads were signs that the dramatic changes in the American economy were creating problems that much of the public considered too important and dangerous to ignore. But the federal government's response to that agitation reflected the continuing weakness of the American state. The government still lacked institutions adequate to perform any significant role in American economic life. And not enough Americans had yet embraced a political ideology that would justify any major expansion of government responsibilities. The effort to create such institutions and to promote such an ideology would occupy much of American public life in the coming decades. Among the first signs of that effort was a dramatic dissident movement that shattered the political equilibrium the nation had experienced for the previous twenty years.

THE AGRARIAN REVOLT

No group watched the performance of the federal government in the 1880s with more dismay than American farmers. Isolated from the urban-industrial society that was beginning to dominate national life, suffering from a long economic decline, afflicted with a painful sense of obsolescence, rural Americans were keenly aware of the problems of the modern economy and particularly eager for government assistance in dealing with them. The result of their frustrations was the emergence of one of the most powerful movements of political protest in American history: what became known as Populism.

The Grangers

According to popular myth, American farmers were the most individualistic of citizens, the least likely to join together in a cooperative economic or political movement. In reality, however, farmers had been making efforts to organize for many decades. There had been occasional cooperative movements in the first decades of the nineteenth century, but the first major farm organization appeared in the 1860s: the Grange. It was less a movement of protest than a social and self-help association. The depression of 1873 turned it into an agency of political change.

"THE GRANGE AWAKENING THE SLEEPERS"
This 1873 cartoon suggests the way the Grange embraced many of the same concerns that the Farmers' Alliances and their People's Party later expressed. A farmer is attempting to arouse passive citizens (lying in place of the "sleepers," or cross ties on railroad tracks), who are about to be crushed by a train. The cars bear the names of the costs of the railroads' domination of the agrarian economy. *(Culver)*

The Grange had its origins shortly after the Civil War in a tour through the South by a minor Agriculture Department official, Oliver H. Kelley. Kelley was appalled by what he considered the isolation and drabness of rural life, and in 1867 he left the government and, with other department employees, founded the National Grange of the Patrons of Husbandry, to which he devoted years of labor as secretary and from which emerged a network of local organizations. At first, the Granges defined their purposes modestly. They attempted to bring farmers together to learn new scientific agricultural techniques—to keep farming "in step with the music of the age." The Granges also hoped to create a feeling of community, to relieve the loneliness of rural life. An elaborate system of initiation and ritual and a strict code of secrecy lent to the organization many of the trappings of urban fraternal organizations.

At first the Grange grew slowly. But when the depression of 1873 caused a major decline in farm prices, membership rapidly increased. By 1875, the Grange claimed over 800,000 members and 20,000 local lodges; it had chapters in almost every state but was strongest, naturally, in the great staple-producing regions of the South and the Midwest.

As membership grew, the lodges in the Midwest began to focus less on the social benefits of organization and more on the economic possibilities. They attempted to organize marketing cooperatives to allow farmers to circumvent the hated middlemen. And they urged cooperative political action to curb the monopolistic practices of the railroads and warehouses. Throughout the Midwest on Independence Day 1873, embittered farmers assembled to hear Granger orators read "The Farmers' Declaration of Independence," which proclaimed that the time had come for farmers, "suffering from long continued systems of oppression and abuse, to rouse themselves from an apathetic indifference to their own interests." The declaration also vowed that farmers would use "all lawful and peaceful means to free [themselves] from the tyranny of monopoly."

The Grangers set up cooperative stores, creameries, elevators, warehouses, insurance companies, and factories that produced machines, stoves, and other items. Some 400 enterprises were in operation at the height of the movement, and some of them forged lucrative relationships with existing businesses. One corporation emerged specifically to meet the needs of the Grangers: the first mail-order business, Montgomery Ward and Company, founded in 1872. Eventually, however, most of the Grange enterprises failed, both because of the inexperience of their operators and because of the opposition of the middlemen whose businesses they were challenging.

The Grangers also worked to elect state legislators pledged to their program. Usually they operated through the existing parties, although occasionally they ran candidates under such independent party labels as "Antimonopoly" and "Reform." At their peak, they managed to gain control of the legislatures in most of the midwestern states. Their purpose, openly and angrily announced, was to subject the railroads to government controls. The Granger laws of the early 1870s, by which many states imposed strict regulations on railroad rates and practices, seemed for a time to vindicate the predictions of those farmers who claimed that their new organization foretold a permanent change in the political status of agriculture. But the new regulations were soon destroyed by the courts. That defeat, combined with the political inexperience of many Grange leaders and above all the temporary return of agricultural prosperity in the late 1870s, produced a dramatic decline in the power of the association. Some of the Granger cooperatives survived as effective economic vehicles for many years, but the movement as a whole dwindled rapidly. By 1880, its membership had shrunk to 100,000.

The Alliances

The successor to the Granges as the leading vehicle of agrarian protest began to emerge even before the Granger movement had faded. As early as 1875, farmers in parts of the South (most notably in Texas) were banding together in so-called Farmers' Alliances. By 1880, the Southern Alliance had more than 4 million members; and a comparable Northwestern Alliance was taking root in the plains states and the Midwest and developing ties with its southern counterpart.

Like the Granges, the Alliances were principally concerned with local problems. They formed cooperatives and other marketing mechanisms. They established stores, banks, processing plants, and other facilities for their members—to free them from dependence on the hated "furnishing merchants" who kept so many farmers in debt. Some Alliance leaders, however, also saw the movement in larger terms: as an effort to build a society in which economic competition might give way to cooperation. They did not advocate rigid collectivism; instead, they argued for a sense of mutual, neighborly responsibility that would enable farmers to resist oppressive outside forces. Alliance lecturers traveled throughout rural areas lambasting the concentration of power in great corporations and financial institutions and promoting cooperation as an alternative economic system.

The Alliances were notable, too, for the prominent role women played within them. From the beginning, women were full voting members in most local Alliances. Many held offices and served as lecturers. A few, most notably Mary E. Lease, went on to become fiery populist orators. (Lease was famous for urging farmers to "raise less corn and more hell.") Most others emphasized issues of particular concern to women, especially temperance. Like women in urban areas concerned about the impact of drinking on family life, agrarian women argued that sobriety was a key to stability in rural society.

Although the Alliances quickly became far more widespread than the Granges had ever been, they suffered from similar problems. Their cooperatives did not always work well, partly because the market forces operating against them were sometimes too strong to be overcome, partly because the cooperatives themselves were often mismanaged. These economic frustrations helped push the movement into a new phase at the end of the 1880s: the creation of a national political organization.

A Populist Gathering

Populism was a response to real economic and political grievances. But like most political movements of its time, it was also important as a cultural experience. For farmers in sparsely settled regions in particular, it provided an antidote to isolation and loneliness. This gathering of Populist farmers in Dickinson County, Kansas, suggests how the political purposes of the movement were tightly bound up with its social purposes. *(Kansas State Historical Society)*

In 1889, the Southern and Northwestern Alliances, despite continuing differences between them, agreed to a loose merger. The next year the Alliances held a national convention at Ocala, Florida, and issued the so-called Ocala Demands, which were, in effect, a party platform. In the 1890 off-year elections, candidates supported by the Alliances won partial or complete control of the legislatures in twelve states. They also won six governorships, three seats in the U.S. Senate, and approximately fifty in the U.S. House of Representatives. Many of the successful Alliance candidates were simply Democrats who had benefited—often passively—from Alliance endorsements. But dissident farmers drew enough encouragement from the results to contemplate further political action, including forming a party of their own.

Sentiment for a third party was strongest among the members of the Northwestern Alliance. But several southern leaders supported the ideas as well—among them Tom Watson of Georgia, the only Southern congressman elected in 1890 openly to identify with the Alliance, and Leonidas L. Polk of North Carolina, per-

haps the ablest mind in the movement. Alliance leaders discussed plans for a third party at meetings in Cincinnati in May 1891 and St. Louis in February 1892—meetings attended by many Northern Alliance members, a smaller but still significant number of Southern Alliance leaders, and representatives of the fading Knights of Labor, whom some farm leaders hoped to bring into the coalition. Then, in July 1892, 1,300 exultant delegates poured into Omaha, Nebraska, to proclaim the creation of the new party, approve an official set of principles, and nominate candidates for the presidency and vice presidency. The new organization's official name was the People's Party, but the movement was more commonly referred to as Populism.

The election of 1892 demonstrated the potential power of the new movement. The Populist presidential candidate—James B. Weaver of Iowa, a former Greenbacker who received the nomination after the death of Leonidas Polk, the early favorite—polled more than 1 million votes, 8.5 percent of the total, and carried six mountain and plains states for 22 electoral votes. Nearly

POPULISM AND THE NEW DAWN
In 1892, when the People's Party ran its first candidate for president, many reformers throughout the United States welcomed it as a healthy challenge to the stale thinking within the two major parties. Later, as conservative opponents began portraying the Populists as ignorant "hayseeds" or dangerous revolutionaries, optimistic images like these became increasingly rare. James B. Weaver, portrayed here standing beside a lion, received 8 percent of the vote in 1892 and 22 electoral votes. *(Kansas State Historical Society)*

1,500 Populist candidates won election to seats in state legislatures. The party elected three governors, five senators, and ten congressmen. It could also claim the support of many Republicans and Democrats in Congress who had been elected by appealing to populist sentiment.

The Populist Constituency

The Populists dreamed of creating a broad political coalition that included many groups. But Populism always appealed principally to farmers, and particularly to small farmers with little long-range economic security—people whose operations were only minimally mechanized, if at all, who relied on one crop, and who had access only to limited and unsatisfactory mechanisms of credit. In the Midwest, the Populists were usually family farmers struggling to hold on to their land (or to get it back if they had lost it). In the South, there were many modest landowners too, but in addition there were significant numbers of sharecroppers and tenant farmers. Whatever their differences, however, most Populists had at least one thing in common: they were engaged in a type of farming that was becoming less viable in the face of new, mechanized, diversified, and consolidated commercial agriculture.

There is evidence, too, that Populists tended to be not only economically but culturally marginal, that the movement appealed above all to geographically isolated farmers who felt cut off from the mainstream of national life and resented their isolation. Populism gave such people an outlet for their grievances; it also provided them with a social experience, a sense of belonging to a community that they had previously lacked.

But the Populists were also notable for the groups they failed to attract. There were energetic efforts to include labor within the coalition. Representatives of the Knights of Labor attended early organizational meetings; the new party added a labor plank to its platform—calling for shorter hours for workers and restrictions on immigration, and denouncing the use of private detective agencies as strikebreakers in labor disputes. On the whole, however, Populism never attracted significant labor support in part because the economic interests of labor and the interests of farmers were often at odds.

One exception was the Rocky Mountain states, where the Populists did have some significant success in attracting miners to their cause. They did so partly because local Populist leaders supported a broader platform than the national party embraced. In particular, they endorsed a demand that the national party only later accepted: "free silver," the idea of permitting silver to become, along with gold, the basis of the currency so as to expand the money supply. In Colorado, Idaho, Nevada, and other areas of the Far West where silver mining was an important activity, the Populist constituency contained more working-class people and more immigrants than it did elsewhere; and the People's Party enjoyed substantial, if temporary, success there.

In the South (and to a lesser degree elsewhere), white Populists struggled with the question of accepting African Americans into the party. Their numbers and poverty made black farmers possibly valuable allies. And indeed there was an important black component to the movement—a network of "Colored Alliances" that by 1890 numbered over one and a quarter million members. But most white Populists were willing to accept the assistance of African Americans only as long as it was clear that whites would remain indisputably in control. When southern conservatives began to attack the Populists for undermining white supremacy, the interracial character of the movement quickly faded.

Most of the Populist leaders were members of the rural middle class: professional people, editors and lawyers, or longtime politicians and agitators. Few were

WHERE HISTORIANS DISAGREE

POPULISM

AMERICAN HISTORY OFFERS FEW examples of successful popular movements operating outside the two major parties. Perhaps that is why Populism, which in its brief, meteoric life became one of the few such phenomena to gain real national influence, has attracted particular attention from historians. It has also produced deep disagreements among them. Scholars have differed in many ways in their interpretations of Populism, but at the heart of most such disagreements have been disparate views of the value of popular, insurgent politics. Some historians have harbored a basic mistrust of such mass uprisings and have therefore viewed the Populists with suspicion and hostility. Others have viewed such insurgency approvingly, as evidence of a healthy resistance to oppression and exploitation; and to them, the Populists have appeared as essentially admirable, democratic activists.

This latter view was the basis of the first, and for many years the only, general history of Populism: John D. Hicks's *The Populist Revolt* (1931). Rejecting the then-prevailing view of the Populists as misguided and unruly radicals, Hicks described them as people reacting rationally and progressively to economic misfortune. Hicks was writing in an era in which the ideas of Frederick Jackson Turner were dominating historical studies, and he brought to his analysis of Populism a strong emphasis on regionalism. Populists, he argued, were part of the democratic West, resisting the pressures from the more aristocratic East. (He explained southern Populism by describing the South as an "economic frontier" region—not newly settled like the West, but prey to many of the same pressures and misfortunes.) The Populists, Hicks suggested, were aware of the harsh, even brutal, impact of eastern industrial growth on rural society. They were proposing reforms that would limit the oppressive power of the new financial titans and restore a measure of control to the farmers. Populism was, he wrote, "the last phase of a long and perhaps a losing struggle—the struggle to save agricultural America from the devouring jaws of industrial America." A losing struggle, perhaps, but not a vain one; for many of the reforms the Populists advocated, Hicks implied, became the basis of later progressive legislation.

This generally approving view of Populism prevailed among historians for more than two decades. But in the early 1950s—when the memory of European fascism and uneasiness about contemporary communism combined to create a general hostility among scholars toward mass popular politics—a harsh new view of the Populist movement appeared in a work by one of the nation's leading historians. Richard Hofstadter, in *The Age of Reform* (1955), admitted that Populism embraced some progressive ideas and advocated some sensible reforms. But the bulk of his effort was devoted to exposing both the "soft" and the "dark" sides of the movement. Populism was "soft," he claimed, because it rested on a nostalgic and unrealistic myth, because it romanticized the nation's agrarian past and refused to confront the realities of modern life. Farmers were, he argued, themselves fully committed to the values of the capitalist system they claimed to abhor. And Populism was "dark," he argued, because it was permeated with bigotry and ignorance. Populists, he claimed, revealed anti-Semitic tendencies, and they displayed animosity toward intellectuals, easterns, and urbanites as well.

Almost immediately, historians more favorably disposed toward mass politics in general,

themselves marginal farmers. Almost all leaders were, like most of their constituents, Protestants. But beyond these basic characteristics there were wide variations. Some Populist leaders were somber, serious theoreticians; others were semihysterical rabble-rousers. In the South, in particular, Populism produced the first generation of what was to become a distinctive and enduring political breed—the "southern demagogue." Tom Watson in Georgia, Jeff Davis in Arkansas, and others attracted widespread popular support by arousing the resentment of poor southerners against the entrenched Bourbon aristocracy.

and Populism in particular, began to challenge what became known as the "Hofstadter thesis." Norman Pollack argued in a 1962 study, *The Populist Response to Industrial America,* and in a number of articles that the agrarian revolt had rested not on nostalgic, romantic concepts but on a sophisticated, farsighted, and even radical vision of reform—one that recognized, and even welcomed, the realities of an industrial economy, but that sought to make that economy more equitable and democratic by challenging many of the premises of capitalism. Walter T. K. Nugent, in *Tolerant Populists* (1963), argued—as his title implies—that the Populists in Kansas were far from bigoted, that they not only tolerated but welcomed Jews and other minorities into their party, and that they offered a practical, sensible program.

Not until 1976, however, did a comprehensive study of Populism emerge that could rival Hicks and Hofstadter in influence. Lawrence Goodwyn, in *Democratic Promise* (and in an abridged version of the same work, *The Populist Moment,* published in 1978), described the Populists as members of a "cooperative crusade," battling against the "coercive potential of the emerging corporate state." Populists were more than the nostalgic bigots Hofstadter described, more even than the progressive reformers portrayed by Hicks. They offered a vision of truly radical change, widely disseminated through what Goodwyn called a "movement culture." They advocated an intelligent, and above all a democratic, alternative to the inequities of modern capitalism.

At the same time that historians were debating the question of what Populism meant, they were also arguing over who the Populists were. Hicks, Hofstadter, and Goodwyn disagreed on many things, but they shared a general view of the Populists as victims of economic distress—usually one-crop farmers in economically marginal agricultural regions victimized by drought and debt. Other scholars, however, have suggested that the problem of identifying the Populists is more complex. Sheldon Hackney, in *Populism to Progressivism in Alabama* (1969), argued that the Populists were not only economically troubled but socially rootless, "only tenuously connected to society by economic function, by personal relationships, by stable community membership, by political participation, or by psychological identification with the South's distinctive myths." Peter Argersinger, Stanley Parsons, James Turner, and others have similarly suggested that Populists were characterized by a form of social and even geographical isolation. Steven Hahn's 1983 study *The Roots of Southern Populism* identifies poor white farmers in the "upcountry" as the core of Populist activity in Georgia; and he argues that they were reacting not simply to the psychic distress of being "left behind," but also to a real economic threat to their way of life—to the encroachments of a new commercial order of which they had never been and could never be a part.

Finally, there has been continuing debate over the legacy of Populism. Historians and politicians alike have argued repeatedly that a populist tradition has survived throughout the twentieth century, influencing movements as disparate as those led by Huey Long in the 1930s, George Wallace in the 1960s, and Ross Perot in the 1990s. Others have maintained that the term "populism" has been used (and misused) so widely as to have become virtually meaningless, that its only real value is in reference to the agrarian insurgents of the 1890s, who first gave meaning to the word.

There were similarly flamboyant leaders in the Midwest: "Sockless" Jerry Simpson of Kansas, for example, and Ignatius Donnelly of Minnesota. Donnelly, in particular, seemed to exemplify the divided character of the movement: sincere idealism combined with crassness and opportunism. A committed, principled man who spoke eloquently on behalf of populist ideals and appeared sincerely to believe in them, Donnelly was also at times something of a charlatan. As a member of Congress, he compiled a shabby legislative record marked, among other things, by a series of seamy, secret deals with railroad companies.

TAKING ARMS AGAINST THE POPULISTS
Kansas was a Populist stronghold in the 1890s, but the new party faced powerful challenges. In 1893 state Republicans disputed an election that the Populists believed had given them control of the legislature. When the Populists occupied the statehouse, Republicans armed themselves, drove out the Populists, and seized control of the state government. Republican members of the legislature pose here with their weapons in a photograph perhaps intended as a warning to any Populists inclined to challenge them. *(Kansas State Historical Society)*

Populist Ideas

The reform program of the Populists was spelled out first in the Ocala Demands of 1890 and then, even more clearly, in the Omaha platform of 1892. It proposed a system of "subtreasuries," which would replace and strengthen the cooperatives with which both the Grangers and Alliances had been experimenting for years. The government would establish a network of warehouses, where farmers could deposit their crops. Using those crops as collateral, growers could then borrow money from the government at low rates of interest and wait for the price of their goods to go up before selling them. In addition, the Populists called for the abolition of national banks, which they believed were dangerous institutions of concentrated power; the end of absentee ownership of land; the direct election of United States senators (which would weaken the power of conservative state legislatures); and

other devices to improve the ability of the people to influence the political process. They called as well for regulation and (after 1892) government ownership of railroads, telephones, and telegraphs. And they demanded a system of government-operated postal savings banks, a graduated income tax, and the inflation of the currency. Eventually, the party as a whole embraced (with varying degrees of enthusiasm) the demand of its western members for the remonetization of silver.

Some Populists were openly anti-Semitic, pointing to the Jews as leaders of the obscure financial forces attempting to enslave them. Others were anti-intellectual, anti-eastern, and anti-urban. A few of the leading Populists gave an impression of personal failure, brilliant instability, and brooding communion with mystic forces. Ignatius Donnelly, for example, wrote one book locating the lost isle of Atlantis, another claiming that Bacon had written Shakespeare's plays, and still another—*Caesar's Column* (1891)—embodying an almost lunatic vision of bloody revolution and the creation of a populist utopia. Tom Watson, once a champion of interracial harmony, ended his career baiting blacks and Jews.

Yet the occasional bigotry of some Populists should not be allowed to dominate the image of Populism as a whole, which was a serious and usually responsible effort to find solutions to real problems. Populists emphatically rejected the laissez-faire orthodoxies of their time, the idea that the rights of ownership are absolute. They raised one of the most overt and powerful challenges of the era to the direction in which American industrial capitalism was moving. Populism was not a challenge to industrialization or to capitalism itself, but a response to what the Populists considered the brutal and chaotic way in which the economy was developing. Progress and growth should continue, they urged, but it should be more strictly defined by the needs of individuals and communities.

THE CRISIS OF THE 1890S

The agrarian protest was only one of many indications of the national political crisis emerging in the 1890s. There was a severe depression, which began in 1893. There was widespread labor unrest and violence, culminating in the tumultuous strikes of 1894. There was the continuing failure of either major party to respond to the growing distress. And there was the rigid conservatism of Grover Cleveland, who took office for the second time just at the moment that the economy collapsed. Out of this growing sense of crisis came some of the most heated political battles in American history, culminating in the dramatic campaign of 1896, on which, many Americans came to believe, the future of the nation hung.

The Panic of 1893

The Panic of 1893 precipitated the most severe depression the nation had yet experienced. It began in March 1893, when the Philadelphia and Reading Railroad, unable to meet payments on loans it had secured from British banks, declared bankruptcy. Two months later, the National Cordage Company (a new corporation that was trying unsuccessfully to establish itself as the dominant force in its industry) failed as well. Together, the two corporate failures triggered a collapse of the stock market. And since many of the major New York banks were heavy investors in the market, a wave of

THE PANIC OF 1893
The floor of the New York stock exchange was a scene of pandemonium on May 5, 1893, when a collapse in stock prices helped usher in the devastating depression of the 1890s. The artist Charles Broughton made sketches of the scene on the spot and later used them as the basis of this drawing. *(Bettmann)*

bank failures soon began. That caused a contraction of credit, which meant that many of the new, aggressive businesses that had recently begun operations soon went bankrupt because they were unable to secure the loans they needed.

There were other, longer-range causes of the financial collapse. Depressed prices in agriculture since 1887 had weakened the purchasing power of farmers, the largest group in the population. Depression conditions that had begun earlier in Europe were resulting in a loss of American markets abroad and a withdrawal by foreign investors of gold invested in the United States. Railroads and other major industries had expanded too rapidly, well beyond market demand. The depression reflected, too, the degree to which the American economy was now interconnected, the degree to which failures in one area affected all other areas. And the depression showed how dependent the economy was on the health of the railroads, which remained the nation's most powerful corporate and financial institutions. When the railroads suffered, as they did beginning in 1893, everything suffered.

Once the panic began, its effects spread with startling speed. Within six months, more than 8,000 businesses, 156 railroads, and 400 banks failed. Already-low agricultural prices tumbled further. Up to 1 million workers, 20 percent of the labor force, lost their jobs—the highest level of unemployment in American history to that point, a level comparable to that of the Great Depression of the 1930s. The leading financial newspaper of the time declared in the summer of 1893: "The month of August will long remain memorable in our industrial history. Never before has there been such a sudden and striking cessation of industrial activity. Nor is any section of the country exempt from the paralysis." The depression was unprecedented not only in its severity but also in its persistence. Although there was slight improvement beginning in 1895, prosperity did not fully return until 1901.

The suffering the depression caused naturally produced social unrest, not least among the enormous numbers of unemployed workers. In 1894, Jacob S. Coxey, an Ohio businessman and Populist, began advocating a massive public works program to create jobs for the unemployed and an inflation of the currency. When it became clear that his proposals were making no progress in Congress, Coxey announced that he would "send a petition to Washington with boots on"—a march of the unemployed to the capital to present their demands to the government. "Coxey's Army," as it was known, numbered only about 500 when it reached Washington, after having marched on foot from Masillon, Ohio. Armed police barred them from the Capitol and arrested Coxey (who was later convicted—of walking on the grass). He and his followers were herded into camps because their presence supposedly endangered public health. Congress took no action on their demands.

There were many signs of union unrest as well during the decade—the Homestead and Pullman strikes, for example. (See above, pp. 497–498.) To many middle-class Americans, the labor turmoil was a sign of a dangerous instability, even perhaps a revolution. La-

bor radicalism—some of it real, much of it imagined by the frightened middle class—was of persistent concern to much of the public, heightening the general sense of crisis.

The Silver Question

The financial panic weakened the government's monetary system. President Cleveland was one of many people who believed that the instability of the currency was the primary cause of the depression. The "money question," therefore, became the basis for some of the most dramatic political conflicts of the era.

The currency issue is a complicated and confusing one, and later generations have often had difficulty understanding the enormous passions the controversy aroused. The heart of the debate was over what would form the basis of the dollar, what would lie behind it and give it value. Today, the value of the dollar rests on little more than public confidence in the government. But in the nineteenth century, currency was assumed to be worthless if there was not something concrete behind it—precious metal (specie), which holders of paper money could collect if they presented their currency to a bank or to the Treasury.

During most of its existence as a nation, the United States had recognized two metals—gold and silver—as a basis for the dollar, a situation known as "bimetallism." In the 1870s, however, that had changed. The official ratio of the value of silver to the value of gold for purposes of creating currency (the "mint ratio") was 16 to 1: sixteen ounces of silver equaled one ounce of gold. But the actual commercial value of silver (the "market ratio") was much higher than that. Owners of silver could get more by selling it for manufacture into jewelry and other objects than they could by taking it to the mint for conversion to coins. So they stopped taking it to the mint, and the mint stopped coining silver.

In 1873, Congress passed a law that seemed simply to recognize the existing situation by officially discontinuing silver coinage. Few objected at the time. But in the course of the 1870s, the market value of silver fell well below the official mint ratio of 16 to 1. (Sixteen ounces of silver, in other words, were now worth *less*, not more, than one ounce of gold.) Silver was available for coinage again. Congress had foreclosed a potential method of expanding the currency. Before long, many Americans concluded that a conspiracy of big bankers had been responsible for the "demonetization" of silver and referred to the law as the "Crime of '73."

Two groups of Americans were especially determined to undo the "Crime of '73." One consisted of the silver-mine owners, now understandably eager to have the government take their surplus silver and pay them much more than the market price. The other group consisted of discontented farmers, who wanted an increase in the quantity of money—an inflation of the currency—as a means of raising the prices of farm products and easing payment of the farmers' debts. The inflationists demanded that the government return at once to "free silver"—that is, to the "free and unlimited coinage of silver" at the old ratio of 16 to 1. But by the time the depression began in 1893, Congress had made no more than a token response to their demands.

At the same time, the nation's gold reserves were steadily dropping. And the panic of 1893 intensified the demands on those reserves. President Cleveland believed that the chief cause of the weakening gold reserves was the Sherman Silver Purchase Act of 1893, which had required the government to purchase (but not to coin) silver, and to pay for it in gold. Early in his second administration, therefore, a special session responded to his request and repealed the Sherman Act—although only after a bitter and divisive battle that helped create a permanent split in the Democratic Party. The president's gold policy had aligned the southern and western Democrats in a solid phalanx against him and his eastern followers.

By now, both sides had invested the currency question with great symbolic and emotional importance. Indeed, the issue aroused passions rarely seen in American politics, culminating in the tumultuous presidential election of 1896. Supporters of the gold standard considered its survival essential to the honor and stability of the nation. Supporters of free silver considered the gold standard an instrument of tyranny. "Free silver" became to them a symbol of liberation. Silver would be a "people's money," as opposed to gold, the money of oppression and exploitation. It would eliminate the indebtedness of farmers and of whole regions of the country. A graphic illustration of the popularity of the silver issue was the enormous success of William H. Harvey's *Coin's Financial School*, published in 1894, which became one of the great best sellers of its age. The fictional Professor Coin ran an imaginary school specializing in finance, and the book consisted of his lectures and his dialogues with his students. The professor's brilliant discourses left even his most vehement opponents dazzled as he persuaded his listeners, with simple logic, of the almost miraculous restorative qualities of free silver: "It means the reopening of closed factories,

the relighting of fires in darkened furnaces; it means hope instead of despair; comfort in place of suffering; life instead of death."

"A Cross of Gold"

Most Populists did not pay much attention to the silver issue at first. But as the party developed strength, the money question became more important to its leaders. The Populists desperately needed funds to finance their campaigns. Silver-mine owners were willing to provide them but insisted on an elevation of the currency plank. And the Populists needed to form alliances with other political groups. The "money question" seemed a way to win the support of many people not engaged in farming but nevertheless starved for currency.

As the election of 1896 approached, Republicans, watching the failure of Cleveland and the Democrats to deal effectively with the depression, were confident of success. Party leaders, led by the Ohio boss Marcus A. Hanna, settled on Governor William McKinley of Ohio, author of the 1890 tariff act, as the party's presidential candidate. The Republican platform opposed the free coinage of silver except by agreement with the leading commercial nations (which everyone realized was unlikely). Thirty-four delegates from the mountain and plains states walked out in protest and joined the Democratic Party.

The Democratic convention of 1896 was the scene of unusual drama. Southern and western delegates, eager to fight off the challenge of the People's Party, were determined to seize control of the party from conservative easterners and incorporate some Populist demands—among them free silver—into the Democratic platform. They wanted as well to nominate a pro-silver candidate. The divided platform committee presented two reports to the convention. The majority report, the work of westerners and southerners, called for tariff reduction, an income tax, "stricter control" of trusts and railroads, and—most prominently—free silver. The minority report, the product of the party's eastern wing, echoed the Republican platform by opposing the free coinage of silver except by international agreement. The debate over the two competing platforms dominated the convention.

Defenders of the gold standard seemed to dominate the debate, until the final speech. Then William Jennings Bryan, a handsome, thirty-six-year-old congressman from Nebraska already well known as an effective orator, mounted the podium to address the convention. His great voice echoed through the hall as he delivered what became one of the most famous political speeches in American history in support of free silver. The closing passage sent his audience into something close to a frenzy: "If they dare to come out in the open and defend the gold standard as a good thing, we will fight them to the uttermost. Having behind us the producing masses of this nation and the world, supported by the commercial interests, the laboring interests and the toilers everywhere, we will answer their demand for a gold standard by saying to them: 'You shall not press down upon the brow of labor this crown of thorns; you shall not crucify mankind upon a cross of gold.'" It became known as the "Cross of Gold" speech.

The convention voted to adopt the pro-silver platform. Perhaps more important, the agrarians had found a leader. And the following day, Bryan (as he had eagerly and not entirely secretly hoped) was nominated for president on the fifth ballot. He was, and remains, the youngest person ever nominated for president by a major party. Republican and conservative Democrats attacked Bryan as a dangerous demagogue. But his many admirers hailed him as the Great Com-

moner. Born in Illinois of typical middle-class stock, he had attended a small sectarian college, had practiced law with only average success, and then, repeating a normal American pattern, had moved to Nebraska, a frontier area, in search of opportunity. He served as a potent symbol of rural, Protestant, middle-class America.

The choice of Bryan and the nature of the Democratic platform created a quandary for the Populists. They had expected both major parties to adopt conservative programs and nominate conservative candidates, leaving the Populists to represent the growing forces of protest. But now the Democrats had stolen much of their thunder. The Populists faced the choice of naming their own candidate and splitting the protest vote or endorsing Bryan and losing their identity as a party. By now, the Populists had embraced the free-silver cause, but somewhat reluctantly. Most Populists still believed that other issues were more important. Many argued that "fusion" with the Democrats—who had endorsed free silver but ignored most of the other Populist demands—would destroy their party. But the majority concluded that there was no viable alternative. Amid considerable acrimony, the convention voted to support Bryan.

The Conservative Victory

The campaign of 1896 produced desperation among conservatives. The business and financial community, frightened beyond reason at the prospect of a Bryan victory, contributed lavishly to the Republican campaign, which may have spent as much as $7 million, as compared to the Democrats' $300,000. From his home at Canton, Ohio, McKinley conducted a dignified "front-porch" campaign before pilgrimages of the Republican faithful, organized and paid for by Hanna.

Bryan showed no such restraint. He became the first presidential candidate in American history to stump every section of the country systematically, to appear in villages and hamlets, indeed the first to say frankly to the voters that he wanted to be president. He traveled 18,000 miles and addressed an estimated 5 million people. But Bryan may have done himself more harm than good. His revivalistic, camp-meeting style pleased old-stock Protestants, but it antagonized many of the immigrant Catholics and other ethnics who normally voted Democratic. By violating a longstanding tradition by which presidential candidates remained aloof from their own campaigns (the tradition by which they "stood" for office rather than "running" for it), Bryan helped establish the modern form of presidential politics. But he also antagonized many voters, who considered his campaign undignified.

On election day, McKinley polled 271 electoral votes to Bryan's 176 and received 51.1 percent of the popular vote to Bryan's 47.7. Bryan carried only those areas of the South and West where miners or struggling staple farmers predominated. The Democratic program, like that of the Populists, had been too narrow to win a national election.

For the Populists and their allies, the election results were a disaster. They had gambled everything on their "fusion" with the Democratic Party and lost. Within months of the election, the People's Party began to dissolve. Never again would American farmers unite so militantly to demand economic reform. And never again would so large a group of Americans raise so forceful a protest against the nature of the industrial economy.

McKinley and Recovery

The administration of William McKinley, which began in the aftermath of turmoil, saw a return to relative calm. One reason was the exhaustion of dissent. By

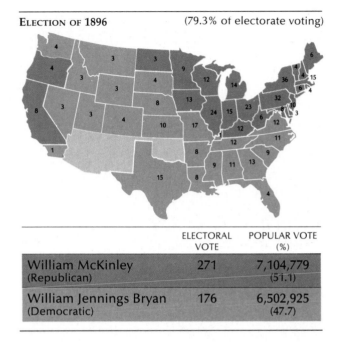

ELECTION OF 1896		(79.3% of electorate voting)

	ELECTORAL VOTE	POPULAR VOTE (%)
William McKinley (Republican)	271	7,104,779 (51.1)
William Jennings Bryan (Democratic)	176	6,502,925 (47.7)

1897, when McKinley took office, the labor unrest that had so frightened many middle-class Americans and so excited working-class people had subsided. With the simultaneous decline of agrarian protest, the greatest destabilizing forces in the nation's politics were—temporarily at least—in retreat. Another reason was the character of the McKinley administration itself, which was politically shrewd and committed to a reassuring stability. Most important, however, was the gradual easing of the economic crisis, a change that undercut many of those who were agitating for change.

McKinley and his allies committed themselves fully to only one issue, one on which they knew virtually all Republicans agreed: the need for higher tariff rates. Within weeks of his inauguration, the administration won approval of the Dingley Tariff, raising the duties to the highest point in American history. The administration dealt more gingerly with the explosive silver question (an issue that McKinley himself had never considered very important in any case). McKinley sent a commission to Europe to explore the possibility of a silver agreement with Great Britain and France. As he and everyone else anticipated, the effort produced no agreement. The Republicans then enacted the Currency, or Gold Standard, Act of 1900, which confirmed the nation's commitment to the gold standard.

And so the "battle of the standards" ended in victory for the forces of conservatism. Economic developments at the time seemed to vindicate the Republi-

SIGNIFICANT EVENTS

1867 National Grange founded	McKinley Tariff enacted
1873 Congress discontinues coinage of silver	Southern and Northwestern Alliances hold national convention at Ocala, Florida
1875 First Farmers' Alliances form in Texas	**1892** Cleveland elected president again
1877 *Munn* v. *Illinois* upholds Granger Laws regulating railroads	People's Party formed in Omaha
1880 James A. Garfield elected president	**1893** Commercial and financial panic launches severe and prolonged depression
1881 Garfield assassinated	Congress repeals Sherman Silver Purchase Act
Chester A. Arthur succeeds him	**1894** Wilson-Gorman Tariff enacted
1883 Congress passes Pendleton Act, first national civil service law	Coxey's Army marches on Washington
	William Harvey publishes *Coin's Financial School*
1884 Grover Cleveland elected president	**1895** *United States* v. *E. C. Knight Co.* weakens Sherman Antitrust Act
1886 Supreme Court in *Wabash* case restricts state regulation of commerce	**1896** William Jennings Bryan wins Democratic nomination after "Cross of Gold" speech at convention
1887 Interstate Commerce Act passed	Populists endorse Bryan for president
Farm prices collapse	William McKinley elected president
1888 Benjamin Harrison elected president	**1898** Economy begins to revive
1890 Sherman Antitrust Act passed	**1900** Gold Standard Act passed
Sherman Silver Purchase Act passed	

cans. Prosperity began to return in 1898. Foreign crop failures sent farm prices surging upward, and American business entered another cycle of expansion. Prosperity and the gold standard, it seemed, were closely allied.

But while the free-silver movement had failed, it had raised an important question for the American economy. In the quarter century before 1900, the countries of the Western world had experienced a spectacular growth in productive facilities and population. Yet the supply of money had not kept pace with economic progress, because the supply was tied to gold and the amount of gold had remained practically constant. Had it not been for a dramatic increase in the gold supply in the late 1890s (a result of new techniques for extracting gold from low-content ores and the discovery of huge new gold deposits in Alaska, South Africa, and Australia), populist predictions of financial disaster might in fact have proved correct. In 1898, two and a half times as much gold was produced as in 1890, and the currency supply was soon inflated far beyond anything Bryan and the free-silver forces had anticipated.

By then, however, Bryan—like many other Americans—was becoming engaged with another major issue: a growing United States presence in world affairs and the possibility of America becoming an imperialist nation.

SUGGESTED READINGS

General Histories. Sean Dennis Cashman, *America and the Gilded Age* (1984). Carl N. Degler, *The Age of the Economic Revolution, 1876–1900,* 2nd. ed. (1977). John H. Dobson, *Politics in the Gilded Age* (1972). Harold U. Faulkner, *Politics, Reform, and Expansion* (1959). John A. Garraty, *The New Commonwealth* (1969). Samuel P. Hays, *The Response to Industrialism, 1885–1914* (1957). Nell Irvin Painter, *Standing at Armageddon: The United States, 1877–1919* (1987). Alan Trachtenberg, *The Intercorporation of America: Culture and Society in the Gilded Age* (1982). Robert Wiebe, *The Search for Order, 1877–1920* (1967). R. Hal Williams, *Years of Decision: American Politics in the 1890s* (1978).

Politics, Reform, and the States. Geoffrey Blodgett, *The Gentle Reformers* (1966). Ruth Bourdin, *Women and Temperance: The Quest for Power and Liberty, 1873–1900* (1980). James Bryce, *The American Commonwealth,* 2 vols. (1888). Ari Hoogenboom, *Outlawing the Spoils: The Civil Service Movement* (1961). Richard Jensen, *The Winning of the Midwest: Social and Political Conflict, 1888–1896* (1971). Matthew Josephson, *The Politicos* (1963). Morton Keller, *Affairs of State* (1977). Paul Kleppner, *The Cross of Culture: A Social Analysis of Midwestern Politics, 1850–1900* (1970); *The Third Electoral System, 1853–1892* (1979). J. Morgan Kousser, *The Shaping of Southern Politics: Suffrage Restriction and the Establishment of the One-Party South, 1880–1910* (1974). Michael P. Malone, *The Battle for Butte: Mining and Politics on the Northern Frontier, 1864–1906* (1981). Robert D. Marcus, *Grand Old Party* (1971). Gerald W. McFarland, *Mugwumps, Morals, and Politics, 1884–1920* (1975). Michael E. McGerr, *The Decline of Popular Politics* (1986). H. Wayne Morgan, *From Hayes to McKinley* (1969). Walter T. K. Nugent, *Money and American Society, 1865–1880* (1968). David J. Rothman, *Politics and Power: The United States Senate, 1869–1901* (1966). Martin J. Sklar, *The Corporate Reconstruction of American Capitalism, 1890–1916* (1988). Stephen Skowronek, *Building a New American State: The Expansion of National Administrative Capacities, 1877–1920* (1982). John Sproat, *"The Best Men": Liberal Reformers in the Gilded Age* (1968). Tom E. Terrill, *The Tariff, Politics, and American Foreign Policy, 1874–1901* (1973). Irwin Unger, *The Greenback Era* (1964). Leonard D. White, *The Republican Era* (1958).

Party Leaders. Harry Barnard, *Rutherford B. Hayes and His America* (1954). Herbert Croly, *Marcus Alonzo Hanna* (1912). Kenneth Davison, *The Presidency of Rutherford B. Hayes* (1972). Lewis L. Gould, *The Presidency of William McKinley* (1981). David Jordan, *Roscoe Conkling of New York* (1971). Margaret Leech, *In the Days of McKinley* (1959). Margaret Leech and Harry J. Brown, *The Garfield Orbit* (1978). Horace Samuel Merrill, *Bourbon Leader: Grover Cleveland and the Democratic Party* (1957). H. Wayne Morgan, *William McKinley and His America* (1963). Allan Nevins, *Grover Cleveland: A Study in Courage* (1933). Allan Peskin, *Garfield* (1978). Thomas C. Reeves, *Gentleman Boss: The Life of Chester Alan Arthur* (1975). Nick Salvatore, *Eugene V. Debs: Citizen and Socialist* (1982). Harry J. Sievers, *Benjamin Harrison,* 3 vols. (1952–1968).

The Depression. Ray Ginger, *Altgeld's America* (1958); *The Bending Cross* (1949). Almot Lindsey, *The Pullman Strike* (1942). Donald McMurray, *Coxey's Army* (1929). Samuel McSeveney, *The Politics of Depression* (1972). Carlos A. Schwantes, *Coxey's Army* (1955).

Populism. Peter Argersinger, *Populism and Politics: William Alfred Peffer and the People's Party* (1974). O. Gene Clanton, *Populism: The Humane Preference in America, 1890–1900* (1991); *Kansas Populism: Ideas and Men* (1969). Robert F. Durden, *The Climax of Populism: The Election of 1896* (1965). Lawrence Goodwyn, *Democratic Promise* (1976); *The Populist Moment* (1978), an abridgement of *Democratic Promise.* Sheldon Hackney, *Populism to Progressivism in Alabama* (1969). Steven Hahn, *The Roots of Southern Populism: Yeoman Farmers and the Transformation of the Georgia Upcountry, 1850–1890* (1983). John D. Hicks, *The Populist Revolt* (1931). Richard Hofstadter, *The Age of Reform* (1954). Robert McMath, *Populist Vanguard* (1975). Theodore R. Mitchell, *Political Education in the Southern Farmers Alliance, 1887–1900* (1987). Walter T. K. Nugent, *The Tolerant Populists* (1960). Bruce Palmer, *Man over Money* (1980). Stanley Parsons, *The Populist Context: Rural Versus Urban Power on a Great Plains Frontier* (1973). Norman Pollack, *The Populist Response to Industrial America* (1962); *The Just Polity: Populism, Law, and Human Welfare* (1987). Martin Ridge, *Ignatius Donnelly: Portrait of a Politician* (1962). Theodore Saloutos, *Farmer Movements in the South, 1865–1933* (1960). Fred Shannon, *The Farmer's Last Frontier* (1945). Barton C. Shaw, *The Wool-Hat Boys: Georgia's Populist Party* (1984). Francis B. Simkins, *Pitchfork Ben Tillman* (1944). Allan Weinstein, *Prelude of Populism: Origins of the Silver Issue* (1970). C. Vann Woodward, *Origins of the New South* (1972); *Tom Watson, Agrarian Rebel* (1938). James E. Wright, *The Politics of Populism: Dissent in Colorado* (1974).

The "Battle of the Standards" and the Election of 1896. Paolo Coletta, *William Jennings Bryan,* 3 vols., (1964–1969). Milton Friedman and Anna J. Schwartz, *A Monetary History of the United States* (1963). Paul Glad, *McKinley, Bryan, and the People* (1964); *The Trumpet Soundeth* (1960). J. Rogers Hollingsworth, *The Whirligig of Politics: The Democracy of Cleveland and Bryan* (1963). Stanley Jones, *The Presidential Election of 1896* (1964).

"MEASURING UNCLE SAM FOR A NEW SUIT," BY J. S. PUGHE, IN *PUCK* MAGAZINE, 1900
President William McKinley is favorably depicted here as a tailor, measuring his client for a
suit large enough to accommodate the new possessions the United States obtained in the
aftermath of the Spanish-American War. The cartoon tries to link this expansion with
earlier, less controversial ones such as the Louisiana Purchase. *(Culver)*

CHAPTER TWENTY

THE IMPERIAL REPUBLIC

HE AMERICAN REPUBLIC HAD been an expansionist nation since the earliest days of its existence. Throughout the first half of the nineteenth century, as the population of the United States grew and pressed westward, the government had continually acquired new territory: the trans-Appalachian West, the Louisiana Territory, Florida, Texas, Oregon, California, New Mexico, Alaska. It was the nation's "Manifest Destiny," many Americans believed, to expand into new realms.

In the last years of the nineteenth century, with little potential left for territorial growth on the North American continent, U.S. expansionism moved into a new phase. In the past, the nation had generally annexed land adjacent to its existing boundaries into which American citizens could move relatively easily and which could ultimately become states of the Union. But the expansionism of the 1890s, the new Manifest Destiny, involved acquiring possessions separate from the continental United States: island territories, many thickly populated, most of which would not attract massive settlement from America, and few of which were likely to become states. The United States was joining England, France, Germany, and others in the great imperial drive that by the end of the century was to bring much of the underdeveloped world under the control of the industrial powers of the West.

STIRRINGS OF IMPERIALISM

For over two decades after the Civil War, the United States expanded hardly at all. By the 1890s, however, some Americans were ready—indeed, eager—to resume the course of Manifest Destiny that had inspired their ancestors to wrest an empire from Mexico in the expansionist 1840s.

The New Manifest Destiny

Several developments helped shift American attention to lands across the seas. The experience of subjugating the Indian tribes had established a precedent for exerting colonial control over dependent peoples. The concept of the "closing of the frontier," widely heralded by Frederick Jackson Turner and many others in the 1890s, produced fears that natural resources would soon dwindle and that alternative sources must be found abroad. The depression that began in 1893 encouraged some businessmen to look overseas for new markets. The bitter social protests of the time—the Populist movement, the free-silver crusade, the bloody labor disputes—led some politicians to urge a more aggressive foreign policy as an outlet for frustrations that would otherwise destabilize domestic life.

IMPERIALISM AT HIGH TIDE: THE WORLD IN 1900

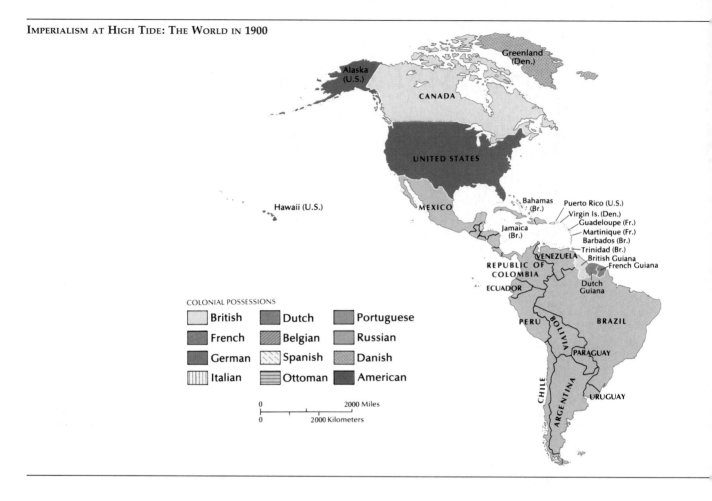

Foreign trade was becoming increasingly important to the American economy in the late nineteenth century. The nation's exports had totaled about $392 million goods in 1870; by 1890, the figure was $857 million; and by 1900, $1.4 billion. Many Americans began to consider the possibility of acquiring colonies that might expand such markets further. "Today," Senator Albert J. Beveridge of Indiana cried in 1899, "we are raising more than we can consume. Today, we are making more than we can use. Therefore, we must find new markets for our produce, new occupation for our capital, new work for our labor."

Americans were, moreover, well aware of the imperialist fever that was raging through Europe and leading the major powers to partition most of Africa among themselves and to turn eager eyes on the Far East and the feeble Chinese Empire. Some Americans feared that their nation would soon be left out, that no territory would remain to be acquired. Senator Henry Cabot Lodge of Massachusetts, a leading imperialist,

warned that the United States "must not fall out of the line of march."

Scholars and others found a philosophic justification for expansionism in Charles Darwin's theories. They contended that nations or "races," like biological species, struggled constantly for existence and that only the fittest could survive. For strong nations to dominate weak ones was, therefore, in accordance with the laws of nature. (This was an application to world affairs of the same distortion of Darwinism that industrialists and others had long been applying to domestic economic affairs in the form of Social Darwinism.)

One of the first to advance this argument was the popular writer John Fiske, who predicted in an 1885 article in *Harper's Magazine* that the English-speaking peoples would eventually control every land that was not already the seat of an "established civilization." The experience of white Americans in subjugating the native population of their own continent, Fiske argued,

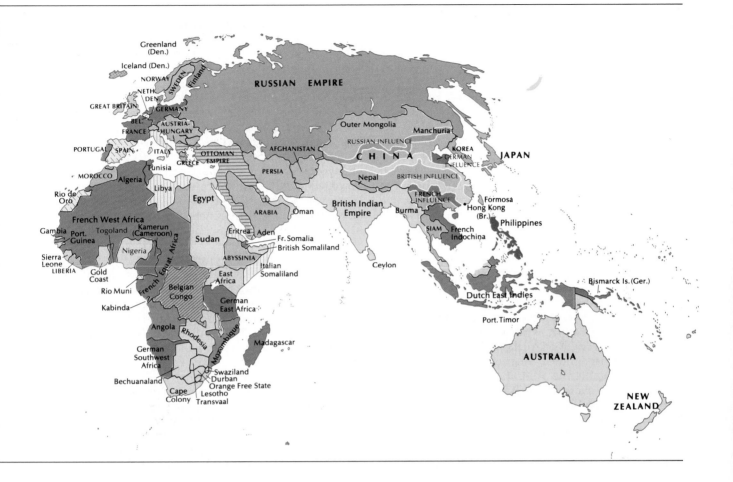

was "destined to go on" in other parts of the world. Support for Fiske's position came the same year from Josiah Strong, a Congregational clergyman and champion of overseas missionary work. In a book entitled *Our Country: Its Possible Future and Its Present Crisis* (1885), Strong declared that the Anglo-Saxon "race," and especially its American branch, represented the great ideas of civil liberty and pure Christianity and was "divinely commissioned" to spread its institutions over the earth. John W. Burgess, founder of Columbia University's School of Political Science, gave a stamp of scholarly approval to imperialism. In his 1890 study *Political Science and Comparative Law*, he flatly stated that the Anglo-Saxon and Teutonic nations possessed the highest political talents. It was their duty, therefore, to uplift less fortunate peoples, even to force superior institutions on them if necessary. "There is," he wrote, "no human right to the status of barbarism."

The ablest and most effective apostle of imperialism was Alfred Thayer Mahan, a captain and later admiral in the United States Navy. Mahan's thesis, presented in *The Influence of Sea Power upon History* (1890) and other works, was simple: Countries with sea power were the great nations of history; the greatness of the United States, bounded by two oceans, would rest on its sea power. The prerequisites for sea power were a productive domestic economy, foreign commerce, a strong merchant marine, a navy to defend trade routes—and colonies, which would provide raw materials and markets and could serve as bases for the navy. Specifically, Mahan advocated that the United States construct a canal across the isthmus of Central America to join the oceans, acquire defensive bases on both sides of the canal in the Caribbean and the Pacific, and take possession of Hawaii and other Pacific islands. "Whether they will or no," he proclaimed, "Americans must now begin to look outward."

Mahan feared the United States did not have a large enough navy to play the great role he envisioned. But during the 1870s and 1880s, the government launched a shipbuilding program that by 1898 had moved the United States to fifth place among the world's naval powers, and by 1900 to third.

Hemispheric Hegemony

James G. Blaine, who served as secretary of state in two Republican administrations in the 1880s, led early efforts to expand American influence into Latin America, where, he believed, the United States must look for markets for its surplus goods. In October 1889, Blaine helped organize the first Pan-American Congress, which attracted delegates from nineteen nations. The delegates agreed to create the Pan-American Union, a weak international organization located in Washington which served as a clearinghouse for distributing information to the member nations. But they rejected Blaine's more substantive proposals: for an inter-American customs union and arbitration procedures for hemispheric disputes.

The Cleveland administration took a similarly active interest in Latin America. In 1895, it supported Venezuela in a dispute with Great Britain over the boundary between Venezuela and British Guiana. When the British ignored American demands that the matter be submitted to arbitration, Secretary of State Richard Olney charged that Britain was violating the Monroe Doctrine. When Britain still did not act, Cleveland created a special commission to determine the boundary line; if Britain resisted the commission's decision, he insisted, the United States should be willing to go to war to enforce it. As war talk raged throughout the country, the British government finally realized that it had stumbled into a genuine diplomatic crisis and agreed to arbitration.

Hawaii and Samoa

The islands of Hawaii in the mid-Pacific had been an important way station for American ships in the China trade since the early nineteenth century. By the 1880s, officers of the expanding American navy were looking covetously at Pearl Harbor on the island of Oahu as a possible permanent base for United States ships. Pressure for an increased American presence in Hawaii was emerging from another source as well: the growing number of Americans who had settled on the islands and who had gradually come to dominate their economic and political life.

In doing so, the Americans were wresting authority away from the leaders of an ancient civilization. Settled by Polynesian people beginning in about 1500 B.C., Hawaii had developed an agricultural and fishing society in which different islands (and different communities on the same islands), each with its own chieftain, lived more or less self-sufficiently. When the first Americans arrived in Hawaii in the 1790s on merchant ships from New England, there were perhaps a half million people living there.

Battles among rival communities were frequent, as ambitious chieftains tried to consolidate power over their neighbors. In 1810, after a series of such battles, King Kamehameha I established his dominance over the other chieftains on Hawaii. He welcomed American traders and helped them develop a thriving trade between Hawaii and China, from which the natives profited along with the merchants. But Americans soon wanted more than trade. Missionaries began settling there in the early nineteenth century; and in the 1830s, William Hooper, a Boston trader, became the first of many Americans to buy land and establish a sugar plantation on the islands.

The arrival of these merchants, missionaries, and planters was devastating to Hawaiian society. The newcomers inadvertently brought infectious diseases to which the Hawaiians, like the American Indians before them, were tragically vulnerable. By the mid-nineteenth century, more than half the native population had died. By the turn of the century, disease had cut the population by more than half again. But the Americans brought other incursions as well. Missionaries worked to undermine native religion. Other white settlers introduced liquor, firearms, and a commercial economy, all of which eroded the traditional character of Hawaiian society. By the 1840s, American planters had spread throughout the islands; and an American settler, G. P. Judd, had become prime minister of Hawaii under King Kamehameha III, who had agreed to establish a constitutional monarchy. Judd governed Hawaii for over a decade.

In 1887, the United States negotiated a treaty with Hawaii that permitted it to open a naval base at Pearl Harbor. By then, growing sugar for export to America had become the basis of the Hawaiian economy—as a result of an 1875 agreement allowing Hawaiian sugar to enter the United States duty-free. The American-dominated sugar plantation system not only displaced native Hawaiians from their lands but relied heavily for workers on Asian immigrants, whom the Americans considered more reliable and more docile than the natives. Indeed, finding adequate labor, and keeping it under control, was the principal concern of many planters. Some deliberately sought to create a mixed-race work force (Chinese, Japanese, native Hawaiian, Filipinos, Portuguese, and others) as a way to keep the workers divided and unlikely to challenge them.

Native Hawaiians did not accept their subordination without protest. In 1891, they elevated a power-

THE CONQUEST OF HAWAII
American planters, with help from the U.S. Navy, worked to depose the nationalist Queen Liliuokalani as ruler of Hawaii in the early 1890s and annex the islands to the United States. Here the queen is shown as a prisoner, being escorted through a rear door of her former palace.
(Hawaii State Archives)

ful nationalist to the throne: Queen Liliuokalani, who set out to challenge the growing American control of the islands. But she remained in power only two years. In 1890, the United States had eliminated the privileged position of Hawaiian sugar in international trade. The result was devastating to the economy of the islands, and American planters concluded that the only way for them to recover was to become part of the United States (and hence exempt from its tariffs). In 1893 they staged a revolution and called on the United States for protection. After the American minister ordered marines from a warship in Honolulu harbor to go ashore to aid the rebels, the queen yielded her authority.

A provisional government, dominated by Americans (who constituted less than 5 percent of the population of the islands), immediately sent a delegation to Washington to negotiate a treaty of annexation. President Harrison signed an annexation agreement in February 1893, just before leaving office. But the Senate, controlled by Democrats after the 1892 election, refused to ratify the treaty, and Grover Cleveland, the new president, refused to support it. Debate over the annexation of Hawaii continued until 1898, when the Republicans returned to power and approved the agreement.

Three thousand miles south of Hawaii, the Samoan islands, had also long served as a way station for American ships in the Pacific trade. As American commerce with Asia increased, business groups in the United States regarded Samoa with new interest, and the American navy began eyeing the Samoan harbor at Pago Pago. In 1878, the Hayes administration extracted a treaty from Samoan leaders for an American naval station at Pago Pago. It bound the United States to arbitrate any differences between Samoa and other nations. Clearly, the United States now expected to have a voice in Samoan affairs.

But Great Britain and Germany were also interested in the islands, and they too secured treaty rights from the native princes. For the next ten years the three powers jockeyed for dominance in Samoa, playing off one native ruler against another and coming dangerously close to war. Finally, the three powers agreed to create a tripartite protectorate over Samoa, with the native chiefs exercising only nominal authority. The three-way arrangement failed to halt the intrigues and rivalries of its members; and in 1899, the United States and Germany divided the islands between them, compensating Britain with territories elsewhere in the Pacific. The United States retained the harbor at Pago Pago.

WAR WITH SPAIN

Imperial ambitions had thus begun to stir within the United States well before the late 1890s. But a war with Spain in 1898 turned those stirrings into overt expansionism. The war transformed America's relationship to the rest of the world, and left the nation with a far-flung overseas empire.

THE DUTY OF THE HOUR:—TO SAVE HER NOT ONLY FROM SPAIN BUT FROM A WORSE FATE.

"THE DUTY OF THE HOUR"
This 1892 lithograph was no doubt inspired by the saying "Out of the frying pan and into the fire." A despairing Cuba, struggling to escape from the frying pan of Spanish misrule, contemplates an even more dangerous alternative: "anarchy" (or home rule). Cartoonist Louis Dalrymple here suggests that the only real solution to Cuba's problems is control by the United States, whose "duty" to Cuba is "To Save Her Not Only from Spain but from a Worse Fate."　*(The Granger Collection)*

Controversy over Cuba

The Spanish-American War emerged out of events in Cuba, which along with Puerto Rico represented virtually all that remained of Spain's once extensive American empire. Cubans had been resisting Spanish rule since at least 1868, when they began a long but ultimately unsuccessful fight for independence. Many Americans had sympathized with the Cubans during that ten-year struggle, but the United States did not intervene.

In 1895, the Cubans rose up again. (Although their goal was an end to Spanish misrule, the island's problems were now in part a result of the Wilson-Gorman Tariff of 1894, whose high duties on sugar had prostrated Cuba's important sugar economy by cutting off exports to the United States, the island's principal market.) This rebellion produced a ferocity on both sides that horrified Americans. The Cubans deliberately devastated the island to force the Spaniards to leave. The Spanish, commanded by General Valeriano Weyler (known in the American press as "Butcher" Weyler), confined civilians in some areas to hastily prepared concentration camps, where they died by the thousands, victims of disease and malnutrition.

The Spanish had used some of these same savage methods during the earlier struggle in Cuba without shocking American sensibilities. But the revolt of 1895 was reported more fully and floridly by the American press, which helped create the impression that the Spaniards were committing all the atrocities, when in fact there was considerable brutality on both sides.

The conflict in Cuba came at a particularly opportune moment for the publishers of some American newspapers. Joseph Pulitzer with his New York *World* and William Randolph Hearst with his New York *Journal* were revolutionizing American journalism in the late nineteenth century by creating a new "penny press," which catered openly to a broad popular au-

THE YELLOW PRESS AND THE WRECK OF THE *MAINE*
No evidence was ever found tying the Spanish to the explosion in Havana harbor that destroyed the American battleship *Maine* in February 1898. Indeed, most evidence indicated that the blast came from inside the ship, a fact that suggests an accident rather than sabotage. Nevertheless, the newspapers of Joseph Pulitzer and William Randolph Hearst ran sensational stories about the incident that were designed to arouse public sentiment in support of a war against the Spanish. This front page from Pulitzer's *New York World* is an example of the lurid coverage the event received. Circulation figures at the top of the page suggest, too, how successful the coverage was in selling newspapers. (*The Granger Collection*)

dience, lower in economic status than the traditional press. Their papers specialized in lurid and sensational news; when such news did not exist, editors were not above creating it. More traditional journalists referred to the new form as "yellow journalism." In the 1890s, Hearst and Pulitzer were engaged in a ruthless circulation war, and they saw the struggle in Cuba as a great opportunity. Both sent batteries of reporters and illustrators to the island with orders to provide accounts of Spanish atrocities. "You furnish the pictures," Hearst supposedly told an overly scrupulous artist, "and I'll furnish the war."

A growing population of Cuban émigrés in the United States—centered in Florida, New York, Philadelphia, and Trenton, New Jersey—gave extensive support to the Cuban Revolutionary Party (whose headquarters was in New York) and helped publicize its leader, José Martí, who was killed in Cuba in 1895. Later, Cuban Americans formed other clubs and associations to support the cause of *Cuba Libre*. In some areas of the country, their efforts were as important as those of the yel-

low journalists in generating popular support for the revolution.

The mounting storm of indignation against Spain did not persuade President Cleveland, who proclaimed American neutrality and tried to stop the agitation by Cuban refugees in New York City. But when McKinley became president in 1897, he took a stronger stand. He formally protested Spain's "uncivilized and inhuman" conduct, causing the Spanish government (fearful of American intervention) to recall Weyler, modify the concentration policy, and grant the island a qualified autonomy. At the end of 1897, with the insurrection losing ground, it seemed that American involvement in the war might be averted.

But whatever chances there were for a peaceful settlement vanished as a result of two dramatic incidents in February 1898. The first occurred when a Cuban agent in Havana stole a private letter written by Dupuy de Lôme, the Spanish minister in Washington, and turned it over to the American press. The letter described McKinley as a weak man and "a bidder for the

THE SPANISH-AMERICAN WAR IN CUBA, 1898

admiration of the crowd." This was no more than many Americans, including some Republicans, were saying about their president. (Theodore Roosevelt described McKinley as having "no more backbone than a chocolate eclair.") But coming from a foreigner, it created intense popular anger. Dupuy de Lôme promptly resigned.

While excitement over the de Lôme letter was still high, the American battleship *Maine* blew up in Havana harbor with a loss of more than 260 people. The ship had been ordered to Cuba in January to protect American lives and property against possible attacks by Spanish loyalists. Many Americans assumed that the Spanish had sunk the ship, particularly when a naval court of inquiry hastily and inaccurately reported that an external explosion by a submarine mine had caused the disaster. (Later evidence suggested that the disaster was actually the result of an accidental explosion inside one of the engine rooms.) War hysteria swept the country, and Congress unanimously appropriated $50 million for military preparations. "Remember the Maine!" became a national chant for revenge.

McKinley still hoped to avoid a conflict. But others in his administration (including Assistant Secretary of the Navy Theodore Roosevelt) were clamoring for war. In March 1898, the president asked Spain to agree to an armistice, negotiations for a permanent peace, and end to the concentration camps. Spain agreed to stop the fighting and eliminate the concentration camps but refused to negotiate with the rebels and reserved the right to resume hostilities at its discretion. That satisfied neither public opinion nor the Congress; and a few days later McKinley asked for and, on April 25, received a congressional declaration of war.

"A Splendid Little War"

Secretary of State John Hay called the Spanish-American conflict "a splendid little war," an opinion that most Americans—with the exception of many of the enlisted men who fought in it—seemed to share. Declared in April, it was over in August. That was in part because Cuban rebels had already greatly weakened the Spanish resistance, which made the American intervention in many respects little more than a "mopping up" exercise. Only 460 Americans were killed in battle or died of wounds, although some 5,200 others perished of disease: malaria, dysentery, and typhoid, among others. Casualties among Cuban insurgents, who continued to bear the brunt of the fighting, were much higher.

And yet the American war effort was not without difficulties. United States soldiers faced serious supply problems: a shortage of modern rifles and ammunition, uniforms too heavy for the warm Caribbean weather, inadequate medical services, and skimpy, almost indigestible food. The regular army numbered only 28,000 troops and officers, most of whom had experience in quelling Indian outbreaks but none in larger-scale warfare. That meant that, as in the Civil War, the United States had to rely heavily on National Guard units, organized by local communities and commanded for the most part by local leaders without military experience. The entire mobilization process was conducted with remarkable inefficiency.

There were also racial conflicts. A significant proportion of the American invasion force consisted of black soldiers. Some were volunteer troops put together by African-American communities (although some governors refused to allow the formation of such units). Others were members of the four black regiments in the regular army, who had been stationed on the frontier to defend white settlements against Indians and were now transferred east to fight in Cuba. As the black soldiers traveled through the South toward the training camps, they chafed at the rigid segregation to which they were subjected and occasionally resisted the restrictions openly. Black soldiers in Georgia deliberately made use of a "whites only" park; in Florida, they beat a soda-fountain operator for refusing to serve them; in Tampa, white provocations and black retaliation led to a nightlong riot that left thirty wounded.

Racial tensions continued in Cuba itself, where American blacks played crucial roles in some of the important battles of the war (including the famous charge at San Juan Hill) and won many medals. Nearly half the Cuban insurgents fighting with the Americans were black, and unlike their American counterparts they were fully integrated into the rebel army. (Indeed, one of the leading insurgent generals, Antonio Maceo, was a black man.) The sight of black Cuban soldiers fighting alongside whites as equals gave American blacks a stronger sense of the injustice of their own position.

Seizing the Philippines

No agency in the American military had clear authority over strategic planning. Only the navy had worked out an objective, and its objective had little to do with freeing Cuba. Assistant Secretary of the Navy Theodore Roosevelt was an ardent imperialist, active proponent of war, and a man uninhibited by the knowledge that he was a relatively minor figure in the military hierarchy. Roosevelt strengthened the navy's Pacific squadron and instructed its commander, Commodore George Dewey, to attack Spanish naval forces in the Philippines, a colony of Spain, in the event of war.

Immediately after war was declared, Dewey sailed for Manila. On May 1, 1898, he steamed into Manila Bay and completely destroyed the aging Spanish fleet stationed there. Only one American sailor died in the battle (of heatstroke), and George Dewey, immediately promoted to admiral, had become the first hero of the war. Several months later, after the arrival of an American expeditionary force, the Spanish surrendered the city of Manila itself. In the rejoicing over Dewey's victory, few Americans paused to note that the character of the war was changing. What had begun as a war to free Cuba was becoming a war to strip Spain of its colonies.

The Battle for Cuba

But Cuba remained the principal focus of American military efforts. At first, the American commanders planned a long period of training before actually sending troops into combat. But when a Spanish fleet under Admiral Pascual Cervera slipped past the American navy into Santiago harbor on the southern coast of Cuba, plans changed quickly. The American Atlantic fleet quickly bottled Cervera up in the harbor. And the U.S. Army's commanding general, Nelson A. Miles, hastily altered his strategy and left Tampa in June with a force of 17,000 to attack Santiago. Both the departure from Florida and the landing in Cuba were scenes of fantastic incompetence. It took five days for this relatively small army to be put ashore, and that with the enemy offering no opposition.

General William R. Shafter, the American commander, moved toward Santiago, which he planned to surround and capture. On the way he met and defeated Spanish forces at Las Guasimas and, a week later, in two simultaneous battles, El Caney and San Juan Hill. At the center of the fighting (and on the front pages of the newspapers) during most of these engagements was a cavalry unit known as the Rough Riders. Nominally commanded by General Leonard Wood, its real leader was Colonel Theodore Roosevelt, who had resigned from the Navy Department to get into the war and who had struggled with an almost desperate fury to ensure that his regiment made it to the front before the fighting ended. Roosevelt rapidly emerged as a hero of the conflict. His fame rested in large part on his role in leading a bold, if perhaps reck-

THE ROUGH RIDERS
Theodore Roosevelt resigned as assistant secretary of the navy to lead a volunteer regiment in the Spanish-American War. They were known as the Rough Riders, and their bold charge during the battle of San Juan Hill made Roosevelt a national hero. Roosevelt is shown here (at center with hat and glasses) posing with the other members of the regiment. *(Bettmann)*

less, charge up Kettle Hill (a charge that was a minor part of the larger battle for the adjacent San Juan Hill) directly into the face of Spanish guns. Roosevelt himself emerged unscathed, but nearly a hundred of his soldiers were killed or wounded. To the end of his life, he remembered the battle as "the great day of my life."

Although Shafter was now in position to assault Santiago, his army was so weakened by sickness that he feared he might have to abandon his position, particularly once the commander of the American naval force blockading Santiago refused to enter the harbor because of mines. Disaster seemed imminent. But unknown to the Americans, the Spanish government

had by now decided that Santiago was lost and had ordered Cervera to evacuate. On July 3, believing the effort to defend the port was hopeless, Cervera tried to escape the harbor. The waiting American squadron destroyed his entire fleet. On July 16, the commander of Spanish ground forces in Santiago surrendered. At about the same time, an American army landed in Puerto Rico and occupied it against virtually no opposition. On August 12, an armistice ended the war.

Under the terms of the armistice, Spain recognized the independence of Cuba. It ceded Puerto Rico (now occupied by American troops) and the Pacific island of Guam to the United States. And it accepted contin-

"SMOKED YANKEES"
Nearly one-fourth of the American invasion force in Cuba consisted of African-American soldiers, many of whom had already served with distinction in campaigns against Indians in the West. Spanish troops called them "smoked Yankees" and often looked on them with more respect than did their American commanders, who kept black troops in rigidly segregated units. In this painting members of the all-black Tenth Cavalry support a charge by the Rough Riders. Members of the Twenty-fourth and Twenty-fifth Negro Infantry Divisions played a crucial role at the Battle of San Juan Hill. *(Library of Congress)*

ued American occupation of Manila pending the final disposition of the Philippines.

Puerto Rico and the United States

The annexation of Puerto Rico produced relatively little controversy in the United States—ironically, since of all the territory America acquired as a result of the Spanish-American war, Puerto Rico would be the most important to the nation's future.

The island of Puerto Rico had been a part of the Spanish Empire since Ponce de León arrived there in 1508, and it had contained Spanish settlements since the founding of San Juan in 1521. The native people of the island, the Arawaks, disappeared almost entirely as a result of infectious diseases, Spanish brutality, and poverty. Puerto Rican society developed, therefore, with a Spanish ruling class and a large African work force for the coffee and sugar plantations that came to dominate its economy.

As Puerto Rican society became increasingly distinctive, resistance to Spanish rule began to emerge, just as it had emerged in Cuba. Uprisings occurred intermittently beginning in the 1820s; the most important of them—the so-called Lares Rebellion—was, like the others, effectively crushed by the Spanish in 1868. But the growing resistance did prompt some reforms: the abolition of slavery in 1873, representation in the Spanish parliament, and other changes. Demands for independence continued to grow, and in 1898, in response to political pressure organized by Luis Muñoz Rivera, Spain granted the island a degree of independence. But before the changes had any chance to take effect, control of Puerto Rico shifted to the United States.

American military forces occupied the island during the war. They remained in control until 1900, when the Foraker Act ended military rule and established a formal colonial government: an American governor, a two-chamber legislature (the members of the upper chamber appointed by the United States, the members of the lower elected by the Puerto Rican people). The United States could amend or veto any legislation the Puerto Ricans passed. Agitation for independence continued. And in 1917, under pressure to clarify the relationship between Puerto Rico and America, Congress passed the Jones Act, which declared Puerto Rico to be United States territory and made all Puerto Ricans American citizens.

The Puerto Rican sugar industry flourished as it took advantage of the American market that was now open to it without tariffs. As in Hawaii, Americans began establishing large sugar plantations on the island and hired natives to work them; many of the planters did not even live in Puerto Rico. The growing emphasis on sugar as a cash crop, and the transformation of many Puerto Rican farmers into paid laborers led to a reduction in the growing of food for the island. Puerto Ricans became increasingly dependent on imported food and hence increasingly a part of the international commercial economy. When international sugar prices were high, Puerto Rico did well. When they dropped, the island's economy sagged, pushing the many plantation workers—already desperately poor—into destitution. Unhappy with the instability, the poverty among natives, and the American threat to Hispanic culture, many Puerto Ricans continued to agitate for independence. Others, however, began to envision closer relations with the United States, even statehood.

The Debate over the Philippines

If the annexation of Puerto Rico produced relatively little controversy, the annexation of the Philippines occasioned a long and impassioned debate. Controlling a nearby Caribbean island fit reasonably comfortably into America's sense of itself as the dominant power in the Western Hemisphere. Controlling a large and densely populated territory thousands of miles away seemed different, and to many Americans more ominous.

McKinley claimed to be reluctant to support annexation. But, according to his own accounts, he came to believe there were no acceptable alternatives. Emerging from what he described as an "agonizing night of prayer," he claimed divine guidance for his decision to accept responsibility for the islands. Returning them to Spain would be "cowardly and dishonorable," he claimed. Turning them over to another imperialist power (France, Germany, or Britain) would be "bad business and discreditable." Granting the islands independence would be irresponsible; the Filipinos were "unfit for self government." The only solution was "to take them all and to educate the Filipinos, and uplift and Christianize them, and by God's grace do the very best we could by them." Growing popular support for annexation and the pressure of the imperialist leaders of his party undoubtedly helped him reach this decision of conscience.

The Treaty of Paris, signed in December 1898, brought a formal end to the war. It confirmed the terms of the armistice concerning Cuba, Puerto Rico, and Guam. But American negotiators startled the Spanish by demanding that they cede the Philippines to the United States, something the original armistice had not included. The Spanish objected briefly, but an American offer of $20 million for the islands softened their resistance. They accepted all the American terms.

In the United States Senate, however, resistance was fierce. During debate over ratification of the treaty, a powerful anti-imperialist movement arose around the country to oppose acquisition of the Philippines. The anti-imperialists included some of the nation's wealthiest and most powerful figures: Andrew Carnegie, Mark Twain, Samuel Gompers, Senator John Sherman, and others. Their motives were various. Some believed simply that imperialism was immoral, a repudiation of America's commitment to human freedom. Some feared "polluting" the American population by introducing "inferior" Asian races into it. Industrial workers feared being undercut by a flood of cheap laborers from the new colonies. Conservatives feared the large standing army and entangling foreign alliances that they believed imperialism would require and that they feared would threaten American liberties. Sugar growers and others feared unwelcome competition from the new territories. The Anti-Imperialist League, established by upper-class Bostonians, New Yorkers, and others late in 1898 to fight against annexation, attracted a widespread following in the Northeast and waged a vigorous campaign against ratification of the Paris treaty.

Favoring ratification was an equally varied group. There were the exuberant imperialists such as Theodore Roosevelt, who saw the acquisition of empire as a way to reinvigorate the nation, and keep alive what they considered the healthy, restorative influence of the war. Some businessmen saw opportunities to profit in the Philippines and believed annexation would position the United States to dominate the Oriental trade. And most Republicans saw partisan advantages in acquiring valuable new territories through a war fought and won by a Republican administration. Perhaps the strongest argument in favor of annexation, however, was the apparent ease with which it could be accomplished. After all, the United States already possessed the islands.

When anti-imperialists warned of the danger of acquiring territories with large populations who might have to become citizens, the imperialists had a ready answer. The nation's longstanding policies toward Indians—treating them as dependents rather than as citizens—had created a precedent for annexing land without absorbing people. Senator Henry Cabot Lodge of Massachusetts, one of the leading imperialists in Congress, made the point explicitly:

> The other day . . . a great Democratic thinker announced that a Republic can have no subjects. He seems to have forgotten that this Republic not only has held subjects from the beginning, . . . but [that we have] acquired them by purchase. . . . [We] denied to the Indian tribes even the right to choose their allegiance, or to become citizens.

Other supporters of annexation argued that the "uncivilized" Filipinos "would occupy the same status precisely as our Indians. . . . They are, in fact, 'Indians'—and the Fourteenth Amendment does not make citizens of Indians."

The fate of the treaty remained in doubts for weeks, until it received the unexpected support of William Jennings Bryan, a fervent anti-imperialist. He backed ratification not because he approved of annexation but because he hoped to move the issue out of the Senate and make it the subject of a national referendum in 1900, when he expected to be the Democratic presidential candidate again. Bryan persuaded a number of anti-imperialist Democrats to support the treaty so as to set up the 1900 debate. The Senate ratified it finally on February 6, 1899.

But Bryan miscalculated. If the election of 1900 was in fact a referendum on the Philippines, as Bryan tried to make it, it proved beyond doubt that the nation had decided in favor of imperialism. Once again Bryan ran against McKinley; and once again McKinley won—even more decisively than in 1896. It was not only the issue of the colonies, however, that ensured McKinley's victory. The Republicans were the beneficiaries of growing national prosperity—and also of the colorful personality of their vice presidential candidate, Colonel Theodore Roosevelt, the hero of San Juan Hill.

THE REPUBLIC AS EMPIRE

The new American empire was small by the standards of the great imperial powers of Europe. But it created large challenges. It embroiled the United States in the politics of both Europe and the Far East in ways the nation had always tried to avoid in the past. It also drew Americans into a brutal war in the Philippines.

Governing the Colonies

Three of the new American dependencies—Hawaii, Alaska, and Puerto Rico—presented relatively few problems. They received territorial status (and their residents American citizenship) relatively quickly: Hawaii in 1900, Alaska in 1912, and Puerto Rico by 1917. The navy took control of Guam and Tutuila. And some of the smallest, least populated Pacific islands now under American control the United States simply left alone.

Cuba was a thornier problem. American military forces, commanded by General Leonard Wood, remained there until 1902 to prepare the island for independence. They built roads, schools, and hospitals, reorganized the legal, financial, and administrative systems, and introduced medical and sanitation reforms. But the United States also laid the basis for years of American economic domination of the island.

When Cuba drew up a constitution that made no reference to the United States, Congress responded by passing the Platt Amendment in 1901 and pressuring Cuba into incorporating its terms into its constitution. The Platt Amendment barred Cuba from making treaties with other nations (thus, in effect, giving the United States control of Cuban foreign policy); gave the United States the right to intervene in Cuba to preserve independence, life, and property; and required Cuba to permit American naval stations on its territory. The amendment left Cuba only nominally independent politically. And American capital, which quickly took over the island's economy, made the new nation an American economic appendage as well. American investors poured into Cuba, buying up plantations, factories, railroads, and refineries. Absentee American ownership of many of the island's most important resources was the source of resentment and agitation for decades. Resistance to "Yankee imperialism" produced intermittent revolts against the Cuban government—revolts that at times prompted U.S. military intervention. American troops occupied the island from 1906 to 1909 after one such rebellion; they returned again in 1912, to suppress a revolt by black plantation workers. As in Puerto Rico and Hawaii,

FILIPINO PRISONERS
American troops guard captured Filipino guerrillas in Manila. The suppression of the Filipino insurrection was a much longer and costlier military undertaking than the Spanish-American War, by which the United States first gained possession of the islands. By mid-1900 there were 70,000 American troops in the Philippines, under the command of General Arthur MacArthur (whose son, Douglas, won fame in the Philippines during World War II). *(Library of Congress)*

sugar production—spurred by access to the American market—increasingly dominated the island's economy and subjected it to the same cycle of booms and busts that so plagued other sugar-producing appendages of the United States economy.

The Philippine War

Americans did not like to think of themselves as imperial rulers in the European mold. Yet like other imperial powers, the United States soon discovered—as it had discovered at home in its relations with the Indians—that subjugating another people required more than ideals; it also required strength and brutality. That, at least, was the lesson of the American experience in the Philippines, where American forces soon became engaged in a long and bloody war with insurgent forces fighting for independence.

The conflict in the Philippines is the least remembered of all American wars. It was also one of the long-est (it lasted from 1898 to 1902) and one of the most vicious. It involved 200,000 American troops and resulted in 4,300 American deaths, nearly ten times the number who had died in combat in the Spanish-American War. The number of Filipinos killed in the conflict is still in dispute, but it seems likely that at least 50,000 natives (and perhaps many more) died. The American occupiers faced guerrilla tactics in the Philippines very similar to those the Spanish occupiers had faced prior to 1898 in Cuba. And they soon found themselves drawn into the same pattern of brutality that had outraged so many Americans when Weyler had used them in the Caribbean.

The Filipinos had been rebelling against Spanish rule even before 1898. And as soon as they realized the Americans had come to stay, they rebelled against them as well. Ably led by Emilio Aguinaldo, who claimed to head the legitimate government of the nation, Filipinos harried the American army of occupation from island to island for more than three years. At first,

THE AMERICAN SOUTH PACIFIC EMPIRE, 1900

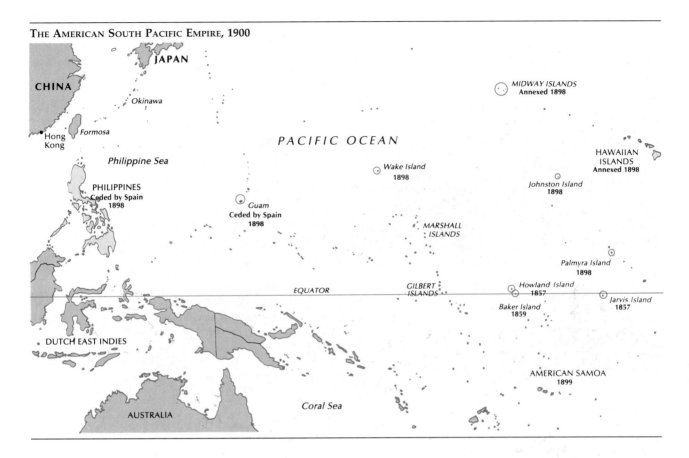

American commanders believed the rebels had only a small popular following. But by early 1900, General Arthur MacArthur (father of General Douglas MacArthur), an American commander in the islands, was writing: "I have been reluctantly compelled to believe that the Filipino masses are loyal to Aguinaldo and the government which he heads."

To MacArthur and others, that realization was not a reason to moderate American tactics or conciliate the rebels. It was a reason to adopt more severe measures. Gradually, the American military effort became more systematically vicious and brutal. Captured Filipino guerrillas were treated not as prisoners of war, but as murderers. Most were summarily executed. On some islands, entire communities were evacuated—the residents forced into concentration camps while American troops destroyed their villages, farms, crops, and livestock. A spirit of savagery grew among some American soldiers, who came to view the Filipinos as almost subhuman and at times seemed to take pleasure in killing almost arbitrarily. One American commander ordered his troops "to kill and burn, the more you kill and burn the better it will please me. . . . Shoot everyone over the age of 10." Over fifteen Filipinos were killed for every one wounded; in the American Civil War—the bloodiest conflict in U.S. history to that point—one person had died for every five wounded.

By 1902, reports of the brutality and of the American casualties had soured the American public on the war. But by then, the rebellion had largely exhausted itself and the occupiers had established control over most of the islands. The key to their victory was the March 1901 capture of Aguinaldo, who later signed a document urging his followers to stop fighting and declaring his own allegiance to the United States. (Aguinaldo then retired from public life and lived quietly until 1964.) Fighting continued in some places for another year, and the war revived intermittently until as late as 1906; but American possession of the Philippines was now secure.

In the summer of 1901, the military transferred authority over the islands to William Howard Taft, who became their first civilian governor. Taft announced that the American mission in the Philippines was to

SIGNIFICANT EVENTS

1868–1878 Cubans revolt against Spanish rule in Ten Years' War

1875 U.S. agrees to allow Hawaii to export sugar to America duty-free

1878 U.S. gains treaty rights for base at Pago Pago in Samoa

1887 U.S. gains treaty rights for base at Pearl Harbor in Hawaii

1889 First Pan-American Congress meets

1890 Alfred Thayer Mahan publishes *The Influence of Sea Power upon History*

U.S. ends favored status of Hawaii in sugar trade, damaging Hawaiian economy

1893 American planters in Hawaii stage revolution

Harrison signs annexation agreement with Hawaii, but Cleveland rejects it

1894 Wilson-Gorman Tariff on sugar ravages Cuban economy

1895 United States and Britain dispute Venezuelan boundary

Insurrection against Spanish begins in Cuba

1896 Alaska gold rush begins

1897 McKinley offers to mediate Cuban conflict, Spain refuses

1898 William Randolph Hearst publishes de Lôme letter

U.S. battleship *Maine* explodes in Havana harbor

Congress declares war on Spain (April 25), Spanish army in Cuba retreats

Dewey captures Philippines

United States and Spain sign armistice (August 12)

Treaty of Paris cedes Puerto Rico, Philippines, and other Spanish possessions to United States and recognizes Cuban independence

United States formally annexes Hawaii

Anti-Imperialist League formed

1898–1902 Philippines revolt against American rule

1899 Senate ratifies Treaty of Paris

Hay releases "Open Door notes"

1900 Foraker Act establishes civil government in Puerto Rico

Hawaii granted territorial status

Boxer Rebellion breaks out in China

McKinley reelected president

1901 Americans capture Emilio Aguinaldo in Philippines

U.S. establishes civil government in Philippines

Congress passes Platt Amendment

1912 Alaska given territorial status

1917 Puerto Ricans granted U.S. citizenship

1946 United States grants Philippines independence

prepare the islands for independence, and he gave the Filipinos broad local autonomy. The Americans also built roads, schools, bridges, and sewers; instituted major administrative and financial reforms; and established a public health system. The Philippine economy—dominated by fishing, agriculture, timber, and mining—also became increasingly linked to the economy of the United States. Americans did not make many investments in the Philippines, and few Americans moved there. But trade with the United States grew to the point that the islands were almost completely dependent on American markets.

In the meantime, a succession of American governors gradually increased Filipino political autonomy.

"Playing the War Game"
Students at the U.S. Army Officer Training School at Fort Leavenworth, Kansas, engage in simulated planning for battle. The school of Fort Leavenworth and other facilities were part of the American effort in the early twentieth century to create a modern command structure for the nation's military. *(Arms Research Library, U. S. Army Command and General Staff College, Fort Leavenworth, Kansas)*

But not until July 4, 1946, did the islands finally gain their independence.

The Open Door

The acquisition of the Philippines greatly increased the already strong American interest in Asia. Americans were particularly concerned about the future of China, with which the United States already had an important trade and which was now so enfeebled that it provided a tempting target for exploitation by stronger countries. By 1900, England, France, Germany, Russia, and Japan were beginning to carve up China among themselves. They pressured the Chinese government for "concessions," which gave them effective control over various regions of China. In some cases, they simply seized Chinese territory and claimed it as their

own. Many Americans feared the process would soon cut them out of the China trade altogether.

Eager for a way to protect American interests in China without risking war, McKinley issued a statement in September 1898 saying the United States wanted access to China, but no special advantages there. "Asking only the open door for ourselves, we are ready to accord the open door to others." Later, Secretary of State John Hay translated those words into policy when he addressed identical messages—which became known as the "Open Door notes"—to England, Germany, Russia, France, Japan, and Italy. He asked them to approve three principles: Each nation with a sphere of influence in China was to respect the rights and privileges of other nations in its sphere; Chinese officials were to continue to collect tariff duties in all spheres (the existing tariff favored the United States);

and nations were not to discriminate against other nations in levying port dues and railroad rates within their own spheres. Together, these principles would allow the United States to trade freely with the Chinese without fear of interference and without having to become militarily involved in the region. They would also retain the illusion of Chinese sovereignty and thus prevent formal colonial dismemberment of China, which might also create obstacles to American trade.

But Europe and Japan received the Open Door proposals coolly. Russia openly rejected them; the other powers claimed to accept them in principle but to be unable to act unless all the other powers agreed. Hay refused to consider this a rebuff. He boldly announced that all the powers had accepted the principles of the Open Door in "final and definitive" form and that the United States expected them to observe those principles. But unless the United States was willing to go to war, it could not prevent any nation that wanted to violate the Open Door from doing so.

No sooner had the diplomatic maneuvering over the Open Door ended than the Boxers, a secret Chinese martial-arts society with highly nationalist convictions, launched a revolt against foreigners in China. The climax of the Boxer Rebellion was a siege of the entire foreign diplomatic corps, which took refuge in the British embassy in Peking. The imperial powers (including the United States) sent an international expeditionary force into China to rescue the diplomats. In August 1900, it fought its way into Peking and broke the siege.

McKinley and Hay had agreed to American participation in quelling the Boxer Rebellion so as to secure a voice in the settlement of the uprising and to prevent the partition of China by the European powers. Hay now won support for his Open Door approach from England and Germany and induced the other participating powers to accept compensation from the Chinese for the damages the Boxer Rebellion had caused. Chinese territorial integrity survived at least in name, and the United States retained access to its lucrative trade.

A Modern Military System

The war with Spain had revealed glaring deficiencies in the American military system. The army had exhibited the greatest weaknesses, but the entire military organization had demonstrated problems of supply, training, and coordination. Had the United States been fighting a more powerful nation, disaster might have resulted. After the war, McKinley appointed Elihu Root, an able corporate lawyer in New York, as secretary of war to supervise a major overhaul of the armed forces. (Root was one of the first of several generations of attorney-statesmen who moved easily between public and private roles and constituted much of what has often been called the American "foreign policy establishment.") Between 1900 and 1903, Root created a new military system.

The Root reforms enlarged the regular army from 25,000 to a maximum of 100,000. They established federal command of the National Guard, ensuring that never again would the nation fight a war with volunteer regiments over which the federal government had limited control. They sparked the creation of a system of officer training schools, including the Army Staff College (later the Command and General Staff School) at Fort Leavenworth, Kansas, and the Army War College at Washington. And in 1903, they established a general staff (which they named the Joint Chiefs of Staff) to act as military advisers to the secretary of war. It was this last reform that Root considered most important: the creation of a central planning agency modeled on the example of European general staffs. The Joint Chiefs were charged with many functions. They were to "supervise" and "coordinate" the entire army establishment, and they were to establish an office that would plan for possible wars. An Army and Navy Board, on which both services were represented, was to foster interservice cooperation. As a result of the new reforms, the United States entered the twentieth century with something resembling a modern military system. The country would make substantial use of it in the turbulent century to come.

SUGGESTED READINGS

General Histories. Robert L. Beisner, *From the Old Diplomacy to the New, 1865–1900,* 2nd ed. (1986). Charles S. Campbell, *The Transformation of American Foreign Relations, 1865–1900* (1976). John Dobson, *America's Ascent: The United States Becomes a Great Power, 1880–1914* (1978). Foster Rhea Dulles, *Prelude to World Power, 1865–1900* (1965). J. A. S. Grenville and George Berkeley Young, *Politics, Strategy and American Diplomacy: Studies in Foreign Policy, 1873–1917* (1966). David F. Healy, *U.S. Expansionism: Imperialist Urge in the 1890s* (1970). Walter LeFeber, *The New Empire* (1963). Ernest May, *Imperial Democracy* (1961); *American Imperialism: A Speculative Essay* (1968). H. Wayne Morgan, *America's Road to Empire* (1965). Milton Plesur, *America's Outward Thrust: Approaches to Foreign Affairs, 1865–1890* (1971). David M. Pletcher, *The Awkward Years: American Foreign Relations under Garfield and Arthur* (1962). Julius W. Pratt, *Expansionists of 1898* (1936). Emily S. Rosenberg, *Spreading the American Dream: American Economic and Cultural Expansion, 1890–1945* (1982). Albert K. Weinberg, *Manifest Destiny: A Study in Nationalist Expansion in American History* (1935). William Appleman Williams, *The Tragedy of American Diplomacy* (rev. ed., 1972).

The Spanish-American War. Richard Challener, *Admirals, Generals, and American Foreign Policy, 1889–1914* (1973). Graham A. Cosmas, *An Army for Empire: The United States Army in the Spanish-American War* (1971). Philip S. Foner, *The Spanish-Cuban-American War and the Birth of American Imperialism,* 2 vols. (1972). Frank Freidel, *The Splendid Little War* (1958). Willard B. Gatewood, Jr., *Black Americans and the White Man's Burden, 1898–1903* (1975); *"Smoked Yankees": Letters from Negro Soldiers, 1898–1902* (1971). Gerald F. Linderman, *The Mirror of War: American Society and the Spanish-American War* (1974). Walter Millis, *The Martial Spirit* (1931). Joyce Milton, *The Yellow Journalists* (1989). Edmund Morris, *The Rise of Theodore Roosevelt* (1979). John L. Offner, *An Unwanted War: The Diplomacy of the United States and Spain over Cuba, 1895–1898* (1992). Louis A. Perez, Jr., *Cuba Between Empires, 1868–1902* (1983). Hyman Rickover, *How the Battleship Maine Was Destroyed* (1976). David F. Trask, *The War with Spain in 1898* (1981). Richard S. West, Jr., *Admirals of the American Empire* (1948).

Imperialism and Anti-Imperialism. Robert L. Beisner, *Twelve Against Empire* (1968). Kendrick A. Clements, *William Jennings Bryan* (1983). James H. Hitchman, *Leonard Wood and Cuban Independence, 1898–1902* (1971). Frederick Merk, *Manifest Destiny and Mission in American History* (1963). Thomas J. Osborne, *"Empire Can Wait": American Opposition to Hawaiian Annexation, 1893–1898* (1891). William J. Pomeroy, *American Neo-Colonialism: Its Emergence in the Philippines and Asia* (1970). Julius W. Pratt, *America's Colonial Empire* (1950). Robert Seager II, *Alfred Thayer Mahan* (1977). E. Berkeley Tompkins, *Anti-Imperialism in the United States, 1890–1920: The Great Debate* (1970).

The Pacific Empire. John Morgan Gates, *Schoolbooks and Krags: The United States Army in the Philippines, 1898–1902* (1971). Stanley Karnow, *In Our Image: America's Empire in the Philippines* (1989). Paul M. Kennedy, *The Samoan Tangle* (1974). Glenn A. May, *Social Engineering in the Philippines* (1980). Stuart Creighton Miller, *"Benevolent Assimilation": The American Conquest of the Philippines, 1899–1903* (1982). Daniel B. Schirmer, *Republic or Empire? American Resistance to the Philippine War* (1972). Peter Stanley, *A Nation in the Making: The Philippines and the United States* (1974). Merze Tate, *The United States and the Hawaiian Kingdom* (1965). Richard E. Welch, Jr., *Response to Imperialism: The United States and the Philippine-American War, 1899–1902* (1979). Leon Wolff, *Little Brown Brother* (1961).

America and Asia. Warren Cohen, *America's Response to China* (rev. ed., 1980). Kenton Clymer, *John Hay: Gentleman as Diplomat* (1975). Patricia Hill, *The World Their Household: The American Women's Foreign Mission Movement and Cultural Transformation* (1985). Michael Hunt, *The Making of a Special Relationship: The United States and China to 1914* (1983). Jane Hunter, *The Gospel of Gentility: American Women Missionaries in Turn-of-the-Century China* (1984). Akira Iriye, *Across the Pacific* (1967); *Pacific Estrangement: Japanese and American Expansion* (1972). Robert McClellan, *The Heathen Chinese: A Study of American Attitudes Toward China* (1971). Thomas J. McCormick, *China Market: America's Quest for Informal Empire, 1893–1901* (1967). Charles Neu, *The Troubled Encounter* (1975). James C. Thomsen, Jr., *Peter W. Stanley, and John Curtis Perry, Sentimental Imperialists: The American Experience in East Asia* (1981). Paul Varg, *The Making of a Myth: The United States and China, 1897–1912* (1968); *Missionaries, Chinese and Diplomats* (1958). Marilyn B. Young, *The Rhetoric of Empire: American China Policy, 1895–1901* (1968).

MᴄCʟᴜʀᴇ's Mᴀɢᴀᴢɪɴᴇ, Mᴀʏ 1903

McClure's was the leading outlet for a form of journalism known as "muckraking," which attempted to expose social and economic scandals in the hope of promoting reform. This issue contains articles by two of the leading muckrakers, Lincoln Steffens and Ida Tarbell.

(Culver)

CHAPTER TWENTY-ONE

THE RISE OF PROGRESSIVISM

WELL BEFORE THE TURN of the century, many Americans had become convinced that the rapid industrialization and urbanization of their society had created intolerable problems, that the nation's most pressing need was to impose order on the growing chaos and to curb industrial society's most glaring injustices. In the early years of the new century, that outlook acquired a name: progressivism.

Not even the progressives themselves could always agree on what the word really meant. Indeed, more than one historian has suggested that the word "progressive" ultimately came to mean so many different things to so many different people that it ceased to mean anything at all. (See "Where Historians Disagree," pp. 574–577.) Yet if progressivism was a phenomenon of great scope and diversity, it was also one that rested on an identifiable set of central assumptions.

THE PROGRESSIVE IMPULSE

Progressivism was, first, an optimistic vision. Progressives believed, as their name implies, in the idea of progress. They believed that society was capable of improvement and that continued growth and advancement were the nation's destiny.

But progressives believed, too, that growth and progress could not continue to occur recklessly, as they had in the late nineteenth century. The "natural laws" of the marketplace, and the doctrines of laissez-faire and Social Darwinism that celebrated those laws, were not sufficient to create the order, stability, and justice their growing society required. Direct, purposeful human intervention in social and economic affairs was essential to ordering and bettering society.

Varieties of Progressivism

Progressives did not always agree on the form their intervention should take, and the result was a variety of reform impulses that sometimes seemed to have little in common.

One powerful impulse was the spirit of "antimonopoly," the fear of concentrated power and the urge to limit and disperse authority and wealth. This impulse, which had much in common with populism, appealed not only to many workers and farmers but to some middle-class Americans as well. And it helped empower government to regulate or break up trusts at both the state and national level.

Another progressive impulse was a belief in the importance of social cohesion: the belief that individuals are not autonomous but part of a great web of social relationships, that the welfare of any single person is dependent on the welfare of society as a whole. That assumption produced a concern about the "victims" of industrialization. A large number of progressive initiatives and reforms involved efforts to help women, children, industrial workers, immigrants, and—to a lesser extent—African Americans.

WHERE HISTORIANS DISAGREE

PROGRESSIVISM

FEW ISSUES IN THE history of twentieth-century America have inspired more disagreement, even confusion, than the nature of progressivism. Until about 1950, most historians were in general accord about the nature of the progressive "movement." It was, they generally agreed, just what it purported to be: a movement by the "people" to curb the power of the "special interests." In particular, it was a protest by an aroused citizenry against the excessive power of urban bosses, corporate moguls, and corrupt elected officials.

In the early 1950s, however, a new interpretation emerged to challenge the traditional view. Without abandoning the earlier view of progressivism as a largely political movement, it offered a new explanation of who the progressives were and what they were trying to do. George Mowry, in *The California Progressives* (1951), described the reform movement in the state not as a protest by the mass of the people, but as an effort by a relatively small and privileged group of business and professional men to limit the over-

bearing power of large corporations and labor unions. Viewing themselves as natural social leaders, they resented their loss of political power to these new economic forces and envisioned reform as a way to restore both their economic fortunes and their social importance and self-esteem. Richard Hofstadter expanded on this idea in *The Age of Reform* (1955), in which he described progressives throughout the country as people suffering from "status anxiety"—old, formerly influential, upper-middle-class families seeking to restore their fading prestige by challenging the powerful new institutions that had begun to displace them. Like the Populists, Hofstadter suggested, the progressives were suffering from psychological, not economic, discontent.

The Mowry-Hofstadter thesis was never without critics. In particular, it received strong challenges from historians who disagreed with two of the basic assumptions of the interpretation. First, these scholars maintained, Mowry and Hofstadter were mistaken in examining progressivism purely in terms of its visible political leaders. It was a movement with a far broader

---

Still another impulse was a deep faith in knowledge—in the possibilities of applying to society the principles of natural and social sciences. To some, those principles seemed a route to organization and efficiency. Many reformers believed that social order was a result of intelligent social organization and rational procedures for guiding social and economic life. To others, knowledge was more important as a vehicle for making society more equitable and humane.

Most progressives believed, too, that a modernized government could—and must—play an important role in the process of improving and stabilizing society. Modern life was too complex to be left in the hands of party bosses, untrained amateurs, and antiquated institutions. It required new and enhanced institutions of government, and a new breed of leaders and experts.

These varied reform impulses were not always as mutually incompatible as they seemed. Many progressives made use of all these ideas (and others), separately or in combination, as they tried to bring order and progress to their turbulent society.

The Muckrakers

Among the first people to articulate the new spirit of reform were crusading journalists who began in the late nineteenth and early twentieth centuries to direct public attention toward social, economic, and political injustices. They became known as the "muckrakers," after Theodore Roosevelt accused one of them of raking up muck through his writings. They were committed to exposing scandal, corruption, and injustice to public view.

WHERE HISTORIANS DISAGREE

social and economic base. Second, they claimed, progressive reformers were not expressing a vague psychological malaise, but a clear recognition of their own self-interest. Beyond that, the new historians of progressivism often disagreed with one another as much as they disagreed with Mowry and Hofstadter.

Perhaps the harshest challenge to earlier interpretations came from Gabriel Kolko, whose influential 1963 study *The Triumph of Conservatism* dismissed the supposedly "democratic" features of progressivism as meaningless rhetoric and examined instead the actual impact of progressive economic reforms. Progressivism was, he agreed, an effort to regulate business. But it was not the "people" who were responsible for this regulation. It was the businessmen who saw in government supervision a way to protect themselves from competition. Regulation, Kolko claimed, was "invariably controlled by the leaders of the regulated industry and directed towards ends they deemed acceptable or desirable."

A somewhat more moderate challenge to the "psychological" interpretation of progressivism came from historians embracing a new "organizational" view of history. Samuel P. Hays was among the first to suggest this approach in *The Response to Industrialism, 1885–1914* (1957) and other writings. Hays argued that progressives were indeed businessmen, as Kolko had suggested. But their impulse was not so much narrow self-interest as a broad desire to bring order and efficiency to political and, hence, economic life. The most important progressives, he claimed, were members of the upper class, who viewed a restoration of stability as essential to the preservation of their privileged position.

Even more influential was a 1967 study by Robert Wiebe, *The Search for Order, 1877–1920.* Wiebe saw progressivism as a response to dislocations in American life that had resulted from rapid changes in the nature of the economy unaccompanied by corresponding changes in social and political institutions. Economic power had moved to large, national organizations, while social and political life remained centered primarily in local communities. The result was widespread disorder and unrest, culminating in the turbulent 1890s. Progressivism, Wiebe argued, was the effort of a "new middle class"—a class

At first, their major targets were the trusts and particularly the railroads, which the muckrakers considered dangerously powerful and deeply corrupt. Exposés of the great corporate organizations began to appear as early as the 1860s, when Charles Francis Adams, Jr., and others uncovered corruption among the railroad barons. Such inquiries continued into the twentieth century. The most notable of them was Ida Tarbell's enormous and influential study of the Standard Oil trust (published first in magazines and then as a two-volume book in 1904).

By the turn of the century, many muckrakers were turning their attention to government and particularly to the urban political machines. The most influential, perhaps, was Lincoln Steffens, a reporter for *McClure's* magazine. His portraits of "machine government" and "boss rule," his exposure of "boodlers" in cities as diverse as St. Louis, Minneapolis, Cleveland, Cincinnati, Chicago, Philadelphia, and New York; his tone of studied moral outrage (as reflected in the title of his series and of the book that emerged from it, *The Shame of the Cities*)—all helped arouse sentiment for urban political reform. The alternative to leaving government in the hands of corrupt party leaders, the muckrakers argued, was for the people themselves to take a greater interest in public life. Indeed, some journalists seemed less outraged at the bosses themselves than at the apathetic public that seemed not to care about the corruption occurring in their midst.

The muckrakers reached the peak of their influence in the first decade of the twentieth century. They investigated governments, labor unions, and corporations. They explored the problems of child labor, immigrant ghettoes, prostitution, and family disorgan-

WHERE HISTORIANS DISAGREE

tied to the emerging national economy—to stabilize and enhance their position in society.

Yet despite all the challenges to the original view of progressivism as a popular democratic movement, some historians continued to produce evidence that the reform phenomenon was indeed a movement of the people against the special interests, although some identified the "people" somewhat differently from earlier such interpretations. J. Joseph Huthmacher argued in 1962 that much of the force behind progressivism came from members of the working class, especially immigrants, who pressed for such reforms as workmen's compensation and wage and hour laws. John Buenker strengthened this argument in *Urban Liberalism and Progressive Reform* (1973), claiming that political machines and urban "bosses" were important sources of reform energy and helped create twentieth-century liberalism.

David P. Thelen, in a 1972 study of progressivism in Wisconsin, *The New Citizenship,* offered an even broader challenge to both the "status anxiety" and the "conservatism-organizational" views. Thelen found a real clash between the "public interest" and "corporate privilege" in Wisconsin. The depression of the 1890s had mobilized a broad coalition of citizens of highly diverse backgrounds behind efforts to make both business and government responsible to the popular will. It marked the emergence of a new "consumer" consciousness that crossed boundaries of class and community, religion and ethnicity.

Other historians writing in the 1970s and 1980s tackled the question of the nature of progressivism less by looking at particular reformers or particular reforms than by trying to identify some of the broad processes of political change that had created the public battles of the era. Richard L. McCormick's *From Realignment to Reform* (1981), for example, studied political change in New York state and argued that the crucial change in this era was the decline of the political parties as the vital players in public life and the rise of interest groups working for particular social and economic goals. Progressivism, he suggested, was not so much a coherent "movement" as part of a broader process of political adaptation to the realities of modern industrial society. At the same time, many histori-

ization. They denounced the waste and destruction of natural resources, the subjugation of women, even occasionally the oppression of blacks. By presenting social problems to the public with indignation and moral fervor, they helped inspire other Americans to take action. In the process they expressed some of the most basic progressive impulses: the opposition to monopoly, the belief in the need for social unity in the face of corruption and injustice, even at times the cry for efficiency and organization.

The Social Gospel

The moralistic tone of the muckrakers' exposés reflected one important aspect of emerging progressive sentiment: a sense of outrage at social and economic injustice. That outrage, combined with a humanitarian sense of social responsibility, helped produce many reformers committed to the pursuit of social justice. A clear expression of that concern was the rise of what became known as the "Social Gospel." By the early twentieth century, it had become a powerful movement within American Protestantism (and, to a lesser extent, within American Catholicism and Judaism). It was chiefly concerned with redeeming the nation's cities.

The Salvation Army, which began in England but soon spread to the United States, was one example of the fusion of religion with reform. A Christian social welfare organization with a vaguely military structure, by 1900 it had recruited 3,000 "officers" and 20,000 "privates" and was offering both material aid and spiritual service to the urban poor. In addition, many ministers, priests, and rabbis left traditional parish work to serve in the troubled cities. Charles Sheldon's *In His*

WHERE HISTORIANS DISAGREE

ans were focusing on the role of women (and the vast network of voluntary associations they created) in shaping and promoting progressive reform and were seeing in these efforts concerns rooted in the female experience. Some progressive battles, these historians argued, were part of an effort by women to protect their interests within the domestic sphere in the face of jarring challenges to that sphere from the new industrial world. That drew them to such issues as temperance, divorce, and prostitution. Many women mobilized behind protective legislation for female and children workers. Other women worked to expand their own roles in the public world. Progressivism cannot be understood, historians of women contend, without understanding the role of women and the importance of issues involving the family and the private world within it.

Given the range of disagreement over the nature of the progressive movement, it is hardly surprising that some historians have despaired of finding any coherent definition for the term at all. Peter Filene, for one, suggested in 1970 that the concept of progressivism as a "movement" had outlived its usefulness. "It is time," he sug-

gested, "to tear off the familiar label and, thus liberated from its prejudice, see the history between 1890 and 1920 for what it was—ambiguous, inconsistent, moved by agents and forces more complex than a [single, uniform] progressive movement." Critics said that Filene's view was an argument for abandoning the search for any historical meaning in the politics of the early twentieth century. But Daniel Rodgers, in an important 1982 article, "In Search of Progressivism," disagreed. His review of the new scholarship on the progressive era concluded:

> Whether historians of the 1980s will call off the search for that great, overarching thing called "progressivism" is hard to predict. Certainly historians in the 1970s manifestly failed to find it. In recompense they found out a vast amount about the world in which the progressives lived and the structures of social and political power shifting so rapidly around them. To acknowledge that these are the questions that matter and to abandon the hunt for the *essence* of the noise and tumult of that era may not be, as Filene's first critics feared, to lose the whole enterprise of historical comprehension. It may be to find it.

Steps (1898), the story of a young minister who abandoned a comfortable post to work among the needy, sold more than 15 million copies and established itself as the most successful novel of the era.

Walter Rauschenbusch, a Protestant theologian with socialist inclinations from Rochester, New York, published a series of influential discourses on the possibilities for human salvation through Christian reform. To him, the message of Darwinism was not that the individual was engaged in a brutal struggle for survival of the fittest, but that all individuals should work to ensure a humanitarian evolution of the social fabric. "Translate the evolutionary themes into religious faith," he wrote, "and you have the doctrine of the Kingdom of God." Some American Catholics seized on the 1893 publication of Pope Leo XIII's encyclical *Rerum Novarum* ("New Things") as justification for their own crusade for social justice. Catholic liberals such as

Father John A. Ryan took to heart the pope's warning that "a small number of very rich men have been able to lay upon the masses of the poor a yoke little better than slavery itself. . . . No practical solution of this question will ever be found without the assistance of religion and the church." For decades, he worked to expand the scope of Catholic social welfare organizations.

The Social Gospel was never the dominant element in the movement for urban reform. Some progressives dismissed it as irrelevant moralization; others viewed it as little more than a useful complement to their own work. But the engagement of religion with reform helped bring to progressivism a powerful moral component and a commitment to redeem the lives of even the least favored citizens. Walter Rauschenbusch captured some of both the optimism and the spirituality of the Social Gospel with his proud comment, after a

THE BOSSES OF THE SENATE.

"THE BOSSES OF THE SENATE" (1889), BY JOSEPH KEPPLER
Keppler was a popular political cartoonist of the late nineteenth century who shared the growing concern about the power of the trusts—portrayed here as bloated, almost reptilian figures standing menacingly over the members of the U.S. Senate, to whose chamber the "people's entrance" is "closed." *(The Granger Collection)*

visit to a New York slum known as Hell's Kitchen, where Christian reformers were hard at work: "One could hear human virtue cracking and crashing all around."

The Settlement House Movement

One of the strongest elements of much progressive thought was the belief in the influence of the environment on individual development. Social Darwinists such as William Graham Sumner had argued that people's fortunes reflected their inherent "fitness" for survival. Many progressive theorists disagreed. Ignorance, poverty, even criminality, they argued, were not the result of inherent moral or genetic failings or of the workings of providence; they were, rather, the effects of an unhealthy environment. To elevate the distressed, therefore, required an improvement of the conditions in which they lived.

Nothing produced more distress, many reformers believed, than the crowded immigrant neighborhoods of American cities, which publicists such as Jacob Riis were exposing through vivid photographs and lurid descriptions. (See pp. 512–514.) One response to the problems of such communities, borrowed from England, was the settlement house. The most famous, and one of the first, was Hull House, which opened in 1889 in Chicago as a result of the efforts of Jane Addams. It became a model for more than 400 similar institutions throughout the nation. Staffed by members of the educated middle class, imbued with ideas derived from the social sciences, settlement houses sought to help immigrant families adapt to the language and customs of their new country. Settlement houses avoided the condescension and moral disapproval of earlier philanthropic efforts. But they generally embraced a belief that middle-class Americans had a responsibility to impart their own values to immigrants and to teach

The settlement houses also helped spawn another important institution of reform: the profession of social work—a profession in which women were also to play a vital role. Workers at Hull House, for example, maintained a close relationship with the University of Chicago's pioneering work in the field of sociology. A growing number of programs for the professional training of social workers began to appear in the nation's leading universities, partly in response to the activities of the settlements. The professional social worker combined a compassion for the poor with a commitment to the values of bureaucratic progressivism: scientific study, efficient organization, reliance on experts. The new profession produced elaborate surveys and reports, collected statistics, and published scholarly tracts on the need for urban reform.

The Allure of Expertise

As the emergence of the social work profession suggests, progressives involved in humanitarian efforts placed a high value on knowledge and expertise. Even nonscientific problems, they believed, could be analyzed and solved scientifically. Many reformers came to believe that only enlightened experts and well-designed bureaucracies could create the stability and order America needed.

This belief found expression in many ways, among them in the writings of a new group of scholars and intellectuals. Unlike the social Darwinists of the nineteenth century, these theorists were no longer content with merely justifying the existing industrial system. They spoke instead of the creation of a new civilization, in which the expertise of scientists and engineers could be brought to bear on the problems of the economy and society. Among the most influential was the social scientist Thorstein Veblen. Harshly critical of the industrial tycoons of the late nineteenth century—the "leisure class" as he satirically described them in his first major work, *A Theory of the Leisure Class* (1899)— Veblen proposed instead a new economic system in which power would reside in the hands of highly trained engineers. Only they, he argued, could fully understand the "machine process" by which modern society must be governed.

In practical terms, the impulse toward expertise and organization helped produce the idea of scientific management, or "Taylorism." (See p. 483.) It encouraged the development of modern mass-production techniques and, above all, the assembly line. But it also inspired a revolution in American education and the creation of a new area of inquiry: social science, the use of scientific techniques in the study of society and its

BAXTER STREET, NEW YORK
The Danish immigrant Jacob Riis rose from modest beginnings to become a successful journalist and a prominent crusader against the miserable living conditions in urban immigrant neighborhoods. He wrote powerfully of those conditions in his famous book *How the Other Half Lives* (1890); equally powerful were the many photographs he took during his investigations. This picture shows conditions in a crowded tenement neighborhood in lower Manhattan. *(Museum of the City of New York)*

them how to create middle-class lifestyles. Even the word "settlement" suggested as much: middle-class people "settling" in the inner city and bringing civilization to the urban frontier.

Central to the settlement houses were the efforts of college women. Indeed, the movement became a training ground for many important female leaders of the twentieth century, including Eleanor Roosevelt. The settlement houses provided these women with an environment and a role that society considered "appropriate" for unmarried women: urban "homes" where settlement workers helped immigrants to become better members of society. (The settlement house was "home" only to some of the reformers; their immigrant constituents did not live there.)

institutions. It produced a generation of bureaucratic reformers concerned with the structure of organizations and committed to building new political and economic institutions capable of managing a modern society. It also helped create a movement toward organization among the expanding new group of middle-class professionals.

The Professions

The late nineteenth century saw a dramatic expansion in the number of Americans engaged in administrative and professional tasks. Industries needed managers, technicians, and accountants as well as workers. Cities required commercial, medical, legal, and educational services. New technology required scientists and engineers who, in turn, required institutions and instructors to train them. By the turn of the century, those performing these services had come to constitute a distinct social group—what some have called a new middle class.

The new middle class placed a high value on education and individual accomplishment. By the early twentieth century, its millions of members were building organizations and establishing standards to secure their position in society. As their principal vehicle, they created the modern, organized professions. The idea of professionalism had been a frail one in America even as late as 1880. When every patent-medicine salesman could claim to be a doctor, when every frustrated politician could set up shop as a lawyer, when anyone who could read and write could pose as a teacher, a professional label by itself carried little weight. There were, of course, skilled and responsible doctors, lawyers, teachers, and others; but they had no way of controlling or distinguishing themselves clearly from the amateurs, charlatans, and incompetents who presumed to practice their trades. As the demand for professional services increased, so did the pressures for reform.

Among the first to respond was the medical profession. Throughout the 1890s, doctors who considered themselves trained professionals began forming local associations and societies. In 1901, they reorganized the American Medical Association into a national professional society. By 1920, nearly two-thirds of all American doctors were members. The AMA quickly called for strict, scientific standards for admission to the practice of medicine, with doctors themselves serving as protectors of the standards. State and local governments responded by passing new laws requiring the licensing of all physicians and restricting licenses to those practitioners approved by the profession.

Accompanying the emphasis on strict regulation of the profession came a concern for rigorous scientific training and research. By 1900, medical education at a few medical schools—notably Johns Hopkins in Baltimore (founded in 1893)—compared favorably with that in the leading institutions of Europe. Doctors such as William H. Welch at Hopkins revolutionized the teaching of medicine by moving students out of the classrooms and into laboratories and clinics. Rigorous new standards forced many inadequate medical schools out of existence, and those that remained were obliged to adopt a strict scientific approach.

There was similar movement in other professions. By 1916, lawyers in all forty-eight states had established professional bar associations; and virtually all of them had succeeded in creating central examining boards, composed of lawyers, to regulate admission to the profession. Increasingly, aspiring lawyers found it necessary to enroll in graduate programs, and the nation's law schools accordingly expanded greatly, both in numbers and in the rigor of their curricula. Businessmen supported the creation of schools of business administration and created their own national organizations: the National Association of Manufacturers in 1895 and the United States Chamber of Commerce in 1912. Even farmers, long the symbol of the romantic spirit of individualism, responded to the new order by forming, through the National Farm Bureau Federation, a network of agricultural organizations designed to spread scientific farming methods, teach sound marketing techniques, and lobby for the interests of their members.

Among the purposes of the new professionalism was guarding entry into the professions. This was only partly an effort to defend the professions from the untrained and incompetent. The admission requirements also protected those already in the professions from excessive competition and lent prestige and status to the professional level. Some professionals used their entrance requirements to exclude blacks, women, immigrants, and other "undesirables" from their ranks. Others used them simply to keep the numbers down, to ensure that demand for the services of existing members would remain high.

Women and the Professions

Both by custom and by active barriers of law and prejudice, American women found themselves excluded from most of the emerging professions. But a substantial number of middle-class women—particularly those emerging from the new women's colleges and from the coeducational state universities—entered professional careers nevertheless.

A few women managed to establish themselves as physicians, lawyers, engineers, scientists, and corporate managers. Several leading medical schools admitted women, and in 1900 about 5 percent of all American physicians were female (a proportion that remained unchanged until the 1960s). Most, however, turned by necessity to those professions that society considered suitable for women. Settlement houses and social work provided two "appropriate" professional outlets for women. The most important, however, was teaching. Indeed, in the late nineteenth century, more than two-thirds of all grammar school teachers were women, and perhaps 90 percent of all professional women were teachers. For educated black women, in particular, teaching was often the only professional opportunity they could hope to find. The existence of segregated black schools in the South created a substantial market for African-American teachers.

Women also dominated other professional activities. Nursing had become primarily a women's field during and after the Civil War, when it was still considered a menial occupation, akin to domestic service. But by the early twentieth century, it was adopting professional standards. Prospective nurses generally needed certification from schools of nursing and could not simply learn on the job. Women also found opportunities as librarians, another field beginning to define itself in professional terms. And many women entered academia—often receiving advanced degrees at such predominantly male institutions as the University of Chicago, MIT, or Columbia, and finding professional opportunities in the new and expanding women's colleges.

The "women's professions" had much in common with other professions: the value they placed on training and expertise, the creation of professional organizations and a professional "identity," the monitoring of admission to professional work. But they also had distinctive qualities. Teaching, nursing, library work, and others were "helping" professions. They usually involved working primarily with other women or with children. Their activities occurred in places that seemed different from the offices that dominated the predominantly male business and professional worlds; such places as schools, hospitals, and libraries had a vaguely "domestic" image.

WOMEN AND REFORM

The prominence of women in reform movements is one of the most striking features of progressivism. In most states in the early twentieth century, women could not vote. They almost never held public office. They had footholds in only a few (and usually primarily female) professions. They lived in a culture in which most people, male and female, believed that women were not suited for the male-dominated public world, that they did, and should, inhabit their own sphere. What, then, explains the prominent role so many women played in the reform activities of the period? In fact, female activism in the progressive era represented both an expansion of women's separate sphere and a confirmation of it.

The "New Woman"

The phenomenon of the "new woman," widely remarked upon at the time, was a product of social and economic changes that affected the private world as much as the public one. By the end of the nineteenth century, almost all income-producing activity had moved out of the home and into the factory or the office. At the same time, children were beginning school at earlier ages and spending more time there. For wives and mothers who did not work for wages, the home was a less all-consuming place. Most women still oversaw the domestic functions of the home. Technological innovations such as running water, electricity, and eventually household appliances made housework less onerous (even if higher standards of cleanliness counterbalanced many of these gains); and for middle-class women with domestic help, housework occupied only a small part of the day. It was not surprising, perhaps, that more and more women were looking for activities outside the home.

Declining family size also changed the lives of many women. Middle-class white women in the late nineteenth century had fewer children than their mothers and grandmothers had borne. They also lived longer than previous generations. Many women thus now spent fewer years with young children in the home and lived more years after their children were grown.

There were also many more women who lived outside traditional families altogether. Some educated women shunned marriage entirely, believing that only by remaining single could they play the roles they envisioned in the public world; approximately 10 percent of all American women in the last decades of the nineteenth century never married—a high proportion of them middle-class women. Single women were among the most prominent female reformers of the time: Jane Addams and Lillian Wald in the settlement house movement; Frances Willard in the temperance movement; Anna Howard Shaw in the suffrage movement; and many others. Some of these women lived alone. Others lived with other women, often in long-term relationships—some of them secretly romantic—that were known at the time as "Boston marriages." The divorce rate also rose rapidly in the late nineteenth century, from one divorce for every twenty-one marriages in 1880 to one in nine by 1916; women initiated the great majority of them.

Higher levels of education also contributed to the prominence of women in reform activities. The proliferation of women's colleges and of coeducational public universities in the late nineteenth-century produced the first generation of women in which significant numbers had education above the high-school level. (See pp. 527–528.) The new colleges also helped create female communities, within which women could find support for their ambitions and companionship for their activities.

There was, in the end, no single profile for the "new woman." But a growing number of American women at the beginning of the twentieth century were defining their lives in ways that included a substantial amount of activity outside the home, and they were deriving from their identity as women a set of distinctive concerns that defined—and limited—their public activities.

The Clubwomen

Among the most visible signs of the increasing public roles of women in the late nineteenth and early twentieth centuries were the women's clubs—a large network of women's associations that proliferated rapidly beginning in the 1880s and 1890s and that became the vanguard of many important reforms.

The women's clubs began largely as cultural organizations to provide middle- and upper-class women with an outlet for their intellectual energies. In 1892, when women formed the General Federation of Wom-

THE SHIRTWAIST STRIKE, 1909
More than 30,000 workers in shirtwaist factories in New York went on strike in November 1909—one of the largest labor actions in American history involving mostly women workers. Members of Local 25 of the International Ladies Garment Workers Union organized the strike. When the ILGWU hesitated to support them, the local turned to the new Women's Trade Union League for help. The strike attracted substantial public support (including support from some of New York's wealthiest women) and soon spread to other cities as well. It ultimately failed to achieve most of its goals, but it did lead to the organization of many garment workers and greatly strengthened both the ILGWU and the WTUL. *(Brown Brothers, courtesy ILGWU)*

en's Clubs to coordinate the activities of local organizations, there were more than 100,000 members in nearly 500 clubs. Eight years later, there were 160,000 members; and by 1917, over 1 million.

By the early twentieth century, the clubs were becoming less concerned with cultural activities and more concerned with contributing to social betterment. Because many club members were from wealthy families, some organizations had substantial funds at their disposal to make their influence felt. And ironically, because women could not vote, the clubs had a nonpartisan image that made them more difficult for politicians to dismiss.

Black women occasionally joined clubs dominated by whites. But most such clubs excluded blacks, and so African Americans formed clubs of their own, some of which affiliated with the General Federation, but more of which became part of the independent National Association of Colored Women. They modeled themselves primarily on their white counterparts, but some black clubs also took positions on issues of particular concern to blacks. Some crusaded against lynch-

ing and called for congressional legislation to make lynching a federal crime. Others protested aspects of segregation.

The women's club movement raised few overt challenges to prevailing assumptions about the proper role of women in society. But it did represent an important effort by women to extend their influence beyond the traditional female sphere within the home and the family. Few clubwomen were willing to accept the arguments of such committed feminists as Charlotte Perkins Gilman, who in her 1898 book *Women and Economics* argued that the traditional definition of gender roles was exploitive and obsolete. The club movement, rather, allowed women to define a space for themselves in the public world without openly challenging the existing, male-dominated order. And it gave many women access to a female community in which they were able to act and express themselves in ways usually impossible in male-dominated institutions. As one Boston clubwoman said, "We need to feel the cheer and inspiration of meeting each other, we gain the courage and fresh life that comes from the mingling of congenial souls, of those working for the same ends."

But the importance of the club movement did not lie simply in what it did for middle-class women. It lay also in what those women accomplished for the working-class people they attempted to help. Much of what the clubs did was uncontroversial: planting trees; supporting schools, libraries, and settlement houses; building hospitals and parks. But clubwomen also supported measures that attracted significant opposition. They were an important force in winning passage of state (and ultimately federal) laws that regulated the conditions of woman and child labor, that established government inspection of workplaces, that regulated the food and drug industries, that reformed policies toward the Indian tribes, and that applied new standards to urban housing. They were instrumental in pressuring state legislatures in most states to provide pensions to widowed or abandoned mothers with small children—a system known as "mother's pensions," which ultimately became absorbed into the Social Security system. In 1912, they pressured Congress into establishing the Children's Bureau in the Labor Department, an agency directed to develop policies to protect children.

In many of these efforts, the clubwomen formed alliances with other women's groups, such as the Women's Trade Union League, founded in 1903 by female union members and upper-class reformers and committed to persuading women to join unions. In addition to working on behalf of protective legislation for women, WTUL members held public meetings on behalf of female workers, raised money to support strikes, marched on picket lines, and bailed striking women out of jail.

Women reformers often worked closely with men; and of course the success of most of their efforts depended on the support of male voters, legislators, and public officials. What made their crusades palatable to men was also what made them appealing to many women: their self-consciously "maternal" character. In campaigning for measures to protect women and children workers and to assist the most powerless members of society, women's clubs emphasized the "nurturing" and "protective" features of their work and fought for "moral uplift." In doing so, they were reflecting contemporary ideas about the natural inclinations of women.

Woman Suffrage

Perhaps the largest single reform movement of the progressive era, indeed one of the largest in American history, was the fight for woman suffrage—a movement that attracted support from both women and men but whose most important leaders were women.

It is sometimes difficult for today's Americans to understand why the suffrage issue could have become the source of such enormous controversy. But at the time, suffrage seemed to many of its critics a very radical demand, in part because of the rationale some of its early supporters used to advance it. Throughout the late nineteenth century, many suffrage advocates presented their views in terms of "natural rights," arguing that women deserved the same rights as men—including, first and foremost, the right to vote. Elizabeth Cady Stanton, for example, wrote in 1892 of woman as "the arbiter of her own destiny. . . . if we are to consider her as a citizen, as a member of a great nation, she must have the same rights as all other members." A woman's role as "mother, wife, sister, daughter" was "incidental" to her larger role as a part of society.

This was an argument that boldly challenged the views of the many men (and even many women) who believed that society required a distinctive female "sphere" in which women would serve first and foremost as wives and mothers. And so a powerful antisuffrage movement emerged, dominated by men but with the active support of many women, which challenged this apparent threat to the existing social order. There were antisuffrage organizations, some with substantial memberships; antisuffrage newspapers; rallies; petitions to legislatures; and widely circulated tracts. Opponents railed against the threat suffrage posed to the "natural order" of civilization. Woman, said one opponent, "was made man's helper, was

SUFFRAGISTS
Suffrage activists hang posters along the boardwalk in the beachfront town of Long Branch, New Jersey. Twenty-nine states had permitted women at least some access to the ballot before ratification of the Nineteenth Amendment in 1920. New Jersey was not one of them. *(Culver)*

given a servient place (not necessarily inferior) and man the dominant place (not necessarily superior) in the division of labor." Antisuffragists associated suffrage with divorce (not without some reason, since many suffrage advocates also supported revising the laws to make it easier for women to obtain a divorce). They linked suffrage with promiscuity, looseness, and neglect of children.

In the first years of the twentieth century, the suffrage movement began to overcome this opposition and win some substantial victories. In part that was because suffragists were becoming better organized and more politically sophisticated than their opponents. Under the leadership of Anna Howard Shaw, a Boston social worker, and Carrie Chapman Catt, a journalist from Iowa, membership in the National American Woman Suffrage Association grew from about 13,000 in 1893 to over 2 million in 1917. The involvement of such well-known and widely admired women as Jane Addams gave added respectability to the cause.

But the movement also gained strength because many of its most prominent leaders began to justify suffrage in "safer," less threatening ways. Suffrage, some supporters began to argue, would not challenge the "separate sphere" in which women resided. It would allow women to bring their special and distinct virtues more widely to bear on society's problems. It was, they claimed, precisely because women occupied a distinct sphere—because as mothers and wives and homemakers they had special experiences and special sensitivities to bring to public life—that woman suffrage could make such an important contribution to politics. Jane Addams expressed this more maternalist justification for suffrage in a 1909 article: "If women would effectively continue their old avocations, they must take part in the slow upbuilding of that code of legislation which is alone sufficient to protect the home from its dangers incident to modern life."

In particular, many suffragists argued that enfranchising women would help the temperance movement, by giving its largest group of supporters a political voice. Some suffrage advocates claimed that once women had the vote, war would become a thing of the past, since women would—by their calming, maternal influence—help curb the belligerence of men. That was one reason why World War I gave a final, decisive push to the movement for suffrage.

Suffrage also attracted support for other, less optimistic reasons. Many middle-class people found persuasive the argument that if blacks, immigrants, and other "base" groups had access to the franchise, then it was not only a matter of justice but of common sense to allow educated, "well-born" women to vote. Some

people, in fact, supported woman suffrage because they believed that it would add to the constituency that supported immigration restriction and racial disfranchisement. Florence Kelley, a prominent social reformer who was later to help organize the NAACP, remarked unhappily in 1906 on this aspect of the suffrage movement: "I have rarely heard a ringing suffrage speech which did not refer to the 'ignorant and degraded' men, or the 'ignorant immigrants' as our masters. This is habitually spoken with more or less bitterness."

Not all suffragists abandoned the more radical rationales. Among working-class, immigrant, and black women in particular, suffrage continued to generate substantial support precisely because it seemed so radical, because it promised to reshape the role of women and reform the social order. But among members of the middle class, the separation of the suffrage movement from more radical feminist goals, and its association with other reform causes of concern to many Americans, helped it gain widespread support.

The principal triumphs of the suffrage movement began in 1910. That year, Washington became the first state in fourteen years to extend suffrage to women. California followed a year later, and four other western states in 1912. This impressive early strength of the suffrage movement in the western states was a result, in part, of the absence of large Catholic communities in the region. In the East, battles over suffrage seemed inevitably to become linked to ethnic battles over cultural issues—most notably temperance—that divided Catholics and Protestants. In the West, the suffrage fight only rarely intersected with other, more divisive issues.

In 1913, Illinois became the first state east of the Mississippi to embrace woman suffrage. And in 1917 and 1918, New York and Michigan—two of the most populous states in the Union—gave women the vote. By 1919, thirty-nine states had granted women the right to vote in at least some elections; fifteen had allowed them full participation. In 1920, finally, suffragists won ratification of the Nineteenth Amendment, which guaranteed political rights to women throughout the nation.

To some feminists, however, the victory seemed less than complete. Alice Paul, head of the militant National Woman's Party (founded in 1916), never accepted the relatively conservative "separate sphere" justification for suffrage. She argued that the Nineteenth Amendment alone would not be sufficient to protect women's rights. Women needed more: a constitutional amendment that would provide clear, legal protection for their rights and would prohibit all discrimination on the basis of sex. But Alice Paul's argument found limited favor even among many of the most important leaders of the recently triumphant suffrage crusade. Jane Addams, Florence Kelley, Carrie Chapman Catt, and others showed no interest in the Equal Rights Amendment. Some, such as Addams, denounced it bitterly, fearing it would invalidate the special protective legislation for women that they had fought so hard to have enacted. It would be many years before the divisions between these two wings of American feminism were healed.

As the controversy over the Equal Rights Amendment suggests, the suffrage movement did not, in the end, produce a coherent movement behind any issue other than securing women the vote. On most other questions, in fact, women were generally no more in agreement than men. Once enfranchised, the new voters did little to support the arguments of those suffragists who had claimed that women would operate in politics as a coherent force for reform.

THE ASSAULT ON THE PARTIES

Sooner or later, most progressive goals required the involvement of government. Only government, reformers agreed, could effectively counter the many powerful private interests that threatened the nation. But American government at the dawn of the new century was, progressives believed, poorly adapted to perform their ambitious tasks. At every level political institutions were outmoded, inefficient, and corrupt. Before they could reform society effectively, they would have to reform government itself. In the beginning, at least, many reformers believed the first step must be an assault on the dominant role the political parties played in the life of the state. They considered the parties corrupt, undemocratic, and reactionary.

Early Attacks

Attacks on party dominance had been frequent in the late nineteenth century. Greenbackism and Populism, for example, had been efforts to break the hammerlock with which the Republicans and Democrats controlled public life. The Independent Republicans (or mugwumps) had attempted to challenge the grip of partisanship; and former mugwumps became important supporters of progressive political reform activity in the 1890s and later.

The early assaults enjoyed some success. In the 1880s and 1890s, for example, most states adopted the secret ballot. Prior to that, the political parties themselves had printed ballots (or "tickets"), with the names of the party's candidates, and no others. They distributed the tickets to their supporters, who then simply went to the polls to deposit them in the ballot box. The old system had made it possible for bosses to monitor the voting behavior of their constituents; it had also made it difficult for voters to "split" their tickets—to vote for candidates of different parties for different offices. The new secret ballot—printed by the government and distributed at the polls to be filled out and deposited in secret—helped chip away at the power of the parties over the voters.

By the late 1890s, critics of the parties were expanding their goals. Party rule could be broken, they believed, in one of two ways. It could be broken by increasing the power of the people, by permitting them to circumvent partisan institutions and express their will directly at the polls. Or it could be broken by placing more power in the hands of nonpartisan, nonelective officials, insulated from political life. Reformers promoted measures that moved along both those paths.

Municipal Reform

Many progressives believed the impact of party rule was most damaging in the cities. Municipal government therefore became the first target of those working for political reform. Muckraking journalists such as Lincoln Steffens were especially successful in arousing public outrage at corruption and incompetence in city politics.

The muckrakers struck a responsive chord among a powerful group of urban middle-class progressives. For several decades after the Civil War, "respectable" citizens of the nation's large cities had avoided participation in municipal government. Viewing politics as a debased and demeaning activity, they shrank from contact with the "vulgar" elements who were coming to dominate public life. By the end of the century, however, a new generation of activists—some of them members of old aristocratic families, others a part of the new middle class—were taking a growing interest in government.

They faced a formidable array of opponents. In addition to challenging the powerful city bosses and their entrenched political organizations, they were attacking a large group of special interests: saloon owners, brothel keepers, and perhaps most significantly, those businessmen who had established lucrative relationships with the urban machines and who viewed reform as a threat to their profits. Allied with these interests were many influential newspapers, which ridiculed the reformers as naive do-gooders. Finally, there was the great constituency of urban working people, many of them recent immigrants, to whom the machines were a source of needed jobs and services. Gradually, however, the reformers gained in political strength—in part because of their own growing numbers, in part because of the failures of the existing political leadership. And in the first years of the twentieth century, they began to score some important victories.

One of the first major successes came in Galveston, Texas, where the old city government proved completely unable to deal with the effects of a destructive tidal wave in 1900. Capitalizing on public dismay, reformers, many of them local businessmen, won approval of a new city charter. The mayor and council were replaced by an elected, nonpartisan commission. In 1907, Des Moines, Iowa, adopted its own version of the commission plan, and other cities soon followed.

Another approach to municipal reform, similarly motivated by the desire to remove city government from the hands of the parties, was the city-manager plan, by which elected officials hired an outside expert—often a professionally trained business manager or engineer—to take charge of the government. The city manager would presumably remain untainted by the corrupting influence of politics. By the end of the progressive era, almost 400 cities were operating under commissions, and another 45 employed city managers.

In most urban areas, and in the larger cities in particular, the enemies of party had to settle for less absolute victories. Some cities made the election of mayors nonpartisan (so that the parties could not choose the candidates) or moved them to years when no presidential or congressional races were in progress (to reduce the influence of the large turnouts that party organizations produced on such occasions). Reformers tried to make city councilors run at large, to limit the influence of ward leaders and district bosses. They tried to strengthen the power of the mayor at the expense of the city council, on the assumption that reformers were more likely to succeed in getting a sympathetic mayor elected than they were to win control of the entire council.

Indeed, some of the most successful reformers emerged not from the new commission and city-manager systems but from conventional political structures that progressives came to control. Tom Johnson, the celebrated reform mayor of Cleveland, waged a long and difficult war against the powerful streetcar interests in his city, fighting to raise the ridiculously low assessments on railroad and utilities properties, to lower streetcar fares to 3 cents, and ultimately to impose municipal ownership on certain basic utilities. After Johnson's defeat and death, his talented aide Newton D. Baker won election as mayor and helped maintain Cleveland's reputation as the best-governed city in America. Hazen Pingree of Detroit, Samuel "Golden Rule" Jones of Toledo, and other mayors effectively challenged local party bosses to bring the spirit of reform into city government.

Statehouse Progressivism

The assault on boss rule in the cities did not, however, always produce results satisfying to reformers. As a result, many progressives turned to state government as an agent for reform. These state-level progressives, like their municipal counterparts, considered existing state governments unfit to answer society's needs. They looked with particular scorn on state legislatures, whose ill-paid, relatively undistinguished members they believed were generally incompetent, often corrupt, and totally controlled by party bosses. Many reformers began looking for ways to circumvent the legislatures (and the party bosses that controlled them) by increasing the power of the electorate.

Two of the most important changes were innovations first proposed by Populists in the 1890s: the initiative and the referendum. The initiative allowed reformers to circumvent state legislatures altogether by submitting new legislation directly to the voters in general elections. The referendum provided a method by which actions of the legislature could be returned to the electorate for approval. By 1918, more than twenty states had enacted one or both of these reforms.

Similarly, the direct primary and the recall were efforts to limit the power of party and improve the quality of elected officials. The primary election was an attempt to take the selection of candidates away from the bosses and give it to the people. In the South, it was also an effort to limit black voting—since primary voting, many white southerners believed, would be easier to control than general elections. The recall gave voters the right to remove a public official from office at a special election, which could be called after a sufficient number of citizens had signed a petition. By 1915 every state in the nation had instituted primary elections for at least some offices. The recall encountered more strenuous opposition, but a few states adopted it as well.

Other reform measures attempted to clean up the legislatures themselves by limiting the influence of corporations on their activities and on the behavior of the parties. Between 1903 and 1908, twelve states passed laws restricting lobbying by business interests in state legislatures. In those same years, twenty-two states banned campaign contributions by corporations, and twenty-four states forbade public officials from accepting free passes from railroads.

ROBERT LA FOLLETTE CAMPAIGNING IN WISCONSIN
After three terms as governor of Wisconsin, La Follette began a long career in the United States Senate in 1906 during which he worked uncompromisingly for advanced progressive reforms—so uncompromisingly, in fact, that he was often almost completely isolated. He entitled a chapter of his autobiography "Alone in the Senate." La Follette had a greater impact on his own state, whose politics he and his sons dominated for nearly forty years and where he was able to win passage of many reforms that the federal government resisted. *(State Historical Society of Wisconsin)*

Reform efforts proved most effective in states that elevated vigorous and committed politicians to positions of leadership. In New York, Governor Charles Evans Hughes exploited progressive sentiment to create a commission to regulate public utilities. In California, Governor Hiram Johnson used the new reforms to limit the political power of the Southern Pacific Railroad. In New Jersey, Woodrow Wilson, the Princeton University president elected governor in 1910, used executive leadership to win reforms designed to end New Jersey's widely denounced position as the "mother of trusts."

But the most celebrated state-level reformer was Robert M. La Follette of Wisconsin. Elected governor in 1900, he helped turn his state into what reformers across the nation described as a "laboratory of progressivism." Under his leadership the Wisconsin progressives won approval of direct primaries, initiatives, and referendums. They regulated railroads and utilities. They passed laws to regulate the workplace and provide compensation for laborers injured on the job. They instituted graduated taxes on inherited fortunes, and they nearly doubled state levies on railroads and other corporate interests.

La Follette brought to progressivism his own fervent, almost evangelical, commitment to reform; and he used his personal magnetism to widen public awareness of progressive goals and to mobilize the energies of many previously passive groups. Reform was not simply the responsibility of politicians, he argued, but of newspapers, citizens' groups, educational institutions, and business and professional organizations. Ultimately, La Follette would be overshadowed by other national progressive leaders. In the early years of the century, however, few men were as effective in publicizing the message of reform. None was as successful in bending state government to that goal.

Parties and Interest Groups

The reformers did not, of course, eliminate parties from American political life. But they did contribute to a decline in party influence. Evidence of that came from, among other things, the decline in voter turnout. In the late nineteenth century, up to 81 percent of eligible voters routinely turned out for national elections. In the early twentieth century, while turnout remained very high by today's standards, the figure declined markedly. In the presidential election of 1900, 73 percent of the electorate voted. By 1912, it had declined to about 59 percent. Never again did voter turnout reach as high as 70 percent.

At the same time that parties were declining, other power centers were beginning to replace them: what

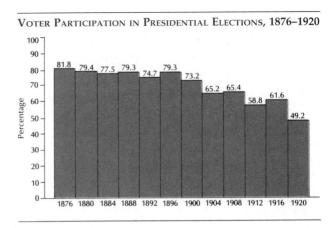

VOTER PARTICIPATION IN PRESIDENTIAL ELECTIONS, 1876–1920

have become known as "interest groups." Beginning late in the nineteenth century and accelerating rapidly in the twentieth, new organizations emerged outside the party system, designed to pressure government to do their members' bidding: professional organizations, trade associations representing particular businesses and industries, labor organizations, farm lobbies, and many others. Social workers, the settlement house movement, women's clubs, and others learned to operate as interest groups to advance their demands. A new pattern of politics, in which many individual interests organized to influence government directly rather than through party structures, was emerging. It would become the characteristic form of American politics in the twentieth century.

SOURCES OF PROGRESSIVE REFORM

Middle-class reformers, most of them from the East, dominated the public image and much of the substance of progressivism in the late nineteenth and early twentieth centuries. But they were not alone in seeking to improve social conditions. Working-class Americans, African Americans, westerners, even party bosses also played crucial roles in advancing some of the important reforms of the era.

Labor, the Machine, and Reform

Although the American Federation of Labor, and its leader Samuel Gompers, remained largely aloof from many of the reform efforts of the time (reflecting Gom-

THE TRIANGLE SHIRTWAIST FIRE
Policemen and investigators stand amid the coffins of victims of the 1911 fire in the Triangle Shirtwaist Factory in New York City, in which 146 workers (almost all of them women) died. Although the proprietors of the factory, who had locked the emergency exits, were acquitted of criminal charges in the deaths, the fire spurred reform and labor groups—most notably the International Ladies Garment Workers Union—to agitate for government action to improve conditions in the sweatshops. *(Culver)*

pers's firm belief that workers should not rely on government to improve their lot), some unions nevertheless played important roles in reform battles. In San Francisco, for example, workers in the Building Trades Council spearheaded the formation of the new Union Labor Party, committed to a program of reform almost indistinguishable from that of middle-class and elite progressives in the city. Corruption and ineptitude within the new party's leadership limited its effectiveness, but the party did manage to elect two of its candidates mayor. Although the workers never controlled enough votes in the state legislature to have much direct influence, other Bay Area politicians supported pro-labor legislation in an effort to appeal to the party's constituency. Between 1911 and 1913, California passed a child labor law, a workmen's compensation law, and a limitation on working hours for women. Union pressures contributed to the passage of similar laws in many other states as well.

One result of the assault on the parties was a change in the party organizations themselves, which attempted to adapt to the new realities so as to preserve their influence. Some party machines emerged from the progressive era almost as powerful as they had entered it. In large part, this was because bosses themselves recognized that they must change in order to survive. Thus they sometimes allowed their machines to become vehicles of social reform. One example was New York's Tammany Hall, the nation's oldest and most notorious city machine. Its astute leader, Charles Francis Murphy, began in the early years of the century to fuse the techniques of boss rule with some of the concerns of social reformers. Murphy did nothing to challenge the fundamental workings of Tammany Hall. But Tammany began to take an increased interest in state and national politics, which it had traditionally scorned; and it used its political power on behalf of legislation to improve working conditions, protect child laborers, and eliminate the worst abuses of the industrial economy.

In 1911, a terrible fire swept through the factory of the Triangle Shirtwaist Company in New York; 146 workers, most of them women, died. Many of them had been trapped inside the burning building because management had locked the emergency exits to prevent malingering. For the next three years, a state commission studied not only the background of the fire but the general condition of the industrial workplace. It was responding to intense public pressure from women's groups and New York City labor unions—and to less-public pressure from Tammany Hall. By 1914, the commission had issued a series of reports calling for major reforms in the conditions of modern labor.

The report itself was a classic progressive document, based on the testimony of experts, filled with statistics and technical data. Yet when its recommendations reached the New York Legislature, its most effective supporters were not middle-class progressives but two Tammany Democrats from working-class backgrounds: Senator Robert F. Wagner and Assemblyman Alfred E. Smith. With the support of Murphy and the backing of other Tammany legislators, they steered through a series of pioneering labor laws that imposed strict regulations on factory owners and established effective mechanisms for enforcement.

Western Progressives

The American West produced some of the most notable progressive leaders of the time: Hiram Johnson of California, George Norris of Nebraska, William Borah of Idaho, and others—almost all of whom spent at least some of their political careers in the United States Senate. That was because for western states, the most important target of reform energies was not state or local governments, which had relatively little power, but the federal government, which exercised a kind of authority in the West that it had never possessed in the East.

That was in part because some of the most important issues to the future of the West required action above the state level. Disputes over water, for example, almost always involved rivers and streams that crossed state lines. The question of who had the rights to the waters of the Colorado River created a political battle that no state government could resolve; the federal government had to arbitrate. More significant, perhaps, the federal government exercised enormous power over the lands and resources of the western states and provided substantial subsidies to the region in the form of land grants and support for railroad and water projects. Huge areas of the West remained (and still remain) public lands, controlled by Washington—a far greater proportion than in any states east of the Mississippi; and much of the growth of the West was (and continues to be) a result of federally funded dams and water projects.

Because so much authority in the region rested in federal bureaucracies which state and local governments could not control, political parties in most of the West were relatively weak. That was one reason why western states could move so quickly and decisively to embrace reforms that parties did not like: the initiative, the referendum, the recall, direct primaries. It is also why aspiring politicians were much quicker to look to Washington as a place from which they could influence the future of their region.

African Americans and Reform

One social question that received relatively little attention from white progressives was race. But among African Americans themselves, the progressive era produced some significant challenges to existing racial norms.

African Americans faced greater obstacles—legal, economic, social, and political—than any other group

W. E. B. Du Bois
Although Du Bois, unlike Booker T. Washington, never developed a large popular following, he was the acknowledged leader of the black elite in the late nineteenth and early twentieth centuries. He was the first African American ever to earn a doctorate at Harvard University, and he published a number of distinguished works of history and sociology during his long career. He also served for more than twenty years as editor of *The Crisis*, the newspaper of the NAACP. He died in 1963, at the age of ninety-five, having lived long enough to see the emergence of a powerful civil rights movement dedicated to achieving many of the goals for which he had fought throughout his life. This pastel portrait was drawn around 1925 by Winhold Reiss. *(National Portrait Gallery)*

in challenging their own oppressed status and seeking reform. Thus it was not surprising, perhaps, that so many embraced the message of Booker T. Washington in the late nineteenth century, to "put down your bucket where you are," to work for immediate self-improvement rather than long-range social change. Not all blacks, however, were content with this approach. And by the turn of the century a powerful challenge was emerging—to the philosophy of Washington and, more important, to the entire structure of race relations. The chief spokesman for this new approach was W. E. B. Du Bois.

Du Bois, unlike Washington, had never known slavery. Born in Massachusetts, educated at Fisk University in Nashville and at Harvard, he grew to maturity with a more expansive view than Washington of the goals of his race and the responsibilities of white society to eliminate prejudice and injustice. In *The Souls of Black Folk* (1903), he launched an open attack on the philosophy of the Atlanta Compromise, accusing Washington of encouraging white efforts to impose segregation and of unnecessarily limiting the aspirations of his race. "Is it possible and probable," he asked, "that nine millions of men can make effective progress in economic lines if they are deprived of political rights, made a servile caste, and allowed only the most meager chance for developing their exceptional men? If history and reason give any distinct answer to these questions, it is an emphatic No."

Rather than content themselves with education at the trade and agricultural schools, Du Bois advocated, talented blacks should accept nothing less than a full university education. They should aspire to the professions. They should, above all, fight for the immediate restoration of their civil rights, not simply wait for them to be granted as a reward for patient striving. In 1905, Du Bois and a group of his supporters met at Niagara Falls—on the Canadian side of the border because no hotel on the American side of the Falls would have them—and launched what became known as the Niagara Movement. Four years later, after a race riot in Springfield, Illinois, they joined with white progressives sympathetic to their cause to form the National Association for the Advancement of Colored People (NAACP). Whites held most of the offices at first, but Du Bois, its director of publicity and research, was the guiding spirit. In the ensuing years, the new organization led the drive for equal rights, using as its principal weapon lawsuits in the federal courts.

Within less than a decade, the NAACP had begun to win some important victories. In *Guinn* v. *United States* (1915), the Supreme Court supported their position that the grandfather clause in an Oklahoma law was unconstitutional. (The statute denied the vote to any citizen whose ancestors had not been enfranchised in 1860.) In *Buchanan* v. *Worley* (1917), the Court struck down a Louisville, Kentucky, law requiring residential segregation. Disfranchisement and segregation would survive through other methods for many decades to come, but the NAACP had established a pattern of black resistance that would ultimately bear important fruits. It had also established itself, particularly after Booker T. Washington's death in 1915, as

one of the nation's leading black organizations, a position it would maintain for many years.

The NAACP was not a radical, or even an egalitarian, organization. It relied, rather, on the efforts of the most intelligent and educated members of the black race, the "talented tenth" as Du Bois called them. And it stressed not so much the elevation of all blacks from poverty and oppression as the opportunity for exceptional blacks to gain positions of full equality. Ultimately, its members believed, such efforts would benefit all blacks. By creating a trained elite, blacks would in effect be creating a leadership group capable of fighting for the rights of the race as a whole.

CRUSADES FOR ORDER AND REFORM

Reformers directed many of their energies at the political process. But they also crusaded on behalf of what they considered moral issues. There were campaigns to eliminate alcohol from national life, to curb prostitution, and to limit divorce. And there were efforts to restrict immigration or curb the power of monopoly in the industrial economy. Proponents of each of those reforms believed that success would help regenerate society as a whole.

The Temperance Crusade

Many progressives considered the elimination of alcohol from American life a necessary step in restoring order to society. Workers in settlement houses and social agencies abhorred the effects of drinking on working-class families: scarce wages vanished as workers spent hours in the saloons. Drunkenness spawned violence, and occasionally murder, within urban families. Women, in particular, saw alcohol as a source of some of the greatest problems of working-class wives and mothers, and hoped through temperance to reform male behavior and thus improve women's lives. Employers, too, regarded alcohol as an impediment to industrial efficiency; workers often missed time on the job because of drunkenness or, worse, came to the factory intoxicated and performed their tasks sloppily and dangerously. Critics of economic privilege denounced the liquor industry as one of the nation's most sinister trusts. And political reformers, who (correctly) looked on the saloon as one of the central institutions of the urban machine, saw an attack on drinking as part of an attack on the bosses. Out of such sentiments emerged the temperance movement.

CRUSADING FOR TEMPERANCE
This unflattering painting by Ben Shahn portrays late-nineteenth-century women demonstrating grimly in front of a saloon. It suggests the degree to which temperance and prohibition had fallen out of favor with liberals and progressives by the 1930s, when Shahn was working. In earlier years, however, temperance attracted the support of some of the most advanced American reformers. *(Museum of the City of New York)*

Temperance had been a major reform movement before the Civil War, mobilizing large numbers of people (and particularly large numbers of women) in a crusade with strong evangelical overtones. Beginning in the 1870s, it experienced a major resurgence. As in the antebellum years, the movement was led and supported primarily by women. In 1873, temperance advocates formed the Women's Christian Temperance Union (WCTU), led after 1879 by Frances Willard. By 1911, it had 245,000 members and had become the single largest women's organization in American history to that point. The WCTU publicized the evils of alcohol and the connection between drunkenness and family violence, unemployment, poverty, and disease. In 1893, the Anti-Saloon League joined the temperance movement and, along with the WCTU, began to press for a specific legislative solution: the legal abolition of saloons. Gradually, that demand grew to include the complete prohibition of the sale and manufacture of alcoholic beverages.

Despite substantial opposition from immigrant and working-class voters, pressure for prohibition grew steadily through the first decades of the new century. By 1916, nineteen states had passed prohibition laws. But since the consumption of alcohol was actually increasing in many unregulated areas, temperance advocates were beginning to advocate a national prohibition law. America's entry into World War I, and the moral fervor it unleashed, provided the last push to the advocates of prohibition. In 1917, with the support of rural fundamentalists who opposed alcohol on moral and religious grounds, progressive advocates of prohibition steered through Congress a constitutional amendment embodying their demands. Two years later, after ratification by every state in the nation except Connecticut and Rhode Island (bastions of Catholic immigrants), the Eighteenth Amendment became law, to take effect in January 1920.

Immigration Restriction

Virtually all reformers agreed that the growing immigrant population had created social problems, but there was wide disagreement on how to best respond.

TOTAL IMMIGRATION, 1900–1920

Some progressives believed that the proper approach was to help the new residents adapt to American society. Others argued that efforts at assimilation had failed and that the only solution was to limit the flow of new arrivals.

In the first decades of the century, therefore, pressure grew to close the nation's gates. New scholarly theories, appealing to the progressive respect for expertise, argued that the introduction of immigrants into American society was polluting the nation's racial stock. The spurious "science" of eugenics spread the belief that human inequalities were hereditary and that immigration was contributing to the multiplication of the unfit. Skillful publicists such as Madison Grant, whose *The Passing of the Great Race* (1916) established him as the nation's most effective nativist, warned of the dangers of racial "mongrelization" and of the importance of protecting the purity of Anglo-Saxon and other Nordic stock from pollution by eastern Europeans, Hispanics, and Asians.

A special federal commission of "experts," chaired by Senator William P. Dillingham of Vermont, issued an elaborate study filled with statistics and scholarly testimony. The Dillingham Report argued that the newer immigrant groups—largely southern and eastern Europeans—had proven themselves less assimilable than earlier immigrants. Immigration, the report implied, should be restricted by nationality. But even many people who rejected these racial arguments supported limiting immigration as a way to solve such urban problems as overcrowding, unemployment, strained social services, and social unrest.

The combination of these concerns gradually won for the nativists the support of some of the nation's leading progressives: Theodore Roosevelt, Henry Cabot Lodge, and others. Powerful opponents—employers who saw immigration as a source of cheap labor, immigrants themselves and their political representatives—managed to block the restriction movement for a time. But by the beginning of World War I (which itself effectively blocked immigration temporarily), the nativist tide was clearly gaining strength.

The Dream of Socialism

At no time in the history of the United States to that point, and seldom after, did radical critiques of the capitalist system attract more support than in the period between 1900 and 1914. Although never a force to rival or even seriously threaten the two major parties, the Socialist Party of America grew during the progressive era into a force of considerable strength. In the election of 1900, it had attracted the support of fewer than 100,000 voters; in 1912, its durable leader and perennial presidential candidate, Eugene V. Debs, received nearly 1 million ballots. Strongest in urban immigrant communities, particularly among Germans and Jews, it also attracted the loyalties of a substantial number of Protestant farmers in the South and Midwest. Socialists won election to over 1,000 state and local offices. And they had the support at times of such intellectuals as Lincoln Steffens, the crusader against municipal corruption, and Walter Lippmann, the brilliant young journalist and social critic. Florence Kel-

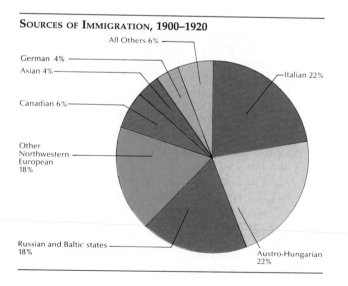

SOURCES OF IMMIGRATION, 1900–1920

SIGNIFICANT EVENTS

1873   Women's Christian Temperance Union (WCTU) founded

1889   Jane Addams opens Hull House in Chicago

1892   General Federation of Women's Clubs founded

1893   Johns Hopkins Medical School established

   Anti-Saloon League founded

1895   National Association of Manufacturers founded

1898   Charles Sheldon publishes *In His Steps*

   Charlotte Perkins Gilman publishes *Women and Economics*

1899   Thorstein Veblen publishes *A Theory of the Leisure Class*

1900   Galveston, Texas, establishes commission government

   Robert La Follette elected governor of Wisconsin

1901   American Medical Association reorganized

1902   Oregon adopts initiative and referendum

   Mississippi adopts direct primary

1903   Women's Trade Union League founded

1904   Ida Tarbell publishes exposé of Standard Oil

1905   National Education Association founded

1909   Herbert Croly publishes *The Promise of American Life*

1911   Fire kills 146 workers at Triangle Shirtwaist Company in New York City

1912   United States Chamber of Commerce founded

1913   Dayton, Ohio, establishes city-manager government

   Louis D. Brandeis publishes *Other People's Money*

1914   Walter Lippmann publishes *Drift and Mastery*

1916   Madison Grant publishes *The Passing of the Great Race*

1919   Eighteenth Amendment (prohibition) ratified

1920   Nineteenth Amendment (woman suffrage) ratified

---

ley, Frances Willard, and other women reformers were attracted to socialism too, in part because of its support for pacifism and labor militancy.

Virtually all socialists agreed on the need for basic structural changes in the economy, but they differed widely on the extent of those changes and the tactics necessary to achieve them. Some endorsed the radical goals of European Marxists; others envisioned a more moderate reform that would allow small-scale private enterprise to survive but would nationalize major industries. Some believed in working for reform through electoral politics; others favored militant direct action.

Most conspicuous among the militants was the radical labor union the Industrial Workers of the World (IWW), known to opponents as the "Wobblies." Under the leadership of William ("Big Bill") Haywood,

the IWW advocated a single union for all workers and abolition of the "wage slave" system; it rejected political action in favor of strikes—especially the general strike. The Wobblies were widely believed to have been responsible for the dynamiting of railroad lines and power stations and other acts of terror, although evidence of their actually engaging in such activities was slim.

The IWW was one of the few labor organizations of the time to champion the cause of unskilled workers, and it had particular strength in the West—where a large group of migratory laborers (miners, timbermen, and others) found it very difficult to organize or sustain conventional unions. The Wobblies created not just a union, but a far-flung social network that became something of a home to workers who were otherwise largely rootless.

In 1917, a strike by IWW timber workers in Washington and Idaho virtually shut down production in the industry. That brought down upon the union the wrath of the federal government, which had just begun mobilizing for war and needed timber for war production. Federal authorities imprisoned the leaders of the union, and state governments between 1917 and 1919 passed a series of laws that effectively outlawed the IWW. The organization survived for a time, but never fully recovered.

More moderate socialists who advocated peaceful change through political struggle dominated the party. They emphasized a gradual education of the public to the need for change and patient efforts within the system to enact it. But by the end of World War I, because the party had refused to support the war effort and because of a growing wave of antiradicalism that subjected the socialists to enormous harassment and persecution, socialism was in decline as a significant political force.

Decentralization and Regulation

Many reformers agreed with the socialists that the greatest threat to the nation's economy was excessive corporate centralization and consolidation, but most progressives retained a faith in the possibilities of reform within a capitalist system. Rather than nationalize basic industries, many reformers hoped to restore the economy to a more human scale. Few envisioned a return to a society of small, local enterprises; some consolidation, they recognized, was inevitable. They did, however, argue that the federal government should work to break up the largest combinations and enforce a balance between the need for bigness and the need for competition. This viewpoint came to be identified particularly closely with Louis D. Brandeis, a brilliant lawyer and later justice of the Supreme Court, who spoke and wrote widely (most notably in his 1913 book *Other People's Money*) about the "curse of bigness." "If the Lord had intended things to be big," Brandeis once wrote, "he would have made man bigger—in brains and character."

Brandeis and his supporters opposed bigness in part because they considered it inefficient. But their opposition had a moral basis as well. Bigness was a threat not just to efficiency but to freedom. It limited the ability of individuals to control their own destinies. It encouraged abuses of power. Government must, Brandeis insisted, regulate competition in such a way as to ensure that large combinations did not emerge.

Other progressives were less enthusiastic about the virtues of competition. More important to them was efficiency, which they believed economic concentration usually encouraged. What government should do, they argued, was not to fight "bigness," but to guard against abuses of power by large institutions. It should distinguish between "good trusts" and "bad trusts," encouraging the good while disciplining the bad. Since economic consolidation was destined to remain a permanent feature of American society, continuing oversight by a strong, modernized government was essential. One of the most influential spokesmen for this emerging "nationalist" position was Herbert Croly, whose 1909 book *The Promise of American Life* became one of the most influential progressive documents.

Increasingly, the attention of nationalists such as Croly focused on some form of coordination of the industrial economy. Society must act, Walter Lippmann wrote in a notable 1914 book, *Drift and Mastery*, "to introduce plan where there has been clash, and purpose into the jungles of disordered growth." To some, that meant businesses themselves learning new ways of cooperation and self-regulation; some of the most energetic "progressive" reformers of the period, in fact, were businessmen searching for ways to bring order to their own troubled world. To others, the solution was for government to play a more active role in regulating and planning economic life. One of those who came to endorse that position (although not fully until after 1910) was Theodore Roosevelt, who once said: "We should enter upon a course of supervision, control, and regulation of those great corporations—a regulation which we should not fear, if necessary, to bring to the point of control of monopoly prices." Roosevelt became for a time the most powerful symbol of the reform impulse at the national level.

SUGGESTED READINGS

Progressivism: Overviews.   John D. Buenker, John C. Burnham, and Robert M. Crunden, *Progressivism* (1977). John W. Chambers II, *The Tyranny of Change: America in the Progressive Era, 1900–1917* (1980). John Milton Cooper, *The Pivotal Decades: The United States, 1900–1920* (1990). Alan Dawley, *Struggles for Justice: Social Responsibility and the Liberal State* (1991). Richard Hofstadter, *The Age of Reform: From Bryan to FDR* (1955). Gabriel Kolko, *The Triumph of Conservatism: A Reinterpretation of American History* (1963). Arthur S. Link and Richard L. McCormick, *Progressivism* (1983). Nell Irvin Painter, *Standing at Armageddon: The United States, 1877–1919* (1987). James Weinstein, *The Corporate Ideal in the Liberal State, 1900–1918* (1969). Robert Wiebe, *The Search for Order, 1877–1920* (1967).

The Muckrakers.   David Chalmers, *The Social and Political Ideas of the Muckrakers* (1964). Louis Filler, *The Muckrakers*, rev. ed. (1980). Leon Harris, *Upton Sinclair* (1975). Justin Kaplan, *Lincoln Steffens* (1974). C. C. Regier, *The Era of the Muckrakers* (1932). Harold S. Wilson, *McClure's Magazine and the Muckrakers* (1970).

Progressive Thought.   Richard Abrams, *The Burdens of Progress* (1978). Carl N. Degler, *In Search of Human Nature: The Decline and Revival of Darwinism in American Social Thought* (1991). Arthur Ekirch, *Progressivism in America* (1974). Charles V. Forcey, *The Crossroads of Liberalism: Croly, Weyl, Lippmann* (1961). Sudhir Kakar, *Frederick Taylor* (1970). D. W. Marcell, *Progress and Pragmatism: James, Dewey, Beard and the American Idea of Progress* (1974). David W. Noble, ed., *The Progressive Mind*, rev. ed. (1981). Jean B. Quandt, *From the Small Town to the Great Community: The Social Thought of Progressive Intellectuals* (1970). Robert Westbrook, *John Dewey and American Democracy* (1991). Morton White, *Social Thought in America* (1949).

Social Work and the Social Gospel.   Jane Addams, *Twenty Years at Hull House* (1910). Paul Boyer, *Urban Masses and Moral Order, 1820–1920* (1978). Mina Carson, *Settlement Folk: Social Thought and the American Settlement Movement, 1885–1930* (1990). Robert M. Crunden, *Ministers of Reform: The Progressives' Achievement in American Civilization, 1889–1920* (1982). Susan Curtis, *A Consuming Faith: The Social Gospel and Modern American Culture* (1991). Allen F. Davis, *Spearheads of Reform: The Social Settlements and the Progressive Movement, 1890–1914* (1968); *American Heroine: The Life and Legend of Jane Addams* (1973). C. H. Hopkins, *The Rise of the Social Gospel in American Protestantism* (1940). William R. Hutchinson, *The Modernist Impulse in American Protestantism* (1982). Rivka Shpak Lissak, *Pluralism and Progressives: Hull House and the New Immigrants, 1890–1919* (1989). Roy Lubove, *The Progressives and the Slums: Tenement House Reform in New York City* (1962). Henry May, *Protestant Churches and Industrial America* (1949). Timothy Miller, *Following in His Steps: A Biography of Charles M. Sheldon* (1987).

Education and the Professions.   Clyde W. Barrow, *Universities and the Capitalist State: Corporate Liberalism and the Reconstruction of American Higher Education, 1894–1928* (1990). Burton Bledstein, *The Culture of Professionalism* (1976). Lawrence A. Cremin, *The Transformation of the Schools: Progressivism in American Education, 1876–1957* (1971). Lynn D. Gordon, *Gender and Higher Education in the Progressive Era* (1990). Samuel Haber, *The Quest for Authority and Honor in the American Professions, 1750–1900* (1991). Barbara Harris, *Beyond Her Sphere: Women and the Professions in American History* (1978). Thomas L. Haskell, *The Emergence of Professional Social Science* (1977). Morton J. Horwitz, *The Transformation of American Law, 1870–1960: The Crisis of Legal Orthodoxy* (1992). Kenneth M. Ludmerer, *Learning to Heal: The Development of American Medical Education* (1985). Regina Markell Morantz-Sanchez, *Sympathy and Science: Women Physicians in American Medicine* (1985). Barbara Miller Solomon, *In the Company of Educated Women: A History of Women in Higher Education in America* (1985). Paul Starr, *The Social Transformation of American Medicine* (1982). David Tyack and Elizabeth Hansot, *Managers of Virtue: Public School Leadership in America, 1820–1980* (1982). Lawrence Veysey, *The Emergence of the American University* (1970).

Municipal Reform.   John D. Buenker, *Urban Liberalism and Progressive Reform* (1973). James B. Crooks, *Politics and Progress: The Rise of Urban Progressivism in Baltimore* (1968). Oscar Handlin, *Al Smith and His America* (1958). Melvin G. Holli, *Reform in Detroit: Hazen S. Pingree and Urban Politics* (1969). J. Joseph Huthmacher, *Senator Robert F. Wagner and the Rise of Urban Liberalism* (1971). Michael Kazin, *Barons of Labor: The San Francisco Building Trades and Union Power in the Progressive Era* (1981). Zane Miller, *Boss Cox's Cincinnati* (1968). Martin J. Schiesl, *The Politics of Efficiency: Municipal Administration and Reform in America, 1880–1920* (1977).

Women, Reform, and Suffrage.   Paula Baker, *The Moral Frameworks of Public Life: Gender, Politics, and the State in Rural New York, 1870–1930* (1991). Karen Blair, *The Clubwoman as Feminist* (1980). Mari Jo Buhle, *Women and American Socialism* (1983). Norman H. Clark, *Deliver Us From Evil: An Interpretation of American Prohibition* (1976). Mark T. Connelly, *The Response to Prohibition in the Progressive Era* (1980). Nancy Cott, *The Grounding of Modern Feminism* (1987). Ellen C. DuBois, *Feminism and Suffrage: The Emergence of an Independent Women's Movement in America, 1848–1869* (1978). Nancy Shrom Dye, *As Equal as Sisters: Feminism, The Labor Movement, and the Women's Trade Union League of New York* (1981). Eleanor Flexner, *Century of Struggle* (1959). Linda Gordon, *Woman's Body, Woman's Right: A Social History of Birth Control* (1976). Alan P. Grimes, *The Puritan Ethic and Woman Suffrage* (1967). Jacquelyn Dowd Hall, *The Revolt Against Chivalry* (1979). David M. Kennedy, *Birth Control in America: The Career of Margaret Sanger* (1970). Aileen S. Kraditor, *Ideas of the*

Woman Suffrage Movement (1965). Ellen C. Lagemann, *A Generation of Women: Education in the Lives of Progressive Reformers* (1979). Elaine Tyler May, *Great Expectations: Marriage and Divorce in Post-Victorian America* (1980). David Morgan, *Suffragists and Democrats: The Politics of Woman Suffrage in America* (1972). Robyn Muncy, *Creating a Female Dominion in American Reform, 1890–1935* (1991). William O'Neill, *Divorce in the Progressive Era* (1967); *Everyone Was Brave: The Rise and Fall of Feminism in America* (1969). Ruth Rosen, *The Lost Sisterhood: Prostitutes in America, 1900–1918* (1982). Rosalind Rosenberg, *Beyond Separate Spheres: Intellectual Roots of Modern Feminism* (1982). Elyce J. Rotella, *From Home to Office: U.S. Women and Work, 1870–1930* (1981). Sheila M. Rothman, *Woman's Proper Place* (1978). Anne F. Scott, *Making the Invisible Woman Visible* (1984).

Racial Issues. John Dittmer, *Black Georgia in the Progressive Era, 1900–1920* (1977). George Fredrickson, *The Black Image in the White Mind* (1968). Paula Giddings, *When and Where I Enter: The Impact of Black Women on Race and Sex in America* (1984). Louis Harlan, *Booker T. Washington: The Making of a Black Leader* (1856); *Booker T. Washington: The Wizard of Tuskegee, 1901–1915* (1983). Charles F. Kellogg, *NAACP* (1970). Jack Temple Kirby, *Darkness at Dawning: Race and Reform in the Progressive South* (1972). Ralph E. Luker, *The Social Gospel in Black and White: American Racial Reform, 1885–1912* (1991). James M. McPherson, *The Abolitionist Legacy: From Reconstruction to the NAACP* (1975). August Meier, *Negro Thought in America, 1880–1915* (1963). Cynthia Neverdon-Morton, *Afro-American Women of the South and the Advancement of the Race, 1885–1925* (1989). Elliott Rudwick, *W. E. B. Du Bois* (1969). Donald Spivey, *Schooling for the New Slavery: Black Industrial Education* (1978). Joel Williamson, *The Crucible of Race: Black-White Relations in the American South Since Emancipation* (1985).

State-Level Reform. Richard M. Abrams, *Conservatism in a Progressive Era: Massachusetts* (1964). Dewey Grantham, *Southern Progressivism: The Reconciliation of Progress and Tradition* (1983). Sheldon Hackney, *Populism to Progressivism in Alabama* (1969). Robert S. Maxwell, *La Follette and the Rise of Progressivism in Wisconsin* (1944). Richard L. McCormick, *From Realignment to Reform: Political Change in New York State, 1893–1910* (1981). George E. Mowry, *California Progressives* (1951). Russel B. Nye, *Midwestern Progressive Politics* (1951). David P. Thelen, *The New Citizenship: Origins of Progressivism in Wisconsin* (1972); *Robert M. La Follette and the Insurgent Spirit* (1976); *Paths of Resistance: Tradition and Dignity in Industrializing Missouri* (1986). Robert F. Wesser, *Charles Evans Hughes: Politics and Reform in New York State, 1905–1910* (1967). C. Vann Woodward, *Origins of the New South* (1951). Irwin Yellowitz, *Labor and the Progressive Movement in New York State* (1965).

National Issues. Ruth Bourdin, *Women and Temperance: The Quest for Power and Liberty, 1873–1900* (1980). Melvyn Dubofsky, *We Shall Be All* (1969). Sidney Fine, *Laissez Faire and the General Welfare State* (1956). Joseph Gusfield, *Symbolic Crusade: Status Politics and the Temperance Movement* (1963). John Higham, *Strangers in the Land* (1955). Michael E. McGerr, *The Decline of Popular Politics: The American North, 1865–1928* (1986). Bruno Ramirez, *When Workers Organize: The Politics of Industrial Relations in the Progressive Era, 1898–1916* (1978). James T. Timberlake, *Prohibition and the Progressive Movement* (1963). James Weinstein, *The Decline of Socialism in America* (1967). Robert Wiebe, *Businessmen and Reform: A Study of the Progressive Movement* (1962). Olivier Zunz, *Making America Corporate, 1870–1920* (1990).

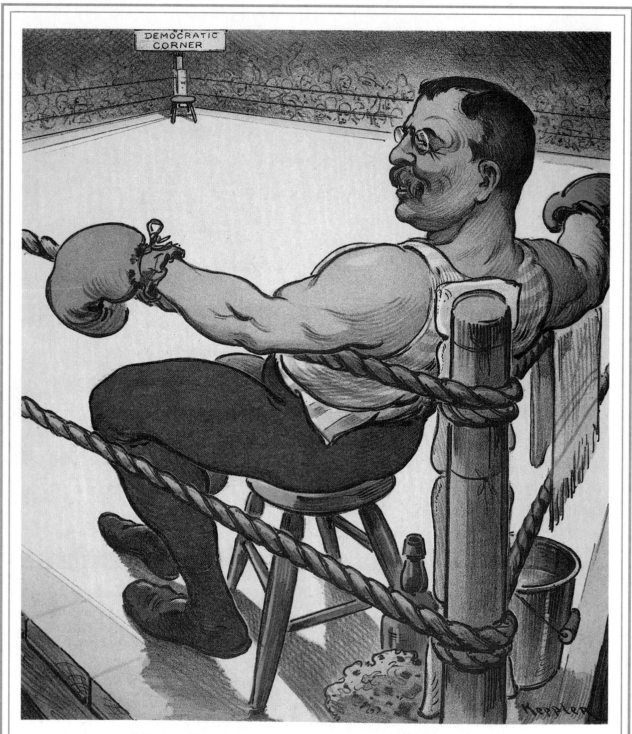

" 'TERRIBLE TEDDY' WAITS FOR 'THE UNKNOWN,' " BY JOSEPH KEPPLER, JR.
This cartoon conveys the widespread (and in the end correct) belief that Theodore Roosevelt
was an unbeatable candidate for election to the presidency in 1904. To oppose him, the
Democrats nominated Alton B. Parker, a New York appeals court judge who was indeed
virtually "unknown" to most of the public. *(The Granger Collection)*

CHAPTER TWENTY-TWO

THE BATTLE FOR NATIONAL REFORM

FFORTS TO REFORM THE industrial economy encountered repeated frustrations at the state and local levels. The great combinations were national in scope, and reformers gradually concluded that only national action could effectively control their power. Beginning early in the twentieth century, they began to look to the federal government.

But like state and local government, the national government—bureaucratically weak and mired in partisan politics—seemed poorly suited to serve as an agent of reform. Progressives attempted to make it more responsive to their demands. Some reformers, for example, urged an end to the system by which United States senators were elected by the members of their state legislatures; they proposed instead a direct popular election, which they believed would force the Senate to react to public demands. The Seventeenth Amendment, passed by Congress in 1912 and ratified by the states in 1913, brought about that change.

Even a reformed Congress, however, could not provide the kind of coherent leadership the progressive agenda required. If the federal government was truly to fulfill its mission, most reformers agreed, it would require leadership from the one office capable of providing it: the presidency.

THEODORE ROOSEVELT AND THE MODERN PRESIDENCY

"Presidents in general are not lovable," the writer Walter Lippmann, who had known many, said near the end of his life. "They've had to do too much to get where they are. But there was one President who was lovable—Teddy Roosevelt—and I loved him."

Lippmann was not alone. To a generation of progressive reformers, Theodore Roosevelt was more than an admired public figure; he was an idol. No president before, and few since, attracted such attention and devotion. Yet for all his popularity among reformers, Roosevelt was in many respects decidedly conservative. He earned his extraordinary popularity less because of the extent of the reforms he championed than because he brought to his office a broad conception of its powers and invested the presidency with something of its modern status as the center of national political life.

The Accidental President

When President William McKinley suddenly died in September 1901, the victim of an assassination, Roosevelt (who had been elected vice president less than a year before) was only forty-two years old, the youngest man ever to assume the presidency. Already, however, he had achieved a considerable reputation within the Republican Party as something of a wild man. Party leaders sensed his independence and despaired of controlling him. "I told William McKinley that it was a mistake to nominate that wild man at Philadelphia," party boss Mark Hanna was reported to have exclaimed. "I asked him if he realized what would happen if he should die. Now look, that damned cowboy is President of the United States!"

Roosevelt's reputation as a wild man was a result less of the substance of his early political career than of its style. As a young member of the New York legislature, he had displayed an energy seldom seen in that lethargic body. As a rancher in the Dakota Badlands (where he retired briefly after the sudden death of his first wife), he had helped capture outlaws. As New York City police commissioner, he had been a flamboyant battler against crime and vice. As assistant secretary of the navy, he had been a bold proponent of American expansion. As commander of the Rough Riders, he had led a heroic, if militarily useless, charge in the battle of San Juan Hill in Cuba during the Spanish-American War.

But Roosevelt as president never openly rebelled against the leaders of his party. He became, rather, a champion of cautious, moderate change. Reform, he believed, was less a vehicle for remaking American society than for protecting it against more radical challenges.

Government, Capital, and Labor

Roosevelt envisioned the federal government not as the agent of any particular interest but as a mediator of the public good, with the president at its center. These attitudes found expression in Roosevelt's poli-

MAKING SAUSAGES
Upton Sinclair's 1906 novel *The Jungle* contained, among other things, nauseating descriptions of the process by which meat factories (such as the one shown here) made sausages. Partly in response to the success of his book, Congress passed the Meat Inspection Act the same year, establishing federal standards for the industry. *(Bettmann)*

ESTABLISHMENT OF NATIONAL PARKS AND FORESTS

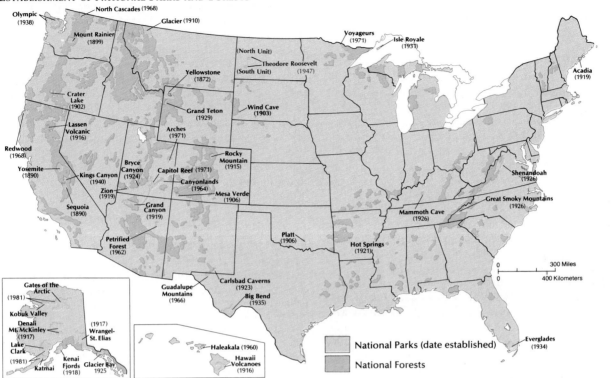

Olympic (1938)
North Cascades (1968)
Glacier (1910)
Mount Rainier (1899)
Voyageurs (1971)
Isle Royale (1931)
Acadia (1919)
Yellowstone (1872)
(North Unit)
Theodore Roosevelt (1947)
(South Unit)
Crater Lake (1902)
Grand Teton (1929)
Wind Cave (1903)
Lassen Volcanic (1916)
Arches (1971)
Redwood (1968)
Rocky Mountain (1915)
Shenandoah (1926)
Yosemite (1890)
Bryce Canyon (1924)
Capitol Reef (1971)
Kings Canyon (1940)
Zion (1919)
Canyonlands (1964)
Mesa Verde (1906)
Great Smoky Mountains (1926)
Sequoia (1890)
Grand Canyon (1919)
Mammoth Cave (1926)
Petrified Forest (1962)
Platt (1906)
Hot Springs (1921)
Gates of the Arctic (1981)
Kobuk Valley
Denali Mt. McKinley (1917)
(1917) Wrangel-St. Elias
Lake Clark (1981)
Kenai Fjords (1918)
Glacier Bay 1925
Katmai
Guadalupe Mountains (1966)
Carlsbad Caverns (1923)
Big Bend (1935)
Haleakala (1960)
Hawaii Volcanoes (1916)
Everglades (1934)

0 — 300 Miles
0 — 400 Kilometers

☐ National Parks (date established)
☐ National Forests

---

cies toward the great industrial combinations. He was not opposed to the principle of economic concentration, but he acknowledged that consolidation produced dangerous abuses of power. He allied himself, therefore, with those progressives who urged regulation (but not destruction) of the trusts.

At the heart of Roosevelt's policy was his desire to win for government the power to investigate the activities of corporations and publicize the results. The pressure of educated public opinion, he believed, would alone eliminate most corporate abuses. Government could legislate solutions for those that remained. The new Department of Commerce and Labor, established in 1903 (later to be divided into two separate departments), was to assist in this task through its investigatory arm, the Bureau of Corporations..

Although Roosevelt was not a trust buster at heart, he made a few highly publicized efforts to break up combinations. In 1902, he ordered the Justice Department to invoke the Sherman Antitrust Act against a great new railroad monopoly in the Northwest, the Northern Securities Company, a $400 million enterprise pieced together by J. P. Morgan, E. H. Harriman,

and James J. Hill. To Morgan, accustomed to a warm, supportive relationship with Republican administrations, the action was baffling. Hurrying to the White House with two conservative senators in tow, he told the president, "If we have done anything wrong, send your man to my man and they can fix it up." Roosevelt proceeded with the case nonetheless, and in 1904 the Supreme Court ruled that the Northern Securities Company must be dissolved. At the same time, however, he assured Morgan and others that the suit did not signal a general campaign to dissolve trusts. Although he filed more than forty additional antitrust suits during the remainder of his presidency, Roosevelt had no serious commitment to reverse the prevailing trend toward economic concentration.

A similar commitment to establishing the government as an impartial regulatory mechanism shaped Roosevelt's policy toward labor. In the past, federal intervention in industrial disputes had almost always meant action on behalf of employers. Roosevelt was willing to consider labor's position as well. When a bitter 1902 strike by the United Mine Workers against the anthracite coal industry dragged on long enough to endanger coal supplies for the coming winter,

Roosevelt asked both the operators and the miners to accept impartial federal arbitration. When the mine owners balked, Roosevelt threatened to send federal troops to seize the mines and resume coal production. The operators finally relented. Arbitrators awarded the strikers a 10 percent wage increase and a nine-hour day, although no recognition of their union—less than they had wanted but more than they would likely have won without Roosevelt's intervention. Despite such episodes, Roosevelt viewed himself as no more the champion of labor than of management. On several occasions, he ordered federal troops to intervene in strikes on behalf of employers.

The Square Deal

Reform was not Roosevelt's top priority during his first years as president. He was principally concerned with winning reelection, which required that he not antagonize the conservative Republican Old Guard. By skillfully dispensing patronage to conservatives and progressives alike, by reshuffling the leadership of unstable Republican organizations in the South, by winning the support of northern businessmen while making adroit gestures to reformers, Roosevelt had all but neutralized his opposition within the party by early 1904. He won its presidential nomination with ease. And in the general election, where he faced a pallid conservative Democrat, Alton B. Parker, he captured over 57 percent of the popular vote and lost no states outside the South. Now, relieved of immediate political concerns, he was free to display the extent—and the limits—of his commitment to reform.

During the 1904 campaign, Roosevelt boasted that he had worked in the anthracite coal strike to provide everyone with a "square deal." In his second term, he tried to extend his square deal further. One of his first targets was the powerful railroad industry. The Interstate Commerce Act of 1887, establishing the Interstate Commerce Commission (ICC), had been an early effort to regulate the industry; but over the years, the courts had sharply limited its influence. Roosevelt asked Congress for legislation to increase the government's power to oversee railroad rates. The Hepburn Railroad Regulation Act of 1906 sought to restore some regulatory authority to the government, although the bill was so cautious that it satisfied few progressives. Some reformers were enraged. Robert La Follette, now a U.S. Senator, never forgave Roosevelt for the concessions he made.

Roosevelt also pressured Congress to enact the Pure Food and Drug Act, which, despite weaknesses in its enforcement mechanisms, restricted the sale of dangerous or ineffective medicines. When Upton Sinclair's powerful novel *The Jungle* appeared in 1906, featuring appalling descriptions of conditions in the meatpacking industry, Roosevelt pushed for passage of the Meat Inspection Act, which ultimately helped eliminate many diseases once transmitted in impure meat. Starting in 1907, he proposed even more stringent measures: an eight-hour day for workers, broader compensation for victims of industrial accidents, inheritance and income taxes, regulation of the stock market, and others. He also started openly to criticize conservatives in Congress and the judiciary who were obstructing these programs. The result was not only a general stalemate in Roosevelt's reform agenda, but a widening gulf between the president and the conservative wing of his party.

ROOSEVELT AND MUIR IN YOSEMITE
John Muir, founder and leader of the Sierra Club, considered Theodore Roosevelt a friend and ally—a relationship cemented by a four-day camping trip the two men took together in Yosemite National Park in 1903. Roosevelt was indeed a friend to the national park and national forest systems and added considerable acreage to both. Among other things, he expanded Yosemite (at Muir's request). But unlike Muir, Roosevelt was also committed to economic development. As a result, he was not always a reliable ally of the most committed preservationists. *(Bettmann)*

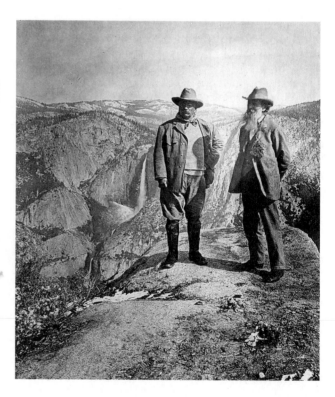

Conservation

Roosevelt's aggressive policies on behalf of conservation contributed to that gulf. An ardent sportsman and naturalist, he had long been concerned about the unregulated exploitation of America's natural resources and its remaining wilderness. Using executive powers, he restricted private development on millions of acres of undeveloped government land—most of it in the West—by adding them to the previously modest national forest system. When conservatives in Congress restricted his authority over public lands in 1907, Roosevelt and his chief forester, Gifford Pinchot, worked furiously to seize all the forests and many of the water power sites still in the public domain before the bill became law.

Roosevelt was the first president to take an active interest in the new and struggling American conservation movement, and his policies had a lasting effect on national environmental policies. More than most public figures, he was sympathetic to the concerns of the naturalists—those within the movement committed to protecting the natural beauty of the land and the health of its wildlife from human intrusion. Early in his presidency, Roosevelt even spent four days camping in the Sierras with John Muir, the nation's leading preservationist and the founder of the Sierra Club. But Roosevelt's actual policies tended to favor another faction within the conservation movement: those who believed in carefully managed development. That was in part a result of the influence of Pinchot, the first director of the National Forest Service (which he had helped create), who supported rational and efficient human use of the wilderness. The Sierra Club might argue for the "aesthetic" value of the forests; Pinchot insisted, in contrast, that "the whole question is a practical one." He and Roosevelt both believed that trained experts in forestry and resource management, such men as Pinchot himself, should apply to the landscape the same scientific standards that others were applying to the management of cities and industries. The president did side with the preservationists on certain issues, but the more important legacy of his conservation policy was to establish the government's role as manager of the continuing development of the wilderness.

The Old Guard may have opposed Roosevelt's efforts to extend government control over vast new lands. But they eagerly supported another important aspect of Roosevelt's natural resource policy: public reclamation and irrigation projects. In 1902, the president backed the National Reclamation Act, better known as the Newlands Act (named for its sponsor, Nebraska congressman Francis Newlands). It was the culmination of years of lobbying by businessmen and others from the West (through the National Irrigation Association). Frustrated by the failure of private capital and state governments to develop their water resources, they wanted the federal government to take over such projects. The Newlands Act provided federal funds for the construction of dams, reservoirs, and canals in the West—projects that would open new lands for cultivation and (years later) provide cheap electric power. It was the beginning of many years of critical federal aid for irrigation and power development in the western states, even though the Newlands Act (and the Bureau of Reclamation it created) had relatively little impact for more than twenty years after passage.

The Panic of 1907

Despite the flurry of reforms Roosevelt was able to enact, the government still had relatively little control over the industrial economy. That became clear in 1907, when a serious panic and recession began. As in 1893, American industrial production had outrun the capacity of either domestic or foreign markets to absorb it. Once again, the banking system and the stock market had displayed pathetic inadequacies. Once again, irresponsible speculation and rampant financial mismanagement had helped shatter a prosperity that many had come to believe was now permanent.

Conservatives blamed Roosevelt's "mad" economic policies for the disaster. And while the president, naturally (and correctly), disagreed, he nevertheless acted quickly to reassure business leaders that he would not interfere with their recovery efforts. J. P. Morgan, in a spectacular display of his financial power, helped construct a pool of the assets of several important New York banks to prop up shaky financial institutions. The key to the arrangement, Morgan told the president, was the purchase by U.S. Steel of the shares of the Tennessee Coal and Iron Company, currently held by a threatened New York bank. He would, he insisted, need assurances that the purchase would not prompt antitrust action. Roosevelt tacitly agreed, and the Morgan plan proceeded. Whether or not as a result, the panic soon subsided.

Roosevelt loved being president. He had made that plain during his first moments in office, when, torn between his excitement at his new position and his distress at McKinley's death, he had written, "It is a dreadful thing to come into the Presidency in this way; but it would be a far worse thing to be morbid about it." As his years in office produced increasing political successes, as his public popularity continued to rise, more and more observers began to assume that he would run for reelection in 1908, despite the long-standing tradition of presidents serving no more than two terms.

But the panic of 1907, combined with Roosevelt's growing "radicalism" during his second term, so alienated conservatives in his own party that he might have had difficulty winning the Republican nomination for another term. In 1904, moreover, he had made a public promise to step down four years later. And so, after nearly eight energetic years in the White House, during which he had transformed the role of the presidency in American government, Theodore Roosevelt, fifty years old, retired from public life—briefly.

The Troubled Succession

William Howard Taft, who assumed the presidency in 1909, had been Theodore Roosevelt's most trusted lieutenant and his hand-picked successor; progressive reformers believed him to be one of their own. But Taft had also been a restrained and moderate jurist, a man with a punctilious regard for legal process; conservatives expected him to abandon Roosevelt's aggressive use of presidential powers. By seeming acceptable to almost everyone, Taft won election to the White House in 1908 with almost ridiculous ease. He received his party's nomination virtually uncontested. His victory in the general election in November—over William Jennings Bryan, running forlornly for the Democrats for the third time—was a foregone conclusion. Taft entered the White House on a wave of good feeling.

Four years later, however, Taft would leave office the most decisively defeated president of the twentieth century, with his party deeply divided and the government in the hands of a Democratic administration for the first time in twenty years.

It had been obvious from the start that Taft and Roosevelt were not at all alike, but not until Taft took office did the real extent of the differences become clear. Roosevelt had been the most dynamic public figure of his age; Taft was stolid and respectable and little more. Roosevelt was an ardent sportsman and athlete; Taft was sedentary and obese—he weighed over 300 pounds and required a special, oversized bathtub to be installed in the White House. Most of all, Roosevelt had taken an expansive view of the powers of his office; Taft, in contrast, was slow, cautious, even lethargic, insistent that the president take pains to observe the strict letter of the law.

Yet even had Taft been the most dynamic of political figures, he would still have had difficulties as president. Having come into office as the darling of pro-

William Howard Taft
Taft could be a jovial companion in small groups, but his public image was of a dull, stolid man who stood in sharp and unfortunate contrast to his dynamic predecessor, Theodore Roosevelt. Taft also suffered public ridicule for his enormous size. He weighed as much as 350 pounds at times, and wide publicity accompanied his installation of a special oversized bathtub in the White House.
(UPI/Bettmann)

gressives and conservatives alike, he soon found that he could not please them both. Gradually he found himself, without really intending it, pleasing the conservatives and alienating the progressives.

Taft and the Progressives

Taft's first problem arose in the opening months of the new administration, when he called Congress into special session to lower protective tariff rates, an old progressive demand. But having proposed the legislation, the president made no effort to overcome the opposition to it of the congressional Old Guard, arguing that to do so would violate the constitutional doctrine of separation of powers. The result was the feeble Payne-Aldrich Tariff, which reduced tariff rates scarcely at all and in some areas actually raised them. Progressives resented the president's passivity and were suspicious of his motives.

With Taft's standing among Republican progressives deteriorating and with the party growing more and more deeply divided, a sensational controversy broke out late in 1909 that helped destroy Taft's popularity with reformers for good. Many progressives had been unhappy when Taft replaced Roosevelt's secretary of the interior, James R. Garfield, an aggressive conservationist, with Richard A. Ballinger, a more conservative corporate lawyer. Suspicion of Ballinger grew when he attempted to invalidate Roosevelt's actions in removing nearly 1 million acres of forests and mineral reserves from the public lands available for private development.

In the midst of this mounting concern, Louis Glavis, an Interior Department investigator, charged the new secretary with having once connived to turn over valuable public coal lands in Alaska to a private syndicate for personal profit. Glavis took the evidence to Gifford Pinchot, still head of the Forest Service and a critic of Ballinger's policies, and Pinchot took the charges to the president. Taft ordered his attorney general to investigate them and eventually decided they were groundless.

But Pinchot was not satisfied, particularly after Taft fired Glavis for his part in the episode. He leaked the story to the press and asked Congress to investigate the scandal. The president discharged him for insubordination, and the congressional committee appointed to study the controversy, dominated by the Old Guard, exonerated Ballinger. But progressives throughout the country supported Pinchot. The controversy aroused as much public passion as any dispute of its time; and when it was over, Taft had alienated the supporters of Roosevelt completely and, it seemed, irrevocably.

To many reformers at the time, the Pinchot-Ballinger controversy was a simple morality tale. In reality, it represented a clash between two competing visions of economic development. Pinchot represented those who wanted carefully supervised economic growth in the American West. Ballinger (himself a westerner) represented many western entrepreneurs who saw federal regulations as an impediment to their own economic ambitions. Progressives portrayed Ballinger as the defender of corporate power; in fact, Pinchot was the more popular among leaders of large corporations, who generally supported his conservation policies, while Ballinger had the support of small businessmen, who had always opposed such policies.

The Return of Roosevelt

During most of these controversies, Theodore Roosevelt was far away: on a long hunting safari in Africa and an extended tour of Europe. To the American public, however, Roosevelt remained a formidable presence. His return to New York in the spring of 1910 was a major public event; and progressives noted that, although he turned down an invitation from Taft to visit the White House, he met at once with Gifford Pinchot (who had already traveled to England to see him several months before).

Roosevelt insisted that he had no plans to return to active politics, but his resolve lasted less than a week. Politicians began flocking immediately to his home at Oyster Bay, Long Island, for conferences. Roosevelt took an active role in several New York political controversies; and within a month, he announced that he would embark on a national speaking tour before the end of the summer. Furious with Taft, who had, he believed, "completely twisted around the policies I advocated and acted upon," he was becoming convinced that he alone was capable of reuniting the Republican Party.

The real signal of Roosevelt's decision to assume leadership of Republican reformers was a speech on September 1, 1910, in Osawatomie, Kansas, where he outlined a set of principles that he labeled the "New Nationalism" and that made clear he had moved a considerable way from the cautious conservatism of the first years of his presidency. Social justice, he argued, was possible only through the vigorous efforts of a strong federal government whose executive acted as the "steward of the public welfare." Those who thought primarily of property rights and personal profit "must now give way to the advocate of human welfare, who rightly maintains that every man holds his property subject to the general right of the community to regulate its use to whatever degree the public welfare may require it." He supported graduated income and inheritance taxes, workers' compensation for industrial accidents, regulation of the labor of women and children, tariff revision, and firmer regulation of corporations.

Spreading Insurgency

The congressional elections of 1910 provided further evidence of how far the progressive revolt had spread. In primary elections, conservative Republicans suffered defeat after defeat while almost all the progres-

ROOSEVELT AT OSAWATOMIE
Roosevelt's famous speech at Osawatomie, Kansas, in 1910 was the most radical of his career and openly marked his break with the Taft administration and the Republican leadership. "The essence of any struggle for liberty," he told his largely conservative audience, "has always been, and must always be to take from some one man or class of men the right to enjoy power, or wealth, or position or immunity, which has not been earned by service to his or their fellows." *(Brown Brothers)*

sive incumbents were reelected. In the general election, the Democrats, who were now offering progressive candidates of their own, won control of the House of Representatives for the first time in sixteen years and gained strength in the Senate. Reform sentiment seemed clearly on the rise. But Roosevelt still denied any presidential ambitions and claimed that his real purpose was to pressure Taft to return to progressive policies. Two events, however, changed his mind.

The first was a 1911 antitrust decision by the Taft administration. Taft had been more active than Roosevelt in enforcing the provisions of the Sherman Antitrust Act and had launched dozens of suits against corporate combinations. And on October 27, 1911, the administration announced a suit against U.S. Steel,

charging, among other things, that the 1907 acquisition of the Tennessee Coal and Iron Company had been illegal. Roosevelt had approved that acquisition in the midst of the 1907 panic, and he was enraged by the implication that he had acted improperly.

But Roosevelt was still reluctant to become a candidate for president, largely because Senator Robert La Follette had been working since 1911 to secure the presidential nomination for himself. La Follette's candidacy stumbled, however, in February 1912, when, exhausted and distraught about his daughter's illness, he appeared to suffer a breakdown during a speech in Philadelphia. With almost indecent haste, many of his supporters abandoned him and turned to Roosevelt, who announced his candidacy on February 22.

The Republican Schism

La Follette retained some diehard support. But for all practical purposes, the campaign for the Republican nomination had now become a battle between Roosevelt, the champion of the progressives, and Taft, the candidate of the conservatives. Roosevelt scored overwhelming victories in all thirteen presidential primaries and arrived at the convention convinced that he was the choice of the party rank and file. Taft, however, remained the choice of most party leaders, whose preference was decisive.

The battle for the nomination at the Chicago convention revolved around an unusually large number of contested delegates: 254 in all. Roosevelt needed fewer than half the disputed seats to clinch the nomination. But the Republican National Committee, controlled by the Old Guard, awarded all but 19 of them to Taft. At a rally the night before the convention opened, Roosevelt addressed 5,000 cheering supporters and announced that if the party refused to seat his delegates, he would continue his own candidacy outside the party. "We stand at Armageddon," he told the roaring crowd, "and we battle for the Lord." The next day, he led his supporters out of the convention, and out of the party. The remaining delegates then quietly nominated Taft on the first ballot.

With financial support from newspaper magnate Frank Munsey and industrialist George W. Perkins, Roosevelt summoned his supporters back to Chicago in August for another convention, to launch the new Progressive Party and nominate him as its presidential candidate. Jane Addams was one of those who placed his name in nomination, and a large number of prominent women reformers played an active role in the new party. Roosevelt approached the battle feeling, as he put it, "fit as a bull moose" (thus giving his new party an enduring nickname). But by then, he was aware that his cause was virtually hopeless. That was partly because many of the insurgents who had supported him during the primaries refused to follow him out of the Republican Party. It was also because of the man the Democrats had nominated for president.

WOODROW WILSON AND THE NEW FREEDOM

The 1912 presidential contest was not simply one between conservatives and reformers. It was also one between two brands of progressivism, expressing two different views of America's future. And it matched

WILSON IN PHILADELPHIA
Wilson spent most of his life as a scholar and university president, but he was a remarkably effective politician once he entered the public world. He is shown here in 1914, speaking to a Fourth of July rally at Independence Hall in Philadelphia. *(UPI/Bettmann)*

the two most important national leaders of the early twentieth century in unequal contest.

The Rise of Wilson

Reform sentiment had been gaining strength within the Democratic as well as the Republican Party in the first years of the century. At the 1912 Democratic convention in Baltimore in June, Champ Clark, the conservative Speaker of the House, was unable to assemble the two-thirds majority necessary to win because of progressive opposition. Finally, on the forty-sixth ballot, Woodrow Wilson, the governor of New Jersey and the only genuinely progressive candidate in the race, emerged as the party's nominee.

Born in Virginia and raised in Confederate Georgia and Reconstruction South Carolina, Wilson had risen to political prominence by an unusual path. An 1879 graduate of Princeton University, he attended law school and for a time engaged unhappily in practice in Atlanta. But he was really more interested in politics and government, and after a few years he enrolled at Johns Hopkins University, where he earned a doctorate in political science. By virtue of his effective teaching and his lucid if unprofound books on the American political system, he rose steadily through the academic ranks until in 1902 he was promoted from the faculty to the presidency of Princeton.

There he displayed some of the strengths and weaknesses that would characterize his later political career. A champion of academic reform, he acted firmly and energetically to place Princeton on the road to becoming a great national university. At the same time, however, he displayed during controversies a self-righteous morality that at times made it nearly impossible for him to compromise.

A series of such stalemates helped propel him out of academia and into politics. Elected governor of New Jersey in 1910, he brought to his new office a commitment to reform that he had already displayed as a university president; and during his two years in the statehouse, he earned a national reputation for winning passage of progressive legislation.

As a presidential candidate in 1912, Wilson presented a brand of progressivism different from Theodore Roosevelt's New Nationalism, a program that came to be called the "New Freedom." The New Freedom differed most clearly from the New Nationalism in its approach to economic policy and the trusts. Roosevelt believed in accepting economic concentration and using government to regulate and control it. Wilson seemed to side with those who (like Brandeis) believed that bigness was both unjust and inefficient, that the proper response to monopoly was not to regulate it but to destroy it.

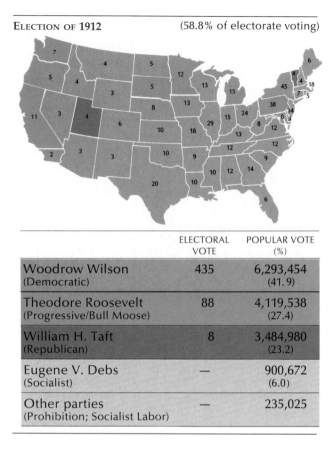

ELECTION OF 1912   (58.8% of electorate voting)

	ELECTORAL VOTE	POPULAR VOTE (%)
Woodrow Wilson (Democratic)	435	6,293,454 (41.9)
Theodore Roosevelt (Progressive/Bull Moose)	88	4,119,538 (27.4)
William H. Taft (Republican)	8	3,484,980 (23.2)
Eugene V. Debs (Socialist)	—	900,672 (6.0)
Other parties (Prohibition; Socialist Labor)	—	235,025

The presidential campaign was something of an anticlimax. William Howard Taft, resigned to defeat, delivered a few desultory conservative speeches and then lapsed into silence. Roosevelt campaigned energetically (until a gunshot wound from a would-be assassin forced him to the sidelines during the last weeks before the election), but he failed to draw any significant numbers of Democratic progressives away from Wilson. In November, Roosevelt and Taft split the Republican vote; Wilson held on to most of the Democrats and won. He polled only a plurality of the popular vote: 42 percent, to 27 percent for Roosevelt, 23 percent for Taft, and 6 percent for the socialist Eugene Debs. But in the electoral college, Wilson won 435 of the 531 votes. Roosevelt had carried only six states, Taft two, Debs none.

The Scholar as President

Wilson was a bold and forceful president. More than William Howard Taft, more even than Theodore Roosevelt, he concentrated the powers of the executive branch in his own hands. He exerted firm control over his cabinet, and he delegated real authority only to those whose loyalty to him was beyond question. Perhaps the clearest indication of his style of leadership was the identity of the most powerful figure in his administration: Colonel Edward M. House, a man who held no office and whose only claim to authority was his personal intimacy with the president.

In legislative matters, Wilson skillfully used his position as party leader and his appointive powers to weld together a coalition of conservatives and progressives who would, he believed, support his program. Democratic majorities in both houses of Congress made his task easier, as did the realization of many Democrats that the party must enact a progressive program in order to maintain those majorities.

Wilson's first triumph as president was a substantial lowering of the protective tariff. The Underwood-Simmons Tariff, passed in a special session of Congress Wilson summoned shortly after his inauguration, provided cuts substantial enough, progressives believed, to introduce real competition into American markets and thus to help break the power of trusts. It passed easily in the House, and despite Senate efforts to weaken its provisions, the bill survived more or less intact. Wilson had succeeded where Roosevelt and Taft had not. To make up for the loss of revenue under the new tariff, Congress approved a graduated income tax, which the recently adopted Sixteenth Amendment to the Constitution now permitted. This first modern income tax imposed a 1 percent tax on individuals and corporations earning over $4,000, with rates ranging up to 6 percent on incomes over $500,000.

Wilson held Congress in session through the summer to work on a major reform of the American banking system. Few doubted the necessity of change, but there were many different opinions about how best to attack the problem. Some legislators, among them Representative Carter Glass of Virginia, wanted to decentralize control of the banking system so as to limit the power of the great Wall Street financiers without substantially increasing the power of government. Others, including William Jennings Bryan and fellow agrarians who had long detested the "money trust," wanted firm government control. Wilson endorsed a plan that divided power in the system. The government would have substantial control at the national level; the bankers would retain control at the local level. The Federal Reserve Act passed both houses of Congress and was signed by the president on December 23, 1913. It was the most important piece of domestic legislation of Wilson's administration.

The Federal Reserve Act created twelve regional banks, each to be owned and controlled by the individual banks of its district. The regional Federal Reserve banks would hold a certain percentage of the assets of their member banks in reserve; they would use those reserves to support loans to private banks at an interest (or "discount") rate that the Federal Reserve system would set; they would issue a new type of paper currency—Federal Reserve notes—which would become the nation's basic medium of trade and would be backed by the government. Most important, perhaps, they would serve as central institutions able to shift funds quickly to troubled areas—to meet increased demands for credit or to protect imperiled banks. Supervising and regulating the entire system was a national Federal Reserve Board, whose members were appointed by the president. All "national" banks were required to join the system; smaller banks were encouraged to do so. Nearly half the nation's banking resources were represented in the system within a year, and 80 percent by the late 1920s.

The Problem of the Trusts

The cornerstone of Wilson's campaign for the presidency had been his promise to attack economic concentration, most notably to destroy monopolistic trusts. By the beginning of his second year in office, however, his approach to the trusts appeared to have changed. He was moving away from his earlier insistence that government dismantle the combinations and toward a commitment to regulating them. On this issue, at least, the New Freedom was beginning to resemble the New Nationalism.

In 1914, he proposed two measures to deal with the problem of monopoly. There was a proposal to create a federal agency through which the government would help business police itself—in other words, a regulatory commission of the type Roosevelt had advocated in 1912. There were, in addition, proposals to strengthen the government's power to prosecute and dismantle the trusts—a decentralizing approach more characteristic of Wilson's campaign. The two measures took shape, ultimately, as the Federal Trade Commission Act and the Clayton Antitrust Act.

The Federal Trade Commission Act created a regulatory agency of the same name that would help businesses determine in advance whether their actions would be acceptable to the government. It would also have authority to launch prosecutions against "unfair trade practices," which the law did not define, and it would have wide power to investigate corporate behavior. The act, in short, increased the government's regulatory authority significantly. Wilson signed it happily. But he seemed to lose interest in the Clayton Antitrust bill and did little to protect it from conservative assaults, which greatly weakened it. The vigorous legal pursuit of monopoly that Wilson had promised in 1912 never materialized. The future, he had apparently decided, lay with government supervision.

Retreat and Advance

By the fall of 1914, Wilson believed that the program of the New Freedom was essentially complete and that agitation for reform should (and would) now subside. As a result, he himself began a conspicuous retreat from activism. Citing the doctrine of states' rights, he refused to support the movement for national woman suffrage. Bowing to the inclinations of the many southerners in his cabinet (and perhaps also to his own southern heritage), he condoned the reimposition of segregation in the agencies of the federal government (in contrast to Theodore Roosevelt, who had ordered the elimination of many such barriers and had even taken the unprecedented step of inviting a black man—Booker T. Washington—to the White House). When congressional progressives attempted to enlist his support for new reform legislation, he dismissed their proposals as unconstitutional or unnecessary.

The congressional elections of 1914, however, shattered the president's complacency. Democrats suffered major losses in the House of Representatives, and voters who in 1912 had supported the Progressive Party began returning to the Republicans. Wilson would not be able to rely on a divided opposition when he ran for reelection in 1916. By the end of 1915, Wilson had begun to support a second flurry of reforms. In January 1916, he appointed Louis Brandeis to the Supreme Court, making him not only the first Jew but the most advanced progressive to serve there. Later, he supported a measure to make it easier for farmers to receive credit and one creating a system of workers' compensation for federal employees.

Much of this renewed effort at reform revealed that Wilson had moved even closer to the New Nationalism. He was sponsoring measures that expanded the role of the national government in important ways, giving it new instruments by which it could regulate the economy and help shape the economic and social structure. In 1916, for example, Wilson supported the Keating-Owen Act, the first federal law regulating child labor. The measure prohibited the shipment, across state lines, of goods produced by underage children, thus giving an expanded importance to the constitutional clause assigning Congress the task of regulating interstate commerce. (It would be some years before the Supreme Court would uphold this interpretation of the clause; the Court invalidated the Keating-Owen Act in 1918.) The president similarly supported measures that used federal taxing authority as a vehicle for legislating social change. When the Court struck down Keating-Owen, a new bill attempted to

LOUIS BRANDEIS
Brandeis graduated from Harvard Law School in 1877 with the best academic record of any student in the school's previous or subsequent history. His success in his Boston law practice was such that by the early twentieth century he was able to spend much of his time in unpaid work for public causes. His investigations of monopoly power soon made him a major figure in the emerging progressive movement. Woodrow Wilson nominated him for the United States Supreme Court in January 1916. He was one of the few nominees in the Court's history never to have held prior public office, and he was the first Jew ever to have been nominated. The appointment aroused five months of bitter controversy in the Senate before Brandeis was finally confirmed. For the next twenty years, he was one of the Court's most powerful members—all the while lobbying behind the scenes on behalf of the many political causes (preeminent among them Zionism, the founding of a Jewish state) to which he remained committed. *(UPI/Bettmann)*

achieve the same goal by imposing a heavy tax on the products of child labor. (The Court later struck it down too.) The Smith-Lever Act of 1914 had used federal spending to change public behavior by offering matching federal grants to states that agreed to support agricultural extension education.

"THE BIG STICK": AMERICA AND THE WORLD, 1901–1917

American foreign policy during the progressive years reflected many of the same impulses that were motivating domestic reform. But more than that, it reflected the nation's new sense of itself as a world power with far-flung economic and political interests. To the general public, foreign affairs remained largely remote. Walter Lippmann once wrote: "I cannot remember taking any interest whatsoever in foreign affairs until after the outbreak of the First World War." But to Theodore Roosevelt and later presidents, that made foreign affairs even more appealing. There the president could act with less regard for the Congress or the courts. There he could free himself from concerns about public opinion. Overseas, the president could exercise power unfettered and alone.

Roosevelt and "Civilization"

Theodore Roosevelt was well suited, by both temperament and conviction, for an activist foreign policy. He believed in the value and importance of using

---

"THE NEW DIPLOMACY"
This 1904 drawing by the famous *Puck* cartoonist Louis Dalrymple conveys the new image of America as a great power that Theodore Roosevelt was attempting to project to the world. Roosevelt the world policeman deals effectively with "less civilized" peoples (Asians and Latin Americans, seen clamoring at left) by using the "big stick" and deals equally effectively with the "civilized" nations (at right) by offering arbitration. *(Culver)*

American power in the world (a conviction he once described by citing the proverb, "Speak softly, but carry a big stick"). And he believed that an important distinction existed between the "civilized" and "uncivilized" nations of the world. "Civilized" nations, as he defined them, were predominantly white and Anglo-Saxon or Teutonic; "uncivilized" nations were generally nonwhite, Latin, or Slavic. But racism was only partly the basis of the distinction. At least as important was economic development. He believed, therefore, that Japan, a rapidly industrializing society, had earned admission to the ranks of the civilized.

Civilized nations were, by Roosevelt's definition, producers of industrial goods; uncivilized nations were sources of raw materials and markets. There was, he believed, an economic relationship between the two parts that was vital to both of them. A civilized society, therefore, had the right and duty to intervene in the affairs of a "backward" nation to preserve order and stability—for the sake of both nations. Accordingly, Roosevelt became an early champion of the development of American sea power, which he considered vital to the nation's ability to exert influence beyond its borders. By 1906, his support had enabled the American navy to attain a size and strength surpassed only by that of Great Britain (although Germany was fast gaining ground).

Protecting the Open Door in Asia

Roosevelt considered the "Open Door" vital for maintaining American trade in the Pacific and for preventing any single nation from establishing dominance there. (See above, pp. 569–570.) He looked with alarm, therefore, at the military rivalries involving Japan, Russia, Germany, and France in Asia.

In 1904 the Japanese attacked the Russian fleet at Port Arthur in southern Manchuria, a province of China that both Russia and Japan hoped to control. Roosevelt, hoping to prevent either nation from becoming dominant there, agreed in 1905 to a Japanese request to mediate an end to the conflict. Russia, faring badly in the war and already plagued by the domestic instability that twelve years later would lead to revolution, had no choice but to agree. At a peace conference in Portsmouth, New Hampshire, Roosevelt extracted from the embattled Russians a recognition of Japan's territorial gains and from the Japanese an agreement to cease the fighting and expand no further. At the same time, he negotiated a secret agreement with the Japanese to ensure that the United States could continue to trade freely in the region.

Roosevelt won the Nobel Peace Prize in 1906 for his work in ending the Russo-Japanese War. But in the years that followed, relations between the United States and Japan steadily deteriorated. Having destroyed the Russian fleet at Port Arthur, Japan now emerged as the preeminent naval power in the Pacific and soon began to exclude American trade from many of the territories it controlled.

A domestic controversy in California soon threatened Japanese-American relations again. In the process of agitating for an extension of the Chinese Exclusion Act, white workers in San Francisco added a demand for the legal exclusion of Japanese immigrants. At first nothing came of these efforts. But in 1906, the school board of San Francisco voted to require all Asian schoolchildren in the city to attend a separate "Oriental School." Anti-Asian riots in California and inflammatory stories in the Hearst papers about the "Yellow Peril" further fanned resentment in Japan.

The president persuaded the San Francisco school board to rescind its edict in return for a Japanese agreement to stop the flow of agricultural immigrants into California. Then, lest the Japanese government interpret his actions as a sign of weakness, he sent sixteen battleships of the new American navy (known as the "Great White Fleet") on an unprecedented voyage around the world that included a call on Japan—to remind the Japanese of the potential might of the United States.

The Iron-Fisted Neighbor

Theodore Roosevelt took a special interest in events in what he (and most other Americans) considered the nation's principal sphere of interest: Latin America. Unwilling to share United States trading rights, let alone military control, with any other nation, Roosevelt embarked on a series of ventures in the Caribbean and South America that established a pattern of American intervention in the region that would long survive his presidency.

Crucial to Roosevelt's thinking was an incident early in his administration. When the government of Venezuela began in 1902 to renege on debts to European bankers, naval forces of Britain, Italy, and Germany blockaded the Venezuelan coast. Then German ships began to bombard a Venezuelan port amid rumors that Germany planned to establish a permanent base in the region. Roosevelt used the threat of American naval power to pressure the German navy to withdraw.

The incident helped persuade Roosevelt that European intrusions into Latin America could result not only from aggression but from instability or irresponsibility (such as defaulting on debts) within the Latin American nations themselves. As a result, in 1904 he

THE UNITED STATES IN LATIN AMERICA, 1895–1941

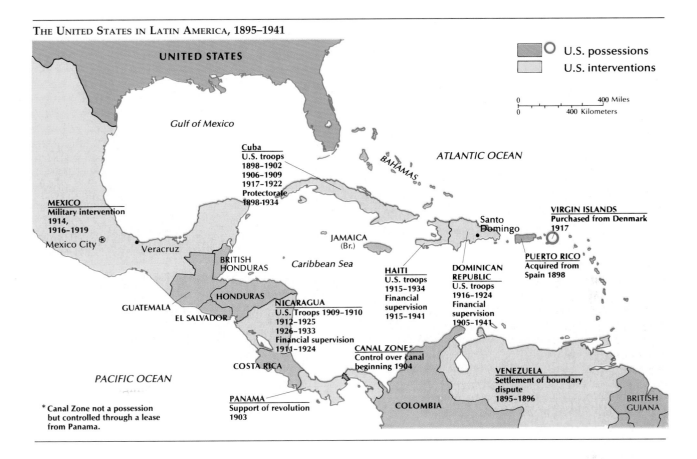

added a new "Roosevelt corollary" to the Monroe Doctrine. The United States, he claimed, had the right not only to oppose European intervention in the Western Hemisphere but to intervene itself in the domestic affairs of its neighbors if they proved unable to maintain order on their own.

The immediate motivation for the Roosevelt corollary, and the first opportunity for using it, was a crisis in the Dominican Republic. A revolution had toppled its corrupt and bankrupt government in 1903, but the new regime proved no better able than the old to make good on the country's $22 million in debts to European nations. Using the "Roosevelt corollary" as a rationale, Roosevelt established, in effect, an American receivership, assuming control of Dominican customs and distributing 45 percent of the revenues to the Dominicans and the rest to foreign creditors. This arrangement lasted, in one form or another, for more than three decades.

In 1902, the United States had granted political independence to Cuba, but only after the new government had agreed to the so-called Platt Amendment to its constitution, giving the United States the right to prevent any foreign power from intruding in the new nation. (See p. 565.) In 1906, when domestic uprisings seemed to threaten the internal stability of the island, Roosevelt reasoned that America must intervene to "protect" Cuba from disorder. American troops landed in Cuba, quelled the fighting, and remained there for three years.

The Panama Canal

The most celebrated accomplishment of Roosevelt's presidency was the construction of the Panama Canal. Creating a channel through Central America linking the Atlantic and the Pacific had been an unfulfilled dream of many nations since the mid-nineteenth century. Roosevelt was determined to achieve it.

The first step was the 1901 Hay-Pauncefote Treaty between America and Britain, canceling an 1850 pact by which the two nations had agreed to construct any canal together. The United States was now free to act alone. The next step was to choose a site for the canal.

OPENING THE PANAMA CANAL
The great Miraflores locks of the Panama Canal open in October 1913 to admit the first ship to pass through the channel.
The construction of the canal was one of the great engineering feats of the early twentieth century. But the heavy-handed
political efforts of Theodore Roosevelt were at least equally important to its completion. *(UPI/Bettmann)*

At first, Roosevelt and many others favored a route across Nicaragua, which would permit a sea-level canal requiring no locks. But they soon turned instead to the narrow Isthmus of Panama in Colombia, the site of an earlier, failed effort by a French company to construct a channel. Although the Panama route was not at sea level (and would thus require locks), it was shorter than the one in Nicaragua. And construction was already about 40 percent complete. When the French company lowered the price for its holdings from $109 million to $40 million, the United States chose Panama.

Roosevelt dispatched John Hay, his secretary of state, to negotiate an agreement with Colombian diplomats in Washington that would allow construction to begin without delay. Under heavy American pressure, the Colombian chargé d'affaires, Tomás Herrán, unwisely signed an agreement giving the United States

perpetual rights to a six-mile-wide "canal zone" across Colombia; in return, it would pay Colombia $10 million and an annual rental of $250,000. The treaty produced outrage in the Colombian Senate, which refused to ratify it. Colombia then sent a new representative to Washington with instructions to demand at least $20 million from the Americans plus a share of the payment to the French.

Roosevelt was furious. The Colombians, he charged, were "inefficient bandits" and "blackmailers." He began to look for ways to circumvent the Colombian government. Philippe Bunau-Varilla, chief engineer of the French canal project, was ready to help. In November 1903, he helped organize and finance a revolution in Panama. There had been many previous revolts, all of them failures. But this one had the support of the United States. Roosevelt landed troops from the *U.S.S. Nashville* in Panama to "maintain order." Their presence prevented Colombian forces from suppressing the rebellion, and three days later Roosevelt recognized Panama as an independent nation. The new Panamanian government quickly agreed to a new treaty. It granted America a canal zone ten miles wide; the United States would pay Panama the $10 million fee and the $250,000 annual rental that the Colombian Senate had rejected. Work on the canal proceeded rapidly, despite the enormous cuts and elaborate locks the construction required. It opened in 1914, three years after Roosevelt had proudly boasted to a university audience: "I took the Canal Zone and let Congress debate!"

Taft and "Dollar Diplomacy"

Like his predecessor, William Howard Taft worked to advance the nation's economic interests overseas. But he showed little interest in Roosevelt's larger vision of world stability. Taft's secretary of state, the corporate attorney Philander C. Knox, worked aggressively to extend American investments into less-developed regions. Critics called his policies "Dollar Diplomacy."

The Taft-Knox foreign policy faced its severest test, and encountered its greatest failure, in the Far East. Ignoring Roosevelt's tacit 1905 agreement with Japan to limit American involvement in Manchuria, the new administration responded to pressure from American bankers and moved aggressively to increase America's economic influence in the region. In particular, Knox worked to include the United States in a consortium of Western powers formed to build railroads in China; and when the Europeans agreed, he went further and tried to exclude the Japanese from any role in Manchuria's railroads. When Japan responded by forming a loose alliance with Russia, the entire railroad project quickly collapsed.

In the Caribbean, the new administration continued and even expanded upon Roosevelt's policies of limiting European and expanding American influence. That meant, Taft and Knox believed, not only preventing disorder but also establishing a significant American economic presence there: replacing the investments of European nations with investments from the United States. But Dollar Diplomacy also had a more violent side. When a revolution broke out in Nicaragua in 1909, the administration quickly sided with the insurgents (who had been inspired to revolt by an American mining company) and sent American troops into the country to seize the customs houses. As soon as peace was restored, Knox encouraged American bankers to offer substantial loans to the new government, thus increasing Washington's financial leverage over the country. When the new pro-American government faced an insurrection less than two years later, Taft again landed American troops in Nicaragua, this time to protect the existing regime. The troops remained there for more than a decade.

Diplomacy and Morality

Woodrow Wilson entered office with little experience or interest in diplomacy. "It would be the irony of fate," he remarked shortly before assuming the presidency, "if my administration had to deal chiefly with foreign affairs." Ironic or not, Wilson faced international challenges of a scope and gravity unmatched by any president before him. Although the greatest test of Wilsonian diplomacy did not occur until after World War I, many of the qualities that he would bring to that ordeal were evident in his foreign policy from his first moments in office, and particularly in his dealings with Latin America—where he continued the interventionist policies of his predecessors.

Having already seized control of the finances of the Dominican Republic in 1905, the United States established a military government there in 1916, when the Dominicans refused to accept a treaty that would have made the country a virtual American protectorate. The military occupation lasted eight years. In Haiti, which shares the island of Hispaniola with the Dominican Republic, Wilson landed the marines in 1915 to quell a revolution in the course of which a mob had murdered an unpopular president. American officers drafted the new Haitian constitution adopted in 1918, and American military forces remained in the country until 1934. When Wilson began to fear that the Danish West Indies might be about to fall into the hands of Germany, he bought the colony from Denmark and renamed it the Virgin Islands. Concerned about the possibility of European influence in Nicaragua, he signed a treaty with that country's government ensuring that no other nation would build a canal there and winning for the United States the right to intervene in Nicaragua's internal affairs to protect American interests.

But Wilson's view of America's role in the Western Hemisphere became clearest in his dealings with Mexico. For many years, under the friendly auspices of the corrupt dictator Porfirio Díaz, American businessmen had been establishing an enormous economic presence in Mexico. In 1910, however, Díaz had been overthrown by the popular leader Francisco Madero, who promised democratic reform but who also seemed hostile to American businesses in Mexico. With American approval, Madero was himself deposed early in 1913 by a reactionary general, Victoriano Huerta.

The Taft administration, in its last weeks in office, prepared to recognize the new Huerta regime and wel-

SIGNIFICANT EVENTS

1898 Theodore Roosevelt elected governor of New York

1900 Roosevelt elected vice president

1901 McKinley assassinated, Roosevelt becomes president

Hay-Pauncefote Treaty ratified

1902 Northern Securities antitrust case filed

Roosevelt intervenes in anthracite coal strike

Newlands Reclamation Act passed

1903 Department of Commerce and Labor created

1904 Roosevelt mediates settlement of Russo-Japanese War

"Roosevelt Corollary" announced

United States orchestrates Panamanian independence; new government signs treaty allowing United States to build Panama Canal

Roosevelt elected president

1906 Hepburn Railroad Regulation Act passed

Upton Sinclair publishes *The Jungle*

Meat Inspection Act passed

American troops intervene in Cuba

1907 Financial panic and recession

1908 William Howard Taft elected president

1909 Payne-Aldrich Tariff passed

Pinchot-Ballinger dispute begins

U.S. troops intervene in Nicaragua

1910 Roosevelt's Osawatomie speech outlines "New Nationalism"

Woodrow Wilson elected governor of New Jersey

Porfirio Díaz overthrown by Francisco Madero in Mexico

1911 Taft administration files antitrust suit against U.S. Steel

1912 Roosevelt challenges Taft for Republican nomination, wins all party primaries

Taft receives Republican nomination, Roosevelt and followers walk out

Roosevelt forms Progressive Party

Woodrow Wilson elected president

1913 Thirteenth Amendment, establishing direct popular election of U.S. senators, ratified

Federal Reserve Act passed

Victoriano Huerta overthrows Madero in Mexico

1914 Federal Trade Commission Act passed

Clayton Antitrust Act passed

Panama Canal opens

U.S. troops intervene in Haiti

Tampico incident strains U.S. relations with Mexico

Venustiano Carranza deposes Huerta in Mexico

1916 Wilson appoints Louis Brandeis to Supreme Court

United States establishes military government in Dominican Republic

U.S. troops pursue Pancho Villa into Mexico

1917 United States recognizes Carranza government

come back a receptive environment for American investments in Mexico. Two things happened before it could do so: agents of the new government murdered Madero, and Woodrow Wilson took office in Washington. The new president instantly announced that he would never recognize Huerta's "government of butchers."

The problem dragged on for years. At first, Wilson hoped that simply by refusing to recognize Huerta he could help topple the regime and bring to power the opposing Constitutionalists, led by Venustiano Carranza. But when Huerta (supported by American business interests in Mexico) established a full military dictatorship in October 1913, the president became more assertive. He pressured the British to stop supporting Huerta. Then he offered to send American troops to assist Carranza. Carranza, aware that such an open alliance with the United States would undermine his popular support in Mexico, declined the offer, but he did secure the right to buy arms in the United States.

In April 1914, a minor naval incident provided the president with an excuse for more open intervention. An officer in Huerta's army briefly arrested several American sailors from the U.S.S. *Dolphin* who had gone ashore in Tampico. The men were immediately released, but the American admiral—unsatisfied with the apology he received—demanded that the Huerta forces fire a twenty-one-gun salute to the American flag as a public display of penance. The Mexicans refused. Wilson seized on the trivial incident as a pretext for seizing the Mexican port of Veracruz.

Wilson had envisioned a bloodless action, but in a clash with Mexican troops in Veracruz, the Americans killed 126 of the defenders and suffered 19 casualties of their own. Now at the brink of war, Wilson began to look for a way out. His show of force, however, had helped strengthen the position of the Carranza faction, which captured Mexico City in August and forced Huerta to flee the country. At last, it seemed, the crisis might be over.

But Wilson was not yet satisfied. He reacted angrily when Carranza refused to accept American guidelines for the creation of a new government, and he briefly considered throwing his support to still another aspirant to leadership: Carranza's erstwhile lieutenant Pancho Villa, who was now leading a rebel army of his own. When Villa's military position deteriorated, however, Wilson abandoned him; finally, in October 1915, he granted preliminary recognition to the Carranza government.

By now, however, he had created yet another crisis. Villa, angry at what he considered an American betrayal, retaliated in January 1916 by taking sixteen Americans from a train in northern Mexico and shooting them. Two months later, he led his soldiers (or bandits, as the United States government called them) across the border into Columbus, New Mexico, where they killed seventeen more Americans. His goal, apparently, was to destabilize relations between Wilson and Carranza and to provoke a war between them, which might provide him with an opportunity to improve his own declining fortunes.

Wilson ordered General John J. Pershing to lead an American expeditionary force across the Mexican border in pursuit of Villa. The American troops never found Villa, but they did engage in two ugly skirmishes with Carranza's army, in which forty Mexicans and twelve Americans died. Again the United States and Mexico stood at the brink of war. But at the last minute, Wilson drew back. He quietly withdrew American troops from Mexico; and in March 1917, having spent four years of effort and gained nothing for it but a lasting Mexican hostility toward the United States, he at last granted formal recognition to the Carranza regime.

By now, however, Wilson's attention was turning elsewhere: to the far greater international crisis engulfing the European continent and ultimately much of the world.

SUGGESTED READINGS

General Histories. John Milton Cooper, Jr., *The Warrior and the Priest: Woodrow Wilson and Theodore Roosevelt* (1983). Arthur Link, *Woodrow Wilson and the Progressive Era, 1910–1917* (1954). George E. Mowry, *The Era of Theodore Roosevelt* (1958). (See also Suggested Readings for Chapter 21.)

Theodore Roosevelt. John Morton Blum, *The Republican Roosevelt* (1954). G. Wallace Chessman, *Theodore Roosevelt and the Politics of Power* (1969). John A. Garraty, *The Life of George W. Perkins* (1960). Lewis L. Gould, *The Presidency of Theodore Roosevelt* (1991). William H. Harbaugh, *Power and Responsibility* (1961); published in paperback as *The Life and Times of Theodore Roosevelt*. Horace S. Merrill and Marion G. Merrill, *The Republican High Command* (1971). Edmund Morris, *The Rise of Theodore Roosevelt* (1979). Henry F. Pringle, *Theodore Roosevelt* (1931).

William Howard Taft. Donald E. Anderson, *William Howard Taft* (1973). Paolo E. Coletta, *The Presidency of William Howard Taft* (1973). George Mowry, *Theodore Roosevelt and the Progressive Movement* (1946). Henry F. Pringle, *The Life and Times of William Howard Taft*, 2 vols. (1939). Norman Wilensky, *Conservatives in the Progressive Era: The Taft Republicans of 1912* (1965).

Woodrow Wilson. John Morton Blum, *Joseph Tumulty and the Wilson Era* (1951); *Woodrow Wilson and the Politics of Morality* (1956). Alexander George and Juliette George, *Woodrow*

Wilson and Colonel House (1956). L. J. Holt, *Congressional Insurgents and the Party System, 1909–1916* (1967). Arthur S. Link, *Woodrow Wilson,* 5 vols. (1947–1965). Edwin A. Weinstein, *Woodrow Wilson: A Medical and Psychological Biography* (1981).

National Issues. O. E. Anderson, *The Health of a Nation* (1958). Stephen R. Fox, *The American Conservation Movement: John Muir and His Legacy* (1981). Samuel P. Hays, *The Gospel of Efficiency: The Progressive Conservation Movement, 1890–1920* (1962). James Holt, *Congressional Insurgents and the Party System* (1969). Susan Kleinberg, *The Shadow of the Mills: Working Class Families in Pittsburgh, 1870–1907* (1989). Naomi Lamoreaux, *The Great Merger Movement in American Business, 1895–1904* (1985). Albro Martin, *Enterprise Denied: Origins of the Decline of the American Railroads, 1897–1917* (1971). Thomas K. McCraw, ed., *Regulation in Perspective* (1981). Roderick Nash, *Wilderness and the American Mind* (1967). James Penick, Jr., *Progressive Politics and Conservation: The Ballinger-Pinchot Affair* (1968). Harold T. Pinkett, *Gifford Pinchot: Private and Public Forester* (1970). Elmo P. Richardson, *The Politics of Conservation* (1962). David Sarasohn, *The Party of Reform: The Democrats in the Progressive Era* (1989). Martin J. Sklar, *The Corporate Reconstruction of American Capitalism, 1890–1916: The Market, the Law, and Politics* (1988). Peter Temin, *Taking Your Medicine: Drug Regulation in the U.S.* (1980). Melvin I. Urofsky, *Louis D. Brandeis and the Progressive Tradition* (1981). Craig West, *Banking Reform and the Federal Reserve, 1863–1923* (1977). Robert Wiebe, *Businessmen and Reform: A Study of the Progressive Movement* (1962).

Roosevelt's Foreign Policy. Howard K. Beale, *Theodore Roosevelt and the Rise of America to World Power* (1956). David H. Burton, *Theodore Roosevelt: Confident Imperialist* (1969). Richard Challener, *Admirals, Generals, and American Foreign Policy, 1898–1914* (1973). Raymond A. Esthus, *Theodore Roosevelt and International Rivalries* (1970). Michael H. Hunt, *The Making of a Special Relationship: The United States and China to 1914* (1983). Akira Iriye, *Pacific Estrangement: Japanese and American Expansion, 1897–1911* (1972). Richard Leopold, *Elihu Root and the Conservative Tradition* (1954). Charles E. Neu, *An Uncertain Friendship: Roosevelt and Japan, 1906–1909* (1967). Bradford Perkins, *The Great Rapprochement: England and the United States, 1895–1914* (1968). Julius W. Pratt, *Challenge and Rejection: The United States and World Leadership, 1900–1921* (1967). Charles Vevier, *United States and China* (1955).

America and the Caribbean. P. Edward Haley, *Revolution and Intervention: The Diplomacy of Taft and Wilson with Mexico, 1910–1917* (1975). David Healy, *The United States in Cuba, 1898–1902* (1963). Walter LaFeber, *The Panama Canal* (1978). Lester E. Langley, *The Banana Wars: An Inner History of American Empire, 1900–1934* (1983). David McCullough, *The Path Between the Seas* (1977). Dwight C. Miner, *Fight for the Panama Route* (1966). Dana G. Munro, *Intervention and Dollar Diplomacy in the Caribbean, 1900–1921* (1964). Louis A. Perez, Jr., *Cuba Under the Platt Amendment* (1988). Walter Scholes and Marie Scholes, *The Foreign Policies of the Taft Administration* (1970). John Womack, *Zapata and the Mexican Revolution* (1968).

Wilson's Foreign Policy. Kenneth Grieb, *The United States and Huerta* (1969). David Healy, *Gunboat Diplomacy in the Wilson Era: The U.S. Navy in Haiti, 1915–1916* (1976). Arthur Link, *Wilson the Diplomatist* (1957); *Woodrow Wilson: Revolution, War, and Peace* (1979). Dana Munro, *Intervention and Dollar Diplomacy in the Caribbean, 1900–1914* (1964). Robert Quirk, *An Affair of Honor: Woodrow Wilson and the Occupation of Veracruz* (1962); *The Mexican Revolution, 1914–1915* (1960). James Reed, *The Missionary Mind and America's East Asian Policy, 1911–1915* (1983). Robert Freeman Smith, *The United States and Revolutionary Nationalism in Mexico, 1916–1932* (1972).

THE AMERICAN ENVIRONMENT

SAVING THE FORESTS

F ROM THE EARLIEST DAYS of European settlement in North America, people depended for their very survival on forests. Lumber was essential not just for houses and farm buildings, but for fences and vehicles as well. Most Americans heated their homes with firewood until late in the nineteenth century, when coal finally gained ascendancy. The nation's early steam engines, including railroad locomotives and steamboats, were fueled mainly with wood, and iron was forged with charcoal. Tree bark was the major source of tannin, which was used in curing leather. When trees were burned to clear land, their ashes were turned into potash, which was used in making soap. Next to food, wood was the most basic resource in the American economy.

It was also the most wasted. The paradox of the American forest was that although its trees were essential to frontier settlements, they were also the chief obstacle to those settlements. East of the Mississippi River, creating new farming communities usually meant cutting down forests. Although trees were cut for lumber and fuel, the main reason for their removal was simply clearing. To prepare land for crops, farmers "girdled" trees by removing a ring of bark from their base, stopping nutrients from reaching leaves and quickly killing them. With the leaves gone, sunlight reached the forest floor and corn could be planted amid the stumps. In time, the dead trees could be cut and burned to fertilize the soil in preparation for plowing. Within a decade or two, few signs would remain that the new cornfield or pasture had ever been a forest at all.

The American forest seemed so endless that few worried about conserving it. As a result, the nineteenth-century inhabitants of the United States destroyed trees at an astonishing rate. By 1850, over 100 million acres of land—an area roughly the size of modern California—had been cleared since the time of the first colonists. Moreover, the rate of forest destruction was increasing, so that over the next ten years another 40 million acres were cleared—as if the entire state of Georgia had been deforested in a single decade. The 1850s saw fully one-third as many trees cut down as had been cleared during the preceding two centuries.

Although most Americans still regarded their forests as limitless, a few began to voice concern about what might happen if deforestation continued at this rapid pace. The most influential of these was a remarkable Vermonter named George Perkins Marsh. A scholar who read a dozen or more European languages, Marsh served as the U.S. ambassador to Turkey from 1849 to 1854, and to Italy from 1860 until his death in 1882. During his many years living on the shores of the Mediterranean, Marsh became interested in the environmental effects of classical civilizations. He gathered evidence from his travels and readings to demonstrate that deforestation had wreaked havoc with the earth.

The result was one of the most important books in the history of American conservation. Published in 1864, Marsh's *Man and Nature* warned of the dangerous consequences that might result if the United States did not stop destroying its forests. Losing access to lumber and fuel was the least of the problems he named. Much more

THE AMERICAN ENVIRONMENT

A NEWLY CLEARED FARM, 1790s
Clearing forests was the essential first step toward establishing a new farm and thereby "improving" land. Farmers killed trees by stripping their bark and then planted crops amid the remaining stumps. Settlers used lumber to build houses and barns, erect fences, and supply fireplaces with fuel. *(Bettmann)*

important, he said, was the forest's role in stabilizing the natural environment. According to Marsh's theories, trees slowed the rate at which water drained from the soil. They prevented erosion, maintained soil fertility, and stabilized the flow of natural springs and streams. Removing them laid the groundwork for environmental disaster. In addition to promoting erosion, drying up rivers, and causing floods, forest destruction decreased the amount of water evaporating into the air and so reduced the total amount of rain that fell in an area. In the end, it would turn the landscape into a desert.

For proof of his claims, Marsh offered evidence from around the world. He described springs he had known as a child in Vermont that had since dried up as the trees around them were cleared. He listed floods that had become more frequent in lumbered areas of the northeastern United States. As evidence that cutting down forests could lead to desertification, he pointed to North Africa and the Middle East, holding them up as examples of what America might become if its citizens refused to heed his warnings. Only

THE AMERICAN ENVIRONMENT

a strong commitment to conserving the forest and other natural resources could save the nation from its folly. "Man has too long forgotten," he wrote, "that the earth was given to him for usufruct alone, not for consumption, still less for profligate waste."

Marsh's book drew wide attention from scientists and politicians all over the United States. From the 1870s forward, increasing numbers of Americans began to express concern about the future of the nation's forests, and laws started to be passed for their protection and restoration. Although many of Marsh's theories about the climatic influence of forests would eventually prove to be overstated or wrong, they became the basis for laws in the 1870s that offered free land on the Great Plains to settlers who planted trees there. Such stands of trees did not increase rainfall as the authors of the laws had hoped, but other early efforts at conserving forests were more effective.

The most important of these occurred in the state of New York. There, people worried that falling water levels in the Erie Canal might threaten the very lifeblood of the state's economy and might foreshadow problems for New York City's water supply as well. Following Marsh's theories, they attributed the problem to deforestation in the state's heavily lumbered Adirondack Mountains. Various citizens began to lobby for

---

EARLY LUMBERING IN MICHIGAN
As pioneer farmers moved west, a parallel migration of woodcutters took place. By the second half of the nineteenth century, pine lumber was being shipped by rail out of the north woods of Maine, New York, Michigan, and Minnesota to supply farmers on the treeless prairies with the construction materials and fuel that were essential to an agricultural economy. *(Bettmann)*

THE AMERICAN ENVIRONMENT

THE ADIRONDACK FOREST: "FOREVER WILD"
By the closing decades of the nineteenth century, Americans had become so worried about
the destruction of eastern forests that they increased their efforts to protect them. One important consequence was the creation of the Adirondack Forest Preserve in northern New
York. A unique provision of the 1894 state constitution mandated that the Adirondacks
were to be left "forever wild." *(The Adirondack Museum, Blue Mountain Lake, N.Y.)*

protection of the Adirondack forests, and the result was a law in 1885 creating a huge
"forest reserve" there. To guarantee that the Adirondacks would remain "forever wild,"
defenders saw that a clause to this effect was inserted into the new state constitution in
1894.

THE AMERICAN ENVIRONMENT

The Adirondack Forest Reserve was a model for the nation as a whole. In 1891, seeking specifically to protect watersheds, Congress passed the Forest Reserve Act, empowering the president to set aside any "public lands wholly or in part covered with timber or undergrowth." The act became the basis for the National Forest system of the United States. Conservation of the forest reserves soon emerged as a chief political objective of Theodore Roosevelt's presidency. Saving the forests had become national policy, in no small measure because of the book Marsh had published four decades earlier.

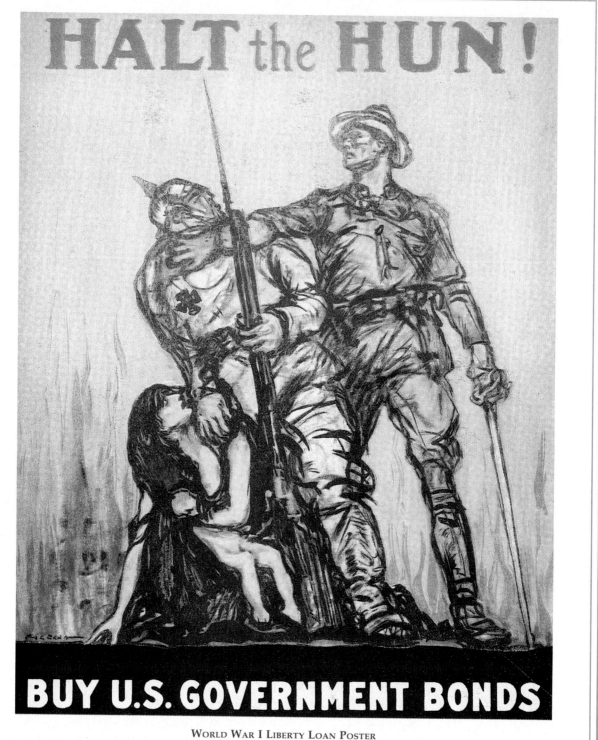

HALT the HUN!

BUY U.S. GOVERNMENT BONDS

WORLD WAR I LIBERTY LOAN POSTER

In this 1918 propaganda poster issued by the U. S. government, an American soldier prevents a "Hun" from ravaging a young woman and her baby—a reference to the widespread and largely erroneous belief that German troops had massacred women and children in Belgium early in the war. *(The Granger Collection)*

CHAPTER TWENTY-THREE

AMERICA AND THE GREAT WAR

HE GREAT WAR, AS it was known to a generation unaware that another, greater war would soon follow, began relatively inconspicuously in August 1914 when forces of the Austro-Hungarian empire invaded the tiny Balkan nation of Serbia. Within weeks, however, it had grown into a widespread conflagration, engaging the armies of almost all the major nations of Europe and shattering forever the delicate balance of power that had maintained a general peace on the Continent since the early nineteenth century. Most Americans looked on with horror as the war became the most savage in history, but also at first with a conviction that the conflict had little to do with them.

After nearly three years of attempting to affect the outcome of the conflict without becoming embroiled in it, the United States formally entered the war in April 1917. In doing so, it joined the most savage conflict in history. The fighting had already dragged on for two and a half years, inconclusive, almost inconceivably murderous, engaging not only the armies of the contending nations but their civilian populations as well. Although the American Civil War had greatly increased the ferocity and extent of combat, World War I was the first truly "total" war. It pitted entire societies against one another, and by 1917 it had left Europe exhausted and on the brink of utter collapse. By the time it ended late in 1918, Germany had lost nearly 2 million soldiers in battle, Russia 1.7 million, France 1.4 million, Great Britain 900,000. A generation of European youth was decimated; centuries of political, social, and economic traditions were damaged and all but destroyed.

For America, however, the war was the source of a very different experience. As a military struggle, it was brief, decisive, and—in relative terms—without great cost. Only 112,000 American soldiers died in the conflict, half of them from influenza and other diseases rather than in combat. Economically, it was the source of a great industrial boom, which helped spark the years of prosperity that would follow. And the war propelled the United States into a position of international preeminence.

In other respects, World War I was a painful, even traumatic experience for the American people. At home, the nation became obsessed with a search not just for victory but also for social unity—a search that continued and even intensified in the troubled years following the armistice, and that helped shatter many of the progressive ideals of the first years of the century. And abroad, once the conflict ended, the United States encountered frustration and disillusionment. The "war to end wars," the war "to make the world safe for democracy," became neither. Instead, it led directly to twenty years of international instability that would ultimately generate another great conflict.

The Road to War

The causes of the war in Europe—indeed the question of whether there were any significant causes at all, or whether the entire conflict was the result of a tragic series of blunders—have been the subject of continued debate for nearly eighty years. What is clear is that the European nations had by 1914 created an unusually precarious international system that careened into war very quickly on the basis of what most historians agree was a minor series of provocations.

The Collapse of the European Peace

The major powers of Europe were organized by 1914 in two great, competing alliances. The "Triple Entente" linked Britain, France, and Russia. The "Triple Alliance" united Germany, the Austro-Hungarian Empire, and Italy. The chief rivalry, however, was not between the two alliances, but between the great powers that dominated them: Great Britain and Germany—the former long established as the world's most powerful colonial and commercial nation, the latter ambitious to expand its own empire and become at least Britain's equal.

The Anglo-German rivalry may have been the most important underlying source of the tensions that led to World War I, but it was not the immediate cause of its outbreak. The conflict emerged most directly out of a controversy involving nationalist movements within the Austro-Hungarian Empire. On June 28, 1914, the Archduke Franz Ferdinand, heir to the throne of the tottering empire, was assassinated while paying a state visit to Sarajevo. Sarajevo was the capital of Bosnia, a province of Austria-Hungary that Slavic nationalists wished to annex to neighboring Serbia; the Archduke's assassin was a Serbian nationalist.

This local controversy quickly escalated through the workings of the system of alliances that the great powers had constructed. With support from Germany, Austria-Hungary launched a punitive assault on Serbia. The Serbians called on Russia to help with their defense. The Russians began mobilizing their army on July 30. Things quickly careened out of control. By August 3, Germany had declared war on both Russia and France and had invaded Belgium in preparation for a thrust across the French border. On August 4, Great Britain—ostensibly to honor its alliance with France, but more importantly to blunt the advance of its principal rival—declared war on Germany. Russia and the Austro-Hungarian Empire formally began hostilities on August 6. Italy, although an ally of Germany in 1914, remained neutral at first and later entered the war on the side of the British and French. The Ottoman Empire (Turkey) and other, smaller nations all joined the fighting later in 1914 or in 1915. Within less than a year, virtually the entire European continent and part of Asia were embroiled in a major war.

Wilson's Neutrality

Wilson called on his fellow citizens in 1914 to remain "impartial in thought as well as deed." But that was impossible, for several reasons. For one thing, many Americans were not, in fact, genuinely impartial. Some

The Sinking of the *Lusitania*
On the afternoon of May 7, 1915, the British passenger liner *Lusitania* sank after having been attacked by German torpedoes. Among those who perished were 150 American passengers. The event was one of many that pushed the United States toward intervention in World War I. *(Bettmann)*

sympathized with the German cause (German Americans because of affection for Germany, Irish Americans because of hatred of Britain). Many more (including Wilson himself) sympathized with Britain. Wilson himself was only one of many Americans who fervently admired England—its traditions, its culture, its political system; almost instinctively, these Americans attributed to the cause of the Allies (Britain, France, Italy, Russia) a moral quality that they denied to the Central Powers (Germany, the Austro-Hungarian Empire, and the Ottoman Empire). Lurid reports of German atrocities in Belgium and France, skillfully exaggerated by British propagandists, strengthened the hostility of many Americans toward Germany.

Economic realities also made it impossible for the United States to deal with the belligerents on equal terms. The British had imposed a naval blockade on Germany to prevent munitions and supplies from reaching the enemy. As a neutral, the United States had the right, in theory, to trade with Germany. A truly neutral response to the blockade would have been to stop trading with Britain as well. But while the United States could survive an interruption of its relatively modest trade with the Central Powers, it could not easily weather an embargo on its much more extensive trade with the Allies, particularly when war orders from Britain and France soared after 1914, helping to produce one of the greatest economic booms in the nation's history. So America tacitly ignored the blockade of Germany and continued trading with Britain. By 1915, the United States had gradually transformed itself from a neutral power into the arsenal of the Allies.

The Germans, in the meantime, were resorting to a new and, in American eyes, barbaric tactic: submarine warfare. Unable to challenge British domination on the ocean's surface, Germany began early in 1915 to use the newly improved submarine to try to stem the flow of supplies to England. Enemy vessels, the Germans announced, would be sunk on sight. Months later, on May 7, 1915, a German submarine sank the British passenger liner *Lusitania* without warning, causing the deaths of 1,198 people, 128 of them Americans. The ship was, it later became clear, carrying not only passengers but munitions; but most Americans considered the attack what Theodore Roosevelt called it: "an act of piracy."

Wilson angrily demanded that Germany promise not to repeat such outrages and that the Central Powers affirm their commitment to neutral rights (among which, he implausibly insisted, was the right of American citizens to travel on the nonmilitary vessels of belligerents). The Germans finally agreed to Wilson's demands, but tensions between the nations continued to grow. Early in 1916, in response to an announcement that the Allies were now arming merchant ships to sink submarines, Germany proclaimed that it would fire on such vessels without warning. A few weeks later it attacked the unarmed French steamer *Sussex*, injuring several American passengers. Again Wilson demanded that Germany abandon its "unlawful" tactics; again the German government relented. Lacking sufficient naval power to enforce an effective blockade against Britain, the Germans decided that the marginal advantages of unrestricted submarine warfare did not yet justify the possibility of drawing America into the war.

Preparedness Versus Pacifism

Despite the president's increasing bellicosity in 1916, he was still far from ready to commit the United States to war. One obstacle was American domestic politics. Facing a difficult battle for reelection, Wilson could not ignore the powerful factions that continued to oppose intervention. His policies, therefore, represented an effort to balance the demands of those who, like Theodore Roosevelt, insisted that the nation defend its "honor" and economic interests against the demands

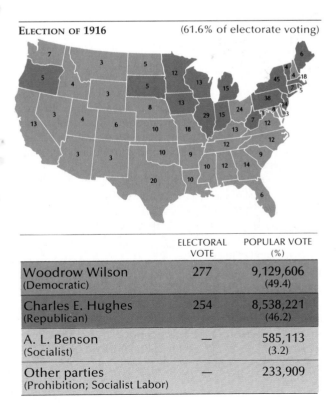

ELECTION OF 1916   (61.6% of electorate voting)

	ELECTORAL VOTE	POPULAR VOTE (%)
Woodrow Wilson (Democratic)	277	9,129,606 (49.4)
Charles E. Hughes (Republican)	254	8,538,221 (46.2)
A. L. Benson (Socialist)	—	585,113 (3.2)
Other parties (Prohibition; Socialist Labor)	—	233,909

of those who, like Bryan, La Follette, and others (including many German Americans and Irish Americans hostile to Britain), denounced any action that seemed to increase the chance of war.

The question of whether America should make military and economic preparations for war provided the first issue over which pacifists and interventionists could openly debate. Wilson at first sided with the anti-preparedness forces, denouncing the idea of an American military buildup as needless and provocative. As tensions between the United States and Germany grew, however, he changed his mind. In the fall of 1915, he endorsed an ambitious proposal by American military leaders for a large and rapid increase in the nation's armed forces. Amid expressions of outrage from pacifists in Congress and elsewhere, he worked hard to win approval of it. He even embarked on a national speaking tour early in 1916 to arouse support for the proposal. By midsummer 1916, armament for a possible conflict was well under way.

Still, the peace faction wielded considerable political strength, as became clear at the Democratic Convention in the summer of 1916. The convention became almost hysterically enthusiastic when the keynote speaker, enumerating Wilson's accomplishments, punctuated his list of the president's diplomatic achievements with the chant, "What did we do? What did we do? . . . We didn't go to war! We didn't go to war!" That speech helped produce one of the most prominent slogans of Wilson's reelection campaign (although one the president himself never used or entirely approved): "He kept us out of war." During the campaign, Wilson did nothing to discourage those who argued that the Republican candidate, the progressive New York governor Charles Evans Hughes (supported by the bellicose Theodore Roosevelt), was more likely than he to lead the nation into war. And when pro-war rhetoric became particularly heated, Wilson spoke defiantly of the nation being "too proud to fight." He ultimately won reelection by one of the smallest margins for an incumbent in American history: fewer than 600,000 popular votes and only 23 electoral votes. The Democrats retained a precarious control over Congress.

A War for Democracy

The election was behind him, and tensions between the United States and Germany were unabated. But Wilson still required a justification for American intervention that would unite public opinion and satisfy his own sense of morality. In the end, he created that rationale himself. The United States, Wilson insisted, had no material aims in the conflict. Rather, the nation was committed to using the war as a vehicle for constructing a new world order, one based on the same progressive ideals that had motivated reform in America. In a speech before Congress in January 1917, he presented a plan for a postwar order in which the United States would help maintain peace through a permanent league of nations—a peace that would ensure self-determination for all nations, a "peace without victory." These were, Wilson believed, goals worth fighting for if there was sufficient provocation. Provocation came quickly.

In January, after months of inconclusive warfare in the trenches of France, the military leaders of Germany decided on one last dramatic gamble to achieve victory. They would launch a series of major assaults on the enemy's lines in France. At the same time, they would begin unrestricted submarine warfare (against American as well as Allied ships) to cut Britain off from vital supplies. The Allied defenses would collapse, they hoped, before the United States could intervene.

The new German policy made American entry into the war virtually inevitable. Two additional events helped clear the way. On February 25, the British gave Wilson a telegram they had intercepted from the German foreign minister, Arthur Zimmermann, to the government of Mexico. It proposed that in the event of war between Germany and the United States, the Mexicans should join with Germany against the Americans. In return, they would regain their "lost provinces" (Texas and much of the rest of the American Southwest) to the north when the war was over. (The Germans understood that anti-American sentiment was still high in Mexico after the interventions of the previous few years.) Widely publicized by British propagandists and in the American press, the Zimmermann telegram inflamed public opinion and helped build popular sentiment for war. A few weeks later, in March 1917, a revolution in Russia toppled the reactionary czarist regime and replaced it with a new, republican government. The United States would now be spared the embarrassment of allying itself with a despotic monarchy. The war for a progressive world order could proceed untainted.

On the rainy evening of April 2, two weeks after German submarines had torpedoed three American ships, Wilson appeared before a joint session of Congress and asked for a declaration of war:

> It is a fearful thing to lead this great peaceful people into war, into the most terrible and disastrous of all wars, civilization itself seeming to be in the balance. But the right is more precious than peace, and we shall fight for the things which we have always carried nearest our hearts—

for democracy, for the right of those who submit to authority to have a voice in their own Governments, for the rights and liberties of small nations, for a universal dominion of right by such a concert of free peoples as shall bring peace and safety to all nations and make the world itself at last free.

Even then, opposition remained. For four days, pacifists in Congress carried on their futile struggle. When the declaration of war finally passed on April 6, fifty representatives and six senators voted against it.

"WAR WITHOUT STINT"

Armies on both sides in Europe were decimated and exhausted by the time of Woodrow Wilson's declaration of war. The German offensives of early 1917 had failed to produce an end to the struggle, and French and British counteroffensives had accomplished little beyond adding to the appalling number of casualties. The Allies looked desperately to the United States for help. Wilson, who had called on the nation to wage war "without stint or limit," was eager to oblige.

Entering the War

American intervention had its most immediate effect on the conflict at sea. By the spring of 1917, Great Britain was suffering such vast losses from attacks by German submarines—one of every four ships setting sail from British ports never returned—that its ability to continue receiving vital supplies from across the Atlantic was in question. Within weeks of joining the war, the United States had begun to alter the balance. A fleet of American destroyers aided the British navy in its assault on the U-boats. Other American warships escorted merchant vessels across the Atlantic. Americans also helped sow antisubmarine mines in the North Sea. The results were dramatic. Sinkings of Allied ships had totaled nearly 900,000 tons in the month of April 1917; by December, the figure had dropped to 350,000; by October 1918, it had declined to 112,000.

Many Americans had hoped that providing naval assistance alone would be enough to turn the tide in the war, but it quickly became clear that a major commitment of American ground forces would also be necessary to shore up the tottering Allies. Britain and France had few remaining reserves. By early 1918, Russia had withdrawn from the war altogether. After the Bolshevik Revolution in November 1917, the new government, led by V. I. Lenin, negotiated a hasty and costly peace with the Central Powers, thus freeing additional German troops to fight on the western front.

The American Expeditionary Force

But the United States did not have a large enough standing army to provide the necessary ground forces in 1917. There were only about 120,000 soldiers in the army and perhaps 80,000 more in the National Guard. Neither group had any combat experience; and except for the small number of officers who had participated in the Spanish American war two decades before and the Mexican intervention of 1916, few commanders had any experience in battle either.

Some urged a voluntary recruitment process to raise the needed additional forces. Among the advocates of this approach was Theodore Roosevelt, now old and ill, who swallowed his hatred of Wilson and called on him at the White House with an offer to raise a regiment to fight in Europe. But the president and his secretary of war, Newton D. Baker, decided that only a national draft could provide the needed men; and despite the protests of those who agreed with House Speaker Champ Clark that "there is precious little difference between a conscript and a convict," he won passage of the Selective Service Act in mid-May. The draft brought nearly 3 million men into the army; another 2 million joined various branches of the armed services voluntarily. Together, they formed what became known as the American Expeditionary Force (AEF).

In some respects, it was the most diverse fighting force the United States had ever assembled. For the first time, women were permitted to enlist in the military—over ten thousand in the navy and a few hundred in the marines. They were not permitted in combat, but they served crucial auxiliary roles in hospitals and offices.

Over 300,000 black soldiers enlisted in or were drafted into the army and navy as well. The marines would not accept them. And while most of them performed relatively menial tasks on military bases in the United States, more than 50,000 went to France. African-American soldiers served in segregated, all-black units under white commanders; and even in Europe, most of them were assigned to non-combat duty. But some black units fought valiantly in the great offensives of 1918.

Most African-American soldiers learned to live with the racism they encountered—in part because they hoped their military service would ultimately improve their status. But a few responded to provocations violently. In August 1917, a group of black soldiers in Houston, subjected to continuing abuse by people in

AMERICA IN WORLD WAR I: THE WESTERN FRONT, 1918

the community, used military weapons to kill seventeen whites. Retribution was quick. Thirteen black soldiers were hanged, and another forty were sentenced to life terms in military jails.

Having assembled this first genuinely national army, the War Department permitted the American Psychological Association to study it. The psychologists gave thousands of them a new test designed to measure intelligence: the "Intelligence Quotient" or "IQ" test. In fact, the tests were less effective in measuring intelligence than in measuring education; and they reflected the educational expectations of the white middle class people who had devised them. It is not surprising, therefore, that the largely working-class and racially mixed group of soldiers the psychologists examined performed poorly. Half the whites and the vast majority of the African Americans taking the test scored at levels that classified them as "morons." In reality, most of them were simply people who had not had very much access to education.

The Military Struggle

The engagement of these forces in combat was intense but brief. Not until the spring of 1918 were significant numbers of American troops available for battle. Eight months later, the war was over. Under the command of General John J. Pershing, the American troops joined the existing Allied forces in turning back a series of new German assaults. In early June, they assisted the French in repelling a bitter German offensive at Chateâu-Thierry, near Paris. Six weeks later, the Americans helped turn away another assault, at Rheims, farther south. By July 18, the Allies had halted the German advance and were beginning a successful offensive of their own.

On September 26, an American fighting force of over 1 million soldiers advanced against the Germans in the Argonne Forest as part of a 200-mile attack (the Meuse-Argonne offensives) that lasted nearly seven weeks. By the end of October, they had helped push

AMERICANS IN FRANCE, 1918
Members of the U.S. Twenty-third Infantry fire at German positions in France in 1918. The scarred landscape reflects the cost of four years of inconclusive trench warfare on the western front. *(U.S. Signal Corps)*

the Germans back toward their own border and had cut the enemy's major supply lines to the front.

Faced with an invasion of their own country, German military leaders now began to seek an armistice—an immediate cease-fire that would, they hoped, serve as a prelude to negotiations among the belligerents. Pershing wanted to drive on into Germany itself; but other Allied leaders, after first insisting on terms that made the agreement little different from a surrender, accepted the German proposal. On November 11, 1918, the Great War shuddered to a close.

THE WAR AND AMERICAN SOCIETY

The American experience in World War I was brief, but it had profound effects on the government, on the economy, and on society. Mobilizing an industrial economy for total war required an unprecedented degree of government involvement in industry, agriculture, and other areas. It also required, many believed, a strenuous effort to ensure the loyalty and commitment of the people.

Organizing the Economy for War

By the time the war ended, the United States government had appropriated $32 billion for expenses directly related to the conflict. This was a staggering sum by the standards of the time. The entire federal budget had seldom exceeded $1 billion before 1915, and as recently as 1910 the nation's entire gross national product had been only $35 billion. To raise the money, the government relied on two devices. First, it launched a major drive to solicit loans from the American people by selling "Liberty Bonds" to the public. By 1920, the sale of bonds, accompanied by elaborate patriotic appeals, had produced $23 billion. At the same time, new taxes were bringing in an additional sum of nearly $10 billion—some from levies on the "excess profits" of corporations, much from new, steeply graduated income and inheritance taxes that ultimately rose as high as 70 percent in some brackets.

An even greater challenge was organizing the economy to meet war needs. The administration tried two very different approaches. In 1916, Wilson established a Council of National Defense, composed of members of his cabinet, and a Civilian Advisory Commission, which set up local defense councils in every state and locality. Economic mobilization, according to this first plan, was to rest on a large-scale dispersal of power to local communities.

But this early administrative structure soon proved completely unworkable. Some members of the Council of National Defense, many of them disciples of the social engineering gospel of Thorstein Veblen and the "scientific management" principles of Frederick Winslow Taylor, urged a more centralized approach. Instead of dividing the economy geographically, they proposed dividing it functionally by organizing a series of planning bodies, each to supervise a specific sector of the economy. Thus one agency would control transportation, another agriculture, another manufacturing. The administrative structure that slowly emerged from such proposals was dominated by a series of "war boards," one to oversee the railroads, one to supervise fuel supplies (largely coal), another to handle food (a board that helped elevate to prominence the brilliant young engineer and business executive Herbert Hoover). The boards were not without weaknesses, but they generally succeeded in meeting essential war needs without paralyzing the domestic economy.

At the center of the effort to rationalize the economy was the War Industries Board, an agency created in July 1917 to coordinate government purchases of military supplies. Casually organized at first, it stumbled badly until March 1918, when Wilson restruc-

FINANCING THE WAR
The Liberty Loan bond-selling drives, heavily promoted by the government in posters such as this one, raised $23 billion for the war effort, an almost unimaginable sum to Americans at the time. Prior to World War I, the total federal budget had seldom exceeded $1 billion. *(Culver)*

tured it and placed it under the control of the Wall Street financier Bernard Baruch. From then on, the board wielded powers greater (in theory at least) than any government agency had ever possessed. Baruch decided which factories would convert to the production of which war materials and set prices for the goods they produced. When materials were scarce, Baruch decided to whom they should go. When corporations were competing for government contracts, he chose among them. He was, it seemed, providing the centralized regulation of the economy that some progressives had long urged.

In reality, the vaunted efficiency of the WIB was something of a myth. The agency was, in fact, plagued by mismanagement and inefficiency. It was less important to the nation's ability to meet its war needs than the sheer extent of American resources and productive capacities. Nor was the WIB in any real sense an example of state control of the economy. Baruch viewed himself, openly and explicitly, as the partner of business; and within the WIB, businessmen themselves—the so-called dollar-a-year men, who took paid leave from their corporate jobs and worked for the government for a token salary—supervised the affairs of the private economy. Baruch ensured that manufacturers who coordinated their efforts in accord with his goals would be exempt from antitrust laws. He helped major industries earn enormous profits from their efforts. Rather than working to restrict private power and limit corporate profits, as many progressives had urged, the government was working to enhance the private sector through a mutually beneficial alliance.

The effort to organize the economy for war produced some spectacular accomplishments: Hoover's efficient organization of domestic food supplies, William McAdoo's success in untangling the railroads, and others. In some areas, however, progress was so slow that the war was over before many of the supplies ordered for it were ready. Even so, many leaders of both government and industry emerged from the experience convinced of the advantages of a close, cooperative relationship between the public and private sectors. Some hoped to continue and extend the wartime experiments in peacetime.

Labor and the War

This growing link between the public and private sectors extended, although in greatly different form, to labor. The National War Labor Board, established in April 1918 to resolve labor disputes, pressured industry to grant important concessions to workers: an eight-hour day, the maintenance of minimal living standards, equal pay for women doing equal work, recognition of the right of unions to organize and bargain collectively. In return, it insisted that workers forgo all strikes and that employers not engage in lockouts. Membership in labor unions increased by more than 1.5 million between 1917 and 1919.

The war provided workers with important, if usually temporary, gains. But it did not stop labor militancy. That was particularly clear in the West, where the Western Federation of Miners staged a series of strikes to improve the terrible conditions in the underground mines. In Ludlow, Colorado, in 1917, workers (mostly Italians, Greeks, and Slavs) walked out of coal mines owned by John D. Rockefeller. Joined by their wives and daughters, they continued the strike even after they had been evicted from company housing and had moved into hastily erected tents. The state militia was called into the town to protect the mines, but in fact (as was often the case in labor actions), it actually worked to help employers defeat the strikers. Joined by strikebreakers and others, the militia attacked the workers' tent colony; and in the battle that followed, 39 people died, among them eleven children. The episode became known as the Ludlow Massacre.

Economic and Social Results of the War

Whatever its other effects, the war helped produce a remarkable period of economic growth in the United States—a boom that began in 1914 (when European demands for American products began to increase) and accelerated after 1917 (when demand from the United States war effort fueled production). Industrial production soared, and manufacturing activity expanded in regions that had previously had relatively little of it. The shipbuilding industry, for example, grew rapidly on the West Coast. Employment increased dramatically; and because so many men were away at war, new opportunities for female, African American, Mexican, and Asian workers appeared. Inflation cut into the wage increases American workers won from employers, but most workers nevertheless experienced a significant growth in income. The agricultural economy profited from the war as well. Farm prices rose to their highest levels in decades, and agricultural production increased dramatically as a result.

One of the most important social changes of the war years was the migration of hundreds of thousands of African Americans from the rural South into northern industrial cities. It became known as the "Great Migration." Like most migrations, it was a result of both a "push" and a "pull." The push was the poverty, indebtedness, racism, and violence most blacks experienced in the South. The pull was the prospect of factory jobs in the urban North and the opportunity to live in communities where blacks could enjoy more freedom and autonomy. In the labor-scarce economy of the war years, northern factory owners dispatched agents to the South to recruit African-American workers. Black newspapers advertised the prospects for employment in the North. And perhaps most important, those who migrated first sent word back to friends and families of the opportunities they encountered—one reason for the heavy concentration of migrants from a single area of the South in certain cities in the North. In Chicago, for example, the more than 70,000 new black residents came disproportionately from a few areas of Alabama and Mississippi.

The result was a dramatic growth in black communities in northern industrial cities such as New York, Chicago, Cleveland, and Detroit. Older, more established black residents of these cities were unsettled by these new arrivals, with their country ways and their revivalistic religion; the existing African-American communities considered the newcomers coarse and feared that their presence would increase their own vulnerability to white racism. But the movement could not be stopped. New churches sprang up in black neighborhoods (many of them simple storefronts, from which self-proclaimed preachers searched for congregations). Low-paid black workers crowded into inadequate housing—small apartments known as kitchenettes, in which several families sometimes lived together. As the black communities expanded, they inevitably began to rub up against white neighborhoods, with occasionally violent results. In East St. Louis, Illinois, a white mob attacked a black neighborhood on July 2, 1917, burned down many houses, and shot the residents of some of them as they fled. As many as forty black people died.

For American women, black and white, the war meant new opportunities for employment. A million or more women worked in a wide range of industrial jobs that, in peacetime, were considered male preserves: steel, munitions, trucking, public transportation. Most of them had been working in other, less well-paying jobs earlier. Among some feminists, the war inspired hopes of a lasting change in the role of women in the economy and the society. Margaret Dreier Robins, an official of the Women's Trade Union

League, said in 1918: "The war has created new values. Men and women are conscious that as citizens they must . . . share in the management of industry and the administration of government." But whatever changes the war brought were temporary ones. As soon as the war was over, almost all of the women working in previously male industrial jobs quit or were fired; in fact, the percentage of women working for wages actually declined between 1910 and 1920.

THE SEARCH FOR SOCIAL UNITY

The idea of unity—not only in the direction of the economy but in the nation's social purpose—had been the dream of many progressives for decades. To them, the war seemed to offer an unmatched opportunity for America to close ranks behind a great common cause. In the process, they hoped, society could achieve a lasting sense of collective purpose. In fact, however, the search for unity produced considerable repression.

The Peace Movement

Government leaders, and many others, realized that public sentiment about American involvement in the war had been deeply divided before April 1917 and remained so even after the declaration of war.

The peace movement in the United States before 1917 had many constituencies: German Americans, who opposed American intervention against Germany; Irish Americans, who opposed any support for the British; religious pacifists (Quakers, Mennonites, and others); intellectuals such as Randolph Bourne and groups on the left such as the Socialist Party and the Industrial Workers of the World, all of whom considered the war a meaningless battle among capitalist nations for commercial supremacy—an opinion many others, in America and Europe, later came to share. But the most active and widespread peace activism came from the women's movement. In 1915, Carrie Chapman Catt, a leader of the fight for woman suffrage, helped create the Woman's Peace Party, with a small but active membership. As the war in Europe intensified, the party's efforts to keep the United States from intervening grew.

Women peace activists were sharply divided once America entered the war in 1917. The National American Woman Suffrage Association, the single largest women's organization, supported the war and, more

WOMEN WAR WORKERS
With much of the male work force fighting overseas, women moved into occupations that in other times would have been considered unsuitable for them. One such occupation, pictured here, was delivering huge blocks of ice daily to households to be used (in this age before electric refrigeration) in wooden iceboxes. *(National Archives)*

than that, presented itself as a patriotic organization dedicated to advancing the war effort. Its membership grew dramatically as a result. Catt, who was among those who abandoned the peace cause, now began calling for woman suffrage as a "war measure," to ensure that women (whose work was essential to the war effort) would feel fully a part of the nation. But many other women refused to support the war even after April 1917. Among them were Jane Addams, who was widely reviled as a result, and Charlotte Perkins Gilman, a leading feminist activist.

Women peace activists shared many of the political and economic objections to the war of the Socialist Party (to which some of them belonged). But some criticized the war on other grounds as well, arguing that as wives and mothers they had a special moral basis for their pacifism. The Woman's Peace Party had claimed to represent the "mother half of humanity," and a similarly maternal opposition to war shaped the position of the many women who remained in opposition after 1917.

Selling the War and Suppressing Dissent

Government leaders were painfully aware of the continuing opposition to the war. Many believed that a crucial prerequisite for victory was to unite public opinion behind the military effort.

The most conspicuous government effort to do that was a vast propaganda campaign to drum up enthusiasm for the conflict. It was orchestrated by the Committee on Public Information (CPI), under the direction of the Denver journalist George Creel, who spoke openly of the importance of achieving social unity:

> When I think of the many voices that were heard before the war and are still heard, interpreting America from a class or sectional or selfish standpoint, I am not sure that, if the war had to come, it did not come at the right time for the preservation and reinterpretation of American ideals.

The CPI supervised the distribution of innumerable tons of pro-war literature (75 million pieces of printed material in all). War posters plastered the walls of offices, shops, theaters, schools, churches, and homes. Newspapers dutifully printed official government accounts of the reasons for the war and the prospects for quick victory. Creel encouraged reporters to exercise "self-censorship" when reporting news about the struggle; and although many people in the press resented the suggestion, the veiled threats that accompanied it persuaded most of them to comply.

The CPI attempted at first to distribute only the "facts," believing that the truth would speak for itself. As the war continued, however, their tactics became increasingly crude. Government-promoted posters and films, at first relatively mild in tone, were by 1918 becoming lurid portrayals of the savagery of the Germans, bearing such titles as *The Prussian Cur* and *The Kaiser: Beast of Berlin,* encouraging Americans to think of the German people as something close to savages.

The government soon began more coercive efforts to suppress dissent. The CPI ran full-page advertisements in popular magazines like the *Saturday Evening Post* urging citizens to notify the Justice Department when they encountered "the man who spreads the pessimistic stories . . . , cries for peace, or belittles our ef-

forts to win the war." The Espionage Act of 1917 gave the government new tools with which to respond to such reports. It created stiff penalties for spying, sabotage, or obstruction of the war effort (crimes that were often broadly defined); and it empowered the post office to ban "seditious" material from the mails, a responsibility Postmaster General Albert Sidney Burleson accepted with great relish. Sedition, he said, included statements that might "impugn the motives of the government and thus encourage insubordination," anything that suggested "that the government is controlled by Wall Street or munitions manufacturers, or any other special interests." He included in that category all publications of the Socialist Party.

More repressive were two measures of 1918: the Sabotage Act of April 20 and the Sedition Act of May 16. These bills expanded the meaning of the Espionage Act to make illegal any public expression of opposition to the war; in practice, it allowed officials to prosecute anyone who criticized the president or the government. Senator Hiram Johnson of California offered a bitter description of the provisions of the law. He said: "You shall not criticize anything or anybody in the Government any longer or you shall go to jail."

The most frequent targets of the new legislation (and one of the reasons for its enactment in the first place) were such anticapitalist groups (and now antiwar) groups as the Socialist Party and the Industrial Workers of the World. Many Americans had favored the repression of socialists and radicals even before the war; the wartime policies now made it possible to move against them with full legal sanction. Eugene V. Debs, the humane leader of the party and an opponent of the war, was sentenced to ten years in prison in 1918. Only a pardon by President Warren G. Harding ultimately won his release in 1921. Big Bill Haywood and members of the IWW were especially energetically prosecuted. Only by fleeing to the Soviet Union did Haywood avoid long imprisonment. In all, more than 1,500 people were arrested in 1918 for the crime of criticizing the government.

State and local governments, corporations, universities, and private citizens contributed as well to the climate of repression. Vigilante mobs sprang up to "discipline" those who dared challenge the war. A dissident Protestant clergyman in Cincinnati was pulled from his bed one night by a mob, dragged to a nearby hillside, and whipped "in the name of the women and children of Belgium." An IWW organizer in Montana was seized by a mob and hanged from a railroad bridge.

A cluster of citizens' groups emerged to mobilize "respectable" members of their communities to root out disloyalty. The American Protective League, probably the largest of such groups, enlisted the services of 250,000 people, who served as "agents"—prying into the activities and thoughts of their neighbors, opening mail, tapping telephones, and in general attempting to impose unity of opinion on their communities. It received government funds to support its work. Attorney General Thomas W. Gregory, a particularly avid supporter of repressing dissent, described them approvingly as "patriotic organizations." Other vigilante organizations—the National Security League, the Boy Spies of America, the American Defense Society—performed much the same function.

There were many victims of such activities: socialists, labor activists, female pacifists (some of whom were arrested and imprisoned simply for criticizing the government or capitalism). But the most frequent targets of repression were immigrants: Irish Americans because of their historic animosity toward the British and because some had, before 1917, expressed hopes for a German victory; Jews because many had expressed opposition to the anti-Semitic policies of the Russian government, until 1917 one of the Allies; and others. "Loyalist" citizens' groups policed immigrant neighborhoods. They monitored meetings and even conversations for signs of disloyalty. Even some settlement house workers, many of whom had once championed ethnic diversity, contributed to such efforts. The director of the National Security League described the origins of the anti-immigrant sentiment, which was producing growing support for what many were now calling "100 percent Americanism":

> . . . the melting pot has not melted. . . . there are vast communities in the nation thinking today not in terms of America, but in terms of Old World prejudices, theories, and animosities. . . . In the bottom of the melting pot there lie heaps of unfused metal.

The greatest target of abuse was the German-American community. Its members had unwittingly contributed to their plight. In the first years of the war in Europe, some had openly advocated American assistance to the Central Powers, and many had opposed United States intervention on behalf of the Allies. But while most German Americans supported the American war effort once it began, public opinion turned bitterly hostile. A campaign to purge society of all things German quickly gathered speed, at times assuming ludicrous forms. Sauerkraut was renamed "liberty cabbage." Hamburger became "liberty sausage." Performances of German music were frequently banned. German books were removed from the shelves of libraries. Courses in the German language were removed from school curricula; the California Board of Education called it "a language that disseminates the

ideals of autocracy, brutality, and hatred." Germans were routinely fired from jobs in war industries, lest they "sabotage" important tasks. Some were fired from positions entirely unrelated to the war—for example Karl Muck, the German-born conductor of the Boston Symphony Orchestra. Vigilante groups routinely subjected Germans to harassment and beatings, including a lynching in southern Illinois in 1918. Relatively few Americans favored such extremes, but many came to agree with the belief of the eminent psychologist G. Stanley Hall that "there is something fundamentally wrong with the Teutonic soul."

The Search for a New World Order

Woodrow Wilson had led the nation into war promising a more just and stable peace at its conclusion. Well before the armistice, he was preparing to lead the fight for what he considered a democratic postwar settlement. That settlement, he believed, must rest on a set of war aims reflecting a philosophy of internationalist relations that became known as Wilsonianism.

The Fourteen Points

On January 8, 1918, Wilson appeared before Congress to present the principles for which he claimed the nation was fighting. The war aims had fourteen distinct provisions, widely known as the Fourteen Points; but they fell into three broad categories. First, Wilson's proposals contained eight specific recommendations for adjusting postwar boundaries and for establishing new nations to replace the defunct Austro-Hungarian and Ottoman Empires. Those recommendations reflected his belief in the right of all peoples to self-determination. Second, there were five general principles to govern international conduct in the future: freedom of the seas, open covenants instead of secret treaties, reductions in armaments, free trade, and impartial mediation of colonial claims. Finally, there was a proposal for a league of nations that would help implement these new principles and territorial adjustments and resolve future controversies.

There were serious flaws in Wilson's proposals. He provided no formula for deciding how to implement the "national self-determination" he promised for subjugated peoples. He said little about economic rivalries and their effect on international relations, even though such economic tensions had been in large part responsible for the war. Nevertheless, Wilson's international vision quickly came to enchant not only much of his own generation (in both America and Europe), but members of generations to come. It reflected his belief, strongly rooted in the ideas of progressivism, that the world was as capable of just and efficient government as were individual nations; that once the international community accepted certain basic principles of conduct, and once it constructed modern institutions to implement them, the human race could live in peace.

The Fourteen Points were also an answer to the new Bolshevik government in Russia. In December 1917, Lenin issued his own statement of war aims strikingly similar to Wilson's own. Wilson's announcement, which came just three weeks later, was, among other things, a last-minute (and unsuccessful) effort to persuade the Bolshevik regime to keep Russia in the war. But Wilson also realized that Lenin was now a competitor in the effort to lead the postwar order. And he announced the Fourteen Points in part to ensure that the world looked to the United States, and not Russia, for guidance. "Liberalism," he said, referring to his own ideals, "is the only thing that can save civilization from chaos—from a flood of ultra-radicalism that will swamp the world . . . Liberalism must be more liberal than ever before, it must even be radical, if civilization is to escape the typhoon."

Early Obstacles

Wilson was confident, as the war neared its end, that popular support would enable him to win Allied approval of his peace plan. But there were ominous signs both at home and abroad that his path might be more difficult than he expected. In Europe, leaders of the Allied powers were preparing to resist him even before the armistice was signed. Most of them resented what they considered Wilson's tone of moral superiority. They had reacted unhappily when Wilson refused to make the United States their "ally" but had kept his distance as an "associate" of his European partners. They had been offended by his insistence on keeping American military forces separate from the Allied armies they were joining. Most of all, however, Britain and France, having suffered incalculable losses in their long years of war, and having stored up an enormous reserve of bitterness toward Germany as a result, were in no mood for a benign and generous peace. The British prime minister, David Lloyd George, insisted for a time that the German Kaiser be captured and executed. He and Georges Clemenceau, president of France, remained determined to the end to gain something from the struggle to compensate them for the catastrophe they had suffered.

At the same time, Wilson was encountering problems at home. In 1918, with the war almost over, Wilson unwisely appealed to the American voters to support his peace plans by electing Democrats to Congress in the November elections. A Republican victory, he declared, would be "interpreted on the other side of the water as a repudiation of my leadership." Days later, the Republicans captured majorities in both houses. Domestic economic troubles, more than international issues, had been the most important factor in the voting; but because of the president's ill-timed appeal, the results damaged his ability to claim broad popular support for his peace plans.

The leaders of the Republican Party, in the meantime, were developing their own reasons for opposing Wilson. Some were angry that he had tried to make the 1918 balloting a referendum on his war aims, especially since many Republicans had been supporting the Fourteen Points. Wilson further antagonized them when he refused to appoint any important Republicans to the negotiating team that would represent the United States at the peace conference in Paris.

But the president considered such matters unimportant. Only one member of the American negotiating party would have any real authority: Wilson himself. And once he had produced a just and moral treaty, he believed, the weight of world and American opinion would compel his enemies to support him. As he sailed for Paris late in 1918, he said:

> In the name of the people of the United States, I have uttered as the objects of this great war ideals and nothing but ideals, and the war has been won by that inspiration. . . . There is a great wind of moral force moving through the world, and every man who opposes that wind will go down in disgrace.

The Paris Peace Conference

Wilson arrived in Europe to a welcome such as few men in history have experienced. To the war-weary people of the Continent, he was nothing less than a savior, the man who would create a new and better world. When he entered Paris on December 13, 1918, he was greeted, some claimed, by the largest crowd in the history of France. The negotiations themselves, however, proved less satisfying.

The principal figures in the negotiations were the leaders of the victorious allied nations: Lloyd George representing Great Britain; Clemenceau representing France; Vittorio Orlando, the prime minister of Italy;

The Big Four in Paris Surface cordiality during the Paris Peace Conference disguised serious tensions among the so-called Big Four, the leaders of the victorious nations in World War I. As the conference progressed, the European leaders developed increasing resentment of Woodrow Wilson's high (and some thought sanctimonious) moral posture in the negotiations. Shown here in the library of the Hotel Crillon are, from left to right, Vittorio Orlando of Italy, David Lloyd-George of Great Britain, Georges Clemenceau of France, and Wilson. *(Bettmann)*

and Wilson, who hoped to dominate them all. Some of Wilson's advisers had warned him that if agreement could not be reached at the "summit," there would be nowhere else to go, and that it would therefore be better to begin negotiations at a lower level. Wilson, however, was adamant; he alone would represent the United States.

From the beginning, the atmosphere of idealism Wilson had sought to create was competing with a spirit of national aggrandizement. There was, moreover, a pervasive sense of unease about the unstable situation in eastern Europe and the threat of communism. Russia, whose new Bolshevik government was still fighting "White" counterrevolutionaries, was unrepresented in Paris; but the radical threat it seemed to pose to Western governments was never far from the minds of any of the delegates, least of all Wilson himself. Indeed, not long before he came to Paris, Wilson ordered the landing of American troops in the Soviet Union. They were there, he claimed, to help a group of 60,000 Czech soldiers trapped in Russia to escape. But the Americans soon became involved, both directly and indirectly, in assisting the White Russians (the anti-Bolsheviks) in their fight against the new regime. Some American troops remained as late as April 1920. Lenin's regime survived these challenges, but Wilson refused to recognize his new government nevertheless. Diplomatic relations between the United States and the Soviet Union were not restored until 1933.

In the tense and often vindictive atmosphere these competing concerns produced in Paris, Wilson was un-able to win approval of many of the broad principles he had espoused: freedom of the seas, which the British refused even to discuss; free trade; "open covenants openly arrived at" (the Paris negotiations themselves were often conducted in secret). Despite his support for "impartial mediation" of colonial claims, he was forced to accept a transfer of German colonies in the Pacific to Japan, to whom the British had promised them in exchange for Japanese assistance in the war. His pledge of "national self-determination" for all peoples suffered numerous assaults. Economic and strategic demands were constantly coming into conflict with the principle of cultural nationalism.

Where the treaty departed most conspicuously from Wilson's ideals was on the question of reparations. As the conference began, the president opposed demanding compensation from the defeated Central Powers. The other Allied leaders, however, were intransigent, and slowly Wilson gave way and accepted the principle of reparations, the specific sum to be set later by a commission. That figure, established in 1921, was $56 billion, supposedly to pay for damages to civilians and for military pensions. There were continued negotiations for a decade, which scaled the sum back considerably. In the end, Germany paid only $9 billion, which was still more than its crippled economy could afford. The reparations, combined with other territorial and economic penalties, constituted an effort to keep Germany not only weak but prostrate for the indefinite future. Never again, the Allied leaders believed, should the Germans be allowed to become powerful enough to threaten the peace of Europe.

Wilson did manage to win some important victories in Paris in setting boundaries and dealing with former colonies. He secured approval of a plan to place many former colonies and imperial possessions (among them Palestine) in "trusteeship" under the League of Nations—the so-called mandate system. He blocked a French proposal to break up western Germany into a group of smaller states. He helped design the creation of two new nations: Yugoslavia and Czechoslovakia, which were welded together out of, among other territories, pieces of the former Austro–Hungarian Empire. Each contained an uneasy collection of ethnic groups that had frequently battled one another in the past.

But Wilson's most visible triumph, and the one most important to him, was the creation of a permanent international organization to oversee world affairs and prevent future wars. On January 25, 1919, the Allies voted to accept the "covenant" of the League of Nations; and with that, Wilson believed, the peace treaty was transformed from a disappointment into a success. Whatever mistakes and inequities had emerged from the peace conference, he was convinced, could be corrected later by the League.

The covenant provided for an assembly of nations that would meet regularly to debate means of resolving disputes and protecting the peace. Authority to implement League decisions would rest with a nine-member Executive Council; the United States would be one of five permanent members of the council, along with Britain, France, Italy, and Japan. The covenant left many questions unanswered, most notably how the League would enforce its decisions. Wilson, however, was confident that once established, the new organization would find suitable answers.

The Ratification Battle

Wilson was well aware of the political obstacles awaiting him at home. Many Americans, accustomed to their nation's isolation from Europe, questioned the wisdom of this major new commitment to internationalism. Others had serious reservations about the specific features of the treaty and the covenant. After a brief trip to Washington in February 1919, during which he listened to harsh objections to the treaty from members of the Senate and others, he returned to Europe and insisted on several modifications in the covenant to satisfy his critics. The revisions limited America's obligations to the League by ensuring that the United States would not be obliged to accept a League mandate to oversee a territory and that the League would not challenge the Monroe Doctrine. But

the changes were not enough to mollify his opponents, and Wilson refused to go further. When Colonel House, his close friend and trusted adviser, told him he must be prepared to compromise more, the president retorted sharply: "I have found that you get nothing in this world that is worth-while without fighting for it." His long friendship with House ended abruptly.

Wilson presented the Treaty of Versailles (which took its name from the palace outside Paris where the final negotiating sessions had taken place) to the Senate on July 10, 1919, asking, "Dare we reject it and break the heart of the world?" In the weeks that followed, he refused to consider even the most innocuous compromise. His deteriorating physical condition—he was suffering from hardening of the arteries and had apparently experienced something like a mild stroke in Paris—may have contributed to his intransigence.

The Senate, in the meantime, was raising many objections. Some senators—the fourteen so-called "irreconcilables," many of them western isolationists—opposed the agreement on principle. But other opponents, with less fervent convictions, were principally concerned with constructing a winning issue for the Republicans in 1920 and with weakening a president whom they had come to despise. Most notable of these was Senator Henry Cabot Lodge of Massachusetts, the powerful chairman of the Foreign Relations Committee. A man of stunning arrogance and a close friend of Theodore Roosevelt (who had died early in 1919, spouting hatred of Wilson to the end), Lodge loathed the president with genuine passion. "I never thought I could hate a man as I hate Wilson," he once admitted. He used every possible tactic to obstruct, delay, and amend the treaty. Wilson, for his part, despised Lodge as much as Lodge despised him. He made his feelings clear when he described his opponents in the Senate (obviously thinking primarily of Lodge) as "contemptible, narrow, selfish, poor little minds that never get anywhere."

Public sentiment clearly favored ratification, so at first Lodge could do little more than play for time. When the document reached his committee, he spent two weeks slowly reading aloud each word of its 300 pages; then he held six weeks of public hearings to air the complaints of every disgruntled minority (Irish Americans, for example, angry that the settlement made no provision for an independent Ireland). Gradually, Lodge's general opposition to the treaty crystallized into a series of "reservations"—amendments to the League covenant limiting American obligations to the organization.

At this point Wilson might still have won approval if he had agreed to some relatively minor changes in the language of the treaty. But the president refused to yield. The United States had a moral obligation, he claimed, to respect the terms of the agreement precisely as they stood. When he realized the Senate would not budge, he decided to appeal to the public.

Wilson's Ordeal

What followed was a political disaster and a personal tragedy. Wilson embarked on a grueling, cross-country speaking tour to arouse public support for the treaty. In a little more than three weeks, he traveled over 8,000 miles by train, speaking as often as four times a day, resting hardly at all. Finally, he reached the end of his strength. After speaking at Pueblo, Colorado, on September 25, he collapsed with severe headaches. Canceling the rest of his itinerary, he rushed back to Washington, where, a few days later, he suffered a major stroke. For two weeks he was close to death; for six weeks more, he was so seriously ill that he could conduct virtually no public business. His wife and his doctor formed an almost impenetrable barrier around him, shielding him from any official pressures that might impede his recovery, preventing the public from receiving any accurate information about the gravity of his condition.

Wilson ultimately recovered enough to resume a limited official schedule, but he was essentially an invalid for the remaining eighteen months of his presidency. His left side was partially paralyzed; more important, like many stroke victims, he had only partial control of his mental and emotional state. His condition only intensified what had already been his strong tendency to view public issues in moral terms and to resist any attempts at compromise. When the Senate Foreign Relations Committee finally sent the treaty to the full Senate for ratification, recommending nearly fifty amendments and reservations, Wilson refused to consider any of them. When the full Senate voted in November to accept fourteen of the reservations, Wilson gave stern directions to his Democratic allies: They must vote only for a treaty with no changes whatsoever; any other version must be defeated. On November 19, 1919, forty-two Democrats, following the president's instructions, joined with the thirteen Republican "irreconcilables" to reject the amended treaty. When the Senate voted on the original version without any reservations, thirty-eight senators, all but one a Democrat, voted to approve it; fifty-five voted no.

There were sporadic efforts to revive the treaty over the next few months. But Wilson's opposition to anything but the precise settlement he had negotiated in Paris remained too formidable an obstacle to sur-

mount. He was, moreover, becoming convinced that the 1920 national election would serve as a "solemn referendum" on the League. By now, however, public interest in the peace process had begun to fade—partly as a reaction against the tragic bitterness of the ratification fight, but more in response to a series of other crises.

A SOCIETY IN TURMOIL

Even during the Paris Peace Conference, many Americans were less concerned about international matters than about turbulent events at home. In the aftermath of the war, various groups of Americans set out to claim the social advances that the idealistic justifications of the conflict seemed to have promised them. But the social environment after 1918 was no longer receptive to progressive reform. The American economy experienced a severe postwar recession. And much of middle-class America responded to demands for change with a fearful, conservative hostility. The aftermath of war brought not the age of liberal reform that progressives had predicted, but a period of repression and reaction.

Industry and Labor

Citizens of Washington, on the day after the armistice, found it impossible to place long-distance telephone calls: the lines were jammed with officials of the war agencies canceling government contracts. The fighting had ended sooner than anyone had anticipated, and without warning, without planning, the nation was launched into the difficult task of economic reconversion.

At first, the wartime boom continued. But the postwar prosperity rested largely on the lingering effects of the war (government deficit spending continued for some months after the armistice) and on sudden, temporary demands (a booming market for scarce consumer goods at home and a strong market for American products in the war-ravaged nations of Europe). The postwar boom was accompanied, moreover, by raging inflation, a result in part of the precipitous abandonment of wartime price controls. Through most of 1919 and 1920, prices rose at an average of more than 15 percent a year.

Finally, late in 1920, the economic bubble burst, as many of the temporary forces that had created it disappeared and as inflation began killing the market for consumer goods. Between 1920 and 1921, the gross na-

UNION MEMBERSHIP, 1900–1920

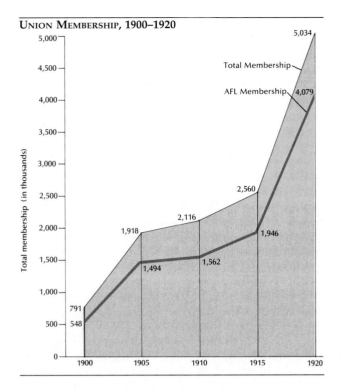

tional product (GNP) declined nearly 10 percent; 100,000 businesses went bankrupt; 453,000 farmers lost their land; nearly 5 million Americans lost their jobs.

In this unpromising economic environment, leaders of organized labor set out to consolidate the advances they had made in the war, which now seemed in danger of being lost. The raging inflation of 1919 wiped out the modest wage gains workers had achieved during the war; many laborers worried about job security as hundreds of thousands of veterans returned to the work force; arduous working conditions—such as the twelve-hour day in the steel industry—continued to be a source of discontent. Employers aggravated the resentment by using the end of the war (and the end of government controls) to rescind benefits they had been forced to concede to workers in 1917 and 1918—most notably recognition of unions.

The year 1919, therefore, saw an unprecedented wave of strikes—more than 3,600 in all, involving over 4 million workers. In January, a walkout by shipyard workers in Seattle, Washington, evolved into a general strike that brought the entire city to a virtual standstill. The mayor requested and received the assistance of U.S. Marines to keep the city running, and eventually the strike failed. But the brief success of a general strike, something Americans associated with European

radicals, made the Seattle incident reverberate loudly throughout the country.

In September, there was a strike by the Boston police force, which was responding to layoffs and wage cuts by demanding recognition of its union. Seattle had remained generally calm; but with its police off the job, Boston erupted in violence and looting. Efforts by local businessmen, veterans, and college students to patrol the streets proved ineffective; and finally Governor Calvin Coolidge called in the National Guard to restore order. (His public statement that "there is no right to strike against the public safety by anybody, anywhere, any time" attracted national acclaim.) Eventually, Boston officials dismissed the entire police force and hired a new one.

In September 1919, the greatest strike in American history began, when 350,000 steelworkers in several eastern and midwestern cities walked off the job, demanding an eight-hour day and recognition of their union. The steel strike was long, bitter, and violent—most of the violence coming from employers, who hired armed guards to disperse picket lines and escort strikebreakers into factories. It climaxed in a riot in Gary, Indiana, in which eighteen strikers were killed. Steel executives managed to keep most plants running with non-union labor, and public opinion was so hostile to the strikers that the AFL—having at first endorsed the strike—soon timidly repudiated it. By January, the strike had collapsed. It was a setback from which organized labor would not recover for more than a decade.

The wave of strikes was a reflection of the high expectations workers had in the aftermath of a war they believed had been fought, in part, to secure their rights. It was also a reflection of the power of the forces arrayed against them. An official of the War Labor Board, observing the dismal postwar experience of unions, said in 1919: "The workers of the Allied world have been told that they were engaged in a democracy. . . . They are asking now, 'Where is that democracy for which we fought?'"

The Demands of African Americans

The black men who had served in the armed forces during the war (367,000 of them) came home in 1919 and marched down the main streets of the industrial cities with other returning troops. And then (in New York and other cities), they marched again through the streets of black neighborhoods such as Harlem, led by jazz bands, cheered by thousands of African Americans, worshiped as heroes. The black soldiers were an inspiration to thousands of urban African Americans, a sign, they thought, that a new age had come, that the

THE GREAT STEEL STRIKE
Mounted police charge a group of striking steelworkers in Philadelphia during the steel strike of 1919. The strike lasted three and a half months and was the greatest single labor action in American history to that point. The strike centered around five demands: recognition of the steelworkers' union, the right of workers to bargain collectively with management through the union, abolition of the twelve-hour day, abolition of company unions, and wage increases. It finally dissolved in failure in early January 1920. *(Culver)*

glory of black heroism in the war would make it impossible for white society ever again to treat African Americans as less than equal citizens.

In fact, that black soldiers had fought in the war had almost no impact at all on white attitudes. But it did have a profound effect on black attitudes: it accentuated African-American bitterness—and increased black determination to fight for their rights. For soldiers, there was an expectation of some social reward for their service. For many other American blacks, the war had raised economic expectations, as they moved into industrial and other jobs vacated by white workers, jobs to which they had previously had no access. Just as black soldiers expected their military service to enhance their social status, so black factory workers regarded their move north as an escape from racial prejudice and an opportunity for economic gain.

By 1919, however, the racial climate had become savage and murderous. In the South, there was a sudden increase in lynchings: more than seventy blacks, some of them war veterans, died at the hands of white mobs in 1919 alone. In the North, black factory workers faced widespread layoffs as returning white veterans displaced them from their jobs. Black veterans found no significant new opportunities for advancement. Rural black migrants to northern cities encountered white communities unfamiliar with and generally hostile to them; and as whites became convinced that black workers with lower wage demands were hurting them economically, animosity grew rapidly.

The wartime riots in East St. Louis and elsewhere were a prelude to a summer of much worse racial violence in 1919. In Chicago, a black teenager swimming in Lake Michigan on a hot July day happened to drift

A BLACK VETERAN
Residents of Harlem watch the 309th Colored Infantry parading through New York on the occasion of their return from Europe in March 1919. One little girl stares intently at a disabled veteran still in uniform, who is standing somberly among the crowd—as if already aware of the disappointments awaiting other black veterans as they reentered civilian life.   *(UPI/Bettmann)*

toward a white beach. Whites on shore allegedly stoned him unconscious; he sank and drowned. Angry blacks gathered in crowds and marched into white neighborhoods to retaliate; whites formed even larger crowds and roamed into black neighborhoods shooting, stabbing and beating passersby, destroying homes and properties. For more than a week, Chicago was virtually at war. In the end, 38 people died—15 whites and 23 blacks—and 537 were injured; over 1,000 people were left homeless. The Chicago riot was the worst but not the only racial violence during the so-called red summer of 1919; in all, 120 people died in such racial outbreaks in the space of little more than three months.

Racial violence, and even racially motivated urban riots, were not new. The deadliest race riot in American history had occurred in New York during the Civil War. But the 1919 riots were different in one respect: they did not just involve white people attacking blacks; they also involved blacks fighting back. The NAACP signaled this change by urging blacks not just to demand government protection, but also to retaliate, to defend themselves. The poet Claude McKay, one of the major figures of what would shortly be known as the Harlem Renaissance, wrote a poem after the Chicago riot called "If We Must Die":

Like men we'll face the murderous cowardly pack.
Pressed to the wall, dying, but fighting back.

At the same time, a black Jamaican, Marcus Garvey, began to attract a wide American following, mostly among poor urban blacks, with an ideology of black nationalism. Garvey encouraged African Americans to

BLACK MIGRATION, 1910–1950

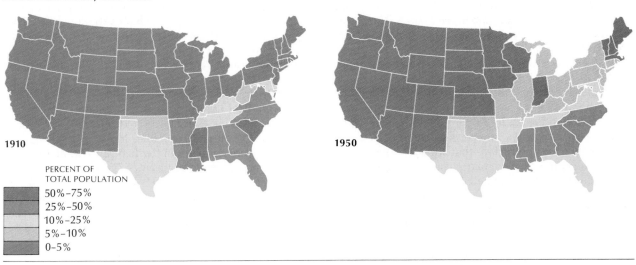

1910

1950

PERCENT OF
TOTAL POPULATION

50%–75%
25%–50%
10%–25%
5%–10%
0–5%

take pride in their own achievements and to develop an awareness of their African heritage—to reject assimilation into white society and develop pride in their own race and culture (which was, he claimed, superior to that of white society). His United Negro Improvement Association (UNIA) launched a chain of black-owned grocery stores and pressed for the creation of other black businesses. Eventually, Garvey began urging his supporters to leave America and return to Africa, where they could create a new society of their own. In the 1920s, the Garvey movement experienced explosive growth for a time; and the UNIA became notable for its mass rallies and parades, for the opulent uniforms of its members, and for the growth of its enterprises. It began to decline, however, after Garvey was indicted in 1923 on charges of business fraud. He was deported to Jamaica two years later. But the allure of black nationalism, which he helped make visible to millions of African Americans, survived in black culture long after Garvey himself was gone.

The Red Scare

To much of the white middle class at the time, the industrial warfare, the racial violence, the demands of feminists all appeared to be frightening omens of instability and radicalism. This was in part because other evidence emerging at the same time seemed likewise to suggest the existence of a radical menace. The Russian Revolution of November 1917 made it clear that communism was no longer simply a theory, but now an important regime. Concerns about the communist threat grew in 1919 when the Soviet government announced the formation of the Communist International (or Comintern), whose purpose was to export revolution around the world. And in America itself, there were, in addition to the great number of imagined radicals, a modest number of real ones. The American Communist Party began its life in 1919, and there were other radical groups (many of them dominated by immigrants from Europe who had been involved in radical politics before coming to America). Some of these radicals were presumably responsible for a series of bombings in the spring of 1919 that produced great national alarm. In April, the post office intercepted several dozen parcels addressed to leading businessmen and politicians that were triggered to explode when opened. Several of them reached their destinations, and one of them exploded, severely injuring a domestic servant of a public official in Georgia. Two months later, eight bombs exploded in eight cities within minutes of one another, suggesting a nation-

Collecting "Subversive" Literature, 1919
Even before the Palmer Raids of 1919–1920 put the federal government behind the effort to suppress radical groups, state and local governments were taking heavy-handed action. Here a group of local law enforcement officials display a stash of "Red" literature they had seized on November 11, 1919, from a Communist Party headquarters in Cambridge, Massachusetts, near Harvard University. *(UPI/Bettmann)*

wide conspiracy. One of them damaged the facade of Attorney General A. Mitchell Palmer's home in Washington. In 1920, there was a terrible explosion in front of the Morgan bank on Wall Street, which killed thirty people (although only one person in the bank itself—a clerk).

The bombings crystallized what was already a growing determination among many middle-class Americans (and some government officials) to fight back against radicalism—a determination steeled by the repressive atmosphere of the war years. This antiradicalism accompanied, and reinforced, the already strong commitment among old-stock Protestants to the idea of "100 Percent Americanism." And it produced what became known as the Red Scare.

Antiradical newspapers and politicians now began to portray almost every form of instability or protest as signs of a radical threat. Race riots, one newspaper claimed, were the work of "armed revolutionaries running rampant through our cities." The steel strike, the *Philadelphia Inquirer* claimed, was "penetrated with the Bolshevik idea . . . steeped in the doctrines of the class struggle and social overthrow." Nearly thirty states enacted new peacetime sedition laws imposing harsh

S I G N I F I C A N T   E V E N T S

1914 Austria invades Serbia

World War I begins

Wilson declares American neutrality

1915 Wartime economic boom begins

Great Migration of blacks to the North begins

Woman's Peace Party founded

Germany begins submarine warfare

Lusitania torpedoed

Wilson launches preparedness program

1916 *Sussex* attacked

Wilson reelected president

1917 Germany announces unrestricted submarine warfare

Germans launch major offensive in France

Zimmermann telegram disclosed

Russian czar overthrown

United States declares war on Central Powers

Selective Service Act passed

War Industries Board created

Espionage Act passed

Race riot in East St. Louis, Illinois

Racial tensions lead to violence among soldiers based in Houston

Coal miners' strike in Ludlow, Colorado, ends in massacre of 39 people

1918 Russia signs a separate peace with Central Powers

Sedition Act passed

U.S. troops repel Germans at Château Thierry and Rheims

U.S. troops launch offensive in Argonne Forest

Bernard Baruch takes over War Industries Board

Wilson announces Fourteen Points

American troops land in Soviet Union

Republicans gain control of Congress

Armistice ends war (November 11)

Paris Peace Conference convenes

1919 Treaty of Versailles signed

Senate proposes modifications to treaty

Wilson suffers stroke

Senate rejects treaty

Economy experiences postwar inflation

Race riots break out in Chicago and other cities

Workers stage steel strike and other actions

Soviet Union creates Comintern

Theodore Roosevelt dies

1920 Nineteenth Amendment gives suffrage to women

Economic recession disrupts economy

United States reacts to "radicalism" with Palmer Raids and Red Scare

Sacco and Vanzetti charged with murder

Warren G. Harding elected president

1924 Woodrow Wilson dies

1927 Sacco and Vanzetti executed

penalties on those who promoted revolution; some 300 people went to jail as a result—many of them people whose "crime" had been nothing more than opposition to the war. There were spontaneous acts of violence against supposed radicals in some communities. A mob

of off-duty soldiers in New York City ransacked the offices of a socialist newspaper and beat up its staff. Another mob, in Centralia, Washington, dragged an IWW agitator from jail and castrated him before hanging him from a bridge. Citizens in many communities removed "subversive" books from the shelves of libraries; administrators in some universities dismissed "radical" members from their faculties. Women's groups such as the National Consumers' League came under attack by antiradicals because so many feminists had opposed American intervention in the fighting in Europe.

Perhaps the greatest contribution to the Red Scare came from the federal government. On New Year's Day, 1920, Attorney General A. Mitchell Palmer and his ambitious assistant, J. Edgar Hoover, orchestrated a series of raids on alleged radical centers throughout the country and arrested more than 6,000 people. The Palmer Raids had been intended to uncover huge caches of weapons and explosives; they netted a total of three pistols and no dynamite. Most of those arrested were ultimately released, but about 500 who were not American citizens were summarily deported.

The ferocity of the Red Scare soon abated, but its effects lingered well into the 1920s, most notably in the celebrated case of Sacco and Vanzetti. In May of 1920, two Italian immigrants, Nicola Sacco and Bartolomeo Vanzetti, were charged with the murder of a paymaster in Braintree, Massachusetts. The evidence against them was questionable; but because both men were confessed anarchists, they faced a widespread public presumption of guilt. They were convicted in a trial of extraordinary injudiciousness, before an openly bigoted judge, Webster Thayer, and were sentenced to death. Over the next several years, public support for Sacco and Vanzetti grew to formidable proportions. But all requests for a new trial or a pardon were denied. On August 23, 1927, amid widespread protests around the world, Sacco and Vanzetti, still proclaiming their innocence, died in the electric chair. Theirs was a cause that a generation of Americans never forgot. Fifty years later, the writer Katherine Anne Porter, who had demonstrated on their behalf, described the case as the "Never-Ending Wrong." It kept the bitter legacy of the Red Scare alive for many years.

The Retreat from Idealism

On August 26, 1920, the Nineteenth Amendment, guaranteeing women the right to vote, became part of the Constitution. To the woman suffrage movement, this was the culmination of nearly a century of struggle. To many progressives, who had seen the inclusion of women in the electorate as a way of bolstering their political strength, it seemed to promise new support for reform. Yet the passage of the Nineteenth Amendment marked not the beginning of an era of reform, but the end of one.

Economic problems, feminist demands, labor unrest, racial tensions, and the intensity of the antiradicalism they helped create—all combined in the years immediately following the war to produce a general sense of disillusionment. That became particularly apparent in the election of 1920. Woodrow Wilson wanted the campaign to be a referendum on the League of Nations, and the Democratic candidates, Ohio Governor James M. Cox and Assistant Secretary of the Navy Franklin D. Roosevelt, tried to keep Wilson's ideals alive. The Republican presidential nominee, however, offered a different vision. He was Warren Gamaliel Harding, an obscure Ohio senator whom party leaders had chosen as their nominee confident that he would do their bidding once in office. Harding offered no ideals, only a vague promise of a return, as he later phrased it, to "normalcy." He won in a landslide. The Republican ticket received 61 percent of the popular vote and carried every state outside the South. The party made major gains in Congress as well.

Woodrow Wilson, who had tried and failed to create a postwar order based on democratic ideals, stood repudiated. Early in 1921, he retired to a house on S Street in Washington, where he lived quietly until his death in 1924. In the meantime, for most Americans, a new era had begun.

SUGGESTED READINGS

The Road to War. Thomas A. Bailey and Paul B. Ryan, *The Lusitania Disaster* (1975). John Coogan, *The End to Neutrality* (1981). John Milton Cooper, Jr., *The Vanity of Power: American Isolation and the First World War* (1969). Patrick Devlin, *Too Proud to Fight: Woodrow Wilson's Neutrality* (1974). Ross Gregory, *The Origins of American Intervention in the First World War* (1971). Manfred Jonas, *The United States and Germany* (1984). C. Roland Marchand, *The American Peace Movement and Social Reform* (1973). Ernest R. May, *The World War and American Isolation* (1959). Emily Rosenberg, *Spreading the American Dream* (1982). Jeffrey J. Sanford, *Wilsonian Maritime Diplomacy* (1978). Daniel Smith, *Robert Lansing and American Neutrality* (1958); *The Great Departure: The United States and World War I, 1914–1920,* (1965). Barbara Tuchman, *The Zimmermann Telegram* (1958); *The Guns of August* (1962).

Military Histories. A. E. Barbeau and Florette Henri, *The Unknown Soldiers: Black American Troops in World War I* (1974). Christopher Campbell, *Aces and Aircraft of World War I* (1981). John Whiteclay Chambers, *To Raise an Army* (1987). J. Garry Clifford, *The Citizen Soldiers* (1972). Edward M. Coffman, *The War to End All Wars* (1969). Harvey A. DeWeerd, *President Wilson Fights His War* (1968). Frank Freidel, *Over There: The Story of America's First Great Overseas Crusade* (1964). Robert Jackson, *Fighter Pilots in World War I* (1977). Herbert M. Mason, Jr., *The Lafayette Escadrille* (1964). Donald Smythe, *Pershing* (1986). Lawrence Stallings, *The Doughboys: The Story of the AEF, 1917–1918* (1963). David Trask, *The United States in the Supreme War Council* (1961). Frank E. Vandiver, *Black Jack: The Life and Times of John J. Pershing* (1977). Russell Weigley, *The American Way of War* (1973).

Wartime Diplomacy. Kathleen Burk, *Britain, America, and the Sinews of War* (1985). W. B. Fowler, *British-American Relations, 1917–1918* (1969). John Lewis Gaddis, *Russia, the Soviet Union and the United States* (1978). George F. Kennan, *Russia Leaves the War* (1956); *Russia and the West Under Lenin and Stalin* (1961). Carl Parrini, *Heir to Empire: United States Economic Diplomacy, 1916–1923* (1969).

Politics and Government in Wartime. Ray H. Abrams, *Preachers Present Arms: The Role of the American Churches and Clergy in World Wars I and II* (1969). Daniel R. Beaver, *Newton D. Baker and the American War Effort, 1917–1919* (1966). George T. Blakey, *Historians on the Homefront* (1970). William J. Breen, *Uncle Sam at Home* (1984). Zechariah Chaffee, Jr., *Free Speech in the United States* (1941). Charles Chatfield, *For Peace and Justice: Pacifism in America, 1914–1941* (1971). Edward M. Coffman, *The Hilt of the Sword: The Career of Peyton C. Marsh* (1966). Valerie Jean Conner, *The National War Labor Board* (1983). Alfred E. Conrebise, *War as Advertised: The Four Minute Men and America's Crusade, 1917–1918* (1984). Wayne Cornelius, *Building the Cactus Curtain: Mexican Migration and U.S. Responses from Wilson to Carter* (1980). Robert D. Cuff, *The War Industries Board: Business-Government Relations During World War I* (1973). Charles DeBenedettis, *Origins of the Modern Peace Movement* (1978). Harvey A. DeWeerd, *President Wilson Fights His War* (1968). Charles V. Forcey, *The Crossroads of Liberalism* (1961). Charles Gilbert, *American Financing of World War I* (1970). Otis L. Graham, Jr., *The Great Campaigns* (1971). Ellis W. Hawley, *The Great War and the Search for a Modern Order* (1979). Sondra Herman, *Eleven Against War* (1969). Donald Johnson, *The Challenge to America's Freedoms* (1963). David M. Kennedy, *Over Here* (1980). Seward Livermore, *Politics Is Adjourned* (1966). J. R. Mock and Cedric Larson, *Words That Won the War* (1939). Paul L. Murphy, *World War I and the Origins of Civil Liberties* (1984). George Nash, *The Life of Herbert Hoover: The Humanitarian, 1914–1917* (1990). Harold C. Peterson, *Propaganda for War: The Campaign Against American Neutrality, 1914–1917* (1968). Harold C. Peterson and Gilbert Fite, *Opponents of War, 1917–1918* (1957). Richard Polenberg, *Fighting Faiths: The Abrams Case, the Supreme Court, and Free Speech* (1987). William Preston, Jr., *Aliens and Dissenters: Federal Suppression of Radicals, 1903–1933* (1963). Ronald Schaffer, *America in the Great War: The Rise of the War Welfare State* (1991). Harry N. Scheiber, *The Wilson Administration and Civil Liberties, 1917–1921* (1960). Jordan Schwarz, *The Speculator: Bernard M. Baruch in Washington, 1917–1965* (1981). John A. Thomas, *Reformers and War* (1987). Stephen Vaughn, *Holding Fast the Inner Lines: Democracy, Nationalism, and the Committee on Public Information* (1979). Neil A. Wynn, *From Progressivism to Prosperity: World War I and American Society* (1986).

Wartime Society and Culture. Allan M. Brandt, *No Magic Bullet: A Social History of Venereal Disease in the United States* (1985). Paul Chapman, *Schools as Sorters* (1988). Stanley Cooperman, *World War I and the American Novel* (1970). Alfred W. Crosby, Jr., *Epidemic and Peace, 1918* (1976). Maurine W. Greenwald, *Women, War, and Work* (1980). Carol S. Gruber, *Mars and Minerva* (1975). John Higham, *Strangers in the Land: Patterns of American Nativism* (1955). Michael T. Isenberg, *War on Film* (1981). Frederick C. Luebke, *Bonds of Loyalty: German-Americans and World War I* (1974). Elizabeth Payne, *Reform, Labor, and Feminism: Margaret Dreier Robins and the Women's Trade Union League* (1988). Michael Pearlman, *To Make Democracy Safe for America: Patricians and Preparedness in the Progressive Era* (1984). Barbara J. Steinson, *American Women's Activism in World War I* (1982).

Wilson and the Peace. Lloyd Ambrosius, *Woodrow Wilson and the American Diplomatic Tradition* (1987). John Morton Blum, *Woodrow Wilson and the Politics of Morality* (1956). Robert H. Ferrell, *Woodrow Wilson and World War I* (1985). Peter Filene, *Americans and the Soviet Experiment* (1967). Denna Fleming, *The United States and the League of Nations* (1932). Inga Floto, *Colonel House at Paris* (1980). John L. Gaddis, *Russia, the Soviet Union, and the United States* (1978). Lloyd C. Gardner, *Safe for Democracy: The Anglo-American Response to Revolution, 1913–1923* (1984). John A. Garraty, *Henry Cabot Lodge* (1953). Robert Jackson, *At War with the Bolsheviks: The*

Allied Intervention into Russia, 1917–1920 (1972). George Kennan, *Decision to Intervene* (1958). Thomas Knock, *To End All Wars: Woodrow Wilson and the Quest for a New World Order* (1992). Warren F. Kuehl, *Seeking World Order* (1969). Christopher Lasch, *The American Liberals and the Russian Revolution* (1962). N. Gordon Levin, Jr., *Woodrow Wilson and World Politics* (1968). Arthur S. Link, *Woodrow Wilson*, 5 vols. (1947–1965); *Wilson the Diplomatist* (1957); *Woodrow Wilson: War, Revolution, and Peace* (1979). Arno Mayer, *Political Origins of the New Diplomacy, 1917–1918* (1963); *Wilson vs. Lenin* (1959); *Politics and Diplomacy of Peacemaking: Containment and Counterrevolution* (1965). Charles L. Mee, Jr., *The End of Order: Versailles 1919* (1980). Robert E. Osgood, *Ideals and Self-Interest in American Foreign Relations* (1953). Klaus Schwabe, *Woodrow Wilson, Revolutionary Germany, and Peacemaking, 1918–1919* (1985). Gene Smith, *When the Cheering Stopped* (1964). Ronald Steel, *Walter Lippmann and the American Century* (1980). Ralph Stone, *The Irreconcilables: The Fight Against the League of Nations* (1970). Arthur Walworth, *Wilson and the Peacemakers* (1986). William C. Widenor, *Henry Cabot Lodge and the Search for an American Foreign Policy* (1980).

Postwar America. Wesley M. Bagby, Jr., *The Road to Normalcy* (1962). David Brody, *Steelworkers in America* (1960); *Labor in Crisis: The Steel Strike of 1919* (1965). Stanley Coben, *A. Mitchell Palmer* (1963). David Cronon, *Black Moses* (1955). Roberta Strauss Feuerlicht, *Justice Crucified: The Story of Sacco and Vanzetti* (1977). Robert L. Friedheim, *The Seattle General Strike* (1965). Amy J. Garvey, *Garvey and Garveyism* (1963). Robert V. Haynes, *A Night of Violence: The Houston Riot of 1917* (1976). Florette Henri, *Black Migration: Movement Northward, 1900–1920* (1975). Kenneth Kusmer, *A Ghetto Takes Shape* (1976). David Montgomery, *The Fall of the House of Labor: The Workplace, the State, and American Labor Activism, 1865–1921* (1987). Robert K. Murray, *The Red Scare: A Study in National Hysteria, 1919–1920* (1955). Burl Noggle, *Into the Twenties* (1974). Stuart I. Rochester, *American Liberal Disillusionment in the Wake of World War I* (1977). Elliot Rudwick, *Race Riot at East St. Louis* (1964). Francis Russell, *A City in Terror* (1975). Alan Spear, *Black Chicago* (1967). Judith Stein, *The World of Marcus Garvey* (1986). William M. Tuttle, Jr., *Race Riot: Chicago in the Red Summer of 1919* (1970). Theodore Vincent, *Black Power and the Garvey Movement* (1971).

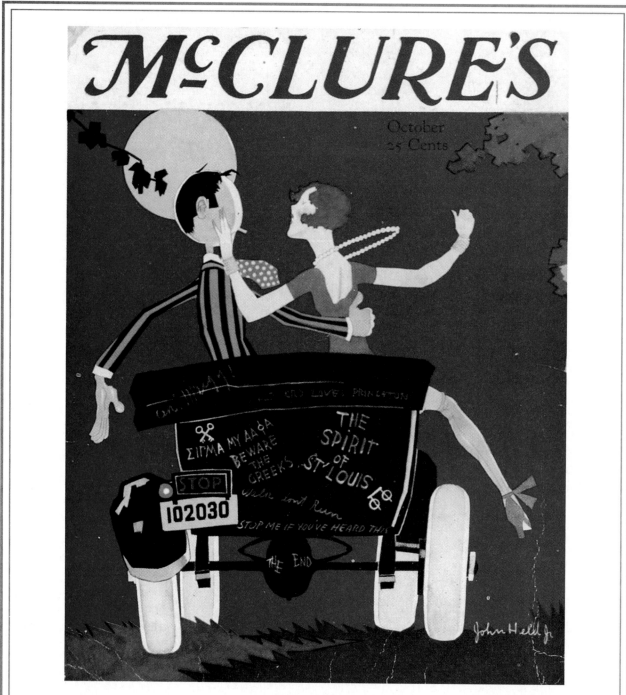

THE "JAZZ AGE"

One of the most popular images of the 1920s, captured here by the magazine illustrator John Held Jr., was of a new, exuberant youth culture in which women—liberated from Victorian constraints—were free to smoke cigarettes, drink alcohol, and socialize with men in ways that had seldom been possible before. The rapid proliferation of the automobile was among many sources of the new freedoms some young people enjoyed. The image of the "Jazz Age," however, reflected mainly the experiences of a small part of the middle-class elite. Most Americans in the 1920s continued to live in ways bound by tradition and economic limits. *(Culver)*

CHAPTER TWENTY-FOUR

THE NEW ERA

HE IMAGE OF THE 1920s in the American popular imagination is of an era of affluence, conservatism, and cultural frivolity: the Roaring Twenties; what Warren G. Harding once called the age of "normalcy." In reality, the decade was a time of significant, even dramatic social, economic, and political change. It was an era in which the American economy not only enjoyed spectacular growth but developed new forms of organization. It was a time in which American popular culture reshaped itself to reflect the urban, industrial, consumer-oriented society America was becoming. And it was a decade in which American government, for all its conservatism, experimented with new approaches to public policy that helped pave the way for the important period of reform that was to follow. Contemporaries liked to refer to the 1920s as the "New Era"—an age in which America was becoming a modern nation.

At the same time, however, the decade saw the rise of a series of spirited and at times effective rebellions against the modern developments that were transforming American life. The intense cultural conflicts that characterized the 1920s were evidence of how many Americans remained outside the reach of the new, affluent consumer culture; and evidence, too, of how some of those inside it remained unreconciled to the modernizing currents of the New Era.

THE NEW ECONOMY

After the recession of 1921–1922, the United States began a long period of almost uninterrupted prosperity and economic expansion. Less visible at the time, but equally significant, was the survival (and even the growth) of serious inequalities and imbalances.

Economic Growth and Organization

No one could deny the remarkable, some believed miraculous, feats of the American economy in the 1920s. The nation's manufacturing output rose by more than 60 percent during the decade. Per capita income grew by a third. Inflation was negligible. A mild recession in 1923 interrupted the pattern of growth, but when it subsided early in 1924, the economy expanded with even greater vigor than before.

The economic boom was a result of many things. An immediate cause was the debilitation of European industry in the aftermath of World War I, which left the United States for a short time the only truly healthy industrial power in the world. More important in the long run was technology, and the great industrial expansion it made possible. The automobile industry, as a result of the development of the assembly line and other innovations, now became one of the most important industries in the nation. It stimulated growth in many related industries as well. Auto manufacturers purchased the products of steel, rubber, glass, and tool companies. Auto owners bought gasoline from the oil corporations. Road construction in response to the proliferation of motor vehicles became an important industry. The increased mobility that the automobile made possible increased the demand for suburban housing, fueling a boom in the construction industry.

Other new industries benefiting from technological innovations contributed as well to the economic growth. Radio expanded rapidly within a few years of its commercial debut in 1920. The motion picture industry grew dramatically, especially after the introduction of sound in 1927. Aviation, electronics, home appliances, plastics, synthetic fibers, aluminum, magnesium, oil, electric power, and other industries fueled by technological advances—all grew impressively and spurred the economic boom. Cheap, readily available energy—from newly discovered oil reserves, from the expanded network of electric power, and from the nation's abundant coal fields—further enhanced the ability of industry to produce.

Large sectors of American business were also accelerating their drive toward national organization and consolidation. Certain industries—notably those, such as steel, dependent on large-scale mass production—seemed naturally to move toward concentrating production in a few large firms; U.S. Steel, the nation's largest corporation, was so dominant that almost everyone used the term "Little Steel" to refer to all of its competitors. Other industries, such as textiles, that were less dependent on technology and less susceptible to great economies of scale, proved more resistant to consolidation, despite the efforts of many businessmen to promote it.

In those areas where industry did consolidate, new forms of corporate organization emerged to advance the trend. General Motors, which by 1920 was not only the largest automobile manufacturer but the fifth largest American corporation, was a classic example. GM's founder, William Durant, had expanded the company dramatically but had never replaced the informal, personal management style with which he began. When GM foundered in the 1920 recession, leadership of the company fell to Alfred P. Sloan, who created a modern administrative system with an efficient divisional organization. The new system not only made it easier for GM to control its many subsidiaries; it also made it simpler for it—and for the many other corporations that adopted similar administrative systems—to expand further.

Some industries less susceptible to domination by a few great corporations attempted to stabilize themselves not through consolidation but through cooperation. An important vehicle was the trade association—a national organization created by various members of an industry to encourage coordination in production and marketing techniques. Trade associations worked reasonably well in the mass-production industries that had already succeeded in limiting competition through consolidation. But in more decentralized industries, such as cotton textiles, their effectiveness was limited.

The strenuous efforts by industrialists throughout the economy to find ways to curb competition through consolidation or cooperation reflected a strong fear of overproduction. Even in the booming 1920s, industrialists remembered how too-rapid expansion had helped produce recessions in 1893, 1907, and 1920. The great, unrealized dream of the New Era was to find a way to stabilize the economy so that such collapses would never occur again.

Labor in the New Era

The remarkable economic growth was accompanied by a continuing, and in some areas even increasing, maldistribution of wealth and purchasing power. More than two-thirds of the American people in 1929 lived at no better than what one major study described as the "minimum comfort level." Half of those languished at or below the level of "subsistence and poverty." Large segments of society, unable to organize, were without power to protect their economic interests.

American industrial workers experienced both the successes and the failures of the 1920s as much as any other group. On the one hand, most workers saw their standard of living rise during the decade; many enjoyed greatly improved working conditions and other benefits. Some employers in the 1920s, eager to avoid disruptive labor unrest and forestall the growth of independent trade unions, adopted paternalistic techniques that came to be known as "welfare capitalism." Henry Ford, for example, shortened the workweek, raised wages, and instituted paid vacations. U.S. Steel made conspicuous efforts to improve safety and sanitation in its factories. For the first time, some workers became eligible for pensions on retirement—nearly 3 million by 1926. When labor grievances surfaced despite these efforts, workers could voice them through the so-called company unions that were emerging in many industries—workers' councils and shop committees, organized by the corporations themselves.

THE STEAMFITTER
Lewis Hine was among the first American photographers
to recognize his craft as an art. In this photograph from the
mid-1920s, Hine made a point that many other artists were
making in other media: The rise of the machine could
serve human beings, but might also bend them to its own
needs. The steamfitter (carefully posed by the photographer) is forced to shape his body to the contours of his machine in order to complete his task. (*International Museum of
Photography at George Eastman House*)

Welfare capitalism brought many workers important economic benefits, but it did not help them gain
any real control over their own fates. Company unions
were feeble vehicles, forbidden in most industries from
raising the issues most important to workers. And welfare capitalism survived only as long as industry prospered. After 1929, with the economy in crisis, the entire system quickly collapsed.

Welfare capitalism affected only a relatively small
number of workers, in any case. Most laborers worked
for employers interested primarily in keeping their labor costs to a minimum. Workers as a whole, therefore, received wage increases that were proportion-
ately far below increases in production and profits.

Unskilled workers, in particular, saw their wages increase almost imperceptibly—by only a little over 2
percent between 1920 and 1926. In the end, American
workers in the 1920s remained a relatively impoverished and powerless group. Their wages rose; but the
average annual income of a worker remained below
$1,500 a year when $1,800 was considered necessary
to maintain a minimally decent standard of living.
Only by relying on the earnings of several family members at once could many working-class families make
ends meet. And almost all such families had to live
with the very real possibility of one or more members'
losing their jobs. Unemployment was lower in the
1920s than it had been in the previous two decades,
and much lower than it would be in the 1930s. But a
large proportion of the work force was out of work for
at least some period during the decade—in part because the rapid growth of industrial technology made
many jobs obsolete. The unemployment rate for the
1920s is difficult to calculate, but scholars estimate that
an average of 5 to 7 percent of the work force was without a job at any given time.

Many laborers continued to regard an effective, independent union movement as their best hope. But the
New Era was a bleak time for labor organization, in
part because the unions themselves were generally
conservative and failed to adapt to the realities of the
modern economy. The American Federation of Labor
remained wedded to the concept of the craft union, in
which workers were organized on the basis of particular skills. It continued to make no provision for the
fastest-growing area of the work force: unskilled industrial workers, many of them immigrants from
southern or eastern Europe. Ignored by the craft
unions, they had few organizations of their own.
William Green, who became president of the AFL in
1924, was committed to peaceful cooperation with employers and to strident opposition to communism and
socialism. He frowned on strikes.

Women and Minorities in the Work Force

A growing proportion of the work force consisted of
women, who were concentrated in what have since become known as "pink-collar" jobs—low-paying service occupations with many of the same problems as
manufacturing employment. Large numbers of women
worked as secretaries, salesclerks, telephone operators,
and other, similarly underpaid jobs. Because techni-
cally such positions were not industrial jobs, the AFL
and other labor organizations were generally uninterested in organizing these workers.

Similarly, the half-million African Americans who
had migrated from the rural South into the cities dur-

ing the Great Migration after 1914 had few opportunities for union representation. The skilled crafts represented in the AFL often worked actively to exclude blacks from their trades and organizations. Most blacks worked in jobs in which the AFL took no interest at all—as janitors, dishwashers, garbage collectors, commercial laundry attendants, domestics, and in other types of service jobs. The Brotherhood of Sleeping Car Porters, founded in 1925 and led for years by A. Philip Randolph, was a notable exception: a vigorous union, led by an African American, and representing a virtually all-black work force. Over time, Randolph won some significant gains for his members—increased wages, shorter working hours, and other benefits. He also enlisted the union in battles for civil rights for African Americans.

In the West and the Southwest, the ranks of the unskilled included considerable numbers of Asians and Hispanics, few of them organized, most actively excluded from white-dominated unions. In the wake of the Chinese Exclusion Acts, Japanese immigrants increasingly took the place of the Chinese in menial jobs in California, despite the continuing hostility of the white population. They worked on railroads, construction sites, farms, and in many other low-paying workplaces. Some Japanese managed to escape the ranks of the unskilled by forming their own small businesses or setting themselves up as truck farmers; and many of the Issei (Japanese immigrants) and Nisei (their American-born children) enjoyed significant economic success—so much so that California passed laws in 1913 and 1920 to make it more difficult for them to buy land. Other Asians—most notably Filipinos—also swelled the unskilled work force and generated considerable hostility. Anti-Filipino riots in California beginning in 1929 helped produce legislation in 1934 virtually eliminating immigration from the Philippines.

Mexican immigrants formed a major part of the unskilled work force throughout the Southwest and California. Nearly half a million Mexicans entered the United States in the 1920s, more than any other national group, increasing the total Mexican population to over a million. Most lived in California, Texas, Arizona, and New Mexico; and by 1930, most lived in cities. Large Mexican barrios—usually raw urban communities, often without even such basic services as plumbing and sewage—grew up in Los Angeles, El Paso, San Antonio, Denver, and many other cities and towns. Some of the residents found work locally in factories and shops; others traveled to mines or did migratory labor on farms, but returned to the cities between jobs. Mexican workers, too, faced hostility and discrimination from the Anglo population of the region; but there were few efforts actually to exclude them. Employers in the relatively underpopulated West needed this ready pool of low-paid, unskilled, and unorganized workers.

The "American Plan"

Whatever the weaknesses of the unions and of unorganized, unskilled workers, the strength of the corporations was the principal reason for the absence of effective labor organization. After the turmoil of 1919, corporate leaders worked hard to spread the doctrine that unionism was somehow subversive, that a crucial element of democratic capitalism was the protection of the open shop (a shop in which no worker could be required to join a union). The crusade for the open shop, euphemistically titled the "American Plan," received the endorsement of the National Association of Manufacturers in 1920 and became a pretext for a harsh campaign of union busting across the country.

When such tactics proved insufficient to counter union power, government assistance often made the difference. In 1921, the Supreme Court upheld a lower-court ruling that declared picketing illegal and supported the right of courts to issue injunctions against strikers. In 1922, the Justice Department intervened to quell a strike by 400,000 railroad workers. In 1924, the courts refused protection to members of the United Mine Workers Union when mine owners launched a violent campaign in western Pennsylvania to drive the union from the coal fields. As a result of these developments, union membership fell from more than 5 million in 1920 to under 3 million in 1929.

The Plight of the Farmer

Like industry, American agriculture in the 1920s was embracing new technologies for increasing production. The number of tractors on American farms, for example, quadrupled during the 1920s, helping to open 35 million new acres to cultivation. At the same time, agricultural production was increasing rapidly in other parts of the world as well. Unlike increased industrial production, increased agricultural production did not stimulate consumer demand. The result was overproduction, a disastrous decline in food prices, and a severe drop in income for farmers beginning early in the 1920s. In 1920, farm income had been 15 percent of the national total; by 1929, it was 9 percent. The average farmer made only about a quarter as much money each year in the 1920s as the average nonfarmer. More than 3 million people left agriculture altogether in the course of the decade. Of those who remained, many were forced into tenancy—los-

FARM TENANCY, 1910 AND 1930

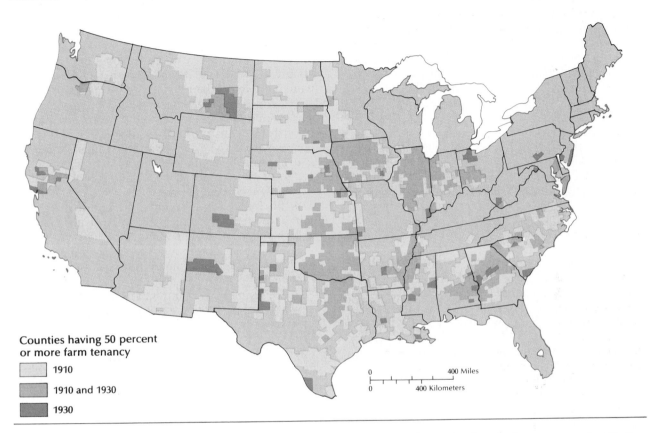

Counties having 50 percent
or more farm tenancy

- 1910
- 1910 and 1930
- 1930

ing ownership of their lands and having to rent instead from banks or other landlords.

In response, some farmers began to demand relief in the form of government price supports. A few gravitated to such vaguely radical organizations as the Nonpartisan League of North Dakota or its successor, the Farmer-Labor Party, which established a foothold as well in Minnesota and other Midwestern states. Most farmers, however, were more moderate. Through such organizations as the American Farm Bureau Federation, they put increasing pressure on Congress (where farmers continued to enjoy disproportionately high representation). And while reform sentiment generally made little headway in the 1920s, farmers' organizational strength boosted the cause of agrarian reform.

One price-raising scheme in particular came to dominate agrarian demands: the idea of parity. "Parity" referred to a formula for guaranteeing farmers a fair price for their crops regardless of how national or international agricultural markets might fluctuate. In the 1920s, the formula was based on the average price of the crop during the half-decade preceding World War I (a good time for farmers) as compared with the general average of all prices during the same period. Champions of parity urged high tariffs against foreign agricultural goods and a government commitment to buy surplus domestic crops at parity and sell them abroad at whatever the market would bring.

The legislative expression of the demand for parity was the McNary-Haugen bill, named after its two principal sponsors in Congress and introduced repeatedly between 1924 and 1928. In 1926, Congress approved a bill requiring parity for grain, cotton, tobacco, and rice, but President Coolidge vetoed it. In 1928, it won congressional approval again, only to succumb to another presidential veto.

THE NEW CULTURE

The increasingly urban and consumer-oriented culture of the 1920s helped many Americans in all regions live their lives and perceive their world in increasingly similar ways. That same culture exposed them to a new

BREAKING DOWN RURAL ISOLATION:
THE EXPANSION OF TRAVEL HORIZONS IN OREGON, ILLINOIS

AREA REACHED IN:

1 hour		3 hours
2 hours		More than 3 hours

++++++++ Railroads (1900)
———— Paved roads (1930)
- - - - - Unpaved roads (1930)

(After Moline)

set of values that reflected the prosperity and complexity of the modern economy. But the new culture could not, of course, erase the continuing, and indeed increasing, diversity of the United States. The relatively uniform mass culture reached Americans divided by region, race, religion, gender, and class, and those characteristics shaped the way individuals responded to national cultural messages.

Consumerism and Communications

Among the many changes industrialization produced in the United States was the creation of a mass consumer culture. By the 1920s, America was a society in which many men and women (although not, of course, all) could afford not merely the means of subsistence, but a considerable measure of additional, discretionary goods and services; a society in which people could buy items not just because of need but for pleasure. Middle-class families purchased such new appliances as electric refrigerators, washing machines, and vacuum cleaners. Men and women wore wristwatches and smoked cigarettes. Women purchased cosmetics and mass-produced fashions. Above all, Americans bought automobiles. By the end of the decade, there were more than 30 million cars on American roads.

No group was more aware of the emergence of consumerism (or more responsible for creating it) than the advertising industry. The first advertising and public relations firms (N. W. Ayer and J. Walter Thompson) had appeared well before World War I; but in the 1920s, partly as a result of techniques pioneered by wartime propaganda, advertising came of age. Publicists no longer simply conveyed information; they sought to identify products with a particular lifestyle, to invest them with glamour and prestige, and to persuade potential consumers that purchasing a commodity could be a personally fulfilling and enriching experience.

Advertisers also encouraged the public to absorb the values of promotion and salesmanship and to admire those who were effective "boosters" and publicists. One of the most successful books of the 1920s was *The Man Nobody Knows,* by advertising executive Bruce Barton. It portrayed Jesus Christ as not only a religious prophet but also a "super salesman," who "picked up twelve men from the bottom ranks of business and forged them into an organization that conquered the world." The parables, Barton claimed, were "the most powerful advertisements of all time." Barton's message was fully in tune with the new spirit of the consumer culture. Jesus had been a man concerned with living a full and rewarding life in this world; twentieth-century men and women should do the same. ("Life is meant to live and enjoy as you go along," Barton once wrote.) Jesus had succeeded because he knew how to make friends, to become popular, to please others; that talent was a prescription for success in the modern era as well.

The advertising industry could never have had the impact it did without the emergence of new vehicles of communication that made it possible to reach large audiences quickly and easily. Newspapers were being absorbed into national chains. New or expanded mass-circulation magazines—*Time, Reader's Digest,* the *Saturday Evening Post,* and others—attracted broad, national, audiences.

At the same time, movies were becoming an ever more popular and powerful form of mass communication. Over 100 million people saw films in 1930, as compared to 40 million in 1922. The addition of sound to motion pictures—beginning in 1927 with the first

THE NEW KITCHEN AND THE NEW WOMAN

Manufacturers attempted to associate their new consumer appliances with the elegant lifestyle of the affluent middle class. Advertisers tried to suggest that modern conveniences could liberate the "new woman" from the drudgery of housework and enable her to enter the glamorous world of society. *(Culver)*

feature-length "talkie," *The Jazz Singer*, with Al Jolson—created nationwide excitement. An embarrassing scandal in 1921 involving the popular comedian Fatty Arbuckle produced public outrage and political pressure to "clean up" Hollywood. In response, the film industry introduced "standards" to its films. Studio owners created the Motion Picture Association, a new trade association, and hired former postmaster general Will Hays to head it. More important, they gave Hays broad powers to review films and to ban anything likely to offend viewers (or politicians). Hays exercised his powers broadly and imposed on the film industry a safe, sanctimonious conformity for many years.

The most important communications vehicle was the only one truly new to the 1920s: radio. The first commercial radio station in America, KDKA in Pittsburgh, began broadcasting in 1920; and the first national radio network, the National Broadcasting Company, was formed in 1927. By 1923, there were more than 500 radio stations, covering virtually every area of the country; by 1929, more than 12 million families owned radio sets. The radio industry, too, feared government regulation and control; the national networks, and most radio stations, monitored program content carefully and excluded controversial or provocative material. But radio was much less centralized than filmmaking. Individual stations had considerable autonomy, and even carefully monitored stations and networks could not control the countless hours of programming as effectively as the Hays office could control films. Radio programming, therefore, was more diverse—and at times more controversial and even subversive—than film.

The influence of the consumer culture, and its increasing emphasis on immediate, personal fulfillment, was visible even in religion. Theological modernists—among them Harry Emerson Fosdick and A. C. McGiffert—taught their followers to abandon some of the traditional tenets of evangelical Christianity (literal interpretation of the Bible, belief in the Trinity, attribution of human traits to the deity) and to accept a faith that would help individuals to live more fulfilling lives in the present world.

Women and the New Culture

In the 1920s college-educated women were no longer pioneers. There were now two and even three generations of graduates of women's or coeducational colleges and universities; and some were making their presence felt in professional areas that in the past they had rarely penetrated. A substantial group of women now combined marriage and careers; 25 percent of all women workers in the 1920s were married. In the progressive era, middle-class women had usually had to choose between work and family. Still, professional opportunities for women remained limited by society's assumptions (assumptions prevalent among many women as well as among most men) about what were suitable female occupations. Although there were notable success stories about female business executives, journalists, doctors, and lawyers, most professional women remained confined to such traditionally "feminine" fields as fashion, education, social work, and nursing, or to the lower levels of business management. The "new professional woman" was a vivid and widely publicized image in the 1920s. In reality, however, most employed women were nonprofessional, lower-class workers. Middle-class married women, in the meantime, remained largely in the home.

Yet the 1920s constituted a new era for middle-class women nonetheless. In particular, the decade saw a redefinition of the idea of motherhood. Shortly after World War I, an influential group of psychologists—the "behaviorists," led by John B. Watson—began to challenge the long-held assumption that women had an instinctive capacity for motherhood. Maternal affection was not, they claimed, sufficient preparation for child rearing. Instead, mothers should rely on the advice and assistance of experts and professionals: doctors, nurses, and trained educators in nursery schools and kindergartens.

For many middle-class women, these changes helped redefine what had been an all-consuming activity. Motherhood was no less important in behaviorist theory than it had been before; if anything it was more so. But for many women it was less emotionally fulfilling, less connected to their instinctive lives, more dependent on (and tied to) people and institutions outside the family. Many attempted to compensate by devoting new attention to their roles as wives and companions, to developing what became known as the "companionate marriage." The middle-class wife shared increasingly in her husband's social life; she devoted more attention to cosmetics and clothing; she was less willing to allow children to interfere with the development of the marital relationship. Most of all, many women now found support for thinking of their sexual relationships with their husbands not simply as a means of procreation, as earlier generations had been taught to do, but as an important and pleasurable experience in its own right, as the culmination of romantic love.

Progress in the development of birth control was both a cause and a result of this change. The pioneer of the American birth-control movement was Margaret Sanger, who had become committed to the cause in part because of the influence of Emma Goldman—a Russian immigrant and political radical who had agitated for birth control before World War I. Sanger began her career promoting the diaphragm and other birth-control devices out of a concern for working-class women, believing that large families were among the major causes of poverty and distress in poor communities. By the 1920s, partly because she had limited success in persuading working-class women to accept her teachings, she was becoming more concerned with persuading middle-class women of the benefits of birth control. Women, she argued, should be free to enjoy the pleasures of sexual activity without any connection to procreation. Birth-control devices began to find a large market among middle-class women, even though some techniques remained illegal in many states (and abortion remained illegal nearly everywhere).

The new, more secular view of womanhood had effects on women beyond the middle class as well. Some women concluded that in the "New Era" it was no longer necessary to maintain a rigid, Victorian female "respectability." They could smoke, drink, dance, wear seductive clothes and makeup, and attend lively parties. They could strive for physical and emotional fulfillment, for release from repression and inhibition.

ALICE PAUL
Alice Paul's National Woman's Party campaigned for, among other things, an Equal Rights Amendment to the Constitution. It provided a strong feminist voice during the years after the victory of the suffrage movement, when many women activists withdrew from politics, believing they had achieved their most important goals. Alice Paul is shown here, in April 1922, speaking to a radio audience about plans for the dedication of the new national headquarters of her party in Washington, D.C.   *(UPI/Bettmann)*

(The wide popularity of Freudian ideas in the 1920s—often simplified and distorted for mass consumption—contributed to the growth of these impulses.)

Such assumptions became the basis of the "flapper"—the modern woman whose liberated lifestyle found expression in dress, hairstyle, speech, and behavior. The "flapper" lifestyle had a particular impact on lower-middle-class and working-class single women, who were flocking to new jobs in industry and the service sector. (The young "Bohemian" women most often associated with the "flapper" image were, in fact, imitating a style that emerged among this larger group.) At night, such women flocked to clubs and dance halls in search of excitement and companionship.

Despite all the changes, most women remained highly dependent on men—both in the workplace, where they were usually poorly paid, and in the home—and relatively powerless when men exploited that dependence. The realization that the "new woman" was as much myth as reality inspired some American feminists to continue their crusade for reform. The National Woman's Party, under the leadership of Alice Paul, pressed on with its campaign for the Equal Rights Amendment, although it found little support in Congress (and met continued resistance from other feminist groups). Nevertheless, women's organizations and female political activities grew in many ways in the 1920s. Responding to the suffrage victory, women organized the League of Women Voters and the women's auxiliaries of both the Democratic and Republican Parties. Female-dominated consumer groups grew rapidly and increased the range and energy of their efforts.

Women activists won a significant triumph in 1921, when they helped secure passage in Congress of a measure in keeping with the traditional feminist goal of securing "protective" legislation for women: the Sheppard-Towner Act. It provided federal funds to states to establish prenatal and child healthcare programs. From the start, however, the bill produced controversy. Alice Paul and her supporters opposed the measure, complaining that it classified all women as mothers. Margaret Sanger complained that the new programs would discourage birth-control efforts. More important, the American Medical Association fought Sheppard-Towner, warning that it would introduce untrained outsiders into the health-care field. In 1929, Congress terminated the program.

The demise of Sheppard-Towner illustrated the power of the medical profession. It also revealed how little woman suffrage had done to support the hopes of many of its supporters (and the fears of many of its foes). When Congress passed Sheppard-Towner in 1921, its members did so in part because they assumed the new female electorate would become a potent political force, generating substantial pressure on behalf of "female" issues. By 1929, it was clear that women voters changed electoral outcomes hardly at all; the female vote distributed itself almost precisely the same as the male vote. As a result, male politicians, in Congress and elsewhere, felt less concern about the consequences of opposing the demands of female reformers.

Education and Youth

The growing secularism of American culture and its expanding emphasis on training and expertise found reflection in the increasingly important role of education in the lives of American youth. The changes were evident in numerous ways. First, more people were going to school in the 1920s than ever before. High-school attendance more than doubled during the decade: from 2.2 million to over 5 million. Enrollment in colleges and universities increased threefold between 1900 and 1930, with much of that increase occurring after World War I. In 1918, there had been 600,000 college students; in 1930, there were 1.2 million, nearly 20 percent of the college-age population. Attendance was increasing as well at trade and vocational schools and in other institutions providing the

specialized training that the modern economy demanded. Schools were also beginning to perform new and more varied functions. Instead of offering instruction only in the traditional disciplines, they were providing training in modern technical skills: engineering, management, economics.

The growing importance of education contributed to the emergence of a separate youth culture. The idea of adolescence as a distinct period in the life of an individual was for the most part new to the twentieth century. In some measure it was a result of the influence of Freudian psychology. But it was a result, too, of society's recognition that a more extended period of training and preparation was necessary before a young person was ready to move into the workplace. Schools and colleges provided adolescents with a setting in which they could develop their own social patterns, their own hobbies, their own interests and activities. An increasing number of students saw school as a place not just for academic training but for organized athletics, other extracurricular activities, clubs, and fraternities and sororities—that is, as an institution that allowed them to define themselves less in terms of their families and more in terms of their peer group.

The Decline of the "Self-Made Man"

The increasing importance of education and the changing nature of adolescence underscored one of the most important changes in American society: the gradual disappearance of the reality, and to some degree even of the ideal, of the "self-made man." The belief that any person could, simply through hard work and innate talent, achieve wealth and renown had always been largely a myth; but it had had enough basis in reality to remain a convincing myth for generations. The ideal of sturdy independence had long been central to the identities of many men, in particular.

Beginning in the late nineteenth century and accelerating in the early twentieth, it became more difficult to believe any longer that success was possible without education and training. "The self-made manager in business," wrote *Century Magazine* in 1925, "is nearing the end of his road. He cannot escape the relentless pursuit of the same forces that have eliminated self-made lawyers and doctors and admirals."

That sense of losing control, of becoming ever more dependent on rules and norms established by large, impersonal bureaucracies, created a crisis of self-identification among many American men. Robbed of the independence and control that had once defined "masculinity," many men looked for other means to do so. Theodore Roosevelt, for example, had glorified warfare and the "strenuous life" as a route to "manhood." Other men turned to fraternal societies, to athletics, and to other settings where they found confirmation of their masculinity.

The "Doom of the Self-Made Man," as *Century* described it, produced marked ambivalence. These mixed feelings were reflected in the identity of three men who became the most widely admired heroes of the New Era: Thomas Edison, the inventor of the electric light bulb and many other technological marvels; Henry Ford, the creator of the assembly line and one of the founders of the automobile industry; and Charles Lindbergh, the first aviator to make a solo flight across the Atlantic Ocean. All received the adulation of much of the American public. Lindbergh, in particular, became a national hero the like of which the country had never seen before.

The reasons for their popularity indicated much about how Americans viewed the new epoch in which they were living. On the one hand, all three men represented the triumphs of the modern technological and industrial society. On the other hand, all three had risen to success without the benefit of formal education and at least in part through their own efforts. They were, their admirers liked to believe, genuinely self-made men. Even many Americans who were happily embracing a new society and a new culture were doing so without entirely diverting their gaze from a simpler past.

The Disenchanted

The generation of artists and intellectuals coming of age in the 1920s found the new society in which they lived especially disturbing. Many were experiencing a disenchantment with modern America so fundamental that they were often able to view it only with contempt. As a result, they adopted a role sharply different from that of most intellectuals of most earlier eras. Rather than trying to influence and reform their society, they isolated themselves from it and embarked on a restless search for personal fulfillment. Gertrude Stein once referred to the young Americans emerging from World War I as a "Lost Generation." For some writers and intellectuals, at least, it was an apt description.

At the heart of the Lost Generation's critique of modern society was a sense of personal alienation, a belief that contemporary America no longer provided individuals with avenues by which they could achieve personal fulfillment. This disillusionment had its roots in many things, but in nothing so deeply as the experience of World War I. To those who had fought in the conflict, and even to many who had not, the aftermath of the war was shattering. The repudiation of Wilsonian idealism, the restoration of "business as usual," the growing emphasis on materialism and consumerism suggested that nothing had been gained. The war had been a fraud; the suffering and the dying had been in vain. Ernest Hemingway, one of the most celebrated (and most commercially successful) of the new breed of writers, expressed the generation's contempt for the war in his novel *A Farewell to Arms* (1929). Its protagonist, an American officer fighting in Europe, decides that there is no justification for his participation in the conflict and deserts the army with a nurse with whom he has fallen in love. Hemingway made it clear that the officer was to be admired for doing so.

But however disillusioning intellectuals found the war, they were equally disturbed by the character of American society in peacetime. To many, it was a society and culture utterly devoid of idealism or vision, steeped in outmoded and priggish morality, obsessed with materialism and consumerism, alienating and dehumanizing.

One result of this alienation was a series of savage critiques of modern society by a wide range of writers, some of whom were known as the "debunkers." Among them was the Baltimore journalist H. L. Mencken. His magazines—first the *Smart Set* and later the *American Mercury*—delighted in ridiculing everything most middle-class Americans held dear: religion, politics, the arts, even democracy itself. Mencken could not believe, he claimed, that "civilized life was possible under a democracy," because it was a form of government that placed power in the hands of the common people, whom he ridiculed as the "booboisie." When someone asked Mencken why he continued to live in a society he found so loathsome, he replied: "Why do people go to the zoo?" Echoing Mencken's contempt was the novelist Sinclair Lewis, the first American to win a Nobel Prize in literature. In a series of savage novels—*Main Street* (1920), *Babbitt* (1922), *Arrowsmith* (1925), and others—he lashed out at one aspect of modern society after another: the small town, the modern city, the medical profession, popular religion.

Intellectuals of the 1920s claimed to reject the "success ethic" that they believed dominated American life (even though many of them hoped for—and a few achieved—commercial and critical success). The novelist F. Scott Fitzgerald, for example, ridiculed the American obsession with material success in *The Great Gatsby* (1925). The novel's title character, Jay Gatsby, spends his life accumulating wealth and social prestige in order to win the woman he loves. The world to which he has aspired, however, turns out to be one of pretension, fraud, and cruelty, and it ultimately destroys him.

Some artists and intellectuals responded to their disillusionment by leaving America to live in France, making Paris for a time a center of American artistic life. Others moved to supposedly more isolated and "natural" communities in the American West; colonies of artists and writers settled in Taos and Santa Fe, New Mexico. Some adopted hedonistic lifestyles, involving drinking, drugs, casual sex, and wild parties. For most of these young men and women, however, the only real refuge from the travails of modern society was art. Only art, they argued, could allow them full individual expression; only the act of creation could offer them fulfillment.

The result of this quest for fulfillment through art was not, for the most part, personal satisfaction for the writers and artists involved. They did, however, produce a body of work that made the decade one of the great eras of American literature. The roster of important American writers who did significant work in the 1920s may have no equal in any other period: Hemingway, Fitzgerald, Lewis, Thomas Wolfe, John Dos Passos, Ezra Pound, T. S. Eliot, Gertrude Stein, Edna Ferber, Willa Cather, William Faulkner, Eugene O'Neill.

Not all intellectuals of the 1920s expressed alienation and despair. Some expressed reservations about their society not by withdrawing from it but by advocating reform. John Dewey, for example, kept alive the philosophical tradition of pragmatism and appealed for "practical" education and experimentation in social policy. Charles and Mary Beard, perhaps the most influential historians of their day, stressed economic factors in tracing the development of modern society and, like other progressive reformers, emphasized the clash of economic interests as central to American history.

To another group of intellectuals, the solution to contemporary problems lay neither in escapism nor in progressivism, but in an exploration of their own cultural or regional origins. In New York City, a new generation of black intellectuals created a flourishing African-American culture widely described as the "Harlem Renaissance." The Harlem poets, novelists, and artists drew heavily from their African roots in an effort to prove the richness of their own racial heritage (and not incidentally, to prove to whites that their race was worthy of respect). The poet Langston Hughes captured much of the spirit of the movement in a single sentence: "I am a Negro—and beautiful." Other black writers in Harlem and elsewhere—James Weldon Johnson, Countee Cullen, Zora Neale Hurston, Claude McKay, Alain Locke—as well as black artists

and musicians helped establish a thriving culture rooted in the historical legacy of their people.

A strangely similar effort was under way among an influential group of white southern intellectuals. Known first as the "Fugitives" and later as the "Agrarians," these young poets, novelists, and critics sought to counter the depersonalization of industrial society by evoking the strong rural traditions of their own region. In their controversial manifesto *I'll Take My Stand* (1930), a collection of essays by twelve southern intellectuals, they issued a simultaneously radical and conservative appeal for a rejection of the doctrine of "economic progress" and the spiritual debilitation that had accompanied it. The supposedly "backward" South, they argued, could serve as a model for a nation drunk with visions of limitless growth and modernization.

A CONFLICT OF CULTURES

The modern, secular culture of the 1920s was not unchallenged. It grew up alongside older, more traditional cultures, with which it continually and often bitterly competed. The older cultures expressed the outlook of generally less affluent, less urban, more provincial Americans—men and women who continued to revere traditional values and customs and who feared and resented the modernist threats to their way of life. Their convictions and their fears resulted in a series of harsh cultural controversies.

Prohibition

When the prohibition of the sale and manufacture of alcohol went into effect in January 1920, it had the support of most members of the middle class and most of those who considered themselves progressives. Within a year, however, it had become clear that the "noble experiment," as its defenders called it, was not working well. Prohibition did substantially reduce drinking, at least in some regions of the country. But it also produced conspicuous and growing violations that made the law an almost immediate source of disillusionment and controversy.

The federal government hired only 1,500 agents to enforce the prohibition laws, and in many places they received little help from local police. Before long, it was almost as easy to acquire illegal alcohol in much of the country as it had once been to acquire legal alcohol. And since an enormous, lucrative industry was now barred to legitimate businessmen, organized crime figures took it over. In Chicago, Al Capone built a criminal empire based largely on illegal alcohol. He guarded it against interlopers with an army of as many as 1,000 gunmen, whose zealousness contributed to the violent deaths of more than 250 people in the city between 1920 and 1927. Other regions produced gangsters and gang wars of their own.

Many middle-class progressives who had originally supported prohibition soon soured on the experiment. But an enormous constituency of provincial, largely rural, Protestant Americans continued vehemently to defend it. To them, prohibition had always carried implications far beyond the issue of drinking itself. It represented the effort of an older America to maintain its dominance in a society in which they were becoming relatively less powerful. Drinking, which they associated with the modern city and with Catholic immigrants, became a symbol of the new culture they believed was displacing them.

As the decade proceeded, opponents of prohibition (or "wets," as they came to be known) gained steadily in influence. Not until 1933, however, when the Great Depression added weight to their appeals, were they finally able effectively to challenge the "drys" and win repeal of the Eighteenth Amendment.

Nativism and the Klan

Like prohibition (which was itself in part a result of old-stock Americans trying to discipline the new immigrant population), agitation for a curb on foreign immigration to the United States had begun in the nineteenth century; and like prohibition, it had gathered strength in the years before the war largely because of the support of middle-class progressives. Such concerns had not been sufficient in the first years of the century to win passage of curbs on immigration; but in the troubled and repressive years immediately following the war, many old-stock Americans began to associate immigration with radicalism. Sentiment on behalf of restriction grew rapidly as a result.

In 1921, Congress passed an emergency immigration act, establishing a quota system by which annual immigration from any country could not exceed 3 percent of the number of persons of that nationality who had been in the United States in 1910. The new law cut immigration from 800,000 to 300,000 in any single year, but the nativists remained unsatisfied and pushed for a harsher law. The National Origins Act of 1924 banned immigration from east Asia entirely. That provision deeply angered Japan, which understood that the Japanese were the principal target; Chinese immigration had been illegal since 1892. The law also reduced the quota for Europeans from 3 to 2 percent. The quota would be based, moreover, not on the 1910 census, but on the census of 1890, a year in which there had been many fewer southern and eastern Europeans in the country. What immigration there was, in other words, would heavily favor northwestern Europeans—people of "Nordic" or "Teutonic" stock. Five years later, a further restriction set a rigid limit of 150,000 immigrants a year. In the years that followed, immigration officials seldom permitted even half that number actually to enter the country.

TOTAL IMMIGRATION, 1920–1960

But the nativism of the 1920s extended well beyond restricting immigration. To defenders of an older, more homogeneous America, the growth of large communities of foreign peoples, alien in their speech, their habits, and their values, came to seem a direct threat to their own embattled way of life. Among other things, this provincial nativism helped instigate the rebirth of the Ku Klux Klan as a major force in American society.

The first Klan, founded during Reconstruction, had died in the 1870s. But in 1915, another group of white southerners met on Stone Mountain near Atlanta and established a modern version of the society. Nativist passions had swelled in Georgia and elsewhere in response to the case of Leo Frank, a Jewish factory manager in Atlanta convicted in 1914 (on very flimsy evidence) of murdering a female employee; a mob stormed Frank's jail and lynched him. The premiere (also in Atlanta) of D. W. Griffith's film *The Birth of a Nation*, which glorified the early Klan, also helped inspire white southerners to join a new one.

At first the new Klan, like the old, was largely concerned with intimidating blacks, who according to Klan leader William J. Simmons were becoming insubordinate. And at first it remained small, obscure, and almost entirely southern. After World War I, however, concern about blacks became secondary to concern about Catholics, Jews, and foreigners. The Klan, its organizers proclaimed, would devote itself to purging American life of impure, alien influences. At that point, membership in the Klan expanded rapidly and dramatically, not just in the small towns and rural ar-

eas of the South, but in industrial cities in the North and Midwest. Indiana had the largest membership of any state, and there were substantial Klans in Chicago, Detroit, and other northern industrial cities as well. The Klan was also strong in the West, with particularly large and active chapters in Oregon and Colorado. By 1923, there were reportedly 3 million members; by 1924, 4 million.

In some communities, where Klan leaders came from the most "respectable" segments of society, the organization operated much like a fraternal society, engaging in nothing more dangerous than occasional political pronouncements. Many Klan units (or "klaverns") tried to present themselves as patriots and defenders of morality. Many established women's and even children's auxiliaries to demonstrate their commitment to the family. Often, however, the Klan also operated as a brutal, even violent, opponent of "alien" groups and as a defender of traditional, fundamentalist morality. Some Klansmen systematically terrorized blacks, Jews, Catholics, and foreigners: boycotting their businesses, threatening their families, and attempting to drive them out of their communities. Occasionally, they resorted to violence: public whipping, tarring and feathering, arson, and lynching.

What the Klan feared, it soon became clear, was not simply "foreign" or "racially impure" groups; it was anyone who posed a challenge to "traditional values," as the Klan defined them. Klansmen persecuted not only immigrants and blacks but those white Protestants they considered guilty of irreligion, sexual promiscuity, or drunkenness. The Klan worked to en-

SOURCES OF IMMIGRATION, 1920–1960

THE KU KLUX KLAN IN WASHINGTON, 1926
So powerful was the Ku Klux Klan in the mid-1920s that its members felt emboldened to march openly and defiantly down the streets of major cities—even down Pennsylvania Avenue in Washington, in the shadow of the Capitol of the United States. *(Culver)*

force prohibition; it attempted to institute compulsory Bible reading in schools; it worked to punish divorce. The Ku Klux Klan, in short, was fighting not just to preserve racial homogeneity but to defend its definition of a traditional culture against the values and morals of modernity.

It also provided its members, many of them people of modest means with little real power in society, with a sense of community and seeming authority. Its bizarre costumes, its elaborate rituals, its "secret" language, its burning crosses—all helped produce a sense of excitement and cohesion. For the many women who joined Klan auxiliaries, the organization served important social functions. The Klan was as committed to defending traditional gender roles as it was to defending white supremacy and Protestant morality, but women found in the Klan opportunities for activism and involvement within the confines of conventional female "spheres."

The organization itself declined quickly after 1925, when a series of internal power struggles and several sordid scandals discredited some of its most important leaders. The most damaging episode involved David Stephenson, head of the Indiana Klan, who raped a young secretary, kidnapped her, and watched her die rather than call a doctor after she swallowed poison. The Klan staggered on in some areas into the 1930s, but by World War II it was effectively dead. (The postwar Ku Klux Klan, which still survives, is modeled on but has no direct connection to the Klan of the 1920s and 1930s.)

Religious Fundamentalism

Another cultural controversy of the 1920s was the result of a bitter conflict over the place of religion in contemporary society. By 1921, American Protestantism was already divided into two warring camps. On one side stood the modernists: mostly urban, middle-class people who had attempted to adapt religion to the teachings of modern science and to the realities of their modern, secular society. On the other side stood the defenders of traditional faith: provincial, largely (although not exclusively) rural men and women, fighting to maintain the centrality of religion in American life. They became known as "fundamentalists," a term

BRYAN AND DARROW IN DAYTON
Clarence Darrow (left) and William Jennings Bryan pose for photographers during the 1925 Scopes trial in Dayton, Tennessee. Both men are in shirtsleeves; Bryan is tieless and holding a fan—testimony to the intense heat that plagued the large crowd throughout the trial. *(Brown Brothers)*

derived from an influential set of pamphlets, *The Fundamentals*, published just before World War I. The fundamentalists were outraged at the abandonment of traditional beliefs in the face of scientific discoveries. They insisted the Bible was to be interpreted literally. Above all, they opposed the teachings of Charles Darwin, who had openly challenged the biblical story of the Creation. Human beings had not evolved from lower orders of animals, the fundamentalists insisted; they had been created by God, as described in *Genesis*.

Fundamentalism was a highly evangelical movement, interested in spreading the doctrine to new groups. Evangelists, among them the celebrated Billy Sunday, a former professional baseball player, traveled from state to state (particularly in the South and parts of the West) attracting huge crowds to their revival meetings. Protestant modernists looked on much of this activity with condescension and amusement. But by the mid-1920s, to their great alarm, evangelical fundamentalism was gaining political strength in some states with its demands for legislation to forbid the teaching of evolution in the public schools. In Tennessee in March 1925, the legislature actually adopted a measure making it illegal for any public school teacher "to teach any theory that denies the story of the divine creation of man as taught in the Bible."

The Tennessee law attracted the attention of the fledgling American Civil Liberties Union, which had

been founded in 1920 by Jane Addams, Norman Thomas, Helen Keller, and others alarmed by the repressive legal and social climate of the war and its aftermath; they had felt the need for an organization to defend (among other things) freedom of speech and belief. The ACLU offered free counsel to any Tennessee educator willing to defy the law and become the defendant in a test case. A twenty-four-year-old biology teacher in the town of Dayton, John T. Scopes, agreed to have himself arrested. And when the ACLU decided to send the famous attorney Clarence Darrow to defend Scopes, the aging William Jennings Bryan (now an important fundamentalist spokesman) announced that he would travel to Dayton to assist the prosecution. Journalists from across the country, among them H. L. Mencken, flocked to Tennessee to cover the trial, which opened in an almost circuslike atmosphere. Scopes had, of course, clearly violated the law; and a verdict of guilty was a foregone conclusion, especially when the judge refused to permit "expert" testimony by evolution scholars. Scopes was fined $100, and the case was ultimately dismissed in a higher court because of a technicality. Nevertheless, Darrow scored an important victory for the modernists by calling Bryan himself to the stand to testify as an "expert on the Bible." In the course of the cross-examination, which was broadcast by radio to much of the nation, Darrow made Bryan's stubborn defense of biblical truths appear foolish and finally tricked him into admitting the possibility that not all religious dogma was subject to only one interpretation.

The Scopes trial was a traumatic experience for many fundamentalists. It isolated and ultimately excluded them from many mainstream Protestant denominations. It helped put an end to much of their political activism. But it did not, of course, change their religious convictions. Even without connection to traditional denominations, fundamentalists continued to congregate in independent churches or new denominations of their own.

The Democrats' Ordeal

The anguish of provincial Americans attempting to defend an embattled way of life proved particularly troubling to the Democratic Party, which suffered during the 1920s as a result of tensions between its urban and rural factions. More than the Republicans, the Democrats were a diverse coalition of interest groups, linked to the party more by local tradition than common commitment. Among those interest groups were prohibitionists, Klansmen, and fundamentalists on one side and Catholics, urban workers, and immigrants on the other.

In 1924, the tensions between them proved devastating. At the Democratic National Convention in New York that summer, bitter conflict broke out over the platform when the party's urban wing attempted to win approval of planks calling for the repeal of prohibition and a denunciation of the Klan. Both planks narrowly failed. More damaging to the party was a deadlock in the balloting for a presidential candidate. Urban Democrats supported Alfred E. Smith, the Irish Catholic Tammanyite who had risen to become a progressive governor of New York. Rural Democrats backed William McAdoo, Woodrow Wilson's Treasury secretary (and son-in-law), later to become a senator from California; he had skillfully positioned himself to win the support of southern and western delegates suspicious of Tammany Hall and modern urban life. The convention dragged on for 103 ballots, until finally, after both Smith and McAdoo withdrew, the party settled on a compromise: the bland corporate lawyer John W. Davis, who had served as solicitor general and ambassador to Britain under Wilson.

A similar schism plagued the Democrats again in 1928, when Al Smith finally secured his party's nomination for president after a much shorter and less acrimonious battle. Smith was not, however, able to unite his divided party—largely because of widespread anti-Catholic sentiment, especially in the South. He was the first Democrat since the Civil War not to carry the entire South. Elsewhere, although he did well in the large

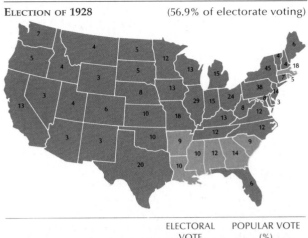

ELECTION OF 1928   (56.9% of electorate voting)

	ELECTORAL VOTE	POPULAR VOTE (%)
Herbert Hoover (Republican)	444	21,391,381 (58.2)
Alfred E. Smith (Democratic)	87	15,016,443 (40.9)
Norman Thomas (Socialist)	—	267,835 (0.7)
Other parties (Socialist Workers, Prohibition)	—	62,890

cities, he carried no states at all except Massachusetts and Rhode Island. Smith's opponent, and the victor in the presidential election, was a man who perhaps more than any other contemporary politician seemed to personify the modern, prosperous, middle-class society of the New Era: Herbert Hoover. The business civilization of the 1920s, with its new institutions, fashions, and values, continued to arouse the animosity of large portions of the population; but the majority of the American people appeared to have accepted and approved it.

REPUBLICAN GOVERNMENT

For twelve years, beginning in 1921, both the presidency and the Congress rested securely in the hands of the Republican Party—a party in which the power of reformers had greatly dwindled since the heyday of progressivism before the war. For most of those years, the federal government enjoyed a warm and supportive relationship with the American business community. Yet the government of the New Era was more than the passive, pliant instrument that critics often described. It also attempted to serve as an active agent of economic change.

Harding and Coolidge

Nothing seemed more clearly to illustrate the unadventurous character of 1920s politics than the characters of the two men who served as president during most of the decade: Warren G. Harding and Calvin Coolidge.

Harding was elected to the presidency in 1920, having spent many years in public life doing little of note. An undistinguished senator from Ohio, he had received the Republican presidential nomination as a result of an agreement among leaders of his party who considered him, as one noted, a "good second-rater." Harding wanted to be a responsible president. He appointed capable men to the most important cabinet offices; he attempted to stabilize the nation's troubled foreign policy; and he displayed on occasion a vigorous humanity, as when he pardoned Socialist Eugene V. Debs in 1921. But even as he attempted to rise to his office, he seemed baffled by his responsibilities, as if he recognized his own unfitness. "I am a man of limited talents from a small town," he reportedly told friends on one occasion. "I don't seem to grasp that I am President." Unsurprisingly, perhaps, Harding soon found himself delegating much of his authority to others: to members of his cabinet, to political cronies, to Congress, to party leaders.

Although Harding appointed several men of real distinction to his cabinet, he lacked the strength to abandon the party hacks who had helped create his political success. One of them, Harry Daugherty, the Ohio party boss principally responsible for his meteoric political ascent, he appointed attorney general. Another, New Mexico Senator Albert B. Fall, he made secretary of the interior. Members of the so-called Ohio Gang filled important offices throughout the administration. Unknown to the public (and perhaps also to Harding), Daugherty, Fall, and others were engaged in fraud and corruption, at least some of which gradually came to light.

The most spectacular scandal involved the rich naval oil reserves at Teapot Dome, Wyoming, and Elk Hills, California. At the urging of Albert Fall, Harding transferred control of those reserves from the Navy Department to the Interior Department. Fall then secretly leased them to two wealthy businessmen and received in return nearly half a million dollars in "loans" to ease his private financial troubles. Fall was ultimately convicted of bribery and sentenced to a year in prison; Harry Daugherty barely avoided a similar fate for his part in another scandal.

In the summer of 1923, only months before Senate investigations and press revelations brought the scandals to light, a tired and depressed Harding left Washington for a speaking tour in the West and a visit to

HARDING AND FRIENDS
President Warren G. Harding (center left, holding a rod) poses with companions during a fishing trip to Miami in 1921. He enjoyed these social and sporting events with wealthy friends and political cronies. Two of his companions here, Attorney General Harry Daugherty (to the left of Harding) and Interior Secretary Albert Fall (at far right) were later principal figures in the scandals that rocked the administration before and after Harding's death. *(UPI/Bettmann)*

Alaska. In Seattle late in July, he suffered severe pain, which his doctors wrongly diagnosed as food poisoning. A few days later, in San Francisco, he died: he had suffered two major heart attacks.

In many ways, Calvin Coolidge, who succeeded Harding in the presidency, was utterly different from his predecessor. Where Harding was genial, garrulous, and debauched, Coolidge was dour, silent, even puritanical. And while Harding was if not personally corrupt then at least tolerant of corruption in others, Coolidge seemed honest beyond reproach. In other ways, however, Harding and Coolidge were similar figures. Both took an essentially passive approach to the presidency.

Like Harding, Coolidge had risen to the presidency on the basis of few substantive accomplishments. Elected governor of Massachusetts in 1919, he had won national attention with his forceful, if laconic, response to the Boston police strike that year. That was enough to make him his party's vice presidential nominee in 1920. Three years later, after news of Harding's death reached him in Vermont, he took the oath of office from his father, a justice of the peace, by the light of a

kerosene lamp on the kitchen table. It was the beginning of a skillful reinvention of Coolidge by party leaders and advisers from the advertising industry (among them Bruce Barton). For the next five years, Coolidge built a reputation as a simple man defending country virtues, even though in reality he was a thoroughly urban man of modern sensibilities.

If anything, Coolidge was an even less active president than Harding, partly as a result of his conviction that government should interfere as little as possible in the life of the nation (and, most importantly, in the life of its economy) and partly as a result of his own personal lassitude. He took long naps every afternoon. He kept official appointments to a minimum and engaged in little conversation with those who did manage to see him. He proposed no significant legislation and took little part in the running of the nation's foreign policy. "He aspired," wrote one of his contemporaries, "to become the least President the country ever had. He attained his desire."

In 1924, he received his party's presidential nomination virtually unopposed. Running against John W. Davis, the 1924 Democratic candidate, he won a com-

SIGNIFICANT EVENTS

1914–1920 Great Migration of black southerners into northern cities

1920 First commercial radio station, KDKA in Pittsburgh, begins broadcasting

Prohibition begins

Warren G. Harding elected president

1921 Sheppard-Towner Act funds maternity assistance

Nation experiences economic recession

1922 Sinclair Lewis publishes *Babbitt*

Motion Picture Association, under Will Hays, founded to regulate film industry

1923 Nation experiences mild recession

Harding dies; Calvin Coolidge becomes president

Teapot Dome and other scandals revealed

Ku Klux Klan reaches peak membership

1924 National Origins Act passed

Coolidge elected president

1925 Congress passes McNary-Haugen bill; Coolidge vetoes it

F. Scott Fitzgerald publishes *The Great Gatsby*

Scopes trial in Dayton, Tennessee

A. Philip Randolph founds Brotherhood of Sleeping Car Porters

1927 First feature-length sound motion picture, *The Jazz Singer,* released

Charles Lindbergh makes solo transatlantic flight

1928 Congress passes, and Coolidge vetoes, McNary-Haugen bill again

Herbert Hoover elected president

1929 Sheppard-Towner program terminated

Anti-Filipino riots in California

William Faulkner publishes *The Sound and the Fury*

---

fortable victory: 54 percent of the popular vote and 382 of the 531 electoral votes. Robert La Follette, the candidate of the reincarnated Progressive Party, received 16.8 percent of the popular vote but carried only his home state of Wisconsin. Coolidge probably could have won renomination and reelection in 1928. Instead, in characteristically laconic fashion, he walked into a press room one day and handed each reporter a slip of paper containing a single sentence: "I do not choose to run for president in 1928."

Government and Business

The story of Harding and Coolidge themselves, however, is only a part—and by no means the most important part—of the story of their administrations. However inept or inert the New Era presidents may have been, much of the federal government was working effectively and efficiently during the 1920s to adapt public policy to the widely accepted goal of the time: helping business and industry operate with maximum efficiency and productivity. The close relationship between the private sector and the federal government that had been forged during World War I continued, although in much altered form.

Secretary of the Treasury Andrew Mellon, the wealthy steel and aluminum tycoon, devoted himself to working for substantial reductions in taxes on corporate profits and personal incomes and inheritances. Largely because of his efforts, Congress cut them all by more than half. Mellon also worked closely with President Coolidge after 1924 on a series of measures to dramatically trim the already modest federal budget. The administration even managed to retire half the nation's World War I debt.

The most prominent member of the cabinet was Commerce Secretary Herbert Hoover, who considered himself, and was considered by others, a notable progressive. During his eight years in the Commerce Department, Hoover constantly encouraged voluntary cooperation in the private sector as the best avenue to stability. But the idea of voluntarism did not require the government to remain passive; on the contrary, Hoover believed public institutions had a duty to play an active role in creating the new, cooperative order. Above all, Hoover championed the concept of business associationalism, the creation of national organizations of businessmen in particular industries. Through these trade associations, Hoover believed, private entrepreneurs could stabilize their industries and promote efficiency in production and marketing. Hoover strongly resisted those who urged that the government sanction collusion among manufacturers to fix prices. But he did believe that shared information and limited cooperation would keep competition from becoming destructive and thus improve the strength of the economy as a whole.

The Supreme Court in the 1920s further confirmed the business orientation of the federal government, particularly after the appointment of William Howard Taft as chief justice in 1921. In one of the most important decisions in its history, *Lochner* v. *New York* (1905), the Court had struck down a New York law limiting the number of hours bakers in New York could be required to work. That law, the justices argued, was an abrogation of the freedom of workers and employers to form contracts; and with that decision, the Court set a nearly impossible standard against which all future economic regulations would have to be measured.

In the 1920s, continuing along the lines the *Lochner* decision had laid out, the Court struck down federal legislation regulating child labor (*Bailey* v. *Drexel Furniture Company*, 1922); nullified a minimum wage law for women in the District of Columbia (*Adkins* v. *Children's Hospital*, 1923); and sanctioned the creation of trade associations, ruling in *United States* v. *Maple Flooring Association* (1925) that such organizations did not violate antitrust statutes as long as some competition survived within an industry. Five years earlier, in *United States* v. *U.S. Steel*, the Court had applied the same doctrine to the monopolistic United States Steel Corporation; there was no illegal "restraint of trade," it ruled, as long as U.S. Steel continued to face any competition, no matter how slight.

The pro-business policies of the Republican administrations were not without their critics. In Congress, progressive reformers of the old school continued to criticize the monopolistic practices of big business, to attack government's alliance with the corporate community, and to decry social injustices. Occasionally, they were able to mobilize enough support to win congressional approval of progressive legislation, most notably the McNary-Haugen plan for farmers and an ambitious proposal to use federal funds to develop public electric power projects on the Tennessee River at Muscle Shoals. But the progressive reformers lacked the power to override the presidential vetoes that their bills almost always received.

Some progressives derived encouragement from the election of Herbert Hoover—widely regarded as the most progressive member of the Harding and Coolidge administrations—to the presidency in 1928. Hoover had easily defeated Alfred Smith, the Democratic candidate. And he entered office promising bold new efforts to solve the nation's remaining economic problems. But Hoover had few opportunities to prove himself. Less than a year after his inauguration, the nation plunged into the severest and most prolonged economic crisis in its history—a crisis that brought many of the optimistic assumptions of the New Era crashing down and launched the nation into a period of unprecedented social innovation and reform.

SUGGESTED READINGS

General Studies. Frederick Lewis Allen, *Only Yesterday* (1931). John Braeman, Robert Bremner, and David Brody, eds., *Change and Continuity in Twentieth Century America: The 1920s* (1968). Ellis Hawley, *The Great War and the Search for a Modern Order* (1979). John D. Hicks, *Republican Ascendancy* (1960). Isabel Leighton, ed., *The Aspirin Age* (1949). William E. Leuchtenburg, *The Perils of Prosperity* (rev. ed. 1994). Donald R. McCoy, *Coming of Age* (1973). Geoffrey Perrett, *America in the Twenties* (1982). Arthur M. Schlesinger, Jr., *The Crisis of the Old Order* (1957). George Soule, *Prosperity Decade: From War to Depression* (1947).

Labor, Agriculture, and Economic Growth. Guy Alchon, *The Invisible Hand of Planning: Capitalism, Social Science, and the State in the 1920s* (1985). Irving Bernstein, *The Lean Years: A History of the American Worker, 1920–1933* (1960). David Brody, *Steelworkers in America* (1960); *Workers in Industrial America* (1980). Alfred Chandler, *Strategy and Structure* (1962). Lisabeth Cohen, *Making a New Deal: Industrial Workers in Chicago, 1919–1939* (1990). Gilbert C. Fite, *George Peek and the Fight for Farm Parity* (1954); *American Farmers: The New Minority* (1981). Louis Galambos, *Competition and Cooperation* (1966). Louis Galambos and Joseph Pratt, *The Rise of the Cor-*

porate *Commonwealth: U.S. Business and Public Policy in the Twentieth Century* (1988). Peter Gottlieb, *Making Their Own Way: Southern Blacks' Migration to Pittsburgh, 1916–1930* (1987). Jim Potter, *The American Economy Between the Wars* (1974). Theodore Saloutos and John D. Hicks, *Twentieth Century Populism* (1951). George Soule, *Prosperity Decade* (1947). Mira Wilkins, *The Maturing of Multinational Enterprise: American Business Abroad from 1914 to 1970* (1974). Leslie Woodcock, *Wage-Earning Women* (1979). Gerald Zahavi, *Workers, Managers, and Welfare Capitalism* (1988). Robert Zieger, *Republicans and Labor* (1969).

The New Culture. Erik Barnouw, *A Tower in Babel: A History of American Radio to 1933* (1966). Daniel Boorstin, *The Americans: The Democratic Experience* (1973). Paul Carter, *The Twenties in America* (1968); *Another Part of the Twenties* (1977). Stanley Coben, *Rebellion Against Victorianism: The Impetus for Cultural Change in 1920s America* (1991). Ed Cray, *Chrome Colossus* (1980). Robert Creamer, *Babe* (1974). Kenneth S. Davis, *The Hero: Charles A. Lindbergh* (1959). Susan J. Douglas, *Inventing American Broadcasting* (1987). Ronald Edsforth, *Class Conflict and Cultural Consensus: The Making of a Mass Consumer Society: Flint, Michigan* (1987). Melvin Patrick Ely, *The Adventures of Amos 'n Andy: A Social History of an American Phenomenon* (1991). Stewart Ewen, *Captains of Consciousness* (1976). James J. Flink, *The Car Culture* (1975); *The Automobile Age* (1988). Stephen Fox, *The Mirror Makers: A History of American Advertising and Its Creators* (1984). Neal Gabler, *An Empire of Their Own: How the Jews Invented Hollywood* (1988). Harvey Green, *Fit for America* (1986). Allen Guttmann, *A Whole New Ball Game* (1988). Sumiko Higashi, *Virgins, Vamps, and Flappers: The American Silent Movie Heroine* (1978). Daniel Horowitz, *The Morality of Spending: Attitudes Toward the Consumer Society in America, 1875–1940* (1985). Robert Lynd and Helen Lynd, *Middletown* (1929). Roland Marchand, *Advertising the American Dream* (1985). Lary May, *Screening Out the Past* (1980). Fred J. McDonald, *Don't Touch That Dial* (1979). Zane Miller, *The Urbanization of America* (1973). Kathy H. Ogren, *The Jazz Revolution: Twenties America and the Meaning of Jazz* (1989). Kathy Peiss, *Cheap Amusements* (1986). Daniel Pope, *The Making of Modern Advertising* (1983). Randy Roberts, *Jack Dempsey, The Manassa Mauler* (1979). Philip T. Rosen, *The Modern Stentors: Radio Broadcasting and the Federal Government, 1920–1933* (1980). Joan Shelley Rubin, *The Making of Middlebrow Culture* (1992). Robert Sklar, *Movie-Made America* (1975). Susan Strasser, *Satisfaction Guaranteed: The Making of the American Mass Market* (1989). Bernard A. Weisberger, *The Dream Maker* (1979).

Women, Family, and Youth. W. Andrew Achenbaum, *Shades of Gray: Old Age, American Values, and Federal Policies Since 1920* (1983). Beth L. Bailey, *From Back Porch to Front Seat* (1988). Lois Banner, *American Beauty* (1983). Susan Porter Benson, *Counter Cultures* (1986). William H. Chafe, *The American Woman: Her Changing Social and Political Roles* (1972). Ellen Chesler, *Woman of Valor: Margaret Sanger and the Birth Control Movement in America* (1992). Howard P. Chudacoff, *How Old Are You? Age in American Culture* (1989). Nancy Cott, *The*

Grounding of American Feminism (1987). Ruth Schwarz Cowan, *More Work for Mother* (1983). John D'Emilio and Estelle B. Friedman, *Intimate Matters: A History of Sexuality in America* (1988). Paula Fass, *The Damned and Beautiful* (1977). David H. Fischer, *Growing Old in America* (1977). Linda Gordon, *Woman's Body, Woman's Right* (1976). Helen Lefkowitz Horowitz, *Campus Life: Undergraduate Cultures from the End of the Eighteenth Century to the Present* (1987). Alice Kessler-Harris, *Out to Work: A History of Wage-Earning Women in America* (1982). J. Stanley Lemons, *The Woman Citizen: Social Feminism in the 1920s* (1973). Sheila Rothman, *Woman's Proper Place* (1978). Lois Scharf, *To Work and to Wed* (1980). Virginia Scharff, *Taking the Wheel* (1991). Susan Strasser, *Never Done: A History of American Housework* (1982). Winifred Wandersee, *Women's Work and Family Values, 1920–1940* (1981). Renold Wilk, *Henry Ford and Grass Roots America* (1972).

Intellectuals and the Arts. Charles C. Alexander, *Here the Country Lies: Nationalism and the Arts in Twentieth Century America* (1980). Houston Baker, Jr., *Modernism and the Harlem Renaissance* (1987). Loren Baritz, ed. , *The Culture of the Twenties* (1970). Cleanth Brooks, *William Faulkner: The Yoknapatawpha Country* (1963). Paul Conkin, *The Southern Agrarians* (1988). Malcolm Cowley, *Exiles Return* (1934). Robert Crunden, *From Self to Society: Transition in American Thought, 1919–1941* (1972). George H. Douglas, *H. L. Mencken* (1978). Frederick J. Hoffman, *The Twenties* (1949). Nathan I. Huggins, *Harlem Renaissance* (1971). Gloria T. Hull, *Color, Sex, and Poetry: Three Women Writers of the Harlem Renaissance* (1987). David L. Lewis, *When Harlem Was in Vogue* (1981). Roderick Nash, *The Nervous Generation: American Thought, 1917–1930* (1969). John Stewart, *The Burden of Time* (1965). Kenneth M. Wheeler and Virginia L. Lussier, eds., *Women, the Arts, and the 1920s in Paris and New York* (1982). Edmund Wilson, *The Twenties* (1975).

Cultural Conflicts. Charles C. Alexander, *The Ku Klux Klan in the Southwest* (1965). Paul Avrich, *Sacco and Vanzetti: The Anarchist Background* (1991). Herbert Asbury, *The Great Illusion* (1950). Kathleen M. Blee, *Women of the Klan: Racism and Gender in the 1920s* (1991). David Chalmers, *Hooded Americanism* (1965). Norman Clark, *Deliver Us from Evil* (1976). Elton C. Fax, *Garvey* (1972). Norman Furniss, *The Fundamentalist Controversy* (1954). Ray Ginger, *Six Days or Forever?* (1958). Joseph Gusfeld, *Symbolic Crusade* (1963). John Higham, *Strangers in the Land* (1963). Kenneth Jackson, *The Ku Klux Klan in the City* (1965). K. Austin Kerr, *Organized for Prohibition: A New History of the Anti-Saloon League* (1985). Don Kirschner, *City and Country: Rural Responses to Urbanization in the 1920s* (1970). Lawrence Levine, *Defender of the Faith, William Jennings Bryan: The Last Decade, 1915–1925* (1965). George M. Marsden, *Fundamentalism and American Culture* (1980). William G. McLoughlin, *Modern Revivalism* (1959). Leonard Moore, *Citizen Klansmen: The Ku Klux Klan in Indiana, 1921-1928* (1991). Andrew Sinclair, *The Era of Excess* (1962). Richard K. Tucker, *The Dragon and the Cross: The Rise and Fall of the Ku Klux Klan in Middle America* (1991). Theodore Vincent, *Black Power and the Garvey Movement* (1971).

Politics and Government. Kristi Andersen, *The Creation of a Democratic Majority, 1928–1936* (1979). LeRoy Ashby, *Spearless Leader* (1972). Christine Bolt, *American Indian Policy and American Reform* (1987). David Burner, *The Politics of Provincialism* (1967). David Burner, *Herbert Hoover* (1979). E. Paula Elder, *Governor Alfred E. Smith: The Politician as Reformer* (1983). Frank Freidel, *Franklin D. Roosevelt: The Ordeal* (1954); *Franklin D. Roosevelt: The Triumph* (1956). James N. Giglio, *H. M. Daugherty and the Politics of Expediency* (1978). James Gilbert, *Designing the Industrial State* (1972). Oscar Handlin, *Al Smith and His America* (1958). William Harbaugh, *Lawyer's Lawyer* (1973). Ellis Hawley, *Herbert Hoover as Secretary of Commerce: Studies in New Era Thought and Practice* (1974). Robert F. Himmelberg, *The Origins of the National Recovery Administration: Business, Government, and the Trade Association Issue, 1921–1933* (1976). Alan Lichtman, *Prejudice and the Old Politics* (1979). Richard Lowitt, *George W. Norris*, vol. 2 (1971). Donald R. McCoy, *Calvin Coolidge* (1967). Robert K. Murray, *The Politics of Normalcy* (1973); *The Harding Era* (1969). Burl Noggle, *Teapot Dome* (1962). Elisabeth Israels Perry, *Belle Moskowitz: Feminine Politics and the Exercise of Power in the Age of Alfred E. Smith* (1987). Francis Russell, *The Shadow of Blooming Grove* (1968). Andrew Sinclair, *The Available Man* (1965). David P. Thelen, *Robert M. La Follette and the Insurgent Spirit* (1978). George B. Tindall, *The Emergence of the New South* (1967). Eugene Trani and David Wilson, *The Presidency of Warren G. Harding* (1977). William Allen White, *A Puritan in Babylon* (1940). John Hoff Wilson, *Herbert Hoover: Forgotten Progressive* (1975).

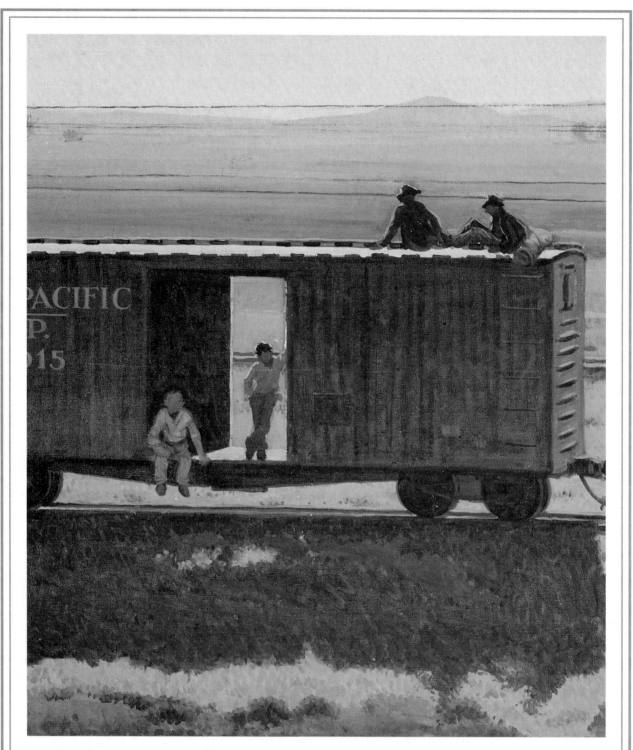

DETAIL FROM *PRIVATE CAR* (1932), BY LECONTE STEWART
Thousands of men left their homes during the Great Depression and traveled from city to city looking for work, often hopping freight trains for a free, if illegal, ride. *(Museum of Church History & Art, Salt Lake City, Utah)*

CHAPTER TWENTY-FIVE

THE GREAT DEPRESSION

W E IN AMERICA TODAY," Herbert Hoover proclaimed in August 1928, not long before his election to the presidency, "are nearer to the final triumph over poverty than ever before in the history of any land. The poorhouse is vanishing from among us." Only fifteen months later those words would return to haunt him, as the nation plunged into the severest and most prolonged economic depression in its history—a depression that continued in one form or another for a full decade, not only in the United States but throughout much of the rest of the world. The Depression was a traumatic experience for individual Americans, who faced unemployment, the loss of land and other property, and in some cases homelessness and starvation. It also placed great strains on the political and social fabric of the nation.

THE COMING OF THE GREAT DEPRESSION

The sudden economic decline that began in 1929 came as an especially severe shock because it followed so closely a period in which the New Era seemed to be performing another series of economic miracles.

The Great Crash

In February 1928, stock prices began a steady rise that continued, with only a few temporary lapses, for a year and a half. Between May 1928 and September 1929, the average price of stocks increased over 40 percent. The stocks of the major industrials—the stocks that are used to determine the Dow Jones Industrial Average—doubled in value in that same period. Trading mushroomed from 2 or 3 million shares a day to over 5 million, and at times to as many as 10 or 12 million. There was, in short, a widespread speculative fever that grew steadily more intense, particularly once brokerage firms began encouraging the mania by recklessly offering easy credit to those buying stocks.

In the autumn of 1929, the market began to fall apart. On October 21 and again on October 23, there were alarming declines in stock prices, in both cases followed by temporary recoveries (the second of them engineered by J. P. Morgan and Company and other big bankers, who conspicuously bought up stocks to restore public confidence). But on October 29, "Black Tuesday," all efforts to save the market failed. Sixteen million shares of stock were traded; the industrial index dropped 43 points; stocks in many companies became virtually worthless. In the months that followed, the market continued to decline. It remained deeply depressed for more than four years and did not fully recover for over a decade.

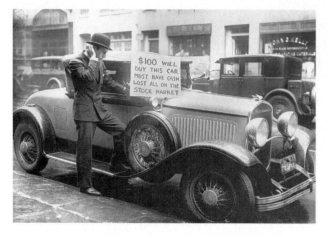

AFTERMATH OF THE CRASH
Walter Thornton, shown here in October 1929 next to an expensive roadster he had bought not long before, was one of many relatively affluent Americans who suffered substantial losses in the crash of the stock market in the fall of 1929. In popular mythology, many such people committed suicide in despair. In reality, almost no one did. Much more common were efforts such as this to sell off assets to make up for the losses. Thornton was more fortunate than many victims of the Depression. Most had few assets to sell. *(UPI/Bettmann)*

Popular folklore has established the stock market crash as the beginning, and even the cause, of the Great Depression. But although October 1929 might have been the first visible sign of the crisis, the Depression had earlier beginnings and more important causes.

Causes of the Depression

Economists, historians, and others have argued for decades about the causes of the Great Depression. But most agree on several things. They agree, first, that what is remarkable about the crisis is not that it occurred; periodic recessions are a normal feature of capitalist economies. What is remarkable is that it was so severe and that it lasted so long. The important question, therefore, is not so much why there was a depression, but why it was such a bad one. Most observers agree, too, that a number of different factors account for the severity of the crisis, even if there is considerable disagreement about which was the most important.

One of those factors was a lack of diversification in the American economy in the 1920s. Prosperity had depended excessively on a few basic industries, no-

tably construction and automobiles. In the late 1920s, those industries began to decline. Expenditures on construction fell from $11 billion to under $9 billion between 1926 and 1929. Automobile sales fell by more than a third in the first nine months of 1929. Newer industries were emerging to take up the slack—among them petroleum, chemicals, plastics, and others oriented toward the expanding market for consumer goods—but had not yet developed enough strength to compensate for the decline in other sectors.

A second important factor was the maldistribution of purchasing power and, as a result, a weakness in consumer demand. As industrial and agricultural production increased, the proportion of the profits going to farmers, workers, and other potential consumers was too small to create an adequate market for the goods the economy was producing. Demand was not keeping up with supply. Even in 1929, after nearly a decade of economic growth, more than half the families in America lived on the edge of or below the minimum subsistence level—too poor to buy the goods the industrial economy was producing.

As long as corporations had continued to expand their capital facilities (factories, warehouses, heavy equipment, and other investments), the economy had flourished. By 1929, however, capital investment had created more plant space than could profitably be used, and factories were producing more goods than consumers could purchase. Industries that were experiencing declining demand (construction, autos, coal, and others) began laying off workers, depleting mass purchasing power further. Even expanding industries often reduced their work forces because of new, less labor-intensive technologies; and in the sluggish economic atmosphere of 1929 and beyond, such workers had difficulty finding employment elsewhere.

A third major problem was the credit structure of the economy. Farmers were deeply in debt—their land mortgaged, crop prices too low to allow them to pay off what they owed. Small banks, especially those tied to the agricultural economy, were in constant trouble in the 1920s as their customers defaulted on loans; many of them failed. Large banks were in trouble too. Although most American bankers were very conservative, some of the nation's biggest banks were investing recklessly in the stock market or making unwise loans. When the stock market crashed, many of these banks suffered losses greater than they could absorb.

A fourth factor contributing to the coming of the Depression was America's position in international trade. Late in the 1920s, European demand for American goods began to decline. That was partly because European industry and agriculture were becoming more productive, and partly because some European

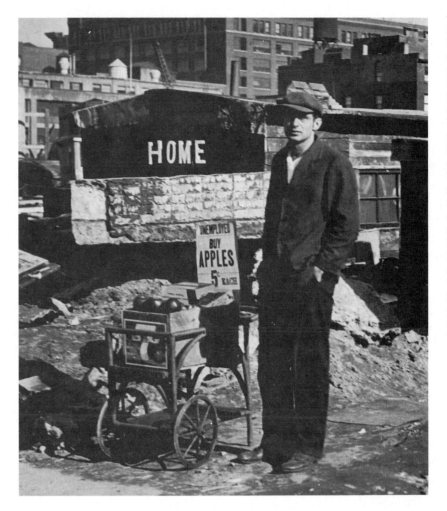

SELLING APPLES, NEW YORK CITY
In the fall of 1931 and again in the fall of 1932, large numbers of the unemployed took to selling apples on the streets of major cities and became in the process a popular symbol of the economic despair of those years. Herbert Hoover later wrote bitterly of the phenomenon: "One incident of these times has persisted as the eternal damnation of Hoover. Some Oregon or Washington growers' association shrewdly appraised the sympathy of the public for the unemployed. They set up a system of selling apples on the street corners in many cities, thus selling their crop and raising their prices. Many persons left their jobs for the more profitable one of selling apples. When any leftwinger wishes to indulge in scathing oratory, he demands, 'Do you want to return to selling apples?' "
(Culver)

nations (most notably Germany, under the Weimar Republic) were having financial difficulties and could not afford to buy goods from overseas. But it was also because the European economy was being destabilized by the international debt structure that had emerged in the aftermath of World War I.

The international debt structure, therefore, was a fifth factor contributing to the Depression. When the war came to an end in 1918, all the European nations that had been allied with the United States owed large sums of money to American banks, sums much too large to be repaid out of their shattered economies. That was one reason why the Allies had insisted (over Woodrow Wilson's objections) on reparation payments from Germany and Austria. Reparations, they believed, would provide them with a way to pay off their own debts. But Germany and Austria were themselves in economic trouble after the war; they were no more able to pay the reparations than the Allies were able to pay their debts.

The American government refused to forgive or reduce the debts. Instead, American banks began making large loans to European governments, with which they paid off their earlier loans. Thus debts (and reparations) were being paid only by piling up new and greater debts. In the late 1920s, and particularly after the American economy began to weaken in 1929, the European nations found it much more difficult to borrow money from the United States. At the same time, high American protective tariffs were making it difficult for them to sell their goods in American markets. Without any source of foreign exchange with which to repay their loans, they began to default. The collapse of the international credit structure was one of the reasons the Depression spread to Europe (and grew much worse in America) after 1931.

Progress of the Depression

The stock market crash of 1929 did not so much cause the Depression, then, as help trigger a chain of events that exposed longstanding weaknesses in the American economy. During the next three years, the crisis steadily worsened.

A collapse of much of the banking system followed the stock market crash. Over 9,000 American banks either went bankrupt or closed their doors to avoid bankruptcy between 1930 and 1933. Depositors lost over $2.5 billion in deposits. Partly as a result of these banking closures, the nation's money supply greatly decreased. The total money supply, according to some measurements, fell by more than a third between 1930 and 1933. The declining money supply meant a decline in purchasing power, and thus deflation. Manufacturers and merchants began reducing prices, cutting back on production, and laying off workers.

Some economists argue that a severe depression could have been avoided if the Federal Reserve system had acted more responsibly. But the members of the Federal Reserve Board, concerned about protecting its own solvency in a dangerous economic environment, raised interest rates in 1931, which contracted the money supply even further.

The collapse was so rapid and so devastating that at the time it created only bewilderment among many of those who attempted to explain it. The American gross national product plummeted from over $104 billion in 1929 to $76.4 billion in 1932—a 25 percent decline in three years. In 1929, Americans had spent $16.2 billion in capital investment; in 1933, they invested only a third of a billion. The consumer price index declined 25 percent between 1929 and 1933, the wholesale price index 32 percent. Gross farm income dropped from $12 billion to $5 billion in four years. By 1932, according to the relatively crude estimates of the time, 25 percent of the American work force was unemployed (some believe the figure was even higher); another third of the work force experienced cuts in wages or hours or both. For the rest of the decade, unemployment averaged nearly 20 percent, never dropping below 15 percent.

THE AMERICAN PEOPLE IN HARD TIMES

Someone asked the British economist John Maynard Keynes in the 1930s whether he was aware of any historical era comparable to the Great Depression. "Yes," Keynes replied. "It was called the Dark Ages, and it lasted 400 years." The Depression did not last 400 years, but it did bring unprecedented despair to the economies of the United States and much of the Western world. And it had far-reaching effects on American society and culture.

Unemployment and Relief

The suffering extended into every area of society. In the industrial Northeast and Midwest, cities were becoming virtually paralyzed by unemployment. For example, Cleveland, Ohio, in 1932 had an unemployment rate of 50 percent; Akron, 60 percent; Toledo, 80 percent. Many industrial workers were accustomed to periods of unemployment, but no one was prepared for the scale and duration of the joblessness of the 1930s. Most Americans had been taught to believe that every individual was responsible for his or her own fate, that unemployment and poverty were signs of personal failure; and even in the face of national distress, many continued to believe it. Many adult men, in particular, felt deeply ashamed of their joblessness; the helplessness of unemployment was a challenge to traditional notions of masculinity. Unemployed workers walked through the streets day after day looking for jobs that did not exist. An increasing number of families were turning to state and local public relief systems, just to be able to eat. But that system, which in the 1920s had served only a small number of indigents, was totally unequipped to handle the new demands being placed on it. In many places, relief simply collapsed. Private charities attempted to supplement the public relief efforts, but the problem was far beyond their capabilities as well. State governments felt pressure to expand their own assistance to the unemployed; but tax revenues were declining along with everything else, and state leaders balked at placing additional strains on already tight budgets. Moreover, many public officials believed that an extensive welfare system would undermine the moral fiber of its clients.

As a result, American cities experienced scenes that a few years earlier would have seemed almost inconceivable. Bread lines stretched for blocks outside Red Cross and Salvation Army kitchens. Thousands of people sifted through garbage cans for scraps of food or waited outside restaurant kitchens in hopes of receiving plate scrapings. Nearly 2 million men, most of them young (and a much smaller number of women), simply took to the roads, riding freight trains from city to city, living as nomads.

In rural areas conditions were in many ways worse. Farm income declined by 60 percent between 1929 and 1932. A third of all American farmers lost their land.

SOUP KITCHEN IN CHICAGO
This soup kitchen offered free food and coffee to about 3,500 unemployed people a day in Chicago, one of many local efforts to deal with the ravages of the Depression. Unlike some such efforts, however, this one had substantial resources behind it. It was run by the famous Chicago gangster Al Capone. *(UPI/Bettmann)*

In addition, a large area of agricultural settlement in the Great Plains of the South and West was suffering from a catastrophic natural disaster: one of the worst droughts in the history of the nation. Beginning in 1930, a large area of the nation, which came to be known as the "Dust Bowl," stretching north from Texas into the Dakotas, began to experience a steady decline in rainfall and an accompanying increase in heat. The drought continued for a decade, turning what had once been fertile farm regions into virtual deserts. In Kansas, the soil in some places was completely without moisture as far as three feet below the surface. In Nebraska, Iowa, and other states, summer temperatures were averaging over 100 degrees. Swarms of grasshoppers were moving from region to region, devouring what meager crops farmers were able to raise, often even devouring fenceposts or clothes hanging out to dry. Great dust storms—"black blizzards," as they were called— swept across the plains, blotting out the sun and suffocating livestock as well as any people unfortunate or foolish enough to stay outside. (See "The American Environment," pp. 696–698.)

It is a measure of how productive American farmers were and how depressed the market for agricultural goods had become that even with these disastrous conditions, the farm economy continued through the 1930s to produce far more than American consumers could afford to buy. Farm prices fell so low that few growers any longer made any profit at all on their crops. As a result, many farmers, like many urban unemployed, left their homes in search of work. In the South, in particular, many dispossessed farmers—black and white—wandered from town to town, hoping to find jobs or handouts. Hundreds of thousands of families from the Dust Bowl (often known as "Okies," since many came from Oklahoma) traveled to California and other states, where they found conditions little better than those they had left. Owning no land of their own, many worked as agricultural migrants, traveling from farm to farm picking fruit and other crops at starvation wages.

Throughout the nation, problems of malnutrition and homelessness grew at an alarming rate. Hospitals pointed to a striking increase in deaths from starvation. On the outskirts of cities, large shantytowns sprang up in which families lived in makeshift shacks constructed of flattened tin cans, scraps of wood, abandoned crates, and other debris. Many homeless Americans simply kept moving—sleeping in freight cars, in city parks, in subways, or in unused sewer ducts.

African Americans and the Depression

African Americans for the most part had not shared very much in the prosperity of the previous decade. But the Depression was devastating for them nevertheless. They experienced more unemployment, home-

BLACK MIGRANTS
The Great Migration of blacks from the rural South into the cities had begun before World War I. But in the 1930s and 1940s the movement accelerated. Jacob Lawrence, an eminent black artist, created a series of paintings entitled, collectively, *The Migration of the Negro,* to illustrate this major event in the history of American blacks. *(Phillips Collection, Washington, D.C.)*

lessness, malnutrition, and disease than they had in the past, and considerably more than most whites.

As the Depression began, over half of all black Americans still lived in the South. Most were farmers. The collapse of prices for cotton and other staple crops left some with no income at all. Many left the land altogether—either by choice or forced by landlords who no longer found the sharecropping system profitable. Some migrated to southern cities. But unemployed whites in the urban South believed they had first claim to all work. Some of them now began to take positions as janitors, street cleaners, and domestic servants, displacing the blacks who formerly had occupied such jobs.

As the Depression deepened, whites in many southern cities began to demand that all blacks be dismissed from their jobs. In Atlanta in 1930, an organization calling itself the Black Shirts organized a campaign with the slogan "No Jobs for Niggers Until Every White Man Has a Job!" In other areas, whites used intimidation and violence to drive blacks from jobs. By 1932, over half the blacks in the South were without employment. And what limited relief there was went almost invariably to whites first.

Unsurprisingly, therefore, many black southerners—perhaps 400,000 in all—left the South in the 1930s and journeyed to the cities of the North. There they generally found less blatant discrimination. But conditions were in most respects little better than in the South. In New York, black unemployment was nearly 50 percent. In other cities, it was higher. Two million African Americans were on some form of relief by 1932.

Traditional patterns of segregation and disfranchisement in the South survived the Depression largely unchallenged. But a few particularly notorious examples of racism did attract national attention. The most celebrated was the Scottsboro case. In March 1931, nine black teenagers were taken off a freight train in Alabama (in a small town near Scottsboro) and arrested for vagrancy and disorder. Later, two white women who had also been riding the train accused them of rape. In fact, there was overwhelming evidence, medical and otherwise, that the women had not been raped at all; they may have made their accusations out of fear of being arrested themselves. Nevertheless, an all-white jury in Alabama quickly convicted all nine of the "Scottsboro boys" (as they were known to both friends and foes) and sentenced eight of them to death.

The Supreme Court overturned the convictions in 1932, and a series of new trials began that attracted increasing national attention. The International Labor Defense, an organization associated with the Communist Party, came to the aid of the accused youths and began to publicize the case. Later, the NAACP provided assistance as well. The trials continued throughout the 1930s. Although the white southern juries who sat on the case never acquitted any of the defendants, all of them eventually gained their freedom—four because the charges were dropped, four because of early paroles, and one because he escaped. But the last of the Scottsboro defendants did not leave prison until 1950.

The Depression was a time of important changes in the role and behavior of leading black organizations. The NAACP, for example, began to work diligently to win a position for blacks within the emerging labor movement, supporting the formation of the Congress of Industrial Organizations and helping to break down racial barriers within labor unions. Walter White, secretary of the NAACP, once even made a personal appearance at an auto plant to implore blacks not to work as strikebreakers. Partly as a result of such efforts, more than half a million blacks were able to join the labor movement. In the Steelworkers Union, for example, African Americans constituted about 20 percent of the membership.

Hispanics and Asians in Depression America

Similar patterns of discrimination confronted Mexicans and Mexican Americans. The Hispanic population of the United States had been growing steadily since early in the century, largely in California and other areas of the Southwest through massive immigration from Mexico (which was specifically excluded from the immigration restriction laws of the 1920s). In the 1930s, there were approximately 2 million Hispanics in the United States. Chicanos (as Mexican Americans are known) filled many of the same menial jobs in the West and elsewhere that blacks filled in other regions. Some farmed small, marginal tracts. Some became agricultural migrants, traveling from region to region harvesting fruit, lettuce, and other crops. But most lived in urban areas—in California, New Mexico, and Arizona, but also in Detroit, Chicago, New York, and other eastern industrial cities— and occupied the lower ranks of the unskilled labor force in such industries as steel, automobiles, and meatpacking. Even during the prosperous 1920s, theirs had been a precarious existence. The Depression made things significantly worse. As in the South, unemployed white Anglos in the Southwest demanded jobs held by Hispanics, jobs that the Anglos had previously considered beneath them. Thus Mexican unemployment rose quickly to levels far higher than those for Anglos. Some Mexicans were, in effect, forced to leave the country by officials who arbitrarily removed them from relief rolls or simply rounded them up and transported them across the border. Perhaps half a million Chicanos left the United States for Mexico in the first years of the Depression.

Those who remained faced persistent discrimination. Most relief programs excluded Mexicans from their rolls or offered them benefits far below those available to whites. Hispanics generally had no access to American schools. Many hospitals refused them admission. American blacks had established educational and social facilities of their own in response to discrimination, but Hispanics generally had fewer institutional supports. Some joined the American Communist Party. Some turned to the Mexican consulates or to the social and economic leaders of Mexican-American communities, but with little effect. Even many who possessed American citizenship found themselves treated like foreigners.

Occasionally, there were signs of organized resistance by Mexican Americans themselves, most notably in California, where some formed a union of migrant farmworkers. But harsh repression by local growers and the public authorities allied with them prevented such organizations from having much impact. Like African-American farm workers, many Hispanics began as a result to migrate to cities such as Los Angeles, where they lived in a poverty comparable to that of urban blacks in the South and Northeast.

For Asian Americans, too, the Depression reinforced longstanding patterns of discrimination and economic marginalization. In California, where the largest Japanese-American and Chinese-American populations were, even educated Asians had always found it difficult, if not impossible, to move into mainstream professions. Japanese-American college graduates often found themselves working in family fruit stands; 20 percent of all Nisei in Los Angeles worked at such stands at the end of the 1930s. For those who found jobs (usually poorly paid) in the industrial or service economy, employment was precarious; like blacks and Hispanics, they often lost jobs to white Americans desperate for work that a few years earlier they would not have considered. Japanese farmworkers, like Chicano farmworkers, suffered from the increasing competition for even these low-paying jobs from white migrants from the Great Plains.

In California, younger Nisei tried to challenge the obstacles facing them through politics. They organized Japanese American Democratic Clubs in several cities, which worked for, among other things, laws protecting racial and ethnic minorities from discrimination. At the same time, some Japanese-American businessmen and professionals tried to overcome obstacles by changing the Nisei themselves, by encouraging them to become more assimilated, more "American." They formed the Japanese American Citizens League in 1930 to promote their goals. By 1940, it had nearly 6,000 members.

Chinese Americans fared no better. The overwhelming majority continued to work in Chinese-owned laundries and restaurants. Those who moved outside the Asian community could rarely find jobs above the entry level. Chinese women, for example, might find work as stock girls in department stores, but almost never as salesclerks. Educated Chinese men and women could hope for virtually no professional opportunities outside the world of the Chinatowns.

Women and Families in the Great Depression

The economic crisis served in many ways to strengthen the widespread belief that a woman's proper place was in the home. Most men and many women believed that with employment so scarce, what work there was should go to men. There was a particularly strong belief that no woman whose husband was employed should accept a job. Indeed, from 1932 until 1937, it was illegal for more than one member of a family to hold a federal civil service job.

But the widespread assumption that married women, at least, should not work outside the home did not stop them from doing so. Both single and married women worked in the 1930s, despite public condemnation of the practice, because they or their families needed the money. In fact, the largest new group of female workers consisted of precisely those people who, according to popular attitudes, were supposed to be leaving the labor market: wives and mothers. By the end of the Depression, 25 percent more women were working than had been doing so at the beginning.

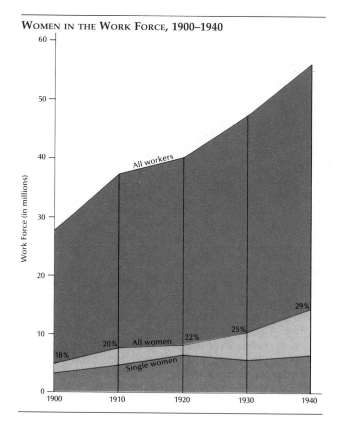

WOMEN IN THE WORK FORCE, 1900–1940

The increase occurred despite considerable obstacles. Professional opportunities for women declined because unemployed men began moving into professions such as teaching and social work that had previously been considered women's fields. Female industrial workers were more likely to be laid off or to experience wage reductions than their male counterparts. But white women also had certain advantages in the workplace. The nonprofessional jobs that women traditionally held—as salesclerks and stenographers, and in other service positions—were less likely to disappear than the predominantly male jobs in heavy industry. Nor were many men, even unemployed men, likely to ask for such jobs.

Black women, however, enjoyed few such advantages. Particularly in the South, they suffered massive unemployment because of a great reduction of domestic service jobs. As many as half of all black working women lost their jobs in the 1930s. Even so, at the end of the 1930s, 38 percent of black women were employed, as compared to 24 percent of white women. That was because black women—both married and unmarried—had always been more likely to work than white women, less out of preference than out of economic necessity.

For American feminists, the Depression years were, on the whole, a time of frustration. Although economic pressures pushed more women into the work force, those same pressures helped to erode the frail support that feminists had won in the 1920s for the idea of women becoming economically and professionally independent. In the difficult years of the 1930s, such aspirations seemed to many to be less important than dealing with economic hardship. The Depression saw the virtual extinction of the National Woman's Party, which had fought throughout the 1920s for the Equal Rights Amendment and other egalitarian goals. Even more moderate feminists, committed to "protective" legislation for women, saw their influence decline—although they did achieve some significant gains in the early years of the New Deal. (See pp. 721–722.) By the end of the 1930s, American feminism had reached its lowest ebb in nearly a century.

The economic hardships of the Depression years placed great strains on American families. Middle-class families that had become accustomed in the 1920s to a steadily rising standard of living now found themselves plunged suddenly into uncertainty, because of unemployment or the reduction of incomes among those who remained employed. Some working-class families, too, had achieved a precarious prosperity in the 1920s and saw their gains disappear in the 1930s.

Such circumstances forced many families to retreat from the consumer patterns they had developed in the 1920s. Women often returned to sewing clothes for themselves and their families and to preserving their own food rather than buying such products in stores. Others engaged in home businesses—taking in laundry, selling baked goods, accepting boarders. Many households expanded to include more distant relatives. Parents often moved in with their children and grandparents with their grandchildren, or vice versa.

But the Depression also eroded the strength of many family units. There was a decline in the divorce rate, but largely because divorce was now too expensive for some. More common was the informal breakup of families, particularly the desertion of families by unemployed men bent on escaping the humiliation of being unable to earn a living. The marriage and birth rates declined simultaneously for the first time since the early nineteenth century.

The Depression and Values

Prosperity and industrial growth had done much to shape American values in the 1920s. Mainstream culture, at least, had celebrated affluence and consumerism and had stressed the importance of personal gratification through both. Many Americans assumed, there-fore, that the experience of hard times would have profound effects on the nation's social values.

In general, however, American social values seemed to change relatively little in response to the Depression. Rather, many people responded to hard times by redoubling their commitment to familiar ideas and goals. The sociologists Robert and Helen Merrell Lynd, who had published a celebrated study of Muncie, Indiana, in 1929 (*Middletown*) returned there in the mid-1930s to see how the city had changed. They described their findings in their 1937 book, *Middletown in Transition*, and they concluded that in most respects "the texture of Middletown's culture has not changed. . . . Middletown is overwhelmingly living by the values by which it lived in 1925." Above all, the men and women of "Middletown"—and by implication many other Americans—remained committed to the traditional American emphasis on the individual.

No assumption would seem to have been more vulnerable to erosion during the Depression than the belief that the individual was in control of his or her own fate, that anyone displaying sufficient talent and industry could become a success. And in some respects, the economic crisis did work to undermine the traditional "success ethic" in America. Many people began to look to government for assistance; many blamed corporate moguls, international bankers, "economic royalists," and others for their distress. Yet the Depression did not, in the end, seriously erode the success ethic.

The survival of the ideals of work and individual advancement was evident in many ways, not least in the reactions of those most traumatized by the Depression: conscientious working people who suddenly found themselves without employment. Some expressed anger and struck out at the economic system. Many, however, seemed to blame themselves. Nothing so surprised foreign observers of America in the 1930s as the apparent passivity of the unemployed, many of whom were so ashamed of their joblessness that they refused to leave their homes. Perhaps that was why people who continued in the 1930s to work and to live more or less as they always had sometimes found it easy to forget that there was an economic crisis. The Depression was sometimes hard to see, because the unemployed tended to hide themselves, unwilling to display to the world what many of them considered their own personal failure.

At the same time, millions responded eagerly to reassurances that they could, through their own efforts, restore themselves to prosperity and success. Dale Carnegie's *How to Win Friends and Influence People* (1936), a self-help manual preaching individual initiative, was one of the best-selling books of the decade. Carnegie's message was not only that personal initiative was the route to success; it was also that the best way for people to make something of themselves was to adapt to the world in which they lived, to understand the values and expectations of others and mold themselves accordingly. The way to get ahead, Carnegie taught, was to fit in and make other people feel important. Similarly, Harry Emerson Fosdick, a Protestant theologian who preached the virtues of positive thinking and individual initiative, attracted large audiences with his radio addresses.

Not all Americans, of course, responded to the crisis of the Depression so self-reflectively. Many men and women believed that the economic problems of their time were the fault of society, not of individuals, and that some collective social response was necessary. Such beliefs found expression in, among other places, American artistic and intellectual life.

The Depression and the Arts

Just as many progressives had become alarmed when, early in the twentieth century, they "discovered" the existence of widespread poverty in the cities, so many Americans were shocked during the 1930s at their discovery of debilitating rural poverty. Perhaps most effective in conveying the dimensions of this poverty was a group of documentary photographers, many of them employed by the federal Farm Security Administration in the late 1930s, who traveled through the South recording the nature of agricultural life. Men such as Roy Stryker, Walker Evans, Arthur Rothstein, and Ben Shahn and women such as Margaret Bourke-White and Dorothea Lange produced memorable studies of farm families and their surroundings, studies designed to reveal the savage impact of a hostile environment on its victims.

Many writers, similarly, turned away from the personal concerns of the 1920s and devoted themselves to exposés of social injustice. Erskine Caldwell's *Tobacco Road* (1932), which later became a long-running play, was an exposé of poverty in the rural South. James Agee's *Let Us Now Praise Famous Men* (1941), with photographs by Walker Evans, was a careful, nonjudgmental description of the lives of three poor rural families in the South. Richard Wright, a major African American novelist, exposed the plight of residents of the urban ghetto in *Native Son* (1940). John Steinbeck's *The Grapes of Wrath* (1939) portrayed the trials of a migrant family in California, concluding with an open call for collective social action against injustice. John Dos Passos's trilogy *U.S.A.* (1930) attacked modern capitalism outright. Playwright Clifford Odets provided an explicit demonstration of the appeal of political radicalism in *Waiting for Lefty* (1935).

But the cultural products of the 1930s that attracted the widest popular audiences were those that diverted attention away from the Depression. The two most powerful instruments of popular culture in the 1930s—radio and the movies—provided mostly light and diverting entertainment. Although radio stations occasionally carried socially and politically provocative programs, the staple of broadcasting was escapism: comedies such as *Amos 'n Andy* (with its humorous but demeaning picture of urban blacks); adventures such as *Superman*, *Dick Tracy*, and *The Lone Ranger*; and other entertainment programs. Hollywood continued to exercise tight control over its products through its resilient censor Will Hays, who ensured that most movies carried only safe, conventional messages.

A few films, such as King Vidor's *Our Daily Bread* (1932) and John Ford's adaptation of *The Grapes of Wrath* (1940), did explore political themes. The director Frank Capra provided a muted social message in several of his comedies—*Mr. Deeds Goes to Town* (1936), *Mr. Smith Goes to Washington* (1939), and *Meet John Doe* (1941)—which celebrated the virtues of the small town and the decency of the common people in contrast to the selfish, corrupt values of the city and the urban rich. Gangster movies portrayed a dark, gritty, violent world with which few Americans were familiar; but their desperate stories were popular nevertheless with those engaged in their own difficult struggles. More often, however, the commercial films of the 1930s were deliberately and explicitly escapist: lavish musicals such as *Gold Diggers of 1933* (whose theme song was "We're in the Money"), "screwball" comedies such as Capra's *It Happened One Night* or the many films of the Marx Brothers—films designed to divert audiences from their troubles and, often, indulge their fantasies about quick and easy wealth.

Popular literature, similarly, offered Americans an escape from the Depression. Two of the best-selling novels of the decade were romantic sagas set in earlier eras: Margaret Mitchell's *Gone with the Wind* (1936) and Hervey Allen's *Anthony Adverse* (1933). Leading magazines, and particularly such popular new photographic journals as *Life*, focused mainly on fashions, stunts, and eye-catching scenery. Even the newsreels distributed to movie theaters across the country tended to give more attention to beauty contests and ship launchings than to the Depression itself.

The Allure of the Left

For a relatively small but important group of Americans—among them some intellectuals, artists, workers, African Americans, Mexican Americans, and others who became disenchanted for various reasons with the

THE JOAD FAMILY
John Steinbeck's 1939 novel *The Grapes of Wrath* was a notable exception to the generally escapist character of popular fiction in the 1930s. It portrayed the travails of the Joad family, who lost their farm in Oklahoma and traveled to California in search of opportunity. In 1940, director John Ford adapted the novel to film. In this still, the Joads sit around a table in their farmhouse shortly before leaving it for California. Tom Joad, played by Henry Fonda, sits to the left of the window, looking at his mother (standing), played by Jane Darwell.   *(Twentieth Century Fox)*

structure and values of the dominant culture—the Depression produced a commitment, for a time at least, to radical politics. Some became members of the American Communist Party, which achieved a size, visibility, and influence in the 1930s that it had never attained before and would never attain again. Others expressed sympathy for communist ideas without joining the party. By the standards of the rest of the world, radicalism in the United States remained relatively limited. By America's own modest standards, however, the 1930s to some degree deserved the label some commentators gave it: the "Red Decade."

For intellectuals, in particular, the left offered an escape from the lonely and difficult stance of detachment and alienation many had embraced in the 1920s. It combined a harsh critique of mainstream American society with an intense commitment to a political movement. The importance of the Spanish Civil War to many American intellectuals was a good example of

how the left helped give meaning and purpose to individual lives. The battle against the Spanish fascists of Francisco Franco (who was receiving support from Hitler and Mussolini) attracted a substantial group of young Americans—more than 3,000 in all—who formed the Abraham Lincoln brigade and traveled to Spain to join in the fight. About a third of its members died in combat; but those who survived remembered the experience with pride, as one of the great moments of their lives. Ernest Hemingway, who spent time as a correspondent in Spain during the conflict, wrote in his novel *For Whom the Bell Tolls* (1940) of how the war provided those Americans who fought in it with "a part in something which you could believe in wholly and completely and in which you felt an absolute brotherhood with others who were engaged in it."

Instrumental in creating the Lincoln brigade, and directing many of its activities, was the American Communist Party. The party's membership peaked at perhaps 100,000 during its heyday in the mid-1930s; and for a time it presented itself as a genuinely American organization, no more threatening or alien than any other political organization. For several years beginning in 1935, the party dropped its insistence on working completely apart from other organizations and began to advocate a democratic alliance of all antifascist groups in the United States, a "Popular Front." It began to praise Franklin Roosevelt and John L. Lewis, a powerful (and strongly anticommunist) labor leader, and it adopted the slogan "Communism is twentieth-century Americanism."

The party was active in organizing the unemployed in the early 1930s and staged a hunger march in Washington, D.C., in 1931. Party members were among the most effective union organizers in some industries. And the party was virtually alone among political organizations in taking a firm stand in favor of racial justice; its active defense of the Scottsboro defendants was but one example of its efforts to ally itself with the aspirations of African Americans. It also helped organize a union of black sharecroppers in Alabama, which resisted—in several instances violently—efforts of white landowners and authorities to displace them from their farms.

But despite its efforts to appear a patriotic organization, the American Communist Party was always under the close and rigid supervision of the Soviet Union. Its leaders took their orders from the Comintern in Moscow. Most members obediently followed the "party line" (although there were many areas in which Communists were active for which there was no party line, areas in which members acted independently). The subordination of the party leadership to the Soviet Union was most clearly demonstrated in 1939, when Stalin signed a nonaggression pact with Nazi Germany. Moscow then sent orders to the American Communist Party to abandon the Popular Front and return to its old stance of harsh criticism of American liberals; and the leaders in the United States immediately obeyed—although thousands of disillusioned members left the party as a result.

The Socialist Party of America, now under the leadership of Norman Thomas, also cited the economic crisis as evidence of the failure of capitalism and sought vigorously to win public support for its own political program. Among other things, it attempted to mobilize support among the rural poor. The Southern Tenant Farmers Union, supported by the party and organized by a young socialist, H. L. Mitchell, attempted to create a biracial coalition of sharecroppers, tenant farmers, and others to demand economic reform. Neither the STFU nor the party itself, however, made any real progress toward establishing socialism as a major

force in American politics. By 1936, in fact, membership in the Socialist Party had fallen below 20,000.

At few times before (and few since) in American history did being part of the left seem so respectable and even conventional among workers, intellectuals, and others. Thus the 1930s witnessed an impressive, if temporary, widening of the ideological range of mainstream politics. But antiradicalism remained a powerful force in the 1930s, just as it had been during and after World War I and would be again in the 1940s and 1950s. Hostility toward the Communist Party, in particular, was intense at many levels of government. Congressional committees chaired by Hamilton Fish of New York and Martin Dies of Texas investigated communist influence wherever they could find it (or imagine it). State and local governments harried and sometimes imprisoned communist organizers. White southerners tried to drive communist organizers out of the countryside, just as growers in California and elsewhere tried (unsuccessfully) to keep communists from organizing Mexican-American and other workers. However strong the radical sentiments of the era, antiradical sentiments were stronger.

THE ORDEAL OF HERBERT HOOVER

Herbert Hoover entered the presidency in March 1929 believing, like most Americans, that the nation faced a bright and prosperous future. For the first six months of his administration, he attempted to expand the policies he had advocated during his eight years as secretary of commerce, policies that he believed would complete a stable system of cooperative individualism and sustain a successful economy. The economic crisis that began before the year was out forced the president to deal with a new set of problems; but for most of the rest of his term, he continued to rely on the principles that had always governed his public life.

The Hoover Program

Hoover's first response to the Depression was to attempt to restore public confidence in the economy. "The fundamental business of this country, that is, production and distribution of commodities," he said in 1930, "is on a sound and prosperous basis." Subsequently, he summoned leaders of business, labor, and agriculture to the White House and urged upon them a program of voluntary cooperation for recovery. He

HERBERT HOOVER RECEIVING A LOAD OF POTATOES
The Maine Potato Growers Association sent a team of oxen to Washington with a load of Maine potatoes in 1931. They presented them as a gift to President Hoover on the White House lawn on November 23, reminding him of the difficulties that faced the agricultural economy as the Great Depression worsened. *(UPI/Bettmann)*

implored businessmen not to cut production or lay off workers; he talked labor leaders into forgoing demands for higher wages or better hours. But by mid-1931, economic conditions had deteriorated so much that this structure of voluntary cooperation collapsed. Frightened industrialists soon began cutting production, laying off workers, and slashing wages. Hoover was powerless to stop them.

Hoover also attempted to use government spending as a tool for fighting the Depression. Rejecting the demands of fiscal conservatives that the government balance its own budget whatever the cost, the president proposed to Congress an increase of $423 million —then a substantial sum—in federal public works programs, and he exhorted state and local governments to engage in the "energetic yet prudent pursuit" of public construction. But Hoover was not willing to spend enough money, or to spend it for a long enough time, to do any good; and while he was not as committed to a balanced budget as some of his advisers, he was not willing to tolerate deficits indefinitely. When economic conditions worsened, he became less willing to increase government spending, worrying instead about maintaining federal solvency. In 1932, at the depth of the Depression, he proposed a tax increase to help the government avoid a deficit.

Even before the stock market crash, Hoover had begun to construct a program to assist the troubled agri-

cultural economy. In April 1929, he proposed the Agricultural Marketing Act, which established for the first time a government bureaucracy to help farmers maintain prices. A federally sponsored Farm Board would administer a budget of $500 million, from which it could make loans to national marketing cooperatives or establish corporations to buy surpluses and thus raise prices. At the same time, Hoover attempted to protect American farmers from international competition by raising agricultural tariffs. The Hawley-Smoot Tariff of 1930 contained protective increases on seventy-five farm products and raised rates to the highest point in American history—to an average of 50 percent on protected commodities.

Neither the Agricultural Marketing Act nor the Hawley-Smoot Tariff ultimately helped American farmers significantly. The Marketing Act relied on voluntary cooperation among farmers and gave the government no authority to do what the agricultural economy most badly needed: limit production. Hoover's call for a reduction of the wheat crop, for example, resulted in a drop in acreage of only 1 percent in Kansas. The Farm Board lacked sufficient funds to deal effectively with the crisis. Prices continued to fall despite its efforts. The Hawley-Smoot Tariff was an unqualified disaster—as 1,000 members of the American Economics Association had warned the president it would be even before he signed it. It provoked foreign governments to enact trade restrictions of their own in reprisal, further diminishing the market for American agricultural goods. And it raised rates on 925 manufactured goods, making industrial products more expensive for farmers to buy.

A Deepening Crisis

By the spring of 1931, Herbert Hoover's political position had deteriorated considerably. In the 1930 congressional elections, Democrats won control of the House and made substantial gains in the Senate. Many Americans held the president personally to blame for the crisis. Shantytowns established on the outskirts of cities were labeled "Hoovervilles," and the president became the target of cruel jokes and vicious attacks. Progressive reformers urged the president to support more vigorous programs of relief and public spending. Instead, Hoover seized on a slight improvement in economic conditions early in 1931 as proof that his policies were working.

The international financial panic of the spring of 1931 destroyed the illusion that the economic crisis was coming to an end. Throughout the 1920s, European nations had depended on loans from American banks to allow them to make payments on their debts. After 1929, when they could no longer get such loans, the financial fabric of several European nations began to unravel. In May 1931, the largest bank in Austria collapsed. Over the next several months, panic gripped the financial institutions of neighboring countries. European governments, desperate for sound assets, withdrew their gold reserves from American banks. European investors, in need of dollars to pay off their loans and protect their solvency, dumped their shares of American stocks onto the market, further depressing prices. Some European nations abandoned the gold standard and devalued their currencies, leaving the United States, which remained tied to gold, at a disadvantage in international trade. The American economy rapidly declined to new lows.

Hoover argued that the economic crisis in the United States was not the result of problems in the American economy but of the collapse of the European financial system. He proposed a moratorium on payment of war debts and reparations, and later on the payment of private debts as well. It was a sound proposal, but it was not enough to stop the downward slide.

By the time Congress convened in December 1931, conditions had grown so desperate that Hoover decided to support a series of measures to keep endangered banks afloat and protect homeowners from fore-

closure on their mortgages. More important was a bill passed in January 1932 establishing the Reconstruction Finance Corporation (RFC), a government agency whose purpose was to provide federal loans to troubled banks, railroads, and other businesses. It even made funds available to local governments to support public works projects and assist relief efforts. Unlike some earlier Hoover programs, it operated on a large scale: in 1932, the RFC had a budget of $1.5 billion for public works alone.

Nevertheless, the new agency failed to deal directly or forcefully enough with the real problems of the economy to produce any significant recovery. Because the RFC was permitted to lend funds only to those financial institutions with sufficient collateral, much of its money went to large banks and corporations, prompting some critics to call it a "bread line for big business." And at Hoover's insistence, it helped finance only those public works projects that promised ultimately to pay for themselves (toll bridges, public housing, and others). Its chairman, the conservative Texas banker Jesse Jones, prided himself on the solvency of his agency and followed sound, prudent banking practices. This meant that the RFC itself remained healthy by refusing to make loans to those institutions that most desperately needed them. Above all, the RFC did not have enough money to make any real impact on the Depression; and it did not even spend all the money it had. Of the $300 million available to support local relief efforts, the RFC lent out only $30 million in 1932. Of its $1.5 billion public works budget, it released only about 20 percent.

Popular Protest

For the first several years of the Depression, most Americans were either too stunned or too confused to raise many effective protests. By the middle of 1932, however, radical and dissident voices were becoming loud and pervasive.

In the Midwest, farmers called for legislation similar to the McNary-Haugen bill of the 1920s by which the government would guarantee them a return on their crops at least equal to the cost of production. Lobbyists from the larger farm organizations pressured members of Congress to act, and some disgruntled farmers staged public protests in the capital. But neither the president nor Congress showed any signs of movement.

In the summer of 1932, a group of unhappy farm owners gathered in Des Moines, Iowa, to establish a new organization: the Farmers' Holiday Association, which endorsed the withholding of farm products

CLEARING OUT THE BONUS MARCHERS
In July 1932, President Hoover ordered the Washington, D.C., police to evict the Bonus Marchers from some of the public buildings and land they had been occupying. The result was a series of pitched battles (one of them visible here), in which both veterans and police sustained injuries. Such skirmishes persuaded Hoover to call out the army to finish the job. (*UPI/Bettmann*)

from the market—in effect a farmers' strike. The strike began in August in western Iowa, spread briefly to a few neighboring areas, and succeeded in blockading several markets; but in the end it dissolved in failure. The scope of the effort was too modest to affect farm prices, and in any case many farmers in the region refused to cooperate. After several violent clashes between strikers and local authorities, the organization's leader, Milo Reno, called off the strike. Nevertheless, the uprising created considerable consternation in state governments in the farm belt and even more in Washington, where the president and much of Congress were facing a national election.

A more celebrated protest movement emerged from a less likely quarter: American veterans. In 1924, Congress had approved the payment of a $1,000 bonus to all those who had served in World War I, the money to be distributed beginning in 1945. By 1932, however, many veterans were demanding that the bonus be paid immediately. Hoover, concerned about balancing the budget, refused to comply. In June, more than 20,000 veterans, members of the self-proclaimed "Bonus Expeditionary Force" (after the "American Expeditionary Force" of World War I, in which the veterans had served) marched into Washington, built crude camps around the city, and promised to stay until Congress approved legislation to pay the bonus. A few of the veterans departed in July, after Congress had voted down their proposal. Most, however, remained where they were.

Their continued presence in Washington was an embarrassment to Herbert Hoover. Finally, in mid-July, he ordered police to clear the marchers out of several abandoned federal buildings in which they had been staying. A few marchers threw rocks at the police, and someone opened fire; two veterans fell dead.

Hoover considered the incident evidence of dangerous radicalism, and ordered the U.S. Army to assist the police in clearing out the buildings.

General Douglas MacArthur, the army chief of staff, carried out the mission himself and greatly exceeded the president's orders. He led the Third Cavalry (under the command of George S. Patton), two infantry regiments, a machine-gun detachment, and six tanks down Pennsylvania Avenue in pursuit of the Bonus Army. By his side was his deputy, Dwight D. Eisenhower. The veterans fled in terror as the troops hurled tear gas canisters and flailed at them with their bayonets. MacArthur followed them across the Anacostia River, where he ordered the soldiers to burn their tent city to the ground. More than 100 marchers were injured. One baby died.

The incident served as perhaps the final blow to Hoover's already battered political standing. Many American newspapers (owned by conservative publishers) applauded the use of troops; but to much of the public, he now stood confirmed as an aloof and insensitive figure, locked in the White House, uncomprehending of the distress around him. Hoover's own cold and gloomy personality did nothing to change the public image, and some of his embattled statements at the time made his plight worse. "Nobody is actually starving," he assured reporters (inaccurately) in 1932. "The hoboes, for example, are better fed than they have ever been." The Great Engineer, the personification of the optimistic days of the 1920s, had become a symbol of the nation's failure to deal effectively with its startling reversal of fortune.

The Election of 1932

As the 1932 presidential election approached, few people doubted the outcome. The Republican Party dutifully renominated Herbert Hoover for a second term in office, but the lugubrious atmosphere of their convention made it clear that few delegates believed he could win. The Democrats, in the meantime, gathered jubilantly in Chicago to nominate the governor of New York, Franklin Delano Roosevelt.

Roosevelt had already been a well-known figure in the party for many years. A Hudson Valley aristocrat, a distant cousin of Theodore Roosevelt (a connection strengthened by his marriage in 1904 to the then-president's niece, Eleanor), and a handsome, charming young man, he had progressed rapidly: from a seat in the New York state legislature, to a position as assistant secretary of the navy under Woodrow Wilson during World War I, to his party's vice presidential nomination in 1920 on the ill-fated ticket with James M.

The Changing of the Guard
Long before the event actually occurred, Peter Arno of the *New Yorker* magazine drew this image of Franklin D. Roosevelt and Herbert Hoover traveling together to the Capitol for Roosevelt's inauguration. It predicted with remarkable accuracy the mood of the uncomfortable ride—Hoover glum and uncommunicative, Roosevelt buoyant and smiling. This was to have been the magazine's cover for the week of the inauguration, but after an attempted assassination of the president-elect several weeks earlier in Florida (in which the mayor of Chicago was killed), the editors decided to substitute a more subdued drawing. *(©1933, 1961 Peter Arno/Franklin D. Roosevelt Library)*

Cox. Less than a year later, he was stricken with polio. And while he was never again able to walk without the use of crutches and braces, he built up sufficient physical strength to return to politics in 1928. When Al Smith received the Democratic nomination for president that year, Roosevelt was elected to succeed him as governor. In 1930, he easily won reelection.

SIGNIFICANT EVENTS

1929 Stock market crash signals onset of Great Depression

Agricultural Marketing Act passed

1930 Hawley-Smoot Tariff enacted

Ten-year drought begins in South and Midwest (the Dust Bowl)

White workers in Atlanta organize Black Shirts to fight African-American competition for jobs

Nisei form Japanese-American Citizens' League

John Dos Passos publishes *U.S.A.* trilogy

1931 Federal Reserve raises interest rates

Depression spreads to Europe and deepens in United States

Scottsboro defendants arrested

Communist Party stages hunger march in Washington

1932 Erskine Caldwell publishes *Tobacco Road*

Glass-Steagall Banking Act passed

Reconstruction Finance Corporation established

Farm Holiday Association formed in Iowa

Bonus Marchers come to Washington, D.C.

Banking crisis

Franklin D. Roosevelt elected president

1934 Southern Tenant Farmers Union organized

1935 American Communist Party proclaims Popular Front

Race riot in Harlem

1936 Dale Carnegie publishes *How to Win Friends and Influence People*

Margaret Mitchell publishes *Gone with the Wind*

1939 John Steinbeck publishes *The Grapes of Wrath*

Nazi-Soviet pact weakens American Communist Party

1940 Richard Wright publishes *Native Son*

Ernest Hemingway publishes *For Whom the Bell Tolls*

1941 James Agee and Walker Evans publish *Let Us Now Praise Famous Men*

Roosevelt worked no miracles in New York, but he did initiate enough positive programs of government assistance to be able to present himself as a more energetic and imaginative leader than Hoover. Equally important, he avoided the inflammatory cultural issues (religion, race, prohibition) that had so divided the party in the 1920s. By emphasizing the economic grievances that most Democrats shared, he assembled a coalition within the party that enabled him to win his party's nomination. In a dramatic break with tradition, he flew to Chicago to address the convention in person and accept the nomination.

In the course of his acceptance speech, Roosevelt roused the delegates with his ringing promise: "I pledge you, I pledge myself, to a new deal for the American people," giving his program a name that would long endure. Neither then nor in the subsequent campaign, however, did Roosevelt give much indica-

tion of what that program would be. But Herbert Hoover's unpopularity virtually ensured Roosevelt's election; his main concern was to avoid offending voters unnecessarily.

There was, however, evidence of important differences between Roosevelt and Hoover. Drawing from the ideas of a talented team of university professors (whom the press quickly dubbed the "Brains Trust"), Roosevelt espoused an amalgam of ideas that combined old progressive reform principles with some of the newer ideas of associationalism that had gained currency in the 1920s. (He also called for a balanced budget and attacked Hoover for his failure to provide one.) Hoover liked to insist that the Depression was international in origin and that any attempt to combat it must be international as well. Roosevelt, in contrast, portrayed the crisis as a domestic (and Republican) problem and argued that the most important solutions

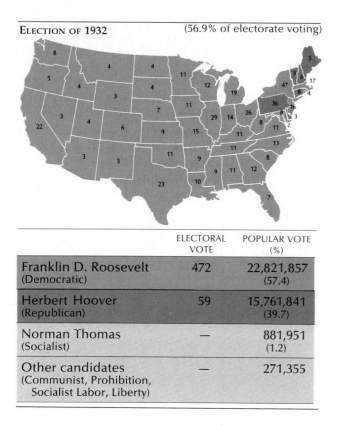

ELECTION OF 1932 — (56.9% of electorate voting)

	ELECTORAL VOTE	POPULAR VOTE (%)
Franklin D. Roosevelt (Democratic)	472	22,821,857 (57.4)
Herbert Hoover (Republican)	59	15,761,841 (39.7)
Norman Thomas (Socialist)	—	881,951 (1.2)
Other candidates (Communist, Prohibition, Socialist Labor, Liberty)	—	271,355

could be found at home. Above all, perhaps, Roosevelt's style—his dazzling smile, his floppy broad-brimmed hat, his cigarette holder poised at a jaunty angle between his teeth, his skillful oratory, his lively wit—all combined to win him a wide personal popularity only vaguely related to the specifics of his programs.

In November, to the surprise of no one, Roosevelt won by a landslide. He received 57.4 percent of the popular vote to Hoover's 39.7. In the electoral college, the result was even more overwhelming. Hoover carried Pennsylvania, Connecticut, Vermont, New Hampshire, and Maine. Roosevelt won everything else. Democrats won majorities in both houses of Congress.

It was a broad and convincing mandate, but it was not yet clear what Roosevelt intended to do with it.

The Interregnum

The period between the election and the inauguration (which until the passage of the Twentieth Amendment to the Constitution in 1933 lasted more than four months) was a season of growing economic crisis. Presidents-elect traditionally do not involve themselves directly in government. But in a series of brittle exchanges with Roosevelt in the months following the election, Hoover tried to exact from the president-elect a pledge to maintain policies of economic orthodoxy. Roosevelt genially refused.

In February, only a month before the inauguration, a new crisis developed when the American banking system began to collapse. Public confidence in the banks was ebbing; depositors were withdrawing their money in panic; and one bank after another was closing its doors and declaring bankruptcy. In mid-February, the governor of Michigan, one of the states hardest hit by the panic, ordered all banks temporarily closed. Other states soon followed, and by the end of the month banking activity was restricted drastically in every state but one. Hoover again asked Roosevelt to give prompt public assurances that there would be no tinkering with the currency, no heavy borrowing, no unbalancing of the budget. "I realize," he wrote a Republican senator at the time, "that if these declarations be made by the president-elect, he will have ratified the whole major program of the Republican Administration." Roosevelt realized the same thing and again refused.

March 4, 1933, was, therefore, a day of both economic crisis and considerable personal bitterness. On that morning, Herbert Hoover, convinced that the United States was headed for disaster, rode glumly down Pennsylvania Avenue with a beaming, buoyant Franklin Roosevelt, who would shortly be sworn in as the thirty-second president of the United States.

SUGGESTED READINGS

The Coming of the Depression. Michael Bernstein, *The Great Depression: Delayed Recovery and Economic Change in America, 1929–1939* (1987). Lester V. Chandler, *America's Greatest Depression* (1970). Milton Friedman and Anna Schwartz, *The Great Contraction* (1965); or Chapter 7 of *A Monetary History of the United States* (1963). John Kenneth Galbraith, *The Great Crash* (1954). Susan E. Kennedy, *The Banking Crisis of 1933* (1973). Charles Kindelberger, *The World in Depression* (1973). Broadus Mitchell, *Depression Decade* (1947). Robert Sobel, *The Great Bull Market* (1968). Peter Temin, *Did Monetary Forces Cause the Great Depression?* (1976).

The Impact of the Depression. Francisco Balerman, *In Defense of La Raza: The Los Angeles Mexican Consulate and the Mexican Community, 1929–1936* (1982). Ann Banks, ed., *First-Person America* (1980). Irving Bernstein, *The Lean Years* (1960). Caroline Bird, *The Invisible Scar* (1966). Glen H. Elder, Jr., *Children of the Great Depression* (1974). Federal Writers' Project, *These Are Our Lives* (1939). James N. Gregory, *American Exodus: The Dust Bowl Migration and Okie Culture in California* (1989). Abraham Hoffman, *Unwanted Mexican-Americans in the Great Depression* (1974). Richard Lowitt and Maurine Beasley, eds., *One-Third of a Nation: Lorena Hickock Reports the Great Depression* (1981). Robert S. McElvaine, ed., *Down and Out in the Great Depression: Letters from the Forgotten Man* (1983). William Mullins, *The Depression and the Urban West Coast, 1929–1933* (1991). Janet Poppendieck, *Breadlines Knee-Deep in Wheat: Food Assistance in the Great Depression* (1986). Arthur M. Schlesinger, Jr., *The Crisis of the Old Order* (1957). Walter Stein, *California and the Dust Bowl Migration* (1973). Bernard Sternsher, *Hitting Home: The Great Depression in Town and Country* (1970). Studs Terkel, *Hard Times* (1970). Tom Terrill and Jerrold Hirsch, *Such as Us: Southern Voices of the Thirties* (1978). Donald Worster, *Dust Bowl: The Southern Plains in the 1930s* (1979).

Depression-Era Culture and Society. Charles C. Alexander, *Nationalism in American Thought, 1930–1945* (1969). Frederick Lewis Allen, *Since Yesterday* (1940). Andrew Bergman, *We're in the Money: Depression America and Its Films* (1971). Anthony Heilbut, *Exiled in Paradise: German Refugee Artists and Intellectuals in America from the 1930s to the Present* (1938). Richard Krickus, *Pursuing the American Dream* (1976). Robert Lynd and Helen Merrell Lynd, *Middletown in Transition* (1935). Alice Goldfarb Marquis, *Hopes and Ashes: The Birth of Modern Times, 1929–1939* (1986). Jeffrey Meikle, *Twentieth Century Limited: Industrial Design in America, 1925–1939* (1979). Gilbert Osofsky, *Harlem: The Making of a Ghetto* (1966). Gilman Ostrander, *American Civilization in the First Machine Age* (1970). David P. Peeler, *Hope Among Us Yet: Social Criticism and Social Thought in the Depression Years* (1987). Richard Pells, *Radical Visions and American Dreams: Culture and Social Thought in the Depression Years* (1973). Thomas Schatz, *The Genius of the System: Hollywood Film Making in the Studio Era* (1988). Ed Sikov, *Screwball: Hollywood's Madcap Romantic Comedies* (1989). Warren Susman, *Culture as History* (1984). (See Suggested Readings at the end of Chapter 26 for more literature on African Americans, Hispanic Americans, Asian Americans, Indians, and labor during the Depression.)

Women and the Depression. Julia K. Blackwelder, *Women of the Depression: Caste and Culture in San Antonio, 1919–1939* (1984). William Chafe, *The American Woman* (1972). Joan Jensen and Lois Scharf, eds., *Decades of Discontent: The Women's Movement, 1920–1940* (1983). Marjorie Rosen, *Popcorn Venus: Women, Movies, and the American Dream* (1971). Vicki Ruiz, *Cannery Women, Cannery Lives: Mexican Women, Unionization, and the California Food Processing Industry, 1930–1950* (1987). Lois Scharf, *To Work and to Wed: Female Employment, Feminism, and the Great Depression* (1980). Susan Ware, *Holding Their Own: American Women in the 1930s* (1982). Jeane Westin, *Making Do: How Women Survived the '30s* (1976). Patricia Zavella, *Women's Work and Chicano Families* (1987).

The Hoover Presidency. William J. Barber, *From New Era to New Deal: Herbert Hoover, The Economists, and American Economic Policy, 1921–1933* (1985). David Burner, *Herbert Hoover* (1978). Martin Fausold, *The Presidency of Herbert C. Hoover* (1985). Martin Fausold and George Mazuzun, eds., *The Hoover Presidency* (1974). Herbert Hoover, *The Great Depression* (1952). James S. Olsen, *Herbert Hoover and the Reconstruction Finance Corporation* (1977); *Saving Capitalism: The Reconstruction Finance Corporation and the New Deal, 1933–1940* (1988). Albert U. Romasco, *The Poverty of Abundance* (1965). Jordan Schwarz, *The Interregnum of Despair* (1970). Harris Warren, *Herbert Hoover and the Great Depression* (1959). Joan Hoff Wilson, *Herbert Hoover: Forgotten Progressive* (1975).

Politics and Protest. David Burner, *The Politics of Provincialism* (1967). Roger Daniels, *The Bonus March* (1971). Frank Freidel, *The Triumph* (1956); *Launching the New Deal* (1973). Donald Grubbs, *Cry from the Cotton* (1971). Dorothy Healey and Maurice Isserman, *Dorothy Healey Remembers: A Life in the American Communist Party* (1990). Irving Howe and Lewis Coser, *The American Communist Party: A Critical History* (1957). Robin D. G. Kelley, *Hammer and Hoe: Alabama Communists During the Great Depression* (1990). Thomas Kessner, *Fiorello H. La Guardia and the Making of Modern New York* (1989). Harvey Klehr, *The Heyday of American Communism: The Depression Decade* (1984). Donald Lisio, *The President and Protest: Hoover, Conspiracy, and the Bonus Riot* (1974). Mark Naison, *Communistis in Harlem During the Depression* (1983). Eliot Rosen, *Hoover, Roosevelt, and the Brains Trust* (1977). Arthur M. Schlesinger, Jr., *The Crisis of the Old Order* (1957). John Shover, *Cornbelt Rebellion* (1965). Rexford G. Tugwell, *The Brains Trust* (1968).

THE AMERICAN ENVIRONMENT

DUST BOWL

T HE DUST BOWL OF the 1930s was one of the great environmental disasters of American history. Although historians have often attributed it solely to an especially severe natural drought, it was in fact a much more complicated event that had as much to do with people as with nature.

The origins of the Dust Bowl stretched back more than half a century. As American settlers moved out onto the western plains after the Civil War, they encountered a more arid climate than any they had known in the East. Farming techniques that had been successful elsewhere failed as rain became scarcer. The biggest problem with the plains was the unreliability of rainfall from year to year: years of above-average rainfall alternated at unpredictable intervals with years of drought. The prosperity farmers enjoyed during good years encouraged them to hang on even if they might face economic ruin when the rains failed.

To deal with the problems of too little rain, farmers experimented with new ways of farming. By plowing the soil deeply, stirring up a fine layer of dust on the surface, and leaving fields bare to gather moisture when not being cropped, they sought to conserve water as best they could. At the same time, they grew less corn and introduced winter wheats from central Europe that were especially well adapted to dry conditions. These techniques worked well enough to encourage farmers to expand into new areas.

DUST STORM, SOUTHWEST PLAINS, 1937
The dust storms of the 1930s were a terrifying experience for all who lived through them. Appearing as a black wall sweeping in from the western horizon, such a storm engulfed farms and towns alike, blotting out the light of the sun and covering everything with fine dirt. *(UPI/Bettmann)*

THE AMERICAN ENVIRONMENT

The great period of expansion for plains farmers came during World War I. European demand and government subsidies sent the price of wheat soaring past $2 per bushel, and other grains rose as well. Farmers responded by planting as never before. By 1919, Colorado, Nebraska, Kansas, Oklahoma, and Texas had expanded their wheat acreage by 13.5 million acres—11 million of which had been covered with native grasses. To handle this vast new cropland, farmers invested in new mechanical equipment: disk plows, combines , and tractors. Tractors quickly replaced horses as the universal power source on Great Plains farms, and their total numbers grew accordingly. In 1915, there had been approximately 3,000 tractors in all of Kansas. Five years later, there were over 17,000, and by 1930 the number had risen to more than 66,000. More and more of the basic work of the farm was performed by internal combustion engines burning gasoline.

The new machinery enabled farm families to produce more grain per capita than ever before, but also exposed them to new risks. Equipment was expensive: a typical tractor in the 1920s cost several hundred dollars, and a typical combine two or three thousand. Most farmers financed such purchases with loans. They also planted larger acreages to take advantage of the new equipment, and incurred additional debts for their new land. Paying off debts was no problem during good years, but could become a nightmare if economic or climatic conditions became unfavorable. Unfortunately, both went bad at once during the 1920s.

By 1930, the world wheat market was in deep trouble, and farmers had no choice but to plant as many acres as possible in a desperate effort to earn enough to pay their debts. At the same time, rain failed up and down the plains. Starting in 1931, areas in the southern plains that ordinarily received eighteen inches of rain each year—the bare minimum for many types of farming—had annual deficits of three to seven inches. Crops died. The parched soil baked and cracked in the sun as thermometers rose above 100 degrees each day for weeks on end. Even many native grasses eventually succumbed. The region was entering its worst drought in recorded history, and it would be a decade before rainfall became abundant once again.

The drought of the 1930s was unprecedented not just in its severity, but also in its human costs. Never before had so many farmers carried so high a burden of debt. The collapse of crop prices meant that thousands of acres, now uncultivated, stood naked in the sun. The native grasses of the plains had once formed a tight natural sod that could withstand a drought even if many individual plants died. Now the sod was gone and nothing remained to protect soil from the wind.

Dust storms had been part of life on the plains for centuries, especially in western Kansas, Oklahoma, and the Texas panhandle, where the soil was sandy and especially susceptible to blowing. Now, however, they fueled themselves in a vicious cycle of ecological and economic disaster. A single famous storm in May 1934 carried 300 million tons of Great Plains soil all the way to the Atlantic Ocean, dropping dust in New York and Washington and even on ships 300 miles at sea. On the southern plains, such storms became a regular occurrence for the better part of the 1930s. They darkened the sky at midday, seeped dust into houses, blew drifts along fencerows, even killed animals and people who were unlucky enough to be caught in their midst. "Three little words," wrote a reporter for the Associated Press in 1935, "achingly familiar on a Western farmer's tongue—rule life today in the dust bowl of the continent. . . . If it rains." And so the southern plains gained a new name: Dust Bowl.

THE AMERICAN ENVIRONMENT

CONTOUR PLOWING
Farmers responded to the dust storms by adopting new cultivation practices designed to prevent soil from blowing away in the wind. Among the most important techniques was contour plowing, which raised furrows in the soil to break the wind's velocity as it moved across the surface. Contour plowing also discouraged water erosion. *(Bettmann)*

There were 22 dust storms in 1934, 40 in 1935, 68 in 1936, 72 in 1937, 61 in 1938, 30 in 1939, and 17 each in 1940 and 1941. Unplanted soil made conditions perfect for dust storms when the drought finally hit, and the combined force of economic depression and too little rain left farmers with few defenses once the cycle got going. Many families eventually abandoned their farms and took to the road, becoming the "Okies" who migrated to California in search of a better life. A number of New Deal agencies stepped in to try to help with a variety of programs. The Resettlement Administration sought to buy up farms on soils that were too marginal for safe agricultural production. The Forest Service planted over 200 million trees as "shelter belts" designed to slow the dusty winds. And the Soil Conservation Service promoted new forms of tillage that held the soil better.

All these things helped, but it was not until 1941, when the rains returned in earnest and World War II began to generate massive new demand for crops, that the Dust Bowl came to an end. New farming techniques, including irrigation systems that tapped underground water supplies, have prevented the return of dust storms on anything like the scale of the 1930s, though lesser storms have from time to time blown through the region. Whether they return in the future depends on whether farmers remember the lessons of the Dust Bowl and adapt their methods to the special needs of their land.

WPA POSTER, 1930s

The Works Progress Administration, which this striking poster celebrates, was the New Deal's most prominent experiment in work relief. In addition to providing jobs for unemployed farmers and industrial workers (as depicted here), it created programs to assist writers, artists, actors, and others. *(Library of Congress)*

CHAPTER TWENTY-SIX

THE NEW DEAL

RANKLIN ROOSEVELT SERVED LONGER as president than anyone else before or since, and during his twelve years in office he became more central to the life of the nation than any chief executive before him. Most important, his administration constructed a series of programs that permanently altered the federal government and its relationship to society.

By the end of the 1930s, the New Deal (as the Roosevelt program was called) had created many of the broad outlines of the political world we know today. It had constructed the foundations of the federal welfare system. It had extended national regulation over new areas of the economy. It had presided over the birth of the modern labor movement. It had made the government a major force in the agricultural economy. It had created a powerful coalition within the Democratic Party that would dominate American politics for most of the next thirty years. And it had produced the beginnings of a new liberal ideology that would govern reform efforts for several decades after the war.

One thing the New Deal had not done, however, was end the Great Depression. It had helped stop the disastrous downward spiral in 1933, and there had been a limited, if erratic, recovery in some areas after that. But by the end of 1939, many of the basic problems of the Depression remained unsolved. An estimated 15 percent of the work force remained unemployed. The gross national product was no larger than it had been ten years before.

LAUNCHING THE NEW DEAL

Roosevelt's first task upon taking office was to alleviate the panic that was threatening to create chaos in the financial system. He did so in part by force of personality and in part by constructing very rapidly an ambitious and diverse program of legislation.

Restoring Confidence

Much of Roosevelt's success was a result of his ebullient personality. Beginning with his inaugural address—in which he assured the American people that "the only thing we have to fear is fear itself"—he projected an infectious optimism that helped alleviate the growing despair. He was the first president to make regular use of the radio, and his friendly "fireside chats," during which he explained his programs and plans to the people, helped build public confidence in the administration. Roosevelt held frequent informal press conferences and won the respect and the friendship of most reporters. Their regard for him was such that by unwritten agreement, no journalist ever photographed the president getting into or out of his car or being wheeled in his wheelchair. Much of the American public remained unaware throughout the Roosevelt years that the president's legs were completely paralyzed.

THE RADIO PRESIDENT
Franklin D. Roosevelt was the first American president to master the use of radio. Beginning in his first days in office, he regularly bypassed the newspapers (many of which were hostile to him) and communicated directly with the people through his famous "Fireside Chats." He is shown here speaking in 1938, urging communities to continue to provide relief work for the unemployed. *(Franklin D. Roosevelt Library)*

But Roosevelt could not rely on image alone. On March 6, two days after taking office, he issued a proclamation closing all American banks for four days until Congress could meet in special session to consider banking-reform legislation. So great was the panic about bank failures that the "bank holiday," as the president euphemistically described it, created a general sense of relief. Three days later, Roosevelt sent to Congress the Emergency Banking Act, a generally conservative bill (much of it drafted by holdovers from the Hoover administration) designed primarily to protect the larger banks from being dragged down by the weakness of smaller ones. The bill provided for Treasury Department inspection of all banks before they would be allowed to reopen, for federal assistance to some troubled institutions, and for a thorough reorganization of those in the greatest difficulty. A confused and frightened Congress passed the bill within four hours of its introduction. "I can assure you," Roosevelt told the public on March 12, in his first fireside chat, "that it is safer to keep your money in a reopened bank than under the mattress." Whatever else the new law accomplished, it helped dispel the panic. Three quarters of the banks in the Federal Reserve system reopened within the next three days, and $1 billion in hoarded currency and gold flowed back into them within a month. The immediate banking crisis was over.

On the morning after passage of the Emergency Banking Act, Roosevelt sent to Congress another measure—the Economy Act—designed to convince fiscally conservative Americans (and especially the business community) that the federal government was in safe, responsible hands. The act proposed to balance the federal budget by cutting the salaries of government employees and reducing pensions to veterans by as much as 15 percent. Otherwise, the president warned, the nation faced a $1 billion deficit. Like the banking bill, this one passed through Congress almost instantly—despite heated protests from some congressional progressives.

Roosevelt also moved in his first days in office to put to rest one of the divisive issues of the 1920s. He supported and then signed a bill to legalize the manufacture and sale of beer with a 3.2 percent alcohol content—an interim measure pending the repeal of prohibition, for which a constitutional amendment (the Twenty-first) was already in process. The amendment was ratified later in 1933.

Agricultural Adjustment

These initial actions were largely stopgaps, to buy time for more comprehensive measures. The first such program was the Agricultural Adjustment Act, which Congress passed in May 1933. It reflected the demands of various farm organizations and the ideas of Henry A. Wallace, Roosevelt's secretary of agriculture, and it included scraps and reworkings of many long-cherished agricultural schemes (including McNary-Haugen). But its most important feature was its provision for reducing crop production to end agricultural surpluses and halt the downward spiral of farm prices.

Under the "domestic allotment" system of the act, producers of seven basic commodities (wheat, cotton, corn, hogs, rice, tobacco, and dairy products) would decide on production limits for their crops. The government, through the Agricultural Adjustment Administration (AAA), would then tell individual farmers how much they should plant and pay them subsidies for leaving some of their land idle. A tax on food processing (for example, the milling of wheat) would provide the funds for the new payments. Farm prices were to be subsidized up to the point of parity.

Because the 1933 agricultural season was already under way by the time the AAA began operations, the agency oversaw a large-scale destruction of existing crops and livestock to reduce surpluses. Six million pigs and 220,000 sows were slaughtered. Cotton farmers plowed under a quarter of their crop. In a society plagued by want, in which many families were suffering from malnutrition and starvation, it was difficult for the government to explain the need for destroying surpluses, and the crop and livestock destruction remained controversial for many years. Beginning in 1934, however, the government used less provocative methods for limiting crop and livestock production.

The results of the AAA efforts were in many ways heartening. Prices for farm commodities did indeed rise in the years after 1933, and gross farm income increased by half in the first three years of the New Deal. The agricultural economy as a whole emerged from the 1930s stabler and more prosperous than it had been in many years. The AAA did, however, tend to favor larger farmers over smaller ones, particularly since local administration of its programs often fell into the hands of the most powerful producers in a community. New Deal farm programs actually dispossessed some struggling farmers, even if unintentionally. In the cotton belt, for example, planters who were reducing their acreage evicted tenants and sharecroppers and fired many field hands.

In January 1936, the Supreme Court struck down the crucial provisions of the Agricultural Adjustment Act, arguing that the government had no constitutional authority to require farmers to limit production. But within a few weeks the administration had secured passage of new legislation (the Soil Conservation and Domestic Allotment Act), which survived judicial scrutiny. It permitted the government to pay farmers to reduce production so as to "conserve soil," prevent erosion, and accomplish other secondary goals. It also attempted to correct one of the injustices of the original act: its failure to protect sharecroppers and tenant farmers. Now landlords were required to share the payments they received for cutting back production with those who worked their land. The new requirements were, however, largely evaded.

The administration launched other efforts to assist poor farmers as well. The Resettlement Administration, established in 1935, and its successor, the Farm Security Administration, created in 1937, provided loans to help farmers cultivating submarginal soil to relocate on better lands. But the programs never moved more than a few thousand farmers. More effective was the Rural Electrification Administration, created in 1935, which worked to make electric power available for the first time to thousands of farmers through utility cooperatives.

Industrial Recovery

The challenge of rescuing the industrial economy from the spiraling deflation of the early 1930s was even more important to the administration. Ever since 1931, leaders of the U.S. Chamber of Commerce and many others had been urging the government to adopt an anti-deflation scheme that would permit trade associations to cooperate in stabilizing prices within their industries. Existing antitrust laws clearly forbade such practices, but businesspeople argued that the economic emergency justified a suspension of the restrictions. Herbert Hoover had refused to endorse suspension of the antitrust laws. But the Roosevelt administration was more receptive.

SALUTING THE BLUE EAGLE
Eight thousand San Francisco schoolchildren assembled on a baseball field in 1933 to form the symbol of the National Recovery Administration: an eagle clutching a cogwheel (to symbolize industry) and a thunderbolt (to symbolize energy). They are evidence of the widespread (if brief) popular enthusiasm the NRA produced. NRA administrators drew from their memories of World War I Liberty Loan drives and tried to establish the Blue Eagle as a symbol of patriotic commitment to recovery. (*UPI/Bettmann*)

In exchange for relaxing antitrust provisions, however, New Dealers insisted on additional provisions that would deal with other economic problems. Businesspeople would have to make important concessions to labor—recognize their right to organize and bargain collectively through unions—to ensure that the incomes of workers would rise along with prices. And to ensure that consumer buying power would not lag behind, the administration added a major program of public works spending designed to pump needed funds into the economy. The result of these and many other impulses was the National Industrial Recovery Act, one of the most complicated pieces of legislation in American history to that point. Congress passed it in June 1933. Roosevelt, signing the bill, called it "the most important and far-reaching legislation ever en-

acted by the American Congress." Businesspeople hailed it as the beginning of a new era of cooperation between government and industry. Labor leaders praised it as a "Magna Carta" for trade unions.

At first the new program appeared to work miracles. At its center was a new federal agency, the National Recovery Administration (NRA). Its director was the flamboyant and energetic Hugh S. Johnson, a retired general and successful businessman. Johnson envisioned himself as a kind of evangelist, whose major mission was to generate public enthusiasm and corporate support for the NRA. He approached his task in two ways.

First, he called on every business establishment in the nation to accept a temporary "blanket code": a minimum wage of between 30 and 40 cents an hour, a max-

WPA WORKERS ON THE JOB
The Works Progress Administration funded an enormous variety of work projects to provide jobs for the unemployed. But most WPA employees worked on construction sites of one kind or another. Here, WPA workers labor on a bridge project in the Bronx, in New York City. *(UPI/Bettmann)*

imum workweek of 35 to 40 hours, and the abolition of child labor. The result, he claimed, would be to raise consumer purchasing power, increase employment, and eliminate the sweatshop. To generate enthusiasm for the blanket code, Johnson devised a symbol—the famous NRA Blue Eagle—which employers who accepted the provisions could display in their windows. Soon Blue Eagle flags, posters, and stickers, carrying the NRA slogan "We Do Our Part," were decorating commercial establishments in every part of the country—just as parents of soldiers or purchasers of war bonds had decorated their homes and offices with patriotic reminders during World War I.

At the same time, Johnson was busy negotiating another, more specific set of codes with leaders of the nation's major industries. These industrial codes set floors below which no company would lower prices or wages in its search for a competitive advantage, and they included agreements on maintaining employment and production. He quickly won agreements from almost every major industry in the country.

From the beginning, however, the NRA encountered serious difficulties, and the entire effort ultimately dissolved in failure. The codes themselves were hastily and often poorly written. Administering them was far beyond the capacities of federal officials with no prior experience in running so vast a program. Large producers consistently dominated the code-writing process and ensured that the new regulations would work to their advantage and to the disadvantage of smaller firms. And the codes at times did more than simply set floors under prices; they actively and artificially raised them—at times to levels higher than was necessary to ensure a profit and far higher than market forces would have dictated.

Attempts to increase consumer purchasing power did not progress as quickly as the efforts to raise prices. Section 7(a) of the National Industrial Recovery Act promised workers the right to form unions and engage in collective bargaining and encouraged many workers to join unions for the first time. But Section 7(a) contained no enforcement mechanisms. Hence recognition of unions by employers (and thus the significant wage increases the unions were committed to winning) did not follow. The Public Works Administration (PWA), established by the bill to administer spending programs and directed by Secretary of the Interior Harold Ickes, only gradually allowed the $3.3 billion in public works funds to trickle out. Not until 1938 was the PWA budget pumping an appreciable amount of money into the economy.

Perhaps the clearest evidence of the NRA's failure was that industrial production actually declined in the months after its establishment—from an index of 101

in July 1933 to 71 in November—despite (some argued because of) the rise in prices that the codes had helped to create. By the spring of 1934, therefore, the NRA was besieged by criticism. Businessmen were flouting its provisions, cutting wages and prices or violating agreements on levels of production—claiming as they did so that the wage requirements of the codes (which many of them were ignoring anyway) were making it impossible to earn adequate profits. Employers were also openly ignoring the provisions requiring them to bargain with unions, and so organized labor grew increasingly hostile toward the NRA. Economists were charging that the price fixing permitted by the codes was undermining efforts to raise purchasing power. Reformers were complaining that the NRA was encouraging economic concentration and monopoly. A national Recovery Review Board, chaired by the famous criminal lawyer Clarence Darrow, reported in the spring of 1934 that the NRA was excessively dominated by big business and unduly encouraging monopoly; and Hugh Johnson's angry, vituperative response served only to undermine the agency's prestige even further. That fall, Roosevelt pressured Johnson to resign and established a new board of directors to oversee the NRA. Then in 1935, the Supreme Court intervened.

The constitutional basis for the NRA had been Congress's power to regulate commerce among the states, a power the administration had interpreted very broadly but that the Court continued to interpret narrowly. The case before the Court involved alleged NRA code violations by the Schechter brothers, who operated a wholesale poultry business confined to Brooklyn, New York. The Court ruled unanimously that the Schechters were not engaged in interstate commerce and, further, that Congress had unconstitutionally delegated legislative power to the president to draft the NRA codes. It nullified the legislation establishing the agency.

Roosevelt denounced the justices for their "horse-and-buggy" interpretation of the interstate commerce clause. He was rightly concerned, for the reasoning in the *Schechter* case threatened many other New Deal programs as well. But the destruction of the NRA itself may have been a blessing for the New Deal, providing it with a face-saving way to abolish the failed experiment.

Regional Planning

The AAA and the NRA reflected the beliefs of New Dealers who favored economic planning but wanted private interests (farmers or business leaders) to dom-

THE TENNESSEE VALLEY AUTHORITY

inate the planning process. In some areas, however, other reformers—those who believed that the government itself should be the chief planning agent in the economy—managed to establish dominance. Their most conspicuous success, and one of the most celebrated accomplishments of the New Deal, was an unprecedented experiment in regional planning: the Tennessee Valley Authority (TVA).

The TVA had its roots in a political controversy of the 1920s. Progressive reformers had agitated for years for public development of the nation's water resources as a source of cheap electric power. In particular, they had urged completion of a great dam at Muscle Shoals on the Tennessee River in Alabama—a dam begun during World War I but left unfinished when the war ended. Opposition from utilities companies, however, had been too powerful to overcome.

But in 1932, one of the great utility empires—that of the electricity magnate Samuel Insull—had collapsed spectacularly, amid widely publicized exposés of corruption. Hostility to the utilities soon grew so intense that the companies were no longer able to block

the public-power movement. The result was legislation supported by the president and enacted by Congress in May 1933 creating the Tennessee Valley Authority. The TVA was intended not only to complete the dam at Muscle Shoals and build others in the region, and not only to generate and sell electricity from them to the public at reasonable rates. It was also to be the agent for a comprehensive redevelopment of the entire region: for stopping the disastrous flooding that had plagued the Tennessee Valley for centuries, for encouraging the development of local industries, for supervising a substantial program of reforestation, and for helping farmers improve productivity.

Opposition by conservatives within the administration ultimately blocked some of the most ambitious social planning projects proposed by the more visionary TVA administrators, but the project revitalized the region in numerous ways. It built dams and waterways. It virtually eliminated flooding in the region. It provided electricity to thousands who had never before had it. Throughout the country, largely because of the "yardstick" provided by the TVA's cheap production of electricity, private power rates declined. Still, the Authority worked no miracles. The Tennessee Valley remained a generally impoverished region despite its efforts. And like many other New Deal programs, it made no serious effort to challenge local customs and racial prejudices.

Financial Reforms

Roosevelt was not an inflationist at heart, but he soon came to consider the gold standard a major obstacle to the restoration of adequate prices. On April 18, 1933, the president made the shift off the gold standard official with an executive order. A few weeks later, Congress passed legislation confirming his decision. By itself, the repudiation of the gold standard meant relatively little. But both before and after the April decision, the administration experimented in various ways with manipulating the value of the dollar—by making substantial purchases of gold and silver and later by establishing a new, fixed standard for the dollar (reducing its gold content substantially from the 1932 amount). The resort to government-managed currency—that is, to a dollar whose value could be raised or lowered by government policy according to economic circumstances—created an important precedent for future federal policies and permanently altered the relationship between the public and private sectors. It did not, however, have any immediate impact on the depressed American economy.

Through other legislation, the early New Deal increased federal authority over previously unregulated or weakly regulated areas of the economy. The Glass-Steagall Act of June 1933 gave the government authority to curb irresponsible speculation by banks. More important, perhaps, it established the Federal Deposit Insurance Corporation, which guaranteed all bank deposits up to $2,500. In other words, even should a bank fail, small depositors would be able to recover their money. Finally, in 1935, Congress passed a major banking act that transferred much of the authority once wielded by the regional Federal Reserve banks to the Federal Reserve Board in Washington.

To protect investors in the stock market, Congress passed the so-called Truth in Securities Act of 1933, requiring corporations issuing new securities to provide full and accurate information about them to the public. Another act of June 1934 established the Securities and Exchange Commission (SEC) to police the stock market. Among other things, the establishment of the SEC was an indication of how far the financial establishment had fallen in public estimation. In earlier years, J. P. Morgan and other important financiers could have wielded enough influence to stop such government interference in the financial world. Now Morgan could not even get a respectful hearing on Capitol Hill. The criminal trials of a number of once-respected Wall Street figures for grand larceny and fraud (including the conviction and imprisonment of Richard Whitney, onetime head of the New York Stock Exchange and a close Morgan associate) eroded the public stature of the financial community still further.

The Growth of Federal Relief

Millions of Americans were unemployed and in desperate need of assistance in 1933, and the relief efforts of private organizations and state and local governments were unable to meet the demand. Although the Roosevelt administration did not consider relief its most important task, it recognized the necessity of doing something to help impoverished Americans survive until the New Deal could revive the economy to the point where relief might not be necessary.

Among Roosevelt's first acts as president was the establishment of the Federal Emergency Relief Administration (FERA), which provided cash grants to states to prop up bankrupt relief agencies. To administer the program, he chose the director of the New York State relief agency, Harry Hopkins. Hopkins disbursed the FERA grants widely and rapidly. But both Hopkins and Roosevelt had misgivings about establishing a government dole. "It is probably going to undermine the independence of hundreds of thousands of families," he once lamented.

They felt somewhat more comfortable with another form of government assistance: work relief. Unlike the dole, Hopkins believed, work relief "preserves a man's morale. It saves his skill. It gives him a chance to do something socially useful." Thus when it became clear that the FERA grants would not be sufficient to pull the country through the winter, the administration established a second program: the Civil Works Administration (CWA). Between November and April, it put more than 4 million people to work on temporary projects. Some of them were of lasting value, such as the construction of roads, schools, and parks; others were little more than make-work. To Hopkins, however, the important thing was pumping money into an economy badly in need of it and providing assistance to people with nowhere else to turn. This use of government spending to stimulate the economy—known at the time as "pump priming" and later as Keynesianism—was one of the New Deal's most important contributions to public policy. But in 1933, at least, members of the administration were only vaguely aware of the broad effects of this spending on the economy as a whole.

Evidence of this limited view of the value of government spending was that most of these early relief programs had short lives. Like the FERA, the CWA was intended to be only a temporary expedient. In the spring of 1934, the president began to dismantle the agency, and ultimately he disbanded it altogether. Most economists now agree that massive and sustained government spending would have been the quickest and most effective way to end the Depression. But few policymakers in the 1930s shared that belief.

Roosevelt's favorite relief project was the Civilian Conservation Corps. Established in the first weeks of the new administration, the CCC was designed to provide employment to the millions of urban young men who could find no jobs in the cities and who, unemployed and restless, were raising fears of urban violence. At the same time, it was intended to advance the work of conservation and reforestation—goals Roosevelt had long cherished. The CCC created a series of camps in national parks and forests and in other rural and wilderness settings. There young men (women were excluded from the program) worked in a semimilitary environment on such projects as planting trees, building reservoirs, developing or maintaining parks, and improving agricultural irrigation. CCC camps were segregated by race—the vast majority reserved for whites, a few open to blacks.

Mortgage relief was a pressing need of millions of farm owners and homeowners. The Farm Credit Administration, which within two years refinanced one-fifth of all farm mortgages in the United States, was one response to that problem. The Frazier-Lemke Farm Bankruptcy Act of 1933 was another. It enabled some farmers to regain their land even after foreclosure on their mortgages. Despite such efforts, however, by 1934 25 percent of all American farm owners had lost their land. Homeowners were similarly troubled, and in June 1933 the administration established the Home Owners' Loan Corporation, which by 1936 had refinanced the mortgages of more than 1 million householders. A year later, Congress established the Federal Housing Administration to insure mortgages for new construction and home repairs—a measure that combined an effort to provide relief with a program to stimulate lasting recovery of the construction industry.

The relief efforts of the first two years of the New Deal were intended to be limited and temporary. But they helped establish the basis of other forms of social protection. Ultimately, the creation of a permanent welfare system would be one of the New Deal's most important and lasting accomplishments.

THE NEW DEAL IN TRANSITION

Seldom has an American president enjoyed such remarkable popularity as Franklin Roosevelt during his first two years in office. But by early 1935, with no end to the Depression yet in sight, the New Deal was beginning to find itself the target of fierce public criticism. In the spring of 1935, partly in response to these growing attacks, Roosevelt launched an ambitious new program of legislation that has often been called the "Second New Deal."

Attacks from Right and Left

Some of the most strident attacks on the New Deal came from critics on the right. Roosevelt had tried for a time to conciliate conservatives and business leaders. By the end of 1934, however, it was clear that the American right in general, and much of the corporate world in particular, had become irreconcilably hostile to the New Deal. So intense was conservative animosity toward the New Deal's "reckless spending," "economic crackpots," and "socialist" reforms that some of Roosevelt's critics could not even bear to say the president's name. They called him, simply and bitterly, "that man in the White House." In August 1934, a group of the most fervent (and wealthiest) Roosevelt opponents, led by members of the Du Pont family, formed the American Liberty League, designed specifically to arouse public opposition to the New Deal's "dictatorial" policies and its supposed attacks on free enterprise. The new organization generated wide publicity and caused some concern within the administration. In fact, however, it was never able to expand its constituency very much beyond the northern industrialists who had founded it. At its peak, membership in the organization numbered only about 125,000.

In 1936, at least, the real impact of the Liberty League and other conservative attacks on Roosevelt was not to undermine the president's political strength, but to convince Roosevelt that there was no longer any point in trying to conciliate the business community. The forces of "organized money," he said near the end of his campaign for reelection, "are unanimous in their hate for me—and I welcome their hatred."

Roosevelt's critics on the left also managed to produce alarm among some supporters of the administration; but like the conservatives, they proved to have only limited strength. The Communist Party, the Socialist Party, and other radical and semiradical organizations were at times harshly critical of Roosevelt.

But they were also sympathetic to some New Deal initiatives. And they were at times uncertain about how best to combine their commitment to radical change with their fervent opposition to the growth of fascism elsewhere in the world. The Communist Party, in particular, spent much of the 1930s tacitly and at times openly supporting the Roosevelt programs.

Popular Protest

More menacing to the New Deal than either the far right or the far left was a group of dissident political movements that defied easy ideological classification. Some were marginal "crackpot" organizations with little popular following. Others gained substantial public support within particular states and regions. Three men, however, succeeded in mobilizing genuinely national followings.

Dr. Francis E. Townsend, an elderly California physician, rose from obscurity to lead a movement of more than 5 million members with his plan for federal pensions for the elderly. According to the Townsend plan, all Americans over the age of sixty would receive monthly government pensions of $200, provided they retired (thus freeing jobs for younger, unemployed Americans) and spent the money in full each month (which would pump needed funds into the economy). By 1935, the Townsend Plan had attracted the support of many older men and women. And while the plan itself made little progress in Congress, the public sentiment behind it helped build support for the Social Security system, which Congress did approve in 1935.

Even greater renown (and eventually great notoriety) came to Father Charles E. Coughlin, a Catholic priest in the Detroit suburb of Royal Oak, Michigan, through his weekly sermons broadcast nationally over the radio. He criticized "rapacious capitalists" for their abdication of social responsibility; and he proposed a series of monetary reforms—remonetization of silver, issuing of greenbacks, and nationalization of the banking system—that he insisted would restore prosperity and ensure economic justice. At first a warm supporter of Franklin Roosevelt, by 1934 he had become disheartened by what he claimed was the president's failure to deal harshly enough with the "money powers." In the spring of 1935, he established his own political organization, the National Union for Social Justice, which some believed was a first step toward forming a new political party. He was also displaying an apparently remarkable influence in Congress. (An avalanche of telegrams inspired by a Coughlin radio sermon was generally believed to have been responsible for the defeat in the Senate of a treaty admitting the United States to the World Court.) And he was attracting public support throughout much of the nation—primarily from Catholics, but from others as well. Father Coughlin was widely believed to have one of the largest regular radio audiences of anyone in America.

Most alarming of all to the administration was the growing national popularity of Senator Huey P. Long of Louisiana. Long had risen to power in his home state through his strident attacks on the banks, oil companies, and utilities, and on the conservative political oligarchy allied with them. Elected governor in 1928, he

HUEY LONG
Few public speakers could arouse a crowd more effectively than Huey Long of Louisiana, known to many as "the Kingfish" (a nickname borrowed from the popular radio show *Amos 'n Andy*). It was Long's effective use of radio, however, that contributed most directly to his spreading national popularity in the early 1930s. *(Culver)*

launched an assault on his opposition so thorough and forceful that soon they were left with virtually no political power at all. Long dominated the legislature, the courts, and the executive departments, and he brooked no interference. When opponents accused him of violating the Louisiana constitution, he brazenly replied, "I'm the Constitution here now." Many claimed that he had, in effect, become a dictator. But he also maintained the overwhelming support of the Louisiana electorate, in part because of his flamboyant personality and in part because of his solid record of conventional progressive accomplishment: building roads, schools, and hospitals; revising the tax codes; distributing free textbooks; lowering utility rates. Barred by law from succeeding himself as governor, he ran in 1930 for a seat in the U.S. Senate, won easily, and left the state government in the hands of loyal, docile allies.

Long, like Coughlin, supported Franklin Roosevelt in 1932. But within six months of Roosevelt's inauguration he had broken with the president. As an alternative to the New Deal, he advocated a drastic program of wealth redistribution, a program he ultimately named the Share-Our-Wealth Plan. The government, he claimed, could end the Depression easily by using the tax system to confiscate the surplus riches of the wealthiest men and women in America, whose fortunes were, he claimed, so bloated that not enough wealth remained to satisfy the needs of the great mass of citizens. That surplus wealth would allow the government to guarantee every family a minimum "homestead" of $5,000 and an annual wage of $2,500.

Long made little effort to disguise his interest in running for president. In 1934, he established his own national organization: the Share-Our-Wealth Society, which soon attracted a large following—not only in Long's native South but in New York, Pennsylvania, parts of the Midwest, and above all California. A poll by the Democratic National Committee in the spring of 1935 disclosed that Long might attract more than 10 percent of the vote if he ran as a third-party candidate, enough to tip a close election to the Republicans.

Long, Coughlin, Townsend, and other dissidents had certain concerns in common. They spoke harshly of the "plutocrats," "international bankers," and other remote financial powers who were, they claimed, not only impoverishing the nation but exercising tyrannical power over individuals and communities. They spoke equally harshly, however, of the dangers of excessive government bureaucracy, attacking the New Deal for establishing a menacing, "dictatorial" state. They envisioned a society in which government would, through a series of simple economic reforms, guarantee prosperity to every American without exercising intrusive control over individuals and communities.

To members of the Roosevelt administration, the dissident politics appeared in 1935 to have become a genuine threat to the president. An increasing number of advisers were warning Roosevelt that he would have to do something dramatic to counter their strength.

The "Second New Deal"

In the spring of 1935, Roosevelt launched a series of important new programs—often called the "Second New Deal"—in response both to the growing political pressures and to the continuing economic crisis. They represented, if not a new direction, at least a change in the emphasis of New Deal policy.

Perhaps the most conspicuous change was in the administration's attitude toward big business. Symbolically at least, the president was now willing openly to attack corporate interests. In March, for example, he asked Congress for a law to break up the great utility holding companies and justified it by speaking harshly of the injustices inherent in their monopolistic position. Congress did indeed pass the Holding Company Act of 1935 (often known as the "death sentence" bill), but furious lobbying by the utilities resulted in amendments that sharply limited its effects.

Equally alarming to affluent Americans was a series of tax reforms proposed by the president in 1935, a program conservatives quickly labeled a "soak the rich" scheme. Apparently designed to undercut the appeal of Huey Long's Share-Our-Wealth Plan, the Roosevelt proposals called for establishing the highest and most progressive peacetime tax rates in history. Rates in the highest brackets reached 75 percent on income, 70 percent on inheritances, and 15 percent on corporate incomes. In fact, the actual impact of these taxes was far less radical than the president liked to claim (as Huey Long quickly pointed out); few people made enough money to qualify for the upper brackets, and most of them were able to find ways to avoid the full tax burden in any case. The next tax laws were more important symbolically than they were economically.

The Supreme Court decision in 1935 to invalidate the National Industrial Recovery Act solved some problems for the administration, but it also created others. Section 7(a) of the now defunct act had guaranteed workers the right to organize and bargain collectively. Supporters of labor, both in the administration and in Congress, advocated quick action to restore that protection. With the president himself slow to respond, a group of progressives in Congress led by Senator Robert F. Wagner of New York introduced what became the National Labor Relations Act of 1935. The new law, popularly known as the Wagner Act, provided workers with more federal protection than Section 7(a) of the National Industrial Recovery Act had offered; it provided a crucial enforcement mechanism, the National Labor Relations Board (NLRB), which would have power to compel employers to recognize and bargain with legitimate unions. The president was not entirely happy with the bill, but he signed it. That was in large part because American workers themselves had become so important and vigorous a force by 1935 that Roosevelt realized his own political future would depend in part on responding to their demands.

Labor Militancy

The emergence of a powerful American trade union movement in the 1930s was one of the most important social and political developments of the decade. It occurred partly in response to government efforts to enhance the power of unions; but it was also a result of the increased militancy of American workers and their leaders.

During the 1920s, most workers had displayed relatively little militancy in challenging employers or demanding recognition of their unions. In the 1930s, however, many of the factors that had impeded militancy vanished or grew weaker. Business leaders and industrialists lost (at least temporarily) the ability to control government policies. Congress passed both Section 7(a) of the National Industrial Recovery Act of 1933 and the Wagner Act of 1935 over the strong objections of most (although not all) corporate leaders. Equally important, new and more militant labor organizations emerged to challenge the established, conservative unions.

The growing militancy first became obvious in 1934, when newly organized workers (many of them inspired by the collective bargaining provisions of the National Industrial Recovery Act) demonstrated a determination and radicalism not seen since 1919 and became involved in militant, occasionally violent, confrontations with employers and local authorities. Industrial workers were, it was clear, becoming too militant to ignore any longer. But it was equally clear that without stronger legal protection, their organizing drives would end in frustration. Once the Wagner Act became law, the search for more effective forms of organization rapidly gained strength in labor ranks.

The American Federation of Labor, now under the leadership of William Green, remained committed to the idea of the craft union: the idea of organizing workers on the basis of their skills. It had little to offer unskilled laborers, who now constituted the bulk of the industrial work force. During the 1930s, therefore, another concept of labor organization challenged the craft union ideal: industrial unionism. Advocates of this approach argued that all the workers in a particular industry should be organized in a single union, regardless of what functions they performed. All auto workers should be in a single automobile union; all steel workers should be in a single steel union. United in this way, workers would greatly increase their power.

Leaders of the AFL craft unions for the most part opposed the new concept. But industrial unionism found a number of important advocates, most prominent among them John L. Lewis, the talented, flamboyant, and eloquent leader of the United Mine Workers—the oldest major union in the country. At first, Lewis and his allies attempted to work within the AFL, but friction between the new industrial organizations Lewis was promoting and the older craft unions grew rapidly.

At the 1935 AFL convention, Lewis became embroiled in a series of angry confrontations (and one celebrated fistfight) with craft union leaders before finally walking out. A few weeks later, he created the Committee on Industrial Organization—a body officially within the AFL but unsanctioned by its leadership. After a series of bitter jurisdictional conflicts, the AFL finally expelled the new committee from its ranks, and along with it all the industrial unions it represented. In response, Lewis renamed the committee the Congress of Industrial Organizations (CIO), established it in 1936 as an organization directly rivaling the AFL, and became its first president. The schism clearly weakened the labor movement in many ways. But by freeing the advocates of industrial unionism from the restrictive rules of the AFL, it gave impetus to the creation of powerful new organizations.

The CIO expanded the constituency of the labor movement. It was more receptive to women and to blacks than the AFL had been, in part because women and blacks were more likely to be relegated to unskilled jobs, in part because CIO organizing drives targeted previously unorganized industries (textiles, laundries, tobacco factories, and others) where women and minorities constituted much of the work force. The CIO was also a more militant organization than the AFL. And by the time of the 1936 schism, it was already engaged in major organizing battles in the automobile and steel industries.

Organizing Battles

The new organizations had been struggling for recognition even before the schism of 1936. Major battles were under way, in particular, in the automobile and steel industries.

Out of several competing auto unions, the United Auto Workers (UAW) was gradually emerging preeminent in the early and mid-1930s. But although it was gaining recruits, it was making little progress in winning recognition from the corporations. Then, in December 1936, auto workers employed a controversial and effective new technique for challenging corporate opposition: the sit-down strike. Employees in several General Motors plants in Detroit simply sat down inside the plants, refusing either to work or to leave, thus preventing the company from using strikebreakers. The tactic spread to other locations, and by February 1937 strikers had occupied seventeen GM plants.

The strikers ignored court orders and local police efforts to force them to vacate the buildings. When Michigan's governor, Frank Murphy, a liberal Democrat, refused to call up the National Guard to clear out the strikers, and when the federal government also refused to intervene on behalf of employers, General Motors relented. In February 1937, GM became the first major manufacturer to recognize the UAW; other automobile companies followed. The sit-down strike proved effective for rubber workers and others as well, but it survived only briefly as a labor technique. Its apparent illegality aroused so much public opposition that labor leaders soon abandoned it.

In the steel industry, the battle for unionization was more difficult. In 1936, the Steel Workers' Organizing Committee (later United Steelworkers of America) began a major organizing drive involving thousands of workers and frequent, often bitter strikes. These conflicts were notable not only for the militancy of the (predominantly male) steelworkers themselves, but for the involvement of thousands of women (many of them wives or relatives of workers), who provided important logistical support for the strikers and who at times took direct action by creating a buffer between strikers and the police.

In March 1937, to the surprise of almost everyone, United States Steel, the giant of the industry, recognized the union rather than risk a costly strike at a time when it sensed itself on the verge of recovery from the Depression. But the smaller companies (known collectively as "Little Steel") remained unyielding in their opposition. On Memorial Day 1937, a group of striking workers from Republic Steel gathered with their families for a picnic and demonstration in South Chicago. When they attempted to march peacefully (and legally) toward the steel plant, police opened fire on them. Ten demonstrators were killed; another ninety were wounded. Despite a public outcry against the "Memorial Day Massacre," the harsh tactics of "Little Steel" were successful. The 1937 strike failed.

But the victory of Little Steel was one of the last gasps of the kind of brutal strikebreaking that had proved so effective in the past. In 1937 alone, there

THE LITTLE STEEL STRIKE, 1937
Al Balant, a leader of the Steel Workers Organizing Committee in Ohio, addresses a rally he has organized at city hall in Cleveland to protest the importation of strikebreakers by Republic Steel. The march to city hall occurred between outbreaks of violence at the Cleveland plants. Similar, and worse, violence was occurring in other cities during the bitter and ultimately unsuccessful strike against the "Little Steel" companies. *(UPI/Bettmann)*

were 4,720 strikes—over 80 percent of them settled in favor of the unions. By the end of the year, more than 8 million workers were members of unions recognized as official bargaining units by employers—as compared with 3 million in 1932. By 1941, that number had expanded to 10 million and included the workers of Little Steel, where employers had finally recognized the SWOC.

Social Security

From the first moments of the New Deal, important members of the administration, most notably Secretary of Labor Frances Perkins, had been lobbying for a system of federally sponsored social insurance for the elderly and the unemployed. In 1935, Roosevelt gave public support to what became the Social Security Act, which Congress passed the same year. It established several distinct programs.

For the elderly, there were two types of assistance. Those who were destitute at the time the bill passed could begin receiving up to $15 a month in federal assistance. More important for the future, many Americans presently working were incorporated into a pension system, to which they and their employers would contribute by paying a payroll tax and which would provide them with an income on retirement. Pension payments would not begin until 1940, and even then would provide recipients only $10 to $85 a month. And broad categories of workers (including domestic servants and agricultural laborers, many of whom were blacks and women) were excluded from the program. But the act was a crucial first step in creating the nation's most important social program for the elderly.

In addition, the Social Security Act created a system of unemployment insurance, to which employers alone would contribute and which made it possible for workers laid off from their jobs to receive government assistance for a limited period of time. It also provided aid to blind and otherwise handicapped people and to dependent children.

The framers of the Social Security Act wanted to create a system of "insurance," not "welfare." And the largest programs (old-age pensions and unemployment insurance) were in many ways similar to private insurance programs, with contributions from participants and benefits available to all. But the act also provided considerable direct assistance based on need—to the elderly poor, to the disabled, to dependent children and their mothers. In 1935, these groups were widely perceived to be small and genuinely unable to support themselves, but in the years to come the programs would expand and assume dimensions that the planners of Social Security neither foresaw nor desired. Aid to Dependent Children, envisioned as a relatively modest program to aid a small number of needy people, would in the 1950s (renamed Aid to Families with Dependent Children) expand to become one of the cornerstones of the modern welfare system.

The distinction built into the Social Security Act between "insurance" and "public assistance" institutionalized a set of cultural biases that would continue to influence the politics of welfare for the rest of the twentieth century. New Dealers, like most other Americans, believed that some people had "earned" social protection—either because they (or their employers) had contributed to the programs from which they drew, as was the case with old-age pensions and unemployment compensation; or because they had performed some special service to the nation, as had been the case

in the past for Civil War and World War I veterans. Other people (many of them women) "needed" benefits because they were incapable of supporting themselves; and while New Dealers (and progressive reformers before them) were willing to provide such benefits, they did so less generously and much more demeaningly (because of elaborate eligibility requirements) than they did for those they believed had earned them. Whatever its limits, however, it is clear that the 1935 act was the most important single piece of social welfare legislation in American history.

New Directions in Relief

Social Security was designed primarily to fulfill long-range goals. But millions of unemployed Americans had immediate needs. To help meet those needs, the administration established in 1935 the Works Progress Administration (WPA). Like the Civil Works Administration and other earlier efforts, the WPA established a system of work relief for the unemployed. But it was much bigger than the earlier agencies, both in the size of its budget ($5 billion at first) and in the energy and imagination of its operations.

Under the direction of Harry Hopkins, the WPA kept an average of 2.1 million workers employed between 1935 and 1941. The agency was responsible ultimately for building or renovating 110,000 public buildings (schools, post offices, public libraries, government office buildings, and others) and for constructing almost 600 airports, more than 500,000 miles of roads, and over 100,000 bridges. In the process, it provided incomes to unemployed workers and stimulated the economy by increasing the flow of money into it.

The WPA also displayed remarkable flexibility and imagination in offering assistance to those whose occupations did not fit into any traditional category of relief. The Federal Writers Project of the WPA, for example, gave unemployed writers a chance to do their work and receive a government salary. The Federal Arts Project, similarly, helped painters, sculptors, and others to continue their careers. The Federal Music Project and the Federal Theater Project oversaw the production of concerts and plays, creating work for unemployed musicians, actors, directors, and others. Other relief agencies emerged alongside the WPA. The National Youth Administration provided work and scholarship assistance to high-school and college-age men and women. The Emergency Housing Division of the Public Works Administration began federal sponsorship of public housing. It cleared some of the nation's most notorious slums and built instead some fifty new housing developments, containing nearly

22,000 units—although most of them were priced too high for those who had been displaced by slum clearance. Not until 1937, when Congress approved Senator Wagner's bill creating the United States Housing Authority, did the government begin to provide a substantial amount of housing for the truly poor.

The hiring practices of the WPA, the NYA, and other work-relief programs—like the character of the Social Security Act—revealed another important, if at the time largely unrecognized, feature of the New Deal welfare system. Men and women alike were in distress in the 1930s (as in all difficult times). But the new welfare system dealt with members of the two sexes in very different ways. For men, the government concentrated mainly on work relief—on such programs as the CCC, the CWA, and the WPA, all of which were overwhelmingly male. The WPA did provide some jobs for women, although usually in such domestic settings as sewing rooms, nursery schools, and handicraft programs. Even these few jobs tended to be quickly eliminated when WPA funds became tight.

The principal government aid to women was not work relief, but cash assistance—most notably through the Aid to Dependent Children program of Social Security, which was designed largely to assist single mothers. This disparity in treatment reflected a widespread assumption, shared even by some of the many women who helped design the programs, that men were the principal "breadwinners" and the bulk of the paid work force and that women should be treated within the context of the family. In fact, millions of women were already employed by the 1930s, and millions of women lived outside the framework of the conventional family and depended on their own earnings for survival.

The 1936 "Referendum"

The presidential election of 1936, it was clear from the start, was to be a national referendum on Franklin Roosevelt and the New Deal. And while in 1935 there had been reason to question the president's political prospects, by the middle of 1936 his reelection was virtually certain. The Republican Party nominated the moderate governor of Kansas, Alf M. Landon, and produced a program that promised, in effect, to continue the programs of the New Deal—but "constitutionally," and without running a deficit. Republican conservatives seemed impotent even within their own party.

Roosevelt's dissident challengers seemed similarly powerless. One reason was the violent death of their most effective leader, Huey Long, who was assassinated in Louisiana in September 1935. Another reason was the ill-fated alliance among several of the remaining dissident leaders in 1936. Father Coughlin, Dr. Townsend, and Gerald L. K. Smith (a henchman of Huey Long) joined forces that summer to establish a new political movement—the Union Party. But the incessant squabbling among them, combined with the colorlessness of their presidential candidate—an undistinguished North Dakota congressman, William Lemke—doomed the new party to ineffectuality. After its demise, two of its embittered leaders, Coughlin and Smith, moved quickly to the right; they also became notorious for their anti-Semitism and, in Coughlin's case, overt fascist sympathies.

The result was the greatest landslide in American history to that point. Roosevelt polled just under 61 percent of the vote, to Landon's 36 percent. The Republican candidate carried only Maine and Vermont. The Democrats increased their already large majorities in both houses of Congress. The Union Party received fewer than 900,000 votes.

The election displayed the party realignment that the New Deal had produced. The Democrats now controlled a broad coalition of western and southern farmers, the urban working classes, the poor and unemployed, and the black communities of the northern cities, as well as traditional progressives and committed new liberals—a coalition that constituted a substantial majority of the electorate. It would be decades before the Republican Party could again produce a true majority coalition of its own.

THE NEW DEAL IN DISARRAY

Roosevelt emerged from the 1936 election at the zenith of his popularity. Within months, however, the New Deal was mired in serious new difficulties—a result of continuing opposition, the president's own political errors, and major economic setbacks.

The Court Fight and the "Purge"

Franklin Roosevelt had become convinced that no program of reform could long survive the obstructionist justices of the Supreme Court who had already struck down the NRA and the AAA and threatened to in-

validate even more legislation. The 1936 mandate, he believed, made it possible for him to do something about the problem. In February 1937, he offered a solution. Without informing congressional leaders in advance, he sent a surprise message to Capitol Hill proposing a general overhaul of the federal court system and including, among many provisions, one to add up to six new justices to the Supreme Court. The courts were "overworked," he claimed, and needed additional manpower and younger blood to enable them to cope with their increasing burdens. But Roosevelt's real purpose, which almost everyone understood, was to give himself the opportunity to appoint new, liberal justices and change the ideological balance of the Court.

Conservatives were outraged at the "Court-packing plan," and even many Roosevelt supporters were disturbed by what they considered evidence of the president's hunger for power. Still, Roosevelt might well have persuaded Congress to approve at least a compromise measure had not the Supreme Court itself intervened. Even before the Court-packing fight began, the ideological balance of the Court had been precarious. Four justices consistently opposed the New Deal, and three generally supported it. Of the remaining two, Chief Justice Charles Evans Hughes often sided with the progressives and Associate Justice Owen J. Roberts usually voted with the conservatives.

On March 29, 1937, Roberts, Hughes, and the three progressive justices voted together to uphold a state minimum-wage law—in the case of *West Coast Hotel* v. *Parrish*—thus reversing a 5-to-4 decision of the previous year invalidating a similar law (and suggesting the first movement away from the narrow interpretation of contracts and the interstate commerce clause that the 1905 *Lochner* decision had helped establish). Two weeks later, again by a 5-to-4 margin, the Court upheld the Wagner Act; and in May, it validated the Social Security Act. The Court had prudently moderated its position to make the Court-packing bill unnecessary. Congress ultimately defeated it.

On one level, the affair was a significant victory for Franklin Roosevelt. The Court was no longer an obstacle to New Deal reforms, particularly after the older justices began to retire, to be replaced by Roosevelt appointees. But the Court-packing episode did lasting damage to the administration. By giving members of his own party an excuse to oppose him, he had helped destroy his congressional coalition. From 1937 on, southern Democrats and other Democratic conservatives voted against his measures much more often than in the past. In combination with Republicans, they constituted a powerful enough force to block many New Deal measures.

One casualty of this newly powerful conservative coalition was an ambitious plan to reorganize the executive branch of government, which Roosevelt also presented to Congress in 1937. The president promoted the measure by emphasizing its potential contribution to governmental "efficiency"; his opponents characterized it, to some degree correctly, as an effort to increase the power of the president over the federal bureaucracy. Executive reorganization, like Court packing, reinforced conservative arguments that the president was aspiring to become a "dictator." The original bill failed, although a much-reduced reorganization plan passed Congress in 1939.

In the spring of 1938, the president's political situation deteriorated further. Determined to regain the initiative in his legislative battles, Roosevelt openly campaigned in several Democratic primary contests against members of his own party who had opposed his programs. Not only was he unable to unseat any of the five Democratic senators against whom he campaigned, but his "purge" efforts drove an even deeper wedge between the administration and its conservative opponents.

But the greatest blow to the administration as it began its second term was an economic one: a serious new recession that threatened to discredit everything the New Deal had done.

Retrenchment and Recession

By the summer of 1937, the national income, which had dropped from $82 billion in 1929 to $40 billion in 1932, had risen to nearly $72 billion. Other economic indices showed similar improvements. Roosevelt seized on these improvements as an excuse to try to balance the federal budget, convinced by Treasury secretary Henry Morgenthau and many economists that the real danger now was no longer depression but inflation. Between January and August 1937, for example, he cut the WPA in half, laying off 1.5 million relief workers.

A few weeks later, the fragile boom collapsed. The index of industrial production dropped from 117 in August 1937 to 76 in May 1938. Four million additional workers lost their jobs. Economic conditions were soon almost as bad as in the bleak days of 1932–1933.

The recession of 1937 came as a terrible shock to New Dealers, and many others, who had convinced themselves that the Depression was already over. It was a result of many factors. But to many observers at the time (including, apparently, Roosevelt), it seemed to be a direct result of the administration's unwise decision to reduce spending. And so the new crisis forced a reevaluation of policies within the administration.

The advocates of government spending as an antidote to the Depression stood vindicated, it seemed; and the notion of using government deficits to stimulate the economy established a frail foothold in American public policy. In April 1938, the president asked Congress for an emergency appropriation of $5 billion for public works and relief programs, and government funds soon began pouring into the economy once again. Within a few months, another tentative recovery seemed to be under way, and the advocates of spending pointed to it as proof of the validity of their approach.

At the same time, a group of younger liberals in the administration, who saw the recession as the result of excessively concentrated corporate power, were urging the president to launch a new assault on monopoly. In April 1938, Roosevelt sent a stinging message to Congress, vehemently denouncing what he called an unjustifiable concentration of economic power and asking for the creation of a commission to examine the problem, with an eye to major reforms in the antitrust laws. In response, Congress established the Temporary National Economic Committee (TNEC), including representatives of both houses of Congress and of several executive agencies. At about the same time, Roosevelt appointed a new head of the antitrust division of the Justice Department: Thurman Arnold, a Yale Law School professor who soon proved to be the most vigorous (and controversial) director ever to serve in that office.

By the end of 1938, however, it was becoming clear that these ambitious new goals faced an uncertain future. For the New Deal had by then essentially come to an end. Congressional opposition now made it difficult for the president to enact any major new programs. But more important, perhaps, the threat of world crisis hung heavy in the political atmosphere, and Roosevelt was gradually growing more concerned with persuading a reluctant nation to prepare for war than with pursuing new avenues of reform.

LIMITS AND LEGACIES OF THE NEW DEAL

In the 1930s, Roosevelt's principal critics were conservatives, who accused him of abandoning the Constitution and establishing a menacing, even tyrannical state. In more recent years, the New Deal's major critics have attacked it from the left, pointing to the major problems it left unsolved and the important groups it failed to represent. A full understanding of the New

MAJOR LEGISLATION OF THE NEW DEAL

1933 Emergency Banking Act	**1935** Works Progress Administration
Economy Act	National Youth Administration
Civilian Conservation Corps	Social Security Act
Agricultural Adjustment Act	National Labor Relations Act
Tennessee Valley Authority	Public Utilities Holding Company Act
National Industrial Recovery Act	Resettlement Administration
Banking Act	Rural Electrification Administration
Federal Emergency Relief Act	Revenue Act ("wealth tax")
Home Owners' Refinancing Act	**1936** Soil Conservation and Domestic Allotment Act
Civil Works Administration	**1937** Farm Security Administration
Federal Securities Act	National Housing Act
1934 National Housing Act	**1938** Second Agricultural Adjustment Act
Securities and Exchange Act	Fair Labor Standards Act
Home Owners' Loan Act	**1939** Executive Reorganization Act

Deal requires examining both its achievements and its limits.

The Idea of the "Broker State"

In 1933, many New Dealers dreamed of using their new popularity and authority somehow to remake American capitalism—to produce new forms of cooperation and control that would create a genuinely harmonious, ordered economic world. By 1939, it was clear that what they had created was in fact something quite different. But rather than bemoan the gap between their original intentions and their ultimate achievements, New Deal liberals, both in 1939 and in later years, chose to accept what they had produced and to celebrate it—to use it as a model for future reform efforts.

What they had created was something that in later years would become known as the "broker state." Instead of forging all elements of society into a single, harmonious unit, as some reformers had once hoped to do, the real achievement of the New Deal was to elevate and strengthen new interest groups so as to allow them to compete more effectively in the national marketplace. And it was to make the federal government a mediator in that continuous competition—a force that could intercede when necessary to help some groups and limit the power of others.

In 1933, there had been only one great interest group (albeit a varied and divided one) with genuine power in the national economy: the corporate world. By the end of the 1930s, American business found itself competing for influence with an increasingly powerful labor movement, with an organized agricultural economy, and with aroused consumers. In later years, the "broker state" idea would expand to embrace other groups as well: racial, ethnic, and religious minorities, women, and many others. Thus, one of the enduring legacies of the New Deal was to make the federal government a protector of interest groups and a supervisor of the competition among them, rather than an instrument attempting to create a universal harmony of interests.

What determines which interest groups receive government assistance in a "broker state"? The experience of the New Deal suggests that such assistance goes largely to those groups able to exercise enough political or economic power to demand it. Thus in the 1930s, farmers—after decades of organization and agitation—and workers—as the result of militant action and mass mobilization—won from the government new and important protections. Other groups, less well organized perhaps but politically important because so numerous and visible, won more limited assistance as well: imperiled homeowners, the unemployed, the elderly.

By the same token, the interest-group democracy that the New Deal came to represent offered much less to those groups either too weak to demand assistance or not visible enough to arouse widespread public support. And yet those same groups were often the ones most in need of help from their government. One of the important limits of the New Deal, therefore, was its very modest record on behalf of several important social groups.

WHERE HISTORIANS DISAGREE

THE NEW DEAL

FOR MANY YEARS, DEBATE among historians over the nature of the New Deal mirrored the debate among Americans in the 1930s over the achievements of the Roosevelt administration. Historians struggled, just as contemporaries had done, to decide whether the New Deal was a good thing or a bad thing. Did it go too far in expanding the size and power of the government? Did it go far enough in helping the dispossessed and reforming capitalism?

The conservative critique of the New Deal has received relatively little scholarly expression. Edgar Robinson, in *The Roosevelt Leadership* (1955), and John T. Flynn, in *The Roosevelt Myth* (1956), attacked Roosevelt as both a radical and a despot; but few historians have ever taken such charges seriously. By far the dominant view of the New Deal among scholars has been an approving, liberal interpretation—one that has appeared in various forms but that rests on several common assumptions. First, liberals maintain, the New Deal was not a radical, socialistic, or communistic program. It was firmly within the mainstream of the American political tradition. Second, they argue, the New Deal represented a powerful (and overdue) response by government to glaring social needs that had long gone unmet. And third, it marked a decisive repudiation of old orthodoxies about the proper relationships among government, business, labor, and other groups in society.

The leading voice in the liberal chorus has long been Arthur M. Schlesinger, Jr. , who argued in the three volumes of *The Age of Roosevelt* (1957–1960) that the New Deal marked a continuation of the long struggle between public power and private interests, but that Roosevelt had moved that struggle to a new level. The unrestrained power of the business community was finally confronted with an effective challenge, and what emerged was a system of reformed capitalism, with far more protection for workers, farmers, consumers, and others than in the past.

Other liberals have gone further. Carl Degler, in *Out of Our Past* (1959), called the Roosevelt years a "Third American Revolution" (the first two being the Revolution of 1776 and the Civil War). It marked, he claimed, "the crossing of a

African Americans and the New Deal

One group the New Deal did relatively little to assist was African Americans. The administration was not hostile to black aspirations. On the contrary, the New Deal was probably more sympathetic to them than any previous government of the twentieth century. Eleanor Roosevelt spoke throughout the 1930s on behalf of racial justice and put continuing pressure on her husband and others in the federal government to ease discrimination against blacks. She was also partially responsibile for what was, symbolically at least, one of the most important events of the decade for African Americans. When the black singer Marian Anderson was refused permission in the spring of 1939 to give a concert in the auditorium of the Daughters of the American Revolution (Washington's only concert hall), Eleanor Roosevelt resigned from the organization and then (along with Interior Secretary Harold Ickes, another champion of racial equality) helped secure government permission for her to sing on the steps of the Lincoln Memorial. Anderson's Easter Sunday concert attracted 75,000 people and became, in effect, the first modern civil-rights demonstration.

The president himself appointed a number of blacks to significant second-level positions in his administration. Roosevelt appointees such as Robert Weaver, William Hastie, and Mary McLeod Bethune created an informal network of officeholders who consulted frequently with one another and who became known as the "Black Cabinet." Eleanor Roosevelt, Harold Ickes, and Harry Hopkins all made efforts to ensure that New Deal relief programs did not exclude blacks; and by 1935, perhaps a quarter of all African Americans were receiving some form of government assistance. One result was a historic change in black electoral behavior. As late as 1932, most American blacks were voting Republican, as they had since the Civil War. By 1936, divide from which, it would seem, there could be no turning back." Eric Goldman, in *Rendezvous with Destiny* (1952) and later works, called the New Deal the culmination of a "Half-Century of Revolution." Although Roosevelt drew heavily on the traditions of the progressive past, "there was something more to New Deal liberalism" because it included unprecedented new departures such as Social Security.

Richard Hofstadter offered a more skeptical assessment of the New Deal in the 1950s, but one that fell largely within the liberal framework. In *The Age of Reform* (1955), he emphasized the New Deal's discontinuities with the past. It was, he said, a "drastic new departure . . . different from anything that had yet happened in the United States"—a program that even many old progressives found alarming, and opposed. The New Deal had largely abandoned the progressive concern about reshaping the corporate world, what Hofstadter called "entrepreneurial" reform. Instead, New Deal liberalism took on a "social-democratic tinge that had never before been present in American reform movements" and raised a new set of issues to prominence: "so-cial security, unemployment insurance, wages and hours, and housing."

Hofstadter not only echoed the view of other liberals that the New Deal marked an important break with the past; he also gave early expression to some of the criticisms that historians in the 1960s would begin to offer. In *The American Political Tradition* (1948) and again in *The Age of Reform*, he complained that the New Deal's fragmented, "pragmatic" aproach had lacked a central, guiding philosophy. James MacGregor Burns, in *Roosevelt: The Lion and the Fox* (1956), raised other objections: that Roosevelt's wily political methods had often led him away from the proper goals to reform; that he had failed to make full use of his potential as a leader but had accommodated himself unnecessarily to existing patterns of political power.

The first systematic "revisionist" interpretation of the New Deal came in 1963, in William Leuchtenburg's *Franklin D. Roosevelt and the New Deal*. Leuchtenburg was a sympathetic critic, arguing that most of the limitations of the New Deal were a result of the restrictons imposed on Roosevelt by the political and ideological realities of

more than 90 percent of them were voting Democratic—the beginnings of a political alliance that would endure for decades.

Blacks supported Franklin Roosevelt because they knew he was not their enemy. But they had few illusions that the New Deal represented a millennium in American race relations. For example, the president was never willing to risk losing the support of southern Democrats by supporting legislation to make lynching a federal crime. Nor would he endorse efforts in Congress to ban the poll tax, one of the most potent tools by which white southerners kept blacks from voting.

New Deal relief agencies did not challenge, and indeed reinforced, existing patterns of discrimination. The Civilian Conservation Corps established separate black camps. The NRA codes tolerated paying blacks less than whites doing the same jobs. Blacks were largely excluded from employment in the TVA. The Federal Housing Administration refused to provide mortgages to blacks moving into white neighborhoods, and the first public housing projects financed by the federal government were racially segregated. The WPA routinely relegated black, Hispanic, and Asian workers to the least-skilled and lowest-paying jobs, or excluded them altogether; when funding ebbed, nonwhites, like women, were among the first to be dismissed.

The New Deal was not hostile to black Americans, and it did much to help them advance. But it refused to make the issue of race a significant part of its agenda.

The New Deal and the "Indian Problem"

In many respects, government policies toward the Indian tribes in the 1930s were simply a continuation of the long-established effort to encourage Native Americans to assimilate. Senator Burton K. Wheeler of Mon-

his time—that the New Deal probably could not have done much more than it did. Nevertheless, Leuchtenburg openly challenged earlier views of the New Deal as a revolution in social policy. He was able to muster only enough enthusiasm to call it a "halfway revolution," one that enhanced the positions of some previously disadvantaged groups (notably farmers and factory workers) but did little or nothing for many others (including blacks, sharecroppers, and the urban poor). Ellis Hawley augmented these moderate criticisms of the Roosevelt record in *The New Deal and the Problem of Monopoly* (1966). In examining 1930s economic policies, Hawley challenged liberal assumptions that the New Deal acted as the foe of private business interests. On the contrary, he argued, New Deal efforts were in many cases designed to enhance the position of private entrepreneurs—even, at times, at the expense of some of the liberal reform goals that administration officials espoused.

Other historians in the 1960s, writing from the perspective of the New Left, expressed much harsher criticisms of the New Deal. Barton Bernstein, in a 1968 essay, compiled a dreary chroni-

cle of missed opportunites, inadequate responses to problems, and damaging New Deal initiatives. The Roosevelt administration may have saved capitalism, Bernstein charged, but it failed to help—and in many ways actually harmed—those groups most in need of assistance. Paul Conkin, in *The New Deal* (1967), similarly chastised the government of the 1930s for its policies toward marginal farmers, its failure to institute meaningful tax reform, and its excessive generosity toward certain business interests. And Ronald Radosh, in 1968, portrayed the New Deal as an effective agent for the consolidation of modern corporate capitalism. Several essays by Thomas Ferguson in the 1980s and Colin Gordon's 1994 book *New Deals* took such argumements further. They cited the close ties between the New Deal and internationalist financiers and industrialists; the liberalism of the1930s was a product of their shared interest in stabilizing capitalism.

Until the work of Ferguson and Gordon, the New Left attack on the New Deal never developed very far beyond preliminary statements. Instead, by the 1970s and 1980s, most scholars seemed largely to have accepted the revised lib-

tana expressed the sentiments of many members of Congress (and many other white Americans) when he said in 1934, in the midst of a hearing on an Indian reform bill, "What we are trying to do is get rid of the Indian problem rather than add to it." By that he meant that the purpose of reforms should be to reduce the numbers of Native Americans who identified themselves as members of tribes and increase the number of those who attempted to become part of the larger society and culture.

But the principal elements of federal policy in the New Deal years worked to advance a very different goal, largely because of the efforts of the extraordinary commissioner of Indian affairs in those years, John Collier. Collier was a former social worker who had become committed to the cause of the Indians after exposure to tribal cultures in New Mexico in the 1920s. More important, he was greatly influenced by the

work of twentieth-century anthropologists who promoted the idea of cultural relativism—the idea that every culture should be accepted and respected on its own terms and that no culture was inherently superior to another. Cultural relativism was a challenge to the three-centuries-old assumption among white Americans that Indians were "savages" and that white society was inherently superior and more "civilized."

Collier promoted legislation that would, he hoped, reverse the pressures on Native Americans to assimilate and would allow them the right to remain Indians. Not all tribal leaders agreed with Collier; indeed, his belief in the importance of preserving Indian culture would not find its broadest support among the tribes until the 1960s. Nevertheless, Collier effectively promoted legislation—which became the Indian Reorganization Act of 1934—to advance his goals. Among other things it restored to the tribes the right to own eral view: that the New Deal was a significant (and most agree valuable) chapter in the history of reform, but one that worked within rigid, occasionally crippling limits. Much of the recent work on the New Deal, therefore, has been less interested in the question of whether it was a "conservative" or "revolutionary" phenomenon than in the question of the constraints within which it was operating. The sociologist Theda Skocpol, in an important series of articles, has emphasized (along with others) the issue of "state capacity" as an important New Deal constraint; ambitious reform ideas often foundered, she argued, because of the absence of a government bureaucracy with sufficient strength and expertise to shape or administer them. James T. Patterson, Barry Karl, Mark Leff, and others have emphasized the political constraints the New Deal encountered. Both in Congress and among the public, conservative inhibitions about government remained strong; the New Deal was as much a product of the pressures of its conservative opponents as of its liberal supporters. Frank Freidel, Ellis Hawley, Herbert Stein, and many others point as well to the ideological constraints

affecting Franklin Roosevelt and his supporters. Alan Brinkley, in *The End of Reform* (1995), has described a transition in New Deal thinking from a regulatory view of government to one that envisioned relatively little direct interference by government in the corporate world; a movement toward an essentially "compensatory" state centered on Keynesian welfare state programs.

The phrase "New Deal liberalism" has come in the postwar era to seem synonymous with modern ideas of aggressive federal management of the economy, elaborate welfare systems, a powerful bureaucracy, and large-scale government spending. The "Reagan Revolution" of the 1980s often portrayed itself as a reaction to the "legacy of the New Deal." Many historians of the New Deal, however, would argue that the modern idea of "New Deal liberalism" bears only a limited relationship to the ideas that New Dealers themselves embraced. The liberal accomplishments of the 1930s can only be understood in the context of their own time; later liberal efforts drew from that legacy but also altered it to fit the needs and assumptions of a very different era.

land collectively (reversing the allotment policy adopted in 1887, which encouraged the breaking up of tribal lands into individually owned plots—a policy that had led to the loss of over 90 million acres of tribal land to white speculators and others). In the thirteen years after passage of the 1934 bill, tribal land increased by nearly 4 million acres, and Indian agricultural income increased dramatically (from under $2 million in 1934 to over $49 million in 1947).

Even with the redistribution of lands under the 1934 act, however, Indians continued to possess, for the most part, only territory whites did not want—much of it arid, some of it desert. And as a group, they continued to constitute the poorest segment of the population. The efforts of the 1930s did not solve what some called the "Indian problem." They did, however, provide Indians with some tools for rebuilding the viability of the tribes.

Women and the New Deal

The New Deal was not hostile to feminist aspirations, but neither did it do a great deal to advance them. That was largely because such aspirations did not have sufficiently widespread support (even among women) to make it politically advantageous for the administration to back them.

There were, to be sure, important symbolic gestures on behalf of women. Roosevelt appointed the first female cabinet member in the nation's history, Secretary of Labor Frances Perkins. He also named more than 100 other women to positions at lower levels of the federal bureaucracy. They created an active female network within the government and cooperated with one another in advancing causes of interest to women. Such appointments were in part a response to pressure from Eleanor Roosevelt, who was a committed advo-

ELEANOR ROOSEVELT AND MARY MCLEOD BETHUNE
Mary McLeod Bethune was one of a small but energetic group of African-American officeholders in the Roosevelt administration. Together they formed an informal network known as the "Black Cabinet." Among their most important allies was Eleanor Roosevelt, who is shown here appearing with Bethune at a 1937 "National Conference on Problems of the Negro and Negro Youth," organized by the National Youth Administration. Bethune was the NYA's Director of Negro Activities. *(UPI/Bettmann)*

cate of women's rights and a champion of humanitarian causes. Molly Dewson, head of the Women's Division of the Democratic National Committee, was also influential in securing federal appointments for women as well as in increasing their role within the Democratic Party. Several women received appointments to the federal judiciary. And one, Hattie Caraway of Arkansas, became in 1934 the first woman ever elected to a full term in the U.S. Senate. (She was running to succeed her husband, who had died in office.)

But New Deal support for women operated within limits, partly because New Deal women themselves had limited views of what their aims should be. Frances Perkins and many others in the administration emerged out of the feminist tradition of the progressive era, which emphasized not so much sexual equality as special protections for women. Perkins herself had been instrumental in fighting for passage of various state laws safeguarding female workers. She opposed the National Woman's Party and its goal of securing the Equal Rights Amendment because she feared the amendment would threaten the protective mechanisms that she had helped to establish. Perkins and other women reformers were instrumental in creating support for, and shaping the character of, the Social Security Act of 1935. But they built into that bill their own notion of women's special place in a male-dominated economy. The principal provision of the bill

UNEMPLOYMENT, 1920–1945

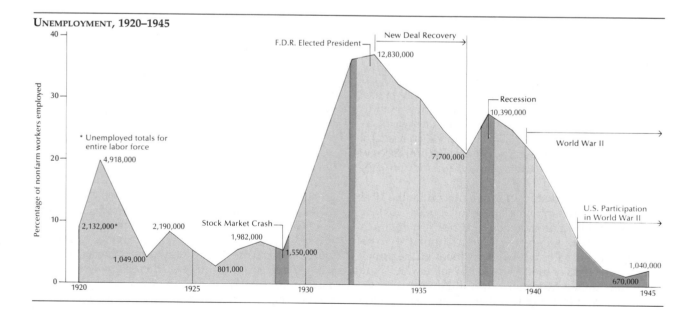

specifically designed for women—the Aid to Dependent Children program—was modeled on the state-level mothers' pensions that generations of progressive women had worked to pass earlier in the century.

The New Deal generally supported the prevailing belief that in hard times women should withdraw from the workplace to open up more jobs for men. Even Frances Perkins spoke out against what she called the "pin-money worker"—the married woman working to earn extra money for the household. New Deal relief agencies offered relatively little employment for women. The NRA sanctioned sexually discriminatory wage practices. The Social Security program at first excluded domestic servants, waitresses, and other predominantly female occupations.

As with blacks, so also with women: the New Deal was not actively hostile; in many ways, it was unprecedentedly supportive. It did, however, accept prevailing cultural norms. There was not yet sufficient political pressure from women themselves to persuade the administration to do otherwise.

The New Deal and the West

One part of American society that did receive special attention from the New Deal was the American West, which benefited disproportionately from New Deal relief and public works programs. The West received more federal funds per capita through New Deal relief programs than any other region.

Most westerners were eager for the assistance New Deal agencies provided, but their political leaders were not always as supportive. In Colorado, for example, the state legislature refused to provide the required matching funds for FERA relief in 1933. When, in response, Harry Hopkins cut Colorado off from the program, unemployed people rioted in Denver and looted food stores. Only then did the legislature reverse course and provide funding.

Just as in the South locally administered relief programs did not challenge prevailing racial norms, so in the West New Deal programs sustained existing racial and ethnic prejudices. In several states, relief agencies paid different groups at different rates: white Anglos received the most generous aid; blacks, Indians, and Mexican American received lower levels of support. In the CCC camps in New Mexico, Hispanics and Anglos sometimes worked in the same camps, but there were frequent tensions and occasional conflicts between them.

But the main reason for the New Deal's particular impact on the West was that conditions in the region

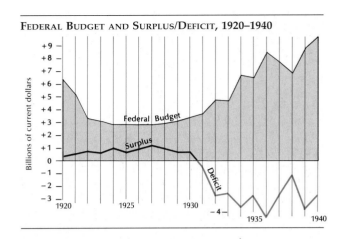

FEDERAL BUDGET AND SURPLUS/DEFICIT, 1920–1940

GROSS NATIONAL PRODUCT, 1920–1940

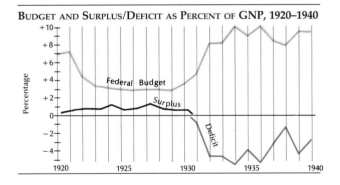

BUDGET AND SURPLUS/DEFICIT AS PERCENT OF GNP, 1920–1940

made the government's programs especially important. Federal agricultural programs had an enormous impact on the West because farming remained so much more central to the economy of the region than it did in much of the East. The largest New Deal public works programs—the great dams and power stations—were mainly in the West, both because the best

SIGNIFICANT EVENTS

1933 Franklin Roosevelt inaugurated

"First New Deal" legislation enacted

United States officially abandons gold standard

Prohibiton ends with repeal of Twenty-first Amendment

Dr. Francis Townsend begins campaign for old-age pensions

1934 Conservatives create American Liberty League

Huey Long establishes Share-Our-Wealth Society

Labor militancy increases

Indian Reorganization Act passed

1935 Supreme Court invalidates NRA

"Second New Deal" legislation passed

Father Charles Coughlin establishes National Union for Social Justice

John L. Lewis and allies break with AFL

Huey Long assassinated

1936 Supreme Court invalidates Agricultural Adjustment Act

CIO established

Sit-down strikes begin

Roosevelt wins reelection by record margin

1937 U.S. Steel recognizes Steel Workers' Organizing Committee

Roosevelt proposes "Court-packing" plan

Supreme Court validates Wagner Act

"Memorial Day Massacre" in Chicago

New Deal spending reduced

Severe recession begins

1938 Roosevelt proposes new spending measures

Temporary National Economic Committee established

Executive reorganization plan proposed

1939 Marian Anderson sings at Lincoln Memorial

locations for such facilities were there and because the West had the most need for new sources of water and power. The Grand Coulee dam on the Columbia River was the largest public works project in American history to that point, and it provided cheap electric power for much of the Northwest. Its construction, and the construction of other, smaller dams and water projects in the region, created a basis for economic development in the region.

Without this enormous public investment by the federal government, much of the economic development that transformed the West after World War II would have been much more difficult, if not impossible, to achieve. But the region paid a price for the government's beneficence. For generations after the Great Depression, the federal government maintained a much greater and more visible bureaucratic presence in the West than in any other region.

The New Deal and the National Economy

The most frequent criticisms of the New Deal involve its failure genuinely to revive or reform the American economy. New Dealers never fully recognized the value of government spending as a vehicle for recovery, and their efforts along other lines never succeeded in ending the Depression. The economic boom sparked by World War II, not the New Deal, finally ended the crisis. Nor did the New Deal substantially alter the distribution of power within American capitalism; and it had only a small impact on the distribution of wealth among the American people.

Nevertheless, the New Deal did have a number of important and lasting effects on both the behavior and the structure of the American economy. It helped elevate new groups—workers, farmers, and others—to positions from which they could at times effectively challenge the power of the corporations. It contributed to the economic development of the West and, to a lesser degree, the South. It increased the regulatory functions of the federal government in ways that helped stabilize previously troubled areas of the economy: the stock market, the banking system, and others. And the administration helped establish the basis for new forms of federal fiscal policy, which in the postwar years would give the government tools for promoting and regulating economic growth.

The New Deal also created the basis of the federal welfare state, through its many relief programs and above all through the Social Security system. The conservative inhibitions New Dealers brought to this task ensured that the welfare system that ultimately emerged would be limited in its impact (at least in comparison with those of other industrial nations), would reinforce some traditional patterns of gender and racial discrimination, and would be expensive and cumbersome to administer. But for all its limits, the new system marked a historic break with the federal government's traditional reluctance to offer public assistance to its neediest citizens.

The New Deal and American Politics

Perhaps the most dramatic effect of the New Deal was on the structure and behavior of American government itself and on the character of American politics. Franklin Roosevelt helped enhance the power of the federal government as a whole. By the end of the 1930s, state and local governments were clearly of secondary importance to the government in Washington; in the past, that had not always been clear. Roosevelt also established the presidency as the preeminent center of authority within the federal government. Never again would Congress be able to wield as much independent power as it had in the years before the New Deal. And never again would it have the same control over presidential authority.

Finally, the New Deal had a profound impact on how the American people defined themselves politically. It took a weak, divided Democratic Party, which had been a minority force in American politics for many decades, and turned it into a mighty coalition that would dominate national party competition for more than forty years. It turned the attention of many voters away from some of the cultural issues that had preoccupied them in the 1920s and awakened in them an interest in economic matters of direct importance to their lives. And it created among the American people greatly increased expectations of government—expectations that the New Deal itself did not always fulfill but that survived to become the basis of new liberal crusades in the postwar era.

SUGGESTED READINGS

General and Biographical Studies. Anthony J. Badger, *The New Deal* (1989). John Braeman et al., eds., *The New Deal*, 2 vols. (1975). James MacGregor Burns, *Roosevelt: The Lion and the Fox* (1956). Blanche Wiesen Cooke, *Eleanor Roosevelt* (1992). Paul Conkin, *The New Deal*, 2nd ed. (1975). Kenneth Davis, *FDR: The New York Years: 1928–1933* (1985); *FDR: The New Deal Years, 1933–1937* (1986); *FDR: Into the Storm, 1937-1940* (1993). Peter Fearon, *War, Prosperity, and Depression* (1987). Steve Fraser and Gary Gerstle, eds., *The Rise and Fall of New Deal Liberalism* (1988). Frank Freidel, *Franklin D. Roosevelt*, 4 vols. (1952–1973); *Franklin D. Roosevelt: A Rendezvous with Destiny* (1990). Joseph P. Lash, *Eleanor and Franklin* (1971). William E. Leuchtenburg, *Franklin D. Roosevelt and the New Deal* (1963); *In the Shadow of FDR* (1983). Katie Louchheim, *The Making of the New Deal* (1983). Richard Lowitt, *The New Deal and the West* (1984). Robert S. McElvaine, *The Great Depression* (1984). Gerald Nash, *The Great Depression and World War II* (1979). Edgar Robinson, *The Roosevelt Leadership* (1955). Arthur M. Schlesinger, Jr., *The Age of Roosevelt*, 3 vols. (1957–1960). Harvard Sitkoff, ed., *Fifty Years Later: The New Deal Evaluated* (1985). Geoffrey Ward, *Before the Trumpet: Young Franklin Roosevelt, 1882–1905* (1985); *A First-Class Temperament: The Emergence of Franklin Roosevelt* (1989). J. H. Wilson and Marjorie Lightman, eds., *Without Precedent: The Life and Career of Eleanor Roosevelt* (1984).

New Deal Politics and Programs. Mimi Abramowitz, *Regulating the Lives of Women* (1988). Bernard Bellush, *The Failure of the NRA* (1975). Donald Brand, *Corporatism and the Rule of Law* (1988). William R. Brock, *Welfare, Democracy, and the New Deal* (1987). Searle Charles, *Minister of Relief* (1963). Ralph F. De Bedts, *The New Deal's SEC* (1964). Herbert Feis, *Characters in Crisis* (1966). Sidney Fine, *The Automobile Under the Blue Eagle* (1963). Frank Freidel, *Launching the New Deal* (1973). Gerald H. Gamm, *The Making of New Deal Democrats: Voting Behavior and Realignment in Boston, 1920–1940* (1989). Otis Graham, *Encore for Reform* (1967). Nancy L. Grant, *TVA and Black Americans: Planning for the Status Quo* (1990). Ellis Hawley, *The New Deal and the Problem of Monopoly* (1966). Peter H. Irons, *The New Deal Lawyers* (1982). Mark Leff, *The Limits of Symbolic Reform: The New Deal and Taxation, 1933–1939* (1984). Thomas K. McCraw, *TVA and the Power Fight* (1971). George McJimsey, *Harry Hopkins: Ally of the Poor and Defender of Democracy* (1987). Raymond Moley and Eliot Rosen, *The First New Deal* (1966). Michael Parrish, *Securities Regulation and the New Deal* (1970). James T. Patterson, *America's Struggle Against Poverty, 1900–1980* (1981). Albert U. Romasco, *The Politics of Recovery: Roosevelt's New Deal* (1983). John Salmond, *The Civilian Conservation Corps* (1967). Bonnie Fox Schwartz, *The Civil Works Administration, 1933–1934* (1984). Jordan Schwarz, *The New Dealers* (1993). Susan Ware, *Beyond Suffrage* (1981); *Partner and I: Molly Dewson, Feminism, and New Deal Politics* (1987).

Agriculture. Christina Campbell, *The Farm Bureaus* (1962). David Conrad, *The Forgotten Farmers* (1965). Lowell K. Dyson,

Red Harvest: The Communist Party and American Farmers (1982). Gilbert Fite, *George M. Peek and the Fight for Farm Parity* (1954). David Hamilton, *From New Day to New Deal: American Farm Policy from Hoover to Roosevelt, 1928–1933* (1991). Richard S. Kirkendall, *Social Scientists and Farm Politics in the Age of Roosevelt* (1966). Paul Mertz, *The New Deal and Southern Rural Poverty* (1978). Van L. Perkins, *Crisis in Agriculture* (1969). Bruce Shulman, *From Cotton Belt to Sunbelt* (1991).

Depression Dissidents. David H. Bennett, *Demagogues in the Depression* (1969). Alan Brinkley, *Voices of Protest: Huey Long, Father Coughlin, and the Great Depression* (1982). Donald Grubbs, *Cry from the Cotton* (1971). Glen Jeansonne, *Gerald L. K. Smith: Minister of Hate* (1988). Abraham Holzman, *The Townsend Movement* (1963). R. Alan Lawson, *The Failure of Independent Liberalism* (1971). Donald McCoy, *Angry Voices: Left-of-Center Politics in the New Deal Era* (1958). Leo Ribuffo, *The Old Christian Right: The Protestant Far Right from the Great Depression to the Cold War* (1983). Arthur M. Schlesinger, Jr., *The Politics of Upheaval* (1960). Charles J. Tull, *Father Coughlin and the New Deal* (1965). T. Harry Williams, *Huey Long* (1969). George Wolfskill, *Revolt of the Conservatives* (1962).

The "Second New Deal". Sidney Baldwin, *Poverty and Politics: The Farm Security Administration* (1968). Paul Conkin, *Tomorrow a New World* (1971). J. Joseph Huthmacher, *Senator Robert Wagner and the Rise of Urban Liberalism* (1968). Roy Lubove, *The Struggle for Social Security* (1968). William F. McDonald, *Federal Relief Administration and the Arts* (1968). Jerre Mangione, *The Dream and the Deal* (1972). Jane deHart Matthews, *The Federal Theater* (1967). W. D. Rowley, *M. L. Wilson and the Campaign for Domestic Allotment* (1970).

The Late New Deal. Leonard Baker, *Back to Back* (1967). Alan Brinkley, *The End of Reform: New Deal Liberalism in Recession and War* (1995); Frank Freidel, *FDR and the South* (1965). Barry Karl, *Executive Reorganization and Reform in the New Deal* (1963). William Leuchtenburg, "The Origins of Franklin D. Roosevelt's 'Court-Packing' Plan," in Philip B. Kurland, ed., *The Supreme Court Review* (1966). Dean May, *From New Deal to New Economics* (1981). James T. Patterson, *Congressional Conservatism and the New Deal* (1967); *The New Deal and the States* (1969). Richard Polenberg, *Reorganizing Roosevelt's Government* (1966). Theodore Rosenof, *Dogma and Depression* (1972); *Patterns of Political Economy in America* (1983). Herbert Stein, *The Fiscal Revolution in America* (1969). Charles Trout, *Boston: The Great Depression and the New Deal* (1977). George Wolfskill and John Hudson, *All But the People* (1969).

Blacks, Hispanics, Indians. Rodolfo Acuna, *Occupied America: A History of Chicanos* (rev. ed. 1988). Francisco E. Balerman, *In Defense of La Raza* (1982). Ralph Bunche, *The Political Status of the Negro in the Age of FDR* (1973). Dan T. Carter, *Scottsboro* (1969). Vine DeLoria, Jr., *The Nations Within* (1984). Sarah Deutsch, *No Separate Refuge: Culture, Class, and*

Gender on the Anglo-Hispanic Frontier in the American Southwest, 1880–1940 (1987). John Dollard, *Caste and Class in a Southern Town*, 3rd ed. (1957). Cheryl Lynn Greenberg, *"Or Does It Explode?": Black Harlem in the Great Depression* (1991). Laurence M. Hauptman, *The Iroquois and the New Deal* (1981). Abraham Hoffman, *Unwanted Mexican Americans in the Great Depression* (1974). Laurence C. Kelly, *The Assault on Assimilation: John Collier and the Origins of Indian Policy Reform* (1983). John B. Kirby, *Black Americans in the Roosevelt Era* (1980). Clifford Lytle, *American Indians, American Justice* (1983). Carey McWilliams, *Factories in the Field* (1939). Donald L. Parman, *The Navajos and the New Deal* (1976). Kenneth R. Philp, *John Collier's Crusade for Indian Reform, 1920–1954* (1977). Harvard Sitkoff, *A New Deal for Blacks* (1978). Graham D. Taylor, *The New Deal and American Indian Tribalism* (1980). Nancy Weiss, *Farewell to the Party of Lincoln: Black Politics in the Age of FDR* (1983); *The National Urban League* (1974). Raymond Wolters, *Negroes and the Great Depression* (1970). Robert L. Zangrando, *The NAACP Crusade Against Lynching* (1980).

Labor. Jerold Auerbach, *Labor and Liberty* (1966). John Barnard, *Walter Reuther and the Rise of the Auto Workers* (1983). Irving Bernstein, *Turbulent Years* (1970); *A Caring Society: The New Deal, the Worker, and the Great Depression* (1985). David Brody, *Workers in Industrial America* (1980). Bert Cochran, *Labor and Communism* (1977). Lizabeth Cohen, *Making a New Deal: Industrial Workers in Chicago, 1919–1939* (1990). Melvyn Dubofsky and Warren Van Tine, *John L. Lewis* (1977). Elizabeth Faue, *Community of Suffering and Struggle: Women, Men, and the Labor Movement in Minnesota, 1915–1945* (1991). Sidney Fine, *Sit-Down* (1969). Steve Fraser, *Labor Will Rule: Sidney Hillman and the Rise of American Labor* (1991). Joshua Freeman, *In Transit: The Transport Workers Union in New York City, 1933–1966* (1989). Peter Friedlander, *The Emergence of a UAW Local* (1975). Gary Gerstle, *Working-Class Americanism: The Politics of Labor in a Textile City 1914–1960* (1989). John W. Hevener, *Which Side Are You On? The Harlan County Coal Miners, 1931–1939* (1978). August Meier and Elliott Rudwick, *Black Detroit and the Rise of the UAW* (1979). David Milton, *The Politics of U.S. Labor: From the Great Depression to the New Deal* (1980). Bruce Nelson, *Workers on the Waterfront: Seamen, Longshoremen, and Unionism in the 1930s* (1988). Daniel Nelson, *American Rubber Workers and Organized Labor, 1900–1941* (1988). Paula F. Pfeffer, *A. Philip Randolph, Pioneer of the Civil Rights Movement* (1990). Ronald W. Schatz, *The Electrical Workers* (1983). George G. Suggs, Jr., *Union Busting in the Tristate: The Oklahoma, Kansas, and Missouri Metal Workers Strike of 1935* (1986). Christopher L. Tomlins, *The State and the Unions* (1985). Robert H. Zieger, *John L. Lewis: Labor Leader* (1988); *American Workers, American Unions, 1920–1985* (1986).

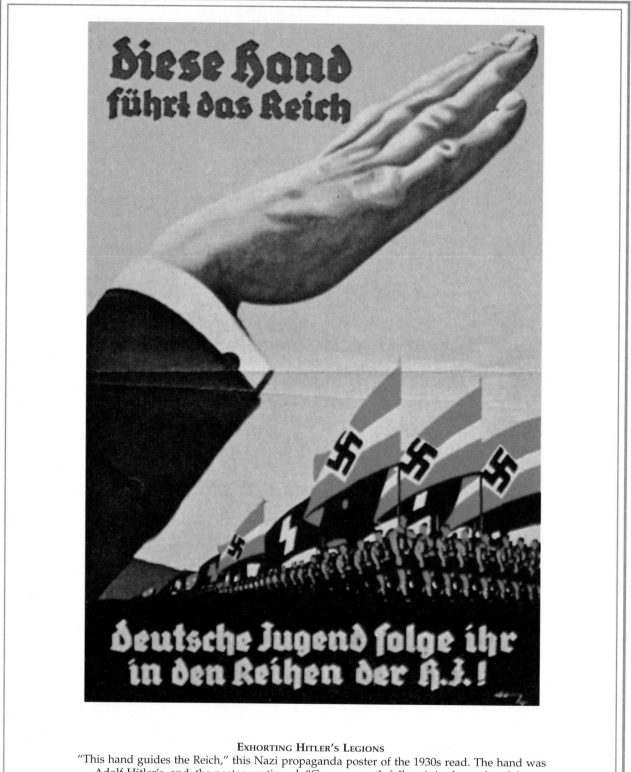

EXHORTING HITLER'S LEGIONS
"This hand guides the Reich," this Nazi propaganda poster of the 1930s read. The hand was
Adolf Hitler's, and, the poster continued, "German youth follow it in the ranks of the
Hitler Youth." *(Institute of Contemporary History and Wiener Library, Ltd., London)*

CHAPTER TWENTY-SEVEN

THE GLOBAL CRISIS, 1921–1941

ENRY CABOT LODGE OF Massachusetts, chairman of the Senate Foreign Relations Committee and one of the most powerful figures in the Republican Party, led the fight against ratification of the Treaty of Versailles in 1918 and 1919. In part because of his efforts, the Senate defeated the treaty; the United States failed to join the League of Nations; and American foreign policy embarked on an independent course that for the next two decades would attempt, but ultimately fail, to expand American influence and maintain international stability without committing the United States to any lasting relationships with other nations.

Lodge was not an isolationist. He recognized that America had emerged from World War I the most powerful nation in the world. He believed the United States should use that power and should exert its influence internationally. But he believed, too, that America's expanded role in the world should reflect the nation's own interests and its own special virtues; it should leave the nation unfettered with obligations to anyone else. He said in 1919:

> We are a great moral asset of Christian civilization. . . . How did we get there? By our own efforts. Nobody led us, nobody guided us, nobody controlled us. . . . I would keep America as she has been—not isolated, not prevent her from joining other nations for . . . great purposes—but I wish her to be master of her own fate.

Lodge was not alone in voicing such sentiments. Throughout the 1920s, those controlling American foreign policy attempted to increase America's role in the world while at the same time keeping the nation free of burdensome commitments that might limit its own freedom of action. In 1933, Franklin Roosevelt became president, and brought his own legacy as a leading Wilsonian internationalist and erstwhile supporter of the League of Nations. But for more than six years, Roosevelt also attempted to keep America the "master of her own fate," to avoid important global commitments that might reduce the nation's ability to pursue its own ends.

In the end, the cautious, limited American internationalism of the interwar years proved insufficient to protect the interests of the United States, to create global stability, or to keep the nation from becoming involved in the greatest war in human history.

THE DIPLOMACY OF THE NEW ERA

Critics of American foreign policy in the 1920s often used a single word to describe the cause of their disenchantment: isolationism. Having rejected the Wilsonian vision of a new world order, they claimed, the nation had turned its back on the rest of the globe and repudiated its international responsibilities. In fact, the United States played a more active role in world affairs in the 1920s than it had at almost any previous time in its history—even if not the role the Wilsonians had prescribed.

Replacing the League

It was clear when the Harding administration took office in 1921 that American membership in the League of Nations was no longer a realistic possibility. As if finally to bury the issue, Secretary of State Charles Evans Hughes secured legislation from Congress in 1921 declaring the war with Germany at an end, and then proceeded to negotiate separate peace treaties with the former Central Powers. Through these treaties, American policymakers believed, the United States would receive all the advantages of the Versailles Treaty with none of the burdensome responsibilities. But Hughes was committed to finding something to replace the League as a guarantor of world peace and stability. He therefore, embarked on a series of efforts to build safeguards against future wars—but safeguards that would not hamper American freedom of action in the world.

The most important such effort was the Washington Conference of 1921—an attempt to prevent what was threatening to become a costly and destabilizing naval armaments race between America, Britain, and Japan. In his opening speech Hughes startled the delegates by proposing a plan for dramatic reductions in the fleets of all three nations and a ten-year moratorium on the construction of large warships. He called for the actual scrapping of nearly 2 million tons of existing shipping. Far more surprising than that proposal was the fact that the conference ultimately agreed to accept most of its terms, something that Hughes himself apparently had not anticipated. The Five-Power Pact of February 1922 established both limits for total naval tonnage and a ratio of armaments among the signatories. For every 5 tons of American and British warships, Japan would maintain 3 and France and Italy 1.75 each. (Although the treaty seemed to confirm the military inferiority of Japan, in fact it sanctioned Japanese dominance in East Asia. America and Britain had to spread their fleets across the globe; Japan was concerned only with the Pacific.) The Washington Conference also produced two other, related treaties: the Nine-Power Pact, pledging a continuation of the Open Door policy in China, and the Four-Power Pact, by which the United States, Britain, France, and Japan promised to respect one another's Pacific territories and cooperate to prevent aggression.

The Washington Conference began the New Era effort to protect the peace (and to protect the international economic interests of the United States) without accepting active international duties. The Kellogg-Briand Pact of 1928 concluded it. When the French foreign minister, Aristide Briand, asked the United States in 1927 to join an alliance against Germany, Secretary of State Frank Kellogg (who had replaced Hughes in 1925) instead proposed a multilateral treaty outlawing war as an instrument of national policy. Fourteen nations signed the agreement in Paris on August 27, 1928, amid great solemnity and wide international acclaim. Forty-eight other nations later joined the pact. It contained no instruments of enforcement but rested, as Kellogg put it, on the "moral force" of world opinion.

Debts and Diplomacy

The first responsibility of diplomacy, Hughes, Kellogg, and others agreed, was to ensure that American overseas trade faced no obstacles to expansion and that, once established, it would remain free of interference. Preventing a dangerous armaments race and reducing the possibility of war were steps to that end. So were the new financial arrangements that emerged at the same time. The United States was most concerned about Europe, on whose economic health American prosperity in large part depended. Not only were the major European industrial powers suffering from the devastation World War I had produced; they were also staggering under a heavy burden of debt. The Allied powers were struggling to repay $11 billion in loans they had contracted with the United States during and shortly after the war, loans that the Republican administrations were unwilling to reduce or forgive. "They hired the money, didn't they?" Calvin Coolidge once replied when asked if he favored offering Europe relief from their debts. At the same time, an even more debilitated Germany was attempting to pay the reparations levied against it by the Allies. With the financial structure of Europe on the brink of collapse, the United States stepped in with a solution.

In 1924 Charles G. Dawes, an American banker and diplomat, negotiated an agreement among France, Britain, Germany, and the United States under which American banks would provide enormous loans to the Germans, enabling them to meet their reparations payments; in return, Britain and France would agree to reduce the amount of those payments. Dawes won the Nobel Peace Prize for his efforts, but in fact the Dawes Plan did little to solve the problems it addressed. It was responsible for a growing American economic presence in Germany. It was also the source of a troubling circular pattern in international finance. America would lend money to Germany, which would use that money to pay reparations to France and England, which would in turn use those funds (as well as large loans they themselves were receiving from American banks) to repay war debts to the United States. The flow was able to continue only by virtue of the enormous debts Germany and the other European nations were accumulating to American banks and corporations.

Those banks and corporations were doing more than providing loans. They were becoming a daily presence in the economic life of Europe. American automobile manufacturers were opening European factories, capturing a large share of the overseas market. Other industries in the 1920s were establishing subsidiaries worth more than $10 billion throughout the Continent, taking advantage of the devastation of European industry and the inability of domestic corporations to recover. Some groups within the American government warned that the reckless expansion of overseas loans and investments, many in enterprises of dubious value, threatened disaster; that the United States was becoming too dependent on unstable European economies. The high tariff barriers that the Republican Congress had erected (through the Fordney-McCumber Act of 1922) were creating additional problems, such skeptics warned. European nations, unable to export their goods to the United States, were finding it difficult to earn the money necessary to repay their loans. Such warnings fell for the most part on deaf ears, and American economic expansion in Europe continued until disaster struck in 1931.

The United States government felt even fewer reservations about assisting American economic expansion in Latin America. After all, the United States had long considered that region its exclusive sphere of influence; and its investments there had been large even before World War I. During the 1920s, American military forces maintained a presence in numerous countries in the region. United States investments in Latin America more than doubled between 1924 and 1929; American corporations built roads and other facilities in many areas—partly, they argued, to weaken the appeal of revolutionary forces in the region, but at least equally to increase their own access to Latin America's rich natural resources. American banks were offering large loans to Latin American governments, just as they were in Europe; and just as in Europe, the Latin Americans were having great difficulty earning the money to repay them in the face of the formidable United States tariff barrier. By the end of the 1920s, resentment of "Yankee imperialism" was growing rapidly. The economic troubles after 1929 would only accentuate such problems.

Hoover and the World Crisis

After the relatively placid international climate of the 1920s, the diplomatic challenges facing the Hoover administration must have seemed ominous and bewildering. The world financial crisis that began in 1929 and greatly intensified after 1931 was not only creating economic distress, it was producing a dangerous nationalism that threatened the weak international agreements established during the previous decade. Above all, the Depression was toppling some existing political leaders and replacing them with powerful, belligerent governments bent on expansion as a solution to their economic problems. Hoover was confronted, therefore, with the beginning of a process that would ultimately lead to war. He lacked sufficient tools for dealing with it.

In Latin America, Hoover worked studiously to repair some of the damage created by earlier American policies. He made a ten-week goodwill tour through the region before his inauguration. Once in office, he tried to abstain from intervening in the internal affairs of neighboring nations and moved to withdraw American troops from Haiti. When economic distress led to the collapse of one Latin American regime after another, Hoover announced a new policy: America would grant diplomatic recognition to any sitting government in the region without questioning the means it had used to obtain power. He even repudiated the Roosevelt corollary to the Monroe Doctrine by refusing to permit American intervention when several Latin American countries defaulted on debt obligations to the United States in October 1931.

In Europe, the administration enjoyed few successes in its efforts to promote economic stability. When Hoover's proposed moratorium on debts in 1931 failed to attract broad support or produce financial stability (see p. 690), many economists and political leaders appealed to the president to cancel all war debts to the United States. Like his predecessors, Hoover refused; and several European nations promptly went into default, severely damaging an already tense international climate. American efforts to extend the disarmament agreements of the 1920s met with similar frustration. At a conference in London in January 1930, American negotiators reached agreement with European and Japanese delegates on extending the limits on naval construction established at the Washington Conference of 1921. But France and England, fearful of German resurgence and Japanese expansionism, insisted on so many loopholes as to make the treaty virtually meaningless. The increasing irrelevance of the New Era approach to diplomacy became even clearer at the World Disarmament Conference that opened in Geneva in January 1932. France rejected the idea of disarmament entirely and called for the creation of an international army to counter the growing power of Germany. Hoover continued to urge major reductions in armaments, including an immediate abolition of all

HITLER AND MUSSOLINI IN BERLIN
The German and Italian dictators (shown here reviewing Nazi troops in Berlin in the mid-1930s) acted publicly as if they were equals. Privately, Hitler treated Mussolini with contempt, and Mussolini complained constantly of being a junior partner in the relationship. *(Bettmann)*

"offensive" weapons (tanks, bombers) and a 30 percent reduction in all land and naval forces. The conference ultimately dissolved in failure.

The ineffectiveness of diplomacy in Europe was particularly troubling in view of some of the new governments coming to power on the Continent. Benito Mussolini's Fascist Party had been in control of Italy since the early 1920s; by the 1930s, the regime was growing increasingly nationalistic and militaristic, and Fascist leaders were loudly threatening an active campaign of imperial expansion. Even more ominous was the growing power of the National Socialist (or Nazi) Party in Germany. By the late 1920s, the Weimar Republic, the nation's government since the end of World War I, had lost virtually all popular support, discredited by, among other things, a ruinous inflation. Adolf Hitler, the stridently nationalistic leader of the Nazis, was rapidly growing in popular favor. Although he

lost a 1932 election for chancellor, Hitler would sweep into power less than a year later. His belief in the racial superiority of the Aryan (German) people, his commitment to providing Lebensraum (living space) for his "master race," his pathological anti-Semitism, and his passionate militarism—all posed a threat to European peace.

More immediately alarming to the Hoover administration was a major crisis in Asia—another early step toward World War II. The Japanese, reeling from an economic depression of their own, were concerned about the increasing strength of the Soviet Union and of Chiang Kai-shek's nationalist China. In particular, they were alarmed at Chiang's insistence on expanding his government's power in Manchuria, which remained officially a part of China but over which the Japanese had maintained effective economic control since 1905. When the moderate government of Japan failed to take forceful steps to counter Chiang's ambitions, Japan's military leaders staged what was, in effect, a coup in the autumn of 1931—seizing control of foreign policy from the weakened liberals. Weeks later, they launched a major invasion of northern Manchuria.

The American government had few options. For a while, Secretary of State Henry Stimson (who had served as secretary of war under Taft) continued to hope that Japanese moderates would regain control of the Tokyo government and halt the invasion. The militarists, however, remained in command; and by the beginning of 1932, the conquest of Manchuria was complete. Stimson issued stern (but essentially toothless) warnings to Japan and tried to use moral suasion to end the crisis. But Hoover forbade him to cooperate with the League of Nations in imposing economic sanctions against the Japanese. Stimson's only real tool in dealing with the Manchurian invasion was a refusal to grant diplomatic recognition to the new Japanese territories. Japan was unconcerned and early in 1932 expanded its aggression farther into China, attacking the city of Shanghai and killing thousands of civilians.

By the time Hoover left office early in 1933, it was clear that the international system the United States had attempted to create in the 1920s—a system based on voluntary cooperation among nations and on an American refusal to commit itself to the interests of other countries—had collapsed. The United States faced a choice. It could adopt a more energetic form of internationalism and enter into firmer and more meaningful associations with other nations. Or it could resort to nationalism and rely on its own devices for dealing with its (and the world's) problems. For the next six years, it experimented with elements of both approaches.

ISOLATIONISM AND INTERNATIONALISM

The administration of Franklin Roosevelt faced a dual challenge as it entered office in 1933. It had to deal with the worst economic crisis in the nation's history, and it had to deal with the effects of a decaying international structure. The two problems were not unrelated. It was the worldwide Depression itself that was producing much of the political chaos throughout the globe.

Through most of the 1930s, however, the United States was unwilling to make more than the faintest of gestures toward restoring stability to the world. Like many other peoples suffering economic hardship, most Americans were turning inward. Yet the realities of world affairs were not to allow the nation to remain isolated for very long—as Franklin Roosevelt realized earlier than many other Americans.

Depression Diplomacy

Roosevelt inherited from Herbert Hoover a foreign policy less concerned with issues of war and peace than with matters of economic policy. And although the New Deal rejected some of the initiatives the Republicans had begun, it continued for several years to base its foreign policy almost entirely on the nation's immediate economic needs.

Perhaps Roosevelt's sharpest break with the policies of his predecessor was on the question of American economic relations with Europe. Hoover had argued that only by resolving the question of war debts and reinforcing the gold standard could the American economy hope to recover. He had therefore, agreed to participate in the World Economic Conference, to be held in London in June 1933, to try to resolve these issues. By the time the conference assembled, however, Roosevelt had already decided to allow the gold value of the dollar to fall to enable American goods to compete in world markets. Shortly after the conference convened, Roosevelt released a famous "bombshell" message repudiating the orthodox views of most of the delegates and rejecting any agreement on currency stabilization. The conference quickly dissolved without reaching agreement, and not until 1936 did the administration finally agree to new negotiations to stabilize Western currencies.

At the same time, Roosevelt abandoned the commitments of the Hoover administration to settle the issue of war debts through international agreement. In effect, he simply let the issue die. Not only did he decline to negotiate a solution at the London Conference, but in April 1934 he signed a bill to forbid American banks from making loans to any nation in default on its debts. The result was to stop the old, circular system by which debt payments continued only by virtue of increasing American loans; within months, war-debt payments from every nation except Finland stopped for good.

If the new administration had no interest in international currency stabilization or settlement of war debts, it did have an active interest in improving America's position in world trade. Roosevelt approved the Reciprocal Trade Agreement Act of 1934, authorizing the administration to negotiate treaties lowering tariffs by as much as 50 percent in return for reciprocal reductions by other nations. By 1939, Secretary of State Cordell Hull, a devoted free-trader, had negotiated new treaties with twenty-one countries. The result was an increase in American exports to them of nearly 40 percent. But most of the agreements admitted only products not competitive with American industry and agriculture, so imports into the United States continued to lag. Thus other nations were not obtaining the American currency needed to buy American products or pay off debts to American banks.

America and the Soviet Union

America's hopes of expanding its foreign trade helped produce efforts by the Roosevelt administration to improve relations with the Soviet Union. The United States and Russia had viewed each other with mistrust and even hostility since the Bolshevik Revolution of 1917, and the American government still had not officially recognized the Soviet regime by 1933. But powerful voices within the United States were urging a change in policy—less because the revulsion with which most Americans viewed communism had diminished than because the Soviet Union appeared to be a possible source of trade. The Russians, too, were eager for a new relationship. They were hoping in particular for American cooperation in containing the power of Japan on Russia's southeastern flank. In November 1933, therefore, Soviet Foreign Minister Maxim Litvinov reached an agreement with the president in Washington. The Soviets would cease their propaganda efforts in the United States and protect American citizens in Russia; in return, the United States would recognize the communist regime.

Despite this promising beginning, however, relations with the Soviet Union soon soured once again. American trade failed to establish a foothold in Russia, disappointing hopes in the United States; and the American government did little to reassure the Soviets that it was interested in stopping Japanese expansion in Asia, dousing expectations in Russia. By the end of 1934, the Soviet Union and the United States were once again viewing each other with considerable mistrust. And Stalin, having abandoned whatever hopes he might once have had of cooperation with America, was beginning to consider making agreements of his own with the fascist governments of Japan and Germany.

The Good Neighbor Policy

Somewhat more successful were American efforts to enhance both diplomatic and economic relations with Latin America through what became known as the "Good Neighbor Policy." Latin America was one of the most important targets of the new policy of trade reciprocity. During the 1930s, the United States succeeded in increasing both exports to and imports from the other nations of the Western Hemisphere by over 100 percent. Closely tied to these new economic relationships was a new American attitude toward intervention in Latin America. The Hoover administration had unofficially abandoned the earlier American practice of using military force to compel Latin American governments to repay debts, respect foreign investments, or otherwise behave "responsibly." The Roosevelt administration went further. At the Inter-American Conference in Montevideo in December 1933, Secretary of State Hull signed a formal convention declaring: "No state has the right to intervene in the internal or external affairs of another." Roosevelt respected that pledge throughout his years in office.

The Good Neighbor Policy did not mean, however, that the United States had abandoned its influence in Latin America. On the contrary, it had simply replaced one form of leverage with another. Instead of military force, Americans now tried to use economic influence. The new reliance on economic pressures eased tensions between the United States and its neighbors considerably, eliminating the most abrasive and conspicuous irritants in the relationship. It did nothing to stem the growing American domination of the Latin American economies.

The Rise of Isolationism

The first years of the Roosevelt administration marked not only the death of Hoover's hopes for international economic agreements, but the end of any hopes for world peace through treaties and disarmament as well.

That the international arrangements of the 1920s were no longer suitable for the world of the 1930s became obvious in the first months of the Roosevelt presidency, when the new administration attempted to stimulate movement toward world disarmament. The arms control conference in Geneva had been meeting, without result, since 1932; and in May 1933, Roosevelt attempted to spur it to action by submitting a new American proposal for arms reductions. Negotiations stalled and then broke down on the Roosevelt proposal; and only a few months later, first Hitler and then Mussolini withdrew from the talks altogether. The Geneva Conference, it was clear, was a failure. Two years later, Japan withdrew from the London Naval Conference, which was attempting to draw up an agreement to continue the limitations on naval armaments negotiated at the Washington Conference of 1921.

Faced with a choice between more active efforts to stabilize the world or more energetic attempts to isolate the nation from it, most Americans unhesitatingly chose the latter. Support for isolationism emerged from many quarters. Old Wilsonian internationalists had grown disillusioned with the League of Nations and its inability to stop Japanese aggression in Asia; internationalism, they were beginning to argue, had failed. Other Americans were listening to the argument (popular among populist-minded politicians in the Midwest and West) that powerful business interests—Wall Street, munitions makers, and others—had tricked the United States into participating in World War I. An investigation by a Senate committee chaired by Senator Gerald Nye of North Dakota revealed exorbitant profiteering and blatant tax evasion by many corporations during the war, and it suggested (on the basis of little evidence) that bankers had pressured Wilson to intervene in the war so as to protect their loans abroad.

Roosevelt himself shared some of the suspicions voiced by the isolationists and claimed to be impressed by the findings of the Nye investigation. Nevertheless, he continued to hope for at least a modest American role in maintaining world peace. In 1935, he asked the Senate to ratify a treaty to make the United States a member of the World Court—a treaty that would have expanded America's symbolic commitment to internationalism without increasing its actual responsibilities in any important way. Nevertheless, isolationist opposition (spurred by unrelenting hostility from the Hearst newspapers and a passionate broadcast by Father Charles Coughlin on the eve of the Senate vote) resulted in the defeat of the treaty. It was a devastating political blow to the president, and he would not soon again attempt to challenge the isolationist tide.

That tide seemed to grow stronger in the following months. Through the summer of 1935, it became clear that Mussolini's Italy was preparing to invade Ethiopia in an effort to expand its colonial holdings in Africa. Fearing that a general European war would result, American legislators began to design legal safeguards to prevent the United States from being dragged into the conflict. The result was the Neutrality Act of 1935.

The 1935 act, and the Neutrality Acts of 1936 and 1937 that followed, were designed to prevent a recurrence of the events that many Americans now believed had pressured the United States into World War I. The 1935 law established a mandatory arms embargo against both victim and aggressor in any military conflict and empowered the president to warn American citizens that they might travel on the ships of warring nations only at their own risk. Thus, isolationists believed, the "protection of neutral rights" could not again become an excuse for American intervention in war. The 1936 Neutrality Act renewed these provisions. And in 1937, with world conditions growing even more precarious, Congress passed a still more stringent measure. The new Neutrality Act established the so-called cash-and-carry policy, by which belligerents could purchase only nonmilitary goods from the United States and had to pay cash and carry the goods away on their own vessels.

The American stance of militant neutrality gained support in October 1935 when Mussolini finally launched his long-anticipated attack on Ethiopia. When the League of Nations protested, Italy simply resigned from the organization, completed its conquest of Ethiopia, and formed an alliance (the "Axis") with Nazi Germany. Most Americans responded to the news with renewed determination to isolate themselves from European instability. Two-thirds of those responding to public opinion polls at the time opposed any American action to deter aggression.

Isolationist sentiment showed its strength once again in 1936–1937 in response to the civil war in Spain. The Falangists of General Francisco Franco, a group much like the Italian fascists, revolted in July 1936 against the existing republican government. Hitler and Mussolini supported Franco, both vocally and with weapons and supplies. Some individual Americans traveled to Spain to assist the republican cause (see p. 687); but the United States government joined with Britain and France in an agreement to offer no assistance to either side—although all three governments were sympathetic to the republicans.

Alarmed by the events of 1935 and 1936, Roosevelt began moving slowly and cautiously to challenge the grip of the isolationists on the nation's foreign policy. For a time, it seemed to be a hopeless cause. The United States was unable to do much more than watch as a series of new dangers emerged that brought the world closer to war.

Particularly disturbing was the deteriorating situation in Asia. Japan's aggressive designs against China had been clear since the invasion of Manchuria in 1931. In the summer of 1937, Tokyo launched an even broader assault, attacking China's five northern provinces. The United States, Roosevelt believed, could not allow the Japanese aggression to go unremarked or unpunished. In a speech in Chicago in October 1937, therefore, the president warned forcefully of the dangers that Japanese aggression posed to world peace. Aggressors, he proclaimed, should be "quarantined" by the international community to prevent the contagion of war from spreading.

The president was deliberately vague about what such a "quarantine" would mean, and there is evidence that he was contemplating nothing more drastic than a break in diplomatic relations with Japan, that he was not considering economic or military sanctions. Nevertheless, public response to the speech was disturbingly hostile. As a result, Roosevelt drew back. Although his strong words encouraged the British government to call a conference in Brussels to discuss the crisis in Asia, the United States refused to make any commitments to collective action, and the conference produced no agreement.

Only months later, another episode gave renewed evidence of how formidable the obstacles to Roosevelt's efforts remained. On December 12, 1937, Japanese aviators bombed and sank the U.S. gunboat *Panay* as it sailed the Yangtze River in China. The attack was almost undoubtedly deliberate. It occurred in broad daylight, with clear visibility, and a large American flag had been painted conspicuously on the *Panay's* deck. Even so, isolationists seized eagerly on Japanese protestations that the bombing had been an accident and pressured the administration into accepting Japan's apologies and overlooking the attack.

The Failure of Munich

In 1936, Hitler had moved the revived German army into the Rhineland, rearming an area that France had, in effect, controlled since World War I. In March 1938, German forces marched into Austria, and Hitler proclaimed a union (or *Anschluss*) between Austria, his native land, and Germany, his adopted one. Neither in America nor in most of Europe was there much more than a murmur of opposition.

The Austrian invasion, however, soon created another crisis; for Hitler had by now occupied territory surrounding three sides of western Czechoslovakia, a region he dreamed of annexing to provide Germany with the Lebensraum he believed it needed. In September 1938, he demanded that Czechoslovakia cede to him part of that region, the Sudetenland, an area on the Austro-German border in which many ethnic Germans lived. Czechoslovakia, which possessed substantial military power of its own, was prepared to fight rather than submit. But it realized it could not hope for success without help from other European nations. It got none. Most Western nations, including the United States, were appalled at the prospect of another war and were willing to pay almost any price to settle the crisis peacefully. On September 29, Hitler met with the leaders of France and Great Britain at Munich in an effort to resolve the crisis. The French and British agreed to accept the German demands in Czechoslovakia in return for Hitler's promise to expand no farther. "This is the last territorial claim I have to make in Europe," the Fuhrer solemnly declared. And Prime Minister Neville Chamberlain returned to England to a hero's welcome, assuring his people that the agree-

THE ANSCHLUSS
Citizens of Graz in Austria welcome Adolf Hitler shortly after the 1938 *anschluss*, by which Germany annexed Austria (Hitler's native land). *(UPI/Bettmann)*

ment ensured "peace in our time." Among those who had cabled him with encouragement at Munich was Franklin Roosevelt.

The Munich accords were the most prominent element of a policy that came to be known as "appeasement" and that came to be identified (not altogether fairly) almost exclusively with Chamberlain. Whoever was to blame, however, it became clear almost immediately that the policy was a failure. In March 1939, Hitler occupied the remaining areas of Czechoslovakia, violating the Munich agreement unashamedly. And in April, he began issuing threats against Poland. At that point, both Britain and France gave assurances to the Polish government that they would come to its assistance in case of an invasion; they even flirted, too late, with the Stalinist regime in Russia, attempting to draw it into a mutual defense agreement. Stalin, however, had already decided that he could expect no protection from the West; after all, he had not even been invited to attend the Munich Conference. Accordingly, he signed a nonaggression pact with Hitler in August 1939, freeing the Germans for the moment from the danger of a two-front war.

For a few months, Hitler had been trying to frighten the Poles into submitting to German demands. When that failed, he staged an incident on the border to allow him to claim that Germany had been attacked; and on September 1, 1939, he launched a full-scale invasion of Poland. Britain and France, true to their pledges, declared war on Germany two days later. World War II had begun.

FROM NEUTRALITY TO INTERVENTION

"This nation will remain a neutral nation," the president declared shortly after the hostilities began in Europe, "but I cannot ask that every American remain neutral in thought as well." It was a statement that stood in stark and deliberate contrast to Woodrow Wilson's 1914 plea that the nation remain neutral in both deed and thought; and it was clear from the start that among those whose opinions were decidedly unneutral in 1939 was the president himself.

Neutrality Tested

There was never any question that both he and the majority of the American people favored Britain, France, and the other Allied nations in the contest. The ques-

tion was how much the United States was prepared to do to assist them. At the very least, Roosevelt believed, the United States should make armaments available to the Allied armies to help them counter the highly productive German munitions industry. In September 1939, he asked Congress for a revision of the Neutrality Acts. The original measures had forbidden the sale of American weapons to any nation engaged in war; Roosevelt wanted the arms embargo lifted. Powerful isolationist opposition forced him to accept a weaker revision than he would have liked; as passed by Congress, the 1939 measure maintained the prohibition on American ships entering war zones. It did, however, permit belligerents to purchase arms on the same cash-and-carry basis that the earlier Neutrality Acts had established for the sale of nonmilitary materials.

For a time, it was possible to believe that little more would be necessary. After the German armies had quickly subdued Poland, the war in Europe settled into a long, quiet lull that lasted through the winter and spring—a "phony war," some called it. The only real fighting during this period occurred not between the Allies and the Axis, but between Russia and its neighbors. Taking advantage of the situation in the West, the Soviet Union overran and annexed the small Baltic republics of Latvia, Estonia, and Lithuania and then, in late November, invaded Finland. Most Americans were outraged, but neither Congress nor the president was willing to do more than impose an ineffective "moral embargo" on the shipment of armaments to Russia. By March 1940, the Soviet advance was complete.

Whatever illusions anyone may have had about the reality of the war in Western Europe were shattered in the spring of 1940 when Germany launched an invasion to the west—first attacking Denmark and Norway, sweeping next across the Netherlands and Belgium, and driving finally deep into the heart of France. Allied efforts proved futile against the Nazi blitzkrieg. One western European stronghold after another fell into German hands. On June 10, Mussolini brought Italy into the war, invading France from the south as Hitler was attacking from the north. On June 22, finally, France fell to the German onslaught. Nazi troops marched into Paris; a new collaborationist regime assembled in Vichy; and in all Europe, only the shattered remnants of the British army, rescued from the beaches of Dunkirk by a flotilla of military and civilian vessels assembled miraculously quickly, remained to oppose the Axis forces.

Roosevelt had already begun to increase American aid to the Allies. He also began preparations to resist a possible Nazi invasion of the United States. On May 16, he asked Congress for an additional $1 billion for defense (much of it for the construction of an enor-

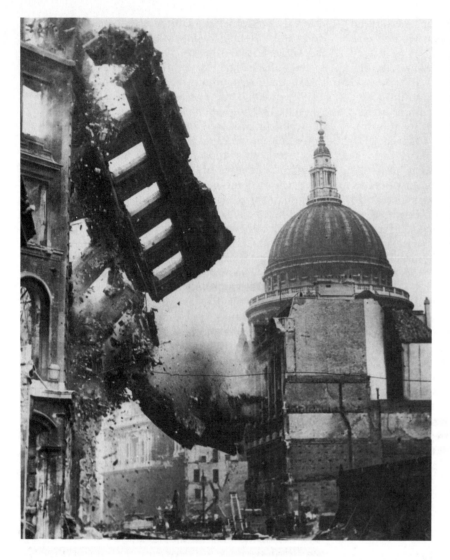

mous new fleet of warplanes) and received it quickly. With France tottering a few weeks later, he proclaimed that the United States would "extend to the opponents of force the material resources of this nation." And on May 15, Winston Churchill, the new British prime minister, sent Roosevelt the first of many long lists of requests for ships, armaments, and other assistance without which, he insisted, England could not long survive. Many Americans (including the United States ambassador to London, Joseph P. Kennedy) argued that the British plight was already hopeless, that any aid to the English was a wasted effort. The president, however, made the politically dangerous decision to "scrape the bottom of the barrel" to make war materials available to Churchill. He even circumvented the cash-and-carry provisions of the Neutrality Act by trading fifty Ameri-

can destroyers (most of them left over from World War I) to England in return for the right to build American bases on British territory in the Western Hemisphere; and he returned to the factories a number of new airplanes purchased by the American government so that the British could buy them instead.

Roosevelt was able to take such steps in part because of a major shift in American public opinion. Before the invasion of France, most Americans had believed that a German victory in the war would not be a threat to the United States. By July, with France defeated and Britain threatened, more than 66 percent of the public (according to opinion polls) believed that Germany posed a direct threat to the United States. Congress was aware of the change and was becoming more willing to permit expanded American assistance to the Allies. It was also becoming more concerned about the need for internal preparations for war, and in September it approved the Burke-Wadsworth Act, inaugurating the first peacetime military draft in American history.

But while the forces of isolation may have weakened, they were far from dead. On the contrary, a spirited and at times vicious debate began in the summer of 1940 between those who advocated expanded American involvement in the war (who were termed, often inaccurately, "interventionists") and those who continued to insist on neutrality. The celebrated journalist William Allen White served as chairman of a new Committee to Defend America, whose members lobbied actively for increased American assistance to the Allies but opposed actual intervention. Others went so far as to urge an immediate declaration of war (a position that as yet had little public support) and in April created an organization of their own, the Fight for Freedom Committee. Opposing them was a powerful new lobby called the America First Committee, which attracted some of America's most prominent leaders. Its chairman was General Robert E. Wood, until recently the president of Sears Roebuck; and its membership included Charles Lindbergh, General Hugh Johnson, Senator Gerald Nye, and Senator Burton Wheeler. It won the editorial support of the Hearst chain and other influential newspapers, and it had at least the indirect support of a large proportion of the Republican Party. (It also, inevitably, attracted a fringe of Nazi sympathizers and anti-Semites.) The debate between the two sides was loud and bitter. Through the summer and fall of 1940, moreover, it was complicated by a presidential campaign.

The Third-Term Campaign

For many months, the politics of 1940 revolved around the question of Franklin Roosevelt's intentions. Would he break with tradition and run for an unprecedented third term? The president himself was deliberately coy and never publicly revealed his own wishes. But by refusing to withdraw from the contest, he made it virtually impossible for any rival Democrat to establish a foothold within the party. Just before the Democratic Convention in July, he let it be known that he would accept a "draft" from his party. The Democrats quickly renominated him and even reluctantly swallowed his choice for vice president: Agriculture secretary Henry A. Wallace, a man too liberal for the taste of many party leaders.

The Republicans, again, faced a far more difficult task. With Roosevelt effectively straddling the center of the defense debate, favoring neither the extreme iso-

lationists nor the extreme interventionists, the Republicans had few viable alternatives. Their solution was to compete with the president on his own ground. Succumbing to a remarkable popular movement (carefully orchestrated by, among others, Henry Luce, the publisher of *Time* and *Life* magazines), they nominated a dynamic and attractive but politically inexperienced businessman, Wendell Willkie. Both the candidate and the party platform took positions little different from Roosevelt's: they would keep the country out of war but would extend generous assistance to the Allies. Willkie was left, therefore, with the unenviable task of defeating Roosevelt by outmatching him in personal magnetism and by trying to arouse public fears of the dangers of an unprecedented third term. An appealing figure and a vigorous campaigner, he managed to evoke more public enthusiasm than any Republican candidate in decades. In the end, however, he was no match for Franklin Roosevelt. The election was closer than it had been in either 1932 or 1936, but Roosevelt nevertheless won decisively. He received 55 percent of the popular vote to Willkie's 45 percent, and won 449 electoral votes to Willkie's 82.

Neutrality Abandoned

In the last weeks of 1940, with the election behind him, Roosevelt began to make subtle but profound changes in the American role in the war. To the public, he claimed that he was simply continuing the now established policy of providing aid to the embattled Allies. In fact, that aid was taking new and more decisive forms.

In December 1940, Great Britain was virtually bankrupt. No longer could the British meet the cash-and-carry requirements imposed by the Neutrality Acts; yet England's needs, Churchill insisted, were greater than ever. The president therefore, suggested a method that would "eliminate the dollar sign" from all arms transactions while still, he hoped, pacifying those who opposed blatant American intervention in the war. The new system was labeled "lend-lease." It would allow the government not only to sell but to lend or lease armaments to any nation deemed "vital to the defense of the United States." In other words, America could funnel weapons to England on the basis of no more than Britain's promise to return or pay for them when the war was over. Isolationists attacked the measure bitterly, arguing (correctly) that it was simply a device to tie the United States more closely to the Allies; but Congress enacted the bill by wide margins.

With lend-lease established, Roosevelt soon faced another serious problem: ensuring that the American supplies would actually reach Great Britain. Shipping

WHERE HISTORIANS DISAGREE

THE QUESTION OF PEARL HARBOR

T HE PHRASE "REMEMBER PEARL Harbor!" became a rallying cry during World War II—reminding Americans of the surprise Japanese attack on the American naval base in Hawaii, and arousing the nation to exact revenge. But within a few years of the end of hostilities, some Americans remembered Pearl Harbor for different reasons and began to challenge the official version of the attack on December 7, 1941. Their charges sparked a debate that has never fully subsided. Was the Japanese attack on Pearl Harbor unprovoked, and did it come without warning, as the Roosevelt administration claimed at the time? Or was it part of a deliberate plan by the president to have the Japanese force a reluctant United States into the war? Most controversial of all, did the administration know of the attack in advance? Did Roosevelt deliberately refrain from warning the commanders in Hawaii so that the air raid's effect on the American public would be more profound?

Among the first to challenge the official version of Pearl Harbor was the historian Charles A. Beard, who maintained in *President Roosevelt and the Coming of the War, 1941* (1948) that the United States had deliberately forced the Japanese into a position where they had no choice but to attack. By cutting off Japan's access to the raw materials it needed for its military adventure in China, by stubbornly refusing to compromise, the United States ensured that the Japanese would stike out into the southwest Pacific to take the needed supplies by force—even at the risk of war with the United States. Not only was American policy provocative in effect, Beard suggested; it was *deliberately* provocative. More than that, the administration, which had some time before cracked the Japanese code, must have known weeks in advance of Japan's plan to attack. Beard supported his argument by citing Secretary of War Henry Stimson's comment in his diary: "The question was how we should maneuver them into the position of firing the first shot."

A partial refutation of the Beard argument appeared in 1950 in Basil Rauch's *Roosevelt from Munich to Pearl Harbor*. The administration did not know in advance of the planned attack on Pearl Harbor, he argued. It did, however, expect an attack somewhere; and it made subtle efforts to "maneuver" Japan into firing the first shot in the conflict. But Richard N. Current, in *Secretary Stimson: A Study in Statecraft* (1954), offered an even stronger challenge to Beard. Stimson did indeed anticipate an attack, Current argued, but not an attack on American territory; rather, he anticipated an assault on British or Dutch possessions in the Pacific. The problem confronting

lanes in the Atlantic had become extremely dangerous; German submarines destroyed as much as a half-million tons of shipping each month. The British navy was losing ships more rapidly than it could replace them and was finding it difficult to transport materials across the Atlantic from America. Secretary of War Henry Stimson (who had been Hoover's secretary of state and who returned to the cabinet at Roosevelt's request in 1940) argued that the United States should itself convoy vessels to England; but Roosevelt decided to rely instead on the concept of "hemispheric defense," by which the United States navy would defend transport ships only in the western Atlantic—which he argued was a neutral zone and the responsibility of the American nations. By July 1941, American ships were patrolling the ocean as far east as Iceland, escorting convoys of merchant ships, and radioing information to British vessels about the location of Nazi submarines.

At first, Germany did little to challenge these obviously hostile American actions. By the fall of 1941, however, events in Europe changed its position. German forces had invaded the Soviet Union in June of that year, shattering the 1939 Nazi-Soviet pact. The Germans drove quickly and forcefully deep into Russian territory. When the Soviets did not surrender, as many had predicted they would, Roosevelt persuaded the administration was not how to maneuver the Japanese into attacking the United States, but how to find a way to make a Japanese attack on British or Dutch territory *appear* to be an attack on America. Only thus, Stimson believed, could Congress be persuaded to approve a declaration of war.

Roberta Wohlstetter took a different approach to the question, in *Pearl Harbor: Warning and Decision* (1962), the most thorough scholarly study to appear to that point. De-emphasizing the question of whether the American government *wanted* a Japanese attack, she undertook to answer the question of whether the administration *knew* of the attack in advance. Wohlstetter concluded that the United States had ample warning of Japanese intentions and should have realized that the Pearl Harbor raid was imminent. But government officials failed to interpret the evidence correctly, largely because their preconceptions about Japanese intentions were at odds with the evidence they confronted. Admiral Edwin T. Layton, who had been a staff officer at Pearl Harbor in 1941, also blames political and bureaucratic failures for the absence of advance warning of the attack. In a 1985 memoir, *And I Was There*, he argues that the Japanese attack was not only a result of "audacious planning and skillful execution" by the Japanese, but of "a dramatic breakdown in our intelligence process . . . related directly to feuding among high-level naval officers in Washington."

The most thorough study of Pearl Harbor to date appeared in 1981: Gordon W. Prange's *At Dawn We Slept*. Like Wohlstetter, Prange concluded that the Roosevelt administration was guilty of a series of disastrous blunders in interpreting Japanese strategy; the American government had possession of enough information to predict the attack, but failed to do so. But Prange dismissed the arguments of the "revisionists" (Beard and his successors) that the president had deliberately maneuvered the nation into the war by permitting the Japanese to attack. Instead, he emphasized the enormous daring and great skill with which the Japanese orchestrated an ambitious operation that few Americans believed possible.

But the revisionist claims have not been laid to rest. John Toland revived the charges of a Roosevelt betrayal in 1982, in *Infamy: Pearl Harbor and Its Aftermath*, claiming to have discovered new evidence (the testimony of an unidentified seaman) that proves the navy knew at least five days in advance that Japanese aircraft carriers were heading toward Hawaii. From that, Toland concluded that Roosevelt must have known that an attack was forthcoming and that he allowed it to occur in the belief that a surprise attack would arouse the nation. But like the many previous writers who have made the same argument, Toland was unable to produce any direct evidence of Roosevelt's knowledge of the planned attack.

Congress to extend lend lease privileges to them—the first step toward creating a new relationship with Stalin that would ultimately lead to a formal Soviet-American alliance. Now American industry was providing crucial assistance to Hitler's foes on two fronts, and the navy was playing a more active role than ever in protecting the flow of goods to Europe.

In September, Nazi submarines began a concerted campaign against American vessels. Early that month, a German U-boat fired on the American destroyer *Greer* (which was radioing the U-boat's position to the British at the time). Roosevelt responded by ordering American ships to fire on German submarines "on

sight." In October, Nazi submarines actually hit two American destroyers and sank one of them, the *Reuben James*, killing many American sailors in the process. Enraged members of Congress now voted approval of a measure allowing the United States to arm its merchant vessels and to sail all the way into belligerent ports. The United States had, in effect, launched a naval war against Germany.

At the same time, a series of meetings, some private and one public, were tying the United States and Great Britain more closely together. In April 1941, senior military officers of the two nations met in secret and agreed on the joint strategy they would follow were the United States to enter the war. In August, Roosevelt met with Churchill aboard a British vessel anchored off the coast of Newfoundland. The president made no military commitments, but he did join the prime minister in releasing a document that became known as the Atlantic Charter, in which the two nations set out "certain common principles" on which to base "a better future for the world." It was, in only vaguely disguised form, a statement of war aims that called openly for, among other things, "the final destruction of the Nazi tyranny."

By the fall of 1941, it seemed only a matter of time before the United States became an official belligerent. Roosevelt remained convinced that public opinion would support a declaration of war only in the event of an actual enemy attack. But an attack seemed certain to come, if not in the Atlantic, then in the Pacific.

The Road to Pearl Harbor

In the meantime, Japan was taking advantage of the crisis (which had preoccupied the Soviet Union and the two most powerful colonial powers in Asia, Britain and France) to extend its empire in the Pacific. In September 1940, Japan signed the Tripartite Pact, a loose defensive alliance with Germany and Italy that seemed to extend the Axis into Asia. (In reality, the European Axis powers never developed a very strong relationship with Japan, and the wars in Europe and the Pacific were largely separate conflicts.)

Roosevelt had already displayed his animosity toward Japanese policies by harshly denouncing their continuing assault on China and by terminating a long-standing American commercial treaty with the Tokyo government. Still the Japanese drive continued. In July 1941, imperial troops moved into Indochina and seized the capital of Vietnam, a colony of France (after having demanded and received a base there a year before). The United States, having broken the Japanese codes, knew that their next target would be the Dutch East Indies; and when Tokyo failed to respond to Roosevelt's stern warnings, the president froze all Japanese assets in the United States and established a complete trade embargo, severely limiting Japan's ability to purchase essential supplies (including oil). American public opinion, shaped by strong anti-Japanese prejudices developed over several decades, generally supported these hostile actions.

Tokyo now faced a choice. It would either have to repair relations with the United States to restore the flow of supplies, or it would have to find those supplies elsewhere, most notably by seizing British and Dutch possessions in the Pacific. At first the Tokyo government seemed willing to compromise. The Japanese prime minister, Prince Konoye, had begun negotiations with the United States even before the freezing of his country's assets, and in August he increased the pace by requesting a personal meeting with President Roosevelt. But the United States rebuffed these overtures. Secretary of State Hull feared that Konoye lacked sufficient power within his own government to be able to enforce any agreement, and he persuaded Roosevelt to say that he would meet with the prime minister only if Japan would give guarantees in advance that it would respect the territorial integrity of China. Konoye could give no such assurances, as Roosevelt and Hull knew, and the negotiations collapsed. In October, militants in Tokyo forced Konoye out of office and replaced him with the leader of the war party, General Hideki Tojo. With Japan's need for new sources of fuel becoming desperate, there now seemed little alternative to war.

For several weeks, the Tojo government kept up a pretense of wanting to continue negotiations. On November 20, 1941, Tokyo proposed a modus vivendi highly favorable to itself and sent its diplomats in Washington to the State Department to discuss it. But Tokyo had already decided that it would not yield on the question of China, and Washington had made clear that it would accept nothing less than a reversal of that policy. Hull rejected the Japanese overtures out of hand; on November 27, he told Secretary of War Henry Stimson, "I have washed my hands of the Japanese situation, and it is now in the hands of you and [Secretary of the Navy Frank] Knox, the Army and Navy." He was not merely speculating. American intelligence had already decoded Japanese messages which made clear that war was imminent, that after November 29 an attack would be only a matter of days.

But Washington did not know where the attack would take place. Most officials were convinced that the Japanese would move first not against American territory but against British or Dutch possessions to the south. American intelligence took note of a Japanese naval task force that began sailing east from the Kurile Islands in the general direction of Hawaii on November 25, and radioed a routine warning to the United States naval facility at Pearl Harbor, near Honolulu. But officials were paying more attention to a large Japanese convoy moving southward through the China Sea. A combination of confusion and miscalculation led the government to overlook indications that Japan intended a direct attack on American forces—partly because Hawaii was so far from Japan that few believed such an attack possible.

At 7:55 A.M. on Sunday, December 7, 1941, a wave of Japanese bombers—taking off from aircraft carriers

SIGNIFICANT EVENTS

1921 Washington Conference leads to reductions in naval armaments

1922 Fordney-McCumber Tariff passed

1924 Dawes Plan renegotiates European debts, reparations

1928 Kellogg-Briand Pact signed

1931 Economic crisis spreads worldwide

Japan invades Manchuria

1932 World Disarmament Conference held in Geneva

1933 Adolf Hitler becomes chancellor of Germany

United States scuttles London Economic Conference

United States establishes diplomatic relations with Soviet Union

Roosevelt proclaims Good Neighbor Policy

1935 Senate defeats World Court treaty

Neutrality Act passed

Italy invades Ethiopia

1936 Spanish Civil War begins

Germany reoccupies Rhineland

Second Neutrality Act passed

1937 Japan launches new invasion of China

Roosevelt gives "quarantine" speech

Japan attacks U.S. gunboat *Panay*

Third Neutrality Act passed

1938 Germany annexes Austria (Anschluss)

Munich Conference

1939 Nazi-Soviet nonaggression pact signed

Germany invades Czechoslovakia

Germany invades Poland

World War II begins

1940 Soviet Union invades Baltic nations, Finland

German blitzkrieg conquers most of Western Europe

Germany, Italy, Japan sign Tripartite Pact

Fight for Freedom Committee founded

America First Committee founded

Roosevelt reelected president

United States makes destroyers-for-bases deal with Britain

1941 Lend-lease plan provides aid to Britain

American ships confront German submarines in North Atlantic

Germany invades Soviet Union

Atlantic Charter signed

Japan attacks Pearl Harbor

United States enters war

---

hundreds of miles away—attacked the United States naval base at Pearl Harbor. A second wave came an hour later. Military commanders in Hawaii had taken no precautions against such an attack and had allowed ships to remain bunched up defenselessly in the harbor and airplanes to remain parked in rows on airstrips. The consequences of the raid were disastrous for America. Within two hours, the United States lost 8 battleships, 3 cruisers, 4 other vessels, 188 airplanes, and several vital shore installations. More than 2,000 soldiers and sailors died, and another 1,000 were injured. The Japanese suffered only light losses.

American forces were now greatly diminished in the Pacific (although by sheer accident, none of the American aircraft carriers—the heart of the Pacific fleet—had been at Pearl Harbor on December 7). Nevertheless, the raid on Pearl Harbor did virtually overnight what more than two years of effort by Roosevelt and others had been unable to do: it unified the American people in a fervent commitment to war. On De-

PEARL HARBOR, DECEMBER 7, 1941
The destroyer U.S.S. *Shaw*, immobilized in a floating drydock in Pearl Harbor in December 1941, survived the first wave of Japanese bombers unscathed. But in the second attack, the Japanese scored a direct hit and produced this spectacular explosion, which blew off the ship's bow. Damage to the rest of the ship, however, was slight. Just a few months later the *Shaw* was fitted with a new bow and rejoined the fleet. *(U.S. Navy Photo)*

cember 8, the president traveled to Capitol Hill, where he grimly addressed a joint session of Congress: "Yesterday, December 7, 1941—a date which will live in infamy—the United States of America was suddenly and deliberately attacked by the naval and air forces of the Empire of Japan." Within four hours, the Senate unanimously and the House 388 to 1 (the lone dissenter being Jeanette Rankin of Montana, who had voted against war in 1917 as well) approved a declaration of war against Japan. Three days later, Germany and Italy, Japan's European allies, declared war on the United States; and on the same day, December 11, Congress reciprocated without a dissenting vote. For the second time in twenty-five years, the United States was engaged in a world war.

SUGGESTED READINGS

The 1920s. Thomas Buckley, *The United States and the Washington Conference* (1970). Warren Cohen, *America's Response to China* (1971); *Empire Without Tears* (1987). Frank Costigliola, *Awkward Dominion: American Political, Economic, and Cultural Relations with Europe, 1919–1933* (1984). Roger Dingman, *Power in the Pacific* (1976). L. Ethan Ellis, *Republican Foreign Policy, 1921–1933* (1968). Robert H. Ferrell, *Peace in Their Time* (1952). Michael J. Hogan, *Informal Entente: The Private Structure of Cooperation in Anglo-American Economic Diplomacy, 1918–1928* (1977). Akira Iriye, *After Imperialism* (1965). William Kamman, *A Search for Stability: United States Diplomacy Toward Nicaragua, 1925-1933* (1968). Melvyn P. Leffler, *The Elusive Quest: America's Pursuit of European Stability and French Security, 1919-1933* (1979). Merlo J. Pusey, *Charles Evans Hughes,* 2 vols. (1963). Joseph Tulchin, *The Aftermath of War* (1971). William Appleman Williams, *The Tragedy of*

American Diplomacy (1962). Joan Hoff Wilson, *American Business and Foreign Policy, 1920–1933* (1968); *Ideology and Economics* (1974).

The Hoover Years. Alexander DeConde, *Hoover's Latin American Policy* (1951). Robert H. Ferrell, *American Diplomacy in the Great Depression* (1970). Elting Morison, *Turmoil and Tradition* (1960). Raymond O'Connor, *Perilous Equilibrium* (1962). Armin Rappaport, *Stimson and Japan* (1963).

New Deal Diplomacy. Edward E. Bennett, *Recognition of Russia* (1970). Dorothy Borg, *The United States and the Far Eastern Crisis of 1933–1938* (1964). Robert Browder, *The Origins of Soviet-American Diplomacy* (1953). Bruce J. Calder, *The Impact of Intervention* (1984). Robert Dallek, *Franklin D. Roosevelt and American Foreign Policy, 1932–1945* (1979). Beatrice Farnsworth, *William C. Bullitt and the Soviet Union* (1967). Peter Filene, *Americans and the Soviet Experiment, 1917–1933* (1967). Frank Freidel, *Launching the New Deal* (1973). Lloyd Gardner, *Economic Aspects of New Deal Diplomacy* (1964). Irwin F. Gellman, *Good Neighbor Diplomacy: United States Policies in Latin America, 1933–1945* (1979). David Green, *The Containment of Latin America* (1971). Warren F. Kimball, *The Juggler: Franklin Roosevelt as Wartime Statesman* (1991). Walter LaFeber, *Inevitable Revolutions* (1983). Lorenzo Meyer, *Mexico and the United States in the Oil Controversy* (1977). Bryce Wood, *The Making of the Good Neighbor Policy* (1961).

Isolationism and Pacifism. Selig Adler, *The Uncertain Giant* (1966); *The Isolationist Impulse* (1957). Charles Chatfield, *For Peace and Justice: Pacifism in America, 1914–1941* (1971). Warren I. Cohen, *The American Revisionists* (1967). Wayne S. Cole, *America First* (1953); *Senator Gerald P. Nye and American Foreign Relations* (1962); *Charles A. Lindbergh and the Battle Against American Intervention in World War II* (1974); *Roosevelt and the Isolationists, 1932–1945* (1983). Charles DeBenedetti, *Origins of the Modern American Peace Movement, 1915–1929* (1978); *The Peace Reform in American History* (1980). Robert Divine, *The Reluctant Belligerent* (1965). Thomas N. Guinsburg, *The Pursuit of Isolation in the United States Senate from Versailles to Pearl Harbor* (1982). Manfred Jonas, *Isolationism in America* (1966). Thomas C. Kennedy, *Charles A. Beard and American Foreign Policy* (1975). William Langer and S. Everett Gleason, *The Challenge to Isolation* (1952); *The Undeclared War* (1953). Richard Lowitt, *George W. Norris,* 3 vols. (1963–1978). John K. Nelson, *The Peace Prophets* (1967). Lawrence Wittner, *Rebels Against War* (1984).

The Coming of World War II. James MacGregor Burns, *Roosevelt: The Soldier of Freedom* (1970). Garry Clifford and Samuel R. Spencer, Jr., *The First Peacetime Draft* (1986). Roger Dingman, *Power in the Pacific* (1976). Bernard F. Donahoe, *Private Plans and Public Dangers* (1965). Herbert Feis, *The Road to Pearl Harbor* (1950). Waldo H. Heinrichs, Jr., *Threshold of War* (1988). Akira Iriye, *Across the Pacific* (1967); *After Imperialism: The Search for a New Order in the Far East, 1921–1933* (1965); *The Origins of the Second World War in Asia and the Pacific* (1987). Manfred Jonas, *The United States and Germany* (1984). Warren Kimball, *The Most Unsordid Act: Lend-Lease, 1939–1941* (1970). Joseph Lash, *Roosevelt and Churchill* (1976). James Leutze, *Bargaining for Supremacy* (1977). Martin V. Melosi, *The Shadow of Pearl Harbor* (1977). Arnold Offner, *The Origins of the Second World War* (1975). Gordon Prange, *At Dawn We Slept* (1981); *Pearl Harbor* (1986). Michael S. Sherry, *The Rise of American Airpower* (1987). David Reynolds, *The Creation of the Anglo-American Alliance, 1937–1941* (1982). David F. Schmitz, *The United States and Fascist Italy, 1922–1944* (1988). Jonathan Utley, *Going to War with Japan* (1985). Roberta Wohlstetter, *Pearl Harbor: Warning and Decision* (1962). David S. Wyman, *Paper Walls: America and the Refugee Crisis, 1938–1941* (1985).

THE THREE-FRONT WAR
Late in the war, during a meeting with Roosevelt and Churchill, Stalin offered a toast: "To American production, without which the war would have been lost." The American government was well aware of how vital production was to the war effort; it was so important that the American industrial economy in effect constituted a "third front" in the fighting. This propaganda poster was one of many designed to boost morale among (and discourage strikes by) industrial workers in America. *(Bettmann)*

CHAPTER TWENTY-EIGHT

AMERICA IN
A WORLD AT WAR

THE ATTACK ON PEARL Harbor thrust the United States into the greatest and most terrible war in the history of humanity. World War I had cost many lives and had destroyed centuries-old European social and political institutions. But World War II created unprecedented carnage and horror in Europe and in much of the rest of the globe. And in the end, it changed the world as profoundly as any event of the twentieth century, perhaps of any century.

Less readily apparent is how profoundly the war changed America—its society, its politics, and its image of itself. Except for the combatants themselves, most Americans experienced the war at a remove of several thousand miles. They endured no bombing, no invasion, no massive dislocations, no serious material shortages. Veterans returning home in 1945 and 1946 found a country that looked very much like the one they had left—something that clearly could not be said of veterans returning home to Britain, France, Germany, Russia, or Japan.

But World War II did transform the United States in profound, if not always in readily visible, ways. As the poet Archibald MacLeish said in 1943: "The great majority of the American people understand very well that this war is not a war only, but an end and a beginning—an end to things known and a beginning of things unknown. We have smelled the wind in the streets that changes weather. We know that whatever the world will be when the war ends, the world will be different." The story of American involvement in the war is not just the story of how the military forces

and the industrial might of the United States helped defeat Germany, Italy, and Japan. It is also the story of the creation of a new world, both abroad and at home.

WAR ON TWO FRONTS

Whatever political disagreements and social tensions may have existed among the American people during World War II, there was striking unity of opinion about the conflict itself—"a unity," as one member of Congress proclaimed shortly after Pearl Harbor, "never before witnessed in this country." America's unity and confidence were severely tested in the first, troubled months of 1942. Despite the impressive display of patriotism and the dramatic flurry of activity, the war was going very badly. Britain appeared ready to collapse. The Soviet Union was staggering. One after another, Allied strongholds in the Pacific were falling to the forces of Japan. The first task facing the United States, therefore, was less to achieve victory than to stave off defeat.

Containing the Japanese

Ten hours after the strike at Pearl Harbor, Japanese airplanes attacked the American airfields at Manila in the Philippines, destroying much of America's remaining air power in the Pacific. Three days later Guam, an American possession, fell to Japan; then Wake Island

WORLD WAR II IN THE PACIFIC

and the British colony, Hong Kong. The great British fortress of Singapore in Malaya surrendered in February 1942, the Dutch East Indies in March, Burma in April. In the Philippines, exhausted Filipino and American troops gave up their defense of the islands on May 6.

American strategists planned two broad offensives to turn the tide against the Japanese. One, under the command of General Douglas MacArthur, would move north from Australia, through New Guinea, and eventually back to the Philippines. The other, under Admiral Chester Nimitz, would move west from

Hawaii toward major Japanese island outposts in the central Pacific. Ultimately, the two offensives would come together to invade Japan itself.

The Allies achieved their first important victory in the Battle of Coral Sea, just northwest of Australia, on May 7–8, 1942, when American forces turned back the previously unstoppable Japanese fleet. A month later, there was an even more important turning point northwest of Hawaii. An enormous battle raged for four days, June 3–6, 1942, near the small American outpost at Midway Island, at the end of which the United States, despite great losses, was clearly victorious. The

GUADALCANAL
Guadalcanal, in the Solomon Islands, was the scene of some of the bloodiest and most protracted fighting between American and Japanese soldiers in the entire Pacific war. U.S. marines are shown here in a jungle outpost in a part of the island that became known as "Hell's Corner." A Navy bomber flies overhead. *(UPI/Bettmann)*

American navy destroyed four Japanese aircraft carriers while losing only one, and regained control of the central Pacific for the United States.

The Americans took the offensive for the first time several months later in the southern Solomon Islands, to the east of New Guinea. In August 1942, American forces assaulted three of the islands: Gavutu, Tulagi, and Guadalcanal. A struggle of terrible ferocity (and, before it was over, terrible savagery) developed at Guadalcanal and continued for six months, inflicting heavy losses on both sides. In the end, however, the Japanese were forced to abandon the island—and with it their last chance of launching an effective offensive to the south.

Thus in both the southern and central Pacific, the initiative had shifted to the United States by mid-1943. The Japanese advance had come to a stop. With aid from the Australians and the New Zealanders, the Americans now began the slow, arduous process of moving toward the Philippines and Japan itself.

Holding Off the Germans

In the European war, the United States had less control over military operations. It was fighting in cooperation with Britain and with the exiled "Free French" forces in the west; and it was trying also to conciliate its new ally, the Soviet Union, which was fighting Hitler in the east. The army chief of staff, General George C. Marshall, supported a plan for a major Allied invasion of France across the English Channel in the spring of 1943. But the American plan faced challenges from the Allies. The Soviet Union, which was absorbing (as it would throughout the war) the brunt of the German war effort, wanted the Allied invasion to proceed at the earliest possible moment. The British, on the other hand, wanted first to launch a series of Allied offensives around the edges of the Nazi empire—in northern Africa and southern Europe—before undertaking the major invasion of France.

Roosevelt was torn, but ultimately decided to support the British plan—in part because he was eager to get American forces into combat quickly and feared a cross-channel invasion would take a long time to prepare. At the end of October 1942, the British opened a counteroffensive against Nazi forces in North Africa under General Erwin Rommel, who was threatening the Suez Canal at El Alamein, and forced the Germans to retreat from Egypt. On November 8, Anglo-American forces landed at Oran and Algiers in Algeria and at Casablanca in Morocco—areas under the Nazi-controlled French government at Vichy—and began moving east toward Rommel. The Germans threw the full weight of their forces in Africa against the inexperienced Americans and inflicted a serious defeat on them at the Kasserine Pass in Tunisia. General George S. Patton, however, regrouped the American troops and began an effective counteroffensive. With the help of Allied air and naval power and of British forces attacking from the east under Field Marshall Bernard Montgomery (the hero of El Alamein), the American offensive finally drove the last Germans from Africa in May 1943.

The North African campaign had tied up so large a proportion of the Allied resources that the planned May 1943 cross-channel invasion of France had to be postponed, despite angry complaints from the Soviet Union. By now, however, the threat of a Soviet collapse seemed much diminished, for during the winter of 1942–1943 the Red Army had successfully held off

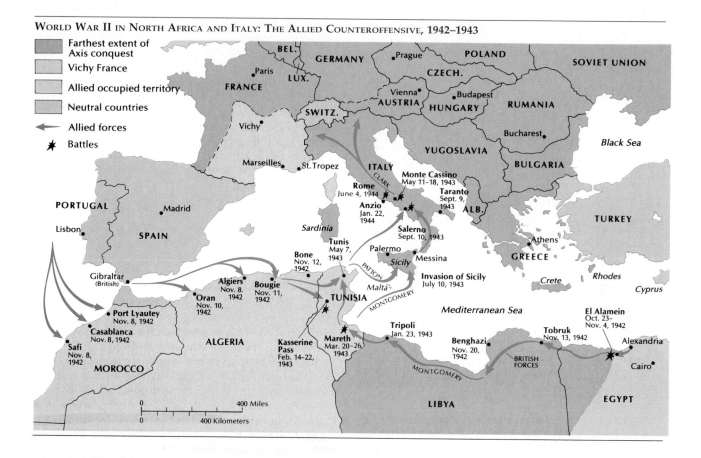

WORLD WAR II IN NORTH AFRICA AND ITALY: THE ALLIED COUNTEROFFENSIVE, 1942–1943

a major German assault at Stalingrad in southern Russia. Hitler had committed such enormous forces to the battle, and had suffered such appalling losses, that he could not continue his eastern offensive.

The Soviet victory had come at a terrible cost. The German siege of Stalingrad had decimated the civilian population of the city and devastated the surrounding countryside. Indeed, throughout the war, the Soviet Union absorbed losses far greater than any other warring nation (up to 20 million casualties)—a fact that continued to haunt the Russian memory and affect Soviet policy generations later. But the Soviet success in beating back the German offensive persuaded Roosevelt to agree, in a January 1943 meeting with Churchill in Casablanca, to a British plan for an Allied invasion of Sicily. General Marshall opposed the plan, arguing that it would further delay the vital invasion of France. But Churchill prevailed with the argument that the operation in Sicily might knock Italy out of the war and tie up German divisions that might otherwise be stationed in France. On the night of July 9, 1943, American and British armies landed in southeast

Sicily; thirty-eight days later they had conquered the island and were moving onto the Italian mainland. In the face of these setbacks, Mussolini's government collapsed and the dictator himself fled north to Germany. But although Mussolini's successor, Pietro Badoglio, quickly committed Italy to the Allies, Germany moved eight divisions into the country and established a powerful defensive line south of Rome. The Allied offensive on the Italian peninsula, which began on September 3, 1943, soon bogged down, especially after a serious setback at Monte Cassino that winter. Not until May 1944 did the Allies resume their northward advance. On June 4, 1944, they captured Rome.

The invasion of Italy contributed to the Allied war effort in several important ways. But it postponed the invasion of France by as much as a year, deeply embittering the Soviet Union, many of whose leaders believed that the United States and Britain were deliberating delaying in order to allow the Russians to absorb the brunt of the fighting. The postponement also gave the Soviets time to begin moving toward the countries of Eastern Europe.

America and the Holocaust

In the midst of this intensive fighting, the leaders of the American government were confronted with one of history's great horrors: the Nazi campaign to exterminate the Jews of Europe—the Holocaust. As early as 1942, high officials in Washington had incontrovertible evidence that Hitler's forces were rounding up Jews and others (including Poles, gypsies, homosexuals, and communists) from all over Europe, transporting them to concentration camps in eastern Germany and Poland, and systematically murdering them. (The death toll would ultimately reach 6 million Jews and approximately 4 million others.) News of the atrocities was reaching the public as well, and public pressure began to build for an Allied effort to end the killing or at least to rescue some of the surviving Jews.

The American government consistently resisted almost all such entreaties. Although Allied bombers were flying missions within a few miles of the most notorious death camp at Auschwitz in Poland, pleas that the planes try to destroy the crematoria at the camp were rejected as militarily unfeasible. So were similar requests that the Allies try to destroy railroad lines leading to the camp. The United States also resisted entreaties that it admit large numbers of the Jewish refugees attempting to escape Europe—a pattern established well before Pearl Harbor. One ship, the *St. Louis*, had arrived off Miami in 1939 carrying nearly 1,000 escaped German Jews, only to be refused entry and forced to return to Europe. Both before and during the war, the State Department did not even use up the number of visas permitted by law; almost 90 percent of the quota remained untouched. This disgraceful record was not a result of inadvertence. There was, it seems clear, a deliberate effort by officials in the State Department—spearheaded by Assistant Secretary Breckinridge Long, a genteel anti-Semite—to prevent Jews from entering the United States. One opportunity after another to assist the imperiled Jews was either ignored or rejected.

After 1941, there was probably little American leaders could have done, other than defeat Germany, to save most of Hitler's victims. But more forceful action by the United States (and Britain, which was even less amenable to Jewish requests for assistance) might well have saved some lives. That they did not take such action, it seems evident in retrospect, constituted a considerable moral failure. Policymakers at the time, however, justified abandoning the Jews to their fate by concentrating their attention solely on the larger goal of winning the war. Any diversion of energy and attention to other purposes, they claimed, would distract them from the overriding goal of victory.

THE AMERICAN IN WARTIME

"War is no longer simply a battle between armed forces in the field," an American government report of 1939 concluded. "It is a struggle in which each side strives to bring to bear against the enemy the coordinated power of every individual and of every material resource at its command. The conflict extends from the soldier in the front line to the citizen in the remotest hamlet in the rear."

The United States had experienced many wars before. But not since the Civil War had the nation undergone so consuming a military experience as World War II. American armed forces engaged in combat around the globe for nearly four years. American society, in the meantime, underwent changes that reached into virtually every corner of the nation.

Prosperity

World War II had its most profound impact on American domestic life by at last ending the Great Depression. By the middle of 1941, the economic problems of the 1930s—unemployment, deflation, industrial sluggishness—had virtually vanished before the great wave of wartime industrial expansion.

The most important agent of the new prosperity was federal spending, which after 1939 was pumping more money into the economy each year than all the New Deal relief agencies combined had done. In 1939, the federal budget had been $9 billion, the highest level it had ever reached in peacetime; by 1945, it had risen to $100 billion. Largely as a result, the gross national product soared: from $91 billion in 1939 to $166 billion in 1945. Personal incomes in some areas grew by as much as 100 percent or more. The demands of wartime production created a shortage of consumer goods, so many wage earners diverted much of their new affluence into savings, which would later help keep the economic boom alive in the postwar years.

The impact of government spending was perhaps most dramatic in the West, which had long relied on federal largesse more than other regions. The West Coast, naturally, became the launching point for most of the naval war against Japan; and the government created large manufacturing facilities in California and elsewhere to serve the needs of its military. Altogether, the government made almost $40 billion worth of capital investments (factories, military and transportation facilities, highways, power plants) in the West during the war, more than in any other region. Ten percent of all the money the federal government spent between 1940 and 1945 went to California alone. Other western states also shared disproportionately in war contracts and government-funded capital investments.

Henry J. Kaiser, whose construction companies had built some of the great western dams in the 1930s and who in the process had become a great favorite of many members of the Roosevelt administration, singlehandedly steered billions of federal dollars into vast capital projects in the West. He then used the infrastructure he had helped build to create major centers for shipbuilding, steel, magnesium, and aluminum production. By the end of the war, the economy of the Pacific Coast and, to a lesser extent, other areas of the West had been transformed. The Pacific Coast had become the center of the growing American aircraft industry. New yards in southern California, Washington State, and elsewhere made the West a center of the shipbuilding industry. Los Angeles, formerly a medium-sized city notable chiefly for its film industry, now became a major industrial center as well.

Once a lightly industrialized region, parts of the West were now among the most important manufacturing areas in the country. Once a region without adequate facilities to support substantial economic growth, the West now stood poised to become the fastest-growing region in the nation after the war.

Labor and the War

Instead of the prolonged and debilitating unemployment that had been the most troubling feature of the Depression economy, the war created a serious labor shortage. The armed forces took more than 15 million men and women out of the civilian work force at the same time that the demand for labor was rising rapidly. Nevertheless, the civilian work force increased by almost 20 percent during the war. The 7 million who had previously been unemployed accounted for some of the increase; the employment of many people previously considered inappropriate for the work force—the very young, the elderly, and most important, several million women—accounted for the rest.

The war gave an enormous boost to union membership, which rose from about 10.5 million in 1941 to over 13 million in 1945. But it also created important new restrictions on the ability of unions to fight for their members' demands. The government was principally interested in preventing inflation and in keeping production moving without disruption. It managed to win important concessions from union leaders on both scores. One was the so-called Little Steel for-

mula, which set a 15 percent limit on wartime wage increases. Another was the "no-strike" pledge, by which unions agreed not to stop production in wartime. In return, the government provided labor with a "maintenance-of-membership" agreement, which ensured that the thousands of new workers pouring into unionized defense plants would be automatically enrolled in the unions. The agreement ensured the continued health of the union organizations, but in return workers had to give up the right to demand major economic gains during the war.

Many rank-and-file union members, and some local union leaders, resented the restrictions imposed on them by the government and the labor movement hierarchy. Despite the no-strike pledge, there were nearly 15,000 work stoppages during the war, mostly wildcat strikes (strikes unauthorized by the union leadership). When the United Mine Workers defied the government by striking in May 1943, Congress reacted by passing, over Roosevelt's veto, the Smith-Connally Act (War Labor Disputes Act), which required unions to wait thirty days before striking and empowered the president to seize a struck war plant. In the meantime, public animosity toward labor rose rapidly, and many states passed laws to limit union power.

Stabilizing the Boom

The fear of deflation, the central concern of the 1930s, gave way during the war to a fear of inflation, particularly after prices rose 25 percent in the two years before Pearl Harbor. In October 1942, Congress grudgingly responded to the president's request and passed the Anti-Inflation Act, which gave the administration authority to freeze agricultural prices, wages, salaries, and rents throughout the country. Enforcement of these provisions was the task of the Office of Price Administration (OPA), led first by Leon Henderson and then by Chester Bowles. In part because of its success, inflation was a much less serious problem during World War II than it had been during World War I.

Even so, the OPA was never popular. There was widespread resentment of its controls over wages and prices. And there was only grudging acquiescence in its complicated system of rationing scarce consumer goods: coffee, sugar, meat, butter, canned goods, shoes, tires, gasoline, and fuel oil. Black-marketing and overcharging grew to proportions far beyond OPA policing capacity.

From 1941 to 1945, the federal government spent a total of $321 billion—twice as much as it had spent in the entire 150 years of its existence to that point, and ten times as much as the cost of World War I. The national debt rose from $49 billion in 1941 to $259 billion in 1945. The government borrowed about half the revenues it needed by selling $100 billion worth of bonds. Much of the rest it raised by radically increasing income taxes through the Revenue Act of 1942, which established a 94 percent rate for the highest brackets and, for the first time, imposed taxes on the lowest-income families as well. To simplify collection, Congress enacted a withholding system of payroll deductions in 1943.

Mobilizing Production

The search for an effective mechanism to mobilize the economy for war began as early as 1939 and continued for nearly four years. One failed agency after another attempted to bring order to the mobilization effort. Finally, in January 1942, the president responded to widespread criticism by creating the War Production Board (WPB), under the direction of former Sears Roebuck executive Donald Nelson. In theory, the WPB was to be a "superagency," with broad powers over the economy. In fact, it never had as much authority as its World War I equivalent, the War Industries Board. And the genial Donald Nelson never displayed the administrative or political strength of his 1918 counterpart, Bernard Baruch.

Throughout its troubled history, therefore, the WPB found itself constantly outmaneuvered and frustrated. It was never able to win control over military purchases; the army and navy often circumvented the board entirely in negotiating contracts with producers. It was never able to satisfy the complaints of small business, which charged (correctly) that most contracts were going to large corporations. Gradually, the president transferred much of the WPB's authority to a new office located within the White House: the Office of War Mobilization, directed by former Supreme Court justice and South Carolina senator James F. Byrnes. But the OWM was only slightly more successful than the WPB.

Despite the administrative problems, the war economy managed to meet almost all the nation's critical war needs. Enormous new factory complexes sprang up in the space of a few months, many of them funded by the federal government's Defense Plants Corporation. An entire new industry producing synthetic rubber emerged, to make up for the loss of access to natural rubber in the Pacific. By the beginning of 1944, American factories were, in fact, producing more than the government needed. Their output was twice that of all the Axis countries combined. There were even complaints late in the war that military production was

becoming excessive, that a limited resumption of civilian production should begin before the fighting ended. The military staunchly and successfully opposed almost all such demands.

African Americans and the War

During World War I, many African Americans had eagerly seized the chance to serve in the armed forces, believing that their patriotic efforts would win them an enhanced position in postwar society. They had been cruelly disappointed. As World War II approached, blacks were again determined to use the conflict to improve their position in society—this time, however, not by currying favor but by making demands.

In the summer of 1941, A. Philip Randolph, president of the Brotherhood of Sleeping Car Porters (a union with a predominantly black membership), began to insist that the government require companies receiving defense contracts to integrate their work forces. To mobilize support for the demand, Randolph planned a massive march on Washington, which would, he promised, bring over 100,000 demonstrators to the capital. Roosevelt was afraid of both the possibility of violence and the certainty of political embarrassment. He finally persuaded Randolph to cancel the march in return for a promise to establish a Fair Employment Practices Commission to investigate discrimination against blacks in war industries. The FEPC's enforcement powers, and thus its effectiveness, were limited, but its creation was a rare symbolic victory for African-Americans making demands of the government.

The demand for labor in war plants greatly increased the migration of blacks from the rural areas of the South into industrial cities—a migration that continued for more than a decade after the war and brought many more African Americans into northern cities than the first Great Migration of 1914–1919 had done. The migration bettered the economic condition of many African Americans, but it also created urban tensions. On a hot June day in Detroit in 1943, a series of altercations between blacks and whites at a city park led to two days of racial violence in which thirty-four people died, twenty-five of them blacks.

Despite such tensions, the leading black organizations redoubled their efforts during the war to challenge the system of segregation. The Congress of Racial Equality (CORE), organized in 1942, mobilized mass popular resistance to discrimination in a way that the older, more conservative organizations had never done. Randolph, Bayard Rustin, James Farmer,

AFRICAN-AMERICAN TROOPS IN GERMANY, 1945
Many black Americans served in the military during World War II, almost all of them in segregated units. Relatively few black soldiers were sent into combat, but those who were fought with distinction. This platoon of the 104th Division—captured twenty-four SS troops near this spot (Scherfide, Germany) in the last weeks of the war. *(UPI/Bettmann)*

and other, younger black leaders helped organize sit-ins and demonstrations in segregated theaters and restaurants. In 1944, they won a much-publicized victory by forcing a Washington, D.C., restaurant to agree to serve blacks. Their defiant spirit would survive into the 1950s and help produce the civil rights movement.

Pressure for change was also growing within the military. At first, the armed forces maintained their traditional practice of limiting blacks to the most menial assignments, keeping them in segregated training camps and units, and barring them entirely from the Marine Corps and the Army Air Forces. Gradually, however, military leaders were forced to make adjustments—in part because of public and political pressures, but also because they recognized that these forms of segregation were wasting manpower. By the end of the war, the number of black servicemen had increased sevenfold, to 700,000; some training camps were being at least partially integrated; blacks were beginning to serve on ships with white sailors; and more black units were being sent into combat. But tensions remained. In some of the partially integrated army bases—Fort Dix, New Jersey, for example—riots occasionally broke out when African Americans protested having to serve in segregated divisions. Substantial discrimination survived in all the services until well after the war. But within the military, as within the society at large, the traditional pattern of race relations was slowly eroding.

Indians and the War

Approximately 25,000 Indians performed military service during World War II. Many of them served in combat (among them Ira Hayes, one of the men who raised the American flag at Iwo Jima and became part of a legendary photograph and, later, war memorial). Others worked as "code-talkers," working in military communications and speaking their own languages (which enemy forces would be unlikely to understand) over the radio and the telephones.

The war had important effects, too, on those Native Americans who remained civilians. Little war work reached the tribes, and government subsidies dwindled. Many talented young people left the reservations, some to serve in the military, even more (more than 70,000) to work in war plants. This brought many Indians into intimate contact with white society for the first time, and awakened in among some of them a taste for the material benefits of life in capitalist America that they would retain after the war. Some never returned to the reservations, but chose to remain in the non-Indian world and assimilate to its ways. Others found that after the war, employment opportunities that had been available to them during the fighting became unavailable once again, leaving them little alternative but to return to the reservations.

The wartime emphasis on national unity undermined support for the revitalization of tribal autonomy that the Indian Reorganization Act of 1934 had launched.

New pressures emerged to eliminate the reservation system and require the tribes to assimilate into white society—pressures so severe that John Collier, the energetic director of the Bureau of Indian Affairs who had done so much to promote the reinvigoration of the reservations, resigned in 1945.

Mexican-American War Workers

Large numbers of Mexican workers entered the United States during the war in response to labor shortages on the Pacific Coast, the Southwest, and eventually almost all areas of the nation. The American and Mexican government agreed in 1942 to a program by which *braceros* (contract laborers) would be admitted to the United States for a limited time to work at specific jobs, and American employers in some parts of the Southwest began actively recruiting Hispanic workers.

During the Depression, many Mexican farmworkers had been deported to make room for desperate white workers. The wartime labor shortage caused farm owners to begin hiring them again. More important, however, Mexicans were able for the first time to find significant numbers of factory jobs. They formed the second largest group of migrants (after blacks) to American cities in the 1940s. Over 300,000 of them served in the United States military.

The sudden expansion of Mexican-American neighborhoods created tensions and occasionally conflict in some American cities. White residents of Los Angeles became alarmed at the activities of Mexican-American teenagers, many of whom were joining street gangs (*pachucos*). The *pachucos* were particularly distinctive because of their members' style of dress, which whites considered outrageous. They wore long, loose jackets with padded shoulders, baggy pants tied at the ankles, long watch chains, broad-brimmed hats, and greased, ducktail hairstyles. (It was a style borrowed in part from fashions in Harlem.) The outfit was known as a "zoot suit." For those who wore them, as for many adolescents, their style of dress became a symbol of rebellion against and defiance toward conventional white, middle-class society.

In June 1943, animosity toward the zoot-suiters produced a four-day riot in Los Angeles, during which white sailors stationed at a base in Long Beach invaded Mexican-American communities and attacked zoot-suiters (in response to alleged attacks by them on servicemen). The city police did little to restrain the sailors, who grabbed Hispanic teenagers, tore off and burned their clothes, cut off their ducktails, and beat them. But when Hispanics tried to fight back, the police moved in and arrested them. In the aftermath of the "zoot suit riots," Los Angeles passed a law prohibiting the wearing of zoot suits.

Women and Children at War

The war drew increasing numbers of women into roles from which, either by custom or law, they had been largely barred. The number of women in the work force increased by nearly 60 percent, and women accounted for a third of paid workers in 1945 (as opposed to a quarter in 1940). These wage-earning women were more likely to be married and were on the whole older than most of those who had entered the work force in the past.

Many women entered the industrial work force to replace male workers serving in the military. But while economic and military necessity eroded some of the popular objections to women in the workplace, obstacles remained. Many factory owners continued to categorize jobs by gender. (Female work, like male work, was also categorized by race: black women were usually assigned more menial tasks, and paid at a lower rate, than their white counterparts.) Employers also made substantial investments in automated assembly lines to reduce the need for heavy labor. Special recruiting materials presented factory work to women through domestic analogies that male employers assumed females would find easily comprehensible: cutting airplane wings was compared to making a dress pattern, mixing chemicals to making a cake. Many employers treated women in the war plants with a combination of solicitude and patronization, which was also an obstacle to winning genuine equality within the work force. Still, women did make important inroads in industrial employment during the war. Women had been working in industry for over a century, but some began now to take on heavy industrial jobs that had long been considered "men's work." The famous wartime image of "Rosie the Riveter" symbolized the new importance of the female industrial work force. Women workers joined unions in substantial numbers, and they helped erode at least some of the prejudice, including the prejudice against mothers' working, that had previously kept many of them from paid employment.

In the end, however, most women workers during the war were employed not in factories but in service-sector jobs. Above all, they worked for the government, whose bureaucratic needs expanded dramatically alongside its military and industrial needs. Washington, D.C., in particular, was flooded with

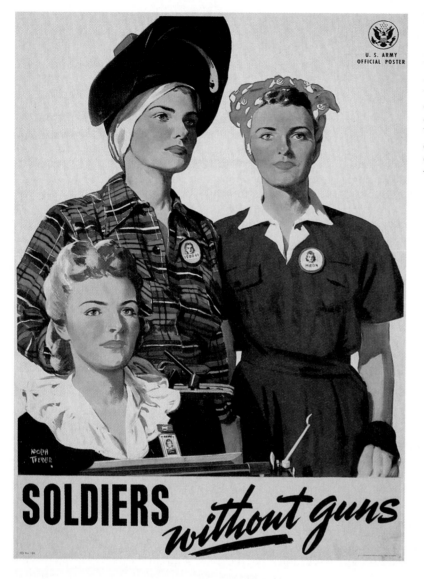

U. S. ARMY
OFFICIAL POSTER

SOLDIERS *without guns*

young female clerks, secretaries, and typists—known as "government girls"—most of whom lived in cramped quarters in boardinghouses, private homes, and government dormitories and worked long hours in the war agencies. Public and private clerical employment for women expanded in other urban areas as well, creating high concentrations of young women in places largely depleted of young men. The result was the development of distinctively female communities, in which women, often separated for the first time from home and family, adjusted to life in the work force through their association with other female workers. Even within the military, which enlisted substantial numbers of women as WAACs (army) and WAVEs (navy), most female work was clerical.

The new opportunities produced new problems. Many mothers whose husbands were in the military had to combine working with caring for their children. The scarcity of child-care facilities or other community services meant that some women had no choice but to leave young children—often known as "latchkey children" or "eight-hour orphans"—at home alone (or sometimes locked in cars in factory parking lots) while they worked.

Perhaps in part because of the family dislocations the war produced, juvenile crime rose markedly in the war years. Young boys were arrested at rapidly increasing rates for car theft and other burglary, vandalism, and vagrancy. The arrest rate for prostitutes, many of whom were teenage girls, rose too, as did the incidence of sexually transmitted disease. For many children, however, the distinctive experience of the war years was not crime but work. More than a third of all teenagers between the ages of fourteen and eighteen were employed late in the war, causing some reduction in high-school enrollments.

The return of prosperity during the war helped increase the rate and lower the age of marriage, but many of these young marriages were unable to survive the pressures of wartime separation. The divorce rate rose rapidly. The rise in the birth rate that accompanied the increase in marriages was the first sign of what would become the great postwar "baby boom."

The Internment of the Japanese Americans

World War I had produced a virtual orgy of hatred, vindictiveness, and hysteria in America, as well as widespread and flagrant violations of civil liberties. World War II did not. The government barred from the mails a few papers it considered seditious, among them Father Coughlin's anti-Semitic and pro-fascist *Social Justice,* but there was no general censorship of dissident publications. A few Nazi agents and American fascists were jailed, but there was no major assault on people suspected of sympathizing with the Axis. The most ambitious effort to punish domestic fascists, a sedition trial of twenty-eight people, ended in a mistrial, and the defendants went free. Unlike during World War I, the government generally left socialists and communists (most of whom strongly supported the war effort) alone.

Nor was there much of the ethnic or cultural animosity that had shaped the social climate of the United States during World War I. Americans continued to eat sauerkraut without calling it "liberty cabbage." They displayed little hostility toward German and Italian Americans. Instead, they seemed to share the view of their government's propaganda: that the enemy was less the German and Italian people than the vicious political systems to which they had succumbed.

But there was a glaring exception to the general rule of tolerance: the treatment of the small, politically powerless group of Japanese Americans. From the beginning, Americans adopted a different attitude toward their Asian enemy than they did toward their European foes. They attributed to the Japanese people certain racial and cultural characteristics that made it easier to hold them in contempt. The Japanese, both government and private propaganda encouraged Americans to believe, were a devious, malign, and cruel people. The infamous attack on Pearl Harbor seemed to many to confirm that assessment.

This racial animosity soon extended to Americans of Japanese descent. There were not many Japanese Americans in the United States—only about 127,000, most of them concentrated in a few areas in California. About a third of them were unnaturalized, first-generation immigrants (Issei); two-thirds were naturalized or native-born citizens of the United States (Nisei). The Japanese in America, like the Chinese, had long been the target of ethnic and racial animosity; and unlike members of European ethnic groups, who had encountered similar resentment, Asians seemed unable to dispel prejudice against them no matter how assimilated they became. Many white Americans continued to consider Asians (even native-born citizens) so "foreign" that they could never become "real" Americans. Partly as a result, much of the Japanese-American population in the West continued to live in close-knit, to some degree even insular, communities, which simply reinforced the belief that they were somehow alien and potentially menacing.

Pearl Harbor inflamed these longstanding suspicions and turned them into active animosity. Wild stories circulated about how the Japanese in Hawaii had helped sabotage Pearl Harbor and how Japanese Americans in California were conspiring to aid an enemy landing on the Pacific coast. There was no evidence to support any of these charges; but according to Earl Warren, then attorney general of California, the apparent passivity of the Japanese Americans was more evidence of the danger they posed. Because they did nothing to allow officials to gauge their intentions, Warren claimed, it was all the more important to take precautions against conspiracies.

Although there was some public pressure in California to remove the Japanese "threat," on the whole popular sentiment was more tolerant of the Nisei and Issei (and more willing to make distinctions between them and the Japanese in Japan) than was official sentiment. The real impetus for taking action came from the government. Secretary of the Navy Frank Knox, for example, said shortly after Pearl Harbor that "the most effective fifth column work of the entire war was done in Hawaii," a statement that later investigations proved to be entirely false. General John L. DeWitt, the senior military commander on the West Coast, claimed to have "no confidence in [Japanese-American] loyalty whatsoever." When asked about the distinction between unnaturalized Japanese immigrants and American citizens, he said, "A Jap is a Jap. It makes no difference whether he is an American citizen or not."

In February 1942, in response to pressure from military officials like DeWitt and Knox and West Coast political leaders like Warren (and over the objections of the attorney general and J. Edgar Hoover, the director of the FBI), the president authorized the army to "intern" the Japanese Americans. He created the War Relocation Authority (WRA) to oversee the project. More than 100,000 people (Issei and Nisei alike) were rounded up, told to dispose of their property however they could (which often meant simply abandoning it), and taken to what the government euphemistically termed "relocation centers" in the "interior." In fact, they were facilities little different from prisons, many of them located in the western mountains and the desert. Conditions in the internment camps were not brutal, but they were harsh and uncomfortable. Government officials talked of them as places where the Japanese could be socialized and "Americanized," much as many officials had at times considered Indian reservations as places for training Native Americans to become more like whites.

But like Indian reservations, the internment camps were more a target of white economic aspirations than of missionary work. The governor of Utah, where many of the internees were located, wanted the federal government to turn over thousands of Japanese Americans to serve as forced laborers. Washington did not comply, but the WRA did hire out many inmates as agricultural laborers.

The internment never produced significant popular opposition. For the most part, once the Japanese were in the camps, other Americans (including their former neighbors on the West Coast) largely forgot about them—except to make strenuous efforts to acquire the property they had abandoned. Even so, beginning in 1943 conditions slowly improved. Some young Japanese Americans left the camps to attend colleges and universities (mostly in the East—the WRA continued to be wary of letting Japanese return to the Pacific Coast). Others were permitted to move to cities to take factory and service jobs (although again, not on the West Coast). Some young men joined and others were drafted into the American military; a Nisei army unit fought with distinction in Europe. In 1944, the Supreme Court ruled in *Korematsu* v. *U.S.* that the relocation was constitutionally permissible. In another case the same year, it barred the internment of "loyal" citizens, but left the interpretation of "loyal" to the discretion of the government. Nevertheless, by the end of 1944 most of the internees had been released; and in early 1945, they were finally permitted to return to the West Coast—where they faced continuing harassment and persecution, and where many found their property and businesses irretrievably lost. Not until 1988

did they win any compensation for their losses, when, after years of agitation by survivors of the camps and their descendants, Congress voted to award them reparations.

Chinese Americans and the War

Just as America's conflict with Japan undermined the position of Japanese Americans, the American alliance with China during World War II significantly enhanced both the legal and social status of Chinese Americans. In 1943, partly to improve relations with the government of China, Congress finally repealed the Chinese Exclusion Acts, which had barred almost all Chinese immigration since 1892. The new quota for Chinese immigrants was miniscule (105 a year), but a substantial number of Chinese women managed to gain entry into the country through other provisions covering war brides and fiancées. Over 4,000 Chinese women entered the United States in the first three years after the war. Permanent residents of the United States of Chinese descent were finally permitted to become citizens.

Racial animosity toward the Chinese did not disappear, but it did decline—in part because government propaganda and popular culture both began presenting positive images of the Chinese (partly to contrast them with the Japanese); in part because Chinese Americans (like African Americans and other previously marginal groups) began taking jobs in war plants and other booming areas suffering from labor shortages and hence moving out of the relatively isolated world of the Chinatowns. A higher proportion of Chinese Americans (22 percent of all adult males) were drafted than of any other national group, and the entire Chinese community in most cities worked hard and conspicuously for the war effort.

The Retreat from Reform

Late in 1943, Franklin Roosevelt publicly suggested that "Dr. New Deal," as he called it, had served its purpose and should now give way to "Dr. Win-the-War." The statement reflected the president's own genuine shift in concern: that victory was now more important than reform. But it also reflected the political reality that had emerged during the first two years of war. Liberals in government were finding themselves unable to enact new programs. They were even finding it difficult to protect existing ones from conservative assault.

Within the administration itself, many liberals found themselves displaced by the new managers of

AMERICANS IN PARIS, 1944
American troop transports roll into Paris in August 1944 to a delirious welcome from French citizens, who had by then
lived under Nazi occupation for more than four years. They had given an even warmer greeting to the Free French
forces under General Charles De Gaulle, which had arrived in the city a few days earlier. *(UPI/Bettmann)*

the wartime agencies, who came overwhelmingly from
large corporations and conservative Wall Street law
firms. But the greatest assault on New Deal reforms
came from conservatives in Congress, who seized on
the war as an excuse to do what many had wanted to
do in peacetime: dismantle many of the achievements
of the New Deal. They were assisted by the end of mass
unemployment, which decreased the need for such relief programs as the Civilian Conservation Corps and
the Works Progress Administration (both of which
were abolished). They were assisted, too, by their own
increasing numbers. In the congressional elections of
1942, Republicans gained 47 seats in the House and 10
in the Senate. Roosevelt continued to talk bravely at
times about his commitment to social progress and liberal reform, in part to bolster the flagging spirits of his
traditional supporters. But increasingly, the president
quietly accepted the defeat or erosion of New Deal
measures in order to win support for his war policies

and peace plans. He also accepted the changes because
he realized that his chances for reelection in 1944 depended on his ability to identify himself less with domestic issues than with world peace.

Republicans approached the 1944 election determined to exploit what they believed was resentment
of wartime regimentation and privation and unhappiness with Democratic reform. They nominated as their
candidate the young and vigorous governor of New
York, Thomas E. Dewey. Roosevelt was unopposed
within his party, but Democratic leaders pressured
him to abandon Vice President Henry Wallace, an advanced New Dealer and hero of the CIO, and replace
him with a more moderate figure. Roosevelt reluctantly acquiesced in the selection of Senator Harry S.
Truman of Missouri. Truman was not a prominent figure in the party, but he had won acclaim as chairman
of the Senate War Investigating Committee (known as
the Truman Committee), which had compiled an im-

WORLD WAR II IN EUROPE: THE ALLIED COUNTEROFFENSIVE, 1943–1945

pressive record uncovering waste and corruption in wartime production.

The conduct of the war was not an issue in the campaign. Instead, the election revolved around domestic economic issues and, indirectly, the president's health. The president was in fact gravely ill, suffering from, among other things, arteriosclerosis. It may not be too much to say that he was dying. But the campaign seemed momentarily to revive him. He made several strenuous public appearances late in October, which dispelled popular doubts about his health and ensured his reelection. He captured 53.5 percent of the popular vote to Dewey's 46 percent, and won 432 electoral votes to Dewey's 99. Democrats lost 1 seat in the Senate, gained 20 in the House, and maintained control of both.

THE DEFEAT OF THE AXIS

By the middle of 1943, America and its allies had succeeded in stopping the Axis advance both in Europe and in the Pacific. In the next two years, the Allies themselves seized the offensive and launched a series of powerful drives that rapidly led the way to victory.

The Liberation of France

By early 1944, American and British bombers were attacking German industrial installations and other targets almost round the clock, drastically cutting production and impeding transportation. Especially devastating was the massive bombing of such German cities as Leipzig, Dresden, and Berlin. A February 1945 incendiary raid on Dresden created a great firestorm that destroyed three-fourths of the previously undamaged city and killed approximately 135,000 people, almost all civilians. Military leaders claimed that the bombing destroyed industrial facilities, demoralized the population, and cleared the way for the great Allied invasion of France in the late spring. In fact, the greatest contribution of the bombing to the military struggle was to force the German air force (the *Luftwaffe*) to relocate much of its strength in Germany itself and to engage Allied forces in the air. The air battles over Germany considerably weakened the *Luftwaffe* and made it a less formidable obstacle to the Allied invasion than it might once have been. Preparations for the invasion were also assisted by the success of the Allies in breaking the most secret German codes—a success made possible by the acquisition of an "Ultra" machine, a sophisticated German coding device.

An enormous invasion force had been gathering in England for two years: almost 3 million troops, and perhaps the greatest array of naval vessels and armaments ever assembled in one place. On the morning of June 6, 1944, D-Day, General Dwight D. Eisenhower, the Supreme Commander of the Allied forces, sent this vast armada into action. The landing came not at the narrowest part of the English Channel, where the Germans had expected and prepared for it, but along sixty miles of the Cotentin peninsula on the coast of Normandy. While airplanes and battleships offshore bombarded the Nazi defenses, 4,000 vessels landed troops and supplies on the beaches. (Three divisions of paratroopers had been dropped behind the German lines the night before, amid scenes of great confusion, to seize critical roads and bridges for the push inland.) Fighting was intense along the beach, but the superior manpower and equipment of the Allied forces gradually prevailed. Within a week, the German forces had been dislodged from virtually the entire Normandy coast.

For the next month, further progress remained slow. But in late July in the Battle of Saint-Lô, General Omar Bradley's First Army smashed through the German lines. George S. Patton's Third Army, spearheaded by heavy tank attacks, then moved through the hole Bradley had created and began a drive into the heart of France. On August 25, Free French forces arrived in Paris and liberated the city from four years of German occupation. And by mid-September the Allied armies had driven the Germans almost entirely out of France and Belgium.

The great Allied drive came to a halt, however, at the Rhine River in the face of a firm line of German defenses and a period of cold weather, rain, and floods. In mid-December, German forces struck in desperation along fifty miles of front in the Ardennes Forest. In the Battle of the Bulge (named for a large bulge that appeared in the American lines as the Germans pressed forward), they drove fifty-five miles toward Antwerp before they were finally stopped at Bastogne. The battle ended serious German resistance in the west.

While the Allies were fighting their way through France, Soviet forces were sweeping westward into central Europe and the Balkans. In late January 1945, the Russians launched a great offensive toward the Oder River inside Germany. In early spring, they were ready to launch a final assault against Berlin. By then, Omar Bradley's First Army was pushing into Germany from the west. Early in March, his forces captured the city of Cologne, on the west bank of the Rhine. The next day, in a remarkable stroke of good fortune, he discovered and seized an undamaged bridge over the river at Remagen; Allied troops were soon pouring across the Rhine. In the following weeks the British Field Marshall Bernard Montgomery, commander of Allied ground operations on D-Day and after, pushed into northern Germany with a million troops, while Bradley's army, sweeping through central Germany, completed the encirclement of 300,000 German soldiers in the Ruhr.

The German resistance was now broken on both fronts. American forces were moving eastward faster than they had anticipated and could have beaten the Russians to Berlin and Prague. Instead, the American and British high commands decided to halt the advance along the Elbe River in central Germany to await the Russians. That decision enabled the Soviets to occupy eastern Germany and Czechoslovakia.

On April 30, with Soviet forces on the outskirts of Berlin, Adolf Hitler killed himself in his bunker in the capital. And on May 8, 1945, the remaining German forces surrendered unconditionally. V-E (Victory in Europe) Day prompted great celebrations in Western Europe and in the United States, tempered by the knowledge of the continuing war against Japan.

The Pacific Offensive

In February 1944, American naval forces under Admiral Chester Nimitz won a series of victories in the Marshall Islands and cracked the outer perimeter of the Japanese Empire. Within a month, the navy had destroyed other vital Japanese bastions. American submarines, in the meantime, were decimating Japanese shipping and crippling the nation's domestic economy. By the summer of 1944, the already skimpy food rations for the Japanese people had been reduced by nearly a quarter; there was also a critical gasoline shortage.

Meanwhile, a frustrating struggle was in progress on the Asian mainland. In 1942, the Japanese had forced General Joseph W. Stilwell of the United States out of Burma and had moved their own troops as far west as the mountains bordering India. For a time, Stilwell supplied the isolated Chinese forces continuing to resist Japan with an aerial ferry over the Himalayas. In 1943, finally, he led Chinese, Indian, and a few American troops back through northern Burma, constructing a road and pipeline across the mountains into China (the Burma Road, also known as the Ledo Road or Stilwell Road), which finally opened in the fall of 1944.

By then, however, the Japanese had launched a major counteroffensive and had driven so deep into the Chinese interior that they threatened the terminus of the Burma Road and the center of Chinese government at Chungking. The Japanese offensive precipitated a long-simmering feud between General Stilwell and Premier Chiang Kai-shek of China. Stilwell was indignant because Chiang (whom he called, contemptuously, the "Peanut") was using many of his troops to maintain an armed frontier against the Chinese communists and would not deploy those troops against the Japanese.

The decisive battles of the Pacific War, however, occurred in the Pacific. In mid-June 1944, an enormous American armada struck the heavily fortified Mariana Islands and, after some of the bloodiest operations of the war, captured Tinian, Guam, and Saipan, 1,350 miles from Tokyo. In September, American forces landed on the western Carolines. And on October 20, General MacArthur's troops landed on Leyte Island in the Philippines. The Japanese now used virtually their entire fleet against the Allied invaders in three major encounters—which together constituted the decisive Battle of Leyte Gulf, the largest naval engagement in history. American forces held off the Japanese onslaught and sank four Japanese carriers, all but destroying Japan's capacity to continue a serious naval war.

Nevertheless, as American forces advanced closer to the Japanese mainland early in 1945, the imperial forces seemed only to increase their resistance. In February 1945, American marines seized the tiny volcanic island of Iwo Jima, only 750 miles from Tokyo, but only after the costliest single battle in the history of the Marine Corps. The marines suffered over 20,000 casualties.

The battle for Okinawa, an island only 370 miles south of Japan, was further evidence of the strength of the Japanese resistance in those last desperate months. Week after week, the Japanese sent kamikaze (suicide) planes against American and British ships, sacrificing 3,500 of them while inflicting great damage. Japanese troops on shore launched desperate nighttime attacks on the American lines. The United States and its allies suffered nearly 50,000 casualties before finally capturing Okinawa in late June 1945. Over 100,000 Japanese died in the siege.

The same kind of bitter fighting seemed to await the Americans in Japan itself. But there were signs early in 1945 that such an invasion might not be necessary. The Japanese had almost no ships or planes left with which to fight. In July 1945, for example, American warships stood off the shore of Japan and shelled industrial targets (many already in ruins from aerial bombings) with impunity. A brutal firebombing of Tokyo in March, in which American bombers dropped napalm on the city and created a firestorm in which over 80,000 people died, further weakened the Japanese will to resist. Moderate Japanese leaders, who had long since decided that the war was lost, were gaining power within the government and were looking for ways to bring the war to an end. After the invasion of Okinawa, Emperor Hirohito appointed a new premier and gave him instructions to sue for peace. Although the new leader could not persuade military leaders to give up the fight, he did try, along with the emperor himself, to obtain mediation through the Soviet Union. The Russians showed little interest in playing the role of arbitrator, but other developments made their participation unnecessary. Whether the moderates could ultimately have prevailed is a question about which historians and others continue to disagree. In any case, the question eventually became moot. In mid-July, American scientists conducted a successful test of a new atomic bomb.

The Manhattan Project

In 1939 reports reached the United States through the Italian physicist Enrico Fermi and the German mathematician Albert Einstein (then living in exile in Amer-

THE MANHATTAN PROJECT
J. Robert Oppenheimer, wearing the broad-brimmed hat, was one of the scientific leaders of the Manhattan Project, which developed the atomic bomb during World War II. The military commander of the project was General Leslie Groves. The two men are shown here after the war, examining the charred landscape of the Trinity site in New Mexico, where the first successful detonation of the new weapon occurred in July 1945. (*UPI/Bettman*)

ica) that Nazi scientists had learned how to produce atomic fission in uranium. Acquiring that knowledge, they warned, was the first step toward the creation of an atomic bomb, a weapon more powerful than any ever previously devised. The United States and Britain immediately began a race to develop the weapon before the Germans did.

Over the next three years, the government secretly poured nearly $2 billion into the so-called Manhattan Project—a massive scientific effort conducted at hidden laboratories in Oak Ridge, Tennessee, Los Alamos, New Mexico, Hanford, Washington, and other sites. (It had gotten its name earlier, when many of the atomic physicists had been working at Columbia University in New York.) Hundreds of scientists, many of them not fully aware of what they were working on, labored feverishly to complete two complementary projects. One (at Oak Ridge and Hanford) was the production

of fissionable plutonium, the fuel for an atomic explosion; the other (at Los Alamos, under the supervision of J. Robert Oppenheimer) was the construction of a bomb that could use the fuel.

The scientists pushed ahead much faster than anyone had predicted. Even so, the war in Europe ended before they were ready to test the first bomb. Just before dawn on July 16, 1945, near Alamogordo, New Mexico, the scientists gathered to witness the first atomic explosion in history: a blinding flash of light brighter than any ever seen on earth, and a huge, billowing mushroom cloud. Some were exhilarated by their success. Others, among them J. Robert Oppenheimer, were already troubled by the implications of what they had done. But by then, control of the atomic bomb had already moved into other hands. The bomb was no longer a scientific project; it was a weapon of war.

Atomic Warfare

News of the explosion reached President Harry S. Truman (who had taken office in April on the death of Roosevelt) in Potsdam, Germany, where he was attending a conference of Allied leaders. He issued an ultimatum to the Japanese (signed jointly by the British) demanding that they surrender by August 3 or face complete devastation. The Japanese premier wanted to accept the Allied demand, but by the time the deadline arrived he had not yet been able to persuade the military leaders to agree. There was a possibility that the government might agree to surrender, in return for a promise that the Japanese could retain their emperor. The American government, firmly committed to the idea of "unconditional surrender," disregarded those overtures. When the Japanese failed to meet the deadline, Truman ordered the air force to use the new atomic weapons against Japan.

Controversy has raged for decades over whether Truman's decision to use the bomb was justified and what his motives were. Some have argued that the atomic attack was unnecessary, that had the United States agreed to the survival of the emperor (which it ultimately did agree to in any case), or waited only a few more weeks, the Japanese would have surrendered. Others argue that nothing less than the atomic bombs could have persuaded the Japanese to surrender without a costly American invasion. Some critics of the decision, including some of the scientists involved in the Manhattan Project, have argued that whatever Japanese intentions, the United States, as a matter of morality, should not have used the terrible new weapon. One horrified physicist wrote the president shortly before the attack: "This thing must not be

SIGNIFICANT EVENTS

1941 A. Philip Randolph proposes march on Washington

Roosevelt establishes Fair Employment Practices Commission

1942 Japanese capture Philippines

Battle of Midway

North Africa campaign begins

News of Holocaust reaches United States

War Production Board created

Japanese-Americans interned

Manhattan Project begins

Temporary Mexican workers allowed entry to U.S.

Congress of Racial Equality (CORE) founded

1943 Americans capture Guadalcanal

Soviets defeat Germans at Stalingrad

Allies launch invasion of Italy

Smith-Connally Act passed

Race riot breaks out in Detroit

Sailors battle Mexican-Americans in "zoot suit" riots in Los Angeles

Chinese Exclusion Act repealed

1944 Allies invade Normandy

Roosevelt reelected president

Americans recapture Philippines

Demonstrators force restaurant in Washington, D.C. to desegregate

1945 Roosevelt dies; Truman becomes president

Hitler kills himself

Allies capture Berlin

Germany surrenders

Americans capture Okinawa

Atomic bomb tested in New Mexico

United States drops atomic bombs on Hiroshima and Nagasaki

Japan surrenders

---

permitted to exist on this earth. We must not be the most hated and feared people in the world."

The nation's military and political leaders, however, showed little concern about such matters. Truman, who had not even known of the existence of the Manhattan Project until he became president, was apparently making what he believed to be a simple military decision. A weapon was available that would end the war quickly; he could see no reason not to use it.

Still more controversy has existed over whether there were other motives at work in Truman's decision. With the Soviet Union poised to enter the war in the Pacific, did the United States want to end the conflict quickly to forestall an expanded communist presence in Asia? Did Truman use the bomb as a weapon to intimidate Stalin, with whom he was engaged in difficult negotiations, so the Soviet leader would accept American demands? Little direct evidence is available to support (or definitively refute) either of these accusations.

On August 6, 1945, an American B-29, the *Enola Gay*, dropped an atomic weapon on the Japanese industrial center at Hiroshima. With a single bomb, the United States completely incinerated a four-square-mile area at the center of the previously undamaged city. More than 80,000 civilians died, according to later American estimates. Many more survived to suffer the crippling effects of radioactive fallout or to pass those effects on to their children in the form of birth defects.

The Japanese government, stunned by the attack, was at first unable to agree on a response. Two days later, on August 8, the Soviet Union declared war on Japan. And the following day, the United States sent another American plane to drop another atomic weapon—this time on the city of Nagasaki—inflicting horrible damage and over 100,000 deaths on another unfortunate community. Finally, the emperor intervened to break the stalemate in the cabinet, and on August 14 the government announced that it was ready to give up. On September 2, 1945, on board the American battleship *Missouri*, anchored in Tokyo Bay, Japanese officials signed the articles of surrender.

The greatest war in the history of mankind had come to an end, and the United States had emerged not only victorious but in a position of unprecedented power, influence, and prestige. It was a victory, however, that few could greet with unambiguous joy. Fourteen million combatants had died in the struggle. Many more civilians had perished, from bombings, from disease and starvation, from genocidal campaigns of extermination. The United States had suffered only light casualties in comparison with many other nations, but the cost had still been high: 322,000 dead, another 800,000 injured. And despite the sacrifices, the world continued to face an uncertain future, menaced by the threat of nuclear warfare and by the emerging antagonism between the world's two strongest nations—the United States and the Soviet Union—that would darken the peace for many decades to come.

SUGGESTED READINGS

War and American Society. John Morton Blum, *V Was for Victory* (1976). Mark J. Harris et al., *The Homefront* (1984). Richard R. Lingeman, *Don't You Know There's a War On?* (1970). Gerald D. Nash, *The American West Transformed: The Impact of the Second World War* (1985). Geoffrey Perrett, *Days of Sadness, Years of Triumph: The American People, 1939–1945* (1974). Richard Polenberg, *War and Society* (1972). Studs Terkel, *"The Good War": An Oral History of World War II* (1984).

War Mobilization and Wartime Politics. Oscar E. Anderson, Jr., *The New World* (1962). Ellsworth Barnard, *Wendell Willkie* (1966). Chester Bowles, *Promises to Keep* (1971). Alan Brinkley, *The End of Reform: New Deal Liberalism in Recession and War* (1995). David Brinkley, *Washington Goes to War* (1987). James MacGregor Burns, *Roosevelt: The Soldier of Freedom* (1970). Bruce Catton, *War Lords of Washington* (1946). Lester V. Chandler, *Inflation in the United States, 1940–1948* (1951). Alan Clive, *State of War: Michigan in World War II* (1979). George Q. Flynn, *The Mess in Washington: Manpower Mobilization in World War II* (1979). Leslie R. Groves, *Now It Can Be Told* (1962). Howell John Harris, *The Right to Manage* (1982). Maurice Isserman, *Which Side Were You On? The American Communist Party During World War II* (1982). Eliot Janeway, *Struggle for Survival* (1951). Paul A. C. Koistinen, *The Military-Industrial Complex: A Historical Perspecive* (1980). Philip Knightley, *The First Casualty* (1975). Nelson Lichtenstein, *Labor's War at Home: The CIO in World War II* (1982). Donald Nelson, *Arsenal of Democracy* (1946). Joel Seidman, *American Labor from Defense to Reconversion* (1953). Bradley F. Smith, *The Shadow Warriors: The OSS and the Origins of the CIA* (1983). Richard Steele, *Propaganda in an Open Society* (1985). Patrick S. Washburn, *A Question of Sedition: The Federal Government's Investigation of the Black Press During World War II* (1986). Michi Weglyn, *Years of Infamy: The Untold Story of America's Concentration Camps* (1976). Alan M. Winkler, *The Politics of Propaganda; The Office of War Information, 1942–1945* (1978).

The War and Race. Domenic J. Capeci, Jr., *The Harlem Riot of 1943* (1977); *Race Relations in Wartime Detroit* (1987). Richard M. Dalfiume, *Desegregation of the U.S. Armed Forces* (1969). Roger Daniels, *The Politics of Prejudice* (1962); *Concentration Camps, USA: Japanese Americans and World War II* (1971). John

W. Dower, *War Without Mercy: Race and Power in the Pacific War* (1986). Mario T. Garcia, *Mexican-Americans: Leadership, Ideology, and Identity, 1930–1960* (1989). Herbert Garfinkel, *When Negroes March* (1959). Audrie Girdner and Anne Loftis, *The Great Betrayal* (1969). Bill Hosokawa, *Nisei* (1969). Peter Irons, *Justice at War* (1983). Thomas James, *Exiles Within: The Schooling of Japanese-Americans, 1942–1945* (1987). Philip McGuire, ed., *Taps for a Jim Crow Army: Letters from Black Soldiers in World War II* (1982). Mauricio Mazon, *The Zoot-Suit Riots* (1984). August Meier and Elliott Rudwick, *CORE* (1973). Louis Ruchames, *Race, Jobs, and Politics* (1953). Holly Cowan Shulman, *The Voice of America* (1991). Neil Wynn, *The Afro-American and the Second World War* (1976).

Women and the War. Karen Anderson, *Wartime Women: Sex Roles, Family Relations, and the Status of Women During World War II* (1981). D'Ann Campbell, *Women at War with America* (1984). Sherna B. Gluck, *Rosie the Riveter Revisited* (1987). Susan Hartmann, *The Homefront and Beyond: American Women in the 1940s* (1982). Margaret R. Higgonet et al., *Behind the Lines: Gender and the Two World Wars* (1987). Maureen Honey, *Creating Rosie the Riveter: Class, Gender, and Propaganda During World War II* (1984). Ruth Milkman, *Gender at Work: The Dynamics of Job Segregation by Sex During World War II* (1987). Susan M. Reverby, *Ordered to Care: The Dilemma of American Nursing, 1850–1945* (1987). Leila Rupp, *Mobilizing Women for War* (1978).

Wartime Military and Diplomatic Experiences. Stephen Ambrose, *The Supreme Commander* (1970); *Eisenhower: Soldier, General of the Army, President-Elect* (1983); *D-Day: June 6, 1944* (1994). Albert Russell Buchanan, *The United States and World War II*, 2 vols. (1962). James MacGregor Burns, *Roosevelt: The Soldier of Freedom* (1970). Winston S. Churchill, *The Second World War*, 6 vols. (1948–1953). Robert Divine, *Roosevelt and World War II* (1969); *Second Chance* (1967). Dwight D. Eisenhower, *Crusade in Europe* (1948). John S. D. Eisenhower, *Allies: Pearl Harbor to D-Day* (1982). Kenneth Greenfield, *American Strategy in World War II* (1963). Max Hastings, *Overlord: D-Day and the Battle for Normandy* (1984). Patrick Heardon, *Roosevelt Confronts Hitler: American Entry into World War II* (1987). Godfrey Hodgson, *The Colonel: The Life and Wars of Henry Stimson, 1967–1950* (1990). Michael Howard, *The*

Mediterranean Strategy in World War II (1968). Margaret Hoyle, *A World in Flames* (1970). D. Clayton James, *A Time for Giants: Politics of the American High Command in World War II* (1987). John Keegan, *Six Armies in Normandy: From D-Day to the Liberation of Paris, June 6–August 25, 1944* (1982). Warren Kimball, *The Juggler: Franklin Roosevelt as Wartime Statesman* (1991). E. J. Kind and W. M. Whitehill, *Fleet Admiral King* (1952). Charles B. McDonald, *The Mighty Endeavor* (1969). William Manchester, *American Caesar* (1979). Samuel Eliot Morison, *Strategy and Compromise* (1958); *History of United States Naval Operations in World War II*, 14 vols. (1947–1960); *The Two Ocean War* (1963). Geoffrey Perret, *There's a War to Be Won: The United States Army in World War II* (1991). Forrest Pogue, *George C. Marshall*, 2 vols. (1963–1966). Gordon W. Prange, *At Dawn We Slept: The Untold Story of Pearl Harbor* (1981). Fletcher Pratt, *War for the World* (1951). Cornelius Ryan, *The Longest Day* (1959); *The Last Battle* (1966). Ronald Schaffer, *Wings of Judgment: American Bombing in World War II* (1985). Michael Schaller, *The United States Crusade in China, 1938–1945* (1979). Michael Sherry, *Preparing for the Next War: American Plans for Postwar Defense, 1941–1945* (1977); *The Rise of American Air Power* (1987). Gaddis Smith, *American Diplomacy During the Second World War* (1964). Ronald H. Spector, *Eagle Against the Sun: The American War with Japan* (1985). Mark A. Stoler, *The Politics of the Second Front: Planning and Diplomacy in Coalition Warfare, 1941–1945* (1977). Christopher Thorne, *Allies of a Kind: The United States, Britain and the War Against Japan, 1941–1945* (1978). John Toland, *The Last Hundred Days* (1966); *The Rising Sun* (1970). Barbara Tuchman, *Stilwell and the American Experience in China* (1971). Russell Weigley, *The American Way of War* (1973); *Eisenhower's Lieutenants: The Campaign of France and Germany, 1944–1945* (1981). Chester Wilmot, *The Struggle for Europe* (1952). David S. Wyman, *The Abandonment of the Jews: America and the Holocaust, 1941–1945* (1984).

Atomic Warfare. Gar Alperovitz, *Atomic Diplomacy* (1965). Nuel Davis, *Lawrence and Oppenheimer* (1969). Robert Donovan, *Conflict and Crisis* (1977). Herbert Feis, *The Atomic Bomb and the End of World War II* (1966). Gregg Herken, *The Winning Weapon: The Atomic Bomb in the Cold War* (1980). John Hersey, *Hiroshima* (1946). Robert Jungk, *Brighter Than a Thousand Suns* (1958). Richard Rhodes, *The Making of the Atomic Bomb* (1987). W. S. Schoenberger, *Decision of Destiny* (1969). Martin Sherwin, *A World Destroyed* (1975). Leon V. Sigal, *Fighting to a Finish* (1988).

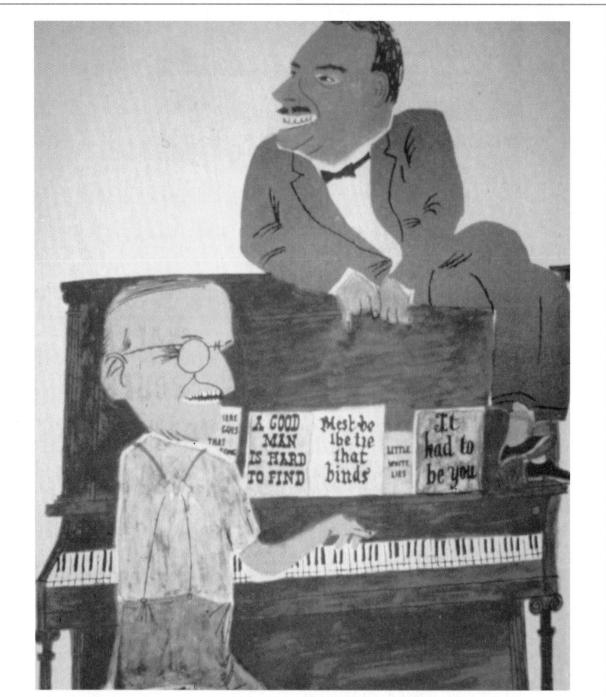

Truman and Dewey, 1948
President Harry S. Truman was once photographed with the actress Lauren Bacall draped across the piano Truman was playing. The artist Ben Shahn satirized that photograph in the unflattering 1948 picture of Truman and his Republican opponent, Governor Thomas E. Dewey of New York. It became a poster for former Vice President Henry A. Wallace, who was running a third-party campaign that year based primarily on opposition to the administration's Cold War foreign policy. *(Harry S. Truman Library)*

CHAPTER TWENTY-NINE

THE COLD WAR

E VEN BEFORE THE END of World War II, in which the United States and the Soviet Union had fought together as allies, there were signs of tension between the two nations. Once the hostilities were over, those tensions quickly grew to create what became known as a "Cold War"—a tense and dangerous rivalry that would cast its shadow over international affairs for decades. The Cold War also had profound effects on American domestic life. Among other things, it helped produce the most corrosive outbreak of antiradical hysteria of the century. America in the postwar years was both powerful and prosperous; but it was also for a time troubled and uncertain about the future.

ORIGINS OF THE COLD WAR

No issue in twentieth-century American history has aroused more debate than the question of the origins of the Cold War. Some have claimed that Soviet duplicity and expansionism created the international tensions, others that American provocations and imperial ambitions were at least equally to blame. Most historians agree, however, that wherever the preponderance of blame may lie, both the United States and the Soviet Union contributed to the atmosphere of hostility and suspicion that quickly clouded the peace. (See "Where Historians Disagree," pp. 770–771.)

Soviet-American Tensions

The wartime alliance between the United States and the Soviet Union was an aberration from the normal tenor of Soviet-American relations, for the two nations had long viewed each other with deep mutual mistrust.

The reasons for American hostility toward the Soviet Union were both obvious and many. There was, of course, the fundamental American animosity toward communism, which had strong roots in the nation's past and had been a powerful force in society since well before the Russian Revolution. But there were more specific reasons as well. Almost the first act of the new Soviet regime had been to negotiate a separate peace with Germany in 1917, leaving the West to fight the Central Powers alone. The Soviet Union had called openly and continually for world revolution and the overthrow of capitalist regimes (even if it did little before World War II actively to advance that goal). The Stalinist purges of the 1930s and 1940s—a savage and brutal campaign of extermination against opponents of the regime, real and imagined, that caused the deaths of millions of people—produced understandable revulsion in the West. Stalin, like Hitler, was one of the great tyrants of modern history; and in 1939, these two tyrants had agreed to the short-lived Nazi-Soviet Pact, freeing Germany to launch World War II.

But Soviet hostility toward the United States had deep roots as well. The United States had opposed the revolution in 1917 and had sent troops into Russia at

ORIGINS OF THE COLD WAR

NO ISSUE IN RECENT American history has pro- duced more controversy than that of the origins of the Cold War between the United States and the Soviet Union. Historians have dis- agreed, often sharply, over the question of who was responsible for the breakdown of American- Soviet relations, and on whether the conflict be- tween the two superpowers was inevitable or could have been avoided.

For more than a decade after the end of World War II, few historians in the United States saw any reason to challenge the official American in- terpretation of the beginnings of the Cold War. Thomas A. Bailey spoke for most students of the conflict when he argued, in *America Faces Russia* (1950), that the breakdown of relations was a di- rect result of aggressive Soviet policies of ex- pansion in the immediate postwar years. Stalin's government violated its solemn promises in the Yalta Accords, imposed Soviet-dominated gov- ernments on the unwilling nations of Eastern Europe, and schemed to spread communism throughout the world. American policy was the logical and necessary response: a firm commit- ment to oppose Soviet expansionism and to keep its own armed forces in a continual state of pre- paredness.

The American involvement in Vietnam disil- lusioned many historians with the premises of the containment policy and, thus, with the tra- ditional view of the origins of the Cold War. But even before the conflict in Asia had reached ma- jor proportions, the first works in what would become known as the "revisionist" interpretation began to appear. William Appleman Williams challenged the accepted wisdom as early as 1952; and in 1959 he published *The Tragedy of Ameri- can Diplomacy*, which placed the Cold War in the context of American foreign policy throughout the twentieth century. The United States had op- erated in world affairs, Williams argued, in re- sponse to one overriding concern: its commit- ment to maintaining an "open door" for American trade in world markets. The confrontation with the Soviet Union, therefore, was less a response to Russian aggressive designs than an expression of the American belief in the necessity of capi- talist expansion.

Later revisionists modified many of Williams's claims, but most accepted some of the basic out- lines of his thesis: that the United States had been primarily to blame for the Cold War; that the Soviet Union had displayed no aggressive de- signs toward the West (and was too weak and exhausted at the end of World War II to be able to pose a serious threat to America in any case); that the United States had used its nuclear mo- nopoly to attempt to threaten and intimidate Stalin; that Harry Truman had recklessly aban- doned the conciliatory policies of Franklin Roo- sevelt and taken a provocative hard line against the Russians; and that the Soviet response had reflected a legitimate fear of capitalist encir- clement. Walter LaFeber, in *America, Russia, and the Cold War, 1945–1967* (1967), maintained that America's supposedly idealistic internationalism at the close of the war—its vision of "One World," with every nation in control of its own destiny—was in reality an effort to ensure a world shaped in the American image, with every nation open to American influence (and Ameri- can trade).

Crucial to many revisionist arguments was the American decision to use atomic weapons against Japan in the closing days of World War II. As early as 1948, a British physicist, P. M. S. Blackett, wrote in *Fear, War, and the Bomb* that the destruction of Hiroshima and Nagasaki was "not so much the last military act of the second World War as the first major operation of the cold diplomatic war with Russia." Gar Alperovitz ex- panded that idea in *Atomic Diplomacy* (1965), in which he claimed that American decision makers used the bombs on an already defeated Japan not to win the war (for the war was already won) but to impress and intimidate the Soviets, to make them more "manageable." In fact, Alperovitz argued, this atomic diplomacy had the opposite effect: it convinced the Soviet Union of America's hostile intentions and helped speed the beginning of the Cold War.

Ultimately, the revisionist interpretation began to produce a reaction of its own, what some have called the "counter-" or "post-revisionist" view of the conflict. Some manifestations of this reaction have consisted of little more than a reaffirmation of the traditional view of the Cold War. Herbert Feis, for example, argued in *The Atomic Bomb and the End of World War II* (1966) that the revisionist claim that the use of nuclear weapons on Japan was a tactic to intimidate the Soviets was unfounded, that Truman had made his decision on purely military grounds—to ensure a speedy American victory and eliminate the need for what was expected to be a long and costly invasion of Japan. Others challenged the revisionists by accepting some of their findings but rejecting their most important claims. Arthur M. Schlesinger, Jr., admitted in a 1967 article that the Soviets may not have been committed to world conquest, as most earlier accounts had claimed. Nevertheless, the Soviets (and Stalin in particular) were motivated by a deep-seated paranoia about the West, which made them insistent on dominating Eastern Europe and rendered any amicable relationship between them and the United States impossible.

But the dominant works of post-revisionist scholarship have attempted to strike a balance between the two camps, to identify areas of blame and misperception on both sides of the conflict. Thomas G. Paterson, in *Soviet-American Confrontation* (1973), viewed Russian hostility and American efforts to dominate the postwar world as equally responsible for the Cold War.

John Lewis Gaddis, in *The United States and the Origins of the Cold War, 1941–1947* (1972), similarly maintained that "neither side can bear sole responsibility for the onset of the Cold War." American policymakers, he argued, had only limited options because of the pressures of domestic politics. And Stalin was immobilized by his obsessive concern with maintaining his own power and ensuring absolute security for the Soviet Union. But if neither side was entirely to blame, Gaddis concluded, the Soviets must be held at least slightly more accountable for the problems, for Stalin was in a much better position to compromise, given his broader power within his own government than the politically hamstrung Truman. Melvyn Leffler's *Preponderance of Power* (1991) argued similarly that American policymakers genuinely believed in the existence of a Soviet threat and were determined to remain consistently stronger than the Soviets in response.

Out of the post-revisionist literature has begun to emerge a new and more complex view of the Cold War, which de-emphasizes the question of who was to blame and adopts a more detached view of the conflict. The Cold War, recent historians suggest, was not so much the fault of one side or the other as it was the natural, perhaps inevitable, result of tensions between the world's two most powerful nations—nations that had been suspicious of, if not hostile toward, one another for nearly a century. As Ernest May wrote in a 1984 essay:

> After the Second World War, the United States and the Soviet Union were doomed to be antagonists. . . . There probably was never any real possibility that the post-1945 relationship could be anything but hostility verging on conflict. . . . Traditions, belief systems, propinquity, and convenience . . . all combined to stimulate antagonism, and almost no factor operated in either country to hold it back.

the end of World War I to work, the Soviets believed, to overthrow their new government. The West had excluded the Soviet Union from the international community throughout the two decades following World War I; Russia had not been invited to participate in either the Versailles Conference in 1919 or the Munich Conference in 1938. The United States had refused to recognize the Soviet government until 1933, sixteen years after the revolution. And just as most Americans viewed communism with foreboding and contempt, so most Russian communists harbored deep suspicions of and a genuine distaste for industrial capitalism. There was, in short, a powerful legacy of mistrust on both sides.

In some respects, the wartime experience helped to abate that mistrust. Both the United States and the Soviet Union tended during the war to focus less on the traditional image of a dangerous potential foe and more on the image of a brave and dauntless ally. Americans expressed open admiration for the courage of Soviet forces in withstanding the Nazi onslaught and began to depict Stalin less as the bloody ogre of the purges than as the wise and persevering "Uncle Joe." The Soviet government, similarly, praised both the American fighting forces and the wisdom and courage of Franklin Roosevelt.

In other respects, however, the war deepened the gulf between the two nations. The Soviet invasion of Finland and the Baltic states late in 1939, once the Allied war with Germany had begun in the west, angered many Americans. So did Soviet wartime brutality—not only toward the fascist enemies but toward supposedly friendly forces such as the Polish resistance fighters. Stalin harbored even greater resentments toward the American approach to the war. Despite repeated assurances from Roosevelt that the United States and Britain would soon open a second front on the European continent, thus drawing German strength away from the assault on Russia, the Allied invasion did not finally occur until June 1944, more than two years after Stalin had first demanded it. In the meantime, the Russians had suffered appalling casualties—some estimates put them as high as 20 million—and it was easy for Stalin to believe that the West had deliberately delayed the invasion to force the Soviets to absorb the brunt of the German strength.

At the heart of the tensions between the Americans and the Soviets in the 1940s, however, was a fundamental difference in the ways the great powers envisioned the postwar world. Many people in the United States embraced a vision first openly outlined in the Atlantic Charter in 1941, and later popularized through a 1943 book by Wendell Willkie, the 1940 Republican presidential candidate, entitled *One World*. In this vision of the world, nations would abandon their traditional belief in military alliances and spheres of influence and govern their relations with one another through democratic processes, with an international organization serving as the arbiter of disputes and the protector of every nation's right of self-determination.

The Soviet Union and to some extent, it gradually became clear, Great Britain held a different vision. Both Stalin and Churchill had signed the Atlantic Charter. But Britain had always been uneasy about the implications of the self-determination ideal for its own enormous empire. And the Soviet Union was determined to create a secure sphere for itself in Eastern Europe as protection against possible future aggression from the West. Both Churchill and Stalin, therefore, tended to envision a postwar structure in which the great powers would control areas of strategic interest to them, in which something vaguely similar to the traditional European balance of power would reemerge.

This difference of opinion was particularly important because the "One World" vision Roosevelt promoted had, by the end of the war, become a fervent commitment among many Americans. Thus when the Soviet Union began to balk at some of the goals the United States was advocating, the debate seemed to become more than a simple difference of opinion; it became an ideological struggle for the future of the world. By the end of the war Roosevelt was able to win at least the partial consent of Winston Churchill to his principles; but although he believed at times that Stalin would similarly relent, he never managed to steer the Soviets from their determination to control Eastern Europe and from their vision of a postwar order in which each of the great powers would dominate its own sphere. Gradually, the differences between these two positions would turn the peacemaking process into a form of warfare.

Wartime Diplomacy

Serious strains began to develop in the alliance with the Soviet Union as early as 1942, a result of Stalin's irritation at delays in opening the second front and his resentment of the Anglo-American decision to invade North Africa before Europe. In this deteriorating atmosphere, Roosevelt and Churchill met in Casablanca, Morocco, in January 1943 to discuss Allied strategy. (Stalin had declined Roosevelt's invitation to attend.) The two leaders could not accept Stalin's most important demand—the immediate opening of a second front. But they tried to reassure him by announcing they would accept nothing less than the unconditional surrender of the Axis powers. It was a signal that the Americans and British would not negotiate a separate peace with Hitler and leave the Soviets to fight on alone.

In November 1943, Roosevelt and Churchill traveled to Teheran, Iran, for their first meeting with Stalin. By now, however, Roosevelt's most effective bargaining tool—Stalin's need for American assistance in his struggle against Germany—was almost gone. The German advance against Russia had failed; Soviet forces were now launching their own westward offensive. Meanwhile, new tensions had emerged in the alliance as a result of the refusal by the British and Americans to allow any Soviet participation in the creation of a new Italian government following the fall of Mussolini. To Stalin, at least, the "One World" doctrine already seemed to be a double standard: America and Britain expected to have a voice in the future of Eastern Europe, but the Soviet Union was to have no voice in the future of the West.

Nevertheless, the Teheran Conference seemed in most respects a success. Roosevelt and Stalin established a cordial personal relationship. Stalin agreed to an American request that the Soviet Union enter the war in the Pacific soon after the end of hostilities in Europe. Roosevelt, in turn, promised that an Anglo-American second front would be established within six months. All three leaders agreed in principle to a postwar international organization and to efforts to prevent a resurgence of German expansionism.

On other matters, however, the origins of future disagreements were already visible. Most important was the question of the future of Poland. Roosevelt and Churchill were willing to agree to a movement of the Soviet border westward, allowing Stalin to annex some historically Polish territory. But on the nature of the postwar government in the portion of Poland that would remain independent, there were sharp differences. Roosevelt and Churchill supported the claims of the Polish government-in-exile that had been functioning in London since 1940; Stalin wished to install another, pro-communist exiled government that had spent the war in Lublin, in the Soviet Union. The three leaders avoided a bitter conclusion to the Teheran Conference only by leaving the issue unresolved.

Yalta

For more than a year after Teheran, the Grand Alliance among the United States, Britain, and the Soviet Union

---

YALTA
Churchill, Roosevelt, and Stalin (known during the war as the "Big Three") meet at Yalta in the Crimea in February 1945 to try to agree on the outlines of the peace that they knew was soon to come. Instead, they settled on a series of vague compromises that ultimately left all parties feeling betrayed. *(Bettmann)*

alternated between high tension and warm amicability. In the fall of 1944, Churchill flew by himself to Moscow for a meeting with Stalin to resolve issues arising from a civil war in Greece. In return for a Soviet agreement to cease assisting Greek communists, who were challenging the British-supported monarchical government, Churchill consented to a proposal whereby control of Eastern Europe would be divided between Britain and the Soviet Union. "This memorable meeting," Churchill wrote Stalin after its close, "has shown that there are no matters that cannot be adjusted between us when we meet together in frank and intimate discussion." To Roosevelt, however, the Moscow agreement was evidence of how little the Atlantic Charter principles seemed to mean to his two most important allies.

In February 1945, Roosevelt joined Churchill and Stalin for a great peace conference in the Soviet city of Yalta. The meeting began in an atmosphere of some gloom. The American president, his health visibly failing, sensed resistance to his internationalist dreams. The British prime minister was already dismayed by Stalin's unwillingness to make concessions and compromises, warning even before the conference met that "I think the end of this war may well prove to be more disappointing than was the last." Stalin, whose armies were now only miles from Berlin, and aware of how much the United States still wanted his assistance in the Pacific, was confident and determined.

On a number of issues, the Big Three reached mutually satisfactory agreements. In return for Stalin's promise to enter the war against Japan, Roosevelt agreed that the Soviet Union should receive the Kurile Islands north of Japan; that it should regain southern Sakhalin Island and Port Arthur, both of which Russia had lost in the 1904 Russo-Japanese War; and that it could exercise some influence (along with the government of China) in Manchuria. The negotiators also agreed to accept a plan for a new international organization, a plan that had been hammered out the previous summer at a conference in Washington, D.C., at the Dumbarton Oaks estate. The new United Nations would contain a General Assembly, in which every member would be represented. But the most important decision-making body would be a Security Council, with permanent representatives of the five major powers (the United States, Britain, France, the Soviet Union, and China), each of which would have veto power. There would also be temporary delegates from several other nations on the Security Council. These agreements became the basis of the United Nations charter, drafted at a conference of fifty nations beginning April 25, 1945, in San Francisco. The United States Senate ratified the charter in July by a vote of 80 to 2

(a striking contrast to the slow and painful defeat it had administered to the charter of the League of Nations twenty-five years before).

On other issues, however, the Yalta Conference either left fundamental differences unresolved or papered them over with weak and unstable compromises. Fundamental disagreement remained about the postwar Polish government. Stalin, whose armies now occupied Poland, had already installed a government composed of the pro-communist "Lublin" Poles. Roosevelt and Churchill insisted that the pro-Western "London" Poles must be allowed a place in the Warsaw regime. Roosevelt wanted a government based on free, democratic elections—which both he and Stalin recognized the pro-Western forces would win. Stalin agreed to a vague compromise by which he would grant an unspecified number of places in the government to pro-Western Poles, and he reluctantly consented to hold "free and unfettered elections" in Poland. But he made no commitment to a date for them. They did not take place for more than forty years.

Nor was there agreement about the future of Germany. Stalin wanted to impose $20 billion in reparations on the Germans, of which Russia would receive half. Roosevelt and Churchill agreed only to leave final settlement of the issue to a future reparations commission. A more important difference was in the way the leaders envisioned postwar German politics and society. In 1944, Roosevelt and Churchill had met in Quebec and agreed on a plan crafted by the American secretary of the treasury, Henry Morgenthau, for the "pastoralization" of Germany—dismantling its industry and turning it into a largely agricultural society. By the time of the Yalta meeting, however, Roosevelt had changed his mind. He seemed now to want a reconstructed and reunited Germany—one that would be permitted to develop a prosperous, modern economy while remaining under the careful supervision of the Allies. Stalin wanted a permanent dismemberment of Germany.

The final agreement was, like the Polish accord, vague and unstable. The United States, Great Britain, France, and the Soviet Union would each control its own "zone of occupation" in Germany—the zones to be determined by the position of troops at end of the war. Berlin, the German capital, was already well inside the Soviet zone, but because of its symbolic importance it would be divided into four sectors, one for each nation to occupy. At an unspecified date, the nation would be reunited, but there was no agreement on how the reunification would occur. As for the rest of Europe, the conference produced a murky accord on the establishment of interim governments "broadly representative of all democratic elements." They would be replaced ultimately by permanent governments "responsible to the will of the people" and created through free elections. Once again, no specific provisions or timetables accompanied the agreements.

The Yalta accords, in other words, were less a settlement of postwar issues than a set of loose principles that sidestepped the most divisive issues. Roosevelt, Churchill, and Stalin each returned home from the conference apparently convinced that he had signed an important agreement. But the Soviet interpretation of the accords differed so sharply from the Anglo-American interpretation that the illusion endured only briefly. In the weeks following the Yalta Conference, Roosevelt watched with growing alarm as the Soviet Union moved systematically to establish pro-communist governments in one Eastern European nation after another and as Stalin refused to make the changes in Poland that the president believed he had promised.

But Roosevelt did not abandon hope. Still believing the differences could be settled, he left Washington early in the spring for a vacation at his retreat in Warm Springs, Georgia. There, on April 12, 1945, he suffered a sudden, massive stroke and died.

THE SOURING OF THE PEACE

Harry S. Truman, who became president on Roosevelt's death, had almost no familiarity with international issues. Nor did he share Roosevelt's faith in the flexibility of the Soviet Union. Roosevelt had believed that Stalin was, essentially, a reasonable man with whom an ultimate accord could be reached—a belief he was beginning to question at the time of his death, but had not yet abandoned. Truman, in contrast, sided with those in the government (and there were many) who considered the Soviet Union fundamentally untrustworthy and viewed Stalin himself with suspicion and loathing.

The Failure of Potsdam

Truman had been in office only a few days before he decided to "get tough" with the Soviet Union. Stalin had made what the new president considered solemn agreements with the United States at Yalta. The United States would insist that he honor them. Dismissing the advice of Secretary of War Stimson that the Polish question was a lost cause and not worth a world crisis, Truman met on April 23 with Soviet Foreign Minister Molotov and sharply chastised him for violations of the Yalta accords. "I have never been talked to like that in my life," a shocked Molotov reportedly replied. "Carry out your agreements and you won't get talked to like that," said the president.

In fact, Truman had only limited leverage with which to compel the Soviet Union to carry out its agreements. Russian forces already occupied Poland and much of the rest of Eastern Europe. Germany was already divided among the conquering nations. The United States was still engaged in a war in the Pacific and was neither able nor willing to engage in a new conflict in Europe. Truman insisted that the United States should be able to get "85 percent" of what it wanted, but he was ultimately forced to settle for much less.

He conceded first on Poland. When Stalin made a few minor concessions to the pro-Western exiles, Truman recognized the Warsaw government, hoping that noncommunist forces might gradually expand their influence there. Until the 1980s, they did not. Other questions remained, above all the question of Germany. To settle them, Truman met in July at Potsdam, in Russian-occupied Germany, with Churchill (who was replaced as prime minister by Clement Atlee in the midst of the negotiations) and Stalin. Truman reluctantly accepted adjustments of the Polish-German border that Stalin had long demanded; but he refused to permit the Russians to claim any reparations from the American, French, and British zones of Germany. The result, in effect, was to confirm that Germany would remain divided, with the western zones eventually united into one nation, friendly to the United States, and the Russian zone surviving as another nation, with a pro-Soviet, communist government. Soon, the Soviet Union would be siphoning between $1.5 and $3 billion a year out of its zone of occupation.

The China Problem

Central to American hopes for an open, peaceful world policed by the great powers was a strong, independent China. But even before the war ended, the American government knew that those hopes faced a major, perhaps insurmountable obstacle: the Chinese government of Chiang Kai-shek. Chiang was generally friendly to the United States, but he had few other virtues. His government was corrupt and incompetent. His popular legitimacy was feeble. And Chiang himself lived in a world of almost surreal isolation, unable or unwilling to face the problems that were threatening to engulf him. Ever since 1927, the nationalist government he headed had been engaged in a prolonged and bitter struggle with the communist armies of Mao Zedong. So successful had the communist challenge grown that by 1945 Mao was in control of one-fourth of the population.

At Potsdam, Truman had managed to persuade Stalin to recognize Chiang as the legitimate ruler of China; but Chiang was rapidly losing his grip on his country. Some Americans urged the government to try to find a "third force" to support as an alternative to either Chiang or Mao. A few argued that America should try to reach some accommodation with Mao himself. Truman, however, decided reluctantly that he had no choice but to continue supporting Chiang. That was in part because of the strength in the United States of forces committed to Chiang, including the formidable publisher of *Time* and *Life* magazines, Henry Luce, the son of Chinese missionaries and an inveterate defender of Chiang. The pro-Chiang forces, known as the "China Lobby," would help shape American policy toward Asia for thirty years.

In the last months of the war, American forces diverted attention from the Japanese long enough to assist Chiang against the communists in Manchuria. For the next several years, as the long struggle between the nationalists and the communists erupted into a full-scale civil war, the United States continued to send money and weapons to Chiang, even as it was becoming clear his cause was lost. But Truman was not prepared to intervene militarily to save the nationalist regime.

Instead, the American government was beginning to consider an alternative to China as the strong, pro-Western force in Asia: a revived Japan. Abandoning the restrictive occupation policies of the first years after the war (when General Douglas MacArthur had governed the nation), the United States lifted all limitations on industrial development and encouraged rapid economic growth in Japan. The vision of an open, united Asia had given way, as in Europe, with an acceptance of the necessity of developing a strong, pro-American sphere of influence.

The Containment Doctrine

By the end of 1945, the Grand Alliance of World War II was in a shambles, and with it any realistic hope of a postwar world constructed according to the Atlantic Charter ideals Roosevelt and others had supported. Instead, a new American policy was slowly emerging. Rather than attempting to create a unified, "open" world, the West would work to "contain" the threat of further Soviet expansion. The United States would be the leading force in that effort.

The new doctrine emerged in part as a response to events in Europe in 1946. In Turkey, Stalin was trying

GEORGE F. KENNAN

Kennan was one of the architects of the policy of containment, which became the basis of foreign policy for over forty years. But almost from the start, he was critical of the United States government's sweeping view of containment. Americans needed, he argued, to define their vital interests more narrowly, to focus their defensive efforts on nations of direct strategic importance to them. That meant, in his view, mainly the industrialized nations of Europe and Japan. In later years, he was outspoken in his attacks on the war in Vietnam. *(Library of Congress)*

to win some control over the vital straits to the Mediterranean. In Greece, communist forces were again threatening the pro-Western government; the British had announced they could no longer provide assistance. Faced with these challenges, Truman decided to enunciate a firm new policy. In doing so, he drew from the ideas of the influential American diplomat George F. Kennan, who warned in a famous telegram from Moscow (and later in an article published under the pseudonym "X") that in the Soviet Union the United States faced "a political force committed fanatically to the belief that with the U.S. there can be no permanent modus vivendi," and that the only answer was "a long-term, patient but firm and vigilant containment of Russian expansive tendencies." On March 12, 1947, Truman appeared before Congress and used Kennan's warnings as the basis of what became known as the Truman Doctrine. "I believe," he argued, "that it must be the policy of the United States to support free peoples who are resisting attempted subjugation by armed minorities or by outside pressures." In the same speech he requested $400 million—part of it to bolster the armed forces of Greece and Turkey, another part to provide economic assistance to Greece. Congress quickly approved the measure.

The American commitment ultimately helped ease Soviet pressure on Turkey and helped the Greek government defeat the communist insurgents. More important, it established a basis for American foreign policy that would survive for over forty years. On the one hand, the Truman Doctrine was a way of accommodating the status quo: it accepted that there was no immediate likelihood of overturning the communist governments Stalin had established in Eastern Europe. On the other hand, it was a strategy for the future: communism was an innately expansionist force, and it must be contained within its present boundaries. Its expansion anywhere could be a threat to democracy everywhere because, as Secretary of State Dean Acheson had argued, the fall of one nation to communism would have a "domino effect" on surrounding nations. It was, therefore, the policy of the United States to assist pro-Western forces in struggles against communism whether those struggles directly involved the Soviet Union or not.

The Marshall Plan

An integral part of the containment policy was a proposal to aid in the economic reconstruction of Western Europe. There were many motives: humanitarian concern for the European people; a fear that Europe would remain an economic drain on the United States if it could not quickly rebuild and begin to feed itself; a desire for a strong European market for American goods. Above all, American policymakers believed that unless something could be done to strengthen the shaky pro-American governments in Western Europe, they might fall under the control of rapidly growing domestic communist parties.

In a June 1947 speech at Harvard, therefore, Secretary of State George C. Marshall announced a plan to provide economic assistance to all European nations (including the Soviet Union) that would join in drafting a program for recovery. Although Russia and its Eastern satellites quickly and predictably rejected the plan, sixteen Western European nations eagerly participated. Whatever domestic opposition there was largely vanished after a coup in Czechoslovakia in February 1948 suddenly established a Soviet-dominated communist government there. In April, Congress approved the creation of the Economic Cooperation Administration, the agency that would administer the Marshall Plan, as it became known. Over the next three years, the Marshall Plan channeled over $12 billion of American aid into Europe, helping to spark a substantial economic revival. By the end of 1950, European industrial production had risen 64 percent, communist strength in the member nations had declined, and opportunities for American trade had revived.

Mobilization at Home

That the United States had fully accepted a continuing commitment to the containment policy became clear in 1947 and 1948 through a series of measures designed to maintain American military power at near-wartime levels. In 1948, at the president's request, Congress approved a new military draft and revived the Selective Service System. In the meantime, the United States, having failed to reach agreement with the Soviet Union on international control of nuclear weapons, redoubled its own efforts in atomic research, elevating nuclear weaponry to a central place in its military arsenal. The Atomic Energy Commission, established in 1946, became the supervisory body charged with overseeing all nuclear research, civilian and military alike.

Particularly important was the National Security Act of 1947, which created several new instruments of foreign policy. A new Department of Defense would oversee all branches of the armed services, combining functions previously performed by the War and Navy Departments. A National Security Council (NSC), operating out of the White House, would advise the president on foreign and military policy. A Central Intelligence Agency (CIA) would be responsible for collecting information through both open and covert methods and, as the Cold War continued, for engaging secretly in political and military operations on behalf of American goals. In other words, the National Security Act gave the government (and particularly the president) expanded powers with which to pursue the nation's international goals. It centralized in the White House control that had once been widely dispersed, enabled the president to take warlike actions without an open declaration of war, and created vehicles by which the government could at times act politically and militarily overseas behind a veil of secrecy.

The Road to NATO

At about the same time, the United States was moving to strengthen the military capabilities of Western Europe. Convinced that a reconstructed Germany was essential to the hopes of the West, Truman reached an

DIVIDED EUROPE AFTER WORLD WAR II

agreement with England and France to merge the three western zones of occupation into a new West German republic (which would include the American, British, and French sectors of Berlin, even though that city lay well within the Soviet zone.) Stalin interpreted the move (correctly) as a direct challenge to his hopes for a subdued Germany and a docile Europe. He was especially alarmed because, at almost the same moment, he was facing a challenge from inside what he considered his own sphere. The government of Yugoslavia, under the leadership of Marshall Josip Broz Tito, broke openly with the Soviet Union and declared the nation an unaligned communist state. The United States offered Tito assistance.

Stalin responded quickly. On June 24, 1948, he imposed a tight blockade around the western sectors of Berlin. If Germany was to be officially divided, he was implying, then the country's Western government would have to abandon its outpost in the heart of the Soviet-controlled eastern zone. Truman refused to comply. Unwilling to risk war through a military response to the blockade, he ordered a massive airlift to supply the city with food, fuel, and supplies. The airlift continued for more than ten months, transporting nearly 2.5 million tons of material, keeping alive a city of 2 million people, and transforming West Berlin into a symbol of the West's resolve to resist communist expansion. In the spring of 1949, Stalin lifted the now in-

BLOCKADING BERLIN
Soviet and East German crews
work to dismantle the rail lines
connecting West Berlin to the rest
of West Germany during the Berlin
blockade of 1949. *(UPI/Bettmann)*

effective blockade. And in October, the division of Germany into two nations—the Federal Republic in the west and the Democratic Republic in the east—became official.

The crisis in Berlin accelerated the consolidation of what was already in effect an alliance among the United States and the countries of Western Europe. On April 4, 1949, twelve nations signed an agreement establishing the North Atlantic Treaty Organization (NATO) and declaring that an armed attack against one member would be considered an attack against all. The NATO countries, moreover, agreed to maintain a standing military force in Europe to defend against what many believed was the threat of a Soviet invasion. The American Senate quickly ratified the treaty, which fused European nations that had been fighting one another for centuries into a strong and enduring alliance. It also spurred the Soviet Union to create an alliance of its own with the communist governments in Eastern Europe—an alliance formalized in 1955 by the Warsaw Pact.

The Enduring Crisis

For a time, Americans believed that these initial achievements had turned the tide of the battle against communism. But a series of events in 1949 eroded that confidence and launched the Cold War in new directions. An announcement in September that the Soviet Union had successfully exploded its first atomic weapon, years earlier than predicted, shocked and frightened many Americans. So did the collapse of Chiang Kai-shek's nationalist government in China, which occurred with startling speed in the last months of 1949. Chiang fled with his political allies and the remnants of his army to the offshore island of Formosa (Taiwan), and the entire Chinese mainland came under the control of a communist government that many Americans believed to be an extension of the Soviet Union. Few policymakers shared the belief of the China Lobby that the United States should now commit itself to the rearming of Chiang Kai-shek. But neither would the United States recognize the new communist regime. The Chinese mainland would remain almost entirely closed to the West for a generation. The United States, in the meantime, would devote increased attention to the revitalization of Japan as a buffer against Asian communism, ending the American occupation in 1952.

In response to these and other setbacks, Truman called for a thorough review of American foreign policy. The result was a National Security Council report, commonly known as NSC-68, which outlined a shift in the American position. The April 1950 document argued that the United States could no longer rely on other nations to take the initiative in resisting communism. It must itself establish firm and active leadership of the noncommunist world. And it must move to stop communist expansion anywhere it occurred, regardless of the intrinsic strategic or economic value

COMMUNIST CHINA
A division of the Red Army marches triumphantly through central China shortly after their 1949 victory in the Chinese civil war. The United States refused to recognize the new government for more than twenty-five years. *(Bettmann)*

of the lands in question. Among other things, the report called for a major expansion of American military power, with a defense budget almost four times the previously projected figure.

AMERICA AFTER THE WAR

The crises overseas were not the only frustrations the American people encountered after the war. The nation also faced serious economic difficulties in adapting to the peace. The resulting instability contributed to an increasingly heated political climate.

The Problems of Reconversion

The bombs that destroyed Hiroshima and Nagasaki ended the war months earlier than almost anyone had predicted and propelled the nation precipitously into a process of reconversion. The lack of planning was soon compounded by a growing popular impatience for a return to normal economic conditions. Under intense public pressure, the Truman administration attempted to hasten that return, despite dire warnings by some planners and economists. The result was a period of economic problems.

They were not, however, the problems that most Americans had feared. There had been many predictions that peace would bring a return of Depression unemployment, as war production ceased and returning soldiers flooded the labor market. But there was no general economic collapse in 1946—for several reasons. Government spending dropped sharply and abruptly, to be sure; $35 billion of war contracts were canceled at a stroke within weeks of the Japanese surrender. But increased consumer demand soon compensated. Consumer goods had been generally unavailable during the war, so many workers had saved a substantial portion of their wages and were now ready to spend. A $6 billion tax cut pumped additional money into general circulation. The Servicemen's Readjustment Act of 1944, better known as the GI Bill of Rights, provided economic and educational assistance to veterans, increasing spending even further.

This flood of consumer demand ensured that there would be no new depression, but it contributed to more than two years of serious inflation, during which prices rose at rates of 14 to 15 percent annually. In the summer of 1946, the president vetoed an extension of the authority of the wartime Office of Price Administration, thus eliminating price controls. (He was not opposed to the controls, but to congressional amendments that had weakened the OPA.) Inflation soared to 25 percent before he relented a month later and signed a bill little different from the one he had rejected.

Compounding the economic difficulties was a sharp rise in labor unrest, driven in part by the impact of inflation. By the end of 1945, there had already been major strikes in the automobile, electrical, and steel industries. In April 1946, John L. Lewis led the United Mine Workers out on strike, shutting down the coal fields for forty days. Fears grew rapidly that without vital coal supplies, the entire nation might virtually grind to a halt. Truman finally forced the miners to return to work by ordering government seizure of the mines. But in the process, he pressured mine owners to grant the union most of its demands, which he had earlier denounced as inflationary. Almost simultaneously, the nation's railroads suffered a total shutdown—the first in the nation's history—as two major unions walked out on strike. By threatening to use the army to run the trains, Truman pressured the workers back to work after only a few days.

Reconversion was particularly difficult for the millions of women and minorities who had entered the work force during the war. With veterans returning home and looking for jobs in the industrial economy, employers tended to push women, blacks, Hispanics, Chinese, and others out of the plants to make room for white males. Some of the war workers, particularly

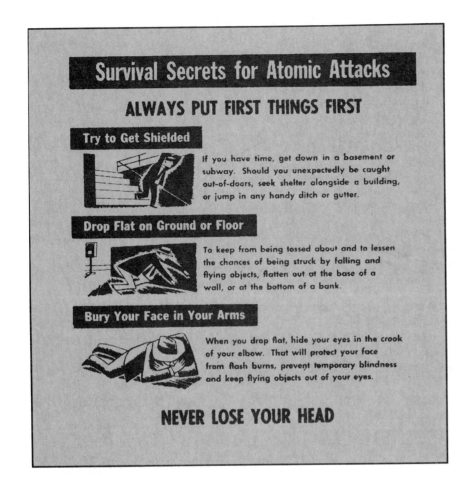

women, left the work force voluntarily, out of a desire to return to their former domestic lives. But as many as 80 percent of women workers, and virtually all black, Hispanic, and Asian males, wanted to continue working. The postwar inflation, the pressure to meet the rising expectations of a high-consumption society, the rising divorce rate, which left many women responsible for their own economic well-being—all combined to create among women a high demand for paid employment. As they found themselves excluded from industrial jobs, therefore, women workers moved increasingly into other areas of the economy (above all, the service sector).

The Fair Deal Rejected

Days after the Japanese surrender, Truman submitted to Congress a twenty-one-point domestic program outlining what he later termed the "Fair Deal." It called for expansion of Social Security benefits; the raising of

the legal minimum wage from 40 to 65 cents an hour; a program to ensure full employment through aggressive use of federal spending and investment; a permanent Fair Employment Practices Act; public housing and slum clearance; long-range environmental and public works planning; and government promotion of scientific research. Weeks later he added other proposals: federal aid to funding for the St. Lawrence Seaway, nationalization of atomic energy, and perhaps most important, national health insurance—a dream of welfare-state liberals for decades, but one deferred in 1935 when the Social Security Act was written. The president was declaring an end to the wartime moratorium on liberal reform. He was also symbolizing, as he later wrote, "my assumption of the office of President in my own right."

But the Fair Deal programs fell victim to the same public and congressional conservatism that had crippled the last years of the New Deal. Indeed, that conservatism seemed to be intensifying, as the November 1946 congressional elections suggested. Using the simple but devastating slogan "Had Enough?", the Republican Party won control of both houses of Congress.

The new Republican Congress quickly moved to reduce government spending and chip away at New Deal reforms. The president bowed to what he claimed was the popular mandate to lift most remaining wage and price controls, and Congress moved further to deregulate the economy. Inflation rapidly increased. When a public outcry arose over the soaring prices for meat, Senator Robert Taft, perhaps the most influential Republican conservative in Congress, advised consumers to "Eat less," and added, "We have got to break with the corrupting idea that we can legislate prosperity, legislate equality, legislate opportunity." True to the spirit of Taft's words, the Republican Congress quickly applied what one congressman described as a "meat-axe to government frills." It refused to appropriate funds to aid education, increase Social Security, or support reclamation and power projects in the West. It defeated a proposal to raise the minimum wage. It passed tax measures that cut rates dramatically for high-income families and moderately for those with lower incomes. Only vetoes by the president finally forced a more progressive bill.

The most notable action of the new Congress was its assault on the Wagner Act of 1935. Conservatives had always resented the new powers the legislation had granted unions; and in the light of the labor difficulties during and after the war, such resentments intensified sharply. The result was the Labor-Management Relations Act of 1947, better known as the Taft–Hartley Act. It made illegal the so-called closed shop (a workplace in which no one can be hired without first being a member of a union). And although it continued to permit the creation of so-called union shops (in which workers must join a union after being hired), it permitted states to pass "right-to-work" laws prohibiting even that. Repealing this provision, the controversial Section 14(b), would remain a goal of the labor movement for decades. The Taft–Hartley Act also empowered the president to call for a "cooling-off" period before a strike by issuing an injunction against any work stoppage that endangered national safety or health. Outraged workers and union leaders denounced the measure as a "slave labor bill." Truman vetoed it, but both houses easily overruled him the same day.

The Taft-Hartley Act did not destroy the labor movement, as many union leaders had predicted. But it did damage weaker unions in relatively lightly organized industries such as chemicals and textiles; and it made more difficult the organizing of workers who had never been union members at all, especially women, minorities, and most workers in the South.

The Election of 1948

Truman and his advisers believed the American public was not ready to abandon the achievements of the New Deal, despite the 1946 election results. As they planned strategy for the 1948 campaign, therefore, they placed their hopes in an appeal to enduring Democratic loyalties. Throughout 1948, Truman proposed one reform measure after another (including, on February 2, the first major civil rights bill of the century). Although Congress ignored or defeated them all, the president was building campaign issues for the fall.

There remained, however, the problem of Truman's personal unpopularity—the assumption among much of the electorate that he lacked stature, that his administration was weak and inept—and the deep divisions within the Democratic Party. At the Democratic Convention that summer, two factions abandoned the party altogether. Southern conservatives reacted angrily to Truman's proposed civil rights bill and to the approval at the convention of a civil rights plank in the platform (engineered by Hubert Humphrey, the mayor of Minneapolis). They walked out and formed the States' Rights (or "Dixiecrat") Party, with Governor Strom Thurmond of South Carolina as its presidential nominee. At the same time, the party's left wing formed a new Progressive Party, with Henry A. Wallace as its candidate. Wallace supporters objected to what they considered the slow and ineffective domestic policies of the Truman administration, but they resented even more the president's confrontational stance toward the Soviet Union.

In addition, many Democratic liberals unwilling to leave the party attempted to dump the president in 1948. The Americans for Democratic Action (ADA), a coalition of liberals, tried to entice Dwight D. Eisenhower, the popular war hero, to contest the nomination. Only after Eisenhower had refused did liberals bow to the inevitable and concede the nomination to Truman. The Republicans, in the meantime, had once again nominated Governor Thomas E. Dewey of New York, whose substantial reelection victory in 1946 had made him one of the nation's leading political figures. Austere, dignified, and competent, he seemed to offer an unbeatable alternative to the president. Polls showed Dewey with an apparently insurmountable lead in September, so much so that some opinion analysts stopped taking surveys. Dewey conducted a subdued, statesmanlike campaign and tried to avoid antagonizing anyone.

Only Truman, it seemed, believed he could win. As the campaign gathered momentum, he became ever more aggressive, turning the fire away from himself and toward Dewey and the "do-nothing, good-for-nothing" Republican Congress, which was, he told the

voters, responsible for fueling inflation and abandoning workers and common people. To dramatize his
point, he called Congress into special session in July
to give it a chance, he said, to enact the liberal measures the Republicans had recently written into their
platform. Congress met for two weeks and, predictably, did almost nothing.

The president traveled nearly 32,000 miles and
made 356 speeches, delivering blunt, extemporaneous
attacks. He had told Senator Alben Barkley of Kentucky, his running mate, "I'm going to fight hard. I'm
going to give them hell." He called for repeal of the
Taft-Hartley act, increased price supports for farmers,
and strong civil rights protection for blacks. (He was
the first president to campaign in Harlem.) He sought,
in short, to re-create much of Franklin Roosevelt's New
Deal coalition. To the surprise of virtually everyone,
he succeeded. On election night, he won a narrow but
decisive victory: 49.5 percent of the popular vote to
Dewey's 45.1 percent (with the two splinter parties dividing the small remainder between them), and an
electoral vote margin of 303 to 189. Democrats, in the
meantime, had regained both houses of Congress by
substantial margins. It was the most dramatic upset in
the history of presidential elections.

The Fair Deal Revived

Despite the Democratic victories, the Eighty-first Congress was no more hospitable to Truman's Fair Deal
reform than its Republican predecessor. Truman did

win some important victories, to be sure. Congress
raised the legal minimum wage from 40 cents to 75
cents an hour. It approved an important expansion of
the Social Security system, increasing benefits by 75
percent and extending them to 10 million additional
people. And it passed the National Housing Act of
1949, which provided for the construction of 810,000
units of low-income housing, accompanied by long-
term rent subsidies. (Inadequate funding plagued the
program for years, and it reached its initial goal only
in 1972.)

But on other issues—among them national health
insurance and aid to education—he made no progress.
Nor was he able to persuade Congress to accept the
civil rights legislation he proposed in 1949, which
would have made lynching a federal crime, provided
federal protection of black voting rights, abolished the
poll tax, and established a new Fair Employment Practices Commission to curb discrimination in hiring (to
replace the wartime commission Roosevelt had established in 1940). Southern Democrats filibustered to kill
the bill.

Truman did proceed on his own to battle several
forms of racial discrimination. He ordered an end to
discrimination in the hiring of government employees.
He began to dismantle segregation within the armed
forces. And he allowed the Justice Department to become actively involved in court battles against discriminatory statutes. In the meantime, the Supreme
Court signaled its own growing awareness of the issue by ruling, in *Shelley* v. *Kraemer* (1948), that the

ELECTION OF 1948   (53% of electorate voting)

	ELECTORAL VOTE	POPULAR VOTE (%)
Harry S. Truman (Democratic)	303	24,105,695 (49.5)
Thomas E. Dewey (Republican)	189	21,969,170 (45.1)
Strom Thurmond (States' Rights)	39	1,169,021 (2.4)
Henry A. Wallace (Progressive)	—	1,156,103 (2.4)
Other candidates (Socialist, Prohibition, Socialist Labor, Socialist Workers)	—	272,713

courts could not be used to enforce private "covenants" meant to bar blacks from residential neighborhoods. The achievements of the Truman years made only minor dents in the structure of segregation, but they were the tentative beginnings of a federal commitment to confront the problem of race.

THE KOREAN WAR

From the beginning, Truman's domestic policies had had a difficult time competing against the growing national obsession with the Soviet threat in Europe. In 1950, a new and more dangerous element of the Cold War emerged and all but killed hopes for further Fair Deal reform. On June 24, 1950, the armies of communist North Korea swept across their southern border in an invasion of the pro-Western half of the Korean peninsula to the south. Within days, they had occu-

pied much of South Korea, including Seoul, its capital. Almost immediately, the United States committed itself to the conflict. It was the nation's first military engagement of the cold war.

The Divided Peninsula

By the end of 1945, both the United States and the Soviet Union had sent troops into Korea, and neither was willing to leave. Instead, they had divided the nation, supposedly temporarily, along the 38th parallel. The Russians finally departed in 1949, leaving behind a communist government in the north with a strong, Soviet-equipped army. The Americans left a few months later, handing control to the pro-Western government of Syngman Rhee, anticommunist but only nominally democratic. He had a relatively small military, which he used primarily to suppress internal opposition.

The relative weakness of the south offered a strong temptation to nationalists in the North Korean government who wanted to reunite the country. The temptation grew stronger when the American government implied that it did not consider South Korea within its own "defense perimeter." The role of the Soviet Union remains unclear; there is some reason to believe that the North Koreans acted without Stalin's approval. But the Soviets supported the offensive once it began.

The Truman administration responded quickly. On June 27, 1950, the president ordered limited American military assistance to South Korea, and on the same day he appealed to the United Nations to intervene. The Soviet Union was boycotting the Security Council at the time (to protest the council's refusal to recognize the new communist government of China) and thus was unable to exercise its veto power. As a result, American delegates were able to win UN agreement to a resolution calling for international assistance to the Rhee government. On June 30, the United States ordered its own ground forces into Korea, and Truman appointed General Douglas MacArthur to command the UN operations there. (Several other nations provided assistance and troops, but the "UN" armies were, in fact, overwhelmingly American.)

The intervention in Korea was the first expression of the newly expansive American foreign policy outlined in NSC-68. But the administration quickly went beyond NSC–68 and decided that the war would be an effort not simply at containment but also at "liberation." After a surprise American invasion at Inchon in September had routed the North Korean forces from the south and sent them fleeing back across the 38th parallel, Truman gave MacArthur permission to pursue the communists into their own territory. His aim, as an American-sponsored UN resolution proclaimed in October, was to create "a unified, independent and democratic Korea."

From Invasion to Stalemate

For several weeks, MacArthur's invasion of North Korea proceeded smoothly. On October 19, the capital, Pyongyang, fell to the UN forces. Victory seemed near—until the new communist government of China, alarmed by the movement of American forces toward its border, intervened. By November 4, eight divisions of the Chinese army had entered the war. The UN offensive stalled and then collapsed. Through December 1950, outnumbered American forces fought a bitter, losing battle against the Chinese divisions, retreating at almost every juncture. Within weeks, communist forces had pushed the Americans back below the 38th parallel once again and had captured the South Korean capital of Seoul a second time. By mid-January 1951 the rout had ceased; and by March the UN armies had managed to regain much of the territory they had recently lost, taking back Seoul and pushing the communists north of the 38th parallel once more. But with that, the war degenerated into a protracted stalemate.

THE KOREAN WAR, 1950–1953

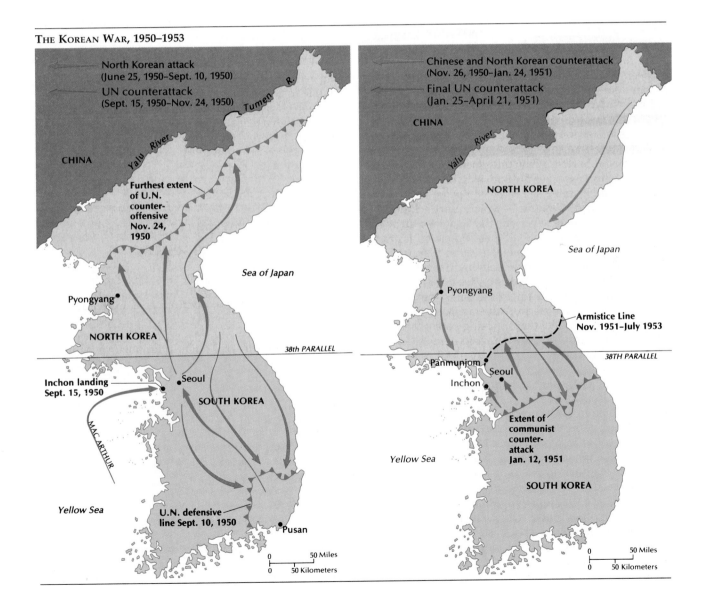

From the start, Truman was determined to avoid a direct conflict with China, which he feared might lead to a new world war. Once China entered the war, he began seeking a negotiated solution to the struggle, and for the next two years he insisted that there be no wider war. But he faced a formidable opponent in General MacArthur, who resisted any limits on his military discretion. The United States was fighting the Chinese, he argued. It should therefore attack China itself, if not through an actual invasion, then at least by bombing communist forces massing north of the Chinese border. In March 1951, he indicated his unhappiness in a public letter to House Republican leader Joseph W. Martin that concluded: "There is no substitute for victory." His position had wide popular support.

The Martin letter came after nine months during which MacArthur had resisted Truman's decisions. More than once, the president had warned the general to keep his objections to himself. The release of the Martin letter, therefore, struck the president as intolerable insubordination. On April 11, 1951, he relieved MacArthur of his command.

There was a storm of public outrage. Sixty-nine percent of the American people supported MacArthur, a Gallup poll reported. When the general returned to the United States later in 1951, he was greeted with wild enthusiasm. His televised farewell appearance before a joint session of Congress—which he concluded by saying "Old soldiers never die, they just fade away"—attracted an audience of millions. Public criticism of Truman finally abated somewhat when a number of prominent military figures, including General Omar Bradley, publicly supported the president's decision. But substantial hostility toward Truman remained.

In the meantime, the Korean stalemate continued. Negotiations between the opposing forces began at Panmunjom in July 1951, but the talks—and the war—dragged on until 1953.

Limited Mobilization

Just as the war in Korea produced only a limited American military commitment abroad, so it created only a limited economic mobilization at home. Still, the government did try to control the wartime economy in several important ways.

First, Truman set up the Office of Defense Mobilization to fight inflation by holding down prices and discouraging high union wage demands. When these cautious regulatory efforts failed, the president took more drastic action. Railroad workers walked off the job in 1951, and Truman ordered the government to seize control of the railroads. That helped keep the trains running, but it had no effect on union demands. Workers ultimately got most of what they had demanded. In 1952, during a nationwide steel strike, Truman seized the steel mills, citing his powers as commander in chief. But in a 6-to-3 decision, the Supreme Court ruled that the president had exceeded his authority, and Truman was forced to relent. A long and costly strike followed, and the president's drastic actions appeared to many to have been both rash and ineffective.

The Korean War gave a significant boost to economic growth by pumping new government funds into the economy at a point when many believed a recession was about to begin. But the war had other, less welcome effects. It came at a time of rising insecurity about America's position in the world and intensified anxiety about communism. As the long stalemate continued, leaving 140,000 Americans dead or wounded, frustration turned to anger. The United States, which had recently won the greatest war in history, seemed unable to conclude what many Americans considered a minor border skirmish in a small country. Many began to believe that something must be deeply wrong—not only in Korea but within the United States as well. Such fears contributed to the rise of the second major campaign of the century against domestic communism.

THE CRUSADE AGAINST SUBVERSION

Why did the American people develop a growing fear of internal communist subversion that by the early 1950s had reached the point of near hysteria? There are many possible answers, but no single definitive explanation.

One factor was obvious. Communism was not an imagined enemy in the 1950s. It had tangible shape, in Joseph Stalin and the Soviet Union. In addition, America had encountered setbacks in its battle against communism: the Korean stalemate, the "loss" of China, the Soviet development of an atomic bomb. Searching for someone to blame, many people were attracted to the idea of a communist conspiracy within American borders. But there were other factors as well, rooted in events in American domestic politics.

HUAC and Alger Hiss

Much of the anticommunist furor emerged out of the Republican Party's search for an issue with which to attack the Democrats, and out of the Democrats' efforts to take that issue away. Beginning in 1947 (with Republicans temporarily in control of Congress), the House Un-American Activities Committee (HUAC) held widely publicized investigations to prove that, under Democratic rule, the government had tolerated (if not actually encouraged) communist subversion. The committee turned first to the movie industry, arguing that communists had infiltrated Hollywood and had tainted America with propaganda. Writers and producers, some of them former communists, were called to testify; and when some of them ("the Hollywood Ten") refused to answer questions about their own political beliefs and those of their colleagues, they were jailed for contempt. Others were barred from employment in the industry when Hollywood, attempting to protect its public image, adopted a blacklist of those of "suspicious loyalty."

More alarming to the public was HUAC's investigation into charges of disloyalty leveled against a former high-ranking member of the State Department: Alger Hiss. In 1948, Whittaker Chambers, a self-avowed former communist agent who had become a conservative editor at *Time* magazine, told the committee that Hiss had passed classified State Department documents through him to the Soviet Union in 1937 and 1938. When Hiss sued him for slander, Chambers produced microfilms of the documents (called the "pumpkin papers," because Chambers had kept them hidden

in a pumpkin in his garden). Hiss could not be tried for espionage because of the statute of limitations (a law that protects individuals from prosecution for most crimes after seven years have passed). But largely because of the relentless efforts of Richard M. Nixon, a freshman Republican congressman from California and a member of HUAC, Hiss was convicted of perjury and served several years in prison. The Hiss case not only discredited a prominent young diplomat; it cast suspicion on a generation of liberal Democrats and made it possible for many Americans to believe that communists had actually infiltrated the government.

The Federal Loyalty Program and the Rosenberg Case

Partly to protect itself against Republican attacks, partly to encourage support for the president's foreign policy initiatives, the Truman administration in 1947 initiated a widely publicized program to review the "loyalty" of federal employees. In August 1950, the president authorized sensitive agencies to fire people deemed no more than "bad security risks." By 1951, more than 2,000 government employees had resigned under pressure and 212 had been dismissed.

The employee loyalty program became a signal throughout the executive branch to launch a major as-

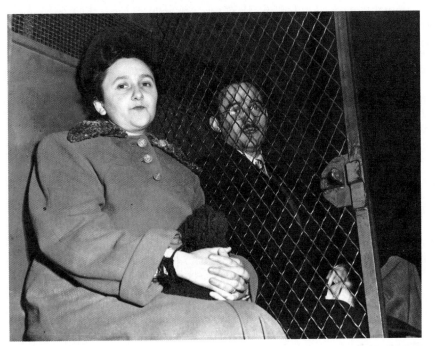

THE ROSENBERGS
Julius and Ethel Rosenberg leave federal court in a police van after being convicted in March 1951 of transmitting atomic secrets to the Soviet Union. A week later, Judge Irving Kaufman sentenced them to death.
(UPI/Bettmann)

sault on subversion. The attorney general established a widely cited list of supposedly subversive organizations. The director of the Federal Bureau of Investigation (FBI), J. Edgar Hoover, investigated and harassed alleged radicals. The anticommunist frenzy quickly grew so intense that even a Democratic Congress felt obliged to bow to it. In 1950, Congress passed the McCarran Internal Security Act, requiring all communist organizations to register with the government and to publish their records and creating other restrictions on "subversive" activity. Truman vetoed the bill. Congress easily overrode his veto.

The successful Soviet detonation of a nuclear weapon in 1949, earlier than generally expected, convinced many people that there had been a conspiracy to pass American atomic secrets to the Russians. In 1950, Klaus Fuchs, a young British scientist, seemed to confirm those fears when he testified that he had delivered to the Russians details of the manufacture of the bomb. The case ultimately settled on an obscure New York couple, Julius and Ethel Rosenberg, members of the Communist Party, whom the government claimed had been the masterminds of the conspiracy. The case against them rested in large part on testimony by Ethel's brother, David Greenglass, a machinist who had worked on the Manhattan Project. Greenglass admitted to channeling secret information to the Soviet Union through other agents (including Fuchs). His sister and brother-in-law had, he claimed, planned and orchestrated the espionage. The Rosenbergs were convicted and, on April 5, 1951, sentenced to death. After two years of appeals and protests by sympathizers, they died in the electric chair on June 19, 1953, proclaiming their innocence to the end.

All these factors—the HUAC investigations, the Hiss trial, the loyalty investigations, the McCarran Act, the Rosenberg case—combined with concern about international events to create a fear of communist subversion that by the early 1950s seemed to have gripped virtually the entire country. State and local governments, the judiciary, schools and universities, labor unions—all sought to purge themselves of real or imagined subversives. A pervasive fear settled on the country—not only the fear of communist infiltration but the fear of being suspected of communism. It was a climate that made possible the rise of an extraordinary public figure, whose behavior at any other time might have been dismissed as preposterous.

McCarthyism

Joseph McCarthy was an undistinguished first-term Republican senator from Wisconsin when, in February 1950, he suddenly burst into national prominence. In the midst of a speech in Wheeling, West Virginia, he raised a sheet of paper and claimed to "hold in my hand" a list of 205 known communists currently working in the American State Department. No person of comparable stature had ever made so bold a charge against the federal government; and in the weeks to come, as McCarthy repeated and expanded on his accusations, he emerged as the nation's most prominent leader of the crusade against domestic subversion.

Within weeks of his charges against the State Department, McCarthy was leveling accusations at other agencies. After 1952, with the Republicans in control of the Senate and McCarthy the chairman of a special subcommittee, he conducted highly publicized investigations of subversion in many areas of the government. His unprincipled assistants, Roy Cohn and David Schine, sauntered arrogantly through federal offices and American embassies overseas looking for evidence of communist influence. One hapless government official after another appeared before McCarthy's subcommittee, where the senator belligerently and often cruelly badgered witnesses and destroyed public careers. McCarthy never produced solid evidence that any federal employee had communist ties. But a growing constituency adored him nevertheless for his coarse, "fearless" assaults on a government establishment that many considered arrogant, effete, even traitorous. Republicans, in particular, rallied to his claims that the Democrats had been responsible for "twenty years of treason," that only a change of parties could rid the country of subversion. McCarthy, in short, provided his followers with an issue into which they could channel a wide range of resentments: fear of communism, animosity toward the country's "eastern establishment," and frustrated partisan ambitions.

For a time, McCarthy intimidated all but a few people from opposing him. Even the highly popular Dwight D. Eisenhower, running for president in 1952, did not speak out against him, even though he disliked McCarthy's tactics and was outraged at, among other things, McCarthy's attacks on General George Marshall.

The Republican Revival

Public frustration over the stalemate in Korea and popular fears of internal subversion combined to make 1952 a bad year for the Democratic Party. Truman, whose own popularity had diminished almost to the vanishing point, wisely withdrew from the presidential contest. The party united instead behind Governor Adlai E. Stevenson of Illinois. Stevenson's dignity, wit, and eloquence made him a beloved figure to many liberals and intellectuals. But those same qualities seemed only to fuel Republican charges that Stevenson lacked

SIGNIFICANT EVENTS

1941 Roosevelt and Churchill draft Atlantic Charter

1943 Wendell Willkie publishes *One World*

Roosevelt, Churchill, and Stalin meet at Teheran

1944 G.I. Bill of Rights enacted

1945 Yalta Conference

Roosevelt dies; Harry S. Truman becomes president

Potsdam Conference

United Nations founded

1946 Atomic Energy Commission established

Postwar inflation

Coal and railroad strikes

Republicans win control of Congress

Crisis in Iran

1947 Truman Doctrine announced

Marshall Plan proposed

National Security Act passed

Taft-Hartley Act passed

HUAC begins investigating Hollywood

Federal employee loyalty program launched

1948 Communists stage coup in Czechoslovakia

Economic Cooperation Administration established

Selective Service System restored

Berlin blockade prompts U.S. airlift

Truman elected president

Hiss case begins

1949 NATO established

Soviet Union explodes atomic bomb

Communists seize power in China

1950 NSC-68 outlines new U.S. policy toward communism

Korean War begins

American troops enter North Korea

Chinese troops enter war

McCarran Act passed

Fuchs-Rosenberg case begins

Joseph McCarthy begins campaign against communists in government

1951 Truman removes MacArthur from command in Korea

Railroad workers strike

Negotiations begin in Korea

1952 American occupation of Japan ends

Steelworkers strike

Dwight D. Eisenhower elected president

---

the strength or the will to combat communism sufficiently. McCarthy described him as "soft" and took delight in deliberately confusing him with Alger Hiss.

Stevenson's greatest problem, however, was the Republican candidate opposing him. Rejecting the efforts of conservatives to nominate Robert Taft or Douglas MacArthur, the Republicans turned to a man who had no previous identification with the party: General Dwight D. Eisenhower, military hero, commander of NATO, president of Columbia University in New York, who won nomination on the first ballot. He chose as his running mate the young California senator who

had gained national prominence through his crusade against Alger Hiss: Richard M. Nixon.

Eisenhower and Nixon were a powerful combination in the autumn campaign. While Eisenhower attracted support through his geniality and his statesmanlike pledges to settle the Korean conflict (at one point dramatically promising to "go to Korea" himself), Nixon effectively exploited the issue of domestic subversion. After surviving early accusations of financial improprieties (which he effectively neutralized in a famous television address, the "Checkers speech"), Nixon went on to launch harsh attacks on Democratic "cowardice," "appeasement," and "treason." He spoke derisively of "Adlai the appeaser" and ridiculed Secretary of State Dean Acheson for running a "cowardly college of communist containment." And he missed no opportunity to publicize Stevenson's early support for Alger Hiss as opposed to Nixon's own role in exposing Hiss. Eisenhower and Nixon both made effective use of allegations of corruption in the Truman administration and pledged repeatedly to "clean up the mess in Washington."

The response at the polls was overwhelming. Eisenhower won both a popular and an electoral landslide: 55 percent of the popular vote to Stevenson's 44 percent, 442 electoral votes to Stevenson's 89. Republicans gained control of both houses of Congress for the first time in two decades. The election of 1952 ended twenty years of Democratic government. And while it might not have seemed so at the time, it also signaled the end of some of the worst turbulence of the postwar era.

SUGGESTED READINGS

Origins of the Cold War. Gar Alperovitz, *Atomic Diplomacy: Hiroshima and Potsdam*, rev. ed. (1985). Stephen Ambrose, *Rise to Globalism*, 5th ed. (1988). Terry H. Anderson, *The United States, Great Britain, and the Cold War, 1944–1947* (1981). H. W. Brands, *Inside the Cold War: Loy Henderson and the Rise of the American Empire, 1918–1961* (1991). Diane Clemens, *Yalta* (1970). Herbert Feis, *Churchill, Roosevelt, and Stalin* (1957); *Between War and Peace: The Potsdam Conference* (1960). John Lewis Gaddis, *Strategies of Containment* (1982); *The United States and the Origins of the Cold War, 1941–1947* (1972); *The Long Peace* (1987). Gregg Herken, *The Winning Weapon: Then Atomic Bomb in the Cold War, 1945–1950* (1980). George C. Herring, Jr., *Aid to Russia* (1973). Timothy P. Ireland, *Creating the Entangling Alliance: The Origins of NATO* (1981). Bruce Kuniholm, *The Origins of the Cold War in the Middle East* (1980). Walter LaFeber, *America, Russia, and the Cold War, 1945–1967* (rev. ed. 1980). Melvyn P. Leffler, *A Preponderance of Power: National Security, the Truman Administration, and the Cold War* (1992). William McNeill, *America, Britain, and Russia* (1953). Wilson D. Miscamble, *George F. Kennan and the Making of American Foreign Policy, 1947–1950* (1992). W. L. Neumann, *After Victory* (1969). Thomas G. Paterson, *Soviet-American Confrontation* (1974); *On Every Front: The Making of the Cold War* (1979); *Meeting the Communist Threat* (1988). Robert A. Pollard, *Economic Security and the Origins of the Cold War* (1985). Martin Sherwin, *A World Destroyed* (1975). Gaddis Smith, *American Diplomacy During the Second World War* (1965); *Dean Acheson* (1972). John L. Snell, *Illusion and Necessity* (1967). William Taubman, *Stalin's American Policy* (1982). Athan G. Theoharis, *The Yalta Myths* (1970). Adam Ulam, *The Rivals: America and Russia Since World War II* (1971). Bernard Weisberger, *Cold War, Cold Peace* (1984). Lawrence Wittner, *American Intervention in Greece, 1943–1949* (1982). Daniel Yergin, *Shattered Peace* (1977).

Truman's Foreign Policy. Dean Acheson, *Present at the Creation* (1970). Hadley Arkes, *Bureaucracy, the Marshall Plan and National Interest* (1973). Richard J. Barnet, *The Alliance* (1983). Robert M. Blum, *Drawing the Line: The Origin of the American Containment Policy in East Asia* (1982). Russell D. Buhite, *Soviet-American Relations in Asia, 1945–1954* (1982). Warren I. Cohen, *America's Response to China* (rev. ed. 1980).

Robert Donovan, *Conflict and Crisis* (1977); *Tumultuous Years* (1982). John King Fairbank, *The United States and China* (rev. ed. 1971). Lloyd Gardner, *Architects of Illusion* (1970). Fraser J. Harbutt, *The Iron Curtain: Churchill, America, and the Origins of the Cold War* (1986). Michael Hogan, *The Marshall Plan* (1987). Akira Iriye, *The Cold War in Asia* (1974). Laurence Kaplan, *The United States and NATO* (1984). George F. Kennan, *American Diplomacy, 1900–1950* (1952); *Memoirs, 1925–1950* (1967). Joyce Kolko and Gabriel Kolko, *The Limits of Power* (1970). Bruce R. Koniholm, *The Origins of the Cold War in the Middle East* (1980). William R. Louis, *The British Empire in the Middle East* (1984). Gary May, *China Scapegoat* (1979). David Mayer, *George Kennan and the Dilemmas of U.S. Foreign Policy* (1988). Edwin O. Reischauer, *The United States and Japan* (rev. ed. 1965). Lisle Rose, *Roots of Tragedy* (1976). Michael Schaller, *The U.S. Crusade in China* (1979); *Communists* (1971); *The American Occupation of Japan: The Origins of the Cold War in Asia* (1985). Howard Schonberger, *Aftermath of War: Americans and the Remaking of Japan,* (1989). Anders Stephanson, *Kennan and the Art of Foreign Policy* (1989). Michael B. Stoff, *Oil, War, and American Security* (1980). Christopher Thorne, *Allies of a Kind* (1978). Imanuel Wexler, *The Marshall Plan Revisited* (1983).

Truman's Domestic Policies. Stephen K. Bailey, *Congress Makes a Law* (1950). Jack S. Ballard, *The Shock of Peace: Military and Economic Demobilization After World War II* (1983). William C. Berman, *The Politics of Civil Rights in the Truman Administration* (1970). Barton J. Bernstein, ed. , *Politics and Policies of the Truman Administration* (1970). Richard Dalfiume, *Desegregation of the U.S. Armed Forces* (1969). Richard O. Davies, *Housing Reform During the Truman Administration* (1966). John P. Diggins, *The Proud Decades* (1988). Robert Donovan, *Conflict and Crisis* (1977); *Tumultuous Years* (1982). Andrew J. Dunar, *The Truman Scandals and the Politics of Morality* (1984). Robert H. Ferrell, *Harry S. Truman and the Modern American Presidency* (1983). Eric Goldman, *The Crucial Decade—and After: America, 1945–1960* (1961). Alonzo Hamby, *Beyond the New Deal: Harry S. Truman and American Liberalism* (1973). Susan Hartmann, *Truman and the 80th Congress* (1971). Roy Jenkins, *Truman* (1986). R. Alton Lee, *Truman and Taft-Hartley* (1967); *Truman and the Steel Seizure Case*

(1977). Arthur F. McClure, *The Truman Administration and the Problems of Postwar Labor* (1969). Donald R. McCoy, *The Presidency of Harry S. Truman* (1984). Donald McCoy and Richard Ruetten, *Quest and Response* (1973). David McCullough, *Truman* (1992). Maeva Marcus, *Truman and the Steel Seizure* (1977). Allen J. Matusow, *Farm Policies and Politics in the Truman Years* (1967). Merle Miller, *Plain Speaking* (1980). Richard L. Miller, *Truman: The Rise to Power* (1986). William O'Neill, *American High* (1986). William E. Pemberton, *Harry S. Truman* (1989). Monte S. Poen, *Harry S. Truman Versus the Medical Lobby* (1979). Gary Reichard, *Politics as Usual: The Age of Truman and Eisenhower* (1988). Christopher L. Tomlins, *The State and the Unions* (1985).

Cold War Politics and Culture. John P. Diggins, *The Proud Decades, 1941–1960* (1989). Steven M. Gillon, *Politics and Vision: The ADA and American Liberalism, 1947–1985* (1987). David Goldfield, *Black, White, and Southern: Race Relations and Southern Culture* (1990). Maurice Isserman, *If I Had a Hammer. . . : The Death of the Old Left and the Birth of the New Left* (1987). Norman Markowitz, *The Rise and Fall of the People's Century: Henry A. Wallace and American Liberalism, 1941–1948* (1973). James T. Patterson, *Mr. Republican* (1972). Richard Pells, *The Liberal Mind in a Conservative Age: American Intellectuals in the 1940s and 1950s* (1985). Irwin Ross, *The Loneliest Campaign* (1968). Richard Norton Smith, *Thomas E. Dewey and His Times* (1982). Allen Yarnell, *Democrats and Progressives* (1974).

The Korean War. Carl Berger, *The Korean Knot* (1957). Ronald Caridi, *The Korean War and American Politics* (1969). Bruce Cumings, *The Origins of the Korean War* (1980); ed., *Child of Conflict: The Korean-American Relationship, 1943–1953* (1983). Charles W. Dobbs, *The Unwanted Symbol* (1981). Joseph C. Goulden, *Korea: The Untold Story of the War* (1982). John Halliday and Bruce Cumings, *Korea: The Unknown War* (1980).

Robert Leckie, *Conflict* (1962). Glenn D. Paige, *The Korean Decision* (1968). Michael Schaller, *Douglas MacArthur* (1989). Robert R. Simmons, *The Strained Alliance* (1975). John Spanier, *The Truman-MacArthur Controversy* (1959). Allen Whiting, *China Crosses the Yalu* (1960).

Countersubversion. Michael R. Belknap, *Cold War Political Justice: The Smith Act, the Communist Party, and American Civil Liberties* (1977). Eric Bentley, ed., *Thirty Years of Treason*. David Caute, *The Great Fear* (1978). Larry Ceplair and Steven Englund, *The Inquisition in Hollywood* (1983). Richard Freeland, *The Truman Doctrine and the Origins of McCarthyism* (1971). Richard Fried, *Men Against McCarthy* (1976); *Nightmare in Red* (1990). Robert Griffith, *The Politics of Fear* (1970). Robert Griffith and Athan Theoharis, eds., *The Specter: Original Essays on the Cold War and the Origins of McCarthyism* (1974). Alan Harper, *The Politics of Loyalty* (1969). Stanley Kutler, *The American Inquisition* (1982). Harvey Levenstein, *Communism, Anticommunism, and the CIO* (1981). Mary Sperling McAuliffe, *Crisis on the Left* (1978). Victor Navasky, *Naming Names* (1980). William O'Neill, *A Better World* (1983). David M. Oshinsky, *A Conspiracy So Immense: The World of Joe McCarthy* (1983). Richard Gid Powers, *Secrecy and Power: The Life of J. Edgar Hoover* (1987). Ronald Radosh and Joyce Milton, *The Rosenberg File* (1983). Thomas C. Reeves, *The Life and Times of Joe McCarthy* (1982). Michael Paul Rogin, *The Intellectuals and McCarthy* (1967). Richard Rovere, *Senator Joe McCarthy* (1959). Walter and Miriam Schneer, *Invitation to an Inquest* (rev. ed. 1983). Ellen Schrecker, *No Ivory Tower* (1986). Edward Shils, *The Torment of Secrecy* (1956). Joseph Starobin, *American Communism in Crisis* (1972). Athan Theoharis, *Seeds of Repression* (1971); *Spying on Americans* (1978). Athan Theoharis and John Stuart Cox, *The Boss: J. Edgar Hoover and the Great American Inquisition* (1988). Allen Weinstein, *Perjury: The Hiss-Chambers Case* (1978). Stephen J. Whitfield, *The Culture of the Cold War* (1991).

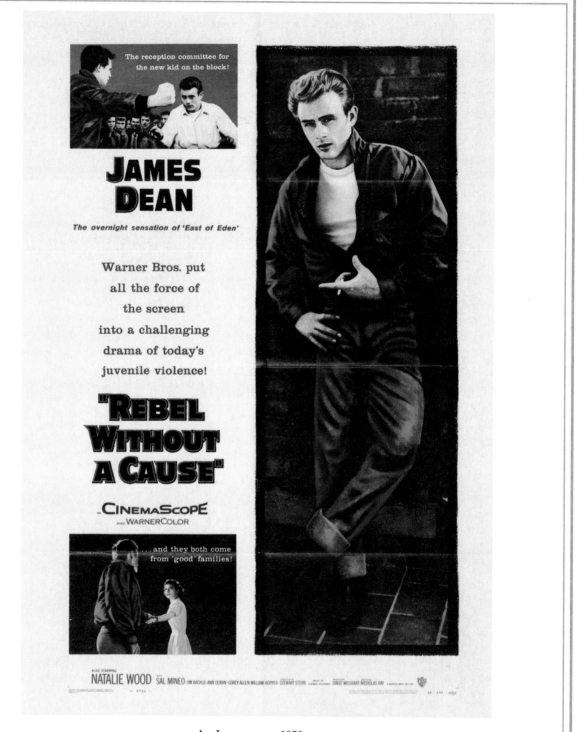

AN ICON OF THE 1950s

The actor James Dean became enormously popular in the 1950s for his portrayal of brooding, sensitive young men rebelling against the stifling conventions of middle-class life. *Rebel Without a Cause* was one of his most successful films, and it suggested something of the restiveness and discontent that lay just below the surface of the seemingly stable culture of the era. *(Warner Brothers)*

CHAPTER THIRTY

THE AFFLUENT SOCIETY

I F AMERICA WAS EXPERIENCING a golden age in the 1950s and early 1960s, as many Americans believed at the time and many continue to believe today, it was largely a result of two developments. One was a booming national prosperity, which profoundly altered the social, economic, and even physical landscape of the United States as well as the way many Americans thought about their lives and their world. The other was the continuing struggle against communism, a struggle that created considerable anxiety but that also encouraged some Americans to look even more approvingly at their own society.

But if these compelling realities created a widespread sense of national purpose and self-satisfaction, they also helped blind many Americans to serious problems plaguing much of their society. More than 30 million Americans, according to some estimates, continued to live in poverty in the 1950s. Significant minorities—most prominently the 10 percent of the American people who were black, but also Hispanics, Asians, Indians, gays and lesbians, and others—continued to suffer social, political, and economic discrimination. Many American women were beginning to chafe at the obstacles to their personal and professional fulfillment. The very things that made America seem so successful in the 1950s also contributed, in the end, to bringing the nation's social problems more sharply into focus.

Gunnar Myrdal, a Swedish sociologist who had spent years studying life in the United States, wrote in 1944: "American affluence is heavily mortgaged. America carries a tremendous burden of debt to its poor people." The efforts to pay that debt, and others, would ultimately help move the nation into the more turbulent era of the 1960s.

THE ECONOMIC "MIRACLE"

Among the most striking features of American society in the 1950s and early 1960s was a booming, almost miraculous, economic growth that made even the heady 1920s seem pale by comparison. But although it was a better balanced and more widely distributed prosperity than that of thirty years earlier, it was not as universal as some Americans liked to believe.

Economic Growth

By 1949, despite the continuing problems of postwar reconversion, an economic expansion had begun that would continue with only brief interruptions for almost twenty years. Between 1945 and 1960, the gross national product grew by 250 percent, from $200 billion to over $500 billion—a striking refutation of the widespread predictions in 1945 that GNP would decline once the demands of war production ended. Unemployment, which during the Depression had averaged between 15 and 25 percent, remained throughout the 1950s and early 1960s at about 5 percent or lower. Inflation, in the meantime, hovered around 3 percent a year or less.

The causes of this growth were varied. Government spending, which had ended the Depression in the 1940s, continued to stimulate growth through public funding of schools, housing, veterans' benefits, welfare, and the $100 billion interstate highway program, which began in 1956. Above all, there was military spending. Economic growth was at its peak (averaging 4.7 percent a year) during the first half of the 1950s, when military spending was highest because of the Korean War. In the late 1950s, with spending on armaments in decline, the annual rate of growth declined by more than half, to 2.25 percent.

Technological progress also contributed to the boom. Because of advances in production techniques and mechanical efficiency, worker productivity increased more than 35 percent in the first decade after the war, a rate far higher than that of any previous era. And technological research and development itself became an increasingly important sector of the economy, expanding the demand for scientists, engineers, and other highly trained experts.

Among the fruits of this scientific and technological research was the development of electronic computers, which first became commercially available in the mid-1950s and which almost immediately began to improve the performance of some American corporations. The first modern computer (the Mark I, developed by the International Business Machines Corporation, or IBM, and scientists at Harvard) emerged as a result of efforts during World War II to decipher enemy codes. For several years after the war, computers continued to develop in response to military needs. By 1954, however, IBM and other companies were developing computers for use by other government agencies and, more important, for private business. Not until the 1980s did most Americans come into direct and regular contact with computers, but the new machines were having a substantial effect on the economy long before that.

The national birth rate reversed a long pattern of decline with the so-called baby boom, which had begun during the war and peaked in 1957. The nation's population rose almost 20 percent in the decade, from 150 million in 1950 to 179 million in 1960. The baby boom meant increased consumer demand and expanding economic growth.

The rapid expansion of suburbs—whose population grew 47 percent in the 1950s, more than twice as fast as the population as a whole—helped stimulate growth in several important sectors of the economy. The number of privately owned cars (more essential for suburban than for urban living) more than doubled in a decade, sparking a great boom in the automobile industry. Demand for new homes helped sustain a

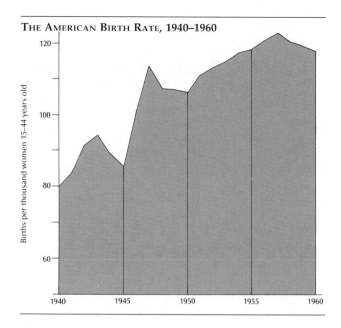

THE AMERICAN BIRTH RATE, 1940–1960

vigorous housing industry. The construction of roads, which was both a cause and a result of the growth of suburbs, stimulated the economy as well.

Because of this unprecedented growth, the economy grew nearly ten times as fast as the population in the thirty years after the war. And while that growth was far from equally distributed, it affected most of society. The average American in 1960 had over 20 percent more purchasing power than in 1945, and more than twice as much as during the prosperous 1920s. By 1960, per capita income (the average income for every individual man, woman, and child) was over $1,800–$500 more than it had been fifteen years before. Family incomes had risen even more. The American people had achieved the highest standard of living of any society in the history of the world.

The Rise of the Modern West

No region of the country experienced more dramatic changes as a result of the new economic growth than the American West. Its population expanded dramatically; its cities boomed; its industrial economy flourished. Before World War II, most of the West had been, economically at least, an appendage of the great industrial economy of the East—providing it with raw materials and agricultural goods. By the 1960s, some parts of the West were among the most important (and populous) industrial and cultural centers of the nation in their own right.

As during World War II, much of the growth of the West was a result of federal spending and investment—on the dams, power stations, highways, and other infrastructure projects that made economic development possible; and on the military contracts that continued to flow disproportionately to factories in California and Texas, many of them built with government funds during the war. But other factors played a role as well. The enormous increase in automobile use after World War II—a result, among other things, of suburbanization and improved highway systems—gave a large stimulus to the petroleum industry and contributed to the rapid growth of oil fields in Texas and Colorado, and of the metropolitan centers serving them: Houston, Dallas, and Denver. State governments in the West invested heavily in their universities. The University of Texas and University of California systems, in particular, became among the nation's largest and best; as centers of research, they helped attract technology-intensive industries to the region. Climate also contributed. Once they had the infrastructure (and, most important, the water supplies) to sustain large populations, southern California, Nevada, and Arizona, in particular, attracted many migrants from the East because of their warm, dry climates. The growth of Los Angeles after World War II was a remarkable phenomenon: more than 10 percent of all new businesses in the United States between 1945 and 1950 began in Los Angeles. Its population rose by over 50 percent between 1940 and 1960.

The New Economics

The exciting (and to some, surprising) discovery of the power of the American economic system was a major cause of the confident, even arrogant tone of much American political life in the 1950s. During the Depression, politicians, intellectuals, and others had often questioned the viability of capitalism. In the 1950s, such doubt virtually vanished. Two features in particular made the postwar economy a source of national confidence.

First was the belief that Keynesian economics made it possible for government to regulate and stabilize the economy without intruding directly into the private sector. The British economist John Maynard Keynes had argued as early as the 1920s that by varying the flow of government spending and managing the supply of currency, the state could stimulate the economy to cure recession, and dampen growth to prevent inflation. The experience of the last years of the Depression and the first years of the war had seemed to confirm this argument. And by the mid-1950s, Keynesian

theory was rapidly becoming a fundamental article of faith—not only among professional economists but among much of the public. The most popular economics textbook of the 1950s and 1960s, Paul Samuelson's *Economics*, imbued a generation of college students with Keynesian ideas. Armed with these fiscal and monetary tools, many economists now believed, it was possible for the government to maintain a permanent prosperity. The dispiriting boom-and-bust cycle long considered a permanent feature of industrial capitalism could now be banished forever. Never again would it be necessary for the nation to experience another Depression.

If any doubters remained, there was ample evidence to dispel their misgivings during the brief recessions the economy experienced during the era. When the economy slackened in late 1953, Secretary of the Treasury George M. Humphrey and the Federal Reserve Board worked to ease credit and make money more readily available. The economy quickly recovered, seeming to confirm the value of Keynesian tactics (even though Humphrey and the Board did not explicitly endorse them). A far more serious recession began late in 1957 and lasted more than a year. This time, the Eisenhower administration ignored the Keynesians and adopted such deflationary tactics as cutting the budget. The slow, halting pace of the recovery, in contrast with the rapid revival in 1954, seemed further to support the Keynesian philosophy. The new economics finally won official acceptance in 1963, when John Kennedy proposed a tax cut to stimulate economic growth. Although it took Kennedy's death and the political skills of Lyndon Johnson to win passage of the measure in 1964, the result seemed to be all that the Keynesians had predicted: an increase in private demand, which stimulated economic growth and reduced unemployment.

Accompanying the belief in the possibility of permanent economic stability was the equally exhilarating belief in permanent economic growth. As the economy continued to expand far beyond what any observer had predicted was possible only a few years before, more and more Americans assumed that such growth was now without bounds—that there were few effective limits to the abundance available to the nation. This was not only a comforting thought in itself; it also made possible a new outlook on social and economic problems. In the 1930s, many Americans had argued that the elimination of poverty and injustice would require a redistribution of wealth—a limitation on the fortunes of the rich and a distribution of wealth to the poor. By the mid-1950s, reformers concerned about economic deprivation were arguing that the solution lay in increased production. The affluent would not have to sacrifice in order to eliminate poverty; the nation would simply have to produce more abundance, thus raising the quality of life of even the poorest citizens to a level of comfort and decency.

The Keynesians never managed to remake federal economic policy entirely to their liking. Political obstacles consistently limited the ability of even the most committed Keynesians to use fiscal and monetary policies as they wished; and the increasingly complex modern economy did not always respond as quickly to Keynesian policies as the theory behind them suggested it should. Still, the new economics gave many Americans a confidence in their ability to solve economic problems that previous generations had never developed.

Capital and Labor

Over 4,000 corporate mergers took place in the 1950s; and more than ever before, a relatively small number of large-scale organizations controlled an enormous proportion of the nation's economic activity. This was particularly true in industries benefiting from government defense spending. As during World War II, the federal government tended to award military contracts to large corporations. In 1959, for example, half of all defense contracts went to only twenty firms. But the same pattern repeated itself in many other areas of the economy, as corporations changed from single-industry firms to diversified conglomerates. By the end of the decade, half the net corporate income in the nation was going to only slightly more than 500 firms, or one-tenth of 1 percent of the total number of corporations.

A similar consolidation was occurring in the agricultural economy. As increasing mechanization reduced the need for farm labor, the agricultural work force declined by more than half in the two decades after the war. Mechanization also endangered one of the most cherished American institutions: the family farm. By the 1960s, relatively few individuals could any longer afford to buy and equip a modern farm, and much of the nation's most productive land had been purchased by financial institutions and corporations.

Corporations enjoying booming growth were reluctant to allow strikes to interfere with their operations, and since the most important labor unions were now so large and entrenched that they could not easily be suppressed or intimidated, business leaders made important concessions to them. As early as 1948, Walter Reuther, president of the United Automobile Workers, obtained a contract from General Motors that included a built-in "escalator clause"—an automatic cost-of-living increase pegged to the consumer price

index. In 1955, Reuther received a guarantee from Ford Motor Company of continuing wages to auto workers even during layoffs. A few months later, steelworkers in several corporations won guarantees of an annual salary. By the mid-1950s, factory wages in all industries had risen substantially, to an average of $80 per week.

By the early 1950s, in other words, large labor unions had developed a new kind of relationship with employers, a relationship sometimes known as the "postwar contract." Workers in steel, automobiles, and other large unionized industries were receiving generous increases in wages and benefits; in return, the unions tacitly agreed to refrain from raising other issues—issues involving control of the workplace and a voice for workers in the planning of production. The postwar "contract" had the support of the National Labor Relations Board, whose mediators (many drawing from their experience in World War II) believed the purpose of labor relations was to maintain industrial peace and promote the general health of the economy, not to defend or expand the "rights" of workers. The contract served the corporations and the union leadership well, but many rank-and-file workers resented the abandonment of efforts to give them more control over the conditions of their labor. By the late 1960s and 1970s, workers in some unions (Teamsters, Mine Workers, and others) were forming dissident organizations in an effort to democratize the unions and increase the scope of their demands. In the meantime, the number of industrial jobs in some major industries was beginning to diminish as a result of new technologies that automated production. Even as the labor movement was enjoying impressive successes in winning better wages for its members, its share of the labor force dropped—from an all-time high of 36 percent in 1953 to 31 percent by the end of the decade.

The economic successes of the 1950s helped pave the way for a reunification of the labor movement. In December 1955, the American Federation of Labor and the Congress of Industrial Organizations ended their twenty-year rivalry and merged to create the AFL-CIO, under the leadership of George Meany.

But success also bred stagnation and corruption in some union bureaucracies. In 1957, the powerful Teamsters Union became the subject of a congressional investigation, and its president, David Beck, was charged with misappropriation of union funds. Beck ultimately stepped down to be replaced by Jimmy Hoffa, whom government investigators pursued for nearly a decade before finally winning a conviction against him (for tax evasion) in 1967. The United Mine Workers, the union that had spearheaded the industrial movement in the 1930s, similarly became tainted

WORKERS REPRESENTED BY UNIONS, 1920–1992

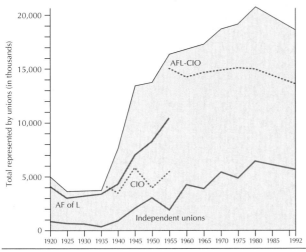

by suspicions of corruption and by violence. John L. Lewis's last years as head of the union were plagued with scandals and dissent within the organization. His successor, Tony Boyle, was ultimately convicted of complicity in the 1969 murder of Joseph ("Jock") Yablonski, the leader of a dissident faction within the union.

While the labor movement enjoyed significant success in winning better wages and benefits for workers already organized in strong unions, the majority of laborers who were as yet unorganized made fewer advances. Total union membership remained relatively stable throughout the 1950s, at about 16 million; and while this was in part a result of a shift in the work force from blue-collar to white-collar jobs, it was also a result of new obstacles to organization. The Taft-Hartley Act and the state right-to-work laws that it spawned made the creation of new unions powerful enough to demand recognition from employers more difficult.

In the American South, in particular, impediments to unionization were enormous. The CIO had launched a major organizing drive in the South shortly after World War II, targeting the poorly paid workers in textile mills in particular. But "Operation Dixie," as it was called, was a failure—as were most other organizing drives for at least thirty years after World War II. Anti-union sentiment was so powerful in the South—not just among employers, but also among politicians, the press, local police, and many others—that almost all organizing drives encountered crushing and usually fatal resistance.

PEOPLE OF PLENTY

Among the most striking social development of the postwar era was the rapid extension of a middle-class lifestyle and outlook to large groups of the population previously insulated from it. The new prosperity of social groups that had previously lived on the margins; the growing availability of consumer products at affordable prices and the rising public fascination with such products; and perhaps above all, the massive population movement from the cities to the suburbs—all helped make the American middle class a larger, more powerful, more homogeneous, and more dominant force than it had ever been before.

The new prosperity, in fact, inspired some Americans to see abundance as the key to understanding the American past and the American character. Leading intellectuals argued that American history had been characterized by a broad "consensus" about the value and necessity of competitive, capitalist growth. "However much at odds on specific issues," the historian Richard Hofstadter wrote in *The American Political Tradition* (1948), Americans have "shared a belief in the rights of property, the philosophy of economic individualism, the value of competition; they have accepted the economic virtues of capitalist culture as necessary qualities of man." David Potter, another leading American historian of the era, published an influential examination of "economic abundance and American character" in 1954. He called it *People of Plenty*. For the American middle class in the 1950s, at least, it seemed an appropriate label.

The Consumer Culture

At the center of middle-class culture in the 1950s, as it had been for many decades before, was a growing absorption with consumer goods. That was a result of increased prosperity, of the increasing variety and availability of products, and of advertisers' adeptness in creating a demand for those products. It was also a result of the growth of consumer credit, which increased by 800 percent between 1945 and 1957 through the development of credit cards, revolving charge accounts, and easy-payment plans. Prosperity fueled such longtime consumer crazes as the automobile, and Detroit responded to the boom with ever-flashier styling and accessories. Consumers also responded eagerly to the development of such new products as dishwashers, garbage disposals, television, hi-fis, and stereos. To a striking degree, the prosperity of the 1950s and 1960s was consumer driven (as opposed to investment driven).

Because consumer goods were so often marketed (and advertised) nationally, the 1950s were notable for the rapid spread of great national consumer crazes. For example, children, adolescents, and even some adults became entranced in the late 1950s with the hula hoop—a large plastic ring kept spinning around the waist. The popularity of the Walt Disney-produced children's television show *The Mickey Mouse Club* created a national demand for related products such as Mickey Mouse watches and hats. It also helped produce the stunning success of Disneyland, an amusement park near Los Angeles that re-created many of the characters and events of Disney entertainment programs. The Disney technique of turning an entertainment success into an effective tool for marketing consumer goods was not an isolated event. Many other entertainers and producers took note and did the same.

The Suburban Nation

By 1960 a third of the nation's population was living in suburbs. The growth of suburbs was a result not only of increased affluence, but of important innovations in home-building, which made single-family houses affordable to millions of new people. The most famous of the postwar suburban developers, William

CHICAGO'S ANNEXATIONS AND THE SUBURBAN NOOSE

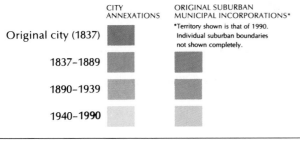

	CITY ANNEXATIONS	ORIGINAL SUBURBAN MUNICIPAL INCORPORATIONS*
		*Territory shown is that of 1990. Individual suburban boundaries not shown completely.
Original city (1837)		
1837–1889		
1890–1939		
1940–1990		

Levitt, came to symbolize the new suburban growth with his use of mass-production techniques to construct a large housing development on Long Island, near New York City. This first "Levittown" (there would later be others in New Jersey and Pennsylvania) consisted of several thousand two-bedroom Cape Cod-style houses, with identical interiors and only slightly varied facades, each perched on its own concrete slab (to eliminate excavation costs), facing curving, treeless streets. Levittown houses sold for under $10,000, and they helped meet an enormous demand for housing that had been growing for more than a decade. Young couples—often newly married war veterans eager to start a family, assisted by low-cost, government-subsidized mortgages provided by the G.I. Bill (see p. 780)—rushed to purchase the inexpensive homes, not only in the Levittowns but in similar developments that soon began appearing throughout the country.

Why did so many Americans want to move to the suburbs? One reason was the enormous importance postwar Americans placed on family life after five years of war in which families had often been separated or otherwise disrupted. Suburbs provided families with larger homes than they could find (or afford) in the cities, and thus made it easier to raise larger numbers of children. They provided privacy. They provided security from the noise and dangers of urban living. They offered space for the new consumer goods—the cars, boats, appliances, outdoor furniture, and other products—that advertisers had helped persuade many middle-class Americans to crave.

For many Americans, suburban life also helped provide a sense of community that was sometimes difficult to develop in large, crowded, impersonal urban areas. In later years, the suburbs would come under attack for their supposed conformity, homogeneity, and isolation. But in the 1950s, many people were attracted by the idea of living in a community populated largely by people of similar age and background, and found it easier to form friendships and social circles there than in the city. Women in particular often valued the presence of other nonworking mothers living nearby to share the tasks of child raising.

Another factor motivating white Americans to move to the suburbs was race. There were some African-American suburbs. But most suburbs were restricted to whites—both because relatively few blacks could afford to live in them and because formal and informal barriers kept out even prosperous blacks. In an era when the black population of most cities was rapidly growing, many white families fled to the suburbs to escape the integration of urban neighborhoods and schools.

Suburban neighborhoods had many things in common with one another. But they were not uniform. A famous study of one Levittown revealed a striking variety of occupations, ethnic backgrounds, and incomes there. Still, the Levittowns and inexpensive developments like them ultimately became the homes of mainly lower-middle-class people one step removed from the inner city. Other, more affluent suburbs became enclaves of wealthy families. In virtually every city, a clear hierarchy emerged of upper-class suburban neighborhoods and more modest ones, just as such gradations had emerged years earlier among urban neighborhoods.

The Suburban Family

For professional men (who tended to work in the city, at some distance from their homes), suburban life generally meant a rigid division between their working and personal worlds. For many middle-class, married women, it meant an increased isolation from the workplace. The enormous cultural emphasis on family life in the 1950s strengthened popular prejudices against women entering the professions, or occupying any paid job at all. Many middle-class husbands considered it demeaning for their wives to be employed. And many women themselves shied away from the workplace when they could afford to, in part because of prevailing ideas about motherhood that seemed to require women to stay at home full-time with their children.

One of the most influential books in postwar American life was a famous guide to child rearing: Dr. Benjamin Spock's *Baby and Child Care*, first published in 1946 and reissued (and revised) repeatedly for decades thereafter. Dr. Spock's approach to raising babies was child-centered, as opposed to the parent-centered theories of many previous child-care experts. The purpose of motherhood, he taught, was to help children learn and grow and realize their potential. All other considerations, including the mother's own physical and emotional requirements, must be subordinated to the needs of the child. Dr. Spock at first envisioned only a very modest role for fathers in the process of child rearing, although he changed his views on this (as on many other issues) over time.

Thus, women who could afford not to work faced heavy pressures—both externally and internally imposed—to remain in the home and concentrate on raising their children. Some women, however, had to balance these pressures against other, contradictory ones. As expectations of material comfort rose, many middle-class families needed a second income to maintain the standard of living they desired. As a result, the number of married women working outside the home actually increased in the postwar years—even as the social pressure for them to stay out of the workplace grew. By 1960, nearly a third of all married women were part of the paid work force.

The experiences of the 1950s worked in some ways to diminish the power of feminism, which for a time ebbed to its lowest point in nearly a century. But they also helped create conditions that only a decade later would create the most powerful feminist movement in American history. The increasing numbers of women in the workplace laid the groundwork for demands for equal treatment by employers that became an important part of the feminist crusades of the 1960s and 1970s. Some middle-class women who were not employed became deeply involved in the public world through work in such organizations as the League of Women Voters, the Red Cross, YWCAs, and PTAs, where they gained organizational and political skills that they would later be able to use in more explicitly feminist causes. And the growing frustrations of other women, who remained in the home, heightened the demand for female professional opportunities, a demand that would also soon help fuel the women's liberation movement.

The Birth of Television

Perhaps the most powerful medium of mass communication in history, television was central to the culture of the postwar era. Experiments in broadcasting pictures (along with sound) had begun as early as the 1920s, but commercial television began only shortly after World War II. Its growth was phenomenally rapid. In 1946, there were only 17,000 sets in the country; by 1957, there were 40 million television sets in use—almost as many sets as there were families. More people had television sets, according to one report, than had refrigerators (a statistic strikingly similar to one in the 1920s that had revealed more people owning radios than bathtubs).

The television industry emerged directly out of the radio industry, and all three of the major networks—The National Broadcasting Company, the Columbia Broadcasting System, and the American Broadcasting Company—had started as radio companies. Like radio, the television business was driven by advertising. The need to attract advertisers determined most programming decisions; and in the early days of television, sponsors often played a direct, powerful, and continuing role in determining the content of the programs they chose to sponsor. Many early television shows bore the names of the corporations that were paying for them: the *GE Television Theater*, the *Chrysler Playhouse*, the *Camel News Caravan*, and others. Some daytime serials (known as "soap operas," because their sponsors were almost always companies making household goods targeted at women) were actually written and produced by Procter and Gamble and other companies.

The impact of television on American life was rapid, pervasive, and profound. By the late 1950s, television news had replaced newspapers, magazines, and radios as the nation's most important vehicle of information. Television advertising helped create a vast market for new fashions and products. Televised athletic events gradually made professional and college sports one of the most important sources of entertainment (and one of the biggest businesses) in America. Television entertainment programming—almost all of it controlled by the three national networks and their corporate sponsors—replaced movies and radio as the principal source of diversion for American families.

Much of the programming of the 1950s and early 1960s created a common image of American life—an image that was predominantly white, middle-class, and suburban, and that was epitomized by such popular situation comedies as *Ozzie and Harriet* and *Leave It to Beaver*. Programming also reinforced the concept of gender roles that most men (and many women) unthinkingly embraced. Most situation comedies, in particular, showed families in which, as the title of one of the most popular put it, *Father Knows Best*, and in which most women were mothers and housewives striving to serve their children and please their husbands.

But television also conveyed other images: the gritty, urban working-class families in Jackie Gleason's *The Honeymooners*; the childless show-business family of the early *I Love Lucy*; the unmarried professional women in *Our Miss Brooks* and *My Little Margie*; the hapless African Americans in *Amos 'n Andy*. Television not only sought to create an idealized image of a homogeneous suburban America. It also sought to convey experiences at odds with that image—but to convey them in warm, unthreatening terms, taking social diversity and cultural conflict and domesticating them, turning them into something benign and even comic.

Yet television also, inadvertently, created conditions that could accentuate social conflict. Even those unable to share in the affluence of the era could, through television, acquire a vivid picture of how the rest of their society lived. Thus at the same time that television was reinforcing the homogeneity of the white middle class, it was also contributing to the sense of alienation and powerlessness among groups excluded from the world it portrayed.

Science and Space

In 1961, *Time* magazine chose as its "man of the year" not an individual but "the American Scientist." It was an indication of the widespread fascination with which Americans in the age of atomic weapons viewed science and technology. Major medical advances accounted for much of that fascination. Jonas Salk's vaccine to prevent polio, which the federal government provided free to the public beginning in 1955, virtually eliminated the disease from American life in a few short years. Other dread diseases such as diphtheria and tuberculosis also all but vanished from society (at least for a time) as new drugs and treatments emerged. Infant mortality declined by nearly 50 percent in the twenty-five years after the war; the death rate among young children declined significantly as well (although both such rates were lower in Western Europe). Average life expectancy in those same years rose by five years, to seventy-one.

But Americans were at least equally impressed by other scientific and technological innovations: the jet plane, the computer, synthetics, new types of commercially prepared foods. And nothing better illustrated the nation's veneration of scientific expertise than the popular enthusiasm for the American space program.

The program began in large part because of the Cold War. When the Soviet Union announced in 1957 that it had launched a satellite—*Sputnik*—which was orbiting the earth in outer space, the American government (and much of the public) reacted with alarm, as if the Soviet achievement was also a massive American failure. Strenuous efforts began to improve scientific education in the schools, to develop more research laboratories, and above all to speed the development of America's own exploration of outer space. The centerpiece of that exploration was the manned space program, established in 1958 with the selection of the first American space pilots, or "astronauts," who quickly became the nation's most revered heroes. On May 5, 1961, Alan Shepard became the first American launched into space (several months after a Soviet "cosmonaut," Yuri Gagarin, had made a similar, and longer, flight). On February 2, 1962, John Glenn (later a United States senator) became the first American to orbit the globe (again, only after Gagarin had already done so).

Interest in the space program remained high in the summer of 1969, when Neil Armstrong and Edwin Aldrin became the first men to walk on the surface of the moon. Not long after that, however, the government began to cut the funding for future missions, and popular enthusiasm for the program began to wane. In the late 1970s and 1980s, the National Aeronautics and Space Administration (NASA) managed to revive some of the earlier enthusiasm for space exploration with the development of a reusable "space shuttle," which performed various commercial functions (such as launching communications satellites) as well as research and military ones. Early in 1986, an explosion destroyed one of the shuttles, the *Challenger*, shortly after it took off. Seven astronauts (one of them a school teacher chosen in a national competition) died. The incident sparked a wave of national grief that made clear the degree to which the space program continued to embody some of the nation's most romantic hopes. But the disaster also revealed serious management problems within the program that stalled its further development.

Organized Society and Its Detractors

Large-scale organizations and bureaucracies increased their influence over American life in the postwar era, as they had been doing for many decades before.

White-collar workers came to outnumber blue-collar laborers for the first time, and an increasing proportion of them worked in corporate settings with rigid hierarchical structures. Industrial workers also confronted large bureaucracies, both in the workplace and in their own unions. Consumers discovered the frustrations of bureaucracy in dealing with the large national companies from whom they bought goods and services. More and more Americans were becoming convinced that the key to a successful future lay in acquiring the specialized training and skills necessary for work in large organizations, where every worker performed a particular, well-defined function.

The American educational system responded to the demands of this increasingly organized society by experimenting with changes in curriculum and philosophy. Elementary and secondary schools gave increased attention to the teaching of science, mathematics, and foreign languages—all of which educators considered important for the development of skilled, specialized professionals. The National Defense Education Act of 1958 (passed in response to the Soviet Union's *Sputnik* success) provided federal funding for development of programs in those areas. Universities in the meantime were expanding their curricula to provide more opportunities for students to develop specialized skills. The idea of the "multiversity"—a phrase first coined by the chancellor of the University of California at Berkeley to describe his institution's diversity—represented a commitment to making higher education a training ground for specialists in a wide variety of fields.

As in earlier eras, many Americans reacted to these developments with ambivalence, even hostility. The debilitating impact of bureaucratic life on the individual slowly became a central theme of popular and scholarly debate. William H. Whyte, Jr., produced one of the most widely discussed books of the decade: *The Organization Man* (1956), which attempted to describe the special mentality of the worker in a large, bureaucratic setting. Self-reliance, Whyte claimed, was losing place to the ability to "get along" and "work as a team" as the most valued trait in the modern character. Sociologist David Riesman had made similar observations in *The Lonely Crowd* (1950), in which he argued that the traditional "inner-directed" man, who judged himself on the basis of his own values and the esteem of his family, was giving way to a new "other-directed" man, more concerned with winning the approval of the larger organization or community.

The most derisive critics of bureaucracy, and of middle-class society generally, were a group of young poets, writers, and artists generally known as the "beats" (or, derisively, as "beatniks"). They wrote harsh critiques of what they considered the sterility and conformity of American life, the meaninglessness of American politics, and the banality of popular culture. Allen Ginsberg's dark, bitter poem *Howl* (1955) decried the "Robot apartments! invincible suburbs! skeleton treasuries! blind capitals! demonic industries!" of modern life. Jack Kerouac produced what may have been the bible of the Beat Generation in his novel *On the Road* (1957)—an account of a cross-country automobile trip that depicted the rootless, iconoclastic lifestyle of Kerouac and his friends.

Other, less starkly alienated writers also expressed misgivings in their work about the enormity and impersonality of modern society. Saul Bellow produced a series of novels—*The Adventures of Augie March* (1953), *Seize the Day* (1956), *Herzog* (1964), and others—that chronicled the difficulties American Jewish men had in finding fulfillment in modern urban America. J. D. Salinger wrote in *The Catcher in the Rye* (1951) of a prep-school student, Holden Caulfield, who was unable to find any area of society—school, family, friends, city—in which he could feel secure or committed.

THE "OTHER AMERICA"

It was relatively easy for white, middle-class Americans in the 1950s to believe that the world they knew— a world of economic growth, personal affluence, and cultural homogeneity—was the world virtually all Americans knew; that the values and assumptions they shared were ones that most other Americans shared too. But such assumptions were false. Even within the middle class, there was considerable restiveness—among women, intellectuals, young people, and others who found the middle-class consumer culture somehow unsatisfying, even stultifying. More importantly, large groups of Americans remained outside the circle of abundance and shared in neither the affluence of the middle class nor its values.

On the Margins of the Affluent Society

In 1962, the socialist writer Michael Harrington created a sensation by publishing a book called *The Other America*, in which he chronicled the continuing existence of poverty in America. The conditions he described were not new. Only the attention he was bringing to them was.

The great economic expansion of the postwar years reduced poverty dramatically but did not eliminate it. In 1960, at any given moment, more than a fifth of all American families (over 30 million people) continued to live below what the government defined as the poverty line (down from a third of all families fifteen years before). Many millions more lived just above the official poverty line, but with incomes that gave them little comfort and no security.

Most of the poor experienced poverty intermittently and temporarily. Eighty percent of those classified as poor at any particular moment were likely to have moved into poverty relatively recently and might move out of it again as soon as they found a job—an indication of how unstable employment could be at the lower levels of the job market. But approximately 20 percent of the poor were people for whom poverty was a continuous, debilitating reality, from which there was no easy escape. That included approximately half the nation's elderly and a large proportion of African Americans and Hispanics. Native Americans constituted the single poorest group in the country, a result of government policies that undermined the economies of the reservations and drove many Indians into cities, where some lived in a poverty worse than that they had left.

This "hard-core" poverty rebuked the assumptions of those who argued that economic growth would eventually lead everyone into prosperity; that, as many claimed, "a rising tide lifts all boats." It was a poverty that the growing prosperity of the postwar era seemed to affect hardly at all, a poverty, as Harrington observed, that appeared "impervious to hope."

Rural Poverty

Among those on the margins of the affluent society were many rural Americans. In 1948, farmers had received 8.9 percent of the national income; in 1956, they received only 4.1 percent. In part, this decline reflected the steadily shrinking farm population; in 1956 alone, nearly 10 percent of the rural population moved into or was absorbed by cities. But it also reflected declining farm prices. Because of enormous surpluses in basic staples, prices fell 33 percent in those years, even though national income as a whole rose 50 percent at the same time. Even most farmers who managed to survive experienced substantial losses of income at the same time that the prices of many consumer goods rose.

Not all farmers were poor. Some substantial landowners weathered, and even managed to profit from, the changes in American agriculture. Others moved from considerable to only modest affluence. But the agrarian economy did produce substantial numbers of genuinely impoverished people. Black sharecroppers and tenant farmers continued to live at or below subsistence level throughout the rural South—in part because of the mechanization of cotton picking beginning in 1944, in part because of the development of synthetic fibers that reduced demand for cotton generally. (Two-thirds of the cotton acreage of the South went out of production between 1930 and 1960.) Migrant farmworkers, a group concentrated especially in the West and Southwest and containing many Mexican-American and Asian-American workers, lived in similarly dire circumstances. In rural areas without much commercial agriculture—such as the Appalachian region in the East, where the decline of the coal economy reduced the one significant source of support for the region—whole communities lived in desperate poverty, increasingly cut off from the market economy. All these groups were vulnerable to malnutrition and even starvation.

The Inner Cities

As white families moved from cities to suburbs in vast numbers, more and more inner-city neighborhoods became vast repositories for the poor, "ghettos" from which there was no easy escape. The growth of these neighborhoods owed much to a vast migration of African Americans out of the countryside (where the cotton economy was in decline) and into industrial cities. More than 3 million black men and women moved from the South to northern cities between 1940 and 1960, many more than had made the same journey during the Great Migration during and after World War I. Chicago, Detroit, Cleveland, New York, and other eastern and midwestern industrial cities experienced a great expansion of their black populations—both in absolute numbers and, even more, as a percentage of the whole, since so many whites were leaving at the same time.

Similar migrations from Mexico and Puerto Rico expanded poor Hispanic neighborhoods in many American cities at the same time. Between 1940 and 1960, nearly a million Puerto Ricans moved into American cities (the largest group to New York). Mexican workers crossed the border in Texas and California and swelled the already substantial Latino communities of such cities as San Antonio, Houston, San Diego, and Los Angeles (which by 1960 had the largest Mexican-American population of any city, approximately 500,000 people).

Why these inner-city communities, populated largely by racial and ethnic minorities, remained so poor in the midst of growing affluence has been the subject of considerable, and very heated, debate. Some critics have argued that the new migrants were victims in part of their own pasts, that the work habits, values, and family structures they brought with them from their rural homes were poorly adapted to the needs of

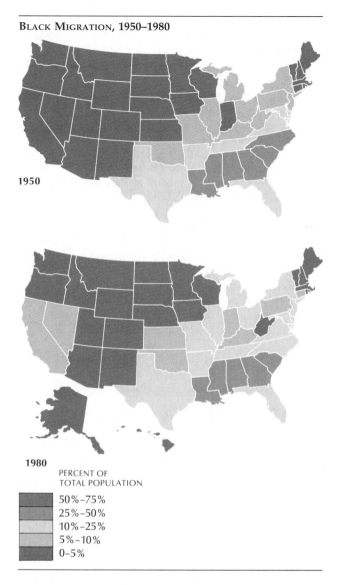

BLACK MIGRATION, 1950–1980

1950

1980

PERCENT OF
TOTAL POPULATION

50%–75%
25%–50%
10%–25%
5%–10%
0–5%

the modern industrial city. Others have argued that the inner city itself—its crippling poverty, its lack of strong educational or service institutions, its crime, its violence, its apparent hopelessness—created a "culture of poverty" that made it more difficult for individuals to advance.

Many others argue that a combination of declining blue-collar jobs, inadequate support for minority-dominated public schools, and barriers to advancement rooted in racism—and not the culture and values of the poor themselves—were the source of inner-city poverty. It is indisputable that inner cities were filling up with poor minority residents at the same time that the unskilled industrial jobs they were seeking were diminishing. Employers were relocating factories and mills from old industrial cities to new locations in suburbs, smaller cities, and even abroad—places where the cost of labor or other things were lower. Even in the factories that remained, automation was reducing the number of unskilled jobs. The economic opportunities that had helped earlier immigrant groups to rise up from poverty were unavailable to most of the postwar migrants. Nor can there be any doubt that historic patterns of racial discrimination in hiring, education, and housing doomed many members of these communities to continuing, and in some cases increasing, poverty.

For many years, the principal policy response to the poverty of inner cities was "urban renewal": the effort to tear down buildings in the poorest and most degraded areas. In the twenty years after World War II, urban renewal projects destroyed over 400,000 buildings, among them the homes of nearly 1.5 million people. In some cases, urban renewal provided new public housing for poor city residents. Some of it was considerably better than the housing they left; some of it was poorly designed and constructed, and deteriorated rapidly into dismal and dangerous slums. Urban renewal was, on the whole, better at eliminating "blights" than at helping the people who lived in them. In many cases, urban renewal projects replaced "slums" with middle- and upper-income housing (part of an often futile attempt to keep middle-class people from leaving), office towers, or commercial buildings; in Los Angeles, a baseball stadium for the Los Angeles Dodgers, recently relocated from Brooklyn, was erected on the site of a Mexican *barrio*.

One result of inner-city poverty was a rising rate of juvenile crime. Indeed, "juvenile delinquency" was one of the few results of poverty that middle-class Americans discussed and worried about with any consistency. A 1955 book, *One Million Delinquents*, called juvenile crime a "national epidemic" and described a troubling subculture of inner-city youth—embittered, rebellious adolescents with no hope of advancement and no sense of having a stake in the structure of their society.

THE RISE OF THE CIVIL RIGHTS MOVEMENT

After decades of skirmishes, an open battle began in the 1950s against racial segregation and discrimination, a battle that would prove to be one of the longest and most difficult of the century. Although white Americans played an important role in the civil-rights movement, pressure from African Americans themselves was the crucial element in raising the issue of race to prominence.

The Brown *Decision and "Massive Resistance"*

On May 17, 1954, the Supreme Court announced its decision in the case of *Brown* v. *Board of Education of Topeka*. In considering the legal segregation of a Kansas public school system, the Court rejected its own 1896 *Plessy* v. *Ferguson* decision, which had ruled that communities could provide blacks with separate facilities as long as the facilities were equal to those of whites.

The *Brown* decision was the culmination of many decades of effort by black opponents of segregation, and particularly by a group of talented NAACP lawyers, many of them trained at Howard University in Washington by the great legal educator Charles Houston. Thurgood Marshall, William Hastie, James Nabrit, and others spent years filing legal challenges to segregation in one state after another, nibbling at the edges of the system, and accumulating precedents to support their assault on the "separate but equal" doctrine itself. The same lawyers filed the suits against the school boards of Topeka, Kansas, and several other cities that became the basis for the *Brown* decision.

The Topeka suit involved the case of an African-American girl who had to travel several miles to a segregated public school every day even though she lived virtually next door to a white elementary school. When the case arrived before the Supreme Court, the justices examined it not simply in terms of legal precedent but in terms of history, sociology, and psychology. They concluded that school segregation inflicted unacceptable damage on those it affected, regardless of the relative quality of the separate schools. Chief Justice Earl Warren explained the unanimous opinion of his colleagues: "We conclude that in the field of public education the doctrine of 'separate but equal' has no place. Separate educational facilities are inherently unequal." The following year, the Court issued another decision (known as "*Brown II*") to provide rules for implementing the 1954 order. It ruled that communities must work to desegregate their schools "with all deliberate speed," but it set no timetable and left specific decisions up to lower courts.

In some communities—for example Washington, D.C.—compliance came relatively quickly and quietly. More often, however, strong local opposition (what came to be known in the South as "massive resistance") produced long delays and bitter conflicts. Some school districts ignored the ruling altogether.

Others attempted to circumvent it with purely token efforts to integrate. More than 100 southern members of Congress signed a "manifesto" in 1956 denouncing the *Brown* decision and urging their constituents to defy it. Southern governors, mayors, local school boards, and nongovernmental pressure groups (including hundreds of "White Citizens' Councils") all worked to obstruct desegregation. Many school districts enacted "pupil placement laws" allowing school officials to place students in schools according to their scholastic abilities and social behavior. Such laws were transparent devices for maintaining segregation; but in 1958, the Supreme Court (in *Shuttlesworth* v. *Birmingham Board of Education*) refused to declare them unconstitutional.

By the fall of 1957, only 684 of 3,000 affected school districts in the South had even begun to desegregate their schools. In those that had complied, white resistance often produced angry mob actions and other violence. Many white parents simply withdrew their children from the public schools and enrolled them in all-white "segregation academies"; some state and local governments diverted money from newly integrated public schools and used it to fund the new, all-white academies. The *Brown* decision, far from ending segregation, had launched a prolonged battle between federal authority and state and local governments, and between those who believed in racial equality and those who did not.

The Eisenhower administration was not eager to commit itself to that battle. The president himself had greeted the *Brown* decision with skepticism (and once said it had set back progress on race relations "at least fifteen years"). But in September 1957, he faced a case of direct state defiance of federal authority and felt compelled to act. Federal courts had ordered the desegregation of Central High School in Little Rock, Arkansas. An angry white mob tried to prevent implementation of the order by blockading the entrances to the school, and Governor Orval Faubus refused to do anything to stop the obstruction. President Eisenhower finally responded by federalizing the National Guard and sending troops to Little Rock to restore order and ensure that the court orders would be obeyed. Only then did Central High School admit its first black students.

The Expanding Movement

The *Brown* decision helped spark a growing number of popular challenges to segregation in the South. On December 1, 1955, Rosa Parks, a black woman, was arrested in Montgomery, Alabama, when she refused to give up her seat on a Montgomery bus to a white passenger (as required by the Jim Crow laws that regulated race relations in the city and throughout most of the South). Parks, an active civil rights leader in the community, had apparently decided spontaneously to resist the order to move. Her feet were tired, she later explained. But black leaders in Montgomery had been waiting for such an incident, which they wanted to use to challenge the segregation of the buses. The arrest of this admired woman produced outrage in the city's African-American community and helped local leaders organize a successful boycott of the bus system to demand an end to segregated seating.

The bus boycott owed much of its success to the prior existence of well-organized black citizens' groups. A black women's political caucus had, in fact, been developing plans for a boycott of the segregated buses for some time. They seized on Rosa Parks as a symbol of the movement. Once launched, the boycott was almost completely effective. Black workers who needed to commute to their jobs (of whom the largest group consisted of female domestic servants) formed car pools to ride back and forth to work, or simply walked, even at times over long distances. The boycott put economic pressure not only on the bus company (a private concern) but on many Montgomery merchants. The bus boycotters found it difficult to get to downtown stores and tended to shop instead in their own neighborhoods. Still the boycott might well have failed had it not been for a Supreme Court decision late in 1956, inspired in part by the protest, that declared segregation in public transportation to be illegal. The buses in Montgomery abandoned their discriminatory seating policies, and the boycott came to a close.

More important than the immediate victories of the Montgomery boycott was its success in establishing a new form of racial protest and in elevating to prominence a new figure in the movement for civil rights. The man chosen to head the boycott movement after its launching was a local Baptist pastor, Martin Luther King, Jr., the son of a prominent Atlanta minister, a powerful orator, and a gifted leader. At first King was reluctant to accept responsibility for the movement. But once he accepted the role, he became consumed by it.

King's approach to black protest was based on the doctrine of non-violence—that is, of passive resistance even in the face of direct attack. He drew from the teachings of Mahatma Gandhi, the Indian nationalist leader; from Henry David Thoreau and his doctrine of civil disobedience; and from Christian doctrine. And he produced an approach to racial struggle that captured the moral high ground for his supporters. He urged African Americans to engage in peaceful demon-

ROSA PARKS IN THE FRONT OF THE BUS
In December 1955 Rosa Parks was arrested in Montgomery, Alabama, for refusing to obey a law that required her to give up her seat to a white passenger and move to the back of the bus. Her defiance sparked an almost total boycott of Montgomery's transit system by black citizens. Just over a year later, the U.S. Supreme Court ruled that racial segregation of public transit systems was unconstitutional, and Mrs. Parks proudly posed for photographers sitting near the front of a city bus. *(UPI/Bettmann)*

strations; to allow themselves to be arrested, even beaten, if necessary; and to respond to hate with love. For the next thirteen years—as leader of the Southern Christian Leadership Conference, an interracial group he founded shortly after the bus boycott—he was the most influential and most widely admired black leader in the country. The popular movement he came to represent soon spread throughout the South and throughout the country.

Pressure from the courts, from northern liberals, and from blacks themselves also speeded the pace of racial change in other areas. One important color line had been breached as early as 1947, when the Brooklyn Dodgers signed the great Jackie Robinson as the first black to play major-league baseball. By the mid-1950s, blacks had established themselves as a powerful force in almost all professional sports. Within the government, President Eisenhower completed the integration of the armed forces, attempted to desegregate the federal work force, and in 1957 signed a civil rights act (passed, without active support from the White House, by a Democratic Congress) providing federal protection for blacks who wished to register to vote. It was a weak bill, with few mechanisms for enforcement, but it was the first civil rights bill of any kind to win passage since the end of Reconstruction, and it served as a signal that the executive and leg-

islative branches were beginning to join the judiciary in the federal commitment to the "Second Reconstruction."

Causes of the Civil Rights Movement

Why did a civil rights movement begin to emerge at this particular moment? The injustices it challenged and the goals it promoted were hardly new; in theory, African Americans could have launched the same movement fifty or a hundred years earlier, or decades later. Why did they do so in the 1950s and 1960s?

Several factors contributed to the rise of African-American protest in these years. The legacy of World War II was one of the most important. Millions of black men and women had served in the military or worked in war plants during the war and had derived from the experience a broader view of the world, and of their place in it, than they had been able to develop in their relatively isolated lives prior to the 1940s.

Another factor was the growth of an urban black middle class, which had been developing for decades but which began to flourish after the war. Much of the impetus for the civil rights movement came from the leaders of urban black communities—ministers, educators, professionals—and much of it came as well from students at black colleges and universities, which had expanded significantly in the previous decades.

Men and women with education and a stake in society were often more aware of the obstacles to their advancement than poorer and more oppressed people, to whom the possibility of advancement may have seemed too remote even to consider. And urban blacks had considerably more freedom to associate with one another and to develop independent institutions than did rural blacks, who were often under the very direct supervision of white landowners.

Television and other forms of popular culture were another factor in the rising consciousness of racism among blacks. More than any previous generation, postwar blacks had constant, vivid reminders of how the white majority lived—of the world from which they were effectively excluded. Television also conveyed the activities of demonstrators to a national audience, ensuring that activism in one community would inspire similar protests in others.

In addition to the forces that were inspiring African Americans to mobilize, other forces were at work mobilizing many white Americans to support the movement once it began. One was the Cold War, which made racial injustice an embarrassment to Americans trying to present their nation as a model to the world. Another was the political mobilization of northern blacks, who were now a substantial voting bloc within the Democratic Party; politicians from northern industrial states could not ignore their views. Labor unions with substantial black memberships also played an important part in supporting (and funding) the civil rights movement.

This great and largely spontaneous social movement emerged, in short, out of an unpredictable combination of broad social changes and specific local grievances. Whatever its causes, it quickly took on a momentum that, by the early 1960s, had made it one of the most powerful forces in America.

EISENHOWER REPUBLICANISM

Dwight D. Eisenhower was the least experienced politician to serve in the White House in the twentieth century. He was also among the most politically successful presidents of the postwar era. At home, he pursued essentially moderate policies, avoiding most new initiatives but accepting the work of earlier reformers. Abroad, he continued and even intensified American commitments to oppose communism, but brought to some of those commitments a measure of restraint that his successors did not always match.

"What's Good for . . . General Motors"

The first Republican administration in twenty years was staffed mostly with men drawn from the same quarter as those who had staffed Republican administrations in the 1920s: the business community. But by the 1950s much of the American business community had acquired a very different social and political outlook from that of their predecessors of earlier decades. Above all, many of the nation's leading businessmen and financiers had reconciled themselves to at least the broad outlines of the Keynesian welfare state the New Deal had launched and, indeed, had come to see it as something that actually benefited them—by helping maintain social order, by increasing mass purchasing power, and by stabilizing labor relations.

To his cabinet, Eisenhower appointed wealthy corporate lawyers and business executives, who were not apologetic about their backgrounds—"eight millionaires and a plumber," the liberal *New Republic* magazine caustically remarked. (The plumber was Secretary of Labor Martin Durkin, president of the plumbers' union, who soon resigned.) Charles Wilson, president of General Motors, assured senators considering his nomination to be secretary of defense that he foresaw no conflict of interest because he was certain that "what was good for our country was good for General Motors, and vice versa." Missing from most members of this business-oriented administration was the deep hostility to "government interference" that had so dominated corporate attitudes three decades before.

Eisenhower's leadership style, which stressed delegation of authority to subordinates, helped enhance the power of his cabinet officers and others. Secretary of State John Foster Dulles was widely believed to be running American foreign policy almost single-handedly (although it has since become clear that the president was far more deeply involved in international decisions than was often apparent at the time). The White House chief of staff, former New Hampshire governor Sherman Adams, exercised broad authority over relations with Congress and strictly controlled access to the president—until he left office in disgrace, near the end of Eisenhower's presidency, after he was discovered to have accepted gifts from a wealthy businessman.

Eisenhower's consistent inclination was to limit federal activities and encourage private enterprise. He supported the private rather than public development of natural resources (and once talked about selling the Tennessee Valley Authority to a private company). To the chagrin of farmers, he lowered federal support for farm prices. He also removed the last limited wage and price controls maintained by the Truman administration. He opposed the creation of new social service programs such as national health insurance and strove constantly to reduce federal expenditures (even during the recession of 1958) and to balance the budget. He ended 1960, his last full year in office, with a $1 billion surplus.

The Survival of Social Welfare

The president took few new initiatives in domestic policy. But he resisted pressure from the right wing of his party and refused to dismantle those welfare policies of the New Deal that had survived the conservative assaults of the war years and after. Indeed, during his term, he agreed to extend the Social Security system to an additional 10 million people and unemployment compensation to an additional 4 million people; and he agreed to increase the minimum hourly wage from 75 cents to $1. Perhaps the most significant legislative accomplishment of the Eisenhower administration was the Federal Highway Act of 1956, which authorized $25 billion for a ten-year effort to construct over 40,000 miles of interstate highways. The program was to be funded through a highway "trust fund," whose revenues would come from new taxes on the purchase of fuel, automobiles, trucks, and tires.

In 1956, Eisenhower ran for a second term, even though he had suffered a serious heart attack the previous year. With Adlai Stevenson opposing him once again, he won by another, even greater landslide, receiving nearly 57 percent of the popular vote and 442 electoral votes to Stevenson's 89. Still, Democrats retained the control of both houses of Congress they had won back in 1954. And in 1958—during a serious recession—they increased that control by substantial margins.

The Decline of McCarthyism

In its first years in office the Eisenhower administration did little to discourage the anticommunist furor that had gripped the nation. Indeed, in many ways it helped sustain it. The president intensified the search for subversives in the government which Truman had begun several years earlier. More than 2,220 federal

---

THE ARMY-MCCARTHY HEARINGS
Senator Joseph McCarthy uses a map to show the supposed distribution of communists throughout the United States during the televised 1954 Senate hearings to mediate the dispute between McCarthy and the U.S. Army. Joseph Welch, chief counsel for the army, remains conspicuously unimpressed. *(UPI/Bettmann)*

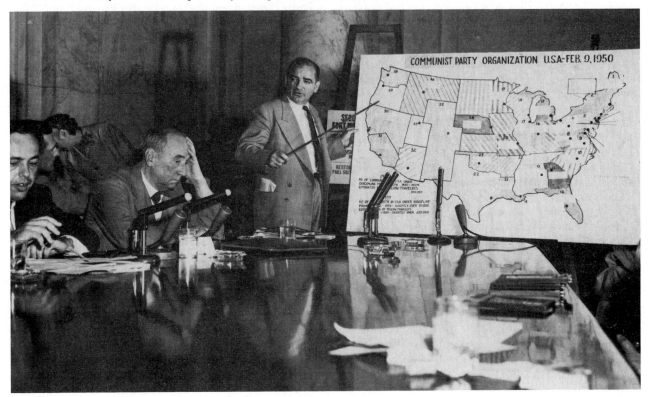

employees resigned or were dismissed as a result of security investigations. Among them were most of the leading Asian experts in the State Department, many of whom were harried from office because they had shown inadequate enthusiasm for the now-exiled regime of Chiang Kai-shek.

Among the most celebrated controversies of the new administration's first year was the case of J. Robert Oppenheimer, director of the Manhattan Project during the war and one of the nation's most distinguished and admired physicists. Although Oppenheimer was now out of government service, he continued as a consultant to the Atomic Energy Commission. But he had angered some officials by his public opposition to development of the new, more powerful hydrogen bomb, which Truman had approved toward the end of his presidency. In 1953, the FBI distributed a dossier within the administration detailing Oppenheimer's prewar association with various left-wing groups. The president responded by ordering a "blank wall" to be placed between Oppenheimer and government secrets. A federal investigation, requested by Oppenheimer himself and conducted in an inflamed and confused atmosphere, revealed no evidence of disloyalty but nevertheless confirmed the decision to deny him a security clearance.

But by 1954, such policies were beginning to produce significant popular opposition—an indication that the anticommunist passions of several years earlier were beginning to abate. The clearest signal of that change was the political demise of Senator Joseph McCarthy.

During the first year of the Eisenhower administration, McCarthy continued to operate with impunity. The president, who privately loathed him, refused to speak out against him in public. Relatively few others —in the political world or in the press—were any more courageous. But McCarthy finally overreached himself in January 1954 when he attacked Secretary of the Army Robert Stevens and the armed services in general. At that point, the administration and influential members of Congress organized a special investigation of the charges, which became known as the Army-McCarthy hearings. They were among the first congressional hearings to be nationally televised.

The result was devastating to McCarthy. Watching McCarthy in action—bullying witnesses, hurling groundless (and often cruel) accusations, evading issues—much of the public began to see him as a villain, even a buffoon. In December 1954, the Senate voted 67 to 22 to condemn him for "conduct unbecoming a senator." Three years later, with little public support left, he died—a victim, apparently, of complications arising from alcoholism.

EISENHOWER, DULLES, AND THE COLD WAR

The threat of nuclear war with the Soviet Union created a sense of high anxiety in international relations in the 1950s. But the nuclear threat had another effect as well. With the potential costs of war now so enormous, both superpowers began to edge away from direct confrontations. The attention of both the United States and the Soviet Union began to turn to the rapidly escalating instability in the nations of the Third World.

Dulles and "Massive Retaliation"

Eisenhower's secretary of state, and (except for the president himself) the dominant figure in the nation's foreign policy in the 1950s, was John Foster Dulles, an aristocratic corporate lawyer with a stern moral revulsion to communism. He entered office denouncing the containment policies of the Truman years as excessively passive, arguing that the United States should pursue an active program of "liberation," which would lead to a "rollback" of communist expansion. Once in power, however, Dulles had to defer to the far more moderate views of the president himself, and he began to develop a new set of doctrines that reflected the impact of nuclear weapons on the world.

The most prominent of those doctrines was the policy of "massive retaliation," which Dulles announced early in 1954. The United States would, he explained, respond to communist threats to its allies not by using conventional forces in local conflicts (a policy that had led to so much frustration in Korea) but by relying on "the deterrent of massive retaliatory power" (by which he clearly meant nuclear weapons).

In part, the new doctrine reflected Dulles's inclination for tense confrontations, an approach he once defined as "brinksmanship"—pushing the Soviet Union to the brink of war in order to exact concessions. But the real force behind the massive-retaliation policy was economics. With pressure growing both in and out of government for a reduction in American military expenditures, an increasing reliance on atomic weapons seemed to promise, as some advocates put it, "more bang for the buck."

At the same time, Dulles intensified the efforts of Truman and Acheson before him to "integrate" the entire noncommunist world into a system of mutual defense pacts modeled on NATO. The new alliances were, without exception, far weaker than the European pact. By the end of the decade, the United States had become a party to almost a dozen such treaties in all areas of the world.

Korea and Vietnam

The most troubling foreign policy concern of the Truman years—the war in Korea—plagued the Eisenhower administration only briefly. On July 27, 1953, negotiators at Panmunjom finally signed an agreement ending the hostilities. Each antagonist was to withdraw its troops a mile and a half from the existing battle line, which ran roughly along the 38th parallel, the prewar border between North and South Korea. A conference in Geneva was to consider means by which to reunite the nation peacefully—although in fact the 1954 meeting produced no agreement and left the cease-fire line as the apparently permanent border between the two countries.

Almost simultaneously, however, the United States faced a difficult choice in Southeast Asia, where France was fighting to retain control of its onetime colony Vietnam. Opposing the French were the powerful nationalist forces of Ho Chi Minh (who was both a committed nationalist and a committed communist), which were determined to win independence for their nation. The Truman administration had supported the French, one of America's most important Cold War allies, and at first the Eisenhower administration did the same.

Early in 1954, however, 12,000 French troops became surrounded in a disastrous siege at the city of Dien Bien Phu. Only American intervention, it was clear, could prevent the total collapse of the French military effort. Yet despite the urgings of Secretary of State Dulles, Vice President Nixon, and others, Eisenhower refused to permit direct American military intervention in Vietnam, claiming that neither Congress nor America's other allies would support such action. Without American aid, the French defense of Dien Bien Phu finally collapsed on May 7, 1954; and France quickly agreed to a settlement of the conflict at a conference in Geneva that summer—the same conference that was considering the settlement of the Korean War. The agreement marked the end of the French commitment to Vietnam and the beginning of an expanded

EISENHOWER AND DULLES
Although President Eisenhower himself was a somewhat colorless television personality, his was the first administration to make extensive use of the new medium to promote its policies and dramatize its actions. The president's press conferences were frequently televised, and on several occasions Secretary of State John Foster Dulles reported to the president in front of the cameras. Dulles is shown here in the Oval Office on May 17, 1955, reporting on the occasion of his return from Europe, where he had signed the treaty restoring sovereignty to Austria. *(AP/Wide World Photos)*

American presence there. (See pp. 834–838 for a more detailed account of the early history of the Vietnam War.)

Israel and the Crises of the Middle East

The establishment of a Jewish state in Palestine had been the dream of a powerful international Zionist movement for more than half a century before World War II. The plight of the homeless Jews uprooted by the war, and the international horror at exposure of the full extent of the Holocaust, gave new strength to Zionist demands in the late 1940s. So did the enormous immigration of European Jews into Palestine after 1945, despite the efforts of Britain (which had governed the region since World War I) to limit them.

THE STATE OF ISRAEL
The prime minister of Israel, David Ben-Gurion, watches the departure of the last British troops from Palestine shortly after the United Nations approved (and the United States recognized) the existence of a new Jewish state in part of the region. *(UPI/Bettmann)*

Finally, Britain brought the problem to the United Nations, which responded by recommending the partition of Palestine into a Jewish state and an Arab state. On May 14, 1948, British rule ended, and Jews proclaimed the existence of the nation of Israel. President Truman recognized the new government the following day. But the creation of Israel, while it resolved some conflicts, created others. Palestinian Arabs, unwilling to accept being displaced from what they considered their own country, rejected the partition and fought determinedly, if unsuccessfully, against the new state in 1948—the first of several Arab-Israeli wars.

Its support of Israel notwithstanding, America was deeply concerned about the stability and friendliness of the Arab regimes in the area. The reason was simple: the region contained the richest oil reserves in the world, reserves in which American companies had already invested heavily, and on which the health of the American (and world) economy would ultimately come to depend. Thus the United States reacted with alarm as it watched Mohammed Mossadegh, the nationalist prime minister of Iran, begin to resist the presence of Western corporations in his nation in the early 1950s. In 1953, the American CIA joined forces with conservative Iranian military leaders to engineer a coup that drove Mossadegh from office. To replace him, the CIA helped elevate the young Shah of Iran, Mohammed Reza Pahlavi, from his position as token constitutional monarch to that of virtually absolute ruler. The Shah remained closely tied to the United States for the next twenty-five years.

American policy was less effective in dealing with the nationalist government of Egypt, under the leadership of General Gamal Abdel Nasser, which in the early 1950s began to develop a trade relationship with the Soviet Union. In 1956, to punish Nasser for his friendliness toward the communists, Dulles withdrew American offers to assist in building the great Aswan Dam across the Nile. A week later, Nasser retaliated by seizing control of the Suez Canal from the British, saying that he would use the income from it to build the dam himself. The repercussions of that seizure were quick and profound.

On October 29, 1956, Israeli forces struck a preemptive blow against Egypt. The next day the British and French landed troops in the Suez to drive the Egyptians from the canal. Dulles and Eisenhower feared that the Suez crisis would drive the Arab states toward the Soviet Union and precipitate a new world war. By refusing to support the invasion, and by joining in a United Nations denunciation of it, the United States helped pressure the French and British to withdraw and helped persuade Israel to agree to a truce with Egypt.

Nasser's continuing flirtation with the Soviet

Union, which offered to assist in building the Aswan Dam once the United States withdrew from the project, strengthened American resolve to resist the growth of communist influence in the Middle East. It also increased the tendency of American officials to equate Arab nationalism with communism. In 1958, as pan-Arab forces loyal to Nasser challenged the government of Lebanon, Eisenhower ordered 5,000 American marines to land on the beaches of Beirut to protect the existing regime; British troops entered Jordan at about the same time to resist a similar threat there. The effect of the interventions was negligible. The governments of both countries managed to stabilize their positions on their own, and within months both the American and British forces withdrew.

Latin America and "Yankee Imperialism"

World War II and the Cold War had eroded the limited initiatives of the Good Neighbor Policy toward Latin America, as American economic aid now flowed increasingly to Europe. Latin American animosity toward the United States grew steadily during the 1950s, as more people in the region came to view the expanding influence of American corporations in their countries as a form of imperialism. Such concerns deepened in 1954, when the Eisenhower administration ordered the CIA to help topple the new, leftist government of Jacobo Arbenz Guzman in Guatemala, a regime that Dulles (responding to the entreaties of the United Fruit Company, a major investor in Guatemala fearful of Arbenz) argued was potentially communist. Four years later, the depths of anti-American sentiment became clear when Vice President Richard Nixon visited the region and was greeted in city after city by angry, hostile, occasionally dangerous mobs.

No nation in the region had been more closely tied to America than Cuba. Its leader, Fulgencio Batista, had ruled as a military dictator since 1952, when with American assistance he had toppled a more moderate government. Cuba's relatively prosperous economy had become a virtual fiefdom of American corporations, which controlled almost all the island's natural resources and had cornered over half the vital sugar crop, and of American organized crime, which controlled much of the lucrative tourist industry. Beginning in 1957, a popular movement of resistance to the Batista regime began to gather power under the leadership of Fidel Castro. By late 1958, the Batista forces were in almost total disarray. And on January 1, 1959, with Batista now in exile in Spain, Castro marched into Havana and established a new government.

At first, the American government reacted warmly to Castro, relieved to be rid of the corrupt and inef-

CASTRO IN MOSCOW, 1963
Fidel Castro, premier of Cuba since the 1959 revolution there, visited Moscow in 1963 to receive public assurances from Soviet premier Khrushchev that the USSR would come to his aid if the United States were to invade the islands again. Khrushchev announced that any American attack on Cuba would be treated as if it were an attack on the Soviet Union. Part of the settlement of the Cuban missile crisis the previous fall involved an American promise not to launch such an attack. *(UPI/Bettmann)*

fective Batista and hopeful that Castro would be a moderate, democratic reformer who would allow American economic activity to continue in Cuba unchallenged. But once Castro began implementing significant land reforms and expropriating foreign-owned businesses and resources, Cuban-American relations rapidly deteriorated. Of particular concern to Eisenhower and Dulles was the Cuban regime's growing interest in communist ideas and tactics. When Castro began accepting assistance from the Soviet Union in 1960, the United States cut back the "quota" by which Cuba could export sugar to America at a favored price. Early in 1961, as one of its last acts, the Eisenhower administration severed diplomatic relations with Castro. The American CIA had already begun secretly training Cuban expatriates for an invasion of the island to topple the new regime. Isolated by the United States, Castro soon cemented an alliance with the Soviet Union.

Europe and the Soviet Union

Although the problems of the Third World were moving slowly to the center of American foreign policy, the direct relationship with the Soviet Union and the effort to resist communist expansion in Europe remained the principal concerns of the Eisenhower administration.

Even as the United States was strengthening NATO and rearming West Germany, however, many Americans continued to hope for negotiated solutions to some of the remaining problems dividing the superpowers. Such hopes grew after the death of Josef Stalin in 1953, especially when the Soviet Union extended a peace overture to the rebellious Tito government in Yugoslavia, returned a military base to Finland, signed a peace treaty with Japan, and ended its long military occupation of Austria by allowing that nation to become an independent, neutral state. In 1955, Eisenhower and other NATO leaders met with the Soviet premier, Nikolai Bulganin, at a cordial summit conference in Geneva. But when a subsequent conference of foreign ministers met to try to resolve specific issues, they could find no basis for agreement.

Relations between the Soviet Union and the West soured further in 1956 in response to the Hungarian Revolution. Inspired by riots in Poland a year earlier, Hungarian dissidents had launched a popular uprising in November 1956 to demand democratic reforms. For several days, they had control of the Hungarian government. But before the month was out, Soviet tanks and troops entered Budapest to crush the uprising and restore an orthodox, pro-Soviet regime. The Eisenhower administration refused to intervene. But the suppression of the uprising convinced many American leaders that Soviet policies had not softened as much as the events of the previous two years had suggested.

The failure of conciliation brought renewed vigor to the Cold War and, among other things, greatly intensified the Soviet-American arms race. Both nations engaged in extensive nuclear testing. Both nations redoubled efforts to develop effective intercontinental ballistic missiles, which could deliver atomic warheads directly from one continent to another. The American military, in the meantime, developed a new breed of atomic-powered submarines, capable of launching missiles from under water anywhere in the world.

The arms race not only increased tensions between the United States and Russia; it increased tensions within each nation as well. In America, public concern about nuclear war was becoming a pervasive national nightmare, a preoccupation never far from popular thought. Movies, television programs, books, popular songs—all expressed the concern. Fear of communism, therefore, combined with fear of atomic war to create a persistent national anxiety.

The U-2 Crisis

In this tense and fearful atmosphere, the Soviet Union raised new challenges to the West in Berlin. The continuing existence of an anticommunist West Berlin inside communist East Germany remained an irritant and embarrassment to the Soviets. In November 1958, Nikita Khrushchev, who had succeeded Bulganin as Soviet premier and Communist Party chief earlier that year, renewed his predecessors' demands that the NATO powers abandon the city. The United States and its allies refused.

Khrushchev declined to force the issue. Instead, he suggested that he and Eisenhower discuss the issue personally, both in visits to each other's countries and at a summit meeting in Paris in 1960. The United States agreed. Khrushchev's 1959 visit to America produced a cool but polite response, and plans proceeded for the summit conference and for Eisenhower's visit to Moscow shortly thereafter. Only days before the scheduled beginning of the Paris meeting, however, the Soviet Union announced that it had shot down an American U-2, a high-altitude spy plane, over Russian territory. Its pilot, Francis Gary Powers, was in captivity. The Eisenhower administration responded clumsily, at first denying the allegations and then, when confronted with proof of them, awkwardly admitting that they were true. Khrushchev lashed back angrily, breaking up the Paris summit almost before it could begin and withdrawing his invitation to Eisenhower to visit the Soviet Union. But the U-2 incident was probably only a pretext. By the spring of 1960, Khrushchev—under heavy pressure from hardliners within his own government—knew that no agreement was possible on the Berlin issue; the U-2 incident may simply have been an excuse to avoid what he believed would be fruitless negotiations.

The events of 1960 provided a somber backdrop for the end of the Eisenhower administration. After eight years in office, Eisenhower had failed to eliminate the tensions between the United States and the Soviet Union. He had failed to end the costly and dangerous armaments race. And he had presided over a transformation of the Cold War from a relatively limited confrontation with the Soviet Union in Europe to a global effort to resist communist subversion. Yet Eisenhower had brought to these matters his own sense of the limits of American power. He had resisted military intervention in Vietnam. And he had placed a measure of restraint on those who urged the creation of an enormous American military establishment, warning in his farewell address in January 1961 of the "unwarranted influence" of a vast "military-industrial complex." His caution, in both domestic and international affairs, stood in marked contrast to the attitudes of his successors, who argued that the United States must act more boldly and aggressively on behalf of its goals at home and abroad.

SIGNIFICANT EVENTS

1946   Dr. Benjamin Spock publishes *Baby and Child Care*

1947   Jackie Robinson becomes first black to play in major leagues

Construction begins on Levittown, New York

1948   UAW and General Motors agree to automatic cost-of-living increases for auto workers

United Nations votes to partition Palestine and create state of Israel

1950   David Riesman publishes *The Lonely Crowd*

1951   J. D. Salinger publishes *The Catcher in the Rye*

1952   Eisenhower elected president

1953   Economic recession begins

Saul Bellow publishes *The Adventures of Augie March*

Department of Health, Education, and Welfare established

Earl Warren becomes chief justice

Truce ends Korean War

CIA helps engineer coup in Iran

Oppenheimer denied security clearance

Stalin dies

1954   Supreme Court rules on *Brown* v. *Board of Education*

Democrats regain control of Congress

Army-McCarthy hearings; Senate censures McCarthy

France surrenders at Dien Bien Phu; Geneva agreement partitions Vietnam

United States helps topple Arbenz regime in Guatemala

1955   Labor organizations reconcile and form AFL-CIO

Supreme Court Announces *"Brown II"* decision

Montgomery bus boycott begins

Ngo Dinh Diem becomes president of South Vietnam

Eisenhower and Bulganin meet in Geneva

1956   Federal Highway Act passed

Eisenhower reelected president

Suez crisis

Hungarian revolution crushed

1957   Postwar baby boom peaks

Economic recession begins

Labor racketeering investigations focus on Teamsters

Soviet Union launches *Sputnik*

Jack Kerouac publishes *On the Road*

Little Rock school desegregation crisis

Civil rights act passed

Germany joins NATO

1958   American manned space program founded

National Defense Education Act passed

American marines land in Lebanon

1959   Castro seizes power in Cuba

Nikita Khrushchev visits United States

1960   U-2 incident precedes collapse of Paris summit

1961   Yuri Gagarin of Soviet Union becomes first man in space

Alan Shepard becomes first American in space

United States breaks diplomatic relations with Cuba

Eisenhower gives farewell address

1962   Michael Harrington publishes *The Other America*

1969   Americans land on moon

UMW president "Jock" Yablonski murdered

SUGGESTED READINGS

General Studies. John Brooks, *The Great Leap* (1966). William Chafe, *The Unfinished Journey* (1986). Carl Degler, *Affluence and Anxiety* (1968). John P. Diggins, *The Proud Decades* (1989). Eric Goldman, *The Crucial Decade and After* (1960). David Halberstam, *The Fifties* (1993). Godfrey Hodgson, *America in Our Time* (1976). William Leuchtenburg, *A Troubled Feast* (1979). Douglas T. Miller and Marion Novak, *The Fifties* (1977). William O'Neill, *American High* (1986).

The Postwar Economy. David P. Calleo, *The Imperious Economy* (1982). Gilbert C. Fite, *American Farmers* (1981). John K. Galbraith, *The Affluent Society* (1958); *The New Industrial State* (1967). Mark I. Gelfand, *A Nation of Cities* (1975). Robert Heilbroner, *The Limits of American Capitalism* (1965). John Hutchinson, *The Imperfect Union* (1970). C. Wright Mills, *The Power Elite* (1956). Loren J. Okroi, *Galbraith, Harrington, Heilbroner* (1986). Joel Seidman, *American Labor from Defense to Reconversion* (1953). Harold G. Vatter, *The U.S. Economy in the 1950s* (1963).

Culture and Ideas. Daniel Bell, *The End of Ideology* (1960); ed., *the Radical Right* (1963). Peter Biskind, *Seeing is Believing: How Hollywood Taught Us to Stop Worrying and Love the Fifties* (1983). Paul Boyer, *By the Bomb's Early Light* (1986). Howard Brick, *Daniel Bell and the Decline of Intellectual Radicalism* (1986). Paul A. Carter, *Another Part of the Fifties* (1983). Ann Charters, *Kerouac* (1973). Bruce Cook, *The Beat Generation* (1971). Edward J. Epstein, *News from Nowhere* (1973). Herbert Gans, *The Levittowners* (1967). William Graebner, *The Age of Doubt: American Thought and Culture in the 1940s* (1991). David Halberstam, *The Powers That Be* (1979). Jeffrey Hart, *When the Going Was Good: American Life in the Fifties* (1982). Dolores Hayden, *Redesigning the American Dream* (1984). Kenneth T. Jackson, *The Crabgrass Frontier: The Suburbanization of the United States* (1985). Marty Jezer, *The Dark Ages: Life in the U.S. 1945–1960* (1982). Landon Y. Jones, *Great Expectations: America and the Baby Boom Generation* (1980). Neil Jumonville, *Critical Crossings: The New York Intellectuals in Postwar America* (1991). George Lipsitz, *Class and Culture in Cold War America* (1981). Mary Sperling McAuliffe, *Crisis on the Left* (1978). Walter A. McDougall, *. . . the Heavens and the Earth: A Political History of the Space Age* (1985). Dennis McNally, *Desolate Angel* (1979). Margaret Marsh, *Suburban Lives* (1990). Douglas T. Miller and Marion Novak, *The Fifties* (1977). Zane L. Miller, *Suburb: Neighborhood and Community in Forest Park, Ohio, 1935–1976* (1981). C. Wright Mills, *White Collar* (1956). Richard H. Pells, *The Liberal Mind in a Conservative Age: American Intellectuals in the 1940s and 1950s* (1985). David Potter, *People of Plenty* (1954). David Riesman, *The Lonely Crowd* (1950). Leila Rupp and Verta Taylor, *Survival in the Doldrums* (1987). Arthur M. Schlesinger, Jr., *The Vital Center* (1949). Lynn Spigel, *Make Room for TV* (1992). Walter Sullivan, ed., *America's Race for the Moon* (1962). John Tytell, *Naked Angels* (1976). Alan M. Wald, *The New York Intellectuals* (1987). Stephen J. Whitfield, *The Culture of the Cold War* (1991). William Whyte, *The Organization Man* (1956). Tom Wolfe, *The Right Stuff* (1979).

Gwendolyn Wright, *Building the American Dream: A Social History of Housing in America* (1981).

Women and Families. William Chafe, *The American Woman: Her Changing Social, Economic, and Political Roles, 1920–1970*, rev. ed. (1988). Ruth Cowan, *More Work for Mother: The Irony of Household Technology* (1983). Eugenia Kaledin, *Mothers and More: American Women in the 1950s* (1984). Susan Estabrook Kennedy, *If All We Did Was to Weep at Home: A History of White Working-Class Women in America* (1979). Alice Kessler-Harris, *Out to Work: A History of Wage-Earning Women in the United States* (1982). Elaine Tyler May, *Homeward Bound: American Families in the Cold War* (1988). Susan Strasser, *Never Done: A History of American Housework* (1982).

Politics in the Eisenhower Years. Sherman Adams, *Firsthand Report* (1961). Charles C. Alexander, *Holding the Line* (1975). Stephen Ambrose, *Eisenhower the President* (1984). Brian Balogh, *Chain Reaction: Expert Debate and Public Participation in American Nuclear Commercial Power, 1945–1975* (1991). Piers Brendon, *Ike* (1986). Jeff Broadwater, *Eisenhower and the Anti-Communist Crusade* (1992). Robert F. Burk, *Dwight D. Eisenhower* (1986). Barbara B. Clowse, *Brainpower for the Cold War: The Sputnik Crisis and the National Defense Education Act of 1958* (1981). Dwight D. Eisenhower, *The White House Years*, 2 vols. (1963–1965). Fred Greenstein, *The Hidden-hand Presidency* (1982). Emmet John Hughes, *The Ordeal of Power* (1963). Peter Lyon, *Eisenhower: Portrait of a Hero* (1974). Richard Nixon, *Six Crises* (1962). Herbert S. Parmet, *Eisenhower and the American Crusades* (1972). Nicol C. Rae, *The Decline and Fall of the Liberal Republicans* (1989). Gary Reichard, *The Reaffirmation of Republicanism* (1975); *Politics as Usual* (1988). David W. Reinhard, *The Republican Right Since 1945* (1983). Elmo Richardson, *The Presidency of Dwight D. Eisenower* (1979). Mark H. Rose, *Interstate: Express Highway Politics, 1941–1956* (1979). R. L. Rosholt, *An Administrative History of NASA* (1966).

Foreign Policy. Stephen Ambrose, *Ike's Spies* (1981). David L. Anderson, *Trapped by Success: The Eisenhower Administration and Vietnam, 1953–1961* (1991). Howard Ball, *Justice Downwind: America's Nuclear Testing Program in the 1950s* (1986). Michael Beschloss, *MAYDAY* (1986). Henry W. Brands, *Cold Warriors* (1988); *The Specter of Neutralism: The United States and the Emergence of the Third World, 1947–1960* (1989). Blanche W. Cooke, *The Declassified Eisenhower* (1981). Chester Cooper, *Lost Crusade* (1970); *The Lion's Last Roar* (1978). Cecil Currey, *Edward Lansdale: The Unquiet American* (1988). Robert A. Divine, *Foreign Policy and U.S. Presidential Elections*, 2 vols. (1974); *Blowing in the Wind: The Nuclear Test Ban Debate, 1954–1960* (1978); *Eisenhower and the Cold War* (1981). Frances Fitzgerald, *Fire in the Lake* (1972). Steven Z. Freiberger, *Dawn over Suez: The Rise of American Power in the Middle East, 1953–1957* (1992). Louis Gerson, *John Foster Dulles* (1967). Gregg Herken, *Counsels of War* (1985). George Herring, *America's Longest War* (1979). Richard G. Hewlett and Jack M. Hall,

Atoms for Peace and War, 1953–1961 (1989). Townsend Hoopes, *The Devil and John Foster Dulles* (1973). Richard Immerman, *The CIA in Guatemala* (1982). Burton Kaufman, *The Oil Cartel Case* (1978). Gabriel Kolko, *Confronting the Third World* (1988). Walter LaFeber, *Inevitable Revolutions* (1983). John T. McAlister, Jr., *Vietnam: The Origins of Revolution* (1969). Richard A. Melanson and David A. Mayers, ed., *Reevaluating Eisenhower* (1986). Stephen G. Rabe, *Eisenhower and Latin America* (1988). Kermit Roosevelt, *Counter-coup* (1980). Andrew Rotter, *The Path to Vietnam* (1987). Richard Smoke, *National Security and the Nuclear Dilemma* (1988). Hugh Thomas, *Suez* (1967). Mira Wilkins, *The Maturing of Multinational Enterprise* (1974).

Legal and Constitutional Issues. Alexander Bickel, *Politics and the Warren Court* (1965); *The Supreme Court and the Idea of Progress* (1970). Phillip Kurland, *Politics, the Constitution, and the Warren Court* (1970). Paul Murphy, *The Constitution in Crisis Times* (1972). Bernard Schwartz, *Super Chief: Earl Warren and His Supreme Court* (1983). Philip Stern, *The Oppenheimer Case* (1969). Michael Straight, *Trial by Television* (1954). John Weaver, *Earl Warren* (1967).

Civil Rights. John W. Anderson, *Eisenhower, Brownell, and the Congress* (1964). Numan V. Bartley, *The Rise of Massive Resistance* (1969). Taylor Branch, *Parting the Waters* (1988). Robert F. Burk, *The Eisenhower Administration and Black Civil Rights* (1984). William Chafe, *Civilities and Civil Rights* (1980).

David Garrow, ed., *The Montgomery Bus Boycott and the Women Who Started It: A Memoir of Jo Ann Gibson Robinson* (1987); *Bearing the Cross* (1986). Elizabeth Huckaby, *Crisis at Central High* (1980). Martin Luther King, Jr., *Stride Toward Freedom* (1958). Richard H. King, *Civil Rights and the Idea of Freedom* (1992). Richard Kluger, *Simple Justice* (1975). Steven Lawson, *Running for Freedom* (1991). Anthony Lewis, *Portrait of a Decade* (1964). Robert J. Norrell, *Reaping the Whirlwind: The Civil Rights Movement in Tuskegee* (1985). Howell Raines, *My Soul Is Rested* (1977). Harvard Sitkoff, *The Struggle for Black Equality, 1954–1980* (1981). Abigail Thernstrom, *Whose Votes Count? Affirmative Action and Minority Voting Rights* (1987). Nancy J. Weiss, *Whitney M. Young, Jr., and the Struggle for Civil Rights* (1989).

Minorities and the Poor. Rodolfo Acuña, *Occupied America: A History of Chicanos* (1981). Larry W. Burt, *Tribalism in Crisis: Federal Indian Policy, 1953–1961* (1982). Donald Fixico, *Termination and Relocation: Federal Indian Policy, 1945–1970* (1986). J. Wayne Flint, *Dixie's Forgotten People: The South's Poor Whites* (1979). Michael Harrington, *The Other America* (1962). Jacqueline Jones, *The Dispossessed: America's Underclasses from the Civil War to the Present* (1992). Nicholas Lemann, *The Promised Land: The Great Black Migration and How It Changed America* (1991). Elena Padilla, *Up from Puerto Rico* (1958). Linda Reed, *Simple Decency and Common Sense* (1992).

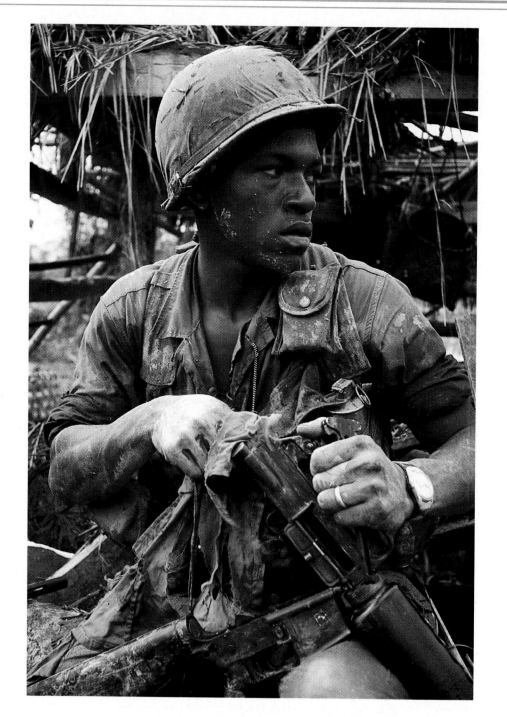

"IN COUNTRY"

This grim 1968 photograph of an American G.I. conveys something of the unhappy character of the nation's military experience in Vietnam. Soldiers serving "in country" (as assignment to Vietnam itself was called) experienced both physical hardship, as they patrolled difficult and unfamiliar territory, and the demoralization of fighting in a confusing, frustrating, and ultimately unsuccessful war. *(John Olson/Black Star)*

CHAPTER THIRTY-ONE

THE ORDEAL OF LIBERALISM

B Y THE LATE 1950s, a growing restlessness was becoming apparent beneath the placid surface of American society. Anxiety about America's position in the world, growing pressures from African Americans and other minorities, the increasing visibility of poverty, the rising frustrations of women, and other long-suppressed discontents were beginning to make themselves felt in the nation's public life. Ultimately, that restlessness would make the 1960s one of the most turbulent eras of the twentieth century. But at first, it contributed to a bold and confident effort by political leaders to attack social and international problems within the framework of conventional liberal politics.

EXPANDING THE LIBERAL STATE

Those who yearned for a more active government in the late 1950s, and who accused the Eisenhower administration of allowing the nation to "drift," looked above all to the presidency for leadership. The political scientist Richard Neustadt, for example, published an influential book in 1960 entitled *Presidential Power,* which stressed the importance of presidential action in confronting national problems. Presidents faced many constraints, he argued, but effective presidents must learn to break free of them. The two men who served in the White House through most of the 1960s—John Kennedy and Lyndon Johnson—seemed for a time to be the embodiment of these liberal hopes.

John Kennedy

The campaign of 1960 produced two young candidates who claimed to offer the nation active leadership. The Republican nomination went almost uncontested to Vice President Richard Nixon, who abandoned the strident anticommunism that had characterized his earlier career and adopted a centrist position in favor of moderate reform. The Democrats, in the meantime, emerged from a hotly contested primary campaign united, somewhat uneasily, behind John Fitzgerald Kennedy, an attractive and articulate senator from Massachusetts who had narrowly missed being the party's vice presidential candidate in 1956.

John Kennedy grew up in a world of ease and privilege, although he himself suffered from a series of grave physical ailments throughout his life. He was the son of the wealthy and powerful Joseph P. Kennedy, controversial American ambassador to Britain at the beginning of World War II. After graduating from Harvard, he served in the navy during World War II, was decorated for bravery, and returned to Massachusetts in 1946 to run for office. By making liberal use of both his own war record and his family's money, he won a seat in Congress. Six years later, he was elected to the United States Senate, and in 1958 was reelected by a record margin. Within days of his triumph, he was planning his campaign for the White House. He premised his campaign, he said, "on the single assumption that the American people are uneasy at the present drift in our national course." But his appealing, and carefully crafted, public image was at least as important as his political positions in attracting his popular support.

A vigorous effort on behalf of Nixon by President Eisenhower in the closing days of the campaign, combined with continuing doubts about Kennedy's youth (he turned forty-three in 1960) and religion (he was a Catholic), almost enabled the Republicans to close what had at one time been a substantial Democratic lead. But Kennedy's strong performance in a series of televised presidential debates helped overcome the doubts. And in the end, he held on to win a tiny plurality of the popular vote—49.9 percent to Nixon's 49.6 percent—and only a slightly more comfortable electoral majority—303 to 219. If a few thousand voters in a few strategic states had voted differently, Nixon would have won.

Kennedy had campaigned promising a program of domestic legislation more ambitious than any since the New Deal, a program he described as the "New Frontier." But the narrowness of his victory limited his political effectiveness, and throughout his brief presidency he had serious problems with Congress. Although Democrats remained in control of both houses, the party's majorities were dependent on conservative southerners, who were far more likely to vote with the Republicans than with Kennedy. Many of those same southerners occupied powerful committee chairmanships. One after another of Kennedy's legislative proposals found themselves hopelessly stalled.

As a result, the president had to look elsewhere for opportunities to display positive leadership. One area where he believed he could do that was the economy. Economic growth was sluggish in 1961 when Kennedy entered the White House, with unemployment hovering at about 6 percent of the work force. Kennedy initiated a series of tariff negotiations with foreign governments—the "Kennedy Round"—in an effort to stimulate American exports. He began to consider an expanded use of Keynesian fiscal and monetary tools—culminating in his 1962 proposal for a substantial federal tax cut to stimulate the economy. And he used his personal prestige to battle inflation. In 1962, several steel companies, led by U.S. Steel, announced that they were raising their prices by $6 a ton, a move certain to trigger similar action by the rest of the steel industry. Kennedy put heavy pressure on U.S. Steel president Roger Blough and other steel executives to rescind the increase. The steel companies soon relented. But it was a fleeting victory. Kennedy's relationship with the corporate community was now permanently strained, and when the steel companies quietly raised prices again a few months later, the president did not protest.

More than any other president of the century (excepting perhaps the two Roosevelts and, later, Ronald Reagan), Kennedy made his own personality an integral part of his presidency and a central focus of national attention. Nothing illustrated that more clearly than the popular reaction to the tragedy of November 22, 1963. Kennedy had traveled to Texas with his wife and Vice President Lyndon Johnson for a series of political appearances. While the presidential motorcade rode slowly through the streets of Dallas, shots rang out. Two bullets struck the president—one in the throat, the other in the head. He was sped to a nearby hospital, where minutes later he was pronounced dead. Lee Harvey Oswald, who appeared to be a confused and embittered Marxist, was arrested for the crime later that day, and then mysteriously murdered by a Dallas nightclub owner, Jack Ruby, two days later as he was being moved from one jail to another.

The popular assumption at the time was that both Oswald and Ruby had acted alone, an assumption endorsed by a federal commission, chaired by Chief Justice Earl Warren, that was appointed to investigate the assassination. In later years, however, many Ameri-

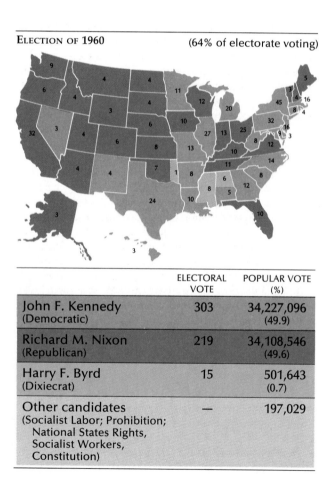

ELECTION OF 1960 (64% of electorate voting)

	ELECTORAL VOTE	POPULAR VOTE (%)
John F. Kennedy (Democratic)	303	34,227,096 (49.9)
Richard M. Nixon (Republican)	219	34,108,546 (49.6)
Harry F. Byrd (Dixiecrat)	15	501,643 (0.7)
Other candidates (Socialist Labor; Prohibition; National States Rights, Socialist Workers, Constitution)	—	197,029

for four days to watch the televised events surrounding the presidential funeral. Images of Kennedy's widow, his small children, his funeral procession, his grave site at Arlington Cemetery with its symbolic eternal flame—all became deeply embedded in the public mind. In later years, when Americans looked back at the optimistic days of the 1950s and early 1960s and wondered how everything had subsequently seemed to unravel, many would think of November 22, 1963, as the beginning of the change.

Lyndon Johnson

At the time, however, much of the nation took comfort in the personality and performance of Kennedy's successor in the White House, Lyndon Baines Johnson. Johnson was a native of the poor "hill country" of central Texas and had risen to eminence by dint of extraordinary, even obsessive effort and ambition. He entered public life in the 1930s as an aide to a Texas congressman, became the Texas director of the New Deal's National Youth Administration, and then, in 1937, was elected to Congress himself, fervently committed to Franklin Roosevelt. He rose steadily in Congress by working hard and by cultivating the favor of party leaders. In 1948, he narrowly won election to the United States Senate; a few years later he became the Senate majority leader, a job in which he displayed a legendary ability to persuade and cajole his colleagues into following his lead. Having failed to win the Democratic nomination for president in 1960, he surprised many who knew him by agreeing to accept the second position on the ticket with Kennedy. The events in Dallas thrust him into the White House.

Johnson's rough-edged, even crude, personality could hardly have been more different from Kennedy's. But like Kennedy, Johnson was a man who believed in the active use of power. And in the end, he proved more effective than his predecessor in translating his goals into reality. Between 1963 and 1966, he compiled the most impressive legislative record of any president since Franklin Roosevelt. He was aided by the tidal wave of emotion that followed the Kennedy assassination, which helped win support for many New Frontier proposals. But Johnson also constructed a remarkable reform program of his own, one that he ultimately labeled the "Great Society." And he won approval of much of it through the same sort of skillful congressional lobbying that had made him an effective majority leader.

Johnson envisioned himself, as well, as a great "coalition builder." He wanted the support of everyone, and for a time he very nearly got it. His first year

JOHN KENNEDY
The new president and his wife, Jacqueline, attend one of the five balls in Washington marking Kennedy's inauguration in 1961. *(Paul Schutzer, Life Magazine, © 1961 Time Warner, Inc.)*

cans—and in 1978 a congressional subcommittee—claimed that the Warren Commission report had not revealed the full story. *JFK*, a popular 1991 film by the director Oliver Stone, endorsed one of the many conspiracy theories advanced over the previous decades to explain the assassination. But no solid evidence has ever appeared to confirm any such theories, and many informed observers continue to believe that the Warren Commission Report (hasty and incomplete as it undoubtedly was) had the story essentially right.

The death of President Kennedy was one of several traumatic public episodes in national history that have left a permanent mark on all who experienced it. Millions of Americans suspended their normal activities

RETROACTIVE I, 1964
Within months of his death, John Kennedy had become transformed in the American imagination to a figure larger than life, a symbol of the nation's thwarted aspirations. The artist Robert Rauschenberg gave evidence of Kennedy's new mythological importance by making him the centerpiece of this evocation of contemporary American society. *(Wadsworth Atheneum, Hartford)*

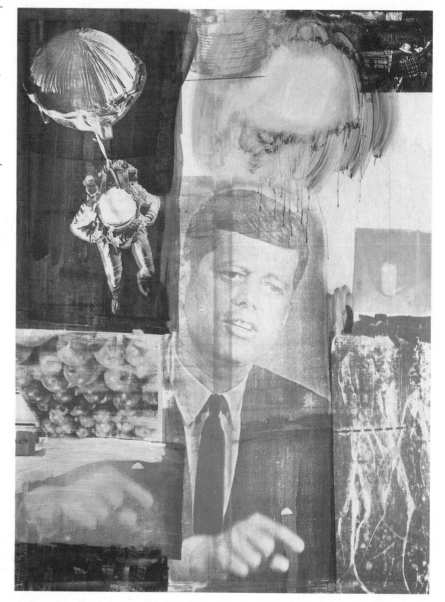

in office was, by necessity, dominated by the campaign for reelection. There was little doubt that he would win—particularly after the Republican Party fell under the sway of its right wing and nominated the conservative Senator Barry Goldwater of Arizona. Liberal Republicans abandoned Goldwater and openly supported Johnson. In the November election, the president received a larger plurality, over 61 percent, than any candidate before or since. Goldwater managed to carry only his home state of Arizona and five states in the Deep South. Record Democratic majorities in both houses of Congress, many of whose members had been

swept into office only because of the margin of Johnson's victory, ensured that the president would be able to fulfill many of his goals. Johnson seemed well on his way to achieving his cherished aim of becoming the most successful reform president of the century.

The Assault on Poverty

The domestic programs of the Kennedy and Johnson administrations had two basic goals: maintaining the strength of the American economy and expanding the

THE "JOHNSON TREATMENT"
Lyndon Johnson was legendary for his powers of persuasion, a combination of charm and intimidation that often worked on even the most experienced politicians. He is shown here meeting in his office with Senate Minority Leader Everett Dirksen of Illinois, who became an ally of the president in 1964 in ending a filibuster against the Civil Rights Act of that year. *(Lyndon Baines Johnson Library)*

responsibilities of the federal government for the general social welfare. In the first, the two presidents were largely continuing a commitment that had been central to virtually every administration since early in the century. In the second, however, they were responding to a marked change in public assumptions. In particular, they were responding to what some described as the "discovery of poverty" in the late 1950s and early 1960s—the realization by Americans who had been glorying in prosperity that there were substantial portions of the population that remained destitute.

For the first time since the 1930s, the federal government took steps in the 1960s to create important new social welfare programs. The largest and probably the most important of these was Medicare: a program to provide federal aid to the elderly for medical expenses. Its enactment in 1965 came after a bitter, twenty-year debate between those who believed in the concept of national health assistance and those who denounced it as "socialized medicine." But the program as crafted by the Kennedy and Johnson administrations removed many objections. For one thing, it avoided the stigma of "welfare" by making Medicare benefits available to all elderly Americans, regardless of need (just as Social Security had done with pensions). That created a large middle-class constituency for the program. The program also defused the opposition of the medical community by allowing doctors serving Medicare patients to practice privately and, in

the beginning, to charge their normal fees; Medicare simply shifted responsibility for paying those fees from the patient to the government. In 1966, Johnson steered to passage the Medicaid program, which extended federal medical assistance to welfare recipients of all ages. Criticism of both programs grew in subsequent years, both from those who thought Medicare and Medicaid were inadequate and from those who thought they were too expensive. But broad public support ensured their survival, and many liberals continued to hope for genuinely universal national health insurance. Not until the 1990s, however, would there be any serious effort to expand the system further.

Medicare and Medicaid were the first steps in a much larger assault on poverty—one that Kennedy had been contemplating in the last months of his life and one that Johnson launched only weeks after taking office. It emerged out of a long debate within the administration, and within Congress, about the nature of poverty and the best way to fight it. And it reflected the views of those who believed that poverty was a result of more than lack of money; it was a product of the institutional and cultural deficiencies of poor communities. By attacking those deficiencies, the planners of the antipoverty effort believed, government would help the poor to help themselves. That, in the end, was the key to the war on poverty: the effort to train the poor to be more successful. It was, as Johnson once put it, a "hand up, not a handout."

The centerpiece of this "war on poverty," as Johnson called it, was the Office of Economic Opportunity (OEO), which created an array of new educational, employment, housing, and health-care programs. But the OEO was controversial from the start, in part because of its commitment to the idea of "community action." Community action was an effort to involve members of poor communities themselves in the planning and administration of the programs designed to help them, to promote what some of its advocates called "maximum feasible participation." The community action programs provided some important benefits. In particular, they provided jobs for many poor people and gave them important experience in administrative and political work.

The community-action programs were also important to Native Americans. They allowed tribal leaders to design and run programs for themselves and to apply for funds from the federal government on an equal basis with state and municipal authorities. Administering these programs helped produce a new generation of tribal leaders who learned much about political and bureaucratic power from the experience.

But despite its achievements, the community-action approach proved impossible to sustain. Many programs fell victim to mismanagement or to powerful opposition from the local governments with which they were at times competing. Some activists in community-action agencies employed tactics that mainstream politicians considered frighteningly radical. The apparent excesses of a few agencies damaged the popular image of the community action program as a whole. And even though community action was a relatively small part of the war on poverty, its growing unpopularity undermined support for the larger program as well.

The OEO spent nearly $3 billion during its first two years of existence, and it helped reduce poverty significantly in certain areas. But it fell far short of eliminating poverty altogether. That was in part because of the weaknesses of the programs themselves and in part because funding for them, inadequate from the beginning, dwindled as the years passed and a costly war in Southeast Asia became the nation's first priority. Still, the war on poverty left a number of significant legacies. A generation of minority men and women became politically active in the community-action programs, and some of them continued to play a major role in public life for many years after. A series of programs—Head Start, a preschool enrichment program to help the children of poor families prepare for their educations; Food Stamps, which provided cash assistance to allow poor families to buy food; and others—were

genuinely successful and had a permanent impact on poverty.

Cities, Schools, and Immigration

Closely tied to the antipoverty program were federal efforts to promote the revitalization of decaying cities and to strengthen the nation's schools. The Housing Act of 1961 offered $4.9 billion in federal grants to cities for the preservation of open spaces, the development of mass transit systems, and the subsidization of middle-income housing. In 1966, Johnson established a new cabinet agency, the Department of Housing and Urban Development (whose first secretary, Robert Weaver, was the first African American ever to serve in a presidential cabinet). Johnson also inaugurated the Model Cities program, which offered federal subsidies for urban redevelopment.

Kennedy had fought long and hard for federal aid to public education, but he had failed to overcome two important obstacles. Many Americans feared aid to education as the first step toward federal control of the schools. Many Catholics insisted federal assistance must extend to parochial as well as public schools, a demand that raised serious constitutional issues and one that Kennedy (a Catholic himself) refused to consider. Johnson managed to circumvent both objections with the Elementary and Secondary Education Act of 1965 and a series of subsequent measures. The bills extended aid to both private and parochial schools and based the aid on the economic conditions of their students, not the needs of the schools themselves. Total federal expenditures for education and technical training rose from $5 billion to $12 billion between 1964 and 1967.

The Johnson administration also supported the Immigration Act of 1965, one of the most important pieces of legislation of the 1960s, even if relatively unnoticed at the time. The law maintained a strict limit on the number of newcomers admitted to the country each year (170,000), but it eliminated the "national origins" system established in the 1920s, which had given preference to immigrants from northern Europe over those from other parts of the world. It continued to restrict immigration from some parts of Latin America, but it allowed people from all parts of Europe, Asia, and Africa to enter the United States on an equal basis. It meant that large new categories of immigrants—and especially large numbers of Asians—would begin entering the United States by the early 1970s and changing the character of the American population. Prior to the 1965 act, 90 percent of immigrants to the United States each year came from European countries; after the act, only 10 percent did.

Legacies of the Great Society

The great surge of reform of the Kennedy-Johnson years reflected a new awareness of social problems in America. It also reflected the confident belief of liberals that America's resources were virtually limitless and that purposeful public effort could surmount any obstacle. By the time Johnson left office, legislation had been either enacted or initiated to deal with a remarkable number of social issues: poverty, health care, education, cities, transportation, the environment, consumer protection, agriculture, science, the arts.

Taken together, the Great Society reforms meant a significant increase in federal spending. For a time, rising tax revenues from the growing economy nearly compensated for the new expenditures. In 1964, Johnson managed to win passage of the $11.5 billion tax cut that Kennedy had first proposed in 1962. The cut increased the federal deficit, but it helped produce substantial economic growth over the next several years that made up for much of the revenue initially lost. As Great Society programs began to multiply, however, and particularly as they began to compete with the escalating costs of America's military ventures, the federal budget rapidly outpaced increases in revenues. In 1961, the federal government had spent $94.4 billion. By 1970, that sum had risen to $196.6 billion.

The high costs of the Great Society programs and the inability of the government to find the revenues to pay for them contributed to a growing disillusionment in later years with the idea of federal efforts to solve social problems. By the 1980s, many Americans had become convinced that the Great Society efforts had not worked and that, indeed, government programs to solve social problems could not work. Others, however, argued equally fervently that social programs had made important contributions both to the welfare of the groups they were designed to help and to the health of the economy as a whole.

Whether because of economic growth or because of government antipoverty efforts—or, as seems most likely, because of both—the decade of the 1960s saw the most substantial decrease in poverty in the United States of any period in the nation's history. In 1959, according to the most widely accepted estimates, 21 percent of the American people lived below the officially established poverty line. By 1969, only 12 percent remained below that line. The improvements affected blacks and whites in about the same proportion: 56 percent of the black population had lived in poverty in 1959, while 32 percent did so ten years later—a 42 percent reduction; 18 percent of all whites had been poor in 1959, but only 10 percent were poor a decade later—a 44 percent reduction.

THE BATTLE FOR RACIAL EQUALITY

The nation's most important domestic initiative in the 1960s was the effort to provide justice and equality to African Americans. It was the most difficult commitment, the one that produced the severest strains on American society. It was also unavoidable. Black Americans were themselves ensuring that the nation would have to deal with the problem of race.

MAJOR ACHIEVEMENTS OF THE GREAT SOCIETY

1964 Civil Rights Act (prohibiting discrimination in public accommodations and hiring)
Twenty-fourth Amendment (abolishing poll tax)
Tax Reduction Act
Urban Mass Transportation Act (subsidizing urban mass transit)
Economic Opportunity Act (creating OEO, Job Corps, VISTA)
Wilderness Preservation Act
1965 Elementary and Secondary Education Act (providing aid to schools)
Medicare
Civil Rights Act (protecting voting rights)
Omnibus Housing Act (providing rent supplements to the poor)

1965 Department of Housing and Urban Development
National Endowments of the Arts and Humanities
Water Quality Act
Immigration law reform
Air Quality Act
Higher Education Act (offering federally financed scholarships)
1966 Medicaid
National Traffic and Motor Vehicle Safety Act
Highway Safety Act
Minimum wage increase
Department of Transportation
Model Cities
1967 Food Stamps
Corporation for Public Broadcasting

Expanding Protests

John Kennedy had long been vaguely sympathetic to the cause of racial justice, but he was hardly a committed crusader. His intervention during the 1960 campaign to help win the release of Martin Luther King, Jr., from a Georgia prison won him a large plurality of the black vote. But like many presidents before him, he feared alienating southern Democratic voters and powerful southern Democrats in Congress. His administration set out to contain the racial problem by expanding enforcement of existing laws and supporting litigation to overturn existing segregation statutes, hoping to make modest progress without creating politically damaging divisions.

But the pressure for more fundamental change could not be contained. In February 1960, black college students in Greensboro, North Carolina, staged a sit-in at a segregated Woolworth's lunch counter; and in the following weeks, similar demonstrations spread throughout the South, forcing many merchants to integrate their facilities. In the fall of 1960, some of those who had participated in the sit-ins formed the Student Nonviolent Coordinating Committee (SNCC), which worked to keep the spirit of resistance alive.

SITTING IN
Black students stage a sit-in at a Woolworth's lunch counter in Charlotte, North Carolina, in 1960, after being refused service by the waitresses there. A similar demonstration at a Woolworth's in Greensboro several weeks earlier sparked a wave of sit-ins across the South. *(Bruce Roberts/Rapho-Photo Researchers)*

In 1961, an interracial group of students, working with the Congress of Racial Equality (CORE), began what they called "freedom rides" (reviving a tactic CORE had tried, without much success, in the 1940s). Traveling by bus throughout the South, the freedom riders tried to force the desegregation of bus stations. In some places, they met with such savage violence at the hands of enraged whites that the president finally dispatched federal marshals to help keep the peace. Kennedy also ordered the integration of all bus and train stations. In the meantime, SNCC workers began fanning out through black communities and even into remote rural areas to encourage blacks to challenge the obstacles to voting that the Jim Crow laws had created and that powerful social custom sustained. The Southern Christian Leadership Conference (SCLC) also created citizen-education and other programs— many of them organized by the remarkable Ella Baker, one of the great grassroots leaders of the movement— to mobilize black workers, farmers, housewives, and others to challenge segregation, disenfranchisement, and discrimination.

Continuing judicial efforts to enforce the integration of public education increased the pressure on national leaders to respond to the civil rights movement. In October 1962, a federal court ordered the University of Mississippi to enroll its first black student, James Meredith; Governor Ross Barnett, a strident segregationist, refused to enforce the order. When angry whites in Oxford, Mississippi, began rioting to protest the court decree, President Kennedy sent federal troops to the city to restore order and protect Meredith's right to attend the university.

Events in Alabama in 1963 helped bring the growing movement to something of a climax. In April, Martin Luther King, Jr., helped launch a series of nonviolent demonstrations in Birmingham, Alabama, a city unsurpassed in the strength of its commitment to segregation. Police Commissioner Eugene "Bull" Connor personally supervised a brutal effort to break up the peaceful marches, arresting hundreds of demonstrators and using attack dogs, tear gas, electric cattle prods, and fire hoses—at times even against small children—as much of the nation watched televised reports in horror. Two months later, Governor George Wallace—who had won election in 1962 pledging staunch resistance to integration—pledged to stand in the doorway of a building at the University of Alabama to prevent the court-ordered enrollment of several black students. Only after the arrival of federal marshals and a visit from Attorney General Robert Kennedy did Wallace give way. His stand won him wide popularity among whites throughout

the nation who were growing uncomfortable with the pace of integration. That same night, NAACP official Medgar Evers was murdered in Mississippi.

A National Commitment

The events in Alabama and Mississippi were a warning to the president that he could no longer contain or avoid the issue of race. In an important television address the night of the University of Alabama confrontation (and the murder of Evers), Kennedy spoke eloquently of the "moral issue" facing the nation. "If an American," he asked, "because his skin is dark, . . . cannot enjoy the full and free life which all of us want, then who among us would be content to have the color of his skin changed and stand in his place? Who among us would then be content with the counsels of patience and delay?" Days later, he introduced a series of new legislative proposals prohibiting segregation in "public accommodations" (stores, restaurants, theaters, hotels), barring discrimination in employment, and increasing the power of the government to file suits on behalf of school integration.

To generate support for the legislation, and to dramatize the power of the growing movement, more than 200,000 demonstrators marched down the Mall in Washington, D.C., in August 1963 and gathered before the Lincoln Memorial for the greatest civil rights demonstration in the nation's history. President Kennedy, who had at first opposed the idea of the march, in the end gave it his open support after receiving pledges from organizers that speakers would not criticize the administration. Martin Luther King, Jr., in one of the greatest speeches of his distinguished oratorical career, roused the crowd with a litany of images prefaced again and again by the phrase "I have a dream." The march was the highwater mark of the peaceful, interracial civil rights movement—and one of the last moments of real harmony within it.

The assassination of President Kennedy three months later gave new impetus to the battle for civil rights legislation. The ambitious measure that Kennedy had proposed in June 1963 had stalled in the Senate after having passed through the House of Representatives with relative ease. Early in 1964, after Johnson applied both public and private pressure, supporters of the measure finally mustered the two-thirds majority necessary to close debate and end a filibuster by southern senators; and the Senate passed the most comprehensive civil rights bill in the nation's history.

The Battle for Voting Rights

Having won a significant victory in one area, the civil rights movement shifted its focus to another: voting rights. During the summer of 1964, thousands of civil rights workers, black and white, northern and southern, spread out through the South, but primarily in Mississippi, to work on behalf of black voter registration and participation. The campaign was known as "freedom summer," and it produced a violent response from some southern whites. Three of the first freedom workers to arrive in the South—two whites, Andrew Goodman and Michael Schwerner, and one black, James Chaney—were murdered by local police and others.

The "freedom summer" also produced the Mississippi Freedom Democratic Party (MFDP), an integrated alternative to the regular state party organiza-

---

KING MARCHES THROUGH SELMA
Martin Luther King, Jr., and his wife, Coretta (right), lead demonstrators on a march through Selma, Alabama, during his turbulent campaign for black voting rights in 1965. Selma was one of the last of the great interracial crusades on behalf of civil rights. Subsequent campaigns, such as King's frustrated effort in Chicago in 1966, attracted much less support from northern whites and far less attention in the media. *(Bruce Davidson/Magnum)*

tion. Under the leadership of Fannie Lou Hamer and others, the MFDP challenged the regular party's right to its seats at the Democratic National Convention that summer. President Johnson, eager to avoid antagonizing anyone (even southern white Democrats who seemed likely to support his Republican opponent), enlisted King's help to broker a compromise. It permitted the MFDP to be seated as observers, with promises of party reforms later on, while the regular party retained its official standing. Both sides grudgingly accepted the agreement. Both were embittered by it.

A year later, in March 1965, King helped organize a major demonstration in Selma, Alabama, to press the demand for the right of blacks to register to vote. Selma sheriff Jim Clark led local police in a brutal attack on the demonstrators—which, as in Birmingham, received graphic television coverage and horrified many viewers across the nation. Two northern whites participating in the Selma march were murdered in the course of the effort there—one, a minister, beaten to death in the streets of the town; the other, a Detroit housewife, shot as she drove along a highway at night with a black passenger in her car. The national outrage that followed the events in Alabama helped push Lyndon Johnson to propose and win passage of the Civil Rights Act of 1965, better known as the Voting Rights Act, which provided federal protection to blacks attempting to exercise their right to vote.

But important as such gains were, they failed to satisfy the rapidly rising expectations of African Americans as the focus of the movement began to move from political to economic issues.

The Changing Movement

For decades, the nation's African-American population had been undergoing a major demographic shift; and by the 1960s, the problem of racial injustice was no longer primarily southern and rural, as it had been earlier in the century. By 1966, 69 percent of American blacks were living in metropolitan areas and 45 percent outside the South. Although the economic condition of much of American society was improving, in the poor urban communities in which the black population was concentrated, things were getting significantly worse. Well over half of all American nonwhites lived in poverty at the beginning of the 1960s; black unemployment was twice that of whites. (See pp. 803–805.)

By the mid-1960s, therefore, the issue of race was moving out of the South and into the rest of the nation. The battle against school desegregation had moved beyond the initial assault on de jure segregation (seg-

regation by law) to an attack on de facto segregation (segregation in practice, as through residential patterns), thus carrying the fight into northern cities. Many African-American leaders (and their white supporters) were demanding, similarly, that the battle against job discrimination move to a new level. Employers should not only abandon negative measures to deny jobs to blacks; they should adopt positive measures to recruit minorities, thus compensating for past injustices. Lyndon Johnson gave his tentative support to the concept of "affirmative action" in 1965. Over the next decade, affirmative action guidelines gradually extended to virtually all institutions doing business with or receiving funds from the federal government (including schools and universities)—and to many others as well.

A symbol of the movement's new direction, and of the problems it would cause, was a major campaign in the summer of 1966 in Chicago, in which King played a prominent role. Organizers of the Chicago campaign hoped to direct national attention to housing and employment discrimination in northern industrial cities in much the same way similar campaigns had exposed legal racism in the South. But the Chicago campaign not only evoked vicious and at times violent opposition from white residents of that city; it failed to arouse the national conscience in the way events in the South had done. It did produce a weak agreement with the city government to end housing discrimination, but little changed as a result. The Chicago campaign was, on the whole, an exercise in frustration.

Urban Violence

Well before the Chicago campaign, the problem of urban poverty had thrust itself into national attention when riots broke out in black neighborhoods in major cities. There were a few scattered disturbances in the summer of 1964, most notably in New York City's Harlem. The first large race riot since the end of World War II occurred the following summer in the Watts section of Los Angeles. In the midst of a seemingly routine traffic arrest, a white police officer struck a protesting black bystander with his club. The incident triggered a storm of anger and a week of violence (and revealed how deeply blacks in Los Angeles, and in other cities, resented their treatment at the hands of local police). As many as 10,000 people were estimated to have participated in the violence—attacking white motorists, burning buildings, looting stores, and sniping at policemen. Thirty-four people died during the Watts uprising, which was eventually quelled by the National Guard; twenty-eight of the dead were black. In the summer of 1966, there were forty-three additional outbreaks, the most serious of them in Chicago and Cleveland. And in the summer of 1967, there were eight major riots, including the largest of them all—a racial clash in Detroit in which forty-three people (thirty-three of them black) died.

Televised reports of the violence alarmed millions of Americans and created both a new sense of urgency and a growing sense of doubt among many of those whites who had embraced the cause of racial justice only a few years before. A special Commission on Civil Disorders, created by the president in response to the riots, issued a celebrated report in the spring of 1968 recommending massive spending to eliminate the abysmal conditions of the ghettoes. "Only a commitment to national action on an unprecedented scale," the commission concluded, "can shape a future compatible with the historic ideals of American society." To many white Americans, however, the lesson of the riots was the need for stern measures to stop violence and lawlessness.

Black Power

Disillusioned with the ideal of peaceful change in co-operation with whites, an increasing number of African Americans were turning to a new approach to the racial issue: the philosophy of "black power." Black power could mean many different things. But in all its forms, it suggested a move away from interracial co-operation and toward increased awareness of racial distinctiveness. It was part of a long nationalist tradition among African Americans that extended back into slavery and that had its most visible twentieth-century expression in the Garvey movement.

Perhaps the most enduring impact of the black-power ideology was a social and psychological one: instilling racial pride in African Americans, who lived in a society whose dominant culture generally portrayed blacks as inferior to whites. It encouraged the growth of black studies in schools and universities. It helped stimulate important black literary and artistic movements. It produced a new interest among many blacks in their African roots. It led to a rejection by some blacks of certain cultural practices borrowed from white society: "Afro" hairstyles began to replace artificially straightened hair; some blacks began to adopt African styles of dress, even to change their names.

But black power had political manifestations as well, most notably in creating a deep schism within the civil rights movement. Traditional black organizations that had emphasized cooperation with sympathetic whites—groups such as the NAACP, the Urban League, and King's Southern Christian Leadership Conference—now faced competition from more radical groups. The Student Nonviolent Coordinating Committee and the Congress of Racial Equality had both begun as relatively moderate, interracial organizations; SNCC, in fact, was originally a student branch of the SCLC. By the mid-1960s, however, these and other groups were calling for more radical and occasionally even violent action against the racism of white society and were openly rejecting the approaches of older, more established black leaders.

Particularly alarming to many whites (and to some African Americans as well) were organizations that existed entirely outside the mainstream civil rights movement. In Oakland, California, the Black Panther Party (founded by Huey Newton and Bobby Seale) promised to defend black rights even if that required violence. Black Panthers organized along semimilitary lines and wore weapons openly and proudly. They were, in fact, more the victims of violence from the police than they were practitioners of violence themselves. But they created an image, quite deliberately, of militant blacks willing to fight for justice, in Newton's words, "through the barrel of a gun."

In Detroit, a once-obscure black nationalist group, the Nation of Islam, gained new prominence. Founded in 1931 by Elijah Poole (who converted to Islam and renamed himself Elijah Muhammed), the movement taught blacks to take responsibility for their own lives, to be disciplined, to live by strict codes of behavior, and to reject any dependence on whites.

The most celebrated of the Black Muslims, as whites often termed them, was Malcolm Little, a former drug addict and pimp who had spent time in prison and had rebuilt his life once joining the movement. He adopted the name Malcolm X ("X" to denote his lost African surname). And he became one of the movement's most influential spokesmen, particularly among younger blacks, as a result of his intelligence, his oratorical skills, and his harsh, uncompromising opposition to all forms of racism and oppression. He did not advocate violence, as his critics often claimed; but he insisted that black people had the right to defend themselves, violently if necessary, from those who assaulted them. Malcolm died in 1965 when black gunmen, presumably under orders from rivals within the Nation of Islam, assassinated him in New York. But a book he had been working on before his death with the writer Alex Haley (*The Autobiography of Malcolm X*) attracted wide attention after its publication in 1965. Malcolm remained an influential figure in many black communities long after his death—as important and revered a symbol to many African Americans as Martin Luther King, Jr.

MALCOLM X
Malcolm X, a leader of the militant Black Muslims, arrives in Washington, D.C., in May 1963 to set up a headquarters for the organization there. Malcolm was hated and feared by many whites during his lifetime. He was assassinated in 1965. In subsequent years, he became a widely revered hero among African Americans. *(UPI/Bettmann)*

"FLEXIBLE RESPONSE" AND THE COLD WAR

In international affairs as much as in domestic reform, the optimistic liberalism of the Kennedy and Johnson administrations dictated a more positive, more active approach to dealing with the nation's problems than in the past. And just as the new activism in domestic reform proved more difficult and divisive than liber-

als had imagined, so too it created frustrations and failures in foreign policy.

Diversifying Foreign Policy

John Kennedy's forceful inaugural address was a clear indication of how central opposition to communism was to his and the nation's thinking. "In the long history of the world," he proclaimed, "only a few generations have been granted the role of defending freedom in its hour of maximum danger. I do not shrink from this responsibility; I welcome 'it." Yet the speech—which, significantly, made no mention whatever of domestic affairs—was also an indication of Kennedy's belief that the United States was not doing enough to counter the communist threat, that it needed to be able to resist aggression in more flexible ways than the atomic weapons-oriented defense strategy of the Eisenhower years permitted.

Kennedy remained committed to the nation's atomic weapons program. Indeed, he ran for president criticizing the Eisenhower administration for allowing an imbalance of nuclear weapons (a "missile gap") to develop between the United States and the Soviet Union. In fact, as Kennedy discovered even before the election, whatever missile gap there was favored the United States. But Kennedy insisted on proceeding with an expansion of the nation's atomic arsenal nevertheless—and the Soviet Union, which several years earlier had slowed the growth of its own nuclear weapons stockpile, responded in kind.

Kennedy's unhappiness with the Eisenhower foreign policy was not that it relied on nuclear weapons; it was that it developed too few other tools and thus had little capacity to respond to problems for which nuclear weapons were inappropriate solutions. In particular, he was unsatisfied with the nation's ability to meet communist threats in "emerging areas" of the Third World. In 1959, the Soviet Union had directed communist movements around the world to shift attention away from direct confrontations with the industrial powers of the West and toward "wars of national liberation" in less developed nations. Kennedy, similarly, concluded that the Third World would be the arena in which the real struggle against communism would be waged in the future. He gave enthusiastic support to the growth of the Special Forces, a small branch of the army created in the 1950s to wage guerrilla warfare in limited conflicts. Kennedy expanded the unit, allowed its members to wear distinctive headgear (thus giving them the informal name "the Green Berets"), and gave them an elite status within the military they had never had before.

Kennedy also favored expanding American influence through peaceful means. To repair the badly deteriorating relationship with Latin America, he proposed an "Alliance for Progress": a series of projects undertaken cooperatively by the United States and Latin American governments for peaceful development and stabilization of the nations of that region. Its purpose was both to spur social and economic development and to inhibit the rise of Castro-like movements in other Central or South American countries. Kennedy also inaugurated the Agency for International Development (AID) to coordinate foreign aid. And he established what became one of his most popular innovations: the Peace Corps, which sent young American volunteers abroad to work in developing areas.

The Bay of Pigs Fiasco

Among the first foreign policy ventures of the Kennedy administration was a disastrous assault on the Castro government in Cuba. The Eisenhower administration had launched the project, and by the time Kennedy took office, the CIA had been working for months in Central America to train a small army of anti-Castro Cuban exiles to invade Cuba and overthrow the Castro regime.

Kennedy had misgivings about the project. But he believed that "communist domination in this hemisphere can never be negotiated" and that Castro represented a threat to the stability of other Latin American nations, and so he accepted the CIA's optimistic assessments of the chances for success and approved the invasion. On April 17, 1961, 2,000 of the armed exiles landed at the Bay of Pigs in Cuba, expecting first American air support and then a spontaneous uprising by the Cuban people on their behalf. They received neither. At the last minute, Kennedy withdrew the air support, fearful of involving the United States too directly in the invasion. (Air support would not likely have changed the result in any case.) And the expected uprising did not occur. Instead, well-armed Castro forces easily crushed the invaders, and within two days the entire mission had collapsed.

Kennedy somberly took responsibility for the fiasco. But he refused to rule out further measures against the

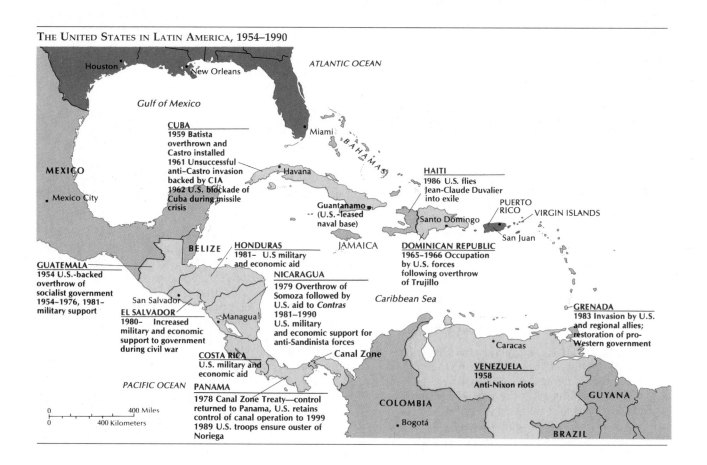

THE UNITED STATES IN LATIN AMERICA, 1954–1990

CUBA
1959 Batista overthrown and Castro installed
1961 Unsuccessful anti-Castro invasion backed by CIA
1962 U.S. blockade of Cuba during missile crisis

HAITI
1986 U.S. flies Jean-Claude Duvalier into exile

GUATEMALA
1954 U.S.-backed overthrow of socialist government
1954–1976, 1981– military support

HONDURAS
1981– U.S military and economic aid

NICARAGUA
1979 Overthrow of Somoza followed by U.S. aid to Contras
1981–1990 U.S. military and economic support for anti-Sandinista forces

DOMINICAN REPUBLIC
1965–1966 Occupation by U.S. forces following overthrow of Trujillo

GRENADA
1983 Invasion by U.S. and regional allies; restoration of pro-Western government

EL SALVADOR
1980– Increased military and economic support to government during civil war

COSTA RICA
U.S. military and economic aid

VENEZUELA
1958 Anti-Nixon riots

PANAMA
1978 Canal Zone Treaty—control returned to Panama, U.S. retains control of canal operation to 1999
1989 U.S. troops ensure ouster of Noriega

Castro regime. "We do not intend to abandon Cuba to the communists," he said only three days after the Bay of Pigs.

Confrontations with the Soviet Union

In the grim aftermath of the Bay of Pigs, Kennedy traveled to Vienna in June 1961 for his first meeting with Soviet Premier Nikita Khrushchev. Their frosty and at times angry exchange of views did little to reduce tensions between the two nations. Nor did Khrushchev's continuing irritation over the existence of a noncommunist West Berlin in the heart of East Germany.

In Vienna, Khrushchev had threatened war if the West did not abandon its defense of the city. Later in the summer, however, he settled on a less dangerous approach to the problem. Particularly embarrassing to the communists was the mass exodus of residents of East Germany to the West through the easily traversed border in the center of Berlin. Before dawn on August 13, 1961, the Soviet Union stopped the exodus by directing East Germany to construct a wall between East and West Berlin. Guards fired on those who continued to try to escape. For nearly thirty years, the Berlin Wall stood as the most potent physical symbol of the conflict between the communist and non-communist worlds.

The rising tensions culminated the following October in the most dangerous and dramatic crisis of the Cold War. During the summer of 1962, American intelligence agencies had become aware of the arrival of a new wave of Soviet technicians and equipment in Cuba and of military construction in progress. On October 14, aerial reconnaissance photos produced clear evidence that the Soviets were constructing sites on the island for offensive nuclear weapons. To the Soviets, placing missiles in Cuba probably seemed a reasonable, and relatively inexpensive, way to counter the presence of American missiles in Turkey (and a way to deter any future American invasion of Cuba). But to Kennedy and most other Americans, the missile sites represented an act of aggression by the Soviets toward the United States. Almost immediately, the president decided that the weapons could not be allowed to remain.

On October 22, after nearly a week of tense deliberations by a special task force in the White House, Kennedy ordered a naval and air blockade around Cuba, a "quarantine" against all offensive weapons. Soviet ships bound for the island slowed down or stopped before reaching the point of confrontation. But work on the missile sites continued. Preparations were under way for an American air attack on Cuba when, late in the evening of October 26, Kennedy received a message from Khrushchev implying that the Soviet

REPAIRING THE BERLIN WALL
First erected in 1961, the Berlin Wall became steadily higher and more elaborately fortified over the next several years. This 1963 photograph shows West Germans, at right, watching East German workers repair a section of wall after an East German mechanic rammed into it with an armored car as he escaped into West Berlin. He was shot by East German police but survived. *(UPI/Bettmann)*

Union would remove the missile bases in exchange for an American pledge not to invade Cuba. Ignoring other, tougher Soviet messages, the president agreed. Privately, he also promised to remove American missiles from Turkey, a decision he had already reached months earlier but had not yet implemented. The crisis was over.

The Cuban missile crisis brought the world closer to nuclear war than at any time since World War II. Both the United States and the Soviet Union had been forced to confront the momentous consequences of war. And in the following months, both seemed ready to move toward a new accommodation. In June 1963, President Kennedy spoke at American University in Washington, D.C., and seemed for the first time to offer hope for a peaceful rapprochement with the Soviet Union. That same summer, the United States and the Soviet Union concluded years of negotiation by agreeing to a treaty to ban the testing of nuclear weapons in the atmosphere—the first step toward mutual arms reduction since the beginning of the Cold War.

In the longer run, however, the missile crisis had more ominous consequences. The humiliating retreat the United States forced upon the Soviet leadership undermined the position of Nikita Khrushchev and contributed to his fall from power a year later. His replacement, Leonid Brezhnev, was a much more orthodox party figure, less interested in reform than Khrushchev had been. Perhaps more important, the graphic evidence the crisis gave the Soviets of their military inferiority helped produce a dramatic Soviet arms buildup over the next two decades, a buildup that contributed to a comparable increase in the United States in the early 1980s and that for a time undermined American support for a policy of rapprochement.

Johnson and the World

Lyndon Johnson entered the presidency lacking even John Kennedy's limited prior experience with international affairs. He was eager, therefore, not only to continue the policies of his predecessor but to prove quickly that he too was a strong and forceful leader.

An internal rebellion in the Dominican Republic gave him an early opportunity to do so. A 1961 assassination had toppled the repressive dictatorship of General Rafael Trujillo, and for the next four years various factions in the country had struggled for dominance. In the spring of 1965, a conservative military regime began to collapse in the face of a revolt by a broad range of groups on behalf of the nationalist reformer Juan Bosch, who had been elected president in

1962 and deposed by the military after only seven months in office. Arguing (without any evidence) that Bosch planned to establish a pro-Castro, communist regime, Johnson dispatched 30,000 American troops to quell the disorder. Only after a conservative candidate defeated Bosch in a 1966 election were the forces withdrawn.

From Johnson's first moments in office, however, his foreign policy was almost totally dominated by the bitter civil war in Vietnam and by the expanding involvement of the United States there. In many respects, Johnson was on this issue simply the unfortunate legatee of commitments initiated by his predecessors. But the determination of the new president, and of others within his administration, to prove their resolve in the battle against communism helped produce the final, decisive steps toward a full-scale commitment.

VIETNAM

George Kennan, who helped devise the containment doctrine in whose name America went to war in Vietnam, once called the conflict "the most disastrous of all America's undertakings over the whole 200 years of its history." In retrospect, few would now disagree. Yet at first, the Vietnam War seemed simply one more Third World struggle on the periphery of the Cold War, a struggle in which the United States would try to tip the balance against communism without becoming too deeply or directly engaged. No president really decided to go to war in Vietnam. Rather, the American involvement there emerged from years of gradually increasing commitments that slowly and imperceptibly expanded.

The First Indochina War

Vietnam had a long history both as an independent kingdom and major power in its region, and as a subjugated province of China; its people were both proud of their past glory and painfully aware of their many years of subjugation. In the mid-nineteenth century, Vietnam became a colony of France. And like other European possessions in Asia, it fell under the control of Japan during World War II. After the defeat of Japan, the question arose of what was to happen to Vietnam in the postwar world. There were two opposing forces attempting to answer that question, both of them appealing to the United States for help. The French wanted to reassert their control over Vietnam. Challenging them was a powerful nationalist movement

THE ORDEAL OF LIBERALISM

within Vietnam committed to creating an independent nation. The nationalists were organized into a political party, the Vietminh, which had been created in 1941 and led ever since by Ho Chi Minh, a communist educated in Paris and Moscow, and a fervent Vietnamese nationalist. The Vietminh had fought against Japan throughout World War II (unlike the French colonial officials who had remained in Vietnam during the war—as representatives of the Vichy regime—and had collaborated with the Japanese). In the fall of 1945, after the collapse of Japan and before the Western powers had time to return, the Vietminh declared Vietnam an independent nation and set up a nationalist government under Ho Chi Minh in Hanoi.

Ho had worked closely during the war with American intelligence forces in Indochina in fighting the Japanese; he apparently considered the United States something like an ally. When the war ended in 1945, he began writing President Truman asking for support in his struggle against the French. He received no reply to his letters, probably because no one in the State Department had heard of him. At the same time, Truman was under heavy pressure from both the British and the French to support France in its effort to reassert its control over Vietnam. The French argued that without Vietnam, their domestic economy would collapse. And since the economic revival of Western Europe was quickly becoming one of the Truman administration's top priorities, the United States did nothing to stop (although, at first, also relatively little to encourage) the French as they moved back into Vietnam in 1946 and began a struggle with the Vietminh to reestablish control over the country.

At first, the French had little difficulty reestablishing control. They drove Ho Chi Minh out of Hanoi and into hiding in the countryside; and in 1949, they established a nominally independent national government under the leadership of the former emperor, Bao Dai—an ineffectual, westernized playboy unable to assert any real independent authority. The real power remained in the hands of the French. But the Vietminh continued to challenge the French-dominated regime and slowly increased its control over large areas of the countryside. The French appealed to the United States for support; and in February 1950, the Truman administration formally recognized the Bao Dai regime and agreed to provide it with direct military and economic aid.

For the next four years, during what has become known as the First Indochina War, Truman and then Eisenhower continued to support the French military campaign against the Vietminh; by 1954, by some calculations, the United States was paying 80 percent of France's war costs. But the war went badly for the French anyway. Finally, late in 1953, Vietminh forces engaged the French in a major battle in the far northwest corner of the country, at Dien Bien Phu, an isolated and almost indefensible site. The French were surrounded, and the battle turned into a prolonged and horrible siege, with the French position steadily deteriorating. It was at this point that the Eisenhower administration decided not to intervene to save the French (see pp. 811–812). The defense of Dien Bien Phu collapsed and the French government decided the time had come to get out. The First Indochina War had come to an end.

Geneva and the Two Vietnams

An international conference at Geneva, planned many months before to settle the Korean dispute and other controversies, now took up the fate of Vietnam as well. The United States was only indirectly involved in the Vietnam phase of the Geneva conference. Secretary of State Dulles, who did not really believe in negotiating with communists, reluctantly attended (described by one observer as a "puritan in a house of ill repute") but left early; the United States never signed the accords. Even so, the Geneva conference produced an agreement to end the Vietnam conflict. There would be an immediate cease-fire in the war; Vietnam would be temporarily partitioned along the 17th parallel, with the Vietminh in control of North Vietnam, and a pro-Western regime in control of the South. In 1956, elections would be held to reunite the country under a single government.

The partition of Vietnam was, therefore, an essentially artificial one. But there were, in fact, real and important differences between North and South Vietnam. North Vietnam, the area now to be controlled by the Vietminh, was the heart of traditional Vietnamese society, the area where French influence had been the weakest. Hence the North had remained a reasonably stable, reasonably homogeneous culture, most of whose people lived in very close-knit, traditional villages. Northern Vietnam was also the poorest region of the country—overpopulated, plagued by a serious maldistribution of scarce land, and hit by a serious famine at the end of the war. The Vietminh had worked effectively to alleviate the great famine and had won strong popular allegiance to the regime as a result. (Later, in the early 1950s, it launched a disastrous land reform policy, which it soon repudiated.) The Hanoi government was also strengthened by the mass exodus, in 1954, at the time of the partition, of many of the Catholics and others in the north who might have opposed them had they stayed. The North Vietnamese were passionately committed to the unification of the

THE WAR IN VIETNAM AND INDOCHINA, 1964–1975

CHINA

Lao Cai

Than Uyen

Red River

Yen Bay

BURMA

Dienbienphu

NORTH VIETNAM

Hanoi
Red River
Delta

Haiphong

Gulf of Tonkin

Pak Seng

Luang Prabang

Ban Ban

Plain of Jars

Hainan

Vang Vieng

L
A
O
S

Vinh

Vientiane

Mekong River

Udon Thani

Phanom

Dong Hoi
Partition Line 1954
Vinh Linh
DMZ (Demilitarized Zone)

QUANG TRI
PROVINCE

Khesanh

Hue
Phu Bai

Da Nang

Hoi An

THAILAND

FRIENDSHIP HIGHWAY

Takhli

Don Muang

Udon Ratchathani

Lop Buri

Ratchasima

Tamky

Chulai

My Lai
Quang Ngai

Dak To

South China Sea

Kontum

Plateau of Kontum

Pleiku

Ankhe

Quinhon

Bangkok

Angkor Wat

Battambang

Tonle Sap

CAMBODIA

Mekong River

Plateau of
Darlac

Ban Me Thout

Nhatrang

Da Lat

Camranh Bay

Phanrang

Kompong
Cham

Bo Duc

SOUTH
VIETNAM

Sattahip

Phnom
Penh

Prey Veng

Tay Ninh

Ben Cat

Gulf of Thailand

1970:
U.S. and South
Vietnam troops
entered Viet Cong
strongholds
inside Cambodia

Tan Son Nhut
Airbase

Bienhua
Saigon

Sihanoukville

Vung Tau

Rach Gia

Cantho

Mekong Delta

Quan Long

Ca Mau
Peninsula

Con Son

0   150 Miles

0   150 Kilometers

■   U.S. bases

←   U.S. and South Vietnam
    invasion of Cambodia

←   Ho Chi Minh Trail
    (communist supply route)

nation, a commitment with deep roots in Vietnamese history.

South Vietnam, by contrast, was a much more recently settled area. Until the early nineteenth century, in fact, very few Vietnamese had lived there; most of the sparse population had consisted of Khmer (Cambodians). Even in the 1950s, most of its people had been there only three generations or less. For many years it had been something like the American West in the nineteenth century—the place where adventurous, or opportunistic, or disenchanted people from the poor, overpopulated North would move in search of a new beginning, and in search of land (which was scarce in the north but plentiful in the south). It was a looser, more heterogeneous, more individualistic society. It was highly factionalized—religiously, politically, and ethnically—with powerful sects (and even a powerful mafia) all competing for power. It was also more prosperous and fertile than the North. It was not overpopulated. It had experienced no famine. It was the only region of the country producing a surplus for export.

South Vietnam had no legacy of strong commitment to the Vietminh and much less fervent commitment to national unification. It was the area where the influence of the French (their language, culture, and values) had been strongest and where there was a substantial, westernized middle class. It was, in other words, a society much more difficult to unite and to govern than the society of the North.

America and Diem

As soon as the Geneva Accords established the partition, the French finally left Vietnam altogether. The United States almost immediately stepped into the vacuum and became the principal benefactor of the new government in the South, led by Ngo Dinh Diem.

Diem was an aristocratic Catholic from central Vietnam, an outsider in the South. But he was also a nationalist, uncontaminated by collaboration with the French. And he was, for a time, apparently successful. With the help of the American CIA, Diem waged an effective campaign against some of the powerful religious sects and the South Vietnamese mafia, which had challenged the authority of the central government. As a result, the United States came to regard Diem as a powerful and impressive alternative to Ho Chi Minh. Lyndon Johnson once called him the "Churchill of Southeast Asia."

The American government supported Diem's refusal in 1956 to permit the elections called for by the Geneva Accords, reasoning, almost certainly correctly,

that Ho Chi Minh would easily win any such election. Ho could count on 100 percent of the vote in the north, with its much larger population, and at least some support in the south. In the meantime, the United States poured military and economic aid into South Vietnam. By 1956, it was the second largest recipient of American military aid in the world, after Korea.

Diem's early successes in suppressing the sects in Vietnam led him in 1959 to begin a similar campaign to eliminate the Vietminh supporters who had stayed behind in the south after the partition. He was quite successful for a time, so successful in fact that the North Vietnamese found it necessary to respond. A new policy emanating from Moscow beginning in 1959, emphasizing communist wars of national liberation (as opposed to direct Soviet confrontations with the United States and NATO), also encouraged Ho Chi Minh to resume his armed struggle for national unification. In 1959, the Vietminh cadres in the south created the National Liberation Front (NLF), known to many Americans as the Viet Cong—an organization closely allied with the North Vietnamese government. It was committed to overthrowing the "puppet regime" of Diem and reuniting the nation. In 1960, under orders from Hanoi, and with both material and manpower support from North Vietnam, the NLF began military operations in the South. This marked the beginning of the Second Indochina War.

By 1961, NLF forces were very successfully destabilizing the Diem regime. They were killing over 4,000 government officials a year (mostly village leaders) and establishing effective control over many areas of the countryside. Diem was also by now losing the support of many other groups in South Vietnam, and he was even losing support within his own military. In 1963, the Diem regime precipitated a major crisis by trying to discipline and repress the South Vietnamese Buddhists in an effort to make Catholicism the dominant religion of the country. The Buddhists began to stage enormous antigovernment demonstrations; and after Diem launched a series of heavy-handed military and police actions against them—which included several massacres of demonstrators and violent government raids on their sacred pagodas—the demonstrations grew much larger. Several Buddhist monks doused themselves with gasoline, sat cross-legged in the streets of downtown Saigon, and set themselves on fire—in view of photographers and television cameras.

The Buddhist crisis was alarming and embarrassing to the Kennedy administration. It caused the American government to reconsider its commitment to Diem—although not to the survival of South Vietnam. Kennedy had greatly increased the number of American personnel and the level of American assis-

THE VIETNAM COMMITMENT

IN 1965 THE DEPARTMENT of Defense released a film intended for American soldiers about to embark for service in Vietnam and designed to explain why the United States had found it necessary to commit so many lives and resources to the defense of a small and distant land. The film was entitled *Why Vietnam?*—a question many Americans have pondered and debated in the three decades since. The debate has proceeded on two levels. At one level is an effort to assess the broad objectives Americans believed they were pursuing in Vietnam. At another is an effort to explain how and why policymakers made the specific decisions that led to the American commitment.

The Defense Department film itself offered one answer to the question of America's broad objectives, an answer that for a time most Americans tended to accept: The United States was fighting in Vietnam to defend freedom and stop aggression; and it was fighting in Vietnam to prevent the spread of communism into a new area of the world, to protect not only Vietnam but also the other nations of the Pacific that would soon be threatened if Vietnam itself were to fall. This explanation—that America intervened in Vietnam to defend its ideals and its legitimate interests—continued to attract support well after the war ended. Journalist Norman Podhoretz's 1982 book *Why We Were in Vietnam* argued that America was in Vietnam "to save the Southern half of that country from the evils of communism" and that the tragic events in Indochina since 1975

have proven the essential morality of the American cause. Political scientist Guenter Lewy contended, in *America in Vietnam* (1978), that the United States entered Vietnam to help an ally combat "foreign aggression." R. B. Smith argued that Vietnam was a vital American interest, that the global concerns of the United States required a commitment there. And historian Ernest R. May stated: "The paradox is that the Vietnam War, so often condemned by its opponents as hideously immoral, may well have been the most moral or at least the most selfless war in all of American history. For the impulse guiding it was not to defeat an enemy or to serve a national interest; it was simply not to abandon friends."

Others argued that America's broad objectives in Vietnam were less altruistic, that the intervention was a form of imperialism—part of a larger effort by the United States after World War II to impose a particular political and economic order on the world. "The Vietnam War," historian Gabriel Kolko wrote in *Anatomy of a War* (1985), "was for the United States the culmination of its frustrating postwar effort to merge its arms and politics to halt and reverse the emergence of states and social systems opposed to the international order Washington sought to establish." Economist Robert Heilbroner, writing in 1967, saw the American intent as somewhat more defensive; the intervention in Vietnam was a response to "a fear of losing our place in the sun," to a fear that a communist victory "would signal the end of capitalism as the dominant world order and would force the acknowledgment that America no longer constituted the model on which the future of world civilization would be mainly based."

---

tance to the anticommunist regime, and he was unwilling to permit South Vietnam to fall. American officials pressured Diem to reform his government, but Diem made no significant concessions. As a result, in the fall of 1963, Kennedy gave his tacit approval to a plot by a group of South Vietnamese generals to topple Diem. In early November 1963, the generals staged

the coup, assassinated Diem and his brother and principal adviser, Ngo Dinh Nhu (killings the United States had not wanted or expected), and established the first of a series of new governments, which were, for over three years, even less stable than the one they had overthrown. A few weeks after the coup, John Kennedy too was dead.

WHERE HISTORIANS DISAGREE

Those who looked less at the nation's broad objectives than at the internal workings of the policymaking process likewise produced competing explanations. Journalist David Halberstam's *The Best and the Brightest* (1972) argued that policymakers deluded themselves into thinking they could achieve their goals in Vietnam by ignoring, suppressing, or dismissing the information that might have suggested otherwise. The foreign policy leaders of the Kennedy and Johnson administrations were so committed to the idea of American activism and success that they refused to consider the possibility of failure; the Vietnam disaster was thus, at least in part, a result of the arrogance of the nation's leaders.

Larry Berman, a political scientist, offered a somewhat different view in *Planning a Tragedy* (1982). Lyndon Johnson never believed that American prospects in Vietnam were bright or that a real victory was within sight, Berman argued. Johnson was not misled by his advisers. He committed American troops to the war in Vietnam in 1965 not because he expected to win but because he feared that allowing Vietnam to fall would ruin him politically. To do otherwise, Johnson believed, would destroy his hopes for winning approval of his Great Society legislation at home.

Leslie H. Gelb (who as an official in the Defense Department in the 1960s directed the writing of the official study of the war that became known as the Pentagon Papers) produced another, related explanation for American intervention, which saw the roots of the involvement in the larger imperatives of the American foreign policy system. In *The Irony of Vietnam: the System Worked*, published in 1979 and written in collaboration with political scientist Richard K. Betts, Gelb argued that intervention in Vietnam was the logical perhaps even inevitable result of a political and bureaucratic order shaped by certain ideological assumptions. The American foreign policy system was wedded to the doctrine of containment and operated, therefore, in response to a single, overriding imperative: the need to prevent the expansion of communism.

The United States, Gelb maintained, stumbled into a commitment to a shaky government in South Vietnam in the 1950s, and the unvarying policy of every subsequent administration until 1975 was to do what was necessary to prevent the collapse of that government. They were doing so not because they anticipated victory but because they saw no alternative. However high the costs of intervention, they believed, the costs of not intervening, of allowing South Vietnam to fall, would be higher. At every step, American presidents did the minimum they thought necessary to stave off the collapse of South Vietnam. In the 1950s and early 1960s, that meant modest economic and military assistance. In the mid-1960s, as the military situation worsened, the same commitment required the introduction of American troops in large numbers. Only when the national and international political situation had shifted to the point where it was possible for American policymakers to reassess the costs of the commitment—to conclude that the costs of allowing Vietnam to fall were less than the costs of continuing the commitment (a shift that began to occur in the early 1970s)—was it possible for the United States to begin disengaging.

From Aid to Intervention

Lyndon Johnson thus inherited what was already a substantial American commitment to the survival of an anticommunist South Vietnam. During his first two years in office, he expanded that commitment into a full-scale American war. Why he did so has long been a subject of debate. (See "Where Historians Disagree," above.)

Many factors played a role in Johnson's decision. But the most obvious explanation is that the new president faced many pressures to expand the American involvement and only a very few to limit it. As the untested successor to a revered and martyred president, he felt obliged to prove his worthiness for the office by continuing the policies of his predecessor. Aid to South Vietnam had been one of the most prominent of those policies. Johnson also felt it necessary to retain in his administration many of the important figures of the Kennedy years. In doing so, he surrounded himself with a group of foreign policy advisers— Secretary of State Dean Rusk, Secretary of Defense Robert McNamara, National Security Adviser McGeorge Bundy, and others—who firmly believed that the United States had an obligation to resist communism in Vietnam. A compliant Congress raised little protest to, and indeed at one point openly endorsed, Johnson's use of executive powers to lead the nation into war. And for several years at least, public opinion remained firmly behind him—in part because Barry Goldwater's bellicose remarks about the war during the 1964 campaign made Johnson seem by comparison to be a moderate on the issue.

Above all, intervention in South Vietnam was fully consistent with nearly twenty years of American foreign policy. An anticommunist ally was appealing to the United States for assistance; all the assumptions of the containment doctrine, as it had come to be defined by the 1960s, seemed to require the nation to oblige. Vietnam, Johnson believed, was a test of American willingness to fight communist aggression, a test he was determined not to fail.

During his first months in office, Johnson expanded the American involvement in Vietnam only slightly, sending an additional 5,000 military advisers there and preparing to send 5,000 more. Then, early in August 1964, the president announced that American destroyers on patrol in international waters in the Gulf of Tonkin had been attacked by North Vietnamese torpedo boats. Later information raised serious doubts as to whether the administration reported the attacks accurately. At the time, however, virtually no one questioned Johnson's portrayal of the incident as a serious act of aggression, or his insistence that the United States must respond. By a vote of 416 to 0 in the House and 88 to 2 in the Senate, Congress hurriedly passed the Gulf of Tonkin Resolution, which authorized the president to "take all necessary measures" to protect American forces and "prevent further aggression" in Southeast Asia. The resolution became, in Johnson's view at least, an open-ended legal authorization for escalation of the conflict.

With the South Vietnamese leadership still in disarray, more and more of the burden of opposition to the Viet Cong fell on the United States. In February 1965, seven marines died when communist forces attacked an American military base at Pleiku. Johnson retaliated by ordering American bombings of the north, which attempted to destroy the depots and transportation lines responsible for the flow of North Vietnamese soldiers and supplies into South Vietnam. The bombing continued intermittently until 1972. A month later, in March 1965, two battalions of American marines landed at Da Nang in South Vietnam. There were now more than 100,000 American troops in Vietnam.

Four months later, the president finally admitted that the character of the war had changed. American soldiers would now, he announced, begin playing an active combat role in the conflict. By the end of the year, there were more than 180,000 American combat troops in Vietnam; in 1966, that number doubled; and by the end of 1967, there were over 500,000 American soldiers there—along with a considerable number of civilian personnel working in various capacities and many American women (some enlisted, some not) who worked as nurses in military hospitals. In the meantime, the air war had intensified; ultimately the tonnage of bombs dropped on North Vietnam would exceed that in all theaters during World War II. And American casualties were mounting. In 1961, 14 Americans had died in Vietnam. By the spring of 1966, more than 4,000 Americans had been killed.

Yet the gains resulting from the carnage were negligible. The United States had finally succeeded in 1965 in creating a reasonably stable government in the south under General Nguyen Van Thieu. But the new regime was hardly less corrupt or brutal than its predecessors, and no more able than they to establish its authority in its own countryside. The Viet Cong, not the Thieu regime, controlled the majority of South Vietnam's villages and hamlets.

The Quagmire

For more than seven years, American combat forces remained bogged down in a war that the United States was never able either to win or fully to understand. Combating a foe whose strength lay less in weaponry than in its infiltration of the population, the United States responded with heavy-handed technological warfare designed for conventional battles against conventional armies. American forces succeeded in winning most of the major battles in which they became engaged. There were astounding (if not always reliable) weekly casualty figures showing that far more communists than Americans were dying in combat. There was a continuous stream of optimistic reports from American military commanders, government officials, and others—including a famous statement of Secretary of Defense McNamara that he could see "the

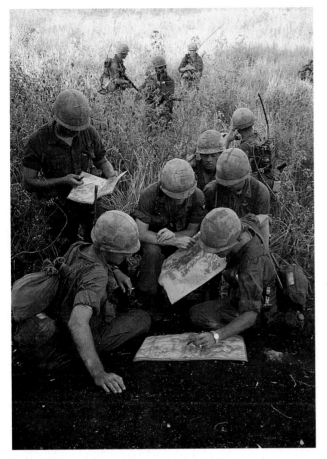

ON PATROL IN VIETNAM
A platoon of American soldiers tries to locate its position as it patrols the Vietnamese countryside in 1966. Among the many things that distinguished the Vietnam War from other conflicts in which Americans have fought was the difficulty of deciphering a terrain unlike any in the United States and the difficulty in locating, or even identifying, the enemy. *(Jim Pickerell/ Black Star)*

light at the end of the tunnel." But if the war was not actually being lost, neither was it being won.

Central to the American war effort was a commitment to what the military called "attrition," a strategy premised on the belief that the United States could inflict so many casualties and so much damage on the enemy that eventually they would be unable and unwilling to continue the struggle. But the attrition strategy failed because the North Vietnamese proved willing to commit many more soldiers to the conflict than the United States had expected (and many more than America itself was willing to send).

It failed, too, because the United States relied heavily on its bombing of the north to eliminate the com-

munists' war-making capacity. American bombers struck at strategic targets (factories, bridges, railroads, shipyards, oil storage depots, etc.) in North Vietnam to weaken the material capacity of the communists to continue the war; and they bombed jungle areas of Vietnam, Laos, and Cambodia to cut off the "Ho Chi Minh Trail," the infiltration routes by which Hanoi sent troops and supplies into the south. In addition, the Americans hoped bombing would weaken the will of North Vietnam to continue the war.

By the end of 1967, virtually every identifiable target of any strategic importance in North Vietnam had been destroyed. The bombing had badly damaged the North Vietnamese economy, killed many soldiers and civilians, and made life difficult for those who survived, but it had produced none of the effects that the United States had expected. North Vietnam was not a modern, industrial society; it had few of the sorts of targets against which bombing is effective. And in any case, the North Vietnamese responded to the air raids with enormous ingenuity: they created a great network of underground tunnels, shops, and factories. They also secured increased aid from the Soviet Union and China. Infiltration of the south was unaffected; the North Vietnamese just kept moving the Ho Chi Minh Trail. Nor did the bombing weaken North Vietnam's will to continue fighting. On the contrary, it seemed to increase the nation's resolve and strengthen its hatred of the United States. As one North Vietnamese leader later explained: "There was extraordinary fervor then. The Americans thought that the more bombs they dropped, the quicker we would fall to our knees and surrender. But the bombs heightened rather than dampened our spirit."

Another crucial part of the American strategy was the "pacification" program, whose purpose was to push the Viet Cong from particular regions and then "pacify" those regions by winning the "hearts and minds" of the people. Routing the Viet Cong was often possible, but the subsequent pacification was more difficult. American forces were not adept at establishing the same kind of rapport with provincial Vietnamese that the Viet Cong had created; and the American military never gave that part of the program a very high priority in any case. Gradually, the pacification program gave way to a more heavy-handed relocation strategy, through which American troops uprooted villagers from their homes, sent them fleeing to refugee camps or into the cities (producing by 1967 more than 3 million refugees), and then destroyed the vacated villages and surrounding countryside. Saturation bombings (using conventional weapons and such inflammatory devices as napalm), bulldozing of settlements, chemical defoliation of fields and jungles—all were designed to eliminate possible Viet Cong sanctuaries. But the Viet Cong responded by moving to new sanctuaries elsewhere. The futility of the United States effort was suggested by the statement of an American officer after flattening one such hamlet that it had been "necessary to destroy [the village] in order to save it."

As the war dragged on and victory remained elusive, some American officers and officials began to urge the president to expand the military efforts. Some argued for heavier bombing and increased troop strength; others insisted that the United States attack communist enclaves in surrounding countries; a few began to urge the use of nuclear weapons. The Johnson administration, however, resisted. Unwilling to abandon its commitment to South Vietnam for fear of destroying American "credibility" in the world, the government was also unwilling to expand the war too far, for fear of provoking direct intervention by the Chinese, the Soviets, or both. In the meantime, the president began to encounter additional obstacles and frustrations at home.

The War at Home

As late as the end of 1965, few Americans, and even fewer influential ones, had protested the American involvement in Vietnam. But as the war dragged on and its futility began to become apparent, political support for it began to erode. A series of "teach-ins" on university campuses, beginning at the University of Michigan in 1965, sparked a national debate over the war before such debate developed inside the government itself. Such pacifist organizations as the American Friends Service Committee and the Women's International League for Peace and Freedom organized early protests. By the end of 1967, American students opposed to the war had become a significant political force. Enormous peace marches in New York, Washington, D.C., and other cities drew broad public attention to the antiwar movement. In the meantime, a growing number of journalists, particularly reporters who had spent time in Vietnam, helped sustain the movement with their frank revelations about the brutality and apparent futility of the war.

The growing chorus of popular protest soon began to stimulate opposition to the war from within the government. Senator J. William Fulbright of Arkansas, chairman of the powerful Senate Foreign Relations Committee, turned against the war and in January 1966 began to stage highly publicized and occasionally televised congressional hearings to air criticisms of it. Distinguished figures such as George F. Kennan and retired General James Gavin testified against the conflict,

giving opposition to the war greater respectability in the minds of many Americans generally unwilling to question the government or the military. Other members of Congress joined Fulbright in opposing Johnson's policies—including, in 1967, Robert F. Kennedy, brother of the slain president, now a senator from New York. Even within the administration, the consensus seemed to be crumbling. Robert McNamara, who had done much to help extend the American involvement in Vietnam, quietly left the government, disillusioned, in 1968. His successor as secretary of defense, Clark Clifford, became a quiet but powerful voice within the administration on behalf of a cautious scaling down of the commitment.

In the meantime, the American economy was beginning to suffer. Johnson's commitment to fighting the war while continuing his Great Society reforms—his promise of "guns and butter"—proved impossible to maintain. The inflation rate, which had remained at 2 percent through most of the early 1960s, rose to 3 percent in 1967, 4 percent in 1968, and 6 percent in 1969. In August 1967, Johnson asked Congress for a tax increase—a 10 percent surcharge that was widely labeled a "war tax"—which he knew was necessary if the nation was to avoid even more ruinous inflation. In return, congressional conservatives demanded and received a $6 billion reduction in the funding for Great Society programs.

THE TRAUMAS OF 1968

By the end of 1967, the twin crises of the war in Vietnam and the deteriorating racial situation at home, crises that fed upon and inflamed each other, had produced profound social and political tensions. In the course of 1968, those tensions seemed suddenly to burst to the surface and to threaten the nation with genuine chaos. Not since World War II had the United States experienced so profound a sense of crisis.

The Tet Offensive

On January 31, 1968, the first day of the Vietnamese New Year (Tet), communist forces launched an enormous, concerted attack on American strongholds throughout South Vietnam. A few cities, most notably Hue, fell to the communists. Others suffered major disruptions. But what made the Tet offensive so shocking to the American people, who saw vivid reports of it on television, was the sight of communist forces in the heart of Saigon, setting off bombs, shooting down

South Vietnamese officials and troops, and holding down fortified areas (including, briefly, the grounds of the American embassy).

The Tet offensive also suggested to the American public something of the brutality of the war in Vietnam. In the midst of the fighting, television cameras recorded the sight of a captured Viet Cong soldier being led up to a South Vietnamese officer in the streets of Saigon. Without a word, the officer pulled out his pistol and shot the young man in the head, leaving him lying dead in the street, his blood pouring onto the pavement. No single event did more to undermine support for the war in the United States.

American forces soon dislodged the Viet Cong from most of the positions they had seized, and the Tet offensive in the end cost the communists such appalling casualties that they were significantly weakened for months to come. Indeed, the Tet defeats permanently depleted the ranks of the NLF and forced North Vietnamese troops to take on a much larger share of the subsequent fighting. But all that had little impact on American opinion. Tet may have been a military victory for the United States; but it was a political defeat for the administration, a defeat from which it would never fully recover.

In the following weeks, opposition to the war grew substantially. Leading newspapers and magazines, television commentators, and mainstream politicians began taking public stands in favor of de-escalation of the conflict. Within weeks of the Tet offensive, public opposition to the war had almost doubled. And Johnson's personal popularity rating had slid to 35 percent, the lowest of any president since Harry Truman.

The Political Challenge

Beginning in the summer of 1967, dissident Democrats (led by the talented activist Allard Lowenstein) tried to mobilize support behind an antiwar candidate who would challenge Lyndon Johnson in the 1968 primaries. When Robert Kennedy declined their invitation, they turned to Senator Eugene McCarthy of Minnesota. A brilliantly orchestrated campaign by Lowenstein and thousands of young volunteers in the New Hampshire primary produced a startling showing by McCarthy in March; he nearly defeated the president.

A few days later, Robert Kennedy finally entered the campaign, embittering many McCarthy supporters, but bringing his own substantial strength among blacks, poor people, and workers to the antiwar cause. Polls showed the president trailing badly in the next scheduled primary, in Wisconsin. Indeed, public animosity toward the president was now so intense that Johnson did not even dare leave the White House to

campaign. On March 31, Johnson went on television to announce a limited halt in the bombing of North Vietnam—his first major concession to the antiwar forces—and, much more surprising, his withdrawal from the presidential contest.

For a moment, it seemed as though the antiwar forces had won. Robert Kennedy quickly established himself as the champion of the Democratic primaries, winning one election after another. In the meantime, however, Vice President Hubert Humphrey, with the support of President Johnson, entered the contest and began to attract the support of party leaders and of the many delegations that were selected not by popular primaries but by state party organizations. He soon appeared to be the front-runner in the race.

The King and Kennedy Assassinations

In the midst of this bitter political battle, in which the war had been the dominant issue, attention suddenly turned back to the nation's bitter racial conflicts. On April 4, Martin Luther King, Jr., who had traveled to Memphis, Tennessee, to lend his support to striking black sanitation workers in the city, was shot and killed while standing on the balcony of his motel. The assassin, James Earl Ray, who was captured days later in London and eventually convicted, had no apparent motive. Later evidence suggested that he had been hired by others to do the killing, but he himself has never revealed the identity of his employers.

King's tragic death produced an outpouring of grief matched in recent memory only by the reaction to the death of John Kennedy. Among American blacks, it also produced anger. In the days after the assassination, major riots broke out in more than sixty American cities. Forty-three people died; more than 3,000 suffered injuries; as many as 27,000 people were arrested.

For two months following the death of King, Robert Kennedy continued his campaign for the presidential nomination. Late in the night of June 6, he appeared in the ballroom of a Los Angeles hotel to acknowledge his victory in that day's California primary. As he left the ballroom after his victory statement, Sirhan Sirhan, a young Palestinian apparently enraged by pro-Israeli remarks Kennedy had recently made, emerged from a crowd and shot him in the head. Early the next morning, Kennedy died.

By the time of his death, Robert Kennedy—who earlier in his career had been widely considered a cold, ruthless agent of his more appealing brother—had emerged as a figure of enormous popular appeal. More than John Kennedy, Robert identified his hopes with the American "underclass"—with blacks, Hispanics, Indians, the poor—and with the many American liberals who were coming to believe that the problems of such groups demanded attention. Indeed, Robert Kennedy, much more than John, shaped what some would later call the "Kennedy legacy," a set of ideas that would for a time become central to American liberalism: the fervent commitment to using government to help the powerless. In addition, Robert had an impassioned following among many people who saw in him (and his family) the kind of glamour and hopefulness they had come, at least in retrospect, to identify with the martyred president. His campaign appearances inspired outbursts of public enthusiasm rarely seen in political life. The passions Kennedy had aroused made his violent death a particularly shattering experience for many Americans.

The presidential campaign continued gloomily during the last weeks before the convention. Hubert Humphrey, who had seemed likely to win the nomination even before Robert Kennedy's death, now faced only minor opposition—despite the embittered claims of many Democrats that Humphrey would simply continue the bankrupt policies of the Johnson administration. The approaching Democratic Convention, therefore, began to take on the appearance of an exercise in futility; and antiwar activists, despairing of winning any victories within the convention, began to plan major demonstrations outside it.

When the Democrats finally gathered in Chicago in August, even the most optimistic observers were predicting a turbulent convention. Inside the hall, delegates bitterly debated an antiwar plank in the party platform that both Kennedy and McCarthy supporters favored. Miles away, in a downtown park, thousands of antiwar protesters were staging demonstrations. On the third night of the convention, as the delegates were beginning their balloting on the now virtually inevitable nomination of Hubert Humphrey, demonstrators and police clashed in a bloody riot in the streets of Chicago. Hundreds of protesters were injured as police attempted to disperse them with tear gas and billy clubs. Aware that the violence was being televised to the nation, the demonstrators taunted the authorities with the chant, "The whole world is watching!" And Hubert Humphrey, who had spent years dreaming of becoming his party's candidate for president, received a nomination that appeared at the time to be almost worthless.

The Conservative Response

The turbulent events of 1968 persuaded many observers that American society was in the throes of revolutionary change. In fact, however, the response of most Americans to the turmoil was a conservative one.

CHICAGO, 1968
Demonstrators climb on a statue in a Chicago park during the 1968 Democratic National Convention, protesting both the Vietnam War and the harsh treatment they themselves had received from Mayor Richard Daley's Chicago police. *(Dennis Brack/Black Star)*

The most visible sign of the conservative backlash was the surprising success of the campaign of George Wallace for the presidency. Wallace had established himself in 1963 as one of the nation's leading spokesmen for the defense of segregation when, as governor of Alabama, he had attempted tc block the admission of black students to the University of Alabama. In 1964, he had run in a few Democratic presidential primaries and had done surprising well, even in several states outside the South. In 1968, he became a third-party candidate for president, basing his campaign on a host of conservative grievances, not all of them connected to race. He denounced the forced busing of students, the proliferation of government regulations and social

SIGNIFICANT EVENTS

1959 Soviet Comintern urges wars of "national liberation" in the Third World

National Liberation Front (NLF) created in Vietnam

1960 John F. Kennedy elected president

Greensboro sit-ins

War resumes in Vietnam

1961 Freedom rides

United States supports failed invasion of Bay of Pigs

Kennedy meets Khrushchev in Vienna

Berlin Wall erected

Peace Corps established

Alliance for Progress established

1962 Steel price increase provokes controversy

Kennedy proposes tax cut to stimulate economy

Desegregation crisis at University of Mississippi

Cuban missile crisis

1963 Martin Luther King, Jr., begins Birmingham campaign

Desegregation crisis at University of Alabama

Kennedy proposes civil rights bill

March on Washington

Test ban treaty signed

Buddhist crisis in Vietnam; Diem toppled by coup

Kennedy assassinated; Lyndon B. Johnson becomes president

1964 Johnson launches war on poverty

Congress passes tax cut

"Freedom summer" campaign in Mississippi

Congress passes Civil Rights Act

Gulf of Tonkin Resolution passed

United States begins bombing of North Vietnam

Johnson elected president by record margin

1965 Medicare enacted

Elementary and Secondary Education Act passed

Selma campaign for voting rights

Race riot breaks out in Watts, Los Angeles

Malcolm X publishes *Autobiography*

Malcolm X assassinated

Congress passes Voting Rights Act

United States intervenes in Dominican Republic

American combat troops sent to Vietnam

Antiwar activities begin on university campuses

Immigration Reform Act passed

1966 Medicaid enacted

King leads Chicago campaign

Senate Foreign Relations Committee holds hearings on Vietnam

1967 Johnson requests tax increase

Race riot breaks out in Detroit

Antiwar movement intensifies

1968 Department of Labor issues affirmative action rules

Viet Cong launch Tet offensive

Johnson withdraws from presidential contest

Martin Luther King, Jr., assassinated

Racial violence breaks out in American cities

Robert Kennedy assassinated

Demonstrators clash with police at Democratic National Convention

George Wallace launches third-party presidential campaign

Richard M. Nixon elected president

programs, and the permissiveness of authorities toward race riots and antiwar demonstrations. There was never any serious chance that Wallace would win the election; but his standing in the polls at times rose to over 20 percent.

A more effective effort to mobilize the "silent majority" in favor of order and stability was under way within the Republican Party. Richard Nixon, whose political career had seemed at an end after his losses in the presidential race of 1960 and a California gubernatorial campaign two years later, reemerged as the preeminent spokesman for what he called "Middle America." Nixon recognized that many Americans were tired of hearing about their obligations to the poor, tired of hearing about the sacrifices necessary to achieve racial justice, tired of judicial reforms that seemed designed to help criminals. By offering a vision of stability, law and order, government retrenchment, and "peace with honor" in Vietnam, he easily captured the nomination of his party for the presidency. And after the spectacle of the Democratic Convention, he enjoyed a commanding lead in the polls as the November election approached.

That lead diminished greatly in the last weeks before the voting. Old doubts about Nixon's character continued to haunt the Republican candidate. A skillful last-minute surge by Hubert Humphrey, who managed to restore a tenuous unity to the Democratic Party, narrowed the gap further. And the Wallace campaign appeared to be hurting the Republicans more than the Democrats. In the end, however, Nixon eked out a victory almost as narrow as his defeat in 1960. He received 43.4 percent of the popular vote to Humphrey's 42.7 percent (a margin of only about 500,000 votes), and 301 electoral votes to Humphrey's 191. George Wallace, who like most third-party candidates faded in the last weeks of the campaign, still managed to poll 13.5 percent of the popular vote

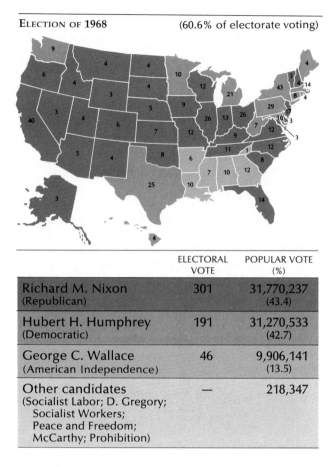

ELECTION OF 1968 (60.6% of electorate voting)

	ELECTORAL VOTE	POPULAR VOTE (%)
Richard M. Nixon (Republican)	301	31,770,237 (43.4)
Hubert H. Humphrey (Democratic)	191	31,270,533 (42.7)
George C. Wallace (American Independence)	46	9,906,141 (13.5)
Other candidates (Socialist Labor; D. Gregory; Socialist Workers; Peace and Freedom; McCarthy; Prohibition)	—	218,347

and to carry five southern states with a total of 46 electoral ballots—the best showing by a third-party candidate since the 1920s. Nixon had not won a decisive personal mandate. But the election made clear that a majority of the American electorate was more interested in restoring stability than in promoting social change.

SUGGESTED READINGS

General Studies. William Chafe, *The Unfinished Journey: America Since World War II*, rev. ed. (1991). Godfrey Hodgson, *America in Our Time* (1976). Allen J. Matusow, *The Unraveling of America: A History of Liberalism in the 1960s* (1984). Charles R. Morris, *A Time of Passion* (1984). Theodore H. White, *America in Search of Itself* (1982).

Kennedy and Johnson. Vaughn D. Bornet, *The Presidency of Lyndon B. Johnson* (1983). Thomas Brown, *JFK: The History of an Image* (1988). David Burner, *John F. Kennedy and a New Generation* (1988). Robert Caro, *The Years of Lyndon B. Johnson: The Path to Power* (1982); *Means of Ascent* (1990). Paul K. Conkin, *Big Daddy from the Pedernales* (1986). Robert Dallek, *Lone Star*

Rising: Lyndon Johnson and His Times, 1908–1960 (1991). Ronnie Dugger, *The Politician* (1982). Edward J. Epstein, *Inquest* (1966); *Legend* (1978). Henry Fairlie, *The Kennedy Promise: The Politics of Expectation* (1973). Eric Goldman, *The Tragedy of Lyndon Johnson* (1968). Richard N. Goodwin, *Remembering America* (1988). Jim Heath, *Decade of Disillusionment* (1975). Henry Hurt, *Reasonable Doubt* (1985). Lyndon B. Johnson, *Vantage Point* (1971). Doris Kearns, *Lyndon Johnson and the American Dream* (1976). Donald Lord, *John F. Kennedy: The Politics of Confrontation and Conciliation* (1977). William Manchester, *The Death of a President* (1967). Bruce Miroff, *Pragmatic Illusions: The Presidential Politics of JFK* (1976). Lewis Paper, *The Promise and the Performance* (1975). Herbert Parmet, *Jack* (1980); *JFK* (1983). George

Reedy, *The Twilight of the Presidency* (1970). Richard Reeves, *President Kennedy* (1992). Thomas Reeves, *A Question of Character: The Life of John F. Kennedy in Image and Reality* (1991). Arthur M. Schlesinger, Jr. , *A Thousand Days* (1965). Theodore Sorensen, *Kennedy* (1965). Anthony Summers, *Conspiracy* (1980). Warren Commission, *The Report of the Warren Commission* (1964). Theodore H. White, *The Making of the President, 1960* (1961). Garry Wills, *The Kennedy Imprisonment* (1982).

Domestic Policies and Politics. Henry J. Aaron, *Politics and the Professors* (1978). Greg J. Duncan, *Years of Poverty, Years of Plenty* (1984). Mark Gelfand, *A Nation of Cities* (1975). James Giglio, *The Presidency of John F. Kennedy* (1991). Hugh Davis Graham, *Uncertain Trumpet* (1984). Robert H. Haveman, ed. , *A Decade of Federal Antipoverty Programs* (1977). Jim Heath, *John F. Kennedy and the Business Community* (1969). Daniel Knapp and Kenneth Polk, *Scouting the War on Poverty* (1971). Sar Levitan, *The Great Society's Poor Law* (1969). Sar Levitan and Robert Taggart, *The Promise of Greatness* (1976). Allen J. Matusow, *The Unraveling of America: A History of Liberalism in the 1960s* (1984). Charles Morris, *A Time of Passion* (1984). Charles Murray, *Losing Ground* (1984). Victor Navasky, *Kennedy Justice* (1971). James T. Patterson, *America's Struggle Against Poverty, 1900–1980* (1981). Frances Fox Piven and Richard Cloward, *Regulating the Poor* (1971). John E. Schwarz, *America's Hidden Success* (1983). James L. Sundquist, *Politics and Policy: The Eisenhower, Kennedy, and Johnson Years* (1968). Tom Wicker, *JFK and LBJ* (1968).

Race Relations. Taylor Branch, *Parting the Waters: America in the King Years* (1988). Carl Brauer, *John F. Kennedy and the Second Reconstruction* (1977). Paul Burstein, *Discrimination, Jobs, and Politics* (1985). James Button, *Black Violence: Political Impact of the 1960s Race Riots* (1978). Stokely Carmichael and Charles Hamilton, *Black Power* (1967). Clayborne Carson, *In Struggle: SNCC and the Black Awakening of the 1960s* (1981). William Chafe, *Civilities and Civil Rights: Greensboro, North Carolina, and the Black Struggle for Freedom* (1980). Joe R. Feagin and Harlan Hahn, *Ghetto Revolts* (1973). Robert Fogelson, *Violence as Protest* (1971). David Garrow, *Protest at Selma* (1978); *The FBI and Martin Luther King* (1981); *Bearing the Cross* (1986). Hugh Davis Graham, *The Civil Rights Era* (1990). Alex Haley, *The Autobiography of Malcolm X* (1966). Martin Luther King, Jr., *Why We Can't Wait* (1964). Steven Lawson, *Black Ballots: Voting Rights in the South, 1966–1969* (1976). Nicholas Lemann, *The Promised Land: The Great Black Migration and How It Changed America* (1991). David L. Lewis, *King: A Critical Biography* (1970). Doug McAdam, *Freedom Summer* (1988). Benjamin Muse, *The American Negro Revolution* (1969). *Report of the National Advisory Commission on Civil Disorders* (1968). Stephen Oates, *Let the Trumpet Sound* (1982). Harvard Sitkoff, *The Struggle for Black Equality, 1954–1992* (1992). Mark Stern, *Calculating Visions: Kennedy, Johnson and Civil Rights* (1992). Abigail Thernstrom, *Whose Votes Count? Affirmative Action and Minority Voting Rights* (1987). Harris Wofford, *Of Kennedy and Kings* (1980). Eugene Wolfenstein, *The Victims of Democracy: Malcolm X and the Black Revolution* (1981).

Foreign Policy. Elie Abel, *The Missile Crisis* (1966). Graham Allison, *Essence of Decision* (1971). Richard Barnet, *Intervention and Revolution* (1968). Michael Bechloss, *The Crisis Years* (1990).

McGeorge Bundy, *Danger and Survival* (1989). Warren Cohen, *Dean Rusk* (1980). Herbert Dinerstein, *The Making of a Missile Crisis* (1976). Bernard Firestone, *The Quest for Nuclear Stability* (1982). Louise Fitzsimmons, *The Kennedy Doctrine* (1972). Philip Geyelin, *Lyndon B. Johnson and the World* (1966). John Girling, *America and the Third World* (1980). Trumbull Higgins, *The Perfect Failure: Kennedy, Eisenhower, and the CIA at the Bay of Pigs* (1987). Roger Hilsman, *To Move a Nation* (1965). Haynes Johnson, *The Bay of Pigs* (1964). Robert Kennedy, *Thirteen Days* (1969). Dan Kurzman, *Santo Domingo* (1966). Walter LaFeber, *Inevitable Revolutions: The United States in Central America* (1985). Thomas J. McCormick, *America's Half Century: United States Foreign Policy in the Cold War* (1989). Richard D. Mahoney, *JFK: Ordeal in Africa* (1983). Gerald T. Rice, *The Bold Experiment: JFK's Peace Corps* (1985). Jerome Slater, *Intervention and Negotiation* (1970). Richard Walton, *Cold War and Counterrevolution* (1972). Peter Wyden, *Bay of Pigs* (1969).

Vietnam. Mark Baker, *Nam* (1982). Lawrence Baskir and William Strauss, *Chance and Circumstance* (1978). Larry Berman, *Planning a Tragedy* (1982); *Lyndon Johnson's War* (1989). Peter Braestrup, *Big Story* (1977; abridged ed. 1978). William Broyles, Jr. , *Brothers in Arms: A Journey from War to Peace* (1986). Philip Davidson, *Vietnam at War* (1991). Gloria Emerson, *Winners and Losers* (1976). Frances Fitzgerald, *Fire in the Lake* (1972). John Galloway, *The Gulf of Tonkin Resolution* (1970). Leslie Gelb and Richard Betts, *The Irony of Vietnam: The System Worked* (1979). David Halberstam, *The Best and the Brightest* (1972). Michael Herr, *Dispatches* (1977). George C. Herring, *America's Longest War*, rev. ed. (1986). George McT. Kahin, *Intervention* (1986). Stanley Karnow, *Vietnam* (1983). Alexander Kendrick, *The Wound Within* (1974). Gabriel Kolko, *The Anatomy of a War* (1985). Robert W. Komer, *Bureaucracy at War* (1986). David Levy, *The Debate over Vietnam* (1991). Guenter Lewy, *America in Vietnam* (1978). Don Oberdorfer, *Tet* (1971). Bruce C. Palmer, Jr., *The 25-Year War* (1984). *The Pentagon Papers*, Senator Gravel edition (1975). Norman Podhoretz, *Why We Were in Vietnam* (1982). Thomas Powers, *Vietnam: The War at Home* (1973). Al Santoli, *Everything We Had* (1981). Herbert Schandler, *The Unmaking of a President: Lyndon Johnson and Vietnam* (1977). Neil Sheehan, *A Bright Shining Lie* (1988). R. B. Smith, *An International History of the Vietnam War: The Kennedy Strategy* (1985). Ronald Spector, *Advice and Support* (1983). Col. Harry Summers, *On Strategy* (1981). Wallace Terry, *Bloods* (1984). Thomas C. Thayer, *War Without Fronts* (1985). Wallace J. Thies, *When Governments Collide* (1980). James Thompson, *Rolling Thunder* (1980). Kathleen J. Turner, *Lyndon Johnson's Dual War: Vietnam and the Press* (1981). Irwin Unger, *The Movement* (1974). Marilyn Young, *The Vietnam Wars* (1991).

1968. David Caute, *The Year of the Barricades* (1988). Lewis Chester, Godfrey Hodgson, and Lewis Page, *American Melodrama* (1969). David Farber, *Chicago '68* (1988). Marshall Frady, *Wallace*, rev. ed. (1976). Godfrey Hodgson, *America in Our Time* (1976). Charles Kaiser, *1968 in America* (1988). Norman Mailer, *Miami and the Siege of Chicago* (1968). Arthur M. Schlesinger, Jr., *Robert Kennedy and His Times* (1978). Ben Stavis, *We Were the Campaign* (1969). Theodore White, *The Making of the President, 1968* (1969).

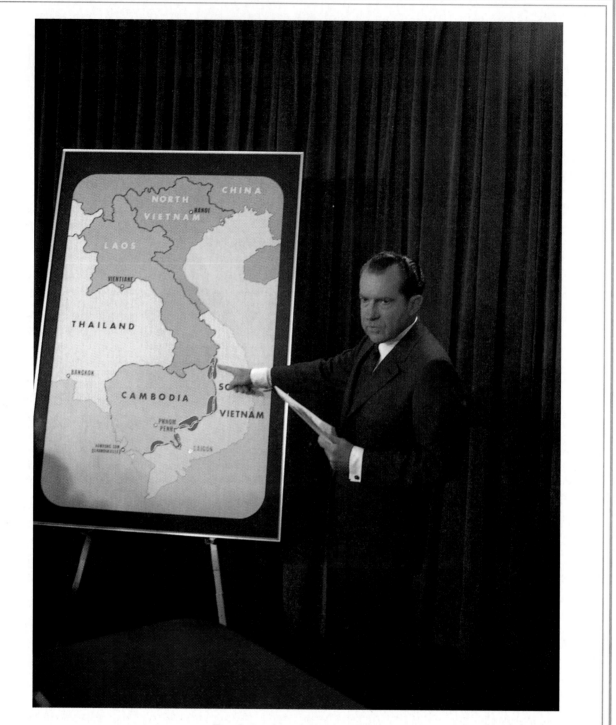

THE CAMBODIAN INVASION, 1970
Richard Nixon precipitated one of the biggest crises of his turbulent presidency in the spring of 1970 when he announced that American troops were invading Cambodia in search of North Vietnamese sanctuaries there. In the days after the president's television address, antiwar protests reached their highest (and most violent) levels ever. *(Dennis Brack/Black Star)*

CHAPTER THIRTY-TWO

THE CRISIS OF AUTHORITY

ICHARD NIXON'S ELECTION IN 1968 was the result of more than the unpopularity of Lyndon Johnson and the war. It was the result, too, of a strong public reaction against what many Americans considered a frontal assault on the foundations of their culture. Throughout the late 1960s and early 1970s, new interest groups were mobilizing to demand protections and benefits. New values and assumptions were emerging to challenge traditional patterns of thought and behavior. The United States was in the throes, some believed, of a genuine cultural revolution.

Some Americans welcomed the changes. But the 1968 election returns suggested that more feared them. There was growing resentment against the attention directed toward minorities and the poor, against the federal social programs that were funneling billions of dollars into the inner cities to help the poor and unemployed, against the increasing tax burden on the middle class, against the "hippies" and radicals who were dominating public discourse with their bitter critiques of values most middle-class Americans held dear. It was time, many men and women believed, for a restoration of stability and a relegitimation of traditional centers of authority.

In Richard Nixon they found a man who seemed to match their mood perfectly. Himself a product of a hardworking, middle-class family, he had risen to prominence on the basis of his own unrelenting efforts, and he projected an image of stern dedication to traditional values. Yet the presidency of Richard Nixon, far from returning calm and stability to American politics, coincided with, and in many ways helped to produce, more years of crisis.

THE YOUTH CULTURE

Perhaps most alarming to conservative Americans in the 1960s and 1970s was a pattern of social and cultural protest that was emerging from younger Americans, who were giving vent to two related impulses. One was the impulse, originating with the political left, to create a great new community of "the people," which would rise up to break the power of elites and force the nation to end the war, pursue racial and economic justice, and transform its political life. The other at least equally powerful impulse was related to, but not entirely compatible with the first: the vision of individual "liberation." It found expression, in part, through the efforts of particular groups—African Americans, Indians, Hispanics, women, gay people, and others—to define and assert themselves and make demands on the larger society. It also found expression through the efforts of individuals to create a new culture—one that would allow them to escape from what they considered the dehumanizing pressures of what some called the modern "technocracy."

The New Left

In retrospect, it seems unsurprising that young Americans became so assertive and powerful in American culture and politics in the 1960s. The postwar baby boom, the unprecedented number of people born in a few years just after World War II, was growing up. By 1970, more than half the American population was under thirty years old; more than 8 million Americans—eight times the number in 1950—were attending college. This was the largest generation of youth in American history, and it was coming to maturity in a time of unprecedented affluence, opportunity, and—for many—frustration. Relatively few of these young people embraced radical political causes or rebelled in any fundamental way against their culture. But those who did were numerous enough, and assertive enough, to have a disproportionate impact on both the cultural and the political climate.

One of the most visible results of the increasingly assertive youth movement was a radicalization of many American college and university students, who in the course of the 1960s formed what became known as the New Left—a large, diverse group of men and women energized by the polarizing developments of their time to challenge the political system. The New Left embraced the cause of African Americans and other minorities, but its own ranks consisted overwhelmingly of white people. Blacks and minorities formed political movements of their own.

The New Left drew from many sources. Some of its members were the children of radical parents (members of the so-called Old Left of the 1930s and 1940s), and had grown up with a critical view of society and politics. Indeed, the New Left drew considerable support, and guidance, from groups and individuals from the Old Left; it was not as entirely "new" as its champions liked to claim. The New Left drew as well from the writings of some of the important social critics of the 1950s—among them C. Wright Mills, a sociologist at Columbia University who wrote a series of scathing and brilliant critiques of modern bureaucracies. And while relatively few members of the New Left were communists, many were drawn to the writings of Karl Marx and such other Marxist theorists as Antonio Gramsci and Herbert Marcuse. Some came to revere Third World Marxists such as Che Guevara, Mao Zedong, and Ho Chi Minh. For a while, left-leaning figures in the labor movement helped nurture the New Left—although relations between the two movements soon deteriorated beyond repair over the New Left's unwillingness to embrace the anti-communism of the AFL-CIO.

But the New Left drew from nothing so much as the civil rights movement, in which many idealistic young white Americans had become involved in the early 1960s. Racism, oppression, and violence were nothing new to the many African Americans fighting for civil rights. But to white college students from mid-dle-class backgrounds, the exposure to social injustice (and personal danger) in the South was shocking and disillusioning, and it led many of them to question their assumptions about the basic values and institutions of American life. Within a few years, some white civil rights activists were beginning to consider broader political commitments.

In 1962, a group of students, most of them from prestigious universities, gathered in Michigan (at a conference center owned by the United Auto Workers) to form an organization to give voice to their demands: Students for a Democratic Society (SDS). Their declaration of beliefs, the Port Huron Statement, expressed their disillusionment with the society they had inherited and their determination to build a new politics. "Many of us began maturing in complacency," the statement (most of it the work of student activist Tom Hayden) declared. "As we grew, however, our comfort was penetrated by events too troubling to dismiss." In the following years, SDS became the principal organization of student radicalism.

Some members of SDS moved into inner-city neighborhoods and tried for a time, without notable success, to mobilize poor, working-class people politically. But most members of the New Left were students, and their radicalism centered for a time on issues related to the modern university. A 1964 dispute at the University of California at Berkeley over the rights of students to engage in political activities on campus gained national attention. The Free Speech Movement, as it called itself, created turmoil at Berkeley as students challenged campus police, occupied administrative offices, and produced a strike in which nearly three quarters of the Berkeley students participated. The immediate issue was the right of students to pass out literature and recruit volunteers for political causes on campus. But the protest quickly became as well an expression of a more basic critique of the university, and the society it seemed to represent. Mario Savio, a Berkeley graduate student and one of the leaders of the Free Speech Movement, captured something of the political anguish in a famous speech on campus, in which he said:

> There is a time when the operation of the machine becomes so odious, makes you so sick at heart, that you can't take part; you can't even passively take part, and you've got to put your bodies upon the gears and upon the wheels, upon the levers, upon all the apparatus and you've got to make it stop. And you've got to indicate to the people who run it, to the people who own it, that unless you're free, the machine will be prevented from working at all.

The revolt at Berkeley was the first outburst of what was to be nearly a decade of campus turmoil.

Students at Berkeley and elsewhere protested the impersonal character of the modern university, and they denounced the role of educational institutions in sustaining what they considered corrupt or immoral public policies. The antiwar movement greatly inflamed and expanded the challenge to the universities; and beginning in 1968, campus demonstrations, riots, and building seizures became almost commonplace. At Columbia University in New York, students seized the offices of the president and other members of the administration and occupied them for days until local police forcibly ejected them. Harvard University had a similar, and even more violent, experience a year later.

Also in 1969, Berkeley became the scene of perhaps the most prolonged and traumatic conflict of any American college campus in the 1960s: a battle over the efforts of a few students to build a "People's Park" on land the university planned to use to build a parking garage. This seemingly minor event precipitated weeks of impassioned and often violent conflicts between the university administration and its students and between students and police.

By the end of the People's Park battle, which lasted for more than a week, the Berkeley campus was completely polarized; even students who had not initially supported or even noticed the People's Park (the great majority) were, by the end, committed to its defense; 85 percent of the 15,000 students voted in a referendum to leave the park alone. Student radicals were, for the first time, winning large audiences for their extravagant rhetoric linking together university administrators, the police, and the larger political and economic system, describing them all as part of one united, oppressive force. As one Berkeley activist said in the midst of the battle: "You've pushed us to the end of your civilization here, against the sea in Berkeley. Then you pushed us into a square-block area called People's Park. It was the last thing we had to defend, this square block of sanity amid all your madness. . . . We are now homeless in your civilized world. We have become the great American gypsies, with only our mythology for a culture." Over the next several years, hardly any major university was immune to some level of disruption.

Most campus radicals were rarely if ever violent (except at times in their rhetoric). But the image of student radicalism in mainstream culture was one of chaos and disorder, based in part on the disruptive actions of relatively small groups of militants. As time went on, moreover, the fringes of the students became increasingly militant. Small numbers of especially dogmatic radicals—among them the "Weathermen," a violent offshoot of SDS—were responsible for a few cases of arson and bombing that destroyed campus buildings and claimed several lives.

Not many people, not even many students, ever accepted the radical political views that lay at the heart of the New Left. But many supported the position of SDS and other groups on particular issues, and above all on the Vietnam War. Student activists tried to drive training programs for military officers (ROTC) and bar military recruiters from college campuses. They attacked the laboratories and corporations that were producing weapons for the war. And between 1967 and 1969, they organized some of the largest political demonstrations in American history. The march on the Pentagon of October 1967, where demonstrators were met by a solid line of armed troops; the "spring mobilization" of April 1968, which attracted hundreds of thousands of demonstrators in cities around the country; the Vietnam "moratorium" of the fall of 1969, during which millions of opponents of the war gathered in major rallies across the nation; and countless other demonstrations, large and small—all helped thrust the issue of the war into the center of American politics.

Closely related to opposition to the war—and another issue that helped fuel the New Left—was opposition to the military draft. The gradual abolition of many traditional deferments—for graduate students, teachers, husbands, fathers, and others—swelled the ranks of those faced with conscription (and thus likely to oppose it). Draft card burnings became common features of antiwar rallies on college campuses. Many draft-age Americans simply refused induction, accepting what occasionally were long terms in jail as a result. Thousands of others fled to Canada, Sweden, and elsewhere (where they were joined by many deserters from the armed forces) to escape conscription. Not until 1977, when President Jimmy Carter issued a general pardon to draft resisters and a far more limited amnesty for deserters, did the Vietnam exiles begin to return to the country in substantial numbers.

The Counterculture

Closely related to the New Left was a new youth culture openly scornful of the values and conventions of middle-class society. The most visible characteristic of the counterculture, as it became known, was a change in lifestyle. As if to display their contempt for conventional standards, young Americans flaunted long hair, shabby or flamboyant clothing, and a rebellious disdain for traditional speech and decorum, which they replaced with their own "hippie" idiom. Also central to the counterculture were drugs: marijuana smoking—which after 1966 became almost as common a youthful diversion as beer drinking—and the less widespread but still substantial use of other, more potent hallucinogens, such as LSD.

WOODSTOCK
In the summer of 1969, more than 400,000 people gathered for a rock concert on a farm in Bethel, New York. Despite mostly terrible weather, the gathering was remarkably peaceful—sparking rapturous talk among some enthusiasts of the new youth culture about the "Woodstock nation." *(Shelly Rustin/Black Star)*

There was also a new, more permissive view of sexual behavior—the beginnings of what some called a "sexual revolution." To some degree, the emergence of more relaxed approaches to sexuality was a result less of the counterculture than of the new accessibility of effective contraceptives, most notably the birth control pill and, after 1973, legalized abortion. Fear of unwanted pregnancy, a powerful force inhibiting female sexuality, declined. But the new sexuality also reflected the counterculture's belief that individuals should strive for release from inhibitions and give vent to their instincts—including the instinct for sensual pleasure.

The counterculture's iconoclasm and hedonism sometimes masked its philosophy, which offered a fundamental challenge to the American middle-class mainstream. Like the New Left, with which it in many ways overlapped, the counterculture challenged the structure of modern American society, attacking its banality, its hollowness, its artificiality, its materialism, its isolation from nature. The most committed adherents of the counterculture—the hippies, who came to dominate the Haight-Ashbury neighborhood of San Francisco and other places, and the social dropouts, many of whom retreated to rural communes—rejected modern society altogether and attempted to find refuge in a simpler, more "natural" existence. But even those whose commitment to the counterculture was less dramatic shared a commitment to the idea of personal fulfillment through rejecting the inhibitions and conventions of middle-class culture. In a corrupt and alienating society, the new creed seemed to suggest, the first responsibility of the individual is cultivation of the self, the unleashing of one's own full potential for pleasure and fulfillment.

Theodore Roszak, whose book *The Making of a Counter Culture* (1969) became a central document of the era, captured much of the spirit of the movement in his frank admission that "the primary project of our counter culture is to proclaim a new heaven and a new earth so vast, so marvelous that the inordinate claims of technical expertise must of necessity withdraw to a subordinate and marginal status in the lives of men." Charles Reich's *The Greening of America* (1970) created a short-lived sensation with its argument that the individual should strive for a new form of consciousness—"Consciousness III," as he called it—in which the self would be the only reality.

The effects of the counterculture reached out to the larger society and helped create a new set of social norms that many young people (and some adults) chose to imitate. Long hair and freakish clothing became the badge not only of hippies and radicals but of an entire generation. The use of marijuana, the freer attitudes toward sex, the iconoclastic (and sometimes obscene) language—all spread far beyond the realm of the true devotees of the counterculture. And perhaps the most pervasive element of the new youth society was one that even the least radical members of the generation embraced: rock music. Rock'n'roll first achieved wide popularity in the 1950s, on the strength of such early performers as Buddy Holly and, above all, Elvis Presley. Early in the 1960s, its influence began to spread, a result in large part of the phenomenal popularity of the Beatles, the English group whose first visit to the United States in 1964 created a remarkable sensation, "Beatlemania." For a time, most rock musicians—like most popular musicians before them—concentrated largely on uncontroversial romantic themes. One of the first great hits of the Beatles was a song with the innocuous title "I Want to Hold Your Hand." By the late 1960s, however, rock had begun to reflect many of the new iconoclastic values of its time. The Beatles, for example, abandoned their once simple and seemingly innocent style for a new, experimental, even mystical approach that reflected the growing popular fascination with drugs and Eastern religions. Other groups, such as the Rolling Stones, turned even more openly to themes of anger, frustration, and rebelliousness. Many popular musicians used their music to express explicit political radicalism as well—especially some of the leading folk singers of the era, such as Bob Dylan and Joan Baez. Rock's driving rhythms, its undisguised sensuality, its often harsh and angry tone—all made it an appropriate vehicle for expressing the themes of the social and political unrest of the late 1960s.

A powerful symbol of the fusion of rock music and the counterculture was the great music festival at Woodstock, New York, in the summer of 1969, where 400,000 people gathered on a farm for nearly a week. Despite heavy rain, mud, inadequate facilities, and impossible crowding, the crowd remained peaceful and harmonious. Champions of the counterculture spoke rhapsodically at the time of how Woodstock represented the birth of a new youth nation, the "Woodstock nation." The Beat poet Allen Ginsberg, revered by many enthusiasts of the counterculture and himself a champion of the "new consciousness," wrote an ecstatic poem proclaiming that at Woodstock "a new kind of man has come to his bliss/to end the cold war he has borne/against his own kind of flesh."

Virtually no Americans could avoid seeing how rapidly the norms of their society were changing in the late 1960s. Those who attended movies saw a gradual

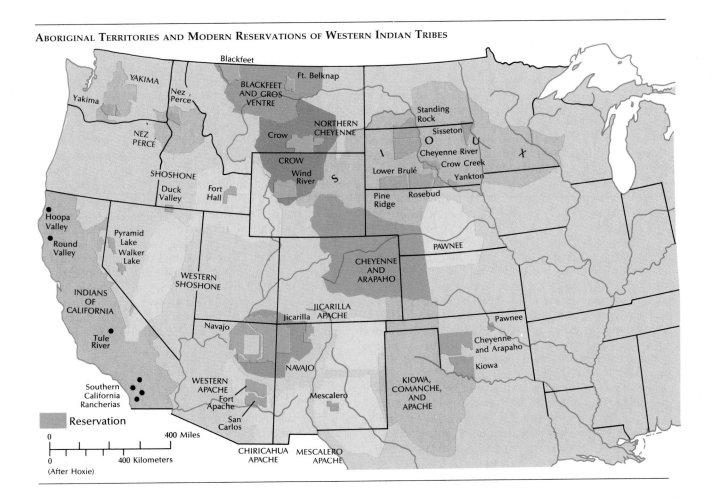

ABORIGINAL TERRITORIES AND MODERN RESERVATIONS OF WESTERN INDIAN TRIBES

Reservation

0   400 Miles

0   400 Kilometers

(After Hoxie)

disappearance of the banal, conventional messages that had dominated films since the 1920s. Instead, they saw explorations of political issues, of new sexual mores, of violence, of social conflict. Television too began to turn (even if more slowly than the other media) to programming that reflected social and cultural conflict—as exemplified by the enormously popular *All in the Family*, whose protagonist, Archie Bunker, was a lower-middle-class bigot.

THE MOBILIZATION OF MINORITIES

The growth of African-American protest, and of a significant white response to it, both preceded the political and cultural upheavals of the 1960s and helped produce them. It also encouraged other minorities to assert themselves and demand redress of their grievances. For Indians, Hispanic Americans, gay men and women, and others, the late 1960s and 1970s were a time of growing self-expression and political activism.

Seeds of Indian Militancy

Few minorities had deeper or more justifiable grievances against the prevailing culture than American Indians—or Native Americans, as some began to call themselves in the 1960s. Indians were the least prosperous, least healthy, and least stable group in the nation. Average annual family income for Indians was $1,000 less than that for blacks. The Native American unemployment rate was ten times the national rate. Joblessness was particularly high on the reservations, where nearly half the Indians lived. But even most Indians living in cities suffered from their limited education and training and could find only menial jobs. Life expectancy among Indians was more than twenty years less than the national average. Suicides among Indian youths were a hundred times more frequent than among white youths. And while black Americans attracted the attention (for good or for ill) of many whites, Indians for many years remained largely ignored.

For much of the postwar era, and particularly after the resignation of John Collier as commissioner of Indian Affairs in 1946, federal policy toward the tribes had been shaped by a determination to incorporate Indians into mainstream American society, whether Indians wanted to assimilate or not. Two laws passed in 1953 established the basis of a new policy, which

became known as "termination." Through termination, the federal government withdrew all official recognition of the tribes as legal entities, administratively separate from state governments, and made them subject to the same local jurisdictions as white residents. At the same time, the government encouraged Indians to assimilate into the larger society and worked to funnel Native Americans into cities, where, presumably, they would adapt themselves to the white world and lose their cultural distinctiveness.

To some degree, the termination and assimilation policies achieved their objectives. The tribes grew weaker as legal and political entities. Many Native Americans adapted to life in the cities, at least to a degree. On the whole, however, the new policies were a disaster for the tribes and a failure for the reformers who had promoted them. Termination led to widespread corruption and abuse. And Indians themselves fought so bitterly against it that in 1958 the Eisenhower administration barred further "terminations" without the consent of the affected tribes. In the meantime, the struggle against termination had mobilized a new generation of Indian militants and had breathed life into the principal Native American organization, the National Congress of American Indians (NCAI), which had been created in 1944.

The Democratic administrations of the 1960s, though they did not disavow the termination policy, made no effort to revive it. Instead, they made modest efforts to restore at least some degree of tribal autonomy. The funneling of OEO money to tribal organizations through the community action program was one prominent example. In the meantime, the tribes themselves were beginning to fight for self-determination—partly because of the inspiration they drew from the black civil rights movement and partly in response to other social and cultural changes (among them, the expanding mobility and rising educational levels of younger Indians, who were becoming more aware of the world around them and of their own anomalous place within it). The new militancy also benefited from the rapid increase in the Indian population, which was growing much faster than that of the rest of the nation (nearly doubling between 1950 and 1970, to a total of about 800,000).

The Indian Civil Rights Movement

In 1961, more than 400 members of 67 tribes gathered in Chicago to discuss ways of bringing all Indians together in an effort to redress common wrongs. The manifesto they issued, the Declaration of Indian Purpose, stressed the "right to choose our own way of life" and

WOUNDED KNEE
Wounded Knee, South Dakota, had been the site of a conflict between American soldiers and Teton Sioux in 1890. The soldiers had attempted to suppress Indian religious rites ("Ghost Dances"), which whites considered threatening. The result had been a substantial massacre of the tribespeople. In 1973 armed members of the new American Indian Movement seized the village of Wounded Knee (now part of a Sioux reservation) and occupied it for over two months to press their demands for reform in federal Indian policy and tribal government. *(Michael Abramson/Black Star)*

the "responsibility of preserving our precious heritage."

The 1961 meeting was only one example of a growing Indian self-consciousness. Indians and others began writing books (for example, Vine Deloria, Jr.'s *Custer Died for Your Sins* and Dee Brown's *Bury My Heart at Wounded Knee*) and otherwise drawing renewed attention to the wrongs inflicted on the tribes by white people in past generations. One result was a gradual change in the way popular culture depicted Indians. By the 1970s, almost no films or television westerns any longer portrayed Indians as brutal savages attacking peaceful white people. And Indian activists even persuaded some white institutions to abandon what they considered demeaning references to them; Dartmouth College, for example, ceased referring to its athletic teams as the "Indians." The National Indian Youth Council, created in the aftermath of the 1961 Chicago meeting, promoted the idea of Indian nationalism and intertribal unity. In 1968, a group of young militant Indians established the American Indian Movement (AIM), which drew its greatest support from those Indians who lived in urban areas but soon established a significant presence on the reservations as well.

The new activism had some immediate political results. In 1968, Congress passed the Indian Civil Rights Act, which guaranteed reservation Indians many of the protections accorded other citizens by the Bill of Rights, but which also recognized the legitimacy of tribal laws within the reservations. But leaders of AIM and other insurgent groups were not satisfied and turned increasingly to direct action. In 1968, Indian fishermen, citing old treaty rights, clashed with Washington State officials on the Columbia River and in Puget Sound. The following year, members of several tribes occupied the abandoned federal prison on Alcatraz Island in San Francisco Bay, claiming the site "by right of discovery."

In response to the growing pressure, the new Nixon administration appointed a Mohawk-Sioux to the position of commissioner of Indian Affairs in 1969; and in 1970, the president promised both increased tribal self-determination and an increase in federal aid. But the protests continued. In November 1972, nearly a thousand demonstrators, most of them Sioux, forcibly occupied the building of the Bureau of Indian Affairs in Washington, D.C., for six days. A more celebrated protest occurred later that winter at Wounded Knee, South Dakota, the site of the 1890 massacre of Sioux by federal troops.

In the early 1970s, Wounded Knee was part of a large Sioux reservation, two-thirds of which had been leased to white ranchers for generations as an outgrowth of the Dawes Act. Conditions for the Indian residents were desperate, and passions grew quickly in 1972 in response to the murder of a Sioux by a group of whites, who were not, many Indians believed, adequately punished. In February 1973, members of AIM seized and occupied the town of Wounded Knee for two months, demanding radical changes in the administration of the reservation and insisting that the government honor its long-forgotten treaty obligations. A brief clash between the occupiers and federal forces left one Indian dead and another wounded. Shortly thereafter the siege came to an end.

More immediately effective than these militant protests were the victories that various tribes were achieving in the 1970s in the federal courts. In *United States* v. *Wheeler* (1978), the Supreme Court confirmed that tribes had independent legal standing and could not be "terminated" by Congress. Other decisions ratified the authority of tribes to impose taxes on businesses within their reservations and to perform other sovereign functions. In 1985, the U.S. Supreme Court, in *County of Oneida* v. *Oneida Indian Nation*, supported Indian claims to 100,000 acres in upstate New York that the Oneida tribe claimed by virtue of treaty rights long forgotten by whites.

The Indian civil rights movement, like other civil rights movements of the same time, fell far short of winning full justice and equality for its constituents. Nor did it ever resolve its own internal conflicts—conflicts similar to those facing other minority groups at the same time. To some Indians, the principal goal was to defend tribal autonomy, to protect the right of Indians (and, more to the point, individual tribal groups) to remain separate and distinct. To others, the goal was equality—to win for Indians a place in society equal to that of other groups of Americans. This latter goal helped produce a new spirit of "pan-Indianism," an effort to persuade Indians to transcend tribal divisions and work together as "a Greater Indian America." But because there was no single Indian culture or tradition in America, pan-Indianism did not flourish.

For all its limits, however, the Indian civil rights movement helped the tribes win a series of new legal rights and protections that gave them a stronger position than they had enjoyed at any previous time in the twentieth century. It helped many Indians gain a renewed awareness of and pride in their identity as Indians and as part of distinct communities within the larger United States. And it challenged patterns of discrimination that had prevented many Native Americans from advancing in the world outside the tribes.

Hispanic-American Activism

More numerous and more visible than Indians were Hispanic-Americans (also known as Latinos), the fastest-growing minority group in the United States. They were no more a single, cohesive group than the Indians were. Some—including the descendants of early Spanish settlers in New Mexico—had roots as deep in American history as those of any other group. Others were men and women who had immigrated since World War II.

Large numbers of Puerto Ricans had migrated to eastern cities, particularly New York. South Florida's substantial Cuban population began with a wave of middle-class refugees fleeing the Castro regime in the early 1960s. These first Cuban migrants quickly established themselves as a successful and increasingly assimilated part of Miami's middle class. In 1980, a second, much poorer wave of Cuban immigrants—the so-called Marielitos, named for the port from which they left Cuba—arrived in Florida when Castro temporarily relaxed exit restrictions. (This group included a large number of criminals, whom Castro had, in effect, expelled from the country.) This second wave was less easily assimilated. Later in the 1980s, large numbers of immigrants (both legal and illegal) began to arrive from the troubled nations of Central and South America—from Guatemala, Nicaragua, El Salvador, Peru, and others. But the most numerous and important Hispanic group in the United States was Mexican Americans.

There had been a significant Mexican-American population in the West throughout the nineteenth and early twentieth centuries—descendants of Spanish and Mexican people who had settled in lands that once belonged to the Spanish Empire and the Republic of Mexico. But their numbers grew rapidly and substantially during and after World War II. Large numbers of Mexican Americans had entered the country during the war in response to the labor shortage, and many had

STRIKING GRAPEWORKERS
Cesar Chavez, founder and leader of the United Farm Workers of America, leads striking Chicano farmworkers in 1978, one of many actions that led to the recognition of the union by most growers in California.   *(George Ballis/Black Star)*

remained in the cities of the Southwest and the Pacific Coast. After the war, when the legal agreements that had allowed Mexican contract workers to enter the country expired, large numbers of immigrants continued to move to the United States illegally. In 1953, the government launched what it called Operation Wetback to deport the illegals, but the effort failed to stem the flow of new arrivals. By 1960, there were substantial Mexican-American neighborhoods (barrios) in American cities from El Paso to Detroit. The largest (with more than 500,000 people, according to Census figures) was in Los Angeles, which by then had a bigger Mexican population than any place except Mexico City.

But the greatest expansion in the Mexican-American population was yet to come. In 1960, the Census reported slightly more than 3 million Hispanics living in the United States (the great majority of them Mexican Americans). In 1970, that number had grown to 9 million, and by 1990 to 20 million. Hispanics constituted more than a third of all legal immigrants to the United States after 1960. Since there was also an uncounted but very large number of illegal immigrants in those years (estimates ranged from 7 million to 12 million), the real percentage of Hispanic immigrants was undoubtedly much larger.

By the late 1960s, therefore, Mexican Americans were one of the largest population groups in the West—outnumbering African Americans—and had established communities in most other parts of the nation as well. They were also among the most urbanized groups

in the population; almost 90 percent lived and worked in cities. Many of them (particularly members of the oldest and most assimilated families of Mexican descent) were affluent and successful people. Wealthy Cubans in Miami filled influential positions in the professions and local government; in the Southwest, Mexican Americans elected their own leaders to seats in Congress and to governorships.

But most newly arrived Mexican Americans and other Hispanics were less well educated than either "Anglo" or black Americans and hence less well prepared for high-paying jobs. The fact that many spoke English poorly or not at all further limited their employment prospects. Some of them found good industrial jobs in unionized industries, and some Mexican Americans became important labor organizers in the AFL-CIO. But many more (including the great majority of illegal immigrants) worked in low-paying service jobs, with few if any benefits and no job security. And like African Americans and other minorities, Mexican Americans encountered almost impossible obstacles when they attempted to move out of blue-collar or low-status service jobs. Almost nowhere were they able to establish themselves as managers or executives in the companies in which they worked; few were able to pursue successful professional careers.

Partly because of language barriers, partly because the family-centered culture of many Hispanic communities discouraged effective organization, and partly because of discrimination, Mexican Americans and others were slower to develop political influence than some other minorities. But some did respond to the highly charged climate of the 1960s by strengthening their ethnic identification and organizing for political and economic power. Young Mexican-American activists began to call themselves "Chicanos" (once a term of derision used by whites) as a way of emphasizing the shared culture of Spanish-speaking Americans; and the term quickly moved into widespread (although never universal) use among Mexican Americans. Some Chicanos advocated a form of nationalism not unlike the ideas of black power advocates. The Texas leaders of *La Raza Unida*, a Chicano political party in the Southwest, called for the creation of something like an autonomous Mexican-American state within a state; it demonstrated significant strength at the polls in the 1970s.

One of the most visible efforts to organize Mexican Americans occurred in California, where an Arizona-born Chicano farmworker, Cesar Chavez, created an effective union of itinerant farmworkers. His United Farm Workers (UFW), a largely Chicano organization, launched a prolonged strike in 1965 against growers to demand, first, recognition of their union and, second, increased wages and benefits. When employers resisted, Chavez enlisted the cooperation of college students, churches, and civil rights groups (including CORE and SNCC) and organized a nationwide boycott, first of table grapes and then of lettuce. In 1968, Chavez campaigned openly for Robert Kennedy. Two years later, he won a substantial victory when the growers of half of California's table grapes signed contracts with his union.

Hispanic Americans were at the center of another controversy of the 1970s and beyond: the issue of bilingualism. It was a question that aroused the opposition not only of many whites but of some Hispanics as well. Supporters of bilingualism in education (which included not just Hispanics, but Asians and others as well) argued that non-English-speaking Americans were entitled to schooling in their own language, that otherwise they would be at a grave disadvantage in comparison with native English speakers. Bilingualism, they argued, was the only way to overcome the language barrier that kept many students from making even minimal academic progress. The United States Supreme Court confirmed the right of non-English-speaking students to schooling in their native language in 1974. Opponents cited not only the cost and difficulty of bilingualism but the dangers it posed to students' ability to assimilate into the mainstream of American culture. Even many Hispanics feared that bilingualism might isolate their communities further from the rest of America and increase resentments toward them.

Challenging the "Melting Pot" Ideal

The efforts of blacks, Hispanics, Indians, Asians, and others to forge a clearer group identity seemed to challenge a longstanding premise of American political thought—the idea of the "melting pot." Older, European immigrant groups liked to believe that they had advanced in American society by adopting the values and accepting the rules of the world to which they had moved and by advancing within it on its own terms. The newly assertive ethnic groups of the 1960s and after were less willing to accept the standards of the larger society and more likely to demand recognition of their own ethnic identity. African Americans, Indians, Hispanics, and Asians all challenged the assimilationist idea. They advocated instead a culturally pluralistic society, in which racial and ethnic groups would preserve a sense of their own heritage and their own social and cultural norms.

To a large degree, the advocates of cultural pluralism succeeded. Recognition of the special character of particular groups was embedded in federal law through a wide range of affirmative action programs, which extended not only to blacks, but to Indians, Hispanics, Asians, and others as well. Ethnic studies programs proliferated in schools and universities. Eventually, this impulse led to an even more assertive (and highly controversial) cultural movement that in the 1980s and 1990s became known as "multiculturalism," which, among other things, challenged the "Eurocentric" basis of American education and culture and demanded that non-European civilizations be accorded equal attention.

Gay Liberation

The last important liberation movement to emerge in the 1960s, and the most surprising to many Americans, was the effort by homosexuals to win political and economic rights and, equally important, social acceptance. Homosexuality had been an unacknowledged reality throughout American history; not until many years after their deaths did many Americans know, for example, that revered cultural figures such as Walt Whitman and Horatio Alger were homosexuals. Non-heterosexual men and women had long been forced either to suppress their sexual preferences, to express them surreptitiously, or to live within isolated and often persecuted communities. But by the late 1960s, the liberating impulses that had affected other groups helped mobilize gay men and lesbians to fight for their own rights.

On June 27, 1969, police officers raided the Stonewall Inn, a gay nightclub in New York City's Greenwich Village, and began arresting patrons simply for frequenting the place. The raid was not unusual; police had been harassing gay bars (and homosexual men and women) for years. It was, in fact, the accumulated resentment of this long history of assaults and humiliations that caused the extraordinary response that summer night. Gay onlookers taunted the police, then attacked them. Someone started a blaze in the Stonewall Inn itself, almost trapping the policemen inside. Rioting continued throughout Greenwich Village (the center of New York's gay community) through much of the night.

The "Stonewall Riot" marked the beginning of the gay liberation movement—one of the most controversial challenges to traditional values and assumptions of its time. New organizations—among them the Gay Liberation Front, founded in New York in 1969—sprang up around the country. Public discussion and media coverage of homosexuality, long subject to an unofficial taboo, quickly and dramatically increased. Gay and lesbian activists had some success in challenging the longstanding assumption that homosexuality was "aberrant" behavior and argued that no sexual preference was any more "normal" than another.

Most of all, however, the gay liberation movement transformed the outlook of gay men and lesbians themselves. It helped them to "come out," to express their preferences openly and unapologetically, and to demand from society a recognition that gay relationships could be as significant and worthy of respect as heterosexual ones. Some gays advocated not only an acceptance of homosexuality as a valid and "normal" preference, but a change in the larger society as well: a redefinition of personal identity to give much greater importance to erotic impulses. There was much resistance to such efforts. But by the early 1980s, the gay liberation movement had made remarkable strides. Even the ravages of the AIDS epidemic (see pp. 912–913), which affected the gay community more disastrously than it affected any other group, failed to halt the growth of gay liberation. In many ways, it strengthened it.

By the early 1990s, gay men and lesbians were achieving some of the same milestones that other oppressed minorities had attained in earlier decades. Some openly gay politicians won election to public office. Universities were establishing gay and lesbian studies programs. And laws prohibiting discrimination on the basis of sexual preference were making slow, halting progress at the local level. But gay liberation produced a powerful backlash as well, as became evident when President Bill Clinton's 1993 effort to lift the ban on gays and lesbians serving in the military met a storm of criticism from members of Congress and from within the military itself.

THE NEW FEMINISM

American women constituted 51 percent of the population. But during the 1960s and 1970s, many women began to identify with minority groups and to demand a liberation of their own. Sexual discrimination was so deeply embedded in the fabric of society that when feminists began to denounce it, many men (and even many women) responded with bafflement and anger. By the 1970s, however, public awareness of the issue had increased dramatically, and the role of women in American life had changed more dramatically than that of any other group in the nation.

The Rebirth

Feminism had been a weak and often embattled force in American life for more than forty years after the adoption of the woman suffrage amendment in 1920. A few determined women kept feminist political demands alive in the National Woman's Party and other organizations. Many more women expanded the acceptable bounds of female activity by entering new areas of the workplace or engaging in political activities. Nevertheless, through the 1950s and early 1960s, active feminism was often difficult to detect. Yet within a very few years, it evolved from an almost invisible remnant to one of the most powerful social movements in American history.

The 1963 publication of Betty Friedan's *The Feminine Mystique* is often cited as the first event of contemporary women's liberation. Friedan had traveled around the country interviewing the women who had graduated with her from Smith College in 1947. Most of these women were living out the dream that postwar American society had created for them: they were affluent wives and mothers living in comfortable suburbs. And yet many of them were deeply frustrated and unhappy. The suburbs, Friedan claimed, had become a "comfortable concentration camp," providing the women who inhabited them with no outlets for their intelligence, talent, and education. The "feminine mystique" was responsible for "burying millions of women alive." The only escape was for them to begin to fulfill "their unique possibilities as separate human beings." By chronicling their unhappiness and frustration, Friedan's book had a powerful impact. But it did not so much cause the revival of feminism as help give voice to a movement that was already stirring.

By the time *The Feminine Mystique* appeared, John Kennedy had established the President's Commission on the Status of Women; and although the president's motives in creating it probably had more to do with deflecting more substantive feminist demands than with real commitment to women's goals, the commission brought national attention to sexual discrimination and helped create important networks of feminist activists who would lobby for legislative redress. Also in 1963, the Kennedy administration helped win passage of the Equal Pay Act, which barred the pervasive practice of paying women less than men for equal work. A year later, Congress incorporated into the Civil Rights Act of 1964 an amendment—Title VII—that extended to women many of the same legal protections against discrimination that were being extended to blacks.

The events of the early 1960s helped expose a contradiction that had been developing for decades between the image and the reality of women's roles in America. The image was what Friedan had called the "feminine mystique"—the ideal of women living happy, fulfilled lives in purely domestic roles. The reality was that increasing numbers of women (including, by 1963, over a third of all married women) had already entered the workplace and were encountering

WOMEN'S HISTORY

T HE REVIVAL OF FEMINISM as a powerful social and political force in the 1960s and 1970s brought with it a dramatic rise of interest in women's history. Indeed, the field of women's history and women's studies has probably been the fastest-growing area of scholarship since the late 1970s. With it has come an effort to make gender a basic category of analysis for history of any kind.

But women's history was not new to the 1960s. Just as women had been challenging traditional gender norms long before the 1960s, so too have women (and some men) been writing women's history for many years. In the nineteenth century, such scholarship generally stressed the unrecognized contributions of women to history—for example, Sarah Hale's 1853 "Record of All Distinguished Women from 'the Beginning' till A.D. 1850." Work of the same sort continued into the twentieth century and, indeed, continues today. But after 1900, people committed to progressive reform movements began to produce a different kind of women's scholarship, in many ways more sociological than historical. It revealed, above all, ways in which women were victimized by a harsh new system of industrialism. In the process, it attempted to raise popular support for reform. Feminist scholars such as Edith Abbott, Margaret Byington, and Katherine Anthony examined the impact of economic change on working-class families, with a special focus on women; and they looked at the often terrible conditions in which women worked in factories, mills, and other people's homes. Their goal was less to celebrate women's contributions than to direct attention to the oppression of women by a rapacious capitalist system.

Feminism receded from prominence after the victory of the suffrage movement in 1920, and women's history entered a half century of relative inactivity as well. Women continued to write important histories in many fields, and some—for example, Eleanor Flexner, whose *Century of Struggle* (1959) became a classic history of the suffrage crusade—wrote explicitly about women. Mary Beard, best known for her work in collaboration with her husband Charles Beard on sweeping historical narratives, published a book of her own in 1946 that suggested some of the directions women's history would later take. In *Women as a Force in History*, she argued for the historical importance of ordinary women as shapers of society.

As modern feminism began to sweep across society in the 1960s and 1970s, interest in women's history revived as well. Gerda Lerner, one of the pioneers of the new women's history, once wrote of the impact of feminism on historical studies: "The recognition that we had been denied our history came to many of us as a staggering insight, which altered our consciousness irretrievably." For a time, the new women's history replicated the pattern of earlier studies of women. Much of the early work was in the "contributionist" tradition, stressing the way in which women had played more notable roles in major historical events than men had usually acknowledged. Other work stressed ways in which women had been victimized by their subordination to men and by their powerlessness within the industrial economy. Many scholars developed their feminist sensibilities under the influence of the civil rights movement; and in the 1960s and 1970s they tended to emphasize the artificiality of gender distinctions, just as early civil rights activists emphasized the artificiality of racial distinctions. The difference between women and men, they argued, was "socially constructed." It was also superficial

WHERE HISTORIANS DISAGREE

and (in the public world, at least) unimportant. The history of women was, therefore, the history of how men (with the unwitting help of many women) had created and maintained a set of fictions about women's capacities that late-twentieth-century women were now attempting to shatter.

By the late 1970s, however, many feminists were beginning to argue that there *were* basic differences between women and men—not just biological differences, but differences in values, sensibilities, and culture. This, of course, is what most men and many women had believed for decades (indeed centuries) before the feminist revolution. But the feminists of the 1970s and 1980s did not see these differences as evidence of women's incapacities. They saw them, rather, as evidence of an alternative female culture capable of challenging (and improving) the male-dominated world. Historians of women, therefore, began exploring areas of female experience that revealed the special character of women's culture and values: family, housework, motherhood, women's clubs and organizations, female literature, the social lives of working-class women, women's sexuality, and many other subjects that suggested "difference" more than "contributions" or "victimization." Partly in response, some historians began to make the same argument about men—that understanding "masculinity" and its role in shaping men's lives is as important as understanding notions of "femininity" in explaining the history of women.

The notion of gender as a source of social and cultural difference was responsible for the most powerful challenge women's history raised to the way in which scholars viewed the past. Gender, they argued, was a critical element of the explanation for many kinds of historical experiences, not just women's experiences. It is not enough simply to expand the existing story to

make room for women, Joan Scott, one of the most influential theorists of gender studies, has written. Feminist history is, rather, a way of reconceptualizing the past to incorporate "ways in which hierarchies of difference—inclusions and exclusions—have been constituted."

There are many examples of the way historians have used gender to reinterpret not just the experience of women, but also the experiences of society as a whole. Carol Karlsen has argued that witchcraft in the seventeenth century was not (as earlier scholars argued) a result simply of religious superstition or of economic tensions within communities. It was an expression of assumptions about gender, and it targeted mostly women who violated the community's beliefs in what was appropriate for women to do. Labor historians such as Alice Kessler-Harris have shown the ways in which women were always present in the work force—despite popular myths to the contrary—and always a force in shaping the workplace, even as male ideas about gender limited their opportunities. Ann Scott, Linda Gordon, Theda Skocpol, and others have revealed ways in which women's political organizations and crusades crucially shaped the character of progressive and New Deal reform.

At the same time, historians of women—like historians in many other fields—have confronted other kinds of "difference": racial, ethnic, religious, regional, class. Many historians believe that these categories (race and class in particular) have in fact been more important in shaping the lives of men and women than has gender. Most women's historians, however, continue to believe that understanding concepts of gender is an essential part of understanding women's (and men's) lives, even if it is not the only, or even always the most important, part.

WOMEN IN THE WORK FORCE, 1940–1992

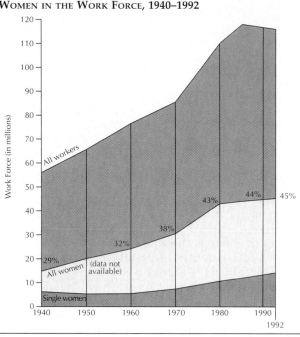

widespread discrimination there; and that many other women were finding their domestic lives suffocating and frustrating. The conflict between the ideal and the reality was crucial to the rebirth of feminism.

In 1966, Friedan joined with other feminists to create the National Organization for Women (NOW), which was to become the nation's largest and most influential feminist organization. "The time has come," the founders of NOW maintained, "to confront with concrete action the conditions which now prevent women from enjoying the equality of opportunity and freedom of choice which is their right as individual Americans and as human beings." Like other movements for liberation, feminism drew much of its inspiration from the black struggle for freedom. "There is no civil rights movement to speak for women," the NOW organizers claimed, "as there has been for Negroes and other victims of discrimination."

The new organization reflected the varying constituencies of the emerging feminist movement. It responded to the complaints of the women Friedan's book had examined—affluent suburbanites with no outlet for their interests—by demanding greater educational opportunities for women and denouncing the domestic ideal and the traditional concept of marriage. But the heart of the movement, at least in the beginning, was directed toward the needs of women in the workplace. NOW denounced the exclusion of women from professions, from politics, and from countless

other areas of American life because of prejudices about women's proper role. It decried legal and economic discrimination, including the practice of paying women less than men for equal work (a practice the Equal Pay Act had not eliminated). The organization called for "a fully equal partnership of the sexes, as part of the worldwide revolution of human rights." By the end of the decade, its membership had expanded to 15,000.

Women's Liberation

By the late 1960s, new and more radical feminist demands were also attracting a large following, especially among younger, affluent, white, educated women—although generally not among the older women whose lives Friedan had studied. The new feminists were mostly younger, the vanguard of the baby-boom generation. Many of them drew inspiration from the New Left and the counterculture. Some were involved in the civil rights movement, others in the antiwar crusade. Many had found that even within those movements, they faced discrimination and exclusion or subordination to male leaders.

By the early 1970s, a significant change was visible in the tone and direction of the organization and of the women's movement as a whole. New books by younger feminists expressed a harsher critique of American society than Friedan had offered. Kate Millett's *Sexual Politics* (1969) signaled the new direction by complaining that "every avenue of power within the society is entirely within male hands." The answer to women's problems, in other words, was not, as Friedan had suggested, for individual women to search for greater personal fulfillment; it was for women to band together to assault the male power structure. Shulamith Firestone's *The Dialectic of Sex* (1970) was subtitled "The Case for Feminist Revolution."

In its most radical form, the new feminism rejected the whole notion of marriage, family, and even heterosexual intercourse (a vehicle, some women claimed, of male domination). Not many women, not even many feminists, embraced such extremes. But by the early 1970s large numbers of women were coming to see themselves as an exploited group organizing against oppression and developing a culture and communities of their own. The women's liberation movement inspired the creation of grassroots organizations and activities through which women not only challenged sexism and discrimination but created communities of their own. In cities and towns across the country, feminists opened women's bookstores, bars, and coffee shops. They founded feminist newspapers and magazines. They created centers to assist victims of rape and abuse, women's health clinics (and, particularly after 1973, abortion clinics), and day-care centers.

Expanding Achievements

By the early 1970s, the public and private achievements of the women's movement were already substantial. In 1971, the government extended its affirmative action guidelines to include women—linking sexism with racism as an officially acknowledged social problem. In the meantime, women were making rapid progress in their efforts to move into the economic and political mainstream. The nation's major all-male educational institutions began to open their doors to women. (Princeton and Yale did so in 1969, and most other all-male colleges and universities soon followed.) Some women's colleges, in the meantime, began accepting male students—although some others remained committed to single-sex education, arguing for the value of the women's communities their campus created.

Women were also becoming an important force in business and the professions. Nearly half of all married women held jobs by the mid-1970s, and almost nine-tenths of all women with college degrees worked. The two-career family, in which both husband and wife maintained active professional lives, was becoming a widely accepted norm; many women were postponing marriage or motherhood for the sake of their careers. There were also important symbolic changes, such as the refusal of many women to adopt their husbands' names when they married and the use of the term "Ms." in place of "Mrs." or "Miss" to denote the irrelevance of a woman's marital status in the public world.

In politics, women were beginning to compete effectively with men by the early 1970s for both elected and appointive positions. By the early 1990s, women were serving in both houses of Congress, in numerous federal cabinet positions, as governors of several states, and in many other positions. Ronald Reagan named the first female Supreme Court Justice, Sandra Day O'Connor, in 1981; in 1993, Bill Clinton named the second, Ruth Bader Ginsburg. In 1984, the Democratic Party chose a woman, Representative Geraldine Ferraro of New York, as its vice presidential candidate. In academia, women were expanding their presence in traditional scholarly fields; they were also creating a field of their own—women's studies, which in the 1980s and early 1990s was the fastest-growing area of American scholarship.

MARCHING FOR WOMEN'S RIGHTS
By the end of the 1960s, the struggle for individual rights— which the African-American civil rights movement had helped push to the center of national consciousness—had helped inspire a broad range of movements. Perhaps the most important in the long run was the drive for women's rights, which was already formidable in the summer of 1970, when thousands of women joined this march through New York City. *(Werner Wolff/Black Star)*

In professional athletics, in the meantime, women were beginning to compete with men both for attention and for an equal share of prize money. Billie Jean King spearheaded the most effective female challenge to male domination of sports. Under her leadership, professional women tennis players established their own successful tours and demanded equal financial incentives when they played in the same tournaments as men. By the late 1970s, the federal government was pressuring colleges and universities to provide women with athletic programs equal to those available to men. Women even joined what had previously been the most celebrated all-male fraternity in American culture: the space program. Sally Ride became the first woman astronaut to travel in space in 1983.

In 1972, Congress approved the Equal Rights Amendment to the Constitution, which some feminists had been promoting since the 1920s, and sent it to the states. For a while ratification seemed almost certain. By the late 1970s, however, the momentum behind the amendment had died. The ERA was in trouble not because of indifference but because of a rising chorus of objections to it from people (including many antifeminist women) who feared it would disrupt traditional social patterns. In 1982, the amendment finally died when the time allotted for ratification expired.

The Abortion Controversy

A vital element of American feminism since the 1920s has been women's effort to win greater control of their own sexual and reproductive lives. In its least controversial form, this impulse helped produce an increasing awareness in the 1960s and 1970s of the problems of rape, sexual abuse, and wife beating. There continued to be some controversy over the dissemination of contraceptives and birth-control information; but that issue, at least, seemed to have lost much of the explosive character it had had in the 1920s, when Margaret Sanger had become a heroine to some and a figure of public scorn to others for her efforts on its behalf. A related issue, however, stimulated as much popular passion as any question of its time: abortion.

Abortion had once been legal in much of the United States, but by the beginning of the twentieth century it was banned by statute in most of the country and remained so into the 1960s (although many abortions continued to be performed quietly, and often dangerously, out of sight of the law). But the women's movement created strong new pressures on behalf of legalizing abortion. Several states had abandoned restrictions on abortion by the end of the 1960s. And in 1973, the Supreme Court's decision in *Roe* v. *Wade*, based on a relatively new theory of a constitutional "right to privacy" first recognized by the Court only a few years earlier in *Griswold* v. *Connecticut* (1965), invalidated all laws prohibiting abortion during the "first trimester"—the first three months of pregnancy. The issue seemed to be settled. But it soon became clear that it was not.

Although in many ways feminism was much like other liberation movements of the 1960s and 1970s, it differed from them in one fundamental respect: its success. The women's movement may not have fulfilled all its goals. But it achieved fundamental and permanent changes in the position of women in American life and promised to do much more.

NIXON, KISSINGER, AND THE WAR

Richard Nixon assumed office in 1969 committed not only to restoring stability at home but to creating a new and more stable order in the world. Central to Nixon's hopes for international stability was a resolution of the stalemate in Vietnam. Yet the new president felt no freer than his predecessor to abandon the American commitment there. He realized that the endless war was undermining both the nation's domestic stability and its position in the world. But he feared that a precipitous retreat would destroy American honor and "credibility."

During the 1968 campaign, Nixon claimed to have formulated a plan to bring "peace with honor" in Vietnam. He had refused to disclose its details. Once in office, however, he soon made clear that the plan consisted of little more than a vague set of general principles, not of any concrete measures to extricate the United States from the quagmire. American involvement in Indochina continued for four more years, during which the war expanded both in its geographic scope and in its bloodiness. And when a settlement finally emerged early in 1973, it produced neither peace nor honor. It succeeded only in removing the United States from the wreckage.

Vietnamization

Despite Nixon's own passionate interest in international affairs, he brought with him into government a man who ultimately seemed to overshadow him in the conduct of diplomacy: Henry Kissinger, a Harvard professor whom the president appointed as his special assistant for national security affairs. Kissinger quickly established dominance over both the secretary of state, William Rogers, and the secretary of defense, Melvin Laird, who were both more experienced in public life. That was in part a result of Nixon's passion for concentrating decision making in the White House. But Kissinger's keen intelligence, his bureaucratic skills, and his success in handling the press were at least equally important. Together, Nixon and Kissinger set out to find an acceptable solution to the stalemate in Vietnam.

The new Vietnam policy moved along several fronts. One was an effort to limit domestic opposition to the war so as to permit the administration more political space in which to maneuver. Aware that the military draft was one of the most visible targets of dissent, the administration devised a new "lottery" system, through which only a limited group—those nineteen-year-olds with low lottery numbers—would be subject to conscription. Later, the president urged the creation of an all-volunteer army. By 1973, the Selective Service System was on its way to at least temporary extinction.

More important in stifling dissent, however, was the new policy of "Vietnamization" of the war—the training and equipping of the South Vietnamese military to assume the burden of combat in place of American forces. In the fall of 1969, Nixon announced the withdrawal of 60,000 American ground troops from Vietnam, the first reduction in U.S. troop strength since the beginning of the war. The withdrawals continued steadily for more than three years, so that by the fall of 1972 relatively few American soldiers remained in Indochina. From a peak of more than 540,000 in 1969, the number had dwindled to about 60,000.

Vietnamization did help quiet domestic opposition to the war. But it did nothing to break the stalemate in the negotiations with the North Vietnamese in Paris. The new administration quickly decided that new military pressures would be necessary to do that.

Escalation

By the end of their first year in office, Nixon and Kissinger had concluded that the most effective way to tip the military balance in America's favor was to destroy the bases in Cambodia from which the American military believed the North Vietnamese were launching many of their attacks. Very early in his presidency, Nixon ordered the air force to begin bombing Cambodian territory to destroy the enemy sanctuaries. He kept the raids secret from Congress and the public. In the spring of 1970, possibly with U.S. encouragement and support, conservative military leaders overthrew the neutral government of Cambodia and established a new, pro-American regime under General Lon Nol. Lon Nol quickly gave his approval to American incursions into his territory; and on April 30, Nixon went on television to announce that he was ordering American troops across the border into Cambodia to "clean out" the bases that the enemy had been using for its "increased military aggression."

Literally overnight, the Cambodian invasion restored the dwindling antiwar movement to vigorous life. The first days of May saw the most widespread and vocal antiwar demonstrations ever. Hundreds of thousands of protesters gathered in Washington to denounce the president's policies. Millions, perhaps, participated in countless smaller demonstrations on campuses nationwide. Antiwar frenzy was reaching so high a level that it was possible briefly for some Americans to believe (incorrectly) that a genuine revolution was imminent. The mood of crisis intensified greatly on May 4, when four college students were killed and nine others injured when members of the National Guard opened fire on antiwar demonstrators at Kent State University in Ohio. Ten days later, police killed two black students at Jackson State University in Mississippi during a demonstration there.

The clamor against the war quickly spread into the government and the press. Congress angrily repealed the Gulf of Tonkin Resolution in December, stripping the president of what had long served as the legal basis for the war. Nixon ignored the action. Then, in June 1971, first the *New York Times* and later other newspapers began publishing excerpts from a secret study of the war prepared by the Defense Department during the Johnson administration. The so-called Pentagon Papers, leaked to the press by former Defense official Daniel Ellsberg, provided confirmation of what many had long believed: that the government had been dishonest, both in reporting the military progress of the war and in explaining its own motives for American involvement. The administration went to court to suppress the documents, but the Supreme Court finally ruled that the press had the right to publish them.

Particularly troubling, both to the public and to the government itself, were signs of decay within the American military. Morale and discipline among U.S. troops in Vietnam, who had been fighting a savage and inconclusive war for more than five years, was rapidly deteriorating. The trial and conviction in 1971 of Lieutenant William Calley, who was charged with overseeing a massacre of more than 100 unarmed South Vietnamese civilians, attracted wide public attention to the dehumanizing impact of the war on those who fought it—and to the terrible consequences for the Vietnamese people of that dehumanization. Less publicized were other, more widespread problems among American troops in Vietnam: desertion, drug addiction, racial hostilities, refusal to obey orders, even the killing of unpopular officers by enlisted men.

The continuing carnage, the increasing savagery, and the social distress at home had largely destroyed public support for the war. By 1971, nearly two-thirds of those interviewed in public opinion polls were urging American withdrawal from Vietnam. But from Richard Nixon there came no sign of retreat. On the contrary, the events of the spring of 1970 left him more convinced than ever of the importance of resisting those who opposed his military policies. With the approval of the White House, both the FBI and the CIA intensified their surveillance and infiltration of antiwar and radical groups, often resorting to blatant illegalities. Administration officials sought to discredit prominent critics of the war by leaking damaging personal information about them. At one point, White House agents broke into the office of a psychiatrist in an unsuccessful effort to steal files on Daniel Ellsberg, the former Defense Department official who had leaked a secret study of the origins of the war (the Pentagon Papers) to the press in 1971. During the congressional campaign of 1970, Vice President Spiro Agnew, using the acid rhetoric that had already made him the hero of many conservatives, stepped up his attack on the "effete" and "impudent" critics of the administration. The president himself once climbed on top of an automobile to taunt a crowd of angry demonstrators.

Meanwhile, the fighting in Indochina raged on. In February 1971, the president ordered the air force to assist the South Vietnamese army in an invasion of Laos—a test, as he saw it, of his Vietnamization program. Within weeks, the South Vietnamese scrambled back across the border in defeat. American bombing in Vietnam and Cambodia increased, despite its apparent ineffectiveness. In March 1972, the North Vietnamese mounted their biggest offensive since 1968 (the so-called Easter Offensive). American and South Vietnamese forces managed to halt the communist advance, but it was clear that without American support the offensive would have succeeded. At the same time, Nixon ordered American planes to bomb targets near Hanoi, the capital of North Vietnam, and Haiphong, its principal port, and called for the mining of seven North Vietnamese harbors (including Haiphong) to stop the flow of supplies from China and the Soviet Union.

"Peace with Honor"

As the 1972 presidential election approached, the administration stepped up its efforts to produce a breakthrough in negotiations with the North Vietnamese. In April 1972, the president dropped his longtime insistence on a removal of North Vietnamese troops from the south before any American withdrawal. Meanwhile, Henry Kissinger was meeting privately in Paris with the North Vietnamese foreign secretary, Le Duc Tho, to work out terms for a cease-fire. On October 26, only days before the presidential election, Kissinger announced that "peace is at hand."

Several weeks later (after the election), negotiations broke down once again. Although both the American and the North Vietnamese governments were ready to accept the Kissinger-Tho plan for a cease-fire, the Thieu regime balked, still insisting on a full withdrawal of North Vietnamese forces from the south. Kissinger tried to win additional concessions from the communists to meet Thieu's objections, but on December 16 talks broke off.

The next day, December 17, American B-52s began the heaviest and most destructive air raids of the entire war on Hanoi, Haiphong, and other North Vietnamese targets. Civilian casualties were high. And fifteen American B-52s were shot down by the North Vietnamese; in the entire war to that point, the United States had lost only one of the giant bombers. On December 30, Nixon terminated the "Christmas

bombing." The United States and the North Vietnamese returned to the conference table. And on January 27, 1973, they signed an "agreement on ending the war and restoring peace in Vietnam." Nixon claimed that the Christmas bombing had forced the North Vietnamese to relent. At least equally important, however, was the enormous American pressure on Thieu to accept the cease-fire.

The terms of the Paris accords were little different from those Kissinger and Tho had accepted in principle a few months before. There would be an immediate cease-fire. The North Vietnamese would release several hundred American prisoners of war, whose fate had become an emotional issue of great importance within the United States. After that the agreement descended into murky and plainly unworkable arrangements. The Thieu regime would survive for the moment—the principal North Vietnamese concession to the United States—but North Vietnamese forces already in the South would remain there. An undefined committee would work out a permanent settlement.

Defeat in Indochina

American forces were hardly out of Indochina before the Paris accords collapsed. During the first year after the cease-fire, the contending Vietnamese armies suffered greater battle losses than the Americans had absorbed during ten years of fighting. Finally, in March 1975, the North Vietnamese launched a full-scale offensive against the now greatly weakened forces of the south. Thieu appealed to Washington for assistance; the president (now Gerald Ford) appealed to Congress for additional funding; Congress refused. Late in April 1975, communist forces marched into Saigon, shortly after officials of the Thieu regime and the staff of the American embassy had fled the country in humiliating disarray. Communist forces quickly occupied the capital, renamed it Ho Chi Minh City, and began the process of reuniting Vietnam under the harsh rule of Hanoi. At about the same time, the Lon Nol regime in Cambodia fell to the murderous communists of Pol Pot and the Khmer Rouge—whose genocidal policies led to the deaths of more than a third of the country's people over the next several years.

That was the dismal end of over a decade of direct American military involvement in Vietnam. More than 1.2 million Vietnamese soldiers had died in combat, along with countless civilians throughout the region. A beautiful land had been ravaged, its agrarian economy left in ruins; for many years after, Vietnam remained one of the poorest and most politically oppressive nations in the world. The United States had paid a heavy price as well. The war had cost the

THE FALL OF SAIGON
Americans and other foreigners scramble to board U.S. helicopters for evacuation from Saigon, only hours before North Vietnamese troops arrive to seize control of the city. Many South Vietnamese officials struggled to find a place on the boats and helicopters as well. *(UPI/Bettmann)*

nation almost $150 billion in direct costs and much more indirectly. It had resulted in the deaths of over 55,000 young Americans and the injury of 300,000 more. And the nation had suffered a blow to its confidence and self-esteem from which it would not soon recover.

NIXON, KISSINGER, AND THE WORLD

The continuing war in Vietnam provided a dismal backdrop to what Nixon considered his larger mission in world affairs: the construction of a new international order. The president had become convinced that old assumptions of a "bipolar" world—in which the United States and the Soviet Union were the only truly great powers—were now obsolete. America must adapt to the new "multipolar" international structure, in which China, Japan, and Western Europe were becoming major, independent forces. "It will be a safer world and a better world," he said in 1971, "if we have a strong, healthy United States, Europe, Soviet Union, China, Japan—each balancing the other, not playing one against the other, an even balance."

Nixon and Kissinger believed it was possible to construct something like the "balance of power" that had permitted nineteenth-century Europe to experience nearly a century of relative stability. To do so, however, required a major change in several longstanding assumptions of American foreign policy.

China and the Soviet Union

For more than twenty years, ever since the fall of Chiang Kai-shek in 1949, the United States had treated China, the second largest nation on earth, as if it did not exist. Instead, America recognized the forlorn regime-in-exile on Taiwan as the legitimate government of mainland China. Nixon and Kissinger wanted to forge a new relationship with the Chinese communists—in part to strengthen them as a counterbalance to the Soviet Union. The Chinese, for their part, were eager to forestall the possibility of a Soviet-American alliance against China and to end China's own isolation from the international arena.

In July 1971, Nixon sent Henry Kissinger on a secret mission to Beijing. When Kissinger returned, the president made the startling announcement that he would visit China himself within the next few months. That fall, with American approval, the United Nations admitted the communist government of China and expelled the representatives of the Taiwan regime, whose claim to be the legitimate government of all China had been a major obstacle to western recognition of the communist regime. Finally, in February 1972, Nixon paid a formal visit to China and, in a single stroke, erased much of the deep American animosity toward the Chinese communists. Nixon did not yet formally recognize the communist regime, but in 1972 the United States and China began low-level diplomatic relations.

The initiatives in China coincided with (and probably assisted) an effort by the Nixon administration to improve relations with the Soviet Union. In 1969, American and Soviet diplomats met in Helsinki, Finland, to begin talks on limiting nuclear weapons. In 1972, they produced the first Strategic Arms Limitation Treaty (SALT I), which froze the nuclear missiles (ICBMs) of both sides at present levels. In May of that year, the president traveled to Moscow to sign the agreement. The next year, the Soviet premier, Leonid Brezhnev, visited Washington, and the two leaders pledged renewed efforts to speed the next phase of arms control negotiations.

The Problems of Multipolarity

The policies of rapprochement with communist China and detente with the Soviet Union reflected Nixon's and Kissinger's belief in the importance of stable

DÉTENTE AT HIGH TIDE
The visit of Soviet Premier Leonid Brezhnev to Washington in 1973 was a high-water mark in the search for détente between the two nations, a search that had begun as early as 1962, that continued through parts of five presidential administrations, and that collapsed in disarray in the late 1970s. Here, Brezhnev and Nixon share friendly words while standing on the White House balcony. *(J. P. Laffont/Sygma)*

relationships among the great powers. But great-power relationships could not alone ensure international stability, for the "Third World" remained the most volatile and dangerous source of international tension.

Central to the Nixon-Kissinger policy toward the Third World was the effort to maintain a stable status quo without involving the United States too deeply in local disputes. In 1969 and 1970, the president described

what became known as the Nixon Doctrine, by which the United States would "participate in the defense and development of allies and friends" but would leave the "basic responsibility" for the future of those "friends" to the nations themselves. In practice, the Nixon Doctrine meant a declining American interest in contributing to Third World development; a growing contempt for the United Nations, where less-developed nations were gaining influence through their sheer numbers; and increasing support to authoritarian regimes attempting to withstand radical challenges from within.

In 1970, for example, the CIA poured substantial funds into Chile to help support the established government against a communist challenge. When the Marxist candidate for president, Salvador Allende, came to power through an honest election, the United States began funneling more money to opposition forces in Chile to help "destabilize" the new government. In 1973, a military junta seized power from Allende, who was subsequently murdered. The United States developed a friendly relationship with the new, repressive military government of General Augusto Pinochet.

In the Middle East, conditions were growing more volatile in the aftermath of the 1967 "Six-Day War," in which Israel routed Egyptian, Syrian, and Jordanian forces, gained control of the whole of the long-divided city of Jerusalem, and occupied substantial new territories: on the west bank of the Jordan River, the Gaza Strip, the Golan Heights, and elsewhere. The war also increased the number of refugee Palestinians—Arabs who claimed the lands now controlled by Israel and who, dislodged from their homes, became a source of considerable instability in Jordan, Lebanon, and the other surrounding countries into which they now moved. Jordan's ruler, King Hussein, was particularly alarmed by the influx of Palestinians and by the activities of the Palestinian Liberation Organization (PLO) and other radical groups, which he feared would threaten Jordan's important relationship with the United States. After a series of uprisings in 1970, Hussein ordered the Jordanian army to expel the Palestinians. Many of them moved to Lebanon, where they became part of many years of instability and civil war.

In October 1973, on the Jewish High Holy Day of Yom Kippur, Egyptian and Syrian forces attacked Israel. For ten days, the Israelis struggled to recover from the surprise attack; finally, they launched an effective counteroffensive against Egyptian forces in the Sinai. At that point, the United States intervened, placing heavy pressure on Israel to accept a cease-fire rather than press its advantage.

CRISES IN THE MIDDLE EAST

ITALY

GREECE

Mediterranean Sea

Tripoli

Gulf of Sidra

LIBYA
1969 Qaddafi seizes power
1977 Abortive border war with Egypt
1986 U.S. responds to Libyan-backed terrorism by bombing Tripoli

TURKEY

Ankara

(Former Soviet Union)

1974 Fighting between Turkey and Greece over Cyprus threatens NATO unity

CYPRUS

SYRIA

LEBANON Beirut • Damascus

Baghdad

IRAQ
1980 Iran-Iraq war

ISRAEL
Jerusalem • Amman
JORDAN

Teheran

IRAN
1953 U.S. supports Shah, helps put down anti-U.S. Socialist government
1979 Shah overthrown
1979–1981 Hostage crisis

AFGHANISTAN
1979 U.S. supports guerillas fighting Soviet invaders

PAKISTAN

Suez Canal —
Cairo
Gulf of Suez

Gulf of Aqaba

EGYPT
1978 Egypt and Israel agree to Camp David accords
1979 Formal peace treaty signed between Egypt and Israel
1981 Sadat assassinated

KUWAIT
1990 Iraq invades Kuwait
1991 U.S. and others drive Iraq out of Kuwait in Gulf War

Kharg Island

Persian Gulf

BAHRAIN

QATAR
Abu Dhabi

Strait of Hormuz

OMAN

Gulf of Oman

Riyadh

SAUDI ARABIA

UNITED ARAB EMIRATES

OMAN

Red Sea

Mecca

SUDAN

YEMEN

San'a

Arabian Sea

ERITREA

Aden

Gulf of Aden

DJIBOUTI

ETHIOPIA

SOMALIA

0   500 Miles

0   500 Kilometers

LEBANON
1958 U.S. intervention supports pro-West government
1981–1984 U.S. joins UN peacekeeping force, suffers series of violent attacks

Tripoli

Beirut

Sidon

Tyre

Damascus

SYRIA

ISRAEL
1993 Israel and PLO sign accords for Palestinian self-rule in Jericho and Gaza Strip

Haifa

Amman

Tel Aviv

Jerusalem

JORDAN

EGYPT
1982 Sinai Peninsula returned to Egypt by Israel

0   50 Miles

0   50 Kilometers

Eilat • Aqaba

U.S. allies

Israel before 1967

Territory occupied by Israel since Six-Day War, 1967

☥ Oilfields (U.S. supporters involved)

The Arab-Israeli Wars
1948 War of Independence
1956 Sinai War
1967 Six-Day War
1973 Yom Kippur War
1982 Invasion of Lebanon
  (occupied 1982-1985)

869

The imposed settlement of the Yom Kippur War demonstrated the growing dependence of the United States and its allies on Arab oil. Permitting Israel to continue its drive into Egypt might have jeopardized the ability of the United States to purchase needed petroleum from the Arab states. A brief but painful embargo by the Arab governments on the sale of oil to supporters of Israel (including America) in 1973 provided an ominous warning of the costs of losing access to the region's resources. The lesson of the Yom Kippur War, therefore, was that the United States could not ignore the interests of the Arab nations in its efforts on behalf of Israel.

A larger lesson of 1973 was that the nations of the Third World could no longer be expected to act as passive, cooperative "client states." The United States could no longer depend on cheap, easy access to raw materials as it had in the past.

POLITICS AND ECONOMICS UNDER NIXON

For a time in the late 1960s, it had seemed to many Americans that the forces of chaos and radicalism were taking control of the nation. The domestic policy of the Nixon administration was an attempt to restore balance: between the needs of the poor and the desires of the middle class, between the power of the federal government and the interests of local communities. In the end, however, economic and political crises—some beyond the administration's control, some of its own making—sharply limited Nixon's ability to fulfill his domestic goals.

Domestic Initiatives

Many of Nixon's domestic policies were a response to what he believed to be the demands of his own constituency—conservative, middle-class people whom he liked to call the "silent majority" and who wanted to reduce federal "interference" in local affairs. He tried, unsuccessfully, to persuade Congress to pass legislation prohibiting the use of forced busing to achieve school desegregation. He forbade the Department of Health, Education, and Welfare to cut off federal funds from school districts that had failed to comply with court orders to integrate. At the same time, he began to reduce or dismantle many of the social programs of the Great Society and the New Frontier. In 1973, for example, he abolished the Office of Economic Oppor-

tunity, the centerpiece of the antipoverty program of the Johnson years.

Yet Nixon's domestic efforts were not entirely negative. One of the administration's boldest efforts was an attempt to overhaul the nation's enormous welfare system. Nixon proposed replacing the existing system, which almost everyone agreed was cumbersome, expensive, and inefficient, with what he called the Family Assistance Plan. It would in effect have created a guaranteed annual income for all Americans: $1,600 in federal grants, which could be supplemented by outside earnings up to $4,000. Even many liberals applauded the proposal as an important step toward expanding federal responsibility for the poor. Nixon, however, presented the plan in conservative terms: as something that would reduce the supervisory functions of the federal government and transfer to welfare recipients themselves daily responsibility for their own lives. Although the FAP won approval in the House in 1970, concerted attacks by welfare recipients (who considered the benefits inadequate), members of the welfare bureaucracy (whose own influence stood to be sharply diminished by the bill), and conservatives (who opposed a guaranteed income on principle) helped kill it in the Senate.

From the Warren Court to the Nixon Court

Of all the liberal institutions that had aroused the enmity of the "silent majority" in the 1950s and 1960s, none had evoked more anger and bitterness than the Supreme Court. Not only had its rulings on racial matters disrupted traditional social patterns in both the North and the South, but its staunch defense of civil liberties had, in the eyes of many Americans, contributed to the increase in crime, disorder, and moral decay. In *Engel* v. *Vitale* (1962), the Court had ruled that prayers in public schools were unconstitutional, sparking outrage among religious fundamentalists and others. In *Roth* v. *United States* (1957), the Court had sharply limited the authority of local governments to curb pornography. In a series of other decisions, the Court had greatly strengthened the civil rights of criminal defendants and, in the eyes of many Americans, had greatly weakened the power of law enforcement officials to do their jobs. For example, in *Gideon* v. *Wainwright* (1963), the Court had ruled that every felony defendant was entitled to a lawyer regardless of his or her ability to pay. In *Escobedo* v. *Illinois* (1964), it had ruled that a defendant must be allowed access to a lawyer before questioning by police. In *Miranda* v. *Arizona* (1966), the Court had confirmed the obligation of authorities to inform a criminal suspect of his or her rights. By 1968, the Warren Court had become the target of Americans of all kinds who felt the balance of power in the United States had shifted too far toward the poor and dispossessed at the expense of the middle class, and toward criminals at the expense of law-abiding citizens.

One of the most important decisions of the Warren Court in the 1960s was *Baker* v. *Carr* (1962), which required state legislatures to apportion electoral districts so that all citizens' votes would have equal weight. In dozens of states, systems of legislative districting had given disproportionate representation to sparsely populated rural areas, hence diminishing the voting power of urban residents. The reapportionment that the decision required greatly strengthened the voting power of African Americans, Hispanics, and other groups concentrated in cities.

Nixon was determined to use his judicial appointments to give the Court a more conservative cast. His first opportunity came almost as soon as he entered office. When Chief Justice Earl Warren resigned early in 1969, Nixon replaced him with a federal appeals court judge of known conservative leanings, Warren Burger. A few months later, Associate Justice Abe Fortas resigned after allegations of financial improprieties. To replace him, Nixon named Clement F. Haynsworth, a respected federal circuit court judge from South Carolina. But Haynsworth came under fire from Senate liberals, black organizations, and labor unions for his conservative record on civil rights and for what some claimed was a conflict of interest in several of the cases on which he had sat. The Senate rejected him. Nixon's next choice was G. Harrold Carswell, a judge of the Florida federal appeals court almost entirely lacking in distinction and widely considered unfit for the Supreme Court. The Senate rejected his nomination too.

Nixon angrily denounced the votes, calling them expressions of prejudice against the South. But he was careful thereafter to choose men of standing within the legal community to fill vacancies on the Supreme Court: Harry Blackmun, a moderate jurist from Minnesota; Lewis F. Powell, Jr., a respected judge from Virginia; and William Rehnquist, a member of the Nixon Justice Department. In the process, he transformed the Warren Court into what some called the "Nixon Court" and others the "Burger Court."

The new Court, however, fell short of what the president and many conservatives had expected. Rather than retreating from its commitment to social reform, the Court in many areas actually moved further. In *Swann* v. *Charlotte-Mecklenburg Board of Education* (1971), it ruled in favor of the use of forced busing to achieve racial balance in schools. Not even the intense and occasionally violent opposition of local communities such as Boston and Louisville, Kentucky, was able to weaken the judicial commitment to integration. In *Furman* v. *Georgia* (1972), the Court overturned existing capital punishment statutes and established strict new guidelines for such laws in the future. In *Roe* v. *Wade* (1973), it struck down laws forbidding abortions.

In other decisions, however, the Burger Court was more moderate. Although the justices approved busing as a tool for achieving integration, they rejected, in *Milliken* v. *Bradley* (1974), a plan to transfer students across district lines (in this case, between Detroit and its suburbs) to achieve racial balance. While the Court upheld the principle of affirmative action in its celebrated 1978 decision *Bakke* v. *Board of Regents of California*, it established restrictive new guidelines for such programs in the future. In *Stone* v. *Powell* (1976), the Court agreed to certain limits on the right of a defendant to appeal a state conviction to the federal judiciary.

The Election of 1972

However unsuccessful his administration may have been in achieving some of its specific goals, Nixon entered the presidential race in 1972 with a substantial reserve of strength. The events of that year improved his position immeasurably. His energetic reelection committee collected enormous sums of money to support the campaign. The president himself used the powers of incumbency with great effect, refraining from campaigning and concentrating on highly publicized international decisions and state visits. Agencies of the federal government dispensed funds and favors to strengthen Nixon's political standing in critical areas.

Nixon was most fortunate in 1972, however, in his opposition. The return of George Wallace to the presidential fray caused some early concern. Nixon was delighted to see Wallace run in the Democratic primaries and quietly encouraged him to do so. But he feared that Wallace would again launch a third-party campaign; Nixon's own reelection strategy rested on the same appeals to the troubled middle class that Wallace was expressing. The possibility of such a campaign vanished in May, when a would-be assassin shot the Alabama governor during a rally at a Maryland shopping center. Paralyzed from the waist down, Wallace was unable to continue campaigning.

The Democrats, in the meantime, were making their own contributions to the Nixon cause by nominating for president a representative of their most liberal wing: Senator George S. McGovern of South Dakota.

An outspoken critic of the war, a forceful advocate of advanced liberal positions on virtually every social and economic issue, McGovern seemed to embody those aspects of the turbulent 1960s that middle-class Americans were most eager to reject. McGovern profited greatly from party reforms (which he himself had helped to draft) that reduced the power of party leaders and gave increased influence to women, blacks, and young people in the selection of the Democratic ticket. But those same reforms helped make the Democratic Convention of 1972 an unappealing spectacle to much of the public. The candidate then disillusioned even some of his own supporters by his indecisive reaction to revelations that his running mate, Senator Thomas Eagleton of Missouri, had undergone treatment for an emotional disturbance. Eagleton finally withdrew from the ticket. The remainder of the Democratic presidential campaign was an exercise in futility.

On election day, Nixon won reelection by one of the largest margins in history: 60.7 percent of the popular vote compared with 37.5 percent for the forlorn McGovern, and an electoral margin of 520 to 17. The Democratic candidate had carried only Massachusetts and the District of Columbia. The new commitments that Nixon had so effectively expressed—to restraint in social reform, to decentralization of political power, to the defense of traditional values, and to a new balance in international relations—had clearly won the approval of the American people. But other problems were already lurking in the wings.

The Troubled Economy

Although it was political scandal that would ultimately destroy the Nixon presidency, the most important national crisis of the early 1970s was the decline of the American economy. For three decades, the American economy had been the envy of the world. It had produced as much as a third of the world's industrial goods and had dominated international trade. The American dollar had been the strongest currency in the world, and the American standard of living had risen steadily from its already substantial heights. Many Americans assumed that this remarkable prosperity was the normal condition of their society. In fact, however, it rested in part on several artificial conditions that were rapidly disappearing by the late 1960s: above all, the absence of significant foreign competition and easy access to raw materials in the Third World.

Inflation, which had been creeping upward for several years when Richard Nixon took office, soon be-

INFLATION, 1960–1992

Annual percentage change in Consumer Price Index

gan to soar; it would be the most disturbing economic problem of the 1970s. Its most visible cause was a significant increase in federal deficit spending in the 1960s, when the Johnson administration tried to fund the war in Vietnam and its ambitious social programs without raising taxes. But there were other, equally important causes of the inflation and of the economic problems that lay behind it. No longer did the United States have exclusive access to cheap raw materials around the globe; not only were other industrial nations now competing for increasingly scarce raw materials; but Third World suppliers of those materials were beginning to realize their value and to demand higher prices for them.

The greatest immediate blow to the American economy was the increasing cost of energy. More than any nation on earth, the United States based its economy on the easy availability of cheap and plentiful fossil fuels. No society was more dependent on the automobile; none was more wasteful in its use of oil and gas in its homes, schools, and factories. Domestic petroleum reserves were no longer sufficient to meet this demand, and the nation was heavily dependent on imports from the Middle East and Africa.

For many years, the Organization of Petroleum Exporting Countries (OPEC) had operated as an informal bargaining unit for the sale of oil by Third World nations, but had seldom managed to exercise any real strength. But in the early 1970s, OPEC began to assert itself, to use its oil both as an economic tool and as a political weapon. In 1973, in the midst of the Yom Kippur War, Arab members of OPEC announced that they would no longer ship petroleum to nations supporting Israel—which meant the United States and its allies in Western Europe. At about the same time, the OPEC nations agreed to raise their prices 400 percent.

These twin shocks produced momentary economic chaos in the West. The United States suffered its first fuel shortage since World War II. And although the boycott ended a few months later, the price of energy continued to skyrocket both because of OPEC's new militant policies and because of the weakening competitive position of the dollar in world markets. No single factor did more to produce the soaring inflation of the 1970s.

But inflation was only one of the new problems facing the American economy. The other, and more important in the long run, was the decline of the nation's manufacturing sector. American industry had flourished in the immediate aftermath of World War II, in part because of the new plant capacity the war had created, in part because the country faced almost no competition from other industrial nations. American workers in unionized industries had profited from this postwar success by winning some of the most generous wage and benefits packages in the world.

By the 1970s, however, the climate for American manufacturing had changed significantly. Many of the great industrial plants were now many decades old, much less efficient than the newer plants that Japan and European industrial nations had constructed after the war. In some industries (notably steel and automobiles), management had become complacent and stultifyingly bureaucratic. Most important, U.S. manufacturing now faced major competition from abroad—not only in world trade (which still constituted only a small part of the American economy) but also at home. Automobiles, steel, and many other manufactured goods from Japan and Europe established major footholds in the United States markets. Some of America's new competitors benefited from lower labor costs than their U.S. counterparts; but that was only one of many reasons for their success.

Thus the 1970s marked the beginning of a long, painful process of deindustrialization, during which thousands of factories across the country closed their gates and millions of workers lost their jobs. New employment opportunities were becoming available in other, growing areas of the economy: technology, information systems, and many other more "knowledge-based" industries. But many industrial workers were poorly equipped to move into those jobs. The result was a growing pool of unemployed and underemployed workers; the virtual disappearance of industrial jobs from many inner cities, where large numbers of minorities lived; and the impoverishment of communities dependent on particular industries. Some of the nation's manufacturing sectors ultimately revived, but few regained the size and dominance they had enjoyed in the 1950s and 1960s; and few employed a work force as large or as relatively well paid as they once had.

The Nixon Response

The Nixon administration responded to these mounting economic problems by focusing on the one thing it thought it could control: inflation. The government moved first to reduce spending and raise taxes. But those policies produced both congressional and popular protest, and Nixon turned increasingly to an economic tool more readily available to him: control of the currency. Placing conservative economists at the head of the Federal Reserve Board, he ensured sharply higher interest rates and a contraction of the money supply. But the tight money policy did little to curb inflation: the cost of living rose a cumulative 15 percent during Nixon's first two and a half years in office. Economic growth, in the meantime, declined. The United States was encountering a new and puzzling dilemma: "stagflation," a combination of rising prices and general economic stagnation.

In the summer of 1971, Nixon imposed a ninety-day freeze on all wages and prices at their existing levels. Then, in November, he launched what he called Phase II of his economic plan: mandatory guidelines for wage and price increases, to be administered by a federal agency. Inflation subsided temporarily, but the recession continued. Fearful that the recession would be more damaging than inflation in an election year, the administration reversed itself late in 1971: interest rates were allowed to drop sharply, and government spending was increased—producing the largest budget deficit since World War II. The new tactics helped revive the economy in the short term, but inflation rose substantially—particularly after the administration abandoned the strict Phase II controls and replaced them with a set of voluntary, and almost entirely ineffective, guidelines. In 1973, prices rose 9 percent; in 1974, after the Arab oil embargo and the OPEC price increases, they rose 12 percent—the highest rate since the relaxation of price controls shortly after World War II. The value of the dollar continued to slide, and the nation's international trade continued to decline. In the meantime, the energy crisis was quickly becoming a national preoccupation. But while Nixon talked often about the need to achieve "energy independence," he offered few concrete proposals.

The erratic economic programs of the Nixon administration were a sign of a broader national confusion about the prospects for American prosperity. The Nixon pattern—of lurching from a tight money policy to curb inflation at one moment, to a spending policy to cure recession at the next—repeated itself during the two administrations that followed.

THE WATERGATE CRISIS

Although economic problems greatly concerned the American people in the 1970s, another stunning development almost entirely preoccupied the nation beginning early in 1973: the fall of Richard Nixon. The president's demise was a result, in part, of his own personality. Defensive, secretive, resentful of his critics, he brought to his office an element of mean-spiritedness that helped undermine even his most important accomplishments. But the larger explanation lay in Nixon's view of American society and the world, and of his own role in both. The president believed the United States faced grave dangers from the radicals and dissidents who were challenging his policies. He came increasingly to consider any challenge to his policies a threat to "national security." By identifying his own political fortunes with those of the nation, Nixon was creating a climate in which he and those who served him could justify almost any tactics to stifle dissent and undermine opposition.

The Scandals

Nixon's outlook was in part a culmination of long-term changes in the presidency. Public expectations of the president had increased dramatically in the years since World War II; yet the constraints on the authority of the office from Congress, the courts, interest groups, the media and elsewhere had grown as well. In response, a succession of presidents had sought new methods for the exercise of power, often stretching the law, occasionally breaking it.

Nixon not only continued but greatly accelerated these trends. Facing a Democratic Congress hostile to his goals, he attempted to find ways to circumvent the legislature whenever possible. Saddled with a federal bureaucracy unresponsive to his wishes, he constructed a hierarchy of command in which virtually all executive power became concentrated in the White House. Operating within a rigid, even autocratic staff structure, the president became a solitary, at times brooding figure, whose contempt for his opponents and impatience with obstacles to his policies festered and grew. Unknown to all but a few intimates, he also became mired in a pattern of illegalities and abuses of power that in late 1972 began to break through to the surface.

Early on the morning of June 17, 1972, police arrested five men who had broken into the offices of the Democratic National Committee in the Watergate office building in Washington, D.C. Two others were seized a short time later and charged with supervising the break-in. When reporters for the *Washington Post* began researching the backgrounds of the culprits, they discovered that among those involved in the burglary were former employees of the Committee for the Re-Election of the President (CRP). One of them had worked in the White House itself. Moreover, they had been paid for the break-in from a secret fund of the re-election committee, a fund controlled by members of the White House staff.

Public interest in the disclosures grew slowly in the last months of 1972. Few Americans questioned the president's assurances that neither he nor his staff had any connection with what he called "this very bizarre incident." Early in 1973, however, the Watergate burglars went on trial; and under relentless prodding from federal judge John J. Sirica, one of the defendants, James W. McCord, agreed to cooperate both with the grand jury and with a special Senate investigating committee recently established under Senator Sam J. Ervin of North Carolina. McCord's testimony opened a floodgate of confessions, and for months a parade of White House and campaign officials exposed one illegality after another. Foremost among them was a member of the inner circle of the White House, counsel to the president John Dean, who leveled allegations against Nixon himself.

Two different sets of scandals were emerging from the investigations. One was a general pattern of abuses of power involving both the White House and the Nixon campaign committee, which included, but was not limited to, the Watergate break-in. The other scandal, and the one that became the major focus of public attention for nearly two years, was the way in which the administration tried to manage the investigations of the Watergate break-in and other abuses—a pattern of behavior that became known as the "cover-up." There was never any conclusive evidence that the president had planned or approved the burglary in advance. But there was mounting evidence that he had been involved in illegal efforts to obstruct investigations of and withhold information about the episode. Testimony before the Ervin committee provided evidence of the complicity of Dean, Attorney General John Mitchell, top White House assistants H. R. Haldeman and John Ehrlichman, and others. As interest in the case grew to something approaching a national obsession, the investigation focused increasingly on a single question: in the words of Senator Howard Baker of Tennessee, a member of the Ervin committee, "What did the President know and when did he know it?"

Nixon accepted the departure of those members of his administration implicated in the scandals. But he continued to insist that he himself was innocent. There the matter might have rested, had it not been for the disclosure during the Senate hearings of a White House taping system that had recorded virtually every conversation in the president's office during the period in question. All the groups investigating the scandals sought access to the tapes; Nixon, pleading "executive privilege," refused to release them. A special prosecutor appointed by the president to handle the Watergate cases, Harvard law professor Archibald Cox, took Nixon to court in October 1973 in an effort to force him to relinquish the recordings. Nixon, clearly growing desperate, then fired Cox and suffered the humiliation of watching both Attorney General Elliot Richardson and his deputy resign in protest. This "Saturday night massacre" made the president's predicament infinitely worse. Not only did public pressure force him to appoint a new special prosecutor, Texas attorney Leon Jaworski, who proved just as determined as Cox to subpoena the tapes; but the episode precipitated an investigation by the House of Representatives into the possibility of impeachment.

The Fall of Richard Nixon

Nixon's situation deteriorated further in the following months. Late in 1973, Vice President Spiro Agnew became embroiled in a scandal of his own when evidence surfaced that he had accepted bribes and kickbacks while serving as governor of Maryland and even as vice president. In return for a Justice Department agreement not to press the case, Agnew pleaded no contest to a lesser charge of income-tax evasion and resigned from the government. With the controversial Agnew no longer in line to succeed to the presidency, the prospect of removing Nixon from the White House became less worrisome to his opponents. The new vice president (the first appointed under the terms of the Twenty-fifth Amendment, which had been adopted in 1967) was House minority leader Gerald Ford, an amiable and popular Michigan congressman.

The impeachment investigation quickly gathered pace. In April 1974, in an effort to head off further subpoenas of the tapes, the president released transcripts of a number of relevant conversations, claiming that they proved his innocence. Investigators and much of the public felt otherwise. Even these edited tapes seemed to suggest Nixon's complicity in the cover-up. In July, the crisis reached a climax. First the Supreme Court ruled unanimously, in *United States* v. *Richard M. Nixon*, that the president must relinquish the tapes to Special Prosecutor Jaworski. Days later, the House Judiciary Committee voted to recommend three articles of impeachment, charging that Nixon had, first, obstructed justice in the Watergate cover-up; second, misused federal agencies to violate the rights of citizens; and third, defied the authority of Congress by refusing to deliver tapes and other materials subpoenaed by the committee.

NIXON'S FAREWELL
Only moments before, Nixon had been in tears saying goodbye to his staff in the East Room of the White House. But as he boarded a helicopter to begin his trip home to California shortly after resigning as president, he flashed his trademark "victory" sign to the crowd on the White House Lawn. *(Bettmann)*

SIGNIFICANT EVENTS

1961 Representatives of sixty-seven tribes draft Declaration of Indian Purpose

1962 Students for a Democratic Society formed at Port Huron, Michigan

Supreme Court decides *Baker* v. *Carr*

1963 Betty Friedan publishes *The Feminine Mystique*

1964 Free Speech Movement begins at UC Berkeley

Beatles come to America

1965 United Farm Workers strike

1966 National Organization for Women (NOW) formed

Miranda v. *Arizona* expands rights of criminal suspects

1967 Antiwar protesters march on Pentagon

Israel and Arabs clash in Six-Day War

1968 Campus riots break out at Columbia University and elsewhere

Antiwar "mobilization" day

American Indian Movement (AIM) launched

Nuclear nonproliferation treaty signed

1969 Antiwar movement stages Vietnam "moratorium"

Theodore Roszak publishes *The Making of a Counter Culture*

People's Park uprising at Berkeley

Nixon orders secret bombing of Cambodia

Nixon begins withdrawing American troops from Vietnam

"Stonewall Riot" in New York City launches gay liberation movement

400,000 people attend rock concert in Woodstock, N.Y.

1970 American troops enter Cambodia

Antiwar protests increase

Students killed at Kent State and Jackson State universities

Palestinians expelled from Jordan

Charles Reich publishes *The Greening of America*

Even without additional evidence, Nixon might well have been impeached by the full House and convicted by the Senate. Early in August, however, he provided at last the "smoking gun"—the concrete proof of his guilt that his defenders had long contended was missing from the case against him. Among the tapes that the Supreme Court compelled Nixon to relinquish were several that offered apparently incontrovertible evidence of his involvement in the Watergate cover-up. Only days after the burglary, the recordings disclosed, the president had ordered the FBI to stop investigating the break-in. Impeachment and conviction now seemed inevitable.

For several days, Nixon brooded in the White House, on the verge, some claimed, of a breakdown. Finally, on August 8, 1974, he announced his resignation—the first president in American history ever to

do so. At noon the next day, while Nixon and his family were flying west to their home in California, Gerald Ford took the oath of office as president.

Many Americans expressed relief and exhilaration that, as the new president put it, "Our long national nightmare is over." Many were relieved to be rid of Richard Nixon, who had lost virtually all the wide popularity that had won him his landslide reelection victory only two years before. And many were also exhilarated that, as some boasted, "the system had worked." But the wave of good feeling could not obscure the deeper and more lasting damage of the Watergate crisis. In a society in which distrust of leaders and institutions of authority was already widespread, the fall of Richard Nixon seemed to confirm the most cynical assumptions about the character of American public life.

SIGNIFICANT EVENTS

1971 Pentagon Papers published

Supreme Court decides *Swann* v. *Charlotte-Mecklenburg Board of Education*

Nixon imposes wage-price freeze and controls

1972 Congress approves Equal Rights Amendment

Nixon visits China

SALT I treaty signed

United States mines Haiphong harbor in North Vietnam

Nixon orders "Christmas bombing" of North Vietnam

Supreme Court decides *Furman* v. *Georgia*

Burglary interrupted in Watergate office building

Nixon reelected president

1973 Indians demonstrate at Wounded Knee

Supreme Court decides *Roe* v. *Wade*

Paris accords produce cease-fire; America withdraws from Vietnam

Israel and Arabs clash in Yom Kippur War

Arab oil embargo produces first American energy crisis

Watergate scandal expands

1974 Impeachment proceedings begin against Nixon

Vice President Spiro Agnew resigns; Gerald Ford appointed to replace him

Nixon resigns; Ford becomes president

1975 South Vietnam falls

Khmer Rouge seize control of Cambodia

1977 President Carter pardons Vietnam draft resisters

1978 Vietnam invades Cambodia

Supreme Court hands down *Bakke* decision

1980 Large numbers of Cubans ("Marielitos") migrate to Florida

1982 Equal Rights Amendment fails to be ratified

SUGGESTED READINGS

General Studies.   John Morton Blum, *Years of Discord: American Politics and Society, 1961–1974* (1991). Peter N. Carroll, *It Seemed Like Nothing Happened* (1982). Allen J. Matusow, *The Unraveling of America* (1984). Kim McQuaid, *The Anxious Years* (1989). William O'Neill, *Coming Apart* (1971).

The New Left and the Counterculture.   Edward Bacciocco, Jr., *The New Left in America* (1974). Ronald Berman, *America in the Sixties* (1968). Wini Breines, *Community and Organization in the New Left* (1983). Peter Clecak, *Radical Paradoxes* (1973). Peter Collier and David Horowitz, *Destructive Generation: Second Thoughts About the Sixties* (1989). Morris Dickstein, *Gates of Eden* (1977). Joan Didion, *Slouching Towards Bethlehem* (1967); *The White Album* (1979). John Diggins, *The American Left in the Twentieth Century* (1973). Sara Evans, *Personal Politics* (1979). Lewis Feuer, *The Conflict of Generations* (1969). Richard Flacks, *Youth and Social Change* (1971). Todd Gitlin, *The Whole World Is Watching* (1981); *The Sixties: Years of Hope, Days of Rage* (1987). Paul Goodman, *Growing Up Absurd* (1960). David Harris, *Dreams Die Hard* (1983). Maurice Isserman, *"If I Had a Hammer. . .": The Death of the Old Left and the Birth of the New Left* (1987). Joseph Kelner and James Munves, *The Kent State Coverup* (1980). Kenneth Keniston, *Young Radicals* (1968); *Youth and Dissent* (1971). Richard King, *The Party of Eros* (1972). James Kunen, *The Strawberry Statement* (1968). Lawrence Lader, *Power on the Left* (1979). Klaus Mehnert, *Twilight of the Young* (1978). James Miller, *"Democracy in the Streets": From Port Huron to the Siege of Chicago* (1987). Charles Reich, *The Greening of America* (1970). W. J. Rorabaugh, *Berkeley at War* (1989). Theodore Roszak, *The*

Making of a Counter Culture (1969). Kirkpatrick Sale, *SDS* (1973). Irwin Unger, *The Movement* (1974). Milton Viorst, *Fire in the Streets* (1979). Jon Wiener, *Come Together: John Lennon in His Time* (1984).

Indians, Hispanics, Asians. Rodolfo Acuña, *Occupied America*, 2nd ed. (1981). Larry W. Burt, *Tribalism in Crisis: Federal Indian Policy, 1953–1961* (1982). Vine Deloria, Jr., *Behind the Trail of Broken Treaties* (1974); *Custer Died for Your Sins* (1969). Ronald Dewing, *Wounded Knee: The Meaning and Significance of the Second Incident* (1985). Douglas E. Foley, *From Peones to Politicos: Class and Ethnicity in a South Texas Town, 1900–1987* (1988). Peter Iverson, *The Navajo Nation* (1981). Oscar Lewis, *La Vida* (1969). D'Arcy McNickle, *Native American Tribalism* (1973). Matt Meier and Feliciano Rivera, *The Chicanos (1972)*. David M. Reimers, *Still the Golden Door: The Third World Comes to America* (1985). Julian Samora, *Los Mojados (1971)*. Stan Steiner, *The New Indians* (1968). Ronald Takaki, *Strangers from a Distant Shore: A History of Asian Americans* (1989); *A Different Mirror: A History of Multicultural America* (1993). Ronald Taylor, *Chavez and the Farm Workers* (1975). Wilcomb Washburn, *Red Man's Land/White Man's Land* (1971). Charles F. Wilkinson, *American Indians, Time, and the Law* (1987).

Feminism. William Chafe, *The American Woman* (1972). Nancy Cott, *The Grounding of Modern Feminism* (1987). Marian Faux, *Roe v. Wade* (1988). Jo Freeman, *The Politics of Women's Liberation* (1975). Betty Friedan, *The Feminine Mystique* (1963). Carol Gilligan, *In A Different Voice* (1982). Cynthia Harrison, *On Account of Sex: The Politics of Women's Issues, 1945–1968* (1988). Susan M. Hartmann, *From Margin to Mainstream: Women and American Politics Since 1960* (1989). Alice Kessler-Harris, *Out to Work: A History of Wage-Earning Women in the United States* (1982). Ethel Klein, *Gender Politics* (1984). Kristin Luker, *Abortion and the Politics of Motherhood* (1984). Robin Morgan, ed., *Sisterhood Is Powerful* (1970). Rosalind Petchesky, *Abortion and Women's Choice* (1984). Sheila Rothman, *Woman's Proper Place* (1978). Winifred Wandersee, *On the Move: American Women in the 1970s* (1988). Gayle Yates, *What Women Want* (1975).

Nixon and the World. Seyom Brown, *The Crisis of Power* (1979). Lloyd Gardner, *A Covenant with Power* (1984); *The Great Nixon Turnaround* (1973). Seymour Hersh, *The Price of Power* (1983). Roger Hilsman, *The Crouching Future* (1975). Arnold Isaacs, *Without Honor: Defeat in Vietnam and Cambodia* (1983). Walter Isaacson, *Kissinger* (1992). Marvin Kalb and Bernard Kalb, *Kissinger* (1974). Henry A. Kissinger, *White House Years* (1979); *Years of Upheaval* (1982); *Diplomacy* (1994). David Landau, *Kissinger: The Uses of Power (1972)*. Robert S. Litwak, *Detente and the Nixon Doctrine: American Foreign Pol-icy and the Pursuit of Stability* (1984). Timothy Lomperis, *The War Nobody Lost—and Won* (1984). Roger Morris, *Uncertain Greatness* (1977). Harland Moulton, *From Superiority to Parity* (1973). John Newhouse, *Cold Dawn* (1973). Michael Oksenberg and Robert Oxnam, eds., *Dragon and Eagle* (1978). Gareth Porter, *A Peace Denied* (1975); *Vietnam* (1979). Thomas Powers, *The Man Who Kept the Secrets* (1979). William Quandt, *Decade of Decision* (1977). Franz Schurman, *The Foreign Policies of Richard Nixon* (1987). William Shawcross, *Sideshow: Nixon, Kissinger, and the Destruction of Cambodia* (1978). Richard Stevenson, *The Rise and Fall of Detente* (1985). John Stockwell, *In Search of Enemies* (1977). Robert Stookey, *America and the Arab States* (1975). Robert D. Schulzinger, *Henry Kissinger: Doctor of Diplomacy* (1989). Tad Szulc, *The Illusion of Peace* (1978).

Nixon and His Presidency. Stephen Ambrose, *Nixon: The Triumph of a Politician, 1962–1972* (1989). Richard Barnet, *The Lean Years* (1980). Fawn Brodie, *Richard Nixon: The Shaping of His Character* (1981). Vincent Burke and Vee Burke, *Nixon's Good Deed* (1974). John Ehrlichman, *Witness to Power* (1982). H.R. Haldeman, *The Haldeman Diaries: Inside the Nixon White House* (1994). Joan Hoff, *Nixon Reconsidered* (1994). J. C. Hurewitz, ed., *Oil, the Arab-Israeli Dispute, and the Industrial World* (1976). R. L. Miller, *The New Economics of Richard Nixon* (1972). Daniel P. Moynihan, *The Politics of a Guaranteed Income* (1973). R. P. Nathan et al., *Monitoring Revenue Sharing* (1975). Richard Nixon, *RN: The Memoirs of Richard Nixon* (1978). Herbert Parmet, *Richard Nixon and His America* (1989). Raymond Price, *With Nixon* (1977). James Reichley, *Conservatives in an Age of Change: The Nixon and Ford Administrations* (1981). William Safire, *Before the Fall* (1975). Joan Edelman Spero, *The Politics of International Economic Relations* (1977). Michael Tanzer, *The Energy Crisis* (1974). Theodore H. White, *The Making of the President, 1972* (1973). Bob Woodward and Scott Armstrong, *The Brethren* (1980).

Nixon and Watergate. Fawn Brodie, *Richard Nixon* (1981). Richard Cohen and Jules Witcover, *A Heartbeat Away* (1974). Len Colodny and Robert Gettlin, *Silent Coup* (1991). John Dean, *Blind Ambition* (1976). James Doyle, *Not Above the Law* (1977). Fred Emery, *Watergate: The Corruption of American Politics* (1994). Stanley J. Kutler, *The Wars of Watergate* (1990). J. Anthony Lukas, *Nightmare: The Underside of the Nixon Years* (1976). Bruce Mazlish, *In Search of Nixon* (1972). Richard M. Nixon, *RN: The Memoirs of Richard Nixon* (1978). Jonathan Schell, *The Time of Illusion* (1975). Arthur M. Schlesinger, Jr., *The Imperial Presidency* (1973). William Sirica, *To Set the Record Straight* (1979). Maurice Stans, *The Terrors of Justice* (1984). Theodore H. White, *Breach of Faith* (1975). Garry Wills, *Nixon Agonistes* (1970). Bob Woodward and Carl Bernstein, *All the President's Men* (1974); *The Final Days* (1976).

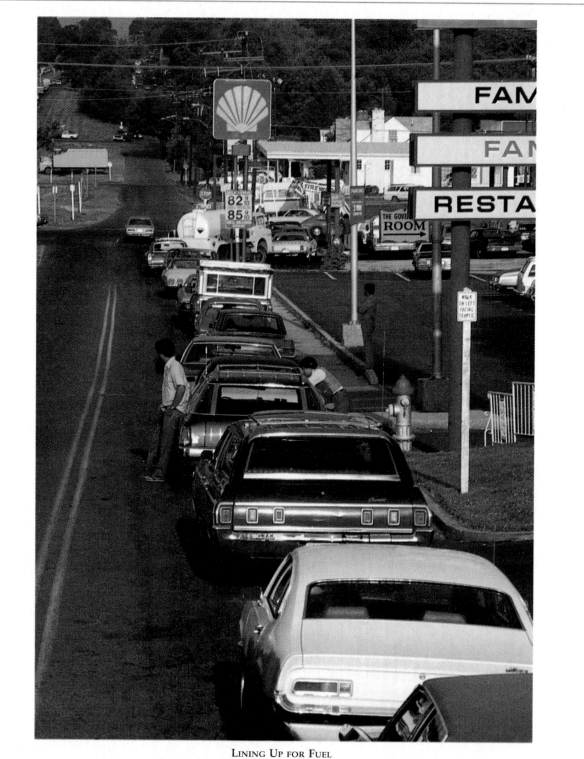

LINING UP FOR FUEL
Motorists line up outside a Virginia gas station in 1979 during one of a series of gasoline shortages that plagued American society during the 1970s.   *(Dennis Brack/Black Star)*

CHAPTER THIRTY-THREE

THE "AGE OF LIMITS"

T HE FRUSTRATIONS OF THE early 1970s—the defeat in Vietnam, the Watergate crisis, the decay of the American economy—inflicted damaging blows to the confident, optimistic nationalism that had characterized so much of the postwar era. At first many Americans responded to these problems by announcing the arrival of an "age of limits," in which America would have to learn to live with increasingly constricted expectations. By the end of the decade, however, the contours of another response to the challenges had become visible in both American culture and American politics. It was a response that combined a conservative retreat from some of the heady visions of the 1960s with a reinforced commitment to the idea of economic growth, international power, and American exceptionalism.

POLITICS AND DIPLOMACY AFTER WATERGATE

In the aftermath of Richard Nixon's ignominious departure from office, many wondered whether faith in the presidency, and in the government as a whole, could easily be restored. The administrations of the two presidents who succeeded Nixon did little to answer those questions.

The Ford Custodianship

Gerald Ford inherited the presidency under unenviable circumstances. He had to try to rebuild confidence in government in the face of the widespread cynicism the Watergate scandals had produced. And he had to try to restore prosperity in the face of major domestic and international challenges to the American economy. He enjoyed some success in the first of these efforts but very little in the second.

The new president's effort to establish himself as a symbol of political integrity suffered a setback only a month after he took office, when he granted Richard Nixon "a full, free, and absolute pardon" for any crimes he may have committed during his presidency. Ford explained that he was attempting to spare the nation the ordeal of years of litigation and to spare Nixon himself any further suffering. But much of the public suspected a secret deal with the former president. The pardon caused a decline in Ford's popularity from which he never fully recovered. Nevertheless, most Americans considered him a decent man; his honesty and amiability did much to reduce the bitterness and acrimony of the Watergate years.

The Ford administration enjoyed less success in its effort to solve the problems of the American economy. In his efforts to curb inflation, the president rejected the idea of wage and price controls and called instead for largely ineffective voluntary efforts. After supporting high interest rates, opposing increased federal spending (through liberal use of his veto power), and resisting pressures for a tax reduction, Ford had to deal with a serious recession in 1974 and 1975. Central to the economic problems was the continuing energy crisis. In the aftermath of the Arab oil embargo of 1973, the OPEC cartel began to raise the price of oil—by 400 percent in 1974 alone. Even so, American dependence on OPEC supplies continued to grow—one of the principal reasons why inflation reached 11 percent in 1976.

At first it seemed that the new administration's foreign policy would differ little from that of its predecessor. Ford retained Henry Kissinger as secretary of state and continued the general policies of the Nixon years. Late in 1974, Ford met with Leonid Brezhnev at Vladivostok in Siberia and signed an arms control accord that was to serve as the basis for SALT II, thus achieving a goal the Nixon administration had long sought. The following summer, after a European security conference in Helsinki, Finland, the Soviet Union and Western nations agreed to ratify the borders that had divided Europe since 1945; and the Soviets pledged to increase respect for human rights within their own country. Meanwhile, in the Middle East, Henry Kissinger helped produce a new accord by which Israel agreed to return large portions of the occupied Sinai to Egypt, and the two nations pledged not to resolve future differences by force. In China, finally, the death of Mao Zedong in 1976 brought to power a new, apparently more moderate government eager to expand its ties with the United States.

Nevertheless, as the 1976 presidential election approached, Ford's policies were coming under attack from both the right and the left. In the Republican primary campaign, Ford faced a powerful challenge from former California governor Ronald Reagan, leader of the party's conservative wing, who spoke for many on the right who were unhappy with any conciliation of communists. The president only barely survived the assault to win his party's nomination. The Democrats, in the meantime, were gradually uniting behind a new and, before 1976, almost entirely unknown candidate: Jimmy Carter, a former governor of Georgia who organized a brilliant primary campaign and appealed to the general unhappiness with Washington by offering honesty, piety, and an outsider's skepticism of the federal government. And while Carter's mammoth lead in opinion polls dwindled to almost nothing by election day, unhappiness with the economy and a general disenchantment with Ford enabled the Democrat to hold on for a narrow victory. Carter emerged with 50 percent of the popular vote to Ford's 47.9 percent and 297 electoral votes to Ford's 240.

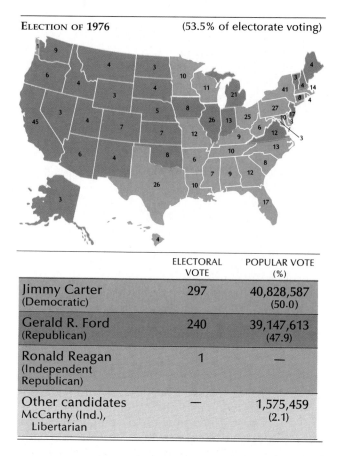

ELECTION OF 1976   (53.5% of electorate voting)

	ELECTORAL VOTE	POPULAR VOTE (%)
Jimmy Carter (Democratic)	297	40,828,587 (50.0)
Gerald R. Ford (Republican)	240	39,147,613 (47.9)
Ronald Reagan (Independent Republican)	1	—
Other candidates McCarthy (Ind.), Libertarian	—	1,575,459 (2.1)

The Trials of Jimmy Carter

Like Ford, Jimmy Carter assumed the presidency at a moment when the nation faced problems of staggering complexity and difficulty. Perhaps no leader could have thrived in such inhospitable circumstances. But Carter seemed at times to make his predicament worse by a style of leadership that many considered self-righteous and inflexible. He left office in 1981 one of the least popular presidents of the century.

Carter had campaigned for the presidency as an "outsider," representing Americans suspicious of entrenched bureaucracies and complacent public officials. He carried much of that suspiciousness with him to Washington. He surrounded himself in the White House with a group of close-knit associates from Georgia; and in the beginning, at least, he seemed deliberately to spurn assistance from more experienced political figures. Carter was among the most intelligent men ever to serve in the White House, but his critics charged that he provided no overall vision or direction to his government. His ambitious legislative agenda included major reforms of the tax and welfare systems; Congress passed virtually none of it.

Carter devoted much of his time to the problems of energy and the economy. Entering office in the midst of a recession, he moved first to reduce unemployment by raising public spending and cutting federal taxes. Unemployment declined, but inflation soared—less because of the fiscal policies he implemented than because of the continuing, sharp increases in energy prices imposed on the West by OPEC. During Carter's last two years in office, prices rose at well over a 10

percent annual rate. Like Nixon and Ford before him, Carter responded with a combination of tight money and calls for voluntary restraint. He appointed first G. William Miller and then Paul Volcker, both conservative economists, to head the Federal Reserve Board, thus ensuring a policy of high interest rates and reduced currency supplies. By 1980, interest rates had risen to the highest levels in American history; at times, they exceeded 20 percent.

The problem of energy also grew steadily more troublesome in the Carter years. In the summer of 1979, instability in the Middle East produced a second major fuel shortage in the United States. In the midst of the crisis, OPEC announced another major price increase, clouding the economic picture still further. Faced with increasing pressure to act (and with public opinion polls showing his approval rating at a dismal 26 percent, lower than Richard Nixon's lowest figures), Carter retreated to Camp David, the presidential retreat in the Maryland mountains. Ten days later, he emerged to deliver a remarkable television address. It included a series of proposals for resolving the energy crisis. But it was most notable for Carter's bleak assessment of the national condition. Speaking with unusual fervor, he complained of a "crisis of confidence" that had struck "at the very heart and soul of our national will." The address became known as the "malaise" speech (although Carter himself had never used that word), and it helped fuel charges that the president was trying to blame his own problems on the American people. Carter's sudden firing of several members of his cabinet a few days later deepened his political problems.

JIMMY AND ROSALYNN CARTER, JANUARY 20, 1977
Jimmy Carter startled the crowds (and alarmed the Secret Service) on his Inauguration Day by walking down Pennsylvania Avenue from the Capitol to the White House after taking the oath of office. Not since Jefferson, whose effort to identify with the "common man" Carter hoped to emulate, had a president walked in his inaugural parade. *(Owen Franken/Sygma)*

Human Rights and National Interests

Among Jimmy Carter's most frequent campaign promises was a pledge to build a new basis for American foreign policy, one in which the defense of "human rights" would replace the pursuit of "selfish interests." Carter spoke out sharply and often about violations of human rights in many countries (including, most prominently, the Soviet Union). Beyond that general commitment, the Carter administration focused on several more traditional concerns. Carter completed negotiations begun several years earlier on a pair of treaties to turn over control of the Panama Canal to the government of Panama. Domestic opposition to the treaties was intense, especially among conservatives who viewed the new arrangements as part of a general American retreat from international power. But the administration argued that relinquishing the canal was the best way to improve relations with Latin America and avoid violence in Panama. After an acrimonious debate, the Senate ratified the treaties by 68 to 32, only one vote more than the necessary two-thirds majority.

Less controversial, within the United States at least, was Carter's stunning success in arranging a peace treaty between Egypt and Israel—the crowning accomplishment of his presidency. Middle East negotiations had seemed hopelessly stalled when a dramatic breakthrough occurred in November 1977. The Egyptian president, Anwar Sadat, accepted an invitation from Prime Minister Menachem Begin to visit Israel. In Tel Aviv, he announced that Egypt was now willing to accept the state of Israel as a legitimate political entity. But translating these good feelings into an actual peace treaty proved more difficult.

When talks between Israeli and Egyptian negotiators stalled, Carter invited Sadat and Begin to a summit conference at Camp David in September 1978, and held them there for two weeks while he and others helped mediate the disputes between them. On September 17, Carter escorted the two leaders into the White House to announce agreement on a "framework" for an Egyptian-Israeli peace treaty. Carter intervened again several months later, when talks stalled once more, and helped produce a compromise on the most sensitive issue between the two parties: the Palestinian refugee issue. On March 26, 1979, Begin and Sadat returned together to the White House to sign a formal peace treaty between their two nations.

In the meantime, Carter continued trying to improve relations with China and the Soviet Union and to complete a new arms agreement. He responded eagerly to the overtures of Deng Xiaoping, the new Chinese leader who was attempting to open his nation to the outside world. On December 15, 1978, Washington and Beijing announced the resumption of formal diplomatic relations between the two nations. A few months later, Carter traveled to Vienna to meet with the aging and visibly ailing Brezhnev to finish drafting the new SALT II arms control agreement. The treaty set limits on the number of long-range missiles, bombers, and nuclear warheads on each side. Almost immediately, however, SALT II met with fierce conservative opposition in the United States. Central to the arguments was a fundamental distrust of the Soviet Union that nearly a decade of detente had failed to destroy; but specific provisions of the treaty—which even some supporters of detente felt were too favorable to the Soviets—also fueled the opposition. By the fall of 1979, with the Senate scheduled to begin debate over the treaty shortly, ratification was already in jeopardy. Events in the following months would provide a final blow, both to the treaty and to the larger framework of detente.

The Year of the Hostages

Ever since the early 1950s, the United States had provided political support and, more recently, massive

SIGNING THE CAMP DAVID ACCORDS
Jimmy Carter experienced many frustrations during his presidency, but his successful efforts in 1978 to negotiate a peace treaty between Israel and Egypt was undoubtedly his finest hour. Egyptian President Anwar Sadat and Israel Prime Minister Menachem Begin join Carter here in the East Room of the White House to sign the accords they had hammered out during two weeks at the president's retreat at Camp David. *(D. B. Owen/Black Star)*

military assistance to the government of the Shah of Iran, hoping to make his nation a bulwark against Soviet expansion in the Middle East. By 1979, however, the Shah was in deep trouble with his own people. Many Iranians resented the repressive, authoritarian tactics through which the Shah had maintained his autocratic rule. At the same time, Islamic clergy (and much of the fiercely religious populace) opposed his efforts to modernize and westernize a fundamentalist society. The combination of resentments produced a powerful revolutionary movement. In January 1979, the Shah fled the country.

The United States made cautious efforts in the first months after the Shah's abdication to establish cordial relations with the succession of increasingly militant regimes that followed. By late 1979, however, revolutionary chaos in Iran was making any normal relations impossible. What power there was resided with a zealous religious leader, the Ayatollah Ruhollah Khomeini, whose hatred of the West in general and the United States in particular was intense.

In late October 1979, the deposed Shah arrived in New York to be treated for cancer. Days later, on November 4, an armed mob invaded the American embassy in Teheran, seized the diplomats and military personnel inside, and demanded the return of the Shah to Iran in exchange for their freedom. Fifty-three Americans remained hostages in the embassy for over a year. Coming after years of international humiliations and defeats, the hostage seizure released a deep well of anger and emotion in the United States.

Only weeks after the hostage seizure, on December 27, 1979, Soviet troops invaded Afghanistan, the mountainous Islamic nation lying between the USSR and Iran. The Soviet Union had in fact been a power in Afghanistan for years, and the dominant force since April 1978, when a coup had established a Marxist government there with close ties to the Kremlin. But while some observers claimed that the Soviet invasion was a Russian attempt to secure the status quo, others—most notably the president—claimed it was a Russian "stepping stone to their possible control over much of the world's oil supplies." It was also the "gravest threat to world peace since World War II." Carter angrily imposed a series of economic sanctions on the Russians, canceled American participation in the 1980 summer Olympic Games in Moscow, and announced the withdrawal of SALT II from Senate consideration.

The combination of domestic economic troubles and international crises created widespread anxiety, frustration, and anger in the United States—damaging President Carter's already low standing with the public, and giving added strength to an alternative political force that had already made great strides.

THE RISE OF THE AMERICAN RIGHT

Much of the anxiety that pervaded American life in the 1970s was a result of jarring public events that left many men and women shaken and uncertain about their leaders and their government. But much of it was a result, too, of significant changes in the character of America's economy, society, and culture. Together these changes disillusioned many liberals, perplexed the already weakened left, and provided the right with its most important opportunity in generations to seize a position of authority in American life.

The Sunbelt and Its Politics

The most widely discussed demographic phenomenon of the 1970s was the rise of what became known as the "Sunbelt"—a term coined by the political analyst Kevin Phillips to describe a collection of regions that together emerged in the postwar era to become the most dynamically growing parts of the country. The Sunbelt included the Southeast (particularly Florida), the Southwest (particularly Texas), and above all, California, which became the nation's most populous state, surpassing New York, in 1964, and continued to grow in the years that followed. By 1980, the population of the Sunbelt had risen to exceed that of the industrial regions of the North and East, which were experiencing not only a relative, but in some cases an absolute, decline in population.

In addition to shifting the nation's economic focus from one region to another, the rise of the Sunbelt helped produce a change in the political climate. The strong populist traditions in the South and the West were capable of producing progressive and even radical politics; but more often in the late twentieth century, they produced a strong opposition to the growth of government and a resentment of the proliferating regulations and restrictions that the liberal state was producing. Many of those regulations and restrictions—environmental laws, land-use restrictions, even the fifty-five-mile-per-hour speed limit created during the energy crisis to force motorists to conserve fuel—affected the West more than any other region. Both the South and the West, moreover, embraced myths about their own pasts that reinforced the hostility to

GROWTH OF THE SUNBELT: POPULATION AND URBAN CENTER SHIFTS, 1970–1990

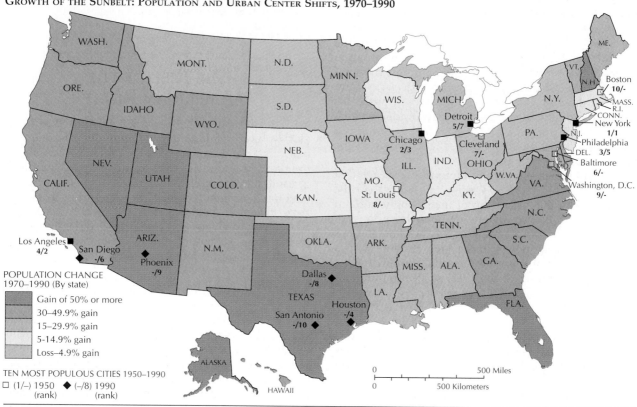

POPULATION CHANGE
1970–1990 (By state)

Gain of 50% or more
30–49.9% gain
15–29.9% gain
5-14.9% gain
Loss–4.9% gain

TEN MOST POPULOUS CITIES 1950–1990
☐ (1/–) 1950   ◆ (–/8) 1990
(rank)   (rank)

the liberal government of the mid- and late-twentieth century. White southerners equated the federal government's effort to change racial norms in the region with what they believed was the tyranny of Reconstruction. Westerners embraced an image of their region as a refuge of "rugged individualism" and resisted what they considered efforts by the government to impose new standards of behavior on them. Thus, the same impulses and rhetoric that populists had once used to denounce banks and corporations, the new conservative populists of the postwar era used to attack the government—and the liberals, radicals, and minorities whom they believed were driving its growth.

If anything, the growth of the Sunbelt seemed to strengthen the hostility toward government in the politics of the regions. In the 1970s and early 1980s, the boom mentality of some of these rapidly growing areas (especially south Florida, Texas, and southern California) conflicted sharply with the concerns of the older industrial states of the Northeast and Midwest. Saddled with declining economic bases, highly congested, home to large, impoverished minority groups, they remained more committed to social programs and

more interested in regulated growth than the relatively wide-open areas of the Sunbelt.

The so-called Sagebrush Rebellion, which emerged in parts of the West in the late 1970s, mobilized conservative opposition to environmental laws and restrictions on development. It also sought to portray the West (which had probably benefited more than any other region from federal investment) as a victim of government control. Its members complained about the very large amounts of land the federal government owned in many western states and demanded that they be opened for development.

The South as a whole was considerably more conservative than other parts of the nation, and its growth served to increase the power of the right in the 1960s and 1970s. The West was not, on the whole, a more conservative region than others; but its rise in the postwar period did help produce some of the most numerous and powerful conservative movements in the nation—particularly in southern California, where Orange County (a large suburban area south of Los Angeles) emerged as one of the most important centers of right-wing politics in the country. When the right rose to power in the 1970s and 1980s, westerners were among its most important leaders and constituents.

Religious Revivalism

In the 1960s, many social critics had predicted the virtual extinction of religious influence in American life. *Time* magazine had reported such assumptions in 1966 with a celebrated cover emblazoned with the question, "Is God Dead?" But religion in America was far from dead. Indeed, in the 1970s the United States experienced the beginning of a major religious revival, perhaps the most powerful since the Second Great Awakening of the early nineteenth century. It continued in various forms into the 1990s.

Some of the new religious enthusiasm found expression in the rise of various cults and pseudo-faiths: the Church of Scientology; the Unification Church of the Reverend Sun Myung Moon; even the tragic People's Temple, whose members committed mass suicide in their jungle retreat in Guyana in 1978. But the most important impulse of the religious revival was the growth of evangelical Christianity.

Evangelicism is the basis of many forms of Christian faith. But evangelicals have in common a belief in personal conversion through direct communication with God. Evangelical religion had been the dominant form of Christianity in America through much of its history, and a substantial subculture since the late nineteenth century. In its modern form, it had been increasingly visible since at least the early 1950s, when evangelicals such as Billy Graham and Pentecostals such as Oral Roberts had begun to attract huge national (and international) followings for their energetic revivalism.

For many years, the evangelicals had gone largely unnoted by much of the media and the secular public, which had dismissed them as a limited, provincial phenomenon. By the early 1980s, it was no longer possible to do so. Earlier in the century, many (although never all) evangelicals had been relatively poor rural people, largely isolated from the mainstream of American culture. But the great capitalist expansion after World War II had lifted many of these people out of poverty and into the middle class, where they were more visible and more assertive. More than 70 million Americans now described themselves as "born-again" Christians—men and women who had established a "direct personal relationship with Jesus." Christian evangelicals owned their own newspapers, magazines, radio stations, and television networks. They operated their own schools and universities. They occupied positions of eminence in the worlds of entertainment and professional sports. And one of their number ultimately occupied the White House itself—Jimmy Carter,

who during the 1976 campaign had talked proudly of his own "conversion experience" and who continued openly to proclaim his "born-again" Christian faith during his years in office.

For Jimmy Carter and for some others, evangelical Christianity had formed the basis for a commitment to racial and economic justice and to world peace. For many evangelicals, however, the message of the new religion was very different—but no less political. In the 1970s, some Christian evangelicals became active on the political and cultural right. They were alarmed by what they considered the spread of immorality and disorder in American life; and they were concerned about the way a secular and, as they saw it, godless culture was intruding into their communities and families—through popular culture, through the schools, and through government policies. Many evangelical men and women feared the growth of feminism and the threat they believed it posed to the traditional family, and they resented the way in which government policies advanced the goals of the women's movement. Particularly alarming to them were Supreme Court decisions eliminating all religious observance from schools and, later, the decision guaranteeing women the right to an abortion.

By the late 1970s, the "Christian right" had become a visible and increasingly powerful political force. Jerry Falwell, a fundamentalist minister in Virginia with a substantial television audience, launched a movement he called the Moral Majority, which attacked the rise of "secular humanism" in American culture. The Moral Majority and other organizations of similar inclination opposed federal interference in local affairs, denounced abortion, divorce, feminism, and homosexuality, defended unrestricted free enterprise, and supported a strong American posture in the world. Some evangelicals reopened issues that had long seemed closed. For example, many fundamentalist Christians denied the scientific doctrine of evolution and instead urged the teaching in schools of the biblical story of the Creation. Others demanded various forms of censorship or control of television, movies, rock music, books, magazines, and newspapers. Their goal was a new era in which Christian values once again dominated American life.

The Emergence of the New Right

Evangelical Christians were an important part, but only a part, of what became known as the New Right—a diverse but powerful movement that enjoyed rapid growth in the 1970s and early 1980s. It had begun to take shape after the 1964 election, in which Barry Goldwater had suffered his shattering defeat. Richard

Viguerie, a remarkable conservative activist and organizer, took a list of 12,000 contributors to the Goldwater campaign and used it to develop a formidable conservative communications and fund-raising organization. By the mid-1970s, he had gathered a list of 4 million contributors and 15 million supporters. Conservative campaigns had for many years been less well funded and organized than those of their rivals. Beginning in the 1970s, largely because of these and other organizational advances, conservatives found themselves almost always better funded and organized than their opponents. Gradually these direct-mail operations helped create a much larger conservative infrastructure, designed to match and even exceed what the right saw as the powerful liberal infrastructure. By the late 1970s, there were right-wing think tanks, consulting firms, lobbyists, foundations, and scholarly centers.

Another factor in the revival of the right was the emergence of a credible right-wing leadership in the late 1960s and early 1970s to replace the discredited conservative hero of the 1950s, Barry Goldwater. Chief among this new generation of conservative leaders was Ronald Reagan. Reagan had grown up in modest circumstances in the Midwest and attended a small college in Illinois. In 1937, at the age of 26, he went to Hollywood and became a moderately successful actor, in westerns at times, but mostly in light romantic comedies. A liberal and a fervent admirer of Franklin Roosevelt as a young man, he moved decisively to the right after his second marriage, to Nancy Davis, a woman of strong conservative convictions; and after, as president of the Screen Actors Guild, he became embroiled in battles with communists in the union. In the early 1950s, he became a corporate spokesman for General Electric and won a wide following on the right with his smooth, eloquent speeches in defense of individual freedom and private enterprise.

In 1964, Reagan delivered a memorable television speech on behalf of Goldwater. After Goldwater's defeat, he worked quickly not only to seize the leadership of the conservative wing of the party but to denounce those Republicans who had repudiated Goldwater. "I don't think we should turn the high command over to leaders who were traitors during the battle just ended," Reagan said in 1965, when other Republicans were trying to push anti-Goldwater moderates into positions of leadership in the party. In 1966, with the support of a group of wealthy conservatives, he won the first of two terms as governor of California—which gave him a much more visible platform for promoting himself and his ideas.

The presidency of Gerald Ford also played an important role in the rise of the right, by destroying the fragile equilibrium that had enabled the right wing and the moderate wing of the Republican Party to coexist. Ford, probably without realizing it, touched on some of the right's rawest nerves. He appointed as vice president Nelson Rockefeller, the liberal Republican governor of New York and an heir to one of America's great fortunes; many conservatives had been demonizing Rockefeller and his family for more than twenty years. (Viguerie attributed the birth of the New Right to this event alone.) Ford proposed an amnesty program for draft resisters, embraced and even extended the hated Nixon-Kissinger policies of detente, presided over the fall of Vietnam, and agreed to cede the Panama Canal to Panama. When Reagan challenged Ford in the 1976 Republican primaries, the president survived, barely, only by dumping Nelson Rockefeller from the ticket, replacing him with Senator Robert Dole of Kansas, and agreeing to a platform largely written by one of Reagan's principal allies, Senator Jesse Helms of North Carolina. Reagan hailed that platform by saying that the party "must raise a banner of no pale pastels, but bold colors which make it unmistakably clear where we stand on all the issues troubling the people."

The Tax Revolt

At least equally important to the success of the new right was a new and potent conservative issue: the tax revolt. It had its public beginnings in 1978, when Howard Jarvis, a conservative activist in California, launched the first successful major citizens' tax revolt in California with Proposition 13, a referendum question on the state ballot rolling back property tax rates. Similar antitax movements soon began in other states and eventually spread to national politics.

The tax revolt became the solution to one of the right's biggest problems. For more than thirty years after the New Deal, Republican conservatives had struggled to halt and even reverse the growth of the federal government. Most of those efforts had ended in futility. Attacking government programs directly, as rightwing politicians from Robert Taft to Barry Goldwater discovered, was not the way to attract majority support. Every federal program had a political constituency. The biggest and most expensive programs had the broadest support. (Goldwater was plagued throughout the 1964 campaign by fears he would dismantle Social Security.)

In Proposition 13 and similar initiatives, members of the right found a better way to undermine government than by attacking specific programs: attacking taxes. By separating the issue of taxes from the issue of what taxes supported, the right found a way to achieve the most controversial elements of its own agenda (eroding the government's ability to expand and launch new programs) without openly antagonizing the millions of voters who supported specific programs. Virtually no one liked to pay taxes, and as the economy grew weaker and the relative burden of paying taxes grew heavier, that resentment naturally rose. The right exploited that resentment and, in the process, expanded its constituency far beyond anything it had known before. The 1980 presidential election propelled it to a historic victory.

The Campaign of 1980

By the time of the crises in Iran and Afghanistan, Jimmy Carter was in desperate political trouble—his standing in popularity polls lower than that of any president in history. Senator Edward Kennedy, younger brother of John and Robert Kennedy and one of the most magnetic (and controversial) figures in the Democratic Party, was preparing to challenge him in the primaries. For a short while, the seizure of the hostages and the stern American response to the Soviet invasion revived Carter's candidacy. But as the hostage crisis dragged on, public impatience grew. Kennedy won a series of victories over the president in the later primaries. Carter managed in the end to stave off Kennedy's challenge and win his party's nomination. But it was an unhappy convention that heard the president's listless call to arms, and Carter's campaign aroused little popular enthusiasm as he prepared to face a powerful challenge.

The Republican Party, in the meantime, had rallied enthusiastically behind the man who, four years earlier, had nearly stolen the nomination from Gerald Ford. Ronald Reagan was a sharp critic of the excesses of the federal government. He linked his campaign to the spreading tax revolt (something to which he had paid relatively little attention in the past) by promising substantial tax cuts. Equally important, he championed a restoration of American "strength" and "pride" in the world. Although he refrained from discussing the issue of the hostages, Reagan clearly benefited from the continuing popular frustration at Carter's inability to resolve the crisis. In a larger sense, he benefited as well from the accumulated frustrations of more than a decade of domestic and international disappointments.

On election day 1980, the anniversary of the seizure of the hostages in Iran, Reagan swept to victory, winning 51 percent of the vote to 41 percent for Jimmy Carter, and 7 percent for John Anderson—a moderate Republican congressman from Illinois who had mounted

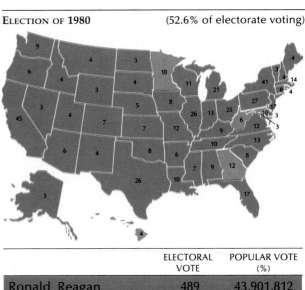

ELECTION OF 1980   (52.6% of electorate voting)

	ELECTORAL VOTE	POPULAR VOTE (%)
Ronald Reagan (Republican)	489	43,901,812 (50.7)
Jimmy Carter (Democratic)	49	35,483,820 (41.0)
John B. Anderson (Independent)	—	5,719,722 (6.6)
Other candidates (Libertarian)	—	921,299 (1.1)

an independent campaign. Carter carried only five states and the District of Columbia, for a total of 49 electoral votes to Reagan's 489. The Republican Party won control of the Senate for the first time since 1952; and although the Democrats retained a modest majority in the House, the lower chamber too seemed firmly in the hands of conservatives.

On the day of Reagan's inauguration, the American hostages in Iran were released after their 444-day ordeal. Jimmy Carter, in the last hours of his presidency, had concluded months of negotiations by agreeing to release several billion dollars in Iranian assets that he had frozen in American banks shortly after the seizure of the embassy. The government of Iran, desperate for funds to support its floundering war against neighboring Iraq, had ordered the hostages freed in return. Americans welcomed the hostages home with demonstrations of joy and patriotism not seen since the end of World War II. But while the celebration in 1945 had marked a great American triumph, the euphoria in 1981 marked something quite different—a troubled nation grasping for reassurance. Ronald Reagan set out to provide it.

THE "REAGAN REVOLUTION"

Ronald Reagan assumed the presidency in January 1981 promising a change in government more fundamental than any since the New Deal of fifty years before. While his eight years in office produced a significant shift in public policy, they brought nothing so fundamental as many of his supporters had hoped or his opponents had feared. But there was no ambiguity about its purely political achievements. Reagan succeeded brilliantly in making his own engaging personality the central fact of American politics in the 1980s.

The Reagan Coalition

Reagan owed his election to widespread disillusionment with Carter and to the crises and disappointments that many voters, perhaps unfairly, associated with him. But he owed it as well to the emergence of a powerful coalition of conservative groups. That coalition was not a single, cohesive movement. It was an uneasy and generally temporary alliance among several very different movements.

The Reagan coalition included a small but highly influential group of wealthy Americans associated with the corporate and financial world—the kind of people who had dominated American politics and government through much of the nation's history until the New Deal began to challenge their preeminence. What united this group was a firm commitment to capitalism and to unfettered economic growth; a deep hostility to most (although not all) government interference in markets; and a belief that most of what is valuable in American life depends on the health and strength of the corporate world, and thus that the corporate world is entitled to a special position of influence and privilege in society. Central to this group's agenda in the 1980s was opposition to what it considered the "redistributive" politics of the federal government (and especially its highly progressive tax structure) and hostility to the rise of what they believed were "antibusiness" government regulations. Reagan courted them carefully and effectively.

A second element of the Reagan coalition was even smaller, but also disproportionately influential: a group of intellectuals commonly known as "neo-conservatives," who gave to the right something it had not had in many years—a firm base among "opinion leaders," people with access to the most influential public forums for ideas. Many of these people had once been liberals and, before that, socialists. But during the turmoil of the 1960s, they had become alarmed by what

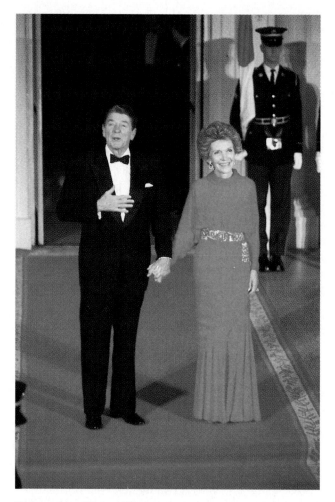

RONALD AND NANCY REAGAN
The president and the first lady greet guests at a White House social event. Nancy Reagan was most visible in her efforts to make the White House, and her husband's presidency, seem more glamorous than those of most recent administrations. But she also played an important, if quiet, policy role in the administration. *(Dirck Halstead/ Gamma Liaison)*

they considered a dangerous and destructive radicalism that was destabilizing American life, and by the weakening of liberal ardor in the battle against communism. Neo-conservatives were sympathetic to the complaints and demands of capitalists, but their principal concern was to reassert legitimate authority and reaffirm Western democratic, anticommunist values and commitments. They considered themselves engaged in a battle to regain control of the marketplace of ideas—to "win back the culture"—from the crass, radical ideas that had polluted it. Some neo-conservative intellectuals went on to become important figures in the battle against multi-culturalism and "political correctness" within academia.

These two groups joined in an uneasy alliance in 1980 with the vast and growing movement known as the "New Right" (or, to some, the populist right). Several things differentiated the New Right from the corporate conservatives and the neo-conservatives. Perhaps the most important was a fundamental distrust of the "eastern establishment": a suspicion of its motives and goals; a sense that it exercised a dangerous, secret power in American life; a fear of the hidden influence of such establishment institutions and people as the Council on Foreign Relations, the Trilateral Commission, Henry Kissinger, and the Rockefellers.

These "populist" conservatives expressed the kinds of concerns that outsiders, non-elites, have traditionally voiced in American society: an opposition to centralized power and influence, a fear of living in a world where distant, hostile forces are controlling society and threatening individual freedom and community autonomy. It was a testament to Ronald Reagan's political skills, and personal charm that he was able to generate enthusiastic support from these populist conservatives while at the same time appealing to more elite conservative groups whose concerns were in many ways antithetical to those of the New Right.

Reagan in the White House

Even many people who disagreed with Reagan's policies found themselves drawn to his attractive and carefully honed public image. Reagan was a master of television, a gifted public speaker, and—in public at least—rugged, fearless, and seemingly impervious to danger or misfortune. He turned seventy weeks after taking office and was the oldest man ever to serve as president. But through most of his presidency, he seemed vigorous, resilient, even youthful. He spent his many vacations on a California ranch, where he chopped wood and rode horses. When he was wounded in an assassination attempt in 1981, he joked with doctors on his way into surgery and appeared to bounce back from the ordeal with remarkable speed. Four years later, he seemed to rebound from cancer surgery with similar zest. He had few visible insecurities. Even when things went wrong, as they often did, the blame seldom seemed to attach to Reagan himself (inspiring some Democrats to begin referring to him as the "Teflon president").

Reagan was not much involved in the day-to-day affairs of running the government; he surrounded himself with tough, energetic administrators who insulated him from many of the pressures of the office and who apparently relied on him largely for general guidance, not specific decisions. At times, the president revealed a startling ignorance about the nature of his own policies or the actions of his subordinates. But Reagan did make active use of his office to generate support for his administration's programs, by appealing repeatedly to the public over television and by fusing his proposals with a highly nationalistic rhetoric.

"Supply-Side" Economics

Reagan's 1980 campaign for the presidency had promised, among other things, to restore the economy to health by a bold experiment that became known as "supply-side" economics or, to some, "Reaganomics." Supply-side economics operated from the assumption that the woes of the American economy were in large part a result of excessive taxation, which left inadequate capital available to investors to stimulate growth. The solution, therefore, was to reduce taxes, with particularly generous benefits to corporations and wealthy individuals, in order to encourage new investments. The result would be a general economic revival that would help everyone. Because a tax cut would reduce government revenues (at least at first), it would also be necessary to reduce government expenses. A cornerstone of the Reagan economic program, therefore, was a dramatic cut in the federal budget.

In its first months in office, accordingly, the new administration hastily assembled a legislative program based on the supply-side idea. It proposed $40 billion in budget reductions and managed to win congressional approval of almost all of them. In addition, the president proposed a bold, three-year rate reduction of 30 percent on both individual and corporate taxes. In the summer of 1981, Congress passed it too, after lowering the reductions slightly, to 25 percent. Not since Lyndon Johnson had a president compiled so impressive a legislative record in his first months in office. Reagan was successful because he had a disciplined Republican majority in the Senate, and because the Democratic majority in the House was weak and riddled with defectors. Shaken by the results of the 1980 election, dozens of Democrats from relatively conservative districts (mostly in the South) deserted the party's leadership; the defectors became known as "boll weevils."

Men and women whom Reagan appointed fanned out through the executive branch of government committed to reducing the role of government in American economic life. "Deregulation," an idea many Democrats had begun to embrace in the Carter years, became the religion of the Reagan administration. Secretary of the Interior James Watt had been a major figure in the Sagebrush Rebellion, a movement among western conservatives to fight federal environmental regulations, which they believed had a particularly devastating effect on their region's economy. Watt opened up public lands and water to development. The Environmental Protection Agency (before its directors were indicted for corruption) relaxed or entirely eliminated enforcement of critical environmental laws and regulations. The Civil Rights Division of the Justice Department eased enforcement of civil rights laws. The Department of Transportation slowed implementation of new rules limiting automobile emissions and imposing new safety standards on cars and trucks. By getting government "out of the way," Reagan officials promised, they were ensuring economic revival.

By early 1982, however, the nation had sunk into the most severe recession since the 1930s. The Reagan economic program was not directly to blame for the problems. It was more a result of the high interest rates the Federal Reserve Board (run by Carter appointee William Volcker) had maintained since the late 1970s as an antidote to inflation. The high interest rates made it difficult for businesses and individuals to borrow money for investment or consumer purchases. They also made the dollar attractive to overseas investors and significantly raised its value—thus making American products more expensive abroad and significantly reducing exports. By 1984, the U.S. trade deficit was $111 billion; in 1980, there had been a $25 billion surplus. The effects of the recession were particularly devastating on American industry, which had already been experiencing serious problems for a decade. Industrialists closed some plants, reduced the labor force in others, and eliminated millions of manufacturing jobs. In 1982 unemployment reached 11 percent, its highest level in over forty years. Farmers, even more dependent than manufacturers on the export trade, fared even worse. Hundreds of thousands of them lost so much money in the early 1980s that they lost their farms.

The recession convinced many people, including some conservatives, that the Reagan economic program (and thus the Reagan presidency) had failed. In fact, however, the economy recovered more rapidly and impressively than almost anyone had expected. By late 1983, unemployment had fallen to 8.2 percent, and it declined steadily for several years after that. The gross national product had grown 3.6 percent in a year, the largest increase since the mid-1970s. Inflation had fallen below 5 percent. The economy continued to grow, and both inflation and unemployment remained low (at least by the new and more pessimistic standards the nation seemed now to have accepted) through most of the decade.

The recovery was a result of many things. The years of tight money policies by the Federal Reserve Board, however painful and destructive they may have been in other ways, had helped lower inflation; equally important, the Board had lowered interest rates early in 1983 in response to the recession. A worldwide "energy glut" and the virtual collapse of the OPEC cartel had produced at least a temporary end to the inflationary pressures of spiraling fuel costs. And stagger-

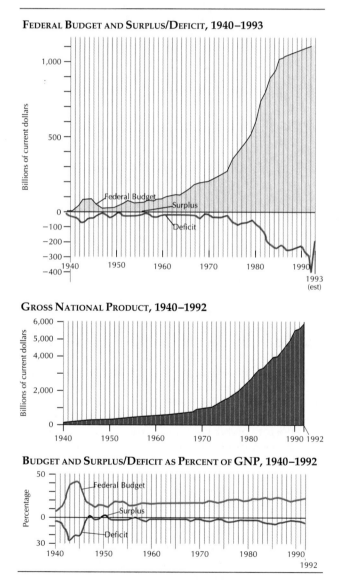

Federal Budget and Surplus/Deficit, 1940–1993

Gross National Product, 1940–1992

Budget and Surplus/Deficit as Percent of GNP, 1940–1992

ing federal budget deficits were pumping billions of dollars into the flagging economy. As a result, consumer spending and business investment both increased. And the stock market rose up from the doldrums of the late 1970s and began a sustained and historic boom. In August 1982, the Dow Jones Industrial Average stood at 777. Five years later it had passed 2,000. Despite a frightening crash in the fall of 1987, the market continued to grow: by 1994, the Dow Jones average was nearing 4,000.

The Fiscal Crisis

The economic revival did little, however, to reduce the staggering, and to many Americans alarming, deficits in the federal budget. By the mid-1980s, this growing fiscal crisis had become one of the central issues in American politics. Having entered office promising a balanced budget within four years, Reagan presided over record budget deficits and accumulated more debt in his eight years in office than the American government had accumulated in its entire previous history. Before the 1980s, the highest single-year budget deficit in American history had been $66 billion (in 1976). Throughout the 1980s, the annual budget deficit consistently exceeded $100 billion (and in 1991 peaked at $268 billion). The national debt rose from $907 billion in 1980 to nearly $3.5 trillion by 1991.

The enormous deficits had many causes, some of them stretching back over decades of American public policy decisions. In particular, the budget suffered from enormous increases in the costs of "entitlement" programs (especially Social Security and Medicare), a result of the aging of the population and dramatic increases in the cost of health care. But some of the causes of the deficit lay in the policies of the Reagan administration. The 1981 tax cuts, the largest in American history, eroded the revenue base of the federal government and accounted for a significant percentage of the deficit. The massive increase in military spending (a proposed $1.6 trillion over five years) on which the Reagan administration insisted added more to the federal budget than its cuts in domestic spending removed.

In the face of these deficits, the administration refused to consider raising income taxes (although it did agree to a major increase in the Social Security tax). It would not agree to reductions in military spending. It could not much reduce the costs of entitlement programs, and it could do nothing to reduce interest payments on the massive (and growing) debt. Its answer to the fiscal crisis, therefore, was further cuts in "discretionary" domestic spending, which included many programs aimed at the poorest (and politically weakest) Americans. There were reductions in funding for food stamps; a major cut in federal subsidies for low-income housing (which became one of many factors contributing to the radical increase in homelessness that by the late 1980s was plaguing virtually all American cities); strict new limitations on Medicare and Medicaid payments; reductions in student loans, school lunches, and other educational programs; and an end to many forms of federal assistance to the states and cities—which helped precipitate years of local fiscal crises as well.

By the end of Reagan's third year in office, funding for domestic programs had been cut nearly as far as Congress (and, apparently, the public) was willing to tolerate, and still no end to the rising deficits was in sight. Congress responded with the so-called Gramm-Rudman bill, passed late in 1985, which mandated major deficit reductions over five years and provided for automatic budget cuts in all areas of government spending should the president and Congress fail to agree on an alternative solution. Under Gramm-Rudman, the budget deficit did decline for several years from its 1983 high. But much of that decline was a result of a substantial surplus in the Social Security trust fund (which the sharply increased Social Security taxes had produced), not of the provisions of the law. By the late 1980s, many fiscal conservatives were calling for a constitutional amendment mandating a balanced budget—a provision the president himself claimed to support. (Congress came within a few votes of passing such an amendment in 1994.)

Reagan and the World

Reagan encountered a similar combination of triumphs and difficulties in international affairs. Determined to restore American pride and prestige in the world, he argued that the United States should once again become active and assertive in opposing communism and in supporting friendly governments whatever their internal policies.

Relations with the Soviet Union, which had been steadily deteriorating in the last years of the Carter administration, grew still more chilly in the first years of the Reagan presidency. The president spoke harshly of the Soviet regime (which he once called the "evil empire"), accusing it of sponsoring world terrorism and declaring that any armaments negotiations must be linked to negotiations on Soviet behavior in other areas. Relations with the Russians deteriorated further after the government of Poland (under strong pressure from

SIGNIFICANT EVENTS

1965 Richard Viguerie launches conservative direct-mail operations

1966 Ronald Reagan elected governor of California

1974 OPEC raises oil prices

"Stagflation" (recession and inflation together) begins

Ford pardons Nixon

Ford meets Brezhnev at Vladivostok summit

1976 Reagan challenges Ford in Republican presidential primaries

Jimmy Carter elected president

Mao Zedong dies

1977 Panama Canal treaties signed

1978 Camp David accords signed

Panama Canal treaties ratified

Voters in California approve Proposition 13, launching tax revolt

1979 Energy crisis jolts United States

U.S. and China restore diplomatic relations

Iranian revolution overthrows Shah

American diplomats taken hostage in Iran

Soviet Union invades Afghanistan

Sandinista revolution triumphs in Nicaragua

SALT II treaty signed

1980 U.S. boycotts Moscow Olympics

Attempt to rescue American hostages in Iran fails; Secretary of State Cyrus Vance resigns in protest

Edward Kennedy challenges Carter in Democratic primaries

Ronald Reagan elected president

1981 American hostages in Iran released

Reagan wins major tax and budget cuts

U.S. military buildup begins

Soviet Union forces imposition of martial law in Poland

United States begins supporting contra rebellion in Nicaragua

Reagan survives assassination attempt

1982 Severe recession

Inflation and interest rates decline

Israel invades Lebanon

1983 U.S. Marines killed in terrorist attack in Beirut

United States invades Grenada

Nuclear freeze movement expands in United States

Unemployment reaches 10.2 percent

Economic recovery begins

1984 Jesse Jackson campaigns for Democratic presidential nomination

Democrats nominate Geraldine Ferraro for vice president

Reagan defeats Walter Mondale in presidential election

Moscow) imposed martial law on the country in the winter of 1981 to crush a growing challenge from an independent labor organization, Solidarity.

Although the president had long denounced the SALT II arms control treaty as unfavorable to the United States, he continued to honor its provisions. But the Reagan administration at first made little progress toward arms control in other areas. In fact, the presi-

dent proposed the most ambitious (and potentially most expensive) new military program in many years: the so-called Strategic Defense Initiative (SDI), widely known as "Star Wars" (after a popular movie of that name). Reagan claimed that SDI, through the use of lasers and satellites, could provide an effective shield against incoming missiles and thus make nuclear war obsolete. The Soviet Union claimed that the new program would elevate the arms race to new and more dangerous levels (a complaint many domestic critics of SDI shared) and insisted that any arms control agreement begin with an American abandonment of SDI.

The escalation of Cold War tensions and the slowing of arms control initiatives helped produce an important popular movement in Europe and the United States calling for an end to nuclear weapons buildups. In America, the principal goal of the movement was a "nuclear freeze," an agreement between the two superpowers not to expand their atomic arsenals. In what many believed was the largest mass demonstration in American history, nearly a million people rallied in New York City's Central Park in 1982 to support the freeze. Perhaps partly in response to this growing pressure, the administration began tentative efforts to revive arms control negotiations in 1983.

It also began, rhetorically at least, to support opponents of communism anywhere in the world, whether or not the regimes or movements they were challenging had any direct connection to the Soviet Union. This new policy became known as the Reagan Doctrine, and it meant, above all, a new American activism in the Third World. The most conspicuous examples of the new activism came in Latin America. In October 1982, the administration sent American soldiers and Marines into the tiny Caribbean island of Grenada to oust an anti-American Marxist regime that showed signs of forging a relationship with Moscow. In El Salvador, where first a repressive military regime and later a moderate civilian one were engaged in murderous struggles with left-wing revolutionaries (who were supported, according to the Reagan administration, by Cuba and the Soviet Union), the president provided increased military and economic assistance. In neighboring Nicaragua, a pro-American dictatorship had fallen to the revolutionary "Sandinistas" in 1979; the new government had grown increasingly anti-American (and increasingly Marxist) throughout the early 1980s. The administration gave both rhetorical and material support to the so-called contras, a guerrilla movement drawn from several antigovernment groups and fighting (without great success) to topple the Sandinista regime. Indeed, support of the contras became a mission of special importance to the president, and later the source of some of his greatest difficulties.

In other parts of the world, the administration's bellicose rhetoric seemed to hide an instinctive restraint. In June 1982, the Israeli army launched an invasion of Lebanon in an effort to drive guerrillas of the Palestinian Liberation Organization from the country. The United States supported the Israelis rhetorically but also worked to permit PLO forces to leave Lebanon peacefully. An American peacekeeping force entered Beirut to supervise the evacuation. American marines then remained in the city, apparently to protect the fragile Lebanese government, which was embroiled in a vicious civil war. Now identified with one faction in the struggle, Americans became the targets in 1983 of a terrorist bombing of a U.S. military barracks in Beirut that left 241 marines dead. Rather than become more deeply involved in the Lebanese struggle, Reagan withdrew American forces.

The tragedy in Lebanon was an example of the changing character of Third World struggles: an increasing reliance on terrorism by otherwise powerless groups to advance their political aims. A series of terrorist acts in the 1980s—attacks on airplanes, cruise ships, commercial and diplomatic posts; the seizing of American and other Western hostages—alarmed and frightened much of the Western world. The Reagan administration spoke bravely about its resolve to punish terrorism; and at one point in 1986, the president ordered American planes to bomb sites in Tripoli, the capital of Libya, whose controversial leader Muammar al-Qaddafi was widely believed to be a leading sponsor of terrorism. In general, however, terrorists remained difficult to identify or control.

The Election of 1984

Reagan approached the campaign of 1984 at the head of a united Republican Party firmly committed to his candidacy. The Democrats, as had become their custom, followed a more fractious course. Former vice president Walter Mondale established an early and commanding lead in the race by soliciting support from a wide range of traditional Democratic interest groups, and survived challenges from Senator Gary Hart of Colorado (who claimed to represent a "new generation" of leadership) and the magnetic Jesse Jackson, who had established himself as the nation's most prominent spokesman for minorities and the poor. Mondale captured the nomination and brought momentary excitement to the Democratic campaign by selecting a woman, Representative Geraldine Ferraro of New York, to be his running mate and the first female candidate ever to appear on a national ticket.

The Republican Party rallied comfortably behind its revered leader, whose triumphant campaign that fall scarcely took note of his opponents and spoke instead of what he claimed was the remarkable revival of American fortunes and spirits under his leadership. His campaign emphasized such phrases as "It's Morning in America" and "America Is Back." Reagan's victory in 1984 was decisive. He won approximately 59 percent of the vote, and carried every state but Mon-

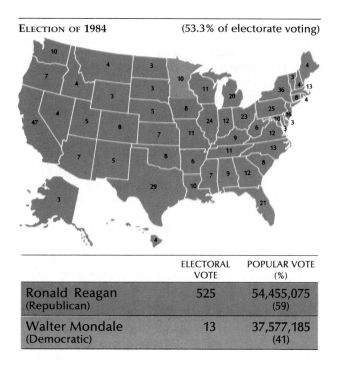

ELECTION OF 1984   (53.3% of electorate voting)

	ELECTORAL VOTE	POPULAR VOTE (%)
Ronald Reagan (Republican)	525	54,455,075 (59)
Walter Mondale (Democratic)	13	37,577,185 (41)

dale's native Minnesota and the District of Columbia. But Reagan was much stronger than his party. Democrats gained a seat in the Senate and maintained only slightly reduced control of the House of Representatives.

The triumphant reelection of Ronald Reagan was the high-water mark of conservative, and Republican, fortunes in the postwar era. It reflected satisfaction with the impressive performance of the economy under the Republican economic program, and pride in the new assertiveness the United States was showing in the world. To many Reagan supporters, the 1984 election seemed to be the dawn of a new conservative era. But almost no one anticipated the revolutionary changes that would change the world, and the United States's place in it, within a very few years. The election of 1984, therefore, was not so much the first of a new era as the last of an old one. It was the final campaign of the Cold War.

SUGGESTED READINGS

The Ford Presidency.   James M. Cannon, *Time and Chance: Gerald Ford's Appointment with History* (1994); Gerald Ford, *A Time to Heal* (1979). John R. Greene, *The Limits of Power: The Nixon and Ford Administrations* (1992). Robert T. Hartmann, *Palace Politics* (1980). Gerald Ter Horst, *Gerald Ford* (1975). Richard Reeves, *A Ford Not a Lincoln* (1976). A. James Reichley, *Conservatives in an Age of Change: The Nixon and Ford Administrations* (1981). Edward and Frederick Schapsmeier, *Gerald R. Ford's Date with Destiny: A Political Biography* (1989). James L. Sundquist, *The Decline and Resurgence of Congress* (1981).

The Carter Presidency.   Jack Bass and Walter Devries, *The Transformation of Southern Politics* (1976). James Bill, *The Eagle and the Lion* (1988). Zbigniew Brzezinski, *Power and Principle* (1983). Jimmy Carter, *Why Not the Best?* (1975); *Keeping Faith* (1982). Rosalynn Carter, *First Lady from Plains* (1984). Steven Gillon, *The Democrats' Dilemma: Walter Mondale and the Liberal Legacy* (1992). Betty Glad, *Jimmy Carter* (1980). Erwin Hargrove, *Jimmy Carter as President* (1989). Steven B. Hunt, *The Energy Crisis* (1978). Haynes Johnson, *In the Absence of Power* (1980). Charles O. Jones, *The Trusteeship Presidency* (1988). Hamilton Jordan, *Crisis* (1982). Walter LaFeber, *Panama Canal* (1978). Clark Mollenhoff, *The President Who Failed* (1980). A. Glenn Mower, Jr. , *Human Rights and American Foreign Policy* (1987). William B. Quandt, *Decade of Decisions* (1977); *Camp David* (1986). Barry Rubin, *Paved with Good Intentions* (1983). Lars Schoultz, *Human Rights and U.S. Policy Toward Latin America* (1981). Gaddis Smith, *Morality, Reason, and Power* (1986). Strobe Talbott, *Endgame* (1979). Jules Witcover, *Marathon* (1977). James Wooten, *Dasher* (1978). Cyrus Vance, *Hard Choices* (1983).

The New Right.   Sidney Blumenthal, *The Rise of the Counter-Establishment* (1986). George Nash, *The Conservative Intellectual Movement in America Since 1945* (1979). Burton Yale Pines, *Back to Basics* (1982). David W. Reinhard, *The Republican Right Since 1945* (1983). Kirkpatrick Sale, *Power Shift: The Rise of the Southern Rim and Its Challenge to the Eastern Establishment* (1975). Peter Steinfels, *The Neo-Conservatives* (1979). John K. White, *The New Politics of Old Values* (1988). John Woodridge, *The Evangelicals* (1975).

The Reagan Presidency.   Frank Ackerman, *Reaganomics* (1982). Laurence I. Barrett, *Gambling with History* (1984). Bill Boyarsky, *The Rise of Ronald Reagan* (1968). Paul Boyer, ed. , *Reagan as President: Contemporary Views of the Man, His Politics, and His Policies* (1990). William J. Broad, *Teller's War: The Top-Secret Story Behind the Star Wars Deception* (1992). Lou Cannon, *Reagan* (1982); *President Reagan: The Role of a Lifetime* (1990). Joan Claybrook, *Retreat from Safety: Reagan's Attack on American Health* (1984). Robert Dallek, *Ronald Reagan: The Politics of Symbolism* (1984). Ronnie Dugger, *On Reagan* (1983). Thomas Byrne Edsall, *The New Politics of Inequality* (1984). Anne Edwards, *Early Reagan* (1987). Rowland Evans and Robert Novak, *The Reagan Revolution* (1981). Benjamin

Friedman, *Day of Reckoning: The Consequences of American Economic Policy Under Reagan and After* (1988). Jack Germond and Jules Witcover, *Blue Smoke and Mirrors: How Reagan Won and Why Carter Lost the Election of 1980* (1981); *Wake Us When It's Over: Presidential Politics of 1984* (1985). George Gildner, *Wealth and Poverty* (1981). Fred I. Greenstein, ed., *The Reagan Presidency* (1983). William Greider, *The Education of David Stockman and Other Americans* (1982). Haynes Johnson, *Sleepwalking Through History: America in the Reagan Years* (1991). Jonathan Lash, *A Season of Spoils: The Story of the Reagan Administration's Attack on the Environment* (1984). Robert Lekachman, *Greed Is Not Enough: Reaganomics* (1982). Jane Mayer and Doyle McManus, *Landslide: The Unmaking of the President, 1984–1988* (1988). Charles Noble, *Liberalism at Work: The Rise and Fall of OSHA* (1986). Peggy Noonan, *What I Saw at the Revolution: A Political Life in the Reagan Era* (1990). John L. Palmer and Isabel V. Sawhill, eds., *The Reagan Experiment* (1982). Michael J. Piore and Charles F. Sabel, *The Second Industrial Divide* (1984). Frances Fox Piven and Richard A. Cloward, *The New Class War: Reagan's Attack on the Welfare State and Its Consequences* (1982). Nancy Reagan, *My Turn* (1989). Richard Reeves, *The Reagan Detour* (1985). Donald T. Regan, *For the Record* (1988). Michael Rogin, *Ronald Reagan: The Movie* (1987). Michael Schaller, *Reckoning with Reagan: America and Its President in the 1980s* (1992). C. Brant Short, *Ronald Reagan and the Public Lands: America's Conservation Debate, 1979–1984* (1989). Hedrick Smith, *The Power Game* (1988). Hedrick Smith et al., *Reagan: The Man, the President* (1980). David A. Stockman, *The Triumph of Politics* (1986). Sidney Weintraub and Marvin Goodstein, eds., *Reaganomics in the Stagflation Economy* (1983). F. Clifton White and William Gil, *Why Reagan Won* (1982). Theodore H. White, *America in Search of Itself* (1982). Garry Wills, *Reagan's America* (1987).

Reagan and the World. Seweryn Bialer and Michael Mandelbaum, eds., *Gorbachev's Russia and American Foreign Policy* (1988). Raymond Bonner, *Weakness and Deceit: U.S. Policy and El Salvador* (1984). Tom Buckley, *Violent Neighbors* (1984). Steven Emerson, *Secret Warriors: Inside the Covert Military Operations of the Reagan Era* (1988). Thomas L. Friedman, *From Beirut to Jerusalem* (1989). Alexander Haig, *Caveat: Realism, Reagan and Foreign Policy* (1984). Jane Hunter et al., *The Iran-Contra Connection* (1987). David E. Kyvig, ed., *Reagan and the World* (1990). Walter LaFeber, *Inevitable Revolutions*, rev. ed. (1984). Richard A. Melanson, *Reconstructing Consensus: American Foreign Policy Since the Vietnam War* (1991). John Newhouse, *War and Peace in the Nuclear Age* (1989). Robert O. Pastor, *Condemned to Repetition: The United States and Nicaragua* (1987). Charles D. Smith, *Palestine and the Arab-Israeli Conflict*, 2nd ed. (1992). Strobe Talbott, *Deadly Gambits* (1984); *The Master of the Game: Paul Nitze and the Nuclear Peace* (1988). Daniel Wirls, *Buildup: The Politics of Defense in the Reagan Era* (1992). Bob Woodward, *Veil: The Secret Wars of the CIA* (1987).

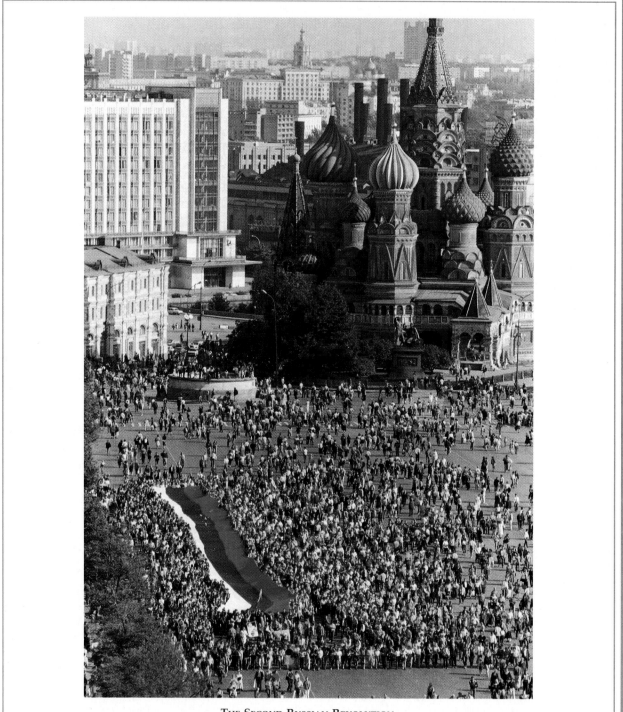

THE SECOND RUSSIAN REVOLUTION
Supporters of Russian President Boris Yeltsin march through Red Square in August 1991 carrying an enormous Russian flag—a symbol of defiance aimed at the Soviet regime, some of whose hardliners were attempting a coup to restore traditional communist rule. Within a few months, the Soviet Union had ceased to exist and its various republics, including Russia, had become independent nations. *(Reuters/Bettmann)*

CHAPTER THIRTY-FOUR

BEYOND THE COLD WAR

O N NOVEMBER 8, 1989, East German soldiers stood guard at the Berlin Wall—keeping westerners out and easterners in—as they had done every day for more than twenty-eight years. The next day they were gone. Within hours, thousands of citizens of both sides of the divided city were swarming over the wall in celebration. Within weeks, bulldozers were tearing it down. Within a year, East and West Germany—divided by the Cold War for forty-five years—had reunited.

The breaching of the Berlin Wall and the reunification of Germany were among the most dramatic of a series of changes between 1986 and 1991 that radically transformed the world order. The Cold War, which as late as 1985 had seemed a permanent fact of international life, came to an end. A new world order, the outlines of which were still only dimly visible, was in the process of being born.

The Cold War had shaped the foreign policy and many aspects of the domestic life of the United States for nearly half a century. Its sudden end changed the character of national politics, economics, and culture. But America in the late 1980s and early 1990s was also encountering a series of other important social and economic changes, many of them unrelated to the Cold War. As the end of the twentieth century approached, most Americans were uncertain whether the changes would bring a better, safer world or a harsher and more dangerous one.

AMERICA AND THE WANING OF THE COLD WAR

In the midst of the turbulent changes that enveloped the world beginning in the late 1980s, it was difficult to identify the point at which it had all begun. Some pointed to the upheavals in Poland in 1981, the first broad challenge to communist rule in Eastern Europe in over a decade. Some pointed to the Soviet war in Afghanistan, a long, stalemated conflict that ultimately proved more disastrous to the Soviet economy and the Soviet government than the Vietnam War had been to the United States. Some pointed to the long-term economic troubles of the Eastern-bloc nations; by the late 1980s, some were experiencing something close to collapse, and even the most successful were falling further and further behind the dynamically expanding economies of Western Europe.

The most frequent explanation, however, centered on a single man: Mikhail Gorbachev, who succeeded to the leadership of the Soviet Union in 1985 and, to the surprise of almost everyone, very quickly became the most revolutionary figure in world politics in at least four decades.

The Fall of the Soviet Union

Benefiting from widespread frustration with the rigid and ineffective policies of the preceding twenty years (which reformers began to call the "time of stagnation"), Gorbachev transformed Soviet politics with two dramatic new initiatives. The first he called *glasnost* (openness). *Glasnost* meant the dismantling of many of the repressive mechanisms that had been among the most conspicuous features of Soviet life for over half a century. Suddenly it became possible for Soviet citizens to express themselves more freely, to criticize the government, even to organize politically in opposition to official policy. The other policy Gorbachev called *perestroika* (reform, or restructuring). Through it, he attempted to remake the rigid and unproductive Soviet economy by introducing, among other things, such elements of capitalism as private ownership and the profit motive. He also began to transform Soviet foreign policy.

The severe economic problems at home evidently convinced Gorbachev that the Soviet Union could no longer sustain its extended commitments around the world. As early as 1987, he began reducing Soviet influence in Eastern Europe. And in 1989, in the space of a few months, the government of every nation in the so-called Soviet bloc—Poland, Hungary, Czechoslovakia, Bulgaria, Romania, and East Germany—was either overthrown or forced to transform itself into an essentially noncommunist (and in some cases, actively anticommunist) regime. The Communist Parties of Eastern Europe all but collapsed. And in every case, Gorbachev and the Soviet Union not only refused to oppose, but actively encouraged, the changes.

The challenges to communism were not successful everywhere. In May 1989, students in China had begun staging large demonstrations calling for greater democratization, which the post-Mao government had long been promising but had never delivered. A visit by Gorbachev to Beijing in late May inspired even greater demonstrations. By the beginning of June, the demonstrations had grown so large and widespread, and had attracted the support of so much of the population, that it seemed possible the communist regime might topple. Instead, hard-line leaders seized control and sent military forces to crush the uprising. The result was a bloody massacre on June 3, 1989, in Tiananmen Square in Beijing, in which a still-unknown number of demonstrators—perhaps several thousand—died. The assault crushed the democracy movement, restored the hard-liners to power, and inaugurated a period of repression and international ostracism. It did not, however, stop China's efforts to modernize and even westernize its economy.

The events in China had no counterpart in the rest of the communist world. The attempt by the Romanian

TIANANMEN SQUARE, 1989
The democracy movement in China accelerated rapidly in the spring of 1989 and was most visible through the vast crowds of students who began demonstrating in Tiananmen Square in Beijing. Some of them fashioned a rough replica of the American Statue of Liberty, which they called the "Goddess of Liberty," an act particularly galling to the conservative leadership of the communist regime. On June 3, the government sent troops into the Square to clear out and arrest the demonstrating students. Hundreds, perhaps thousands, were killed in the violence that resulted from that decision. *(Forrest Anderson/Gamma Liaison)*

dictator Nicolae Ceausescu to crush a dissident revolt in his country in December 1989 produced a popular revolution that drove him from power, led to his capture and execution, and culminated in the installation of a new, noncommunist (although still authoritarian) regime. In all other Eastern European nations, the toppling of communist regimes was remarkably peaceful.

There were even signs of democratization in parts of the world far removed from the Soviet empire. Early in 1990, the government of South Africa, long an international pariah for its rigid enforcement of white supremacy through the "apartheid" system, began a cautious retreat from its traditional policies. Among other things, it legalized the major black opposition movements, most prominently the African National Congress, which had been banned for decades. And on February 11, 1990, it released from prison the leader of the ANC, Nelson Mandela, a revered hero to black South Africans who had been in jail for twenty-seven years. Over the next several years, the South African government repealed its apartheid laws. And in 1994, there were national elections in which all South Africans could participate. As a result, Nelson Mandela became the first black president of South Africa.

In 1991, communism began to collapse at the site of its birth: the Soviet Union itself. An unsuccessful coup by hard-line Soviet leaders on August 19 precipitated a dramatic unraveling of communist power. Within days, not only did the coup itself collapse in the face of resistance from the public and, more important, crucial elements within the military; not only did Mikhail Gorbachev return to power; but the forces of disunion that had been gathering strength for several years made a great leap forward. It soon became evident that the legitimacy of both the Communist Party and the central Soviet government had been fatally injured. By the end of August, almost every republic in the Soviet Union had declared independence; the Soviet government was clearly powerless to stop the fragmentation. At the same time, Boris Yeltsin, the president of the Russian Republic, in effect outlawed the Communist Party—barring it from owning property or playing any significant role in the life of the largest and most important republic in the Soviet Union. Gorbachev himself finally resigned as leader of the now virtually powerless communist party and Soviet government, and the Soviet Union ceased to exist.

Reagan and Gorbachev

In the face of these dramatic changes, American foreign policy, which for over four decades had remained securely tied to the premises of "containment," suddenly seemed obsolete. And while a new strategic doctrine to replace containment did not quickly emerge, the pattern of American international behavior began inevitably to change. The last years of the Reagan administration coincided with the first years of the Gorbachev regime; and while Reagan was skeptical of Gorbachev at first, he gradually became convinced (by, among others, British Prime Minister Margaret Thatcher) that the Soviet leader was sincere in his desire for reform.

That the Gorbachev regime was committed to a new relationship with the West had been clear almost from the start, when the new leader began reaching out to Washington for major arms control agreements. At a summit meeting with Reagan in Reykjavik, Iceland, in 1986, Gorbachev proposed reducing the nuclear arsenals of both sides by 50 percent or more, although continuing disputes over Reagan's commitment to the SDI program derailed agreements. But in 1988, after Reagan and Gorbachev exchanged cordial visits to each other's capitals, the two superpowers signed a treaty eliminating American and Soviet intermediate-range nuclear forces (INF) from Europe—the most significant arms control agreement of the nuclear age. At about the same time, Gorbachev ended the Soviet Union's long and frustrating military involvement in Afghanistan, removing one of the principal irritants in the relationship between Washington and Moscow.

The Fading of the Reagan Revolution

For a time, the dramatic changes around the world and Reagan's personal popularity deflected attention from a series of scandals that might well have destroyed another administration. Top officials in the Environmental Protection Agency resigned when it was disclosed that they were flouting the laws they had been appointed to enforce. Officials of the CIA and the Defense Department resigned after revelations of questionable stock transactions. Reagan's secretary of labor left office after being indicted for racketeering (although he was later acquitted). Edwin Meese, the White House counsel and later attorney general, finally resigned in 1988 after years of attacks for controversial financial arrangements that many believed had compromised his office.

Unnoticed at first were several larger scandals that surfaced only as Reagan was about to leave office. One involved misuse of funds by the Department of Housing and Urban Development, abuses so widespread that by 1990 the survival of the agency itself was in question. Another, more serious scandal involved the savings and loan industry. The Reagan administration had sharply reduced regulatory controls over the troubled savings and loans. Many savings banks responded by rapidly, often recklessly, and sometimes corruptly, expanding. By the end of the decade the industry was in chaos, and the government was forced to step in to prevent a complete collapse. The government insured the assets of most savings and loan depositors; and as the banks failed, it found itself saddled with large debts. Predictions of eventual cost to the public of the debacle ran to more than half a trillion dollars.

But the most politically damaging scandal of the Reagan years came to light in November 1986. After reports of the episode had begun appearing in foreign newspapers, the White House conceded that it had sold weapons to the revolutionary government of Iran, apparently as part of a largely unsuccessful effort to secure the release of several Americans being held hostage by radical Islamic groups in the Middle East. Even more damaging was the administration's revelation that some of the money from the arms deal with Iran had been covertly and illegally funneled into a fund to aid the contras in Nicaragua.

In the months that followed, aggressive reporting and a highly publicized series of congressional hearings exposed a remarkable and previously unsuspected feature of the Reagan White House: the existence within it of something like a "secret government," largely unknown to the State Department, the Defense Department, even parts of the CIA, dedicated to advancing the administration's foreign policy aims through secret and at times illegal means. The principal figure in this covert world appeared at first to be an obscure marine lieutenant colonel assigned to the staff of the National Security Council, Oliver North. But gradually it became clear that North was acting in concert with other, more powerful figures in the administration. The Iran-contra scandal, as it became known, did serious damage to the Reagan presidency—even though the investigations were never able decisively to tie the president himself to the most serious violations of the law.

There were other signs in the late 1980s that the glow of the "Reagan Revolution" was beginning to fade. In October 1987, the American stock market—whose spectacular success had been one of the most conspicuous features of the economic boom—experienced the greatest single-day decline in its history; and although stock prices recovered and continued to rise over the next two years, the crash eroded confidence in the financial markets. At about the same time, one of the most popular financial innovations of the 1980s, the "leveraged buyout," which had permitted a wave of corporate takeovers financed by huge loans (many of them in the form of risky "junk bonds"), began to unravel. Some of the nation's largest corporations, un-

able to carry the enormous debt they had acquired in their takeover efforts, began to flounder or collapse. And some of the financial managers who had engineered the buyouts and takeovers were convicted of insider trading and other fraudulent activities.

The Election of 1988

The fraying of the Reagan administration helped the Democrats regain control of the United States Senate in 1986 and fueled hopes in the party for a presidential victory in 1988. Even so, several of the most popular figures in the Democratic Party refused to run. The early favorite, Senator Gary Hart of Colorado,

THE BUSH CAMPAIGN, 1988
Vice President George Bush had never been an effective campaigner, but in 1988 he helped his candidacy revive with an unabashed attack on his opponent's values and patriotism. Bush himself missed no chance to surround himself with patriotic symbols, including this red, white, and blue hot-air balloon in Kentucky. *(L. Johnson/Gamma Liaison)*

ELECTION OF **1988**   (50% of electorate voting)

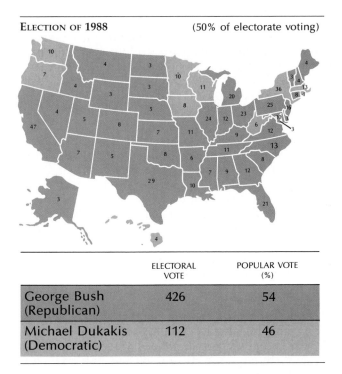

	ELECTORAL VOTE	POPULAR VOTE (%)
George Bush (Republican)	426	54
Michael Dukakis (Democratic)	112	46

withdrew from the race in May 1987 after embarrassing revelations of an extramarital relationship with a young model. That left the field to a group of lesser-known candidates and to the civil rights leader Jesse Jackson, whose fervent support among African Americans made him a major force in the party.

The man who emerged victorious from the crowded field was relatively little known: Michael Dukakis, a three-term governor of Massachusetts who claimed to have helped produce a dramatic revival in the New England economy (a revival frequently described as "the Massachusetts miracle"). Dukakis was a dry, even dull campaigner. But Democrats remained optimistic about their prospects in 1988, largely because of the identity of their opponent, Vice President George Bush—who had been an ineffective campaigner in 1980 when he ran unsuccessfully for president, and who had attracted derision for his performance in the 1984 campaign, when he was running for reelection as vice president. Bush captured the Republican nomination without great difficulty, but he entered the last months of the campaign substantially behind Dukakis.

Beginning at the Republican convention, however, Bush staged a remarkable turnaround by making his campaign into a long, relentless attack on Dukakis, tying him to all the unpopular social and cultural stances Americans had come to identify with "liberals." Indeed, the Bush campaign was almost certainly the most savage of the twentieth century. It was also,

apparently, one of the most effective, although the listless, indecisive character of the Dukakis effort contributed to the Republican cause as well. Bush won a substantial victory in November: 54 percent of the popular vote to Dukakis's 46, and 426 electoral votes to Dukakis's 111. But Bush carried few Republicans into office with him; the Democrats retained secure majorities in both houses of Congress.

The Bush Presidency

The Bush presidency was notable for a series of dramatic developments in international affairs and an almost complete absence of initiatives or ideas on domestic issues. For a time, Bush's achievements in foreign policy managed to obscure the absence of a domestic agenda. By early 1992, however, with the nation in the second year of a serious recession, the president's once overwhelming popularity had begun to fray.

The broad popularity Bush enjoyed during his first three years in office was partly because of his subdued, unthreatening public image. But it was primarily because of the wonder and excitement with which Americans viewed the dramatic events in the rest of the world. Bush profited both passively and actively from the nation's satisfaction at having "won" the Cold War. He took credit for the international changes, even though he had played a relatively small role in most of them. But he also launched initiatives of his own. Late in 1989, he dispatched American troops to Panama to overthrow the unpopular military leader Manuel Noriega, who was under indictment in the United States for drug trafficking and whose contemptuous defiance of American pressures had embarrassed the government in Washington for two years. The Panama invasion—which installed an elected, pro-American, civilian government in Panama—was highly popular within the United States.

Bush moved cautiously at first in dealing with the changes in the Soviet Union. But like Reagan, he eventually embraced Gorbachev and reached a series of significant agreements with the Soviet Union in its waning years. The Gorbachev regime had all but repudiated the arms race with the United States in the late 1980s and had been working energetically to produce arms control agreements well before Bush entered office. In the three years after the INF agreement in 1988, the United States and the Soviet Union moved rapidly toward even more far-reaching arms reduction agreements, including major troop reductions in Europe and the dismantling of new categories of strategic weapons. At the same time, the Soviet Union and the new, noncommunist governments in Eastern Europe were appealing to the West for economic assistance through subsidies, loans, and investments; the United States, beset with its own fiscal and economic difficulties, was slow to respond.

On domestic issues, the Bush administration was less successful—partly because the president himself seemed to have little interest in promoting a domestic agenda and partly because he faced serious obstacles. His administration inherited a staggering burden of debt and a federal deficit that had been out of control for nearly a decade. Any domestic agenda that required significant federal spending was, therefore, incompatible with the president's pledge to reduce the deficit and his 1988 campaign promise of "no new taxes." President Bush also faced a Democratic Congress, which was not, on the whole, disposed to cooperate with him. And while the president himself was at heart a nonideological pragmatist, he was deeply concerned about the right wing of his own party and, in his eagerness to ingratiate himself with them, took divisive positions on such cultural issues as abortion and affirmative action that further damaged his ability to work with Congress.

Despite this political stalemate, Congress and the White House managed on occasion to agree on significant measures. They cooperated in producing a plan to salvage the floundering savings and loan industry. In 1990, the president bowed to congressional pressure and agreed to a significant tax increase as part of a multiyear "budget package" designed to reduce the deficit. In 1991, after almost two years of acrimonious debate, the president and Congress agreed on a civil rights bill to combat job discrimination.

But the most serious domestic problem facing the Bush administration was one to which neither the president nor Congress had any answer: a recession that began late in 1990 and slowly increased its grip on the national economy in 1991 and 1992. Because of the enormous level of debt that corporations (and individuals) had accumulated in the 1980s, the recession caused an unusual number of bankruptcies. It also created growing fear and frustration among middle- and working-class Americans and increasing pressure on the government to address such problems as the rising cost of health care.

The Gulf War

The events of 1989–1991 had left the United States in the unanticipated position of being the only real superpower in the world. The Soviet Union was too embroiled in its own problems to play a major international role any longer. Germany and Japan, the new economic superpowers, had no significant military strength. China remained largely isolated in international affairs. The Bush administration, therefore, had to consider what to do with America's formidable political and military power in a world in which the major justification for that power—the Soviet threat—was now gone.

The events of 1990–1991 suggested two possible answers, both of which had some effect on policy. One was that the United States would reduce its military strength dramatically and concentrate its energies and resources on pressing domestic problems. And, indeed, there was considerable movement in that direction both in Congress and within the administration. The other was that America would continue to use its power actively, not to fight communism but to defend its economic interests. Once again, that drew the United States into the turbulent politics of the Middle East.

On August 2, 1990, the armed forces of Iraq invaded and quickly overwhelmed their small, oil-rich neighbor, the emirate of Kuwait. Saddam Hussein, the militaristic leader of Iraq, soon announced that he was annexing Kuwait and set out to entrench his forces there. After some initial indecision, the Bush administration agreed to join with other nations to force Iraq out of Kuwait—through the pressure of economic sanctions if possible, through military force if necessary. Within a few weeks, Bush had persuaded virtually every important government in the world, including the Soviet Union and almost all the Arab and Islamic states, to join in a United Nations-sanctioned trade embargo of Iraq. That meant the Iraqis, whose economy was already weak, would be unable to sell any oil on world markets and would be unable to buy any products from abroad or generate hard currency with which to pay their massive debts.

At the same time, the United States and its allies (including the British, French, Egyptians, and Saudis) began deploying a massive military force along the border between Kuwait and Saudi Arabia, a force that ultimately reached 690,000 troops (425,000 of them American) and that assembled the largest and most sophisticated collection of military technology ever used in warfare.

By late 1990, the Bush administration was clearly losing patience with the sanctions and was preparing for war. On November 29, the United Nations, at the request of the United States, voted to authorize military action to expel Iraq from Kuwait if Iraq did not leave by January 15, 1991. On January 12, both houses of Congress voted to authorize the use of force against Iraq, although many Democrats opposed the resolution, arguing that sanctions should be given more time to work. And on January 16, American and allied air forces began a massive bombardment of Iraqi forces in Kuwait and of military and industrial installations in Iraq itself.

The allied bombing continued for six weeks, meeting only token resistance from the small Iraqi air force and Iraqi ground defenses. And on February 23, allied (primarily American) forces under the command of General Norman Schwarzkopf began a major ground offensive—not primarily against the heavily entrenched Iraqi forces along the Kuwait border, as expected, but into Iraq itself. The allied armies encountered almost no resistance and suffered only light casualties (141 fatalities). There were no reliable figures for the number of Iraqi military casualties, but some estimates of deaths (most as a result of the bombing) ranged as high as 100,000. There were also a significant, if unverifiable, number of civilian casualties. On February 28, Iraq announced its acceptance of allied terms for a cease-fire, and the brief war came to an end.

The quick and (for America) relatively painless victory over Iraq was highly popular in the United States. But the longer-range results of the Gulf War were more difficult to assess. The tyrannical regime of Saddam Hussein survived, in a weakened form but showing no signs of retreat from its militaristic ambitions. And Kuwait returned to the control of its prewar government, an undemocratic monarchy increasingly unpopular with its own people.

The Election of 1992

President Bush's popularity reached a record high in the immediate aftermath of the Gulf War. For a time, over 90 percent of those polled claimed to approve of the way he was handling his office, the highest approval rating in the history of opinion surveys. But the president received much lower approval ratings for his handling of domestic issues. As the recession worsened in late 1991, and as the administration declined to propose any policies for combatting it, the president's popularity rapidly eroded.

Because the early maneuvering for the 1992 presidential election occurred when President Bush's popularity remained high, many leading Democrats declined to run. That gave Bill Clinton, the young and energetic five-term governor of Arkansas, the opportunity to emerge early as the front-runner, as a result of a skillful campaign that emphasized broad economic issues over the racial and cultural questions that had so divided the Democrats in the past. Clinton survived a bruising primary campaign and a series of damaging personal controversies to win his party's nomination. And George Bush withstood an embarrassing primary challenge from the conservative journalist Pat Buchanan to become the Republican nominee again.

Complicating the campaign was the emergence of Ross Perot, a blunt, forthright Texas billionaire who became an independent candidate by tapping popular resentment of the federal bureaucracy and by promising tough, uncompromising leadership to deal with the fiscal crisis and other problems of government. Particularly appealing to many voters were Perot's attacks on corruption in the political system and his insistence that his own campaign (funded by his personal fortune, not by special-interest lobbies) was a

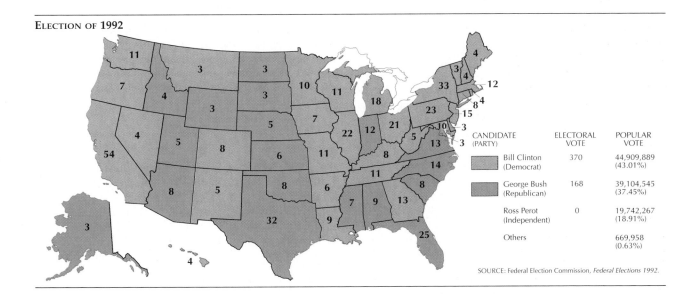

ELECTION OF 1992

CANDIDATE (PARTY)	ELECTORAL VOTE	POPULAR VOTE
Bill Clinton (Democrat)	370	44,909,889 (43.01%)
George Bush (Republican)	168	39,104,545 (37.45%)
Ross Perot (Independent)	0	19,742,267 (18.91%)
Others		669,958 (0.63%)

SOURCE: Federal Election Commission, *Federal Elections 1992.*

pure reflection of the will of the people. At several moments in the spring, Perot led both Bush and Clinton in public opinion polls. In July, as he began to face hostile scrutiny from the media, he abruptly withdrew from the race. But early in October, he reentered and soon regained much (although never all) of his early support.

After a campaign in which the economy and the president's unpopularity were the principal issues, Clinton won a clear, but hardly overwhelming, victory over Bush and Perot. He received 43 percent of the vote in the three-way race, to the president's 38 percent and Perot's 19 percent (the best showing for a third-party or independent candidate since Theodore Roosevelt in 1912). Clinton won 370 electoral votes to Bush's 168; Perot won none. Democrats retained control of both houses of Congress.

Launching the Clinton Presidency

Bill Clinton was the first Democratic president since Jimmy Carter, and the first liberal activist to be president since Lyndon Johnson. He entered office carrying the extravagant expectations of liberals who had spent a generation in exile. He also had significant political weaknesses. Having won the votes of well under half the electorate, he enjoyed no powerful mandate. Democratic majorities in Congress were frail, and Democrats in any case had grown unaccustomed to bowing to presidential leadership. The Republican leadership in Congress was highly adversarial and opposed the president with unusual unanimity on many issues.

The new administration compounded its problems with a series of missteps and misfortunes in its first months. The president's effort to end the longtime ban on gay men and women serving in the military met with ferocious resistance from the armed forces themselves and from many conservatives in both parties. He was forced to settle for a pallid compromise. Several of his early appointments—to the Justice Department, in particular—became sources of controversy and were eventually withdrawn. A longtime friend of the president from Arkansas serving in the office of the White House counsel committed suicide in the summer of 1993. His death helped spark an escalating inquiry into some banking and real estate ventures involving the President and his wife in the early 1980s; and the clumsy actions of some administration officials raised suspicions that the White House was attempting to interfere with the investigation into what became known as the Whitewater affair. A special prosecutor began investigating these issues in 1993. His first reports (on the actions of figures in President Clinton's administration accused of trying to cover up evidence) revealed no evidence of illegality.

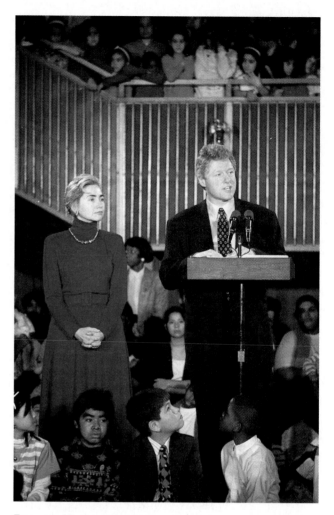

BILL AND HILLARY CLINTON
Hillary Clinton quickly established herself as the most active and powerful first lady in American history—as she demonstrated by her stewardship of the president's most important domestic initiative: health care reform. President and Mrs. Clinton often appeared together to speak to citizen and student groups about their health plan and other initiatives. *(Brad Markel/Gamma Liaison)*

Despite its many problems, the Clinton administration could boast of some significant achievements in its first year. The president narrowly (by a single vote in the Senate) won approval of a budget that marked a significant turn away from the policies of the Reagan-Bush years. It included a substantial tax increase on the wealthiest Americans, a significant reduction in many areas of government spending, and a major expansion of tax credits to low-income families, designed to help lift many struggling families out of poverty. Clinton also signed legislation requiring employers to give both male and female employees unpaid leaves to deal with such urgent family responsibilities as the birth of a child or the illness of a relative. And after a long and difficult battle against, among others, Ross Perot, the AFL-CIO, and most Democrats in Congress, he won approval of the North American Free Trade Agreement, which eliminated most trade barriers among the United States, Canada, and Mexico.

The fate of the president's most ambitious initiatives remained unclear well into his second year. A task force chaired by the president's wife, Hillary Rodham Clinton, proposed a sweeping reform of the nation's health-care system designed to guarantee coverage to every American and hold down the costs of medical care. (In the process of heading the task force, Mrs. Clinton emerged as the most important figure in the administration after the president, and the most powerful First Lady in American history). Opposition from (among others) insurance companies, drug companies, doctors, and small businesses—who balked at the proposed requirement that they provide insurance to their employees—clouded the prospects for reform. By late 1994, the prospects for any comprehensive reform seemed dim.

The foreign policy of the Clinton administration was, on the whole, cautious and even tentative—a reflection, perhaps, of the president's relative inexperience in international affairs, but also of the rapidly changing character of the world order. Clinton presided over (although his administration had played a small role in creating) a historic agreement between Israel and the Palestinian Liberation Organization to end their long struggle over the lands Israel had occupied in 1967. His administration reached an agreement with Ukraine for an elimination of the nuclear weapons that had been positioned there when the republic had been part of the Soviet Union. And after months of resisting involvement in a bloody civil war in Bosnia (part of the former Yugoslavia), he agreed early in 1994 to NATO air strikes and other military actions against the aggressors in the conflict. But there was as yet no clear outline for a new American foreign policy to replace containment.

MODERN TIMES

The widespread popular suspicion of politics and government that characterized American life in the 1980s and 1990s was in part a result of decades of crises and scandals in public life. But it reflected, too, a series of major changes in the character and behavior of the American economy and American society, which were changing more rapidly—and more jarringly—than at any time in the twentieth century.

The New Economy

Foremost among the changes that challenged and perplexed Americans in the last years of the twentieth century was a difficult transformation of the national economy. The changes had begun in earnest in the early 1970s, when the Arab oil embargo and the rapid increase in energy prices first shook the stability of the American economy. But the energy crisis was only one of many changes that affected the United States. More important in the long run was the rise of powerful economic competitors in Western Europe (especially Germany) and Asia (above all, Japan), who successfully challenged the United States in world trade and penetrated deeply into the American domestic market. Automobiles, steel, and other manufactured goods imported from abroad—often priced lower than their American counterparts—cut into the market share of major industries in the United States and contributed to the contraction of heavy manufacturing (and hence of industrial jobs) that characterized the nation's economy in the 1980s and 1990s.

The result of these and other factors was a series of fundamental changes in the behavior of the economy. Economic growth continued, but at a much slower rate. In the twenty years after World War II, the Gross National Product grew, on average, by 3.8 percent a year. In the last two decades, the GNP has grown by an average of less than 2.6 percent. Productivity grew 2.6 percent a year in the 1950s and 1960s; in the 1970s and 1980s it grew by less than 1 percent. The national savings rate—the rate at which individuals and institutions saved income, which then became available for investment—peaked at around 10 percent between 1948 and 1973. In the 1980s, at its highest, the rate was 3.2 percent.

For families and individuals, the results of these contractions were often devastating. In the first twenty years after World War II, it was possible for many, perhaps most, Americans, to sustain themselves on a single (usually male) income. In later years, more and more families required two incomes to sustain their standards of living, and even that was often not enough. In the 1950s and 1960s, most Americans could expect to live more comfortably as adults than their parents had; in the 1980s and 1990s, increasing numbers of Americans were finding it impossible even to live as well as the generation before them. From 1973 to 1989, median family income increased less than 2 percent (from $33,656 a year to $34,213), even though many families added a second income in those years. Poverty in America declined steadily and at times dramatically in the years after World War II, so that by the end of the 1960s the percentage of people living in poverty had declined to 12 percent (from about 20 percent in preceding decades). By the late 1980s, the poverty rate had climbed back to its old levels—and beyond—to over 24 percent. As always, this increase in poverty affected women, children, and minorities far more than any other groups.

The increasingly unequal distribution of wealth and income in the United States accentuated these changes. Over 94 percent of the new wealth created by the American economy in the 1980s went to the wealthiest 20 percent of the population; over 50 percent went to the top 1 percent. In the meantime, the middle 40 percent of the population experienced an actual decline in wealth. It was little wonder that the economic anxieties of the middle class became one of the central issues in American politics in the late 1980s and early 1990s.

The Graying of America

One of the most fundamental changes in American life in the post-liberal era was the new profile of the American population. After decades of steady growth, the nation's birth rate began to decline in the 1970s and remained low through the 1980s and early 1990s. In 1970, there were 18.4 births for every 1,000 people in the population. By 1975, the rate had declined to 14.6, the lowest in the twentieth century. And despite a modest increase in the 1980s, the rate remained below 16

throughout the decade. The declining birth rate and a significant rise in life expectancy produced a substantial increase in the proportion of elderly citizens. Over 12 percent of the population was more than sixty-five years old by 1990, as compared with 8 percent in 1970. That figure was projected to rise to over 20 percent by the end of the century. In 1990 the median age was 32.9 years, as compared with 28.0 in 1970.

The aging of the population had important, if not entirely predictable, implications. It was, for example, a cause of the increasing costliness of Social Security pensions. It meant rapidly increasing health costs, both for the federal Medicare system and for private hospitals and insurance companies. It also ensured that the elderly, who already formed one of the most powerful interest groups in America, would remain politically formidable well into the twenty-first century.

The Changing Profile of Immigration

Perhaps the most striking demographic change in America in the 1970s and 1980s, and the one likely to have the farthest-reaching consequences, was the enormous change in both the extent and the character of

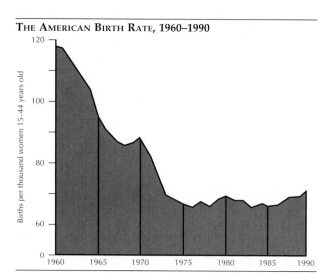

THE AMERICAN BIRTH RATE, 1960–1990

TOTAL IMMIGRATION, 1960–1990

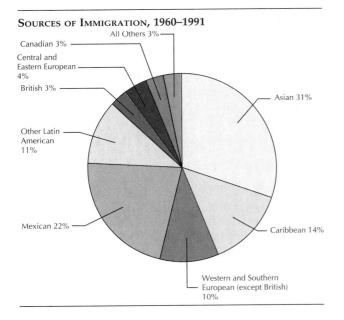

SOURCES OF IMMIGRATION, 1960–1991

All Others 3%
Canadian 3%
Central and Eastern European 4%
British 3%
Other Latin American 11%
Mexican 22%
Western and Southern European (except British) 10%
Caribbean 14%
Asian 31%

nificant segments of the American population for many decades—Hispanics since the very beginning of the nation's history, Asians since the waves of Chinese and Japanese immigration in the nineteenth century. But both groups experienced enormous, indeed unprecedented, growth after 1965.

People from Latin America constituted more than a third of the total number of legal immigrants to the United States in every year since 1965—and a much larger proportion of the total number of illegal immigrants. In California and the Southwest, in particular, they became an increasingly important presence. There were also substantial Hispanic populations in Illinois, New York, and Florida. High birth rates among Hispanic communities already in the United States further increased their numbers. In the 1980 census, 6 percent of the population was listed as being of Hispanic origin. The 1990 census showed an increase to 9 percent—or 20 million people. (Twenty years earlier, the number had been 7 million.) Economic problems and political repression in Mexico and other Latin American and Caribbean nations propelled the new immigrants to the United States; but in most of the areas to which they moved, opportunities were also hard to find. Mexican Americans had an official poverty rate of 20 percent in 1990 (and a real poverty rate that was probably much higher, given the number of illegal immigrants who evaded official statistics). The poverty rate among Puerto Ricans was 30 percent. For illegal immigrants, conditions were particularly dire. Because they were subject to deportation if they came to the attention of the government, they had no legal recourse to being exploited by employers. Most worked for subsistence wages in menial jobs, constantly fearful of exposure.

The growing Hispanic presence became a political issue of increasing importance in the 1980s and 1990s, both to "Anglos" and, of course, to Hispanics themselves. The Immigration Reform and Control (or Simpson-Mazzoli) Act of 1987 reflected the political power of both groups. Its principal goal was to respond to the demands of whites in the Southwest and California by stemming the flow of illegal immigrants (mostly from Mexico). To that end, it placed the burden on employers for the first time to confirm the legal status of their employees. Those who failed to do so faced economic and even criminal penalties. Hispanics charged that the bill would increase discrimination in hiring, and in the first years after its passage there was considerable evidence that such charges were well founded. At the same time, the act responded to the growing political influence of Hispanics by offering amnesty to all undocumented workers who had entered the country before 1982. By the early 1990s, how-

immigration. The nation's immigration quotas expanded significantly in those years (partly to accommodate refugees from Southeast Asia and other nations), allowing more newcomers to enter the United States legally than at any point since the beginning of the twentieth century. In the 1970s, more than 4 million legal immigrants entered the United States. In the 1980s, that number rose to more than 6 million. When the uncounted but very large numbers of illegal immigrants in those years are included, the wave of immigration in the twenty years after 1970 is the largest of the twentieth century.

Equally striking was the character of the new immigration. The Immigration Reform Act of 1965 (see p. 824) had eliminated quotas based on national origin; from then on, newcomers from regions other than Latin America were generally admitted on a first-come, first-served basis. In 1965, 90 percent of the immigrants to the United States came from Europe. Twenty years later, only 10 percent of the new arrivals were Europeans. The extent and character of the new immigration was causing a dramatic change in the composition of the American population. Already by the early 1990s, people of white European background constituted under 80 percent of the population (as opposed to 90 percent a half century before). It seemed likely that by the middle of the twenty-first century, whites of European heritage would constitute less than 50 percent of the population.

Particularly important to the new immigration were two groups: Hispanics and Asians. Both had been sigever, it seemed clear that the law was failing. Illegal immigration from Mexico and elsewhere was continuing at near record levels.

White residents of areas in which the Hispanic populations were growing rapidly often reacted with alarm, fearing that they would soon become a minority in what they considered their own cities. Such fears lay behind efforts to bar the use of the Spanish language in public schools and other measures to force Hispanic immigrants to assimilate more quickly and completely. And while the strenuous effort to combat Hispanic street gangs in Los Angeles and other cities was motivated mainly by the desire to fight crime, it was also an effort to halt the creation of an "alien" culture within America (much like the efforts to eliminate the "zoot-suiters" in the 1940s; see p. 755). These white fears prompted angry and defiant responses from many Hispanics. "You hear all the ravings and complaints like, 'In the year 2000 Los Angeles is going to become a minority city! The Mexicans are going to take over!'" a Mexican-American film producer said in 1989. "I'd like to remind them that we're just going to reinstate the original composition of the city—like it was a hundred years ago, before they showed up."

In the 1980s and early 1990s, Asian immigrants arrived in even greater numbers than Hispanics, constituting more than 40 percent of the total of legal newcomers. They swelled the already substantial Chinese and Japanese communities in California and elsewhere. And they created substantial new communities of immigrants from Vietnam, Thailand, Cambodia, Laos, the Philippines, Korea, and India. By 1990, there were more than 7 million Asian Americans in the United States, more than twice the number of ten years before. Like Hispanics, they were concentrated mainly in large cities and in the West.

Many of the new Asian immigrants were refugees, including Vietnamese driven from their homes in the aftermath of the disastrous war in which the United States had so long been involved. Large numbers of "boat people"—Vietnamese refugees who put to sea in crowded boats without any clear destination—ultimately found their way to the United States, usually after enduring terrible dangers and hardships. But many Asian immigrants were highly educated professionals seeking greater opportunities in the United States.

Like most new immigrant groups, Asian Americans found adjustment to the very different culture of the United States difficult and disorienting. "When I think how lonely I am in America," a Vietnamese immigrant wrote in the late 1980s, "I wonder why I am here, and what I have to live for." They also experienced resentment and discrimination. Whites feared Asian competition in economic activities that they had been accustomed to controlling. For example, there were heated disputes between white and Vietnamese shrimpers on the Gulf Coast in Texas, Mississippi, and Louisiana. Some African Americans resented the success of Asian merchants in black neighborhoods (as the black filmmaker Spike Lee noted in his 1989 film *Do the Right Thing*). In New York, racial tensions led to a black boycott of some Korean grocery stores in African American neighborhoods in 1990. Resentment of Asian-Americans may have been a result, in part, of their remarkable success. Indeed, some Asian groups (most notably Indians, Japanese, and Chinese) were by the 1980s earning larger average annual incomes than whites. Chinese and Japanese Americans consistently ranked at or near the top of high school and college classes in the 1980s. That was in part because Asian-American communities contained significant numbers of people who had been involved in business and the professions before coming to America and had arrived with a high degree of expertise. They also placed an unusually high value on education.

Black America in the Post-Liberal Era

The civil rights movement and the other liberal efforts of the 1960s had two very different effects on African Americans. On the one hand, there were increased opportunities for advancement available to those in a position to take advantage of them. On the other hand, as the industrial economy declined and government services dwindled, there was a growing sense of helplessness and despair among the large groups of nonwhites who continued to find themselves barred from upward mobility.

For the black middle class, which by the late 1970s constituted nearly a third of the entire black population of America, the progress was at times astonishing. Economic disparities between black and white professionals did not vanish, but they diminished substantially. Black families moved into more affluent urban communities and, in many cases, into suburbs—at times as neighbors of whites, more often into predominantly black communities. The number of blacks attending college rose by 350 percent in the decade following the passage of the civil rights acts (in contrast to a 150 percent increase among whites); African Americans made up 12 percent of the college population in 1990 (up from 5 percent twenty-five years earlier). The percentage of black high-school graduates going on to college was by then virtually the same as that of white high-school graduates (although a far smaller proportion of blacks than whites managed to complete high school). And African Americans were making rapid strides in many professions from

COMPARISON OF BLACK AND WHITE OCCUPATIONAL DISTRIBUTION, 1992

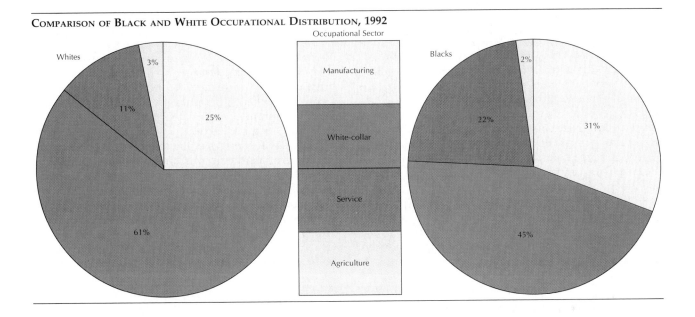

which, a generation earlier, they had been barred or within which they had been segregated. They were becoming partners in major law firms, joining the staffs of major hospitals and the faculties of major universities. Nearly half of all employed blacks in the United States had white-collar jobs. There were few areas of American life from which blacks were any longer entirely excluded. Middle-class blacks, in other words, had realized great gains from the legislation of the 1960s, from the changing national mood on race, and from the creation of controversial affirmative action programs.

But the rise of a black middle class also accentuated (and perhaps even helped cause) the increasingly desperate plight of other black Americans, whom many of the liberal programs of the 1960s had never reached. This growing "underclass" made up about a third of the nation's black population. It felt the impact of the economic troubles of the 1970s and 1980s with special force. And as more successful blacks moved out of the inner cities, the poor were left virtually alone in their decaying neighborhoods. By the late 1980s, more than one-third of all black families lived in poverty; at the same time, just under 11 percent of white families could be officially classified as poor. Fewer than half of young inner-city blacks finished high school; more than 60 percent were unemployed.

The black family structure suffered as well from the dislocations of urban poverty. There was a radical increase in the number of single-parent, female-headed black households in the 1970s and 1980s. In the early 1990s, over 60 percent of all black children were born into single-parent families, as opposed to only 15 percent of white children. In 1960, only 20 percent of black children had lived in single-parent homes.

Nonwhites were disadvantaged by many things in the changing social and economic climate of the 1980s. Among them was a growing impatience with affirmative action and other programs designed to advance their fortunes, as symbolized by the Bakke case in 1978 and by a growing reluctance among federal officials after 1980 to move aggressively to enforce affirmative action guidelines. Nonwhites suffered as well from a steady decline in the number of unskilled jobs in the economy. They suffered from the deterioration of public education and of other social services, which made it more difficult for them to find opportunities for advancement. And they suffered, in some cases, from a sense of futility and despair, born of years of entrapment in brutal urban ghettoes.

By the early 1990s, whole generations of nonwhites had grown to maturity living in destitute neighborhoods where welfare, drug dealing, and other crimes were virtually the only means of support for many people. Violence was increasingly a part of daily life. While rates of violent crime were declining nationally in the late 1980s and early 1990s, violence (much of it entirely random) was escalating in many inner-city communities—a result of the drug trade, gang wars, and the proliferation of guns.

The anger and despair such conditions were creating among inner-city residents became clear in the summer of 1992 in Los Angeles. The previous year, a bystander had videotaped several Los Angeles police officers beating an apparently helpless black man whom they had captured after an auto chase. Broadcast repeatedly around the country, the tape evoked outrage among whites and blacks alike. But an all-white jury in a suburban community just outside Los Angeles acquitted the officers when they were tried for assault. Black residents of South Central Los Angeles, one of the poorest communities in the city, erupted in anger—precipitating the largest racial disturbance of the twentieth century. There was widespread looting and arson. More than fifty people died.

In the 1960s, urban uprisings had helped produce a major (if ultimately inadequate) government effort to deal with the problems of the inner city. But in the fiscally starved 1990s, the Los Angeles riot produced no such response.

Modern 'Plagues: Drugs, AIDS, and Homelessness

The new immigrants of the 1980s and 1990s arrived in cities being ravaged not just by economic decline but by two new and deadly epidemics. One was a dramatic increase in drug use, which penetrated nearly every community in the nation. The enormous demand for drugs, and particularly for "crack" cocaine, spawned what was in effect a multibillion-dollar industry; and those reaping the enormous profits of the illegal trade fought strenuously and often savagely to protect their positions.

Political figures of both parties spoke heatedly about the need for a "war on drugs"; but in the absence of significant funding for such programs, government efforts appeared to be having little effect. Drug use declined significantly among middle-class people beginning in the late 1980s, but the epidemic showed no signs of abating in the poor urban neighborhoods where it was doing the most severe damage.

The drug epidemic was directly related to another scourge of the 1980s and 1990s: the epidemic spread of a new and lethal disease first documented in 1981 and soon named AIDS (acquired immune deficiency syndrome). AIDS is the product of the HIV virus, which is transmitted by the exchange of bodily fluids (blood or semen). The virus gradually destroys the body's immune system and makes its victims highly vulnerable to a number of diseases (particularly to various forms of cancer and pneumonia) to which they would otherwise have a natural resistance. Although those infected with the virus (i.e., HIV positive) can live for many years without developing AIDS, once they do become ill they are virtually certain to die. The first American victims of AIDS, (and in the early 1990s the group among whom cases remained the most numerous) were homosexual men. But by the late 1980s, as the gay community began to take preventive measures, the most rapid increase in the spread of the disease occurred among heterosexuals, many of them intravenous drug users, who spread the virus by sharing contaminated hypodermic needles. By the early 1990s,

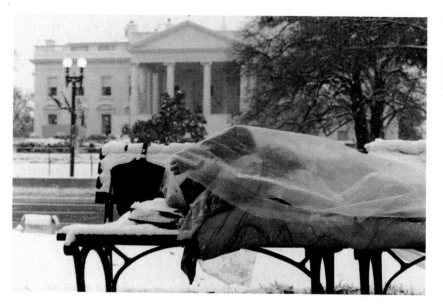

HOMELESS IN WASHINGTON
A homeless man sleeps through a snowstorm on a bench in Lafayette Park, directly across the street from the White House. *(UPI/Bettmann)*

U.S. government agencies were estimating that between 1 and 1.5 million Americans were infected with the HIV virus. (Worldwide, the figure was approximately 10 million). Over 200,000 Americans had actually contracted AIDS, and over 130,000 had died. Although by the 1990s researchers had discovered several drugs that could delay or limit the effects of AIDS, neither a cure nor a vaccine seemed imminent. Governments and private groups, in the meantime, began promoting AIDS awareness in increasingly visible and graphic ways—urging young people, in particular, to avoid "unsafe sex" through abstinence or the use of latex condoms.

The spread of AIDS had a chilling effect on the sexual revolution that had transformed behavior beginning in the 1960s. Fear of infection caused many people to avoid casual sexual relations; but the more puritanical sexual standards against which many Americans had rebelled in the 1960s did not return.

The increasing scarcity of housing for low-income people contributed to another urban crisis of the 1980s and 1990s: homelessness. There had always been homeless men and women in most major cities; but their numbers were clearly increasing at an alarming rate in the face of rising housing costs, severe cutbacks in federal support for public housing, reduced welfare assistance, deinstitutionalization of the mentally ill, the declining availability of unskilled jobs, and the increasing weakness of family structures. The phenomenon of tens of thousands of homeless people at large in the cities put pressure on municipal governments to provide shelter and assistance for the indigent; but in an age of fiscal stringency and greatly reduced federal aid, cities found it difficult to respond adequately to the dimensions of the crisis.

Battles Against Feminism and Abortion

Among the principal goals of the New Right as it became more powerful and assertive in the 1980s and 1990s was to challenge feminism and its achievements. Leaders of the New Right had campaigned successfully against the proposed Equal Rights Amendment to the Constitution. And they played a central role in the most divisive issue of the late 1980s and early 1990s: the controversy over abortion rights.

For those who favored allowing women to choose to terminate unwanted pregnancies, the Supreme Court's decision in *Roe* v. *Wade* (1973) had seemed to settle the question. By the 1980s, abortion was the most commonly performed surgical procedure in the country. But at the same time, opposition to abortion was creating a powerful grassroots movement. The right-

to-life movement, as it called itself, found its most fervent supporters among Catholics; and indeed, the Catholic Church itself lent its institutional authority to the battle against legalized abortion. Religious doctrine also motivated the anti-abortion stance of Mormons, fundamentalist Christians, and other groups. The opposition of some other anti-abortion activists had less to do with religion than with their commitment to traditional notions of family and gender relations. To them, abortion was a particularly offensive part of a much larger assault by feminists on the role of women as wives and mothers. It was also, many foes contended, a form of murder. Fetuses, they claimed, were human beings who had a "right to life" from the moment of conception.

Although the right-to-life movement was persistent in its demand for a reversal of *Roe* v. *Wade* or, barring that, a constitutional amendment banning abortion, it also attacked abortion in more limited ways, at its most vulnerable points. In the 1970s, Congress and many state legislatures began barring the use of public funds to pay for abortions, thus making them almost inaccessible for many poor women. The Reagan and Bush administrations imposed further restrictions on federal funding and even on the right of doctors in federally funded clinics to give patients any information on abortion. Extremists in the right-to-life movement began picketing, occupying, and at times bombing abortion clinics. One anti-abortion activist murdered a doctor in Florida who performed abortions; other physicians were subject to campaigns of terrorism and harassment—part of an effort to force them to abandon serving women who wanted abortions.

The changing composition of the Supreme Court in the 1980s to early 1990s (when five new conservative justices were named by Presidents Reagan and Bush) renewed the right-to-life movement's hopes for a reversal of *Roe* v. *Wade*. In *Webster* v. *Reproductive Health Services* (1989), the Court upheld a Missouri law that forbade any institution receiving state funds from performing abortions, whether or not those funds were used to finance the abortions. But the Court stopped short of overturning its 1973 decision.

Through much of the 1970s and 1980s, defenders of abortion had remained confident that *Roe* v. *Wade* protected their right to choose abortion and that the anti-abortion movement was unlikely to prevail. But the changing judicial climate of the late 1980s mobilized defenders of abortion as never before. They called themselves the "pro-choice" movement, because they were defending not so much abortion itself as every woman's right to choose whether and when to bear a child. It quickly became clear that the pro-choice movement was in many parts of the country at least as strong as, and in some areas much stronger than, the right-to-life movement. With the election of President Clinton in 1992, the immediate threat to *Roe* v. *Wade* seemed to fade. In his first two years in office, Clinton named two pro-choice justices to the Court—Ruth Bader Ginsburg and Stephen Breyer.

At times the pro-choice campaign overshadowed other efforts by feminists to protect and expand the rights of women. But such efforts continued. Women's organizations and many individual women worked strenuously in the 1980s and 1990s to improve access to child care for poor women, and to win the right to caregiver leaves for parents. They also worked to raise awareness of sexual harassment in the workplace, with considerable success. Colleges, universities, government agencies, even many corporations established strict new standards of behavior for their employees in dealing with members of the opposite sex and created grievance procedures for those who believed they had been harassed.

Both the achievements and the limits of their progress on this issue were evident in the sensational controversy in 1991 over Judge Clarence Thomas, President Bush's nominee for a seat on the Supreme Court. Late in the confirmation proceedings, accusations of sexual harassment from Anita Hill, a law professor and former employee of Thomas, became public. Hill's testimony before the Senate Judiciary Committee dramatically polarized both the Senate and the nation. Feminists and others tended to believe the accusations and hailed the accuser for drawing national attention to the issue of harassment; but many Americans (and most members of the virtually all-male Senate) apparently did not believe her—or at least concluded that the alleged activities should not disqualify Thomas from serving on the Court. Thomas was ultimately confirmed by a narrow margin.

The Changing Left and the New Environmentalism

The New Left of the 1960s and early 1970s did not disappear after the end of the war in Vietnam, but it faded rapidly. Many of the students who had fought in its battles grew up, left school, and entered conventional careers. Some radical leaders, disillusioned by the unresponsiveness of American society to their demands, resignedly gave up the struggle and chose instead to work "within the system." Marxist critiques continued to flourish in academic circles, but to much of the public they came to appear dated and irrelevant—particularly as, beginning in 1989, Marxist governments collapsed in disrepute.

PRINCE WILLIAM SOUND, ALASKA
The giant oil tanker *Exxon Valdez* hit a reef in Prince William Sound in April 1989, and the result was the largest oil spill in American history. In this photograph, a tugboat pulls the tanker across the sound after it finally floated off the reef thirteen days after running aground. *(UPI/Bettmann)*

Yet a left of sorts did survive, giving evidence in the process of how greatly the nation's political climate had changed. Where 1960s activists had rallied to protest racism, poverty, and war, their counterparts in the 1980s and 1990s more often fought to stop the proliferation of nuclear weapons and power plants, to save the wilderness, to protect endangered species, to limit reckless economic development, and to otherwise protect the environment.

Public concerns about the environment had arisen intermittently since the beginning of the industrial era and had been growing in intensity since 1962, when the publication of Rachel Carson's *Silent Spring* aroused widespread public concern about the effect of insecticides on the natural world. (See "The American Environment," pp. 919–922.) Several highly visible environmental catastrophes in the 1960s and 1970s greatly increased that concern. Among them were a major oil spill off Santa Barbara, California, in 1969; the discovery of large deposits of improperly disposed toxic wastes in a residential community in upstate New York in 1978; and a frightening accident at the nuclear power plant on Three Mile Island, Pennsylvania in 1979. These and other revelations of the extent to which human progress threatened the natural world helped produce a major popular movement.

In the spring of 1970, a nationwide "Earth Day" signaled the beginning of the environmental movement. It differed markedly from the "conservation" movements of earlier years. Modern environmentalists shared the concerns of such earlier figures as John Muir and Gifford Pinchot about preserving some areas of the wilderness and carefully managing the exploitation of resources. But the new activists went much further, basing their positions on the developing field of ecology, the study of the interconnections among all components of an environment. Toxic wastes, air and water pollution, the destruction of forests, the extinction of species—these were not separate, isolated problems. All elements of the earth's environment were intimately and delicately linked, ecologists claimed. Damaging any one of those elements risked damaging all the others. Only by adopting a new social ethic, in which economic growth became less important than ecological health, or a new economics, in which environmental costs were factored into economic analyses, could the human race hope to survive in a healthy world.

In the twenty years after the first Earth Day, environmental issues gained increasing attention and support. Although the federal government generally displayed limited interest in the subject, environmentalists won a series of significant battles, mostly at the local level. They blocked the construction of roads, airports, and other projects (including American development of the supersonic transport airplane, or SST) that they claimed would be ecologically dangerous. By the end of the decade, the sense of urgency had grown, as scientists began warning that the release of certain industrial pollutants (most notably chlorofluorocarbons) into the atmosphere was depleting the ozone layer of the earth's atmosphere, which protects the globe from the sun's most dangerous rays. They warned, too, of the related danger of global warming, a rise in the earth's temperature as a result of emissions from the burning of fossil fuels (coal and oil).

The concern for the environment, the opposition to nuclear power, the resistance to economic development—all were reflections of a more fundamental characteristic of the post-Vietnam left. In a sharp break from the nation's long commitment to growth and progress, many dissidents argued that only by limiting growth and curbing traditional forms of progress could society hope to survive. Some of these critics of the "idea of progress" expressed a gloomy resignation, urging a lowering of social expectations and predicting an inevitable deterioration in the quality of life. Other advocates of restraint believed that change did not require decline: human beings could live more comfortably and more happily if they learned to respect the limits imposed on them by their environment. But in either case, such arguments evoked strong opposition from conservatives and others, who ridiculed the no-growth ideology as an expression of defeat-

ism and despair. Ronald Reagan, in particular, made an attack on the idea of "limits" central to his political success.

Turning Inward

For many Americans, the answer to the dilemmas of living in uncertain times lay not in religion or politics but in the cultivation of the self. No aspect of the culture of the 1980s and early 1990s aroused more comment than this tendency of individuals to "turn inward," that is, to replace social concerns with personal ones. Among affluent Americans, at least, there emerged

ELECTRONIC LEARNING
These students at the Clara Barton School in Minneapolis, photographed in 1991, were among millions of young people throughout the nation whose educational experience was being transformed by the proliferation of computers and other electronic devices. Among other things, the computer revolution increased the gulf separating affluent schools from poor ones; many schools in underfunded districts lacked the money to purchase the new equipment. *(Ed Bock/Stock Market)*

SIGNIFICANT EVENTS

1979 Nuclear accident at Three Mile Island

1981 Existence of AIDS reported in United States

Solidarity movement leads revolt against communist regime in Poland

1985 Mikhail Gorbachev chosen as leader of the Soviet Union

Reagan and Gorbachev meet in Geneva

Congress passes Gramm-Rudman bill to limit deficits

Homeless crisis worsens

Crack cocaine appears in American cities

1986 U.S. planes bomb targets in Libya

Reagan and Gorbachev meet in Reykjavik, Iceland

Insider trading scandals on Wall Street

Democrats regain control of U.S. Senate

Iran-contra scandal revealed

Glasnost and perestroika expand in Soviet Union

1987 Gorbachev visits Reagan in Washington

Congress investigates Iran-contra scandal

Stock market falls by record 508 points

Televangelist scandals begin

Congress passes Immigration Reform and Control Act

1988 INF Treaty signed

Gorbachev announces Soviet troop reductions in Europe

George Bush elected president

1989 Berlin Wall dismantled, German reunification begins

Communist regimes collapse throughout Eastern Europe

Chinese government suppresses student uprising with assault on demonstrators in Tiananmen Square

American troops invade Panama

Supreme Court's *Webster* decision limits, but does not overturn, *Roe* v. *Wade*

1990 South Africa begins dismantling *apartheid* system

Bush agrees to tax increase

Recession begins

Iraq invades Kuwait; United Nations imposes sanctions

1991 Failed coup precipitates collapse of Soviet regime and disintegration of Soviet Union

Civil rights bill reinforces laws against job discrimination

United States drives Iraq out of Kuwait in Gulf War

Controversy surrounds confirmation of Clarence Thomas to Supreme Court

1992 Bill Clinton elected president

Ross Perot polls 19 percent of popular vote in independent campaign for presidency

Major race riot in Los Angeles

1993 Congress approves tax increase as part of deficit reduction

Congress ratifies North American Free Trade Agreement

Clinton proposes national health care system

1994 U.S. participates in air strikes in Bosnia

---

a pervasive concern with personal "lifestyles." In the booming 1980s, which greatly increased the affluence of the upper middle class, such concerns became a central theme of popular culture. The "yuppie"—the young, urban professional with a large disposable income, intent on ever greater material comforts—became a common image of the Reagan years (often as a contrast to the ever more desperate poverty that was becoming visible in the same urban communities the "yuppies" were "gentrifying").

The American Future

The American people had suffered many trials and disappointments since the heady days at the end of World War II, when an "American Century" seemed about to dawn; and since the mid-1950s, when the country appeared poised for a prolonged era of domestic tranquility, economic abundance, and international preeminence. By the mid-1990s, America, like many other nations, was faced with the problems of a changing industrial economy, an increasingly diverse and contentious population, growing dangers to the environment that threatened the health of the entire world, and a declining popular faith in the ability of the nation's leaders and institutions to deal with these problems.

The dramatically different world order that was emerging from the upheavals of the late twentieth century was filled with dangers, both at home and abroad. But the United States, despite its many problems, remained what it had been for over two centuries: one of the stablest, wealthiest, and most resilient societies in modern history. At the dawn of a new millennium and a new era, the United States—whose example had done much to fuel the forces of change—was challenged with preserving and extending its own democracy in the face of major new perils and great new opportunities.

SUGGESTED READINGS

The Post Cold-War World. Bernard Gwertzman and Michael T. Kaufman, eds., *The Collapse of Communism* (1990). Paul Kennedy, *The Rise and Fall of the Great Powers* (1987). Robert Kuttner, *The End of Laissez Faire: National Purpose and the Global Economy After the Cold War* (1991). Henry R. Nau, *The Myth of America's Decline: Leading the World Economy in the 1990s* (1990). Joseph Nye, *Bound to Lead: The Changing Nature of American Power* (1990). H. Norman Schwarzkopf, *It Doesn't Take a Hero* (1992).

Politics After Reagan. E. J. Dionne, *Why Americans Hate Politics* (1991). Thomas Ferguson and Joel Rogers, *Right Turn* (1986). William Greider, *Who Will Tell the People?* (1992). Robert S. McElvaine, *The End of the Conservative Era: Liberalism After Reagan* (1987). Kevin Phillips, *The Politics of Rich and Poor: Wealth and the American Electorate in the Reagan Aftermath* (1990). Adolph L. Reed, Jr., *The Jesse Jackson Phenomenon (1986).* Bob Woodard, *The Agenda* (1994)

Post-Liberal Culture. Peter N. Carroll, *It Seemed Like Nothing Happened* (1982). Peter Clecak, *America's Quest for the Ideal Self* (1983). Jim Hougan, *Decadence: Radical Nostalgia, Narcissism, and Decline in the Seventies* (1975). Christopher Lasch, *The Culture of Narcissism* (1978). Edwin Schur, *The Awareness Trap* (1976). Daniel Yankelovich, *New Rules: Search for Self-Fulfillment in a World Turned Upside Down* (1981).

Economy and Society. Carl Abbott, *The New Urban America: Growth and Politics in the Sunbelt Cities* (1981). Michael A. Bernstein and David E. Adler, *Understanding American Economic Decline* (1994). Barry Bluestone and Bennett Harrison, *The Deindustrializing of America* (1982). Connie Bruck, *The Predator's Ball: The Junk Bond Raiders and the Man Who Staked Them* (1988). Bryan Burroughs and John Helyar, *Barbarians at the Gate: The Fall of RJR Nabisco* (1990). Elizabeth Fee and Daniel M. Fox, eds., *AIDS: The Burdens of History* (1988); *AIDS: The Making of a Chronic Disease* (1992). Gerald N. Grob, *From Asylum to Community: Mental Health Policy in Modern Amer-*ica (1991). Robert Heilbroner and Lester Thurow, *Five Economic Challenges* (1983). John Langone, *AIDS: the Facts* (1988). Frank Levy, *Dollars and Dreams: The Changing American Income Distribution* (1987). Michael Lewis, *Liar's Poker* (1989). Eric Marcus, *Making History: The Struggle for Gay and Lesbian Equal Rights, 1945–1990* (1992). Robert Reich, *The Work of Nations: Preparing Ourselves for Twenty-first-Century Capitalism* (1991). Kirkpatrick Sale, *Power Shift* (1975). Jonathan Schell, *The Fate of the Earth* (1982). Bruce J. Schulman, *From Cotton Belt to Sunbelt: Federal Policy, Economic Development, and the Transformation of the South, 1938–1980* (1991). Randy Shilts, *And the Band Played On: Politics, People, and the AIDS Epidemic* (1987). James B. Stewart, *Den of Thieves* (1991). Studs Terkel, *The Great Divide* (1988). John Woodridge, *The Evangelicals* (1975). Daniel Yergin, *The Prize* (1991).

Gender and Family. Mary Francis Berry, *Why ERA Failed* (1986). Susan M. Bianchi, *American Women in Transition* (1987). Nancy Caraway, *Segregated Sisterhood: Racism and the Politics of American Feminism* (1991). Andrea Dworkin, *Right-Wing Women* (1983). Barbara Ehrenreich, *The Hearts of Men: American Dreams and the Flight from Commitment* (1983). Jonathan Kozol, *Rachel and Her Children: Homeless Families in America* (1988). Kristin Luker, *Abortion and the Politics of Motherhood* (1984). Jane Mansbridge, *Why We Lost the ERA* (1986). Donald G. Mathews and Jane Sherron De Hart, *Sex, Gender, and the Politics of E.R.A.: A State and the Nation* (1990). Rosalind Pechesky, *Abortion and Woman's Choice* (1984). Harrell R. Rodgers, Jr., *Poor Women, Poor Families* (1986). Hilda Scott, *Working Your Way to the Bottom: The Feminization of Poverty* (1985). Ruth Sidel, *Women and Children Last* (1986). Suzanne Staggenborg, *The Pro-Choice Movement: Organization and Activism in the Abortion Conflict* (1991). Winifred D. Wandersee, *On the Move: American Women in the 1970s* (1988).

Nonwhites in the 1970s and 1980s. Ken Auletta, *The Underclass* (1981). Frank D. Bean and Marta Tienda, *The Hispanic Population of the United States* (1987). Derrick Bell, *And We Are*

Not Saved: The Elusive Quest for Racial Justice (1987). James D. Cockcroft, *Outlaws in the Promised Land: Mexican Immigrant Workers and America's Future* (1986). John Crewden, *The Tarnished Door: The New Immigrants and the Transformation of America* (1983). Vine Deloria, Jr., *American Indian Policy in the Twentieth Century* (1985). Leslie W. Dunbar, ed., *Minority Report* (1984). Marian Wright Edelman, *Families in Peril* (1987). Douglas Glasgow, *The Black Underclass* (1980). Andrew Hacker, *Two Nations: Black and White, Separate, Hostile, Unequal* (1992). Michael Katz, *The Undeserving Poor: From the War on Poverty to the War on Welfare* (1989). Nicholas Lemann, *The Promised Land: The Great Black Migration and How It Changed America* (1989). David M. Reimers, *Still the Golden Door* (1985). Carol B. Stack, *All Our Kin: Strategies for Survival in a Black Community* (1975). Stan Steiner, *The New Indians* (1968). William Julius Wilson, *The Truly Disadvantaged* (1987).

THE AMERICAN ENVIRONMENT

SILENT SPRING

ONE SUMMER DAY IN 1957, a small plane flew over the nature sanctuary behind Olga Huckins's house in Duxbury, Massachusetts. It sprayed the land below with an oily mist and then vanished. The next day, Huckins found seven dead songbirds, their beaks gaping in apparent agony. She was so furious that she wrote an angry letter to a local paper; as an afterthought, she sent a copy to her friend Rachel Carson. It was one of those small events that alters the course of history.

Carson was a biologist and a gifted writer. Educated at Johns Hopkins University at a time when few women became scientists, she had gone to work for the government as an aquatic biologist. Although she was extremely shy, her skills as a writer quickly led her colleagues to rely on her to communicate their work to a wider public. Even-

PESTICIDE SPRAYING
When pesticides first became available to farmers, they proved so effective against agricultural pests that soon they were being sprayed on most crops. Although scientists and consumers have raised many questions about the safety of such chemicals, they continue to play an important role in the farm economy. Most foods grown in the United States are still treated with pesticides to some degree, although the growing popularity of organic foods (cultivated without artificial fertilizers or pesticides) testifies to the durability of the concerns Carson raised. *(Bettmann)*

THE AMERICAN ENVIRONMENT

tually, in 1949, she became chief editor for the U.S. Fish and Wildlife Service. In the meantime, she began to write popular essays about her special love, the ocean. A first book proved only marginally successful, but in 1951 she published *The Sea Around Us*. It instantly became an international best seller, bringing Carson a fame she never imagined and enough income to retire. By 1957, she was one of the most popular nature writers of her generation. Huckins's letter would turn her life onto an entirely new path.

The mist that the plane had sprayed behind Huckins's house was a mixture of ordinary fuel oil and a chemical called dicholoro-diphenyl-trichloroethane: DDT. In 1939, a Swiss chemist named Paul Muller had discovered that although DDT seemed harmless to human beings and other mammals, it was extremely toxic to insects. American scientists learned of Muller's discovery in 1942, just as the army was grappling with the special problems of tropical warfare. Unless something could be done to exterminate the mosquitoes that carried malaria and the lice that carried typhus, thousands of soldiers seemed likely to die from disease.

Under these circumstances, DDT seemed a godsend. It was first used on a large scale in Italy in 1943–1944 during a typhus outbreak, which it quickly helped end. Soon it was being sprayed in mosquito-infested areas of Pacific islands where American troops were fighting the Japanese. No soldiers suffered any apparent ill effects from the sprayings, and the incidence of malaria dropped precipitously. DDT quickly gained a reputation as a miraculous tool for controlling insects, and it undoubtedly saved thousands of lives. For its discovery, Paul Muller was awarded the Nobel Prize in medicine in 1948.

With so many benefits and no obvious drawbacks, the new chemical was first released for public use in 1945. Scientists in the Food and Drug Administration noted only one disturbing fact about DDT: it tended to accumulate in the fatty tissues of large animals, including humans, and was passed on in the milk of cows and humans alike. In large doses, it damaged the central nervous system. But data on the effects of chronic exposure were lacking, and the FDA could not legally restrict its use while waiting for further research. DDT thus entered the marketplace billed as an extraordinarily safe and effective poison, the ultimate weapon against destructive insects.

For the next decade, the new chemical continued to live up to its early billing. It helped farmers eliminate chronic pests and was widely used to control mosquitoes. One of its most impressive successes was against the gypsy moth, a voracious insect that had been stripping the leaves from northeastern forests ever since being accidentally introduced to the Boston area in 1868. All previous efforts to control the destructive moth had come to naught, but it virtually vanished from forests that were sprayed with DDT.

By the time Rachel Carson received Olga Huckins's letter, however, signs of trouble were beginning to appear in areas that had been sprayed with the chemical. For one, its effectiveness against certain insects declined as they developed resistance to its effects, so that higher doses were needed to produce the same lethal effect. A resistant housefly had appeared as early as 1948, and a resistant mosquito by 1949.

More worrisome were the chemical's effects on larger animals. Some were killed outright, like the birds in Olga Huckins's back yard. But DDT also seemed to inhibit some animals' ability to reproduce. It would later be learned that the eggshells of certain birds

THE AMERICAN ENVIRONMENT

RACHEL CARSON
Rachel Carson, who began her career as a marine biologist, became the world's best-selling author about the ocean environment in the 1950s. Carson's abiding love for the creatures of shore and surf led to her concern about the harm pesticides might do them.   *(Bettmann)*

were so thinned by the chemical that young birds were crushed in their nests even before they hatched. The extraordinary persistence of DDT in the environment, and its tendency to accumulate in fatty tissues, meant that animals could concentrate surprising quantities in their flesh. This was especially true of those at the top of food chains— eagles, trout, and, not least, people. What this meant remained unclear, but many bird lovers were noting a general reduction in bird populations, and people who fished were catching fewer fish. As the woods became emptier and more silent, DDT seemed the mostly likely culprit.

THE AMERICAN ENVIRONMENT

Rachel Carson had worried about pesticides for years, but it was not until reading Olga Huckins's letter that she decided to do something about them. Meticulously gathering the best available data, she wrote a book that was published in 1962, *Silent Spring*. In it, she warned that the indiscriminate use of pesticides was wreaking havoc with the web of life, destroying wildlife populations, and even threatening human health. She wrote of a landscape in which sickness and death threatened animals and people alike, and "a strange stillness" had replaced the familiar songs of birds. Her eloquence was made all the more urgent by her private knowledge as she finished the book that she herself was dying of cancer.

Silent Spring became one of the most controversial books of the 1960s. It sold nearly half a million copies within six months of its publication and was discussed everywhere. The chemical industry responded with cries of outrage. After first trying to suppress the book's publication altogether and threatening lawsuits against its author and publisher, pesticide manufacturers began a long campaign to discredit Carson and repair the damage her book had done. They attacked her, often unfairly, for being unscientific, for distorting facts, and for being hostile to technological progress. In the end, though, Carson won at least a partial victory: the U.S. finally banned the sale of DDT in 1972. More important, her book raised public awareness about the threats human activities pose to the natural environment. Although she died in 1964, no single person would be more important in shaping environmental policies over the next thirty years.

APPENDICES

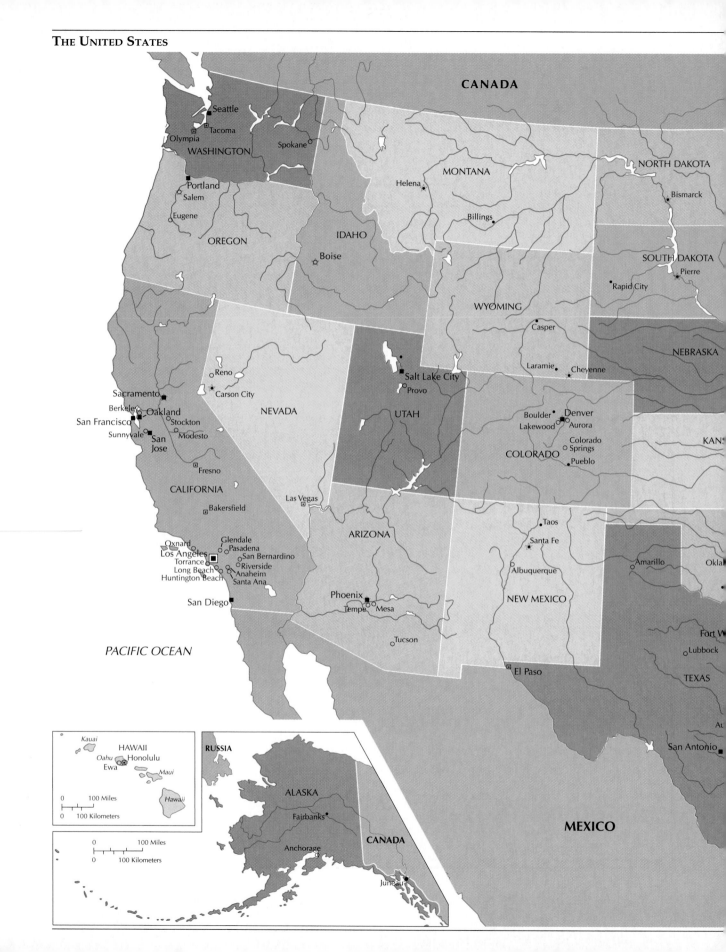

CANADA

Seattle
Tacoma
Olympia
WASHINGTON
Spokane

Portland
Salem
Eugene

OREGON

IDAHO

Boise

MONTANA

Helena

Billings

NORTH DAKOTA

Bismarck

SOUTH DAKOTA

Pierre

Rapid City

WYOMING

Casper

Laramie
Cheyenne

NEBRASKA

Reno
Carson City

Sacramento
Berkeley
San Francisco
Sunnyvale
San Jose

NEVADA

Oakland
Stockton
Modesto

Fresno

CALIFORNIA

Bakersfield

Las Vegas

Salt Lake City
Provo

UTAH

Boulder
Lakewood

Denver
Aurora

Colorado
Springs
Pueblo

COLORADO

KAN

ARIZONA

Taos

Santa Fe

Albuquerque

Amarillo

Okla

Oxnard
Glendale
Pasadena
Los Angeles
Torrance
San Bernardino
Long Beach
Riverside
Anaheim
Huntington Beach
Santa Ana

San Diego

Phoenix
Tempe
Mesa

Tucson

NEW MEXICO

El Paso

Fort W

Lubbock

TEXAS

PACIFIC OCEAN

A

San Antonio

Kauai

HAWAII

Oahu
Ewa

Honolulu

Maui

Hawaii

0   100 Miles
0   100 Kilometers

RUSSIA

ALASKA

Fairbanks

Anchorage

CANADA

Juneau

MEXICO

0   100 Miles
0   100 Kilometers

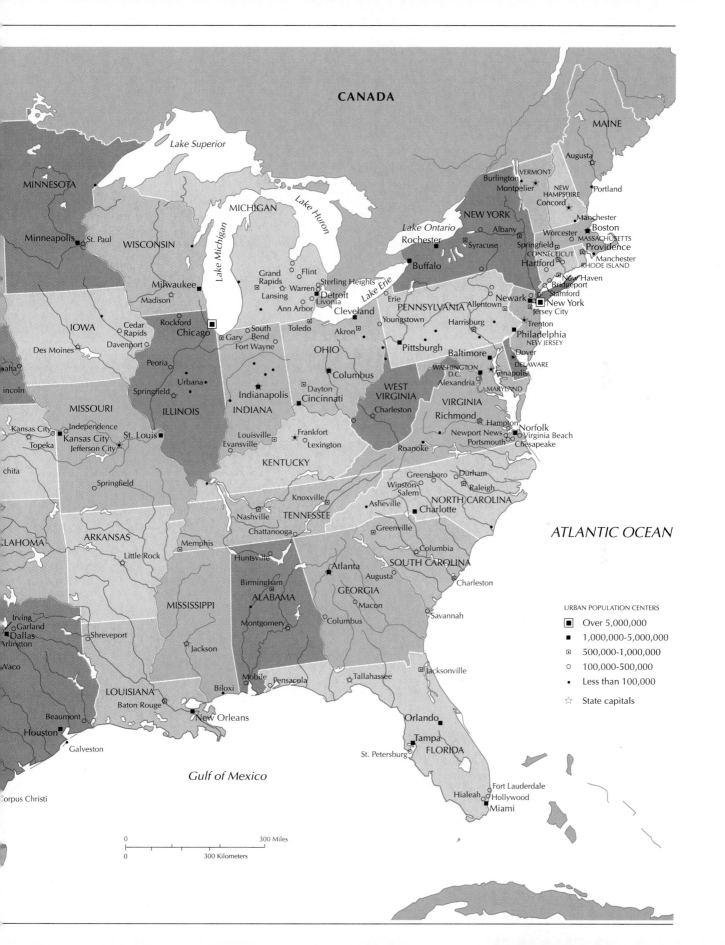

CANADA

Lake Superior

MINNESOTA

Minneapolis • St. Paul

MICHIGAN

Lake Huron

WISCONSIN

Madison

Milwaukee

IOWA
Cedar
Rapids
Davenport

Des Moines

Rockford
Chicago

Peoria
Urbana
Springfield

ILLINOIS

INDIANA

Gary
South
Bend
Fort Wayne

Grand
Rapids • Flint
Warren • Sterling Heights
Lansing
Detroit
Ann Arbor Livonia
Cleveland

Toledo
Akron

OHIO

Columbus

Dayton
Cincinnati

Indianapolis

Lake Ontario
Rochester
Albany
Buffalo Syracuse

Lake Erie
Erie

Youngstown

PENNSYLVANIA

Harrisburg
Pittsburgh
Allentown

NEW YORK

Burlington VERMONT
Montpelier NEW
HAMPSHIRE
Concord

Worcester Boston
MASSACHUSETTS
Springfield Providence
CONNECTICUT
Hartford Manchester
RHODE ISLAND

New Haven
Bridgeport
Stamford
Newark
New York
Jersey City

Trenton
Philadelphia
NEW JERSEY
Dover
DELAWARE

Baltimore

WASHINGTON
D.C.
Alexandria
MARYLAND

Annapolis

MAINE

Augusta

Portland

Manchester

WEST
VIRGINIA

Charleston

VIRGINIA

Richmond

Hampton
Newport News Norfolk
Portsmouth Virginia Beach
Roanoke Chesapeake

MISSOURI

Kansas City
Independence
Kansas City
Topeka
Jefferson City
St. Louis

aha
incoln

Springfield

KENTUCKY

Louisville
Evansville
Frankfort
Lexington

Omaha
Lincoln

ARKANSAS

Little Rock

Springfield

Memphis

Nashville
TENNESSEE

Knoxville
Asheville
Chattanooga
Greenville

Greensboro Durham
Winston- Raleigh
Salem
NORTH CAROLINA
Charlotte

Columbia

SOUTH CAROLINA

OKLAHOMA

MISSISSIPPI

Jackson

ALABAMA

Birmingham

Montgomery

Huntsville

GEORGIA

Atlanta
Augusta

Macon

Columbus

Charleston

Savannah

ATLANTIC OCEAN

Irving
Garland
Dallas
Arlington

Waco

Shreveport

LOUISIANA
Baton Rouge

Beaumont

Houston

Galveston

Corpus Christi

Mobile Pensacola
Biloxi

New Orleans

Tallahassee

Jacksonville

FLORIDA

Orlando

Tampa
St. Petersburg

Fort Lauderdale
Hialeah Hollywood
Miami

Gulf of Mexico

URBAN POPULATION CENTERS

■ Over 5,000,000
■ 1,000,000–5,000,000
⊡ 500,000–1,000,000
○ 100,000–500,000
• Less than 100,000
☆ State capitals

0   300 Miles

0   300 Kilometers

TOPOGRAPHICAL MAP OF THE UNITED STATES

Puget Sound

Ranges

Columbia R.

Columbia R.

Snake R.

Cascade Range

Coast

Willamette R.

Columbia Plateau

Owyhee R.

Snake R.

Kootenai R.

Marias R.

Milk R.

Missouri R.

ROCKY

Yellowstone R.

Tongue R.

Bighorn R.

Powder R.

Belle Fourche R.

Black Hills

Cheyenne R.

G R E A T

Assiniboine R.

Red River of the North

Little Missouri R.

James R.

Missouri R.

Humboldt R.

GREAT BASIN

Great Salt Lake

M O U N T A I N S

White R.

Yampa R.

N. Platte R.

Laramie R.

Lodgepole Cr.

Niobrara R.

Loup R.

N. Platte R.

Platte R.

Republican R.

Sacramento R.

Sierra Nevada

Central Valley

San Joaquin R.

Death Valley

GREAT BASIN

Virgin R.

Sevier R.

Green R.

Colorado R.

Gunnison R.

Rio Grande

S. Platte R.

P L A I

Smoky Hill R.

Kansas R.

Arkansas R.

Coast Ranges

Mohave Desert

Colorado R.

Colorado Plateau

ROCKY MOUNTAINS

Rio Grande

Pecos R.

Cimarron R.

Canadian R.

N. Canadian R.

N S

Red R.

Trinity R.

Gila R.

Verde R.

PACIFIC OCEAN

Rio Grande

Pecos R.

Nueces R.

Rio Grande

Colorado R.

Brazos R.

G U

125°

120°

115°

110°

105°

100°

ARCTIC OCEAN

Brooks Range

70°

PACIFIC OCEAN

20°

Arctic Circle

Yukon R.

Alaska Range ▲ Mt. McKinley

60°

160°

180°

170°

BERING SEA

PACIFIC OCEAN

170°

160°

150°

140°

50°

65°

45°

Lake Superior

St. Lawrence R.

Kennebeck R.

Mississippi R.

St. Croix R.

Minnesota R.

Lake Huron

Lake Michigan

Adirondack Mts.

Mohawk R.

Hudson R.

Connecticut R.

40°

Des Moines R.

Iowa R.

Cedar R.

Rock R.

Fox R.

Lake Ontario

Lake Erie

Allegheny R.

APPALACHIAN MOUNTAINS

Delaware R.

Susquehanna R.

COASTAL PLAIN

Illinois R.

Kankakee R.

Wabash R.

Scioto R.

Ohio R.

Potomac R.

CENTRAL PLAINS

Missouri R.

Osage R.

Mississippi R.

Ohio R.

Mts. Kanawha R.

Shenandoah Valley

James R.

Chesapeake Bay

35°

70°

Ozark Plateau

White R.

S. Francis R.

Cumberland R.

Allegheny

APPALACHIAN MOUNTAINS

Blue Ridge Mountains

Roanoke R.

ATLANTIC COASTAL

Arkansas R.

Tennessee R.

Saluda R.

Ouachita R.

Yazoo R.

Tombigbee R.

Savannah R.

Red R.

Pearl R.

Alabama R.

Chattahoochee R.

Altamaha R.

30°

Sabine R.

Mississippi R.

ATLANTIC OCEAN

C O A S T A L   P L A I N

Galveston Bay

Gulf of Mexico

25°

95°

90°

85°

80°

75°

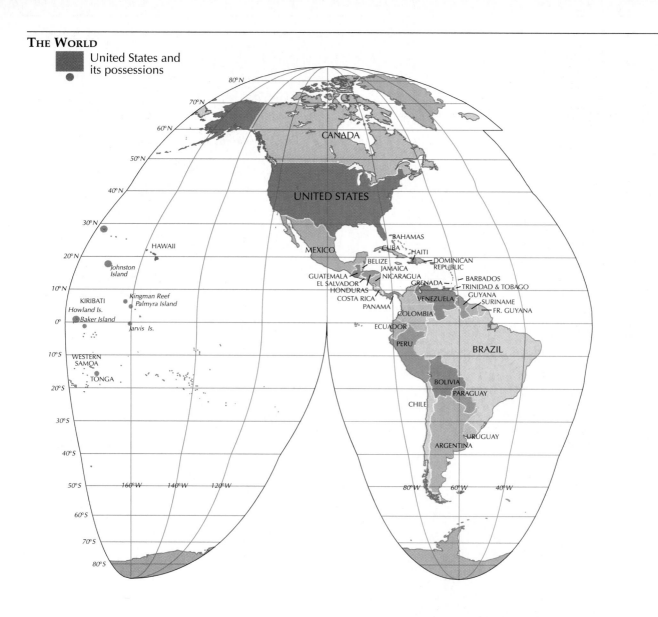

United States and
its possessions

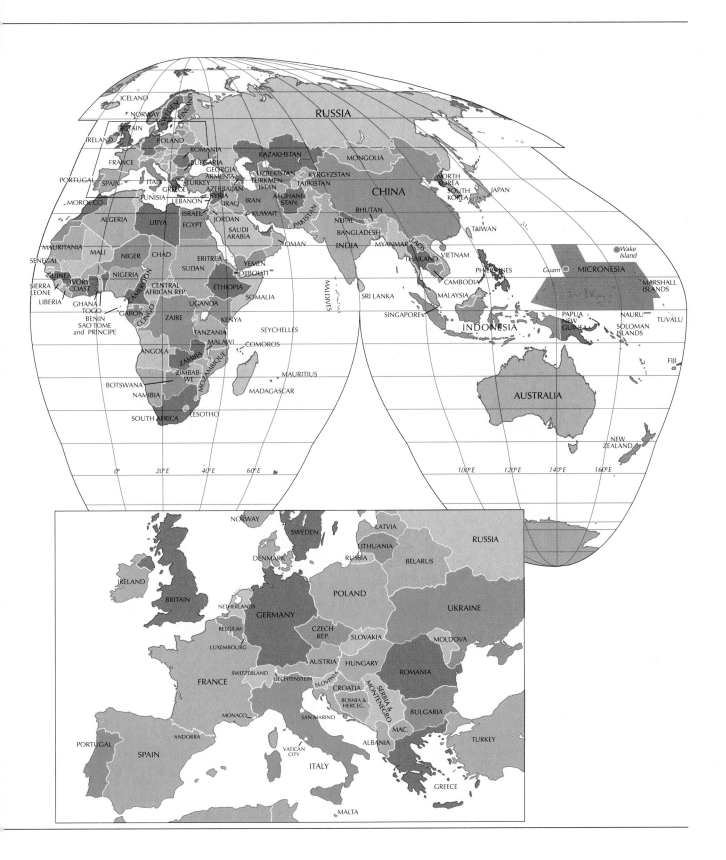

ICELAND
NORWAY
SWEDEN
FINLAND
BRITAIN
IRELAND
POLAND
FRANCE
ROMANIA
BULGARIA
GEORGIA
ARMENIA
PORTUGAL
SPAIN
ITALY
GREECE
TURKEY
AZERBAIJAN
TUNISIA
LEBANON
SYRIA
MOROCCO
ALGERIA
LIBYA
ISRAEL
EGYPT
JORDAN
IRAQ
IRAN
KUWAIT
SAUDI
ARABIA
MAURITANIA
MALI
NIGER
CHAD
ERITREA
YEMEN
SENEGAL
SUDAN
DJIBOUTI
GUINEA
NIGERIA
SIERRA
LEONE
IVORY
COAST
CAMEROON
CENTRAL
AFRICAN REP.
ETHIOPIA
SOMALIA
LIBERIA
GHANA
UGANDA
TOGO
BENIN
SAO TOME
and PRINCIPE
GABON
CONGO
ZAIRE
KENYA
TANZANIA
SEYCHELLES
ANGOLA
MALAWI
COMOROS
ZAMBIA
MOZAMBIQUE
ZIMBAB-
WE
MAURITIUS
BOTSWANA
MADAGASCAR
NAMIBIA
SOUTH AFRICA
LESOTHO

RUSSIA
KAZAKHSTAN
MONGOLIA
UZBEKISTAN
KYRGYZSTAN
TURKMEN-
ISTAN
TAJIKISTAN
CHINA
NORTH
KOREA
SOUTH
KOREA
JAPAN
AFGHANI-
STAN
PAKISTAN
BHUTAN
TAIWAN
NEPAL
BANGLADESH
OMAN
INDIA
MYANMAR
LAOS
VIETNAM
MALDIVES
THAILAND
PHILIPPINES
Guam
MICRONESIA
Wake
Island
SRI LANKA
CAMBODIA
MARSHALL
ISLANDS
MALAYSIA
SINGAPORE
INDONESIA
PAPUA
NEW
GUINEA
NAURU
TUVALU
SOLOMAN
ISLANDS
FIJI
AUSTRALIA
NEW
ZEALAND

0° 20°E 40°E 60°E 100°E 120°E 140°E 160°E

NORWAY
SWEDEN
LATVIA
RUSSIA
LITHUANIA
DENMARK
RUSSIA
BELARUS
IRELAND
BRITAIN
NETHERLANDS
POLAND
UKRAINE
BELGIUM
GERMANY
LUXEMBOURG
CZECH
REP.
SLOVAKIA
MOLDOVA
AUSTRIA
HUNGARY
ROMANIA
FRANCE
SWITZERLAND
LIECHTENSTEIN
SLOVENIA
CROATIA
SERBIA &
MONTENEGRO
BULGARIA
MONACO
BOSNIA &
HERCEG.
SAN MARINO
MAC.
PORTUGAL
ANDORRA
ALBANIA
TURKEY
SPAIN
VATICAN
CITY
ITALY
GREECE
MALTA

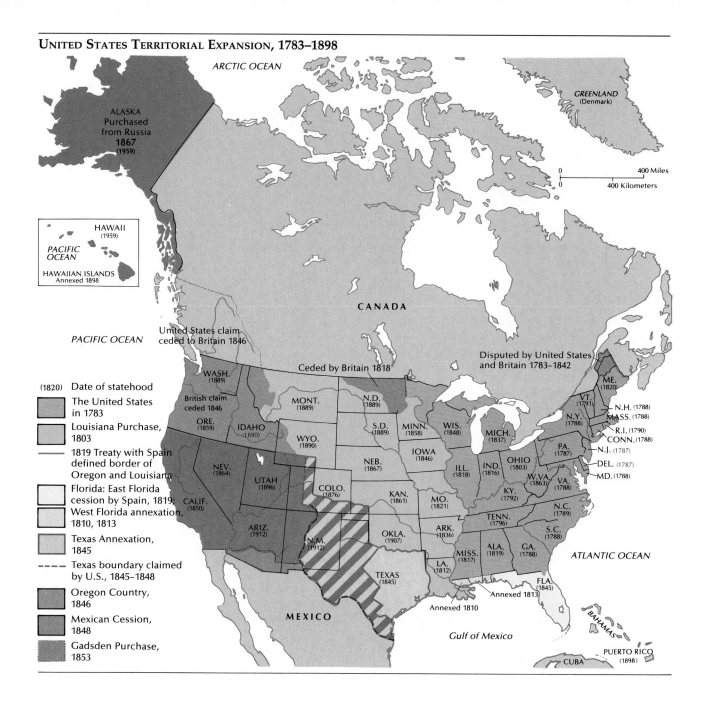

ARCTIC OCEAN

GREENLAND
(Denmark)

ALASKA
Purchased
from Russia
1867
(1959)

400 Miles

400 Kilometers

HAWAII
(1959)

PACIFIC
OCEAN

HAWAIIAN ISLANDS
Annexed 1898

CANADA

PACIFIC OCEAN

United States claim
ceded to Britain 1846

Ceded by Britain 1818

Disputed by United States
and Britain 1783–1842

(1820)   Date of statehood

The United States
in 1783

Louisiana Purchase,
1803

1819 Treaty with Spain
defined border of
Oregon and Louisiana

Florida: East Florida
cession by Spain, 1819;
West Florida annexation,
1810, 1813

Texas Annexation,
1845

Texas boundary claimed
by U.S., 1845–1848

Oregon Country,
1846

Mexican Cession,
1848

Gadsden Purchase,
1853

WASH.
(1889)

British claim
ceded 1846

ORE.
(1859)

IDAHO
(1890)

MONT.
(1889)

N.D.
(1889)

WYO.
(1890)

S.D.
(1889)

MINN.
(1858)

WIS.
(1848)

MICH.
(1837)

ME.
(1820)

VT.
(1791)

N.H. (1788)

N.Y.
(1788)

MASS. (1788)

R.I. (1790)

CONN. (1788)

PA.
(1787)

N.J. (1787)

DEL. (1787)

MD. (1788)

NEV.
(1864)

UTAH
(1896)

COLO.
(1876)

NEB.
(1867)

IOWA
(1846)

ILL.
(1818)

IND.
(1816)

OHIO
(1803)

W.VA.
(1863)

VA.
(1788)

CALIF.
(1850)

ARIZ.
(1912)

N.M.
(1912)

KAN.
(1861)

MO.
(1821)

KY.
(1792)

TENN.
(1796)

N.C.
(1789)

S.C.
(1788)

OKLA.
(1907)

ARK.
(1836)

MISS.
(1817)

ALA.
(1819)

GA.
(1788)

ATLANTIC OCEAN

LA.
(1812)

TEXAS
(1845)

MEXICO

Annexed 1810

Annexed 1813

FLA.
(1845)

BAHAMAS

Gulf of Mexico

PUERTO RICO
(1898)

CUBA

THE DECLARATION OF INDEPENDENCE

In Congress, July 4, 1776,

THE UNANIMOUS DECLARATION OF THE THIRTEEN UNITED STATES OF AMERICA

When, in the course of human events, it becomes necessary for one people to dissolve the political bands which have connected them with another, and to assume, among the powers of the earth, the separate and equal station to which the laws of nature and of nature's God entitle them, a decent respect to the opinions of mankind requires that they should declare the causes which impel them to the separation.

We hold these truths to be self-evident, that all men are created equal; that they are endowed by their Creator with certain unalienable rights; that among these, are life, liberty, and the pursuit of happiness. That, to secure these rights, governments are instituted among men, deriving their just powers from the consent of the governed; that, whenever any form of government becomes destructive of these ends, it is the right of the people to alter or to abolish it, and to institute a new government, laying its foundation on such principles, and organizing its powers in such form, as to them shall seem most likely to effect their safety and happiness. Prudence, indeed, will dictate that governments long established, should not be changed for light and transient causes; and, accordingly, all experience hath shown, that mankind are more disposed to suffer, while evils are sufferable, than to right themselves by abolishing the forms to which they are accustomed. But, when a long train of abuses and usurpations, pursuing invariably the same object, evinces a design to reduce them under absolute despotism, it is their right, it is their duty, to throw off such government and to provide new guards for their future security. Such has been the patient sufferance of these colonies, and such is now the necessity which constrains them to alter their former systems of government. The history of the present King of Great Britain is a history of repeated injuries and usurpations, all having, in direct object, the establishment of an absolute tyranny over these States. To prove this, let facts be submitted to a candid world:

He has refused his assent to laws the most wholesome and necessary for the public good.

He has forbidden his governors to pass laws of immediate and pressing importance, unless suspended in their operation till his assent should be obtained; and, when so suspended, he has utterly neglected to attend to them.

He has refused to pass other laws for the accommodation of large districts of people, unless those people would relinquish the right of representation in the legislature; a right inestimable to them, and formidable to tyrants only.

He has called together legislative bodies at places unusual, uncomfortable, and distant from the depository of their public records, for the sole purpose of fatiguing them into compliance with his measures.

He has dissolved representative houses repeatedly for opposing, with manly firmness, his invasions on the rights of the people.

He has refused, for a long time after such dissolutions, to cause others to be elected; whereby the legislative powers, incapable of annihilation, have returned to the people at large for their exercise; the state remaining, in the meantime, exposed to all the danger of invasion from without, and convulsions within.

He has endeavored to prevent the population of these States; for that purpose, obstructing the laws for naturalization of foreigners, refusing to pass others to encourage their migration hither, and raising the conditions of new appropriations of lands.

He has obstructed the administration of justice, by refusing his assent to laws for establishing judiciary powers.

He has made judges dependent on his will alone, for the tenure of their officers, and the amount and payment of their salaries.

He has erected a multitude of new offices, and sent hither swarms of officers to harass our people, and eat out their substance.

He has kept among us, in time of peace, standing armies, without the consent of our legislatures.

He has affected to render the military independent of, and superior to, the civil power.

He has combined, with others, to subject us to a jurisdiction foreign to our Constitution, and unacknowledged by our laws; giving his assent to their acts of pretended legislation:

For quartering large bodies of armed troops among us:

For protecting them by a mock trial, from punishment, for any murders which they should commit on the inhabitants of these States:

For cutting off our trade with all parts of the world:

For imposing taxes on us without our consent:

For depriving us, in many cases, of the benefit of trial by jury:

For transporting us beyond seas to be tried for pretended offences:

For abolishing the free system of English laws in a neighboring province, establishing therein an arbitrary government, and enlarging its boundaries, so as to render it at once an example and fit instrument for introducing the same absolute rule into these colonies:

For taking away our charters, abolishing our most valuable laws, and altering, fundamentally, the powers of our governments:

For suspending our own legislatures, and declaring themselves invested with power to legislate for us in all cases whatsoever.

He has abdicated government here, by declaring us out of his protection, and waging war against us.

He has plundered our seas, ravaged our coasts, burnt our towns, and destroyed the lives of our people.

He is, at this time, transporting large armies of foreign mercenaries to complete the works of death, desolation, and tyranny, already begun, with circumstances of cruelty and perfidy scarcely paralleled in the most barbarous ages, and totally unworthy the head of a civilized nation.

He has constrained our fellow citizens, taken captive on the high seas, to bear arms against their country, to become the executioners of their friends, and brethren, or to fall themselves by their hands.

He has excited domestic insurrections amongst us, and has endeavored to bring on the inhabitants of our frontiers, the merciless Indian savages, whose known rule of warfare is an undistinguished destruction of all ages, sexes, and conditions.

In every stage of these oppressions, we have petitioned for redress, in the most humble terms; our repeated petitions have been answered only by repeated injury. A prince, whose character is thus marked by every act which may define a tyrant, is unfit to be the ruler of a free people.

Nor have we been wanting in attention to our British brethren. We have warned them, from time to time, of attempts made by their legislature to extend an unwarrantable jurisdiction over us. We have reminded them of the circumstances of our emigration and settlement here. We have appealed to their native justice and magnanimity, and we have conjured them, by the ties of our common kindred, to disavow these usurpations, which would inevitably interrupt our connections and correspondence. They, too, have been deaf to the voice of justice and consanguinity. We must, therefore, acquiesce in the necessity, which denounces our separation, and hold them as we hold the rest of mankind, enemies in war, in peace, friends.

We, therefore, the representatives of the United States of America, in general Congress assembled, appealing to the Supreme Judge of the world for the rectitude of our intentions, do, in the name, and by the authority of the good people of these colonies, solemnly publish and declare, that these united colonies are, and of right ought to be, free and independent states: that they are absolved from all allegiance to the British Crown, and that all political connection between them and the state of Great Britain is, and ought to be, totally dissolved; and that, as free and independent states, they have full power to levy war, conclude peace, contract alliances, establish commerce, and to do all other acts and things which independent states may of right do. And, for the support of this declaration, with a firm reliance on the protection of Divine Providence, we mutually pledge to each other our lives, our fortunes, and our sacred honor.

The foregoing Declaration was, by order of Congress, engrossed, and signed by the following members:

JOHN HANCOCK

New Hampshire
Josiah Bartlett
William Whipple
Matthew Thornton

Massachusetts Bay
Samuel Adams
John Adams
Robert Treat Paine
Elbridge Gerry

Rhode Island
Stephen Hopkins
William Ellery

Connecticut
Robert Sherman
Samuel Huntington
William Williams
Oliver Wolcott

New York
William Floyd
Philip Livingston
Francis Lewis
Lewis Morris

New Jersey
Richard Stockton
John Witherspoon
Francis Hopkinson
John Hart
Abraham Clark

Pennsylvania
Robert Morris
Benjamin Rush
Benjamin Franklin
John Morton
George Clymer
James Smith
George Taylor
James Wilson
George Ross

Delaware
Caesar Rodney
George Read
Thomas McKean

Maryland
Samuel Chase
William Paca
Thomas Stone
Charles Carroll,
    of Carrollton

Virginia
George Wythe
Richard Henry Lee
Thomas Jefferson
Benjamin Harrison
Thomas Nelson, Jr.
Francis Lightfoot Lee
Carter Braxton

North Carolina
William Hooper
Joseph Hewes
John Penn

South Carolina
Edward Rutledge
Thomas Heyward, Jr.
Thomas Lynch, Jr.
Arthur Middleton

Georgia
Button Gwinnett
Lyman Hall
George Walton

Resolved, That copies of the Declaration be sent to the several assemblies, conventions, and committees, or councils of safety, and to the several commanding officers of the continental troops; that it be proclaimed in each of the United States, at the head of the army.

THE CONSTITUTION OF THE UNITED STATES OF AMERICA[1]

We the People of the United States, in Order to form a more perfect Union, establish Justice, insure domestic Tranquility, provide for the common defence, promote the general Welfare, and secure the Blessings of Liberty to ourselves and our Posterity, do ordain and establish this CONSTITUTION for the United States of America.

Article 1

Section 1.

All legislative Powers herein granted shall be vested in a Congress of the United States, which shall consist of a Senate and House of Representatives.

Section 2.

The House of Representatives shall be composed of Members chosen every second Year by the People of the several States, and the Electors in each State shall have the Qualifications requisite for Electors of the most numerous Branch of the State Legislature.

No Person shall be a Representative who shall not have attained to the Age of twenty-five Years, and been seven Years a Citizen of the United States, and who shall not, when elected, be an Inhabitant of that State in which he shall be chosen.

[Representatives and direct Taxes[2] shall be apportioned among the several States which may be included within this Union, according to their respective Numbers, which shall be determined by adding to the whole Number of free Persons, including those bound to Service for a Term of Years, and excluding Indians not taxed, three fifths of all other Persons.][3] The actual Enumeration shall be made within three Years after the first Meeting of the Congress of the United States, and within every subsequent Term of ten Years, in such Manner as they shall by Law direct. The Number of Representatives shall not exceed one for every thirty Thousand, but each State shall have at Least one Representative; and until such enumeration shall be made, the State of New Hampshire shall be entitled to chuse three, Massachusetts eight, Rhode-Island and Providence Plantations one, Connecticut five, New York six, New Jersey four, Pennsylvania eight, Delaware one, Maryland six, Virginia ten, North Carolina five, South Carolina five, and Georgia three.

When vacancies happen in the Representation from any State, the Executive Authority thereof shall issue Writs of Election to fill such Vacancies.

The House of Representatives shall chuse their Speaker and other Officers; and shall have the sole Power of Impeachment.

Section 3.

The Senate of the United States shall be composed of two Senators from each State, chosen by the Legislature thereof, for six Years; and each Senator shall have one Vote.

Immediately after they shall be assembled in Consequence of the first Election, they shall be divided as equally as may be into three Classes. The Seats of the Senators of the first Class shall be vacated at the Expiration of the second Year, of the second Class at the Expiration of the fourth Year, and of the third Class at the Expiration of the sixth Year, so that one-third may be chosen every second Year; and if Vacancies happen by Resignation, or otherwise, during the Recess of the Legislature of any State, the Executive thereof may make temporary Appointments until the next Meeting of the Legislature, which shall then fill such Vacancies.

No Person shall be a Senator who shall not have attained to the Age of thirty Years, and been nine Years a Citizen of the United States, and who shall not, when elected, be an Inhabitant of that State for which he shall be chosen.

The Vice President of the United States shall be President of the Senate, but shall have no vote, unless they be equally divided.

The Senate shall chuse their other Officers, and also a President pro tempore, in the absence of the Vice President, or when he shall exercise the office of President of the United States.

The Senate shall have the sole Power to try all Impeachments. When sitting for that purpose they shall be on Oath or Affirmation. When the President of the United States is tried, the Chief Justice shall preside: And no person shall be convicted without the Concurrence of two thirds of the Members present.

Judgment in Cases of Impeachment shall not extend further than to removal from Office, and disqualification to hold and enjoy any Office of honor, Trust, or Profit under the United States: but the Party

---

[1] This version, which follows the original Constitution in capitalization and spelling, was published by the United States Department of the Interior, Office of Education, in 1935.
[2] Altered by the Sixteenth Amendment.
[3] Negated by the Fourteenth Amendment.

convicted shall nevertheless be liable and subject to Indictment, Trial, Judgment, and Punishment, according to Law.

Section 4.

The Times, Places and Manner of holding Elections for Senators and Representatives, shall be prescribed in each State by the Legislature thereof; but the Congress may at any time by Law make or alter such Regulations, except as to the Places of Chusing Senators.

The Congress shall assemble at least once in every Year, and such Meeting shall be on the first Monday in December, unless they shall by Law appoint a different day.

Section 5.

Each House shall be the Judge of the Elections, Returns and Qualifications of its own Members, and a Majority of each shall constitute a Quorum to do Business; but a smaller number may adjourn from day to day, and may be authorized to compel the Attendance of absent Members, in such Manner, and under such Penalties, as each House may provide.

Each House may determine the Rules of its Proceedings, punish its Members for disorderly Behaviour, and, with the Concurrence of two thirds, expel a Member.

Each House shall keep a Journal of its Proceedings, and from time to time publish the same, excepting such Parts as may in their Judgment require Secrecy; and the Yeas and Nays of the Members of either House on any question shall, at the Desire of one fifth of those Present, be entered on the Journal.

Neither House, during the Session of Congress, shall, without the Consent of the other, adjourn for more than three days, nor to any other Place than that in which the two Houses shall be sitting.

Section 6.

The Senators and Representatives shall receive a Compensation for their Services, to be ascertained by Law, and paid out of the Treasury of the United States. They shall in all Cases, except Treason, Felony, and Breach of the Peace, be privileged from Arrest during their Attendance at the Session of their respective Houses, and in going to and returning from the same; and for any Speech or Debate in either House, they shall not be questioned in any other Place.

No Senator or Representative shall, during the Time for which he was elected, be appointed to any civil Office under the Authority of the United States, which shall have been created, or the Emoluments whereof shall have been increased, during such time; and no Person holding any Office under the United States shall be a Member of either House during his continuance in Office.

Section 7.

All Bills for raising Revenue shall originate in the House of Representatives; but the Senate may propose or concur with Amendments as on other bills.

Every Bill which shall have passed the House of Representatives and the Senate, shall, before it become a Law, be presented to the President of the United States; If he approve he shall sign it, but if not he shall return it, with his Objections, to that House in which it shall have originated, who shall enter the Objections at large on their Journal, and proceed to reconsider it. If after such Reconsideration two thirds of that House shall agree to pass the bill, it shall be sent, together with the objections, to the other House, by which it shall likewise be reconsidered, and if approved by two thirds of that House, it shall become a Law. But in all such Cases the Votes of both Houses shall be determined by Yeas and Nays, and the Names of the Persons voting for and against the Bill shall be entered on the Journal of each House respectively. If any Bill shall not be returned by the President within ten Days (Sundays excepted) after it shall have been presented to him, the Same shall be a Law, in like Manner as if he had signed it, unless the Congress by their Adjournment prevent its Return, in which Case it shall not be a Law.

Every Order, Resolution, or Vote to which the Concurrence of the Senate and House of Representatives may be necessary (except on a question of Adjournment) shall be presented to the President of the United States; and before the Same shall take Effect, shall be approved by him, or being disapproved by him, shall be repassed by two thirds of the Senate and House of Representatives, according to the Rules and Limitations prescribed in the Case of a Bill.

Section 8.

The Congress shall have Power To lay and collect Taxes, Duties, Imposts and Excises, to pay the Debts and provide for the common Defence and general Welfare of the United States; but all Duties, Imposts and Excises shall be uniform throughout the United States;

To borrow money on the credit of the United States;

To regulate Commerce with foreign Nations, and among the several States, and with the Indian Tribes;

To establish an uniform rule of Naturalization, and uniform Laws on the subject of Bankruptcies throughout the United States;

To coin Money, regulate the Value thereof, and of foreign Coin, and fix the Standard of Weights and Measures;

To provide for the Punishment of counterfeiting the Securities and current Coin of the United States;

To establish Post Offices and post Roads;

To promote the Progress of Science and useful Arts, by securing for limited Times to Authors and Inventors the exclusive Right to their respective Writings and Discoveries;

To constitute Tribunals inferior to the Supreme Court;

To define and punish Piracies and Felonies committed on the high Seas, and Offenses against the Law of Nations;

To declare War, grant Letters of Marque and Reprisal, and make Rules concerning Captures on Land and Water;

To raise and support Armies, but no Appropriation of Money to that Use shall be for a longer Term than two Years;

To provide and maintain a Navy;

To make Rules for the Government and Regulation of the land and naval forces;

To provide for calling forth the Militia to execute the Laws of the Union, suppress Insurrections and repel Invasions;

To provide for organizing, arming, and disciplining the Militia, and for governing such Part of them as may be employed in the Service of the United States, reserving to the States respectively, the Appointment of the Officers, and the Authority of training the Militia according to the discipline prescribed by Congress;

To exercise exclusive Legislation in all Cases whatsoever, over such District (not exceeding ten Miles square) as may, by Cession of particular States, and the acceptance of Congress, become the Seat of the Government of the United States, and to exercise like Authority over all Places purchased by the Consent of the Legislature of the State in which the Same shall be, for the Erection of Forts, Magazines, Arsenals, Dockyards, and other needful Buildings;—And

To make all Laws which shall be necessary and proper for carrying into Execution the foregoing Powers, and all other Powers vested by this Constitution in the Government of the United States, or in any Department or Officer thereof.

Section 9.

The Migration or Importation of such Persons as any of the States now existing shall think proper to admit, shall not be prohibited by the Congress prior to the Year one thousand eight hundred and eight, but a tax or duty may be imposed on such Importation, not exceeding ten dollars for each Person.

The privilege of the Writ of Habeas Corpus shall not be suspended, unless when in Cases of Rebellion or Invasion the public Safety may require it.

No bill of Attainder or ex post facto Law shall be passed.

No capitation, or other direct, Tax shall be laid unless in Proportion to the Census or Enumeration herein before directed to be taken.

No Tax or Duty shall be laid on Articles exported from any State.

No Preference shall be given by any Regulation of Commerce or Revenue to the Ports of one State over those of another: nor shall Vessels bound to, or from, one State, be obliged to enter, clear, or pay Duties in another.

No Money shall be drawn from the Treasury, but in Consequence of Appropriations made by Law; and a regular Statement and Account of the Receipts and Expenditures of all public Money shall be published from time to time.

No Title of Nobility shall be granted by the United States: And no Person holding any Office of Profit or Trust under them, shall, without the Consent of the Congress, accept of any present, Emolument, Office, or Title, of any kind whatever, from any King, Prince, or foreign State.

Section 10.

No State shall enter into any Treaty, Alliance, or Confederation; grant Letters of Marque and Reprisal; coin Money; emit Bills of Credit; make any Thing but gold and silver Coin a Tender in Payment of Debts; pass any Bill of Attainder, ex post facto Law, or Law impairing the Obligation of Contracts, or grant any Title of Nobility.

No State shall, without the Consent of the Congress, lay any Imposts or Duties on Imports or Exports, except what may be absolutely necessary for executing its inspection Laws; and the net Produce of all Duties and Imposts, laid by any State on Imports or Exports, shall be for the use of the Treasury of the United States; and all such Laws shall be subject to the Revision and Control of the Congress.

No state shall, without the Consent of Congress, lay any duty of Tonnage, keep Troops, or Ships of War in time of Peace, enter into any Agreement or Compact with another State, or with a foreign Power, or engage in War, unless actually invaded, or in such imminent Danger as will not admit of delay.

Article II

Section 1.

The executive Power shall be vested in a President of the United States of America. He shall hold his Office during the Term of four years, and, together with the Vice President, chosen for the same Term, be elected, as follows:

Each State shall appoint, in such Manner as the Legislature thereof may direct, a Number of Electors, equal to the whole Number of Senators and Representatives to which the State may be entitled in the Congress: but no Senator or Representative, or Person holding an Office of Trust or Profit under the United States, shall be appointed an Elector.

[The Electors shall meet in their respective States, and vote by Ballot for two persons, of whom one at least shall not be an Inhabitant of the same State with themselves. And they shall make a List of all the Persons voted for, and of the Number of Votes for each; which List they shall sign and certify, and transmit sealed to the Seat of the Government of the United States, directed to the President of the Senate. The President of the Senate shall, in the Presence of the Senate and House of Representatives, open all the Certificates, and the Votes shall then be counted. The Person having the greatest Number of Votes shall be the President, if such Number be a Majority of the whole Number of Electors appointed; and if there be more than one who have such Majority, and have an equal Number of Votes, then the House of Representatives shall immediately chuse by Ballot one of them for President; and if no Person have a Majority, then from the five highest on the list the said House shall in like Manner chuse the President. But in chusing the President, the Votes shall be taken by States, the Representation from each State having one Vote; a quorum for this Purpose shall consist of a Member or Members from two-thirds of the States, and a Majority of all the States shall be necessary to a Choice. In every Case, after the Choice of the President, the Person having the greatest Number of Votes of the Electors shall be the Vice President. But if there should remain two or more who have equal votes, the Senate shall chuse from them by Ballot the Vice President.][4]

---

[4] Revised by the Twelfth Amendment.

The Congress may determine the Time of chusing the Electors, and the Day on which they shall give their Votes; which Day shall be the same throughout the United States.

No person except a natural-born Citizen, or a Citizen of the United States, at the time of the Adoption of this Constitution, shall be eligible to the Office of President; neither shall any Person be eligible to that Office who shall not have attained to the Age of thirty-five years, and been fourteen Years a Resident within the United States.

In Case of the Removal of the President from Office, or of his Death, Resignation, or Inability to discharge the Powers and Duties of the said Office, the same shall devolve on the Vice President, and the Congress may by Law provide for the Case of Removal, Death, Resignation, or Inability, both of the President and Vice President, declaring what Officer shall then act as President, and such Officer shall act accordingly, until the disability be removed, or a President shall be elected.

The President shall, at stated Times, receive for his Services a Compensation, which shall neither be increased nor diminished during the Period for which he shall have been elected, and he shall not receive within that Period any other Emolument from the United States, or any of them.

Before he enter on the execution of his Office, he shall take the following Oath or Affirmation:—"I do solemnly swear (or affirm) that I will faithfully execute the Office of President of the United States, and will, to the best of my Ability, preserve, protect, and defend the Constitution of the United States."

Section 2.

The President shall be Commander in Chief of the Army and Navy of the United States, and of the Militia of the several States, when called into the actual Service of the United States; he may require the Opinion, in writing, of the principal Officer in each of the executive Departments, upon any subject relating to the Duties of their respective Offices, and he shall have Power to Grant Reprieves and Pardons for Offenses against the United States, except in Cases of Impeachment.

He shall have Power, by and with the Advice and Consent of the Senate, to make Treaties, provided two-thirds of the Senators present concur; and he shall nominate, and by and with the Advice and Consent of the Senate, shall appoint Ambassadors, other public Ministers and Consuls, Judges of the supreme Court, and all other Officers of the United States, whose

Appointments are not herein otherwise provided for, and which shall be established by Law: but the Congress may by Law vest the Appointment of such inferior Officers, as they think proper, in the President alone, in the Courts of Law, or in the Heads of Departments.

The President shall have Power to fill up all Vacancies that may happen during the Recess of the Senate, by granting Commissions which shall expire at the End of their next Session.

Section 3.

He shall from time to time give to the Congress Information of the State of the Union, and recommend to their Consideration such Measures as he shall judge necessary and expedient; he may, on extraordinary occasions, convene both Houses, or either of them, and in Case of Disagreement between them, with respect to the Time of Adjournment, he may adjourn them to such Time as he shall think proper; he shall receive Ambassadors and other public Ministers; he shall take care that the Laws be faithfully executed, and shall Commission all the Officers of the United States.

Section 4.

The President, Vice President and all civil Officers of the United States, shall be removed from Office on Impeachment for, and Conviction of, Treason, Bribery, or other high Crimes and Misdemeanors.

Article III

Section 1.

The judicial Power of the United States, shall be vested in one supreme Court, and in such inferior Courts as the Congress may from time to time ordain and establish. The Judges, both of the supreme and inferior Courts, shall hold their Offices during good Behaviour, and shall, at stated Times, receive for their Services, a Compensation, which shall not be diminished during their Continuance in Office.

Section 2.

The judicial Power shall extend to all Cases, in Law and Equity, arising under this Constitution, the Laws of the United States, and Treaties made, or which shall be made, under their Authority;—to all Cases affecting ambassadors, other public ministers and consuls;—to all cases of admiralty and maritime Jurisdiction;—to Controversies to which the United States shall be a Party;—to Controversies between two or more States;—between a State and Citizens of another State;[5]—between Citizens of different States—between Citizens of the same State claiming Lands under Grants of different States, and between a State, or the Citizens thereof, and foreign States, Citizens, or Subjects.

In all Cases affecting Ambassadors, other public Ministers and Consuls, and those in which a State shall be Party, the supreme Court shall have original Jurisdiction. In all the other Cases before mentioned, the supreme Court shall have appellate Jurisdiction, both as to Law and Fact, with such Exceptions, and under such Regulations as the Congress shall make.

The trial of all Crimes, except in Cases of Impeachment, shall be by Jury; and such Trial shall be held in the State where the said Crimes shall have been committed; but when not committed within any State, the Trial shall be at such Place or Places as the Congress may by Law have directed.

Section 3.

Treason against the United States, shall consist only in levying War against them, or in adhering to their Enemies, giving them Aid and Comfort. No Person shall be convicted of Treason unless on the Testimony of two Witnesses to the same overt Act, or on Confession in open Court.

The Congress shall have power to declare the Punishment of Treason, but no Attainder of Treason shall work Corruption of Blood, or Forfeiture except during the Life of the Person attained.

Article IV

Section 1.

Full Faith and Credit shall be given in each State to the public Acts, Records, and judicial Proceedings of every other State. And the Congress may by general Laws prescribe the Manner in which such Acts, Records and Proceedings shall be proved, and the Effect thereof.

Section 2.

The Citizens of each State shall be entitled to all Privileges and Immunities of Citizens in the several States.

A Person charged in any State with Treason, Felony, or other Crime, who shall flee from Justice, and be found in another State, shall on demand of the

---

[5] Qualified by the Eleventh Amendment.

executive Authority of the State from which he fled, be delivered up, to be removed to the State having Jurisdiction of the crime.

No Person held to Service or Labour in one State, under the Laws thereof, escaping into another, shall, in Consequence of any Law or Regulation therein, be discharged from such Service or Labour, but shall be delivered up on Claim of the Party to whom such Service or Labour may be due.

Section 3.

New States may be admitted by the Congress into this Union; but no new State shall be formed or erected within the Jurisdiction of any other State; nor any State be formed by the Junction of two or more States, or parts of States, without the Consent of the Legislatures of the States concerned as well as of the Congress.

The Congress shall have Power to dispose of and make all needful Rules and Regulations respecting the Territory or other Property belonging to the United States; and nothing in this Constitution shall be so construed as to Prejudice any Claims of the United States, or of any particular State.

Section 4.

The United States shall guarantee to every State in this Union a Republican Form of Government, and shall protect each of them against Invasion; and on Application of the Legislature, or of the Executive (when the Legislature cannot be convened) against domestic violence.

Article V

The Congress, whenever two-thirds of both Houses shall deem it necessary, shall propose Amendments to this Constitution, or, on the Application of the Legislatures of two-thirds of the several States, shall call a Convention for proposing Amendments, which, in either Case, shall be valid to all Intents and Purposes, as part of this Constitution, when ratified by the Legislatures of three-fourths of the several States, or by Conventions in three-fourths thereof, as the one or the other Mode of Ratification may be proposed by the Congress; Provided that no Amendment which may be made prior to the Year One thousand eight hundred and eight shall in any Manner affect the first and fourth Clauses in the Ninth Section of the first Article; and that no State, without its Consent, shall be deprived of its equal Suffrage in the Senate.

Article VI

All Debts contracted and Engagements entered into, before the Adoption of this Constitution, shall be as valid against the United States under this Constitution, as under the Confederation.

This Constitution, and the Laws of the United States which shall be made in Pursuance thereof; and all Treaties made, or which shall be made, under the Authority of the United States, shall be the supreme Law of the Land; and the Judges in every State shall be bound thereby, any Thing in the Constitution or Laws of any State to the Contrary notwithstanding.

The Senators and Representatives before mentioned, and the Members of the several State Legislatures, and all executive and judicial Officers, both of the United States and of the several States, shall be bound by Oath or Affirmation to support this Constitution; but no religious Tests shall ever be required as a qualification to any Office or public Trust under the United States.

Article VII

The Ratification of the Conventions of nine States shall be sufficient for the Establishment of this Constitution between the States so ratifying the same.

Done in Convention by the Unanimous Consent of the States present the Seventeenth Day of September in the Year of our Lord one thousand seven hundred and Eighty seven, and of the Independence of the United States of America the Twelfth. In Witness whereof We have hereunto subscribed our Names.[6]

George Washington
President and deputy from Virginia

New Hampshire
John Langdon
Nicholas Gilman

Massachusetts
Nathaniel Gorham
Rufus King

Connecticut
William Samuel
  Johnson
Roger Sherman

New York
Alexander Hamilton

New Jersey
William Livingston
David Brearley
William Paterson
Jonathan Dayton

---

[6] These are the full names of the signers, which in some cases are not the signatures on the document.

Pennsylvania
Benjamin Franklin
Thomas Mifflin
Robert Morris
George Clymer
Thomas FitzSimons
Jared Ingersoll
James Wilson
Gouverneur Morris

Delaware
George Read
Gunning Beford, Jr.
John Dickinson
Richard Bassett
Jacob Broom

Maryland
James McHenry
Daniel of St. Thomas
    Jenifer
Daniel Carroll

Virginia
John Blair
James Madison, Jr.

North Carolina
William Blount
Richard Dobbs
    Spaight
Hugh Williamson

South Carolina
John Rutledge
Charles Cotesworth
    Pinckney
Charles Pinckney
Pierce Butler

Georgia
William Few
Abraham Baldwin

Articles in Addition to, and Amendment of, the Constitution of the United States of America, Proposed by Congress, and Ratified by the Legislatures of the Several States, Pursuant to the Fifth Article of the Original Constitution[7]

[Article I]

Congress shall make no law respecting an establishment of religion, or prohibiting the free exercise thereof; or abridging the freedom of speech, or of the press; or the right of the people peaceably to assemble, and to petition the Government for a redress of grievances.

[Article II]

A well regulated Militia, being necessary to the security of a free State, the right of the people to keep and bear Arms shall not be infringed.

[Article III]

No Soldier shall, in time of peace, be quartered in any house, without the consent of the Owner, nor in time of war, but in a manner to be prescribed by law.

---

[7] This heading appears only in the joint resolution submitting the first ten amendments.

[Article IV]

The right of the people to be secure in their persons, houses, papers, and effects, against unreasonable searches and seizures, shall not be violated, and no Warrants shall issue, but upon probable cause, supported by Oath or affirmation, and particularly describing the place to be searched, and the persons or things to be seized.

[Article V]

No person shall be held to answer for a capital or otherwise infamous crime, unless on a presentment or indictment of a Grand Jury, except in cases arising in the land or naval forces, or in the Militia, when in actual service in time of War or public danger; nor shall any person be subject for the same offence to be twice put in jeopardy of life or limb; nor shall be compelled in any criminal case to be a witness against himself, nor be deprived of life, liberty, or property, without due process of law; nor shall private property be taken for public use, without just compensation.

[Article VI]

In all criminal prosecutions, the accused shall enjoy the right to a speedy and public trial, by an impartial jury of the State and district wherein the crime shall have been committed, which district shall have been previously ascertained by law, and to be informed of the nature and cause of the accusation; to be confronted with the witnesses against him; to have compulsory process for obtaining witnesses in his favour, and to have the Assistance of Counsel for his defence.

[Article VII]

In suits at common law, where the value in controversy shall exceed twenty dollars, the right of trial by jury shall be preserved, and no fact tried by a jury, shall be otherwise reexamined in any Court of the United States, than according to the rules of the common law.

[Article VIII]

Excessive bail shall not be required, nor excessive fines imposed, nor cruel and unusual punishments inflicted.

[Article IX]

The enumeration of the Constitution, of certain rights, shall not be construed to deny or disparage others retained by the people.

[Article X]

The powers not delegated to the United States by the Constitution, nor prohibited by it to the States, are reserved to the States respectively, or to the people.
[Amendments I-X, in force 1791.]

[Article XI][8]

The Judicial power of the United States shall not be construed to extend to any suit in law or equity, commenced or prosecuted against one of the United States by Citizens of another State, or by Citizens or Subjects of any Foreign State.

[Article XII][9]

The Electors shall meet in their respective States and vote by ballot for President and Vice-President, one of whom, at least, shall not be an inhabitant of the same State with themselves; they shall name in their ballots the person voted for as President, and in distinct ballots the person voted for as Vice-President, and they shall make distinct lists of all persons voted for as President, and of all persons voted for as Vice-President, and of the number of votes for each, which lists they shall sign and certify, and transmit sealed to the seal of the government of the United States, directed to the President of the Senate;—The President of the Senate shall, in the presence of the Senate and House of Representatives, open all the certificates and the votes shall then be counted;—The person having the greatest number of votes for President, shall be the President, if such number be a majority of the whole number of Electors appointed; and if no person have such majority, then from the persons having the highest numbers not exceeding three on the list of those voted for as President, the House of Representatives shall choose immediately, by ballot, the President. But in choosing the President, the votes shall be taken by states, the representation from each state having one vote; a quorum for this purpose shall consist of a member or members from two-thirds of the states, and a majority of all the states shall be necessary to a choice. And if the House of Representatives shall not choose a President whenever the right of choice shall devolve upon them, before the fourth day of March next following, then the Vice-President shall act as President, as in the case of the death or other constitutional disability of the President.—The person having the greatest number of votes as Vice-President, shall be the Vice-President, if such number be a majority of the whole number of Electors appointed, and if no person have a majority, then from the two highest numbers on the list, the Senate shall choose the Vice-President; a quorum for the purpose shall consist of two-thirds of the whole number of Senators, and a majority of the whole number shall be necessary to a choice. But no person constitutionally ineligible to the office of President shall be eligible to that of Vice-President of the United States.

[Article XIII][10]

Section 1.

Neither slavery nor involuntary servitude, except as a punishment for crime whereof the party shall have been duly convicted, shall exist within the United States, or any place subject to their jurisdiction.

Section 2.

Congress shall have power to enforce this article by appropriate legislation.

[Article XIV][11]

Section 1.

All persons born or naturalized in the United States, and subject to the jurisdiction thereof, are citizens of the United States and of the State wherein they reside. No State shall make or enforce any law which shall abridge the privileges or immunities of citizens of the United States; nor shall any State deprive any person of life, liberty, or property, without due process of law; nor deny to any person within its jurisdiction the equal protection of the laws.

---

[8] Adopted in 1798.
[9] Adopted in 1804.

[10] Adopted in 1865.
[11] Adopted in 1868.

Section 2.

Representatives shall be apportioned among the several States according to their respective numbers, counting the whole number of persons in each State, excluding Indians not taxed. But when the right to vote at any election for the choice of electors for President and Vice-President of the United States, Representatives in Congress, the Executive and Judicial officers of a State, or the members of the Legislature thereof, is denied to any of the male inhabitants of such State, being twenty-one years of age, and citizens of the United States, or in any way abridged, except for participation in rebellion, or other crime, the basis of representation therein shall be reduced in the proportion which the number of such male citizens shall bear to the whole number of male citizens twenty-one years of age in such State.

Section 3.

No person shall be a Senator or Representative in Congress, or elector of President and Vice-President, or hold any office, civil or military, under the United States, or under any State, who, having previously taken an oath, as a member of Congress, or as an officer of the United States, or as a member of any State legislature, or as an executive or judicial officer of any State, to support the Constitution of the United States, shall have engaged in insurrection or rebellion against the same, or given aid or comfort to the enemies thereof. But Congress may by a vote of two-thirds of each House, remove such disability.

Section 4.

The validity of the public debt of the United States, authorized by law, including debts incurred for payment of pensions and bounties for services in suppressing insurrection or rebellion, shall not be questioned. But neither the United States nor any State shall assume or pay any debts or obligation incurred in aid of insurrection or rebellion against the United States, or any claim for the loss or emancipation of any slave; but all such debts, obligations, and claims shall be held illegal and void.

Section 5.

The Congress shall have the power to enforce, by appropriate legislation, the provisions of this article.

[Article XV][12]

Section 1.

The right of citizens of the United States to vote shall not be denied or abridged by the United States or by any State on account of race, color, or previous condition of servitude—

Section 2.

The Congress shall have power to enforce this article by appropriate legislation.

[Article XVI][13]

The Congress shall have power to lay and collect taxes on incomes, from whatever source derived, without apportionment among the several States, and without regard to any census or enumeration.

[Article XVII][14]

The Senate of the United States shall be composed of two Senators from each State, elected by the people thereof, for six years; and each Senator shall have one vote. The electors in each State shall have the qualifications requisite for electors of the most numerous branch of the State legislatures.

When vacancies happen in the representation of any State in the Senate, the executive authority of such State shall issue writs of election to fill such vacancies: *Provided,* That the legislature of any State may empower the executive thereof to make temporary appointments until the people fill the vacancies by election as the legislature may direct.

This amendment shall not be so constructed as to affect the election or term of any Senator chosen before it becomes valid as part of the Constitution.

[Article XVIII][15]

Section 1.

After one year from the ratification of this article the manufacture, sale, or transportation of intoxicating liquors within, the importation thereof into, or the

---

[12] Adopted in 1870.
[13] Adopted in 1913.
[14] Adopted in 1913.
[15] Adopted in 1918.

exportation thereof from the United States and all territory subject to the jurisdiction thereof for beverage purposes is hereby prohibited.

Section 2.

The Congress and the several States shall have concurrent power to enforce this article by appropriate legislation.

Section 3.

This article shall be inoperative unless it shall have been ratified as an amendment to the Constitution by the legislatures of the several States, as provided in the Constitution, within seven years from the date of the submission hereof to the States by the Congress.

[Article XIX][16]

The right of citizens of the United States to vote shall not be denied or abridged by the United States or by any State on account of sex.

Congress shall have power to enforce this article by appropriate legislation.

[Article XX][17]

Section 1.

The terms of the President and Vice-President shall end at noon on the 20th day of January, and the terms of Senators and Representatives at noon on the 3d day of January, of the years in which such terms would have ended if this article had not been ratified; and the terms of their successors shall then begin.

Section 2.

The Congress shall assemble at least once in every year, and such meeting shall begin at noon on the 3d day of January, unless they shall by law appoint a different day.

Section 3.

If, at the time fixed for the beginning of the term of the President, the President elect shall have died, the Vice-President elect shall become President. If a President shall not have been chosen before the time fixed for the beginning of his term or if the President elect shall

have failed to qualify, then the Vice-President elect shall act as President until a President shall have qualified; and the Congress may by law provide for the case wherein neither a President elect nor a Vice-President elect shall have qualified, declaring who shall then act as President, or the manner in which one who is to act shall be selected, and such person shall act accordingly until a President or Vice-President shall have qualified.

Section 4.

The Congress may by law provide for the case of the death of any of the persons from whom the House of Representatives may choose a President whenever the right of choice shall have devolved upon them, and for the case of the death of any of the persons from whom the Senate may choose a Vice-President whenever the right of choice shall have devolved upon them.

Section 5.

Sections 1 and 2 shall take effect on the 15th day of October following the ratification of this article.

Section 6.

This article shall be inoperative unless it shall have been ratified as an amendment to the Constitution by the legislatures of three-fourths of the several States within seven years from the date of its submission.

[Article XXI][18]

Section 1.

The eighteenth article of amendment to the Constitution of the United States is hereby repealed.

Section 2.

The transportation or importation into any State, Territory, or possession of the United States for delivery or use therein of intoxicating liquors, in violation of the laws thereof, is hereby prohibited.

Section 3.

This article shall be inoperative unless it shall have been ratified as an amendment to the Constitution by conventions in the several States, as provided in the Constitution, within seven years from the date of the submission hereof to the States by the Congress.

[16] Adopted in 1920.
[17] Adopted in 1933.

[18] Adopted in 1933.

[Article XXII][19]

No person shall be elected to the office of the President more than twice, and no person who has held the office of President, or acted as President, for more than two years of a term to which some other person was elected President shall be elected to the office of the President more than once.

But this Article shall not apply to any person holding the office of President when this Article was proposed by the Congress, and shall not prevent any person who may be holding the office of President, or acting as President, during the term within which this Article becomes operative from holding the office of President or acting as President during the remainder of such term.

This article shall be inoperative unless it shall have been ratified as an amendment to the Constitution by the legislatures of three-fourths of the several states within seven years from the date of its submission to the states by the Congress.

[Article XXIII][20]

Section 1.

The District constituting the seat of Government of the United States shall appoint in such manner as the Congress may direct:

A number of electors of President and Vice-President equal to the whole number of Senators and Representatives in Congress to which the District would be entitled if it were a State, but in no event more than the least populous State; they shall be in addition to those appointed by the States, but they shall be considered, for the purposes of the election of President and Vice-President, to be electors appointed by a State; and they shall meet in the District and perform such duties as provided by the twelfth article of amendment.

Section 2.

The Congress shall have power to enforce this article by appropriate legislation.

[Article XXIV][21]

Section 1.

The right of citizens of the United States to vote in any primary or other election for President or Vice President, for electors for President or Vice President, or for Senator or Representative in Congress, shall not be denied or abridged by the United States or any state by reason of failure to pay any poll tax or other tax.

Section 2.

The Congress shall have the power to enforce this article by appropriate legislation.

[Article XXV][22]

Section 1.

In case of the removal of the President from office or of his death or resignation, the Vice President shall become President.

Section 2.

Whenever there is a vacancy in the office of the Vice President, the President shall nominate a Vice President who shall take office upon confirmation by a majority vote of both Houses of Congress.

Section 3.

Whenever the President transmits to the President Pro Tempore of the Senate and the Speaker of the House of Representatives his written declaration that he is unable to discharge the powers and duties of his office, and until he transmits to them a written declaration to the contrary, such powers and duties shall be discharged by the Vice President as Acting President.

Section 4.

Whenever the Vice President and a majority of either the principal officers of the executive departments or of such other body as Congress may by law provide, transmit to the President Pro Tempore of the Senate

---

[19] Adopted in 1951.
[20] Adopted in 1961.

[21] Adopted in 1964.
[22] Adopted in 1967.

and the Speaker of the House of Representatives their written declaration that the President is unable to discharge the powers and duties of his office, the Vice President shall immediately assume the powers and duties of the office as Acting President.

Thereafter, when the President transmits to the President Pro Tempore of the Senate and the Speaker of the House of Representatives his written declaration that no inability exists, he shall resume the powers and duties of his office unless the Vice President and a majority of either the principal officers of the executive departments or of such other body as Congress may by law provide, transmit within four days to the President Pro Tempore of the Senate and the Speaker of the House of Representatives their written declaration that the President is unable to discharge the powers and duties of his office. Thereupon Congress shall decide the issue, assembling within forty-eight hours for that purpose if not in session. If the Congress, within twenty-one days after receipt of the latter written declaration, or, if Congress is not in session, within twenty-one days after Congress is required to assemble, determines by two-thirds vote of both Houses that the President is unable to discharge the powers and duties of his office, the Vice President shall continue to discharge the same as Acting President; otherwise, the President shall resume the powers and duties of his office.

[Article XXVI][23]

Section 1.

The right of citizens of the United States, who are eighteen years of age or older, to vote shall not be denied or abridged by the United States or by any State on account of age.

Section 2.

The Congress shall have power to enforce this article by appropriate legislation.

---

[23] Adopted in 1971.

[Amendment XXVII][24]

No law varying the compensation for the services of Senators and Representatives shall take effect until an election of Representatives shall have intervened.

PRESIDENTIAL ELECTIONS

Year	Candidates	Parties	Popular Vote	Percentage of Popular Vote	Electoral Vote	Percentage of Voter Participation
1789	**GEORGE WASHINGTON (Va.)***				69	
	John Adams				34	
	Others				35	
1792	**GEORGE WASHINGTON (Va.)**				132	
	John Adams				77	
	George Clinton				50	
	Others				5	
1796	**JOHN ADAMS (Mass.)**	Federalist			71	
	Thomas Jefferson	Democratic-Republican			68	
	Thomas Pinckney	Federalist			59	
	Aaron Burr	Dem.-Rep.			30	
	Others				48	
1800	**THOMAS JEFFERSON (Va.)**	Dem.-Rep.			73	
	Aaron Burr	Dem.-Rep.			73	
	John Adams	Federalist			65	
	C. C. Pinckney	Federalist			64	
	John Jay	Federalist			1	
1804	**THOMAS JEFFERSON (Va.)**	Dem.-Rep.			162	
	C. C. Pinckney	Federalist			14	
1808	**JAMES MADISON (Va.)**	Dem.-Rep.			122	
	C. C. Pinckney	Federalist			47	
	George Clinton	Dem.-Rep.			6	
1812	**JAMES MADISON (Va.)**	Dem.-Rep.			128	
	De Witt Clinton	Federalist			89	
1816	**JAMES MONROE (Va.)**	Dem.-Rep.			183	
	Rufus King	Federalist			34	
1820	**JAMES MONROE (Va.)**	Dem.-Rep.			231	
	John Quincy Adams	Dem.-Rep.			1	
1824	**JOHN Q. ADAMS (Mass.)**	Dem.-Rep.	108,740	30.5	84	26.9
	Andrew Jackson	Dem.-Rep.	153,544	43.1	99	
	William H. Crawford	Dem.-Rep.	46,618	13.1	41	
	Henry Clay	Dem.-Rep.	47,136	13.2	37	
1828	**ANDREW JACKSON (Tenn.)**	Democratic	647,286	56.0	178	57.6
	John Quincy Adams	National Republican	508,064	44.0	83	
1832	**ANDREW JACKSON (Tenn.)**	Democratic	687,502	55.0	219	55.4
	Henry Clay	National Republican	530,189	42.4	49	
	John Floyd	Independent			11	
	William Wirt	Anti-Mason	33,108	2.6	7	
1836	**MARTIN VAN BUREN (N.Y.)**	Democratic	765,483	50.9	170	57.8
	W. H. Harrison	Whig			73	
	Hugh L. White	Whig	739,795	49.1	26	
	Daniel Webster	Whig			14	
	W. P. Magnum	Independent			11	

*State of residence at time of election.

A-24

Year	Candidates	Parties	Popular Vote	Percentage of Popular Vote	Electoral Vote	Percentage of Voter Participation
1840	**WILLIAM H. HARRISON (Ohio)**	Whig	1,274,624	53.1	234	80.2
	Martin Van Buren	Democratic	1,127,781	46.9	60	
	J. G. Birney	Liberty	7,069		—	
1844	**JAMES K. POLK (Tenn.)**	Democratic	1,338,464	49.6	170	78.9
	Henry Clay	Whig	1,300,097	48.1	105	
	J. G. Birney	Liberty	62,300	2.3	—	
1848	**ZACHARY TAYLOR (La.)**	Whig	1,360,967	47.4	163	72.7
	Lewis Cass	Democratic	1,222,342	42.5	127	
	Martin Van Buren	Free-Soil	291,263	10.1	—	
1852	**FRANKLIN PIERCE (N.H.)**	Democratic	1,601,117	50.9	254	69.6
	Winfield Scott	Whig	1,385,453	44.1	42	
	John P. Hale	Free-Soil	155,825	5.0	—	
1856	**JAMES BUCHANAN (Pa.)**	Democratic	1,832,955	45.3	741	78.9
	John C. Frémont	Republican	1,339,932	33.1	114	
	Millard Fillmore	American	871,731	21.6	8	
1860	**ABRAHAM LINCOLN (Ill.)**	Republican	1,865,593	39.8	180	81.2
	Stephen A. Douglas	Democratic	1,382,713	29.5	12	
	John C. Breckinridge	Democratic	848,356	18.1	72	
	John Bell	Union	592,906	12.6	39	
1864	**ABRAHAM LINCOLN (Ill.)**	Republican	2,213,655	55.0	212	73.8
	George B. McClellan	Democratic	1,805,237	45.0	21	
1868	**ULYSSES S. GRANT (Ill.)**	Republican	3,012,833	52.7	214	78.1
	Horatio Seymour	Democratic	2,703,249	47.3	80	
1872	**ULYSSES S. GRANT (Ill.)**	Republican	3,597,132	55.6	286	71.3
	Horace Greeley	Democratic; Liberal Republican	2,834,125	43.9	66	
1876	**RUTHERFORD B. HAYES (Ohio)**	Republican	4,036,298	48.0	185	81.8
	Samuel J. Tilden	Democratic	4,300,590	51.0	184	
1880	**JAMES A. GARFIELD (Ohio)**	Republican	4,454,416	48.5	214	79.4
	Winfield S. Hancock	Democratic	4,444,952	48.1	155	
1884	**GROVER CLEVELAND (N.Y.)**	Democratic	4,874,986	48.5	219	77.5
	James G. Blaine	Republican	4,851,981	48.2	182	
1888	**BENJAMIN HARRISON (Ind.)**	Republican	5,439,853	47.9	233	79.3
	Grover Cleveland	Democratic	5,540,309	48.6	168	
1892	**GROVER CLEVELAND (N.Y.)**	Democratic	5,556,918	46.1	277	74.7
	Benjamin Harrison	Republican	5,176,108	43.0	145	
	James B. Weaver	People's	1,041,028	8.5	22	
1896	**WILLIAM McKINLEY (Ohio)**	Republican	7,104,779	51.1	271	79.3
	William J. Bryan	Democratic-People's	6,502,925	47.7	176	
1900	**WILLIAM McKINLEY (Ohio)**	Republican	7,207,923	51.7	292	73.2
	William J. Bryan	Dem.-Populist	6,358,133	45.5	155	
1904	**THEODORE ROOSEVELT (N.Y.)**	Republican	7,623,486	57.9	336	65.2
	Alton B. Parker	Democratic	5,077,911	37.6	140	
	Eugene V. Debs	Socialist	402,283	3.0	—	
1908	**WILLIAM H. TAFT (Ohio)**	Republican	7,678,908	51.6	321	65.4
	William J. Bryan	Democratic	6,409,104	43.1	162	
	Eugene V. Debs	Socialist	420,793	2.8	—	

Year	Candidates	Parties	Popular Vote	Percentage of Popular Vote	Electoral Vote	Percentage of Voter Participation
1912	**WOODROW WILSON (N.J.)**	Democratic	6,293,454	41.9	435	58.8
	Theodore Roosevelt	Progressive	4,119,538	27.4	88	
	William H. Taft	Republican	3,484,980	23.2	8	
	Eugene V. Debs	Socialist	900,672	6.0	—	
1916	**WOODROW WILSON (N.J.)**	Democratic	9,129,606	49.4	277	61.6
	Charles E. Hughes	Republican	8,538,221	46.2	254	
	A. L. Benson	Socialist	585,113	3.2	—	
1920	**WARREN G. HARDING (Ohio)**	Republican	16,152,200	60.4	404	49.2
	James M. Cox	Democratic	9,147,353	34.2	127	
	Eugene V. Debs	Socialist	919,799	3.4	—	
1924	**CALVIN COOLIDGE (Mass.)**	Republican	15,725,016	54.0	382	48.9
	John W. Davis	Democratic	8,386,503	28.8	136	
	Robert M. LaFollette	Progressive	4,822,856	16.6	13	
1928	**HERBERT HOOVER (Calif.)**	Republican	21,391,381	58.2	444	56.9
	Alfred E. Smith	Democratic	15,016,443	40.9	87	
	Norman Thomas	Socialist	267,835	0.7	—	
1932	**FRANKLIN D. ROOSEVELT (N.Y.)**	Democratic	22,821,857	57.4	472	56.9
	Herbert Hoover	Republican	15,761,841	39.7	59	
	Norman Thomas	Socialist	881,951	2.2	—	
1936	**FRANKLIN D. ROOSEVELT (N.Y.)**	Democratic	27,751,597	60.8	523	61.0
	Alfred M. Landon	Republican	16,679,583	36.5	8	
	William Lemke	Union	882,479	1.9	—	
1940	**FRANKLIN D. ROOSEVELT (N.Y.)**	Democratic	27,244,160	54.8	449	62.5
	Wendell L. Willkie	Republican	22,305,198	44.8	82	
1944	**FRANKLIN D. ROOSEVELT (N.Y.)**	Democratic	25,602,504	53.5	432	55.9
	Thomas E. Dewey	Republican	22,006,285	46.0	99	
1948	**HARRY S. TRUMAN (Mo.)**	Democratic	24,105,695	49.5	304	53.0
	Thomas E. Dewey	Republican	21,969,170	45.1	189	
	J. Strom Thurmond	State-Rights Democratic	1,169,021	2.4	38	
	Henry A. Wallace	Progressive	1,156,103	2.4	—	
1952	**DWIGHT D. EISENHOWER (N.Y.)**	Republican	33,936,252	55.1	442	63.3
	Adlai E. Stevenson	Democratic	27,314,992	44.4	89	
1956	**DWIGHT D. EISENHOWER (N.Y.)**	Republican	35,575,420	57.6	457	60.6
	Adlai E. Stevenson	Democratic	26,033,066	42.1	73	
	Other	—	—		1	
1960	**JOHN F. KENNEDY (Mass.)**	Democratic	34,227,096	49.9	303	62.8
	Richard M. Nixon	Republican	34,108,546	49.6	219	
	Other	—			15	
1964	**LYNDON B. JOHNSON (Tex.)**	Democratic	43,126,506	61.1	486	61.7
	Barry M. Goldwater	Republican	27,176,799	38.5	52	
1968	**RICHARD M. NIXON (N.Y.)**	Republican	31,770,237	43.4	301	60.6
	Hubert H. Humphrey	Democratic	31,270,533	42.7	191	
	George Wallace	American Indep.	9,906,141	13.5	46	
1972	**RICHARD M. NIXON (N.Y.)**	Republican	47,169,911	60.7	520	55.2
	George S. McGovern	Democratic	29,170,383	37.5	17	
	Other	—	—		1	
1976	**JIMMY CARTER (Ga.)**	Democratic	40,828,587	50.0	297	53.5
	Gerald R. Ford	Republican	39,147,613	47.9	241	
	Other	—	1,575,459	2.1	—	
1980	**RONALD REAGAN (Calif.)**	Republican	43,901,812	50.7	489	52.6
	Jimmy Carter	Democratic	35,483,820	41.0	49	
	John B. Anderson	Independent	5,719,722	6.6	—	
	Ed Clark	Libertarian	921,188	1.1	—	

Year	Candidates	Parties	Popular Vote	Percentage of Popular Vote	Electoral Vote	Percentage of Voter Participation
1984	**RONALD REAGAN (Calif.)**	Republican	54,455,075	59.0	525	53.3
	Walter Mondale	Democratic	37,577,185	41.0	13	
1988	**GEORGE BUSH (Texas)**	Republican	47,946,422	54.0	426	50.2
	Michael S. Dukakis	Democratic	41,016,429	46.0	112	
1992	**WILLIAM J. CLINTON (Ark.)**	Democratic	44,908,233	43.3	370	55.2
	George Bush	Republican	39,102,282	37.7	168	
	Ross Perot	Independent	19,721,433	19.0	—	

VICE PRESIDENTS AND CABINET MEMBERS

The Washington Administration (1789–1797)

Vice President	John Adams	1789–1797
Secretary of State	Thomas Jefferson	1789–1793
	Edmund Randolph	1794–1795
	Timothy Pickering	1795–1797
Secretary of Treasury	Alexander Hamilton	1789–1795
	Oliver Wolcott	1795–1797
Secretary of War	Henry Knox	1789–1794
	Timothy Pickering	1795–1796
	James McHenry	1796–1797
Attorney General	Edmund Randolph	1789–1793
	William Bradford	1794–1795
	Charles Lee	1795–1797
Postmaster General	Samuel Osgood	1789–1791
	Timothy Pickering	1791–1794
	Joseph Habersham	1795–1797

The John Adams Administration (1797–1801)

Vice President	Thomas Jefferson	1797–1801
Secretary of State	Timothy Pickering	1797–1800
	John Marshall	1800–1801
Secretary of Treasury	Oliver Wolcott	1797–1800
	Samuel Dexter	1800–1801
Secretary of War	James McHenry	1797–1800
	Samuel Dexter	1800–1801
Attorney General	Charles Lee	1797–1801
Postmaster General	Joseph Habersham	1797–1801
Secretary of Navy	Benjamin Stoddert	1798–1801

The Jefferson Administration (1801–1809)

Vice President	Aaron Burr	1801–1805
	George Clinton	1805–1809
Secretary of State	James Madison	1801–1809
Secretary of Treasury	Samuel Dexter	1801
	Albert Gallatin	1801–1809
Secretary of War	Henry Dearborn	1801–1809
Attorney General	Levi Lincoln	1801–1805
	Robert Smith	1805
	John Breckinridge	1805–1806
	Caesar Rodney	1807–1809
Postmaster General	Joseph Habersham	1801
	Gideon Granger	1801–1809
Secretary of Navy	Robert Smith	1801–1809

The Madison Administration (1809–1817)

Vice President	George Clinton	1809–1813
	Elbridge Gerry	1813–1817
Secretary of State	Robert Smith	1809–1811
	James Monroe	1811–1817
Secretary of Treasury	Albert Gallatin	1809–1813
	George Campbell	1814
	Alexander Dallas	1814–1816
	William Crawford	1816–1817
Secretary of War	William Eustis	1809–1812
	John Armstrong	1813–1814
	James Monroe	1814–1815
	William Crawford	1815–1817
Attorney General	Caesar Rodney	1809–1811
	William Pinkney	1811–1814
	Richard Rush	1814–1817
Postmaster General	Gideon Granger	1809–1814
	Return Meigs	1814–1817
Secretary of Navy	Paul Hamilton	1809–1813
	William Jones	1813–1814
	Benjamin Crowninshield	1814–1817

The Monroe Administration (1817–1825)

Vice President	Daniel Tompkins	1817–1825
Secretary of State	John Quincy Adams	1817–1825
Secretary of Treasury	William Crawford	1817–1825
Secretary of War	George Graham	1817
	John C. Calhoun	1817–1825
Attorney General	Richard Rush	1817
	William Wirt	1817–1825
Postmaster General	Return Meigs	1817–1823
	John McLean	1823–1825

Secretary of Navy	Benjamin Crowninshield	1817–1818
	Smith Thompson	1818–1823
	Samuel Southard	1823–1825

The John Quincy Adams Administration (1825–1829)

Vice President	John C. Calhoun	1825–1829
Secretary of State	Henry Clay	1825–1829
Secretary of Treasury	Richard Rush	1825–1829
Secretary of War	James Barbour	1825–1828
	Peter Porter	1828–1829
Attorney General	William Wirt	1825–1829
Postmaster General	John McLean	1825–1829
Secretary of Navy	Samuel Southard	1825–1829

The Jackson Administration (1829–1837)

Vice President	John C. Calhoun	1829–1833
	Martin Van Buren	1833–1837
Secretary of State	Martin Van Buren	1829–1831
	Edward Livingston	1831–1833
	Louis McLane	1833–1834
	John Forsyth	1834–1837
Secretary of Treasury	Samuel Ingham	1829–1831
	Louis McLane	1831–1833
	William Duane	1833
	Roger B. Taney	1833–1834
	Levi Woodbury	1834–1837
Secretary of War	John H. Eaton	1829–1831
	Lewis Cass	1831–1837
	Benjamin Butler	1837
Attorney General	John M. Berrien	1829–1831
	Roger B. Taney	1831–1833
	Benjamin Butler	1833–1837
Postmaster General	William Barry	1829–1835
	Amos Kendall	1835–1837
Secretary of Navy	John Branch	1829–1831
	Levi Woodbury	1831–1834
	Mahlon Dickerson	1834–1837

The Van Buren Administration (1837–1841)

Vice President	Richard M. Johnson	1837–1841
Secretary of State	John Forsyth	1837–1841
Secretary of Treasury	Levi Woodbury	1837–1841
Secretary of War	Joel Poinsett	1837–1841
Attorney General	Benjamin Butler	1837–1838
	Felix Grundy	1838–1840
	Henry D. Gilpin	1840–1841
Postmaster General	Amos Kendall	1837–1840
	John M. Niles	1840–1841
Secretary of Navy	Mahlon Dickerson	1837–1838
	James Paulding	1838–1841

The William Harrison Administration (1841)

Vice President	John Tyler	1841
Secretary of State	Daniel Webster	1841
Secretary of Treasury	Thomas Ewing	1841
Secretary of War	John Bell	1841
Attorney General	John J. Crittenden	1841
Postmaster General	Francis Granger	1841
Secretary of Navy	George Badger	1841

The Tyler Administration (1841–1845)

Vice President	None	
Secretary of State	Daniel Webster	1841–1843
	Hugh S. Legaré	1843
	Abel P. Upshur	1843–1844
	John C. Calhoun	1844–1845
Secretary of Treasury	Thomas Ewing	1841
	Walter Forward	1841–1843
	John C. Spencer	1843–1844
	George Bibb	1844–1845
Secretary of War	John Bell	1841
	John C. Spencer	1841–1843
	James M. Porter	1843–1844
	William Wilkins	1844–1845
Attorney General	John J. Crittenden	1841
	Hugh S. Legaré	1841–1843
	John Nelson	1843–1845
Postmaster General	Francis Granger	1841
	Charles Wickliffe	1841
Secretary of Navy	George Badger	1841
	Abel P. Upshur	1841
	David Henshaw	1843–1844
	Thomas Gilmer	1844
	John Y. Mason	1844–1845

The Polk Administration (1845–1849)

Vice President	George M. Dallas	1845–1849
Secretary of State	James Buchanan	1845–1849
Secretary of Treasury	Robert J. Walker	1845–1849
Secretary of War	William L. Marcy	1845–1849
Attorney General	John Y. Mason Nathan Clifford Isaac Toucey	1845–1846 1846–1848 1848–1849
Postmaster General	Cave Johnson	1845–1849
Secretary of Navy	George Bancroft John Y. Mason	1845–1846 1846–1849

The Taylor Administration (1849–1850)

Vice President	Millard Fillmore	1849–1850
Secretary of State	John M. Clayton	1849–1950
Secretary of Treasury	William Meredith	1849–1850
Secretary of War	George Crawford	1849–1850
Attorney General	Reverdy Johnson	1849–1850
Postmaster General	Jacob Collamer	1849–1850
Secretary of Navy	William Preston	1849–1850
Secretary of Interior	Thomas Ewing	1849–1850

The Fillmore Administration (1850–1853)

Vice President	None	
Secretary of State	Daniel Webster Edward Everett	1850–1852 1852–1853
Secretary of Treasury	Thomas Corwin	1850–1853
Secretary of War	Charles Conrad	1850–1853
Attorney General	John J. Crittenden	1850–1853
Postmaster General	Nathan Hall Sam D. Hubbard	1850–1852 1852–1853
Secretary of Navy	William A. Graham John P. Kennedy	1850–1852 1852–1853

Secretary of Interior	Thomas McKennan Alexander Stuart	1850 1850–1853

The Pierce Administration (1853–1857)

Vice President	William R. King	1853–1857
Secretary of State	William L. Marcy	1853–1857
Secretary of Treasury	James Guthrie	1853–1857
Secretary of War	Jefferson Davis	1853–1857
Attorney General	Caleb Cushing	1853–1857
Postmaster General	James Campbell	1853–1957
Secretary of Navy	James C. Dobbin	1853–1857
Secretary of Interior	Robert McClelland	1853–1857

The Buchanan Administration (1857–1861)

Vice President	John C. Breckinridge	1857–1861
Secretary of State	Lewis Cass Jeremiah S. Black	1857–1860 1860–1861
Secretary of Treasury	Howell Cobb Philip Thomas John A. Dix	1857–1860 1860–1861 1861
Secretary of War	John B. Floyd Joseph Holt	1857–1861 1861
Attorney General	Jeremiah S. Black Edwin M. Stanton	1857–1860 1860–1861
Postmaster General	Aaron V. Brown Joseph Holt Horatio King	1857–1859 1859–1861 1861
Secretary of Navy	Isaac Toucey	1857–1861
Secretary of Interior	Jacob Thompson	1857–1861

The Lincoln Administration (1861–1865)

Vice President	Hannibal Hamlin Andrew Johnson	1861–1865 1865
Secretary of State	William H. Seward	1861–1865
Secretary of Treasury	Samuel P. Chase William P. Fessenden Hugh McCulloch	1861–1864 1864–1865 1865
Secretary of War	Simon Cameron Edwin M. Stanton	1861–1862 1862–1865

Attorney General	Edward Bates	1861–1864
	James Speed	1864–1865
Postmaster General	Horatio King	1861
	Montgomery Blair	1861–1864
	William Dennison	1864–1865
Secretary of Navy	Gideon Welles	1861–1865
Secretary of Interior	Caleb B. Smith	1861–1863
	John P. Usher	1863–1865

The Andrew Johnson Administration (1865–1869)

Vice President	None	
Secretary of State	William H. Seward	1865–1869
Secretary of Treasury	Hugh McCulloch	1865–1869
Secretary of War	Edwin M. Stanton	1865–1867
	Ulysses S. Grant	1867–1868
	Lorenzo Thomas	1868
	John M. Schofield	1868–1869
Attorney General	James Speed	1865–1866
	Henry Stanbery	1866–1868
	William M. Evarts	1868–1869
Postmaster General	William Dennison	1865–1866
	Alexander Randall	1866–1869
Secretary of Navy	Gideon Welles	1865–1869
Secretary of Interior	John P. Usher	1865
	James Harlan	1865–1866
	Orville H. Browning	1866–1869

The Grant Administration (1869–1877)

Vice President	Schuyler Colfax	1869–1873
	Henry Wilson	1873–1877
Secretary of State	Elihu B. Washburne	1869
	Hamilton Fish	1869–1877
Secretary of Treasury	George S. Boutwell	1869–1873
	William Richardson	1873–1874
	Benjamin Bristow	1874–1876
	Lot M. Morrill	1876–1877
Secretary of War	John A. Rawlins	1869
	William T. Sherman	1869
	William W. Belknap	1869–1876
	Alphonso Taft	1876
	James D. Cameron	1876–1877
Attorney General	Ebenezer Hoar	1869–1870
	Amos T. Ackerman	1870–1871
	G. H. Williams	1871–1875
	Edwards Pierrepont	1875–1876
	Alphonso Taft	1876–1877

Postmaster General	John A. J. Creswell	1869–1874
	James W. Marshall	1874
	Marshall Jewell	1874–1876
	James N. Tyner	1876–1877
Secretary of Navy	Adolph E. Borie	1869
	George M. Robeson	1869–1877
Secretary of Interior	Jacob D. Cox	1869–1870
	Columbus Delano	1870–1875
	Zachariah Chandler	1875–1877

The Hayes Administration (1877–1881)

Vice President	William A. Wheeler	1877–1881
Secretary of State	William M. Evarts	1877–1881
Secretary of Treasury	John Sherman	1877–1881
Secretary of War	George W. McCrary	1877–1879
	Alex Ramsey	1879–1881
Attorney General	Charles Devens	1877–1881
Postmaster General	David M. Key	1877–1880
	Horace Maynard	1880–1881
Secretary of Navy	Richard W. Thompson	1877–1880
	Nathan Goff, Jr.	1881
Secretary of Interior	Carl Schurz	1877–1881

The Garfield Administration (1881)

Vice President	Chester A. Arthur	1881
Secretary of State	James G. Blaine	1881
Secretary of Treasury	William Windom	1881
Secretary of War	Robert T. Lincoln	1881
Attorney General	Wayne MacVeagh	1881
Postmaster General	Thomas L. James	1881
Secretary of Navy	William H. Hunt	1881
Secretary of Interior	Samuel J. Kirkwood	1881

The Arthur Administration (1881–1885)

| Vice President | None | |
| Secretary of State | F. T. Frelinghuysen | 1881–1885 |

Secretary of Treasury	Charles J. Folger	1881–1884
	Walter Q. Gresham	1884
	Hugh McCulloch	1884–1885
Secretary of War	Robert T. Lincoln	1881–1885
Attorney General	Benjamin H. Brewster	1881–1885
Postmaster General	Timothy O. Howe	1881–1883
	Walter Q. Gresham	1883–1884
	Frank Hatton	1884–1885
Secretary of Navy	William H. Hunt	1881–1882
	William E. Chandler	1882–1885
Secretary of Interior	Samuel J. Kirkwood	1881–1882
	Henry M. Teller	1882–1885

The Cleveland Administration (1885–1889)

Vice President	Thomas A. Hendricks	1885–1889
Secretary of State	Thomas F. Bayard	1885–1889
Secretary of Treasury	Daniel Manning	1885–1887
	Charles S. Fairchild	1887–1889
Secretary of War	William C. Endicott	1885–1889
Attorney General	Augustus H. Garland	1885–1889
Postmaster General	William F. Vilas	1885–1888
	Don M. Dickinson	1888–1889
Secretary of Navy	William C. Whitney	1885–1889
Secretary of Interior	Lucius Q. C. Lamar	1885–1888
	William F. Vilas	1888–1889
Secretary of Agriculture	Norman J. Colman	1889

The Benjamin Harrison Administration (1889–1893)

Vice President	Levi P. Morton	1889–1893
Secretary of State	James G. Blaine	1889–1892
	John W. Foster	1892–1893
Secretary of Treasury	William Windom	1889–1891
	Charles Foster	1891–1893
Secretary of War	Redfield Proctor	1889–1891
	Stephen B. Elkins	1891–1893
Attorney General	William H. H. Miller	1889–1891
Postmaster General	John Wanamaker	1889–1893

Secretary of Navy	Benjamin F. Tracy	1889–1893
Secretary of Interior	John W. Noble	1889–1893
Secretary of Agriculture	Jeremiah M. Rush	1889–1893

The Cleveland Administration (1893–1897)

Vice President	Adlai E. Stevenson	1893–1897
Secretary of State	Walter Q. Gresham	1893–1895
	Richard Olney	1895–1897
Secretary of Treasury	John G. Carlisle	1893–1897
Secretary of War	Daniel S. Lamont	1893–1897
Attorney General	Richard Olney	1893–1895
	James Harmon	1895–1897
Postmaster General	Wilson S. Bissell	1893–1895
	William L. Wilson	1895–1897
Secretary of Navy	Hilary A. Herbert	1893–1897
Secretary of Interior	Hoke Smith	1893–1896
	David R. Francis	1896–1897
Secretary of Agriculture	Julius S. Morton	1893–1897

The McKinley Administration (1897–1901)

Vice President	Garret A. Hobart	1897–1901
	Theodore Roosevelt	1901
Secretary of State	John Sherman	1897–1898
	William R. Day	1898
	John Hay	1898–1901
Secretary of Treasury	Lyman J. Gage	1897–1901
Secretary of War	Russell A. Alger	1897–1899
	Elihu Root	1899–1901
Attorney General	Joseph McKenna	1897–1898
	John W. Griggs	1898–1901
	Philander C. Knox	1901
Postmaster General	James A. Gary	1897–1898
	Charles E. Smith	1898–1901
Secretary of Navy	John D. Long	1897–1901

Secretary of Interior	Cornelius N. Bliss	1897–1899
	Ethan A. Hitchcock	1899–1901
Secretary of Agriculture	James Wilson	1897–1901

The Theodore Roosevelt Administration (1901–1909)

Vice President	Charles Fairbanks	1905–1909
Secretary of State	John Hay	1901–1905
	Elihu Root	1905–1909
	Robert Bacon	1909
Secretary of Treasury	Lyman J. Gage	1901–1902
	Leslie M. Shaw	1902–1907
	George B. Cortelyou	1907–1909
Secretary of War	Elihu Root	1901–1904
	William H. Taft	1904–1908
	Luke E. Wright	1908–1909
Attorney General	Philander C. Knox	1901–1904
	William H. Moody	1904–1906
	Charles J. Bonaparte	1906–1909
Postmaster General	Charles E. Smith	1901–1902
	Henry C. Payne	1902–1904
	Robert J. Wynne	1904–1905
	George B. Cortelyou	1905–1907
	George von L. Meyer	1907–1909
Secretary of Navy	John D. Long	1901–1902
	William H. Moody	1902–1904
	Paul Morton	1904–1905
	Charles J. Bonaparte	1905–1906
	Victor H. Metcalf	1906–1908
	Truman H. Newberry	1908–1909
Secretary of Interior	Ethan A. Hitchcock	1901–1907
	James R. Garfield	1907–1909
Secretary of Agriculture	James Wilson	1901–1909
Secretary of Labor and Commerce	George B. Cortelyou	1903–1904
	Victor H. Metcalf	1904–1906
	Oscar S. Straus	1906–1909
	Charles Nagel	1909

The Taft Administration (1909–1913)

Vice President	James S. Sherman	1909–1913
Secretary of State	Philander C. Knox	1909–1913
Secretary of Treasury	Franklin MacVeagh	1909–1913
Secretary of War	Jacob M. Dickinson	1909–1911
	Henry L. Stimson	1911–1913

Attorney General	George W. Wickersham	1909–1913
Postmaster General	Frank H. Hitchcock	1909–1913
Secretary of Navy	George von L. Meyer	1909–1913
Secretary of Interior	Richard A. Ballinger	1909–1911
	Walter L. Fisher	1911–1913
Secretary of Agriculture	James Wilson	1909–1913
Secretary of Labor and Commerce	Charles Nagel	1909–1913

The Wilson Administration (1913–1921)

Vice President	Thomas R. Marshall	1913–1921
Secretary of State	William J. Bryan	1913–1915
	Robert Lansing	1915–1920
	Bainbridge Colby	1920–1921
Secretary of Treasury	William G. McAdoo	1913–1918
	Carter Glass	1918–1920
	David F. Houston	1920–1921
Secretary of War	Lindley M. Garrison	1913–1916
	Newton D. Baker	1916–1921
Attorney General	James C. McReynolds	1913–1914
	Thomas W. Gregory	1914–1919
	A. Mitchell Palmer	1919–1921
Postmaster General	Albert S. Burleson	1913–1921
Secretary of Navy	Josephus Daniels	1913–1921
Secretary of Interior	Franklin K. Lane	1913–1920
	John B. Payne	1920–1921
Secretary of Agriculture	David F. Houston	1913–1920
	Edwin T. Meredith	1920–1921
Secretary of Commerce	William C. Redfield	1913–1919
	Joshua W. Alexander	1919–1921
Secretary of Labor	William B. Wilson	1913–1921

The Harding Administration (1921–1923)

Vice President	Calvin Coolidge	1921–1923
Secretary of State	Charles E. Hughes	1921–1923
Secretary of Treasury	Andrew Mellon	1921–1923
Secretary of War	John W. Weeks	1921–1923

Attorney General	Harry M. Daugherty	1921–1923
Postmaster General	Will H. Hays Hubert Work Harry S. New	1921–1922 1922–1923 1923
Secretary of Navy	Edwin Denby	1921–1923
Secretary of Interior	Albert B. Fall Hubert Work	1921–1923 1923
Secretary of Agriculture	Henry C. Wallace	1921–1923
Secretary of Commerce	Herbert C. Hoover	1921–1923
Secretary of Labor	James J. Davis	1921–1923

The Coolidge Administration (1923–1929)

Vice President	Charles G. Dawes	1925–1929
Secretary of State	Charles E. Hughes Frank B. Kellogg	1923–1925 1925–1929
Secretary of Treasury	Andrew Mellon	1923–1929
Secretary of War	John W. Weeks Dwight F. Davis	1923–1925 1925–1929
Attorney General	Harry M. Daugherty Harlan F. Stone John G. Sargent	1923–1924 1924–1925 1925–1929
Postmaster General	Harry S. New	1923–1929
Secretary of Navy	Edwin Derby Curtis D. Wilbur	1923–1924 1924–1929
Secretary of Interior	Hubert Work Roy O. West	1923–1928 1928–1929
Secretary of Agriculture	Henry C. Wallace Howard M. Gore William M. Jardine	1923–1924 1924–1925 1925–1929
Secretary of Commerce	Herbert C. Hoover William F. Whiting	1923–1928 1928–1929
Secretary of Labor	James J. Davis	1923–1929

The Hoover Administration (1929–1933)

Vice President	Charles Curtis	1929–1933
Secretary of State	Henry L. Stimson	1929–1933
Secretary of Treasury	Andrew Mellon Ogden L. Mills	1929–1932 1932–1933

Secretary of War	James W. Good Patrick J. Hurley	1929 1929–1933
Attorney General	William D. Mitchell	1929–1933
Postmaster General	Walter F. Brown	1929–1933
Secretary of Navy	Charles F. Adams	1929–1933
Secretary of Interior	Ray L. Wilbur	1929–1933
Secretary of Agriculture	Arthur M. Hyde	1929–1933
Secretary of Commerce	Robert P. Lamont Roy D. Chapin	1929–1932 1932–1933
Secretary of Labor	James J. Davis William N. Doak	1929–1930 1930–1933

The Franklin D. Roosevelt Administration (1933–1945)

Vice President	John Nance Garner Henry A. Wallace Harry S. Truman	1933–1941 1941–1945 1945
Secretary of State	Cordell Hull Edward R. Stettinius, Jr.	1933–1944 1944–1945
Secretary of Treasury	William H. Woodin Henry Morgenthau, Jr.	1933–1934 1934–1945
Secretary of War	George H. Dern Henry A. Woodring Henry L. Stimson	1933–1936 1936–1940 1940–1945
Attorney General	Homer S. Cummings Frank Murphy Robert H. Jackson Francis Biddle	1933–1939 1939–1940 1940–1941 1941–1945
Postmaster General	James A. Farley Frank C. Walker	1933–1940 1940–1945
Secretary of Navy	Claude A. Swanson Charles Edison Frank Knox James V. Forrestal	1933–1940 1940 1940–1944 1944–1945
Secretary Interior	Harold L. Ickes	1933–1945
Secretary of Agriculture	Henry A. Wallace Claude R. Wickard	1933–1940 1940–1945
Secretary of Commerce	Daniel C. Roper Harry L. Hopkins Jesse Jones Henry A. Wallace	1933–1939 1939–1940 1940–1945 1945
Secretary of Labor	Frances Perkins	1933–1945

The Truman Administration (1945–1953)

Vice President	Alben W. Barkley	1949–1953
Secretary of State	Edward R. Stettinius, Jr.	1945
	James F. Byrnes	1945–1947
	George C. Marshall	1947–1949
	Dean G. Acheson	1949–1953
Secretary of Treasury	Fred M. Vinson	1945–1946
	John W. Snyder	1946–1953
Secretary of War	Robert P. Patterson	1945–1947
	Kenneth C. Royall	1947
Attorney General	Tom C. Clark	1945–1949
	J. Howard McGrath	1949–1952
	James P. McGranery	1952–1953
Postmaster General	Frank C. Walker	1945
	Robert E. Hannegan	1945–1947
	Jesse M. Donaldson	1947–1953
Secretary of Navy	James V. Forrestal	1945–1947
Secretary of Interior	Harold L. Ickes	1945–1946
	Julius A. Krug	1946–1949
	Oscar L. Chapman	1949–1953
Secretary of Agriculture	Clinton P. Anderson	1945–1948
	Charles F. Brannan	1948–1953
Secretary of Commerce	Henry A. Wallace	1945–1946
	W. Averell Harriman	1946–1948
	Charles W. Sawyer	1948–1953
Secretary of Labor	Lewis B. Schwellenbach	1945–1948
	Maurice J. Tobin	1948–1953
Secretary of Defense	James V. Forrestal	1947–1949
	Louis A. Johnson	1949–1950
	George C. Marshall	1950–1951
	Robert A. Lovett	1951–1953

The Eisenhower Administration (1953–1961)

Vice President	Richard M. Nixon	1953–1961
Secretary of State	John Foster Dulles	1953–1959
	Christian A. Herter	1959–1961
Secretary of Treasury	George M. Humphrey	1953–1957
	Robert B. Anderson	1957–1961
Attorney General	Herbert Brownell, Jr.	1953–1958
	William P. Rogers	1958–1961
Postmaster General	Arthur E. Summerfield	1953–1961
Secretary of Interior	Douglas McKay	1953–1956
	Freed A. Seaton	1956–1961

Secretary of Agriculture	Ezra T. Benson	1953–1961
Secretary of Commerce	Sinclair Weeks	1953–1958
	Lewis L. Strauss	1958–1959
	Frederick H. Mueller	1959–1961
Secretary of Labor	Martin P. Durkin	1953
	James P. Mitchell	1953–1961
Secretary of Defense	Charles E. Wilson	1953–1957
	Neil H. McElroy	1957–1959
	Thomas S. Gates Jr.	1959–1961
Secretary of Health, Education, and Welfare	Oveta Culp Hobby	1953–1955
	Marion B. Folsom	1955–1958
	Arthur S. Flemming	1958–1961

The Kennedy Administration (1961–1963)

Vice President	Lyndon B. Johnson	1961–1963
Secretary of State	Dean Rusk	1961–1963
Secretary of Treasury	C. Douglas Dillon	1961–1963
Attorney General	Robert F. Kennedy	1961–1963
Postmaster General	J. Edward Day	1961–1963
	John A. Gronouski	1963
Secretary of Interior	Stewart L. Udall	1961–1963
Secretary of Agriculture	Orville L. Freeman	1961–1963
Secretary of Commerce	Luther H. Hodges	1961–1963
Secretary of Labor	Arthur J. Goldberg	1961–1962
	W. Willard Wirtz	1962–1963
Secretary of Defense	Robert S. McNamara	1961–1963
Secretary of Health, Education, and Welfare	Abraham A. Ribicoff	1961–1962
	Anthony J. Celebrezze	1962–1963

The Lyndon Johnson Administration (1963–1969)

Vice President	Hubert H. Humphrey	1965–1969
Secretary of State	Dean Rusk	1963–1969
Secretary of Treasury	C. Douglas Dillon	1963–1965
	Henry H. Fowler	1965–1969

Attorney General	Robert F. Kennedy	1963–1964
	Nicholas Katzenbach	1965–1966
	Ramsey Clark	1967–1969
Postmaster General	John A. Gronouski	1963–1965
	Lawrence F. O'Brien	1965–1968
	Marvin Watson	1968–1969
Secretary of Interior	Stewart L. Udall	1963–1969
Secretary of Agriculture	Orville L. Freeman	1963–1969
Secretary of Commerce	Luther H. Hodges	1963–1964
	John T. Connor	1964–1967
	Alexander B. Trowbridge	1967–1968
	Cyrus R. Smith	1968–1969
Secretary of Labor	W. Willard Wirtz	1963–1969
Secretary of Defense	Robert F. McNamara	1963–1968
	Clark Clifford	1968–1969
Secretary of Health, Education, and Welfare	Anthony J. Celebrezze	1963–1965
	John W. Gardner	1965–1968
	Wilbur J. Cohen	1968–1969
Secretary of Housing and Urban Development	Robert C. Weaver	1966–1969
	Robert C. Wood	1969
Secretary of Transportation	Alan S. Boyd	1967–1969

The Nixon Administration (1969–1974)

Vice President	Spiro T. Agnew	1969–1973
	Gerald R. Ford	1973–1974
Secretary of State	William P. Rogers	1969–1973
	Henry A. Kissinger	1973–1974
Secretary of Treasury	David M. Kennedy	1969–1970
	John B. Connally	1971–1972
	George P. Shultz	1972–1974
	William E. Simon	1974
Attorney General	John N. Mitchell	1969–1972
	Richard G. Kleindienst	1972–1973
	Elliot L. Richardson	1973
	William B. Saxbe	1973–1974
Postmaster General	Winton M. Blount	1969–1971
Secretary of Interior	Walter J. Hickel	1969–1970
	Rogers Morton	1971–1974

Secretary of Agriculture	Clifford M. Hardin	1969–1971
	Earl L. Butz	1971–1974
Secretary of Commerce	Maurice H. Stans	1969–1972
	Peter G. Peterson	1972–1973
	Frederick B. Dent	1973–1974
Secretary of Labor	George P. Shultz	1969–1970
	James D. Hodgson	1970–1973
	Peter J. Brennan	1973–1974
Secretary of Defense	Melvin R. Laird	1969–1973
	Elliot L. Richardson	1973
	James R. Schlesinger	1973–1974
Secretary of Health, Education, and Welfare	Robert H. Finch	1969–1970
	Elliot L. Richardson	1970–1973
	Caspar W. Weinberger	1973–1974
Secretary of Housing and Urban Development	George Romney	1969–1973
	James T. Lynn	1973–1974
Secretary of Transportation	John A. Volpe	1969–1973
	Claude S. Brinegar	1973–1974

The Ford Administration (1974–1977)

Vice President	Nelson A. Rockefeller	1974–1977
Secretary of State	Henry A. Kissinger	1974–1977
Secretary of Treasury	William E. Simon	1974–1977
Attorney General	William Saxbe	1974–1975
	Edward Levi	1975–1977
Secretary of Interior	Rogers Morton	1974–1975
	Stanley K. Hathaway	1975
	Thomas Kleppe	1975–1977
Secretary of Agriculture	Earl L. Butz	1974–1976
	John A. Knebel	1976–1977
Secretary of Commerce	Frederick B. Dent	1974–1975
	Rogers Morton	1975–1976
	Elliot L. Richardson	1976–1977
Secretary of Labor	Peter J. Brennan	1974–1975
	John T. Dunlop	1975–1976
	W. J. Usery	1976–1977
Secretary of Defense	James R. Schlesinger	1974–1975
	Donald Rumsfeld	1975–1977
Secretary of Health, Education, and Welfare	Caspar Weinberger	1974–1975
	Forrest D. Mathews	1975–1977

Secretary of Housing and Urban Development	James T. Lynn	1974–1975
	Carla A. Hills	1975–1977
Secretary of Transportation	Claude Brinegar	1974–1975
	William T. Coleman	1975–1977

The Carter Administration (1977–1981)

Vice President	Walter F. Mondale	1977–1981
Secretary of State	Cyrus R. Vance	1977–1980
	Edmund Muskie	1980–1981
Secretary of Treasury	W. Michael Blumenthal	1977–1979
	G. William Miller	1979–1981
Attorney General	Griffin Bell	1977–1979
	Benjamin R. Civiletti	1979–1981
Secretary of Interior	Cecil D. Andrus	1977–1981
Secretary of Agriculture	Robert Bergland	1977–1981
Secretary of Commerce	Juanita M. Kreps	1977–1979
	Philip M. Klutznick	1979–1981
Secretary of Labor	F. Ray Marshall	1977–1981
Secretary of Defense	Harold Brown	1977–1981
Secretary of Health, Education and Welfare	Joseph A. Califano	1977–1979
	Patricia R. Harris	1979
Secretary of Health and Human Services	Patricia R. Harris	1979–1981
Secretary of Education	Shirley M. Hufstedler	1979–1981
Secretary of Housing and Urban Development	Patricia R. Harris	1977–1979
	Moon Landrieu	1979–1981
Secretary of Transportation	Brock Adams	1977–1979
	Neil E. Goldschmidt	1979–1981
Secretary of Energy	James R. Schlesinger	1977–1979
	Charles W. Duncan	1979–1981

The Reagan Administration (1981–1989)

Vice President	George Bush	1981–1989
Secretary of State	Alexander M. Haig	1981–1982
	George P. Shultz	1982–1989
Secretary of Treasury	Donald Regan	1981–1985
	James A. Baker III	1985–1988
	Nicholas F. Brady	1988–1989
Attorney General	William F. Smith	1981–1985
	Edwin A. Meese III	1985–1988
	Richard Thornburgh	1988–1989
Secretary of Interior	James Watt	1981–1983
	William P. Clark, Jr.	1983–1985
	Donald P. Hodel	1985–1989
Secretary of Agriculture	John Block	1981–1986
	Richard E. Lyng	1986–1989
Secretary of Commerce	Malcolm Baldrige	1981–1987
	C. William Verity, Jr.	1987–1989
Secretary of Labor	Raymond Donovan	1981–1985
	William Brock	1985–1987
	Ann D. McLaughlin	1987–1989
Secretary of Defense	Caspar Weinberger	1981–1987
	Frank C. Carlucci	1987–1989
Secretary of Health and Human Services	Richard Schweiker	1981–1983
	Margaret Heckler	1983–1985
	Otis R. Bowen	1985–1989
Secretary of Education	Terrel H. Bell	1981–1985
	William J. Bennett	1985–1988
	Laura F. Cavazos	1988–1989
Secretary of Housing and Urban Development	Samuel Pierce	1981–1989
Secretary of Transportation	Drew Lewis	1981–1983
	Elizabeth Dole	1983–1987
	James H. Burnley	1987–1989
Secretary of Energy	James Edwards	1981–1982
	Donald P. Hodel	1982–1985
	John S. Herrington	1984–1989

The Bush Administration (1989–1993)

Vice President	J. Danforth Quayle	1989–1993
Secretary of State	James A. Baker III	1989–1992
	Lawrence S. Eagleburger	1992–1993
Secretary of Treasury	Nicholas F. Brady	1989–1993

Attorney General	Richard Thornburgh William P. Barr	1989–1991 1991–1993
Secretary of Interior	Manuel Lujan	1989–1993
Secretary of Agriculture	Clayton K. Yeutter Edward Madigan	1989–1991 1991–1993
Secretary of Commerce	Robert A. Mosbacher Barbara H. Franklin	1989–1992 1992–1993
Secretary of Labor	Elizabeth Dole Lynn M. Martin	1989–1991 1991–1993
Secretary of Defense	Richard B. Cheney	1989–1993
Secretary of Health and Human Services	Louis W. Sullivan	1989–1993
Secretary of Education	Laura F. Cavazos Lamar Alexander	1989–1991 1991–1993
Secretary of Housing and Urban Development	Jack F. Kemp	1989–1993
Secretary of Transportation	Samuel K. Skinner Andrew H. Card	1989–1992 1992–1993
Secretary of Energy	James D. Watkins	1989–1993
Secretary of Veterans Affairs	Edward J. Derwinski	1989–1993

Attorney General	Janet Reno	1993–
Secretary of Interior	Bruce Babbitt	1993–
Secretary of Agriculture	Mike Espy	1993–
Secretary of Commerce	Ronald H. Brown	1993–
Secretary of Labor	Robert B. Reich	1993–
Secretary of Defense	Les Aspin William Perry	1993–1994 1994–
Secretary of Health and Human Services	Donna E. Shalala	1993–
Secretary of Education	Richard W. Riley	1993–
Secretary of Housing and Urban Development	Henry G. Cisneros	1993–
Secretary of Energy	Hazel R. O'Leary	1993–
Secretary of Transportation	Federico Pena	1993–
Secretary of Veterans Affairs	Jesse Brown	1993–

The Clinton Administration (1993–   )

Vice President	Albert Gore, Jr.	1993–
Secretary of State	Warren M. Christopher	1993–
Secretary of Treasury	Lloyd M. Bentsen, Jr.	1993–

POPULATION OF THE UNITED STATES, 1790–1993

Year	Population	Percent Increase	Population per Square Mile	Percent Urban/ Rural	Percent White/ Nonwhite	Median Age
1790	3,929,214		4.5	5.1/94.9	80.7/19.3	NA
1800	5,308,483	35.1	6.1	6.1/93.9	81.1/18.9	NA
1810	7,239,881	36.4	4.3	7.3/92.7	81.0/19.0	NA
1820	9,638,453	33.1	5.5	7.2/92.8	81.6/18.4	16.7
1830	12,866,020	33.5	7.4	8.8/91.2	81.9/18.1	17.2
1840	17,069,453	32.7	9.8	10.8/89.2	83.2/16.8	17.8
1850	23,191,876	35.9	7.9	15.3/84.7	84.3/15.7	18.9
1860	31,443,321	35.6	10.6	19.8/80.2	85.6/14.4	19.4
1870	39,818,449	26.6	13.4	25.7/74.3	86.2/13.8	20.2
1880	50,155,783	26.0	16.9	28.2/71.8	86.5/13.5	20.9
1890	62,947,714	25.5	21.2	35.1/64.9	87.5/12.5	22.0
1900	75,994,575	20.7	25.6	39.6/60.4	87.9/12.1	22.9
1910	91,972,266	21.0	31.0	45.6/54.4	88.9/11.1	24.1
1920	105,710,620	14.9	35.6	51.2/48.8	89.7/10.3	25.3
1930	122,775,046	16.1	41.2	56.1/43.9	89.8/10.2	26.4
1940	131,669,275	7.2	44.2	56.5/43.5	89.8/10.2	29.0
1950	150,697,361	14.5	50.7	64.0/36.0	89.5/10.5	30.2
1960	179,323,175	18.5	50.6	69.9/30.1	88.6/11.4	29.5
1970	203,302,031	13.4	57.4	73.5/26.5	87.6/12.4	28.0
1980	226,545,805	11.4	64.0	73.7/26.3	86.0/14.0	30.0
1990	248,709,873	9.8	70.3	77.5/22.5	80.3/19.7	32.9
1993	259,383,000	4.3	73.3	NA/NA	NA/NA	NA

NA = Not Available.

EMPLOYMENT, 1870–1992

Year	Number of Workers (in millions)	Male/Female Employment Ratio	Percentage of Workers in Unions
1870	12.5	85/15	—
1880	17.4	85/15	—
1890	23.3	83/17	—
1900	29.1	82/18	3
1910	38.2	79/21	6
1920	41.6	79/21	12
1930	48.8	78/22	7
1940	53.0	76/24	27
1950	59.6	72/28	25
1960	69.9	68/32	26
1970	82.1	63/37	25
1980	108.5	58/42	23
1985	108.9	57/43	19
1992	117.6	55/45	16

PRODUCTION, TRADE, AND FEDERAL SPENDING/DEBT, 1790–1992

Year	Gross National Product (GNP) (in billions $)	Balance of Trade (in millions $)	Federal Budget (in billions $)	Federal Surplus/Deficit (in billions $)	Federal Debt (in billions $)
1790	—	−3	.004	+0.00015	.076
1800	—	−20	.011	+0.0006	.083
1810	—	−18	.008	+0.0012	.053
1820	—	−4	.018	−0.0004	.091
1830	—	+3	.015	+0.100	.049
1840	—	+25	.024	−0.005	.004
1850	—	−26	.040	+0.004	.064
1860	—	−38	.063	−0.01	.065
1870	7.4	−11	.310	+0.10	2.4
1880	11.2	+92	.268	+0.07	2.1
1890	13.1	+87	.318	+0.09	1.2
1900	18.7	+569	.521	+0.05	1.2
1910	35.3	+273	.694	−0.02	1.1
1920	91.5	+2,880	6.357	+0.3	24.3
1930	90.7	+513	3.320	+0.7	16.3
1940	100.0	−3,403	9.6	−2.7	43.0
1950	286.5	+1,691	43.1	−2.2	257.4
1960	506.5	+4,556	92.2	+0.3	286.3
1970	992.7	+2,511	196.6	+2.8	371.0
1980	2,631.7	+24,088	579.6	−59.5	914.3
1985	4,087.7	−148,480	946.3	−212.3	1,827.5
1990	5,524.5	−101,012	1,251.8	−220.5	3,233.3
1992	5,961.9	−84,501	1,381.9	−290.2	4,064.6

ILLUSTRATIONS

MAPS

CHARTS

NOTE: Some pages are in *italics* and are preceded by letters. These refer to *i* illustrations and their captions, *m* maps, and *c* charts.

Hearst, William Randolph, 522, 558, 559, *i559*
Heilbroner, Robert, 838
Helms, Jesse, 888
Helsinki, Finland: Helsinki accords (1975), 882; SALT talks (1969), 867
Hemingway, Ernest, 663, 664, 687
Hemispheric defense, 740
Henderson, Leon, 752
Hepburn Railroad Regulation Act of 1906, 604
Herrán, Tomás, 616
Herzog (Bellow), 803
Hewitt, Abram S., 482
Hicks, John D., 542, 543
Highest Stage of White Supremacy, The (Cell), 439
Hill, Anita, 914
Hill, James J., 483, 603
Hine, Lewis, *i492, i493, i514, i655*
Hippies, 851, 852
Hirohito, emperor of Japan, 762, 764–765
Hiroshima, bombing of, 764
Hispanic Americans:
—activism of, 856–858; unions in Great Depression, 683; United Farm Workers (UFW) and, *i857*, 857–858
—*barrios* and, 454, 656, 857
—bilingualism and, 858
—*Californios, i453*, 454
—in cities, 510, 857, 909
—employment of: competition for jobs, 492; as migrant farmworkers, 683, *i857*, 857–858; racial assumptions and, 459–460; in unskilled jobs, 656; as war workers, 755, 856–857; in West, 459
—Great Depression and, 683–684
—immigration of Hispanics and: from Cuba, 856, 857; growth in, 909–910; illegal, 857, 909–910; from Latin America, 856, 909; from Mexico, 453, 491, 509, 656, 683; from Puerto Rico, 563–564, 856
—Immigration Reform Act of 1965 and, 909
—institutional supports for, 683
—migration to cities, 453, 804, 856, 857
—Operation Wetback and, 857
—poverty rates of, 909
—Puerto Rican, 563–564, 856, 909
—racial prejudice against, 510, 594, 683, 910
—Simpson-Mazzoli Act of 1987 and, 909
—in Southwest: aftermath of Mexican War and, 452; California and Texas, *i453*, 453–454; cattle ranching and, 462; interaction with Indian tribes, 450; migration to Colorado, 453; New Mexico, 452–453; population growth during World War II, 856–857; Spanish mission society and, 453–454
—in street gangs, 910
—unionization of, 683, *i857*, 857–858
—zoot suit riots and, 755, 910
—*See also* Cuba; Latin America
Hiss, Alger, 787, 789, 790
Historians' disagreements: on frontier and west, 466–467; on New Deal, 718–721; on origins of Cold War, 770–771; on origins of segregation, 438–439; on Pearl Harbor, 740–741;

on Populism, 542–543; on Progressivism, 574–577; on Reconstruction, 432–433; on Vietnam War, 838–839; on women's history, 860–861
History, 526
Hitler, Adolf, 687, 732, *i732*, 734, 769; *Anschluss*, 736, *i736*; suicide of (1945), 761
HIV virus, 912
Ho Chi Minh, 811, 835, 837, 850
Ho Chi Minh City (Saigon), 866
Ho Chi Minh Trail, 841
Hoffa, Jimmy, 796
Hofstadter, Richard, 542, 574, 719, 797
Hofstadter thesis, 542–543
Holding companies, 486
Holding Company Act of 1935, 710
Holly, Buddy, 852
Holocaust, 751, 812
Home industries, 582
Homelessness, 893, *i912*, 913
Home Owners' Loan Corporation, 708
Homer, Winslow, 523
Homestake company, 461
Homestead Act of 1862, 457
Homestead strike (1892), 497, 546
Homosexuals, 858–859
Honeymooners, The, 801
Hooper, William, 556
Hoover, Herbert, 633, 634, 669, 688–694; Commerce Secretary, 672–673; economic crises and, 690; economic programs, 688–690, *i689*; election of 1932 and, *i692*, 692–694, *m694*; popular protest and, 690–692, *i691*; prevents sanctions against Japanese, 733; refusal to suspend antitrust laws, 703
Hoover, J. Edgar, 648, 758, 788
Hopkins, Harry, 707, 713, 718, 722
Hopper, Edward, 523
Horizontal corporate integration, 485–486
Hostage crises, 884–885; effect on election of 1980, 889; Iran-contra scandal and, 902; Reagan Doctrine and, 895
House, Colonel Edward M., 611, 641
House Judiciary Committee, 875
House Un-American Activities Committee (HUAC), 786–787
Housing, in cities, 512–514, *m513, i514*
Housing Act of 1961, 824
Houston, Charles, 805
Howard, General Oliver O., 415
Howard University, 805
Howells, William Dean, 523
Howl (Ginsberg), 803
How the Other Half Lives (Riis), 514, *i579, i580*
How to Win Friends and Influence People (Carnegie), 685–686
Huckins, Olga, 919, 920, 922
Huerta, Victoriano, 617–619
Hughes, Charles Evans, 589, 630, 715, 730
Hughes, Langston, 664
Hula hoop, 798
Hull, Cordell, 734, 742
Hull House, 578–579
Humphrey, George M., 795
Humphrey, Hubert, 782, 843, 844, 846
Hungarian Revolution, 814
Huntington, Collis P., 483
Hurston, Zora Neale, 664
Hussein, King of Jordan, 868
Hussein, Saddam, 904, 905

Huthmacher, J. Joseph, 576
Hydrogen bomb, 810

ICC (Interstate Commerce Commission), 537–538, 604
Iceboxes, 518
Ickes, Harold, 718
Idaho becomes state (1890), 457
"If We Must Die" (McKay), 645
"I have a dream" speech (King), 827
ILGWU (International Ladies Garment Workers Union), *i583, i590*
I'll Take My Stand (1930), 664
I Love Lucy, 801
Immigrant ghettoes, 510
Immigrants: assimilation of, 511; ethnic diversity of, 491–492, 510; illegal, amnesty for, 909–910; predictors of success of, 510–511; racial prejudice against, 510; in 1920s, 665–667, *c666, i667*; targets of repression in World War I, 638; urban population growth and, 509, *c510*; Western settlement and, 457; in work force, *c491*, 491–492, *i492*
Immigration:
—changes in, *c908*, 908–910, *c909*
—restriction of, 512, 593–594, *c594*, 665, *c666*; woman suffrage and, 585
—shift in sources of, 491
—*See also specific countries of origin*
Immigration Reform Act of 1965, 824, 909
Immigration Reform and Control Act of 1987, 909
Immigration Restriction League, 512
Immunizations, 801
Impeachment attempts: of Andrew Johnson, 420–421, *i421*; of Nixon, 875–876
Imperialism, 553–570
—governing colonies, 565–566
—in Hawaii and Samoa, 556–557, *i557*
—modern military system, *i569*, 570
—new Manifest Destiny, 553–556, *m554–555*
—Open Door policy, 569–570
—Philippine War, *i566*, 566–569
—philosophic justification for, 554–555
—Spanish-American War and: battle for Cuba, 561–563, *i562, i563*; controversy over Cuba, *i558*, 558–560, *i559*; debate over Philippines, 564–565; Puerto Rico, 563–564; seizure of Philippines, 561; support for, *m560*, 560–561
—in western hemisphere, 556
Incandescent light bulb, 482
Inchon, Korea, 784, *m785*
Income, 425, 794
Income tax, 611, 633
Independent Republicans (Mugwumps), 534, 586
Independent treasury system, 544
Indian Civil Rights Act (1968), 855
Indian Peace Commission, 468
Indian Reorganization Act of 1934, 720–721, 754
Indian ring scandal, of Grant administration, 428
Indian Territory (Oklahoma), 450, 468
Indian tribes:
—dispersal from West: Dawes Act, 470–471; Indian wars, 469–471, *i470, i472*; white tribal policies, 468–469

Keynesianism, 707–708
Khmer Rouge, 866
Khomeini, Ayatollah Ruholla, 885
Khruschev, Nikita, *i813*, 814, 833–834
Kicking Bear, *i470*
King, Billie Jean, 863
King, Coretta Scott, *i828*
King, Martin Luther, Jr., 806; assassination of, 843; Birmingham demonstrations, 827; failure of Chicago campaign, 829; "I have a dream" speech, 827; march through Selma, Alabama, *i828*; MFDP compromise, 829; released from prison, 826
Kinship networks among Plains Indians, 451
Kirkland, Caroline, 502, 504
Kissinger, Henry, 864–867, 882, 891
Kitty Hawk, North Carolina, 482
Klaverns, 666
Knights of Labor, 495, 540, 541
Knights of the White Camellia, 430
Knowledge-based industries, 873
Knox, Frank, 742, 757–758
Kolko, Gabriel, 575, 838
Konoye, Prince of Japan, 742
Korean War, 784–786; American mobilization for, 786; Cold War and, 811; conduct of, *m785*, 785–786; division of Korea, 784–785; Panmunjom agreement (1953), 811
Korematsu v. *United States*, 758
Ku Klux Klan: Reconstruction era, 426, 430; of 1920s, 666–667, *i667*
Kuwait, 904

Labor (*see* Labor unions)
"Labor and Monopoly" (cartoon), *i536*
Labor Contract Law, 491
Labor Department, Children's Bureau of, 583
Labor force:
—on Hawaiian sugar plantations, 556
—Homestead strike and, 497
—immigrant work force, *c491*, 491–492, *i492*
—minorities in, 655–656
—multiracial nature of, 459–460
—Pullman strike and, 497–498, *i498*
—recruitment of, 436
—shortages during World War II, 751
—sources of labor weakness, 498–500
—struggle to unionize, 495–496
—women in, 655–656, 861; children and, 492, *i493*, 494; married, 684; in World War II, 751, 755–757, *i756*. *See also* Women, employment of
—working conditions for (*see* Working conditions)
—*See also* Industry; Labor unions; Manufacturing
Labor-Management Relations Act of 1947, 782, 797
Labor-management relationship, 496
Labor unions, 796–797; American Federation of Labor (AFL), 495–497, *i496*; attempts to organize, 494–495, 797; civil rights movement and, 808; dissident organizations in, 796; effect of World War II on membership, 751; Knights of Labor, 495; membership in, 635, 797, *c797*; middle-class hostility toward, 494–495; of migrant farmworkers, 683; militancy of, 711; orga-

nizing, 711–712, *i712*; Theodore Roosevelt's policy toward, 603–604; weakness in late 1800s, 498–500; in World War I, 635; World War I and, 643. *See also* Industry; Labor force; Manufacturing; Working conditions; *specific unions and union leaders*
Ladies' Home Journal, 522
LaFeber, Walter, 770
La Follette, Robert, 604, 630, 672; as reform governor, *i588*, 589; withdrawal from politics, 608, 609
Laird, Melvin, 864
Lamar, Howard, 467
Land-grant institutions, 526–527
Land grants in western states, 591
Landon, Alfred M., 714, 715
Landownership: changing distribution of, 454; Reconstruction and, 423–425, *m424*
Lange, Dorothea, 686
Laos, invasion of (1971), 866
La Raza Unida, 857
Lares Rebellion (1868), 563
Las Guasimas, Battle of (1898), 561
Last of the Mohicans, The (Cooper), 465
Latchkey children, 756
Latin America, 556, 731; "alliance for progress" in, 832; Good Neighbor Policy in, 734; growth in immigration from, 909; Reagan Doctrine and, 895; Theodore Roosevelt's intervention in, 614–615, *m615*; Woodrow Wilson's intervention in, 617–619; "Yankee imperialism" and, 813, *i813*
Laundries, 456
Lawrence, Jacob, *i682*
Laws of incorporation, 484
Lawyers, 581
Layton, Admiral Edwin T., 741
Leadville, Colorado, 461
League of Nations, 641, 729, 735; 1920 election campaign and, 648; Fourteen Points and, 638; replacing, 730. *See also* United Nations
League of Women Voters, 800
Lease, Mary E., 539
Leave It to Beaver, 801
Lebanon, 813, 895
Lebensraum, 732, 736
Le Duc Tho, 866
Lee, Spike, 910
Leff, Mark, 721
Leffler, Melvyn, 771
Leisure time, 519–521, *i520*
Lemke, William, 715
Lena, Maggie, 440
Lenin, Vladimir I., 631, 640
León, Ponce de, 563
Leo XII (Pope), 577
Lerner, Gerda, 860
Lesbians, 858–859
Let Us Now Praise Famous Men (Agee), 686
Leuchtenburg, William, 719, 720
Leveraged buyouts, 902
Levitt, William, 798–799, *i800*
Levittown, 799, *i800*
Lewis, John L., 711, 781, 797
Lewis, Sinclair, 663, 664
Lewy, Guenter, 838
Leyte Gulf, Battle of (1944), 762
Liberalism:
—assault on poverty, 822–824

—cities, schools, and immigration, 824
—conservative hostility to, 885–886
—in international affairs: Bay of Pigs fiasco, 832–833; confrontations with Soviet Union, *i833*, 833–834; diversifying foreign policy, 831–832, *m832*; Lyndon Johnson and, 834
—John Kennedy and, 819–821, *m820*, *i821*, *i822*
—legacies of Great Society, 825, *c825*
—Lyndon Johnson and, 821–822, *i823*
—of New Deal, 721
—racial equality and, 825–830; black power, 830, *i831*; demographic shift, 829; expanding protests, *i826*, 826–827; national commitment, 827, *i828*; urban violence and, 829–830; voting rights, 828–829
Liberty Bonds, *i626*, 633, *i634*
Liberty Loan posters, *i626*, *i634*
Life magazine, 686, 739, 776
Liliuokalani, Queen of Hawaii, 556–557, *i557*
Limerick, Patricia Nelson, 467
Limited liability, 484
Lincoln, Abraham, 415, *i416*; death of, 416–417; readmission of Southern states and, 413; Reconstruction plan of, 416
Lincoln, Edward, *i416*
Lincoln, Mary Todd, 416, *i416*
Lincoln, Robert Todd, *i416*
Lincoln, Thomas (Tad), *i416*
Lincoln, "Willie," *i416*
Lincoln Memorial, 718, 827
Lindbergh, Charles, 663, 739
Lippmann, Walter, 594, 596, 601
Literacy requirement for immigrants, 512
"Literacy" tests, 442, 443
Literature, 476; popular, 435, 465, 686; of urban America, 523
Little Big Horn, Battle of (1876), 470, *i470*
Little Crow, 469
Little Rock, Arkansas, 806
"Little Steel," 654, 712, *i712*
Little Steel formula, 751
Little Women (Alcott), 522
Litvinov, Maxim, 734
Litwack, Leon, 433
Lloyd George, David, 639, *i640*
Lochner v. *New York* (1905), 673, 715
Locke, Alain, 664
Lodge, Henry Cabot, 554, 565, 594, 641–642, 729
Logging, deforestation and, *i623*
Lôme, Dupuy de, 559–560
London Blitz, *i738*
London Naval Conference (1935), 734
Lonely Crowd, The (Riesman), 802
Lone Ranger, The, 686
Long, Breckinridge, 751
Long, Huey P., 543, *i709*, 709–710, 715
Long drives (cattle drives), *m462*, *i463*, 463–464
Lon Nol, 865, 866
Looking Backward (Bellamy), 490
Los Angeles, California: growth after World War II, 795; Hispanic population of, 857; riots, 829, 911–912
Los Angeles Dodgers, 805
Lost Generation, 663

Motion picture industry, 654; focus of HUAC on, 787; growth of, 658–659
Motion pictures, 521–522; during Great Depression, 686, i687; social conflict in, 853–854
Mount Holyoke College, 528
Movie palaces, 522
Mowry, George, 574
Mowry-Hofstadter thesis, 574–575
Mr. Deeds Goes to Town (Capra), 686
Mr. Smith Goes to Washington (Capra), 686
Muck, Karl, 638
Muckrakers, i572, 574–576, i578, 586
Mugwumps (Independent Republicans), 534, 586
Muhammed, Elijah (Poole), 830
Muir, John, i604, 605, 915
Muller, Paul, 920
Multiculturalism, 858
Multiversities, 802
Munich accords, i736, 736–737
Munich Conference (1938), 736–737, 772
Municipal governments, 586–588, i587
Munsey, Frank, 609
Murder, 516
Murphy, Charles Francis, 590
Murphy, Frank, 712
Muscle Shoals dam, 706
Music: rock 'n roll, i852, 852–853; WPA and, 713
Musical comedy, 521
Mussolini, Benito, 687, 732, i732, 734, 773; flees to Germany, 750; invasion of Ethiopia, 735; invasion of France (1940), 737
Mutual defense pacts, 810
My Lai massacre, 865
My Little Margie, 801
Myrdal, Gunnar, 793

Nabrit, James, 805
NAFTA (North American Free Trade Agreement), 907
Nagasaki, bombing of, 764
Naismith, Dr. James A., 521
NASA (National Aeronautics and Space Administration), 802
Nasser, Gamal Abdel, 812–813
Nation, The, 427
National Aeronautics and Space Administration (NASA), 802
National American Woman Suffrage Association, 585, 636
National Association for the Advancement of Colored People (NAACP), i591, 592, 645, 683, 805, 827
National Association of Colored Women, 583
National Association of Manufacturers, 581, 656
National (baseball) League, 520
National Broadcasting Company, 659–660, 801
National College Athletic Association, 521
National Congress of American Indians (NCAI), 853
National Consumers' League, 519, 648
National Cordage Company, 545
National Defense Education Act of 1958, 802
National elections, 531–532. *See also* Presidential elections
National Farm Bureau Federation, 581

National Forest Service, 605, 607
National Forest system, 625
National government, 532–533, 574, 591. *See also* Congress; Foreign policy; Government spending; *specific aspects of national government*
National Grange of the Patrons of Husbandry, 538
National Greenback Party, 429
National Guard: in Boston police strike, 643; federal command of, 570; formation of urban groups, 516; Homestead strike and, 497; at Kent State University, 865; in Spanish-American War, 561; in Watts uprising, 829
National Housing Act of 1949, 783
National Indian Youth Council, 855
National Industrial Recovery Act of 1933, 704, 705, 710, 711
National Irrigation Association, 605
Nationalism, 490, 610, 646
Nationalist Clubs, 490
National Labor Relations Act (Wagner Act) of 1935, 710–711, 715, 782
National Labor Relations Board (NLRB), 711, 796
National Labor Union, 494
National Liberation Front (NLF), 837, 843
National Organization for Women (NOW), 862
National Origins Act of 1924, 665
National press services, 522
National Reclamation Act (Newlands Act, 1902), 605
National Recovery Administration (NRA), i703, 704–705
National reform:
—in foreign policy: activist policy, i613, 613–614; "Dollar Diplomacy," 617; in Latin America, 614–615, m615; "Open Door" in Asia, 614; Panama Canal, 615–617, i616; Wilsonian diplomacy, 617–619
—under Theodore Roosevelt: "accidental president," 602; capital and labor, 602–604; conservation, m603, i604, 605; Panic of 1907, 605–606; "square deal," i602, 604
—under William Howard Taft: progressives and, 606–607; Republican Party split, 609; Roosevelt's return to politics, 607, i608; spreading insurgency, 607–608
—under Woodrow Wilson: additional reforms, i612, 612–613; legislation, 610–611; trusts and, 611–612; Wilson's entry into politics, 610, m610
—See also Progressivism
National Security Act of 1947, 777
National Security Council (NSC), 777
National Security League, 638
National Socialist (Nazi) Party, 732
National Union for Social Justice, 709
National War Labor Board, 635
National Woman's Party, 585, 661, i661, 685, 722, 859
National Woman Suffrage Association, 420
National Youth Administration (NYA), 713, i722, 821
Nation of Islam, 830
Native Americans (*see* American Indians)

Native Son (Wright), 686
Nativism: immigration restriction and, 594; Ku Klux Klan and, 666–667, i667
NATO (North Atlantic Treaty Organization), 777–779, m778, i779
Natural resources, 553
Natural selection, 524
Navajo Indians, 450
Naval blockades, 629
Naval conflict in World War I, 631
Naval disarmament, 730
Naval power, 555–556
Navy Department, 670
Nazi-Soviet Pact (1939), 769
NCAI (National Congress of American Indians), 853
Nebraska becomes state (1867), 457
Nelson, Donald, 753
Neo-conservatives, 890
Netherlands, 737
Neustadt, Richard, 819
Neutrality
—World War I and, i628, 628–629
—World War II and, 734–744; abandonment of, 739–742; prelude to Pearl Harbor and, 742–744, i744; presidential election of 1940 and, 739; tests of, 737–739, i738
Neutrality Acts (1935–1937), 735, 737
Nevada becomes state (1864), 457
New Citizenship, The (Thelen), 576
New Deal, 693; African Americans and, 718–719; agricultural adjustment and, 702–703; American politics and, 725; assistance to Dust Bowl farmers, 698; attacks on, 708–709; "broker state," 717; "court-packing plan," 715–716; disagreements of historians on, 718–721; effects in West, 722–724; election of 1936 and, 714–715; federal relief in, 707–708; financial reforms, 707; Indians and, 719–721; industrial recovery and, i703, 703–705, i704; labor militancy and, 711; liberalism of, 721; major legislation of, c717; national economy and, c723, 724–725; popular protest and, i709, 709–710; recession of 1937 and, 716; regional planning, 705–707, m706; relief projects of, 713–714, i714; restoring confidence, 701–702, i702; "Second New Deal," 710–711; Social Security, 712–713; union organization and, 711–712, i712; women and, 721–722, i722. *See also* Economy; Great Depression; Roosevelt, Franklin D.
New Deal, The (Conklin), 720
New Deal and the Problem of Monopoly (Hawley), 720
New Deals (Gordon), 720
"New Diplomacy, The" (Dalrymple), i613
New Era (1920s): "American Plan" in, 656; composition of work force, 655–656; consumerism and communications, 658–660, i659; decline of self-made man, 662–663; Democratic party conflict in, 669, m669; disenchanted artists and intellectuals, 663–664; education and youth, 662; farmers and, 656–657, m657, m658; government helping business and industry, 672–673; growth and organization of economy, 653–654; Harding and Coolidge, i670, 670–672, i671;

I-13

Weathermen (SDS), 851
Weaver, James B., 537, 540–541, *i542*
Weaver, Robert, 718, 824
Webb, Walter Prescott, 466
Webster v. *Reproductive Health Services* (1989), 913
Weimar Republic, 679, 732
Welch, Joseph, *i809*
Welch, William H., 581
Welfare capitalism, 654, 655
Wells, Ida B., 443
West:
—agriculture in: "agrarian malaise," 476; commercial agriculture, 475–476; farmers, 464, 472–476; farming on Great Plains, 473–475
—Anglo-American easterners in, 457–458, *i458*
—boom towns in, *i460,* 461; women in, 461–462
—buffalo hunting in, *i450,* 451, 468; from railroad trains, *i473,* 502–504
—cattle ranching, *m462,* 462–464, *i463*; cattle drives, *m462, i463,* 463–464; plains ecology and, 503–504; in southern California, 454; techniques of Mexican ranchers, 462
—changing economy of, 458–468
—Chinese in, 454–456; anti-Chinese sentiments and, *i455,* 456–457; attracted by Gold Rush, 455; benevolent societies and tongs, 456; "coolies," 454, 456; foreign miners tax on, 455; in mining, 455, 459; as railroad workers, 455, 491; settlement in West, 454–456; "Six Companies" (San Francisco), 456, 457; in unskilled jobs, 459–460, 656
—colleges and universities in, 795, 802, 850, 851
—conservatism in, 886
—disagreement of historians on, 466–467
—economy after World War II, 794–795
—gold rush: in Black Hills, 461; in Colorado, *i460,* 461
—Great Plains, commercial agriculture, 475–476; ecological changes in, 468–469; farming on, 473–475; fences and, 473–474; railroads and, 502
—Hispanics in: California and Texas, *i453,* 453–454; New Mexico, 452–453;
—Homestead Act and, 457
—Indian tribes in, *i450,* 450–452, 468–472; Dawes Act and, 470–471; *genizaros,* 450; Indian wars, 469–470, *i470, i472*; white policies, 468–469
—labor force in, 459–460
—land grants in, 591
—migration from East, 457–458, *i458*; —mining in, *m459, i460,* 460–462; Chinese in, 455, 459
—New Deal and, 722–724
—progressive movement in, 591
—romantic appeal of: historians and, 465–468; in literature, 465, 476; "Rocky Mountain School" of painting, 464
—shipbuilding industry on west coast, 751
—Southwest, *see* Southwest
—World War II and, 751–752, 794–795
West Berlin, 814
West Coast Hotel v. *Parrish* (1937), 715
Western Federation of Miners strike (1917), 635

Western (football) Conference (Big Ten), 521
West German Republic, 777–778
Westward Expansion (Billington), 466
Weyler, General Valeriano "Butcher," 558
Wheat market, 697
Wheeler, Burton K., 719–720, 739
Whiskey ring scandal, 428
Whistler, James McNeil, 523
White, Richard, 467
White, Walter, 683
White, William Allen, 739
White Bird Canyon, Battle of (1877), 471
White Citizens' Councils, 806
White collar workers: African-American, 911, *c911*; incomes of, 518
White Leagues, 430
Whitman, Walt, 858
Whitney, Richard, 707
Whyte, William H., Jr., 802
Why Vietnam? (Defense Dept. film), 838
Why We Were in Vietnam (Podhoretz), 838
Wiebe, Robert, 575
Wildcat strikes, 751
Willard, Frances, 582, 593, 595
Williams, William Appleman, 770
Williamson, Joel, 438, 439
Williams v. *Mississippi* (1898), 443
Willkie, Wendell, 739, 772
Wilson, Charles, 808
Wilson, Woodrow, *m610, i612,* 642, 669, 692; anti-trust legislation as governor, 589; national reform under, *i609,* 609–613; neutrality and, *i628,* 628–629, 737; objections to reparations, 679; organizing economy for World War I, 633; at Paris Peace Conference (1918), 639–641, *i649;* Princeton University president, 610; "Wilsonianism," 638
Wilson-Gorman Tariff of 1894, 537, 558
Wilsonianism, 638
Wister, Owen, 465
Witchcraft, 861
Wohlstetter, Roberta, 741
Wolfe, Thomas, 664
Woman's Bureau of the Knights of Labor, 495
Woman's Peace Party, 636, 637
Woman suffrage, *i584,* 584–586; decline of feminism and, 860; first granted by Wyoming, 464; Wilson refuses support of, 612
Women:
—economy and: cattle ranching, 464; Farmers' Alliances, 539; Great Depression, *c684,* 684–685; post-war reconversion, 780–781; symbolic gestures by New Deal and, 721–722, *i722*
—education of, 527–528
—employment of: in academia, 581; as clerks and waitresses, 519; in factory work, 492, 494; migration to industrial cities, 508; in post-Reconstruction South, 436; pressure for second income and, 800; in World War I, 635; in World War II, 751, 755–757, *i756*
—freedoms and, 660–661
—greatly outnumbered in mining towns, 461–462
—growth of political activities in 1920s, 661–662
—ignored by Fifteenth Amendment, 420
—isolation of, 800

—labor unions and, 494–496, 711
—in professions, 579, 581–582, 863
—reform and, 577, 582–586
—rights and protections of, 863, *i863*
—roles of: family, 426, i426; motherhood, 660; in Plains Indian society, 451; as primary consumers, 519; in 1920s, 660–662, *i661*
—sports for, 521
—working conditions for, 860
—*See also* Feminism; Gender; Men
Women and Economics (Gilman), 583
Women as a Force in History (Beard), 860
Women's Christian Temperance Union (WCTU), 593
Women's clubs, 582–584, *i583*
Women's colleges, 528
Women's history, 860–861
Women's International League for Peace and Freedom, 842
Women's Liberation, 862–863
Women's organizations, growth in 1920s, 661–662; political reform and, 861
"Women's professions," 479, 581–582, 660
Women's Trade Union League (WTUL), 498, *i583,* 583–584, 635–636
Wood, General Leonard, 561, 565
Wood, General Robert E., 739
Woodstock, *i852,* 853
"Woodstock nation," *i852,* 853
Woodward, C. Vann, 432, 438
Woolworth's lunch counter sit-ins, 826, *i826*
Workers, in industry (*see* Labor force)
Working conditions, 492; for children in factory work, 494; for Chinese railroad workers, 455; federal legislation to regulate, 583; for laborers in West, 459; for miners, 462; wages and, 492, 860; for women, 860. *See also* Industry; Labor force; Labor unions; Manufacturing
Workingmen's Party of California, 456
Working Women's Association, 420
Work Relief, 707
Works Progress Administration (WPA), *i700, i704,* 713–714, *i714,* 759
World Court treaty (1935), 735
World Disarmament Conference (1932), 731–732
World Economic Conference (1933), 733
World Series, 520
World War I:
—American Expeditionary Force, 631–632
—beginning of, 631
—business interests blamed for, 735
—collapse of peace in Europe, 628
—combat, *m632,* 632–633, *i633*
—debt produced by, 730
—economic and social results of, 635–636, *i636*
—economic organization for, 633–634, *i634*
—effect on woman suffrage, 585
—effects on Europe, 627
—justification for intervention, 630–631
—labor unions and, 635
—neutrality and, *i628,* 628–629
—peace movement, 636–637
—postwar settlement, 638–642, *i640*
—postwar society: African-American demands, 643–646, *i645,* m645; indus-